ART

A BRIEF HISTORY

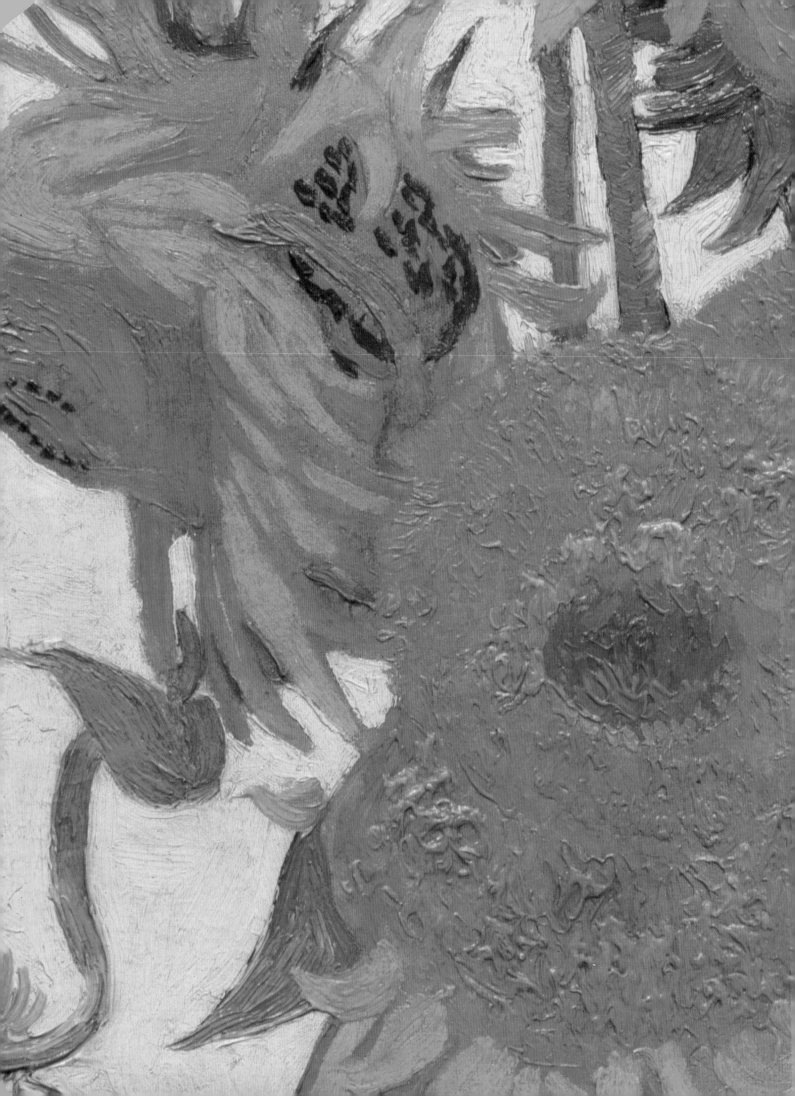

ART
A BRIEF HISTORY

Marilyn Stokstad

The University of Kansas

with the collaboration of Margaret A. Oppenheimer

and with contributions by Stephen Addiss, Bradford R. Collins, Chu-tsing Li, Marylin M. Rhie, and Christopher D. Roy

Prentice Hall, Inc., and Harry N. Abrams, Inc., Publishers

DEDICATED TO MY SISTER, KAREN L.S. LEIDER, AND MY NIECE, ANNA J. LEIDER

Publishers: *Paul Gottlieb, Bud Therien*
Director, Textbook Publishing: *Julia Moore*
Project Manager and Editor: *Katherine Rangoon Doyle*
Assistant Editor: *Jungha Oh*
Design, art direction, and production: *Lydia Gershey and Yonah Schurink of Communigraph*
Photo editing, rights and reproduction: *Janice Ackerman, Lauren Boucher, Jennifer Bright, Helen Lee,*
    Diana Gongora.Pilar, Catherine Ruello
Senior Marketing Manager, Prentice Hall: *Sheryl Adams*
Marketing assistance: *Darcy Betts*
New Media: *Alison Prendergast*
Market Research, Prentice Hall: *Seth Reichlin*
Illustration: *John McKenna, Paulo Suzuki*
Project assistance, Prentice Hall: *Mary Amoon*
Indexing: *Peter and Erica Rooney*

Library of Congress Cataloging-in-Publication Data

Stokstad, Marilyn, 1929–
    [Art History]
    Art : a brief history / Marilyn Stokstad in collaboration with Margaret A.
Oppenheimer ; with chapters by Stephen Addiss . . . [et al.].
        p. cm.
    Simultaneously published: Art History. New York : Harry N. Abrams, 2000.
    Includes bibliographical references and index.
    ISBN 0–13–085364–X (pb.)
    1. Art—History. I. Oppenheimer, Margaret A. II. Addiss, Stephen, 1935–
III. Title.
    N5300 .S923 1999b
    709—dc21   99–32187

This is a concise edition of *Art History* by Marilyn Stokstad, published by Harry N. Abrams, Inc., in first and revised editions in 1995 and 1999 respectively.

Copyright © 2000 Harry N. Abrams, Inc.
Published in 2000 by Harry N. Abrams, Incorporated, New York

 Prentice-Hall, Inc.
A Division of Pearson Education
Upper Saddle River, NJ 07458

Send inquiries to:
    Marketing Manager
    Humanities and Social Sciences, Prentice Hall, Inc.
    One Lake Street
    Upper Saddle River, N.J. 07458
    http://www.prenhall.com

Printed and bound in Japan

On the cover and pages 2–3: Vincent van Gogh. *Sunflowers* (detail of fig. 17). 1888. Oil on canvas. The National Gallery, London

Preface to Art: A Brief History

Over the more than forty years I have been introducing the history of art to students and to the public, this long-held conviction of mine has only deepened: the first purpose of an introductory course should be to nurture an educated, enthusiastic public for the arts. In the five years since the publication of Art History and, more recently, the Revised Edition of Art History, I have seen resounding evidence that when a book responds to the needs of its audience, that book can make a great difference in the role art assumes in the lives of individuals.

I firmly believe students and the lay reader can and should be able to *enjoy* their introduction to art history. Only then will they learn to appreciate art as the most tangible creation of the human imagination. That is why the authors and publishers in 1995 made Art History a sensitive, accessible, engaging, large textbook survey. Art: A Brief History preserves those goals and most of the features of Art History, while offering a more abbreviated and slightly more popular account.

Art: A Brief History is contextual, in the best sense of the term. This book, like its parents, balances formalist traditions with the newer interests of contextual art history while supporting specific needs of a diverse and fast-changing student population. Throughout the text we treat the visual arts not in a vacuum but within the real-world contexts of history, geography, politics, religion, and culture; we carefully define the parameters—social, religious, political, and cultural—that either constrained or liberated individual artists. And bearing in mind that there is no substitute for experiencing works of art firsthand, we have whenever feasible included works on view in many different museums and collections around the United States, including college and university museums.

Art: A Brief History is wide-ranging and inclusive. We have reached beyond the West to the arts of other regions and cultures, presenting a global view of art through the millennia. We regard art as more than the world's most significant paintings and works of sculpture and architecture, and so we include drawings, photographs, works in metal and ceramics, textiles, and jewelry. We pay due respect to the canon of great monuments of the history of art, but we also treat artists and artworks not previously acknowledged in surveys. We incorporate the best and most recent scholarship, including new discoveries (the prehistoric cave paintings of Chauvet cave in southern France, for example), and bring new works to the forefront.

This book is a pleasure to read and use. Every chapter opens with visually supported, two-page explanations of **Key Terms of Art History**. Chapter introductions, graphically set off from the main text, offer inviting, sometimes anecdotal vignettes that raise interest for the material to come. While the text carries the central narrative of Art: A Brief History, set-off boxes present interesting and instructive material that enriches the text. A number of thought-provoking boxes focus on such critical issues as the use of the word *primitive* as an art historical label and the way the titles given to works of art may affect our perception of them. Other boxes provide insights into contextual influences, such as women as art patrons, the lives of major religious leaders, and the intersection of art and politics. **Elements of Architecture** boxes explicate basic architectural forms and terminology. **Technique** boxes explore how artworks have been made, from prehistoric cave paintings to Renaissance frescoes to how a camera works. Finally, Art: A Brief History includes **a rich illustration program** of some 550 photographs—most in full color—as

well as around 70 original line drawings (including architectural plans and cutaways) that have been universally acclaimed in Art History.

In addition, a complete **ancillary package** is available for Art: A Brief History. This package includes two slide sets, videos, a student Study Guide, an Instructor's Resource Manual with Test Bank, and the publication Art and the Internet.

Art: A Brief History is also supported by the most effective art textbook interactive website available today at www.prenhall.com/stokstad.

Art: A Brief History represents the cumulative efforts of a distinguished team of scholars and educators. Even in a book of this size, single authorship is no longer a fully responsible proposition. Our world has become too complex, our coverage too wide, and our research on art too sophisticated to entrust the world's art to a single author. An individual view of art may be very persuasive—even elegant—but it remains personal. Now, however, we no longer look for a single "truth," nor do we venerate a static canon of artworks. Art: A Brief History incorporates the work of the original team of scholar-teachers, all with independent views and the ability to treat the art they write about on its own terms and in its own cultural context. The overarching viewpoint—the controlling imagination—is mine, but the original book would not have been successful without the work of the following distinguished contributing authors:

Stephen Addiss, Tucker Boatwright Professor in the Humanities at the University of Richmond, Virginia

Bradford R. Collins, Associate Professor in the Art Department, University of South Carolina, Columbia

Chu-tsing Li, Professor Emeritus at the University of Kansas, Lawrence

Marylin M. Rhie, Jessie Wells Post Professor of Art and Professor of East Asian Studies at Smith College

Christopher D. Roy, Professor of Art History at the University of Iowa in Iowa City

Finally, Art: A Brief History would not have been possible without the substantial efforts of independent scholar and editor Margaret Oppenheimer. Her clearheaded suggestions for condensing the original work almost by half and her well-tuned ear for narrative have resulted in a book that is entirely self-sufficient. This book, too, has benefited from the invaluable assistance and advice of scores of other scholars and teachers who have generously answered my questions, given their recommendations on organization and priorities, and provided specialized critiques. I am especially grateful to my colleagues at the University of Kansas, Amy McNair and Marsha Weidner, for their expert advice on aspects of Asian art; and to Charles Eldredge and David Cateforis for modern art. Patricia Darish and David Binkley of the National Museum of African Art, Smithsonian Institution reread the chapter on African art; and Roger Ward of The Nelson-Atkins Museum of Art worked with me on the Renaissance and Baroque periods.

I hope all of you will enjoy this concise edition of Art History and that you will continue to share your comments and suggestions with me.

Acknowledgments to Art: A Brief History

A note: Art: A Brief History is a concise version of Art History, which was first published in 1995 by Harry N. Abrams, Inc., and Prentice Hall. Everyone who contributed to the original and revised editions of Art History deserves to be recognized and thanked for step-parenting this book, Art: A Brief History. For that reason, Acknowledgments from both the first edition and the revised edition of Art History appear here.

On this concise edition, I worked again with my editor at Abrams, Julia Moore, to create a book that would cohesively incorporate effective, and highly successful, pedagogical features into this shortened narrative of Art History. Kathy Doyle managed the project and edited the manuscript, ably supported by assistant editor Jungha Oh. Janice Ackerman was the photo researcher. Lydia Gershey and Yonah Schurink of Communigraph once again have my deepest respect for the disciplined creativity shown in the intelligent, approachable design and layout of this book. My research assistants at the University of Kansas, Amy Fowler and Jill Vessely, have my everlasting gratitude. So do all my graduate teaching assistants at the University of Kansas. To all of you, my heartfelt thanks.

Marilyn Stokstad
Lawrence, Kansas
June 1999

Acknowledgments to the First Edition of Art History

Writing and producing this book has been a far more challenging undertaking than any of us originally thought it would be. Were it not for the editorial and organizational expertise of Julia Moore, we never would have pulled it off. She inspired, orchestrated, and guided the team of editors, researchers, photo editors, designers, and illustrators who contributed their talents to the volume you now hold. Paul Gottlieb and Bud Therien convinced me to undertake the project, and with Phil Miller were unfailingly supportive throughout its complex gestation. A team of developmental editors led by David Chodoff at Prentice Hall and Jean Smith at Abrams refined the final manuscript to make it clear and accessible to students. Special thanks are due to Ellyn Childs Allison, Sheila Franklin Lieber, and Steve Rigolosi for their careful developmental work during the crucial early stages; to Mark Getlein for his extraordinary care in developing the chapters on Asian and African art; and to Gerald Lombardi for his work on the chapters on Western art since the Renaissance. Photo researchers Lauren Boucher, Jennifer Bright, Helen Lee, and Catherine Ruello performed miracles in finding the illustrations we needed—and, because of their zeal in finding the best pictures, sometimes helped us see what we wanted. John McKenna's drawings have brought exactly the right mix of information, clarity, and human presence to the illustration program. Special thanks also to Nancy Corwin, who was an essential resource on the history of craft, and to Jill Leslie Furst for her assistance on the chapters on the art of Pacific cultures and the art of the Americas. Designer Lydia Gershey and associate Yonah Schurink have broken new ground with their clear and inviting design and layout. Alison Pendergast, marketing manager, contributed many helpful insights as the book neared completion. My research assistants at the University of Kansas, Katherine Giele, Richard Watters, and Michael Willis, have truly earned my everlasting gratitude.

Every chapter has been read by one or more specialists: Barbara Abou-El-Haj, SUNY Binghamton; Jane Aiken, Virginia Polytechnic; Vicki Artimovich, Bellevue Community College; Elizabeth Atherton, El Camino College; Ulku Bates, Hunter College, CUNY; Joseph P. Becherer, Grand Rapids Community College; Janet Catherine Berlo, University of Rochester; Roberta Bernstein, SUNY Albany; Edward Bleiberg, University of Memphis; Daniel Breslauer, University of Kansas; Ronald Buksbaum, Capital Community Technical College; Petra ten-Doesschate Chu, Seton Hall University; John Clarke, University of Texas, Austin; Robert Cohon, The Nelson-Atkins Museum of Art; Frances Colpitt, University of Texas, San Antonio; Lorelei H. Corcoran, University of Memphis; Ann G. Crowe, Virginia Commonwealth University; Pamela Decoteau, Southern Illinois University; Susan J. Delaney, Mira Costa College; Walter B. Denny, University of Massachusetts, Amherst; Richard DePuma, University of Iowa; Brian Dursam, University of Miami; Ross Edman, University of Illinois, Chicago; Gerald Eknoian, DeAnza State College; Mary S. Ellett, Randolph-Macon College; James D. Farmer, Virginia Commonwealth University; Craig Felton, Smith College; Mary F. Francey, University of Utah; Joanna Frueh, University of Nevada, Reno; Mark Fullerton, Ohio State University; Anna Gonosova, University of California, Irvine; Robert Grigg; Glenn Harcourt, University of Southern California; Sharon Hill, Virginia Commonwealth University; Mary Tavener Holmes, New York City; Paul E. Ivey, University of Arizona; Carol S. Ivory, Washington State University; Nina Kasanof, Sage Junior College of Albany; John F. Kenfield, Rutgers University; Ruth Kolarik, Colorado College; Jeffrey Lang, University of Kansas; William A. Lozano, Johnson County Community College; Franklin Ludden, retired; Lisa F. Lynes, North Idaho College; Joseph Alexander MacGillivray, Columbia University; Janice Mann, Wayne State University; Michelle Marcus, The Metropolitan Museum of Art; Virginia Marquardt, University of Virginia; Peggy McDowell, University of New Orleans; Sheila McNally, University of Minnesota; Victor H. Miesel, University of Michigan; Vernon Minor, University of Colorado, Boulder; Anta Montet-White, University of Kansas; Anne E. Morganstern, Ohio State University; William J. Murnane, University of Memphis; Lawrence Nees, University of Delaware; Sara Orel, Truman State University; John G. Pedley, University of Michigan; Elizabeth Pilliod, Oregon State University; Nancy H. Ramage, Ithaca College; Ida K. Rigby, San Diego State University; Howard Risatti, Virginia Commonwealth University; Ann M. Roberts, University of Iowa; Stanley T. Rolfe, University of Kansas; Wendy W. Roworth, University of Rhode Island; James H. Rubin, SUNY Stony Brook; John Russell, Columbia University; Patricia Sands, Pratt Institute; Thomas Sarrantonio, SUNY New Paltz; Diane G. Scillia, Kent State University; Linda Seidel, University of Chicago; Nancy Sevcenko, Cambridge, Massachusetts; Tom Shaw, Kean College; Jan Sheridan, Erie Community College; Anne R. Stanton, University of Missouri, Columbia; Thomas Sullivan, OSB, Benedictine College (Conception Abbey); Janis Tomlinson, Columbia University; the late Eleanor Tufts; Dorothy Verkerk, University of North Carolina, Chapel Hill; Roger Ward, The Nelson-Atkins Museum of Art; Mark Weil, Washington University, St. Louis; Alison West, New York City; Randall White, New York University; and David Wilkins, University of Pittsburgh.

Others who have tried to keep me from errors of fact and interpretation—who have shared ideas and course syllabi, read chapters or sections of chapters, and offered suggestions and criticism—include: Janetta Rebold Benton, Pace University; Elizabeth Gibson Broun, National Museum of America Art; Robert G. Calkins, Cornell University; William W. Clark, Queens College, CUNY; Jaqueline Clipsham; Alessandra Comini, Southern Methodist University; Susan Craig, University of Kansas; Charles Cuttler, retired; Ralph T. Coe, Santa Fe; Nancy Corwin, University of Kansas; Patricia Darish, University of Kansas; Lois Drewer, Index of Christian Art; Edmund Eglinski, University of Kansas; Charles Eldredge, University of Kansas; James Enyeart, University of New Mexico; Ann Friedman, Oakland University, Rochester; Mary D. Garrard, American University; Walter S. Gibson, retired; Paula Gerson, Florida State University; Dorothy Glass, SUNY Buffalo; Stephen Goddard, University of Kansas; the late Jane Hayward, The Cloisters, The Metropolitan Museum of Art; Robert Hoffmann, retired; Luke Jordan, University of Kansas; Charles Little, The Metropolitan Museum of Art; Karen Mack, University of Kansas; Richard Mann, San Francisco State University; Bob Martin, Arizona State University; Amy McNair, University of Kansas; Sara Jane Pearman, The Cleveland Museum of Art; Michael Plante, H. Sophie Newcomb Memorial College; John Pultz, University of Kansas; Virginia Raguin, College of the Holy Cross; James Seaver, University of Kansas; Pamela Sheingorn, Baruch College, CUNY; Caryle K. Smith, retired; Walter Smith, Ball State University; Lauren Soth, Carleton College; Linda Stone-Ferrier, University of Kansas; Michael Stoughton, University of Minnesota; Elizabeth Valdez del Alamo, Montclair State College; and Ann S. Zielinski, retired.

Finally, the book was class tested with students under the direction of these teachers: Fred C. Albertson, University of Memphis; Betty J. Crouther, University of Mississippi; Linda M. Gigante, University of Louisville; Cynthia Hahn, Florida State University; Jennifer Haley, University of Nebraska, Lincoln; Lawrence R. Hoey, University of Wisconsin, Milwaukee; Delane O. Karalow, Virginia Commonwealth University; Charles R. Mack, University of South Carolina, Columbia; Brian Madigan, Wayne State University; Merideth Palumbo, Kent State University; Sharon Pruitt, East Carolina State University; J. Michael Taylor, James Madison University; Marcilene K. Wittmer, University of Miami; and Marilyn Wyman, San Jose State University.

A FINAL WORD

As each of us develops a genuine appreciation of the arts, we come to see them as the ultimate expression of human faith and integrity as well as creativity. I have tried here to capture that creativity, courage, and vision in such a way as to engage and enrich even those encountering art history for the very first time. If I have done that, I will feel richly rewarded.

Marilyn Stokstad
Spring 1995

Acknowledgments to the Revised First Edition of Art History

Many people reviewed the original edition of Art History and helped with the changes and revisions to the Revised Edition. By period, they are Jean Middleton James, the entire text; Judith Oliver (Colgate University), the European Middle Ages; Edward Olszewski (Case Western Reserve University) and Edmund Eglinski (The University of Kansas), Renaissance and Baroque; David Cateforis (The University of Kansas) and Grace Flam (Salt Lake City Community College), modern art and architecture; and Marta Braun (Ryerson Polytechnic University), photography.

Others whose comments were especially helpful include James Adams (Manchester College), Anthony Alofsin (University of Texas at Austin), Larry Beck, Sara Blick (Kenyon College), Nancy Corwin (Tulane University), Stephen Goddard (The University of Kansas), Wendy Kindred (University of Maine, Fort Kent), Aileen Laing (Sweet Briar College), and Amy Ogata (Cleveland Institute of Art).

Many of those acknowledged in the original edition assisted with the Revised Edition, especially Robert Calkins, Robert Cohon, Susan Craig, Charles Cuttler, Charles Eldredge, Eileen Fry, Walter Gibson, Dorothy Glass, Charles Little, Bob Martin, Amy McNair, Anta Montet-White, Sara Orel, Sarajane Pearman, John Pultz, James Seaver, Pamela Sheingorn, Linda Stone-Ferrier, Elizabeth Valdez del Alamo, Roger Ward, and Ann Zielinski.

Again, thanks to my wonderful editor at Abrams, Julia Moore, and to those who worked with her so competently, Jean Smith and Jungha Oh. Photo researchers Diana Pilar Gongora and Janice Ackerman have my gratitude and so do Lydia Gershey and Yonah Schurink, designers extraordinary.

Marilyn Stokstad
June 1998

Brief Contents

Contents

Starter Kit

This section is a very compact quick-reference guide to concepts and working assumptions used in the study of art history. It supplements this book and may help you as you encounter and interact with art in museums and elsewhere. Most of the topics you will find here are developed further on the first two pages of each chapter. Two of this book's special-feature boxes—Technique boxes and Elements of Architecture boxes—are introduced here to alert you to the way they convey information.

What Art History Is

Art history is a humanistic field of inquiry that concentrates on visual culture—works created to inform, express, and inspire through what we see. Increasingly, art history seeks to understand the role of visual culture in societies around the world and, through a multidimensional study of the art itself, to learn more about the people and cultures who created individual artworks.

The field of art history embraces many different approaches to visual culture. CONTEXTUAL ART HISTORY seeks to understand art as one expression of complex social, economic, political, philosophical, and religious influences on culture and individuals. Another approach is FORMALISM, or FORMAL ANALYSIS, in which the examination of the formal elements of works of art in and of themselves are the primary focus. A third approach, one requiring the study of the actual work of art, not merely photographs of it, is CONNOISSEURSHIP, the almost intimate appreciation and evaluation of works of art for their intrinsic attributes, including genuineness and quality. Connoisseurship necessarily involves AESTHETICS, a branch of philosophy concerned with the nature of beauty and taste. This book focuses on contextual art history, with formal analysis in a strong supporting role, while acknowledging other approaches in special features and extended captions.

What Art Is

The word *art* can embrace a very wide range of creations, which conventionally are assigned to broad categories. In reading about art, you will come across a number of these classifications. FINE ARTS, or FINE ART, generally means painting, sculpture, and architecture. The notion of the fine arts as having superior status arose in Europe as an expression of Renaissance ideals, which exalted individual artists within society as well as their one-of-a-kind aesthetic expressions and interpretations of ideas. Before the Renaissance in the West and within other cultures throughout the rest of the world, art has not been stratified along these lines.

Architecture is sometimes referred to as one of the APPLIED ARTS or PRACTICAL ARTS. The so-called DECORATIVE ARTS are also referred to as APPLIED ARTS, MINOR ARTS, and occasionally FUNCTIONAL ARTS and include ceramic or pottery wares of both practical and decorative intent; textiles and needlework; objects of glass; metalwork, including arms and armor; furniture; jewelry; and creations such as fancy bookbindings. (*Industrial design* is a term for objects made by machine and includes items produced in multiples, especially of metal and plastic.) FOLK ART, sometimes called TRADITIONAL ART, encompasses art made by people not trained in art schools but working in popular traditions specific to their cultures.

Two-dimensional arts include painting, drawing, the graphic arts, and photography. **Three-dimensional arts** are sculpture, architecture, and most of the decorative arts. Other categories of art are treated later, under MEDIUM.

The philosopher Suzanne Langer wrote, "Art is the creation of forms symbolic of human feeling" (*Feeling and Form*, 1990); and the painter Georgia O'Keeffe wrote, "I found that I could say things with color and shapes that I couldn't say any other way—things that I had no words for" (cited in *Alfred Stieglitz Presents One Hundred Pictures: Oils, Watercolors, Pastels, Drawings by Georgia O'Keeffe, American*, The Anderson Galleries, New York, exhibition brochure, January 29–February 10, 1923). Beyond specific categories, which seem more and more arbitrary as time goes on, we may say in basic, nonphilosophical terms that art has two components: FORM and CONTENT. We may also discuss its STYLE or PERIOD, or the artist's TECHNIQUE or use of the MEDIUM.

FORM. Referring to purely visual aspects of art and architecture, form includes LINE, SHAPE

COLOR, TEXTURE, SPATIAL QUALITIES, and COMPOSITION. These attributes are often referred to as formal elements. The study of formal elements is known as *formalism* or *formal analysis*.

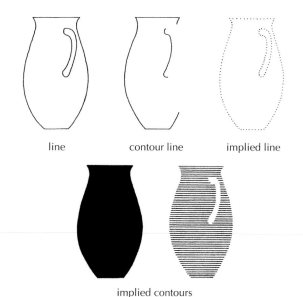

a. Aspects of line

Line is an element—usually drawn or painted—that creates *shape* with a more or less continuous mark (fig. a). *Contour* is the *outline*, whether actual or implied, that defines the outside borders of a shape. From a fixed viewpoint, even three-dimensional objects can be perceived as shapes with contours. The movement of the viewer's eyes over the surface of a work of art may follow a path determined by the artist and so create imaginary lines.

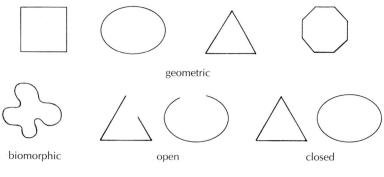

b. Shape

Shapes are often a kind of visual shorthand for the rendering of three-dimensional objects and can be *geometric, biomorphic, closed,* or *open* (fig. b). Biomorphic shapes are irregular in form and suggest living things.

Color has several attributes. These include HUE, VALUE, and INTENSITY.

HUE is what we think of when we hear the word *color,* and the terms are interchangeable. Colors are the result of differing wavelengths of the sun's electromagnetic energy. (That is why darkness is essentially colorless.) The visible spectrum, which you see in a bright rainbow, runs from red through violet and includes red, orange, yellow (which are warm hues) and green, blue, and violet (which are cool hues). We perceive warm hues as coming forward and cool hues as receding. Red, yellow, and blue are PRIMARY COLORS; the SECONDARY COLORS of orange, green, and violet occur in the visible spectrum between the primary hues. Instead of being hues, white and black are neutral.

VALUE is the relative degree of lightness or darkness in the range from white to black and is created by the amount of light reflected from an object's surface. A dark green has a deeper value than a light green, for example, and light gray has a lighter value than dark gray.

INTENSITY is the degree of purity or brightness of a hue and is also called *saturation* or *chroma.*

Texture is the tactile quality of a surface. It is perceived and described with words like *smooth, polished, satiny, rough, coarse,* or *oily.* Texture takes two forms: the texture of the actual surface of the work of art and the implied (imaginary) surface of the object the artist is representing.

Spatial qualities include MASS, VOLUME, and SPACE.

MASS and VOLUME are properties of three-dimensional objects that exist in space.

SPACE may be three-dimensional and actual, as with sculpture and architecture, or may be represented in two dimensions. Unfilled space is referred to as negative space; solids are referred to as positive space.

Composition is the organization, or arrangement, of form in a work of art.

PICTORIAL DEPTH (spatial recession) is a specialized aspect of composition in which the three-dimensional world is represented in two dimensions in paintings and drawings. Artists have used many methods to depict objects as

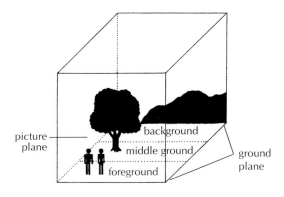

c. Schematic drawing of picture space

seeming to recede from the two-dimensional surface, called the PICTURE PLANE. The area "behind" the picture plane is called the PICTURE SPACE and conventionally contains three "zones": FOREGROUND, MIDDLE GROUND, and BACK-GROUND (fig. c). Perpendicular to the picture plane, forming the "floor" of the space, is the GROUND PLANE.

Various techniques for conveying a sense of pictorial depth have been preferred by artists in different cultures and at different times (fig. d).

CONTENT. Content is a less specific aspect of a work of art than is form. Content includes subject matter, which quite simply is what is represented, even when that consists strictly of lines and formal elements—lines and color without recognizable subject matter, for example. Content includes the ideas contained in a work. When used inclusively, the term *content* can embrace the social, political, and economic contexts in which a work was created, the intention of the artist, the reception of the be-holder (the audience) to the work, and ulti-mately the meaning in the work of art.

Iconography is the study of the art of rep-resentation by pictures, the "what" of subject

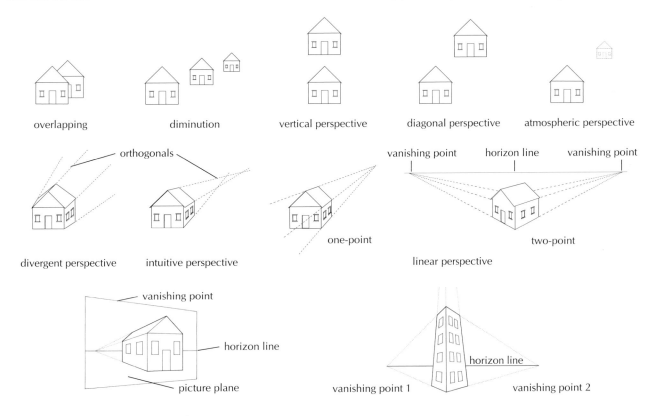

d. Pictorial devices for depicting recession in space

Among the simpler devices are OVERLAPPING, in which partially covered elements are meant to be seen as located behind those covering them, and DIMINUTION, in which smaller elements are meant to be perceived as being farther away than larger ones. In VERTICAL and DIAGONAL PERSPECTIVE, elements are stacked vertically or diagonally, with the higher elements meant to be perceived as deeper in space. Another way of suggesting depth is through ATMOSPHERIC PERSPECTIVE, which depicts objects in the far distance with less clarity than nearer objects, often in bluish gray hues, and treats the sky as paler near the horizon. For many centuries, DIVERGENT PERSPECTIVE, in which forms widen slightly and lines diverge as they recede in space, was used by East Asian artists. INTUITIVE PERSPECTIVE, such as that in some late medieval European art, uses the opposite: forms become more narrow and lines converge the farther away they are from the viewer, approximating the optical experience of spatial recession. LINEAR PERSPECTIVE, also called SCIENTIFIC, MATHEMATICAL, ONE-POINT, or RENAISSANCE PERSPECTIVE, is an elaboration and standardization of intuitive perspective and was developed in fifteenth-century Italy. It uses mathematical formulas to con-struct illusionistic images in which all elements are shaped by imaginary lines called ORTHOGONALS that converge in one or more VANISHING POINTS on a HORIZON LINE. Linear perspective is the system that most people in Euro-American cultures think of as perspective. Because it is the visual code they are accustomed to reading, they accept as "truth" the distortions it imposes, including FORESHORTENING, in which, for instance, the soles of the feet in the foreground are the largest element of a figure lying on the ground.

TECHNIQUE

LOST-WAX CASTING

The lost-wax casting process (also called *cire perdue*, the French term) has been used for many centuries. It probably started in Egypt. By 200 BCE the technique was known in China and ancient Mesopotamia and was soon after used by the Benin peoples in Africa. It spread to ancient Greece sometime in the sixth century BCE and came to be widespread in Europe. The usual metal is bronze, an alloy of copper and tin, or sometimes brass, an alloy of copper and zinc.

The progression of drawings here shows the steps used by Benin and other sculptors. A heat-resistant "core" of clay—approximating the shape of the sculpture-to-be (and eventually becoming the hollow inside the sculpture)—was covered by a layer of wax about the thickness of the final sculpture. The sculptor modeled the details in wax. Rods and a pouring cup made of wax were attached to the model. A thin layer of fine, damp sand was pressed very firmly into the surface of the wax model, and then model, rods, and cup were encased in thick layers of clay. When the clay was completely dry, the mold was heated to melt out the wax. The mold was then turned upside down to receive the molten metal, which, for the Benin, was brass, heated to the point of liquification. The cast was placed in the ground. When the metal was completely cool, the outside clay cast and the inside core were broken up and removed, leaving the cast brass sculpture. Details were polished to finish the piece of sculpture, which could not be duplicated because the mold had been destroyed in the process.

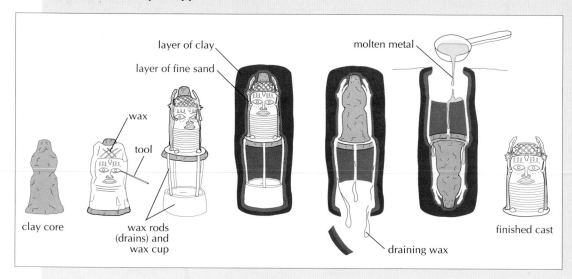

layer of clay

layer of fine sand

molten metal

wax

tool

clay core

wax rods (drains) and wax cup

draining wax

finished cast

matter. Iconology has come to mean the study of art in its cultural context, the study of the "why" of subject matter.

STYLE. Expressed very broadly, style is the consistent use of form and composition. Style does not depend on subject matter or content. Through style we recognize individual artists, places, and times.

Representational and **nonrepresentational style** (also called NONOBJECTIVE) refer to whether the subject matter is or is not recognizable.

Linear and **painterly** describe techniques and styles of painting. In the *linear* style, an artist uses line as the primary means of definition and a smooth sculptural modeling in which brushstrokes nearly disappear. When shadows and highlights brushed in freely with vigorous, defined strokes dominate, the style may be called *painterly*. Architecture and sculpture may be linear or painterly, too, as artists calculate the even or flickering play of light over surfaces.

Realistic, naturalistic, and **idealized** are often-found descriptions of style. REALISM is the attempt to depict objects as they are in actual, visible reality. NATURALISM is a style of depiction in which the physical appearance of the rendered image in nature is the primary inspiration. A work in a naturalistic style

resembles the original but not with the same exactitude and literalness as a work in a realistic style. IDEALIZATION strives for perfection that is grounded in prevailing values of a culture. Classical Greek sculpture is an example of art that is both naturalistic and idealized. In **abstract** art, the artist tries to capture the essence of an object or idea. Abstract artists observe nature or work from a memory image of forms in nature, often simplifying these forms to enhance their clarity and geometric simplicity. Prehistoric and Egyptian art is abstract in this way. When artists exaggerate formal expression to appeal to the subjective responses of beholders or to express their own subjective feelings, the art may be referred to as **expressionistic**.

PERIOD. A word often found in art historical writing, *period* means the historical era from which a work of art comes. It is good practice not to use the words *style* and *period* interchangeably. Style is the sum of many influences and characteristics, including the period of its creation. An example of good usage is: "an American house from the Colonial period built in the Georgian style."

MEDIUM (plural **media** or **mediums**). The materials and technical processes (TECHNIQUES) used to create works of art are important areas of study. Today, almost anything can be used by artists, including not only traditional paints and inks but rubbish, food, and the earth itself. When several media are used in a single work of art, we use the term *mixed-media.*

Mixed-media includes categories such as collage and assemblage in which the two-dimensional surface is built up from elements that may or may not be painted, such as pieces of paper or metal or garments.

Ephemeral arts include processions and festival decorations and costumes, performance art, earthworks, cinema, video art, and computer art, all of which have a central temporal aspect in that the artwork is viewable for a finite period of time and then disappears forever, is in a constant state of change, or must be replayed to be experienced.

Painting includes wall painting and fresco, illumination (decoration of books with paintings), panel painting (paintings on wood panels), miniature painting, handscroll and hanging scroll painting. One other kind, easel painting, can be easily transported to a variety of different settings because of the mobility of its support.

Drawings may be sketches (quick visual notes for larger drawings or paintings); studies (more carefully drawn analyses of details or entire compositions); cartoons (full-scale drawings made in preparation for work in another medium, such as fresco); or complete artworks in themselves.

Graphic arts refers to those branches of the arts that utilize paper as a primary support, such as drawing, writing, and printmaking (engraving, etching, lithography). Today, *graphic arts* often implies commercial design.

Sculpture is a three-dimensional work of art that is carved, modeled, or assembled. Carved sculpture is reductive in the sense that the image is created by taking material away. Wood and stone are carved. Modeled sculpture is considered additive, meaning that the object is built up from a material such as clay that is soft enough to be molded and shaped. Metal sculpture is usually cast (see "Lost-Wax Casting," page 14) or is assembled by welding or similar means of joining.

Sculpture is either FREESTANDING (sculpture in the round) or in RELIEF, which means projecting from the surface of which it is a part. Relief may be HIGH RELIEF, with parts of the

sculpture projecting far off the background, or LOW RELIEF, in which the projections are only slightly raised.

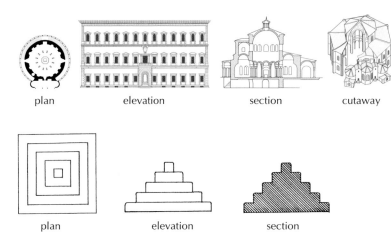

e. Schematic architectural drawings of different structures (*top*) and the same structure (*bottom*)

Architecture is three-dimensional and highly spatial, and it is closely bound up with developments in technology and materials. An example of the relationship among technology, materials, and function is illustrated by the box showing how space is spanned (see "Elements of Architecture," page 16).

Buildings are represented by a number of two-dimensional schematic drawings, including PLANS, ELEVATIONS, SECTIONS, and CUTAWAYS (fig. e). PLANS are imaginary slices through a building at approximately waist height. Everything below the slice is drawn as if looking straight down from above. ELEVATIONS are exterior sides of a building as if seen from a moderate distance but without any perspective distortion. SECTIONS are imaginary vertical slices from top to bottom through a building that reveal elements "cut" by the slice. CUT-AWAYS show both inside and outside elements from an oblique angle.

Other media. Besides painting, drawing, graphic arts, photography, sculpture, and architecture, works of art can be made in the media of ceramic and glass, textile and stitchery, metalwork and enamel, and many other materials.

Museums, Galleries, Art Centers, and Commercial Galleries

The museum, or "house of muses," originally sheltered books as well as works of art and provided space for scholars to study. Today, museums may be devoted to natural history, history, aviation, jazz, folklore—every kind of

Elements of Architecture

SPACE-SPANNING CONSTRUCTION DEVICES

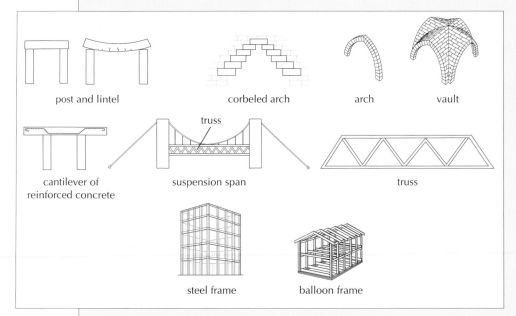

post and lintel corbeled arch arch vault

truss

cantilever of
reinforced concrete suspension span truss

steel frame balloon frame

Gravity presents great challenges to builders needing to cover spaces. The simplest space-spanning device is post-and-lintel construction, in which uprights are spanned by a horizontal element. However, a horizontal element over a wide span breaks under the pressure of its own weight and the weight it carries. The cantilever, in which one end of the horizontal element is weighted, is a variant of post-and-lintel construction.

Vaults, which are more difficult to build but more effective in spanning space, are essentially extended arches. Arches may be corbeled or built of trapezoidal blocks called *voussoirs*. Corbeling, the building up of overlapping stones, is a simple method of enclosing space. Vaulting requires highly skilled masons. Vaults, raised on walls or piers, like the arches of which they are formed, exert an outward thrust from voussoirs as well as reacting to the downward pull of gravity. Barrel vaults are tunnel-like. Cross or groin vaults consist of two barrel vaults meeting at right angles so that weight and outward thrust are concentrated at the outer corners. The dome, essentially an arch spun on its axis, is used today as much for its symbolic associations as for its structure.

Today, buildings are usually built of reinforced concrete or timber and wallboard. Steel-frame construction relies on steel's properties of strength and flexibility to bear great loads. When concrete is reinforced with steel or iron rods, the inherent brittleness of cement and stone is then overcome because of metal's flexible qualities. The timber balloon frame, an American innovation, is based on post-and-lintel principles and exploits the lightweight, flexible properties of wood.

collection—as well as to art. The word *gallery* is often reserved for collections of fine art. Originally, galleries were long rooms or corridors in European palaces where paintings and works of sculpture were displayed. You may find sections of museums called *galleries*, not all of which contain paintings and works of sculpture. Sometimes, the art collections you see are permanently owned or on permanent loan to a museum or gallery; sometimes the exhibition is temporary, with pieces on loan from other museums, collectors, or commercial galleries. Commercial galleries also show art. The difference is that they are in business to sell the art they show as well as the work of artists they represent. Many communities have art centers, where children and adults can see temporary exhibitions or take courses in art. Today, almost all museums, galleries, and art centers have an educational mission.

You do not need special training to visit an art museum, although planning can increase your enjoyment and deepen your rewards. This is especially true when you have only a little time available. Most museums provide information about their collections and programs in the form of brochures or guides to the collections, floor plans, and guided tours led by museum staff persons or trained volunteers—called *docents*—or even by portable audio devices. Increasing numbers of museums now have interactive programs that offer information about their holdings and help visitors find what they are looking for. Most major museums and many smaller ones now have websites that are very helpful in planning a museum visit.

Artworks are almost always labeled (see Reading Museum Labels, pages 434–435), and museums increasingly provide large-type wall texts that give general information about specific works. You may find that you experience a work of art more directly if you look at it before you read about it. Reading about art—whether in books, catalogs, on-line, or on museum walls and labels—supplements looking at art but never substitutes for experiencing the real work.

Use Notes

The various features of this book reinforce each other, helping you to become comfortable with terminology and concepts specific to art history.

Starter Kit and Introduction The Starter Kit is a concise primer of basic concepts and tools. The outside margins of the Starter Kit pages are tinted to make them easy to find. The Introduction that follows these Use Notes is an invitation to the pleasures of art history.

Captions There are two kinds of captions in this book: short and long. Short captions identify information specific to the work of art or architecture illustrated:

> artist (when known)
> title or descriptive name of work
> date
> original location
> material or materials a work is made of
> size (height before width) in feet and
>   inches, with centimeters and
>   meters in parentheses
> present location (if moved to a museum
>   or other site)

Dimensions are not given for architecture, for most wall painting, or for architectural sculpture. Some captions have one or more lines of small print below the identification section of the caption that gives museum or collection information.

Long captions contain information that complements the main text.

Definitions of Terms You will encounter the basic terms of art history in three places:

> IN THE TEXT, where words appearing in **boldface** type are defined, or used in context, on first use; some terms are explained more than once, especially those that experience shows are hard to remember.

> IN BOXED FEATURES on techniques and other subjects and in Elements of Architecture boxes, where labeled drawings and diagrams visually reinforce the use of terms.

IN THE GLOSSARY at the end of the volume, which contains all the words in **boldface** type in the text and boxes. The Glossary begins on page *Glossary* 1, and the outside margins are tinted to make the Glossary easy to find.

Chapter Opener Spreads The first two pages of every chapter are devoted to explaining topics and terms that are central to the study of art history. By using images from the chapter or from the period covered in the chapter to illustrate points, you will be able to see how terms and ideas are actually applied in art history. **Keys to Art History**, a boxed section, is a general discussion of the given topic in relation to the image or images.

Boxes Special material that complements, enhances, explains, or extends the text is set off in three types of tinted boxes. Elements of Architecture boxes clarify specifically architectural features, such as "Space-Spanning Construction Devices" in the Starter Kit (page 16). Technique boxes (see "Lost-Wax Casting," page 14) describe the way in which a given type of artwork is created. Other boxes treat special-interest material related to the text.

Selected Bibliography The Selected Bibliography, at the end of this book beginning on page *Bibliography* 1, contains books in English, organized by general works and by chapter, that are basic to the study of art history today.

Dates, Abbreviations, and Other Conventions This book uses the designations BCE and CE, abbreviations for "before the Common Era" and "Common Era," instead of BC ("before Christ") and AD ("Anno Domini," "the year of our Lord"). The first century BCE is the period from 99 BCE to 1 BCE; the first century CE is from the year 1 CE to 99 CE.

Circa ("about" or "approximately") is used with dates, spelled out in the text and abbreviated to "c." in the captions, when an exact date is not known.

An illustration is called a "figure," or "fig." Figure 6-25 is the twenty-fifth numbered illustration in Chapter 6. Figures 1 through 17 are in the Introduction (the Starter Kit illustrations are labeled with lowercase letters).

When introducing artists, we use the words *active* and *documented* with dates—in addition to "b." (for "born") and "d." (for "died"). "Active" means that an artist worked during the years given. "Documented" means that documents link the person to the date.

Accents are used for words in Spanish, Italian, French, and German only.

With few exceptions, names of museums and other cultural bodies in Western European countries are given in the form used in that country.

Titles of Works of Art Most paintings and sculpture created in Europe and the United States in the last 500 years have been given formal titles, either by the artist or by critics and art historians. Such formal titles are printed in italics. In other traditions and cultures, a single title is not important or even recognized. In this book we use formal titles of artworks in cases where they are established and descriptive titles of artworks where titles are not established. If a work is best known by its non-English title, such as Manet's *Le Déjeuner sur l'Herbe* (*The Luncheon on the Grass*), the original language precedes the translation.

INTRODUCTION

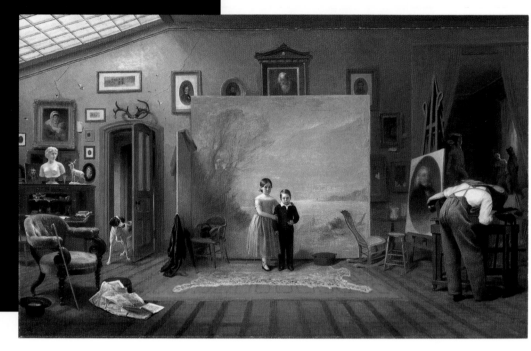

1. **Thomas LeClear.**
Interior with Portraits.
c. 1865. Oil on canvas,
25⁷/₈ x 40¹/₂"
(65.7 x 102.9 cm).
National Museum of
American Art,
Smithsonian Institution,
Washington, D.C.
Museum purchase made
possible by the
Pauline Edwards Bequest

Art and Reality

What is art? And what is reality? Today, when one can capture an image with a camera, why should one bother to draw or paint or carve? In the nineteenth-century painting *Interior with Portraits* (fig. 1), by the American artist Thomas LeClear (1818–1882), two children stand painfully still while a photographer prepares to take their picture. The paintings and sculpture that fill the studio have been moved aside to make way for the preparation of a new kind of art—the photograph. As the photographer adjusts the lens of his camera, we see his baggy pants but not his head. Is LeClear suggesting that the artist and the camera have become a single recording eye? Or is this painting a witty commentary on the nature of reality? Art history leads us to ask such questions.

LeClear's painting resembles a snapshot in its recording of studio clutter, but the artist made subtle changes to what he saw. He directed light on the girl and boy to focus attention on them rather than on the interesting and distracting objects that surround them. The light intensifies the brilliant coral and green color of the cloth on the floor; softer coral shades in the curtain and the upholstered chair frame the image. LeClear reminds us that art can also participate in illusion: the photograph will show the children in a vast landscape, but the painting reveals that the setting is only a two-dimensional painted backdrop. These observations make us realize that the painting is more than a portrait. The painting has become a commentary on the idea of the artist as a faithful recorder of reality.

Certainly there is more to this painting— and to most paintings—than first meets the eye. We can simply enjoy *Interior with Portraits* as a visually interesting record of nineteenth-century America, or we can study the history of the painting to probe deeper into its meaning. Who are the children? Why was their portrait painted? Who owned the painting? The answers to these questions lead us to doubt the reality of this seemingly "realistic" work.

Thomas LeClear worked in Buffalo, New York, from 1847 to 1863. The painting, which is now in the National Museum of American Art in Washington, D.C., once belonged to the Sidway family of Buffalo. Family records show that the girl in the painting, Parnell Sidway, died in 1849; the boy, her younger brother James Sidway, died in 1865. Evidence suggests that the painting was not made until the 1860s, well after Parnell's death and when James was a grown man, or possibly after his death, too. How do experts arrive at a date in the 1860s for the painting? LeClear moved to New York City in 1863, and the studio seen in the painting resembles the one he borrowed from his son-in-law there. Another clue to the painting's date is the camera, which is a type that was not used before 1860. The Sidway children, then, could never have

2. **Titian (formerly attributed to Giorgione).** *Pastoral Concert.* c. 1509–10. Oil on canvas, 43¹/₄ x 54³/₈" (109.9 x 138.1 cm). The Louvre, Paris

posed for this painting. It must, instead, be a memorial portrait, perhaps painted by LeClear from a photograph. In short, this image of "reality" does not correspond to real events in time and cannot be "real." Art historical research reveals a different story entirely from what uninformed observation of the painting alone suggests.

This new knowledge leads us to further speculate on the nature of art and the intentions of the artist. If this is a memorial portrait re-creating a vanished childhood, is it also a reflection on life and death, on the passage of time? The ambiguities we noticed before—the contrast between the reality of the studio and the painted landscape, the juxtaposition of the new medium of photography with the old-fashioned painted portrait on an easel—take on deeper significance. LeClear seems to be commenting on the tension between nature and art, on art and reality, and on the role of the artist as a recording eye and controlling imagination.

But what about the reality of photographs? Today the camera has become a universal tool for picture making. Even though we know that film can be manipulated and photographs made to lie, we generally accept the idea that the camera tells the truth. We forget that in a photograph a vibrant, moving, three-dimensional world has been immobilized, reduced to two dimensions, and often recorded in black and white.

An artist's vision can turn the everyday world into a superior reality—more imaginative, per-

haps more focused or intense, than we know it. Artists often try to paint even more than the eye can see, relying on the viewer to understand the messages they convey through the use of symbols or other visual clues. Thus even apparently "realistic" paintings can present challenges to viewers unfamiliar with the artist's intent.

Art and the Idea of Beauty

For thousands of years, people have sought to create objects of beauty and significance that did more than simply help them survive. The concept of beauty has found expression in a variety of **styles**, or manners of representation. The painting of horses, bison, and other animals recently discovered in a limestone cavern near the Ardèche River in France exhibits an **abstract** style (see fig. 1-6). These remarkable images, preserved over time in their remote cavern, were created some 30,000 years ago. The painters have simplified the shapes, eliminated all but the essentials, and emphasized the abstract beauty of the animal silhouettes against the walls of the cave. But of the artists' intention as they worked, we have no idea. That such representations were made at all is evidence of a uniquely human trait, the ability to engage in impractical activities (such as playing games) that are nonessential to daily life.

In contrast to the wall painting, the painting by LeClear exemplifies a style or mode of expression known as **realism**. Realistic art, even if it represents an imagined or supernatural sub-

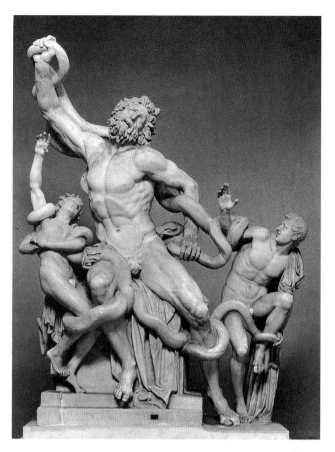

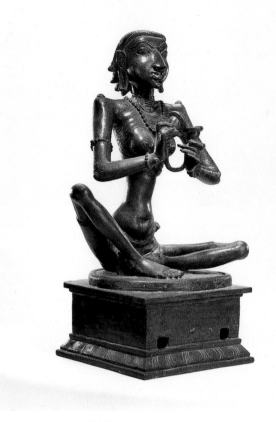

3. Hagesandros, Polydoros, and Athanadoros of Rhodes. *Laocoön and His Sons,* perhaps the original of the 2nd or 1st century BCE or a Roman copy of the 1st century CE. Marble, height 8' (2.44 m). Musei Vaticani, Museo Pio Clementino, Cortile Ottagono, Rome

4. *Punitavati (Karaikkalammaiyar),* Shiva saint, from Karaikkal, India. 15th century. Bronze, height 16¼" (41.3 cm). The Nelson-Atkins Museum of Art, Kansas City, Missouri
Purchase: Nelson Trust (33-533)

ject, has a surface reality; the artist appears, with greater or lesser accuracy, to be recording exactly what he or she sees. Realistic art, as we have noted, can carry complex messages and be open to individual interpretation.

Realism and abstraction represent opposite approaches to the representation of beauty. In a third style, called **idealism**, artists represent things not as they are but as they ought to be. In ancient Greece and Rome, artists observed the world around them and then subjected their findings to mathematical analysis in an effort to define perfect forms. The term *Classical,* which refers to the period in ancient Greek history when this type of idealism emerged (480–320 BCE), has come to be used broadly (and with a lowercase *c*) to mean the peak of perfection in any period.

Sixteenth-century Italian artists also created ideal images in their works of art. The Venetian Renaissance painter Titian (c. 1478?–1576) imagined a new classical age of innocence and idealism when he painted his *Pastoral Concert* (fig. 2). Elegantly dressed musicians and voluptuous women engage in idle activities in a utopian landscape. Their graceful poses and elegant drapery seem at the same time ideally perfect and perfectly natural. The lush foliage of the setting reflects the opulence of flesh and drapery. The painting defies complete explanation. Evok-

ing a golden age of love and innocence, Titian's painting style seems perfectly suited to capturing such an idyllic time and space.

The flawless perfection of classical idealism could be dramatically modified by artists more concerned with emotion than pure form. This can be seen in a melodramatic representation of a story from the ancient Greek legend of the Trojan War. The priest Laocoön, who attempted to warn the Trojans about the Greeks, was strangled by serpents, along with his two sons (fig. 3). In the sculpture, his features are twisted in agony, and the muscles of his superhuman torso and arms extend and knot as he struggles. This work, rediscovered in Rome in the 1500s at least sixteen centuries after its creation, inspired artists such as Michelangelo to develop a heroic style.

Through the centuries, people have returned again and again to the ideals of classical art. In the United States, official sculpture and architecture are often modeled on classical forms. Even the National Museum of American Art is housed behind a Greek pediment and Doric columns (see fig. 8).

How different from this ideal of physical beauty the perception and representation of spiritual beauty can be. A fifteenth-century bronze sculpture from India represents Punitavati, a beautiful and generous woman who was deeply devoted to the Hindu god Shiva (fig. 4).

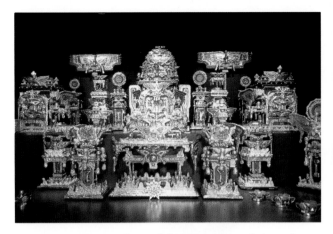

5. James Hampton. *Throne of the Third Heaven of the Nations' Millennium General Assembly*. c. 1950–64. Gold and silver aluminum foil, colored Kraft paper, and plastic sheets over wood, paperboard, and glass, 10'6" x 27' x 14'6" (3.20 x 8.23 x 4.42 m). National Museum of American Art, Smithsonian Institution, Washington, D.C.

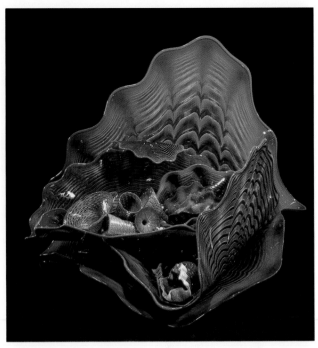

6. Dale Chihuly. *Violet Persian Set with Red Lip Wraps*. 1990. Glass, 26 x 30 x 25" (66.0 x 76.2 x 63.5 cm). Spencer Museum of Art, University of Kansas, Lawrence Peter T. Bohan Acquisition Fund

Abandoned by her greedy husband because she fed the beggars, Punitavati offered her beauty to Shiva. Shiva accepted her offering but turned her into an emaciated, fanged hag. According to legend, Punitavati, with clanging cymbals, provides the music for Shiva as he dances the cosmic dance of destruction and creation that keeps the universe in motion. To the followers of Shiva, Punitavati became a saint. The bronze sculpture, although it depicts Punitavati after her transformation, is nevertheless beautiful both for its formal qualities and for its message of generosity and self-sacrifice.

Some works of art defy simple categories, especially when artists go to extraordinary lengths to represent their visions. James Hampton (1909–1964) composed his *Throne of the Third Heaven of the Nations' Millennium General Assembly* (fig. 5) using discarded furniture, spent flashbulbs, and all sorts of trash, tacked together and wrapped in silver and gold foil and purple paper. Hampton's inspiration, whether divine or not, knew no bounds. The critic Robert Hughes called Hampton's work "the finest piece of visionary art produced by an American." Hampton worked as a janitor to support himself while he built this monument to Christ. Thrones and altars to Jesus and Moses rise in tiers: the New Testament at the right, the Old Testament at the left. Hampton labeled and described everything in a language and writing system of his own invention. Although this language is still not fully understood, its major source is the Bible, especially the Book of Revelation. On one of many placards he wrote his artist's credo: "Where there is no vision, the people perish" (Proverbs 29:18).

These divergent ideas of art and beauty remind us that as viewers we enter into an agreement with artists, who, in turn, make special demands on us. We re-create works of art for ourselves as we bring to them our own experiences. Without our participation they are only hunks of stone or metal or pieces of paper or canvas covered with ink or colored paints.

In this book we study the history of art from around the world from earliest times to the present. Although we treat Western art in the most detail, we also look extensively at the art of other regions. The qualities of a work of art, the artist who made it, the patron who paid for it, the audiences who have viewed it, and the places in which it has been displayed—all are considered in our study of art's history.

Artists

We have focused so far on works of art. What of the artists who make the art? Originally artists were considered artisans. Often they worked in anonymous teams to produce great buildings, paintings, and such adornments as stained glass. The head of the workshop was the controlling intellect, the organizer, and the inspiration for others. The same spirit is evident today in the creations of Dale Chihuly (b. 1941), who has a team of artist-craftspeople skilled in the ancient art of glassmaking but remains his studio's guiding imagination. Once created, his pieces can be transformed by their owners. *Violet Persian Set with Red Lip Wraps* (fig. 6) has twenty separate pieces whose relationship to each other depends on the whim and eye of the assembler. Artists, artisans, and patrons unite in an ever-changing individual yet communal act of creation.

During the Renaissance, around the time of Titian (see fig. 2), artists in western Europe, especially in Italy, began to think of themselves as inspired creative geniuses rather than as

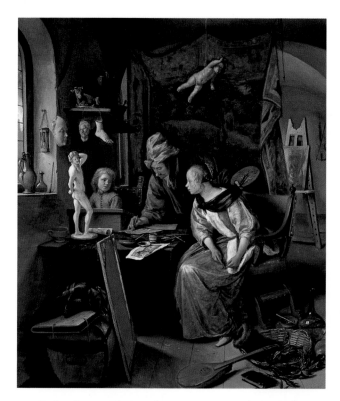

7. Jan Steen. *The Drawing Lesson*. 1665. Oil on wood, 19⅜ x 16¼" (49.2 x 41.3 cm). The J. Paul Getty Museum, Los Angeles, California

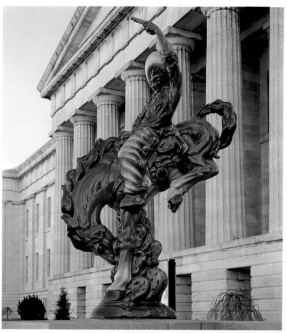

8. Luis Jimenez. *Vaquero*. Modeled 1980, cast 1990. Cast fiberglass and epoxy, height 16'6" (5.03 m). National Museum of American Art, Smithsonian Institution, Washington, D.C.

This white-hatted, gun-slinging bronco buster whoops it up in front of the stately, classical colonnade of the Old Patent Building (now the National Museum of American Art, the National Portrait Gallery, and the Archives of American Art). The Old Patent Office was designed in 1836 and finished in 1867. One of the finest Neoclassical buildings in the United States and the site of Abraham Lincoln's second inaugural ball, it was supposed to be destroyed for a parking lot, but it was acquired by the Smithsonian in 1958.

team workers. But even the most inspired artists had to learn their trade through study or years of apprenticeship to a master. In his painting *The Drawing Lesson* (fig. 7), Dutch artist Jan Steen (1626–1679) takes us into an artist's studio where an apprentice watches his master teaching a young woman. The woman has been drawing from a sculpture because women then were not permitted to work from live nude models. Like Thomas LeClear's painting of the photographer's studio, *The Drawing Lesson* is a valuable record of an artist's workplace and equipment, including such things as the musical instruments, furniture, glass, ceramics, and basketry used in the seventeenth century.

The painting is more than a realistic **genre painting** (scene from daily life) or **still life** (arrangement of objects). *The Drawing Lesson* is also an **allegory**, or symbolic representation, of the arts. The objects in the studio symbolize painting, sculpture, and music. The bookend on the high shelf is in the form of an ox, the symbol of Saint Luke, the patron saint of painters. The basket in the foreground holds not only a woman's fur muff but also a laurel wreath, the classical symbol for excellence. Today many viewers may not recognize these symbols or understand the sense that Steen wanted to convey. It has always been true that an artist's motivation or intention may be quite different from the public perception of his or her creations.

Artists and Art History

Artists draw on their predecessors in ways that make each work a very personal interpretation of

the history of art. The influence of Jan Steen's genre paintings, for example, can be seen in Thomas LeClear's *Interior with Portraits* (see fig. 1). Titian called on his knowledge of earlier classical and Italian Renaissance art in his painting of the *Pastoral Concert* (see fig. 2). In his sculpture *Vaquero* (Cowboy), Luis Jimenez (b. 1940), an artist of Mexican and Texan heritage, draws in part on the tradition of Hispanic-American art to revitalize a sculptural form with roots in antiquity—the equestrian monument, or statue of a horse and rider (fig. 8). Traditionally, equestrian statues have stood as symbols of power and authority. The rider's command over the animal is emblematic of human control over lesser beings, nature, and human passions. Jimenez's bucking bronco turns this tradition, or at least the horse, on its head. The horse and cowboy, united in a single exuberant and dynamic force, can be seen as a witty satire on sober bronze monuments to generals and monarchs. At the same time, the sculpture reminds us that real *vaqueros* included hardworking African Americans and Hispanic Americans who had as little in common with the cowboys of popular fiction as they did with monumental bronzes.

Jimenez surprises us with his choice of material for his equestrian monument: fiberglass

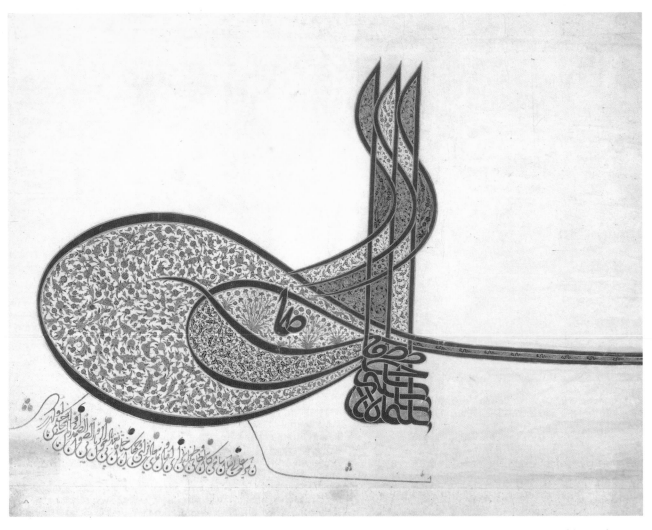

9. Illuminated *tugra* of Sultan Suleyman, from Istanbul, Turkey. c. 1555–60. Ink, paint, and gold on paper, removed from a firman (official document) and trimmed to 20¹/₂ x 25³/₈" (52.1 x 64.5 cm). The Metropolitan Museum of Art, New York
Rogers Fund, 1938 (38.149.1)

rather than the traditional bronze or marble. He first models a sculpture in a plastic paste called Plasticine on a steel armature. Then he makes a fiberglass mold, from which he casts the final sculpture, also in fiberglass. The materials and processes are the same as those used to make automobile bodies. After assembling and polishing a sculpture, Jimenez sprays it with the kind of acrylic urethane used to coat the outside of jet airplanes. Then he applies colors with an airbrush and finally coats the finished sculpture with three more layers of acrylic urethane to protect the color and play up its distinctive, sleek, gleaming surface. When asked how to care for the outdoor piece, he recommended a wash-and-wax job, just as one would care for a car. In *Vaquero* Jimenez has created a true popular art that appeals to every kind of viewer from the rancher to the connoisseur.

When artists appropriate and transform images from the past in the way Jimenez appropriated the equestrian form, they enrich the **aesthetic** vocabulary of the arts in general. *Vaquero* resonates through the ages with associations to cultures distant in time and place, giving it added meaning.

Art and Society

The arts can also be enlisted to serve social ends, in ways that range from heavy-handed propaganda to more subtle forms of persuasion. In sixteenth-century Turkey, the Ottoman Turks put calligraphy (the art of writing) to political use by making the design of imperial emblems, or *tugras*, into a specialized art form. Ottoman *tugras* symbolized the authority of the sultan (ruler) by combining the ruler's name, title, father's name, and the motto "Eternally Victorious" into a monogram. *Tugras* appeared on seals, coins, and buildings, as well as on official documents and imperial edicts.

The rare, oversized *tugra* of the powerful Ottoman sultan Suleyman (fig. 9) required unusual skill to execute. The underlying structure consists of three long, vertical strokes to the right of two horizontal teardrops, one inside the other. The sweeping, fluid lines had to be drawn with perfect control according to set proportions, and a mistake meant starting over. The delicate floral interlace enclosed by the sweeping calligraphic lines was inspired by similar patterns on ceramics and textiles. The Ottoman *tugra* is a sophisticated merging of abstract calligraphy and natural plant forms. As a symbol of political power it served a utilitarian function, while its graceful ornament suggested an informed patronage. This *tugra* authenticated a document endowing an institution in Jerusalem that had been established by Suleyman's wife, Sultana Hurrem.

Of course, the visual arts shape and are shaped by the social context in which they find expression. We might consider, for example, the fifteenth-century *Ghent Altarpiece* (fig. 10), by Jan van Eyck (c. 1370/90–1441). The altarpiece, designed to stand above and behind an altar in a Catholic church, is made up of a group of painted wooden panels in a frame. The panels visible here can be opened outwards to show more painted scenes inside (see fig. 11-3). While we can enjoy the painting, colors, and arrangement of shapes in this altarpiece without any prior knowledge, we must study the work's cultural context if we want to understand it fully.

Jan van Eyck lived in the wealthy city of Bruges, in what is now Belgium, in the first half of the fifteenth century. The niches, with their decorative arches and the room portrayed in the closed altarpiece, reflect the architecture Jan van Eyck saw around him in Bruges. The man and woman in the lower left and right panels wear fashionable contemporary dress, but other figures seem to have wandered in from other times and places. The two central figures in the bottom row are statues on pedestals rather than real people. Above them kneel two apparently supernatural figures—a winged angel and a young woman who has a dove with a halo hovering above her head. Four more figures in exotic dress crown the work. Scrolls bearing words in Latin float above each of these personages, curling decoratively to fit within the boundaries of the frame.

Clearly something strange and wonderful is happening, but only if we know something about the symbols, or **iconography**, of Christian art does the meaning of this painting become clear. The scene in the middle row of panels is the Annunciation, the moment when the angel

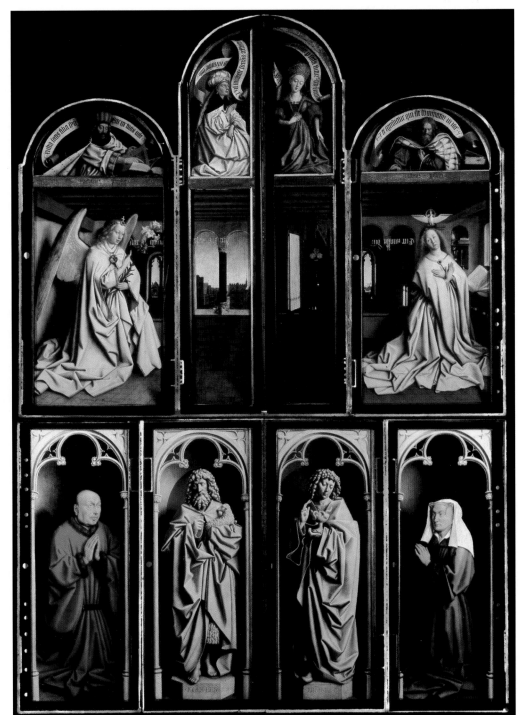

10. Jan van Eyck. *Ghent Altarpiece* (closed), Cathedral of Saint-Bavo, Ghent, Flanders (Belgium). 1432. Oil on panel, 11'5¾" x 7'6¾" (3.5 x 2.3 m)

Gabriel tells the Virgin Mary that she will bear Jesus, the Son of God (recounted in the New Testament of the Christian Bible, Luke 1:26–38). In the panels above are ancient sibyls (prophetesses) and Old Testament prophets who foretold the coming of Christ. The Latin inscriptions above them are lines from their prophecies. On the lowest row of outer panels are the donors, Jodocus Vijd and his wife, who paid for daily masses to be celebrated at the altar. They kneel in prayer on either side of statues of Saint John the Baptist and Saint John the Evangelist, the patron saints of the church for which the artwork was made.

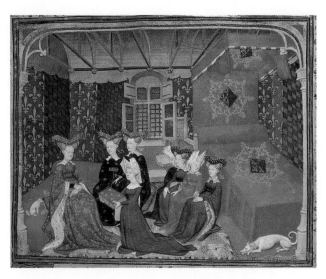

11. *Christine Presenting Her Book to the Queen of France.* 1410–15. Tempera and gold on vellum, image approx. 5¹/₂ x 6³/₄" (14 x 17 cm). The British Library, London MS. Harley 4431, folio 3

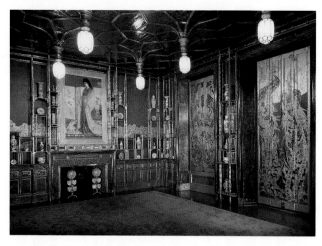

12. James McNeill Whistler. *Harmony in Blue and Gold.* The Peacock Room, northeast corner, from a house owned by Frederick Leyland, London. 1876–77. Oil paint and metal leaf on canvas, leather, and wood, 13'11⁷/₈" x 33'2" x 19'11¹/₂" (4.26 x 10.11 x 6.08 m). Freer Gallery, Smithsonian Institution, Washington, D.C. (04.61)

All the details have a meaning. The lamb Saint John the Baptist holds is a reference to Jesus, who is sometimes called the Lamb of God (John 1:29). Saint John the Evangelist, one of Jesus' apostles, holds a cup with a snake, a symbol of his escape from poisoning. According to legend, when the Roman emperor Domitian ordered John to drink poisoned wine, the poison disappeared from the liquid in the form of a snake. The dove above the Virgin's head symbolizes the Holy Spirit and Mary's role as the mother of God, and the lilies Gabriel holds are symbols of Mary's purity. The fifteenth-century architectural setting suggests that Mary also represents the new Christian Church.

Artists and Patrons

Patrons of art constitute a very special kind of audience for the artist. Patrons provide economic support for art and vicariously participate in its creation. Rare, valuable, beautiful, and strange things appeal to human curiosity. People who are not artists "use" art, too. They have collected special objects since prehistoric times, when people buried the dead with necklaces of fox teeth. Collections of "curiosities" were passed along from one generation to the next, gaining luster or mysterious power with age. Art enhanced the owner's prestige, created an aura of power and importance, and impressed others. Many collectors truly love the arts. When collectors diligently study the art they collect, they become scholars. When their expertise turns to questions of refined evaluation, of taste and aesthetics, they become what we call **connoisseurs**.

In earlier periods, artists depended on the patronage of the individuals and the institutions they represented. An illustrated book contemporary with the Ghent altarpiece shows the French writer Christine de Pisan presenting her work to Isabeau of Bavaria, the queen of France (fig. 11). Christine was a patron herself, for she hired painters and scribes to assist her. She especially admired the painting of a woman named Anastaise, whose work she considered unsurpassed in the city of Paris. Christine believed Paris had the world's best painters of miniatures.

Christine, Isabeau, the Vijds (donors of the Ghent altarpiece) all appear as generous and pious patrons. Relations between artists and patrons are not always harmonious. In the late nineteenth century, the Liverpool shipping magnate Frederick Leyland asked James McNeill Whistler (1834–1903), an American painter living in London, what color to paint the shutters in the dining room where he planned to hang Whistler's painting *The Princess from the Land of Porcelain.* The room had been decorated with expensive embossed and gilded leather as well as special shelves to show off Leyland's collection of Asian blue-and-white porcelain. Whistler, inspired by the porcelain and by the Japanese theme of his own painting, painted the window shutters with splendid turquoise, blue, and gold peacocks. Then, while Leyland was away, he painted the entire room (fig. 12), replacing the gilded leather on the walls with turquoise peacock feathers.

Leyland was shocked and angry when he returned and saw the results. Whistler memorialized the confrontation with his employer by painting a pair of fighting peacocks on one wall of the room. One of the peacocks, standing on a pile of coins, represents the tightfisted patron. The Peacock Room, which Whistler called *Harmony in Blue and Gold,* is an extraordinary example of total design, and Leyland did not change it. The American collector Henry Freer, who sought to unite the aesthetics of East Asia and the

West, later acquired the room and donated it on his death to a museum in the Smithsonian Institution in Washington, D.C., where it can now be appreciated by all. Today museums are the primary collectors and preservers, and even patrons, of art.

The Keepers of Art: Museums

An art museum can be thought of in two ways: as a scholarly research institution where curators, or keepers, care for and study their collections and teach new scholar-curators, and as a public institution dedicated to exhibiting and explaining the collections. Today museums with good collections are widespread, and one does not have to live in a major population center to experience wonderful art. Of the works illustrated in this chapter, five are located in midwestern American museums. No one would assert that Kansas City, for example, is the art capital of the world; the point is that encounters with works of art are not out of most people's range. And no matter how faithful the quality of reproductions, there is no substitute for a "live interview" with an actual work of art or architecture.

The display of artworks is a major challenge for curators. Art must be put on public view in a way that ensures its safety and also enhances its qualities and clarifies its significance. At the Nelson-Atkins Museum of Art in Kansas City, a polychromed and gilded wooden bodhisattva, or enlightened being, sits majestically in front of a mural painting of the Buddha (fig. 13). Together, the sculpture and painting form a magnificent ensemble of Chinese art, placed in a re-created temple setting with screens from the seventeenth century. The curators established an environment that recalls the religious context of the art, subtly emphasizes its importance, and provides it with a measure of security.

The Seattle Art Museum took a different tack; it had different problems to solve. Its carved-stone Chinese tomb figures were weather-beaten and moss-covered after standing outdoors in a park for years. The museum's new building, designed by Robert Venturi (b. 1925) and Denise Scott Brown (b. 1931) and finished in 1991, has a monumental staircase that unites the museum interior with the steep city street outside. The figures, cleaned and restored, now stand on the stairs like welcoming guardians for the galleries above (fig. 14). Set under colorful festive arches, they provide a grand and semi-serious contrast to the witty, theatrical, and "irreverent" architecture (the museum coffee shop interrupts their stately procession). They also serve as an appropriate symbol for a city that prides itself as a link between East and West.

Equally witty and irreverent is the way the Swedish-born Claes Oldenburg (b. 1929) has turned the Nelson-Atkins Museum of Art in

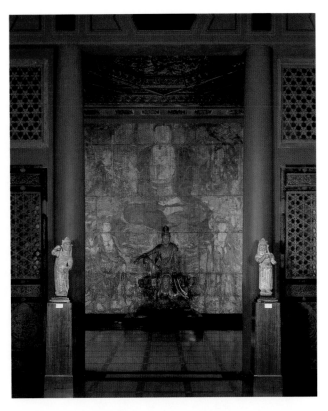

13. *The Water and Moon Kuan-yin Bodhisattva.* Northern Sung or Liao dynasty, 11th–12th century. Wood with paint, height 7'11" (2.41 m). Mural painting, 14th century; wooden screens, 17th century. The Nelson-Atkins Museum of Art, Kansas City, Missouri
Purchase: Nelson Trust (34.10)

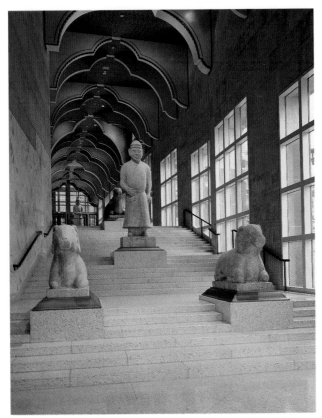

14. Robert Venturi and Denise Scott Brown. Stair Hall with Ming dynasty tomb figures, Seattle Art Museum. 1986–91

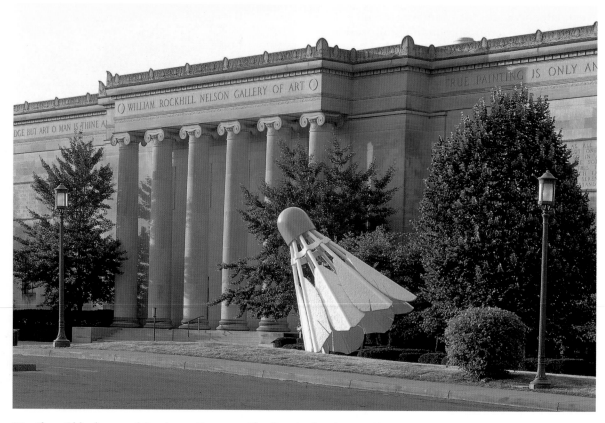

15. **Claes Oldenburg and Coosje van Bruggen. Shuttlecocks**, detail, one of four. 1994. Aluminum and fiberglass-reinforced plastic, painted with polyurethane enamel, height of each figure 17'10½" (5.45 m). The Nelson-Atkins Museum of Art, Kansas City, Missouri
Purchase: acquired through the generosity of the Sosland Family

Kansas City, Missouri, into a giant badminton net. Oldenburg both embraces and parodies popular culture with immensely oversized renditions of common objects—a lipstick, a trowel, a clothespin. Badminton birdies provided the inspiration for *Shuttlecocks* (fig. 15), made with Coosje van Bruggen (b. 1942), Oldenburg's wife and collaborator since 1977. The museum itself takes the place of a badminton net between the four colossal shuttlecocks arranged on its front and back lawns. Many have seen in the shuttlecocks a reflection of the Native Amerindian art of the region; the array of feathers recalls the eagle-feather headdresses of Plains Indian warriors. Finally, *Shuttlecocks* unites art, architecture, and the city, luring people into the museum building with an implied promise of relaxed recreation.

"I Know What I Like"

In our involvement with art, at first we may react instinctively to a painting or building or photograph. This level of "feeling" about art—"I know what I like"—ultimately can never be fully satisfying. Our opinions about art change over time, as we learn and understand more about what we see. Agreement as to what constitutes a work of art also changes over time. Impressionist paintings of the late nineteenth century,

now among the most avidly sought and widely collected, were laughed at when first displayed. They seemed like rough and unfinished "impressions" rather than the careful depictions of the visible world of nature people then expected to see. Claude Monet (1840–1926) in his *Boulevard des Capucines, Paris* (fig. 16) recorded immediate visual sensations with flecks of color rather than by drawing the forms of branches and leaves and dark-clothed figures. When the critic Louis Leroy reviewed this painting the first time Monet exhibited it, he sneered: "Only, be so good as to tell me what those innumerable black tongue-lickings in the lower part of the picture represent?" (*Le Charivari*, April 25, 1874). Today we easily see—not "black tongue-lickings"—but a street in early spring filled with horse-drawn cabs, strolling men and women, and a balloon seller.

Art history, in contrast with art criticism, combines analysis of visual elements in the work of art with the study of the work's broad historical context. Art historians draw on biography to learn about artists' lives; social history to understand the economic and political forces shaping artists, their patrons, and their public; and the history of ideas to gain an understanding of the intellectual currents influencing artists' works. They also study the history of other arts, includ-

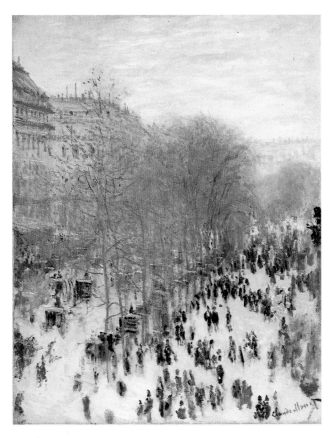

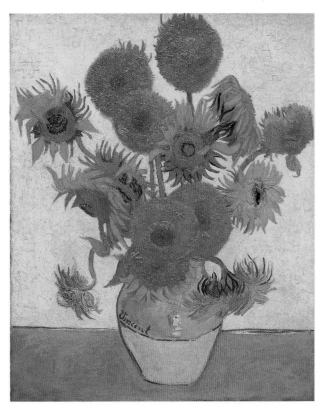

16. Claude Monet. *Boulevard des Capucines, Paris.* 1873–74. Oil on canvas, 31¼ x 23¼" (79.4 x 59.1 cm). The Nelson-Atkins Museum of Art, Kansas City, Missouri
Purchase: the Kenneth A. and Helen F. Spencer Foundation Acquisition Fund (F72-35)

17. Vincent van Gogh. *Sunflowers.* 1888. Oil on canvas, 36¼ x 28¾" (92.1 x 73 cm). The National Gallery, London

ing music, drama, and literature, to gain a richer sense of the context of the visual arts. Every artwork presents a new challenge. Even a glowing painting like *Sunflowers* (fig. 17), by Vincent van Gogh (1853–1890)—to which we may react with spontaneous enthusiasm—forces us to think about art, as well as our feelings about it.

Our first reaction is that *Sunflowers* is a joyous and colorful painting of a simple subject. Art history makes us search for more. The brilliant yellow ground that looks flat in a reproduction of the painting is actually richly built up with thick paint. So carefully placed are the small brushstrokes that the surface resembles a tightly woven basket or textile. Van Gogh suggested the space by two bands of yellow ocher of different intensity, separated by just the narrowest blue line, the color of maximum contrast with the golden orange. In fact, there is no sense of space, no setting; we imagine a table, a sun-filled room. But did Van Gogh see a pot of flowers on a table—or did he see them on a windowsill, against the blazing, shimmering heat and light of the true sun? He had a troubled life, and that knowledge makes us reflect on the possible meaning of the painting to him, for despite its brightness, it seems to reveal something ominous, a foreboding of the artist's loneliness and despair to come.

As viewers, we re-create a work of art as we bring to it our own experiences, and its meaning changes from individual to individual, from era to era. Once we welcome the arts into our life, we have a ready source of sustenance and challenge that grows, changes, mellows, and enriches our daily experience. No matter how much we study or read about art and artists, eventually we return to the contemplation of the work of art itself, for art is the tangible evidence of the ever-questing human spirit.

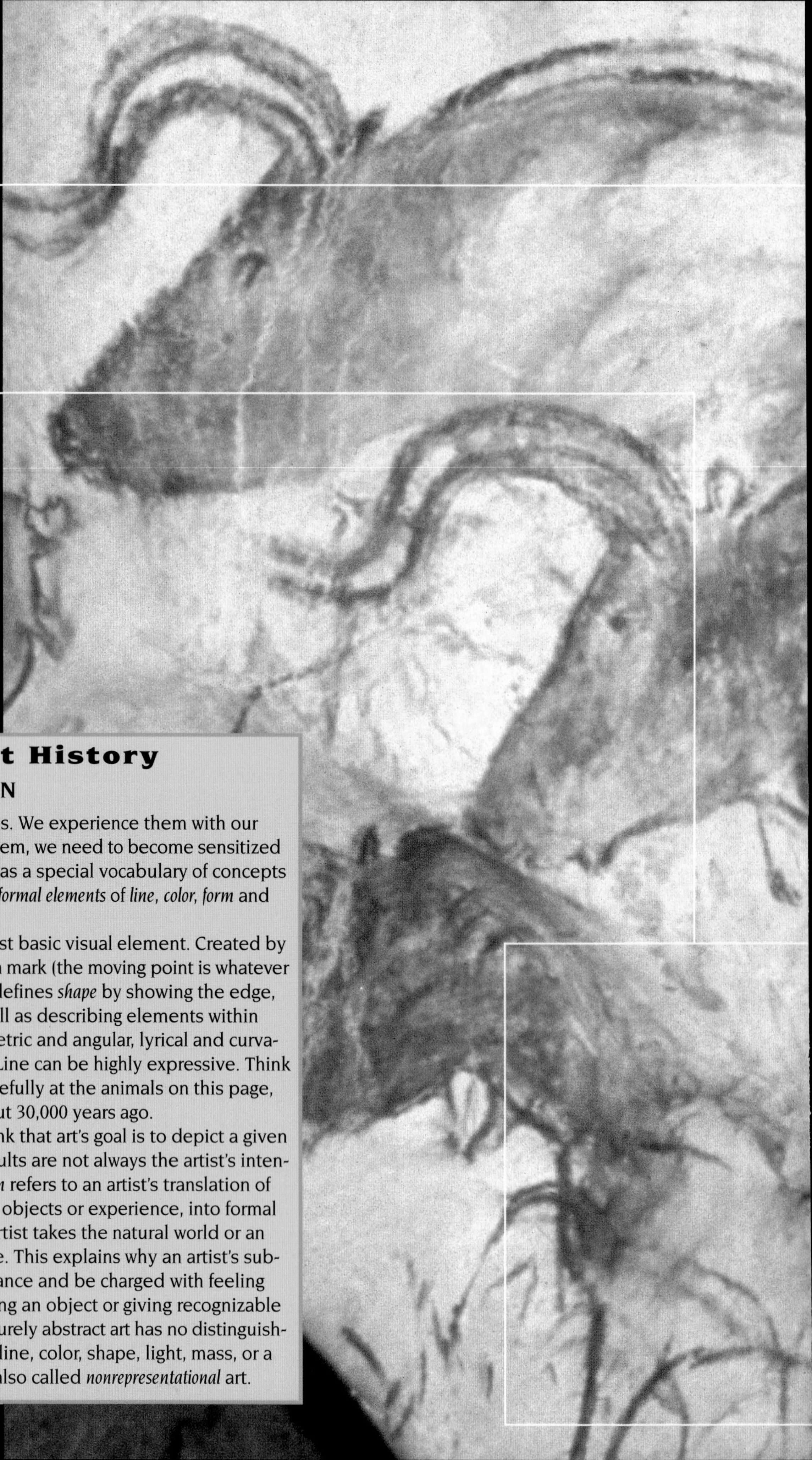

Representational Images

The artist or artists who painted on the walls of Chauvet cave 30,000 years ago made very recognizable pictures of animals. We see here rhinos, horses, and aurochs (extinct European wild oxen, the ancestors of domesticated cattle).

Abstraction

These painters have used an abstract style: they drew and painted profiles without fine details or imitative color. Note, however, that horns and legs are staggered so we can see each animal's most important features or attributes. Artists employed *abstraction* to create *memory images* of these wild creatures. Memory images are the generalized, collective impressions agreed on by a society.

K E Y S to Art History

LINE & ABSTRACTION

Artworks are visual creations. We experience them with our eyes and mind. To "read" them, we need to become sensitized to their "language," which has a special vocabulary of concepts and terms that include the *formal elements* of *line, color, form* and *shape, mass* and *volume.*

Line is probably the most basic visual element. Created by a moving point that leaves a mark (the moving point is whatever the artist draws with), line defines *shape* by showing the edge, or *outline,* of an object as well as describing elements within a shape. Line can be geometric and angular, lyrical and curvaceous, restless or languid. Line can be highly expressive. Think of comic strips and look carefully at the animals on this page, painted on a cave wall about 30,000 years ago.

While some people think that art's goal is to depict a given object or scene, lifelike results are not always the artist's intention. Very broadly, *abstraction* refers to an artist's translation of "reality," whether of visible objects or experience, into formal elements. Actually, every artist takes the natural world or an idea as a point of departure. This explains why an artist's subject matter may have relevance and be charged with feeling while not faithfully mimicking an object or giving recognizable form to an idea or feeling. Purely abstract art has no distinguishable subject matter—only line, color, shape, light, mass, or a combination of these. It is also called *nonrepresentational* art.

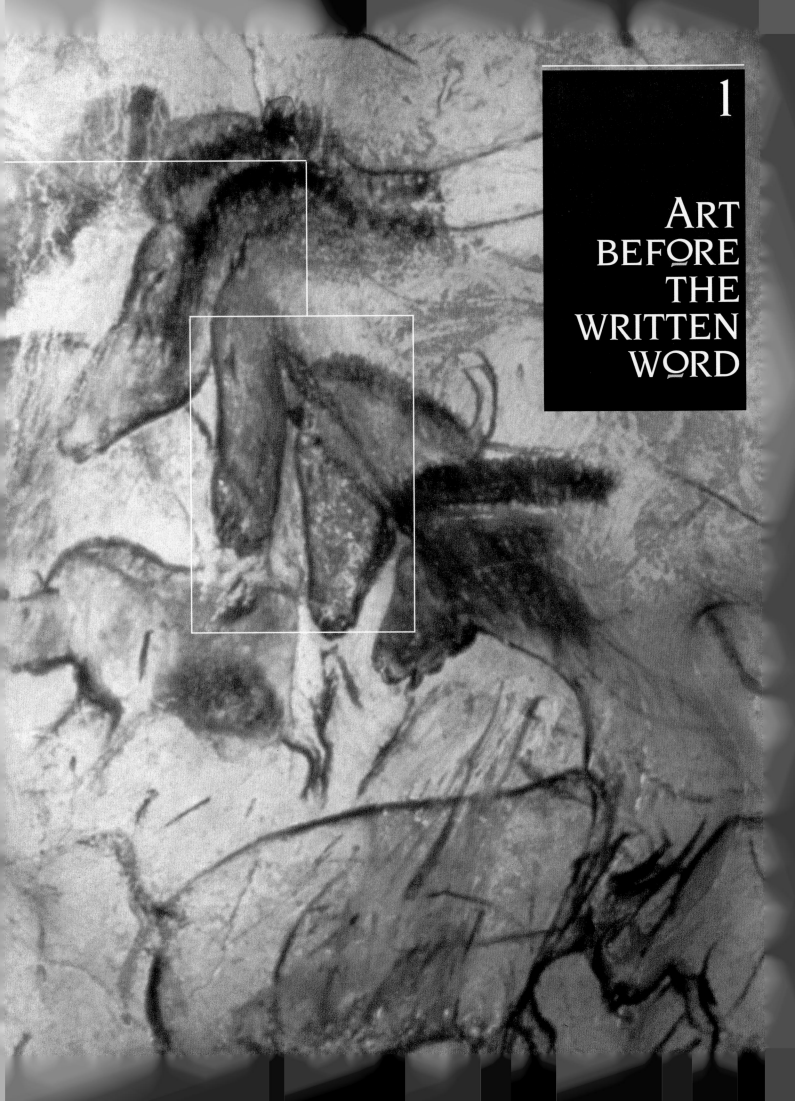

ART BEFORE THE WRITTEN WORD

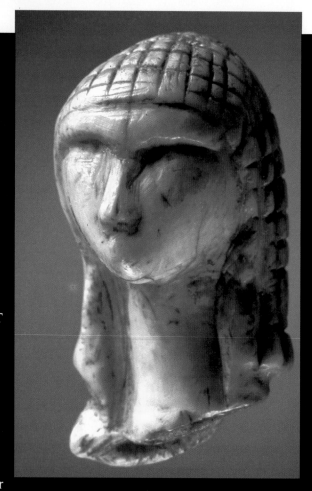

1-1. **Woman from Brassempouy**, Grotte du Pape, Brassempouy, Landes, France. c. 22,000 BCE. Ivory, height ¼" (3 cm). Musée des Antiquités Nationales, St.-Germain-en-Laye

ELEGANT and remote yet warmly human, the *Woman from Brassempouy* seems to contemplate her world with equanimity, her once-painted pupils made sightless by more than 24,000 years of lying in the soil of central France (fig. 1-1). The subtle arch of her brows, the graceful lines of her neck and nose, even the neat pattern of her hair or headdress capture the living presence of a mature young woman. Her image in ivory by a long-dead sculptor still speaks to us of our essential humanity, of our need to make images of ourselves and our kind, of our status as the only creatures who both make useful tools (the great apes do that too) *and* create works of art. We make things of beauty, however we may define such elusive concepts as "art" and "beauty."

We do not know what moved someone to carve this piece, of which only the head survives. Perhaps the maker associated the woman with spiritual or magical power: ancestor, goddess, or perhaps a ruler of the natural world or of the spirit world of the hereafter. Perhaps she ensured her tribe's continuity as a fertility figure controlling the abundance of nature; perhaps she presided over some dark unknown world.

Our speculations are fruitless, for the *Woman from Brassempouy* and her kin left no written record to share with us their thoughts and deeds. She is indeed prehistoric. And therein lies part of our fascination with this art. Whereas new studies of physical remains—from fossils to Stone Age hunting sites—tell us about the physical life, appearance, and capabilities of our distant ancestors, only their painting and sculpture— what we choose to call art—can lead us to some understanding of their creative, spiritual, and intellectual life. We begin our study of the history of art with many great questions and a mission of understanding.

Archeological evidence indicates that the earliest upright human species came into being about 4.4 million years ago in Africa. How and when modern humans evolved is the subject of lively debate, but it seems that the hominids called *Homo sapiens* (wise humans) appeared about 200,000 years ago and that the species to which we belong, *Homo sapiens sapiens*, evolved about 120,000 to 100,000 years ago. From Africa, modern humans spread across Asia, into Europe, and finally to Australia and the Americas. Among these people were those whom today we call artists.

Scholars began to study prehistory systematically—that is, to examine the thousands of years of human civilization before the invention of written historical records—less than 200 years ago. Struck by the wealth of stone tools, weapons, and figures found at ancient living sites, nineteenth-century archeologists named the whole period of early human development the Stone Age. Today's researchers further divide the time span into the Paleolithic, or Old Stone Age (from the Greek *paleo-*, "old," and *lithos*, "stone"), which has Lower (earliest), Middle, and Upper phases; and the Neolithic, or New Stone Age (from the Greek *neo-*, "new"). The term Mesolithic, or Middle Stone Age, is used also, primarily in Europe, to refer to a transitional period after the Paleolithic during which some, but not all, Neolithic technologies were adopted or developed.

Upper Paleolithic Art

Our hunter-gatherer ancestors lived in small nomadic groups and created works of art and architecture as early as the Upper (later) Paleolithic period (c. 42,000–8000 BCE). During this time, the glaciers of the last ice age still covered northern stretches of Europe, North America, and Asia. Some of the most ancient examples of Paleolithic art are small figures, or figurines, of people and animals, made of bone, ivory, stone, and clay. An early and puzzling example is a human figure with a feline head (fig. 1-2), made circa 30,000 to 26,000 BCE. Archeologists excavating at Hohlenstein-Stadel, Germany, found broken pieces of ivory from the tusk of the now-extinct woolly mammoth, which they could reassemble into a figure. Nearly a foot tall, this remarkable statue surpasses in size and complexity most early figurines. Instead of copying what he or she saw in nature, the sculptor created a unique imagined creature, part human and part beast. Was it intended to represent a person wearing a lion mask and taking part in some ritual? Was it a shaman who has taken the appearance of his animal guardian? One of the few indisputable things that can be said about the *Lion-Human* is that it shows the sculptor's highly sophisticated thinking and creative imagination: the ability to conjure a creature never before seen in nature.

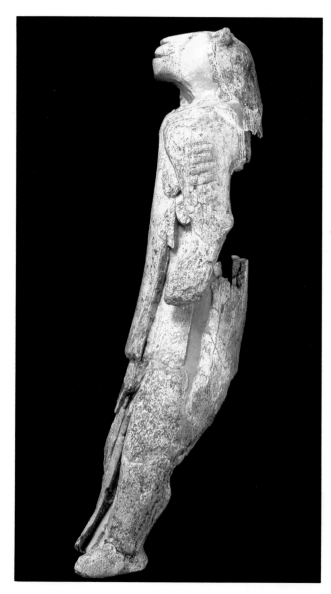

1-2. **Lion-Human,** from Hohlenstein-Stadel, Germany. c. 30,000–26,000 BCE. Mammoth ivory, height 11⅝" (29.6 cm). Ulmer Museum, Ulm, Germany

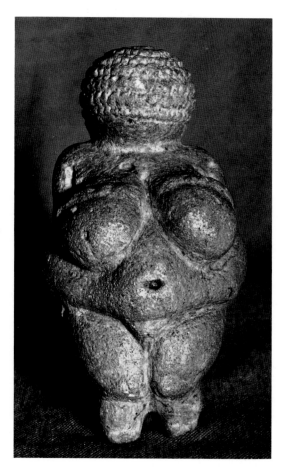

1-3. **Woman from Willendorf,** Austria. c. 22,000–21,000 BCE. Limestone, height 4⅜" (11 cm). Naturhistorisches Museum, Vienna

One of three Paleolithic female figurines discovered in 1908 at Willendorf in the Wachau region of the Danube River in Austria. These figurines were the first Paleolithic works of sculpture to be found.

THE POWER OF NAMING

Figures such as the *Woman of Willendorf* are sometimes termed "goddess" or "Venus" figurines: this statuette, discovered near Willendorf, Austria, was originally called the "Venus of Willendorf." Because Venus was the Roman goddess of love and beauty, the use of this name sent a message that the statuette was associated with religious belief, that it represented an ideal of womanhood, and that it was one in a long line of images of "classical" feminine beauty. Yet there is no proof that figures such as the *Woman from Willendorf* had any religious associations. They can be interpreted as representations of actual women, fertility symbols, expressions of ideal beauty, erotic images, ancestor figures, or even dolls meant to help young girls learn women's roles. Current research from studies done on Neanderthal skeletons has even postulated that a body type like that of the *Woman of Willendorf* might actually be the result of deformation due to gross insufficiency of iodine.

Our ability to understand and interpret works of art creatively is easily compromised by labels with embedded assumptions. Calling a prehistoric figure a "woman" instead of "Venus" frees us to think about it in new and different ways.

Paleolithic sculptors depicted women more frequently than other subjects. The carver of the *Woman from Brassempouy* (see fig. 1-1) captured the essence of a head, that is, what psychologists call the "memory image"—those elements that reside in our generalized memory of a human head. An egg shape rests atop a long neck: a wide nose and a strongly defined browline suggest deep-set eyes, and an engraved squared patterning may be hair or a headdress. This is an example of **abstraction**: the reduction of shapes and appearances to basic forms that do not faithfully reproduce those of the thing represented. The result in this case looks uncannily modern to the contemporary viewer. Today, when such a piece is isolated in a museum case—or as a book illustration—we enjoy the ivory head as an aesthetic object, but we lose its cultural context.

Another early female figurine, the *Woman from Willendorf* (fig. 1-3), dates from about 22,000–21,000 BCE (see "The Power of Naming," above). Carved from limestone and originally colored with red ocher, the statuette's swelling, rounded forms make it seem much larger than its actual 4⅜-inch height. The sculptor exaggerated the figure's female attributes, giving it pendulous breasts, a big belly with deep navel (a natural hole in the stone), wide hips, dimpled knees and buttocks, and solid thighs. Sculptures of women, from slender adolescents to old women, have been found at dozens of sites from France to Ukraine. By carving a woman with a well-nourished body, the artist expresses the condition of health, which could guarantee both longevity and the ability to produce strong children for the survival of the clan.

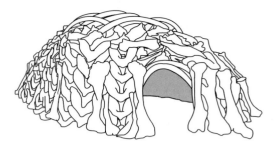

1-4. Reconstruction drawing of mammoth-bone house from Ukraine. c. 16,000–10,000 BCE

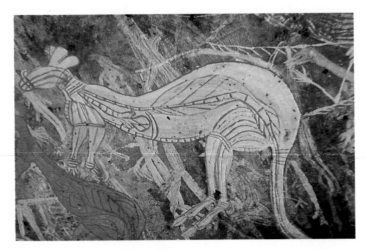

1-5. *Mimis and Kangaroo*, prehistoric rock art, Oenpelli, Arnhem Land, Australia. Older painting 16,000–7000 BCE. Red and yellow ocher and white pipe clay

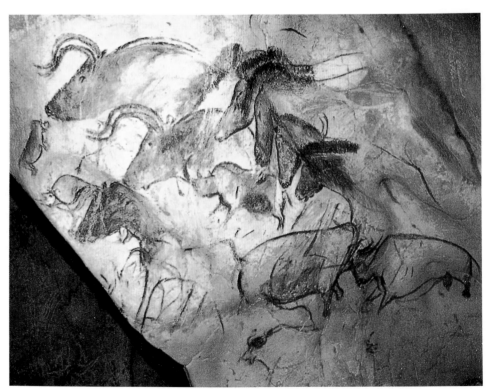

1-6. Wall painting with four horses, Chauvet cave, Vallon-Pont-d'Arc, Ardèche gorge, France. c. 28,000 BCE. Paint on limestone

Whatever their original significance, Paleolithic works of sculpture show an aesthetic sense and the ability to pose and solve problems. Both of these faculties are among the characteristics unique to human beings. Similar talents are revealed in structures of the period. Their builders sometimes seem to have had a feel for what we now call architecture—enclosure of spaces with at least some measure of aesthetic intent—rather than simple building construction.

Some well-preserved examples of Upper Paleolithic dwellings have been found in Russia and Ukraine. The people of those treeless grasslands built settlements of up to ten houses using the bones and hide of the woolly mammoth (fig. 1-4). One such village, dating from 16,000–10,000 BCE, was discovered near the Ukrainian village of Mezhirich. Its turf-and-hide-covered houses were cleverly constructed of dozens of skulls, shoulder blades, pelvis bones, jawbones, and tusks. The largest house was an impressive 24 by 33 feet, and inside, archeologists found fifteen small hearths containing ashes and charred bones left by its last occupants. Clearly, life revolved around the hearth, the source of light and heat.

Cave and rock paintings from the Upper Paleolithic period provide another means of connection to our early ancestors. Rock art survives in many places around the world, but the oldest known examples come from Australia and western Europe, beginning around 30,000 BCE. In Australia, the hunter-gatherer ancestors of today's Aborigines practiced both rock painting and rock engraving (pecking designs into rock with stone tools). They sometimes returned to a single location over many centuries to renew a fading painting or add new images. The ritual of making the painting may have been more important than the finished work. An ornately decorated rock surface, located on the northern coast of Australia in Oenpelli, Arnhem Land, contains two superimposed **compositions** (fig. 1-5). The first, painted around 16,000–7000 BCE, shows the skinny, sticklike humans that later Aborigines believed had been painted by *mimis* (ancestral spirits). Long after this imagery was abandoned, the figures were painted over with a kangaroo image in the so-called x-ray style, in which the bones and internal organs are drawn inside the silhouetted outline of the animal. Bark painters in Australia today still use the x-ray style.

In European caves, people began to paint, carve, and model images about 30,000 years ago. They produced many cave paintings in southern France and northern Spain between about 28,000 and 10,000 BCE. Artists painted images of animals, such as wild horses, bison, mammoths, aurochs (ancestors of domestic cattle), and a few people; many handprints; and hundreds of

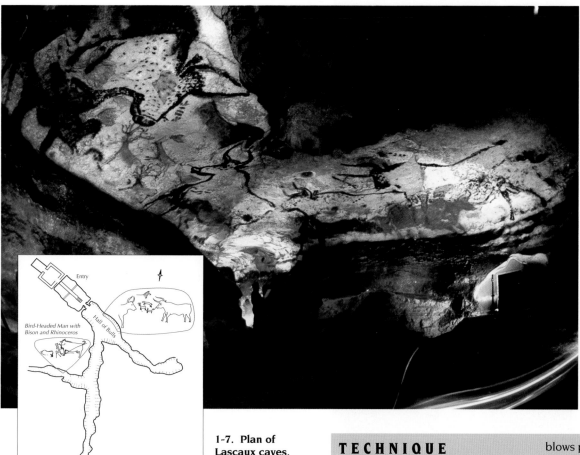

1-8. **Hall of Bulls,** Lascaux caves. c. 15,000–13,000 BCE. Paint on limestone

Discovered in 1940 and opened to the public after World War II, the prehistoric "museum" at Lascaux soon became one of the most popular tourist sites in France. Too popular, for many visitors sowed the seeds of the paintings' destruction in the form of heat, humidity, exhaled carbon dioxide, and other insidious contaminants from the outside world. The cave was closed to the public in 1963, so that conservators might battle with an aggressive fungus that had attacked the paintings. Eventually they won, but instead of re-opening the site, the authorities created a facsimile of it. Visitors at what is called Lascaux II may now view copies of the painted images without harming the precious originals.

1-7. **Plan of Lascaux caves,** Dordogne, France

geometric markings, such as grids, circles, and dots. In some caves, painters decorated not only large caverns but also tiny chambers and recesses whose natural surfaces inspired images resembling low-relief sculpture. They worked in the light of small stone lamps fueled by animal fat, using red and brown pigments ultimately derived from manganese dioxide (see "Prehistoric Wall Painting," right).

The oldest securely dated European cave paintings are found in the Chauvet cave in southeastern France, which was discovered in 1994 (fig. 1-6). These paintings were made around 28,000 BCE, which seems remarkable given the accomplished appearance of the animals depicted. It is impossible to know whether the horses shown here represent the beginnings of early painting or some other stage in early artistic development. Because we have no records predating this time, we have no way of knowing whether early artists had actually been practicing for thousands of years. The significance of such cave paintings is unknown, but many theories have been suggested (see "Why Did They Do It? The Meaning(s) of Prehistoric Paintings," page 36).

The best-known cave paintings remain those at Lascaux, in southern France (figs. 1-7, 1-8). The Lascaux paintings of cows, bulls, horses,

TECHNIQUE
PREHISTORIC WALL PAINTING

In a dark cave, working by the light of an animal-fat lamp, an artist chews a piece of charcoal to dilute it with saliva and water. Then he blows out the mixture on the surface of a wall, using his hand as a stencil. Cave archeologist Michel Lorblanchet is showing us how the original artists of a cave at Pech-Merle in France created a complex design of spotted horses. By turning himself into a human spray can, he can produce clear lines on the rough stone surface much more easily than he could with a brush. To create the line of a horse's back, with its clean upper edge and blurry lower one, he blows pigment below his hand; to capture its angular rump, he places his hand vertically against the wall, holding it slightly curved; to produce the sharpest lines, such as those of the upper hind leg and tail, he places his hands side by side and blows between them. The forelegs and the hair on the horses' bellies he executes with finger painting, and a hole punched in a piece of leather serves as a stencil for the horses' spots. It takes Lorblanchet only thirty-two hours to reproduce the Pech-Merle painting of spotted horses, his speed suggesting that a single artist created the original (perhaps with the help of an assistant to mix pigments and tend the lamp).

and deer date from about 15,000–13,000 BCE. The animals appear singly, in rows, face-to-face, tail-to-tail, and even painted on top of one another. As in other caves, horns, eyes, and hooves are shown as seen from the front, while heads and bodies are rendered in profile. The artists used the contours of the rock as part of their compositions. This sculptural dimension is seen perhaps most clearly in photographs of the cave ceiling at Altamira, Spain. This site is another of the important sites of cave paintings (fig. 1-9).

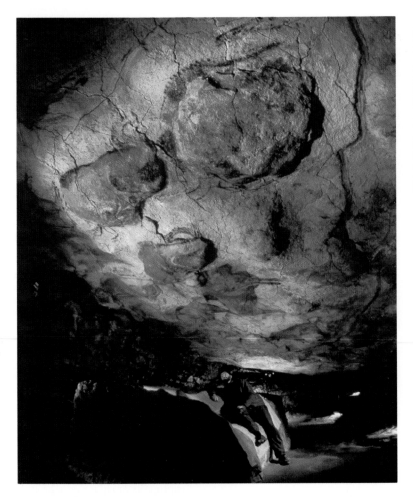

1-9. Bison, on the ceiling of a cave at Altamira, Spain. c. 12,000 BCE. Paint on limestone, length approx. 8'3" (2.5 m)

No one knew of the existence of prehistoric cave painting until one day in 1879, when a young girl exploring with her father on the family estate in Altamira crawled through a small opening in the ground and found herself in a cave chamber whose ceiling was covered with painted animals. Her father searched the rest of the cave, then told authorities about the remarkable find. Few people believed that these amazing works could have been done by "primitive" people, and the scientific community declared the paintings a hoax. They were accepted as authentic only in 1902, after many other cave paintings, drawings, and engravings had been discovered at other spots in northern Spain and France.

Why Did They Do It?

The Meaning(s) of Prehistoric Paintings

Why did people thousands of years ago paint images on cave walls and ceilings? Anthropologists and art historians have put forward countless theories to explain this early artistic activity, often telling us as much about themselves and their times as about the art. Here are two early theories.

In the nineteenth century, the idea that human beings have an inherent desire to decorate themselves and their surround-ings—an innate "aesthetic sense"—found ready acceptance. Some artists at the time promoted the idea of "art for art's sake," believing that people create works of art for the sheer love of beauty. However, the effort and organization required to accomplish the great paintings of Lascaux suggest that their creators were motivated by more than simple pleasure.

Early in the twentieth century, scholars rejected the idea of "art for art's sake" as a dated, romantic expla-nation. Led by Salomon Reinach, who believed that art fulfills a social function, they proposed that prehis-toric cave paintings might be the end products of rites performed to enhance the fertility of the animals on which people depended for food. In 1903 Reinach proposed that cave paint-ings were expressions of "sympathetic magic." He posited that the painters may have thought that producing a picture of a bison lying down would ensure that hunters found their prey asleep, or that the symbolic killing of the picture of a bison would guarantee the hunters' triumph over the beast itself.

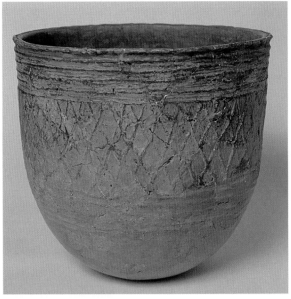

1-10. Jomon vessel. c. 10,000 BCE. Ceramic, reconstructed from sherds. Height 8⅝" (21.9 cm); mouth diameter 9¼" (23.5 cm). Yamato-shi Board of Education, Kanagawa-ken

The archeologist's best friend is the potsherd, or piece of broken pottery. Ceramic vessels are easily broken, yet the fragments are almost indestructible. The discovery of early sherds at a site marks the time when people in the region first began producing ceramics. Pottery styles, like automobile designs and fashions in clothing, change over time. Archeologists are able to determine the chronological order of such changes. By matching the potsherds excavated at a site with the types in this sequence, they can determine the relative date of the site.

Pottery cooking vessels, which first appeared in the Paleolithic period, also display the artistry of early humankind. Recent scientific dating methods have shown that Japanese potters made the oldest-known fired pottery vessels more than 12,000 years ago. The people of the Japan-ese Jomon culture who made the cooking pots, or *fukabachi*, decorated virtually all their ceramic wares, even utilitarian cooking vessels like this one (fig. 1–10). They pressed slender ribs of clay onto the body of the pot in a diamond pattern, set off above and below with bands of horizontal grooves. The round base of the vessel was prob-ably buried in sand to steady it when cooking food over an open fire. Beginning about 7500 BCE, potters decorated *fukabachi* with *jomon*, or marks of cords pressed into damp clay, a pottery style that gives the Jomon period its name.

Art in the Neolithic Period

Fundamental social and cultural changes mark the beginning of the Neolithic period. These include the development of organized agricul-ture; the practice of animal husbandry (the main-tenance of herds of domesticated animals); and the foundation of permanent, year-round settle-ments. These shifts, which took place as the Ice Age ended, occurred in some regions earlier than others and first in the Near East, where farmers began to cultivate native grains about 9000 BCE.

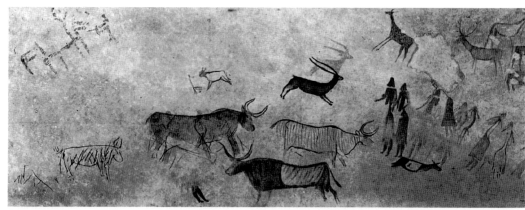

1-11. Women and Animals, facsimile of detail of rock-shelter painting in Cogul, Lérida, Spain. c. 4000–2000 BCE. Museo Arqueológico, Barcelona

The transition from the Paleolithic to the Neolithic began later in Europe, around 8000 BCE; about 7000 BCE in China; circa 3000 BCE in Africa south of the Sahara; and later yet in most parts of the Americas, where widespread human occupation had only begun around 10,000 BCE. The Neolithic period ended with the introduction of metalworking—the Bronze Age—around 3400 BCE in the Near East, about 2300 BCE in Europe, and about 1500 BCE in China. In other parts of the world, this Paleolithic-Neolithic-Bronze Age chronology based on technological development in Europe and Asia is somewhat less useful. For example, Africa south of the Sahara went straight from the Neolithic to the Iron Age without an intervening Bronze Age. In Australia, the hunter-gatherer culture developed by the Aborigines was so efficient and well adapted to the environment that the Aborigines never adopted Neolithic agriculture and the domestication of animals, even though they knew of these developments through contacts with Papua New Guinea.

Much of what we know of Neolithic life comes from ancient art and architecture. Rock-shelter paintings found at Cogul, in northeastern Spain, suggest some of the day-to-day activities of these Neolithic peoples. Dating from circa 4000–2000 BCE, the paintings show women leading children, carrying baskets, gathering food, and digging the earth with sticks. In the detail reproduced here (fig. 1-11), skirted women with large breasts are standing near several long-horned cattle. Above, grazing animals include the Spanish ibex, red deer, a pig, and more cows. Animals are also represented in motion; they leap forward with fully extended legs. (The pose is called the "flying gallop.") Unnatural as it is, this pose has been the conventional way to indicate speed from prehistory to our own time.

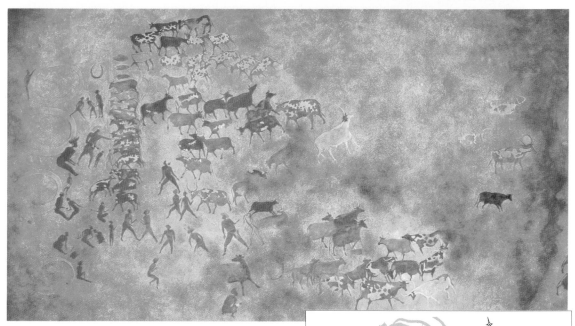

1-12. Cattle Gathered Next to a Group of Huts, detail of *The Herders' Village*, rock-wall painting, Tassili-n-Ajjer, Algeria. c. 2500–1500 BCE. Watercolor facsimile painted by students of Henri Lhote. Musée de l'Homme, Paris

These wall paintings contain so much information that it is tempting to imagine them as records of daily life. But like all early art, they probably served a greater social function. Perhaps they had an educational or religious use, for in some places the images were repainted many times. People were still coming to the sites in Roman times when, scribbling on the walls, they left **graffiti**.

An even more detailed portrayal of village life was painted at Tassili-n-Ajjer, Algeria, about 2500–1500 BCE (fig. 1-12). In front of round, thatched houses, men are tending cattle, and women are preparing a meal and caring for children. The cattle, some tethered to a long rope, have mottled, white, red, or black hides. Many have graceful lyre-shaped horns.

A Neolithic settlement preserved in the sea sands at Skara Brae, in the Orkney Islands off the northern coast of Scotland, gives a vivid picture of village life (fig. 1-13). The excavated village (built by 3100 BCE) consists of a compact cluster

1-13. Plan, village of Skara Brae, Orkney Islands, Scotland. By c. 3100 BCE

of stone dwellings linked together by covered passageways. The largest house measures 20 x 21 feet, the smallest 13 x 14 feet. The interiors, such as the one shown (fig. 1-14), were equipped with space-saving built-in furniture. Rectangular stone beds, some of them engraved with simple markings, flank the walls on either side of the large rectangular hearth. These boxlike beds would probably have been filled with heather "mattresses" and covered with warm furs. On the back wall is a sizable storage niche and a two-shelf cabinet erected using **post-and-lintel construction.** In this structural system, two or more vertical elements (posts) are used to support a bridging horizontal one (lintel). The principle has been used throughout history, whether for simple structures like these shelves or for huge stone monuments such as the temples of Egypt (Chapter 2) and Greece (Chapter 4).

boulders but also artists and engineers to devise methods to shape and align them. They also called for powerful political and religious leaders to dictate a society's need for such edifices, as well as a coordinated workforce to build them.

Many megalithic tombs are preserved in Europe, where they were used for both single and multiple burials. In the simplest type, the **dolmen**, a tomb chamber was formed of huge upright stones supporting one or more tablelike rocks, or **capstones**. Smaller rocks and dirt were mounded on top of the chamber to form an artificial hill called a **cairn** (see "Dolmen and Passage Grave," below).

More elaborate burial sites, called **passage graves**, had one or more corridors leading into a large room at the cairn's center. Many still command the landscape in Ireland. One example (fig. 1-15) discovered at Newgrange, Ireland, was constructed around 3000 to 2500 BCE. Rings, spirals, diamond shapes, and other linear designs enrich the stones at its entrance and along its 62-foot-long passageway. These patterns must have been marked out using strings or compasses, then carved by pecking at the rock surface with tools made of antlers and hard stones. A cairn that measured about 280 feet in diameter concealed the tomb chamber and passage. The ritual use of the tomb/cairn is still a mystery; however, some powerful solar symbolism must have played a part. The builders oriented the passage to the rising sun in midsummer, at which time the sun shines through a semiconcealed opening down the length of the passage to the tomb chamber and falls on a shallow, scooped out, platterlike stone.

Besides tombs, Neolithic and post-Neolithic cultures built megalithic monuments and sculptures for ritual purposes that are still not fully understood by today's scholars. The best-known megalithic monument, and another solar structure, is Stonehenge in southern England (figs. 1-16, 1-17, 1-18). Its name comes from the word *henge*, meaning a circle formed by stones or wooden posts, often surrounded by a ditch with built-up embankments. While Stonehenge is not the largest such circle from the Neolithic period, it is the most complex. Reworked over at least four major

Elements of Architecture
DOLMEN AND PASSAGE GRAVE

The **dolmen**—a late eighteenth-century term derived from the Breton *dol* (table) and *men* (stone)—was made up of a **post-and-lintel** frame of large, stone slabs "roofed" with one or more **capstones**, then mounded over with dirt and smaller stones to from a **cairn**. This construction created a small, fully enclosed burial chamber. Today, most dolmens are exposed, giving the erroneous impression that they were built as open-air monuments.

The **passage grave** was a burial chamber, also covered over by an earth-and-pebble cairn that was entered through a long, slab-lined passageway or passageways. The central space was sometimes segmented into several chambers and usually held multiple burials.

The oldest megalithic tombs have been found in Brittany.

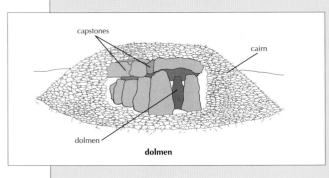

dolmen

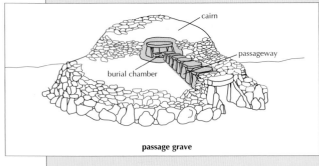

passage grave

MEGALITHIC ARCHITECTURE

Massive tombs and monuments built from huge stones first appeared in the Neolithic period, as human societies became more stratified and complex. These structures are known as megalithic architecture, after the Greek terms *mega-* for "large" and *lithos* for "stone." Their construction required not only laborers to transport the giant

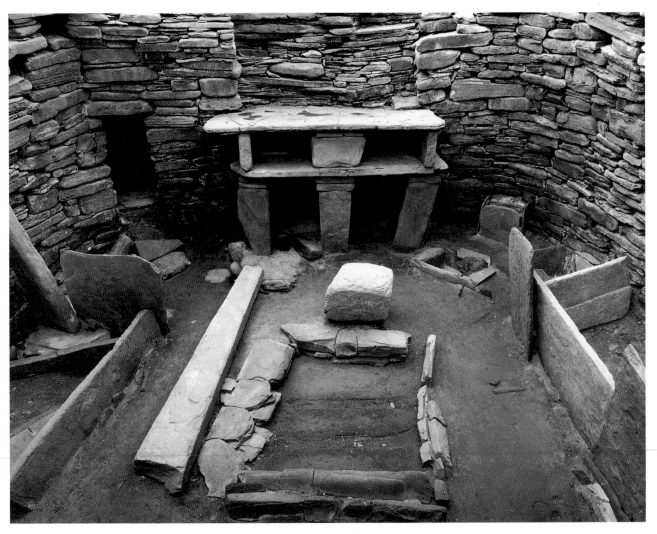

1-14. House interior, Skara Brae (house 7 in fig. 1-13)

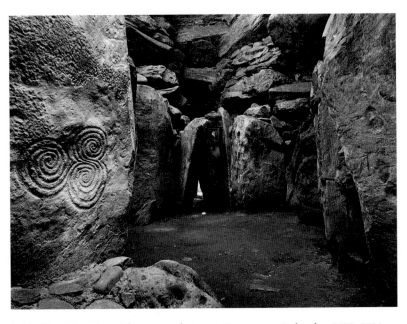

1-15. Tomb interior with engraved stones, Newgrange, Ireland. c. 3000–2500 BCE

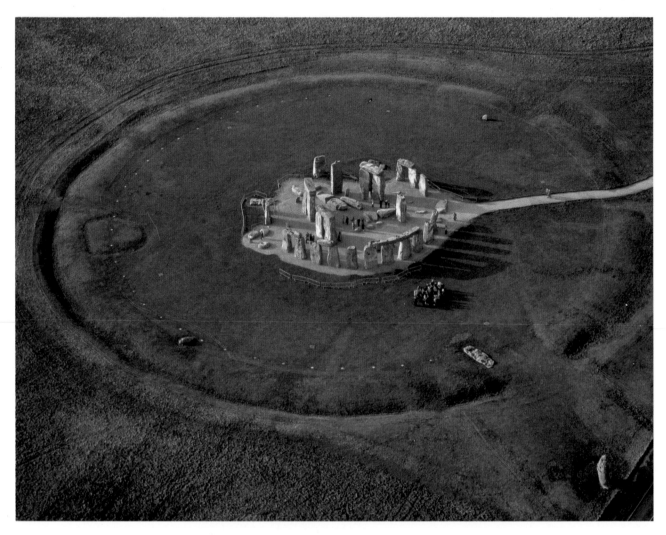

1-16. Stonehenge, Salisbury Plain, Wiltshire, England. c. 2750–1500 BCE

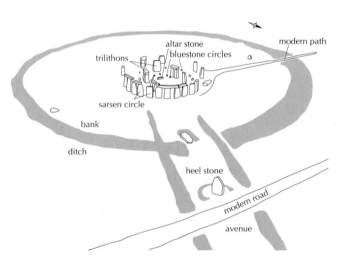

1-17. Diagram of Stonehenge, showing elements discussed in text

building phases between about 2750 and 1500 BCE, Stonehenge must have had extraordinary importance in its region.

The main elements of Stonehenge are illustrated in the accompanying aerial photograph and diagram (figs. 1-16, 1-17). The earliest circle was a ditch with a 6-foot embankment, about 330 feet in diameter, with a surrounding circle of white chalk marks in the earth. A single 35-ton sarsen (sandstone) megalith, known today as the "heel stone," was moved from quarries 23 miles away and placed outside the circles. Later people added a more complex structure. They built a ring of gray sarsen uprights about 20 feet tall and topped by a continuous lintel. Inside the sarsen circle they placed a ring of smaller bluestones, made of a bluish dolerite that they transported from Welsh quarries 150 miles away. These circles surround a horseshoe-shaped arrangement of five trilithons, or pairs of

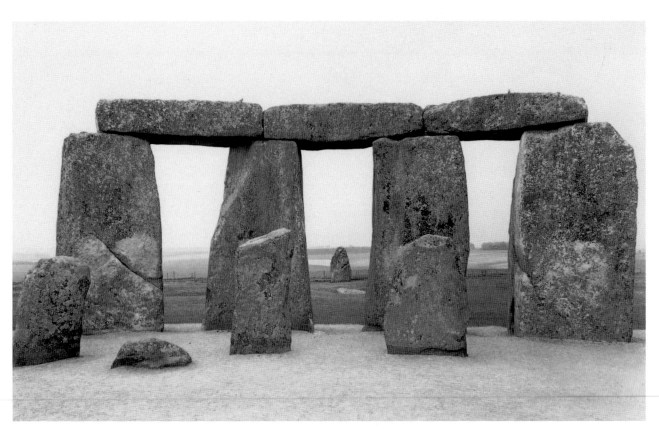

1-18. *Within Circle, Looking Toward Heel Stone, Stonehenge,* 1967. Photograph by Paul Caponigro

Caponigro, a great enthusiast of megalithic architecture, spent twenty years photographing prehistoric structures all over Europe. He admirably captures the harmonious grace and simplicity of Stonehenge by positioning his camera directly above the large "altar stone" at the heart of the complex and aiming it toward the heel stone outside the monument's perimeter. It is from this spot that a dawn visitor to the site at the time of the summer solstice can see the sun rise directly over that distant marker.

unlinked stones topped by lintels, and a second horseshoe of bluestones. The largest of the trilithons stood 24 feet high. At the very center of this complex lies the so-called altar stone, a modern designation. (No religious meaning should be assumed; we have seen the problems modern terms can present in the context of the "Venus" name discussed in "The Power of Naming," page 33.) The opening of the horseshoe focuses on the "heel stone," which stands outside the henge to the northeast and connects to the opening by a causeway.

One aspect of this megalithic monument more than any other has captured the public's imagination. Anyone standing at the exact center of Stonehenge on the morning of the summer solstice 4,000 years ago would have seen the sun rise directly over the heel stone (fig. 1-18). Even today, the midsummer sunrise

inspires hundreds of people to gather at Stonehenge. Given the relationship between the monument's orientation and the sun, some scholars think it may have been a kind of observatory that helped astronomers to track cosmic events. Aside from its possible astronomical significance, anthropologists suspect that Stonehenge was an important site for major public ceremonies, possibly planting or harvest rituals.

Neolithic culture persisted in northern Europe until about 2000 BCE. Metals had made their appearance about 2300 BCE, although gold and copper had been used in southern Europe and the Near East much earlier. The period that follows the introduction of metalworking is commonly called the Bronze Age. A remarkable sculpture found in Denmark depicts a wheeled horse pulling a cart laden with a large, upright

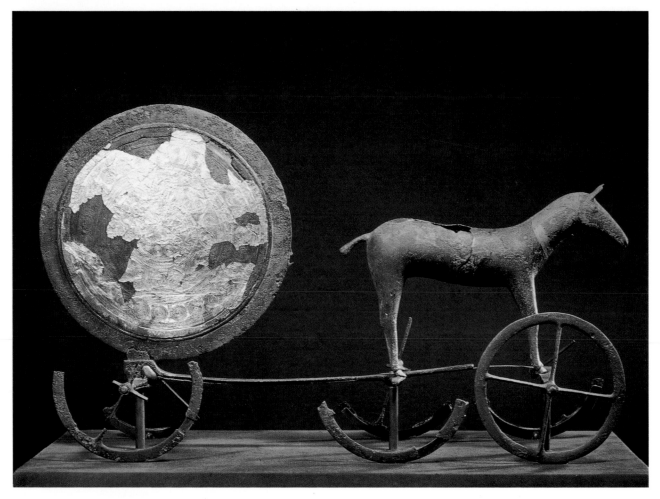

1-19. *Horse and Sun Chariot*, from Trundholm, Zealand, Denmark. c. 1800–1600 BCE. Bronze, length 23¼" (59.2 cm). National Museum, Copenhagen

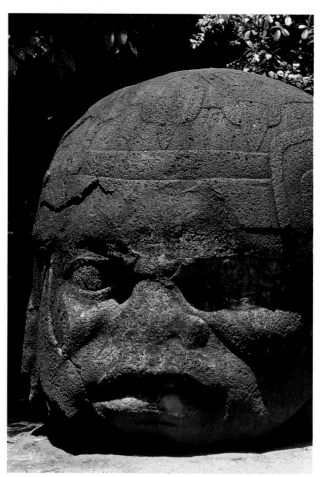

disk, thought to represent the sun (fig. 1-19). A widespread sun cult seems to have existed in the north, as our discussion of Stonehenge suggests. The horse, with its gleaming load, could have been rolled from place to place in a ritual reenactment of the sun's passage across the sky.

The *Horse and Sun Chariot* dates from between 1800 and 1600 BCE. The valuable materials from which the sculpture was made attest to its importance. The horse, cart, and disk were cast in bronze and delicately engraved with an abstract design of concentric rings, zigzags, circles, spirals, and loops. A thin sheet of beaten gold was then applied to the bronze disk and pressed into the incised patterns. The continuous and curvilinear patterns suggest the movement of the sun itself. The sculpture hints at a rich and complex ritual life among the people of the far north.

Megalithic art was not limited to Europe. The Olmec peoples in the area that is now southern Mexico near the Gulf quarried and carved stone of a massive size. With basalt transported from the Tuxtla Mountains to an area near the Gulf coast, the La Venta Olmec carved heads that are

1-20. Colossal head (no. 4), from La Venta, Mexico. Olmec culture, c. 900–500 BCE. Basalt, height 7'5" (2.26 m). La Venta Park, Villahermosa, Tabasco, Mexico

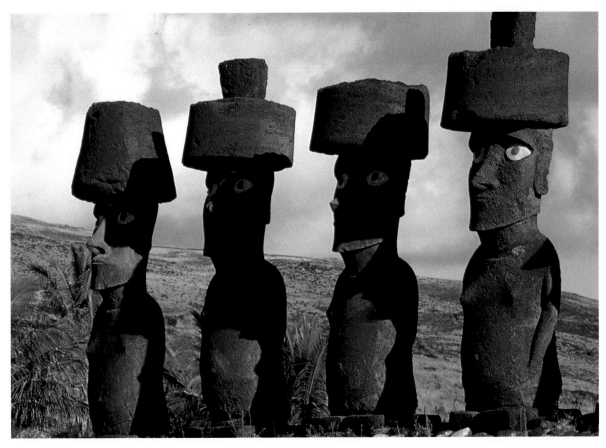

1-21. Ancestor figures (*moai*?) Ahu Nau Nau, Easter Island, Polynesia. c. 1000–1500 CE, restored 1978. Volcanic stone (tufa), average height approx. 36' (11 m)

up to 12 feet tall and 20 tons in weight (fig. 1-20). Dating from circa 900 to 500 BCE, these heads represent men wearing close-fitting caps with chin straps, and large, round earplugs. Each face is different, suggesting that the heads may represent specific individuals. At present, most scholars consider them to be portraits of rulers. Obviously, the difficulty of transporting these boulders (it might have taken up to 200 people to drag the quarried stone) indicates strong motivation. To traverse water distances, the raw basalt was presumably floated both along the Gulf coast and navigable streams and rivers. Scholars do not know whether the driving force behind such arduous labor was religious in nature. As with Stonehenge, however, large groups of people united to accomplish a common goal.

Regardless of geographic location, megalithic sculpture offers some of the greatest art historical conundrums. For instance, many people have wondered about the towering stone figures known as *moai* that were erected on Easter Island (fig. 1-21), which lies in the Pacific Ocean. Carved from a yellowish brown volcanic stone called tufa, they have coral and stone eyes and red tufa topknots. Not only do the figures stand some 36 feet tall; their topknots alone can measure up to 9 feet. The remains of nearly 1,000 *moai* have been found, including some unfin-

ished examples discovered in quarries where they were being made. All probably date from around 1000 to 1500 CE. After that period, warfare broke out on Easter Island, and many of the *moai* were knocked down and destroyed. Their original meaning has been lost over the centuries, but they may have been memorials to dead chiefs.

It is so tempting to see history, and art history, as a series of cumulative developments: this perspective goes hand in hand with the notion that human beings have always strived toward ever-more-perfect expressions of artistic and cultural values. Yet there is much evidence to the contrary, and nowhere is the notion of systematic improvement shakier than when dealing with prehistoric periods and cultures.

Around the globe, many developments occurred at the same time in geographically unrelated and unconnected places. Conversely, some of the same innovations have happened on very different timetables from place to place. Instead of thinking of early art and architecture in terms of a rigid chronology and dominant culture (especially given the very incomplete record of that art and architecture), it seems more productive to continue revising our understanding of general patterns as the evidence continues, quite literally, to come to light.

Funerary mask of Tutankhamun (ruled 1336/35–1327 BCE), from the tomb of Tutankhamun, Valley of the Kings, Deir el-Bahri, Egypt, photographed the day it was discovered—October 28, 1925

Funerary mask of Tutankhamun as it appears today. Gold inlaid with glass and semiprecious stones, height 21¼" (54.0 cm). Egyptian Museum, Cairo

Archeology's Role

Staring out for all eternity, the young king wears a funerary mask with a deep collar of dried flowers and beads. With linen cloths packed around his head and his mummified body wrapped in linen strips, he lay inside three nested, finely decorated coffins, themselves placed in a quartzite stone box within three more nested wooden containers. Carter raised the lid of the innermost coffin two years and eleven months after opening King Tut's tomb, and he excavated the tomb for another seven years. The Carter team's excavation was careful, painstaking, and thoroughly documented. The findings are still being published.

Art in Context

On the right-hand page is the same mask as it appears today in a museum case. The inner-most funerary mask, which covered the king's skull, is gold, decorated with inlaid glass and semiprecious stones. The coffins and their contents are the highlights of the royal trove, which also included as *material culture* couches, chairs, chests, carts, sculpture, musical instruments, and even food. The thoughtful and lavish furnishing of the king's final resting place speaks tellingly about the values of Egyptian kings and of the society as a whole.

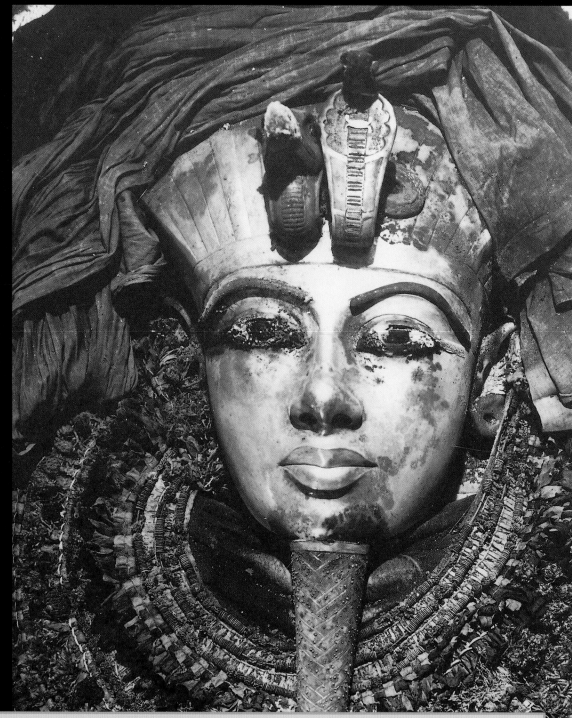

K E Y S to Art History

ARCHEOLOGY, ART & MATERIAL CULTURE

The English archeologist Howard Carter (1873–1939) was also an epigrapher (decipherer of ancient inscriptions) and an artist. His singularly rich discovery, made thirty-one years after he began his archeological research in Egypt, was the intact tomb of King Tutankhamun (King Tut, who reigned 1336/35–1327 BCE). The photograph shows what Carter saw when his team opened the third, inner-most coffin on October 28, 1925.

We know about early art mostly because of excavations on land and discoveries undersea by archeologists, men and women who study the human past by revealing its material remains, its *material culture*. In fact, from before about 3000 BCE, when the first written languages evolved, the only information we have is archeological. Because its subject is human society, *archeology* is classified with anthropology in social sciences, although classical archeology is often grouped with the humanities. As a science, archeology involves accurate records, analysis, and interpretation of data before drawing conclusions. Dating of material remains is an important aspect of archeology. The study of material culture—physical remains, especially tools and shelter—overlaps with and certainly enlivens our understanding of *art*, for material culture gives us the contexts in which artists worked.

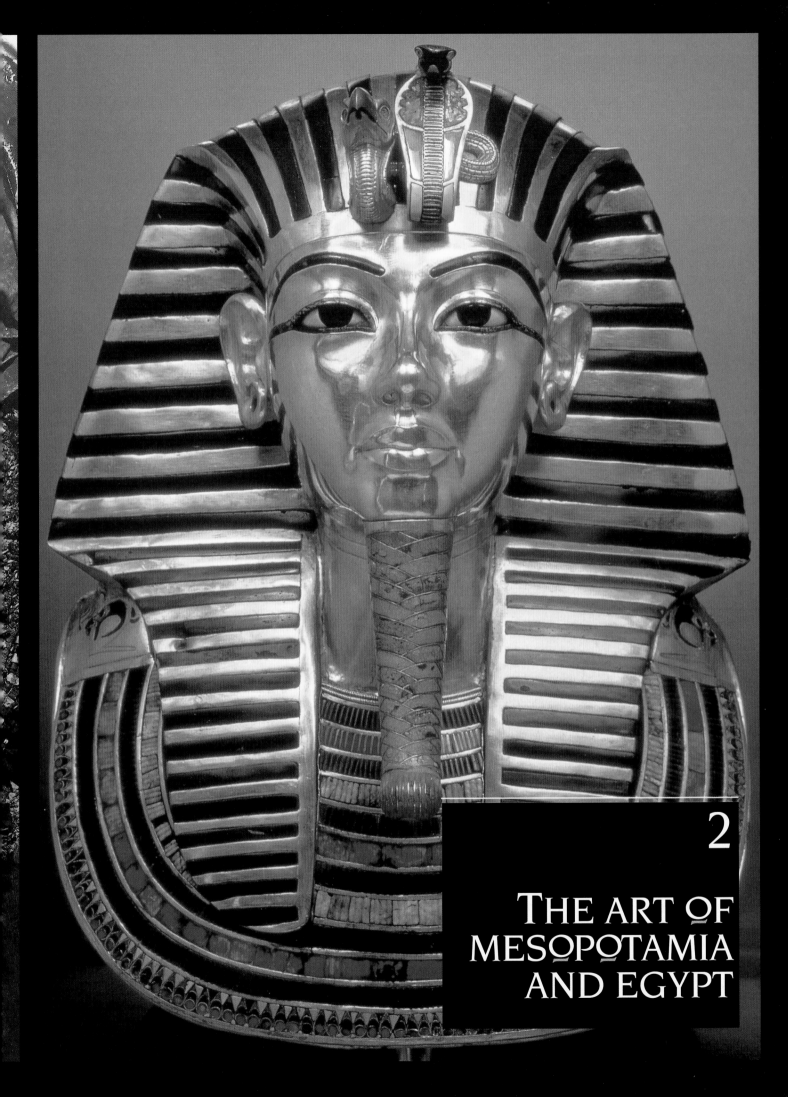

2

THE ART OF MESOPOTAMIA AND EGYPT

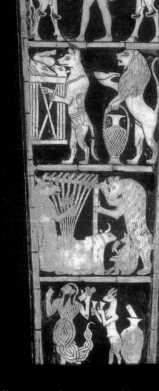

2-1. Mythological figures,
detail of the sound box of
the bull lyre, from the tomb
of Queen Pu-abi, Ur
(modern Muqaiyir, Iraq).
c. 2680 BCE. Wood with shell
inlay, 12¼ x 4½" (31.1 x
11 cm). University Museum,
University of Pennsylvania,
Philadelphia

As in the animal fables of the legendary Greek author Aesop, the animals in the panels that decorate a very early (c. 2680 BCE) harp from Sumer personify humans: a donkey, assisted by a bear, plays the harp, accompanied by a fox with a rattle; a lion and a wolf, imitating the upright posture of humans, march in stately procession carrying offerings. The top and bottom **registers**—bands—are particularly intriguing, because they seem to illustrate scenes that are found in the *Epic of Gilgamesh*, a 3,000-line epic poem that is Sumer's great contribution to world literature. What is especially interesting is that the poem was first written down nearly 700 years after the harp was decorated, suggesting a very long oral tradition.

The *Epic of Gilgamesh* probes the question of mortality, or immortality. Its hero undertakes a voyage to the netherworld, the Land of No Return, and declares it a bad place. In the depths of the ocean, Gilgamesh encounters scorpion-men, like the one pictured in the lowest register of figure 2-1. Gilgamesh's story also expresses the heroic aim to understand surroundings that were hostile and a longing to find meaning in human existence. The almost-human, bearded figure in the top register masterfully controls two rearing human-headed bulls— a recurring theme in art of the ancient Near East. So vivid were the imagined hybrid ancestors' strange adventures with fabulous friends and adversaries that early Mesopotamians actually thought they might have to confront these composite creatures during their lifetimes. (Other early civilizations also had human-animal composite power figures: sphinxes in Egypt; human-headed bulls and lions in Akkadia, Babylonia, and Assyria; and cat-faced humans in Japan, to name three.) About 3300 BCE, Sumerians invented markings to keep records, to make lists, and eventually to write stories. We can study the **iconography**, or imagery, of Sumerian works of art with some confidence, for beginning with inscribed clay tablets and decorated seals from Sumer we are no longer dealing with the speculations of prehistory.

Earth's great river valleys nourished and united people: water and waterways made possible agriculture and a settled way of life. The Tigris and Euphrates rivers in Mesopotamia (which means "between the rivers") and the Nile in Egypt—and, as we shall see, the Indus and the Yellow rivers in Asia, the Danube in Europe, and the Mississippi in North America—were the most important waterways. The rivers also formed transportation corridors linking the farmers along the banks. The land constituting ancient Mesopotamia, now Iraq and part of southwestern Iran, was the wide alluvial plain created by the Tigris and the Euphrates. It was home to many early cultures over the millennia.

More than 5,000 years ago, men and women in the ancient Near East and Egypt laid the foundations for Western civilization. Political and religious hierarchies evolved as people banded together in community projects: digging irrigation and drainage ditches, planting and reaping crops, storing and distributing the harvest. The families and clans that had come together in communities eventually created cities, places known today by such fabled names as Jericho and Babylon, Memphis and Thebes. By about 3500 BCE, rulers, priests, and laborers— and eventually artists—lived and worked together in real cities in the service of the community and of gods and goddesses. The objects we now call art include weavings, ceramics, **monumental** sculpture, and statuettes. About 500 years later, another important breakthrough occurred in the ancient Near East. Around 3000 BCE, Sumerian artists became expert metalworkers. They created bronze, a hard, strong alloy of tin and copper. The Mesopotamian Bronze Age replaced the Stone Age a thousand years before this development occurred in northern Europe (see fig. 1-19), and it was followed by the Iron Age.

In some ways, life in Mesopotamia and Egypt followed a similar course. People farmed in both the valleys of the Tigris and the Euphrates in Mesopotamia and along the Nile in Egypt. In both places, agriculture became the basis of wealth. Community leaders consolidated their power until kingship became the dominant form of government. Religion played a central role in government and daily life. People worshiped many gods and goddesses, each of whom had different powers and features. Rulers often identified closely with the gods, sometimes through symbolic marriage to a god or goddess. The responsibilities of rulers included ceremonial as well as political duties. The priests who honored and communicated with the gods joined the rulers to mediate between these deities and the people. Some individuals, freed from the necessity of daily work in the fields, became administrative assistants to these intermediaries, and eventually people settled into stratified social groups.

These complex, hierarchical societies could no longer depend on oral communication. People needed records, and this led to the development of writing—first, simple **pictographs** and then a complex system of **hieroglyphic** or **cuneiform** signs. Today, these records, and the history and literature that were soon recorded, help us to interpret the visual arts that were produced at that time.

In ways that life and culture in Mesopotamia and Egypt differed, so did art. Mesopotamia's wealth and agricultural resources, as well as its few natural defenses, made its peoples vulnerable to repeated invasions and to internal conflicts between rival powers. Over the centuries, the balance of power in Mesopotamia shifted between north and south and between local powers and outside invaders. The seemingly unending rise and fall of cities like Babylon, Nineveh, and Ur has given Mesopotamia a varied and rich concentration of archeological remains. Its art and architecture continued to be based on the earliest Sumerian traditions but changed subtly with each of many successive cultures.

In contrast, mountains and deserts protected the Nile Valley. With only a few interruptions, Egypt remained a unified state for some 3,000 years. This cohesion made possible an unprecedented continuity in artistic and cultural development. Strikingly, Egypt's great artistic resources were directed toward the decoration and outfitting of tombs. Since the Egyptians imagined life after death as a continuation of life, much of what we know about ancient Egypt today we owe to their funerary art.

Early Neolithic Communities

The world's first settled farming communities emerged in an area of the ancient Near East long referred to as the Fertile Crescent. Rising along the Mediterranean coast through modern Jordan, Israel, Lebanon, and Syria, the "crescent" arched into central Turkey and descended along the plains of Mesopotamia through Iraq and western Iran to the Persian Gulf. Agriculture first began in this region around 9000 BCE, with farming villages forming nearly four thousand years later.

One of the earliest Near Eastern cities, Jericho, located in the West Bank territory, was home to about 2,000 people by around 7000 BCE. Its houses, made of mud brick (bricks shaped from clay and dried in the sun), covered 6 acres, an enormous size for that time. Ain Ghazal (Spring of Gazelles), located just outside present-day Amman, Jordan, was even larger. The settlement, dating from about 7200 to 5000 BCE, occupied 30 acres on a slope that was shaped into terraces stabilized by stone retaining walls. Its houses may have resembled the adobe pueblos that native peoples in the American Southwest began to build more than 7,000

years later (see fig. 14-22). The concentration of people and resources in cities such as Jericho and Ain Ghazal was an early step toward the formation of larger city-states. These larger city-states first arose in Mesopotamia and later were common in the ancient Near East.

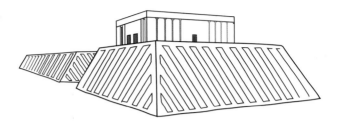

2-2. Reconstruction drawing of the Anu Ziggurat and White Temple, Uruk (modern Warka, Iraq). c. 3100 BCE

Mesopotamia

The prosperous Mesopotamian cities and their surrounding territories developed around 3500 BCE into independently governed city-states. Eventually the most powerful city-states absorbed their neighbors to form larger kingdoms and empires.

One powerful cluster of cities in the southern region was known collectively as Sumer. The Sumerians have been credited with many "firsts": inventing the wagon wheel and the plow, casting objects in copper and bronze, and—perhaps the Sumerians' greatest contribution to later civilizations—inventing a system of writing known as cuneiform script between 3300 and 3000 BCE (see "Origins of Writing," page 48).

In architecture, the Sumerians' most imposing buildings were **ziggurats**, stepped pyramidal structures with a temple or shrine on top. Towering over the flat plains, ziggurats proclaimed the wealth, prestige, and stability of a city's rulers and glorified the city's gods. The peoples of the ancient Near East were polytheistic; they worshiped many gods and goddesses, attributing to them power over human activities and the forces of nature. Each city had one special protective deity for whom the people worked and from whom they received benefits. Religious specialists, eventually developing into a priest class, controlled rituals and sacred sites, ensuring that the gods were honored properly. **Temple complexes**—clusters of religious, administrative, and service buildings—filled each city's center.

Two large temple complexes at Uruk (modern Warka, Iraq), mark the first independent Sumerian city-state. One complex was dedicated to Inanna, the goddess of fertility, the other probably to the sky god Anu. The Anu Ziggurat, built up in stages over the centuries, ultimately rose to a height of about 40 feet. Around 3100 BCE, the people of Uruk built a temple of white-washed brick on top. Modern archeologists call it the White Temple (fig. 2-2).

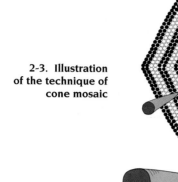

2-3. Illustration of the technique of cone mosaic

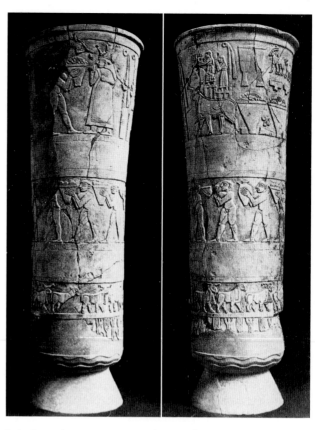

2-4. Carved vase (two views), from Uruk (modern Warka, Iraq). c. 3500–3000 BCE. Alabaster, height 36"(91 cm). Iraq Museum, Baghdad

Origins of Writing

The Sumerians developed the first known system of writing, recorded on clay tablets, in the late third millennium BCE. The earliest preserved tablets, dating to around 3300 BCE, bear an accounting system for products traded at the city of Uruk. The symbols, which were drawn in the wet clay with a pointed tool, are simple pictures, or **pictographs**, that represent a thing or concept. The head of a bull, for example, means "bull." Between 2900 and 2400 BCE, the symbols evolved from pictures into phonograms—representations of the sounds of syllables in the Sumerian language—thus becoming a true writing system. During the same centuries, scribes (specialists in writing and maintaining records) developed a writing instrument called a **stylus**, shaped like a triangular wedge. Mesopotamian writing is termed **cuneiform** (from the Latin "wedge-shaped") after the shape of the marks made by the stylus.

Ancient Egypt developed three types of writing. The earliest system employed symbols called **hieroglyphs**. Like cunei-form, these were either pictographs or phonograms. Later, scribes evolved **hieratic** writing, a shorthand version of hieroglyphs. The simplified forms, used for record keeping, correspondence, and manuscripts of all sorts, could be written quickly in script on scrolls made of papyrus (a plant that grew along the Nile). The third type of Egyptian writing came into use only in the eighth century BCE, as written communication ceased to be restricted exclusively to priests and scribes. It was less formal and was easier to master, and the Greeks referred to it as **demotic writing** (from *demos*, "the people").

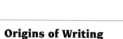

stylus

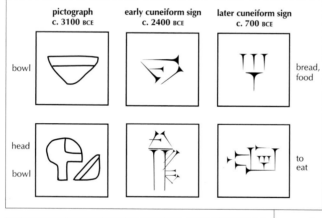

	pictograph c. 3100 BCE	early cuneiform sign c. 2400 BCE	later cuneiform sign c. 700 BCE	
bowl				bread, food
head / bowl				to eat

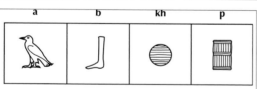

a	b	kh	p

Four hieroglyphs with the sounds they represent. Used in combinations, such phonogramic hieroglyphs were especially useful in rendering foreign names.

Courtyards and interior walls in both the Inanna and the Anu compounds were decorated with **cone mosaics**, a decoration apparently invented at Uruk (fig. 2-3). Artisans pressed thousands of baked clay cones like thumbtacks into the wet plaster walls so that the flat colored "heads" created shimmering, multicolored designs. They decorated the exterior surfaces of ziggurats with paint and patterns of plain or colored bricks.

Inanna had her devotees in Uruk. A tall vase of carved alabaster (a fine, white stone), found near her temple, shows her accepting an offering from a naked priest (fig. 2-4). Inanna stands in front of her shrine, indicated by two reed door-poles. Through the doorway her wealth is displayed, and behind the priest come other offering bearers. Plants and animals in horizontal bands decorate the base of the vase. Medical historians have identified the plants as the pomegranate and the now-extinct silphium, plants used by early people both to control fertility and as fertility symbols. The scene is usually interpreted as the ritual marriage between the goddess and a human to ensure the fertility of crops, animals, and people, and thus the continued survival of Uruk.

The ziggurat reached its final form (about a thousand years after the completion of the White Temple), in Ur, a city on the Euphrates south of Uruk. The people of Ur built a mud-brick ziggurat dedicated to the moon god Nanna, also called Sin (fig. 2-5). Here three staircases converge at an imposing entrance gate atop the first platform. Each platform is angled outward from top to base, probably to prevent rainwater from forming puddles and eroding the pavement. The first two levels of the Nanna Ziggurat and their

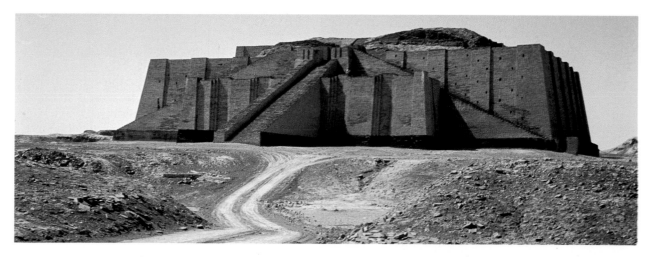

2-5. Nanna Ziggurat, Ur (modern Muqaiyir, Iraq). c. 2100–2050 BCE

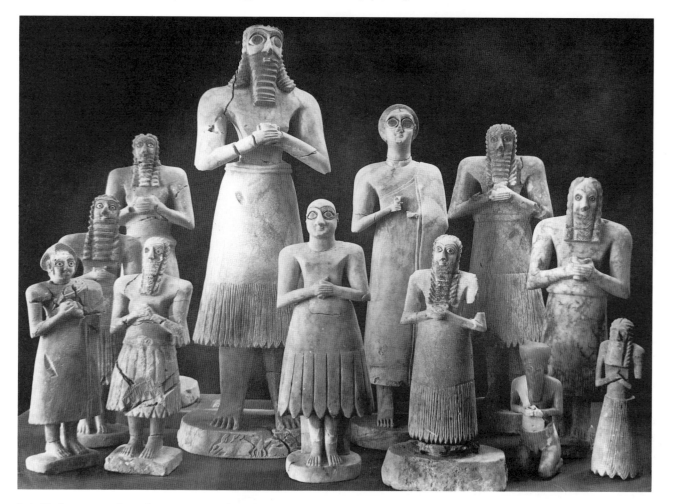

2-6. Votive statues, from the Square Temple, Eshnunna (modern Tell Asmar, Iraq). c. 2900–2600 BCE. Limestone, alabaster, and gypsum, height of largest figure approx. 30" (76.3 cm). The Oriental Institute of the University of Chicago; Iraq Museum, Baghdad

retaining walls were reconstructed in recent times, but little remains of the upper level and the temple. Such temples were known as "the offering table of heaven" and "the waiting room of the gods," but we know nothing of the rituals performed in them.

Sculpture during this period was associated with religion, and large statues were commonly placed in temples as objects of devotion. In addition, individual worshipers set up **votive** figures— small statues that they sometimes identified as portraits of themselves. Apparently, anyone who

could afford to might commission a votive figure and place it in the god's shrine. A simple inscription might identify the figure as "one who offers prayers." Larger inscriptions might recount all the things accomplished in the god's honor.

Marble votive statues dating from about 2900 to 2600 BCE (fig. 2-6) were found in the ruins of a temple at Eshnunna (modern Tell Asmar, Iraq). The carvers, following the conventions of Sumerian art—that is, traditional ways of representing forms—simplified the faces, bodies, and dress to emphasize the cylindrical

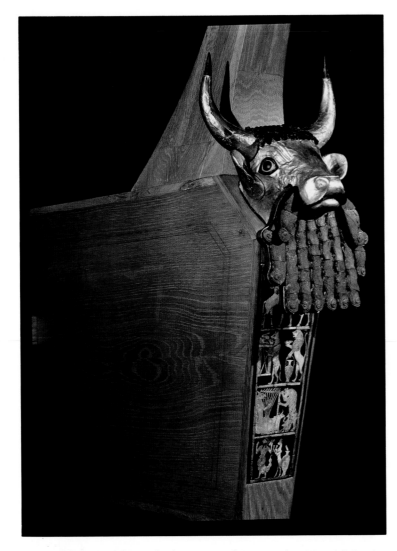

2-7. Bull lyre, from the tomb of Queen Pu-abi, Ur (modern Muqaiyir, Iraq). c. 2680 BCE. (Detail shown in fig. 2-1.) Wood with gold, lapis lazuli, and shell, reassembled in modern wood support

those that human visitors used during ritual activities. The statues' wide, staring eyes indicate communication between the votive figures and the god of the temple. The figures stand at respectful attention for all eternity.

The artists of Ur became accomplished in many arts—music, storytelling (which later became literature), work in precious materials, as well as stone sculpture and architecture. They used great skill to make a superb lyre (c. 2680 BCE), a kind of harp (fig. 2-7), one of two found in the tomb of Queen Pu-abi of Ur. Archeologists have restored the lost wooden parts of the lyre and reassembled the surviving pieces. On one end of the sound box, surmounting the inlaid shell images of animals (see fig. 2-1), sits the head of a magnificent bearded bull created out of gold and the semiprecious gemstone lapis lazuli.

Sumerian temple staff and merchants not only invented cuneiform writing, they developed flat stamps and more elaborate cylinder-form seals for securing and identifying documents and signaling property ownership. **Cylinder seals,** usually less than 2 inches high, were made of hard and sometimes semiprecious stones with designs **incised** (cut) into the surface. Rolled across a damp clay surface, the seal leaves a mirror image of its design that cannot be easily altered once dry. The seals were used for signing documents or marking container lids or storage-room doorways. One fine example shows an "animal combat" theme (fig. 2-8). A lone, nude male tries to stop a long-maned lion from mauling a frightened stag, while another lion attacks the stag's mate.

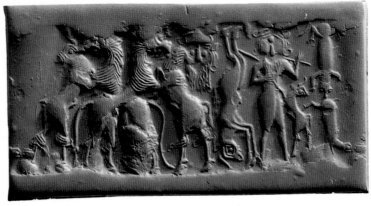

2-8. Cylinder seal from Sumer and its impression. c. 2500 BCE. Marble, height approx. 1³/₄" (4.5 cm). The Metropolitan Museum of Art, New York.   Gift of Walter Hauser, 1955 (55.65.4)

The distinctive design on the stone cylinder seal on the left belonged to its owner, like a coat of arms in the European Middle Ages or a modern cattle-rancher's brand. When rolled across soft clay applied to the closure to be sealed—a jar lid, the knot securing a bundle, or the door to a room—the cylinder left a raised image, or band of repeated raised images, of the design. Sealing discouraged unauthorized people from secretly gaining access to goods or information.

Such animal and human combats remind us that kings were expected to protect their people from both human and animal enemies. They also intervened with the gods to exert control over the natural world. The Akkadians, warring invaders who settled the area north of Uruk near modern Baghdad, are an example of such a hostile group. Unlike the Sumerians, the Akkadians spoke a Semitic language (a language in the same family as Arabic and Hebrew). Under the powerful military and political figure Sargon I (ruled c. 2332–2279 BCE), they conquered the Sumerian cities and brought most of Mesopotamia under their control. Sargon I even elevated himself to the status of a god, setting a precedent followed by later Akkadian rulers. Soon after, the Akkadians adopted Sumerian culture.

shapes of the figures. The men in this group wear sheepskin kilts, while the tall female figure to the right of center wears a dress wrapped diagonally to expose one breast. Some of the figures hold small vessels, probably similar to

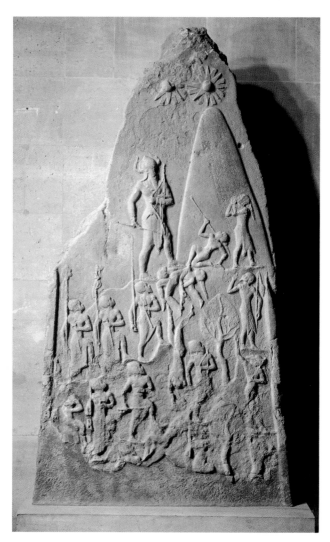

2-9. *Stela of Naramsin*. c. 2254–2218 BCE. Limestone, height 6'6" (1.98 m). Musée du Louvre, Paris

The *Stela of Naramsin*, about 2254–2218 BCE (fig. 2-9), commemorates a military victory of Naramsin, Sargon's grandson and successor. The king, wearing the horned crown associated with deities, stands above his soldiers and fallen foes near the top of the stone. The shape of the **stela** (upright stone slab) is used as a dynamic part of the **composition**. Its pointed shape accommodates the carved mountain within it. Naramsin is also larger than the other figures. In the art of many peoples, greater size is an indication of greater relative importance. Art historians call this convention **hieratic scale**.

The Akkadian empire fell around 2180 BCE to the Guti, a mountain people from the northeast. For a brief time the Guti controlled most of the Mesopotamian plain, except for the city-state of Lagash, which remained independent under its ruler, Gudea. The tradition of votive statues continued in the art of Lagash, circa 2100 BCE. Gudea presented votive statues of himself, made of a hard, durable stone called diorite, to many temples he built or restored. The cuneiform inscription on the statue shown here (fig. 2-10) relates that Gudea dedicated himself, the sculpture, and the temple in which the sculpture resided to the goddess Geshtinanna, the divine poet and

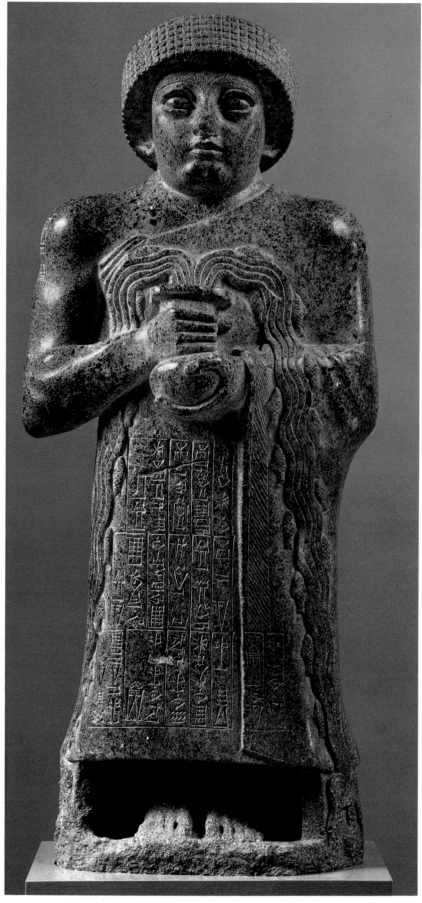

2-10. Votive statue of Gudea, from Lagash (modern Telloh, Iraq). c. 2120 BCE. Diorite, height 29" (73.7 cm). Musée du Louvre, Paris

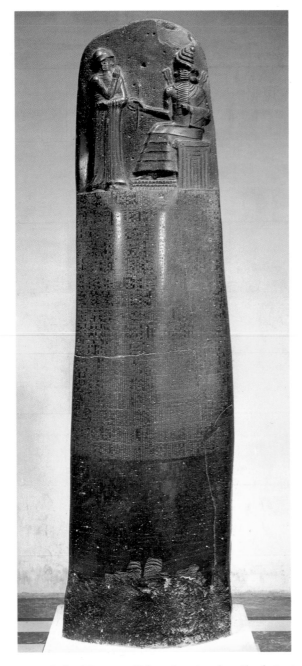

and reunited Sumer under Hammurabi (ruled 1792–1750 BCE). Their capital city was Babylon, and its residents were called Babylonians.

Among Hammurabi's achievements was a written legal code that recorded the laws of his realm and the penalties for breaking them. The code is incised in cuneiform script on a stela, under a portrait of the ruler—himself depicted standing before the supreme judge, the sun god Shamash (fig. 2-11). As in the *Stela of Naramsin*, the relative importance of the figures is indicated by hieratic scale. Hammurabi, the earthly law enforcer, is smaller than Shamash, who wears a four-horned headdress that marks him as a deity. Rays of light rise from the god's shoulders as he holds a rod and ring, Babylonian symbols of justice and power.

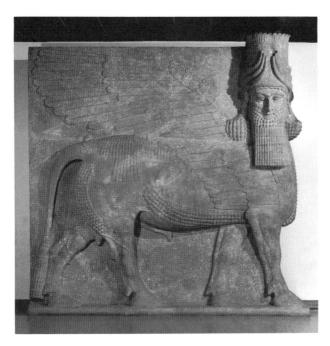

2-11. Stela of Hammurabi, from Susa (modern Shush, Iran). c. 1792–1750 BCE. Basalt, height of stela approx. 7' (2.13 m), height of relief 28" (71.1 cm). Musée du Louvre, Paris

In the introductory section of the stela's long cuneiform inscription, Hammurabi declared that with this code of law he intended "to cause justice to prevail in the land and to destroy the wicked and the evil, that the strong might not oppress the weak nor the weak the strong." Most of the 300 or so entries that follow deal with commercial and property matters. Only sixty-eight relate to domestic problems, and a mere twenty deal with physical assault. Punishments depended on the gender and social standing of the offender.

2-12. Guardian figure, from the entrance to the throne room, palace of Sargon II. c. 720 BCE. Limestone, height 16' (4.86 m). The Oriental Institute of the University of Chicago

interpreter of dreams. Gudea is shown clothed in a long garment similar to that worn by the female votive figure from Eshnunna (see fig. 2-6). He holds a vessel from which life-giving water flows in two streams filled with leaping fish.

The land between the rivers remained a much fought-over prize. Periods of political turmoil and stable government alternated until the Amorites, a Semitic-speaking people from the Arabian Desert to the west, moved into the area

Around 1400 BCE, a people called the Assyrians rose to dominance in northern Mesopotamia. Known for their military prowess, they controlled most of Mesopotamia by the end of the ninth century BCE. By the early seventh century BCE, they had extended their influence as far west as Egypt. Strongly influenced by Sumerian culture, the Assyrians adopted the ziggurat form and preserved Sumerian texts. The most complete surviving version of the *Epic of Gilgamesh*, the best-known literary work of ancient Sumer, was found in the library of the powerful Assyrian king Assurbanipal (ruled 669–c. 627 BCE).

The Assyrians built fortified cities and vast palaces decorated with wall paintings and stone reliefs. The capital at Dur Sharrukin (modern Khorsabad, Iraq), built by Sargon II (ruled 721–

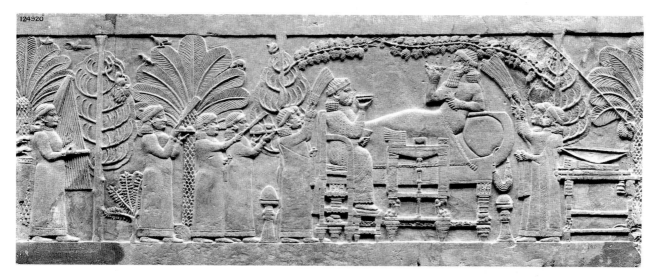

2-13. *Assurbanipal and His Queen in the Garden,* from the palace at Nineveh (modern Kuyunjik, Iraq). c. 647 BCE. Alabaster, height approx. 21" (53.3 cm). The British Museum, London

705 BCE), featured a walled citadel, or fortress, containing 200 rooms, 30 courtyards, and an immense ziggurat. Inside the citadel, a palace complex was raised on a fortified platform about 52 feet high. Deep inside it, the king's throne room was protected by a stone gate carved with colossal guardian figures, such as the human-headed bull illustrated here (fig. 2-12). These hybrid creatures, ranging from 13 to 16 feet tall, also flanked the gates of the citadel.

Assurbanipal, king of the Assyrians three generations after Sargon II, had his own capital at Nineveh (modern Kuyunjik, Iraq). His palace was decorated with panels of alabaster, carved with a pictorial narrative in low relief. One panel shows the king and queen in a pleasure garden (fig. 2-13). The ruler, reclining on a couch, and his queen, seated, are surrounded by servants bringing trays of food and whisking away flies. The king has taken off his rich necklace and laid aside his weapons, seen on the table behind him. This tranquil domestic scene is actually a victory celebration. A grisly trophy, the upside-down severed head of his vanquished enemy, hangs from a tree at the far left.

Assurbanipal's conquests, which stretched as far as Egypt, were short-lived. Soon after his reign, the Assyrians succumbed to internal weakness and external enemies, and by 600 BCE their empire had collapsed. Before another century passed, Mesopotamia was absorbed by the Persian Empire under Cyrus II, called the Great (ruled 559–530 BCE). Under Persian rule, Mesopotamia became part of an empire that eventually stretched from India to Egypt.

Egypt

While city-states such as Sumer began to develop in Mesopotamia, a rich civilization arose in Egypt in the fertile valley and delta of the Nile. The Predynastic period, which lasted roughly from 4500 to 3300 BCE, was a time of social and political transformation when Egypt was unified under a succession of powerful families or dynasties.

An Egyptian priest and historian named Manetho drew up a list of rulers in the third century BCE. He based his work on temple records and inscriptions written in hieroglyphs or hieratic writing (see "Origins of Writing," page 48). Manetho grouped the kings into thirty dynasties that ruled the country between its unification around 3150 BCE and its conquest by Alexander the Great of Macedonia in 332 BCE. Egyptologists have since grouped these dynasties into larger time spans reflecting broad historical developments. The Early Dynastic period (c. 3150–2700 BCE, Dynasties 1–2) was followed by three major periods: the Old Kingdom (c. 2700–2190 BCE, Dynasties 3–6), the Middle Kingdom (c. 2040–1674 BCE, Dynasties 11–14), and the New Kingdom (c. 1552–1069 BCE, Dynasties 18–20). These phases alternated with politically turbulent intermediate periods. After the conquest of Egypt by Alexander the Great, and Macedonian rule (332–305 BCE), Greek Ptolemaic rulers (fifteen rulers in succession were named Ptolemy), reigned until the country became part of the Roman Empire in 31 BCE. The line ended with the famous queen, Cleopatra.

EARLY DYNASTIC AND OLD KINGDOM EGYPT

With the start of the Early Dynastic period, Egypt became a consolidated state along the banks of the Nile River. According to Egyptian tradition, the country had previously evolved into two kingdoms, Upper Egypt in the south and Lower Egypt in the north. (Upper and Lower Egypt refer to the flow of the Nile, not their position on modern maps.) An Upper Egyptian ruler, referred to in an ancient document as "Menes king–Menes god," finally conquered Lower Egypt and merged the lands into a single kingdom.

Egyptian Symbols

Crowned figures, symbolizing kingship, are everywhere in Egyptian art. The false beard of a dead king is long, braided, and ends in a knob. A living king is portrayed with a shorter, squared-off beard (see fig. 2-17). The cobra, "she who rears up," was equated with the sun, the king, and some deities.

The god Horus, king of the earth and a force for good, is represented most characteristically as a falcon. Horus's eyes (*wedjat*)

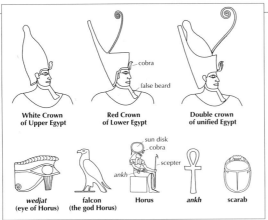

White Crown of Upper Egypt

Red Crown of Lower Egypt

Double crown of unified Egypt

cobra
false beard

sun disk
cobra
ankh
scepter

wedjat (eye of Horus)

falcon (the god Horus)

Horus

ankh

scarab

were regarded as symbolic of the sun and moon. The *wedjat* here is the solar eye. The *ankh* is symbolic of everlasting life. The scarab (beetle) was associated with the creator god Atum and the rising sun.

Mummies

No actual ancient recipes for preserving the dead have been found, but the basic process can be gleaned from several sources, including images found in tombs, the descriptions of later Greek writers, scientific analysis of mummies, and modern experiments. The process was roughly as follows.

The dead body was taken to a mortuary, a special structure used exclusively for embalming. Under the supervision of a priest, workers removed the brain, generally through the nose, and emptied the body cavity through an incision in the left side. They then placed the body, together with its major internal organs, in a vat of natron, a naturally occurring salt. It was left to steep in this solution for a period of a month or more. This caused the skin to blacken, so once the workers had retrieved a body from the vat and carefully dried it, they often dyed it to restore something of its color, using red ocher for a man, yellow ocher for a woman. They then packed the body cavity with clean linen, provided by the family of the deceased and soaked in various herbs and ointments. They wrapped the major organs in separate packets, either putting them in special containers to be placed in the tomb chamber or stuffing them back into the body.

The tedious ritual of wrapping the body could now begin. They first wound the trunk and each of the limbs separately with cloth strips, then wrapped the whole body in a shroud. They then wound it in additional strips of cloth, layer after layer, to produce the familiar mummy shape. The linen winders often inserted good luck charms and other small objects among the wrappings. If the family happened to have furnished a Book of the Dead, a selection of magic spells meant to help the deceased survive a "last judgment" and win everlasting life, it was tucked in between the mummy's legs.

This legendary king-god Menes may have been an actual king named Narmer (Dynasty 1, ruled c. 3150–3125 BCE), known from a famous stone plaque, the *Palette of Narmer* (fig. 2-14), found at Hierakonpolis. **Palettes**, flat stones with a circular depression on one side, were used to mix paint that was applied to the eyelids to help prevent eye infections and perhaps to reduce the glare of the sun. The *Palette of Narmer* has the same form as these common objects but is much larger and probably had a ceremonial function.

King Narmer appears as the main character on the palette, and his name appears at the top in pictographs, or picture writing: a horizontal fish (*nar*) above a vertical chisel (*mer*). Following the convention of hieratic scale, he is shown larger than the other human figures on the palette to indicate his importance. On one side of the palette (fig. 2-14, left), Narmer, wearing the White Crown of Upper Egypt (see "Egyptian Symbols," above), holds the hair of a captive

who may be the conquered ruler of Lower Egypt. On the other side of the palette (fig. 2-14, right), Narmer is shown at the top left wearing the Red Crown of Lower Egypt, making it clear that he rules both lands now. The decapitated bodies of Lower Egyptian warriors have been placed in two neat rows, their heads between their feet.

Many of the figures on the palette are shown in poses that would be impossible to assume in real life. Heads are shown in profile, to best capture the subject's identifying features, while eyes, most expressive when seen from the front, are rendered in frontal view. The shoulders are represented frontally, but the hips, legs, and feet are drawn in profile. These conventions of Egyptian painting and relief sculpture were followed especially in the depiction of royalty and other dignitaries, while persons of lesser social rank tended to be represented slightly more **naturalistically** (compare the figure of Narmer with those of his standard-bearers in figure 2-14, right).

Central to ancient Egyptian religious belief was the notion that an essential part of every human being was its life force—the *ka*, or spirit. The *ka* lived on after the death of the body, forever engaged in the activities it had enjoyed during its earthly existence. It needed a body to live in, however, such as a carved likeness of the deceased and/or his or her actual corpse, preserved by mummification (see "Mummies," left).

The need to fulfill the requirements of the *ka* led not only to the creation of *ka* statues, but also to the development of elaborate funerary rites and tombs filled with supplies and furnishings that the *ka* might require throughout eternity. In the Early Dynastic period, the most common type of tomb structure in Egypt was the **mastaba**, a flat-topped, one-story building with slanted walls erected above an underground burial chamber. The kings of Dynasties 3 and 4, the first dynasties of the Old Kingdom, devoted huge sums to the construction of extensive funerary complexes. These structures tended to be grouped together in a **necropolis**—literally, a city of the dead—at the edge of the desert on the west bank of the Nile. The land of the dead was believed to be situated in the direction of the setting sun. Two of the most extensive of these early necropolises are those at Saqqara and Giza, near modern Cairo.

For his tomb complex at Saqqara, King Djoser (Dynasty 3, ruled c. 2681–2662 BCE) commissioned the earliest truly monumental architecture in Egypt. The designer of the complex, a man called Imhotep, laid out Djoser's tomb as a stepped pyramid consisting of six mastaba-like elements placed on top of each other, and originally covered with a limestone facing, or veneer (fig. 2-15). Although the final structure superficially resembles the ziggurats of Mesopotamia, it differs in both concept and purpose. It is built of

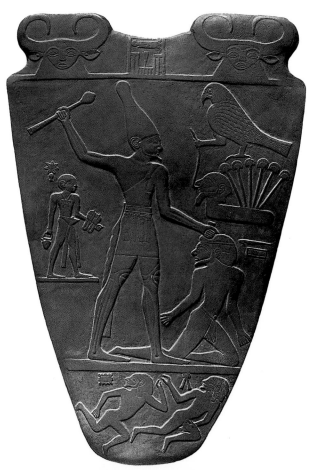
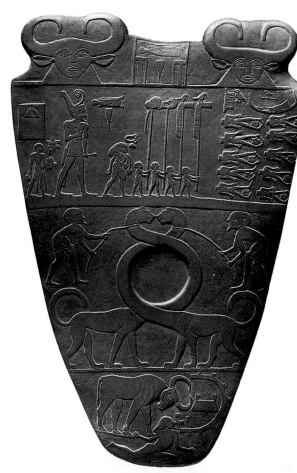

2-14. **Palette of Narmer,** from Hierakonpolis. Dynasty 1, c. 3150–3125 BCE. Slate, height 25" (63.5 cm). Egyptian Museum, Cairo

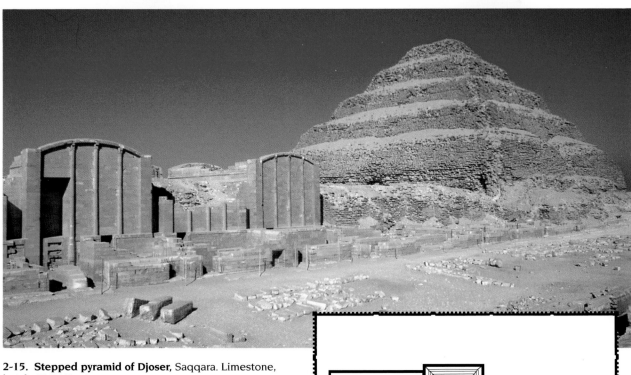

2-15. **Stepped pyramid of Djoser,** Saqqara. Limestone, height 204' (62 m)

finely cut stone, not mud brick; it rises in stages and does not have ramps; and it protects a tomb. From its top, a 92-foot shaft descended to a granite-lined burial vault. Adjacent to the stepped pyramid, a funerary temple was used for continuing worship of the dead king, and sham buildings—simple masonry shells filled with debris—represented chapels, palaces with courtyards, and other structures (fig. 2-16).

2-16. **Plan of Djoser's funerary complex,** Saqqara. Dynasty 3, c. 2681–2662 BCE

large court

sham buildings

funerary temple

ka statue

court of the statue room

North Palace

entrance   festival courtyard   South Palace

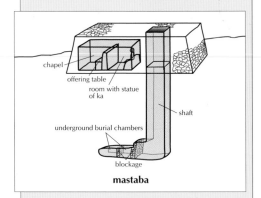

mastaba

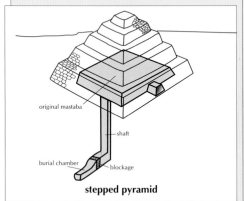

stepped pyramid

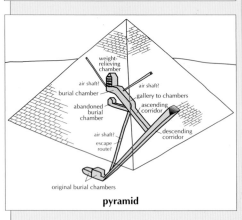

pyramid

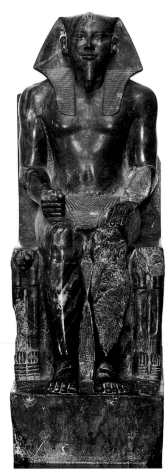

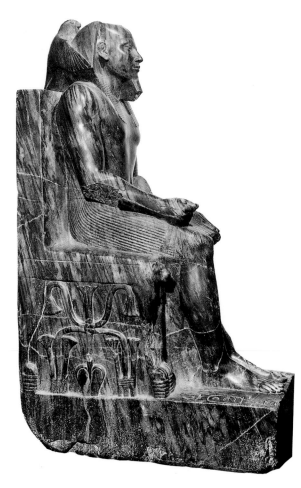

2-17. Khafre, from Giza. Dynasty 4, c. 2570–2544 BCE. Diorite, height 5'6 1/8" (1.68 m). Egyptian Museum, Cairo

Designed as a miniature replica of the king's earthly realm, these buildings were intended for the use of his *ka* in the hereafter.

In three-dimensional sculpture, artists were capable of sculpting figures naturalistically, as they are in life. Nevertheless a rigidly frontal, simple conception continued to control the sculpted forms. Egyptian sculpture is rectilinear and blocklike, in contrast to the cylindrical forms of early Mesopotamian sculpture. An over-lifesize *ka* statue of the Old Kingdom, the Dynasty 4 King Khafre (ruled c. 2570–2544 BCE), represents the ruler enthroned and protected by the falcon-god Horus (fig. 2-17). The god Horus/ falcon merges with the king's headdress as he protectively enfolds the king's head with his wings.

In his *ka* statue, Khafre wears the traditional royal costume: a short kilt, a false beard symbolic of kingship, and a linen headdress with an *uraeus*, the cobra symbol of the sun god

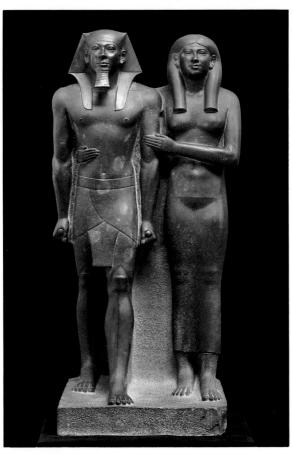

2-18. Menkaure and His Wife, Queen Khamerernebty, from Giza. Dynasty 4, c. 2515 BCE. Slate, height 54 1/2" (142.3 cm). Museum of Fine Arts, Boston
Harvard University–MFA Expedition

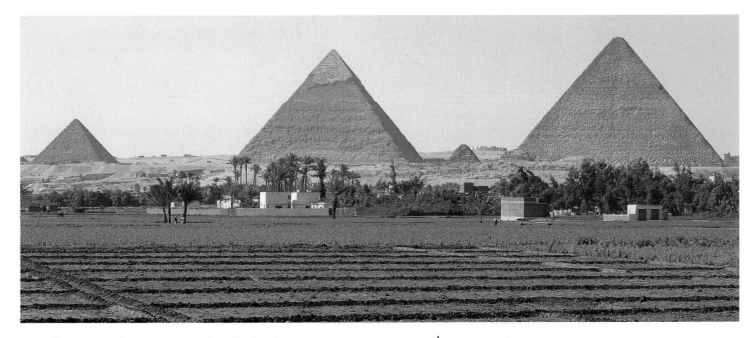

2-19. Great Pyramids, Giza. Dynasty 4, c. 2601–2515 BCE. Erected by (from left) Menkaure, Khafre, and Khufu. Granite and limestone, height of pyramid of Khufu 450' (137 m)

For many centuries it was not known that the pyramids were the tombs of early Egyptian rulers. One theory was that they were gigantic silos for storing grain during periods of drought and famine. This notion was fostered in part by the discovery that the pyramids' accessible interior spaces were empty. The designers of the pyramids tried to ensure that the king and the tomb "home" would never be disturbed. Khufu's builders placed his tomb chamber in the very heart of the mountain of masonry, at the end of a long, narrow, steeply rising passageway, sealed off after the king's burial by a 50-ton stone block. Three false passageways, either deliberately meant to mislead or the result of changes in plan as construction progressed, obscured the location of the tomb. Despite such precautions, early looters managed to penetrate to the tomb chamber and make off with Khufu's funeral treasure.

Ra, and the Horus falcon, on the back of the throne. The symbols of united Egypt, the lotus and papyrus, also decorate the throne. Like the votive statue of Gudea of Lagash (see fig. 2-10), this statue was carved in durable diorite, ensuring that the figure would provide a home for the king's *ka* for eternity.

A double portrait of Khafre's son and daughter-in-law, King Menkaure (ruled c. 2533–2515 BCE) and Queen Khamerernebty (fig. 2-18), was discovered in the funerary temple built by Menkaure. The figures, carved from a single block of stone, are visually joined by the queen's symbolic gesture of embrace. The king, depicted in accordance with cultural ideals as an athletic, youthful figure nude to the waist, stands in a typically Egyptian balanced pose with one foot in front of the other, his arms straight at his sides and his fists clenched. His equally youthful queen mimics his striding pose with a smaller step forward, her sheer, tight-fitting garment revealing the curves of her body.

The architectural form most closely identified with Egypt is the true pyramid with a square base and four sloping triangular sides (see "Mastaba

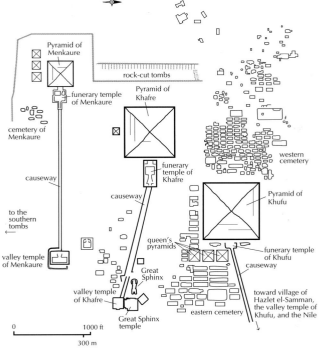

2-20. Plan of the funerary complex, Giza

to Pyramid," opposite). Egypt's most famous funerary structures are the three Great Pyramids at Giza (fig. 2-19), part of tomb complexes built by the Dynasty 4 kings Khufu (ruled c. 2601–2578 BCE), Khafre (ruled c. 2570–2544 BCE), and Menkaure (ruled c. 2533–2515 BCE). The oldest and largest of the Giza pyramids is that of Khufu, which covers 13 acres at its base and rises to a height of about 450 feet even in its deteriorated state. It was originally finished with a sheath of polished limestone that lifted its apex some 30 feet above the present summit, to roughly the height of a 48-story skyscraper.

Next to each of the pyramids was a funerary temple connected by a causeway, or elevated road, to a valley temple on the bank of the Nile (fig. 2-20). When a king died, his body was ferried across the Nile from the royal palace to his valley temple, where it was received with elaborate ceremony. It was then carried up the causeway to his funerary temple and placed in its chapel, where further rites took place. Finally, the body was entombed in a well-hidden vault inside the pyramid.

Tombs of royalty and wealthy individuals were often decorated on the interior with paintings and reliefs. These images frequently show the dead person going about the duties and pleasures of earthly life. The paintings might also have symbolic or religious meanings. A scene in the mastaba of a Dynasty 5 government official named Ti shows him supervising a hippopotamus hunt from a shallow boat (fig. 2-21). As dictated by Egyptian hieratic scale, Ti stands much larger than his men. Space is indicated in registers, with the nearest elements at the bottom of the composition. The river is seen from above, a band of parallel wavy lines below the boats. The fish, a crocodile, and hippopotamuses are shown in profile for easy identification. The boats skim the surface of the water unhampered by the papyrus stalks, shown as parallel vertical lines. The hunt had symbolic value: The companions of Seth, god of darkness, were believed to disguise themselves as hippopotamuses, so depictions of such hunts illustrate not only the valor of the deceased and the eradication of a troublesome beast that destroyed crops, but also the triumph of good over evil.

THE MIDDLE KINGDOM

During the Middle Kingdom, political authority became less centralized. Provincial governors claimed increasing power, limiting the king's responsibilities to national concerns such as the defense of Egypt's frontiers, the control of water, and related matters such as agricultural wealth and trade. Cities along the Nile grew up along the river's banks, with long streets laid out parallel to the river (that is, running north and south) and short crossing streets leading in from the water. This grid pattern became the first logical city plan. At Kahun, for example, archeologists found the rectangular blocks formed by the streets further subdivided into lots for houses much like modern cities. The size of the houses and the arrangement of the rooms indicate three distinct economic and social levels within the population, each having its own quarter: the governmental and ceremonial center with the palace of the king, the quarter with large dwellings probably for court officials and priests, and a large district with smaller mud-brick homes for the workers.

During Dynasties 11 and 12, wealthy members of the nobility and high-level officials commissioned labor-intensive rock-cut tombs that proclaimed their status. The tombs were carved

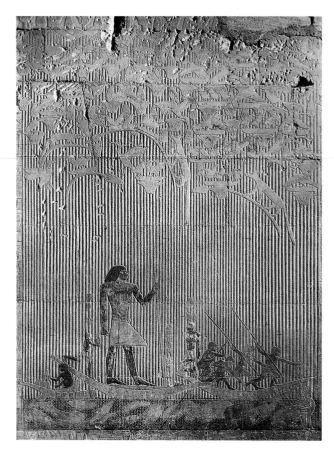

2-21. Ti *Watching a* Hippopotamus Hunt. Tomb of Ti, Saqqara. Dynasty 5, c. 2510–2460 BCE. Painted limestone relief, height approx. 45" (114.3 cm)

This relief forms part of the decoration of a mastaba tomb discovered by the French archeologist Auguste Mariette in 1865. Among Mariette's many other famous finds was the *ka* statue of Khafre (see fig. 2-17). A pioneer Egyptologist, Mariette was a man of great heart, intellect, and diverse talents. It was he who provided the composer Giuseppe Verdi with the scenario for the opera *Aida*, set in ancient Egypt. He pressed the Egyptians to establish the National Antiquities Service to protect, preserve, and study the country's art monuments. In gratitude, they later placed a statue of him in the new Egyptian Museum in Cairo. At his death, his remains were brought back to his beloved Egypt for burial.

out of faces of cliffs, and the walls were commonly painted with scenes of daily life. The Dynasty 12 tomb of a local lord named Khnumhotep in the necropolis at Beni Hasan on the east bank of the Nile has a painting in which two men picking figs compete for the fruit with three baboons seated in the trees (fig. 2-22). Like the hunters in the Old Kingdom relief of Ti, and the standard-bearers of Narmer, these active farmworkers are shown with their shoulders in profile, not in the twisted pose prescribed for royalty.

There is little indication of how ancient Egyptians viewed the artists who created portraits of kings and nobles and recorded so many details of contemporary life, but they must have been admired and respected. Some certainly had a high opinion of themselves, as we learn from an inscription on the tombstone of a Middle Kingdom sculptor: "I am an artist who excels in my art, a man above the common herd in knowledge. I know the proper attitude for a statue [of a man]; I know how a woman holds herself, [and how] a spearman lifts his arm. . . . There is no man famous for this knowledge other than I myself and my eldest son" (cited in Montet, page 159).

The patron's and the artist's desire for clarity permeates Egyptian art. A pectoral, or chest ornament on a necklace (fig. 2-23), also made during Dynasty 12 (c. 1895–1878 BCE), incorporates clearly recognizable human and animal imagery. The pectoral suggests the splendor of royal dress and tomb furnishings during this period. Executed in gold and inlaid with perfectly cut and fitted semiprecious stones, it was discovered in the funerary complex of Senwosret II (Dynasty 12, ruled c. 1895–1878 BCE), in the tomb of the king's daughter Sithathoryunet. Two Horus falcons and coiled cobras of the sun god Ra support a **cartouche**—an oval figure or tablet—enclosing the hieroglyphs (symbols) of the king's name. Around their necks, the cobras wear the *ankh*, the symbol of life. Below, a male figure helps to support a double arch of notched palm ribs, a hieroglyph meaning "millions of years." Decoded, the pectoral's combination of images yields the message: "May the sun god give eternal life to Senwosret II."

THE NEW KINGDOM

During the New Kingdom, Egypt prospered both politically and economically, its kings surpassing in wealth and power the Mesopotamian rulers. One of the most dynamic kings of Dynasty 18, Tuthmose III (ruled 1479–1425 BCE), even extended Egypt's influence along the eastern Mediterranean coast as far as modern Syria. Tuthmose III was the first ruler to refer to himself as "pharaoh," a term that simply meant "great house." (Egyptians used it in the same way that people in the United States speak of

"the White House" when they really mean the current president.) The successors of Tuthmose III continued to use the term, and it ultimately found its way into the Hebrew Bible—and modern usage—as the title for the kings of Egypt.

At the height of the New Kingdom, rulers undertook extensive building programs along the Nile. One of the most spectacular surviving architectural complexes is the funerary temple

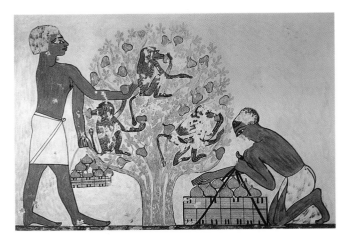

2-22. *Harvest Scene*, tempera facsimile by Nina de Garis Davies of a wall painting in the tomb of Khnumhotep, Beni Hasan. Dynasty 12, c. 1928–1895 BCE

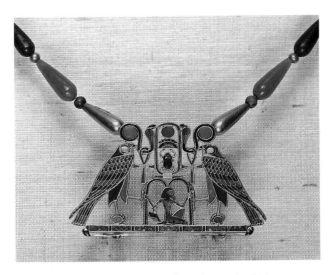

2-23. Pectoral of Senwosret II, from the tomb of Princess Sithathoryunet, el-Lahun. Dynasty 12, c. 1895–1878 BCE. Gold and semiprecious stones, length 3¼" (8.2 cm). The Metropolitan Museum of Art, New York
Purchase, Rogers Fund and Henry Walters Gift, 1916 (16.1.3)

of the female ruler Hatshepsut (Dynasty 18, ruled c. 1478–1458 BCE). Like the temples adjacent to the Old Kingdom pyramids at Giza, the structure, located at Deir el-Bahri, across the Nile from the New Kingdom capital city of Thebes, was designed for funeral rites and

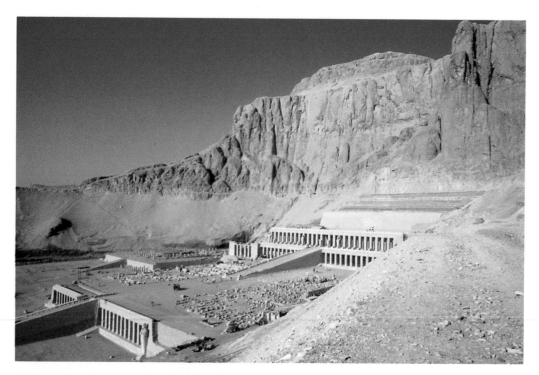

2-24. Funerary temple of Hatshepsut, Deir el-Bahri. Dynasty 18, c. 1478–1458 BCE. At the far left, ramp and base of the funerary temple of Mentuhotep III. Dynasty 11, c. 2009–1997 BCE

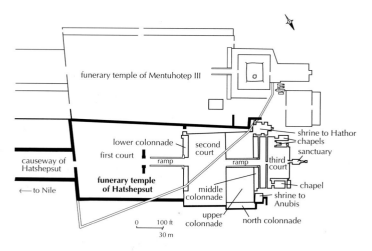

2-25. Plan of the funerary temple of Hatshepsut, Deir el-Bahri

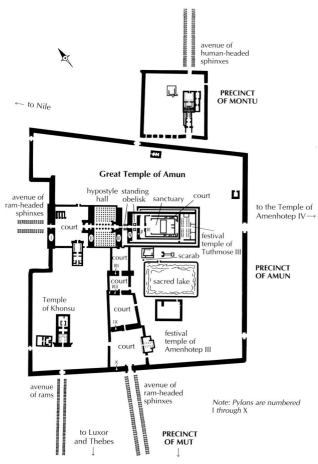

2-26. Plan of the Great Temple of Amun, Karnak. New Kingdom

commemorative ceremonies (fig. 2-24). Hatshepsut's actual tomb was hidden in the hills.

Magnificently positioned against high cliffs, Hatshepsut's temple was constructed on three levels, which were connected by ramps and adorned with rows of **columns**, or **colonnades** (fig. 2-25). The colonnade on the top level was fronted by colossal royal statues; behind it was a **hypostyle** hall, or vast column-filled space, with chapels to Hatshepsut, her father Tuthmose I, and the gods Amun and Ra-Horakhty. At the back of the hall, the temple's innermost sanctuary was cut deep into the cliff in the manner of Middle Kingdom rock-cut tombs. Rare myrrh trees brought from Nubia and pools of water decorated the temple's terraces, and an elevated causeway lined with

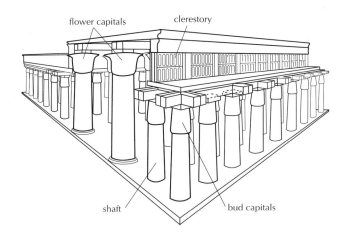

flower capitals | clerestory

shaft | bud capitals

2-27. **Reconstruction drawing** of the hypostyle hall, Great Temple of Amun, Karnak. Dynasty 19, c. 1294–1212 BCE

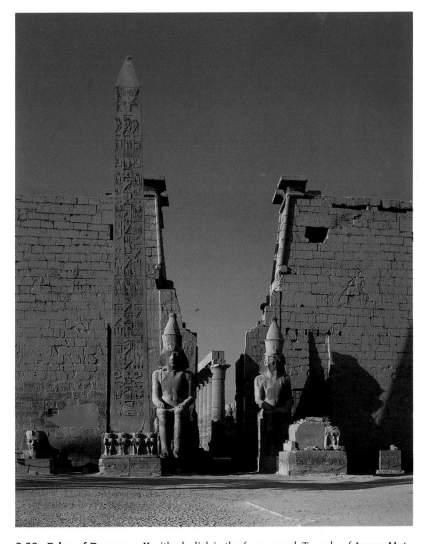

2-28. **Hypostyle hall,** Great Temple of Amun, Karnak

sphinxes once connected the complex to a valley temple on the Nile.

Other important New Kingdom building campaigns took place at Karnak, to the north of Thebes, and Luxor, to its south. Both sites had temple districts consecrated primarily to three Theban deities: Amun, his wife Mut, and their son Khonsu. At Karnak, remains of the Great Temple of Amun still dominate the landscape. Access to the heart of the temple, a sanctuary containing the statue of Amun, was through a series of **pylons** (massive gateways) and courtyards (fig. 2-26). The principal structure, a hypostyle hall, still amazes visitors by its overwhelming size.

The hypostyle hall (figs. 2-27, 2-28) was erected in the reigns of Dynasty 19 rulers Sety I (ruled 1294–1279 BCE) and his son Ramesses II (ruled c. 1279–1212 BCE), whom some believe to be the "pharaoh" of the biblical story of Moses and the Exodus. Known as the "Temple of the Spirit of Sety, Beloved of Ptah in the House of Amun," the hall may have been used for royal coronation ceremonies. Ramesses II referred to it in more mundane terms as "the place where the common people extol the name of his majesty." Extending 170 feet long and 340 feet wide, the hall roof was supported by 134 closely spaced columns, their **shafts** decorated with hieroglyphic inscriptions and images of kings and gods. The columns were topped with **capitals** shaped like lotus flowers or lotus buds, a flower symbolic of Upper Egypt.

Ramesses II, who constructed more temples than any other Egyptian king, also undertook a building campaign in the sacred district at Luxor. He enlarged the existing Temple of Amun, Mut, and Khonsu with the addition of a pylon and a **peristyle** court, or open courtyard ringed with columns and covered walkways (fig. 2-29).

2-29. **Pylon of Ramesses II** with obelisk in the foreground, Temple of Amun, Mut, and Khonsu, Luxor. Dynasty 19, c. 1279–1212 BCE

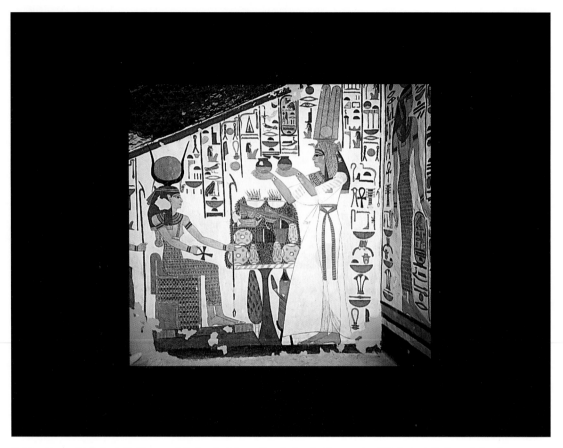

2-30. Queen Nefertari Making an Offering to Isis, wall painting in the tomb of Nefertari, Valley of the Queens, near Deir el-Bahri. Dynasty 19, c. 1279–1212 BCE

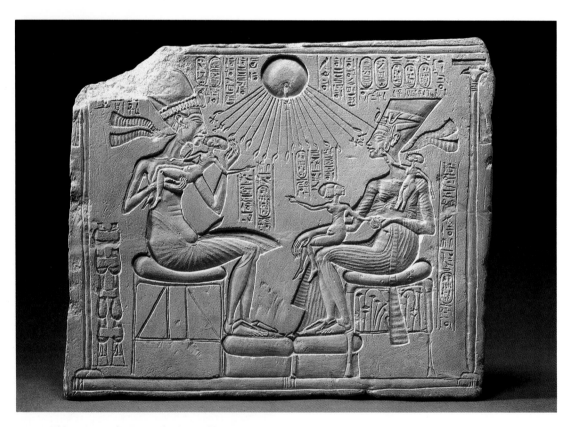

2-31. Akhenaten and His Family, from Akhetaten (modern Tell el-Amarna). Dynasty 18, 1348–1336/5 BCE. Painted limestone relief, 12¼ x 15¼" (31.1 x 38.7 cm). Staatliche Museen zu Berlin, Preussischer Kulturbesitz, Ägyptisches Museum

Egyptian relief sculptors often employed the technique seen here, called sunken relief. In ordinary reliefs, the background is carved away so that the figures project out from the finished surface. In sunken relief, the original flat surface of the stone is the background, and the outlines of the figures are deeply incised, permitting the development of three-dimensional forms within them. If an ordinary relief became badly worn, a sculptor might restore it by recarving it as a sunken relief.

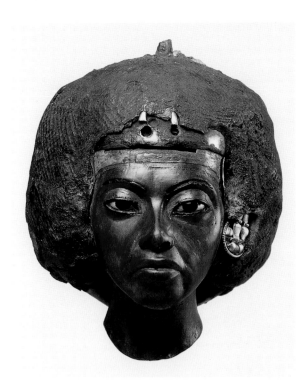

2-32. Queen Tiy, from Kom Mendinet Ghurab (near el-Lahun). Dynasty 18, c. 1390–1352 BCE. Boxwood, ebony, glass, gold, lapis lazuli, cloth, clay, and wax, height 3³/₄" (9.4 cm). Staatliche Museen zu Berlin, Preussischer Kulturbesitz, Ägyptisches Museum

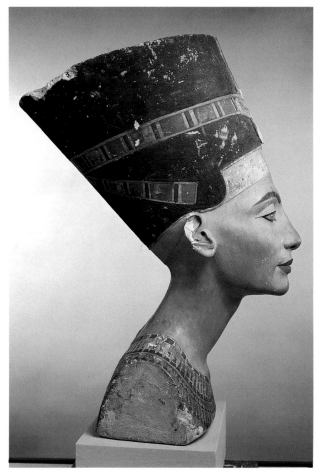

2-33. Nefertiti, from Akhetaten (modern Tell el-Amarna). Dynasty 18, c. 1348–1336/5 BCE. Limestone, height 20" (51 cm). Staatliche Museen zu Berlin, Preussischer Kulturbesitz, Ägyptisches Museum

In front of his pylon stood two colossal statues of himself and a pair of **obelisks**—slender, slightly tapered shafts of stone capped by a pyramidal shape. The faces of the pylon are ornamented with reliefs detailing the king's military exploits.

The tomb of Nefertari, the best known of Ramesses II's eight wives, is among the wonders of the Valley of the Queens necropolis, near Deir el-Bahri. In one of the tomb's many beautiful, large-figured scenes, Nefertari offers jars of perfumed ointment to the goddess Isis (fig. 2-30). The queen wears the vulture-skin headdress of royalty, a royal collar, and a long, transparent white gown. The outline drawing and use of clear colors reflect traditional practices of depicting figures. The artists used particular care in placing the hieroglyphic inscriptions around these figures in order to create a harmonious overall design.

The veneration of traditional Egyptian deities, and especially the worship of the Theban gods Amun, Mut, and Khonsu, which spread throughout the country during the New Kingdom, was interrupted briefly during the reign of the unusual ruler Amenhotep IV (Dynasty 18, 1352–c. 1348 BCE). This king founded a new religion demanding belief in a single god, the life-giving sun disk Aten, and accordingly changed his own name to Akhenaten ("One Who Is Effective on Behalf of Aten"). Such concern for directness also found expression in art. In portraits of the king, such as a relief of him with his queen, Nefertiti, playing with three of their daughters (fig. 2-31), artists candidly emphasized his unusual physical characteristics—long, thin arms and legs, protruding stomach, and a thin neck supporting an elongated head. Above the royal couple, the sun god Aten is depicted as a solar disk sending down long rays ending in human hands. Some of the hands hold *ankhs*, the symbol of life. The base of the queen's throne is adorned with the stylized symbol of a unified Egypt, which has led some historians to conclude that Nefertiti, who was sometimes called "the lady of the two lands," acted as coruler with her husband.

Akhenaten's mother, Queen Tiy, also played a significant role in affairs of state during his reign. Her personality emerges from a miniature portrait head that reveals the exquisite bone structure of her powerful face (fig. 2-32). One of Queen Tiy's formal titles, "The Woman Who Knows," here seems particularly apt. This portrait contrasts sharply with a head of Nefertiti, in which the heavy-lidded eyes and half smile divulge almost nothing about her personal qualities (fig. 2-33). Nefertiti's subjects referred to her as "Fair of Face," "Mistress of Happiness," and "Endowed with Favors," suggesting that she indeed possessed the great beauty seen in this sculpture, which is heightened by the artist's dramatic use of color.

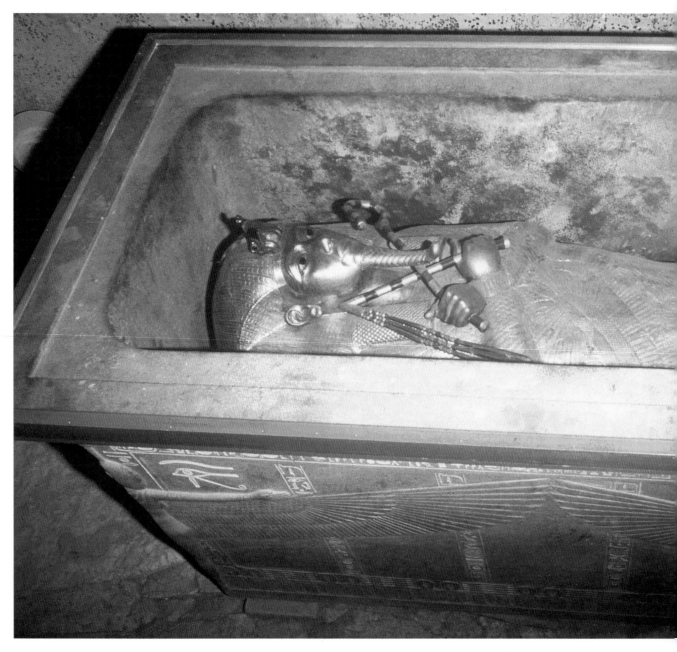

2-34. Inner coffin of Tutankhamun's sarcophagus, from the tomb of Tutankhamun, Valley of the Kings. Dynasty 18, 1336/5–1327 BCE. Gold inlaid with glass and semiprecious stones, height 6'7/8" (1.85 m). Egyptian Museum, Cairo

The English archeologist Howard Carter had worked in Egypt for more than twenty years before he undertook a last expedition, sponsored by the wealthy British amateur Egyptologist Lord Carnarvon, after World War I. In November 1922 Carter discovered the entrance to the tomb of King Tutankhamun, the only Dynasty 18 royal burial place as yet unidentified. By November his workers had cleared their way down to its antechamber, which was found to contain unbelievable treasures: jewelry, textiles, gold-covered furniture, a carved and inlaid throne, four gold chariots, and other precious objects. In February 1923, they pierced through the wall separating the antechamber from the actual burial chamber, and in early January of the following year—having taken great care to catalog all the intervening riches and prepare for their safe removal—they finally reached the king's astonishing sarcophagus.

Akhenaten's new religion outlived him by only a few years, and the priesthood of Amun quickly regained its former power. The young king Tutankhaten (ruled 1336/35–1327 BCE) returned to traditional religious beliefs, changing his name, which meant "Living Image of the Aten," to Tutankhamun, or "Living Image of Amun." He died at a young age and was buried in the Valley of the Kings near Thebes, a necropolis used by New Kingdom rulers.

The sealed inner chamber of his tomb, discovered in 1922, was found to contain amazing treasures: jewelry, textiles, gold-clad furniture, a carved and inlaid throne, four gold chariots, and other precious objects. The king's body lay inside three nested coffins that identified him with Osiris, the god of the dead. The innermost coffin (fig. 2-34) of the **sarcophagus** (rectangular stone coffin), made of solid gold, is decorated with colored **enamelwork** and semiprecious gemstones, as well as very finely incised linear designs and hieroglyphic inscriptions. The king holds a crook and a flail—agricultural harvest instruments associated with Osiris, a fertility and vegetation god who presided over the dead and the underworld.

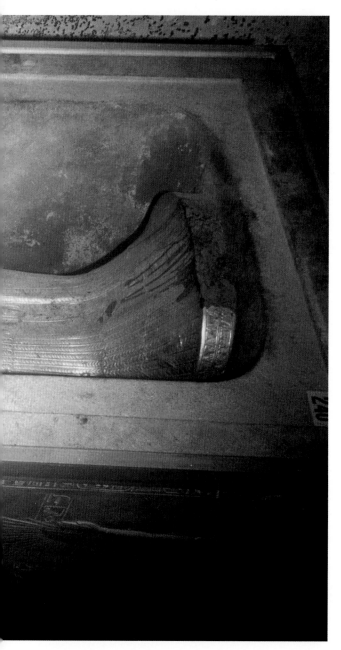

Egyptian funerary practices revolved around Osiris, his resurrection, and a belief in the continuity of life after death by Egyptians of all ranks. The dead were thought to undergo a "last judgment" consisting of two tests presided over by Osiris and supervised by Anubis, the overseer of funerals and cemeteries, represented as a man with a jackal's head. The deceased were first questioned by a delegation of deities about their behavior in life. Then their hearts, which the Egyptians believed to be the seat of the soul, were weighed on a scale against an ostrich feather, the symbol of Maat, goddess of truth. A monster waited beside the scale to devour those who tipped the balance.

These beliefs gave rise to additional funerary practices especially popular among the non-royal classes. Family members commissioned papyrus scrolls containing magical texts or spells to help the dead survive the tests (see "Mummies," page 54). Early collectors of Egyptian artifacts referred to such scrolls as Books of the Dead. A scene from a Dynasty 19 example, created for a man named Hunefer, shows him at successive stages in his introduction into the afterlife (fig. 2-35). At the left, Anubis leads him to the spot where he will weigh his heart in a tiny jar. After passing the test, Hunefer is presented by the god Horus to the enthroned Osiris, who holds his usual crook and flail.

Although we cannot know how Hunefer and other ancient Egyptians actually fared in the afterlife, the art produced to commemorate their lives and support them after death has assured them of immortality. The creativity of the Egyptians over many centuries was acknowledged and admired by contemporary peoples—as it was by their eventual conquerors.

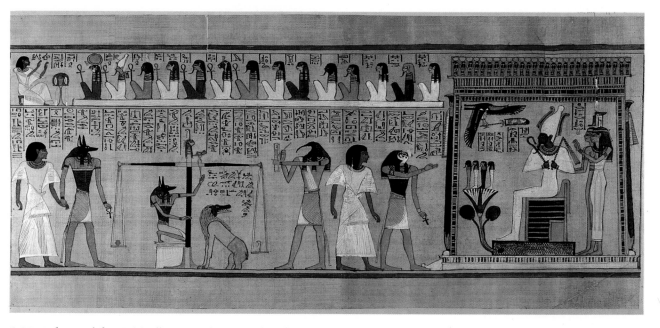

2-35. Judgment before Osiris, illustration from a Book of the Dead. Dynasty 19, c. 1285 BCE. Painted papyrus, height 15⅝" (39.8 cm). The British Museum, London

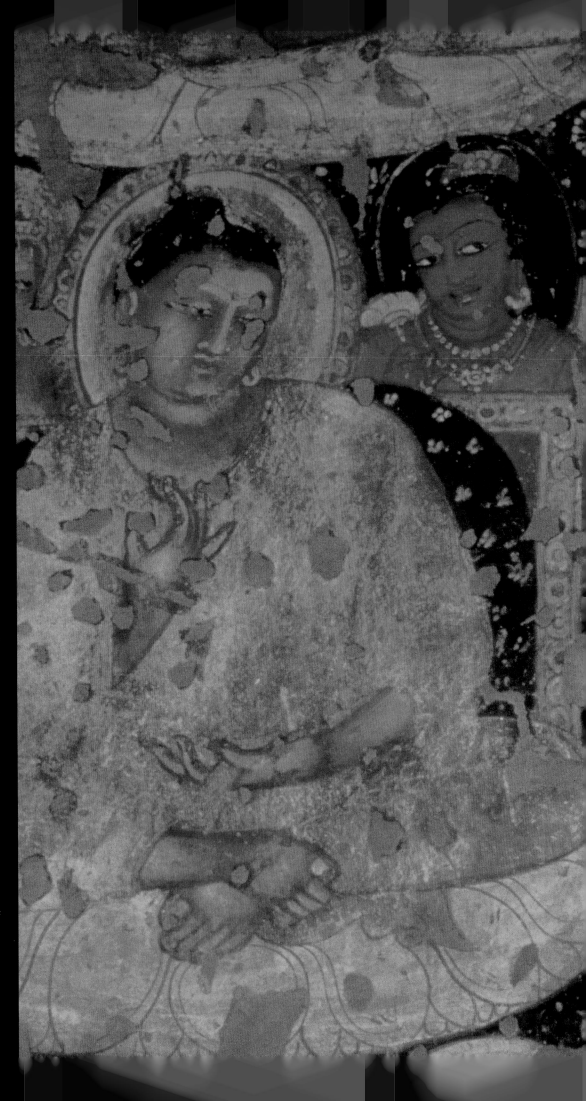

Seated Buddhas, wall painting in Cave 2, Ajanta, India. First half of the 6th century CE

Iconography

Besides the two large seated male figures, we see the heads and upper torsos of three jewel-adorned figures, behind the patterned back cushions. Each holds a flywhisk in his right hand, a Buddhist reference to nonharming. All the figures have halos around their heads, signaling that they are sacred, not profane.

Symbols

Symbols identify the two large figures: both are the Buddha. Both wear simple, unadorned monk's robes; they sit with legs crossed in two different ways: the "noble" posture on the left, and the "full lotus" posture on the right. Some of the thirty-two signs of the Buddha seen here include: long earlobes of royalty, tight hair curls, a bulge on the top of the head (enlightenment), the small tuft of hair between the eyebrows, the rings visible on the necks, and the spoked wheels of Life and the Law painted on the upturned feet and hand on the right. The halos, also called aureoles, indicate holiness. What look like large cushions are, in fact, lotus-flower thrones, symbolic of purity, cosmic harmony, and sponta-neous origin, or divine birth.

Meaning

The key to the meaning of this scene on the monastery wall lies in understanding the symbols and in knowing the artistic con-ventions and styles of sixth-century India. This painting is about the importance and holi-ness of the Buddha's teachings. Both images of the Buddha refer to this, specifically in the hand gestures (*mudras*). Even the crowd of flywhisk bearers reminded the resident monks of the importance of undisturbed concentration.

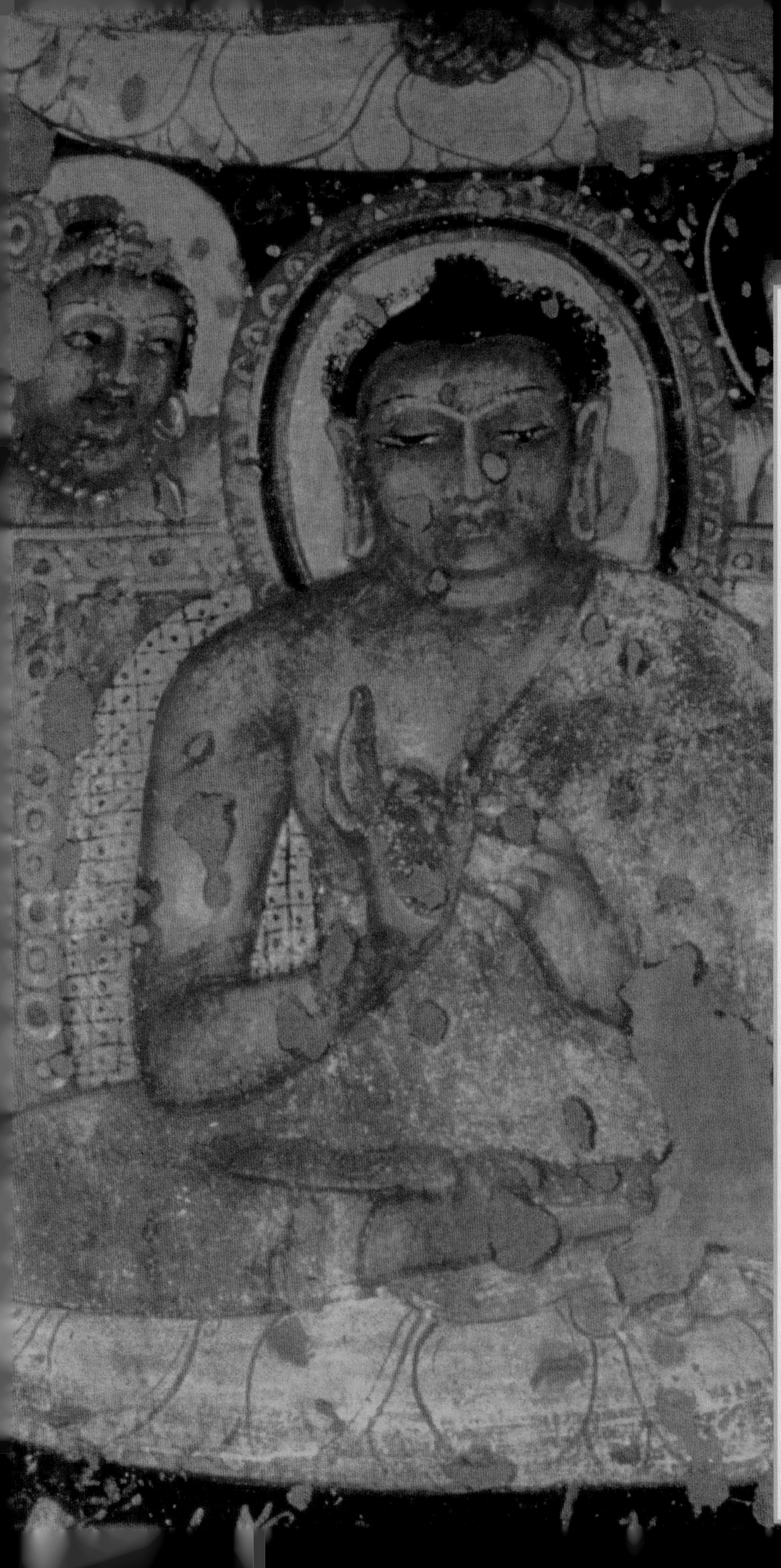

EARLY ASIAN ART

KEYS to Art History

ICONOGRAPHY, SYMBOLISM & MEANING

The study of subject matter and themes in works of art is broadly referred to as iconography. *Iconography* looks at the subject matter—that which is represented—and examines the significance and varying interpretations of art in its cultural context. *Meaning* is derived through a wide understanding of subjects like history, religion, and literature and also from a knowledge of symbolism. *Symbolism* is the use of signs and images to represent ideas that are not easily depicted.

Here we are looking at a section of a wall painted in the first half of the sixth century CE in Ajanta, India (see also fig. 3-9), when Buddhism was flourishing there. It is one of a number of paintings decorating a *vihara*, a monastery where Buddhist monks lived and studied. What we see is two male figures with very long earlobes, gesturing with their hands and sitting cross-legged on cushionlike forms that have patterned back supports. Both have roundish disks or circles behind their heads. In a row behind the back cushions are ornamented figures, each holding an object in his right hand. Clearly there is more going on here than meets the eye. This is a complex image, filled with symbols.

Making sense of iconography requires a knowledge of symbols. The attributes shown here—the long ears, the painting on hands and feet, the protuberance on the top of the heads, the circle form behind the heads, and the pattern on the floor cushions—tell us that both large figures are images of the Buddha. One meaning of this image is that the Buddha was a supreme teacher whose presence could inspire the monks who lived and studied in the cave where this painting is found.

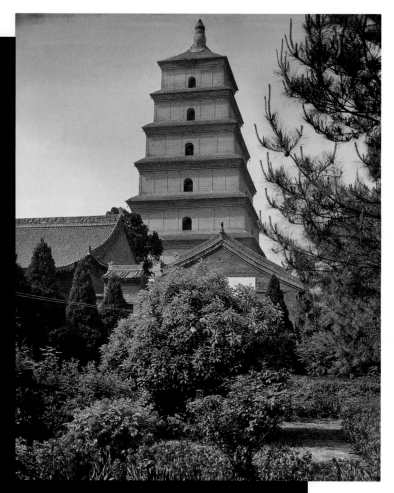

3-1. Great Wild Goose Pagoda at Ci'en Temple, Xi'an, Shanxi. Tang dynasty, first erected 645 CE; rebuilt mid-8th century CE

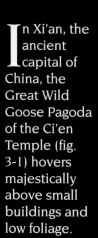

In Xi'an, the ancient capital of China, the Great Wild Goose Pagoda of the Ci'en Temple (fig. 3-1) hovers majestically above small buildings and low foliage. Massive walls, punctuated by roof after horizontal roof, dominate the surroundings with grace and power.

This **pagoda** holds special meaning for students. For over a thousand years (roughly 618–1644 CE), from the Tang through the Ming dynasties, when students passed their official examinations, they went to the pagoda and inscribed their names on the rafters. Thus the Great Wild Goose Pagoda houses a remarkable collection of inscriptions, a veritable history of Chinese calligraphy. This long association with scholarly success invokes the pagoda's original builder, the seventh-century scholar-monk Xuanzang. He built the Ci'en Temple pagoda to store the Sanskrit Buddhist scriptures he brought back from India.

Pagodas, towers associated with East Asian Buddhist temples, serve as reminders of the extent and influence of Buddhist belief. Buddhism, a religion both persuasive and adaptable, inspired artists and millions of believers. The art of Buddhism contributed recurring themes to the otherwise disparate art of Asia.

The civilizations of South and East Asia, among the world's oldest, also rank among the most culturally rich. Together, the South Asian subcontinent and the East Asian countries of China and Japan witnessed the birth of six great, still-living religions and/or philosophies: Buddhism, Hinduism, and Jainism in India; Confucianism and Daoism in China; and Shinto in Japan. The eastward spread of Buddhism from India through Central Asia, to China, Korea, and Japan, united these regions culturally through its philosophy and art. At the same time, India, China, and Japan proudly point to the profound differences in their aesthetic traditions.

The Indian Subcontinent

The South Asian, or Indian, subcontinent includes present-day India, southeastern Afghanistan, Pakistan, Nepal, Bangladesh, and the island of Sri Lanka. Throughout the history of the area, these places have been culturally linked, and the art they have produced shares several overarching traits. It is known for full forms and a profusion of ornament, pattern, and color. This visual generosity is considered auspicious, and it reflects a hope for the abundance and favor of the gods. The pervasive use of symbolism and a concrete familiarity with the divine imbue the art with intellectual and emotional depth. Gods and humans, ideas and abstractions come forth as sensuous forms, radiant with inner spirit.

The earliest civilization of South Asia arose in the lower reaches of the Indus River (in present-day Pakistan and in northwestern India). This Indus Valley, or Harappan, civilization (after Harappa, the first discovered site) flourished from approximately 2600 to 1900 BCE, during roughly the same time as the Old Kingdom in Egypt and the dynasty of Ur in Mesopotamia. Indeed, with Egypt and Mesopotamia it is one of the world's four earliest urban river-valley civilizations.

Stone seals (more than 2,000 small stone seals and impressions have been found) offer an intriguing window on Indus Valley civilization (fig. 3-2). Many of the images carved on the seals suggest continuities with later South Asian culture. Seal (f) in figure 3-2, for example, depicts a man in the meditative posture associated in Indian culture with a yogi, one who seeks mental, physical, and spiritual purification and self-control. In seal (d), people in a procession walk single file under a kneeling worshiper and a figure, possibly a goddess, standing in a tree. This scene may offer some insight into the religious customs of Indus Valley peoples, whose deities may have been the prototypes of later Indian gods and goddesses. The function of the seals, beyond sealing packets, remains a mystery, and their pictographic script has yet to be deciphered.

Around 1500 BCE, after the Indus Valley civilization declined for unknown reasons, a seminomadic warrior people known as the Aryans entered India from the northwest, bringing with them an Indo-European language called Sanskrit and a hierarchical social order. The Vedic period that followed, named for the Vedas, a body of sacred writing, lasted from about 1500 BCE until

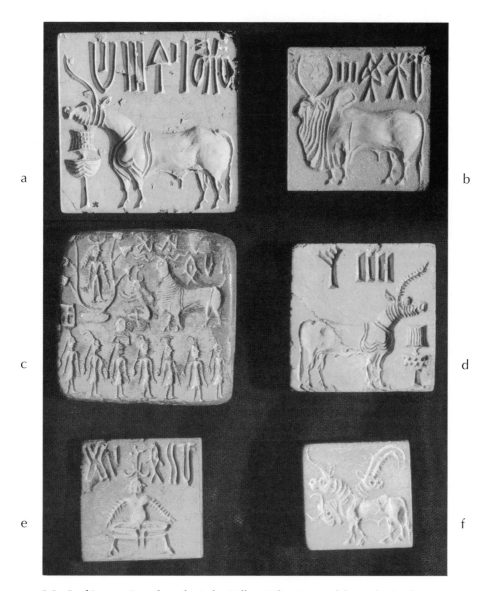

3-2. Seal impressions, from the Indus Valley civilization: a., d. horned animal; b. buffalo; c. sacrificial rite to a goddess(?); e. yogi; f. three-headed animal. c. 2500–1500 BCE. Seals: steatite, each approx. 1¼ x 1¼" (3.2 x 3.2 cm)

Usually carved from steatite stone, seals were coated with alkali and then fired to produce a lustrous, white surface. A perforated knob on the back of each may have been for suspending them. The most popular subjects are animals, the most common being a one-horned bovine standing before an altarlike object (a, d). Animals on Indus Valley seals are often portrayed with remarkable naturalism, their taut, well-modeled surfaces implying their underlying skeletal structures.

the rise of the first unified empire in the South Asian subcontinent in the late fourth century BCE. The Vedic period is marked by the development of religiously sanctioned social classes or castes, which became hereditary, and by the beginnings of Buddhism, Hinduism, and Jainism—three of the four (the fourth is Islam) great religions of India. The metaphysical texts known as the *Upanishads* were also written during this period. Examining the meaning of earlier, more cryptic Vedic hymns, the *Upanishads* focus on the relationship between the individual soul and the universal soul, or *Brahman*. The *Upanishads* advanced concepts that became central to subsequent Indian philosophy, including the assertions that the material world is illusory and only the *Brahman* is

real and eternal; that an existence is cyclical; and that all beings are caught in a relentless cycle of birth, life, death, and rebirth. The goal of religious life is to attain *nirvana*—liberation from this cycle—by uniting our individual soul with the eternal, universal *Brahman*. These philosophical ideas are expressed in a more accessible and popular way in India's great literary epics, the *Mahabharata* and the *Ramayana*. Appearing toward the end of the Vedic period, these texts related stories of gods and humans that later became immensely important in Hinduism.

The Buddhist and Jain religions arose in India with two great teachers, Shakyamuni Buddha (traditionally 563–483 BCE) and Mahavira (599–527 BCE). The Buddha, or "enlightened

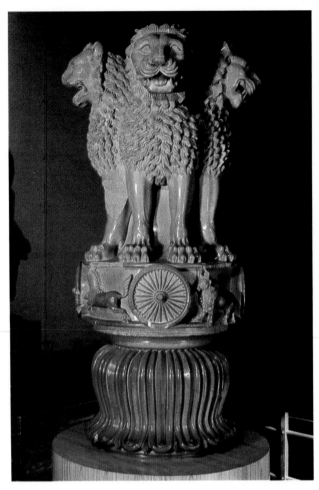

3-3. Lion capital, from an Ashokan pillar at Sarnath, Uttar Pradesh, India. Maurya period, c. 250 BCE. Polished sandstone, height 7' (2.13 m). Archaeological Museum, Sarnath

one," lived and taught in India (see "Buddhism," opposite). Both Shakyamuni Buddha and Mahavira espoused such basic Upanishadic tenets as the cyclical nature of existence and the desirability of escape from it. However, they rejected the authority of the Vedas and the hereditary class structure of Vedic society, with its powerful, exclusive priesthood. Buddhism and Jainism were open to all, regardless of social position.

Buddhism provided the impetus for much of the major art created between the third century BCE and the fifth century CE. Under the Maurya dynasty (c. 322–185 BCE), whose rule extended over all but the southernmost regions of the subcontinent, Buddhism became the state religion. For many centuries, the painting and sculpture of India were associated with imperial sponsorship of the religion. The Mauryan lion **capital**, circa 250 BCE, is a prime example of one emperor's promotion of Buddhism (fig. 3-3). This capital once topped a 50-foot-high pillar of highly polished sandstone located on the grounds of the monastery at Sarnath, site of the Buddha's first teaching. One of many so-called Ashokan pillars, it was erected by the king who first sponsored Buddhism as the state religion. The capital rises with a cushion of downturned lotus petals, on which rests a deep, round collar carved with four animals (symbolizing the earth's four great rivers), alternating with four

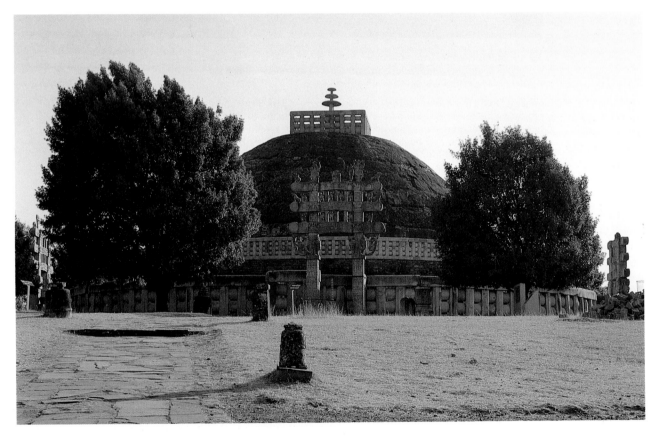

3-4. Great Stupa, Sanchi, Madhya Pradesh, India. Founded 3rd century BCE, enlarged c. 150–50 BCE

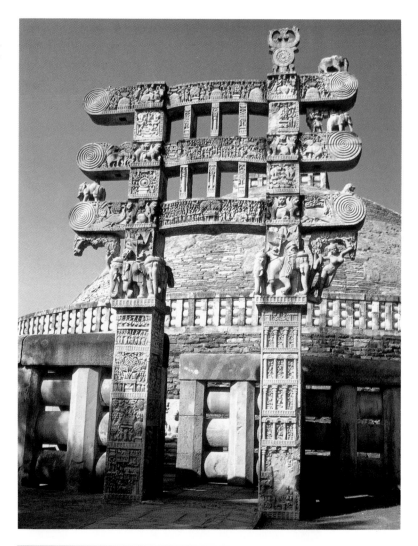

3-5. North torana of the Great Stupa at Sanchi. Early Andhra period, mid-1st century BCE. Stone, height 35' (10.66 m)

wheels (*chakras*)—symbols closely bound to Vedic and Buddhist thought. Among other things, the lions represent the four cardinal directions. Their heraldic stance and the strong stylization of actual elements, such as leg tendons and veins, claws, manes, and toothy muzzles, endow them with almost supernatural presence. When India gained its independence in 1947, it made this capital the national emblem.

Between the second century BCE and the early first century CE, Buddhism continued as the main inspiration for art, and some of the most important and magnificent early Buddhist structures were created. Perhaps no early Indian monument is more famous than the Great Stupa at Sanchi in central India (fig. 3-4). **Stupas** derive from burial mounds and contain **relics**, that is, material remains associated with a holy person, within their solid, dome-shaped earthen core. The first Buddhist stupas, holding the remains of the Buddha after his cremation, were venerated as his body and, by extension, his enlightenment and attainment of *nirvana*. Rituals of veneration included circumambulation, walking around the stupa in a clockwise direction, following the sun's path across the sky.

Originally built during the Maurya period and enlarged circa 150 to 50 BCE, the Great Stupa at Sanchi was part of a large monastery complex crowning a hilltop. The stupa's brick dome, once covered with shining white plaster, is topped by a square stone railing defining the domain of the gods atop the cosmic mountain. The railing encloses the top of a mast bearing three stone disks, or "parasols," of decreasing size, which signal high rank and status. The mast itself is an **axis mundi**, axis of the world, assumed to connect the cosmic waters below the earth with the celestial realm above it and to anchor everything in its proper place.

An 11-foot-tall stone railing, punctuated by four stone gateways, or **toranas** (fig. 3-5), rings the entire stupa. As in much religious architecture, the railing provides a physical and symbolic boundary between the inner, sacred area and the outer, profane world. Each gateway is decorated with a profusion of carved scenes of Buddha's life and past lives, as well as figural sculpture depicting such subjects as *yakshis* (wild and demonic female nature deities) and riders on real and mythical animals. As in all known early Buddhist art, the Buddha himself is not shown in human form. Instead, he is represented by symbols such as his footprints, an empty "enlightenment" seat, or a stupa.

Buddhism

The Buddhist religion developed from the teachings of Shakyamuni Buddha (traditionally dated c. 563–483 BCE, though some scholars now put his death at c. 400 BCE), who lived and taught in the present-day regions of Nepal and northeast India. Born Prince Siddhartha Gautama in a small kingdom of the Shakya clan, he left his family and home at the age of twenty-nine to live as an ascetic in the wilderness. He was deeply troubled by the inevitable sufferings of the human condition—old age, sickness, and death—and the repetitions of these sufferings through the continual cycle of rebirth. But after six long years of meditation, while sitting under a pipal (bodhi) tree at Bodh Gaya, he attained complete enlightenment, or understanding of true reality.

In his teachings Shakyamuni Buddha expounded the Four Noble Truths, which are the foundation of Buddhism: (1) life is suffering; (2) this suffering has a cause, which is desire; (3) desire can be overcome and extinguished; and (4) the way to overcome desire is by following the eightfold path of right view, right resolve, right speech, right action, right livelihood, right effort, right mindfulness, and right concentration.

A buddha is not a god but rather one who sees the ultimate nature of the world and is therefore no longer subject to *samsara*, the cycle of birth, death, and rebirth. The early form of Buddhism, known as Theravada, stresses self-cultivation for the purpose of attaining *nirvana*, which is release from the wheel of *samsara*. In Mahayana Buddhism, which developed later and became popular in northern India, China, Korea, and Japan, the goal was expanded from attaining *nirvana* for oneself to the attainment of buddhahood for all beings. Compassion for all became a primary motivating force.

Mahayana Buddhism recognizes not only Shakyamuni Buddha but also numerous other buddhas, such as Maitreya, the buddha of the future, and Amitabha (called Amida in Japan), the Buddha of Infinite Light and Infinite Life (that is, incorporating all space and time). Mahayana Buddhism developed the concept of bodhisattvas, saintly beings on the brink of buddhahood who have vowed to help others become buddhas before crossing over themselves. The appearance of bodhisattvas in art is based on the princely image of Shakyamuni before he became the Buddha. They wear the princely garb of India, jewelry, and long hair. They are easily distinguished from buddhas, who wear a monk's robe, no jewelry, and have short hair.

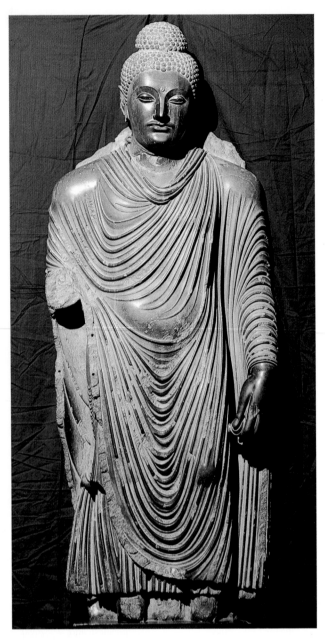

3-6. *Standing Buddha*, from Gandhara (Pakistan). Kushan period, c. 2nd–3rd century CE. Schist, height 7'6" (2.28 m). Lahore Museum, Lahore

During the first century CE, the regions of present-day Afghanistan, Pakistan, and North India came under the control of the Kushans, a nomadic people from Central Asia. During this period Buddhism underwent profound change resulting in the development of a form of Buddhism known as Mahayana, or Great Vehicle (see "Buddhism," page 71). Closely related to this new movement was the appearance of the first Buddha images. The two earliest styles of Buddha images arose in Kushan-ruled areas: Gandhara in the northwest (present-day Pakistan and Afghanistan) and Mathura in central India. Slightly later, a third stylistic tradition, known as the Amaravati school after its most famous site, developed to the south in the region ruled by the Andhra dynasty.

In images from all three schools and throughout Asian art, the Buddha is readily recognized by certain visual characteristics. He wears a simple monk's robe, and because he had been a prince in his youth and had worn the customary heavy earrings, his earlobes are distended. The top of his head has a protuberance (*ushnisha*), which in images often resembles a bun or topknot, a symbol of his enlightenment. Between his eyes is a tuft of white hair from which the light of wisdom emanates.

A typical image from the Gandhara school portrays the Buddha as a powerful, over-lifesize figure (fig. 3-6). His robe is carved in tight, riblike folds alternating with delicate creases, setting up a clear, rhythmic pattern of heavy and shallow lines. This complex fold pattern resembles the treatment of togas in some sculptural works from ancient Rome (see fig. 6-8), a stylistic influence resulting from this region's long history of contact with the Western world. The Gandhara style, transmitted across Central Asia, exerted a strong influence on portrayals of the Buddha in East Asia.

At Mathura, the image of Buddha developed within the indigenous sculptural tradition as represented by statues of *yakshas*, the native male nature deities. In one of the finest of the early Mathura images of Buddha (fig. 3-7), the robe is pulled tightly over the body, allowing the fleshy form to be seen as almost nude. The Buddha is seated in a yogic posture, and his right hand is raised in a **mudra**, or symbolic gesture, meaning "have no fear." His distinctive features and the impressions of *chakras*, or wheels, on his feet and right hand are all clearly visible. An ancient sun symbol, the *chakra* symbolizes both the various states of existence (the Wheel of Life) and the Buddhist doctrine (the Wheel of the Law). In the background are the branches of the pipal, or bodhi, tree, under which the Buddha was sitting when he achieved enlightenment.

As noted above, events from the Buddha's life were popular subjects in reliefs decorating Buddhist stupas and temples. One example from the Great Stupa of Nagarjunakonda, a site of the Amaravati school, depicts a scene from the Buddha's life when he was a prince called Siddhartha, before his renunciation and subsequent quest for enlightenment (fig. 3-8). Shown in his father's palace, surrounded by adoring women, Siddhartha seems worlds away from the sobering burden of the reflections that were to profoundly change his life. Typical of the Amaravati school, the figures on this relief are thinner than those of the Gandhara and Mathura schools. They seem sinuous and mobile, even while at rest.

Buddhism reached its greatest influence in India during the Gupta period (c. 320–500 CE), named for the founders of a dynasty that ruled much of India at that time. Some of the finest surviving artworks of the Gupta period are

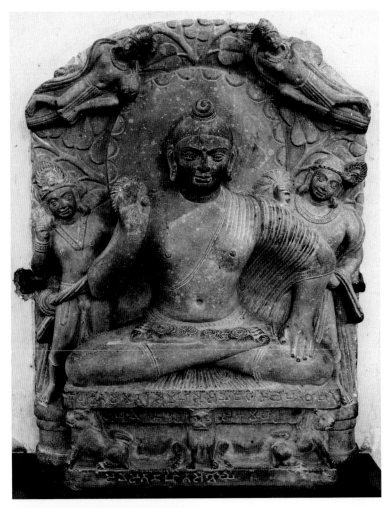

3-7. Buddha and Attendants, from Katra Keshavdev, Mathura, Madhya Pradesh, India. Kushan period, c. late 1st–early 2nd century CE. Red sandstone, height 27¼" (69.2 cm). Government Museum, Mathura

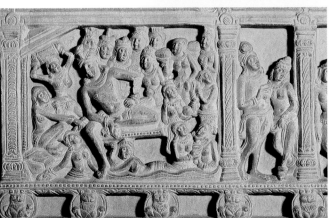

3-8. Siddhartha in the Palace, detail of a relief from Nagarjunakonda, Andhra Pradesh, India. Later Andhra period, c. 3rd century CE. Limestone. National Museum, New Delhi

Hinduism

Hinduism is not one integral religion but many related beliefs and innumerable sects. Resulting from the mingling of Vedic culture (first appearing around 1500 BCE) with indigenous, local beliefs, each Hindu sect takes its particular deity as supreme. In Vaishnavism the supreme deity is Vishnu, in Shaivism it is Shiva, and in Shaktism it is the Goddess Devi—a deity worshiped under many different names. Each deity is revealed and depicted in multiple ways. Vishnu, for example, has ten major incarnations in which he manifests himself in the world. Devi has forms indicative of beauty, wealth, and auspiciousness, but also forms of wrath, pestilence, and power.

All three major Hindu sects draw upon the texts of the Vedas, which are believed to be sacred revelation set down circa 1200–800 BCE. Central to Hindu practice is ritual sacrifice, generally performed to obtain a diety's favor and in the hope that this favor will lead to liberation from *samsara's* endless cycle. Because desire for the fruits of our actions traps us, the ideal is to consider all earthly endeavors as sacrificial offerings to a god. Pleased with our devotion, he or she may grant us an eternal state of pure being, pure consciousness, and pure bliss.

murals (wall paintings) from the Buddhist rock-cut temples and halls of Ajanta, in western India (see pages 66–67). From ancient times, caves, frequently the abode of holy ones and ascetics, were considered hallowed places in India. During the second century BCE, Buddhist monks began to excavate two types of rock-cut halls out of the plateaus in the Deccan region. The type known as the *vihara* was used for the living quarters of the monks, and that known as *chaitya,* meaning "sacred," usually enshrined a stupa. Cave I at Ajanta, carved around 475 CE, is a *vihara* with monks' chambers around the sides and a shrine chamber in the back. Flanking the entrance of the shrine are **fresco** paintings of two **bodhisattvas**, beings who are in the process of becoming buddhas and who have reached a high level of spiritual attainment already. The bodhisattvas are distinguishable from Buddhas because the former wears princely garments lavishly adorned with delicate ornaments and a crown festooned with pearls

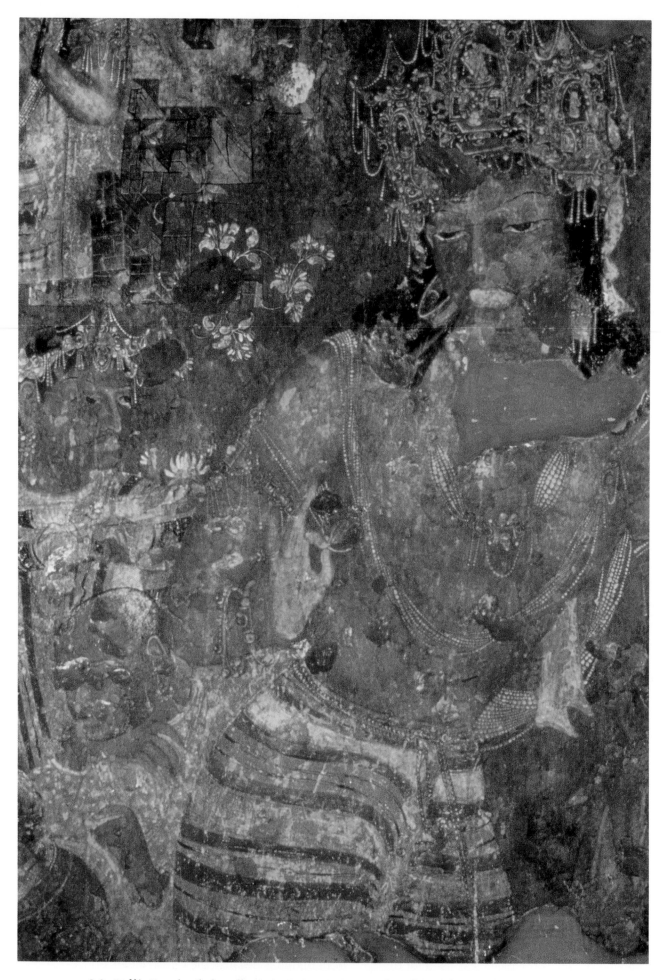

3-9. *Bodhisattva,* detail of a wall painting in Cave I, Ajanta, Maharashtra, India. Gupta period, c. 475 CE

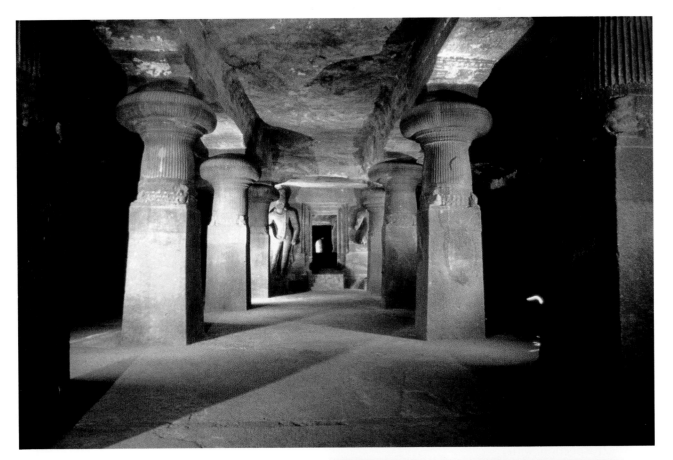

3-10. Cave-Temple of Shiva at Elephanta, Maharashtra, India. Mid-6th century CE. View along the east-west axis to the Shiva shrine

(fig. 3-9), rather than the simple monk's robe. The graceful bending posture conveys his sympathetic attitude, while his spiritual power is suggested by his large size in comparison with the surrounding figures. In no other known example of Indian painting do bodhisattvas appear so magnanimous and graciously divine yet at the same time so human.

Even as Buddhism flourished, Hinduism, sponsored by Gupta monarchs, began the ascendancy that led to its eventual domination of Indian religious life (see "Hinduism," page 73). Hindu temples and sculpture of the Hindu gods rose with increasing frequency during the Gupta period and the post-Gupta era of the sixth to mid-seventh century.

In the mid-sixth century, a rock-cut cave-temple devoted to the major Hindu god Shiva was carved on the island of Elephanta, off the coast of Bombay in western India (fig. 3-10). Shiva (meaning "the auspicious one") exhibits a wide range of aspects or forms, both gentle and wild: he is the Great Yogi who dwells for vast periods of time in meditation in the Himalaya; he is also the husband par excellence who makes love to the goddess Parvati for eons at a time; he is the Slayer of Demons; and he is the Cosmic Dancer, who dances the destruction and re-creation of the world.

Many of these forms of Shiva appear in monumental relief panels adorning the cave-

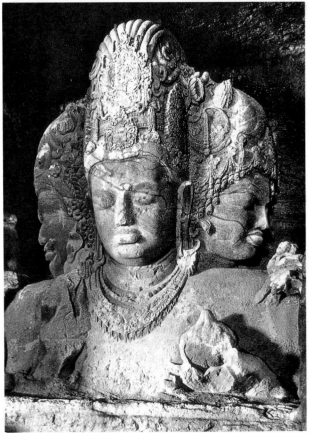

3-11. Eternal Shiva, rock-cut relief in the Cave-Temple of Shiva at Elephanta. Mid-6th century CE. Height approx. 11' (3.4 m)

temple at Elephanta. A huge bust of the deity represents his Sadashiva, or Eternal Shiva, aspect (fig. 3-11). Three heads are shown resting upon the broad shoulders of the upper body, but five are implied: the fourth in back and the fifth, never depicted, on top. The heads summarize Shiva's fivefold nature as creator (back), protector (left shoulder), destroyer (right shoulder), obscurer (front), and releaser (top). On his left shoulder, his protector nature is depicted as female, with curled hair and a pearl-festooned crown. On his right, the wrathful destroyer nature wears a fierce expression, and in front, the god is shown in deep introspection, with

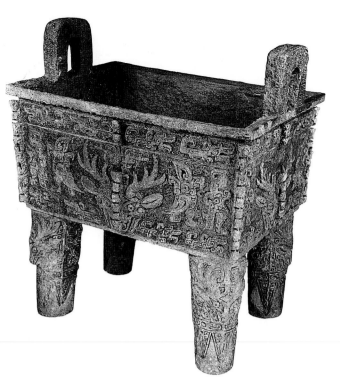

3-12. *Fang ding*, from Tomb 1004, Houjiazhuang, Anyang, Henan. Shang dynasty, Anyang period, c. 12th century BCE. Bronze, height 24¹/₂" (62.2 cm). Academia Sinica, Taipei, Taiwan

the piled-up hair of a yogi. Indian artists often convey the many aspects or essential nature of a deity through multiple heads or arms. Their gift is to portray these additions with such convincing naturalism that we readily accept them. Here, for example, the artist has united three heads onto a single body so skillfully that we still relate to the statue as an essentially human presence.

China

Among the cultures of the world, China is distinguished by its long, uninterrupted development, which has been traced back some 8,000 years. Even more remarkably, while rulers have come and gone, the country has been, with only a few breaks, unified since 221 BCE. Geographically, China is notable for its size, occupying a landmass slightly larger than the continental United States. Within its borders lives one-fifth of the human race.

The country's historical and cultural heart—sometimes called Inner China—is the land watered by its three great rivers, the Yellow, the Yangzi, and the Xi. Just as in South Asia civilization first arose by the Indus River, and in Egypt by the banks of the Nile, Chinese towns and cities first emerged in the Neolithic period in fertile river valleys, especially around the deep southern bend of the Yellow River, nicknamed "China's Sorrow" because of its disastrous floods.

The first Chinese kingdoms date to the Bronze Age, which began in China before 1600 BCE. Traditional histories tell of three Bronze Age dynasties: the Xia, the Shang, and the Zhou.

Modern scholars once dismissed the Xia and Shang as legends, not actual civilizations, but recent archeological discoveries have now established the historical existence of the Shang (c.16th–11th c. BCE), and point strongly to the historical existence of the Xia as well.

Shang kings ruled from a succession of capitals in the Yellow River valley, where archeologists have found walled cities, palaces, and vast royal tombs. Society seems to have been highly stratified, with a ruling group that possessed the bronze technology needed to make weapons. They maintained their authority in part by claiming power as shamans, intermediaries between the supernatural and human realms. Nature and fertility spirits were also honored, and regular sacrifices were made to the spirits of dead ancestors so that they might help the living.

Bronze vessels are the most admired and studied of Shang artifacts. They were connected with shamanistic practices, serving as containers for ritual offerings of food and wine. The illustrated bronze *fang ding*, a square vessel with four legs (fig. 3-12), is one of the largest of hundreds of vessels recovered from royal tombs near the last of the Shang capitals, Yin (present-day Anyang). In typical Shang style its surface is decorated with a complex array of images based on animal forms. A large deer's head (*taotie*) adorns the center of each side; more deer appear on the legs; and the rest of the surface is filled with images resembling birds, dragons, and other fantastic creatures. Such images seem to be related to the hunting life of the Shang, but their deeper significance is unknown.

In the eleventh century BCE, the Shang were conquered by the Zhou from western China. During the Zhou dynasty (1100–256 BCE), a feudal society developed, with a king and his relatives ruling over numerous small states. The supreme deity became known as Tian, or Heaven, and the king ruled as the Son of Heaven. Tian remained the personal cult of China's sovereigns until the end of imperial rule in the early twentieth century.

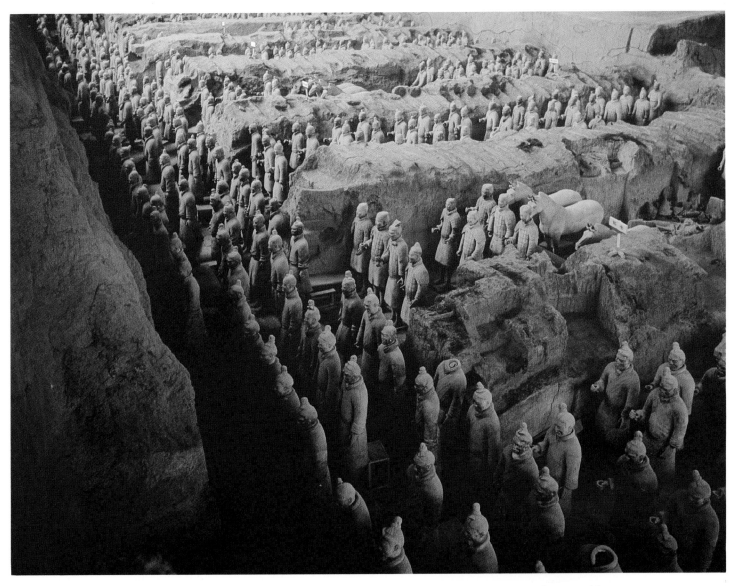

3-13. Soldiers, from the mausoleum of the first emperor of Qin, Lintong, Shaanxi. Qin dynasty, c. 210 BCE. Earthenware, lifesize

Many of China's great philosophers lived during the Zhou dynasty, thinkers such as Confucius, Laozi, and Mozi. During the lifetime of Confucius (551–479 BCE)—a scholar born into an aristocratic family—warfare for supremacy among the various states of China had begun, and the traditional social fabric seemed to be breaking down. Looking back to the early Zhou dynasty as a golden age, Confucius thought about how a just and harmonious society could again emerge (see "Confucianism," right). He never found a ruler who would put his ideas into effect, but his philosophy, Confucianism, eventually became central to Chinese thought and culture.

Toward the middle of the third century BCE, the state of Qin (pronounced "chin," and the source for the English name "China") launched military campaigns that led to its triumph over the other Chinese states by 221 BCE. For the first time, China was united under a single ruler, the powerful emperor Shihuangdi, the first emperor of Qin.

Anxious to ensure personal immortality, Shihuangdi built his own **mausoleum** (a building used as a tomb) at Lintong, near the city of Xi'an in Shaanxi Province. Archeologists who began

---

Confucianism

Confucianism is based on the teachings of the Chinese scholar Confucius (551–479 BCE). His words have come down to us through a book known in English as the *Analects*, which records sayings of the great philosopher collected by his disciples and their followers. At the heart of Confucian thought is the concept of *ren*, or humanheartedness. *Ren*, which emphasizes morality and empathy as the basic standards for all human interactions, is most fully realized in the Confucian ideal of the *junzi*, or gentleman. Originally indicating noble birth, the term was redirected to mean one who through education and self-cultivation had become a superior person, right-thinking and right-acting in all situations.

Confucius also emphasized the importance of *li*, ritual or etiquette. The formalities of social interaction—scrupulous manners as well as ritual, ceremony, and protocol—choreographed life so that an entire society moved in harmony.

Both *ren* and *li* operated in the realm of the Five Constant Relationships defining Confucian society: ruler and subject, parent and child, husband and wife, elder sibling and younger sibling, elder friend and younger friend. Deference based on age and sex is built into this view, as is the deference to authority that made Confucianism popular with emperors. Yet responsibilities flow the other way as well: the duty of a ruler is to earn the loyalty of subjects, of a husband to earn the respect of his wife, of age to guide youth wisely.

---

to excavate a pit near the tomb in 1974 were stunned by what they found: a vast underground army composed of more than 7,000 lifesize clay soldiers and horses standing in military formation ready for battle (fig. 3-13). Skillfully

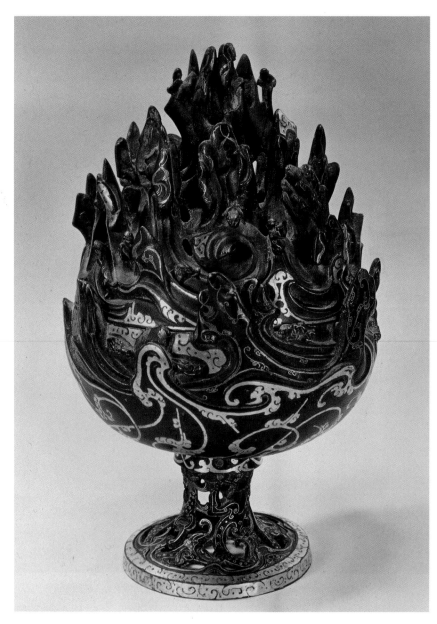

3-14. Incense burner, from the tomb of Prince Liu Sheng, Mancheng, Hebei. Han dynasty, 113 BCE. Bronze with gold inlay, height 10¼" (26 cm). Hebei Provincial Museum, Shijiazhuang

Under the Han dynasty, the philosophies of Daoism and Confucianism flourished. Daoism emphasizes the close relationship between humans and nature. On the philosophical level, it is concerned with bringing the quiet and humble individual life into harmony with the *Dao*, or Way, of the universe. On a popular level Daoism developed into an organized religion, absorbing many traditional folk practices such as shamanism and the search for immortality.

A popular Daoist legend, which told of the Isles of the Immortals in the Eastern Sea, is depicted on a bronze incense burner from the tomb of Prince Liu Sheng, who died in 113 BCE (fig. 3-14). Gold inlays on the base outline the **stylized** waves of the sea. Above them rises the mountainous island, crowded with birds, animals, and people who have discovered the secret of immortality. The techniques used in the manufacturing of this piece represent the ultimate development of the long tradition of bronze casting in China.

In contrast to the metaphysical focus of Daoism, Confucianism is concerned with the human world, and its goal is the attainment of harmony. To this end, it offers an ethical system based on correct relationships among people. Attracted by this emphasis on social order and respect for authority, the Han emperor Wu (ruled 141–87 BCE) made Confucianism the official philosophy. It remained the state ideology of China until the end of imperial rule in the twentieth century and eventually assumed the form and force of a religion.

Confucian subjects appear frequently in Han art. Among the most famous examples are the reliefs from the Wu family shrines built in 151 CE in Jiaxiang. Carved and engraved in low relief on stone slabs, the scenes were meant to teach such basic Confucian tenets as respect for the emperor, filial piety, and wifely devotion. One relief (fig. 3-15) seems to depict homage to the first emperor of the Han dynasty, who is sheltered in a two-story building and distinguished by his larger size. The birds and small figures on the roof may represent mythical creatures and immortals, while to the left the legendary archer Yi shoots at one of the sun-crows. (Traditional myths tell how Yi shot all but one of the ten crows of the ten suns so that the earth would not dry out.) Across the lower register, a procession brings more dignitaries to the reception.

With the fall of the Han dynasty in 220 CE, China splintered into warring kingdoms. A period of almost constant turmoil broadly known as the period of the Northern and Southern Dynasties lasted until 579 CE. Many intellectuals turned to Daoism, which contained a strong escapist element. Yet ultimately it was a new system of belief, Buddhism, that brought the greatest comfort to people of the time. Bud-

modeled from clay and then fired, the figures were originally painted in vivid colors. Literary sources suggest that the tomb itself, which has not yet been opened, may reproduce the world as it was known to the Qin people, with stars overhead and rivers and mountains below.

While harsh and repressive as rulers, the Qin emperors established a centralized bureaucracy and administrative framework, aspects of which are still used in China today. The country was divided into provinces and prefectures; the writing system and coinage were standardized; and forts on the northern frontier were connected to form the Great Wall. During the peaceful and prosperous Han dynasty that followed (206 BCE–220 CE), the country's borders were extended and secured. Chinese control over strategic stretches of Central Asia led to the opening of the famous Silk Road, actually a network of land and sea routes that linked China by trade to Europe.

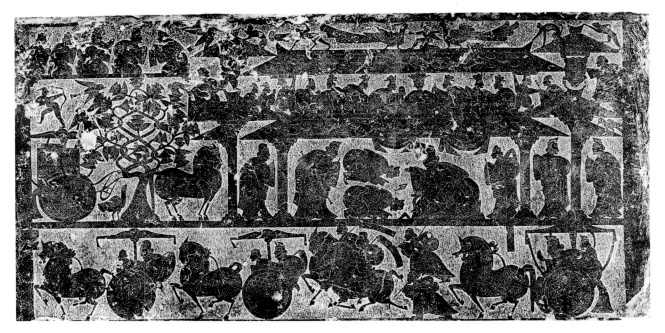

3-15. Detail from a rubbing of a relief in the Wu family shrine (Wuliangci), Jiaxiang, Shandong. Han dynasty, 151 CE. Stone, 27¹/₂ x 66¹/₂" (70 x 169 cm)

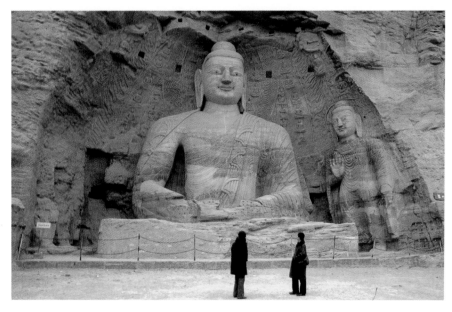

3-16. Seated Buddha, Cave 20, Yungang, Datong, Shanxi. Northern Wei dynasty, c. 460 CE. Stone, height 45' (13.7 m)

dhism spread gradually north from India into Central Asia. With the opening of the Silk Road during the Han dynasty, it reached China (see "The Silk Road and the Making of Silk," page 80). To the Chinese of the post-Han period, beset by constant warfare and social devastation, Buddhism offered consolation in life and the promise of life after death.

The most impressive surviving works of Buddhist art from the Northern and Southern Dynasties period are hundreds of caves carved from the solid rock of cliffs. The rock-cut caves at Yungang in Shanxi Province, for instance, contain many impressive examples of early Chinese Buddhist sculpture. The monumental seated Buddha illustrated here was carved in the latter part of the fifth century (fig. 3-16). Because the front part of the cave has crumbled away, the 45-foot statue is now exposed to the open air. As we've seen, the elongated ears, protuberance on the head (ushnisha), and monk's robe are traditional attributes of the Buddha. The masklike face, massive shoulders, and shallow, stylized drapery indicate a strong Central Asian influence.

In 589 CE a northern general reunified China and established a short-lived dynasty of his own, the Sui. The Sui paved the way for one of the greatest dynasties in Chinese history, the

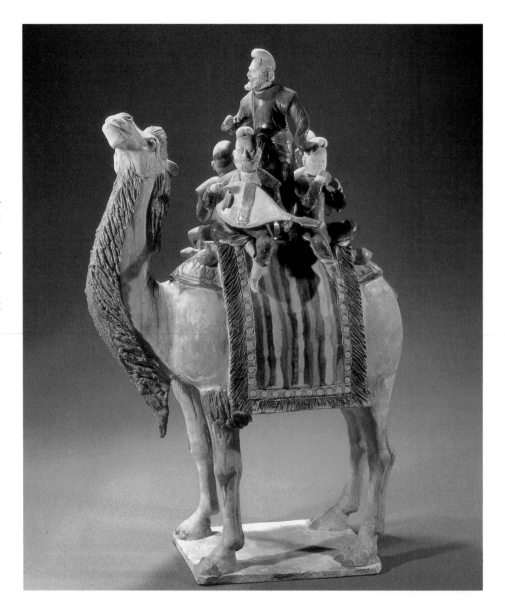

3-17. *Camel Carrying a Group of Musicians,* from a tomb near Xi'an, Shanxi. Tang dynasty, c. mid-8th century CE. Earthenware with three-color glaze, height 26¹/₈" (66.5 cm). Museum of Chinese History, Beijing

---

The Silk Road and the Making of Silk

The fabled trade route between East Asia and the West, called the Silk Road, was a 5,000-mile-long network of caravan and sea routes stretching from Chang'an to the westernmost point of the Great Wall of China—then all the way to Rome. Caravans carrying Chinese luxury goods to the West—and bringing back gold in payment—passed through some of the most hostile regions in Asia and the Middle East, although no one caravan had to make the entire trip; goods were passed from trader to trader on both the overland and sea portions of the route. The Silk Road's importance fluctuated with the politics of the region, as did its safety. Only twice in its long history was it entirely open and comparatively safe.

One of the precious goods carried along the Silk Road, along with spices, was silk. The cultivation and weaving of silk had been a closely guarded secret in China since about 2640 BCE, and it was not until circa 550 CE, when two Christian missionaries smuggled a few silkworm larvae to Constantinople, that the Chinese lost their virtual monopoly. From as early as the third century BCE, silk cloth was exported to Europe. It was treasured in Greece and Rome. In the sixth century, silk was a protected palace industry in the Byzantine Empire. Eventually, sericulture (the cultivation of silkworms) and luxury textile weaving took hold in southern Europe. For this and many other reasons, use of the Silk Road declined. By the sixteenth century, it was no longer in use.

Tang (618–907 CE). Even today many Chinese living abroad still call themselves "Tang people." To them, Tang implies that part of the Chinese character that is strong and vigorous, noble and idealistic, but also realistic and pragmatic. Cosmopolitan and tolerant, the Tang Chinese were both self-confident and curious about the world. As many foreigners came to the splendid new capital, Chang'an (present-day Xi'an), the Chinese depicted them in witty detail. A ceramic statue of a camel carrying a troupe of musicians reflects the Tang fascination with the "exotic" Turkic cultures of Central Asia (fig. 3-17).

Ceramic figurines produced by the thousands for tombs were decorated using a three-color **glaze** technique that was a specialty of Tang ceramists. The glazes—usually chosen from a restricted palette of amber, yellow, green, and white—were splashed freely and allowed to run over the surface during firing to convey a feeling of spontaneity. Stylistically, the ceramic camel statue shows an interest in naturalistic gesture and expression, compared with the rigid, staring ceramic soldiers of the first emperor of Qin (see fig. 3-13).

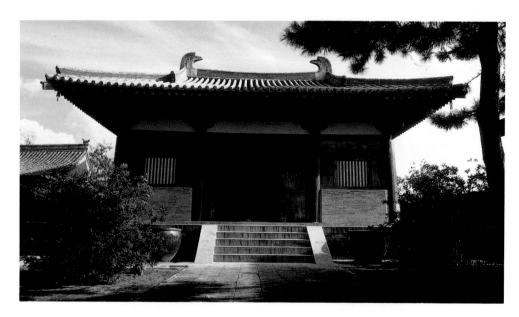

3-18. Nanchan Temple, Wutaishan, Shanxi. Tang dynasty, 782 CE

Buddhism flourished in China during the Tang dynasty. The early Tang emperors proclaimed a policy of religious tolerance, and virtually the entire country adopted the Buddhist faith. However, thousands of temples, shrines, and monasteries were destroyed and innumerable bronze statues melted down when Confucianism was reasserted during the ninth century and Buddhism was briefly persecuted as a "foreign" religion.

Nanchan Temple, located on Mount Wutai in the eastern part of Shanxi Province, is not only one of the rare wooden Buddhist structures surviving from the Tang dynasty but also the first important surviving example of Chinese woodframe architecture (fig. 3-18). Constructed in 782 CE, its curved

Elements of Architecture
STUPAS AND PAGODAS

Stupas began in India as simple, solid dome-shaped structures containing Buddhist relics. Later, a multistoried form of the stupa developed in India's Gandhara region during the Kushan dynasty (c. 50–250 CE). As Buddhism spread northeastward along the Silk Road, the form of the multilevel stupa was merged with that of the watchtower of Han dynasty China, leading to the creation of multistoried masonry structures with projecting tiled roofs. In China, Korea, and Japan, this transformation culminated in wooden pagodas with upward-curving roofs supported by elaborate bracketing.

Like the stupas of South Asia, early East Asian pagodas were nearly solid, with small spaces for relics. Later examples often provided access to the ground floor and sometimes to upper levels. Most pagodas were associated with Buddhism and retain the **axis mundi** masts of stupas.

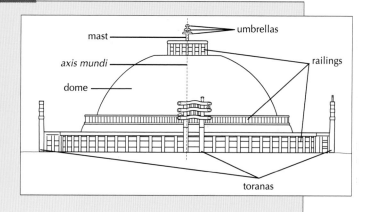

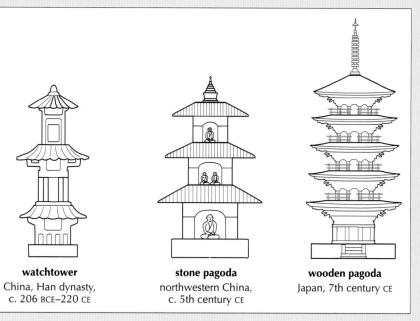

watchtower
China, Han dynasty, c. 206 BCE–220 CE

stone pagoda
northwestern China, c. 5th century CE

wooden pagoda
Japan, 7th century CE

and tiled roof has broad overhanging eaves supported by **brackets** (architectural supports projecting from the walls). Bracketing became a standard element of East Asian architecture, especially in palaces and temples. Also typical is the **bay** system of construction, in which a cubic unit of space, a bay, is formed by four posts and their lintels. To create larger structures, an architect multiplied the number of bays. Thus the three-bayed Nanchan Temple, modest in scope, gives an idea of the vast, multistoried, lost palaces of the Tang.

The Great Wild Goose Pagoda at the Ci'en Temple in Xi'an, the Tang capital, is another important monument of Tang architecture (see fig. 3-1). The pagoda, or reliquary tower, originated in the Indian Buddhist stupa (see "Stupas and Pagodas," page 81). Chinese builders combined the idea of the stupa reliquary, which developed in India around the first century CE, with Han watchtowers to produce the tall pagoda.

Originally built of mud bricks between 645 and 652, and rebuilt at the beginning of the eighth century of brick with wooden floors and steps, the Great Wild Goose Pagoda imitates the forms of wooden architecture of the time. The walls are decorated in low relief to resemble bays, and bracket systems are reproduced under the projecting roofs of each story. The pagoda preserves the essence of Tang architecture in its simplicity, proportions, and grace.

Japan

Human habitation in Japan dates back at least 30,000 years, to a time when its islands were still linked to the East Asian landmass and the Sea of Japan was only a lake. Some 15,000 years ago, melting Ice Age glaciers caused the sea level to rise, creating the islands we know today. A distinctive Japanese culture began to emerge during the Jomon period (c. 12,000–300 BCE), which was remarkable for its creation of the world's earliest surviving fired pottery vessels (Chapter 1).

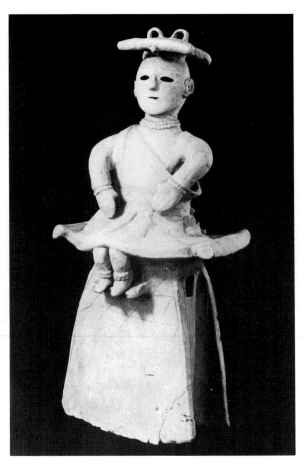

3-19. Haniwa, from Kyoto. Kofun period, 6th century CE. Earthenware, height 27" (68.5 cm). Tokyo National Museum

From ancient times, indigenous Japanese taste has been distinguished by a respect for and delight in natural materials. Wooden architecture such as Shinto shrines and farmhouses, for example, is often left unpainted, and ceramics frequently are only partly glazed in order to display all or some of their clay bodies. The Japanese aesthetic has a taste for asymmetry, evidenced by paintings and prints that seem off-balance but are actually adroitly composed. In addition, a sense of humor and playfulness can surface in unexpected contexts, such as religious art of great power and depth. Finally, the Japanese have preserved their cultural heritage while welcoming and creatively transforming foreign influences—first from China and Korea and more recently from Europe and America.

Immigrants from Korea during the Yayoi (300 BCE–300 CE) and Kofun (300–552 CE) periods helped to transform Japan into an agricultural nation, where rice cultivation became widespread. The emergence of a class structure can be dated to the Yayoi period, as can the development of metal technology—first bronze and then iron.

The ensuing Kofun, or "old tombs" period, named for the large royal tombs that were built then, was distinguished by a pattern of veneration of leaders that grew into the beginnings of an imperial system. This system, still in existence today in Japan, eventually equated the emperor (or, very rarely, empress) with the all-powerful sun goddess.

When a Kofun emperor died, chamber tombs furnished with pottery and other grave goods were constructed. Tomb sites might extend over more than 400 acres, with artificial hills built over the tombs themselves. The hills were topped with hollow ceramic works of sculpture called *haniwa* to further distinguish the tomb sites.

The first *haniwa* were simple cylinders that may have held jars with ceremonial offerings. Gradually these cylinders came to be made in the shapes of ceremonial objects, houses, and

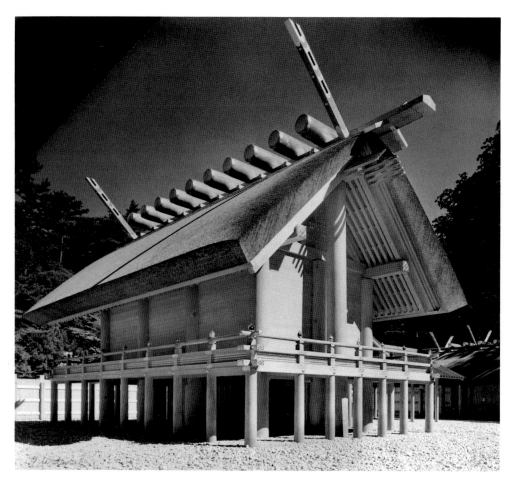

3-20. Inner shrine, Ise, Mie Prefecture. Early 1st century CE; rebuilt 1993

boats, and later, birds and animals. Finally, *haniwa* in human shapes were crafted, of both sexes and all professions and classes. The *haniwa* illustrated here (fig. 3-19) has been identified as a seated female shaman. In early Japan, shamans acted as agents between the natural and supernatural worlds. Similarly, *haniwa* figures seem to have served as some kind of link between the world of the dead and the world of the living.

Haniwa figures may also reflect some of the beliefs of Shinto. Shinto, the indigenous religion of Japan, can be characterized as a loose confederation of beliefs in deities (*kami*). *Kami* were thought to inhabit many different aspects of nature, including particularly hoary and magnificent trees, rocks, waterfalls, and living creatures such as deer. Shinto also represents the ancient Japanese belief in purification through the ritual use of water. In response to the arrival of Buddhism in Japan in the sixth century CE, Shinto became somewhat more systematized, with shrines, a hierarchy of deities, and more strictly regulated ceremonies.

One of the great Shinto sites is at Ise, on the coast southwest of Tokyo (fig. 3-20). The Inner Shrine is dedicated to the sun goddess, the legendary ancestor of Japan's imperial family. It was originally constructed in the early first century CE,

and it has been ritually rebuilt at intervals over nearly 2,000 years. Stylistically and technically, the shrine is typical of Shinto architecture in the builder's use of wooden piles to raise the building off the ground, unpainted cypress wood as a construction material, and a thatched roof held in place by horizontal logs. These traditional features, which convey a sense of natural simplicity, ultimately derive from the architecture of ancient (first century CE) raised granaries used to store food. The Inner Shrine at Ise houses spiritual rather than corporal nourishment—a sword, a mirror, and a jewel—the three sacred symbols of Shinto.

Buddhism, introduced from China and Korea during the Asuka period (552–646 CE), soon coexisted with Shinto in Japan. During this time of intense cultural transformation, the Japanese also adopted a system of writing and a centralized governmental structure from China. Buddhism, which reached Japan in Mahayana form, with its many buddhas and bodhisattvas (see "Buddhism," page 71), soon became a state religion.

Buddhism introduced not only different gods but an entirely new concept of religion itself. Where Shinto had found deities in nature, Buddhism introduced a complex pantheon of anthropomorphic gods. The most significant

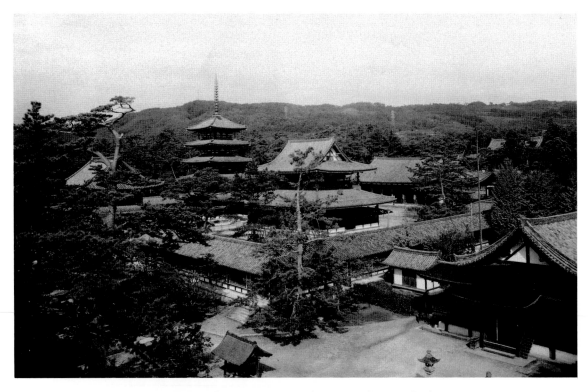

3-21. Main compound, Horyu-ji, Nara Prefecture. Asuka period, 7th century CE

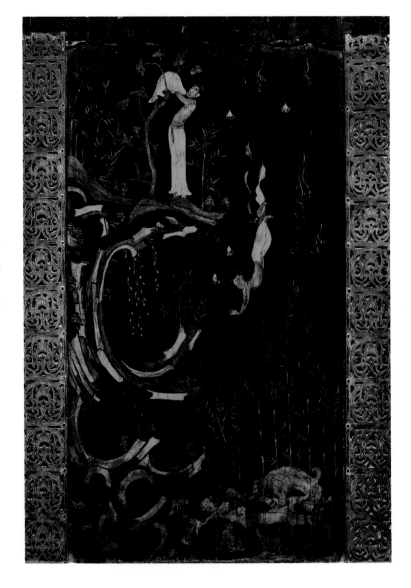

3-22. *Hungry Tigress Jataka,* panel of the Tama-mushi Shrine, Horyu-ji. Asuka period, 7th century CE. Lacquer on wood, height of shrine 7'7¾" (2.33 m). Horyu-ji Treasure House

surviving early Japanese temple is Horyu-ji (fig. 3-21), located on Japan's central plain not far from Nara. Founded in 607 CE and rebuilt after a fire in 670, Horyu-ji includes the oldest surviving documented wooden structure in the world.

The main compound of Horyu-ji consists of a rectangular courtyard surrounded by covered corridors. Only two buildings stand within the compound, a large *kondo*, or golden hall, and a slender, five-story pagoda. Both are Chinese-style woodframe buildings with tile roofs. The *kondo* is filled with Buddhist images and is used for worship and ceremonies. The pagoda also serves primarily as a **reliquary** (that is, it holds relics). Other monastery buildings, such as a repository for sacred texts and dormitories for monks, lie outside the main compound.

Among the many treasures preserved in Horyu-ji is a miniature shrine decorated with paintings in **lacquer** (a type of hard, glossy surface varnish) (fig. 3-22). It is known as the Tamamushi Shrine after the tamamushi beetle, whose iridescent wings were originally affixed to the shrine to make it glitter. The shrine may have been crafted in Korea or Japan, or perhaps by Korean artisans working in Japan, testifying to the international range of Buddhist art at this period.

The paintings ornamenting the Tamamushi Shrine are among the few two-dimensional works of art to survive from the Asuka period. The painting illustrated here tells a story from a former life of the Buddha. In this painting, he is shown nobly sacrificing his life in order to feed his body to a starving tigress and her cubs. The tigers are at first too weak to eat him, so he jumps off a cliff to break open his flesh. The elegantly slender rendition of the Buddha's figure, shown three times in the three stages of the story, and the abstract treatment of the cliff, trees, and bamboo, represent a Buddhist style shared during this time by China, Korea, and Japan.

During the seventh and eighth centuries Buddhism so thoroughly permeated the upper levels of society that an empress wanted to cede her throne to a Buddhist monk. Her advisers intervened, but Buddhism remained the single most significant element in Japanese culture, comfortably coexisting with Shinto, just as it had with Hinduism in India and with Confucianism and Daoism in China.

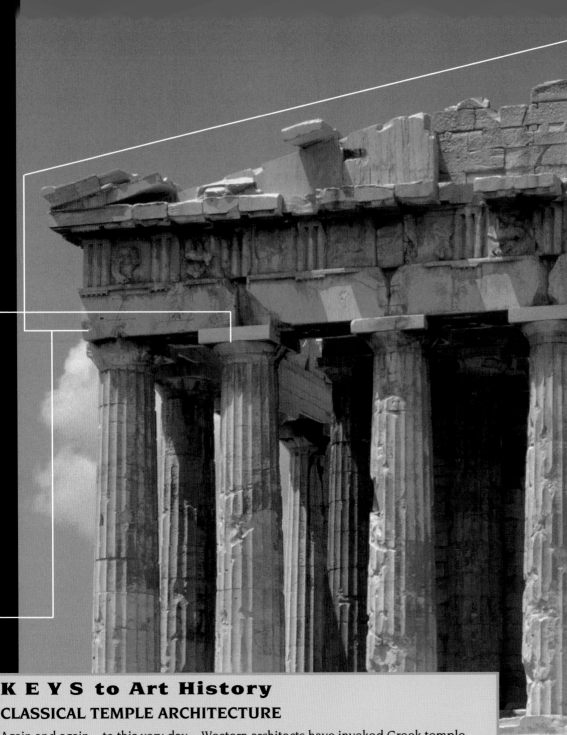

Kallikrates and Iktinos.
Parthenon, Acropolis, Athens.
447–438 BCE.
View from the west

Temple Design

All Greek temples are based on post-and-lintel construction. The plan consists of two main elements: an interior space (*cella*), where the cult statue stood and where priests and other special people assembled, and the *peristyle*, the space outside the cella wall, including rows of columns. Some of the front and side walls of the Parthenon cella are visible here. The roof is gone, which makes the peristyle appear to stand free.

Doric Order

The columns that support the lintel and once supported the roof are of the Doric order. Rising directly from the top step (*stylobate*) and carved in place from a stack of cylindrical marble pieces (*drums*), the Doric columns are cut in channels (*fluted*) and topped with a capital consisting of a cushionlike form (*echinus*) and square block (*abacus*). They swell slightly near the middle (*entasis*) to compensate for the optical illusion that makes a straight column appear to curve inward. Columns at the ends of rows are a bit thicker than the others and lean inward slightly to give an illusion of greater weight and strength at the corners of the building.

Entablature & Pediment

Resting on the capitals of the columns is a typical Doric *entablature*: a row of plain slabs (*architraves*) topped by a row (frieze) of pictorial reliefs (*metopes*) alternating with vertically grooved blocks (*triglyphs*). Above the frieze is the *cornice*. The triangular area between the peaked roof and the top of the entablature is the *pediment*, a deeply recessed, stagelike gable that was once filled with sculpture. Much of the Parthenon's pedimental sculpture, many of its metopes, and an inner frieze on the cella wall (not visible here) were destroyed in an explosion in 1687.

K E Y S to Art History

CLASSICAL TEMPLE ARCHITECTURE

Again and again—to this very day—Western architects have invoked Greek temple design to express rationality, restraint, and physical and moral perfection. No building is identified more closely with these ancient Classical values than the Parthenon, which was built nearly 2,400 years ago at the summit of Athens's acropolis (Greek for "hill"+"city"). The great Athenian leader Perikles (c. 495–429 BCE) ordered the construction of this temple about 447 BCE, and it became Athens's most important center for civic and religious celebrations to honor the city's patron goddess, Athena.

The builders of the Parthenon used the Doric order, the earliest of the three great Greek orders. (An *order* is a system of proportions derived from the diameter of the column shaft and used in the ensemble of *entablature*, *capital*, *column*, and *base*.) The Parthenon's proportions and technical refinements seem to respond to its lofty site and give it an understated grandeur. Its decoration, directed by the great sculptor Pheidias, once included some of the most beautiful sculpture of all time. Originally, the white marble columns and inner walls supported bands of brightly painted low-relief sculpture (*friezes*), with scenes depicting battles of mythical gods and heroes and processions of the men and women of Athens. In the triangular pediments, the goddess Athena was portrayed at her birth and claiming the city as her own.

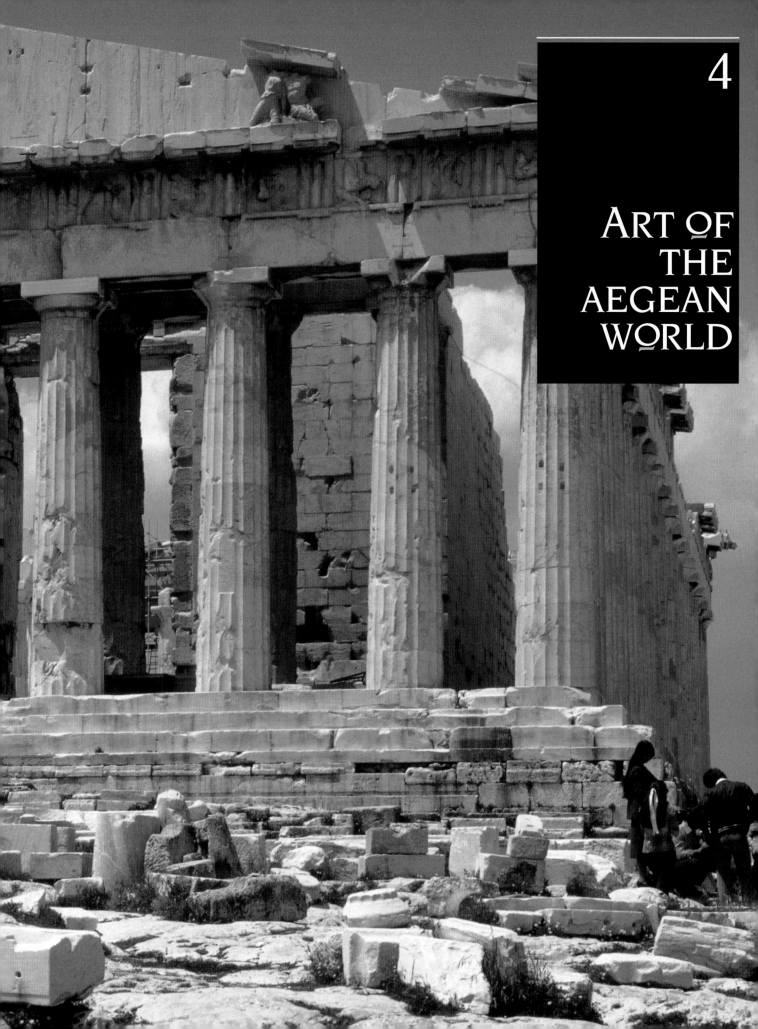

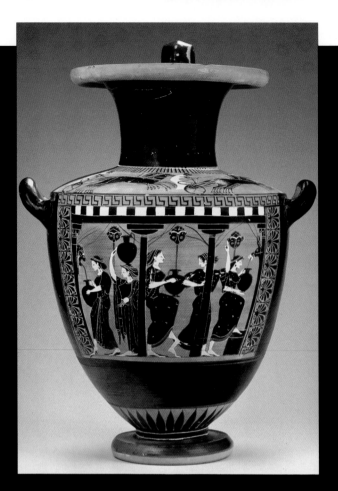

4-1. "A.D." Painter. *Women at a Fountain House,* black-figure decoration on a hydria. 520–510 BCE. Ceramic, height of hydria 20⅞" (53 cm). Museum of Fine Arts, Boston William Francis Warden Fund

Throughout the ancient Greek world, archeologists have unearthed thousands of ceramic vessels, a high proportion of them painted with complex designs depicting scenes from mythology or daily life. The **hydria**, or water jug, shown in figure 4-1 depicts Greek women performing a common chore: collecting water at a communal well. While earlier art historians tended to cite the fineness of vase painting as the height of Greek art, more recently scholars have pointed to the vessels' relevance as functional objects and as evidence of what subjects the Greeks cared about. Obviously, the Greek myths and legends were believed and enjoyed. The details of ordinary life were also considered worthy subject matter.

To meet the practical need for jugs, storage vessels, pitchers, and bowls, potters and painters produced them in great numbers, sometimes in a setting that would be called a small factory today. The wares were inexpensive to make and own. By comparison, few large-scale mural paintings survive intact, and only the most affluent Greeks could afford to commission them. The painters of large-scale murals were probably held in higher esteem than the painters of vases, in spite of the fact that these apparently common household objects often contain designs of infinite elegance and skill.

Natives of the islands and coast, the people of the Cyclades, Crete, and Greece became seafaring and adventurous by necessity. They created visual arts of striking originality, beginning in the third millennium BCE and culminating in the Classical art of fifth-century BCE Athens. Most of the early civilizations we have already considered arose in fertile river valleys: the Tigris and Euphrates, the Nile, the Indus, and the Yellow River. In the Aegean region, the surrounding seas provided the needed security and resources.

The Aegean region of Europe is an area composed of mainland Greece, a cluster of nearby islands in the Aegean Sea called the Cyclades, and the large southern island of Crete. Cycladic peoples were established as early as 6000 BCE. Because they left no written records, the prosperous society they developed in the Bronze Age, about 3000 BCE, is obscure. Their art is one of our main sources of information about them.

South of the Cyclades, on the island of Crete, the culture now known as Minoan took shape at the beginning of the Aegean Bronze Age, which lasted from about 3100 BCE to 1100 BCE, and was marked technologically by the use of bronze to make weapons and tools. Strategically located, Minoan Crete became a great sea power, reaching its height between 1750 and 1470 BCE, the so-called New Palace period. Excavations in and around immense architectural complexes, built from about 1900 BCE, have revealed the richness of Minoan art and ceremony and have uncovered ceramics, sculpture, wall paintings, and spectacular craftwork in ivory and gold.

Minoan Crete declined after 1500 BCE, although the main center, Knossos, functioned until the mid-thirteenth century BCE. Dominance in the Aegean region then shifted to a mainland Greek culture known as Helladic and/or Mycenaean, after one of its major cities, Mycenae. The Mycenaeans, who spoke an early form of the Greek language, built fortified strongholds ruled by local princes or kings, warlords whose exploits were memorialized in later Greek epics such as the *Iliad* and the *Odyssey*.

The Aegean Bronze Age ended about 1100 BCE, when Mycenaean civilization collapsed for unknown reasons. A period of disorganization followed, and not until around 900 BCE did the inhabitants of the Aegean region begin to flourish again. These were the people who came to be called the Greeks. Linked by language—most spoke some form of Greek by then—they lived in self-sufficient, close-knit communities scattered throughout the region, which eventually developed into independently governed city-states.

For at least 700 years, the Greeks were unimaginably creative. We still credit them with groundbreaking experiments in science, mathematics, and herbal medicine; for the implementation of representative government, that is, democracy; and for an astounding legacy of art and architecture that influences the Western world to this day. The works of Greek poets, dramatists, and philosophers have endured for more than two millennia. Homer, Aeschylus, Sophocles, Euripides, and Plato are only a few of the Greek authors whose works are still studied today.

Greek philosophers sought to define the ideal community, the actions of responsible citizenship, and the meaning of a good life. They asked, What is the Good, the True, the Beautiful? Artists responded by trying to capture such intangible concepts as "truth" and "beauty" in the material forms of sculpture, architecture, and painting. "Know thyself" and "Nothing in excess" are maxims inscribed in the sun god Apollo's sanctuary at Delphi in the mountains above the Gulf of Corinth, and they seem to have been imprinted on the heart and hands of every Greek artist. Know thyself: study the world around you; observe the variety found in nature; focus on human beings, for the gods and goddesses have human form. Then attempt to simplify and clarify these impressions in order to capture the essence of life.

The Cycladic Islands

During the late Neolithic and early Bronze Ages, the people who lived on the Cycladic islands, like their contemporaries in the ancient Near East and Egypt (Chapter 2) farmed, made crafts, and engaged in trade. They used local stone to build fortified towns and hillside burial chambers, and they produced ceramic pottery and clay figurines of humans and animals.

Human figurines made of a fine white marble, abundant especially on the islands of Naxos and Paros, have been unearthed in and around graves. A few male statuettes have been found, including depictions of musicians and acrobats, but they are greatly outnumbered by representations of women. Female figures like the two illustrated in figure 4-2 have become the best-known type of Cycladic art. Made between 2500–2200 BCE, their elegant, pared-down forms, which convey the essence of the human figure, contrast sharply with the volumetric shapes seen in Egyptian statues from the same time period (see fig. 2-17). Their tilted-back heads, folded arms, and down-pointed toes indicate that the figures were intended to lie on their backs, not to stand. Now starkly white, originally they had painted faces, hair, and jewelry. They may have been used in religious or burial rituals since they have been found in graves. The largest—examples as tall as 5 feet have been found—might have been set up for communal worship. The female figures recall Paleolithic fertility figures (Chapter 1), though the people of

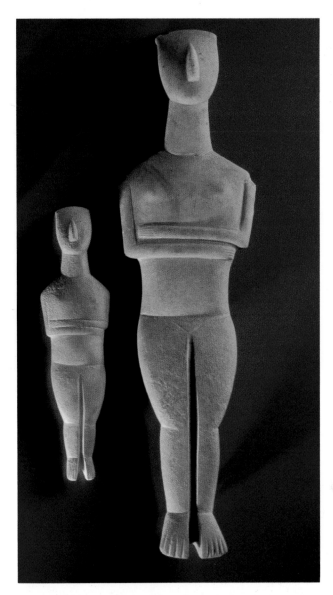

4-2. Two figures of women, from the Cyclades. c. 2500–2200 BCE. Marble, heights 13" (33 cm) and 25" (63.4 cm). Museum of Cycladic Art, Athens
Courtesy of the N. P. Goulandris Foundation

the Cyclades may have thought of them as ancestors or divinities.

Minoan Crete

The culture of the island of Crete, called Minoan by twentieth-century archeologists, came into being around 3000 BCE. The word *Minoan* comes from a much later Greek legend about King Minos of Crete, who was said to keep a human-eating monster called a Minotaur (half human and half bull) at the center of a labyrinth, or maze. (This legend inspired later artists as diverse as Titian and Picasso.)

Crete is the largest of the Aegean islands, 150 miles long and 36 miles wide. The earliest Minoans were self-sufficient agriculturally, producing grains, fruit, cattle, and sheep, which they traded for the copper and tin ores they needed to make bronze and for various luxury goods. Incredibly, the Minoan traders sailed to ports in places as distant as Egypt, the Near East, and Anatolia (western Turkey).

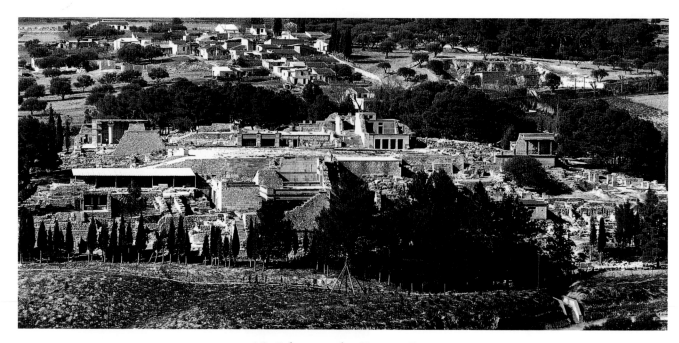

4-3. Palace complex, Knossos, Crete

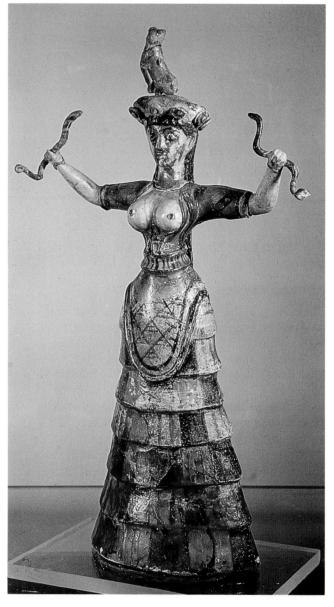

4-4. *Woman or Goddess with Snakes,* from the palace complex, Knossos, Crete. c. 1700–1550 BCE. Faience, height 11⅝" (29.5 cm). Archeological Museum, Iráklion, Crete

Relatively little is known about daily life during the Minoan period, although a number of written records have been found. The two earliest forms of Cretan writing, hieroglyphs and a script called Linear A, still defy translation, but the surviving documents in a later script, Linear B—a very early form of Greek imported from the mainland—have proven to be invaluable. The documents incorporating this script include administrative records and inventories: lists of animals, olive trees, chariots, and weapons. Minoan civilization remained very much a mystery until a British archeologist, Sir Arthur Evans (1851–1941), excavated the buried ruins of an extraordinary palace complex at Knossos, on Crete's north coast, in the early twentieth century.

Great palace complexes such as Knossos were the dominant kind of architectural structure on Crete from roughly 1900 to 1300 BCE. Safeguarded by watchtowers and stone walls, they were simultaneously used as administrative, commercial, and religious centers. The builders devised an almost earthquake-proof flexible wall system of timber supports and braces with light, mud-brick fill. Facades and lower walls were faced with **dressed stone** (cut and highly finished), in this case, limestone.

After a major earthquake about 1750 BCE, several palaces, including Knossos, were repaired and enlarged. The resulting "new palaces"—multistoried, flat-roofed, and with many columns—were designed with staggered levels, open stairwells, and strategically placed air shafts and light wells to maximize air and light. Religious, residential, manufacturing, and warehouse areas surrounded a large, central courtyard.

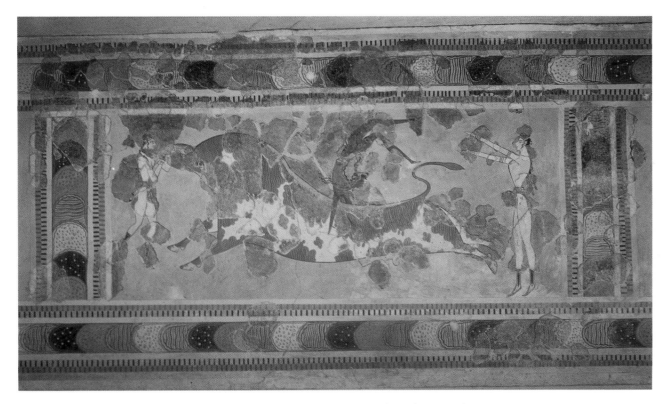

4-5. Bull Jumping, wall painting with areas of modern reconstruction, from the palace complex, Knossos, Crete. c. 1550–1450 BCE. Height approx. 24½" (62.3 cm). Archeological Museum, Iráklion, Crete

Careful sifting during excavation preserved many fragments of the paintings that once covered the palace walls. The pieces were painstakingly sorted and cleaned by restorers and reassembled into puzzle pictures that still had more pieces missing than found. The next step was to fill in the gaps with colors similar to the original ones, but lighter and grayer in tone. It is therefore obvious which are the restored portions, but the eye can still read and enjoy the image.

During Knossos's heyday, the palace complex covered 6 acres (fig. 4-3). Its residential quarters had many assets: sunlit courtyards, richly colored murals, and an extraordinarily sophisticated plumbing system consisting of bathrooms and a network of terra-cotta pipes laid beneath the palace. Extensive workshops in and around Knossos and other complexes suggest that arts and crafts were officially sponsored. Huge storerooms point to the centralized management of trade in foodstuffs. In a single storeroom at Knossos, excavators found enough large ceramic jars to hold 20,000 gallons of olive oil.

The palace complexes in Crete included areas for ritual activities. Priestesses are believed to have overseen the worship of a goddess who controlled the natural world and who is associated with the **iconography** (subject matter and its symbolic meaning) of serpents, bulls, and the double ax. This Aegean deity may have inspired the later Greeks to venerate goddesses such as Artemis and Athena. Female images made of ivory or ceramic found in caves, hilltop sacred sites, and palace shrines may represent goddesses, priestesses, or worshipers.

A figurine of a woman (or goddess) brandishing two snakes (fig. 4-4) survived the destruction of the palace at Knossos. Along with other ceremonial objects, she was found in a storeroom pit. She wears a typically Minoan,

long and flounced skirt and an overskirt decorated with geometric patterns resembling the scales of a snake. Her headdress supports a cat. In addition, she holds a snake in each hand. Female figurines incorporating serpents were fashioned on Crete as early as 6000 BCE and may have been associated—as they were elsewhere—with water, with regenerative power, and with protection of the home. This example is made from a glassy paste called **faience**, developed in Egypt, which when fired acquires a lustrous shine and smooth texture.

Many early cultures associated their gods and god-rulers with powerful animals, especially the lion and the bull. Depictions of bulls appear often in Minoan art, rendered with an intensity not seen since the prehistoric cave paintings at Chauvet, Lascaux, and Altamira (Chapter 1). While neither the images nor later myths offer any proof that the Minoans worshiped a bull god, the animals apparently were sacrificed; horn shapes decorated outdoor altars. They also figured in a rite called bull jumping practiced by men and women who must have been trained acrobats.

The palace at Knossos has wall paintings and painted low reliefs showing bulls. In one painting two women and a man engage in the dangerous ritual of bull jumping (fig. 4-5). (Minoan painters followed the convention of depicting figures with pale skin to represent

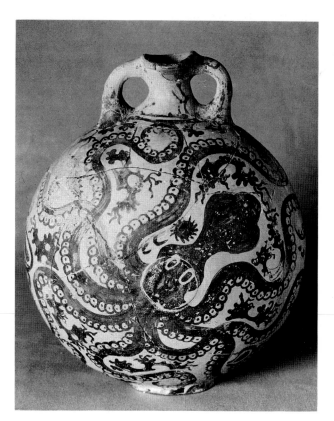

4-6. *Octopus Flask,* from Palaikastro, Crete. c. 1500–1450 BCE. Ceramic, height 11" (28 cm). Archeological Museum, Iráklion, Crete

women and dark skin to represent men.) The woman at the right is either beginning or finishing her vault, the man is in the midst of his, and the woman at the left grasps the bull by its horns, ready to leap. The painting may show an initiation or fertility ritual or it may honor a god or goddess by displaying human courage.

Painting on a smaller scale decorated ceramics made in palace workshops, where the potter's wheel was in use from the early second millennium BCE. A striking vessel from the eastern site of Palaikastro, a bottle known as the *Octopus Flask,* was made about 1500–1450 BCE (fig. 4-6). This is one of a group of pieces decorated with sea creatures and plants and probably celebrates Cretan maritime power. Like microscopic life teeming in a drop of seawater, sea creatures float among an octopus's curling, sucker-covered tentacles. The painter captures the grace and energy of natural forms while presenting them as a stylized design in harmony with the vessel's shape.

The skills of Minoan artists, particularly those of metalsmiths, made their work highly sought after in mainland Greece. Jewelers

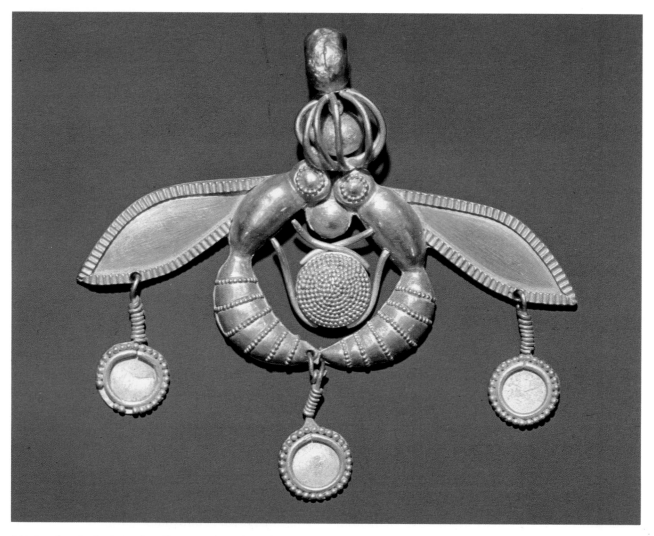

4-7. Pendant in the form of two bees or wasps, from Chryssolakkos, near Mallia, Crete. c. 1700–1550 BCE. Gold, height approx. 1¹³/₁₆" (4.6 cm). Archeological Museum, Iraklion, Crete

became adept at decorating their goldwork with minute granules, or balls, of the precious metal fused to the surface, a technique known as **granulation**. This type of ornamentation is visible on a pendant perhaps made for a necklace in about 1700–1550 BCE (fig. 4-7). The artist arched a pair of bees or wasps around a granulated drop of honey. Their sleek bodies, decorated with parallel rows of granules, are framed by a single pair of outspread wings.

For reasons not entirely clear, Minoan civilization declined after about 1500 BCE, although Knossos continued as an administrative center until about 1250 BCE. Mainland Greece became the center of political power and cultural influence in the Aegean by 1400 BCE.

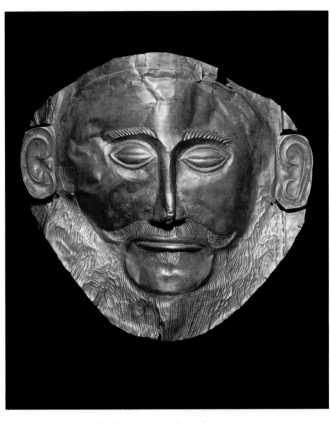

4-8. Funerary mask, from the royal tombs at Mycenae, Greece. c. 1550–1500 BCE. Gold, height approx. 12" (30.5 cm). National Archeological Museum, Athens

Mycenaean (Late Bronze Age) Civilization

Archeologists have used the term *Helladic* (from *Hellas*, the Greek word for Greece) to designate the Bronze Age in mainland Greece. The Helladic period extends from about 3000 to 1000 BCE, overlapping with the Minoan chronology of Crete. Like the time frames for Cycladic and Minoan cultures, dates are now debated. Sometime in the early part of this period, Greek-speaking peoples invaded the mainland. They brought advanced metalworking, ceramic, and architectural techniques and displaced the indigenous Neolithic culture.

Life in fortified Mycenaean strongholds such as Mycenae probably contrasted sharply with life in the open palace complexes on Crete ninety-two miles away. The communities centered around these strongholds were controlled by local princes or kings. Evidence from shaft graves—deep vertical pits used for burial—dating from between 1600 and 1500 BCE, suggests a society that became increasingly wealthy and stratified. Magnificent swords, daggers, scepters, jewelry, and drinking cups mark the burials of an elite class of warriors. Masks of gold or a silver-gold alloy called electrum covered rulers' faces as if to preserve their heroic features forever.

In a gold funerary mask dated about 1550–1500 BCE, the combination of a strong chin, broad cheekbones, and thin nose produce an effect uncannily like a death mask molded over the actual face of the deceased (fig. 4-8). This mask is often called the Mask of Agamemnon, as it was once mistakenly believed to have belonged to that Mycenaean king. The German archeologist Heinrich Schliemann (1822–1890), who excavated the shaft graves in 1876, understandably wanted to associate the burial with one of the great epics of Greek history and literature, the *Iliad* by the Greek poet Homer.

Homer, who probably lived in the eighth century BCE, left us two epic tales called the *Iliad* and the *Odyssey*. In the *Iliad* he tells of a ten-year siege by the Greeks of the city of Troy, which is generally believed to have stood on the site of Hissarlik, in modern Turkey. Inspired by the goddess Aphrodite, Paris, son of the Trojan king, abducted Helen, the most beautiful woman in the world and wife of King Menelaus of Sparta. King Menelaus and his brother King Agamemnon of Mycenae, both sons of Atreus, led the Greek troops in a siege of Troy. Human warriors, gods, and goddesses took sides in a ten-year war to avenge Menelaus and regain Helen. It is not clear whether Helen, Menelaus, Agamemnon, or Atreus really existed, or even if the Trojan War really took place, although the story probably had roots in some actual battle or raid. Ancient Greek historians, accepting the Trojan War as history, dated it anywhere from 1334 BCE to 1150 BCE, certainly long before Homer turned it into a legendary combat. In any case, the so-called Mask of Agamemnon dates from several centuries before any plausible date for the Trojan War, so it could not possibly have been Agamemnon's even if he was an actual person.

A tomb, popularly and incorrectly designated as the "Treasury of Atreus," built around

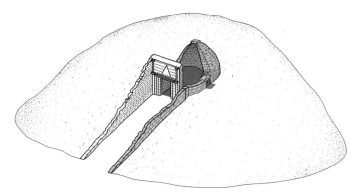

4-9. Cutaway drawing of the beehive tomb called the Treasury of Atreus, Mycenae, Greece. c. 1300–1200 BCE

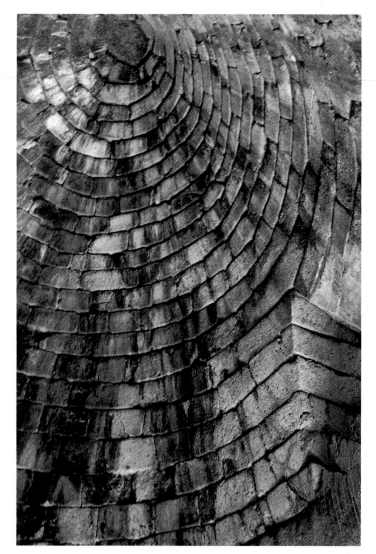

4-10. Corbeled vault, interior of the Treasury of Atreus. Stone, height of vault approx. 43' (13 m), diameter 47'6" (14.48 m)

1300–1200 BCE (fig. 4-9), is close to the Trojan War in date, but it is no more likely than the "Mask of Agamemnon" to be connected to Homer's kings of Mycenae. Other legends tell of a race of giants, the Cyclops, who moved the huge stones and gave the name **cyclopean** to the large-stone masonry seen in Mycenaean citadels and tombs. More than a hundred such tombs have been found on mainland Greece,

nine of them, like this one, in the vicinity of Mycenae. They were constructed for members of Helladic ruling families and were used later than shaft graves.

An uncovered, walled passageway about 120 feet long and 20 feet wide led to the door of a conical structure, the beehive-shaped tomb. The circular main chamber, 43 feet high, is formed by a **corbeled vault:** a vault built up in regular **courses** (layers) of dressed stone in overlapping and ever-decreasing rings carefully calculated to meet in a single **capstone** at the peak (fig. 4-10). The great size of the vaulted chamber—47 feet in diameter and 43 feet high—made the tomb the largest unobstructed interior space built before the Roman Pantheon (see fig. 6-21). Like the Neolithic passage graves constructed in western Europe (see "Dolmen and Passage Grave," page 38), the stone structure was covered by earth to form an artificial mountain.

Megalithic walls, broken by a monumental entrance and one or two secret emergency exits, encircled the Mycenaean fortress-palaces (fig. 4-11). The imposing Lioness Gate (c. 1300–1200 BCE) led into the citadel of Mycenae (fig. 4-12). The gate consists of a **post-and-lintel** frame that once held massive wood and metal doors, topped by a **relieving arch**, in this case, a **corbel arch** spanning the open space with layers of stones, each layer projecting over the lower level. In the opening over the door, a pair of lionesses nearly 9 feet tall flank a Minoan-style column that may symbolize the king's inner retreat and audience chamber. The animals have lost their heads, but holes in the stones suggest the heads were removable and probably fashioned of some precious material. If they were indeed made of bronze or gold, they must have created an imposing presence. From this gate, a long, stone passageway pierces the citadel proper, at the center of which stood the king's palace.

Mycenaean civilization does not have a long history. By 1200 BCE, invaders are believed to have crossed into mainland Greece and taken control of the major cities and citadels. The period between about 1100 and 900 BCE became a "dark age" in the Aegean, marked by political and economic instability and upheaval and producing very little art. But a new culture emerged, one that looked back to the exploits of the Helladic warrior princes and the glories of a heroic age and at the same time formed the basis of a truly new Greek civilization.

The Emergence of Greek Civilization

In the ninth and eighth centuries BCE, the people we know as Greeks, the offspring of ancient inhabitants of the Aegean region and newer migrants, began to form independently governed city-states. Whenever possible, cities were built

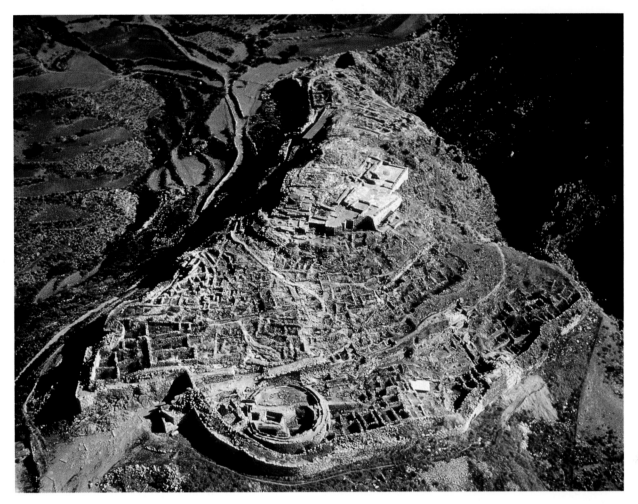

4-11. Mycenae, Greece. c. 1600–1200 BCE

The citadel's hilltop position and fortified ring wall are clearly visible. The Lioness Gate (fig. 4-12) is at the lower left, approached by a dirt path.

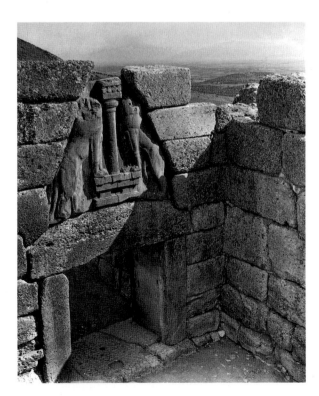

4-12. Lioness Gate, Mycenae. c. 1300–1200 BCE.
Limestone relief, height of sculpture approx. 9'6" (2.9 m)

on a hilltop that could be fortified, an **acropolis** (*acro* means "high," and *polis* means "city"). Eventually the hill became a fortified religious sanctuary with the commercial, governmental, and domestic areas constructed in the plain or valley below. The most famous acropolis is in Athens.

As population expansions eventually outstripped crop yields, outlying colonies were established to alleviate food shortages. The new communities, like their Bronze Age predecessors, depended on trade with other regions to meet the needs of their growing populations. Many city-states developed sizable merchant fleets that sailed as far as the Black Sea and Africa. They established colonies, some of which became influential commercial centers in their own right.

The Greek city-states were at first ruled by aristocratic councils. Then, beginning around 700 BCE and extending into the sixth century BCE, self-appointed leaders called tyrants imposed a dictatorial form of rule, often with popular support. At their most beneficent, they fostered urban development at home and sought economic rather than military influence abroad.

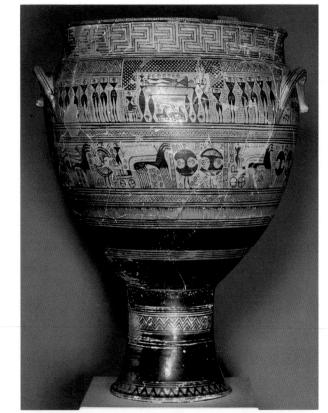

4-13. Vase, from the Dipylon Cemetery, Athens. c. 750 BCE. Terra-cotta, height 42⅝" (108 cm). The Metropolitan Museum of Art, New York
Rogers Fund, 1914 (14.130.14)

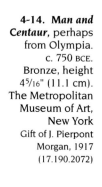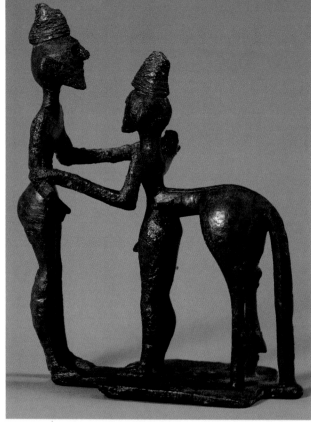

4-14. Man and Centaur, perhaps from Olympia. c. 750 BCE. Bronze, height 4⁵⁄₁₆" (11.1 cm). The Metropolitan Museum of Art, New York
Gift of J. Pierpont Morgan, 1917 (17.190.2072)

The idea that all citizens should share in the rights and responsibilities of government began to emerge in the city-state of Athens in the sixth century BCE, although only a few privileged males were citizens. In the late sixth century, a leader called Kleisthenes, often called the father of democracy, instituted reforms that broadened the representative base of Athenian government. Although the system of rulership

Kleisthenes developed was democratic in principle, it was open only to citizens. Women took no official part in government, nor did slaves or men born outside Athens.

Athens and the other Greek city-states, in spite of their different governments and frequent rivalries, shared a common language and culture and developed a distinctively Greek art, as compared with Minoan or Mycenaean art. Over a remarkably brief time span, the early Greek artists developed ideals of human beauty and a vocabulary of architecture that continue to have a profound influence today. From about 900 BCE to about 100 BCE, they explored a succession of new ideas and produced an impressive body of work that exhibits clear stylistic and technical traits. Periods of Greek art are named for these styles: Geometric, Archaic, and Classical.

The most important early Greek style is the Geometric, which became widespread after about 900 BCE and lasted until about 700 BCE. A vase found in Athens exemplifies the complex linear decoration of the Geometric style (fig. 4-13). Triangles were used to represent torsos and heads in profile, round dots stand for eyes, and long, thin rectangles were used to represent arms. Dated to about 750 BCE, the vessel was a grave marker made to hold offerings. Funerary rituals are recorded in two bands, or **registers**, of decoration. In the top register, the body of the deceased is shown on its side on a platform. Accompanying figures with their hands on their heads may be tearing their hair with grief. Below, a procession of horse-drawn chariots and foot soldiers, who look like walking shields, recall the athletic competitions or funeral games held to honor dead men. Figures are shown neither in fully frontal nor in full-profile views but from a subtly twisted perspective.

Besides vases, Greek artists of the Geometric period produced many small figurines of wood, ivory, clay, and especially cast bronze. A tiny bronze of this type, *Man and Centaur*, dates to about 750 BCE (fig. 4-14). Like the painter of the vase from the Dipylon Cemetery (see fig. 4-13), the sculptor reduced the body parts to simple geometric shapes in a composition of solid forms and open, or negative, spaces. Nevertheless the figures seem charged with energy. The identity of the two figures is unknown, but they might be the legendary hero Achilles and the centaur Chiron, his teacher. Figurines such as *Man and Centaur*, which possibly served as a votive offering, have been found in **sanctuaries**, sites sacred to one or more of the Greek gods.

THE ARCHAIC PERIOD

The Archaic period lasted from about 600 to 480 BCE. Its name, meaning "old" or "old-fashioned," reflects a presumed contrast between the art of that time and the art of the following Classical

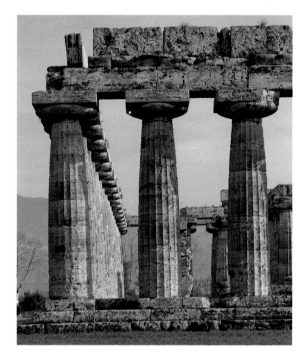

4-15. Corner view of the Temple of Hera I, Paestum, Italy. c. 550 BCE

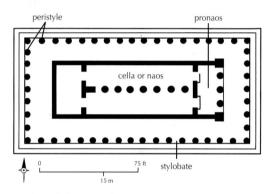

4-16. Plan of the Temple of Hera I, Paestum

period, which for many centuries was regarded as the most admirable and highly developed—a view no longer universally accepted. In fact, the Archaic period was a time of great achievement during which the Greek city-states and their colonies flourished. The poet Sappho on the island of Lesbos wrote poetry during the Archaic period. Her poetry would later inspire the geographer Strabo, near the end of the millennium, to write: "Never within human memory has there been a woman to compare with her as a poet." On another island, the legendary slave Aesop told animal fables of human folly that are still recounted today. Artists shared in the growing prosperity by competing for commissions from city councils and from wealthy individuals who sponsored the creation of sculpture; fine ceramic wares; and civic buildings such as council chambers, public fountains, and temples.

The earliest standing Greek temples date from the Archaic period. The temple was conceived both as an earthly home and as a treasury for gods and goddesses; it is in effect the ideal shelter. Generally temples have a main room, called the **cella** or **naos**, and a vestibule, called the **pronaos**. This room is surrounded by a single

or double row of columns, known as a **peristyle** (see fig. 4-16). Architects developed standardized systems of proportions and ornament known as "orders" for temple plans and **elevations**—the arrangement, proportions, and appearance of the temple foundation, the columns, and the lintels. The posts and lintels we have seen up until now

Elements of Architecture
THE GREEK ARCHITECTURAL ORDERS

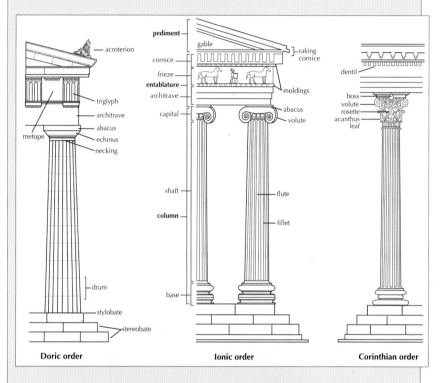

Doric order   Ionic order   Corinthian order

The three classical Greek architectural orders are the Doric, the Ionic, and the Corinthian. The Doric and Ionic orders were well developed by about 600 BCE. The Doric order is the oldest and plainest of the three orders. The Ionic order is named after Ionia, a region occupied by Greeks on the west coast of Anatolia and the islands off that coast. The Corinthian order, a variation of the Ionic, began to appear around 450 BCE and was initially used by the Greeks in interiors. Later, the Romans appropriated the Corinthian order and elaborated it, as we shall see in Chapter 6.

The basic components of the Greek orders are the **column** and the **entablature**, which function as post and lintel. All types of columns have a **shaft** and a **capital**; some also have a **base**. Columns are formed of round sections, or **drums**, which are joined inside by metal pegs. In Greek temple architecture, columns stand on the **stylobate**, the "floor" of the temple; the levels below the stylobate form the **stereobate**.

in the history of ancient architecture (see "Dolmen and Passage Grave," page 38) became **columns** and **entablatures** (see "The Greek Architectural Orders," above).

It is often the case that buildings are better preserved in outlying regions than in the homeland of a culture. A well-preserved Archaic period temple built about 550 BCE still stands at Paestum (Poseidonia), a Greek colony founded about 50 miles south of the modern city of Naples, Italy. Dedicated to Hera, queen of the gods, the temple (figs. 4-15, 4-16) is known today as Hera I to distinguish it from a second temple to Hera built adjacent to it about a century later. The builders used the Doric order, the earliest Greek order. Fluted columns without **bases**, resting directly on the **stylobate**, or floor of the temple, rise to unadorned, cushionlike **capitals**, formed of a rounded **echinus** and a tabletlike **abacus**. The especially robust columns of Hera I, topped with widely flaring capitals, create an impression of great permanence and

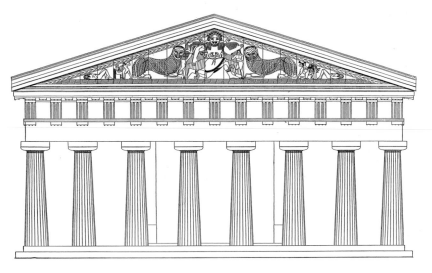

4-17. Reconstruction of the west pediment of the Temple of Artemis, Korkyra (Corfu), after G. Rodenwaldt. c. 600–580 BCE

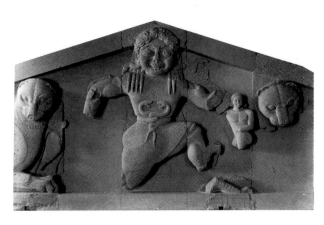

4-18. *Medusa*, fragment of sculpture from the west pediment of the Temple of Artemis, Korkyra. c. 580 BCE. Limestone, height of pediment at the center 9'2" (2.79 m). Archeological Museum, Korkyra

stability. But because the columns swell in the middle and contract toward the top (an attribute known as **entasis**) the building retains a sense of energy and upward lift. Above the columns, a horizontal entablature (composed of **architrave**, **frieze**, and **cornice**) and the triangular **pediments** (forming the triangular gable ends) support the temple's roof. In the frieze, flat panels (**metopes**) alternate with vertically grooved panels (**triglyphs**).

Sculpture often decorated the metopes of the frieze and the pediments. Perhaps among the earliest surviving examples of Greek pedimental sculpture are fragments of the ruined Temple of Artemis on the island of Korkyra (Corfu), which date from about 600–580 BCE (fig. 4-17). The figures in this sculpture were carved in high relief on slabs, which were then installed in the pediment space. At the center is the snake-haired Medusa, a female monster who had the power to turn humans into stone if they looked upon her face (fig. 4-18). The hero Perseus avoided this fate by looking at her in the mirror-like surface of his shield as he beheaded her. On either side of Medusa are her offspring: the flying horse Pegasus on the left (only part of his rump and tail remain) and the giant Chrysaor on the right. Flanking them are crouching felines and dying human warriors tucked into the corners of the pediment. Men, animals, and monster are all depicted in simple volumetric forms, once brightly painted in reds and blues.

In addition to carving sculpture for temple exteriors, artists of the Archaic period created freestanding statues. Usually lifesize or larger, most were made of white marble and originally were painted in bright, naturalistic colors. Some bore inscriptions indicating that they had been commissioned by individual men or women for a commemorative purpose. While some marked graves, most stood in sanctuaries, where they lined the sacred way from the entrance to the main temple in perpetual attendance to the god or goddess.

Traditionally, a female statue of this type is called a **kore** (plural, **korai**), Greek for "young woman," and a male statue is called a **kouros** (plural, **kouroi**), meaning "young man." The Archaic korai, wearing long, sleeveless garments and earrings, represented deities, priestesses, or nymphs. The kouroi, nearly always nude, have been variously identified as gods, warriors, and victorious athletes. Because the Greeks associated young athletic males with fertility and familial regeneration, the kouroi may also have been looked upon as symbolic ancestor figures.

A kouros dating from about 600 BCE (fig. 4-19) exemplifies the early Greek ideal. Superficially reminiscent of standing males in Egyptian sculpture (see fig. 2-18), this young Greek is shown frontally, arms at his sides, fists clenched, and one leg slightly in front of the other. Quite un-Egyptian, however, is the figure's athletic build. The sculptor removed the stone from around the body and between the legs, making the figure seem light and energetic. He depicted anatomy carefully, although tradition required that the ridges and grooves of bones and muscles form simple, balanced patterns. The eyes are relatively large and wide open, and the mouth forms a characteristic closed-lip smile, known as the **Archaic smile**, apparently used to enliven the expressions of figures. Unlike his

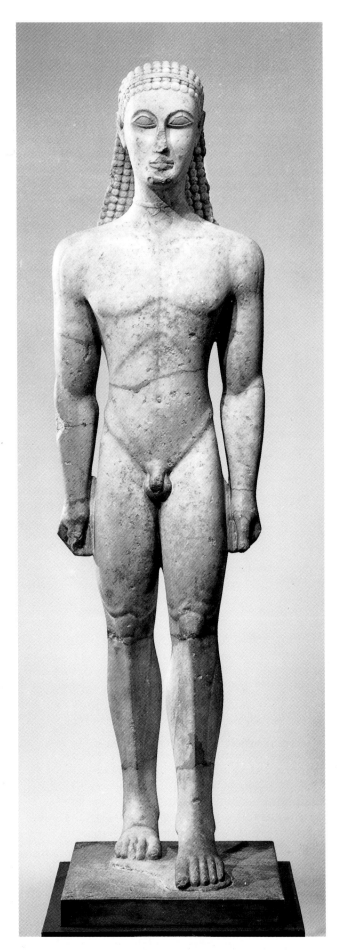

4-19. *Kouros.* c. 600 BCE. Marble, height 6'4" (1.93 m). The Metropolitan Museum of Art, New York
Fletcher Fund, 1932 (32.11.1)

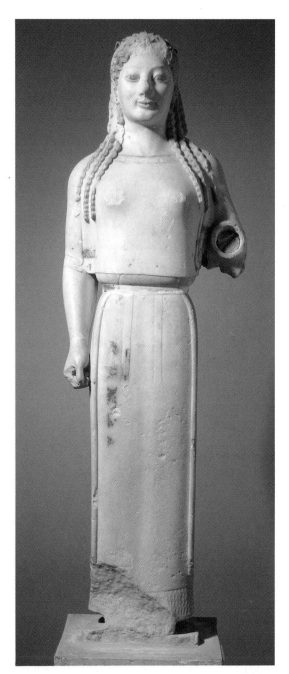

4-20. *Peplos Kore*, from the Acropolis, Athens. c. 530 BCE. Marble, height 48" (123 cm). Acropolis Museum, Athens

partially clothed Egyptian counterpart, the young Greek wears only a ribbon around his neck and another band on his beaded hair. Here nudeness serves to remove the figure from a specific place, time, or social class.

With remarkable rapidity, Greek sculptors triumphed in the art of creating lifelike human figures. The *Peplos Kore* (fig. 4-20), dated about seventy years after the youth, exhibits swelling, rounded body forms. Her arms and head convey a greater sense of soft flesh covering a real bone structure. Her smile and hair seem almost natural, and color must have made her seem even more lifelike. She also once wore a metal crown and earrings. The figure is carved to indicate that she wears the distinctive Athenian garment

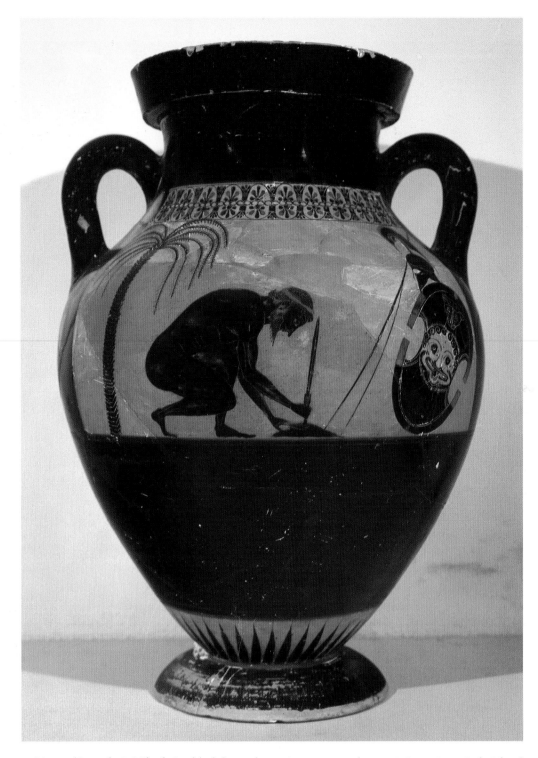

4-21. Exekias. *The Suicide of Ajax,* black-figure decoration on an amphora. c. 540 BCE. Ceramic, height of amphora 27" (69 cm). Château-Musée, Boulogne-sur-Mer, France

known as a *peplos*—a draped rectangle of woolen cloth, folded over the top, fastened at the shoulders, and belted to give a bloused effect. Traces of paint on the lower area of the sculpture suggest that the carved *peplos* may have been decorated with a pattern of rich embroidery.

In vase painting, artists presented not just a single figure, but a story, or narrative. Abandoning the narrow bands of decoration characteristic of the Geometric period (see fig. 4-13), vase painters, especially in Athens, gradually increased the size of figures until one or two scenes filled the body of the vessel. A mid-sixth-century BCE

amphora—a large, all-purpose storage jar—illustrates this development (fig. 4-21). One side shows *The Suicide of Ajax*, an episode from the legends of the Trojan War. Ajax, a Greek warrior, was second only to Achilles in bravery. After the death of Achilles, the Greeks awarded the hero's armor to Odysseus rather than to Ajax; the latter, humiliated, committed suicide. With typical Greek restraint yet sense of drama, Exekias, the potter and painter who signed this vase, captures the impending moment of tragedy rather than the instant of the hero's death. Ajax plants his sword upright in a mound of dirt so that he can

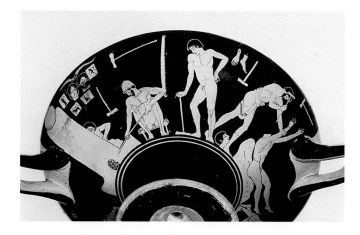

4-22. Foundry Painter. *A Bronze Foundry,* red-figure decoration on a kylix from Vulci, Italy. 490–480 BCE. Ceramic, diameter of kylix 12" (31 cm). Staatliche Museen zu Berlin, Preussischer Kulturbesitz, Antikensammlung

fling himself upon it. Two in-curving elements— the tree on the left and the shield that the warrior has set aside on the right—echo the swelling shape of the amphora and the rounding of the hero's back. Thus the painter recalls a complex story in a single image, adding to its solemnity by creating a clear, easily readable **composition.**

Exekias has used a technique known as **black-figure** painting. This technique became the principal mode of vase painting throughout Greece in the sixth century BCE. The painter used a **slip** (a mixture of clay and water) to silhouette figures against the reddish, unpainted clay of the background. Details are incised with a sharp tool inside the silhouetted shapes. The color contrast is created in the firing process.

Touches of white and reddish purple gloss, made of metallic pigments mixed with slip, enhance the black-figure decoration on some pieces, such as an Athenian **hydria**, or water jug, made about 510 BCE (see fig. 4-1). Painted by an artist who signed the work with the initials "A.D.," the hydria, as mentioned earlier, depicts women gathered at a communal fountain housed in a splendid Doric building. Columns with flaring Doric capitals support a brightly painted frieze. Water flows from carved animal-head water spouts. Three women fill hydrias like the one on which they are painted, while a fourth balances a jug on her head for the trip home. A fifth woman appears to be waving to someone in greeting. The women's skin is painted white, a convention for female figures also found in Egyptian and Minoan art. Incised marks and touches of reddish purple gloss were used to create fine details in the architecture and in the figures' clothing and hair. In ancient Greece, communal fountains supplied water to the cities, and the daily meeting of the women at the fountain house provided opportunities for social interaction in a society that restricted most women to their homes.

In the last third of the sixth century BCE, while "A.D." and others were still creating handsome black-figure wares, some painters turned away from this meticulous process to a new technique called **red-figure** decoration, so called because red figures stand out against a black background. In the red-figure technique, the painter covered the vase with slip but left figures unpainted to reveal the reddish body of the vessel. Instead of engraving details, the painter drew with a fine brush dipped in the slip. The result was a lustrous dark vessel with light-colored figures painted with dark-painted details (see fig. 4-23). The greater ease, speed, and flexibility of this technique led artists to adopt it quickly.

An early-fifth-century red-figure **kylix**, or two-handled drinking cup, displays the painter's virtuosity at adapting a scene to the shape of the vessel (fig. 4-22), as well as in the drawing of individual figures in action. The artist known as the Foundry Painter used the circular underside of the cup to illustrate the workings of a foundry for casting bronze figures. The walls of the pictured workshop are filled with tools and other paraphernalia: hammers, an ax and saw, molds of a human foot and hand, and several sketches. A seated worker attends to a furnace at left, while a second man, perhaps the supervisor, leans on a staff. A third worker assembles the already-cast parts of a figure; they are braced against a molded support. The painter has created a successful decoration in an awkward space and also gives us insight into the working methods of sculptors using the cast-bronze medium.

THE TRANSITIONAL OR EARLY CLASSICAL PERIOD

Historically, the early fifth century BCE was a violent period marked by a series of invasions from Persia (Chapter 5). The Greek cities banded together against their common foe, and by 479 BCE an alliance of city-states led by Athens and Sparta had driven out the advancing Persians. Perhaps the Greeks' success against the Persians gave them a self-confidence that accelerated the development of their art. In any event within thirty years they created a new style. This period of marked change and evolution, called the Transitional or Early Classical period, lasted from the end of the Persian Wars to about 450 BCE.

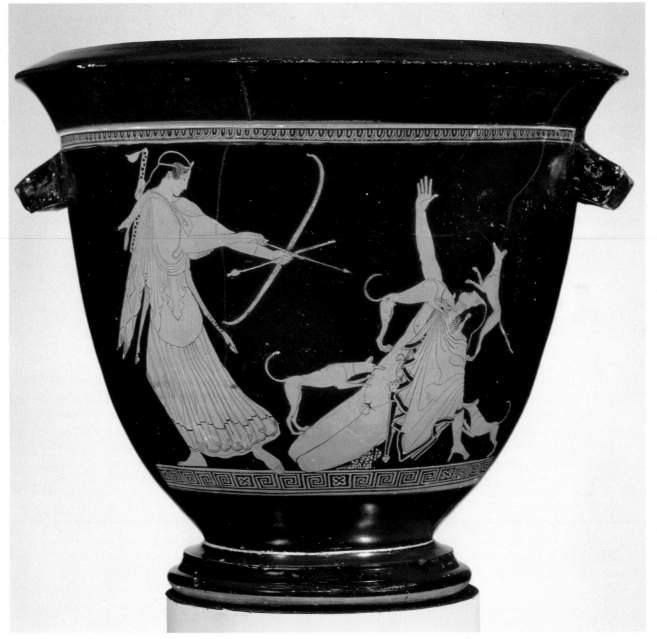

**4-23. Pan Painter.
Artemis Slaying
Actaeon,** red-figure
decoration on a
bell krater. c. 470
BCE. Ceramic,
height of krater
14⅝" (37 cm).
Museum of Fine
Arts, Boston
James Fund and by
Special Contribution

A red-figured bell **krater** (bell-shaped bowl
for mixing wine and water) shows the increasing
naturalism (semblance to visible nature) that
differentiates the Early Classical from the
Archaic style. Here, the painter, called the Pan
Painter, depicted *Artemis Slaying Actaeon* (fig. 4-23).
When Actaeon, out hunting, surprised the goddess Artemis at her bath, she retaliated by causing his dogs to mistake him for a stag and to
tear him apart. Here the hounds swarm over the
fallen hunter, whom Artemis prepares to finish
off with an arrow. The death seems melodramatic compared with the suicide of Ajax, but the

Greek artist's sense of balance and order still
successfully adjusts the actions of the figures to
the vase shape.

In freestanding sculpture, the Greeks shifted
in only a few generations from the rigid, frontal
presentation of the human figure embodied in
the Archaic *kouroi* to more natural, lifelike figures
such as the so-called *Kritios Boy* (fig. 4-24). (When
the *Kritios Boy* was excavated from debris at the
Acropolis of Athens, the statue was thought by
its finders to be by the Greek sculptor Kritios,
whose work was known only from Roman
copies.) In contrast to the over-lifesize Archaic

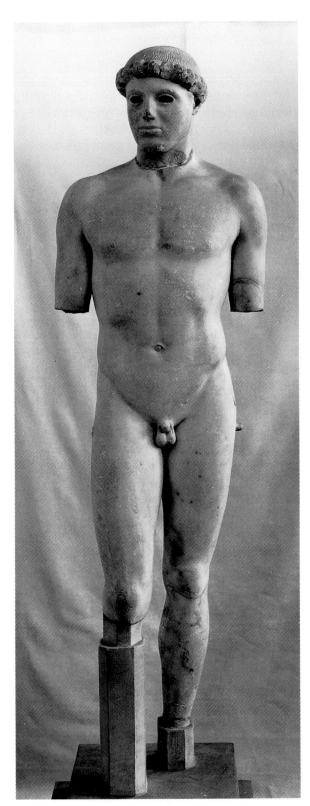
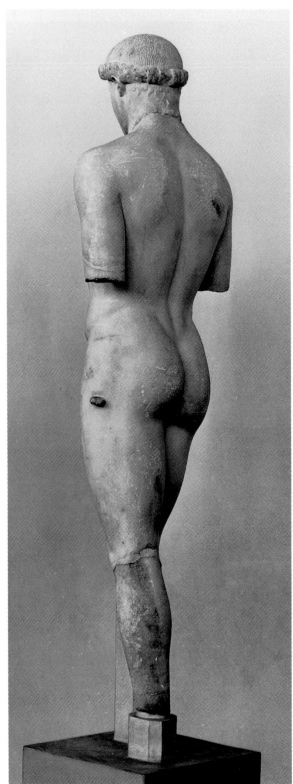

4-24. Kritios Boy. c. 480 BCE. Marble, height 33⁴/₅" (86 cm). Acropolis Museum, Athens

period *kouroi*, the *Kritios Boy* originally stood only a little over 3 feet tall. The solid, rounded body forms, broad facial features, and thoughtful expression—which lacks even a trace of the Archaic smile—give the figure an air of extraordinary solemnity. The easy pose contrasts markedly with the more rigid bearing of Archaic *kouroi*. The boy's weight rests on his left leg (the

"engaged" leg), and his unengaged right leg bends slightly at the knee. The curve in his spine counters the slight shifting of his hips and the subtle drop of one shoulder. The ability to capture life and movement, first implied in the Archaic *kouroi*, here is taken one step further.

The technique of modeling and **hollow-casting** bronze, developed at the end of the

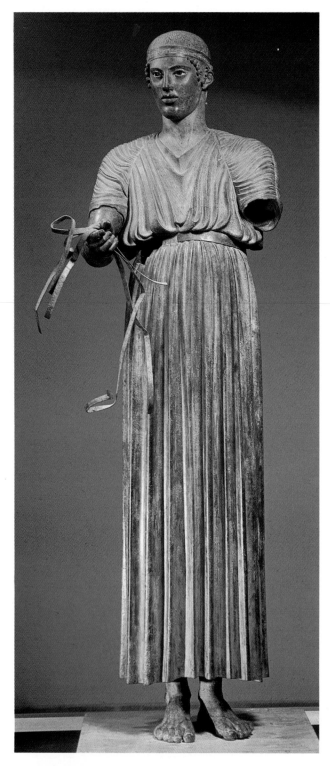

4-25. Charioteer, from the Sanctuary of Apollo, Delphi. c. 470 BCE. Bronze, height 5'11" (1.8 m). Archeological Museum, Delphi

The setting of a work of art affects the impression it makes. Today, this stunning figure is exhibited on a low base in the peaceful surroundings of a museum, isolated from other works and spotlighted for close examination. Its effect would have been very different in its original outdoor location, standing in a horse-drawn chariot atop a tall monument. Viewers in ancient times, exhausted from the steep climb to the sanctuary, possibly jostled by crowds of fellow pilgrims, could have absorbed only its overall effect, not the fine details of the face, robe, and body visible to today's viewers.

Archaic period, made possible more complex and even off-balance action poses, which would be difficult to carve in stone. A lifesize bronze *Charioteer* (fig. 4-25), cast about 470 BCE and found in the Sanctuary of Apollo at Delphi together with fragments of a bronze chariot and horses, illustrates the skill of Greek metalworkers. According to its inscription, the sculpture commemorates a victory by the driver sponsored by King Polyzalos of Gela (Sicily) in the Pythian Games (an event like the Olympics but held at Delphi and honoring Apollo) of 478 or 474 BCE. The idealized features of a handsome youth could almost be those of a particular individual. The single remaining hand and the feet are so realistic that they seem to have been cast from molds made from an actual person. The robe falls neatly into folds, yet the garment seems capable of swaying and rippling if the charioteer moved slightly or encountered a sudden breeze. The lifelike quality of the *Charioteer* calls to mind the claim by the Roman historian and naturalist Pliny the Elder (in the first century BCE), that three-time winners in Greek competitions had their features memorialized in statues.

A pair of over-lifesize bronze figures known as the *Riace Warriors* illustrate sculptors' skill in depicting the nude figure. Found by a diver on the seabed near Riace, a city on the southern coast of Italy, they may have been thrown from a sinking ship by sailors trying to lighten the load. One of the pair, the so-called *Young Warrior* (fig. 4-26), dating from about 460–450 BCE, reveals a striking balance between anatomical forms based on arbitrary standards of perfection and details corresponding to visible nature. The athletic musculature suggests a youthfulness belied by the maturity of the heavy beard and almost haggard face. Minutely detailed touches, such as the swelling veins in the backs of the hands, contrast with the idealized smoothness of the rest of the body. The sculptor heightened the lifelike quality of the sculpture by adding eyes of bone and colored glass, silver plating on the teeth, and eyelashes and eyebrows of separately cast strands of bronze. Such intense study of the human figure prepared the way for the achievements of artists in the High Classical period.

THE HIGH CLASSICAL PERIOD

The High Classical period of Greek art, dating from about 450 to 400 BCE, is known also as the golden age. Yet this period saw turmoil and destruction resulting from the Peloponnesian War: Sparta and Athens, without a common enemy, turned on each other. Sparta dominated

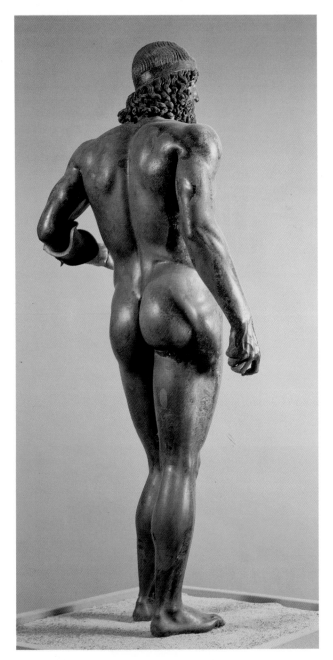
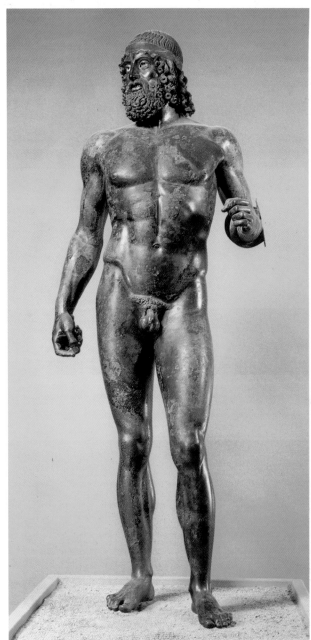

4-26. *Young Warrior,* found in the sea off Riace, Italy. c. 460–450 BCE. Bronze with bone and glass eyes, silver teeth, and copper lips and nipples, height 6'8" (2.03 m). Museo Archeològico Nazionale, Reggio Calabria, Italy

the Peloponnese peninsula and much of the rest of mainland Greece, while Athens controlled the Aegean and became the wealthy and influential center of a maritime empire. Today we remember Athens for its cultural and intellectual brilliance and its experiments with democratic government, which reached their zenith in the fifth century BCE under the charismatic leader Perikles.

The Acropolis of Athens, the hill that formed the city's ceremonial center, visually expressed both the city's values and civic pride. The Persians originally destroyed the buildings and statues in 480 BCE, but the Athenians rebuilt their monuments on the Acropolis during the second half of the fifth century BCE. Athens was the patron city of the goddess Athena. Her temple, the Parthenon, dedicated to the Virgin Athena

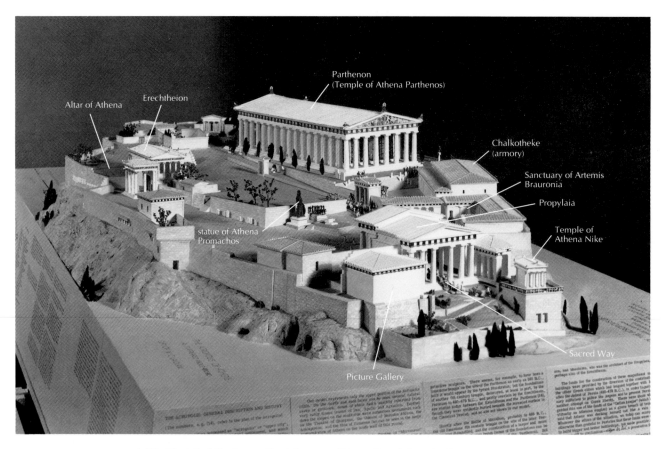

4-27. Model of the Acropolis, Athens, c. 400 BCE. Royal Ontario Museum, Toronto

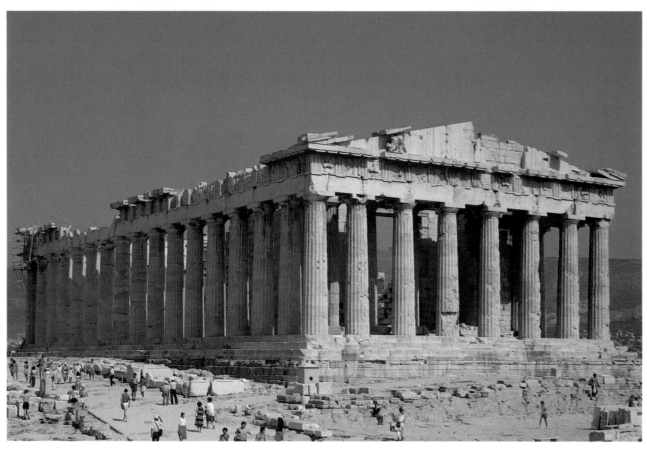

4-28. Kallikrates and Iktinos. Parthenon, Acropolis, Athens. 447–438 BCE. View from the northwest

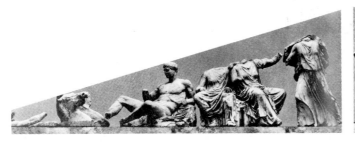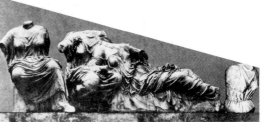

| Apollo and horses of his chariot team | Dionysos | Persephone Demeter | Iris | Hestia (?) | Dione | Aphrodite | Selene and one horse of her chariot team |

4-29. Photographic mock-up of the east pediment of the Parthenon (using photographs of the extant marble sculpture c. 438–432 BCE). The blank vertical spaces represent the missing sculptures.

At the beginning of the nineteenth century, Thomas Bruce, the British earl of Elgin and ambassador to Constantinople, acquired much of the surviving sculpture from the Parthenon, which was being used for military purposes. He shipped it back to London in 1801 to decorate a lavish mansion for himself and his wife. By the time he returned to England a few years later, his wife had left him and the ancient treasures were at the center of a financial dispute. Finally, he sold the sculpture for a very low price. Referred to as the *Elgin Marbles*, most of the sculpture is now in the British Museum, including all the elements seen here except the torso of *Selene*, which is in the Acropolis Museum, Athens. The Greek government has tried unsuccessfully in recent times to have the *Elgin Marbles* returned.

(*Athena Parthenos* in Greek), rose triumphantly over the city. It dominated the other structures on the hilltop site (fig. 4-27), where there had been an earlier, unfinished, and destroyed temple to the goddess. The Parthenon was designed and built by the architects Kallikrates and Iktinos. The builders used the finest white marble everywhere on the building, even replacing the customary terra-cotta roof with marble slabs. The renowned sculptor Pheidias designed the sculptural decorations and in addition supervised the entire building project of the Acropolis. The building was completed in 438 BCE, and its sculpture, executed by Pheidias and other sculptors in his workshop, was finished in 432 BCE.

The Parthenon illustrates the refinement of Greek architecture in its structure and design (fig. 4-28). It follows the typical cella and peristyle plan and uses the Doric order. To counteract the optical illusions that would distort its appearance when seen from a distance, the architects made many subtle adjustments. Usually, long horizontal lines appear to sag in the center, but here they do not because the architects designed both the base of the temple and the entablature to curve slightly upward toward the center. The columns have a subtle swelling, or entasis, and tilt inward slightly from bottom to top. In addition, the space between columns is less at the corners than elsewhere. These subtle modifications in the arrangement of elements give the Parthenon a buoyant organic appearance and prevent it from looking like a heavy, lifeless stone box. The building becomes, in effect, a gigantic marble sculpture.

Sculpture carved in the round filled the pediments of the Parthenon. Figures also stood

on the projecting shelves of the horizontal cornice—the top of the entablature—secured to the pediment wall with metal pins. Most of the works of sculpture have been damaged or lost over the centuries, but using the locations of the pinholes, scholars have determined the placement of the surviving statues and can infer the poses of the missing ones (fig. 4-29).

The figures on the east pediment illustrate the birth of Athena, the goddess of wisdom. The statues in the center of the composition, missing, probably showed Zeus seated on a throne, and standing next to him, Athena, who according to mythology had emerged fully grown from his head. Flanking the central figures were groups of goddesses, then single reclining male figures, and finally, in either corner, the sun god Apollo in his chariot and the moon goddess Selene in hers. The standing female figure left of center is Iris, messenger of the gods, already spreading the news of Athena's birth. The three female figures on the right side are perhaps Hestia (a sister of Zeus and the goddess of the hearth), Aphrodite (goddess of love), and her mother Dione (one of Zeus's many consorts). The sculptor, whether Pheidias or someone working in the Pheidian style, expertly rendered the human form beneath the draperies. The clinging fabric creates circular patterns rippling with a life of their own over torsos, breasts, and knees and uniting the three figures into a single mass.

The Doric frieze of the Parthenon has carved metopes with scenes of human, as opposed to divine, victory. On the south side, the metopes depict the fight between the half-human centaurs and a legendary Greek tribe known as the Lapiths. The Lapith victory over the centaurs

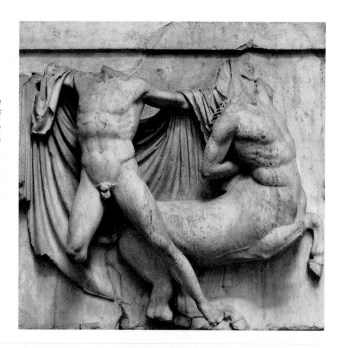

4-30. *Lapith Fighting a Centaur,* metope relief from the Doric frieze on the south side of the Parthenon. c. 440 BCE. Marble, height 56" (1.42 m). The British Museum, London

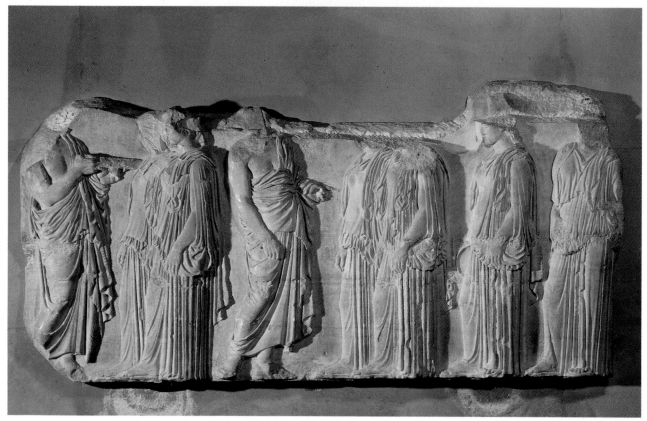

4-31. *Marshals and Young Women,* detail of the *Procession,* from the Ionic frieze on the east side of the Parthenon. c. 438–432 BCE. Marble, height 43" (109 cm). Musée du Louvre, Paris

may have symbolized the triumph of reason over animal passions. In one relief (fig. 4-30), what should be a death struggle seems more like a choreographed, athletic ballet, displaying the Lapith's muscles and graceful movements against the implausible backdrop of his carefully draped cloak. In Greek art, a single image can stand for an entire historical episode.

Inside the Parthenon's Doric peristyle, an Ionic frieze (see "The Greek Architectural Orders," page 97) decorates the upper temple wall. Unlike the episodic Doric frieze, the Ionic frieze consisted

of a continuous band of sculpture. Here the 525-foot-long frieze shows a procession, traditionally believed to celebrate the Great Panathenaic festival. In this procession, the women of Athens carried a new wool *peplos* to the Acropolis sanctuary to clothe an ancient wooden cult statue of Athena housed there. In the frieze, carefully planned rhythmic variations enliven the composition: the horses plunge ahead at full gallop; women proceed with a slow, stately step (fig. 4-31); parade marshals pause to look back at the progress of those behind them; and the gods

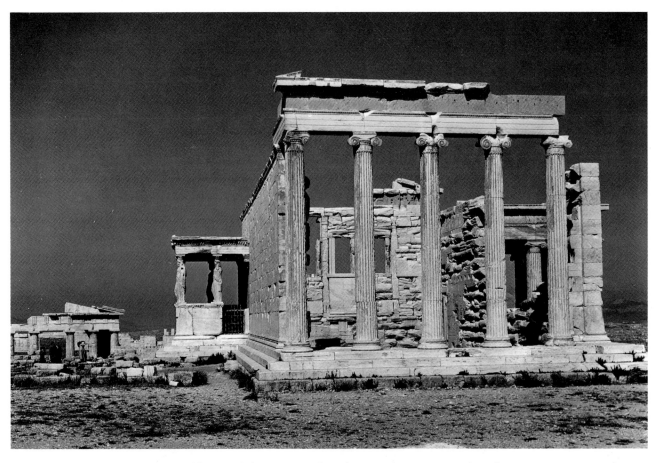

4-32. Mnesikles. Erechtheion, Acropolis, Athens. 430s–405 BCE. View from the east

and goddesses seated on benches await the arrival of the marchers.

The maidens who walk with such grace and dignity represent the Greek ideal of young womanhood, and their procession is an ideal procession outside time and place. The marble sculpture of the frieze was originally painted in dark blue, red, and ocher, and details such as the bridles and reins on the horses were added in bronze. To make up for the dim lighting inside the peristyle, the top of the frieze band is carved in slightly higher relief than the lower part, tilting the figures outward to catch reflected light from the pavement. The procession of maidens attended by parade marshals, although only a fragment of the architectural decoration, provides an indication of the extraordinary quality of every detail of the temple.

Construction of another temple on the Acropolis, the Erechtheion (fig. 4-32), began in the 430s BCE and continued until 405 BCE. The Erechtheion precinct was thought to have been the site of a mythical contest between Athena and the sea god Poseidon for patronage of Athens. For this important spot, the architect (believed to be Mnesikles) designed a temple with porches on three sides, the most famous of which is the Porch of the Maidens (fig. 4-33). Six stately **caryatids** (sculpted women serving as columns) topped with simple Doric capitals stand on a high base. Assuming a pose

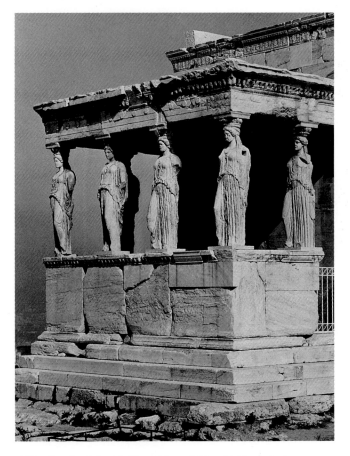

4-33. Porch of the Maidens (Caryatid Porch), Erechtheion, Acropolis, Athens. 421–405 BCE

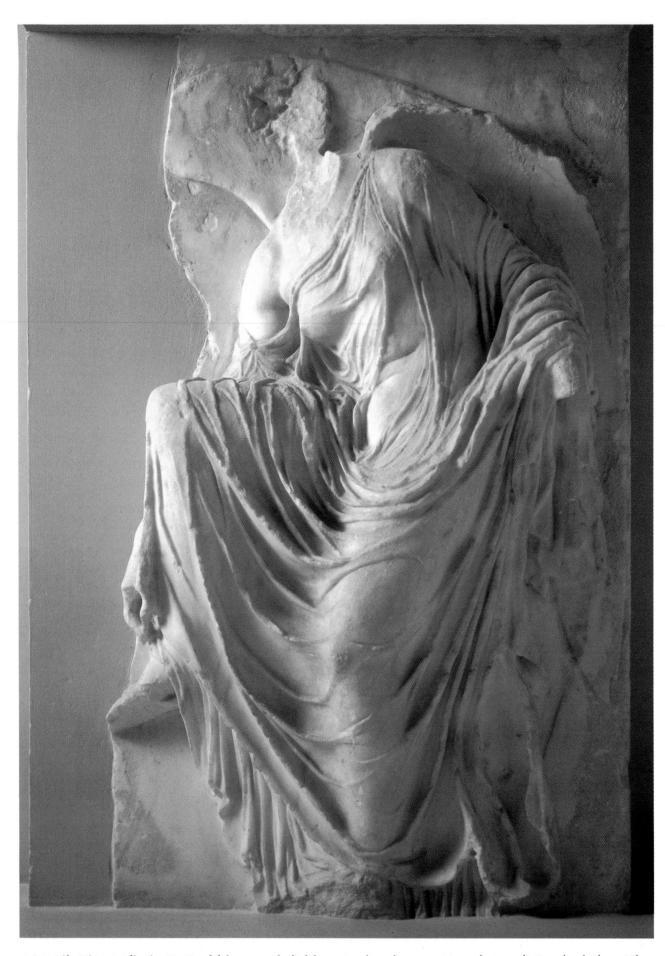

4-34. *Nike (Victory) Adjusting Her Sandal,* fragment of relief decoration from the parapet (now destroyed), Temple of Athena Nike, Acropolis, Athens. 410–407 BCE. Marble, height 42" (107 cm). Acropolis Museum, Athens

characteristic of Classical figures, each caryatid's weight is supported on one engaged leg, while the free leg, bent at the knee, rests on the ball of the foot. The vertical fall of the drapery on the engaged side resembles the fluting of a column shaft and provides a sense of stability, whereas the bent leg gives an impression of relaxed grace and effortless support, like the entasis of the Doric shaft.

The building was constructed using the Ionic order, and the north and east porches of the Erechtheion epitomize the Ionic form. Taller and more slender in proportion than the Doric, the Ionic order also has richer and more elaborately carved decoration (see "The Greek Architectural Orders," page 97). The columns rise from molded bases and end in **volute** (spiral) capitals. The frieze consists of a continuous band of sculpture.

A second Ionic temple, dedicated to Athena Nike, stands near the entrance to the Acropolis precinct. It was surrounded by a low wall faced with narrative relief panels of Athena presiding over her winged attendants, called Victories, as they prepared for a victory celebration. The Victories contrast with the restrained caryatids of the Erechtheion. One of the most admired panels depicts Nike adjusting her sandal (fig. 4-34). The figure bends forward gracefully, causing her ample robe to slip off one shoulder. Her large wings, one open and one closed, effectively balance this unstable pose. Unlike the decorative swirls of heavy fabric covering the Parthenon goddesses or the weighty pleats of the robes of the Erechtheion caryatids, the textile covering this *Nike* appears delicate and light, clinging to her body like wet silk. The artist's vision, and/or the patron's wish, has changed dramatically since the creation of the *Peplos Kore*.

Just as Greek architects defined and followed a set of standards for ideal temple design, Greek sculptors sought an ideal of human beauty. Studying human appearances closely, the sculptors of the High Classical period selected those attributes they considered the most desirable, such as regular facial features, smooth skin, and certain body proportions, and combined them into a single ideal of physical perfection. For example, a thousand like events must have been observed and distilled to achieve the rhythmic harmony presented in the *Procession* frieze, where each form is distinct and individual yet all are united into an utterly satisfying whole. This quest for the ideal can also be seen in the philosophy of Socrates (c. 470–399 BCE) and his disciple Plato (c. 429–347 BCE), both of whom argued that all objects in the physical world were reflections of ideal forms that could be discovered through reason.

About 450 BCE, the sculptor Polykleitos of Argos developed a set of mathematical rules for constructing the ideal human form, which he set

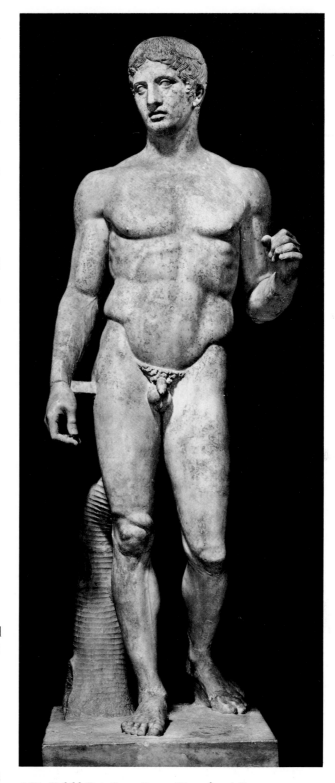

4-35. Polykleitos. *Spear Bearer* **(Doryphoros),** Roman copy after the original bronze of c. 450–440 BCE. Marble, height 6'6" (2 m). Museo Archeològico Nazionale, Naples, Italy

down in a treatise, now lost, called *The Canon* (*kanon* is Greek for "measure," "rule," or "law"). To illustrate his theory, Polykleitos created a larger-than-lifesize bronze statue, the *Spear Bearer* (*Doryphoros*). The original statue has not survived, but later Roman artists made copies of it, such as the marble replica illustrated here (fig. 4-35). The pose is more dynamic than that of the *Kritios Boy* or the *Riace Warrior* of a generation earlier.

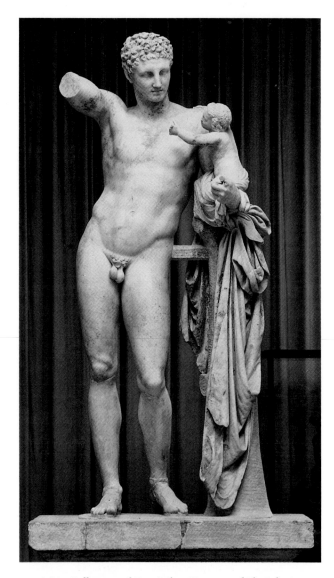

4-36. Followers of Praxiteles. *Hermes and the Infant Dionysos,* probably a Roman copy after an original of c. 300–250 BCE. Marble, with remnants of red paint on the lips and hair, height 7'1" (2.16 m). Archeological Museum, Olympia

The whole weight of the upper body is supported on the straight right leg; only the ball of the left foot touches the ground. This pattern of tension and relaxation is reversed in the arms, with the right arm relaxed and the left bent to support the weight of the (missing) spear. The tilt of the hipline is pronounced, and the head is tilted and turned toward the right. The young man appears to have paused for a moment in perfect equilibrium, ready to step forward. Greek artists achieved such ideal figures through a combination of close observation of nature, seen in Transitional period art, and generalization based on ideal mathematical proportions. The resulting idealism inspired artists and their patrons for centuries afterward.

LATE CLASSICAL ART OF THE FOURTH CENTURY BCE

In 404 BCE, the Peloponnesian War concluded with the defeat of Athens by Sparta. Athens never regained its dominant political and military status, yet Sparta failed to establish a lasting preeminence over the rest of Greece. The quarreling city-states finally fell under the dominance of Philip II of Macedonia in 338 BCE. After Philip's assassination two years later, his son, Alexander the Great, incorporated the Greek city-states into an empire.

Remarkably, Greek art continued to evolve during this turbulent period. Architects preferred the elegant Ionic order and introduced the even more decorative Corinthian order (see "The Greek Architectural Orders," page 97). In their search for an ideal human form, sculptors, most notably Praxiteles and Lysippos in the fourth century BCE, developed a new canon of proportions for figures. Polykleitos's fifth-century BCE canon had produced a figure 6½ or 7 times the height of the head. Praxiteles, who worked in Athens from about 370 to 335 BCE or later, created figures about 8 or more "heads" tall. A marble sculpture of *Hermes and the Infant Dionysos* (fig. 4-36)—probably a Hellenistic or Roman copy but so fine that generations of scholars believed it to be an original statue by Praxiteles—has a smaller head and a more youthful and graceful body than Polykleitos's *Spear Bearer.* Its off-balance, S-curve pose contrasts sharply with that of the earlier work. The subject is less dignified: Hermes teases the infant god of wine with a bunch of grapes. Soft modulations in the musculature, deep folds in the draperies, and rough locks of hair create a sensuous play of light over the figure's surface.

Around 350 BCE Praxiteles created a daring statue of Aphrodite, the goddess of love. For the first time, a well-known Greek sculptor depicted a goddess as a completely nude woman (fig. 4-37). The citizens of Knidos in Asia Minor purchased the sculpture and displayed it proudly in a shrine open on all four sides. The original sculpture is lost, but in the version of the statue seen here, actually a composite of two Roman copies, the goddess is preparing to take a bath. Her hand, posed in a gesture of modesty, paradoxically seems to emphasize her nudity. She leans forward slightly with one knee in front of the other in a seductive pose that emphasizes the swelling forms of her thighs and abdomen. According to an old legend, Praxiteles' original statue depicted her so accurately that Aphrodite herself made a journey to Knidos to see it and cried out in shock, "Where did Praxiteles see me naked?"

The other major sculptor of the fourth century BCE whose name and fame come down to us was Lysippos. He became famous for his monumental statues of Zeus. He also carved Alexander the Great standing and holding a scepter in the same way he is believed to have represented the king of the gods, though neither of these statues still exists. A sculpted head found at Pergamon (in Turkey), once part of a standing figure, is believed

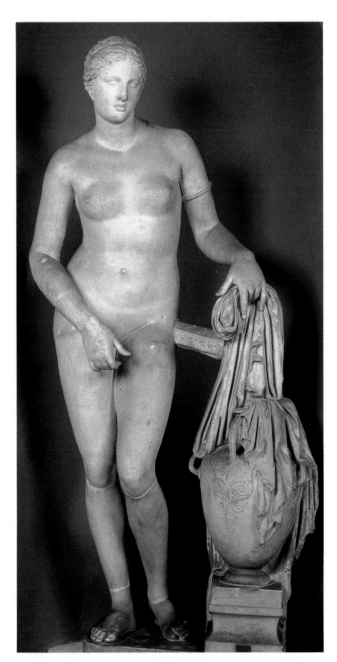

to come from one of several copies of Lysippos's *Alexander the Great* (fig. 4-38). According to the Roman historian Plutarch, the sculptor depicted Alexander with his head slightly turned and his face raised upward toward the sky, a description

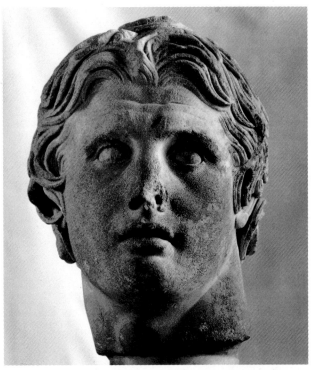

4-38. Alexander the Great, head from a Hellenistic copy (c. 200 BCE) of a statue, possibly after a 4th-century BCE original by Lysippos. Marble fragment, height 16¹/₈" (41 cm). Archeological Museum, Istanbul, Turkey

4-37. Praxiteles. Aphrodite of Knidos, composite of two similar Roman copies after the original marble of c. 350 BCE. Marble, height 6'8" (2.03 m). Musei Vaticani, Museo Pio Clementino, Gabinetto delle Maschere, Rome

In this composite of two Roman copies, the head is from one copy and the body from another. Seventeeth- and eighteenth-century restorers added the nose, the neck, the right forearm and hand, most of the left arm, and the feet and parts of the legs. This kind of restoration would rarely be undertaken today, but it was frequently done and considered quite acceptable in the past, when archeologists were trying to put together a body of work documenting the appearances of lost Greek statues. It was also done to create a piece suitable for sale to a private individual or for display in a museum.

that fits this head well. The deep-set eyes are gazing upward and the low forehead is lined, as though the ruler, contemplating grave decisions, is waiting to receive divine advice.

Alexander is typically portrayed in Greek art as young and godlike. After conquering an empire stretching from Greece south to Egypt, and as far east as India, he died of a fever in Babylon at the age of thirty-three in 323 BCE. Alexander's premature death, and the subsequent breakup of his vast empire, marks the end of the Classical period in Greek art.

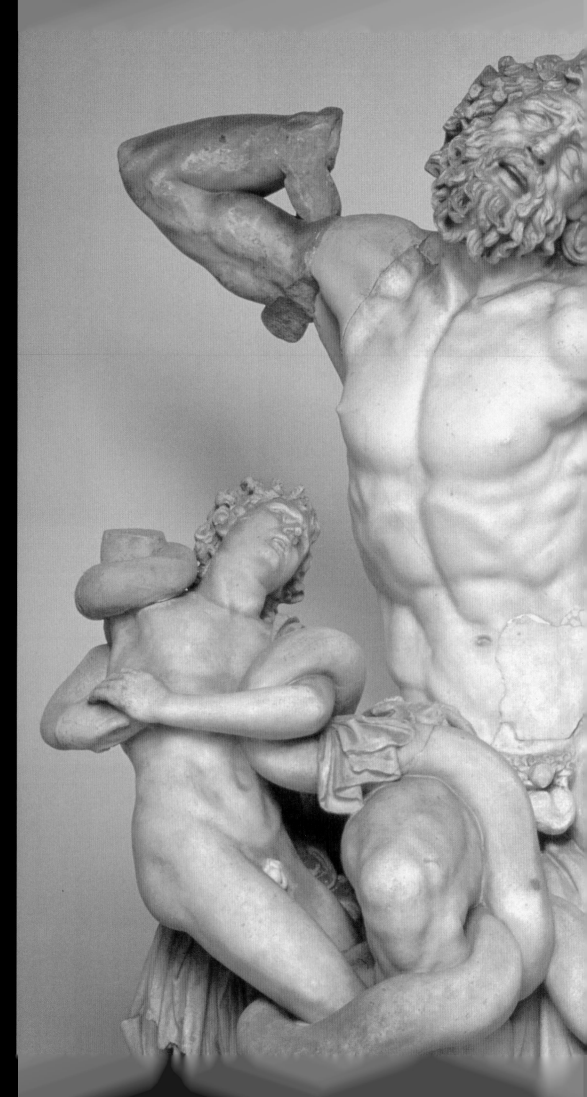

Hagesandros, Polydoros, and Athanadoros of Rhodes. *Laocoön and His Sons* (detail), perhaps the original of the 2nd or 1st century BCE or a Roman copy of the 1st century CE. Marble, height 8' (2.44 m). Musei Vaticani, Museo Pio Clementino, Cortile Ottagono, Rome

The Myth of Laocoön

Laocoön, Trojan priest of the god Apollo, angered the gods by marrying and fathering children (breaking his vow of chastity). His punishment came at the end of the Trojan War, when the Greeks defeated Troy by trickery. The Greeks built a huge wooden horse, large enough to hold many warriors. When the Greek army appeared to sail away, the delighted Trojans decided to take the horse into their city to Athena's temple. Laocoön, who had the ability to know the future, warned the Trojans against the "gift" of the Greeks. The Greek sea god Poseidon, who hated the Trojans and Laocoön, sent two serpents to crush the priest and his sons. Taking this tragedy as a sign of Laocoön's error, the Trojans brought the horse into Troy. That night, the hidden Greeks came out and destroyed the city.

Images of Laocoön

For a story as well known as Laocoön's, there are only a few extant early depictions of the subject—two vases and two mural paintings. By far the most affecting and influential representation is this one, found by excavators in Rome during the Renaissance, in 1506. The Roman historian Pliny the Elder (23–79 CE) describes the marble statue as being carved by Hagesandros, Polydoros, and Athanadoros— Greek sculptors working in Rome—and as decorating the palace of the Roman emperor Titus (39–81 CE). The heroic figures of the struggling father and sons inspired Renaissance and Baroque artists as different as Michelangelo, El Greco, and Bernini.

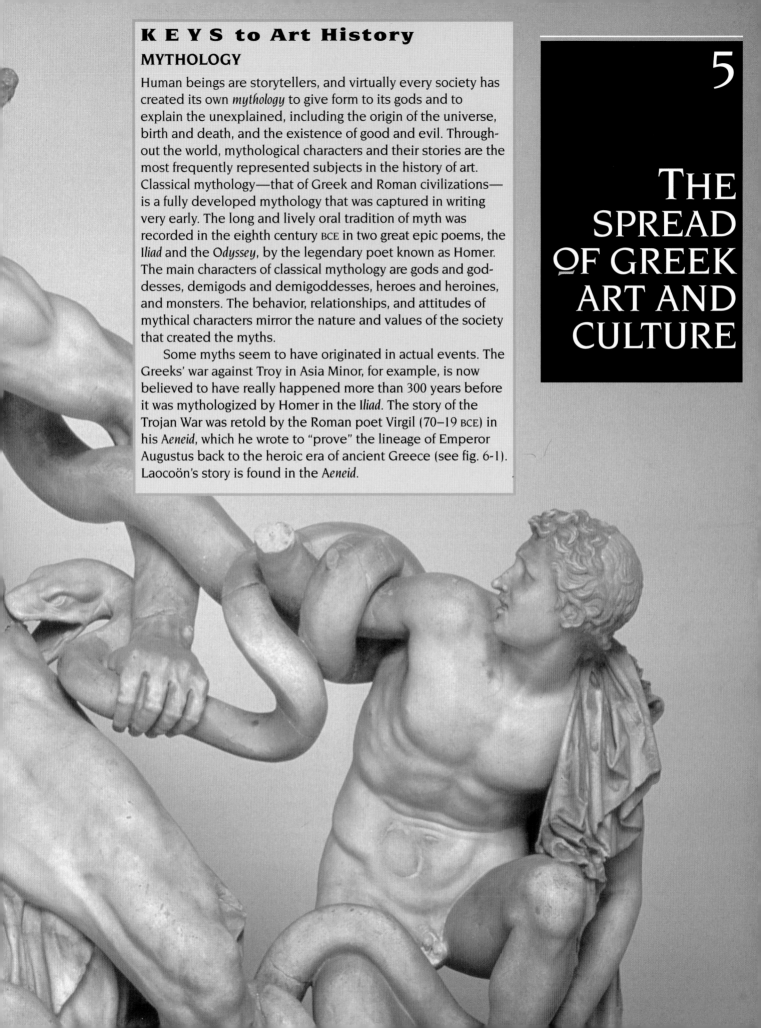

KEYS to Art History

MYTHOLOGY

Human beings are storytellers, and virtually every society has created its own *mythology* to give form to its gods and to explain the unexplained, including the origin of the universe, birth and death, and the existence of good and evil. Throughout the world, mythological characters and their stories are the most frequently represented subjects in the history of art. Classical mythology—that of Greek and Roman civilizations— is a fully developed mythology that was captured in writing very early. The long and lively oral tradition of myth was recorded in the eighth century BCE in two great epic poems, the *Iliad* and the *Odyssey*, by the legendary poet known as Homer. The main characters of classical mythology are gods and goddesses, demigods and demigoddesses, heroes and heroines, and monsters. The behavior, relationships, and attitudes of mythical characters mirror the nature and values of the society that created the myths.

Some myths seem to have originated in actual events. The Greeks' war against Troy in Asia Minor, for example, is now believed to have really happened more than 300 years before it was mythologized by Homer in the *Iliad*. The story of the Trojan War was retold by the Roman poet Virgil (70–19 BCE) in his *Aeneid*, which he wrote to "prove" the lineage of Emperor Augustus back to the heroic era of ancient Greece (see fig. 6-1). Laocoön's story is found in the *Aeneid*.

5

THE SPREAD OF GREEK ART AND CULTURE

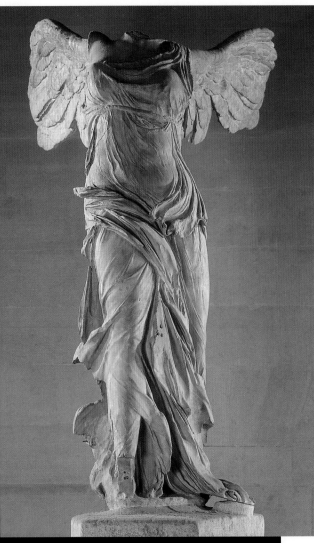

5-1. _Nike (Victory) of Samothrace,_ from the Sanctuary of the Great Gods, Samothrace. c. 190 BCE (?). Marble, height 8' (2.44 m). Musée du Louvre, Paris

Victory! Throughout history, warriors and athletes, leaders and mobs, men and women— shouting, dancing, embracing—have expressed the joy of winning. Yearning to capture that supreme yet fleeting sense of achievement, the victors have taken steps to make sure that their accomplishments would not be easily forgotten. In expressions intrinsic to the arts—songs, epic tales of their exploits, and visible monuments, such as stelae, huge freestanding arches, and memorials—the triumphant have chosen material objects to commemorate their successes and to guarantee their immortality.

In the late second century BCE, Greek artists personified victory as a supremely beautiful and powerful woman who swept through the air on the wings of an eagle, alighting where she chose to bestow the leafy crown of victory on a chosen mortal. Nowhere was she more magnificently portrayed than in Samothrace, a city on the coast of what is now modern Turkey. Here, to celebrate a naval victory, sculptors captured the goddess's idealized form in an imposing and subtly carved and polished marble sculpture.

The _Nike of Samothrace_ (fig. 5-1) exemplifies the spreading of Greek culture through the ancient world. Greek art and thought could be accepted, rejected, or modified, but it had to be considered, not only in the wake of Alexander's triumphant armies, but also in the more mundane reality of seafaring merchants who carried the products of Greek artistry around the Mediterranean. From energetic Etruscans to sophisticated Persians, from "barbarian" Scythians to the Hellenized population of the classical homelands, ancient peoples adapted Hellenistic culture. By blending Greek Classical style with indigenous traditions, they created distinctive new art forms.

Alexander the Great (356–323 BCE) of Macedonia did not live to rule the lands he conquered. In fact, for much of the first millennium BCE, many states and kingdoms rose and fell, playing out a delicate balance of power.

In the western Mediterranean, the Etruscans controlled the northern half of the Italian Peninsula from the seventh century BCE until the rise of Rome in the third century BCE. Renowned both as metalworkers and sailors, the Etruscans maintained close trading relationships with the Greeks and Phoenicians. The Phoenicians, based in the coastal area of modern Lebanon, sailed and traded as far as the western coast of Africa. They founded colonies in North Africa and Spain by the eighth century BCE. During the same period, the Greeks (Chapter 4) ruled far-flung colonies, including southern Italy and Anatolia (western Asia Minor, forming modern Turkey). From coastal outposts in what is now the Crimean region of Ukraine, the Greeks also traded with the Scythians, nomadic horse- and cattle-breeders who lived north of the Black Sea on the semi-arid, grass-covered plains, or steppes.

To the east, the Assyrian Empire in Mesopotamia remained a significant force until around 625 BCE (Chapter 2). Harassed periodically by the Scythians, the Assyrians were overthrown in 612 BCE by an alliance of the southern Mesopotamian state of Babylonia (now Iraq) and an Iranian people known as the Medes. Neo-Babylonia—so-named because it recaptured the splendor that had marked Babylon twelve centuries earlier under Hammurabi— flourished for less than one century before being taken over by the Persians, vassals of the Medes who obtained their independence in 549 BCE.

Beginning in the mid-sixth century BCE, the Persians, who occupied an area that is now southwestern Iran, began a vigorous campaign of military expansion. Under a dynasty of kings known as the Achaemenids, the Persian Empire became the dominant power in an area reaching from Asia Minor to Bactria (modern Afghanistan). They also conquered Egypt, Arabia, and Syria and attempted, but failed, to overcome mainland Greece (as we learned in Chapter 4).

The vast region ruled by the Persians fell to Alexander the Great in the late fourth century BCE. Although his empire disintegrated, Alexander's lasting legacy can be seen in the impact of Greek culture far beyond its original borders. Under Alexander and his successors, non-Greek people produced Hellenistic ("Greek-like") art in Egypt and in the former Persian lands of Asia as far east as the Indus River.

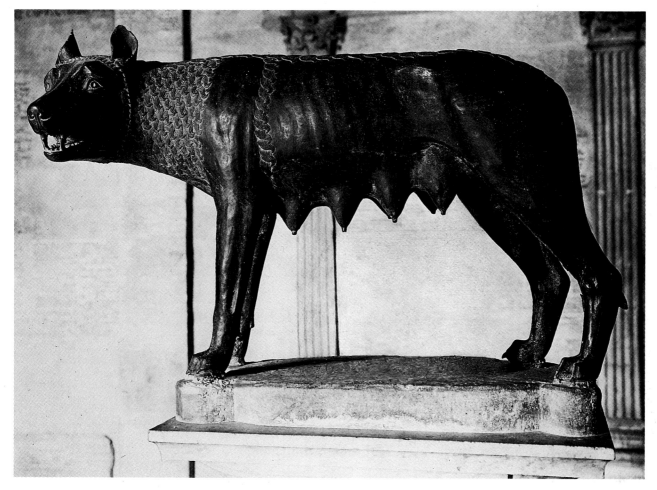

5-2. She-Wolf. c. 500–480 BCE. Bronze, height 33¹/₂" (85 cm). Museo Capitolino, Rome

Although this sculpture was almost certainly the work of an Etruscan artist, it has long been associated with Rome. According to an ancient Roman legend, twin infants named Romulus and Remus, who had been abandoned on the banks of the Tiber River by a wicked uncle and left there to die, were suckled by a she-wolf that had come to the river to drink. The twins were raised by a shepherd, and when they grew up, they decided to build a city near the spot where they had been rescued by the wolf. They quarreled, however, about its exact location. Romulus killed Remus and then established a small settlement that would become the great city of Rome, an event that, according to tradition, occurred in 753 BCE.

The Etruscans

The boot-shaped Italian peninsula, shielded on the north by the formidable Alps, juts into the Mediterranean Sea, exposing its inhabitants in ancient times to the interplay among Near Eastern, Egyptian, and Greek civilizations. Etruscan society, deeply influenced by the Greek, emerged in the seventh century BCE in Etruria (modern Tuscany). The Etruscans may have descended from a people called the Villanovans, who had occupied the northern and western regions of Italy since the Bronze Age. The fifth-century BCE Greek historian Herodotus claimed that the Etruscans originated in the kingdom of Lydia in Asia Minor in the twelfth century BCE. The Etruscans reached the height of their power in the sixth century BCE, when they formed a loose federation of a dozen cities. The fertile soil of Etruria and its rich lodes of metal ore formed the basis of their wealth.

The skill of Etruscan bronzeworkers was widely known in ancient times. Only a few examples of large-scale cast-bronze sculpture in the round have survived the wholesale recycling of bronze objects over the centuries. One

such sculpture, which dates to about 500 BCE, portrays a she-wolf with heavy, milk-filled teats—evidence that she has recently given birth (fig. 5-2). The sculpture may represent the legendary she-wolf who nurtured the twins

---

A Global Golden Age

The term *golden age* refers to a period of fruitful activity in a country or a culture—a time when everything flourishes simultaneously: statecraft, economy, art, philosophy, literature, even social conditions. Greek civilization from about 500 to roughly 300 BCE represents such a golden age. So heroic were its achievements and so pervasive its influence on Western cultures that Western historians customarily capitalize the term:

the Golden Age.

But ponder this. During the same 200 years, in places vastly separated by geography, extraordinary individuals left legacies that have profoundly affected the course of human history. There was very little direct contact among most of these cultures, so cross-fertilization is not a credible explanation. And since these cultures began at different times, their golden eras cannot be attributed to a parallel "coming of age." Perhaps there is no justifi-

cation for this "global golden age" except coincidence. In any case, the following list of locations and names is something to marvel at:

- In Greece, the philosophers Plato, Aristotle, and Socrates; the playwrights Sophocles, Aeschylus, and Euripides; Alexander the Great of Macedonia
- In China, Confucius
- In India, the Buddha and the prophet Mahariva, founder of Jainism
- In Persia, Cyrus II, Darius I, and Xerxes

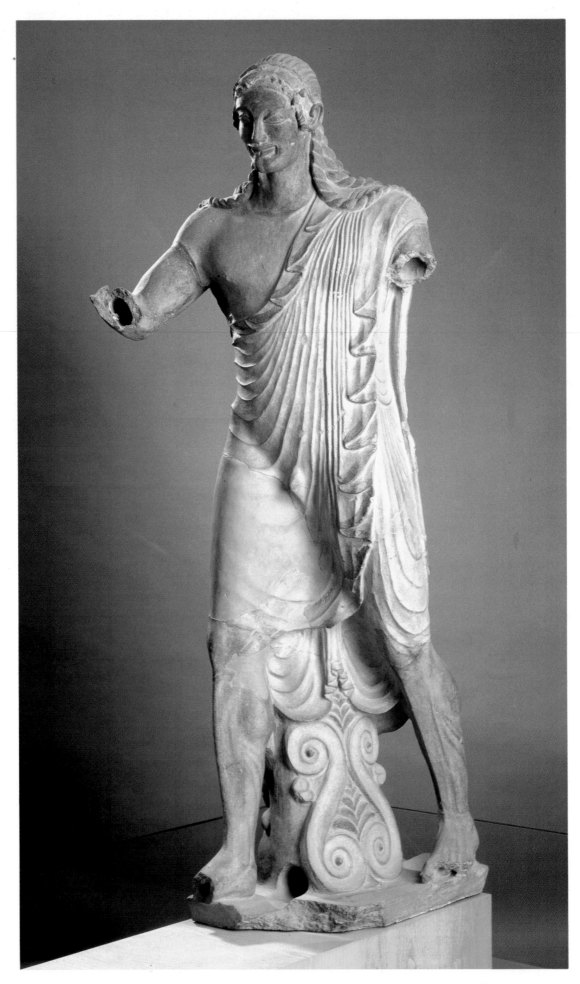

5-3. *Apollo*, from Veii. c. 500 BCE. Painted terra-cotta, height 5'10" (1.8 m). Museo Nazionale di Villa Giulia, Rome

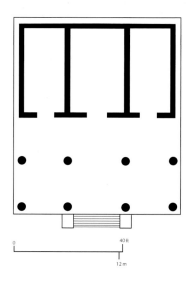

5-4. Plan of an Etruscan temple, based on descriptions by Vitruvius

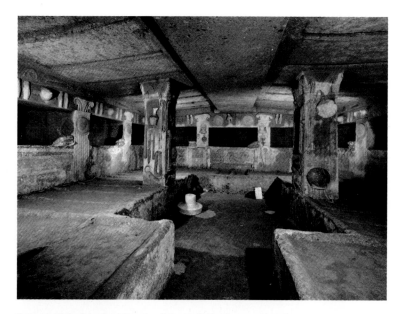

5-5. Burial chamber, Tomb of the Reliefs, Cerveteri. 3rd century BCE

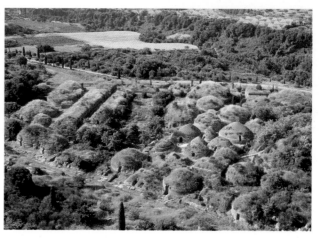

5-6. Etruscan cemetery of La Banditaccia, Cerveteri. 7th–4th century BCE

Romulus and Remus, the founders of Rome. Stylistically, the naturalistic rendering of the animal's body contrasts with the stylized rendering of the tightly curled ruff of fur around the neck.

Etruscan artists also excelled at making monumental terra-cotta sculpture, a task requiring great technical and physical skill. The artist had to construct the figures so that they would not collapse under their own weight while the clay was still heavy with moisture. In addition, the artist also had to regulate the **kiln** temperature during the long firing process. The lifesize sculpture of the sun god Apollo illustrated in figure 5-3 was made about 500 BCE. The well-developed body and the Archaic smile of this figure, known as *Apollo from Veii*, demonstrate that Etruscan sculptors knew Greek Archaic *kouroi* and *korai* (see figs. 4-19, 4-20). But while the Greeks represented men nude, the Etruscans often represented men partially clothed. Here the figure of Apollo is partly concealed by a robe. The striding pose—the figure was originally placed along the ridge of an Etruscan temple at Veii as part of a four-figure scene—has a vigor that contrasts with the quieter stance of Archaic Greek figures (Chapter 4). Apollo looks as if he has just stepped over the decorative scroll that actually helped support the sculpture when it was atop a temple. This quality of energy expressed in purposeful movement is characteristic of both Etruscan sculpture and painting.

The scene from which this figure is drawn comes from Greek mythology. Apollo fought with the hero Herakles for the possession of a deer sacred to Artemis, goddess of the moon and of the hunt. Artemis watched over the struggle with Hermes, the messenger of the gods. From early on, the Etruscans incorporated Greek mythology into their religion.

According to the Roman architect Vitruvius, Etruscan temples had only a superficial resemblance to those of the Greeks. They used the post-and-lintel structure and gable roofs, but the plan was different. The Etruscans built their temples on a high base with a single flight of stairs leading to a columned porch. The deep porch led in turn to a cella, which was divided into three parallel rooms (fig. 5-4).

The typical Etruscan home was a rectangular mud-brick structure built either around a central courtyard or around an **atrium**, a room with a shallow indoor pool for drinking, cooking, and bathing, fed by rainwater through a large opening in the roof. The burial chamber of the Tomb of the Reliefs at Cerveteri was carved to imitate such a house in the third century BCE (fig. 5-5). Its walls were plastered and painted, and it was provided with a full selection of furnishings, some real, others simulated in **stucco**, a slow-drying type of plaster that can easily be modeled or molded.

Like the Greeks, the Etruscans employed both cremation and burial to dispose of the dead. The Etruscan cemetery at Cerveteri (fig. 5-6) was

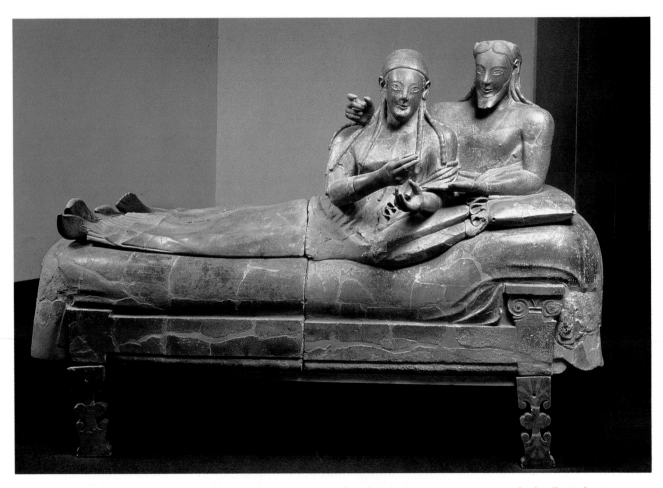

5-7. Sarcophagus, from Cerveteri. c. 520 BCE. Terra-cotta, length 6'7" (2.06 m). Museo Nazionale di Villa Giulia, Rome.

laid out like a small town, with "streets" running between the grave mounds. The tomb chambers were partially or entirely excavated below the ground, and some were hewn out of rock to resemble the rooms in a house.

Surprisingly, sarcophagi (large carved tomb chests) also provided a domestic touch. Figural sculptures resembling the dead seem to recline comfortably on a terra-cotta sarcophagus made to look like a couch, from Cerveteri, circa 520 BCE (fig. 5-7). Rather than a cold, somber memorial to the dead, we see two lively, happy individuals rendered in sufficient detail to convey contemporary hair and clothing styles. They might almost be attending a banquet or enjoying a performance of music or dance, convivial festivities often recorded in paintings on tomb walls.

In the Tomb of the Lionesses at Tarquinia, a detail of a frieze painted about 480–470 BCE shows a couple energetically dancing to the music of a double flute beneath a pediment ornamented with a leopardess (fig. 5-8). Both images of couples (that on the sarcophagus and that in the wall painting) are striking in that the female is represented on equal footing with her male partner. This suggests that some women were well educated and active in Etruscan society. The immediacy of this wall painting is striking. The dancers and musicians seem to be performing for us in the here and now, not enacting the formal rituals of a remote, long-dead civilization.

The Scythians

About 1000 BCE, as the Phoenicians (a Near Eastern seafaring people) began to dominate trade along the Mediterranean coast, new migrations began in Central Asia. The Medes and the Persians, nomads who spoke Indo-European languages, moved southward into Iran. Earlier Aryan migrants had already established themselves on the Indian subcontinent (Chapter 3). By the late seventh century BCE, another Aryan people, called Scythians, who may have come originally from Siberia, settled north of the Black Sea. They bred cattle and horses on the grass-covered plains and sold livestock and grain to the Greeks and to Near Eastern kingdoms in Mesopotamia and Iran. In return, they received metal ores and textiles, gold- and silverwork, and other luxury goods, such as Egyptian amulets.

Much of our knowledge of Scythian culture comes from burial mounds, known in Russian as *kurgans*, that the Scythians built for their rulers. The burial chamber beneath a *kurgan* was a large wood or stone structure, designed to shelter the ruler's body and those of his servants, horses, and concubines who were sacrificed and buried with him. Many tombs were furnished with valuable burial goods, especially vessels, jewelry, and weapons made of gold and silver.

The golden stag illustrated in figure 5-9, dating from the late seventh or the early sixth

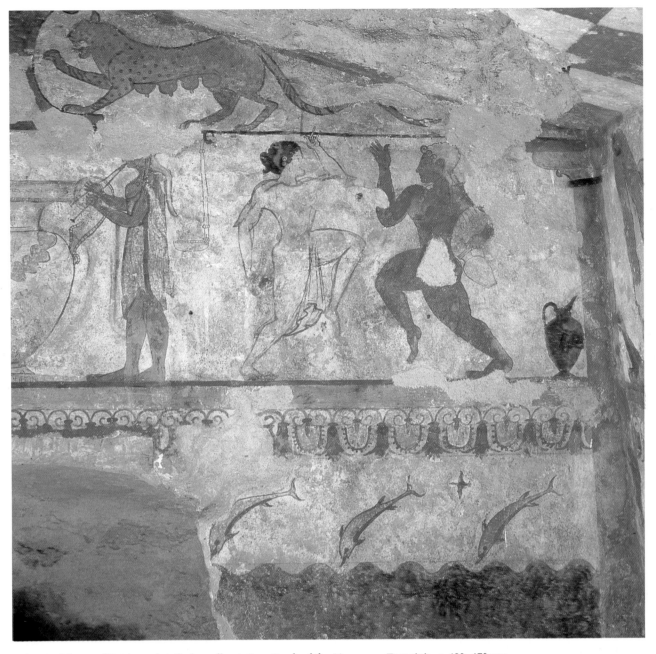

5-8. Musicians and Dancers, detail of a wall painting, Tomb of the Lionesses, Tarquinia. c. 480–470 BCE

The Etruscan method of painting decoration on walls has often been called fresco, but there are continuing doubts as to whether that designation is correct. Fresco is essentially painting with water-based pigments on a still-damp layer of fresh plaster applied in sections over a finished wall surface. The pigment soaks in and becomes an integral part of the plaster coating. Laboratory analyses to determine whether or not Etruscan wall paintings are true frescoes have been inconclusive. Some investigators think they are frescoes, while others claim that sections that appear to be fresco resulted from the artist's accidentally painting on a wall before the plaster had dried.

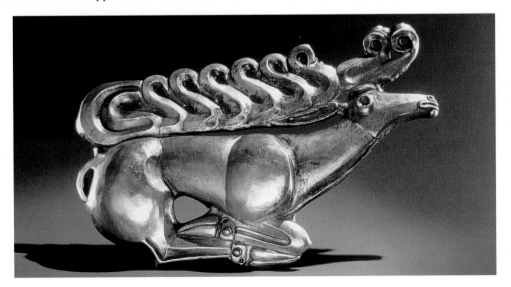

5-9. Scythian Stag, shield plaque. Late 7th–early 6th century BCE. Gold, length 12½" (31.7 cm). Hermitage Museum, St. Petersburg

Human figures are represented relatively infrequently in native Scythian art, but gold vessels and weapons of Greek workmanship, commissioned by Scythian customers, reveal aspects of daily life among the nomads of the steppes.

The Neo-Babylonians

In the seventh century BCE, the Scythian raiders joined the Medes from western Iran to invade the northern and eastern parts of Assyria. Meanwhile, in 615 BCE, the Babylonians, under a new royal dynasty, rebelled against Assyrian rule and formed a treaty with the Medes. In 612 BCE, an allied army of Medes and Neo-Babylonians captured and sacked Nineveh, the capital of Assyria (Chapter 2). When the dust settled, Assyria was no longer the power it was. The Medes controlled a large strip of land south of the Black and Caspian Seas, and the Neo-Babylonians dominated the lowlands of Mesopotamia.

The most famous Neo-Babylonian ruler was Nebuchadnezzar II (ruled 604–562 BCE). A great patron of architecture, he built temples throughout his realm dedicated to the Babylonian gods and transformed Babylon—the cultural, political, and economic hub of his empire—into one of the most splendid cities of its day. The eastern sector of the city was crossed by a broad avenue named May the Enemy Not Have Victory, also called the Processional Way because it was the route taken by religious processions honoring the city's patron god, Marduk (fig. 5-10). Up to 66 feet wide at some points, the street was paved with large stone slabs. Walls on both sides along the route were faced with colorful glazed bricks. These bricks were covered with the same type of coating applied to smaller ceramics and then fired to produce a shiny, waterproof surface. The Processional Way ended at the Ishtar Gate, a main entrance to the city (fig. 5-11). Named after the goddess known as Inanna in Sumer (see pages 47–48) and Ishtar in the Semitic-speaking regions of Mesopotamia, the gate was a symbol of Babylonian power. Guarded by four **crenellated** (notched) towers, the glazed-brick gate was decorated with tiers of the dragons sacred to Marduk and the bulls with blue forelocks and tails associated with a number of other deities.

Now reconstructed in a Berlin State Museum, the Ishtar Gate is installed next to a panel from the outer wall of the throne room of Nebuchadnezzar's palace (seen on the right in fig. 5-11).

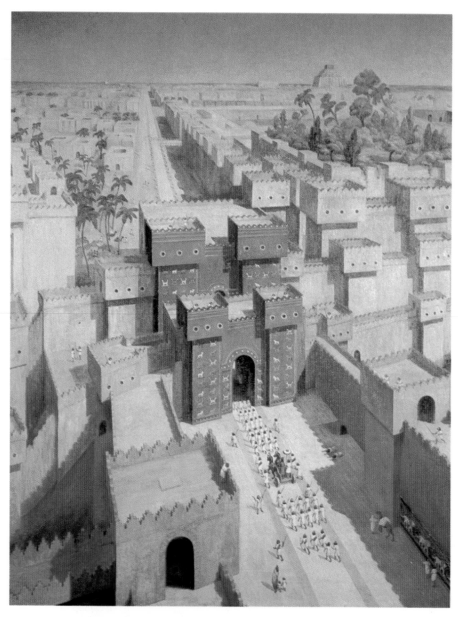

5-10. Reconstruction drawing of Babylon in the 6th century BCE. The Oriental Institute of the University of Chicago

In this view, the palace of Nebuchadnezzar II, with its famous Hanging Gardens, can be seen just behind and to the right of the Ishtar Gate, to the west of the Processional Way. The Marduk Ziggurat looms up in the far distance on the east bank of the Euphrates. This structure was at times believed to be the biblical Tower of Babel—Bab-il was an early form of the city's name.

century BCE, was found in a *kurgan* at Kostromskaya, not far from the Black Sea. The tautly stretched neck and alert head belie the reclining pose, hinting that the animal could actually be in full flight, its legs tucked up not in sleep or death, but perhaps in midleap. Inlays, possibly made of turquoise, once decorated the animal's eye and ear. This lavish work, made to decorate a warrior's shield, represents the **animal style** found across the steppes of Asia and eastern Europe. The Scythian raiders based their exploits from regions that are now part of Russia and Ukraine. Birds and animals are commonly shown locked in combat or curled up with their legs under them. Characteristic features may be exaggerated, such as the antlers on this stag.

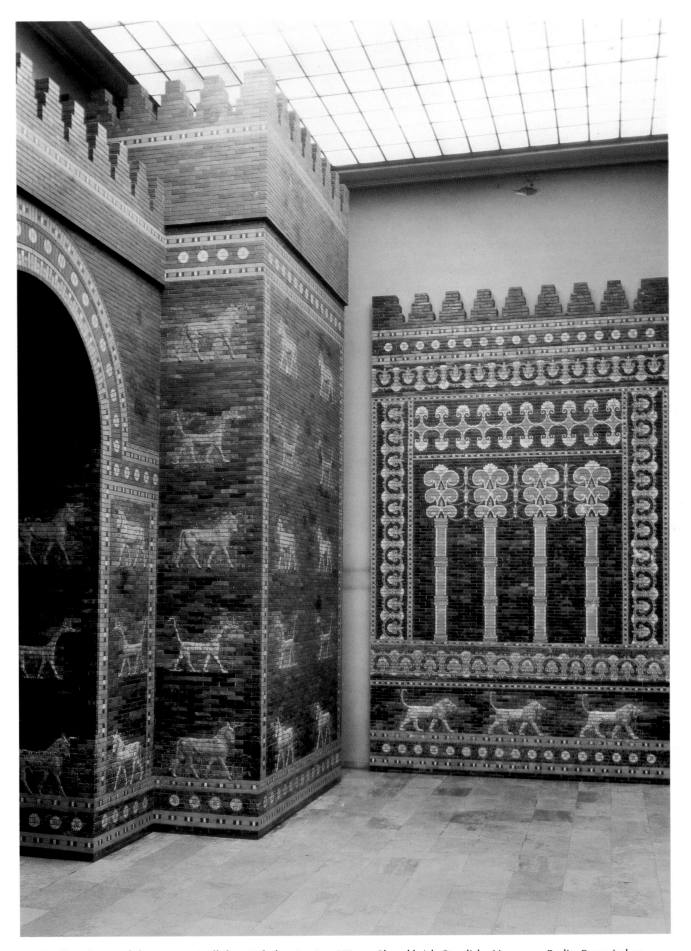

5-11. Ishtar Gate and throne room wall, from Babylon (Iraq). c. 575 BCE. Glazed brick. Staatliche Museen zu Berlin, Preussischer Kulturbesitz, Vorderasiatisches Museum

On this panel, lions made of molded and glazed brick walk in single file beneath stylized palm trees. Lions were often associated with royal power in the Near East, and in Mesopotamia the goddess Ishtar is sometimes shown on cylinder seals with her foot resting on a lion.

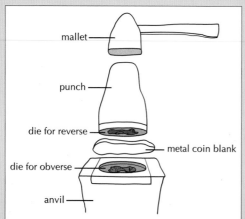
The Persians

Farther east, the Persians settled in southwestern Iran at the beginning of the first millennium BCE. Originally subservient to the Medes, the Persians obtained their independence in 549 BCE under a dynamic chieftain, Cyrus II, called the Great (ruled 559–530 BCE). Cyrus led the Persians in an astonishing series of conquests. By the time of his death, the Persian Empire included Babylonia, vanquished by Persia in 539 BCE; the land of the Medes, which stretched from Iran into Anatolia; the kingdom of Lydia, in western Asia Minor; and some of the Aegean islands. Cyrus's son Cambyses II (ruled 529–522 BCE) added Egypt and Cyprus to the empire. By the time Darius I (ruled 521–486 BCE) took the throne, he could boast: "I am Darius, great King, King of Kings, King of countries, King of this earth." Darius and his successors were known as

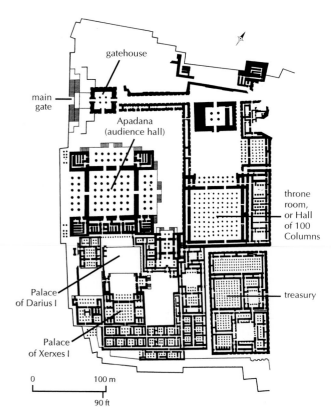

5-12. Plan of the ceremonial complex, Persepolis, Iran. 518–c. 460 BCE

the Achaemenid monarchs after a semilegendary ancestor, Achaemenes. They ruled for nearly two centuries, expanding the Achaemenid Empire both eastward and westward.

An able administrator, Darius organized the Persian lands into twenty tribute-paying areas under Persian governors, and he often left local rulers in place. This practice, along with a tolerance for diverse native customs and religions, won the Persians the loyalty of many of their subjects. Darius also developed a system of fair taxation, issued a standardized currency, and improved communication throughout the empire.

Darius, like many powerful rulers, created monuments to serve as visible symbols of his authority. About 518 BCE, he began building a new capital in the Persian homeland, today known by its Greek name Persepolis (fig. 5-12). He imported materials, workers, and artists from all over his empire. The result was a new style of art that combined many different cultural traditions—Persian, Mede, Mesopotamian, Egyptian, and Greek.

In Assyrian fashion, the imperial complex at Persepolis was set on a raised platform, 40 feet high, and like Egyptian and Greek cities, it was

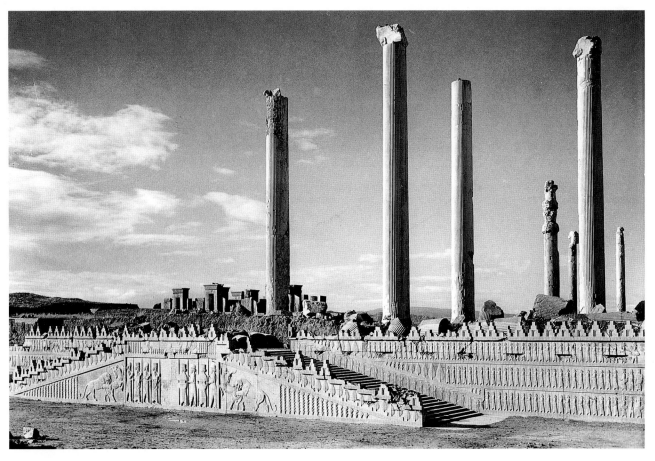

5-13. Apadana (audience hall) of Darius I and Xerxes I, ceremonial complex, Persepolis, Iran. 518–c. 460 BCE

The ancient historian Cleiarchus of Alexandria relates that Alexander the Great and his troops accidentally torched the royal compound at Persepolis during a wild banquet in celebration of their victory over the Persians. It is more probable that Alexander had it destroyed deliberately. The site was never rebuilt, and its ruins were never buried. Scholars have been measuring, mapping, and studying what remains of the complex for the past 200 years. Various pieces of architectural ornament have been stripped from Persepolis for display in museums around the world.

laid out on a rectangular grid. The platform was accessible only from a single ramp made of wide, shallow steps to allow equestrians to ride up rather than dismount and climb on foot. Construction extended over nearly 60 years, and Darius lived to see the erection of only a treasury, the *Apadana* (audience hall), and a very small palace for himself. His son Xerxes I (ruled 484–465 BCE) added a sprawling palace complex, enlarged the treasury building, and began a vast new public reception space, the Hall of 100 Columns.

Darius's Apadana (fig. 5-13), set above the rest of the complex on a second terrace, had open porches on three sides and a square hall large enough to hold several thousand people.

The sides of the staircases and walls of the **parapet** (low wall at the edge of the balcony) are covered with sculpture in low relief. Architectural low relief provides an important example in studying Persian art, since large-scale sculpture in the round from this era and region are rare and little known.

The sides of the Apadana staircase shown in figure 5-13 include two scenes of animal combat, an ancient and ubiquitous theme in the Near East (see fig. 2-8). Most of the reliefs at Persepolis are concerned with displays of allegiance or economic prosperity. In one example, Darius holds an audience while his son and heir, Xerxes, listens from behind the throne

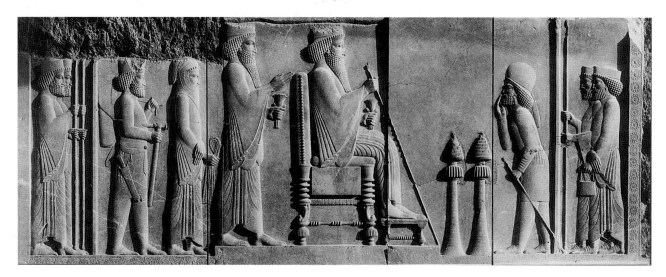

5-14. _Darius and Xerxes Receiving Tribute_, detail of a relief from the stairway leading to the Apadana, ceremonial complex, Persepolis, Iran. 491–486 BCE. Limestone, height 8'4" (2.54 m). Iranbastan Museum, Tehran

(fig. 5-14). The Persian reliefs, like Greek friezes, were once brightly painted, and metal objects, such as Darius's crown, were covered in **gold leaf** (thin sheets of hammered gold).

When Cyrus the Great defeated the ancient country of Lydia's fabulously wealthy King Croesus (ruled 560–546 BCE) in 546 BCE, Persia gained control over its gold. (Croesus's name has come down to us in the lasting expression "rich as Croesus.") The Persians learned from the Lydians to mint coins in standard weights. One type of Persian coin, the gold daric, named for Darius and first minted during his reign, is among the most sought-after coins in the world today (fig. 5-15). Commonly called an archer, it shows the well-armed emperor wearing his crown and carrying a lance in his right hand: he lunges forward as if he had just loosed an arrow from his bow. Besides their function as economic standard, coins also served as propaganda, carrying the ruler's portrait throughout the empire.

At its height, the empire conquered by Darius and his successors extended from Africa to India. Only mainland Greeks successfully resisted the armies of the Achaemenids, and it was a Greek who ultimately put an end to their rule. In 334 BCE, Alexander the Great of Macedonia crossed into Anatolia and swept through Mesopotamia, defeating Darius III and sacking Persepolis in 331 BCE. The lands of Persia became part of the Greek world.

The Hellenistic Period in Greece

At his death in 323 BCE, Alexander left a vast empire with no administrative structure and no appointed successor. Almost immediately, his

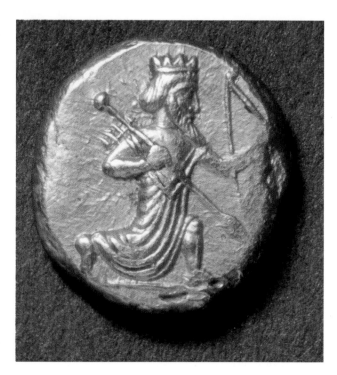

5-15. Daric, a coin first minted under Darius I of Persia. 4th century BCE. Gold. Heberden Coin Room, Ashmolean Museum, Oxford

generals turned against one another, and local leaders tried to regain their lost autonomy. The Greek city-states formed a new mutual-protection league but never again achieved significant power.

By the early third century BCE, three major powers had emerged out of the chaos, ruled by three of Alexander's generals and their heirs: Antigonus, Ptolemy, and Seleucus. The Antigonids controlled Macedonia and mainland Greece; the Ptolemies ruled Egypt; and the Seleucids controlled Anatolia, Syria, Mesopotamia, and Persia. Each of these regions followed a different political course, but they were unified artistically

5-16. *Aphrodite of Melos* (also called *Venus de Milo*). c. 150 BCE. Marble, height 6'10" (2.1 m). Musée du Louvre, Paris

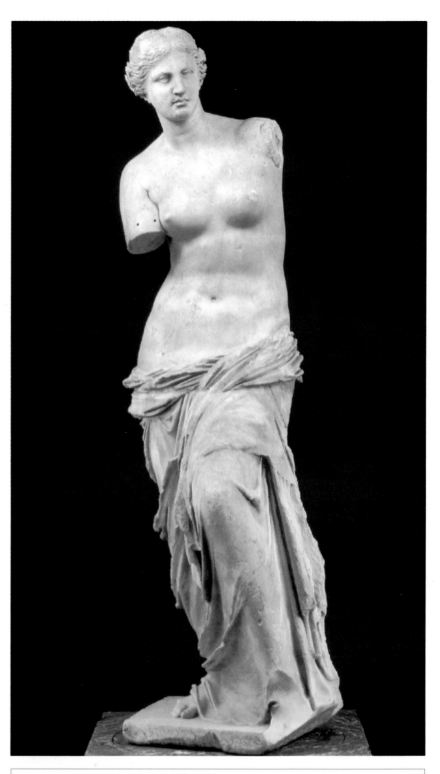

and culturally by the spread of Greek ideas and forms. Therefore all are considered a part of the Hellenistic world (a term deriving from *Hellas*, the Greek word for Greece), which lasted until the rise of Rome in the second and first centuries BCE.

Greek artists of the Hellenistic period had a vision discernibly different from that of their predecessors. Where earlier artists sought to capture the ideal and the all-encompassing in art, Hellenistic artists sought the individual and the specific. They turned increasingly from the heroic to the everyday, from aloof serenity to individual emotion, and from high drama to melodramatic pathos. They appealed to the senses through lustrous or glittering surface treatments and to the emotions by dramatic subjects and poses—two trends that were introduced in the fourth century BCE and that became more pronounced in the Hellenistic period. Hellenistic artists also reexamined the past, creating eclectic works by borrowing elements from earlier Classical styles. Not surprisingly, they often used the Corinthian order in architecture. Based on the Ionic order, the Corinthian order, with its richly carved **acanthus** (leaflike) capitals, was the most highly decorative of the three traditional Greek orders (see "The Greek Architectural Orders," page 97).

Certain popular sculptors, no doubt encouraged by nostalgic patrons, looked back especially to Praxiteles and Lysippos for their models. This renewed interest in the style of the fourth century BCE is exemplified by the *Aphrodite of Melos* (fig. 5-16), found on the Aegean island of Melos by French excavators in the early nineteenth century. The sculpture was intended by its maker to recall the *Aphrodite of Knidos* by Praxiteles (see fig. 4-37), and indeed the head, with its dreamy gaze, suggests Praxiteles' work. But the twisting stance and strong projection of the knee, as well as the rich, three-dimensional quality of the drapery, are typical of Hellenistic art of the third century BCE and later. Moreover, the sensuous juxtaposition of flesh with the texture of draperies, which seem about to slip off the figure, adds an insistent note of erotic tension that is thoroughly Hellenistic in concept and intent.

The idealized beauty of the *Aphrodite of Melos* contrasts sharply with the realistic depiction of an old woman, also made in the second century

Aphrodite's Arms

Aphrodite of Melos (fig. 5-16), better known as the *Venus de Milo*, has traditionally been synonymous with female beauty in the Western world.

Perhaps some of the figure's enduring hold is attributable to her very incompleteness. What was she doing, and where were her hands placed? Was she clutching the drapery slipping so seductively off her hips? Or was she temptingly holding out an apple in her right hand, as fragments of sculpture found near her suggest? When the sculpture was dug up in a field in 1820, many judged the loose fragments to be part of a later restoration and not part of the original statue.

The image of Aphrodite admiring herself in the highly polished shield of her lover, the war god Ares, became popular in the second century BCE, so this figure could have been holding a shield. If so, it would have been positioned off to one side, tilted at an angle, and probably resting on the goddess's left thigh. Today many archeologists compare the figure to the similar image of a Victory writing the name of a hero on a shield. Whether admiring herself or recording and memorializing a hero, these theories offer an explanation for the position of the shoulders, the pronounced S-curve of the pose, and the otherwise unnatural forward projection of the knee.

In ancient Greece, the theater offered more than mere entertainment; it was a vehicle for the communal expression of religious belief through music, poetry, and dance. During the fifth century BCE, the plays shown were primarily tragedies in verse based on popular myths and were performed at a festival dedicated to

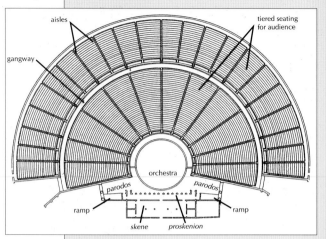

Plan of the theater at Epidauros

Dionysos. At this time, the three great Greek tragedians—Aeschylus, Sophocles, and Euripides— were creating the works that would define tragedy for centuries.

Because theaters were used continuously and were frequently modified over many centuries, no early theaters have survived in their original form. The largely intact theater at Epidauros, however, which dates from the early third century BCE, presents a good example of the characteristics of early theaters. A semicircle of tiered seats built into the hillside overlooked the circular performance area, called the orchestra, at the center of which was an altar to Dionysos. Rising behind the orchestra was a two-tiered stage structure made up of the vertical *skene* (scene)— an architectural backdrop for performances and a screen for the backstage area—and the *proskenion* (proscenium), a raised platform in front of the *skene* that was increasingly used over time as an extension of the orchestra. Ramps connecting the *proskenion* with lateral passageways (*parodoi*; singular *parodos*) provided access to the stage for performers. Steps gave the audience access to the fifty-five rows of seats and divided the seating area into uniform wedge-shaped sections. The tiers of seats above the wide corridor, or gangway, were added at a much later date. This design provided uninterrupted sight lines, good acoustics, and efficient crowd control for some 12,000 spectators. Greek theater plans have not been greatly improved upon since.

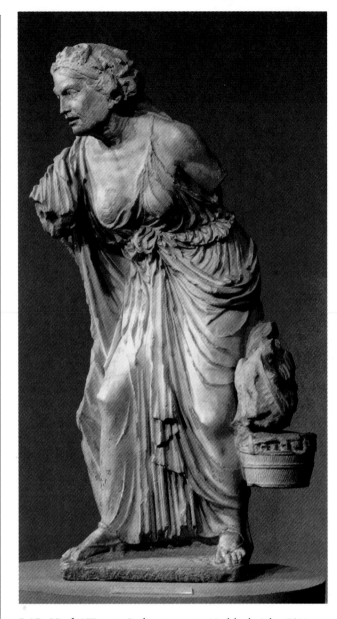

5-17. *Market Woman.* 2nd century BCE. Marble, height 49½" (125.7 cm). The Metropolitan Museum of Art, New York Rogers Fund, 1909 (09.39)

BCE (fig. 5-17). The representation of people from all levels of society, as well as unusual physical types, became popular during the Hellenistic period. This marble statue, once thought to represent a peasant woman on her way to the market, has also been identified in relation to Dionysus, god of wine. The disarray of her dress and her unfocused stare suggest that she represents an aging, dissolute follower of the wine god. We may assume that she is on her way to make an offering, since she seems to step out assertively into the space around her.

Dramatic poses, such as that of the *Market Woman*, are often found in Hellenistic art. The *Nike* (*Victory*) *of Samothrace*, for instance, is almost theatrically still (see fig. 5-1). The wind-whipped robe and raised wings of this victory goddess indicate that she has just landed on the prow of

the stone ship that formed the original base of the statue. The 8-foot-high Victory originally stood in a hillside niche high above the sanctuary of the Samothracian gods, perhaps drenched with spray from a fountain. The fact that victory in real life does often seem miraculous makes this image of a goddess alighting suddenly on a ship breathtakingly appropriate for a war memorial.

Some of the best-known examples of Hellenistic art were made in the third and second centuries BCE in the kingdom of Pergamon, a Greek state on the west coast of Asia Minor. After gaining independence in the early third century BCE, Pergamon quickly became a leading center of the arts and the hub of a new sculptural style that had far-reaching influence. That style is illustrated by sculpture from a monument commemorating the victory in 230 BCE of Attalos I (ruled 241–197 BCE) over the Gauls, a Celtic people who invaded from the north. These figures, originally in bronze but known today from Roman copies in marble, were mounted on a large pedestal. One of them, with the name Epigonos inscribed on the base, shows the agonizing demise of a wounded soldier-trumpeter (fig. 5-18). His wiry, unkempt hair and neck ring, or torque (the only item of dress the Gauls wore in battle), identify him as a "barbarian." But the sculpture also depicts dignity and heroism in defeat, and the artist has sought to inspire the viewer's admiration and pity for his subject. The viewer experiences a sense of arrested motion seeing the trumpeter supporting himself on his right arm, struggling to remain upright. One can see that his elbow is buckling, his body about to collapse. This kind of deliberate attempt to elicit a specific emotional response in the viewer, "expressionism," became a characteristic of Hellenistic art.

The style and approach seen in the monument to the defeated Gauls culminated in a monumental frieze, which stretched around the base of a huge altar on a mountainside at Pergamon (fig. 5-19). The frieze, which runs beneath the altar's Ionic colonnade, was probably executed during the reign of Eumenes II (197–159 BCE). It depicts the battle between the Gods and the Giants, a mythical struggle that the Greeks are thought to have used as a metaphor for contemporary conflict—in this case, Pergamon's victory over the Gauls.

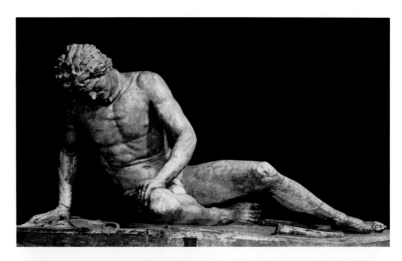

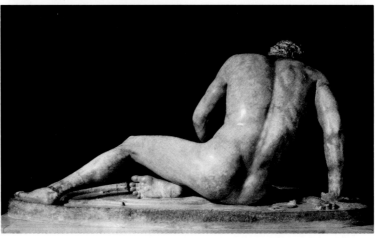

5-18. Epigonos (?). *Dying Gallic Trumpeter,* Roman copy after the original bronze of c. 220 BCE. Marble, lifesize. Museo Capitolino, Rome

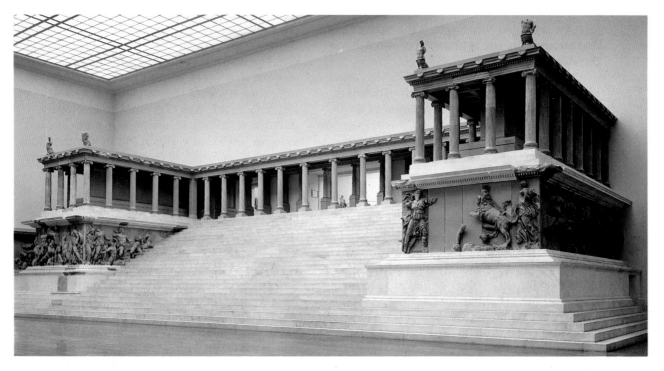

5-19. Reconstructed west front of the altar from Pergamon, Turkey. c. 166–159 BCE. Marble. Staatliche Museen zu Berlin, Preussischer Kulturbesitz, Pergamonmuseum

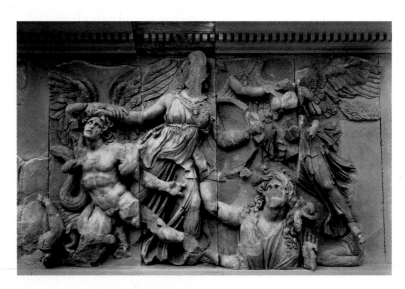

5-20. *Athena Attacking the Giants,* detail of the frieze from the east front of the altar from Pergamon. Marble, frieze height 7'6" (2.3 m). Staatliche Museen zu Berlin, Preussischer Kulturbesitz, Pergamonmuseum

The panels, about 7½ feet high, show Greek gods fighting human-looking Giants and grotesque hybrids emerging from the bowels of the earth. In one section of the frieze, the goddess Athena has forced a winged monster to his knees (fig. 5-20). Inscriptions along the base of the sculpture identify him as Alkyoneos, a son of the earth goddess Ge, who rises in maternal wrath from the ground on the right. At the far right, a winged Nike foretells the outcome of this struggle, as she is about to crown Athena the victor.

The Pergamon frieze is carved in high relief with deep undercutting that prompts dramatic contrasts of light and shade to play over the complex forms. Compositionally, the Pergamene sculptors sought to balance opposing forces in three-dimensional space along diagonal lines, whereas Greek artists of the fifth century BCE sought equilibrium and control through balanced horizontals and verticals. Some of the figures in the Pergamon frieze even crawl out of their architectural settings onto the steps, where visitors had to pass them on their way up to the shrine. Many consider this theatrical and complex interaction of space and form to be a hallmark of the Hellenistic style, just as they consider the balanced restraint of the Parthenon sculpture to characterize the High Classical style. Similarly, the emotional composure admired in Classical art gives way in the Hellenistic period to extreme expressions of pain, stress, wild anger, fear, and despair. All of these emotions characterize the sculpture of *Laocoön*

and His Sons (see fig. 3 and pages 114–115).

Hellenistic painting, like sculpture, reflects the new taste for dramatic narrative subject matter. Little remains of original Greek wall paintings, but in antiquity later patrons greatly admired Greek murals and commissioned copies in the form of wall paintings or mosaics. The second-century BCE mosaic illustrated in figure 5-21, showing a battle between Alexander the Great and Darius III of Persia, is a Roman copy of a wall painting of about 310 BCE. The historian Pliny the Elder attributed the original to a Greek painter named Philoxenos of Eretria; a recent theory claims it as a work of Helen of Egypt, one of a number of women painters recorded as having worked in ancient Greece. The mosaic was found in a home in the ancient Roman city of Pompeii, a city strongly influenced by Greek culture during the Hellenistic period.

The scene is one of violent action and radical foreshortening, both working to elicit the viewer's response to a dramatic situation. Astride a horse at the left, his hair blowing free and his neck bare, Alexander challenges the helmeted and armored Persian leader, who stretches out his arm in a gesture of defeat and apprehension as his charioteer whisks him back toward safety in the Persian ranks. Presumably in close imitation of the original painting, the mosaicist created the illusion of solid figures through **modeling**, mimicking the play of light on three-dimensional surfaces by highlighting protrusions and **shading** receding areas.

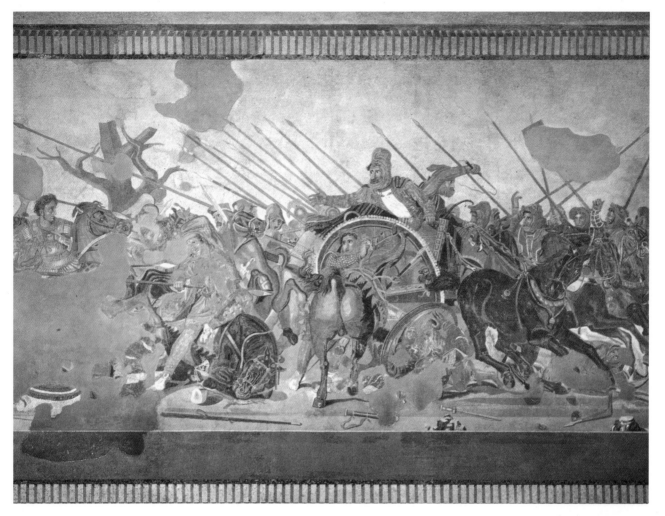

5-21. ***Alexander the Great Confronts Darius*** **III** ***at the Battle of Issos,*** Roman mosaic copy after a Greek painting of c. 310 BCE, perhaps by Philoxenos or Helen of Egypt. Museo Archeològico Nazionale, Naples

By the late first century BCE, the influence of Greek painting, sculpture, and architecture was paramount in communities such as Pompeii, which was dominated by the emerging Roman civilization. As Romans conquered the lands around the Mediterannean Sea, they inherited the artistic legacy of the Hellenistic world. Near Eastern and Egyptian components of Hellenism played a role in the Roman Empire, but Greek forms were valued above all others. Roman patrons and artists were so enthusiastic about Greek art that they made replicas of Greek artworks and wrote careful descriptions of Greek buildings, paintings, and sculpture. The art of Rome, built on Greek foundations, is marked indelibly by this rich Hellenistic heritage.

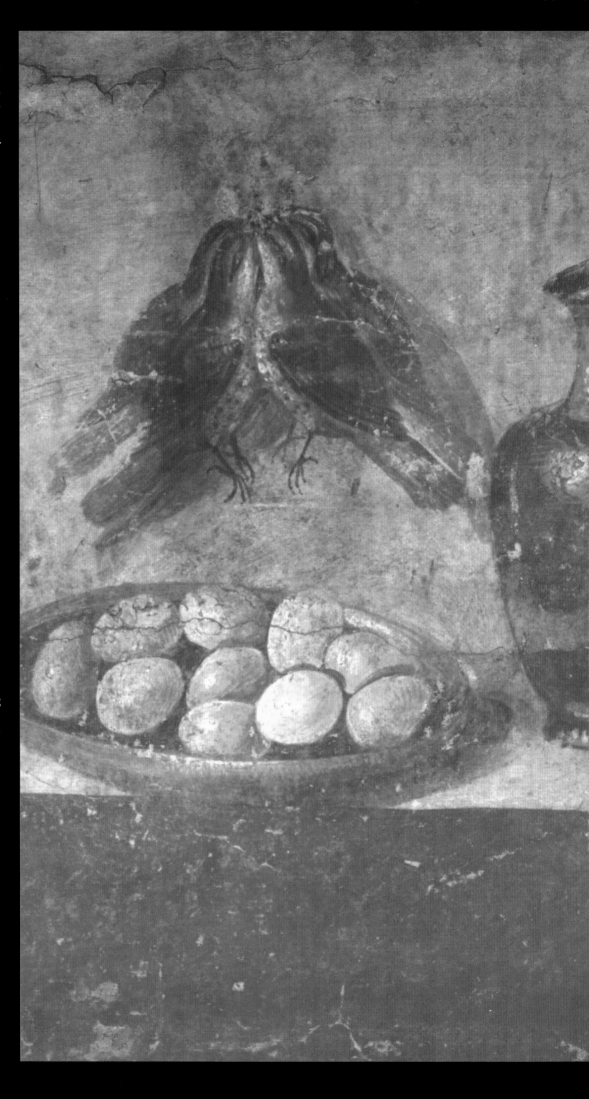

Still Life, detail of a wall painting from the House of Julia Felix, Pompeii, Italy. Late 1st century CE. Museo Archeòlogico Nazionale, Naples

Roman Wall Painting

Although not *buon fresco* as it is now understood, Roman wall painting is not strictly *fresco a secco*, either. The *intonaco* layer was applied in broad bands that paralleled the scaffolding on which the artist worked. The painting was done while the *intonaco* still contained some amount of moisture. The painted surface was sometimes burnished with a hard tool to achieve a look of glazed transparency, or it might be covered with a coat of wax.

Still Life

The beauty, richness, and sophistication that a skilled painter can achieve is seen in this still life. A *still life* is a grouping of inanimate objects. This detail pictures a low table or shelf on which rest a plate of eggs and a pewter wine jug. Hanging on the back wall are a brace of thrushes and a fringed cloth. A small flask rests against the shelf. Made to decorate the house of an independently wealthy Pompeian landowner, Julia Felix, this image celebrates the good life. (Little did the artist or house-owner know that very soon Mount Vesuvius would bury the seaside resort town under mud and lava.) Unlike still lifes made for Egyptian tombs, in which the objects depicted were expected to serve in the afterlife, the painting of these Roman foods and vessels ostensibly had no symbolic or religious purpose. They were pleasant decoration. The cast shadows are a sophisticated Roman visual illusion that lend the objects a three-dimensional quality.

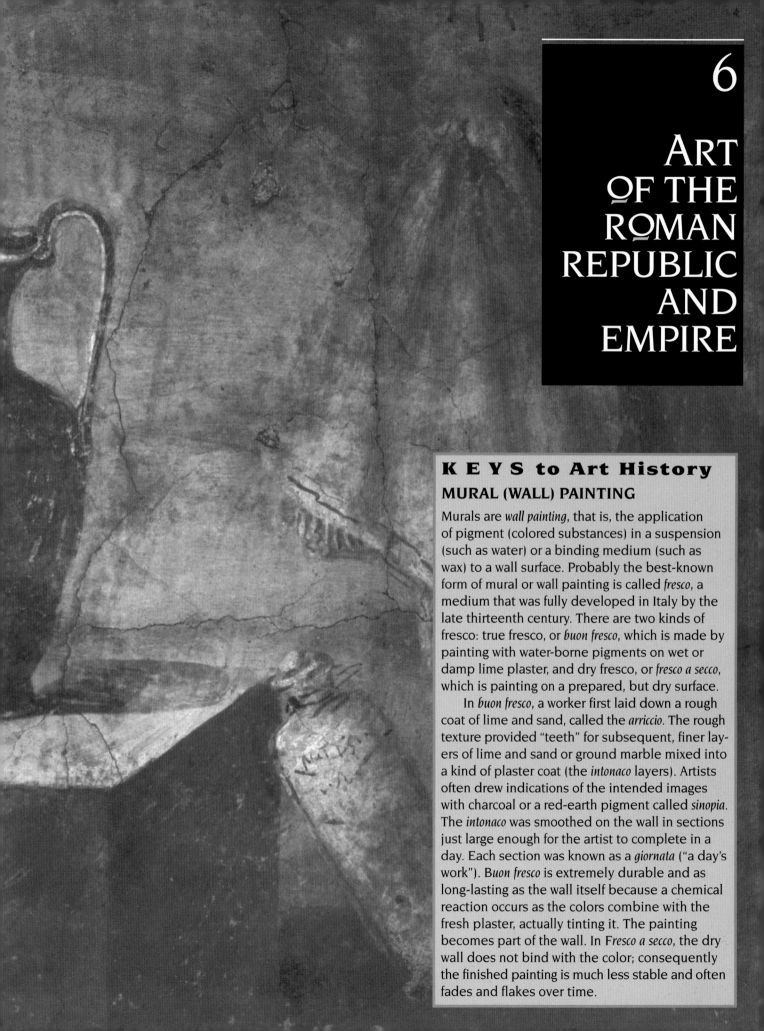

KEYS to Art History
MURAL (WALL) PAINTING

Murals are *wall painting*, that is, the application of pigment (colored substances) in a suspension (such as water) or a binding medium (such as wax) to a wall surface. Probably the best-known form of mural or wall painting is called *fresco*, a medium that was fully developed in Italy by the late thirteenth century. There are two kinds of fresco: true fresco, or *buon fresco*, which is made by painting with water-borne pigments on wet or damp lime plaster, and dry fresco, or *fresco a secco*, which is painting on a prepared, but dry surface.

In *buon fresco*, a worker first laid down a rough coat of lime and sand, called the *arriccio*. The rough texture provided "teeth" for subsequent, finer layers of lime and sand or ground marble mixed into a kind of plaster coat (the *intonaco* layers). Artists often drew indications of the intended images with charcoal or a red-earth pigment called *sinopia*. The *intonaco* was smoothed on the wall in sections just large enough for the artist to complete in a day. Each section was known as a *giornata* ("a day's work"). B*uon fresco* is extremely durable and as long-lasting as the wall itself because a chemical reaction occurs as the colors combine with the fresh plaster, actually tinting it. The painting becomes part of the wall. In *Fresco a secco*, the dry wall does not bind with the color; consequently the finished painting is much less stable and often fades and flakes over time.

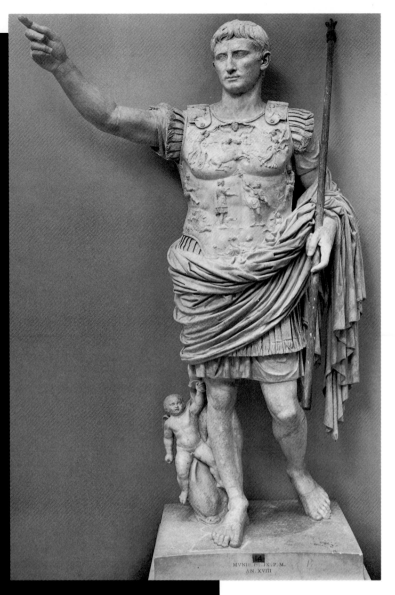

6-1. *Augustus of Primaporta.*
Early 1st century CE (perhaps a copy of a bronze statue of c. 20 BCE). Marble, height 6'8" (2.03 m). Musei Vaticani, Braccio Nuovo, Rome

The first Roman emperor was born Gaius Octavius (Octavian) in 63 BCE into a minor branch of the Caesar family. When he was only eighteen years old, Octavian was adopted as son and heir by his brilliant great-uncle, Julius Caesar, who recognized qualities in him that would make him a worthy successor. That was in 45 BCE. Early in 44 BCE, Julius Caesar refused the Roman Senate's offer of the imperial crown, which amounted to saying no to being the first Roman emperor. By March 15 of that year he was dead, murdered by a group of conspirators. Octavian stepped up. Over the next seventeen spectacular years, as general, politician, statesman, and public relations genius, Octavian vanquished warring internal factions and brought peace to fractious provinces. By 27 BCE, the Senate conferred on him the title Augustus (meaning "exalted, sacred"). For the West, Augustus defined the concepts of empire and imperial rule as he led the state and the empire for another forty-one years of peace and prosperity (the great *Pax Romana,* or Roman Peace) until his death in 14 CE.

The statue found in the villa of his wife, Livia, at Primaporta near Rome embodies the complex character and creative conservatism of the man (fig. 6-1). We see Augustus as he wanted to be seen and remembered, an image depicting him in his prime and inspired by heroic Greek figures like the *Spear Bearer* (see fig. 4-35). At the same time, the *Augustus of Primaporta* is one of the most successful imperial images of all time. The emperor extends his hand in an orator's gesture, as if convincing his people through his superior intellect rather than commanding them by force of arms. Yet imperial power is evident in the idealization of the figure, both in his bare feet, a sign of divine status, and in the parade armor, with its defeated "barbarians" and scenes of victory. Nonetheless, this convincing image is rendered with the skill in naturalistic representation demanded by Roman patrons and public. Augustus's staggering accomplishments are evoked through this work of art.

As early as the Iron Age, small groups of people who spoke a common language, Latin, settled on the central Italian plains south of the Tiber River. They also built small settlements on seven hills near the Tiber, which eventually joined to become the city of Rome. By the sixth century BCE, Rome had developed into a major transportation and trading center. At this time central Italy was also home to the Etruscans (Chapter 5). The Romans soon challenged the Etruscan presence, and by the end of the first millennium BCE, Rome had unified Italy. At the height of their power, Romans ruled all the lands around the Mediterranean Sea, which they proudly referred to as *mare nostrum,* or "our sea." In the early second century CE, the Roman Empire stretched east to the Euphrates River, south to Egypt, and northwest as far as Scotland.

To spur growth and simplify administration of the empire, as well as to make city life comfortable and attractive to its citizens, the Roman government undertook building programs of unprecedented scale and complexity, mandating the construction of central administrative centers (**basilicas**), racetracks, theaters, public baths, **aqueducts** to carry water, middle-class housing, and even entire new towns. To speed communication and facilitate commerce and the movement of troops, the Romans built a vast and sophisticated network of roads between their capital and the farthest reaches of the empire. Many modern European highways still follow the routes laid down by Roman engineers, and Roman-era foundations underlie the streets of many European cities.

Culturally, the Romans borrowed heavily from the Greek and Hellenistic world. They used Greek orders to decorate their architecture, imported Greek art, and employed Greek artists. Like the Etruscans, they adopted the Greek gods and heroes as their own, giving them Latin names (see "Roman Counterparts of Greek Gods," right). The sophisticated legal, administrative, and cultural systems that the Romans imposed on the people they conquered endured for some five hundred years in the West. In the eastern Mediterranean, classical traditions and styles survived into the fifteenth century as an important element of Byzantine art.

The Republican Period

Early Rome was governed by a series of kings and an advisory body called the Senate, made up of upper-class citizens. The last kings of Rome were overthrown in 509 BCE, marking the beginning of what is known as the period of the Republic.

Lasting from 509 to 27 BCE and governed by the Senate, Rome gradually incorporated neighboring territories. By 275 BCE, it dominated the entire Italian peninsula. During the next two centuries Rome extended its rule over the western Mediterranean, into Macedonia and Greece, and throughout most of Gaul (modern France).

Art and architecture during the Republic initially reflected both Etruscan and Greek influences. In religious architecture, the Romans favored urban temples set in the Etruscan manner in the midst of congested commercial centers. An early example is a small, rectangular temple built in the late second century BCE, perhaps dedicated to Portunus, the god of harbors and ports (figs. 6-2, 6-3). The structure, which stands beside the Tiber River in Rome, rests on a raised platform, or **podium**, almost like a piece

ROMAN COUNTERPARTS OF GREEK GODS	
Roman Name	**Greek God**
Jupiter	Zeus, king of the gods
Juno	Hera, Zeus's wife and sister, queen of the gods
Minerva	Athena, goddess of wisdom
Mars	Ares, god of war
Apollo; also Phoebus	Apollo, god of the sun and reason
Venus	Aphrodite, goddess of love
Diana	Artemis, goddess of the moon and hunting
Mercury	Hermes, messenger of the gods
Pluto	Hades, god of the underworld
Bacchus	Dionysos, god of wine
Vulcan	Hephaistos, god of fire
Vesta	Hestia, goddess of hearth and family
Ceres	Demeter, goddess of agriculture
Neptune	Poseidon, god of the sea
Cupid or Amor	Eros, god of love
Hercules	Herakles

Although sometimes worshiped as a god, strictly speaking Hercules is a hero known for his physical strength.

of sculpture. It has a rectangular cella (main room) and a colonnaded porch at one end. To this Etruscan plan, the Romans applied the Greek orders. Here the Ionic columns are freestanding on the porch and **engaged** (attached to the wall) around the cella. The entablature above the porch columns continues around the cella as a frieze. This design, with variations in the orders used with it, was to become standard for Roman temples.

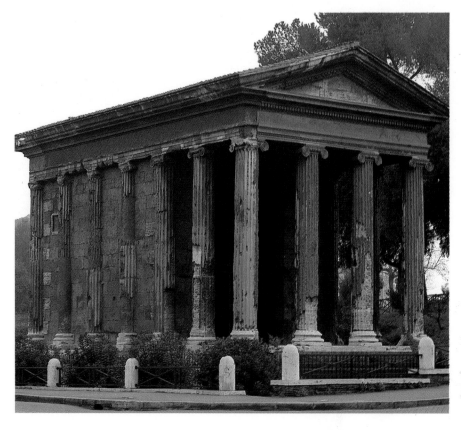

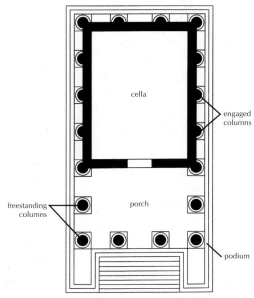

6-2. (*left*) **Temple perhaps dedicated to Portunus,** Forum Boarium (cattle market), Rome. Late 2nd century BCE

6-3. (*above*) **Plan of the temple perhaps dedicated to Portunus**

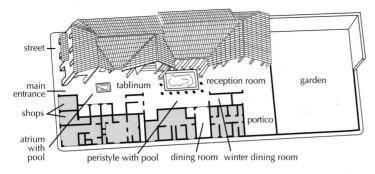

6-4. Reconstruction drawing and plan of the House of Pansa, Pompeii. 2nd century BCE

Roman Funerary Practices

The early Romans generally cremated their dead and placed the ashes in special cinerary (ash) urns or vases. They frequently kept the ash containers, together with busts and casts from death masks of their ancestors, on view in their homes, often in a room called a tablinum. Every February, they left small offerings at grave sites of family members.

In Rome, related individuals or members of social clubs or other organizations established private group cemeteries. When a group's members had used up the ground-level space in their cemetery, they tunneled underground to create a burial area known as a **hypogeum**, or **catacomb**. The tunnels of the catacomb extended from one edge of the cemetery property to the other, descending to another level as space filled up. They were lined with niches for urns and busts of the dead.

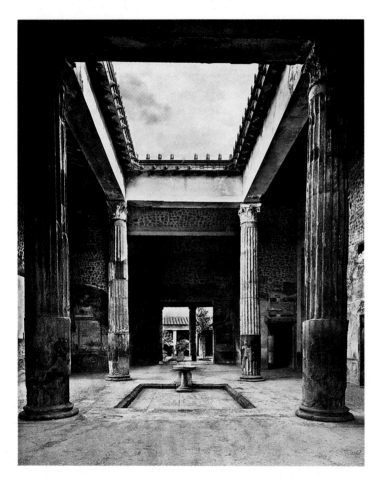

6-5. Atrium, House of the Silver Wedding, Pompeii. Early 1st century CE

Ancient Roman houses excavated at Pompeii and elsewhere are usually named after the families or individuals who once lived in them. In many cases, however, the owner is unknown. This house received its unusual name as a commemorative gesture. It was excavated in 1893, the year of the silver wedding anniversary of Italy's King Humbert and his wife, Margaret of Savoy, who had supported archeological fieldwork at Pompeii.

As city dwellers, Romans devoted their ingenuity and resources to secular architecture. In large cities they built two- or three-story apartment buildings with shared walls, and in the towns they lived in houses behind or above rows of shops. Wealthy people built gracious private residences with one or more gardens (fig. 6-4). These large, elegant houses had rooms opening onto a central atrium, an unroofed space with a pool (impluvium) for catching the rainwater. In dry climates the rainwater coming through the open roof might instead be drained into a deep cistern.

Many fine examples of Republican dwellings can be seen at Pompeii, near modern Naples. Located near Mount Vesuvius, Pompeii was buried in volcanic ash after the mountain's eruption in 79 CE and remained remarkably well preserved until its rediscovery in the eighteenth century. The "House of the Silver Wedding" is typical (fig. 6-5). Behind the atrium and its surrounding rooms lay the reception room, called the tablinum, where portrait busts of the family's ancestors were displayed (see "Roman Funerary Practices," left). The tablinum opened into a peristyle court, an interior garden courtyard surrounded by a colonnaded walkway or **portico**. The more private family quarters, such as the bedrooms, dining room, and servants' quarters, were usually entered through the peristyle court.

Public building projects to allow for the storage of food and water also made possible the expansion of cities. In many areas of Europe and the Mediterranean, impressive examples of Roman engineering still stand. The Pont du Gard near Nîmes in southern France (fig. 6-6), spanning 900 feet, was designed to carry water over the Gard River. This aqueduct, as such structures with water conduits are called, was part of a system that brought water to Nîmes from springs 30 miles to the north. At the time it was built, probably about 20 BCE, the aqueduct could provide 100 gallons of water a day for every person in Nîmes.

The Pont du Gard was constructed of precisely cut stones from a nearby quarry. It consists of three **arcades** (walls with a series of regularly spaced arched openings). The top arcade supports the water trough. The fundamental element of all three arcades is the round **arch** (see "Arch and Vault," opposite), formed by fitting together wedge-shaped pieces, called **voussoirs**, which are locked together at the top center by a final piece, called a **keystone**. A utilitarian structure, the aqueduct was left undecorated, and the projecting blocks that supported scaffolding during construction were left to provide easy access for repairs. The Pont du Gard nevertheless conveys a sense of proportion and rhythm: it harmonizes with its natural setting as it visually links the hilly riverbanks.

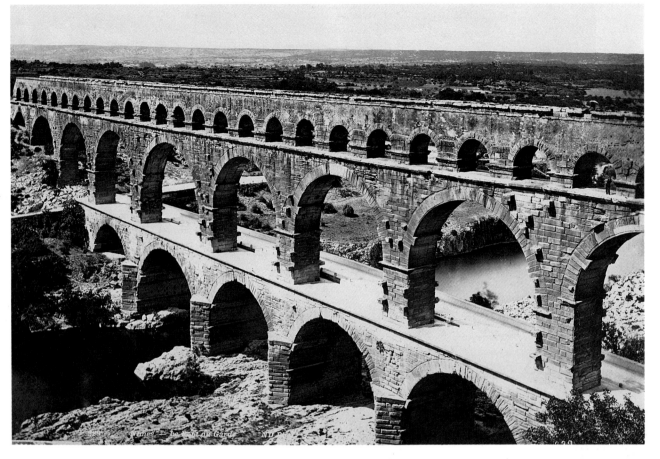

6-6. **Pont du Gard,** Nîmes, France. Late 1st century BCE

Elements of Architecture

ARCH AND VAULT

The round arch is the basic arch of Western architecture. It is designed to displace most of the weight of the masonry above it to its curving sides, and from there to the ground through supporting upright elements (**piers,** columns, or door or window **jambs**). In a succession of arches (an **arcade**), the space encompassed by each arch and its supports is called a **bay**. Wall areas adjacent to curves of an arch are called **spandrels**.

A round arch can be extended to form a **barrel vault**. A barrel vault is constructed in the same manner as a round arch, but the outside pressure exerted by its curving sides usually requires added support, called **buttressing**. When two barrel-vaulted spaces intersect each other on the perpendicular, the result is a **groin vault**, or cross vault. The round arch and barrel vault were known and were put to limited use by the Mesopotamians and the Egyptians. They were employed more extensively by the Etruscans. But it was the Romans who realized the potential strength and versatility of these architectural elements and exploited them to the fullest degree.

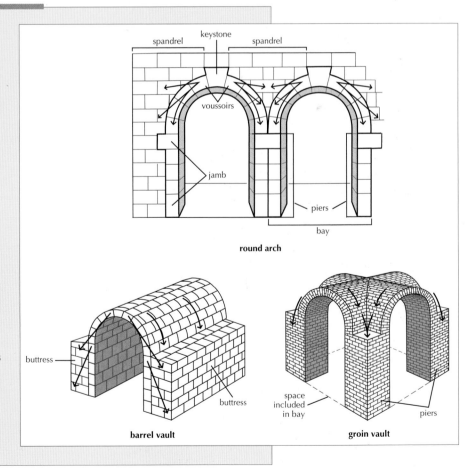

round arch

barrel vault

groin vault

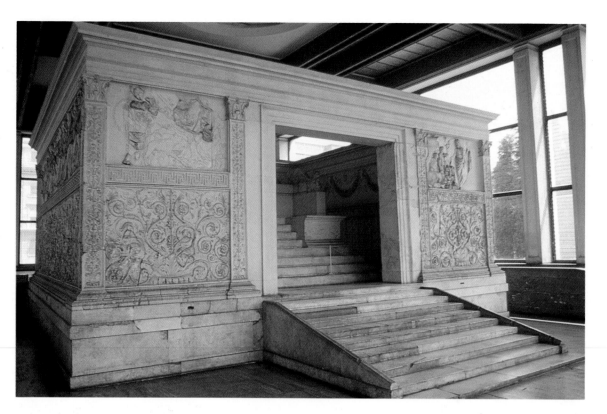

6-7. Ara Pacis.
13–9 BCE. Marble, approx. 34'5" (10.5 m) x 38' (11.6 m). Rome

The Early Empire

Rome's conquest of lands outside the Italian peninsula strained its political system, weakening the authority of the Senate and leading to a series of civil wars among powerful generals. In 46 BCE Julius Caesar emerged victorious over his rivals; he ruled Rome as dictator until his assassination in 44 BCE. After Caesar's death and a period of renewed fighting, his great-nephew and adopted son, Octavian, assumed power.

Although Octavian kept the forms of Republican government, he retained the real authority for himself, and his ascension marks the end of the Republic. Under Augustus Caesar, as Octavian was titled in 27 BCE, the Romans began to use imperial portraiture as political propaganda. As we have seen, an over-lifesize statue of the emperor, the *Augustus of Primaporta* (see fig. 6-1), exemplifies this form of portraiture. Augustus wears a cuirass (torso armor) and holds a commander's baton, but his feet are bare, suggesting to some scholars that the work was made after his death to commemorate his apotheosis, or elevation to divine status. Recently it has been suggested that the marble sculpture was made after Augustus's death in 14 BCE and copies an earlier bronze figure. After Augustus, Roman emperors were deified in part to unify the culturally diverse populations that had come under Roman rule. Worship of ancient gods was mingled with homage to past rulers and oaths of allegiance to the living ones.

Roman sculptors contributed unabashedly to imperial propaganda by recording contemporary events on commemorative arches, columns, and tombs. A monument erected by Augustus, the Ara Pacis, or Altar of Augustan Peace (fig. 6-7),

was as famous in its day as the Vietnam Veterans Memorial is in ours. The rectangular structure is a Roman adaptation of earlier Greek and Hellenistic altars. It was constructed in Rome between 13 and 9 BCE to memorialize Augustus's triumphal return to the city following the successful establishment of Roman rule in France and Spain.

Whenever a general or emperor returned to Rome after a significant campaign, he paraded through the city with his troops, captives, and booty in a victory celebration known as a "triumph." The route of the procession was ornamented with temporary structures such as triumphal arches and altars, which afterward might be re-created in stone as permanent memorials. The interior of the Ara Pacis, decorated with carved garlands suspended in **swags**, or loops, is a kind of marble imitation of the flower-swagged temporary altar that would have been set up during Augustus's triumphal procession. Relief panels along the exterior of the north and south sides of the Ara Pacis depict senators and members of the imperial family who would have attended the victory celebrations (fig. 6-8). Unlike the Greek sculptors who created the procession on the frieze of the Parthenon (see fig. 4-31), the Roman sculptors of the Ara Pacis depicted actual individuals. They also attempted to suggest spatial depth by carving the closest elements in high relief and those farther back in increasingly lower relief. Using a device reminiscent of the Altar of Zeus at Pergamon (see fig. 5-19), the sculptors visually draw the spectator into the event by making the feet of the nearest figures project from the architectural **groundline** into our space.

The second foreground adult figure from the left in the detail shown in figure 6-8 is probably

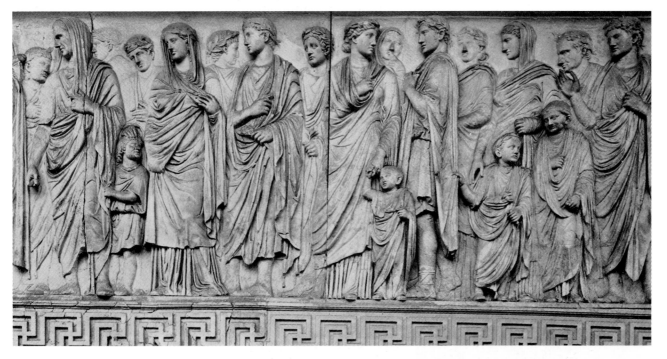

6-8. Imperial Procession, detail of a relief on the Ara Pacis. Height 5'2" (1.6 m)

The middle-aged man with the shrouded head at the far left is Marcus Agrippa, who would have been Augustus's successor had he not died in 12 CE, the year after the Ara Pacis was dedicated. The bored but well-behaved youngster pulling at Agrippa's robe—and being restrained gently by the hand of the man behind him—is probably Agrippa's son, Gaius Caesar. The heavily swathed woman next to Agrippa on the right is probably Augustus's wife, Livia, followed by the elder of her two sons, Tiberius, who would become the next emperor. Behind Tiberius is Antonia, the niece of Augustus, looking back at her husband, Drusus, Livia's younger son. She grasps the hand of Germanicus, one of her younger children. Behind their uncle Drusus are Gnaeus and Domitia, children of Antonia's older sister, who can be seen standing quietly beside them. The depiction of children in an official relief was new to the Augustan period and reflects Augustus's desire to promote private family life.

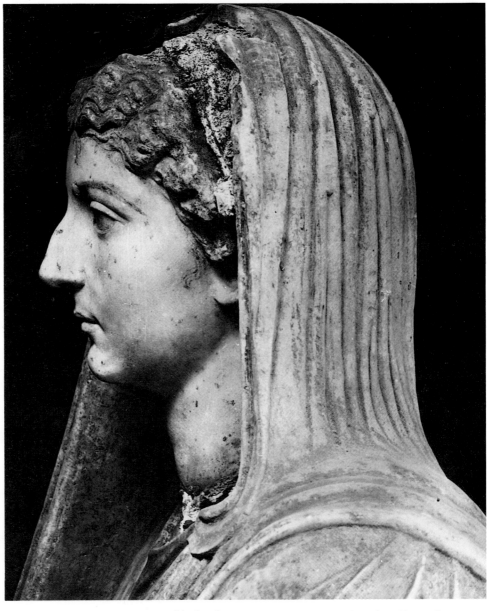

Augustus's second wife, Livia, who remained at his side for more than fifty years. She supported laws that favored marriage and family, provided increased legal protection for married women, and penalized bachelors, unmarried women, and childless wives or widows. These laws made family life not only a desirable state but a patriotic duty and were aimed at increasing the Roman birthrate.

A portrait bust of Livia, dated about 20 BCE, when she was in her mid-thirties, reveals a striking woman with strong features and a serene expression (fig. 6-9). During Rome's Republican period,

6-9. Livia. c. 20 BCE. Marble, height approx. 15" (38.5 cm). Antiquarium, Pompeii

a taste for strongly realistic portraiture developed, influenced by Etruscan models. The bust of Livia represents a continuation of that **veristic**, or realistic, tradition, in contrast to the *Augustus of Primaporta*, which displays a more **idealized** style of portraiture.

Because the marriage of Augustus and Livia was childless, the emperor's successor was Tiberius, one of Livia's two sons by her first marriage, to Tiberius Claudius Nero. The sequence of related rulers that begins with Tiberius is known as the Julio-Claudian dynasty (14–68 CE). It ended with the reign of the despotic and capricious emperor Nero. A powerful general named Vespasian seized control of the government

6-10. Colosseum, Rome. 72–80 CE

after Nero's death. The dynasty he founded, the Flavian, ruled from 69 to 96 CE. The Flavian emperors, Vespasian (ruled 69–79 CE), Titus (ruled 79–81 CE), and Domitian (ruled 81–96 CE), restored imperial finances and stabilized the empire's frontiers.

The Colosseum (fig. 6-10), one of Rome's most influential monuments, was built during the reign of Vespasian. Construction began in 72 CE, and the Colosseum was dedicated by Titus in 80 CE, after Vespasian's death. In this enormous entertainment center, Roman audiences watched blood sports and spectacles. These included animal hunts, fights to the death between gladiators or between gladiators and wild animals, performances of trained animals and acrobats, and even mock sea battles, for which the arena was flooded by a built-in mechanism. The Flavians erected the structure to bolster their popularity in Rome, and its name then was the Flavian Amphitheater. The name "Colosseum," by which it came to be known, derived from the Colossus, a bigger-than-life statue of Nero that had been left standing next to it. The opening performance in 80 CE lasted 100 days, during which time, it

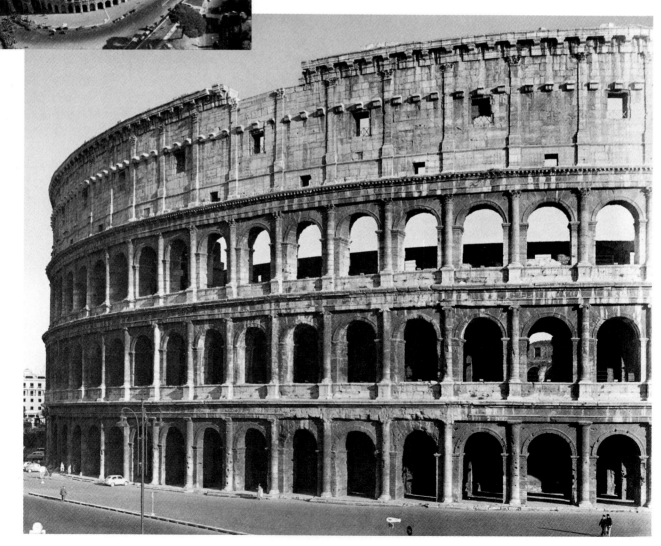

6-11. Colosseum

was claimed, 9,000 wild animals and 2,000 gladiators died. For its ease of crowd movement and unobstructed views, the design of the Colosseum has never been improved upon. Architects still copy it today.

The Colosseum was built entirely of masonry—**concrete** faced with stone. Barrel vaults over corridors and stairs radiate from the center and intersect the barrel ring vaults of the perimeter passageways to form groin vaults (see "Arch and Vault," page 137). These complex curved shapes could be formed of concrete faster and more cheaply than of stone blocks that had to be cut by trained masons. The concrete consisted of stone rubble in a binder made from a natural cement and water. This rough but strong core was faced with finer, worked stone. (In very fine buildings, the core might be covered with a marble veneer, or exterior facing.)

The curving outer wall of the Colosseum consists of three levels of arcade surmounted by a wall-like top, or **attic story** (fig. 6-11). Every arch in the arcades is framed by engaged columns, which support entablature-like friezes marking the division between levels. Each level uses a different architectural order. The ground floor is ornamented with columns in the Tuscan order (generally similar to the Greek Doric order except that the columns have bases). The Ionic order is used on the second level, the Corinthian on the third, and flat Corinthian **pilasters** (engaged columnar elements) adorn the fourth story. All of these elements are purely decorative and serve no structural function. The systematic use of the orders in a logical succession from sturdy Tuscan to decorative Corinthian follows a tradition inherited from Hellenistic architecture. It is still popular as a way of articulating and organizing the facades of large buildings.

When Domitian assumed the throne in 81 CE, he immediately commissioned a triumphal arch to honor his brother and deified predecessor,

Elements of Architecture

ROMAN ARCHITECTURAL ORDERS

Greek and Roman orders—columns with their entablatures—are known as classical orders. Each order is made up of a system of interdependent parts whose proportions are based on mathematical ratios. In Greek and Roman architecture, no element of an order could be changed without producing a corresponding change in the other elements.

The Etruscans and Romans adapted Greek architectural orders to their own tastes and uses. For example, the Etruscans modified the Greek Doric order by adding a base to the column. The Romans created the **Composite order** by incorporating the **volute** motif of the Greek Ionic capital with other forms from the Greek Corinthian order. The sturdy, unfluted **Tuscan order**, also a Roman development, derived from the Greek Doric order by way of Etruscan models. In this diagram, the two Roman orders are shown on **pedestals**, which consist of a **plinth**, a **dado**, and a **cornice**.

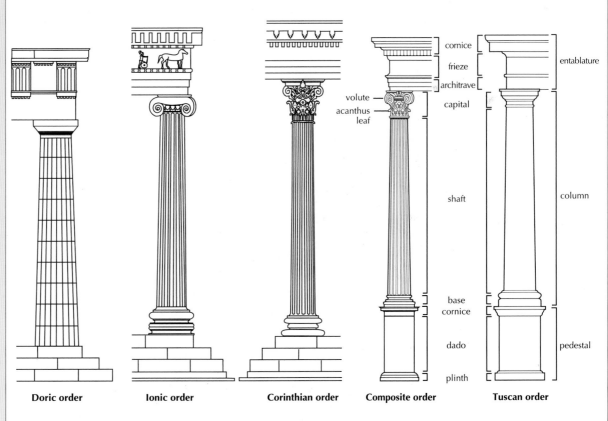

Doric order   Ionic order   Corinthian order   Composite order   Tuscan order

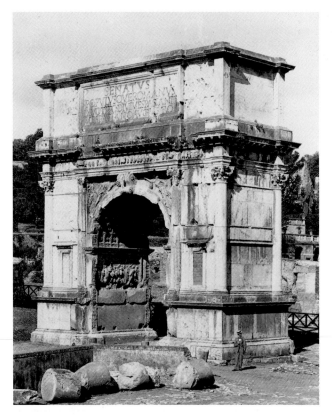

6-12. Arch of Titus, Rome. c. 81 CE. Concrete and white marble, height 50' (15 m)

The dedication inscribed across the tall attic story above the arch opening reads: "The Senate and the Roman People to the Deified Titus Flavius Vespasianus Augustus, son of the Deified Vespasian." The Romans typically recorded historic occasions and identified monuments with solemn prose and beautiful inscriptions in stone. The use by the sculptors of elegant Roman capital letters—perfectly sized and spaced to be read from a distance and cut with sharp terminals (serifs) to catch the light—established a standard that calligraphers and alphabet designers still follow.

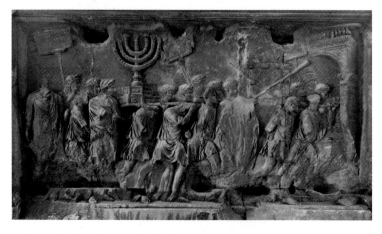

6-13. Spoils from the Temple of Solomon, Jerusalem, relief in the passageway of the Arch of Titus. Marble, height 6'8" (2.03 m)

Titus (fig. 6-12). The Arch of Titus, which commemorates Titus's capture of Jerusalem in 70 CE, is essentially a freestanding gateway pierced by a barrel-vaulted passageway. Originally the whole arch served as a giant base, 50 feet tall, for a statue of a four-horse chariot and driver, a typical Roman triumphal symbol. The exterior of the arch is ornamented with engaged Composite columns.

The Romans added the Composite order, along with the Tuscan order, to the repertory of forms they adopted from Greek architecture (see "Roman Architectural Orders," page 141). Capitals of the Composite order are formed by superimposing Ionic volutes on a Corinthian capital.

Titus's capture of Jerusalem ended a fierce campaign to crush a revolt of the Jews in Palestine. His troops looted and destroyed the Second Temple of Jerusalem and carted off its sacred treasures. These spoils were displayed in Rome during Titus's triumphal procession. According to the Jewish eyewitness and historian Flavius Josephus (*The Jewish War*), the prizes included: "the law of the Jews"; a gold table; and a seven-branched gold lamp, or menorah.

The reliefs on the inside walls of the arch depict Titus's soldiers carrying this booty through the streets of Rome (fig. 6-13). Viewing them, the observer can easily imagine the boisterous army on the march. The artist creates a window on the world through which we observe the crowd. The varying height of the relief elements creates the impression that the marchers are moving toward the viewer and then turning to move away through a distant arch. Spatial relationships, achieved by rendering close elements in higher relief than those more distant, produce a sense of atmosphere. The mood and the illusion of space go beyond the formal solemnity and neutral background of the Ara Pacis.

The development of art in Rome depended on private as well as public patronage. For their homes, wealthy individuals might commission portraits in marble or bronze, or wall paintings, or mosaics. At Pompeii, many wall paintings were preserved beneath the ashes from the volcano Vesuvius.

In the earliest paintings, artists created the illusion that the walls were actually covered with thin slabs of colored marble set off by real architectural details such as plaster columns. In the first century BCE they extended the space of a room visually with painted scenes of figures on a shallow "stage" or with a landscape or cityscape seen close-up. Architectural details were painted on rather than molded in plaster. Sometimes artists reemphasized the wall surface by painting it a solid color and decorating it with whimsical architecture. In these representations, delicate vignettes sometimes appear. By the first century CE, painters combined narrative paintings, especially mythological scenes, with ever more fantastic and realistic renderings of buildings.

Paintings dating to the mid-first century CE, found in the House of M. Lucretius Fronto in Pompeii, emphasize the walls in panels of black and red (fig. 6-14). Three rectangular pictures seem to be mounted on the panels, but they are

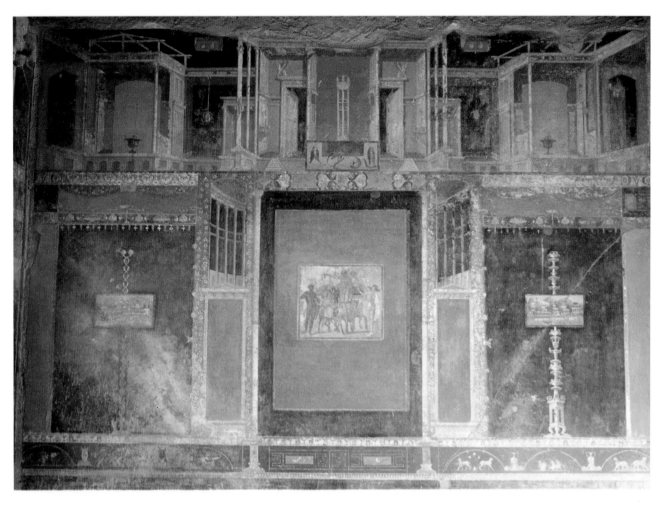

6-14. **Detail of a wall painting in the House of M. Lucretius Fronto**, Pompeii. Mid-1st century CE

actually painted on the wall. The artistic device of architectural illusionism can be seen in the simulated window openings protected by grilles and the suggestion of an upper level, but these elements show no logical layout or significant depiction of depth.

The pictures that adorned the walls featured every kind of subject, including historical and mythological scenes, landscapes, and exquisitely rendered **still lifes** (compositions of inanimate objects). Portraits, perhaps imaginary ones, were also popular in wall paintings. A late-first-century CE **tondo** (circular panel) from a house in Pompeii contains a portrait known as *Young Woman Writing* (fig. 6-15). Perhaps, like some Roman women, she was a professional writer. In a convention popular among women patrons, she is shown with the tip of a writing stylus raised to her lips. She holds a set of wood tablets coated with wax that were used in much the same way we might use a small chalkboard; letters engraved with a stylus could be smoothed over and rewritten. When a text or letter was considered ready, it was copied onto expensive papyrus or parchment. As in a modern studio photograph, with its careful lighting and retouching, the young woman in this painting is portrayed in an idealized fashion.

Mosaics became enormously popular as decoration for Roman floors and fountains, places not suitable for paintings. Mosaic designs

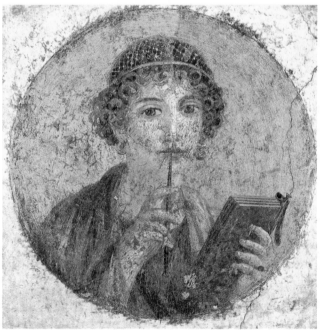

6-15. *Young Woman Writing*, detail of a wall painting, from Pompeii. Late 1st century CE. Diameter 14⅝" (37 cm). Museo Archeològico Nazionale, Naples

were created with pebbles or with small, regularly shaped pieces of colored stone, or marble, called **tesserae**. The tesserae were pressed into a kind of soft cement called **grout**.

So accomplished were some mosaicists that they could create works that looked like paintings. In fact, at the request of patrons, they often copied well-known paintings employing a technique in which very small tesserae created subtle shadings and color changes. In a work called *The*

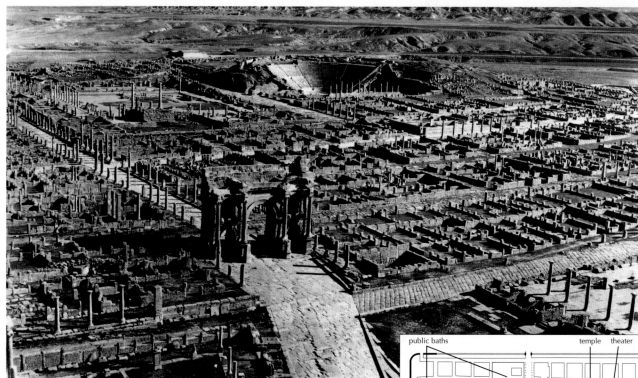

6-16. Heracleitus. The Unswept Floor, mosaic variant of a 2nd-century BCE painting by Sosos of Pergamon. 2nd century CE. Musei Vaticani, Museo Gregoriano Profano, ex Lateranense, Rome

6-17. (*right*) **Plan of Timgad,** Algeria (construction begun c. 100 CE)

6-18. (*above*) **Ruins of Timgad**

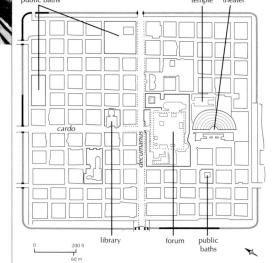

Unswept Floor (fig. 6-16), the Roman mosaicist Heracleitus adapted the design of an earlier Hellenistic painter named Sosos. In Pergamon, in the second century BCE, Sosos had created a large painting that included a **trompe l'oeil** ("fool the eye") representation of a floor littered with droppings from a table. Heracleitus's mosaic version, made three centuries later, shows a mouse among

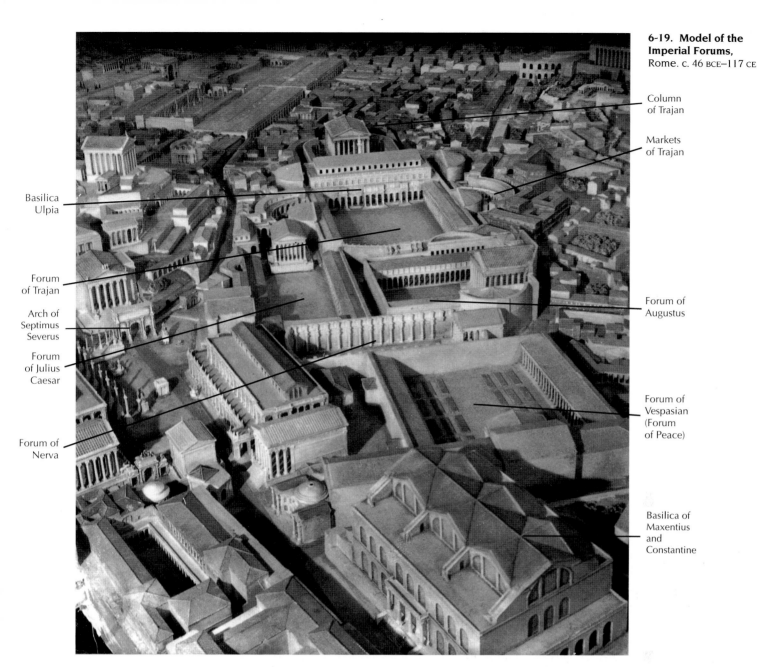

Column of Trajan

Markets of Trajan

Basilica Ulpia

Forum of Trajan

Arch of Septimus Severus

Forum of Julius Caesar

Forum of Nerva

Forum of Augustus

Forum of Vespasian (Forum of Peace)

Basilica of Maxentius and Constantine

table scraps, which are tossed aside for the family pets. Bones of fish and foul, fruit, and nuts are all re-created in meticulous detail, even to the extent of capturing the shadows they cast on the floor.

The "Good Emperors"

The arts flourished during the first and second centuries CE. Five very competent rulers succeeded the Flavians: Nerva (ruled 96–98 CE), Trajan (ruled 98–117 CE), Hadrian (ruled 117–138 CE), Antoninus Pius (ruled 138–161 CE), and Marcus Aurelius (ruled 161–180 CE). Known as the "Five Good Emperors," they oversaw a long period of stability and prosperity. Under Trajan, the empire reached its greatest extent, annexing Dacia (roughly modern Romania) in 106 CE and expanding the empire's boundaries in the Middle East.

Wherever they went, Romans built roads, bridges, and cities. Typical of these new towns was Timgad in the Algerian desert (figs. 6-17, 6-18). Once home to 15,000 people, it was a community planned for former soldiers and their families as a form of pension. (The emperors

established provincial cities such as Timgad as land became scarce in Italy.)

Roman architects designed these new cities using the grid plan. They divided towns into four quarters defined by intersecting north-south and east-west arteries, called, respectively, the *cardo* and the *decumanus*. A **forum** (a main square surrounded by temples and government buildings) was usually located at this intersection. As initially laid out, Timgad was a square of about 30 acres. The forum and a theater straddled the *cardo* just south of the intersection with the *decumanus* at the town center. Other amenities included a library and several public baths. Elaborate triumphal arches marked the main entrances to the town, and its streets, paved with precisely cut and fitted ashlar blocks, were once lined with colonnades.

Individual projects, such as the Imperial Forums, show the value put on logic in Roman building. Trajan had a forum constructed on a large piece of property next to the earlier forums of Augustus and Julius Caesar. These so-called Imperial Forums (fig. 6-19) were part of a

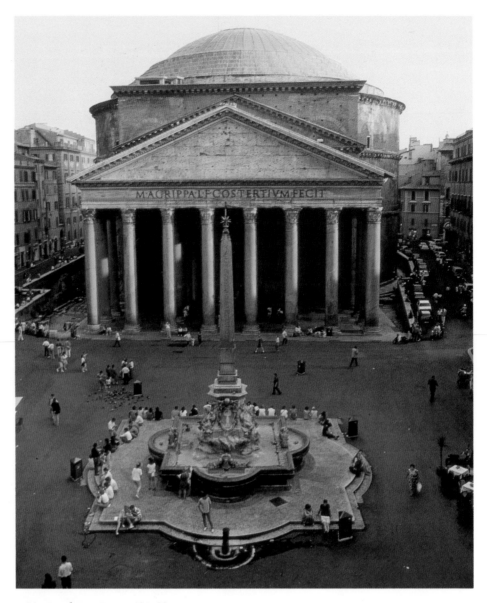

6-20. Pantheon, Rome. 125–28 CE

It is not clear what the early Romans themselves thought of this architectural monument, so well known to travelers and students today, because it was rarely mentioned by any contemporary writers. An exception was Ammianus Marcellinus, who described it in 357 CE with restrained praise as being "rounded like the boundary of the horizon, and vaulted with a beautiful loftiness."

continuing effort to transform the capital into a magnificent monument to imperial rule. The large open square of the forum was generally surrounded by colonnades leading to a temple and sometimes a basilica. In Trajan's Forum, the Basilica Ulpia, dedicated in 113 CE, was named for the family to which Trajan belonged. It was a large, rectangular building with a rounded extension, called an **apse**, at each end. (More typically, basilicas have a single apse at one end.) A general-purpose administrative structure, a basilica could be adapted to many uses. The Basilica Ulpia was a court of law. Other basilicas served as imperial audience chambers, army drill halls, and schools. The spacious and adaptable interior made the basilica form attractive to Christians, who would later appropriate it for churches.

The Basilica Ulpia was entered through several doors on the long sides of the building facing the open square. The interior space was partitioned into a large central area bordered by two lower colonnaded aisles. This tall central space was able to accommodate a **clerestory**, or windowed wall area, that extended above the abutting aisle roofs and brought light into the interior. A timber-raftered roof covered the space. The semicircular vaulted apses at each end might be hung with portraits of the emperor, providing imposing settings for judges when the court was in session.

Beyond the Basilica Ulpia stood two libraries, one for Greek texts and the other for Latin. Trajan's tomb, surmounted by a column carved with reliefs depicting his victory over the Dacians, stood between the libraries. Later the complex was completed with a temple to the deified emperor. The Forum of Trajan exemplifies the finest in imperial city planning, satisfying both the needs of the citizens and the imperial desire for impressive public works and propaganda.

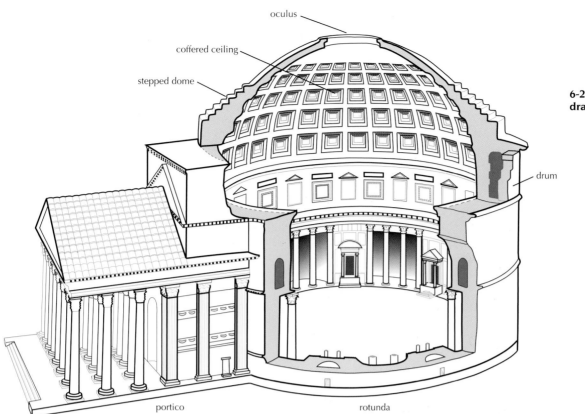

oculus

coffered ceiling

stepped dome

drum

portico

rotunda

6-21. Reconstruction drawing of the Pantheon

Trajan's successor, Hadrian, was well educated and widely traveled. His admiration for Greek culture spurred new building programs throughout the empire. To the splendid architecture of Rome itself he added the remarkable temple to the Olympian gods known as the Pantheon ("all the gods"), built between 125 and 128 CE (fig. 6-20). The entrance porch, made to resemble the facade of a typical Roman temple, was raised on a podium (now covered by centuries of dirt and street construction). Behind this porch, a giant **rotunda** (circular room) is surmounted with a huge, bowl-shaped dome, 143 feet in diameter and 143 feet from the floor at its summit (fig. 6-21).

Although the Pantheon has inspired hundreds of copies, variants, and eclectic borrowings, only recently has the true complexity of its construction been fully understood. The circular wall, or drum, of the rotunda, which supports and buttresses the dome, is formed of brick arches and concrete. These structural elements are hidden beneath a marble veneer. Structurally a dome works as an arch pivoted 360° around the top of the drum. In the Pantheon the usual keystone is replaced by a central circular opening, or **oculus**, a daring concept. The repetition of square against circle, established on a large scale by juxtaposing the rectilinear portico against the circular rotunda, is found throughout the building's ornament. Seven niches, rectangular alternating with semicircular, originally held statues of the gods. The square, boxlike **coffers** (sunken ceiling panels) inside the dome, which help lighten the weight of the masonry, may once have contained gilded bronze **rosettes** or stars suggesting the heavens.

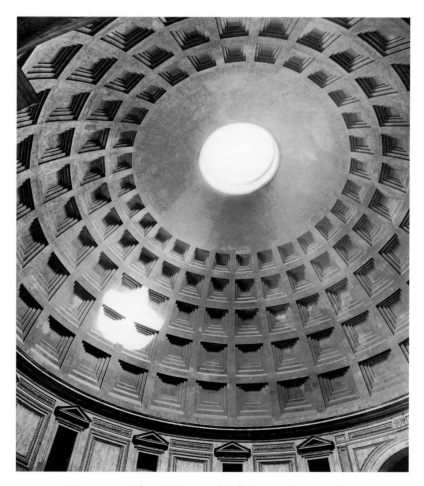

6-22. Dome of the Pantheon with light from oculus on coffering

Inside, the eye is drawn upward over the patterns made by the coffers to the light entering the 29-foot-wide oculus (fig. 6-22). Clouds can be seen through this opening on clear days; rain falls through it on wet ones, then drains off as

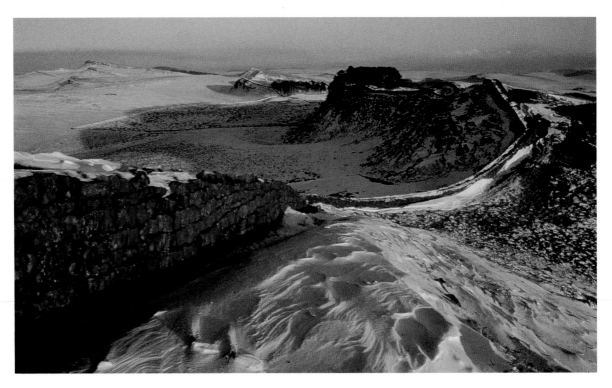

6-23. Hadrian's Wall, seen near Housesteads, England. 2nd century CE

planned by the original engineer; and occasionally a bird flies through it. But the empty, luminous space also imparts a sense that one could rise buoyantly upward to escape the spherical hollow of the building and commune with the gods.

Hadrian consolidated the empire's borders and imposed far-reaching social, administrative, and military reforms. He ordered the construction of a monumental stone wall in England to protect his northern frontier. Known as Hadrian's Wall, this barrier stretches from coast to coast across a 73.5-mile-wide strip of England (fig. 6-23). Some 8 to 10 feet thick and 20 feet high, it created a symbolic as well as a physical boundary between Roman territory and that of the Picts and Scots to the north. Towers were located at every mile mark. Seventeen larger camps housed auxiliary forces ready to respond to any trouble the sentries might spot. These camps were laid out in a grid pattern, like Roman cities, with main streets dividing them into blocks. In the center were the hospital, granaries, and the commander's house

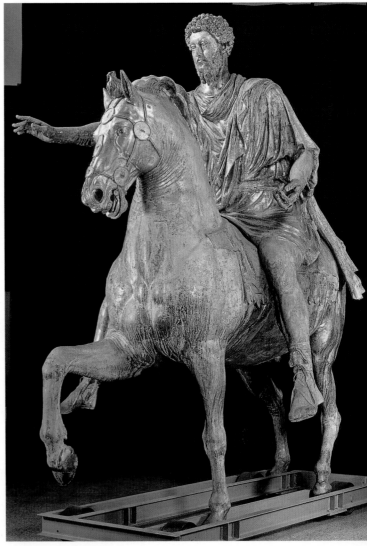

6-24. Marcus Aurelius. 161–80 CE. Bronze, originally gilded; height of statue 11'6" (3.5 m). Capitoline Museum, Rome

and administrative headquarters. Surrounding these structures were barracks. Similarly designed camps were built from one end of the Roman Empire to the other, wherever military troops were quartered.

Hadrian's successor, Marcus Aurelius, was also renowned for both his intellectual and military achievements. In a gilded bronze equestrian statue, the emperor appears as a commander dressed in a tunic and short, heavy cloak (figs. 6-24, 6-25). The raised foreleg of his horse is poised to trample a defeated foe (now lost). The emperor wears no armor and carries no weapons; like the Egyptian kings, he conquers effortlessly by the will of the gods. And like his illustrious predecessor Augustus (see fig. 6-1), he assumes a gesture symbolic of addressing an assembly. In a lucky error, or twist of fate, this statue came mistakenly to be revered as a portrait of Constantine, the first Christian emperor. Consequently, it escaped being melted down, a fate that befell many other bronze statues from antiquity.

Marcus Aurelius was succeeded by his son Commodus, a man without political skill, administrative competence, or intellectual distinction.

During his unfortunate reign (180–192 CE), he devoted himself to luxury and frivolous pursuits. He did, however, attract some of the finest artists of the day for his commissions. A marble bust of Commodus posing as Hercules displays skillful chiseling and **drillwork** (fig. 6-26). With a drill, a sculptor can rapidly cut deep grooves with straight sides that look like dark lines at a distance—for example, the holes in Comodus's curls. With a combination of carving and drillwork, the sculptor exploited the play of light and shadow on the figure and brought out the textures of the hair, beard, and drapery. The portrait conveys the illusion of life and movement, but it also captures its subject's vanity and weakness through the grand pretensions of his costume.

The Late Empire

The reign of Commodus marked the beginning of a period of political and economic decline. During the rule of the Severan emperors (193–235 CE) who succeeded Commodus, migrating peoples from the north and east began to cross Rome's frontiers, disrupting provincial government. Imperial rule became increasingly autocratic, and soon the army controlled the government.

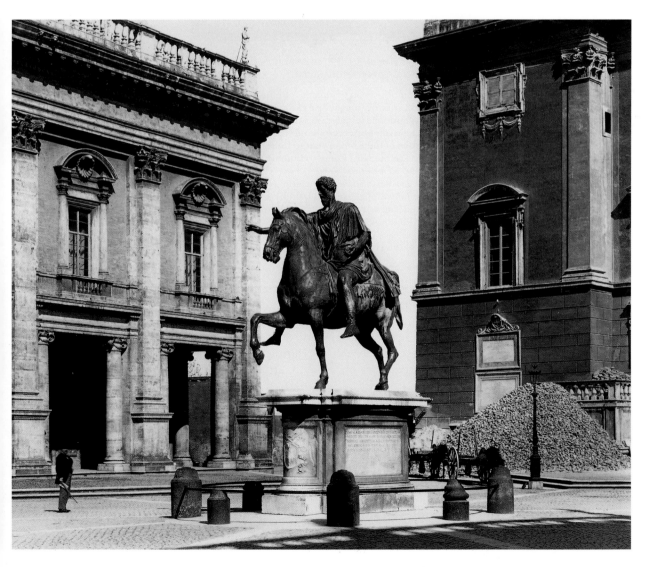

6-25. Marcus Aurelius, in the Piazza del Campidoglio

This statue stood for centuries in the piazza fronting on the palace and church of Saint John Lateran in Rome. In January 1538 Pope Paul III had it moved to the Capitoline Hill, where it became the focus of a renovation and building program that created the Piazza del Campidoglio as it looks today. The statue is shown here in its second location, in the center of the piazza with the Palazzo Senatorio behind it and the Palazzo Nuovo (New Palace, today the Capitoline Museum) at the left. After being removed from its base for cleaning and restoration some years ago, it was taken inside the Capitoline Museum to preserve it from the continued effects of Rome's polluted air (see fig. 6-24).

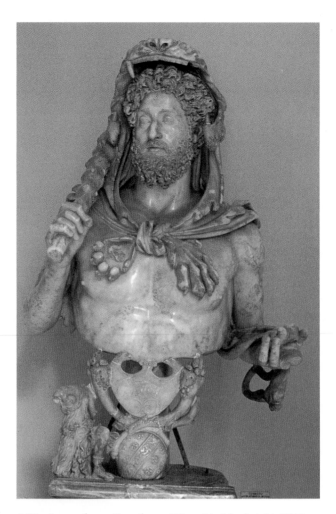

6-26. *Commodus as Hercules.* c. 190 CE. Marble, height 46½" (118 cm). Palazzo dei Conservatori, Rome

The emperor Commodus, son of Marcus Aurelius, was not just decadent, he was probably insane. He claimed at various times to be the reincarnation of Hercules and the incarnation of the god Jupiter, and he even appeared in public as a gladiator. He ordered the months of the Roman year to be renamed after him and changed the name of Rome to Colonia Commodiana. When he proposed to assume the consulship dressed and armed as a gladiator, his associates, including his mistress, arranged to have him strangled in his bath by a wrestling partner. In this portrait, the emperor is shown in the guise of Hercules, adorned with references to the hero's legendary labors: his club, the skin of the Nemean Lion, and the golden apples from the garden of the Hesperides.

The death of the last Severan emperor in 235 CE began a half century of anarchy that ended with the rise to power of Emperor Diocletian (ruled 284–305 CE). This brilliant politician and general reversed the empire's declining fortunes, but he also initiated an increasingly dictatorial form of rule and toward the end of his reign approved the persecution of Christians, begun under Emperor Nero more than 200 years earlier.

To share in the task of defending and administering the empire, Diocletian devised a form of government called the Tetrarchy, or rule by four. He divided the empire into eastern and western sections, each with an emperor and a designated assistant and heir. Joint rule lasted only until Diocletian abdicated in 305 CE. From the battle for succession in the west, Constantine I, known as The Great (ruled 306–337 CE), emerged victorious. In a decisive battle in 312 CE, Constantine vanquished his rival Maxentius just outside Rome at the Battle of the Milvian Bridge.

During the turmoil of the third century, Roman artists lost interest in representing the natural world, emphasizing instead the symbolic or general characters of their subjects and expressing them in increasingly simplified, geometric forms. A further turn toward abstraction and symbolic representation can be seen in *The Tetrarchs,* a depiction of Diocletian and his three corulers from the early fourth century CE (fig. 6-27). Hardly a realistic depiction of the men, the sculpture is a symbolic representation of four-man rule. The nearly identical figures embrace one another in a show of imperial unity, but

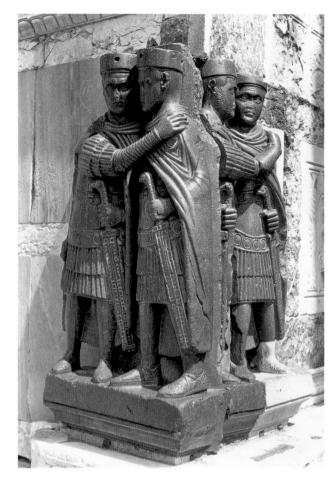

6-27. The Tetrarchs. c. 305 CE. Porphyry, height of figures 51" (129 cm). Installed in the Middle Ages at the corner of the facade of the Cathedral of San Marco, Venice

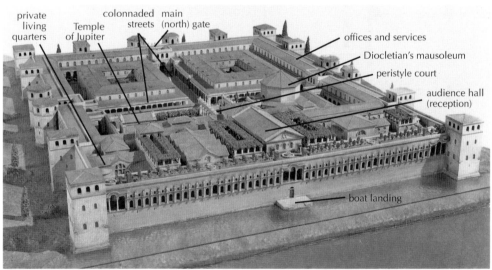

6-28. Model of Palace of Diocletian, Split, Croatia. c. 300 CE. Museo della Civiltà Romana, Rome

each also grasps his sword. Dressed in military garb, they proclaim a kind of peace through concerted strength and vigilance.

The sculpture is made of porphyry, a purple stone from Egypt reserved for imperial use. The hardness of the stone—which makes it difficult to carve—and perhaps the sculptor's familiarity with Egyptian artistic conventions may have contributed to the extremely abstract style of the work. But the simplification of natural forms to geometric shapes, the disregard for normal human proportions, and the emphasis on message or idea are also characteristics of Roman art made by the end of the third century.

After Diocletian retired from active rule, he built a huge and well-fortified imperial residence at Split, on the Adriatic coast of what is now Croatia. Revolutionary in design, the building recalled the compact, regular plan of a Roman army camp (fig. 6-28). It consisted of a rectangular enclosure 650 by 550 feet crossed by two colonnaded streets that divided it into quarters.

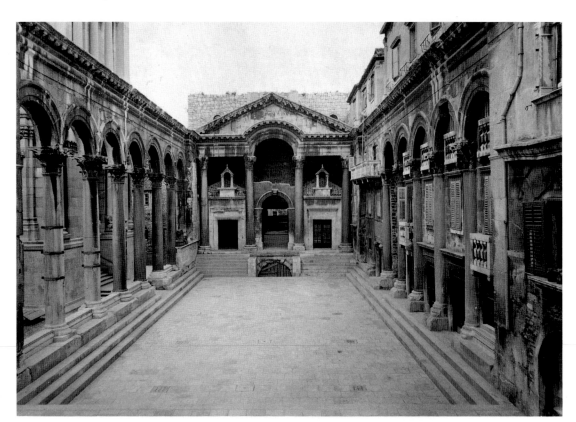

6-29. Peristyle court, Palace of Diocletian

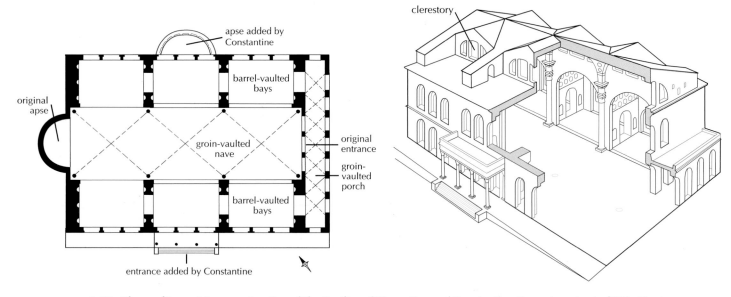

6-30. Plan and isometric reconstruction of the Basilica of Maxentius and Constantine, Rome (constructed 306–13 CE)

The emperor's residential complex, which included the reception hall on the main, north-south axis of the palace, faced the sea and was constructed with a narrow boat landing. The main gate was on the opposite (north) side of the palace. A colonnaded avenue extended from this entrance to a peristyle court that ended in a grand facade with an enormous arched doorway through which the emperor made his ceremonial appearances (fig. 6-29). In contrast to earlier examples of Roman architecture, the columns of the peristyle court support arches rather than entablatures, a more formal and elaborate arrangement that stresses the vertical height of the colonnade.

Thereafter Rome declined in importance, but building did not end altogether. Maxentius (ruled 306–312 CE) ordered the repair of many buildings

in Rome and had others built there during his short reign. In 330, Constantine (ruled as sole emperor 324–337 CE) made the port city of Byzantium his new capital, renaming it Constantinople. Maxentius's most impressive undertaking in Rome was a huge new basilica called the Basilica Nova, or New Basilica (fig. 6-30). Now known as the Basilica of Maxentius and Constantine because Constantine's architects modified and completed it, this was the last important imperial government building erected in Rome itself. It functioned, like all basilicas, as an administrative center and provided a magnificent setting for the emperor when he appeared as supreme judge.

Three brick-and-concrete barrel vaults of the side aisle still loom over the streets of modern Rome (fig. 6-31). The central hall was covered

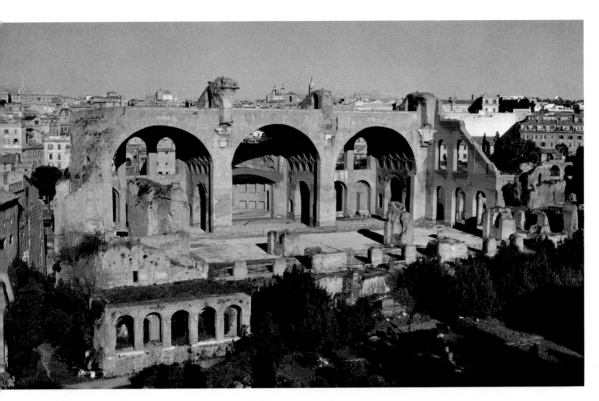

6-31. (*left*) **Basilica of Maxentius and Constantine**

6-32. (*below*) **Arch of Constantine**, Rome. 312–15 CE (dedicated July 25, 315 CE)

This massive, triple-arched monument to Emperor Constantine's victory over Maxentius in 312 CE is a wonder of recycled sculpture. On the attic story, flanking the inscription over the central arch, are relief panels taken from a monument celebrating the victory of Marcus Aurelius over the Germans in 174 CE. On the attached piers framing these panels are large statues of prisoners made to celebrate Trajan's victory over the Dacians in the early second century CE. On the inner walls of the central arch (not seen here) are reliefs also commemorating Trajan's conquest of Dacia. Over each of the side arches are pairs of giant roundels taken from a monument to Hadrian. The rest of the decoration is contemporary with the arch.

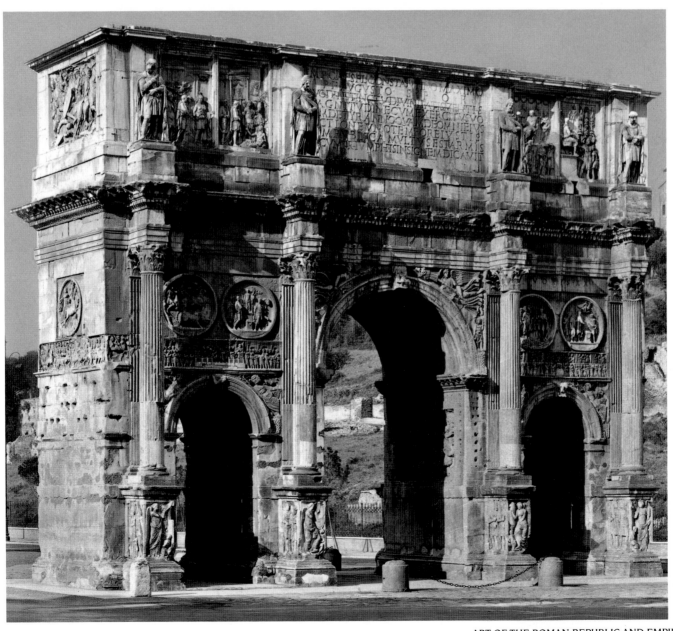

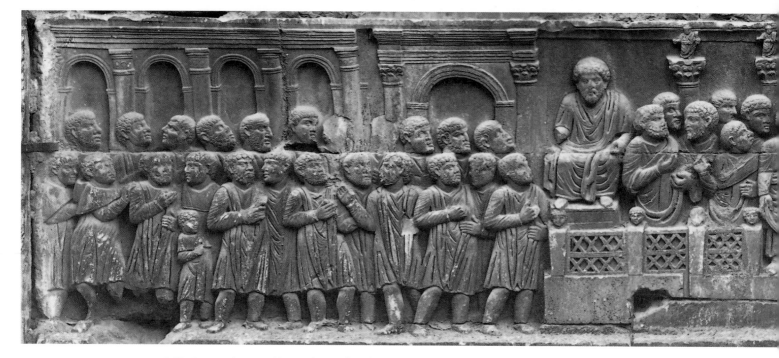

6-33. *Constantine Speaking to the People,* relief panel from the Arch of Constantine. Marble

with groin vaults (see "Arch and Vault," page 137). The side aisles were covered with barrel vaults that acted as buttresses, or projecting supports, for the central groin vault and allowed generous window openings in the clerestory areas of the central aisle. A groin-vaulted porch extended across the short side and sheltered a triple entrance to the central hall. At the opposite end of the long axis of the hall was an apse nearly as wide as the nave, which acted as a focal point for the interior. The directional focus along a central axis from the entrance to the apse emphasized the imperial presence of the emperor, or his statue.

One of the last major pre-Christian Roman monuments to be constructed was a triumphal arch erected by the Senate to commemorate Constantine's defeat of Maxentius in 312 CE. This memorial, placed next to the Colosseum in Rome, took the form of a huge triple arch (fig. 6-32) that dwarfs the nearby Arch of Titus (see fig. 6-12). Three barrel-vaulted passageways are flanked by columns on high pedestals and surmounted by a large attic story bearing a

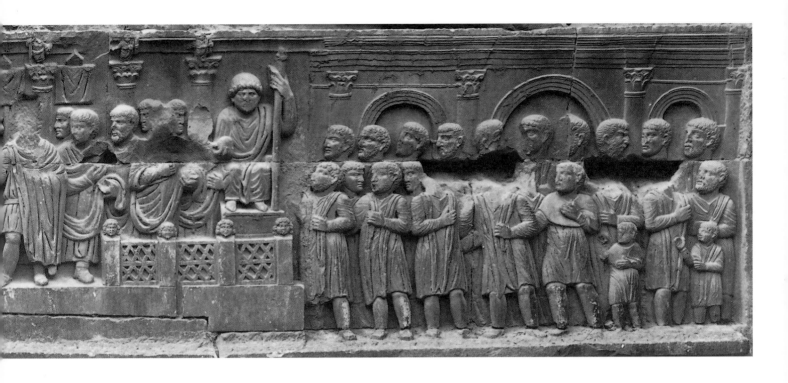

laudatory inscription indicating that the arch was dedicated to Constantine by the Senate and the Roman people. Some of the sculpture decorating it was looted from other monuments made for Constantine's illustrious predecessors, the "good emperors" Trajan, Hadrian, and Marcus Aurelius. The reused items in effect transferred to Constantine the virtues of strength, courage, and piety associated with these earlier emperors. New reliefs made for the arch recount the story of Constantine's victory and remind the viewers of his power and generosity. A panel in one of the **lintels** above the arches depicts his first public speech after he defeated Maxentius (fig. 6-33). Toward the center of the panel, the emperor (his head is missing) stands on a temporary speaker's platform in front of a monument to the Tetrarchs (the columns with statues on top of them). He is flanked by seated images of Marcus Aurelius and Hadrian. In the background, the Basilica Julia and the Arch of Tiberius are to the left and the Arch of Septimus Severus is to the right, identifying the site of the speech as the Republican Forum.

Although the new reliefs reflect the long-standing Roman fondness for depicting important events with realistic detail, in style and subject matter they contrast with the reused elements in the arch. The stocky, mostly frontal figures, each one resembling the next, are compressed into the foreground plane. The participants below the standing Constantine look so uniform that they seem to isolate "the new Augustus" and connect him visually with his illustrious predecessors on each side of him. This two-dimensional, hierarchical approach, with its emphasis on authority, ritual, and symbolism rather than outward form, was adopted by the emerging Christian Church.

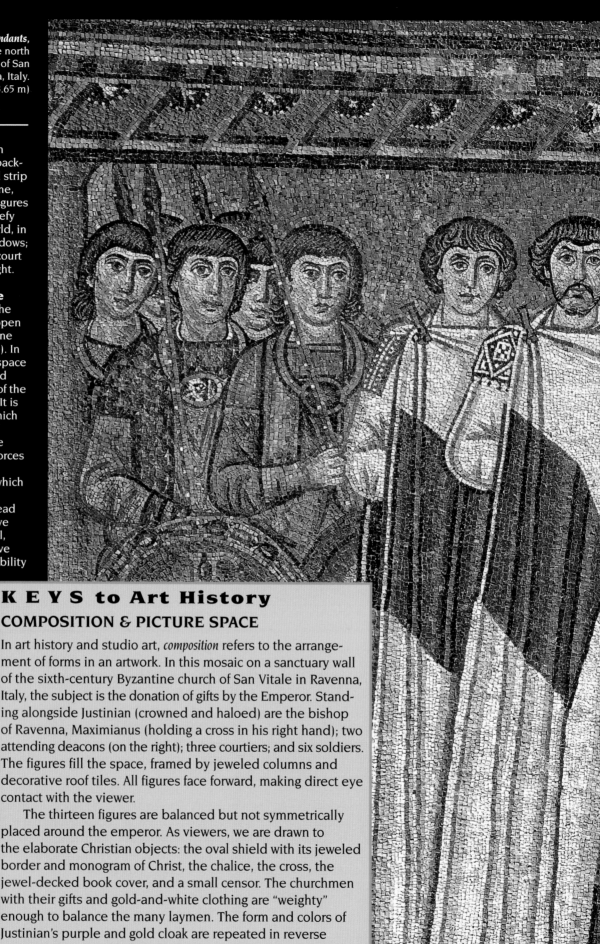

Emperor Justinian and His Attendants, detail of a mosaic on the north wall of the apse. Church of San Vitale, Ravenna, Italy. c. 547. 8'8" x 12' (2.64 x 3.65 m)

Ground Plane

The figures seem to float in front of a gold-and-green back-drop. The green horizontal strip represents the ground plane, which extends under the figures and columns. The artists defy the logic of the natural world, in which objects cast dark shadows; instead, Justinian and his court stand in pools of yellow light.

The Depiction of Space

In Western European art, the picture space appears to open out behind the picture plane (the image bearing surface). In Byzantine art, the picture space lies between the image and the viewer; that is, in front of the wall, panel, or parchment. It is an active space through which sight lines—like beams of light—move, joining image and viewer. This concept forces artists to create so-called "reverse perspective," in which lines perpendicular to the picture plane seem to spread apart. Images seem to move forward, away from the wall, rather than sink into a fictive space behind it. The possibility of intimate contact between the viewer and image gives Byzantine art great immediacy and power.

KEYS to Art History
COMPOSITION & PICTURE SPACE

In art history and studio art, *composition* refers to the arrange-ment of forms in an artwork. In this mosaic on a sanctuary wall of the sixth-century Byzantine church of San Vitale in Ravenna, Italy, the subject is the donation of gifts by the Emperor. Stand-ing alongside Justinian (crowned and haloed) are the bishop of Ravenna, Maximianus (holding a cross in his right hand); two attending deacons (on the right); three courtiers; and six soldiers. The figures fill the space, framed by jeweled columns and decorative roof tiles. All figures face forward, making direct eye contact with the viewer.

The thirteen figures are balanced but not symmetrically placed around the emperor. As viewers, we are drawn to the elaborate Christian objects: the oval shield with its jeweled border and monogram of Christ, the chalice, the cross, the jewel-decked book cover, and a small censor. The churchmen with their gifts and gold-and-white clothing are "weighty" enough to balance the many laymen. The form and colors of Justinian's purple and gold cloak are repeated in reverse in Maximianus's gold chasuble and in the purple panels on the courtiers' cloaks. Seen in its architectural context, the composi-tion of the mosaic leads the viewer's eye from left to right, from the great shield to the censing deacon, and so focuses on the center of the sanctuary and the image of Christ above the altar.

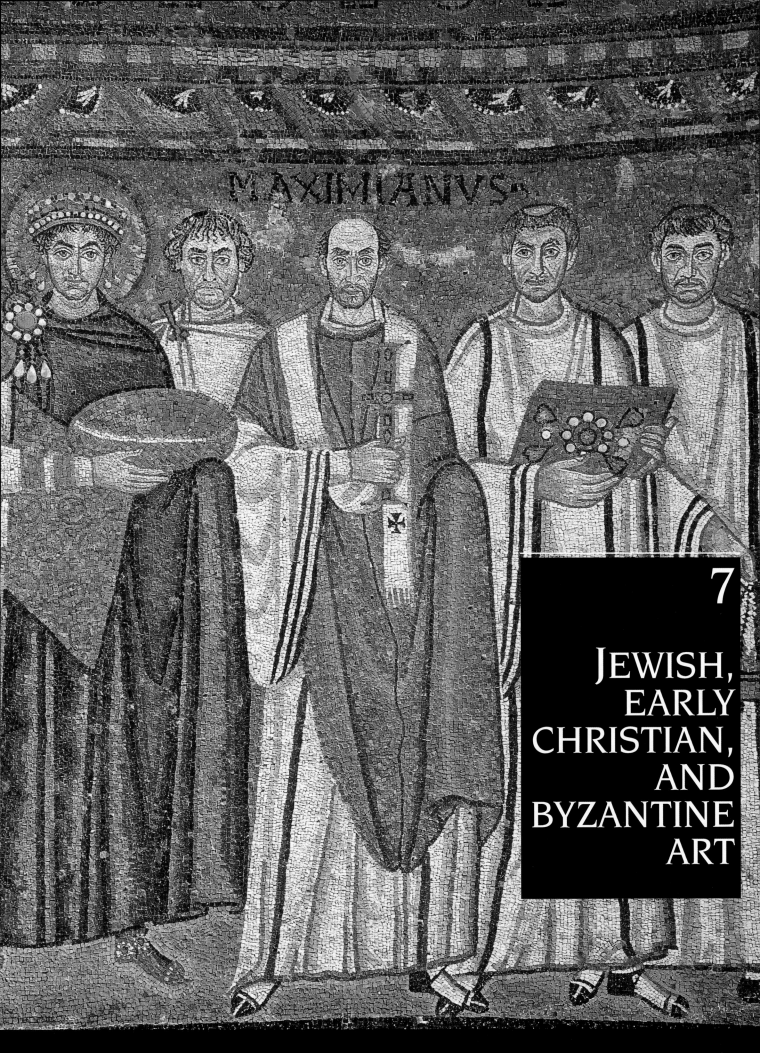

MAXIMIANVS

7

JEWISH,
EARLY
CHRISTIAN,
AND
BYZANTINE
ART

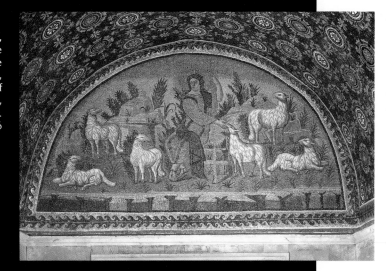

7-1. Good Shepherd, mosaic in the lunette over the west entrance, Mausoleum of Galla Placidia, Ravenna, Italy. c. 425–26

Few images have such great appeal as the Good Shepherd, with associations at once loving, caring, protective, and strong (fig. 7-1). Originating in agrarian societies, the theme of the shepherd watching over a flock of sheep or carrying home a weak or lost lamb develops as a powerful and positive motif even in urban cultures. If today the Good Shepherd is thought of as a Christian symbol, it was not always conceived as such. Among ancient Greeks and Romans, Hermes could be represented as a shepherd carrying a lamb or calf, and Orpheus charmed the flocks and even defied death with his music. Jewish patriarchs measured their wealth in herds of sheep and camels, and one of the greatest and best known of the songs of King David envisions God as an all-providing shepherd (Psalm 23). Not surprisingly, Christians adopted this imagery for Jesus, who used it himself in his parables as an effective way to make God's love understandable to his listeners (Luke 15:3–7 and Matthew 18:12–14). According to John (10:10–11), Jesus called himself the good shepherd who lays down his life for his sheep. And so the imagery contributed to a common theme for Jews and Christians alike in both West and East.

By the fifth century, with Christianity relatively secure as an established religion, the artist might add, or the patron might request, specifically Christian symbols. In the Ravenna mosaic, Jesus sits with his sheep in a luxuriant landscape, like a young Orpheus. But his shepherd's crook has become a golden cross. Not dressed as a simple peasant, he wears imperial robes of purple and gold and embodies the Byzantine ideal of majesty. Nearly a century had passed since the last official persecution of Christians, and at the time this mosaic was made, Christianity had been the official state religion for forty-five years. The patrons of the Ravenna mosaic chose to assert the glory of Jesus Christ in gold and purple mosaic, the richest medium of decoration known, and to present Jesus in the guise of a young emperor, an imperial image still imbued with pagan spirit but now glorying in the triumph of the new faith.

Three religions that arose in the Near East dominate the spiritual life of the Western world: Judaism and Christianity, discussed in this chapter, and Islam, treated in Chapter 8. All three religions are monotheistic, meaning that their followers believe that only one god created and rules the universe. They are known as "religions of the book" because they have written records of their god's will and words: the Hebrew Scriptures of the Jews; the Christian Bible, which includes both the Hebrew Scriptures as its Old Testament and the Christian New Testament; and the Muslim Koran, the word of God (Allah) revealed directly to the prophet Muhammad. Each religion builds on the beliefs and traditions of the earlier. Traditional Jews believe that God made a covenant, or pact, with their ancestors and that they are God's chosen people. They await the coming of a savior, the Messiah, "the anointed one." Traditional Christians maintain that Jesus of Nazareth was that Messiah (the title *Christ* is derived from the Greek term meaning "Messiah"). They believe that God took human form, preached among men and women, was put to death on a cross, and then rose from the dead and went to heaven after establishing the Christian Church under the leadership of the apostles (his closest disciples). Muslims, while accepting the Hebrew prophets and Jesus as divinely inspired, believe Muhammad to be Allah's last and greatest prophet, through whom Islam was revealed some six centuries after Jesus' earthly lifetime.

Jewish, Christian, and Muslim art combine in varying degrees Greek, Roman, and Near Eastern forms and styles. Jews and Christians use the visual arts to educate their followers through narratives and to glorify their religious services through ornamental enrichment of buildings and books. Muslims also incorporate these forms and styles but use words, not images, to convey meaning.

Early Judaism

The Jewish people trace their ancestry to a Semitic people called the Hebrews, who lived in the land of Canaan. Canaan, known from the 2nd century CE by the Roman name of Palestine, was located between the Mediterranean Sea and the Jordan River. According to the Torah (the first five books of the Hebrew Scriptures), God promised the patriarch Abraham that Canaan would be a homeland for the Jewish people (Genesis 17:8), a belief that remains important among Jews to this day.

Jewish settlement of Canaan probably began sometime in the second millennium BCE. According to Exodus, the second book of the Torah, the prophet Moses led the Hebrews out of slavery in Egypt to the promised land of Canaan. At one crucial point during the journey, Moses climbed alone to the top of Mount Sinai, where God gave him the Ten Commandments, the cornerstone of Jewish law. The Commandments, inscribed on tablets, were kept in a gold-covered wooden box, the Ark of the Covenant.

In the tenth century BCE, the Jewish king Solomon built a temple in Jerusalem to house the Ark of the Covenant. The Temple consisted of courtyards, a porch, a hall, and the holy of holies housing the Ark with its guardian cherubim. King Solomon sent to nearby Phoenicia for cedar, cypress, and sandalwood, and for a master craftsman to supervise the Temple's construction (II Chronicles 2:2–15). The Temple was the spiritual center of Jewish life.

In 586 BCE, the Babylonians, under King Nebuchadnezzar II, conquered Jerusalem. They destroyed the Temple, exiled the Jews, and carried off the Ark of the Covenant. When Cyrus the Great of Persia conquered Babylonia in 538 BCE, the Jews were permitted to return to Jerusalem and rebuild the Temple, but from that time forward Canaan existed primarily under foreign rule and eventually became part of the Roman Empire. In 70 CE Roman forces led by the future emperor, Titus, destroyed the Second Temple and Jerusalem (Chapter 6).

Jews continued to live in dispersed communities throughout the Roman Empire. Most of the earliest surviving examples of Jewish art date from the Hellenistic and Roman periods. Six Jewish **catacombs**, or underground burial chambers (see "Roman Funerary Practices," page 136), discovered just outside the city of Rome and in use from the first to fourth century CE, display wall paintings with Jewish themes. In one example, from the third century CE, two **menorahs**, or seven-branched lamps, flank the long-lost Ark of the Covenant (fig. 7-2). The conspicuous representation of the menorah looted from the Second Temple of Jerusalem on the Arch of Titus in Rome (see fig. 6-13) kept the memory of these treasures alive. The menorah form probably derives from the ancient Near Eastern Tree of Life, symbolizing both the end of exile and the paradise to come.

The destroyed Temple in Jerusalem had been a special, central holy place for all Jews, but synagogues could be constructed in any Jewish community. Judaism has always emphasized religious learning. Jews gather in synagogues for study and worship; a synagogue can be any large room where the Torah scrolls are kept and read publicly. Far less Jewish art than Christian or Islamic art has survived, but a num-ber of synagogues have been discovered or excavated. Their architecture and ornament reflect late Roman artistic traditions melded with specifically Jewish symbolism. In the Roman city of Dura-Europos, in modern Syria, excavators discovered a Jewish **house-synagogue**, or synagogue built within a private home; a Christian **house-church**; shrines to the Persian gods Mithras and Zoroaster; and temples to Roman gods.

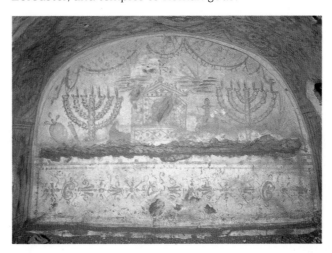

7-2. Menorahs and Ark of the Covenant, wall painting in a Jewish catacomb, Villa Torlonia, Rome. 3rd century. 3'11" x 5'9" (1.19 x 1.8 m)

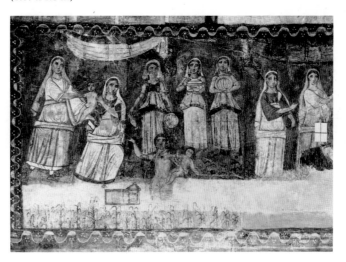

7-3. Finding of the Baby Moses, detail of a wall painting from a house-synagogue, Dura-Europos, Syria. Second half of 3rd century. Tempera on plaster. National Museum, Damascus, Syria

The synagogue at Dura-Europos is especially interesting because its walls are covered with paintings depicting scenes from Jewish history. One panel illustrates the early life of Moses, who was born into a Jewish family in Egypt (fig. 7-3). Moses' mother set him afloat in a reed basket in the shallows of the Nile River in an attempt to save him from the decree of the reigning pharaoh that all Jewish male infants be put to death (Exodus 1:8–2:10). He was found by the pharaoh's daughter when she came down to the river to bathe. Compassionately, she raised Moses as her own child. The painting shows these events unfolding in a continuous narrative

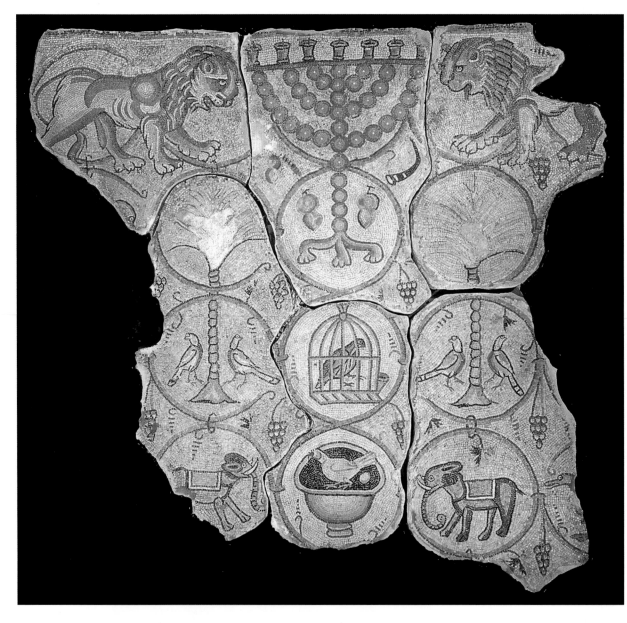

7-4. Synagogue floor, Maon, West Bank. c. 530. Mosaic. The Israel Museum, Jerusalem

set in a narrow foreground space. At right, the princess sees the child's cradle floating among the bulrushes; at the center, she sends her servant into the water to save him; and at the left, she hands him to a nurse (actually Moses' true mother). The vivid continuous narrative follows the Roman tradition of historical representation; however, the frontal poses, strong outlines, and flat colors are pictorial devices that are associated with Near Eastern art.

The Dura-Europos synagogue had originally been built as a house, but Jews also built synagogues designed like Christian churches on the model of the ancient Roman basilica. A typical basilica synagogue had a central **nave**; an aisle on both sides, separated from the nave by a line of columns; a mosaic floor; a semicircular apse in the wall facing Jerusalem; and perhaps an atrium (courtyard) and porch, or **narthex.** A Torah was kept in a shrine in the apse.

Synagogues contained almost no representational sculpture because Jewish law forbade praying to images or idols. Paintings and mosaics, on the other hand, often decorated walls and floors. A fragment of a mosaic floor from a sixth-century synagogue at Maon (Menois) features traditional Jewish symbols along with a variety of stylized plants, birds, and animals (fig. 7-4). Two lions of Judah flank a menorah. Beneath it is a *shofar*, or ram's horn, blown on ceremonial occasions, and three *etrogs*, or citrons, used to celebrate the harvest festival of Sukkoth. Palm trees refer to another Sukkot emblem, the *lulav*, a sheaf of palm, myrtle, and willow branches, and an etrog, used to symbolize the bounty of the earth and unity of all Jews. The variety of placid animals may symbolize the universal peace as prophesied by Isaiah (11:6–9; 65:25). The pairing of images around a central element, as in the birds flanking the palm trees, or the lions facing the menorah, is characteristic of Near Eastern art. In contrast, the grapevine forming circular **medallions** as a frame for the images was popular in Roman mosaics.

In 395 the Roman Empire split permanently in two, becoming the Western (Roman) Empire, which collapsed in 476, and the Eastern, or Byzantine, Empire, which lasted until 1453, when it fell to the Ottoman Turks. By this time most Jews lived outside Palestine, in communities spread across the Middle East, North Africa, and Europe. Because their religious practice set them apart, and their numbers made them a minority, they faced special taxes, restrictions on the occupations they could enter, and sometimes violent persecution. The history of Jewish art is fragmented because many artworks were destroyed when Jewish homes and synagogues were attacked and burned. The artworks that survive reflect the interplay of many styles, centuries, and regions.

Early Christianity

Christianity began with the life and teachings of Jesus of Nazareth, a Jew born sometime between 8 and 4 BCE and crucified at the age of thirty-three. Christians believe that Jesus was the son of God, born in a human body to a virgin woman, Mary, and resurrected after death. They believe in one God manifest in three Persons, a Trinity of Father (God), Son (Jesus Christ), and Holy Spirit. In later years Christians also began to acknowledge saints: holy individuals canonized, or officially honored, by the Church for upholding and practicing Christian beliefs, often at the cost of martyrdom, or execution. Worshipers may ask the saints, who must also be connected with a verifiable miracle, to intercede for them with God, but saints are not worshiped as gods in their own right.

The life of Jesus is described in the Christian New Testament, in the first four books, known as the Gospels (the Good News). The Gospels relate that Jesus was a descendant of the Jewish royal house of King David and that he was born in Bethlehem in Judaea, where his mother, Mary, and her husband, Joseph, had gone to be registered in the Roman census. He grew up in Nazareth in Galilee (in what is now northern Israel), where Joseph was a carpenter. At the age of thirty, Jesus began his public ministry. He gathered about him a group of disciples, male and female, preaching love and charity, a personal relationship with God, the forgiveness of sins, and the promise of life after death. He chose twelve as his apostles to carry on his work after his death (see "Iconography of the Life of Jesus," pages 162–163).

Jesus limited his ministry primarily to Jews; his apostles, including Paul, who joined the group later, took Jesus' teachings to non-Jews. Despite sporadic persecutions, Christianity persisted and spread throughout the Roman Empire. The Roman emperor Constantine permitted the Christians freedom of worship with the Edict of Milan in 313 CE. By the end of the fourth century, Christianity had become

the official religion of the empire, and non-Christians became the targets of persecution.

In Rome, even before their religion was recognized, Christians met in private houses for worship. Several private patrons also owned cemeteries and funeral basilicas. The congregations used the burial grounds as places to gather for worship, commemorative meals, and funeral rituals, and they excavated catacombs below ground for burials. Painted walls and ceilings in catacombs provide some of the earliest examples of Christian art. The domed ceiling of a **cubiculum**, or small room, in a fourth-century catacomb is painted with a central medallion and four **lunettes** (semicircular compartments)

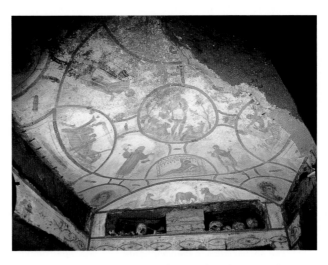

7-5. Good Shepherd, Orants, and Story of Jonah, painted ceiling of the Catacomb of Saints Peter and Marcellinus, Rome. 4th century

The underground cemeteries, or catacombs, of which this image is an example, consist of narrow passages and small burial chambers lined with rectangular burial niches. These niches were filled with stone sarcophagi or sealed with tiles or stone slabs. In this room a later niche cuts through the painting of sheep in a pasture. The bones and skulls, as well as the brick support in the center of the niche, are not part of the original room.

linked by the arms of a cross (fig. 7-5). The pose of the shepherd in the central **roundel** (circular decorative element) derives from Greek sculpture. In its new context, the image reminded viewers of Jesus' promise: "I am the good shepherd. A good shepherd lays down his life for the sheep" (John 10:11). The words refer to the Christian belief that Jesus died to redeem the sins of the world.

The Old Testament story of Jonah and the Whale (Jonah 1–2) fills the lunettes. According to the Old Testament, God caused Jonah to be thrown overboard during a storm, swallowed by a whale, and released alive three days later. Christians interpreted the story as a prefiguring of Christ's death and resurrection. In a larger sense, the story symbolized the everlasting life awaiting true believers. On the left, Jonah is

Iconography of the Life of Jesus

Iconography is the study of subject matter in art. It involves identifying both what a work of art represents—what it depicts—and the deeper significance of what is represented—its symbolic meaning. Stories about the life of Jesus, grouped in "cycles," form the basis of Christian iconography. What follows is an outline of those cycles and the main events of each.

The Incarnation Cycle and the Childhood of Jesus

This cycle is the events surrounding the conception and birth of Jesus.

The Annunciation: The archangel Gabriel informs the Virgin Mary that God has chosen her to bear his son. A dove represents the Incarnation, her miraculous conception of Jesus through the Holy Spirit.

The Visitation: Mary visits her older cousin Elizabeth, pregnant with the future Saint John the Baptist. Elizabeth is the first to recognize and acknowledge the divinity of the child Mary is carrying.

The Nativity: Jesus is born to Mary in Bethlehem. The Holy Family—Jesus, Mary, and her husband, Joseph—is shown in a house, a stable, or, in Byzantine art, in a cave.

The Annunciation to the Shepherds and **The Adoration of the Shepherds:** An angel announces Jesus' birth to humble shepherds. They hurry to Bethlehem to honor him.

The Adoration of the Magi: The Magi—wise men from the East—follow a bright star to Bethlehem to honor Jesus as King of the Jews, presenting him with precious gifts: gold (symbolizing kingship), frankincense (divinity), and myrrh (death). In the European Middle Ages the Magi were identified as three kings.

The Presentation in the Temple: Mary and Joseph bring the infant Jesus to the Temple in Jerusalem, where he is presented to the high priest. It is prophesied that Jesus will redeem humankind and that Mary will suffer great sorrow.

The Massacre of the Innocents and **The Flight into Egypt:** An angel warns Joseph that King Herod—to eliminate the threat of a newborn rival king—plans to murder all the babies in Bethlehem. The Holy Family flees to Egypt.

Jesus among the Doctors: In Jerusalem for the celebration of Passover, Joseph and Mary find the twelve-year-old Jesus in serious discussion with Temple scholars, a sign of his coming ministry.

The Public Ministry Cycle

In this cycle Jesus preaches his message.

The Baptism: At age thirty Jesus is baptized by John the Baptist in the Jordan River. He sees the Holy Spirit and hears a heavenly voice proclaiming him God's son. This marks the beginning of his ministry.

The Calling of Matthew: Passing by the customhouse, Jesus sees Matthew, a tax collector, to whom he says, "Follow me." Matthew complies, becoming one of his disciples.

Jesus and the Samaritan Woman at the Well: Jesus rests by a spring called Jacob's Well. Contrary to Jewish custom, he asks a local Samaritan woman for a drink of water. The disciples are surprised to find them conversing.

Jesus Walking on the Water: The disciples, in a storm-tossed boat, see Jesus walking toward them on the water. Peter tries to go out to meet Jesus, but begins to sink, and Jesus saves him. When Jesus reaches the boat, the storm stops.

The Raising of Lazarus: Jesus brings his friend Lazarus back to life four days after he has died. Lazarus emerges from the tomb wrapped in his shroud.

The Delivery of the Keys to Peter: Jesus designates Peter as his successor, symbolically turning over to him the keys to the kingdom of heaven.

The Transfiguration: Jesus is transformed into a dazzling vision on Mount Tabor in Galilee as his closest disciples—Peter, James, and John the Evangelist—look on. A cloud overshadows them, and a heavenly voice proclaims Jesus to be God's son.

The Cleansing of the Temple: Jesus, in anger, drives money changers and animal traders from the Temple.

The Passion Cycle

This cycle contains events surrounding Jesus' death and resurrection. (*Passio* is Latin for "suffering.")

The Entry into Jerusalem: Jesus, riding an ass, and his disciples enter Jerusalem in triumph. Crowds honor them, spreading clothes and palm fronds in their path.

The Last Supper: During the Jewish Passover seder, Jesus reveals his impending death to his disciples. Instructing them to drink wine (his blood) and eat bread (his body) in remembrance of him, he lays the foundation for the Christian Eucharist (Mass).

Jesus Washing the Disciples' Feet: After the Last Supper, Jesus humbly washes the disciples' feet to set an example of humility. Peter, embarrassed, protests.

---

thrown from the boat; on the right, the monster spews him up; and at the center, he reclines in the shade of a gourd vine, a symbol of paradise. Between the medallions, **orant** figures—worshipers with arms uplifted in prayer—pray for the souls of the departed.

The era of religious toleration, which began with the Edict of Milan and Constantine's active support of Christianity, spurred the building of Christian churches and shrines. Constantine ordered a monumental basilica constructed at the place where Christians believed Saint Peter, the leader of Jesus' apostles, to be buried. Peter (died c. 64 CE) had established the first Christian community in Rome. As the city's first bishop (spiritual and administrative leader of the Church), he was later recognized as the precursor of the popes—the heads of the Christian Church in the West. Old Saint Peter's Church (called "old" because it was completely replaced by a new building in the sixteenth century) became the pope's church and came to signify his authority over all Christendom.

Old Saint Peter's Church (see "Basilica-Plan and Central-Plan Churches," page 164) included architectural elements arranged in a way that has characterized Christian basilica-plan churches ever since (fig. 7-6). A narthex across the width of the building protected the doorways, which opened into the nave and the four side aisles, two on each side of the nave. As in Roman secular basilicas, which inspired its

The Agony in the Garden: In the Garden of Gethsemane on the Mount of Olives, Jesus struggles between his human fear of pain and death and his divine strength to overcome them (*agon* is Greek for "contest"). The apostles sleep nearby, oblivious.

The Betrayal (The Arrest): Judas Iscariot, one of the disciples, accepts a bribe to point Jesus out to his enemies. Judas brings an armed crowd to Gethsemane. He kisses Jesus, a pre-arranged signal. Peter makes a futile attempt to defend Jesus from the Roman soldiers who seize him.

The Denial of Peter: Jesus is brought to the palace of the Jewish high priest, Caiaphas, to be interrogated for claiming to be the Messiah. Peter follows, and there he three times denies knowing Jesus, as Jesus predicted he would.

Jesus before Pilate: Jesus is taken to Pontius Pilate, the Roman governor of Judaea, and charged with treason for calling himself King of the Jews. He is sent to Herod Antipas, ruler of Galilee, who scorns him. Pilate proposes freeing Jesus but is shouted down by the mob, which demands that he be crucified. Pilate washes his hands before the crowd to signify that Jesus' blood is on its hands, not his.

The Flagellation (The Scourging): Jesus is whipped by his Roman captors.

Jesus Crowned with Thorns (The Mocking of Jesus): Pilate's soldiers torment Jesus. They dress him in royal robes, crown him with thorns, and kneel before him, hailing him as King of the Jews.

The Bearing of the Cross (The Road to Calvary): Jesus bears the cross from Pilate's house to Golgotha, where he is executed. Medieval artists depicted this event and its accompanying incidents in fourteen images known as the Stations of the Cross: (1) Jesus is condemned to death; (2) Jesus picks up the cross; (3) Jesus falls for the first time; (4) Jesus meets his grieving mother; (5) Simon of Cyrene is forced to help Jesus carry the cross; (6) Veronica wipes Jesus' face with her veil; (7) Jesus falls again; (8) Jesus admonishes the women of Jerusalem; (9) Jesus falls a third time; (10) Jesus is stripped; (11) Jesus is nailed to the cross; (12) Jesus dies on the cross; (13) Jesus is taken down from the cross; (14) Jesus is entombed.

The Crucifixion: The earliest representations of the Crucifixion are abstract, showing either a cross alone or a cross and a lamb. Later depictions include some or all of the following narrative details: two criminals (one penitent, the other not) are crucified on either side of Jesus; the Virgin Mary, John the Evangelist, Mary Magdalen, and other followers mourn at the foot of the cross; Roman soldiers torment Jesus—one extends a sponge on a pole with vinegar instead of water for him to drink, another stabs him in the side with a spear, and others gamble for his clothes; a skull identifies the execution ground as Golgotha, "the place of the skull," where Adam was buried. The association symbolizes the promise of redemption: the blood flowing from Jesus' wounds will wash away Adam's Original Sin.

The Descent from the Cross (The Deposition): Jesus' followers take his body down from the cross. Joseph of Arimathea and Nicodemus wrap it in linen with myrrh and aloe. Also present are the grief-struck Virgin, John the Evangelist, and sometimes Mary Magdalen, other disciples, and angels.

The Lamentation (Pietà): Jesus' sorrowful followers gather around his body. An image of the Virgin mourning alone with Jesus across her lap is known as a pietà (from the Latin *pietas*, "pity").

The Entombment: Jesus' mother and friends place his body in a nearby sarcophagus, or rock tomb. This is done hastily because of the approaching Jewish Sabbath.

The Descent into Limbo (The Harrowing of Hell): No longer in mortal form, Jesus, now called Christ, descends into limbo, or hell, to free deserving souls, among them Adam, Eve, and Moses.

The Resurrection (The Anastasis): Three days after his death, Christ walks out of his tomb while the soldiers guarding it sleep.

The Marys at the Tomb (The Holy Women at the Sepulchre): Christ's female followers—usually including Mary Magdalen and the mother of the apostle James, also named Mary—discover his empty tomb. An angel announces Christ's resurrection. The soldiers guarding the tomb look on, terrified.

Noli Me Tangere ("Do Not Touch Me"), The Supper at Emmaus, and **The Doubting of Thomas:** Christ makes a series of appearances to his followers in the forty days between his resurrection and his ascension. He first appears to Mary Magdalen, as she weeps at his tomb. She reaches out to him, but he warns her not to touch him. In the Supper at Emmaus, he shares a meal with his apostles. In the Doubting of Thomas, Christ invites Thomas to touch the wound in his side to convince the doubting apostle of his resurrection.

The Ascension: Christ ascends to heaven from the Mount of Olives, disappearing in a cloud. His apostles, often accompanied by the Virgin, watch.

---

design, a clerestory with windows in the tall central nave lit the interior, and the nave was lined with columns supporting an entablature. At Old Saint Peter's, because of its size and double aisles, the columns of the side aisles supported a series of round arches. At the end of the nave and aisles was another special feature of Old Saint Peter's, a **transept**—a wing that crossed the nave and aisles at a right angle. The transept met the need for more space near the tomb of the saint. A large number of clergy and pilgrims gathered near the altar and tomb for elaborate rituals. Christians believed that Saint Peter's bones lay beneath the high altar; indeed early Christian and pagan catacombs lay under the church. Clearly, Old Saint Peter's had to

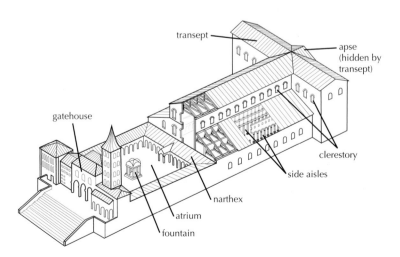

7-6. Reconstruction drawing of Old Saint Peter's, Rome. c. 320–27; atrium added in later 4th century

Elements of Architecture
BASILICA-PLAN AND CENTRAL-PLAN CHURCHES

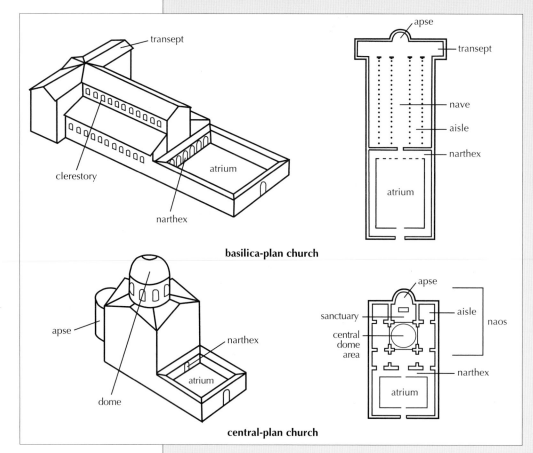

basilica-plan church

central-plan church

narthex, spanning one of the building's short ends. Doorways—known collectively as the church's **portal**—lead from the narthex into a long central area called a **nave**. The high-ceiling nave is separated into aisles on either side by rows of columns. The nave is lit by windows along its upper story—called a **clerestory**—that rises above the side aisles' roofs. At the opposite end of the nave from the narthex is a semicircular projection, the **apse**. The apse functions as the building's symbolic core where the altar, raised on a platform, is located. Sometimes there is also a **transept**, a horizontal wing that crosses the nave in front of the apse, making the building T-shaped; this is known as a *Tau plan*. When additional space (a choir) separates the transept and the apse, the plan is called a **Latin cross**.

Central-plan buildings were first used by Christians as tombs, baptism centers, and shrines to martyrs. (The **Greek-cross plan**, in which two similarly sized "arms" intersect at their centers, is a type of central plan.) Instead of the longitudinal axis of basilican churches, which draws worshipers forward toward the apse, central-plan churches such as Ravenna's San Vitale (see figs. 7-13, 7-14) have a more vertical axis. This makes the **dome**, a symbolic "vault of heaven," a natural focus over the main worship area. Like basilicas, central-plan churches generally have an atrium, a narthex, and an apse. The naos is the space containing the central dome, sanctuary, and apse.

The forms of early Christian buildings were based on two classical prototypes: rectangular Roman basilicas (see fig. 6-19) and round-domed structures—rotundas—such as the Pantheon (see figs. 6-20, 6-21). As in Old Saint Peter's in Rome (fig. 7-6), **basilica-plan** churches are characterized by a forecourt, the **atrium**, leading to a porch, the

---

St. Peter's, Notre Dame, and Sta. Maria Maggiore (Traditional Usage and Abbreviations)

Christian churches always have a dedication, for example, St. Peter's Church or the Church of St. Mary. When we omit the word *church*, we should add an apostrophe s to the saint's name; thus St. Peter's or St. Mary's. Mary is often called Our Lady, *Notre Dame* in French. Although many churches are dedicated to Our Lady, the words alone now refer to the Cathedral of Paris (not to be confused with Notre Dame University in the United States). *Saint* is abbreviated *St.* in English; *Sta.* for female saints and *S.* for male saints (plural *SS.*) in Italian; and *Ste.* or *St.* (and joined to the name with a hyphen) in French. Relics, material remains of the saint to whom the church is dedicated, must lie in, on, or under the main altar of the church. The church of Sta. Maria Maggiore in Rome has as its chief relic a piece of wood from the manger.

Only one church in each diocese can be called a cathedral, and it must have a bishop's throne (Latin, *cathedra*). Other churches, regardless of their size or splendor, are simply churches. St. John's, where the pope acts as bishop of Rome—not St. Peter's—is the Cathedral of Rome.

---

serve a variety of functions: it was a congregational church, a burial place, and a pilgrimage shrine containing the relics of a holy person. Old Saint Peter's could hold at least 14,000 worshipers, and it remained the largest of all Christian churches until the eleventh century.

Old Saint Peter's is gone, but some idea of its splendor can be gained from the Church of Santa Maria Maggiore, built in Rome in the fifth century, shortly after a church council awarded Mary the title "Bearer (Mother) of God"(see "St. Peter's, Notre Dame, and Sta. Maria Maggiore," left). Like Old Saint Peter's, Santa Maria Maggiore is a basilica with columns supporting an entablature and a clerestory (fig. 7-7). The altar is located in an apse set off from the nave by a **triumphal arch**, replacing the end wall of the nave. Mosaics along the nave walls, in framed panels high above the worshipers, illustrate Old Testament stories of Jewish patriarchs and heroes whom Christians accepted as part of their own history. One mosaic, *Parting of Lot and Abraham* (fig. 7-8), illustrates a story told in the first book of the Old Testament (Genesis 13:1–12). The people of Abraham and his nephew Lot, dwelling together, had grown too numerous, so the two agreed to separate and

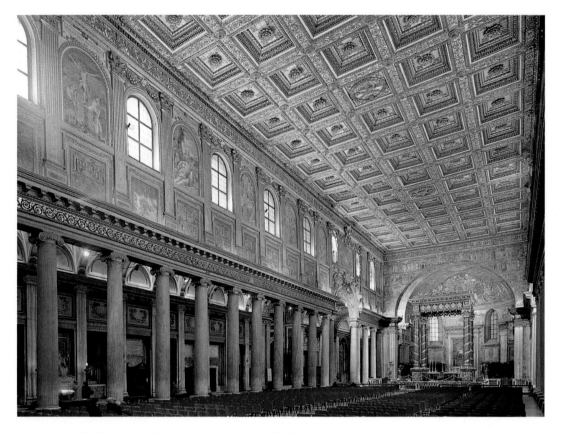

7-7. Nave, Church of Santa Maria Maggiore, Rome. 432–40

Changes in public taste and patrons' desires for the enrichment and redecoration of churches make it very difficult to imagine the original appearance of these early places of worship. In the Church of Santa Maria Maggiore, the underlying architectural plan and structure, including the columns with their Ionic capitals, remain the same. Of the original mosaic decoration, only the mosaics just below the windows and on the end wall of the nave remain. The later, elaborately gilded ceiling tends to dominate modern photographs, and electric lighting also changes the effect of the interior. Chairs are another modern addition; the seated people visible in the lower left corner, however, give an idea of the enormous size of this early Christian church.

lead their followers in different directions. On the right, Lot and his daughters turn toward Jordan, while Abraham and his wife stay in Canaan. This parting is meaningful to Christians since Abraham was the founder of the Jewish nation from which Jesus descended. The solid, three-dimensional rendering of the toga-clad foreground figures and the hint of perspective in the buildings reflect a continuation of the earlier naturalistic style of Roman art, even as the sheen of the gold tesserae tends to flatten the forms and reduce the illusion of space.

By the time the Roman Church of Santa Maria Maggiore was completed, Rome had lost its political, although not its spiritual, importance. The capital of the Western Roman Empire was moved to Milan in the late fourth century, and then to Ravenna at the beginning of the fifth century. Ravenna had an important naval base, Classis, and offered direct access by sea to Constantinople, the capital of the Eastern, or Byzantine, Empire. Ravenna became the capital of the Byzantine state in Italy.

One of the earliest surviving Christian structures in Ravenna is a small, cross-shaped chapel attached to the church of the imperial palace. It

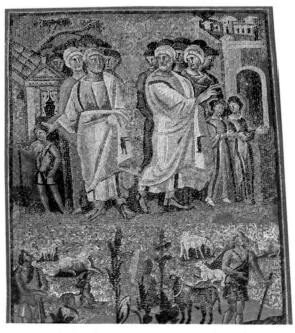

7-8. *Parting of Lot and Abraham,* mosaic in the nave arcade, Church of Santa Maria Maggiore. Panel approx. 4'11" x 6'8" (1.49 x 2.03 m)

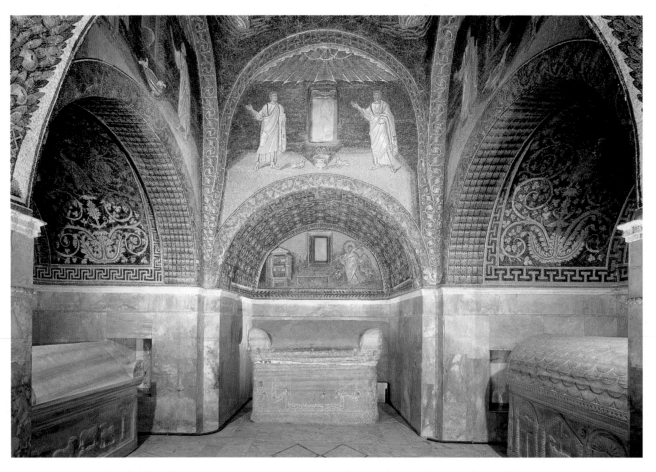

7-9. Mausoleum of Galla Placidia, Ravenna, Italy. c. 425–26. Eastern bays with sarcophagus niches and lunette mosaic of the *Martyrdom of Saint Lawrence*

is called the Mausoleum of Galla Placidia after one of the most remarkable women of the fifth century (although she was not buried there). Galla Placidia was the daughter of the Western Roman emperor, wife of the Gothic king, sister of Emperor Honorius, and mother of Emperor Valentinian. As regent for her son after 425, she ruled the Western empire. The vaults of "her" tiny chapel are richly decorated with mosaics, and panels of veined marble cover the walls below (fig. 7-9). Floral designs derived from funeral garlands cover the four central arches, and the walls above them are filled with the figures of standing apostles gesturing like orators. Saint Lawrence, to whom the building was probably dedicated, is represented in the central lunette in figure 7-9. The saint holds a cross and gestures toward the metal grill on which he was literally roasted. At the left stands a tall cabinet containing the books of the Gospels, signifying the faith for which Lawrence was martyred.

In another lunette is a mosaic depicting the *Good Shepherd* (see fig. 7-1). In a fourth-century painting of the same subject (see fig. 7-5), Jesus was a simple shepherd boy carrying an animal on his shoulders. In contrast, in this mosaic he is a young adult wearing imperial robes. There is a halo, or circle of light, behind his head—a device artists used to distinguish rulers and holy personages from ordinary people. The rocky band at the bottom of the lunette scene, resembling a cliff

face riddled with clefts, separates the divine image from worshipers. This visual device illustrates an increasing tendency in Christian art to differentiate the sacred and secular worlds.

Early Byzantine Art

During the fifth and sixth centuries, the Italian peninsula was invaded by the Visigoths, Vandals, and Ostrogoths—Germanic peoples from the north. Rome was sacked twice, in 410 and 455. The Western Roman Empire collapsed in 476, and Italy fell to the Ostrogoths.

During the same period, the Eastern Empire and its capital city of Constantinople flourished. Byzantine political power, wealth, and culture reached its height in the sixth century, under Emperor Justinian I (ruled 527–565), ably seconded by Empress Theodora (c. 500–548). At the height of its powers under Justinian, the Byzantine Empire included the areas that are now Greece, the Balkans, and Turkey; the Levant from Syria south to Arabia; Egypt; part of Spain; and a long strip along the Mediterranean coast of Africa. Justinian also reconquered Italy and Sicily from the Ostrogoths, establishing Ravenna as the administrative capital of Byzantine Italy.

In Constantinople, Justinian began a campaign of building and renovation, but little remains of his architectural projects or of the old imperial city. The Church of Hagia Sophia (Holy Wisdom) is a magnificent exception

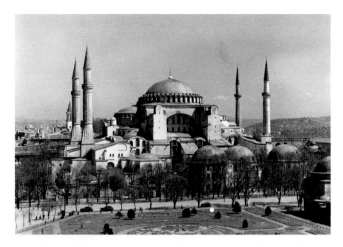

7-10. Anthemius of Tralles and Isidorus of Miletus. Church of Hagia Sophia, Istanbul, Turkey. 532–37. View from the southwest

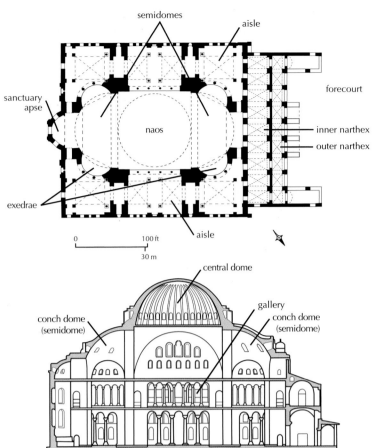

7-11. Plan and section of the Church of Hagia Sophia

(fig. 7-10). Designed by two scholar-theoreticians, Anthemius of Tralles and Isidorus of Miletus, it embodies both imperial power and Christian glory. Anthemius was a specialist in geometry and optics, and Isidorus was a specialist in physics who had studied vaulted construction. Their crowning achievement was the dome of Hagia Sophia, which provided a golden, light-filled canopy high above a processional space. Procopius of Caesarea, who chronicled Justinian's reign, claimed poetically that the dome seemed to hang suspended on a "golden chain from heaven." It was rumored that Hagia Sophia was constructed by angels, but mortal builders achieved the feat in only five years (532–537) (see "Pendentives and Squinches," below).

Hagia Sophia is based on a central plan with a dome inscribed in a square (fig. 7-11). To form a longitudinal nave, **conches**—semidomes—expand outward from the central dome to con-

nect with the narthex on one end and the conch of the sanctuary apse on the other. This central core, called the naos in Byzantine architecture, is flanked by side aisles; above the aisles, galleries overlook the naos. The Byzantine church required **galleries** to accommodate female worshipers, who were not allowed to stand directly on the church floor.

Elements of Architecture
PENDENTIVES AND SQUINCHES

Pendentives and **squinches** are two methods of supporting a round dome or its drum over a square or rectangular space. Pendentives are structural elements between arches that form a circular opening on which the dome sits. Squinches are bracketlike constructions or **corbels**, fitted into the walls' upper corners beneath the dome. Because squinches create an octagon, which is close in shape to a circle, they provide a solid base on which a dome may rest. Byzantine builders experimented with both pendentives (as at Hagia Sophia, see fig. 7-12) and squinches. Elaborate squinch-supported domes became a hallmark of Islamic interiors (as at Córdoba's Great Mosque, see fig. 8-18).

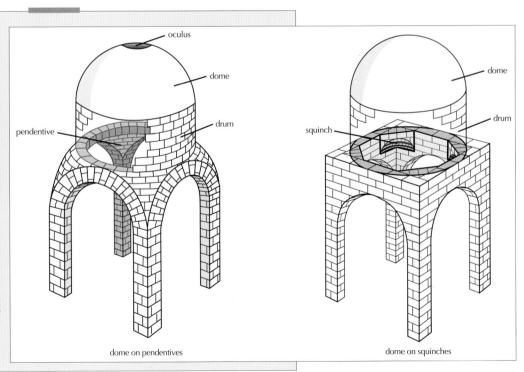

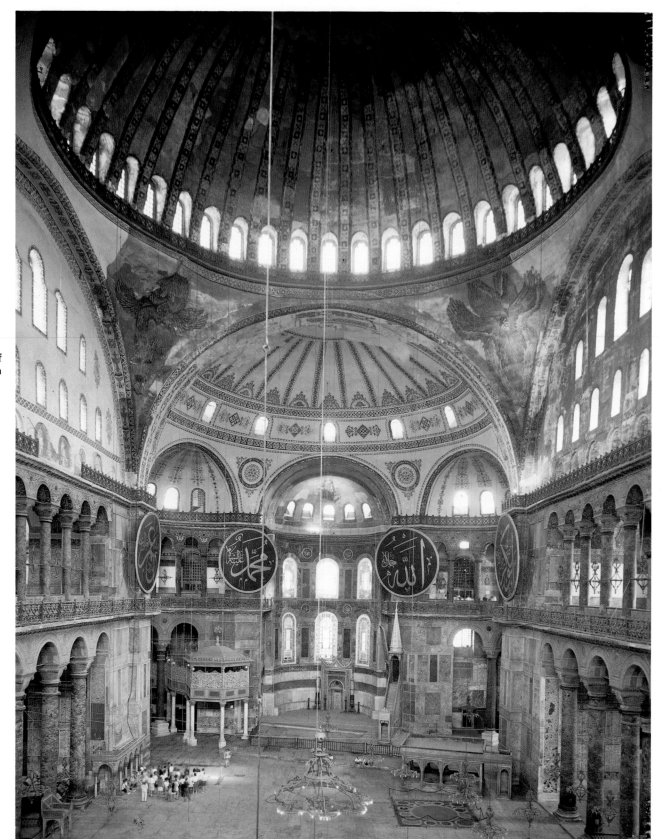

7-12. Church of Hagia Sophia

The main dome of Hagia Sophia is supported on pendentives, triangular curving wall sections built between the four huge arches that spring from **piers** (large columnar supports) at the corners of the dome's square base (fig. 7-12). The origin of the dome on pendentives, which became the preferred method for supporting domes in Byzantine architecture, is obscure, but Hagia Sophia represents its earliest use in a major building. Unlike the Pantheon's dome, which rises as a solid form from a circular drum and opens with an oculus at the top (see fig. 6-21), the dome of Hagia Sophia has a band of forty windows around its base. This daring concept challenged architectural logic by weakening the integrity of the masonry but created the all-important circle of light that makes the dome appear to float.

Among the sixth-century Byzantine churches built outside of Constantinople, San Vitale in Ravenna and Sant'Apollinare in Classe were two of the most important structures. Both were commissioned by a local bishop, Ecclesius, when Italy was under Ostrogothic rule, but they were only completed after Justinian's conquest of Ravenna.

The Church of San Vitale was dedicated in 547 to the fourth-century Italian martyr, Saint Vitalis. Its design is basically a dome-covered octagon extended by eight **exedrae**, or semicircular **niches** (hollows or recesses in a wall or other architectural element)(fig. 7-13). A rectangular sanctuary and apse, flanked by circular rooms, project through one of the octagonal sides of the shell. A narthex once led to the palace.

The floor plan of San Vitale only begins to convey the effect of the complex, interpenetrating interior spaces of the church. The dome rests on eight large piers that frame the exedrae and the sanctuary. These two-story exedrae open through arches into outer aisles on the ground floor and into galleries on the second floor. They expand the circular central space physically and create an airy, floating sensation, reinforced by the liberal use of colored veined marble veneer and colored glass and gold tesserae in the surface decoration. In the vault over the altar, angels support the Lamb of God, and in the conch of the sanctuary apse, an image of Christ enthroned is flanked by Saint Vitalis and by Bishop Ecclesius, who presents a model of the church to Christ (fig. 7-14).

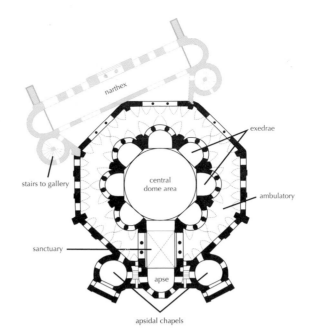

7-13. Plan and cutaway drawing of the Church of San Vitale, Ravenna, Italy. 526–47

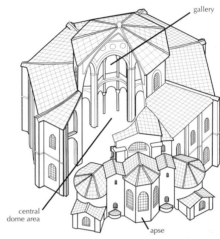

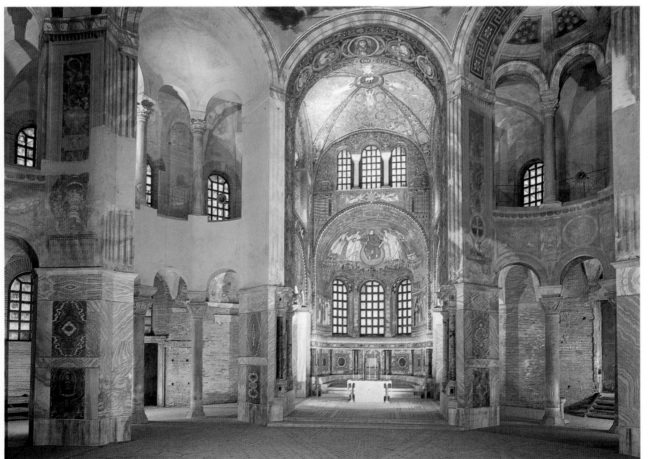

7-14. Church of San Vitale. View across the central space toward the sanctuary apse with mosaic showing Christ enthroned and flanked by Saint Vitalis and Bishop Ecclesius

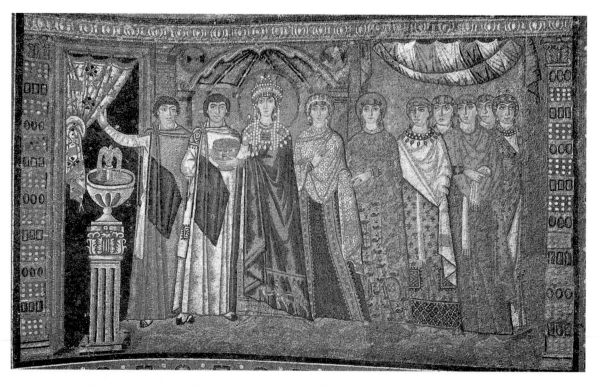

7-15. Empress Theodora and Her Attendants, mosaic on south wall of the apse, Church of San Vitale. c. 547. 8'8" x 12' (2.64 x 3.65 m)

Theodora's head is adorned with a huge pearled crown and golden halo. Because of these ornaments, she seems almost like a holy image. She may well have worn the extraordinary pearls in her ostentatious imperial regalia as protection, for pearls were believed to be an antidote for poison and disease. Theodora died, probably of cancer, in 548, only a year after the dedication of this church and its mosaics.

Justinian and Theodora may never have set foot in Ravenna, but two large mosaic panels that face each other across the apse make their presences known. Theodora, followed by her sisters and ladies of the court, carries a huge golden chalice, or cup, studded with jewels (fig. 7-15). She presents this as a precious offering to Christ—emulating the Magi, wise kings from the East, whom Christians believe brought valuable gifts to Jesus at his birth. The three Magi are depicted in the embroidered panel at the bottom of her purple robe. The chalice, in its function as a wine goblet, also represents an offering for the Mass, the religious ceremony performed during communal Christian worship. At the central core of the Mass, the ritual of Eucharist identifies the body and blood of Christ with the substances of bread and wine, which Jesus had instructed his followers to eat and drink in remembrance of him.

The empress and her ladies stand beside a fountain at the entrance to the women's gallery. The open door and curtain are classical **illusionistic** devices, but here the mosaicists deliberately avoided making them space-creating elements and instead turned them into flat two-dimensional patterns. Even nature plays tricks, for the figures cast no shadows but stand in pools of yellow light. By the sixth century, the early interest Christian artists had shown in capturing the appearance of the material world had given way to a newer, hieratic style: a formal, stately, and static mode of presenting religious imagery with which artists sought to convey a timeless, supernatural world.

The Church of Sant'Apollinare in Classe was consecrated two years after San Vitale, in 549. Designed on a simple basilica plan, its layout emphasizes the forward processional movement from the entrance to the semicircular apse at the end of the nave. In the grand mosaic that decorates the conch of the apse (fig. 7-16), a jeweled cross with the face of Christ at its center symbolizes the Transfiguration—the moment when Jesus revealed his divinity to the apostles Peter, John, and James (here represented as three sheep). The Hand of God reaches down from glowing clouds and the Old Testament prophets Moses and Elijah emerge from clouds at each side, symbolically linking the Old Testament with the New and attesting to the coming of the Messiah. Saint Apollinaris, the first bishop of Ravenna, is shown below the cross as an orant; the twelve lambs flanking him, and the twelve sheep emerging from the buildings represented on the wall above, represent Jesus' twelve apostles.

The mosaics on the wall above the apse were added in the seventh and ninth centuries. Christ, holding the Gospels, is portrayed with a cross inscribed in his halo, an indication of his sacrifice as a human being. He is flanked by figures symbolizing the Four Evangelists—Matthew, Mark, Luke, and John—the authors of the four Gospels. Saint Matthew is represented by an angel, Saint Mark by a lion, Saint Luke by an ox,

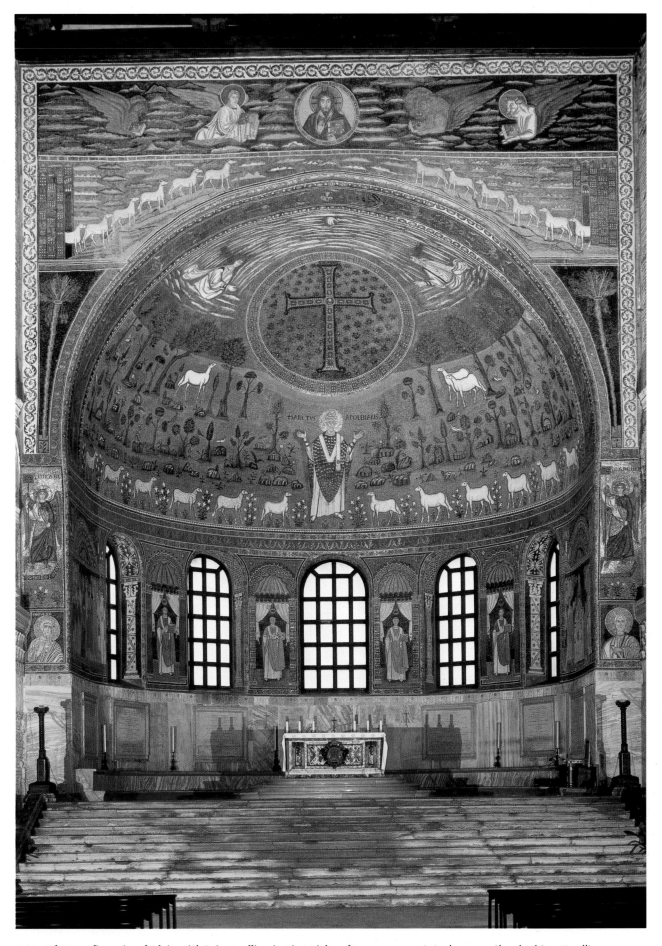

7-16. *The Transfiguration of Christ with Saint Apollinaris, First Bishop of Ravenna,* mosaic in the apse, Church of Sant'Apollinare in Classe, the former part of Ravenna (Classis), Italy. 533–49. Mosaic on the wall above the arch leading to the apse, 7th and 9th centuries

Christian Symbols

Symbols have always played an important part in Christian art. Some were devised just for Christianity, but most were borrowed from pagan and Jewish traditions and adapted for Christian use.

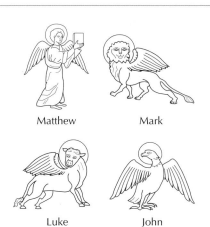

Matthew   Mark

Luke   John

Dove

The Old Testament dove is a symbol of purity, representing peace when it is shown bearing an olive branch. In Christian art a white dove is the symbolic embodiment of the Holy Spirit.

Four Evangelists

The evangelists who wrote the New Testament Gospels are traditionally associated with the following creatures: Saint Matthew, a man (or angel); Saint Mark, a lion; Saint Luke, an ox; and Saint John, an eagle.

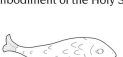

Fish

The fish was one of the earliest symbols for Jesus Christ. Because of its association with baptism in water, it came to stand for all Christians.

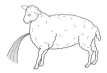

Lamb (Sheep)

The lamb, an ancient sacrificial animal, symbolizes Jesus' sacrifice on the cross as the Lamb of God, its pouring blood redeeming the sins of the world. A flock of sheep represents the apostles—or all Christians—cared for by their Good Shepherd, Jesus Christ.

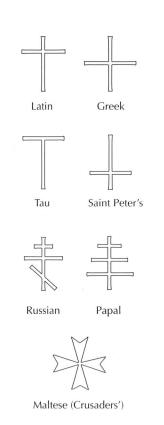

Latin   Greek

Tau   Saint Peter's

Russian   Papal

Maltese (Crusaders')

Cross

The primary Christian emblem, the cross, symbolizes the suffering and triumph of Jesus' crucifixion and resurrection as Christ. It also stands for Jesus Christ himself, as well as the Christian religion as a whole. Crosses have taken various forms, the two most common in Christian art being the Latin and the Greek.

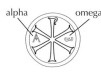

alpha   omega

alpha and omega
I and X

Monograms

Alpha (the first letter of the Greek alphabet) and omega (the last) signify God as the beginning and end of all things. This symbolic device was popular from Early Christian times through the Middle Ages.

and Saint John by an eagle (see "Christian Symbols," left).

Christians required large numbers of books for religious services, for education, and for study and meditation. Until the invention of printing, all books were **manuscripts**—that is, they were written by hand on **parchment**, specially prepared animal skin. If they were decorated or illustrated, today we say that they were *illuminated*. During the Byzantine period and the European Middle Ages, many illuminated manuscripts were made in monasteries and convents, religious communities where devout men and women (monks and nuns) withdrew from the secular world to devote their lives to study and prayer.

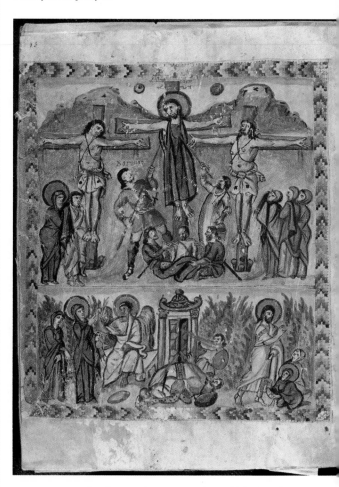

7-17. Page with *The Crucifixion*, from the *Rabbula Gospels*, from Beth Zagba, Syria. 586. 13¼ x 10½" (33.7 x 26.7 cm). Biblioteca Medicea Laurenziana, Florence

The manuscript page (called a **folio**) illustrated in figure 7-17 comes from an illuminated manuscript of the Gospels signed by a monk named Rabbula and completed in February 586, at a monastery in Beth Zagba, Syria. It depicts crucial events from the life of Jesus. Both upper and lower illustrations incorporate the convention of narrative. The upper illustration tells the story of the Crucifixion. Jesus was said to be crucified in the company of two criminals, one penitent and the other not. As he died, he was

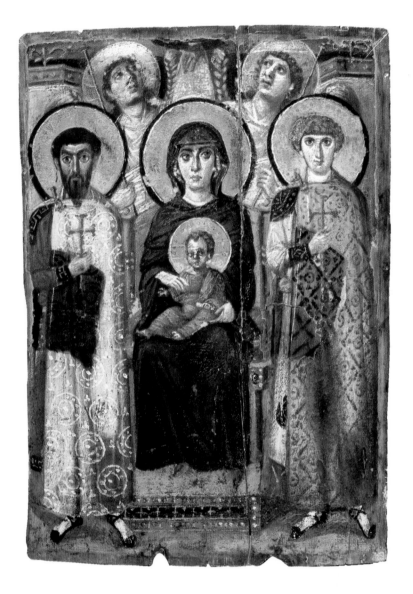

7-18. *Virgin and Child with Saints and Angels,* icon, Monastery of Saint Catherine, Mount Sinai, Egypt. Second half of 6th century. Encaustic on wood, 27 x 18⁷⁄₈" (69 x 48 cm)

tormented by Roman soldiers: one extending a sponge on a pole with vinegar instead of water for him to drink, another stabbing him in the side with a spear, and others gambling for his clothes. Jesus is dressed in a long purple robe, called a colobium, signifying royal status in the Byzantine world. Jesus' mother, the Virgin Mary, and Saint John the Evangelist watch the Crucifixion from the far left.

In the lower register, Jesus' empty tomb stands with open doors, proving that Christ rose from the dead. The soldiers guarding his burial place have fallen asleep. At left, an angel announces the Resurrection to the Marys, and at right, Jesus appears to female followers who came to his tomb. That events take place in an otherworldly setting is indicated by the lush foliage and glowing bands of color in the sky.

Many Eastern Christians prayed to Christ, Mary, and the saints while looking at images of them in manuscripts or on painted panels known as **icons.** Church doctrine toward the veneration of icons distinguished between idolatry—the worship of images—and the veneration of an idea or holy person depicted in a work of art. Icons were thus accepted as aids to meditation and prayer: the images were thought to act as intermediaries between worshipers and the holy personages they depicted.

In the eighth century, in a reaction against the veneration of images known as **iconoclasm**, conservative churchmen destroyed the icons. A few very beautiful examples survived in isolated places like the Monastery of Saint Catherine on Mount Sinai, Egypt. Among the finest is the *Virgin and Child with Saints and Angels* (fig. 7-18). The humble, earthly mother of Jesus, the Virgin Mary as Theotokos, bearer of God, was viewed as a powerful intercessor, or go-between, who could appeal to her Divine Son for mercy on behalf of repentant Christians. She was also called the Seat of Wisdom, and many images of her, like this one, show her holding Jesus on her lap in a way that suggests that she has become an imperial throne for her son. She is flanked by the Christian warrior-saints Theodore (left) and George (right)—legendary figures said to have slain dragons. Symbolically the warrior-saints represent the triumph of the Church over the "evil serpent" of paganism. The artist who painted the Christ Child, the Virgin, and the angels worked in an illusionistic, Roman-derived manner and created almost realistic figures. The male saints are much more stylized, and the artist barely hints at real bodies beneath the richly

Pillar-Sitting Saints

Determined to avoid the temptations and distractions of the material world, some deeply religious men and women left their homes and went to live in the wilderness. They led solitary lives dedicated to prayer and self-mortification either as hermits living entirely alone or as monks or nuns in a religious community. They looked to Saint Anthony of Egypt (c. 250–355 CE) as their spiritual role model.

Well-known hermits might find their solitude interrupted or disturbed by people wanting to join them or hoping to learn from the spiritual benefits of the hermits. Some hermits took extreme measures to ensure their privacy. Saint Simeon Stylites, finding life as a monk not rigorous enough, climbed to the top of a pillar where he lived for the rest of his life (increasing the height of the pillar to "40 cubits" high). Since many pilgrims flocked to see this wonder, Saint Simeon preached as well as prayed from the top of his column. At his death a church and monastery were constructed around the pillar.

Saint Simeon had many emulators. Men who lived on the tops of pillars were known as *stylites,* from the Greek word for pillar. Their pillars varied in size and height, and some stylites even built huts on top. They received food from disciples below, sent up in a basket. Stylites could be found in Egypt, the Near East, and Greece in the Early Middle Ages.

Saint Anthony of Egypt organized a community of hermits at the beginning of the fourth century. Later, in the sixth century, Saint Benedict drew up a set of practical rules for community living in the service of religion (the Benedictine Rule). These precepts became the foundation for organized Western monasticism.

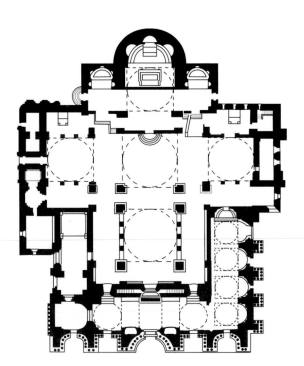

7-19. Plan of the Cathedral of San Marco, Venice. Begun 1063

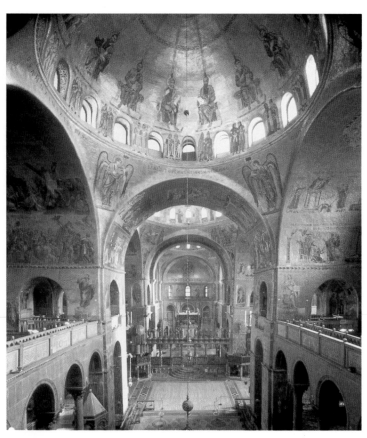

7-20. Cathedral of San Marco. View looking toward apse

The church is the third one built on the site. It is both the palace chapel and the martyrium where the bones of the patron of Venice, Saint Mark, are preserved. This great multidomed structure, consecrated as the Venice Cathedral in 1807, has been reworked continually, right to the present day.

patterned textiles of their cloaks. From their emergence in early Byzantine art, icons play an increasingly important role in later periods.

Later Byzantine Art

The first great age of Byzantine art, which began with the reign of Justinian I in the sixth century, ended with a period of iconoclasm in the eighth century. In 726, Emperor Leo III decreed that all religious images were idols and should be destroyed. Innumerable examples of devotional art were demolished before this policy was reversed, first in 787 by Empress Irene and then finally in 843 by Empress Theodora. A second golden age of Byzantine art began in 867 under the leadership of an imperial dynasty from Macedonia and lasted until Christian Crusaders from the West occupied Constantinople in 1204. Byzantine culture flourished once more in the fourteenth and early fifteenth centuries up to the time that Muslim Ottoman Turks conquered Constantinople in 1453.

While little Byzantine art survives from Constantinople, the northeastern Italian city of Venice holds rich treasures of middle and late Byzantine art. At the end of the tenth century, Constantinople granted Venice a special trade status that allowed its merchants to control much of the commercial exchange between western Europe and the Eastern Empire. With untold wealth flowing into the city's coffers, Venice's ruler, the doge, in 1063 commissioned a splendid church to replace an older chapel, holding the relics of the martyred patron saint of Venice, Saint Mark the Apostle. Venetian architects looked to the Byzantine domed church for inspiration, especially the no longer extant Church of the Holy Apostles in Constantinople. The plan of the Cathedral of San Marco (fig. 7-19) is based on the Greek cross (a cross with four arms of the same length). Each of its five square units is covered with a great dome. Separated by barrel vaults and supported by pendentives, these domed compartments, covered with golden mosaics, produce a complex space in which each individual dome vies for attention in seeming competition with the high altar and choir (fig. 7-20). As at Hagia Sophia (see fig. 7-12), windows encircle the bases of the domes, and gold mosaics sweep over the vast spaces.

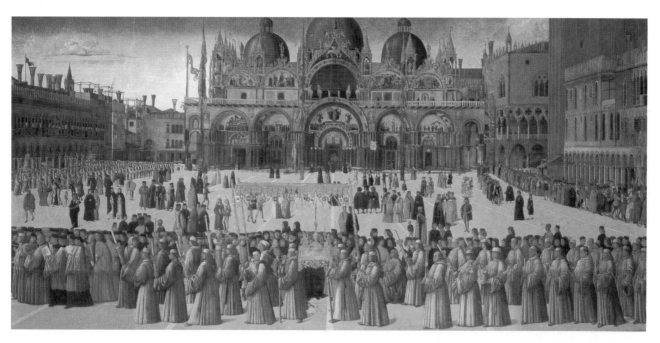

7-21. Gentile Bellini. *Procession of the Relic of the True Cross before the Church of San Marco.* 1496. Oil on canvas, 10'7" x 14' (3.23 x 4.27 m). Galleria dell'Accademia, Venice

Over the centuries the masonry exterior of the church was encrusted with marble and mosaics. An early Renaissance painting by the Venetian artist Gentile Bellini (Chapter 11) shows the facade of San Marco as it appeared in 1496 (fig. 7-21). The four bronze horses, probably Greek, over the central door were looted from Constantinople in 1204. The bulbous shells encasing the domes were added in the twelfth or thirteenth century, and the frothy Gothic curlicues and pinnacles adorning the second story date to the fifteenth century. The doge's palace stands immediately to the right of the church.

The religious procession depicted in the painting was a contemporary historical event. In 1444 a relic of the True Cross (believed by devout Christians to be a fragment of the cross on which Jesus was crucified) was carried in a procession around the piazza of St. Mark's. A miraculous healing occurred, which was attributed to the holy relic. The golden reliquary (protective case) housing the relic can be seen under the canopy carried in the center of the procession.

All over the Byzantine world, eleventh-century artists looked with renewed interest at models from the past, studying both classical art and the art of Justinian's era. A stark mosaic image of *Christ Pantokrator*, ruler of the world, fills the central dome of the Church of the Dormition at Daphni, Greece (fig. 7-22). This awe-inspiring effigy, hovering in golden glory, is a powerful evocation of the promised Last Judgment, when Christ will reward the faithful

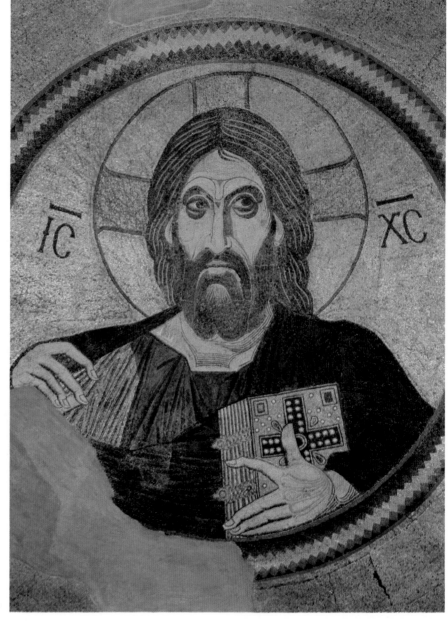

7-22. Christ Pantokrator, mosaic in the central dome, Church of the Dormition, Daphni, Greece. Central dome, c. 1080–1100

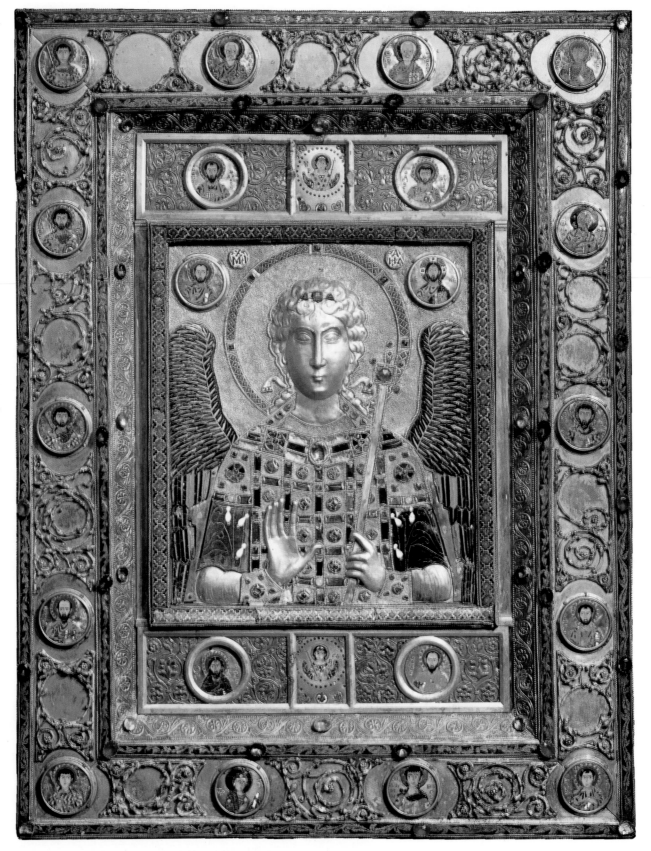

7-23.
*Archangel
Michael,*
icon. 10th
century.
Silver gilt
and enamel,
19 x 14"
(48 x 36 cm).
Treasury
of the
Cathedral of
San Marco,
Venice

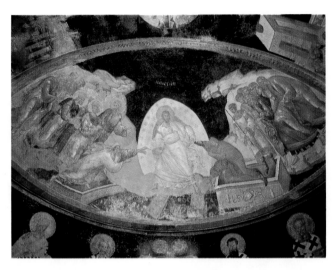

7-24. Anastasis, painting in the apse of the funerary chapel, Church of the Monastery of Christ in Chora (now Kariye Muzesi), Istanbul, Turkey. Chapel, c. 1315–21

and punish the sinners. The artists conceived their composition in terms of an intellectual rather than a physical ideal. They eliminated all unnecessary detail and focus on the huge eyes and clawlike hand grasping the jeweled Bible. The linearity of the face, hair, and robe is a far cry from the art of the classically inspired mosaicists at Santa Maria Maggiore in Rome more than six centuries before.

During the tenth, eleventh, and twelfth centuries, artists also produced luxury items for the Byzantine church and court, using precious materials such as silver and gold, jewels and enamels, and working them with impeccable skill and aesthetic sensibility. One of the prizes the Crusaders took back to Venice in 1204 was a silver gilt-and-enamel icon of the archangel Michael (fig. 7-23). The angel's head and hands are executed in relief in the **repoussé** technique (pounded out from the back of the plate). Halo, wings, and garments are detailed in delicate **cloisonné** enamel, and the framing borders are inset with enamel roundels. (Cloisonné is produced by soldering fine wires in the desired pattern to a metal plate and then filling the cells—**cloisons**—with powdered colored glass. When the object is heated, the glass powder melts and fuses onto the surface of the metal to create small, jewel-like sections.) Although the angel is portrayed in timeless youthfulness, the dazzling patterns remove the image from the physical world. The sheer artistry of this icon seems to lift the image to a plane where light and color supplant form, and material substance becomes pure spirit.

A third flowering of Byzantine art began after Western Crusaders, who occupied Constantinople in 1204, were expelled from the city in 1261. The patronage of emperors, wealthy courtiers, and the Church stimulated renewed church building and renovation. In the early fourteenth century, an elaborately painted funerary chapel was added to the former Church of the Monastery of Christ in Chora, Constantinople (later a mosque and now a museum, Kariye Muzesi). A painting symbolic of the Resurrection of Christ, known as the *Anastasis*, is situated in the apse conch (fig. 7-24). Artists in western Europe usually depicted the Resurrection as the triumphant Christ emerging in glory from his tomb. The Eastern Church, as we see in this example, instead depicts Christ descending into hell to rescue Adam and Eve (the first humans) and other devout people from Satan. Christ, dressed in white, is backed by a star-studded **mandorla,** or almond-shaped light. He has trampled down the doors of hell; tied Satan into a helpless bundle; and shattered locks and chains, which lie scattered over the ground. He drags the elderly Adam and Eve from their open sarcophagi with such force that their bodies almost seem airborne.

The third great age of Byzantine art coincided with a time of close commercial ties with Russia, where Christianity had been introduced in the late tenth century. Eastern churches in Russia followed the traditional Byzantine plan of a dome over a Greek cross, but over the centuries this led to a spectacular architectural style epitomized by the Cathedral of Saint Basil the Blessed in

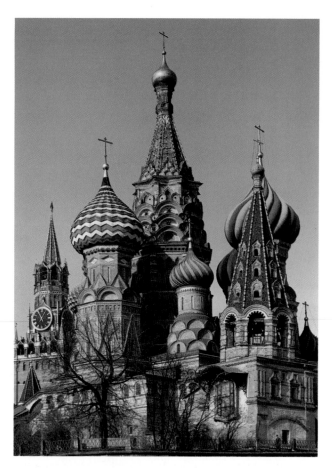

7-25. Barma and Postnik. Cathedral of Saint Basil the Blessed, Moscow. 1555–61

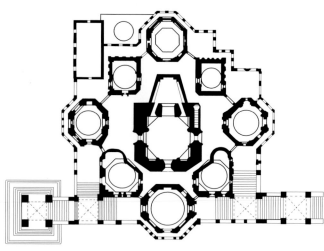

7-26. Plan of the Cathedral of Saint Basil the Blessed

Moscow (fig. 7-25). The first Russian czar, Ivan IV, known as Ivan the Terrible (1530–1584), commissioned the church, and the architects Barma and Postnik designed and constructed it (1555–1561). One of its most striking features is the combination of a Byzantine domed church plan with the traditional Russian, steeply pitched tent roof called a **shater**, developed to keep dangerously large accumulations of snow from piling up on the roof. The large, central *shater* seems to have spawned a brood of lesser, budlike domes, each with its own tall drum. The multiplication of shapes and sizes and the layering of the surfaces with geometric relief elements all work to distract us from the underlying design—a central building plan surrounded by four arms ending in domed octagons and four domed cubical areas (fig. 7-26). This dramatic building shows the evolution of Byzantine art into a distinctly national style.

The use of icons, so significant in Byzantine art, assumed great importance in Russia. Many icons were believed to have been created miraculously and were thought to have magical protective and healing powers. The remarkable icon of *The Old Testament Trinity (Three Angels Visiting Abraham)* was painted between about 1410 and 1420 by the famed artist-monk Andrey Rublyov (fig. 7-27). The theme represents the dogma of

the Trinity—one God in three Persons—a great challenge for artists. One solution used in late medieval works was to show three identical divine individuals—here, three angels—to suggest the idea of the Trinity. The subject was inspired by an Old Testament story of the Hebrew patriarch Abraham and his wife, Sarah, who entertained three strangers who were in fact God represented by three divine beings in human form (Genesis 18). Abraham and Sarah's home and the oak of Mamre are barely visible above the angels; their food becomes a chalice on an altarlike table. Rublyov conveys a sense of spirituality in this work by using Byzantine conventions, including simple contours, elongation of the body, and a focus on a limited number of figures. The sweet, poetic mood, however, is his own invention.

In the fifteenth century, the Byzantine style took on a new life just as western European artists were also beginning to look anew at the world around them. In 1453, however, the troops of the Ottoman sultan Muhammad II broke through the walls of Constantinople, and the last Byzantine emperor died in the onslaught. The Eastern Empire became part of the Islamic world, which had its own sumptuous yet refined aesthetic heritage.

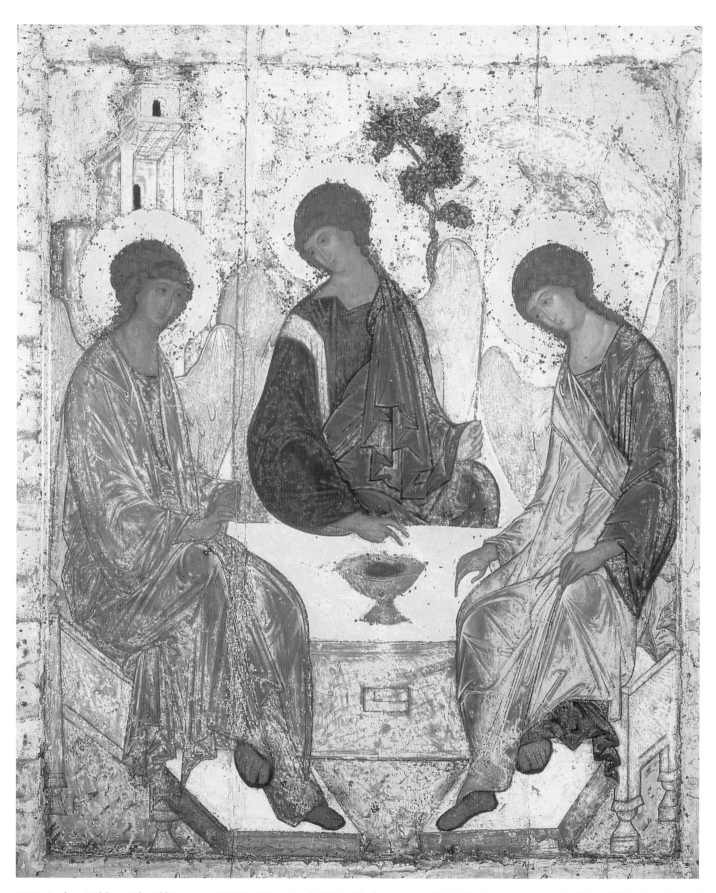

7-27. Andrey Rublyov. *The Old Testament Trinity* (*Three Angels Visiting Abraham*), icon. c. 1410–20. Tempera on panel, 55¹/₂ x 44¹/₂" (141 x 113 cm). Tretyakov Gallery, Moscow

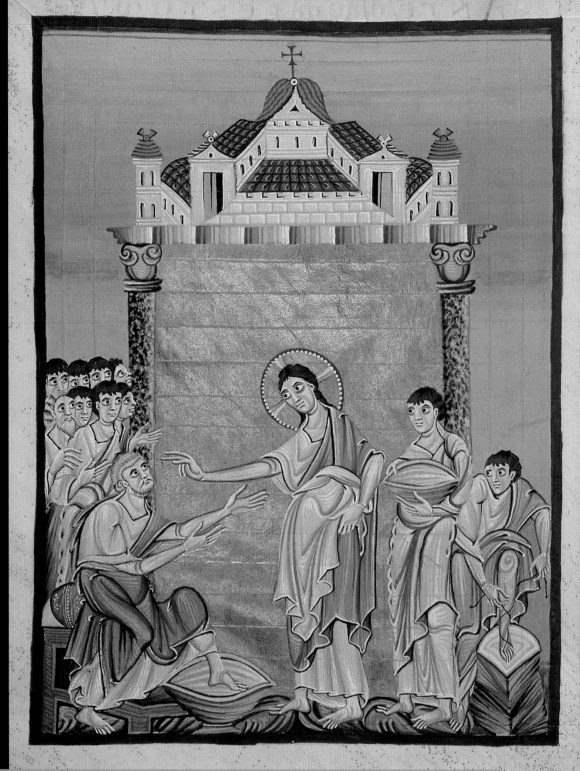

(*left*) **Page with *Christ Washing the Feet of His Disciples***, *Gospels of Otto III*. c. 1000. Staatsbibliothek, Munich

(*right*) **Page from Koran (*surah 47:36*)** in kufic script, from Syria. 9th century. Ink, pigments, and gold on vellum, 9³⁄₈ x 13¹⁄₈" (23.8 x 33.3 cm). The Metropolitan Museum of Art, New York Rogers Fund, 1937 (37.99.2)

Illuminated Manuscripts

Most early surviving books in the West are *codices* (singular *codex*), many of them hand-painted with scenes and decorative elements called *illuminations*. The scene shown here was created on a leaf of an *illuminated manuscript* made for the German Emperor Otto III nearly 1,000 years ago. Its tempera-paint colors are still fresh, and the section of burnished gold behind the main figures lends the scene a sense of shimmering otherworldliness. The pores of the animal skin give a rich texture to the margins of this vellum leaf.

Calligraphy

The page of script seen here, from a ninth-century Koran, the holy book of Islam, was written on vellum in an early Arabic script called *kufic*. The writing is calligraphic, meaning that it is handwritten and highly ornamental. *Calligraphy* is the highest art in the Islamic tradition, for it carries the word of God as revealed to the Prophet Muhammad and set forth in the Koran. The small red marks are pronunciation guides (or diacritics). The chapter title is embedded in the burnished gold pattern at the bottom of the sheet. Calligraphy is a major art form of the cultures of East Asia.

K E Y S to Art History

EARLY BOOKS

Whether written and decorated by hand or produced from a printing press, books are portable repositories of thoughts, ideas, sentiments, and facts. The physical definition of a book is a set of sheets on which there may be writing or illustration. Sheets may be formed of *papyrus* (a marsh plant cut into strips and pressed to make a writing surface), *palm leaf* (dried, cut strips of certain palm leaves), or other vegetable fibers (flax or cotton) used to make paper; *parchment* (goatskin or sheepskin prepared to receive writing); *vellum* (kidskin, lambskin, or calfskin treated to be written on and finer than parchment); linen, silk, or other fabrics; and even *tablets* of wood or ivory bound together. The very earliest books were kept in the form of *rolls* for protection and storage, with the sheets pasted or stitched together. Today, the most common kind of book is the *codex*, in which a number of folded sheets are stitched together (*a gathering*). The codex was probably derived from the tablet form that was common in classical Mediterranean civilizations (see fig. 6-15). About 400 CE, the codex began to assume greater favor than other book forms in Europe. The scroll remained popular in Asia.

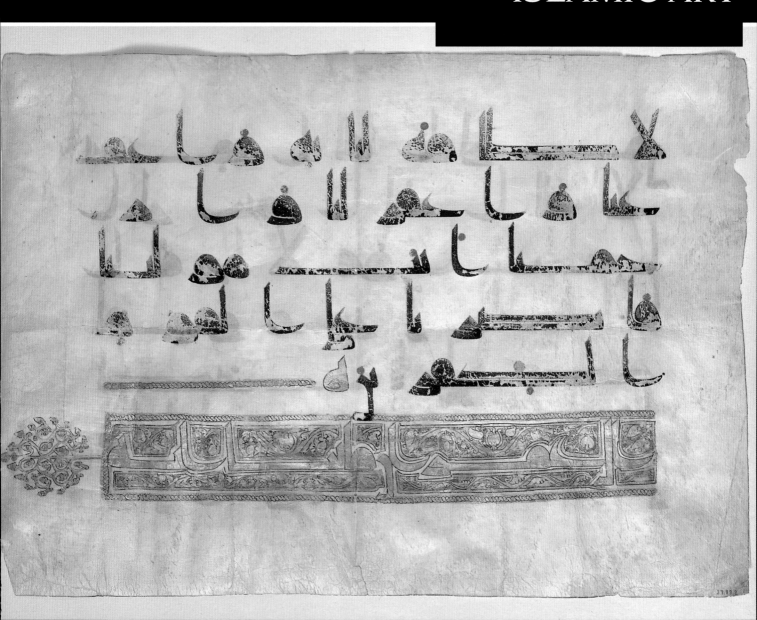

8-1. Emeterius and Ende, with the scribe Senior. Page with *Battle of the Bird and the Serpent,* *Commentary on the Apocalypse* by Beatus and *Commentary on Daniel* by Jerome, made for Abbot Dominicus, probably at the Monastery of San Salvador at Tábara, León, Spain. Completed July 6, 975. Tempera on parchment, 15¾ x 10¼" (40 x 26 cm). Cathedral Library, Gerona, Spain, MS 7[11], fol. 18v

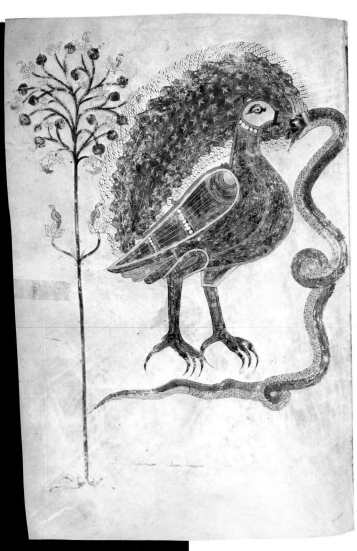

In a dazzling display of pure color, an eaglelike bird attacks a serpent, a Christian **allegory** (representation of an abstract idea using specific objects or human figures) of the triumph of Christ (fig. 8-1). The artists painted in a style called Mozarabic, which combines Christian and Muslim aesthetic traditions. Mozarabs were Christians living under Muslim rule in Spain, from which Muslim armies had driven the Visigoths who had occupied the Iberian peninsula during the last years of the Roman Empire. Christians and Muslims confronted each other not only in Spain, but also in the Holy Land, where Christians, Muslims, and Jews all laid claim to the same territory— especially to Jerusalem—as sacred to their faiths. This image of the bird and snake draws together the disparate threads of this chapter on the emergence of early medieval and Islamic art.

The dominance of **decoration** in Muslim art—pure line and color—over visual naturalism (style in which the physical appearance of the rendered image in nature is the primary inspiration) can be seen in the way the serpent is represented as a glittering, curling ribbon, and the bird as a series of red and yellow-bordered green shapes set against brilliant penwork, like cloisonné enamels in a filigree frame. The tree, with its symmetrical pattern of branches, leaves, and birds seems plucked from an Oriental carpet. The illusion of nature, so prized in Greek and Roman art and still hinted at by the Byzantines, has disappeared to be replaced by a manner of expression based on ornament alone. When adopted by Christian painters, the forms and sensibility of Islamic art seem almost shocking. Yet, European art also had a long **aniconic** (anti-image) creative tradition of Celtic spirals and interlocking, abstracted animal forms. Although medieval art emerged from this background, artists gradually began to use images as an effective teaching tool. In support of this idea, churchmen argued that since God had chosen to take on a visible human shape, the representation of material forms must be justifiable. Conservative Islamic and Jewish religious thought banned imagery; God had spoken to Muhammad, and earlier to Moses, but in their view he had chosen not to reveal himself visibly. Thus, in Islamic art words but not images came to be treasured, glorified, and adorned. These different points of view led to dramatically different arts that came together in the painting of Emeterius and Ende in tenth-century Spain.

Early Medieval Art in Western Europe

At the outset of the Middle Ages, as Roman authority crumbled, political power in western Europe passed to various Germanic and other barbarian groups, as well as to the Christian Church, the repository of tradition and learning. As patrons of the arts, clergymen sponsored the building of churches and the creation of liturgical objects, including altars, altar vessels, crosses, vestments, reliquaries (shrines for holy relics), copies of sacred books, holy images, and portrayals of the events of Christian history. At the same time, the nobility built manor houses and castles and commissioned the making of secular works of art such as jewelry, textiles, and armor, little of which survives. Stylistically, early medieval art reflects the fusion of Germanic and late Roman traditions in the former Western Empire, as well as the influence of both pre-Christian art from northern Europe and the Islamic art of Spain.

The fall of the Western Roman Empire in the fifth century left various Celtic and Germanic peoples, including the Angles, Saxons, Ostrogoths, Visigoths, Franks, and Alemani, settled in and ruling many formerly Roman territories. The artists among these groups worked in abstract patterns inherited from the Bronze and Iron Ages, often in a manner known as the animal style. This style incorporated an impressive array of generally symmetrical designs, emphasizing fantastic animal forms. The Gummersmark brooch (fig. 8-2), a large silver-gilt pin made in Denmark in the sixth century, displays intricate animal-style **motifs** (discrete elements of a design). Probably one of a pair, it was used to fasten a cloak around the wearer's shoulders. Individual motifs include spirals, birds, humans, and dragonlike animals so interlaced that one has to look carefully to make them out.

Christianity gained steadily in strength in the vacuum left by the collapse of the Empire. The Church helped to unify Europe's heterogenous population, and Christianity spread into lands such as Scandinavia and Ireland, which had never been ruled by Rome. In the eighth century, the German emperor Charlemagne sought to revive the glory of the old Roman Empire of Constantine and to reestablish an explicitly Christian regime in the West. Charlemagne's Empire united Germany and Italy under a single ruler and became a major power in medieval Europe. Other monarchies gradually assumed control in the British Isles and France, and by the year 1000, Christian Europe, formerly on the defense against Islam, was ready to become the aggressor.

Western Europeans in the early medieval period looked with dismay on the rapid advance of Islam. The presence of Muslims in Spain from the eighth century on raised fears among Christians of further Islamic inroads into Europe. Muslim rulers were often tolerant of Christians and Jews in their territories, but western and northern European leaders were rarely so broadminded. Predominantly Christian, they viewed Muslims not only as unwanted foreigners, but also as dangerous infidels.

BRITISH ISLES AND SCANDINAVIA

Another clash of cultures occurred in the British Isles. The Romans subjugated the native Celtic inhabitants of Britain in 43 CE but did not invade Ireland. During the period of Roman rule, which lasted until 406, Christianity took root in Britain and spread to Ireland, which remained under Celtic rule. After the fall of the Roman Empire, powerful Romanized British chieftains took control of different areas of Britain, vying for dominance with the help of mercenary soldiers from continental Europe. This period of struggle gave rise to the legends of King Arthur and the Round Table. The mercenaries from the Continent—Angles, Saxons, and Jutes—soon established kingdoms of their own, and the people under their rule adopted Anglo-Saxon speech and customs. Over the next 200 years, Anglo-Saxon and Hiberno-Saxon culture (*Hibernia* was the Roman name for Ireland) formed out of a fusion of these Celtic, Germanic, and Romanized British traditions.

Metalworking was one of the glories of Anglo-Saxon art. Anglo-Saxon literature, such as the epic poem *Beowulf*, is filled with references to splendid jewelry and military equipment decorated with gold and silver. An early-seventh-century burial mound, excavated in the English region of East Anglia at a site called Sutton Hoo (*hoo* means "hill"), concealed a hoard of such treasures. The grave's still-unidentified occupant was buried in an 86-foot-long ship. The vessel held weapons, armor, other equipment for the

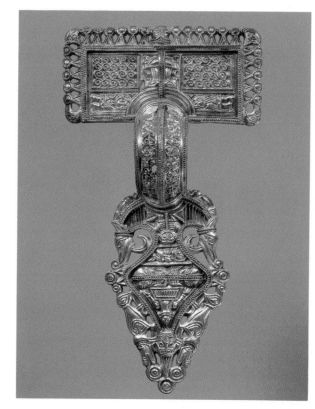

8-2. Gummersmark brooch, Denmark. 6th century. Silver gilt, height 5¾" (14.6 cm). Nationalmuseet, Copenhagen

The faceted surface of this pin seems to seethe with abstract human, animal, and grotesque forms such as the eye-and-beak motif that frames the headplate, the man compressed between dragons just below the bridge element, and the pair of crouching dogs with snapping tongues that forms the top of the foot plate.

The Medieval Scriptorium

Today presses can produce hundreds of thousands of identical copies of any book. In Europe in the Middle Ages, however, before the invention of printing from movable type in the mid-1400s, books were made by hand, one at a time, with pen, ink, brush, and paint. Each one was a time-consuming and expensive undertaking.

At first, medieval books were usually made by monks and nuns in a workshop called a **scriptorium** (plural, scriptoria), usually in a monastery or convent. As the demand for books increased, rulers set up palace workshops of both religious and lay scribes, supervised by scholars.

Before paper came into common use in the early 1400s, books were written on animal skin—either **vellum**, which was fine and soft, or parchment, which was heavier and shinier. The skins were cleaned and scraped to create a smooth surface that would absorb ink and paint, which also required time and experience to prepare. Many pigments—particularly blues and greens—were as costly as semi-precious stones. In early manuscripts, bright yellow was used to suggest gold, but later, artists used actual gold in the form of gold leaf or gold paint.

Sometimes work on a book was divided between a scribe, who copied the text, and one or more artists, who painted illustrations, large initials, or other decorations. More often in the Early Middle Ages, scribe and artist were one. Although most books were produced anonymously, scribes and illustrators sometimes signed their work or provided background information on a **colophon** (page containing information related to a book's production).

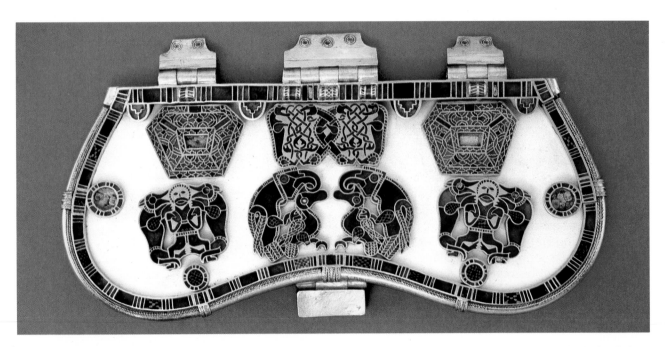

8-3. Purse cover, from the Sutton Hoo burial ship, Suffolk, England. c. 615–25. Cloisonné plaques of gold, garnet, and checked millefiore enamel, length 8" (20.3 cm). The British Museum, London

Only the decorations on this purse cover are original. The lid itself, of a rich tan-colored ivory or bone, deteriorated and disappeared centuries ago, and the white backing is a modern replacement. The purse was designed to hang at the waist, and the plaques were positioned on the cover for the wearer to enjoy from his or her vantage point.

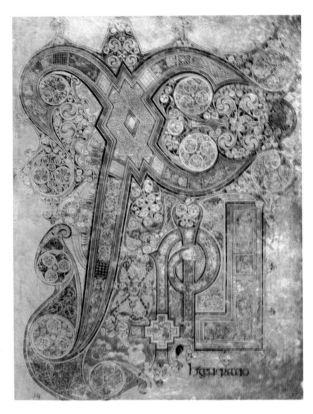

8-4. *Chi Rho Iota* **page,** Book of Matthew, *Book of Kells,* probably made at Iona, Scotland. Late 8th or early 9th century. Tempera on vellum, 13 x 9½" (33 x 24 cm). The Board of Trinity College, Dublin, MS 58 (A.1.6.), fol. 34v

The Greek letters *chi rho iota* (*XPI,* or *chri*) form the abbreviation for *Christi,* the first word in the Latin sentence *Christi autem generatio,* meaning: "Now this is how the birth of Jesus Christ came about" (Matthew 1:18). The word *autem* appears as another Latin abbreviation resembling an *h,* which is followed by *generatio* written out. The text continues on the next page. Medieval scribes had to learn a long list of standard abbreviations for Latin words, which were used like modern shorthand to save time and space in transcribing long documents or copying texts. Scribes in the courts of popes and secular rulers were even given the official title of "abbreviator."

afterlife, and such luxury items as an exquisitely worked lid for a purse (fig. 8-3).

The purse lid is decorated with intricate cloisonné enamel. The decorations on the lid come from wide-ranging sources. The designs in the top center are a form of **animal interlace**. In this type of design, growing out of the animal style popular in Scandinavia, the bodies of animals and birds are elongated into interwoven serpentine ribbons.

The pairs of animals flanking human figures at the lower right and left recall the "animal combat" theme prevalent throughout the ancient Near East (see fig. 2-8). In the center of the lid, Norse curved-beak hawks attack Celtic ducks. The rich blend of motifs on the purse heralds a complex style adopted by the Church and known as Hiberno-Saxon, which flourished in England and Ireland during the seventh and eighth centuries.

Hiberno-Saxon art is particularly well represented by large, lavishly decorated gospel books produced in monasteries in Ireland, Scotland, and England (see "The Medieval Scriptorium," page 183). The *Book of Kells*, one of the most original and inventive of the surviving Hiberno-Saxon Gospel books, was probably made in the late eighth century in a monastery on Iona, an island off the west coast of Scotland. The most celebrated folio (manuscript page) in the *Book of Kells* may be the one from the Book of Matthew that begins the account of Jesus' birth (fig. 8-4). The Greek letters *chi*, *rho*, and *iota* dominate the page. The letters create an irregularly shaped form that resembles a cluster of gold and enamel brooches. At first glance, the page seems filled with completely abstract ornament. But hidden in the dense thicket of spirals and interlaces are human and animal forms. The curve of the *rho* in the center of the page ends in the head of a red-headed youth, possibly representing Christ. Three angels hold the left vertical edge of the *chi*, and below them, just to the right of the long stroke of the letter, an otter catches a salmon and pairs of cats capture mice. The cat-and-mouse scene signals the triumph of good (embodied in the cats) over evil (embodied in the mice who try to eat the host—the Communion wafer, the mystical body of Christ). Even as monks finished the *Book of Kells*, Hiberno-Saxon culture came under threat from abroad. Seafaring bands of Scandinavians known as Vikings began to appear on the coasts of the British Isles, carrying warriors lured by the church treasuries and fertile land. The monks of Iona retreated, taking their precious Gospels to the inland Irish monastery of Kells.

At the end of the eighth century, the Vikings descended on the rest of Europe. Intermittently looting and destroying coastal and inland river communities, they were a terrifying presence in Europe for nearly 300 years. Viking bands settled in Iceland, Greenland, Ireland, England, France, Scotland, and Russia. They even established a short-lived outpost in North America after 1000.

Most Viking art is made of wood, metal, or textile; however, large memorial stones, erected both at home and abroad, are the best-preserved Viking monuments. They are called **rune stones** when covered with inscriptions in the twiglike writing of the north; those with figural decorations are called **picture stones**. Traces of pigments on both rune and picture stones suggest that they were originally painted in bright colors.

The eighth-century picture stone illustrated in figure 8-5 comes from Larbro Saint Hammers on the Swedish island of Gotland. Borders ornamented with a band of **ribbon interlace**, a complex pattern of knotted lines, surround scenes of battles and rituals associated with the cult of Odin. The bottom panel of the stone shows a large Viking ship with a broad sail cruising over foamy waves. To the Vikings, ships recalled their daring journeys and the dead warrior's passage to Valhalla, the hall where heroic souls were received by Odin, the chief Norse god. This rich Norse-Germanic mythology eventually succumbed to a militant Christianity, however, as strong monastic rule began to take hold in Scandinavia during the eleventh century. These developments, in conjunction with the rise of powerful monarchies in England and France, ended the Viking era.

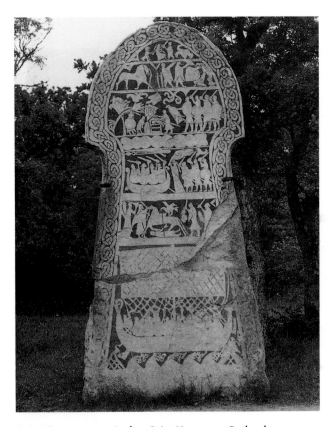

8-5. Picture stone, Larbro Saint Hammers, Gotland, Sweden. 8th century

CHRISTIAN SPAIN

The Christian and Islamic worlds met in medieval Spain. When Muslim armies arrived in the early eighth century, Spain was governed by a Germanic people known as the Visigoths, who had ruled over the indigenous Spanish population since the fall of the Western Roman Empire. The Visigoths were Arian Christians who rejected the doctrine of the Trinity and believed that Jesus was coeternal with God but not fully divine, having been made by God. Arians were considered heretics by other Christians, and eventually they adopted mainstream Trinitarian beliefs.

The Islamic conquest of Spain in 711 ended Visigothic rule. With some exceptions, Christians and Jews who did not convert to Islam but

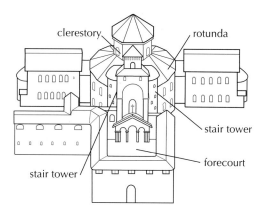

8-6. Reconstruction drawing of the Palace Chapel of Charlemagne, Aachen (Aix-la-Chapelle), Germany. Constructed 792–805

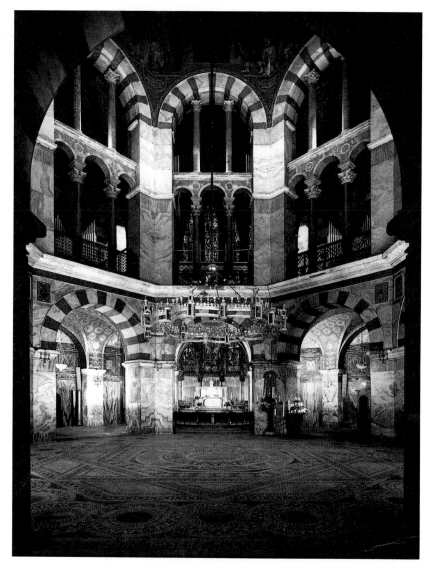

8-7. Palace Chapel of Charlemagne

paid the taxes required of non-Muslims were left free to follow their own religious practices. Christian artists adapted many features of Islamic style to fit their traditional themes. The hybrid Mozarabic style was a feature of the monasteries of northern Spain, in lands reconquered by the Christians.

Writing biblical commentaries to refute heretical beliefs became a major task of the monasteries of northern Spain. The antagonisms among Muslims, orthodox Christians, and the followers of various Christian beliefs such as Arianism provided fertile material for Spanish theologians such as Beatus. The abbot of a monastery in the north Spanish kingdom of Asturias, Beatus compiled an influential commentary on the Book of Revelation—the book of the New Testament that describes the Apocalypse, the final and fiery destruction of the world before the Last Judgment and triumph of Christ.

A copy of Beatus's *Commentary on the Apocalypse* was made for an abbot named Dominicus in the late tenth century at the Monastery of San Salvador at Tábara, in the Spanish kingdom of León. The scribe for the project was named Senior, and the illustrators were a monk named Emeterius and a nun named Ende, who signed herself "painter and servant of God." A full-page painting from this book (see fig. 8-1) illustrates Beatus's metaphorical description of the triumph of Christ over Satan. According to the text next to the illustration, a bird with a powerful beak and beautiful plumage (Christ) covers itself with mud to trick the snake (Satan). Just when the snake decides the bird is harmless, the bird swiftly attacks and kills it. Allegories such as this were popular among artists, writers, and theologians in the Middle Ages. Because allegories translate abstract ideas into concrete events and images, they communicate directly with people of almost any level of education. The painters followed an honorable tradition, for Jesus himself spoke to the people with parables.

FRANCE AND GERMANY

The Franks, another Germanic tribe, settled in northern Gaul (modern France) by the end of the fifth century. In 732 Frankish warriors turned back the Muslim invasion of Gaul, and their leaders established a dynasty of rulers known as the Carolingians, after their greatest member, Charlemagne, or Charles the Great (ruled 768–814). Charlemagne consolidated an empire in continental Europe during the second half of the eighth century, which at its greatest extent encompassed western Germany, France, part of Spain, and the Low Countries (modern Belgium and Holland). Charlemagne imposed Christianity, sometimes brutally, throughout this territory and promoted church reform through his support of the Benedictine order of monks and nuns. In 800, Pope Leo III (ruled 795–816) granted Charlemagne the title of emperor, declaring him the rightful successor to the first Christian Roman emperor, Constantine. This event served to reinforce Charlemagne's authority over his realm and strengthened the bonds between the papacy and secular government in the West.

To proclaim the glory of the new empire, Charlemagne's architects, painters, and sculptors turned to the two former Western imperial capitals, Rome and Ravenna, for inspiration. The chapel of Charlemagne's palace at Aachen (in Germany) has a central octagonal plan (fig. 8-6), as does the Church of San Vitale in Ravenna (see fig. 7-13); however, it lacks San Vitale's sophistication. The structure served as the emperor's private chapel, the church of his imperial court, a **martyrium** to house certain precious relics of saints, and, after Charlemagne's death, his mausoleum, or tomb.

The core of the building is an octagon surrounded on the first story by an **ambulatory** (passage) and ringed by a **gallery** (opening overlooking the nave) on the second floor (fig. 8-7). Alternating square and triangular bays convert the inner octagon to a sixteen-sided building. In the gallery, bays divided by diaphragm arches (arches supporting walls) support transverse barrel-vaulted bays. Columns and grilles at the gallery level form a screen and reemphasize the flat, pierced walls of the octagon. These features create a powerful vertical visual pull from the floor of the central area to the top of the vault. Another architectural feature created by Carolingian architects is the **westwork,** or monumental entrance section. Above a projecting porch, a throne room and chapel face the apse, giving the emperor an unobstructed view of the ceremonies at the high altar, and at the same time ensuring his privacy and safety. Twin towers flank this entrance complex and create a distinctive western facade. The vertical emphasis of the western towers and the equally upward rising thrust of the interior were northern contributions to Christian architecture, in marked contrast to the more horizontal treatment of Roman and Early Christian basilicas.

Charlemagne turned to the Church to help stabilize his empire and to educate his people. He called the Benedictine monks his "cultural army." One of the sources he looked to was Saint Benedict of Nursia (c. 480–c. 547), who had written his *Rule for Monasteries*, a set of practical guidelines for community life that combined work, prayer, and participation in religious services, in the sixth century. Benedictine monasticism quickly became dominant, displacing earlier forms. In the ninth century, Abbot Haito of Reichenau developed a general plan for the construction of monasteries, which survives in the library of the Abbey of Saint Gall in modern

Switzerland (fig. 8-8). The Saint Gall plan shows a basilican church with western towers and apses to house altars and relics at both ends, presumably along the traditional east-west axis (fig. 8-9). The monks' quarters lie at the south, with dormitory, refectory (dining room), and workrooms; at the east are the cemetery, hospital, and school for young monks and novices; and at the north stand the abbot's residence, guest quarters, and a hospice for the poor. Buildings for lay farmworkers and shelter for animals surrounded this central core. So efficient and functional was this plan that the Benedictine order still follows the layout today.

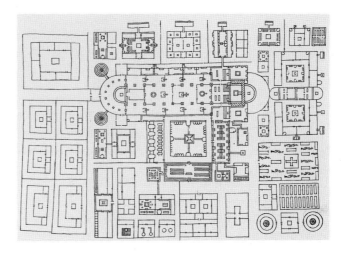

8-8. Plan of the Abbey of Saint Gall (redrawn). c. 817. Original in red ink on parchment, 28 x 44½" (71.1 x 112.1 cm). Stiftsbibliothek, St. Gallen, Switzerland, Cod. Sang. 1092

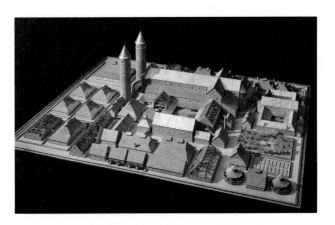

8-9. Model after the Saint Gall monastery plan (fig. 8-8), constructed by Walter Horn and Ernst Born, 1965

One of the most important kinds of work performed by the monks and nuns was the production of books. Scrupulously edited versions of key religious texts written with beautiful, clear penmanship are among the lasting achievements of the Carolingian period. The monasteries of northeastern France, around Reims, became a brilliant center of book production during the reign of Louis the Pious (ruled 814–840), Charlemagne's son and successor.

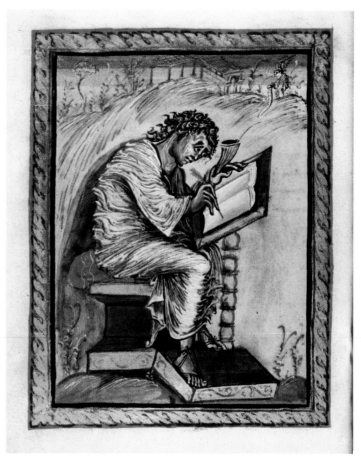

8-10. Page with *Matthew the Evangelist*, Book of Matthew, *Ebbo Gospels.* c. 816–40. Ink and colors on vellum, 10¼ x 8¾" (26 x 22.2 cm). Bibliothèque Municipale, Epernay, France, MS 1, fol.18v

A portrait of Saint Matthew from a gospel book made for Archbishop Ebbo of Reims, begun after 816 at the Abbey of Hautevillers near Reims, demonstrates the unique style that emerged there (fig. 8-10). The figure of Saint Matthew vibrates with intensity, and the acanthus leaves in the frame seem blown by a violent wind. The rapid, calligraphic style focuses attention on the evangelist's spiritual excitement as he hastens to transcribe the Word of God delivered by the angel (Matthew's symbol) in the upper-right corner. As if to echo the saint's turbulent emotions, the footstool tilts precariously, and the top of the desk seems about to detach itself from the pedestal. Following an ancient tradition, a portrait of the author introduces each Gospel, as photographs on book jacket flaps introduce the author to the reader today.

Magnificent manuscripts such as the Ebbo Gospel represent an enormous investment in time, talent, and materials. For example, hundreds of sheep were slaughtered to make the parchment on which the books were written. Books were protected with heavy, leather-covered wooden, and sometimes jeweled, covers. The elaborate book cover shown in figure 8-11 was probably made between 870–880 at one of the workshops of Charles the Bald (ruled 840–877), the son of Louis the Pious. It is not known what book it was made for, but sometime before the sixteenth century it became the cover of a late-ninth-century Carolingian manuscript known as the *Lindau Gospels.*

The Crucifixion scene on the front cover of the *Lindau Gospels* features gold figures in relief. They are formed by the repoussé technique, which we saw in the archangel Michael icon (see fig 7-23). Angels hover above the arms of the cross, and mourners twist in agony below. Over Jesus' head, hiding their faces, are figures representing the sun and moon. Jesus has been modeled in a rounded, naturalistic style suggesting a Classical influence. He stands straight and wide-eyed with outstretched arms, announcing his triumph over death and welcoming believers into the faith. The jewels, cut to form cabochons (polished, not faceted, stones), stand on tiny raised feet allowing light to penetrate and enhance their luster. The colored light of jewels recalled to the medieval viewer the description of the Heavenly Jerusalem.

THE OTTONIAN PERIOD

The heirs of Louis the Pious divided the Carolingian Empire into three parts, setting the stage for the modern division of Europe. In the tenth century, control of the eastern portion of the empire, which corresponded roughly to modern Germany and Austria, passed to a dynasty of Saxon rulers known as the Ottonians, after its three principal figures, Otto I (ruled 936–973), Otto II (ruled 973–983), and Otto III (ruled 983–1002). Otto I, who took control of Italy in 951, was crowned emperor by the pope in 962. Thereafter he and his successors dominated the papacy and appointments to other high Church offices. This union of Germany and Italy under a German ruler came to be known in the twelfth century as the Holy Roman Empire. It survived in modified form until 1806 (having lost most Italian territories by the sixteenth century).

An ivory panel shows Otto I presenting a model of a church to Christ (fig. 8-12). The ivory may once have been part of the decoration of an altar or pulpit in the cathedral of Magdeburg. For all his earthly power, Otto is a tiny figure in the company of Christ and the saints, who include Saint Peter, holding the keys to heaven, and Saint Maurice, who presents Otto to Christ.

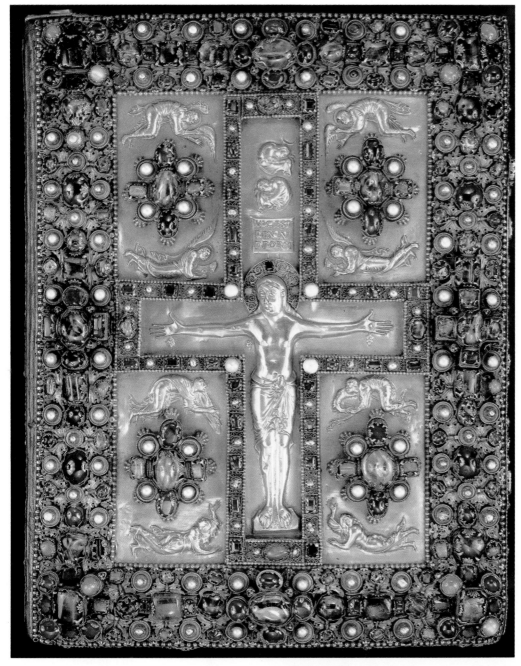

8-11. Crucifixion with Angels and Mourning Figures, outer cover, *Lindau Gospels.* c. 870–80. Gold, pearls, and gems, 13³/₄ x 10³/₈" (34.9 x 26.7 cm). The Pierpont Morgan Library, New York, MS 1

8-12. Otto I Presenting Magdeburg Cathedral to Christ, one of a series of nineteen ivory plaques, known as the *Magdeburg Ivories.* German or North Italian. c. 962–73. Ivory plaque, 5 x 4¹/₂" (12.7 x 11.4 cm). The Metropolitan Museum of Art, New York

Bequest of George Blumenthal, 1941 (41.100.157)

During the reign of Otto I, Magdeburg was on the edge of a buffer zone between the Ottonian Empire and the pagan Slavs. In the 960s, Otto established a religious center there from which the Slavs could be converted.

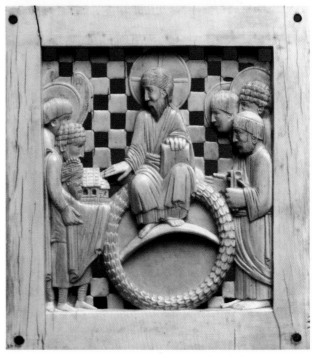

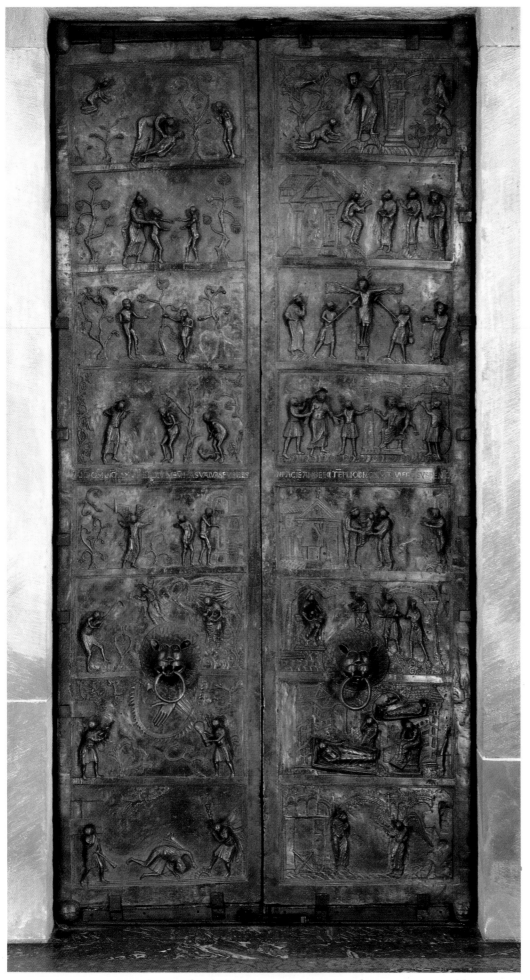

8-13. Doors of Bishop Bernward, Cathedral (Abbey Church of Saint Michael), Hildesheim, Germany.1015. Bronze, height 16'6" (5 m)

Saint Maurice was a third-century Roman Christian commander of African troops who is said to have suffered martyrdom for refusing to worship in pagan rites. In the Middle Ages he was often represented as a dark-skinned African. Christ, seated on a heavenly wreath, his feet on the arc of the earth, graciously extends his hand to receive the offering.

In the tenth and eleventh centuries, Ottonian artists in northern Europe, drawing on Roman, Byzantine, and Carolingian models, began a new tradition of large sculpture in wood and bronze that would have a significant influence on later medieval art. An important patron of these sculptural works was Bishop Bernward of Hildesheim, Germany, who was himself a skilled goldsmith. A pair of bronze doors made under his direction for his Abbey Church of Saint Michael represents the most ambitious and complex bronze-casting project since antiquity (fig. 8-13). The inscription in the band running across the center of the doors states that Bishop Bernward installed them in 1015.

The doors, standing more than 16 feet tall, are decorated with Old Testament scenes on the left and New Testament scenes on the right. The Old Testament scenes read down from the top to the bottom panel; the New Testament narrative continues on the right, upward from the bottom panel, the Annunciation, to the top one, the *Noli me tangere* (see "Iconography of the Life of Jesus," pages 162–163). In each pair of scenes, the Old Testament event can be interpreted as a prefiguration of the New Testament event. Such elaborate parallels characterize the Christian use of images. The third panel down, for example, shows on the left Adam and Eve picking the forbidden fruit of Knowledge in the Garden of

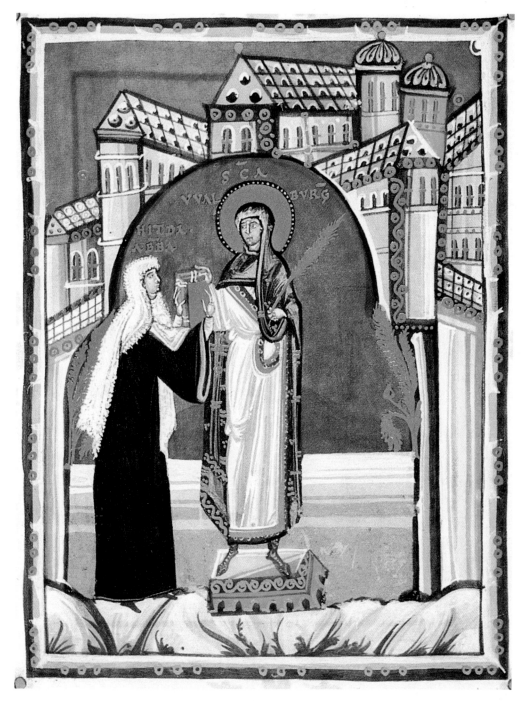

8-14. Presentation page with Abbess Hitda and Saint Walpurga, *Hitda Gospels.* Early 11th century. Ink and colors on vellum, 11³/₈ x 5⁵/₈" (29 x 14.2 cm). Hessische Landes- und Hochschul-Bibliothek, Darmstadt, Germany

Eden and thus bringing down on humankind the evils of sin, suffering, and death. This scene is paired on the right with the Crucifixion of Jesus, whose sacrifice was believed to have atoned for Adam and Eve's Original Sin. At the center of the doors six panels down, Eve and Mary sit side by side, each holding her first born son. Cain (who murdered his brother) and Jesus signify the opposition of evil and good, damnation and salvation.

Women held positions of considerable authority in the Ottonian Empire. Not long after Bernward installed his doors, Abbess Hitda

(d. 1041), the abbess of the convent at Meschede, near Cologne, commissioned a manuscript book of the Gospels. The illustration on the presentation page of the book (fig. 8-14) shows Hitda offering the volume to Saint Walpurga, her convent's patron saint. The artist has arranged the architectural lines of the convent in the background to frame the figures and draw attention to the transaction. The size of the convent underscores the abbess's position of authority. The foreground setting—a rocky, uneven strip of landscape—is meant to be understood as holy

The Life of the Prophet Muhammad

Muhammad, the prophet of Islam, was born about 570 in Mecca, a city in west-central Arabia. Mecca was a pilgrimage center to pre-Muslim Arabs, the site of the Kaaba, an ancient, cube-shaped stone building, which had been venerated by pilgrims for centuries. As a young man, Muhammad became a trader's agent, accompanying caravans across the desert. At the age of twenty-five, he married his employer, Khadija, a well-to-do widow.

Muhammad received his first revelations from God in 610, and soon thereafter was accepted as the Prophet of God first by his wife, and then by a few friends and other members of his family. As the number of his converts grew, Muhammad encountered increasing opposition from the ruling families of Mecca, who objected not only to his religious teachings, but also to the threat that they posed to the trade brought to the city by pilgrims coming to venerate the Kaaba. In 622, Muhammad and his companions fled Mecca for the oasis town of Yathrib, which they later renamed Medina, the Prophet's City. It is to this event, called the *hijra* (emigration), that Muslims date the beginning of their history. After years of fighting, Muhammad and his followers won control of Mecca in 630, and the city's inhabitants converted to the new religion, Islam, which soon spread throughout Arabia. The Kaaba in Mecca became its sacred center, toward which Muslims around the world still turn to pray.

Muslims believe in a single, all-powerful God—Allah, in Arabic—and that Muhammad is the last in a succession of true prophets of God that includes Abraham, Moses, and Jesus. Islam teaches the all-pervading immateriality of God and bans any veneration of images. In Islam, women gained rights where they had had none before, although the degree of freedom granted to women has varied considerably from country to country and from period to period.

After making a final pilgrimage to Mecca, Muhammad died in Medina in 632. His tomb there is an important Muslim pilgrimage site. A generation after Muhammad's death his revelations, which he continued to receive throughout his life, were written down and assembled in 114 chapters, or *surahs*, each divided into verses, which make up the Koran (recitation), the sacred scripture of Islam. Another body of work, the Hadith (account), compiled over the centuries, contains sayings of the Prophet, anecdotes

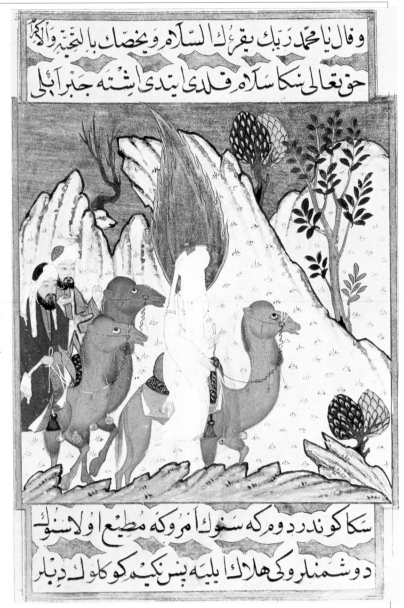

The Prophet Muhammad and His Companions Traveling to the Fair, from a later copy of the *Siyar-i Nabi* (Life of the Prophet) of al-Zarir (14th century), Istanbul, Turkey. 1594. Pigments and gold on paper, 10⅝ x 15" (27 x 38 cm). New York Public Library, New York. Spencer Collection

about him, and additional revelations. The Koran and the Hadith together form the foundation of Islamic law.

This painting shows Muhammad traveling by camel to a desert market fair in the hope of making converts. He is accompanied by his father-in-law, Abu Bakr, and his son-in-law, the warrior Ali. Abu Bakr was to become the first caliph, or successor to the Prophet, after Muhammad's death; Ali was to become the fourth caliph. The power struggle that ended in Ali's death led to the rise of one branch of Islam, the Shiite sect. Although the faces of Abu Bakr and Ali are shown, that of Muhammad, in keeping with the Islamic injunction against the making of religious images, is not. The degree of representation permitted in Islamic art varied with the place and period, depending on how this rule was interpreted.

ground, separated from the rest of the world by golden trees and the huge arch-shaped aura that silhouettes Saint Walpurga. The simple contours of the stately figures give them a monumental quality that recalls Byzantine precedents. The German court in Rome gave northern artists access to the artistic heritage of Italy, which they reinterpreted in light of their own local materials and techniques. From this groundwork during the early medieval period emerged the arts of European Romanesque culture.

The Franks beat back the Muslim armies in the eighth century and so secured Europe to develop as a Christian land. By the end of the eleventh century Christians were on the offensive, mounting crusades against the Muslims in return. Yet the Muslims were also "people of the book": monotheistic, they accepted Judaism and Christianity as forerunners of their own prophet, Muhammad. Jews, Christians, and Muslims, for all they had in common, seemed doomed to conflict.

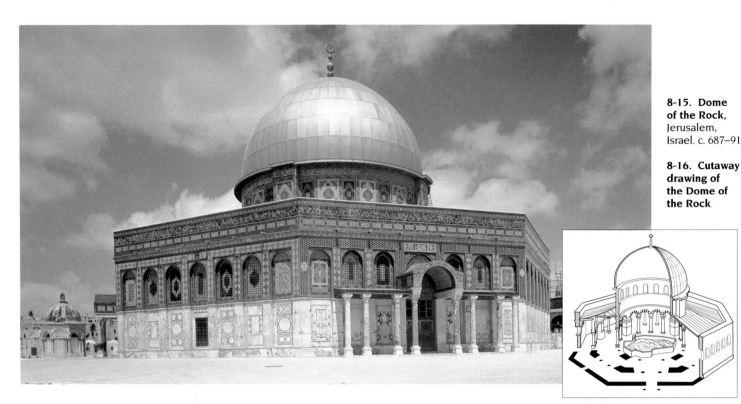

8-15. Dome of the Rock, Jerusalem, Israel. c. 687–91

8-16. Cutaway drawing of the Dome of the Rock

The Emergence of Islam

The religion called Islam ("submission to God's will") was born in Arabia in the early seventh century CE. Under the leadership of its founder, the Prophet Muhammad, as well as his successors, Islam spread rapidly, encompassing much of Africa, Europe, and Asia. Islamic art reflects these far-reaching influences, especially the Roman-Byzantine and Persian traditions. Because Islam discouraged the use of figural images, particularly in religious contexts, Islamic artists developed a rich vocabulary of nonfigural ornament, including complex geometric designs and the scrolling vines known outside the Islamic world as **arabesques**. They excelled in surface decoration, manipulating an infinite variety of highly controlled patterns and often highlighting the interplay between pure abstraction and organic form. For Muslims, abstraction helps to free the mind from the contemplation of material form, opening it to the enormity of divine presence.

MUHAMMAD

Muhammad, the prophet of Islam, was born about 570 in Mecca, in west-central Arabia. His family traced their ancestry to Ishmael, a son of the Hebrew patriarch Abraham. One night in 610 CE, since called by Muslims "The Night of Power and Excellence," Muhammad, at that time named al-Amin (the Trusted One), sought solitude in a cave on Mount Hira, a few miles north of Mecca. There the angel Gabriel is believed to have appeared to him and commanded him to recite revelations from God. At that moment, al-Amin became Muhammad, the Messenger of God (see "The Life of the Prophet Muhammad," opposite).

Islamic practice emphasizes the believer's direct, personal relationship with God through prayer. Every Muslim must observe the Five Pillars, or duties of faith. The most important of these is the statement of faith: "There is no god but God and Muhammad is his messenger." Next come ritual prayer five times a day, charity to the poor, fasting during the month of Ramadan, and, if possible, a pilgrimage to Mecca—Muhammad's birthplace and the site of the Kaaba, Islam's holiest structure. Muslims are also expected to participate in congregational worship at a **mosque** (prayer hall) on Friday. When not at a mosque, the faithful simply kneel wherever they may find themselves to pray, facing the Kaaba in Mecca.

Islam continued to expand dramatically after Muhammad's death in 632. Under four of Muhammad's closest associates, who assumed in turn the title of caliph, or successor, Muslim armies conquered Persia, Egypt, and the Byzantine provinces of Syria and Palestine. The last of these caliphs, Ali (ruled 656–661), was succeeded by a rival, Muawiya (ruled 661–680), who founded a caliphate, or dynasty, called the Umayyad. By the early eighth century, the aggressively expansionist Umayyads had reached India, conquered all of North Africa and Spain, and penetrated France to within 100 miles of Paris before being turned back.

ART DURING THE EARLY CALIPHATES

The caliphs of the Umayyad dynasty (661–750) ruled from a capital at Damascus (in modern Syria). They built shrines and mosques that reflected both their own authority and the growing public acceptance of Islam. The Dome of the Rock in Jerusalem, constructed by the Umayyads about 687–691, is the oldest surviving Islamic sanctuary (fig. 8-15). After Mecca and Medina, it is the holiest site in Islam. The building encloses a rock outcrop (fig. 8-16) that Muslims identify as

Elements of Architecture

MOSQUE PLANS

The earliest mosques were **hypostyle halls** (interior gathering rooms filled with tall, closely spaced columns) such as the Great Mosque at Córdoba (see fig. 8-17). Approached through an open courtyard called a *sahn*, their interiors are divided by rows of columns. The columns lead to a *qibla* wall, oriented toward Mecca.

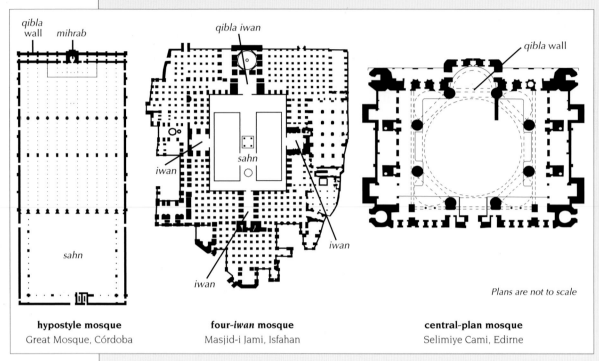

A second variety, the four-*iwan* mosque, developed in Persia in buildings like Isfahan's Masjid-i Jami (see fig. 8-23). Iwans—barrel-vaulted halls with monumental arched openings—faced each other across a central *sahn*. Related structures spread out and behind the *iwans*.

Central-plan mosques, the last type to develop, were derived from Istanbul's Church of Hagia Sophia (see fig. 7-12). They are typical of Ottoman Turkish architecture. Central-plan interiors are dominated by a large domed space uninterrupted by structural supports.

Plans are not to scale

hypostyle mosque
Great Mosque, Córdoba

four-*iwan* mosque
Masjid-i Jami, Isfahan

central-plan mosque
Selimiye Cami, Edirne

---

the site from which Muhammad ascended to the presence of God on the Night Journey. The same rock face is also associated with the creation of Adam and the place where the patriarch Abraham prepared to sacrifice his son Isaac at the command of God, making it holy to Jews and Christians, as well as to Muslims. As the area is also the site of the Temple of Solomon, it is exceptionally important to Jews.

The Dome of the Rock was built by Syrian artisans trained in the Byzantine tradition. Its centralized plan—an octagon surrounding a circular core—is derived from both Byzantine and local Christian architecture. Muslim patrons and builders delighted in complex mathematical forms; for example, the octagonal structure is based on the Arabic eight-pointed star, formed of two intersecting squares. Later Islamic architects built similar octagonal sanctuaries and saints' tombs from Morocco to China. The central space is covered by a dome on a tall drum supported by an arcade. Concentric aisles enclose the rock.

As at San Vitale in Ravenna (see fig. 7-14), the interior surfaces were originally decorated with marble at ground level and glass mosaics above. Glass mosaics also covered the upper half of the octagon's exterior but were replaced

by the Ottoman Turks in the sixteenth century with magnificent, colorful ceramic tiles. Because little stone was available for construction in much of the Islamic world, tiles became an important decorative element to conceal brick walls. Persian and Turkish tiled wall coverings remain the finest architectural use of the medium. The lower part of the octagon retains its original white marble facings, inset with patterns in colored stone.

The Dome of the Rock is a special shrine. Mosques, in contrast, provide a place for regular public worship. Mosques are built on various plans (see "Mosque Plans," above), but they typically include a **sahn**, a consecrated space or courtyard, and a large covered space to accommodate Friday prayers. The mosque is oriented toward Mecca, and worshipers pray facing the **qibla**, the wall facing Mecca. A niche called a **mihrab** differentiates the *quibla* wall from the others.

In 750, caliphs of the Abbasid dynasty overthrew the Umayyads and ruled the eastern lands of Islam until 1258. They governed in the grand manner of the ancient Persian emperors (Chapter 5) from their capitals at Baghdad and Samarra (in modern Iraq). Their long and cosmopolitan reign saw achievements in medicine, mathematics, the natural sciences, philosophy, literature, music, and art.

While the Abbasids ruled most of Islam, the Umayyads kept their authority in the West. In 750, when the Abbasid caliphs took power, a survivor of the Umayyad dynasty, Abd ar-Rahman I (ruled 756–788), fled across North Africa into southern Spain (known as *al-Andalus* in Arabic). He established himself there as the provincial ruler, or amir. From a new capital at Córdoba, the Umayyads governed al-Andalus until 1031. Beginning with Abd ar-Rahman III (ruled 912–961), the Umayyads set themselves up as equal rivals to the Abbasids by claiming for themselves the title of caliph. Their court at Córdoba became a renowned center for scholars, scientists, poets, and musicians. They maintained close contacts not just with the Islamic world but also with the Byzantine Empire.

The finest surviving example of Spanish Umayyad architecture is the Great Mosque of Córdoba. This sprawling structure was begun on the site of a Christian church in 785 and was repeatedly enlarged. The marble columns and capitals in the first **hypostyle** prayer hall (fig. 8-17; see "Mosque Plans," opposite) were recycled from the ruins of classical buildings in the region, formerly a wealthy Roman province. Two tiers of arches, one above the other, surmount the columns. The double-tiered design creates a light and airy impression and increases the height of the interior space. The distinctively shaped **horseshoe arches**—a form known from Roman times and favored by the Visigoths—came to be closely associated with Islamic architecture in the West. At the Great Mosque, these arches are distinguished by the alternation of pale stone and red brick voussoirs (oblong, wedge-shaped stone blocks). While the alternating colors and textures are decorative, the use of contrasting materials is also functional. The stone gives strength, and the brick lends flexibility and ease in achieving the circular form of the arch. Roman and Byzantine builders also used the technique, but only in utilitarian structures like defensive walls. The Muslims saw its decorative possibilities and utilized it for purposes of ornamentation.

In the tenth century, the Umayyad caliph Al-Hakam II (ruled 961–976) commissioned luxurious renovations in the Great Mosque, including enlargements and a new *mihrab* with a richly decorated space for the ruler. In front of the *mihrab*, a melon-shaped, ribbed dome seems to float over a web of intersecting arches that emerge from their supporting piers (fig. 8-18). The dome is supported by squinches—arches or brackets placed diagonally over the corners of a space to provide a base for a round or polygonal dome. Byzantine builders experimented with both pendentives (as at Hagia Sophia, see fig. 7-12) and squinches, but elaborate squinch-supported

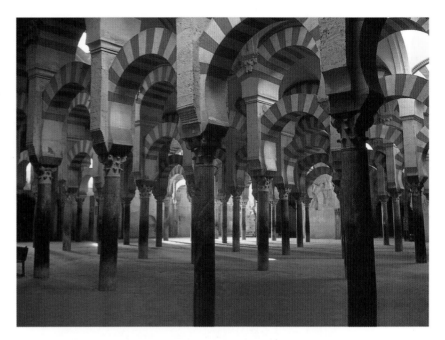

8-17. Prayer hall, Great Mosque, Córdoba, Spain. Begun 785–86

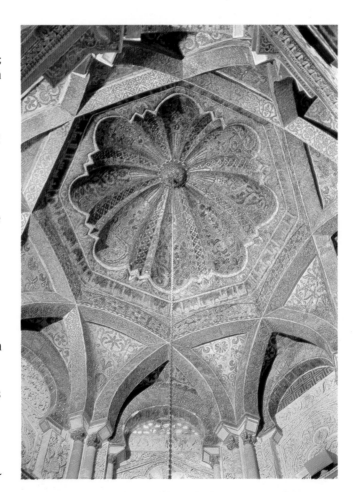

8-18. Dome in front of the *mihrab*, Great Mosque. 965

domes became a particular hallmark of Islamic interiors. At Córdoba, the squinch dome is lined with arabesques, inscriptions, geometric motifs, and stylized vegetation.

Arabic language and script have always held a unique place in Islamic society and art. As the language of the Koran and Muslim liturgy, Arabic

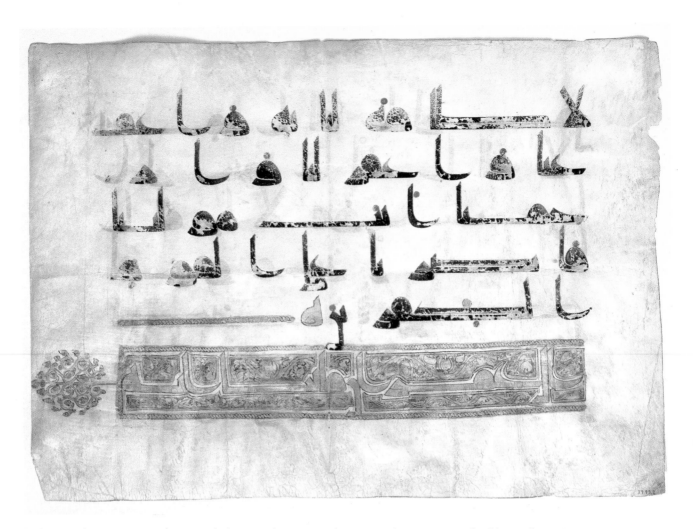

8-19. Page from Koran (*surah* 47:36) in kufic script, from Syria. 9th century. Ink, pigments, and gold on vellum, 9³/₈ x 13¹/₈" (23.8 x 33.3 cm). The Metropolitan Museum of Art, New York
Rogers Fund, 1937 (37.99.2)

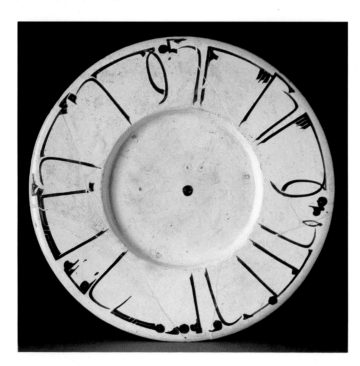

8-20. Bowl with kufic border, Samarkand, Uzbekistan. 9th–10th century. Earthenware with slip, pigment, and glaze, diameter 14¹/₂" (37 cm). Musée du Louvre, Paris

The white ground of this piece imitated prized Chinese porcelains made of fine white kaolin clay. Samarkand was connected to the Silk Road (Chapter 3), the great caravan route to China, and was influenced by Chinese culture.

is a powerful unifying force within Islam. Reverence for the Koran as the word of God extends by association to the act of writing. **Calligraphy**—the art of fine writing—is one of the glories of Islamic art.

The earliest formal script, called *kufic* (from the city of Kufa in modern Iraq), was angular and probably evolved from inscriptions on stone monuments. A page from a ninth-century Syrian Koran exemplifies a style of kufic writing common from the eighth to tenth century (fig. 8-19). Red diacritical marks (pronunciation guides) accent the dark brown ink. Horizontal strokes are elongated, and fat-bodied letters are emphasized. This Koran is written on vellum, an especially fine parchment. Rag-based paper, a Chinese invention, was imported into the Islamic world by the mid-eighth century but did not fully replace vellum and parchment there until after the year 1000, and even later in western Europe.

Arabic script was used decoratively not only in manuscripts but also in architecture and on smaller-scale objects such as textiles, ceramics, and glass. For instance, kufic-style letters decorate the white ceramics made in the ninth and tenth centuries in and around Nishapur (in modern northeastern Iran) and Samarkand

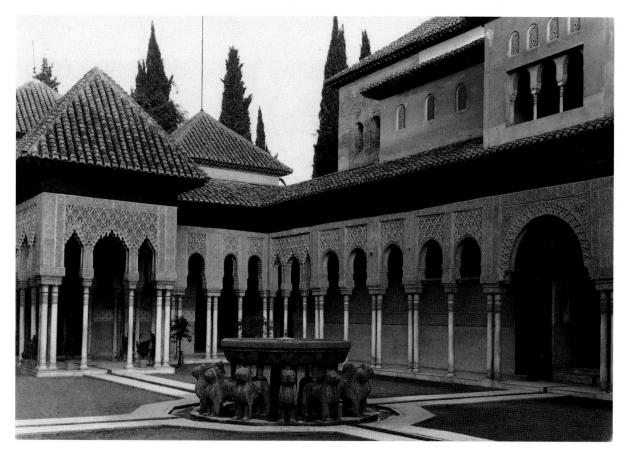

8-21. Court of the Lions, Palace of the Lions (Palacio de los Leones), Alhambra, Granada, Spain. Begun c. 1380

Granada, with its ample water supply, had long been known as a city of gardens. The twelve stone lions in the fountain in the center of this court were salvaged from the ruins of an earlier palatial complex on the Alhambra hill. The earlier structure was begun in the late eleventh century by a high Granadan official of Jewish heritage named Samuel ibn Naghralla and completed by his son Yusuf in the early twelfth century. Commentators of the time praised this complex, with its pools, fountains, and gardens. No doubt it was a source of inspiration for the builders of the later palaces.

(in modern Uzbekistan in Central Asia). Now known as *Samarkand ware*, these pieces exhibit a clear lead glaze applied over a black inscription on a white, slip-painted ceramic ground (fig. 8-20). The figures have been elongated to fill the bowl's rim, stressing their verticality. The inscription translates: "Knowledge, the beginning of it is bitter to taste, but the end is sweeter than honey." Inscriptions on Samarkand ware provide a storehouse of such popular sayings and folk wisdom.

ISLAMIC ART UNDER THE SELJUKS AND THE NASRIDS

In the ninth century, power in the Islamic world began to be broken up among more or less independent regional rulers. As the Abbasid caliphate disintegrated, one branch of the Seljuks, a Turkic people who converted to Islam in the tenth century, ruled Persia and most of Mesopotamia. Another branch of the dynasty governed much of Anatolia (modern Turkey). In Egypt, the Mamluks, the descendants of slave soldiers (*mamluk* means "slave" in Arabic) founded a dynasty that reigned from 1250 to 1517. The Umayyad dynasty in Spain ended in 1031, and small kingdoms formed around major cities such as Saragossa, Málaga, Granada, and

Seville. By the late eleventh century, the Muslims in Spain were threatened from the north by Christian armies intent upon expelling them from the Iberian peninsula. This military reconquest, as it was called, continued over a 400-year period. It ended only in 1492, with the overthrow of the Nasrid dynasty in the kingdom of Granada, the last Islamic outpost in Spain.

One of the best-preserved Islamic monuments, and the finest surviving palace in Spain, is the Alhambra, a fortified hilltop palace complex in Granada. The Alhambra was the seat of the Nasrids, who ruled the provinces of Almería, Málaga, and Granada from 1232 to 1492. The Alhambra, begun in 1238, took its present form in the fourteenth century. Literally a small town extending for about half a mile along the crest of a high hill overlooking Granada, it included government buildings, workshops, gardens, mosques, baths, servants' quarters, barracks, stables, a mint, and royal residences such as the so-called Palace of the Lions.

The Palace of the Lions was a private retreat within the Alhambra—a palace within a palace—built by Muhammad V (ruled 1362–1391) in the late fourteenth century. At its heart is the Court of the Lions (fig. 8-21), named for a marble

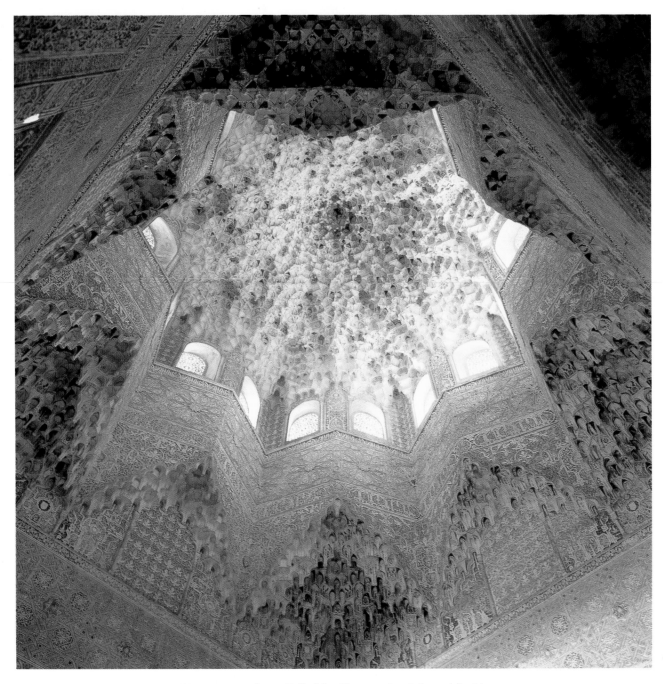

8-22. Muqarnas dome, Hall of the Abencerrajes, Palace of the Lions

fountain surrounded by stone lions. Although filled with sand today, it was originally a sunken garden. Aromatic shrubs, flowers, and small citrus trees were planted between the water channels that radiate from the fountain, dividing the courtyard into quarters evocative of the rivers of Paradise. The architectural focus of the Alhambra was largely directed inward, toward the lushly planted courtyards. They embodied the Muslim vision of paradise as a well-watered, walled garden. Indeed, the English word *paradise* comes from the Persian term for an enclosed park, *faradis*.

Four pavilions used for dining and performances of music, poetry, and dance open onto the Court of the Lions. One of these, the two-storied Hall of the Abencerrajes on the south side, may have been used year-round as a music room. Like the other pavilions (all of which had good acoustics), it is covered by a spectacularly intricate domed ceiling (fig. 8-22). The star-shaped dome rests on clusters of small squinches or nichelike cells called **muqarnas**. A honeycomb of *muqarnas* likewise covers the apex of the dome. The effect is of architectural lace, material form made immaterial.

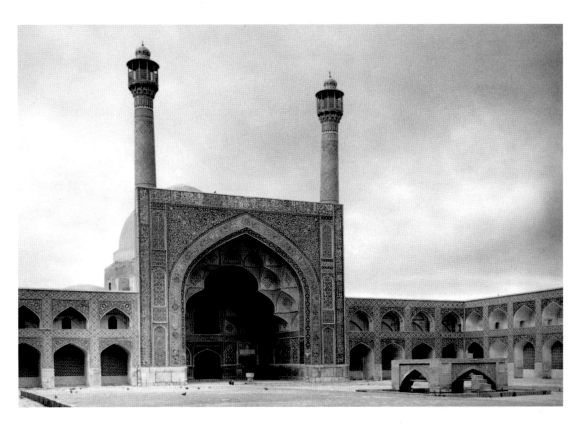

8-23. Courtyard, Masjid-i Jami (Great Mosque), Isfahan, Persia (Iran). 11th–18th century. View from the northeast

In the eastern Islamic world, the Seljuk rulers proved themselves enlightened patrons of the arts. One far-reaching development during their reign was the introduction of the four-**iwan** mosque (see "Mosque Plans," page 194). *Iwans* first appeared in **madrasas**, schools for advanced study that were the precursors of the modern university. Hundreds of these institutions were founded beginning in the eleventh century, and many are still in existence. The four-*iwan* mosque may have evolved from the need to provide separate quarters for four schools of thought within *madrasas*.

The Masjid-i Jami (Great Mosque) in the Seljuk capital of Isfahan (in modern Iran) displays the four-*iwan* layout that became standard in Persia. The building was originally a hypostyle mosque, but in the twelfth century it was refurbished with *iwans* and a monumental gate (fig. 8-23). The *muqarnas* beneath the *qibla iwan* on the south are fourteenth-century additions, and the paired **minarets** (tall, slender towers) date from the seventeenth century. Brilliant blue architectural tiles sheathe the brick facades. Also added in the seventeenth century, they are

an Islamic characteristic for which this monument is justly famous.

In the early fourteenth century, a group of Muslim Turks known as the Ottomans replaced the Seljuks in northwestern Anatolia. The Ottomans eventually conquered most of the Near East, Egypt, and the Sudan, as well as the Balkans in eastern Europe. In 1453 they captured Constantinople (renaming it Istanbul) and brought the Byzantine Empire to an end. The Church of Hagia Sophia (see fig. 7-10) became a mosque framed by graceful cylindrical towers, Ottoman minarets. The church's mosaics were destroyed or whitewashed over, and Turkish Islamic paintings were added to the interior. The huge discs, visible on the clerestory level, are preserved today as masterpieces of Ottoman calligraphy. At present, Hagia Sophia is neither a church nor a mosque, but a state museum.

For many years the largest and most powerful political entity in the Islamic world, the Ottoman Empire lasted until the end of World War I. It was not until 1918 that the modern country of Turkey was founded in Anatolia, the former heart of the empire.

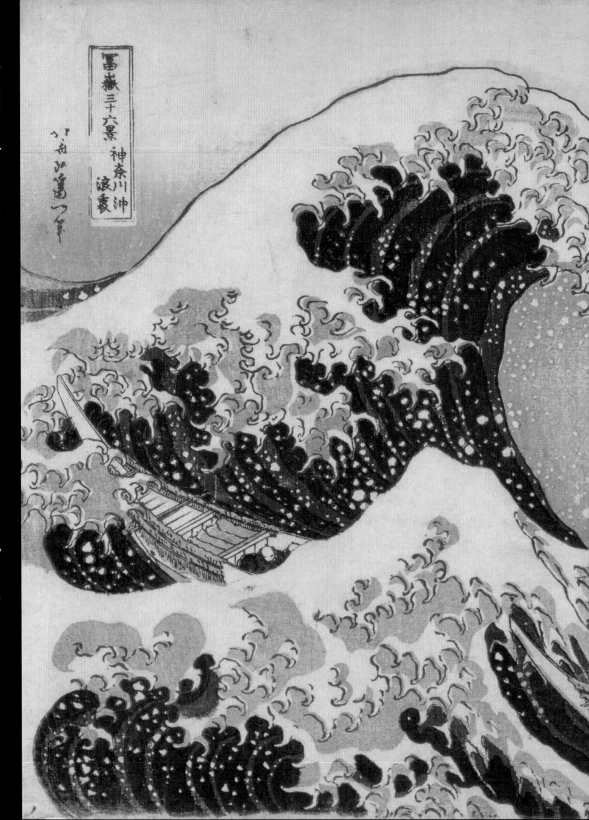

Katsushika Hokusai.
The Great Wave. Japan,
Edo period, c. 1831. Polychrome
woodblock print on paper,
9⁷⁄₈ x 14⁵⁄₈" (25 x 37.1 cm). Honolulu
Academy of Arts, Honolulu, Hawaii

Polychromy

Because this woodcut was
printed using color inks, it is a
polychrome (meaning "many
color") print. If no color from the
visible spectrum had been
used, it would be *monochromatic*
and would read as light and
dark *values*.

Flat color

The color in this print may be
described as *flat color*: it does
not have shading or modeling
to suggest a light source and
three-dimensionality. The waves
have two *hues* and three *values*:
dark blue, light blue, and white.
Only the lower part of the
sky, where the broad gray band
is inked in soft vertical streaks,
is not printed in flat color.
The effect suggests falling rain.

Palette

Artists mix their colors on a
board called a palette, so the
word palette has come to mean
the general range of colors in
a work. Hokusai uses a subdued,
predominantly cool palette of
blues with a few warm beiges.
He uses a limited palette
as well, that is, he uses very few
colors to achieve a rich effect.

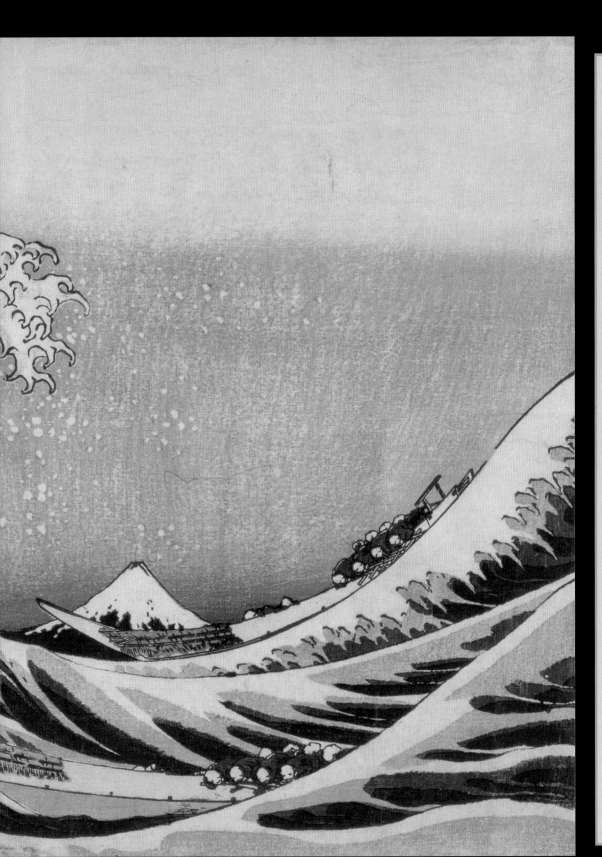

KEYS to Art History

COLOR

Color is so basic to art that we often take it for granted. But color has many properties and qualities that are important to recognize. The simplest property, perhaps, is hue: the color we think of when someone says "red" or "yellow" or "rose." The visible chromatic (color) spectrum, which can be seen in a rainbow, is traditionally divided into six hues: red, orange, yellow, green, blue, and violet. Warm colors are those between red and yellow; cool colors are those between green and violet. White, black, and the grays between them create tones or values. Value describes the degree of lightness ("high value") or darkness ("low value"). A hue raised in value by the addition of white is a tint. Correspondingly, a color mixed with black to achieve a lower, darker value is a shade. The intensity or saturation is the vividness or purity of a hue. Local color refers to the hue of an object in normal daylight, unaffected by cast shadows or reflected light from nearby objects.

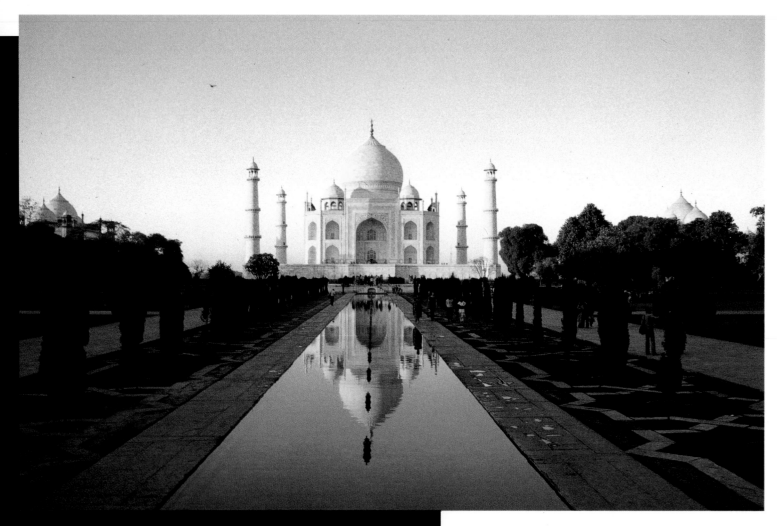

9-1. **Taj Mahal,** Agra, India. Mughal period, Mughal, reign of Shah Jahan, c. 1632–48

Visitors catch their breath. Ethereal and weightless, the building seems barely to touch the ground. Its white marble dome catches each shift of light—flushing rose at dawn, dissolving into its own brilliance in the noonday sun. Its reflection shimmers in the long pools of the garden, itself intended to invoke the paradise described in the Koran, the sacred book of Islam.

One of the most celebrated buildings in the world, the Taj Mahal (pronounced "tazh ma-**hell**," and meaning "Crown of the Palace") was built in northern India by the Mughal ruler Shah Jahan. It was constructed as a tomb for his favorite wife, Mumtaz Mahal, who died giving birth to one of their children. A guest at the splendid dedication ceremonies left us this description: "The master of all slaves, the emperor himself, honored the gathering with his presence. By his prayers and blessing he contributed to the mind of the Chaste One, now at rest in the Gardens of Paradise." In fact, the unidentified architects of the Taj Mahal (fig. 9-1) had designed a walled-in paradise on the bank of one of India's holy rivers and were following the Indian custom of providing the dead with some of the same things that had given meaning to their lives. The Mughal culture was an imported one—Turkic peoples newly converted to Islam had invaded and taken control of northern India in the eleventh century—but its rulers were open to Indian sensibilities and showed great respect for Indian artisans and artists.

The long Indian Medieval period (c. 650–1526) was a time of transition in the South Asian subcontinent. Buddhism declined as a cultural force, while artistic achievement under Hinduism soared. Hindu temples, in particular, developed monumental forms that were rich in symbolism and ritual function, with each region of India developing its own variation. Later in the Medieval period, Islam became a part of the artistic heritage of the subcontinent. Around the year 1000, Turkic peoples began military campaigns into North India. From 1206, various Turkic kingdoms, called sultanates, and dynasties ruled portions of the Indian subcontinent from several northern cities. Islamic influence reached its height under the Mughals (1526–1857).

During roughly the same period that Hinduism began to displace Buddhism in India, Buddhism reached its height in China under the Tang dynasty (618–907) (Chapter 3). Reaction to this flowering of a foreign religion on Chinese soil began during the late Tang and continued under the Song dynasty (960–1279). Cultural and artistic openness to foreign influence gave way to greater cultivation of China's own traditions, including the revival of Confucianism. Landscape emerged as a premier painting **genre** (category of artistic form), a medium that could be used to express both philosophical and personal concerns.

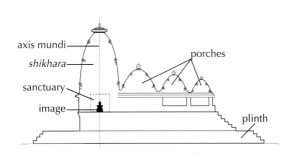

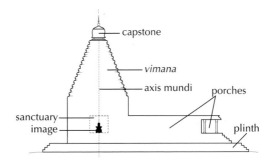

9-2. Schematic drawing of the two main Indian temple forms: northern style (left), and southern style (right)

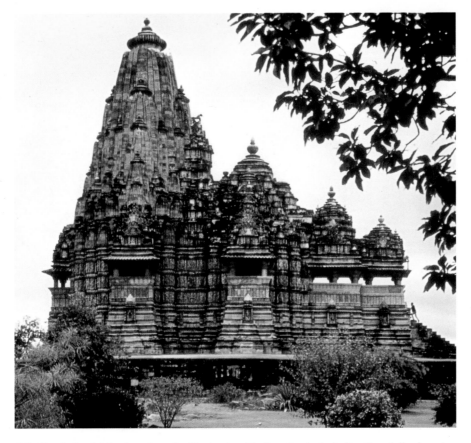

9-3. Kandariya Mahadeva temple, Khajuraho, Madhya Pradesh, India. Chandella dynasty, Early Medieval period, c. 1000 CE

In Japan, Buddhism maintained a large following. Introduced from India by way of China and Korea, Buddhism was an important force in Japanese culture by the beginning of the Heian period (794–1185). New forms of Buddhism became popular: first Esoteric Buddhism and Pure Land Buddhism, and later, Zen. Toward the end of the fourteenth century, Zen Buddhism began to influence many aspects of Japanese life and culture. Works of painting and calligraphy of great sophistication represent major forms of Zen expression.

The South Asian Subcontinent

Hinduism flourished in the Indian subcontinent during the Early Medieval period, which extended roughly from the mid-seventh to the eleventh century. With the increasing popularity of Hindu sects came the rapid development of Hindu temples. Local kings rivaled each other in the building of temples to their favored deities, and by around 1250 CE the Hindu temple had reached unparalleled heights of grandeur and engineering.

Hindu temples can be classified broadly into two types, northern and southern (fig. 9-2). The northern type, exemplified by the Kandariya Mahadeva temple (c. 1000 CE) dedicated to the god Shiva at Khajuraho in central India (fig. 9-3), is chiefly distinguished by a superstructure called a **shikhara**. The *shikhara* rises from the flat, stone roof of a windowless sanctuary, which houses an image of the temple's "resident" deity. Crowning the temple is a circular, cushionlike element from which rises a **finial** that takes the eye to the point where earthly and cosmic worlds are thought to meet and join. An imaginary axis mundi (line connecting the center of

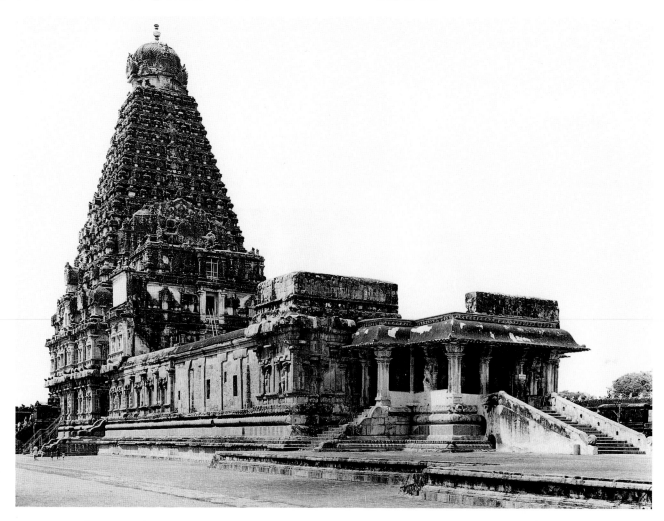

9-4. Rajarajeshvara Temple to Shiva, Thanjavur, Tamil Nadu, India. Chola dynasty, Early Medieval period, 1003–1010 CE

the earth to the heavens) runs from the finial down through the temple into the ground below, making the temple a conduit between celestial realms and earth, a concept familiar from Buddhist stupas (Chapter 3).

At the Kandariya Mahadeva temple, the *shikhara* is bolstered by the addition of many smaller *shikhara* motifs bundled around it. Below, the body of the temple is surrounded by porches on the sides and back. In the front (to the right in fig. 9-3), a steep flight of stairs leads to a series of three halls preceding the sanctuary, each with a pyramidal roof. The halls symbolically represent the Subtle Body stage of Shiva's threefold emanation (see "Hinduism," page 73).

Another temple to Shiva, known as the Rajarajeshvara Temple (1003–1010 CE), represents the supreme achievement of the southern style of Hindu architecture (fig. 9-4). Southern and northern temples are most clearly distinguished by their superstructures (compare figs. 9-3 and 9-4). The Rajarajeshvara does not culminate in the paraboloid shape of the northern *shikhara*, but in a pyramidal tower called a *vimana*. Its halls have flat roofs rather than the pyramidal roofs seen in the north. The

temple culminates in a huge, dome-shaped capstone. Crowning the *vimana*, the capstone is exactly above, and the same size as, the sanctuary housed thirteen stories below. It thus evokes the presence of the shrine as it points the viewer toward the heavens.

During the Early Medieval period, when these temples were built, a major devotional bhakti movement affected Hindu practice and its art. The movement, based on ideas expressed in ancient texts, especially the Bhagavad Gita, is centered in the ideal relationship between humans and deities. Bhakti involves an intimate, personal, and loving relation with god, and the complete devotion and giving up of oneself to god. The movement was especially influential to the Chola dynasty, who ruled the far south of India from the mid-ninth into the late thirteenth century.

Chola bronzes, such as this Shiva Nataraja, or King of the Dance (fig. 9-5), express the bhakti movement at its most fervent. No longer does the deity appear self-absorbed and introspective (see fig. 3-11). Instead, he generously displays himself to the devotee in full awareness of his benevolent powers. Dancing within a ring of fire,

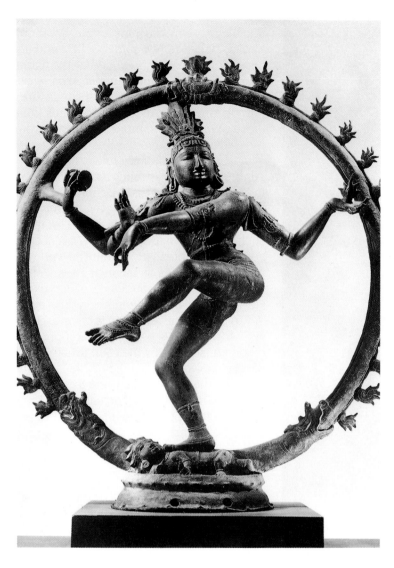

9-5. Nataraja: *Shiva as King of Dance*. South India, Chola dynasty, 11th century. Bronze, height 43⁷/₈" (111.4 cm). The Cleveland Museum of Art
© The Cleveland Museum of Art, 1998, Purchase from the J. H. Wade Fund, 1930.331

The fervent religious devotion of the bhakti movement was fueled in no small part by the sublime writings of a series of poet-saints who lived in the south of India. One of these poet-saints, Appar, who lived from the late sixth to mid-seventh century, wrote this tender, personal vision of the Shiva Nataraja. The ash the poem refers to is one of many symbols associated with the deity. In penance for having lopped off one of the five heads of Brahma, the first created being, Shiva smeared his body with ashes and went about as a beggar.

> If you could see
> the arch of his brow,
> the budding smile
> on lips red as the kovvai fruit,
> cool matted hair,
> the milk-white ash on coral skin,
> and the sweet golden foot
> raised up in dance,
> then even human birth on this wide earth
> would become a thing worth having.

(Translated by Indira Vishvanathan Peterson)

Shiva's extended left hand holds a spray of flames, emblematic of the destruction of the universe as well as of our ego-centered concepts. Shiva's back right hand holds a drum, whose ceaseless beat represents the unstoppable rhythms of creation and destruction, birth and death. With his right front hand, he makes the "have no fear" gesture. His left front arm, gracefully stretched across his body with the hand pointing to his raised foot and leg, symbolizes the promise of liberation. The earlier Hindu emphasis on ritual and the depiction of the gods' heroic feats is here subsumed into a pervasive and humanizing quality of grace.

The bhakti movement spread to North India during the ensuing Late Medieval period (c. 1100–1526) and flourished in the courts of local Hindu princes of the Rajputs, Indian warrior clans. This period also witnessed the incursion of Islam, an outside religious culture. The conquerors built forts, mausoleums, monuments, and mosques. These early dynasties introduced Islamic architectural design to the subcontinent, but it was the Mughal dynasty that made the most inspired and lasting Islamic contribution to the art and architecture of India.

The first Mughal emperor, Babur (ruled 1494–1530), conquered an empire stretching from Afghanistan to Delhi. Akbar (ruled 1556–1605), the third ruler, extended Mughal control over most of North India: by 1658, Akbar and his two successors, Jahangir and Shah Jahan, had unified all of northern India. Emperor Akbar was an avid patron of the arts, especially painting. He created an imperial painting workshop, which he placed under the direction of two artists from the Persian court. The Indian painters of this workshop soon transformed the borrowed Persian styles into the vigorous, naturalistic styles that mark the Mughal school (see "Indian Painting on Paper," page 206).

One of the most remarkable works produced for Emperor Akbar is an illustrated manuscript of the *Hamza-nama*, a Persian classic about the adventures of Hamza, uncle of the prophet Muhammad. The illustrations, painted on cotton cloth, are each 2¹/₂ feet high. The entire project gathered 1,400 illustrations into twelve volumes and took fifteen years to complete. One illustration shows Hamza's spies scaling a fortress wall and surprising some men as they sleep

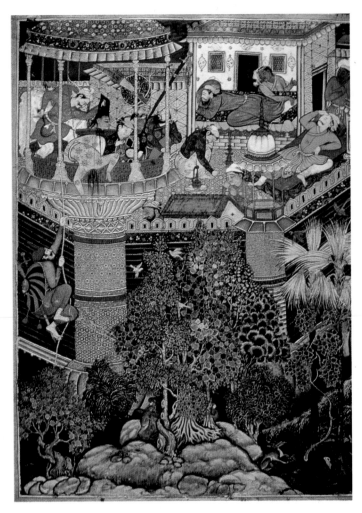

9-6. Page with *Hamza's Spies Scale the Fortress*, from the *Hamza-nama*, North India. Mughal period, Mughal, reign of Akbar, c. 1567–82. Gouache on cotton, 30 x 24" (76 x 61 cm). Museum of Applied Arts, Vienna

Indian Painting on Paper

Before the fourteenth century, most painting in India was made on walls or palm leaves. With the introduction of paper and the painting techniques adapted from Persia, later Indian artists produced jewel-toned paintings of unsurpassed beauty on paper. They used brushes made from the curved hairs of a squirrel's tail, arranged to taper from a thick base to a single hair at the tip. Their paint came from mineral and vegetable pigments, ground to a paste with water, then bound with a solution of gum from the acacia plant.

Artists frequently worked from a collection of sketches in a master painter's studio. Sometimes sketches were pricked with small holes, and wet color dabbed over the holes to transfer the drawing to a blank sheet beneath. The dots were connected into outlines, and the painting began. First, the painter applied a **wash**, or thin coat, of chalk-based white, which sealed the surface of the paper while allowing the underlying sketch to show through. Next, the artist filled the outlines with opaque color. When the colors dried, the painting was placed face-down on a smooth marble surface and burnished (rubbed) with a rounded agate stone. The indirect pressure against the marble polished the pigments to a high luster. Then outlines, details, and modeling were added with a fine brush. Raised details such as the pearls of a necklace were made with thick, chalk-based paint, each pearl a single droplet hardened into a tiny raised mound.

(fig. 9-6). One man climbs a rope; another has already beheaded a figure in yellow and lifts his head aloft. The energy exuded by the figures is characteristic of painting under Akbar—even the sleepers seem active. In the sensuous foreground landscape, monkeys and birds inhabit a grove of trees that shimmer and glow against the darkened background like precious gems.

Akbar's son Jahangir (ruled 1605–1627) admired painting as much as did his father. Indeed, he boasted that he could recognize the hand of each of his artists even in collaborative paintings. The paintings produced for Jahangir, such as *Jahangir in Darbar* (fig. 9-7), reflect his admiration for realistic detail. The work, probably part of a series on Jahangir's reign, shows the emperor holding an audience, or *darbar*, at court. He sits on a balcony beneath an ornate canopy at top center. The audience is composed of individuals, portrayals possibly taken from albums meticulously kept by the court artists. Some are people known to have died before Jahangir's reign, so the painting may represent a symbolic gathering rather than an actual event. The black robe of a Jesuit priest from Europe stands out amid the bright array of garments. Both Akbar and Jahangir were known for their interest in things foreign, and many foreigners flocked to the courts of these open-minded rulers.

Jahangir's son and heir, Shah Jahan (ruled 1628–1658), was the emperor who commissioned the Taj Mahal (see fig. 9-1). Shah Jahan is believed to have taken a major part in overseeing the design and construction of this memorial to one of his wives. As visitors enter through a monumental, hall-like gate, originally a guest house, the tomb looms before them, raised on a white marble platform, across a spacious formal garden set with long reflecting pools. In Shah Jahan's time, fountains played in the pools, and fruit trees and cypresses—symbolic of life and death, respectively—lined the garden's walkways. A lucid geometric symmetry pervades the entire design. Each facade of the main structure is identical, with a central *iwan*, or vaulted opening characteristic of eastern Islamic architecture (see fig. 8-23), flanked by two stories of smaller *iwans*. By creating voids in the facades, these *iwans* contribute to the building's sense of weightlessness. Four minarets surround the central structure, each crowned with a pavilion. Traditional embellishments of Indian palaces, these pavilions quickly passed into the vocabulary of Islamic architecture in India. Four more pavilions, this time on the roof, create a visual transition to the lofty, bulb-form dome. The Indian worldview is deeply embedded in the Taj Mahal, an "imported" structure that hovers between earth and sky like an apparition of pure form and that captures the essence of the sacredness of everything as pulsating, living energy.

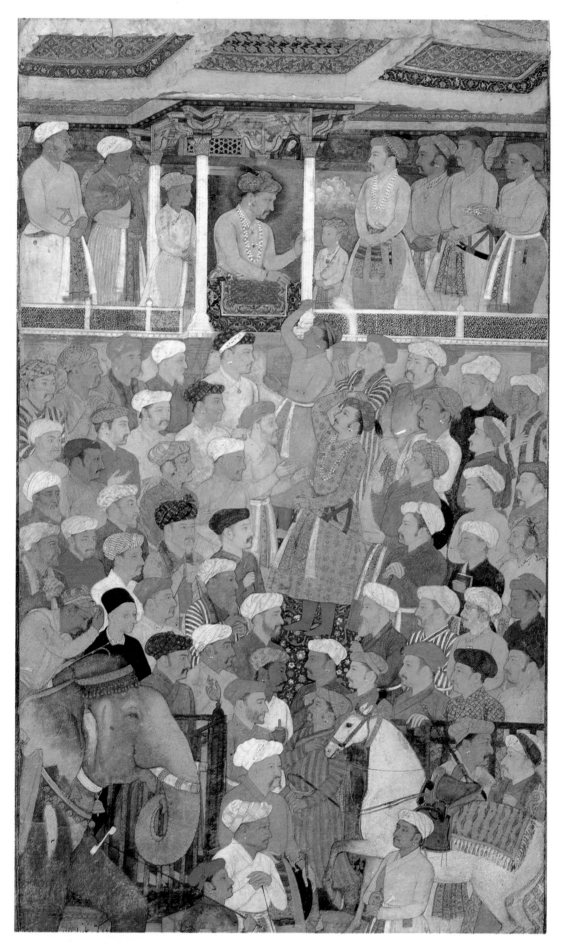

9-7. Abul Hasan and Manohar. Page with *Jahangir in Darbar*, from the *Jahangir-nama*, North India. Mughal period, Mughal, reign of Jahangir, c. 1620. Gouache on paper, 13⅝ x 7⅝" (34.5 x 19.5 cm). Museum of Fine Arts, Boston

Frances Bartlett Donation of 1912 and Picture Fund

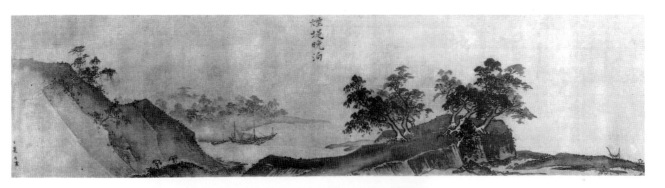

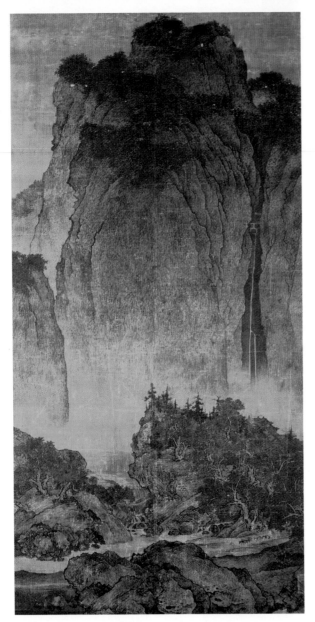

9-8. Fan Kuan. _Travelers among Mountains and Streams_. Northern Song dynasty, early 11th century. Hanging scroll, ink and colors on silk, height 6'9¼" (2.06 m). National Palace Museum, Taipei, Taiwan

China

Outside invaders threatened China during the Song dynasty (960–1279). In 1126, Ruzhen (Jin) invaders from the north sacked the Song capital at Bian (present-day Kaifeng) and occupied much of the northern part of the country. Song forces withdrew southward and established a new capital at Hangzhou. The dynasty from this point on is known as Southern Song (1127–1279). The earlier years are called Northern Song (960–1126).

During the Song period, the martial vigor of the Tang (Chapter 3) gave way to a culture of increasing refinement and scholarship. It was a great period for history, literature, and philosophy. Song philosophers engaged in a revival of Confucianism, drawing on both Buddhism and Daoism to provide Confucianism with a metaphysical basis, an all-embracing explanation of the universe. This new system of thought is called Neo-Confucianism.

Neo-Confucianism teaches that the universe consists of two interacting forces known as _li_ (principle or idea) and _qi_ (matter). All pine trees, for instance, consist of an underlying _li_ we might call the "pine tree idea," brought into the world through _qi_, the living tree. All the _li_ of the universe, including humans, are but aspects of an eternal first principle known as the Great Ultimate. The task of humans is to rid our _qi_ of impurities through education and self-cultivation so that our _li_ may realize its oneness with the Great Ultimate.

Neo-Confucian ideas found visual expression in landscape painting. Northern Song artists studied nature closely to master its many appearances—the way each species of tree grew, the distinctive character of rock formations, the changing of the seasons, the myriad birds, blossoms, and insects. This study was the artist's form of self-cultivation; mastering outward forms showed an understanding of the principles behind them.

Yet despite the convincing representation of forms, the paintings do not record specific views. The artist's goal was to paint the eternal aspect of a mountain, for example, not to reproduce the particular appearance of a mountain. Over the centuries, landscape also became a vehicle for conveying human emotions, even for expressing one's deepest feelings.

One of the first great masters of Song landscape was Fan Kuan (active c. 990–1030), whose _Travelers among Mountains and Streams_ is generally regarded as one of the great monuments in the history of Chinese art (fig. 9-8). The composition unfolds in three stages, comparable to the three acts of a drama. A low-lying group of rocks at

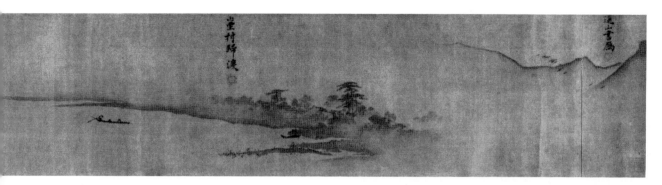

9-9. Xia Gui. Detail of *Twelve Views from a Thatched Hut.* Southern Song dynasty, early 13th century. Handscroll, ink on silk, height 11" (28 cm), length of extant portion 7'7¼" (2.31 m). The Nelson-Atkins Museum of Art, Kansas City, Missouri. Purchase, Nelson Trust (32–159/2)

the bottom establishes the extreme foreground, anticipating, on a small scale, the shape and substance of the mountains to come. In the middle ground, travelers and their mules enter from the right. We realize the discrepancies in relative scale—how small we are, how vast nature is! This middle ground, like the second act of a play, shows variation and development. Instead of a solid mass, the rocks here are separated into two groups by a waterfall. At right, the rooftops of a temple stand out above the trees.

Mist veils the transition to the background, so the mountain seems to loom up suddenly. This background area, almost twice as large as the foreground and middle ground combined, is the climactic third act of the drama. As our eyes begin their ascent, the mountain solidifies, its ponderous weight increasing as it billows upward. The whole painting summons the feeling of climbing a high mountain, leaving the human world behind to come face-to-face in a spiritual communion with the Great Ultimate.

The ability of Chinese landscape painters to let us wander freely through their recorded sites is closely linked to the absence of **linear perspective** as it has been understood in the West since the fifteenth century. Fifteenth-century European painters developed a "scientific" system for recording exactly the view that could be seen from a single, fixed vantage point (Chapter 11). The goal of Chinese painting is to show a totality beyond what we are normally given to see. If we can imagine the ideal viewpoint of Western painters as a photograph that shows only what can be seen from a fixed spot, we can imagine the ideal for Chinese artists as a video camera aloft in a balloon: distant, all-seeing, and mobile.

Landscape painting took a very different course after the fall of the Northern Song and the removal of the court to Hangzhou. The work of Xia Gui (c. 1180–1230), a member of a reestablished imperial painting academy, is representative of this change. His *Twelve Views from a Thatched Hut* (fig. 9-9), in sharp contrast to the majestic, austere landscapes of the Northern Song painters, presents an intimate and lyrical view of nature. In the surviving four of the twelve views that originally made up this long **handscroll** (narrow, horizontal painting), subtle ink

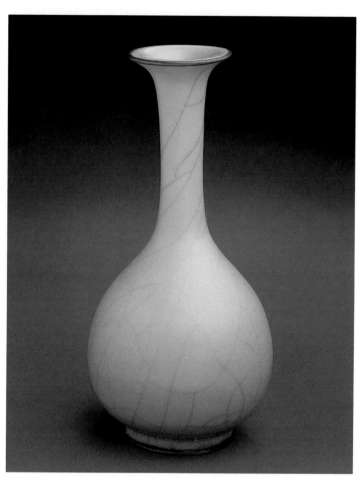

9-10. Guan Ware vase. Southern Song dynasty, 13th century. Porcelaneous stoneware with crackled glaze, height 6⅝" (16.8 cm). Percival David Foundation of Chinese Art, London

washes describe a landscape veiled in mists. A few deft brushstrokes suffice to evoke fishermen at their work, trees laden with moisture, and two bent figures carrying their heavy loads along a path that skirts the hill. Simplified forms, stark contrasts of light and dark, asymmetrical compositions, and great expanses of blank space suggest a fleeting world that can be captured only in glimpses.

The highly cultivated audience that appreciated the subtle and sophisticated paintings of the Song was equally discerning in other arts, such as ceramics. Of the many types of Song ceramics, one of the most prized was Guan Ware, made mainly for imperial use (fig. 9-10). The form of this graceful vase flows without interruption from base to lip, but the potter intentionally

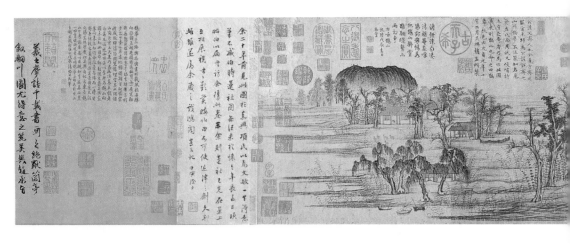

9-11 Zhao Mengfu. Section of *Autumn Colors on the Qiao and Hua Mountains.* Yuan dynasty, 1296. Handscroll, ink and color on paper, 11¼ x 36¾" (28.6 x 93.3 cm). National Palace Museum, Taipei, Taiwan

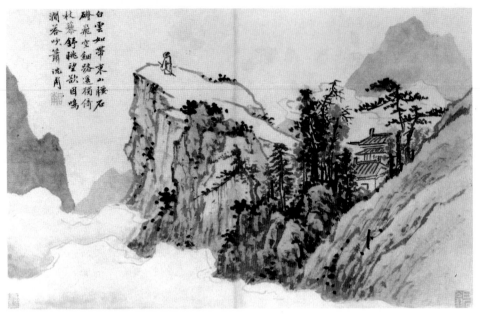

9-12. Shen Zhou. *Poet on a Mountain Top,* leaf from an album of landscapes; painting mounted as part of a handscroll, Ming dynasty, c. 1500. Ink and color on paper, 15¼ x 23¾" (38.1 x 60.2 cm). The Nelson-Atkins Museum of Art, Kansas City, Missouri
Purchase, Nelson Trust (46–51/2)

allowed a pattern of irregular, spontaneous cracks to develop in the lustrous off-white glaze. This piece, with its careful interplay of ordered and unplanned elements, has an understated quality as eloquent as the blank spaces in Xia Gui's painting.

In 1279, the Southern Song dynasty fell to the armies of the Mongol leader Kublai Khan, and China became part of the vast Mongol Empire. Kublai founded the Yuan dynasty (1279–1368), setting up his capital in the northeast, in what is now Beijing. The center of Chinese culture remained in the south, however, and southern Chinese scholars found themselves alienated from the Mongol court. Denied normal access to the government positions for which they were educated, these scholars, or literati, searched for other outlets for their talents, including the arts.

The southerner Zhao Mengfu (1254–1322), a descendant of the imperial line of Song, is somewhat typical in this regard. Unlike many of his southern contemporaries, he eventually served the Yuan government in Beijing and was made a high official. Nevertheless, as a painter, calligrapher, and poet, he also produced works for cultivated southern literati. Zhao painted *Autumn Colors on the Qiao and Hua Mountains* (fig. 9-11), for instance, for a friend living in the south. The painting supposedly depicts the friend's ancestral home, Jinan, the present-day capital of Shandong province, in the north. However, the mountains are not painted in the naturalistic mode perfected before Zhao's time but rather in an archaic yet oddly elegant manner that recalls the art of the much earlier Tang dynasty. Through his painting, Zhao evoked a feeling of nostalgia, not only for his friend's distant homeland but also for China's past.

This educated taste for archaic styles became an important aspect of **literati painting** in later periods. Also typical of the literati tradition are the unassuming brushwork, the subtle colors sparingly used, and even the intended audience—a close friend. The literati painted

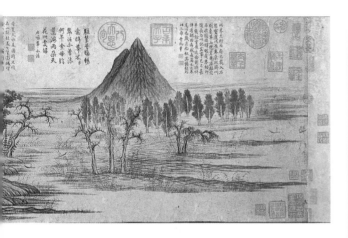

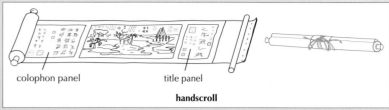

colophon panel   title panel

handscroll

not for public display but for each other. They favored formats such as handscrolls, **hanging scrolls**, or **album leaves** (book pages), which could easily be transported to show to friends or small gatherings (see "Formats of Chinese Painting," right).

The contrast between the opulent display and the austere aesthetic ideals of the literati is a defining feature of Ming dynasty (1368–1644) painting. Where court painters revived academic traditions of the Song dynasty, many literati painters built on the styles created by their predecessors, of the Yuan. One of the major literati artists of the Ming period is Shen Zhou (1427–1509), who spent most of his life in the southern city of Suzhou, far from the court in Beijing. Shen Zhou studied the Yuan painters avidly and tried to recapture their spirit in such works as *Poet on a Mountain Top* (fig. 9-12). Here the poet has climbed a mountain and surveys the landscape. Before his gaze, a poem hangs in the air, like a projection of his thoughts. Like the poem, the landscape is a vehicle for self-expression, having more to do with the artist's response to nature than with the physical world itself. With its perfect synthesis of poetry, calligraphy, and painting, and its harmony of mind and landscape, *Poet on a Mountain Top* represents the very essence of literati painting.

The cities of the south, such as Suzhou, where Shen Zhou painted, were full of newly wealthy merchants who collected paintings, antiques, and art objects. The court, too, was prosperous and patronized the arts on a lavish scale. In such a setting, the decorative arts thrived.

Like the Song dynasty before it, the Ming became famous the world over for its exquisite ceramics, especially **porcelain**. Porcelain is made from kaolin, an extremely refined white clay, and petuntse, a variety of the mineral feldspar. When properly combined and fired at a high temperature, the two materials fuse into a glasslike, translucent ceramic that is far stronger than it looks.

The porcelain flask in figure 9-13 came from the imperial kilns in Jingdezhen, in Jiangxi province, the most renowned center for porcelain in Ming China. The blue decoration—made

TECHNIQUE
FORMATS OF CHINESE PAINTING

Aside from wall paintings that decorated palaces, temples, and tombs, most Chinese paintings were done in ink and water-based colors on silk or paper. Finished works usually were mounted on silk as **handscrolls**, **hanging scrolls**, **albums**, or fans.

An **album** comprises a set of paintings of similar size, and usually of related subject matter, mounted in an accordion-fold book. Typically the paintings are square or rectangular, but fan paintings were sometimes collected in albums. Album-size paintings could also be mounted as a handscroll, a horizontal format generally about 12 inches high and anywhere from a few feet to dozens of feet long. More typically, however, a handscroll would be a single continuous painting, generally preceded by a

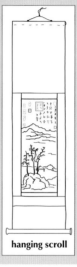

hanging scroll

panel giving the work's title and often followed by a long panel bearing colophons—inscriptions such as poems in praise of the work or comments by its owners over the centuries. Handscrolls were not meant to be displayed all at once, the way they are commonly presented today in museums. Rather, they were kept rolled up and only occasionally taken out for viewing. The viewer would unroll the scroll a couple of feet at a time, moving gradually through the entire scroll from right to left, lingering over favorite details.

Like handscrolls, hanging scrolls were not displayed permanently but were taken out for a limited time, whether a day, a week, or a season. Unlike a handscroll, however, the hanging scroll was viewed as a whole, unrolled and put up on a wall, with the wooden roller at the lower end acting as a weight to help the scroll hang flat.

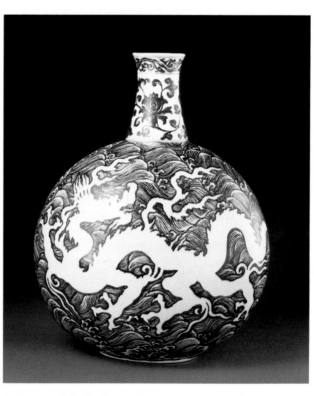

9-13. Porcelain flask with decoration in blue underglaze. Ming dynasty, c. 1425–35. Palace Museum, Beijing

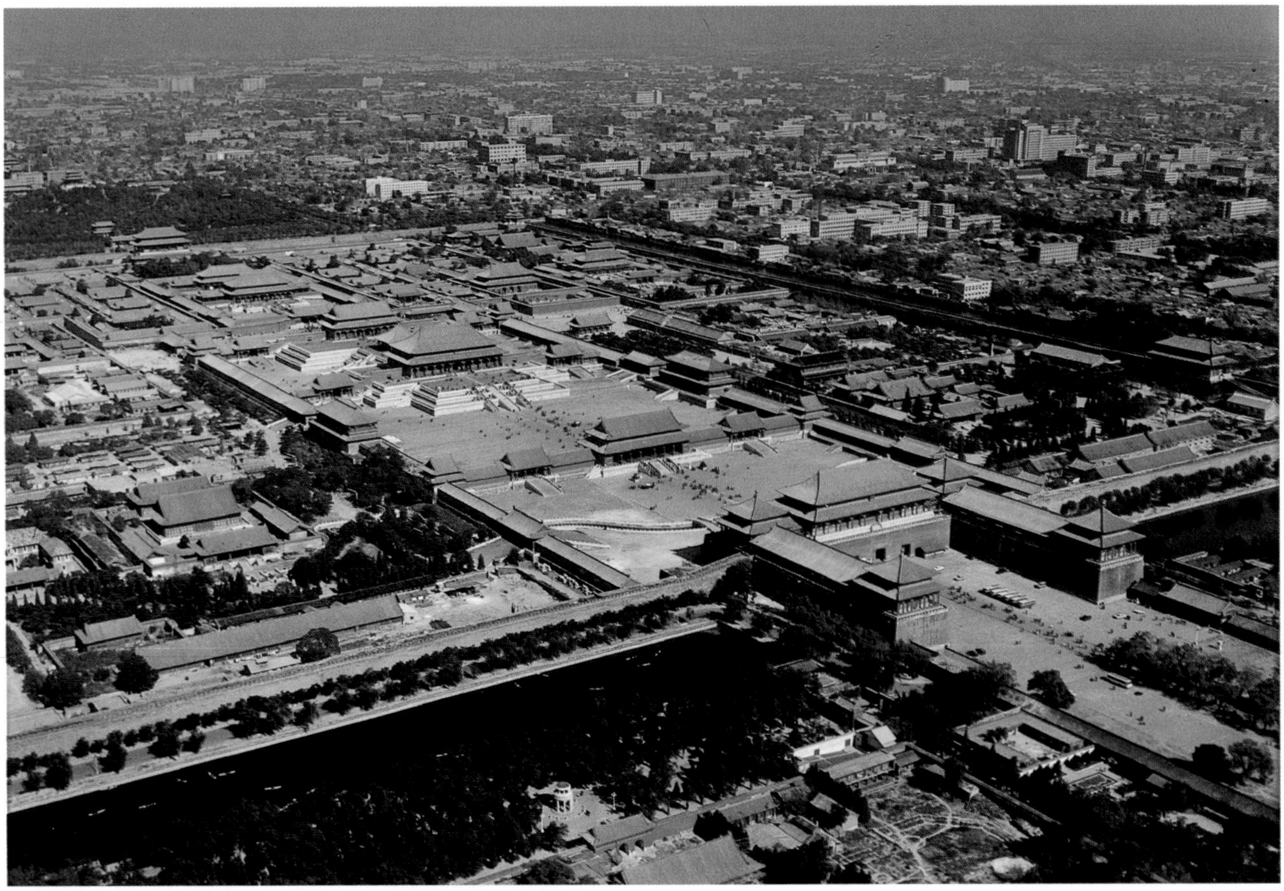

9-14. The Forbidden City, now the Palace Museum, Beijing. Mostly Ming dynasty. View from the south-west

from cobalt oxide, finely ground and mixed with water—was painted directly onto the unfired porcelain vessel in a technique known as **under-glaze**. Next, the painter applied a white glaze over the blue designs. The piece was then fired, emerging from the kiln with its clear blue decoration set sharply against a snowy white background. The subtle shape, the refined yet vigorous decoration of dragons writhing in the sea, and the flawless glazing embody the high achievement of Ming artisans.

Ming architects created the most important remaining example of traditional Chinese architecture: the Forbidden City, the imperial palace compound in Beijing (fig. 9-14). The basic plan of Beijing was the work of the Mongols, who laid out their capital city according to Chinese principles, creating a walled rectangle with gates oriented to the four cardinal directions and streets running north-south and east-west arranged on a grid. The palace enclosure occupied the center of the northern part of the city. Under the third Ming emperor, the Yongle emperor (ruled 1402–1424), the Forbidden City was rebuilt as we see it today.

Visitors to the Forbidden City entered on the south and passed through the Meridian (south) Gate, the monumental U-shaped gate seen at right in figure 9-14. Inside the gate, a bow-shaped canal spanned by five arched marble bridges crosses a broad courtyard. On the north side of the courtyard is the Gate of Supreme Harmony, opening into an even larger courtyard that houses three ceremonial halls raised on a

broad platform. Classic examples of Chinese palatial architecture, with brilliant yellow tile roofs and red lacquered columns, these are the Halls of Supreme Harmony, Central Harmony, and Protecting Harmony. In the first and largest, the Hall of Supreme Harmony, the emperor sat on his throne on important state occasions. He faced south, looking out toward his city and, by extension, his realm. His back was to the north, the source of evil spirits, not to mention military threats from non-Chinese peoples beyond the Great Wall.

Continuing on to the north in the Forbidden City, the visitor encounters an inner court that also has a progression of three buildings, this time more intimate in scale. In its directional orientation and symmetrical arrangement, the plan of the Forbidden City reflects ancient Chinese beliefs about the harmony of the universe and emphasizes the emperor's role as the Son of Heaven, whose duty was to maintain the cosmic order from his throne in the middle of the world.

Japan

By the Heian period (794–1185), Buddhism was practiced throughout Japan, although it did not completely supplant the country's indigenous religion, Shinto (Chapter 3). One offers paradisaical realms and enlightenment; the other, the intercession of the gods in the affairs of this world. Since these ideals did not fundamentally clash, modes of mutual accommodation were found. To this day, most Japanese see nothing inconsistent about having Shinto weddings and Buddhist funerals.

The generally peaceful Heian period was marked by a new cultural self-reliance on the part of the Japanese. Ties to China were severed in the mid-ninth century, and the imperial government was sustained by support from aristocratic families. During these four centuries of splendor and refinement, two new schools of Buddhism became prominent: first, Esoteric, or secret, Buddhism and later, Pure Land Buddhism.

In Esoteric Buddhism, the historical Shakyamuni Buddha became less important. Teaching centered instead on a universal or cosmic Buddha (called Dainichi, "Great Sun," in Japanese) of whom all other buddhas are emanations. Esoteric Buddhism gave rise to a huge pantheon of buddhas, bodhisattvas, and fierce guardian deities. The process of learning all the gods and their interrelationships was eased by works of art, especially **mandalas**, cosmic diagrams of the universe that represent the deities in schematic order (fig. 9-15). Esoteric Buddhism was favored by the leisured aristocracy: its network of deities, hierarchy, and ritual found a parallel in the elaborate social divisions of the Heian court.

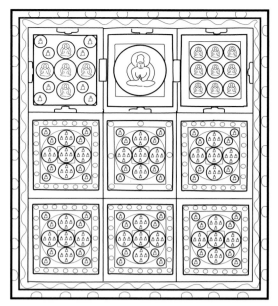

9-15. Schematic drawing of a Japanese Buddhist mandala

Pure Land Buddhism came to prominence in the latter half of the Heian period, as a rising military class threatened the peace and tranquillity of court life. In those uncertain years, many Japanese were ready for a form of Buddhism that would offer a means of salvation more direct than through the elaborate rituals of Esoteric sects. Pure Land Buddhism taught that the Western Paradise (the Pure Land) of Amida (Amitabha) Buddha (see "Buddhism," page 71) could be reached through faith alone. In its ultimate form, Pure Land Buddhism held that the mere chanting of a mantra—the phrase Namu Amida Butsu ("Hail to Amida Buddha")—would lead to rebirth in Amida's Pure Land, his Western Paradise. This doctrine, spread by traveling monks who took the chant to all parts of the country, has made Pure Land Buddhism the most popular form of Buddhism in Japan.

One of the most beautiful temples of Pure Land Buddhism is the Phoenix Hall at the Byodo-in (built c. 1053), located by the Uji River southeast of Kyoto (fig. 9-16). Originally the summer retreat of a powerful aristocrat, it was

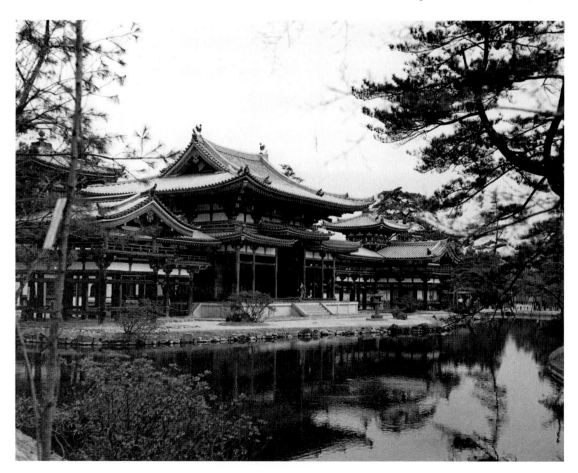

9-16. Byodo-in, Uji, Kyoto Prefecture. Heian period, c. 1053

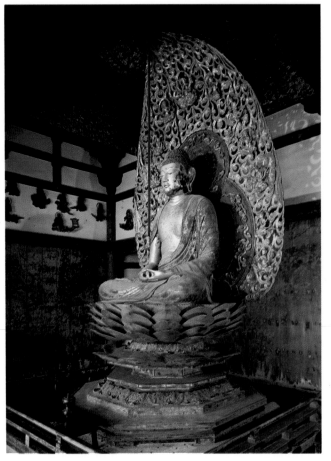

9-17. Jocho.
Amida Buddha,
Byodo-in. Heian
period, c. 1053.
Gold leaf and
lacquer on
wood, height
9'8" (2.95m)

later converted into a temple. The hall and its garden combine to evoke the palace of Amida in the Western Paradise. The lightness of its thin columns gives the Phoenix Hall a sense of airiness, as though the entire structure could easily rise up through the sky to the Western Paradise. In front of the hall is an artificial pond created in the shape of the Sanskrit letter A, the sacred symbol for Amida.

The Phoenix Hall's central image of Amida (fig. 9-17) was constructed out of individually carved blocks of wood by the master sculptor Jocho (d. 1057). This **joined-wood** method, developed by Jocho, allowed sculptors to create sculpture larger but lighter than those formerly carved from a single block of wood.

Reflected in the water of the pond before it, the Amida image, heightened with gold leaf and **lacquer** (a hard, glossy surface varnish), seems to shimmer in its private retreat. The Buddha sits on an open lotus, a Buddhist symbol of purity. The flower's stem is an axis mundi, connecting the earthly and celestial realms. This timeless image exemplifies the compassion of the Buddha, who welcomes the souls of all believers to his paradise, nirvana.

While Buddhism dominated the Heian era, a refined secular culture that has never been equaled in Japan also arose at court. A new system of writing in Japanese developed, known as *kana* script (see "Writing, Language, and Culture," left). With its simple, flowing symbols interspersed with more complex Chinese characters, *kana* allowed Japanese writers to create a distinctive calligraphy quite unlike that of China.

Kana was used during the Heian period to write down a large body of literature, including many *tanka*, or five-line love poems. The poems in one famous Heian anthology, the *Thirty-Six Immortal Poets,* are still familiar to educated Japanese today. This anthology was produced in sets of albums, the *Ishiyama-gire,* which display elegantly written *tanka* on high-quality papers decorated with painting, **block printing**, scattered gold and silver, and sometimes paper **collage** (pasted colored papers). The page shown here reproduces two *tanka* by the courtier Ki no Tsurayuki (fig. 9-18). Both poems express sadness for the loss of a lover, the first lamenting:

> Until yesterday
> I could meet her,
> But today she is gone—
> Like clouds over the mountain
> She has been wafted away.

> (Translated by Stephen Addiss)

The spiky, flowing calligraphy, the patterning of the papers, the rich use of gold, and the suggestion of natural imagery epitomize courtly Japanese taste.

Writing, Language, and Culture

Written Chinese was the international language of scholarship in East Asia, much as Latin was in medieval Europe. Educated Koreans, for example, wrote almost exclusively in Chinese until the fifteenth century. In Japan, Chinese continued to be used for certain kinds of writing, such as philosophical and legal texts, into the nineteenth century.

When the Japanese first began to write, they borrowed Chinese characters, which they refer to as *kanji.* However, differences between the Chinese and Japanese languages made this system extremely unwieldy, so during the ninth century the Japanese developed two syllabaries (*kana*), *katakana* and *hiragana,* to transcribe the sounds of their own language. (A syllabary is a system in which each symbol stands for a syllable.) *Katakana,* now generally used for foreign words, consists of mostly angular symbols, while *hiragana,* which is used for Japanese words, has graceful, cursive symbols.

Below is a stanza of a poem written three ways. At the right, it appears in *katakana* glossed with the original phonetic value of each symbol. (Modern pronunciation has shifted slightly). In the center, the stanza appears in flowing *hiragana.* At left is the mixture of Chinese characters and *kana* that eventually became standard. This alternating rhythm of simple *kana* symbols and more complex Chinese characters gives a special flavor to Japanese calligraphy. In all three versions of the stanza, the text is written, like Chinese, in columns from top to bottom and across the page from right to left. Chinese and Japanese handscrolls also read from right to left.

常ならむ
我世誰ぞ
散りぬるを
色は匂へど

kanji and kana

わかよたれそ
つねならむ
いろはにほへと
ちりぬるを

hiragana

ツネナラム
ワカヨタレソ
チリヌルヲ
イロハニホヘト

Tsu- ne
Wa- ka yo ta- re
Chi- ri- nu- ru wo
I- ro ha- ni- ho- he to
na- ra- mu
so

katakana

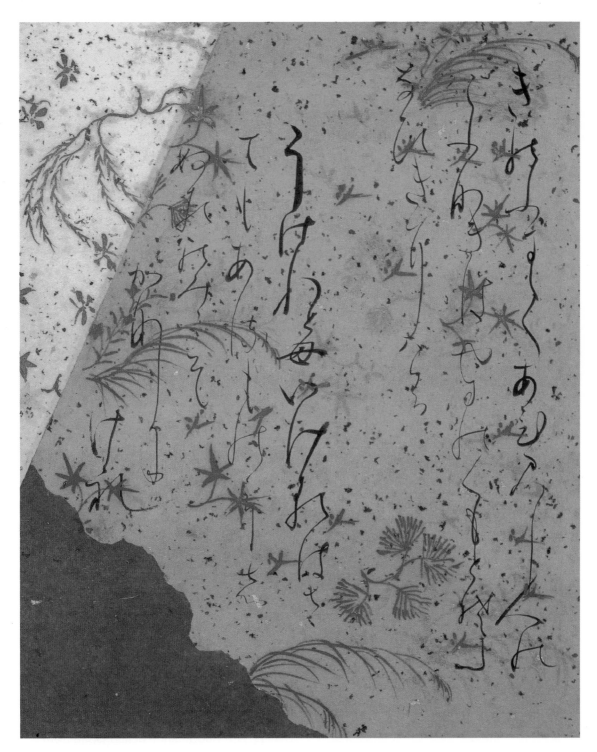

9-18. Album leaf from the Ishiyama-gire. Heian period, early 12th century. Ink with gold and silver on decorated and collaged paper, 8 x 6³/₈" (20.3 x 16.1 cm). Freer Gallery of Art, Smithsonian Institution, Washington, D.C.

The world's first known novel, *The Tale of Genji*, written in Japanese at the beginning of the eleventh century by Lady Murasaki, immortalizes the lifestyle of the Heian court. Underlying the story of the love affairs of Prince Genji and his companions is the Japanese conception of fleeting pleasures and ultimate sadness in life, an echo of the Buddhist view of the vanity of earthly pleasures.

Among the earliest extant secular paintings from Japan are illustrations for *The Tale of Genji*, done in the twelfth century by unknown artists in a style sometimes described as "women's hand." This style was characterized by emphasis on shapes rather than lines, strong if sometimes muted colors, and asymmetrical compositions in which interiors of buildings are viewed from above through invisible, "blown-away" roofs. The painters convey feelings by colors and poses rather than through movement or facial expressions. One evocative scene portrays a seemingly happy Prince Genji holding a baby boy borne

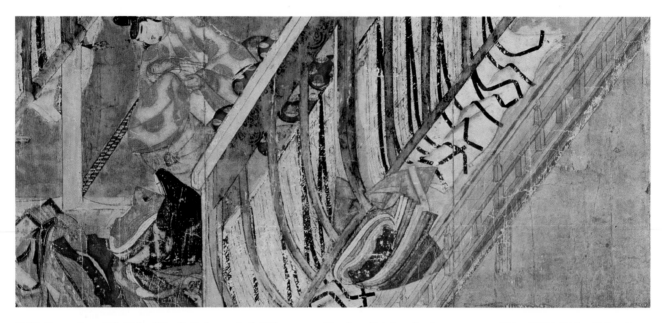

9-19. Scene from *The Tale of Genji*. Heian period, 12th century. Handscroll, ink and colors on paper, 8⁵/₈ x 18⁷/₈" (21.9 x 47.9 cm). Tokugawa Art Museum, Nagoya

Twenty chapters from *The Tale of Genji* have come down to us in illustrated scrolls such as this one. Scholars assume, however, that the entire novel of fifty-four chapters must have been written out and illustrated—a truly monumental project. Each scroll seems to have been produced by a team of artists. One was the calligrapher, most likely a member of the nobility. Another was the master painter, who outlined two or three illustrations per chapter in fine brushstrokes and indicated the color scheme. Next, colorists went to work, applying layer after layer of color to build up patterns and textures. After they had finished, the master painter returned to reinforce outlines and apply the finishing touches, among them the details of the faces.

by his wife, Nyosan (fig. 9-19). In fact, the baby was fathered by another court noble. Since Genji himself has not been faithful to Nyosan, who appears in profile below him, he cannot complain; meanwhile the true father of the child has died, unable to acknowledge his only son. The irony is even greater because Genji himself is the illegitimate son of an emperor. Thus what should be a joyous scene has undercurrents of sorrow. This is underscored visually by the muted colors of Genji's clothing, which contrast with the bright colors around him, and by the uncomfortable space he occupies.

The courtiers of the Heian era became so engrossed in their own search for refinement that they neglected their responsibilities for governing the country. Clans of warriors, known as samurai, grew increasingly strong, and samurai leaders soon became the real powers in Japan.

The Kamakura era (1185–1392) began when the samurai Minamoto Yoritomo (1147–1199) assumed power in Japan as shogun (general-in-chief). He established a military capital at the seaside town of Kamakura, far from Kyoto. While paying respects to the emperor, Yoritomo kept both military and political power for himself. He thus began a tradition of rule by shogun that lasted in various forms until 1868.

Toward the latter part of the Kamakura period, Zen Buddhism reached Japan from China. In some ways, Zen resembles the original teachings of the historical Buddha in stressing that individuals must achieve their own enlightenment through meditation, without the devotional practices or elaborate rituals promoted by other schools of Buddhism. In line with this emphasis on self-reliance, Zen monks grow and cook their own food, clean their temples, and are held as responsible for their own lives as for their spiritual growth. This approach appealed to the self-disciplined spirit of the samurai.

An abbot named Kao at an early Zen temple was a pioneer in a kind of rough and simple painting in black ink that so directly expresses the Zen spirit. In a remarkable portrait of a monk

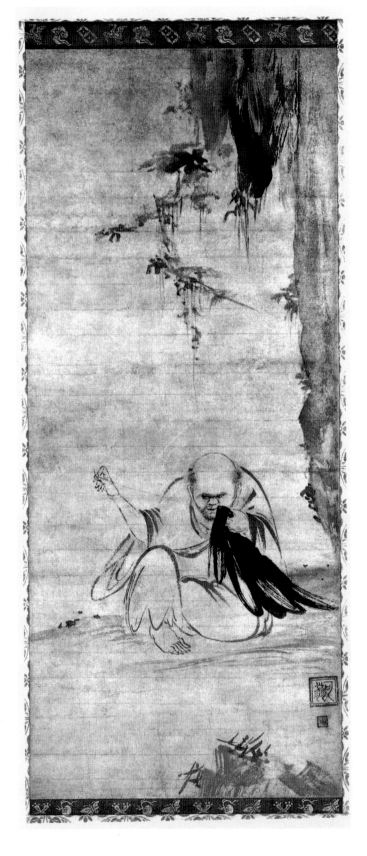

9-20. Attributed to Kao. _Monk Sewing._ Kamakura period, early 14th century. Ink on paper, 32⅞ x 13¾" (83.5 x 35.4 cm). The Cleveland Musuem of Art

John L. Severance Fund, 62.163

sewing his robe (fig. 9-20), we are drawn into the activity of the painting rather than merely sitting back and enjoying it as a work of art. The almost humorous compression of the monk's face, coupled with the position of the darker robe, focuses our attention on his eyes, which then lead us out to his hand pulling the needle.

By the beginning of the Muromachi period (1392–1568), Zen dominated many aspects of Japanese culture. One of the most renowned Zen creations in Japan, built during the Muromachi era, is the "dry landscape garden" at the

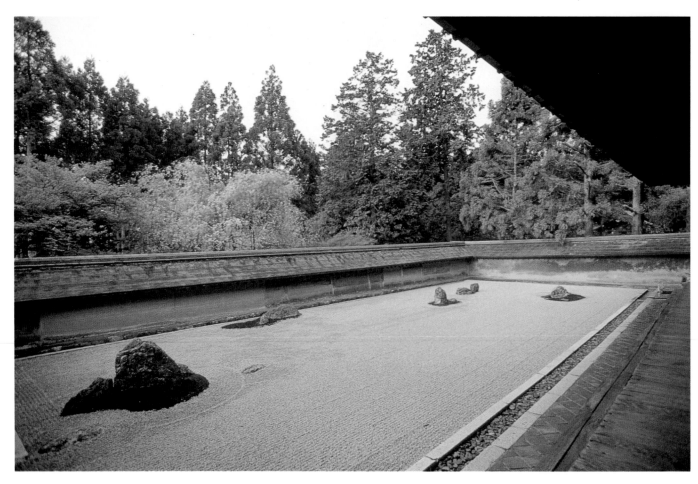

9-21. Stone and gravel garden, Ryoan-ji, Kyoto. Muromachi period, c. 1480

The American composer John Cage once exclaimed that every stone at Ryoan-ji was in just the right place. He then said, "and every other place would also be just right." His remark is thoroughly Zen in spirit. There are many ways to experience Ryoan-ji. For example, we can imagine the rocks as having different visual "pulls" that relate them to one another. Yet there is also enough space between them to give each one a sense of self-sufficiency and permanence.

9-22. Kano Eitoku.
Fusuma depicting pine and cranes (left) and plum tree (right), from the central room of the Juko-in, Daitoku-ji, Kyoto. Momoyama period, c. 1563–73. Ink and gold on paper, height 5'9¹/₈" (1.76 m)

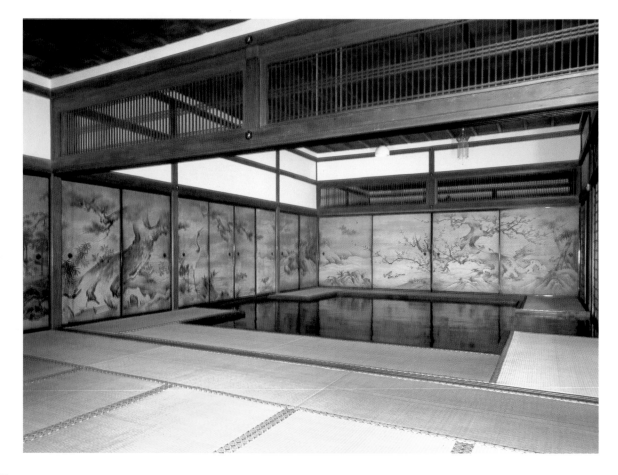

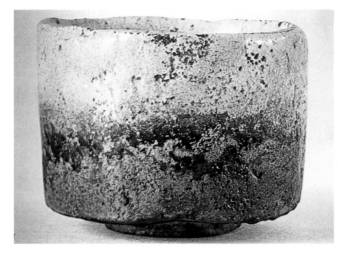

9-23. Hon'ami Koetsu. Teabowl, called *Mount Fuji*. Edo period, early 17th century. Raku ware, height 3³/₈" (8.5 cm). Sakai Collection, Tokyo.

temple of Ryoan-ji in Kyoto (fig. 9-21). There is a record of a famous cherry tree at this spot, so the completely severe nature of the garden may have come about some time after its original founding in the late fifteenth century. Nevertheless, today the garden is celebrated for its serene sense of space and emptiness. Fifteen rocks are set in a long rectangle of raked white gravel. Temple verandas border the garden on the north and east sides, while clay-and-tile walls define the south and west. Only a part of the larger grounds of Ryoan-ji, the garden has provoked so much interest and curiosity that there have been numerous attempts to "explain" it. Some people see the rocks as land and the gravel as sea. Others imagine animal forms in certain of the rock groupings. However, perhaps it is best to see the rocks and gravel as simply what they represent—rocks and gravel. The asymmetrical balance in the placement of the rocks and the austere beauty of the raked gravel have led many people to meditation.

During the Momoyama period (1568–1603), civil wars swept through Japan, fought among samurai loyal to their own feudal lords rather than to the central government. Portuguese explorers and traders arrived, and with them European muskets and cannons, which soon changed the nature of Japanese warfare. In response to the new weapons, monumental fortified castles were built in the early seventeenth century. Many were sumptuously decorated, offering artists unprecedented opportunities to work on a grand scale. Large murals on *fusuma*—paper-covered sliding doors—were particular features of Momoyama design, as were folding screens with gold-leaf backgrounds. Temples, too, commissioned large-scale decorative paintings for rebuilding projects after the devastation of the civil wars.

Daitoku-ji, a celebrated Zen monastery in Kyoto, has a number of subtemples that are treasure troves of Japanese art. One, the Juko-in, features *fusuma* by Kano Eitoku (1543–1590). Eitoku was one of the most brilliant painters from the Kano school, a professional school of artists patronized by government leaders for

several centuries. The illustration here shows two of three walls of *fusuma* panels painted when the artist was in his mid-twenties (fig. 9-22). The subject to the left is a popular Kano-school theme of cranes and pines, both symbols of long life; to the right is a great gnarled plum tree, symbol of spring and renewal. An island situated where two walls meet in a corner provides a focus for the outreaching trees. Ingeniously, it belongs to both compositions at the same time, thus uniting them into a single organic whole.

During the Momoyama period, there continued to be interest in the quiet, the restrained, and the natural. This introspective mood found expression in the tea ceremony. "Tea ceremony" is an unsatisfactory characterization of *cha no yu*, the Japanese ritual preparing and drinking of tea, for which there is no counterpart in Western culture. The most famous tea master in Japanese history, Sen no Rikyu (1521–1591), conceived of the tea ceremony as an intimate gathering in which a few people would enter a small, rustic room, drink tea carefully prepared in front of them by their host, and quietly discuss the tea utensils or a work of art displayed for their enjoyment.

The age-old Japanese admiration for the natural and the asymmetrical is reflected in certain types of tea ceramics. A teabowl would be judged by such factors as how well it fit into the hands, how subtly its shape and texture appealed to the eye, and who had previously used and appreciated it. If a bowl had been given a name by a leading tea master, it was especially treasured by later generations. One of the finest teabowls extant was crafted by Hon'ami Koetsu (1558–1637). Named *Mount Fuji* after Japan's most sacred peak (fig. 9-23), it is an example of **raku**—a hand-built, low-fired ceramic developed especially for use in the tea ceremony. With its small foot, straight sides, slightly irregular shape, and crackled texture, this bowl exemplifies the entire ceremony. Merely looking at it suggests the feeling one would get from holding it, warm with tea, in one's hands.

During the Edo period (1603–1868), when the *Mount Fuji* bowl was made, peace and

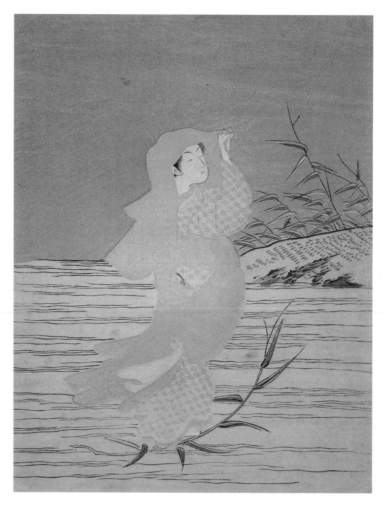

9-24. Suzuki Harunobu. *Geisha as Daruma Crossing the Sea.* Edo period, mid-18th century. Color woodcut, 10⁷/₈ x 8¹/₄" (27.6 x 21 cm). Philadelphia Museum of Art
Gift of Mrs. Emile Geyelin, in memory of Anne Hampton Barnes

prosperity came to Japan at the price of an increasingly rigid and often repressive form of government. Zen Buddhism was replaced as the prevailing intellectual force by a form of Neo-Confucianism, a philosophy formulated in Song dynasty China that emphasized loyalty to the state. The government discouraged foreign ideas and foreign contacts, forbidding Japanese from traveling abroad and barring outsiders from Japan, with the exception of small Chinese and Dutch trading communities on an island off the southern port of Nagasaki.

Across Japan, and especially in the bustling new capital of Edo (modern Tokyo), people savored the delights of their peaceful society. Wealthy merchants patronized painters in the middle and later Edo period, and even artisans and tradespeople could purchase less costly works of art—above all, **woodblock prints**.

Ukiyo-e ("pictures of the floating world"), as these prints are called in Japanese, represent the combined expertise of three people: the artist, the carver, and the printer. The artist supplied the master drawing for the print, executing its outlines in ink on tissue-thin paper. The carver pasted the drawing facedown on a hardwood block and cut around the lines with a sharp knife. The rest of the block was chiseled away, leaving the outlines standing in relief. This block, which reproduced the master drawing, was called the **key block**. If the print was to be **polychrome** (having multiple colors), the carver made a separate block for each color. A printer brushed water-based ink or color over the blocks, beginning with the key block; placed a piece of paper on top; and then rubbed with a smooth, padded device called a *baren* to make an impression. A publisher coordinated and funded the endeavor and distributed the prints to stores or itinerant peddlers.

The first artist to design polychrome prints was Suzuki Harunobu (1724–1770). One print that displays the charm and wit of Harunobo's art is *Geisha as Daruma Crossing the Sea* (fig. 9-24), in which a gracefully robed young woman is shown crossing the water on a reed. This is a playful ref-

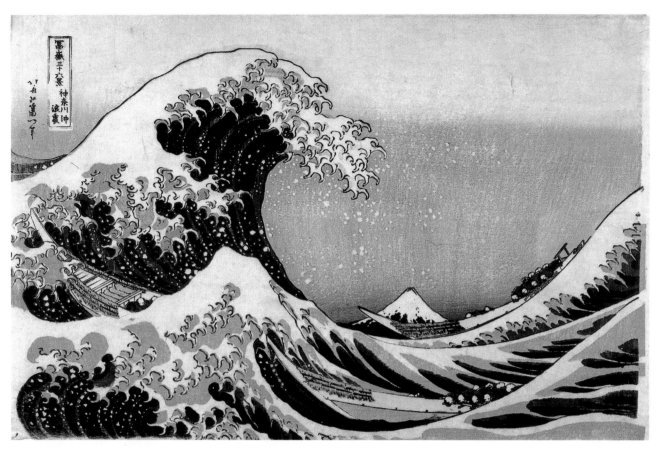

9-25. Katsushika Hokusai. *The Great Wave.* Edo period, c. 1831. Polychrome woodblock print on paper, 9⁷/₈ x 14⁵/₈" (25 x 37.1 cm). Honolulu Academy of Arts, Honolulu, Hawaii
James A. Michener Collection (HAA 13, 695)

erence to one of the legends about Bodhidharma, a semilegendary Indian monk, known in Japan as Daruma, and recognized as the founder of the Zen tradition in China. Many paintings were made of this monk standing on a reed to cross the Yangzi River. To see a young woman rather than a grizzled Zen master peering ahead to the other shore must have greatly amused the Japanese populace. There was also another layer of meaning in this image because geishas, or courtesans, were sometimes compared with Buddhist teachers or deities in their ability to bring ecstasy, akin to enlightenment, to humans.

Popular *ukiyo-e* subjects included courtesans, actors, and, beginning in the nineteenth century, landscapes. *Thirty-Six Views of Fuji*, by Katsushika Hokusai (1760–1849), became one of the most successful works of graphic art the world has ever known. The blocks were printed again and again until they were worn out. Then they were recarved, and still more copies were printed.

The Great Wave (fig. 9-25) may be the most famous scene from *Thirty-six Views of Fuji*. The great wave rears up like a dragon with claws of foam, ready to crash down on the figures huddled in the boats below. Far in the distance rises Japan's most sacred peak, Mount Fuji, whose slopes, we suddenly realize, swing up like waves and whose snowy crown is like foam—comparisons the artist makes clear in the wave nearest us, caught just at the moment of greatest resemblance.

When first seen in Europe and America, these and other Japanese prints were immediately acclaimed, and they strongly influenced late-nineteenth- and early-twentieth-century Western art (Chapter 17). Not only was the first book on Hokusai published in France, but the value of these prints as collectable works of art was recognized in the West before it was in Japan. Only within the past fifty years or so have Japanese museums and connoisseurs fully recognized the value of this originally "plebian" form of art.

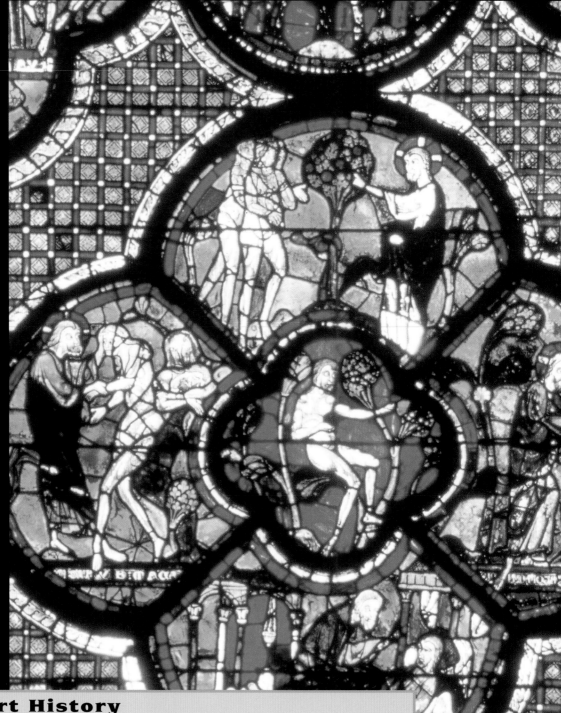

(*left*) **The Good Samaritan,** south aisle window, Chartres Cathedral. c. 1210. Stained glass

(*right*) **Charlemagne,** ambulatory window, Chartres Cathedral. c. 1225. Stained glass

Technique

The process of making a stained-glass window is complex. The artist drew the design on a board identical in size and shape to the window opening. The lead strips (cames) that would hold individual pieces of glass were drawn with bold lines, giving the glass workers (glaziers) a pattern for the glass pieces they had to cut. Glass blowers created sheets of glass, and by dipping their rods into different pots of colored glass, they created the many layers of color that give medieval glass its intensity and subtlety. Master craftsmen then cut the colored-glass pieces and fit them together. They painted details such as drapery, facial features, and foliage on the glass with black or dark-brown enamel, then heated the painted pieces to a point that set the enameled details. The stained- and painted-glass pieces were fit together with cames. The masters secured this rather flexible panel with iron bars and then installed it in the stone tracery of the window. The final effect of the window is of glowing paintings (glass) combined with a pattern of black lines (lead, iron, and stone).

KEYS to Art History

STAINED GLASS

Stained glass is one of the West's most important ecclesiastical (church) arts. Other ecclesiastical arts include church furniture, such as carved choir stalls; vestments (special garments worn by priests and other clerics); reliquaries for holding objects (relics) associated with saints and other holy persons; and articles associated with the rite of Mass (liturgical equipment). Stained glass is a monumental art; it actually forms and defines the walls of Gothic churches.

Because stained glass is a translucent (light-transmitting) material, its effect is dependent on the presence of light. In bright daylight, stained-glass panels glow with color, bringing an otherworldly atmosphere to the interiors of buildings. As the intensity and direction of the light changes from morning to evening, or as clouds pass over the sun, the stained-glass windows also change. As light passes through the windows it becomes colored, and as colored beams of light fall on architecture or on people, they make these shapes also seem to dissolve in color.

Like murals, stained-glass windows were painted as well as stained. Biblical events; stories of saints; the heroes of the church, such as Charlemagne; even complex points of church doctrine could be depicted. In the Middle Ages, light coming through glass symbolized the Virgin Mary and the virgin birth of Jesus.

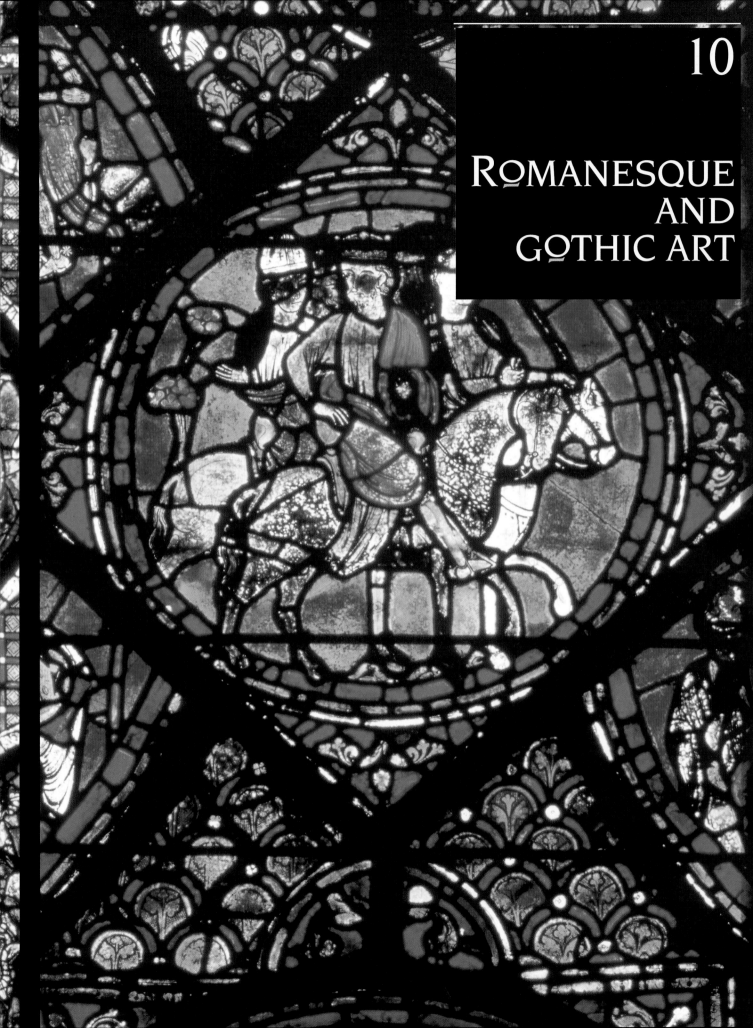

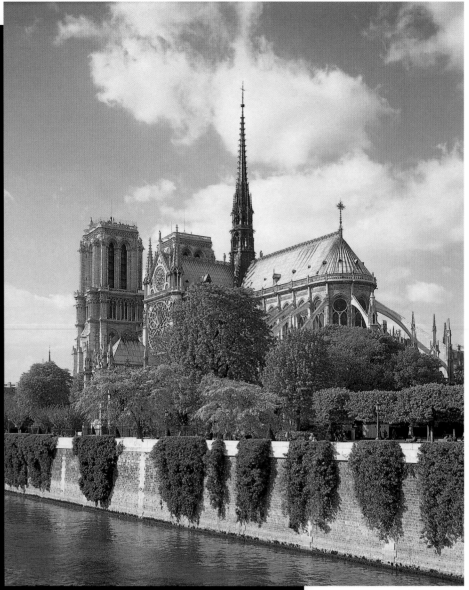

10-1. Cathedral of Notre-Dame, Paris. Begun 1163. View from the southeast

Unprecedented resources were devoted to Christian art in the late Middle Ages. Within 100 years an estimated 2,700 churches were built in the Île-de-France region around Paris alone. These new churches shimmered with stained glass, sumptuous altars, sculpture, crosses, and reliquaries, paid for by clergy, monarchs, aristocrats, and wealthy merchants. Private patrons commissioned innumerable other works of art for personal use as well, such as luxurious clothing, jewels, armor, and castles.

The art produced during the period from the eleventh to the fifteenth century is divided into two chronologic and stylistic periods: the Romanesque and the Gothic. Nineteenth-century art historians coined the word *Romanesque* ("in the Roman manner") to describe the appearance of eleventh- and twelfth-century churches, because these structures display the solid masonry walls, rounded arches, and masonry vaults characteristic of ancient Roman architecture. Soon the term *Romanesque* was applied to all of the arts produced from roughly the mid-eleventh to the late twelfth century.

The Gothic style prevailed from about 1150 to 1400 and lingered past 1500 in some regions, overlapping the Romanesque style at the beginning of the period and the Renaissance style at the end. In its own day, Gothic architecture was called "modern art" or the "French style." The sixteenth-century Italian artist and historian Giorgio Vasari introduced the word *Gothic* as a disparaging term. Vasari attributed the design of buildings such as the Cathedral of Notre-Dame to the "barbarous Goths," Germanic peoples who had destroyed the classical civilization of the Roman Empire that he and his contemporaries admired. But tastes change, and today we consider the Gothic style Vasari despised one of the most radiant manifestations of Western culture.

Think of medieval art. Chances are, the image that springs to mind is that of a soaring cathedral like Notre-Dame of Paris (fig. 10-1). Its nave, bridging the twelfth and thirteenth centuries, rose to a lofty 115 feet, soon to be surpassed by the cathedrals in Chartres (120 feet) and Reims (125 feet), which were also dedicated to "Our Lady," the Virgin Mary. For all its spiritual and technological glory, the Cathedral Church of Notre-Dame of Paris barely survived the French Revolution, when it was turned into a secular "Temple of Reason." Still, traditional Christians who continued to believe that Mary's church would be restored to her proved to be right, as Notre-Dame was soon returned to Christian use. Napoleon crowned himself emperor at its altar in 1804. In the twentieth century, the liberation of Paris from the Nazis in August 1944 was celebrated in Notre-Dame. Today, boats filled with tourists circle the island on which the cathedral stands, the Île de la Cité, drifting under its bridges and past its tree-lined streets to approach the beautiful building. The Cathedral of Notre-Dame has become more than a house of worship and a work of art; it is a symbol of Paris and part of the shared culture of humankind.

The Romanesque Period

Europe's society was predominantly agricultural during the Romanesque period. In many regions, a system governing social and political relations called feudalism had evolved in the Early Middle Ages (roughly 500–900). In this system, land belonged to the ruler (kings claimed to hold their territories in trust for God), who granted some of his property to a lesser nobleman, called a vassal. In exchange, the vassal promised to the ruler his allegiance and military service, which included a troop of armed knights and warhorses to protect the land when necessary. These vassals regranted portions of their land to vassals of their own under similar terms. Landless but free peasants living in villages performed farmwork and other manual labor on the estates. At the same time, cities with populations of merchants and artisans developed outside the feudal system, often directly under a royal charter. By granting charters to cities, kings could create a power base outside the feudal system.

The nations we know today did not exist in medieval Europe. In Germany and northern Italy, local rulers and towns resisted attempts by the successors of the Ottonian emperors to impose a central authority. Although these regions were called the Holy Roman Empire in the twelfth century, they remained politically fragmented until the nineteenth century. In eleventh-century France, the north was dominated by the powerful feudal duchy of Normandy, a region on the northwest coast that had been settled by Vikings. Southern France had close linguistic and cultural ties to northern Spain. In 1066, Duke William of Normandy (1035–1087) invaded England and, as William I ("the Conqueror"), became that country's king. William replaced the Anglo-Saxon nobility with Norman nobles, and England began to emerge as a nation politically and culturally allied to northern France. In France itself, where powerful dukes controlled the richest lands, the kings of the Capetian dynasty began to consolidate their authority from their personal stronghold around Paris. By the end of the twelfth century, they had laid the foundation for a powerful national monarchy.

In 1054, the Christian Church split into two major parts, the Roman Catholic Church, led by the pope in western Europe, and the Eastern Orthodox Church, led by the Patriarch of Constantinople in the Byzantine Empire. The Church became an international force, as the pope and the Patriarch acted as important players in European politics, often forging fruitful alliances with the rulers of Christian Europe. Pilgrimages to the holy places of Christendom dramatically increased in the eleventh century, despite the great financial and physical hardships they entailed. In 1095, Pope Urban II called for the first of several medieval Crusades to free Jerusalem and the Holy Land from Islamic rule. Although the Crusades were for the most part military failures, the West's encounters with the sophisticated Byzantine and Islamic worlds created a demand for goods from the East. Trade led to the rise of an increasingly urban society, and foreign contacts helped to nourish a period of intellectual and artistic ferment that has been termed the twelfth-century *renaissance*, or rebirth of classical learning.

CHURCH ARCHITECTURE AND DECORATION IN FRANCE AND SPAIN

In the eleventh and twelfth centuries, churches and monasteries multiplied across Europe. As one eleventh-century monk put it, the world was "clothed everywhere in a white garment of churches" (Raduldphus Glaber, cited in Holt, *A Documentary History of Art*, I, page 18). Romanesque

---

Elements of Architecture
RIB VAULTING AND FLYING BUTTRESSES

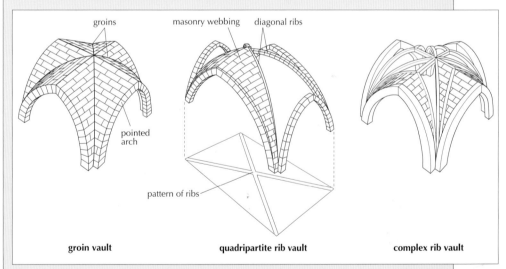

groin vault

quadripartite rib vault

complex rib vault

Rib vaulting was one of the chief technical contributions of Romanesque and Gothic builders. Rib vaults are a form of **groin vault** (see "Arch and Vault," page 137) in which the ridges (groins) formed by the intersecting vaults are supported by curved moldings called ribs. These ribs were usually structural as well as decorative, helping to support the weight of the vault. Thus, they simplified construction, strengthened the joins, and helped (although not as much as early architects believed) channel the vaults' thrust outward and downward. Ribs developed over time into an intricate masonry "skeleton," filled with an increasingly lightweight "skin," the web of the vault, or webbing.

In the Gothic period, builders developed a further structural component, the **flying buttress,** to help support their high rib-vaulted naves. The flying buttress, a gracefully arched, skeletal exterior support, carries the outward thrust of the nave vaulting over the aisles to massive buttresses, which are freestanding above the aisle roofs (see "The Gothic Church," page 237).

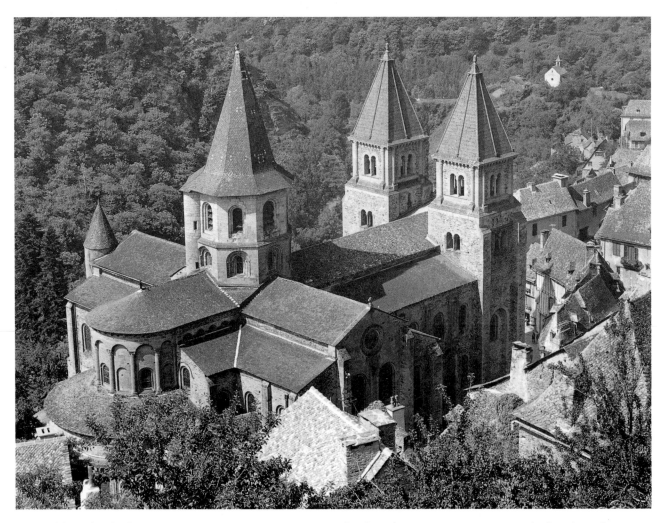

10-2. Abbey Church of Sainte-Foy, Conques, Rouergue, France. Mid-11th–12th century. Western towers rebuilt in the 19th century; crossing tower rib-vaulted in the 14th century, restored in the 19th century. View from the northeast

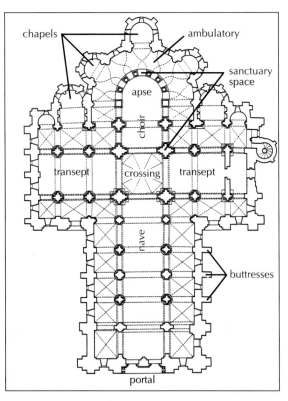

10-3. Plan of Abbey Church of Sainte-Foy

churches, like early medieval ones, were built on Early Christian basilica plans, but they featured significant structural innovations. Instead of wooden roofs, in some regions they were roofed with stone barrel vaults or groin (sectional) vaults reinforced by powerful supporting arches called ribs. These new styles of vaulting permitted builders more flexibility in laying out interior space (see "Rib Vaulting and Flying Buttresses," page 225). **Buttresses**—thick masses of masonry—reinforced walls at critical points and made taller buildings and masonry vaults possible. Towers emphasized the **crossing** (where the nave and transept intersect) and the west facade, which contained the entrance to the church (and by extension, to the City of God, the Heavenly Jerusalem).

The Abbey Church of Sainte-Foy (fig. 10-2), at Conques in south-central France, exhibits these architectural developments. The monastery possessed a golden reliquary containing the remains of an Early Christian child saint, Saint Foy ("Faith"), which attracted many religious pilgrimages. To accommodate these visitors, construction of a new, larger church at Conques began in the mid-eleventh century and continued into the next century. Its original **cruciform**

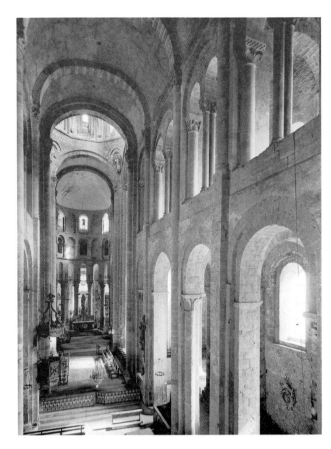

10-4. **Nave, Abbey Church of Sainte-Foy.** c. 1120

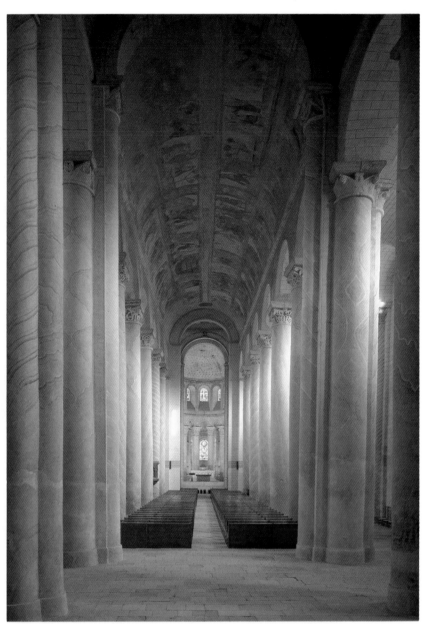

10-5. **Nave, Abbey Church of Saint-Savin-sur-Gartempe**, Poitou, France. c. 1100

(cross-shaped) plan with a wide transept is typical of Romanesque pilgrimage churches (fig. 10-3). In the west facade, a portal, or large doorway, opens directly into a broad nave. The sanctuary at the east end is made up of the apse, containing the altar, and the **choir**, an area where the clergy celebrated the mass apart from the congregation, who remained in the nave. Behind the apse, a wide ambulatory, or walkway, permitted visitors to reach chapels and view relics displayed there.

On entering the church, the viewer's attention is focused on the altar but is also to some extent drawn upward (fig. 10-4). A ribbed barrel vault covers the high nave; the ribs continue the vertical line of the piers. In the upper-level galleries, half-barrel vaults, called **quadrant vaults**, help strengthen the building by carrying the outward thrust of the nave vaults to the outer walls and buttresses. Above the church's square crossing, a windowed, octagonal tower, or **lantern**, admits daylight. The light streaming in from the lantern and apse windows acted as a beacon, directing the worshipers' attention forward to the altar. The piers supporting the nave arcade have attached half-columns on all four sides, and for this reason are known as **compound piers**. The sculptural form they give to church interiors was a major contribution of Romanesque builders to architectural structure and aesthetics.

Richly painted decoration, most of it now faded or lost, covered the interiors of many Romanesque churches. It took the place of the expensive mosaics and marble veneers popular in Early Christian and Byzantine buildings. At the Abbey Church of Saint-Savin-sur-Gartempe, in the Poitou region of western France, the nave columns are painted to resemble veined marble (fig. 10-5). Painted Old Testament scenes cover the entire length of the tunnel-like barrel vault; scenes from the New Testament and from the lives of two local saints, Savin and Cyprian, appear in the transept, ambulatory, and chapels. Several artists or teams of artists worked in different parts of the Church of Saint-Savin, and the painters were inspired by models available to them locally. Some must have seen examples of Byzantine art; others may have had Carolingian or even Early Christian models. While the paintings of the nave vault are energetic, suggesting the work of Carolingian artists like those

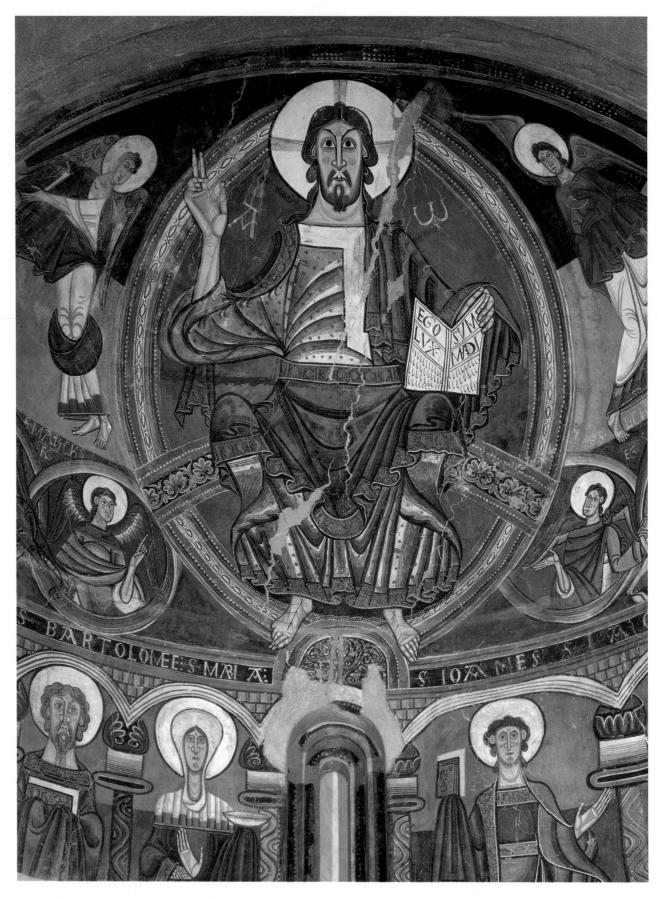

10-6. *Christ in Majesty,* detail of apse painting from the Church of San Clemente, Tahull, Lérida, Spain. c. 1123. Museu Nacional d'Art de Catalunya, Barcelona

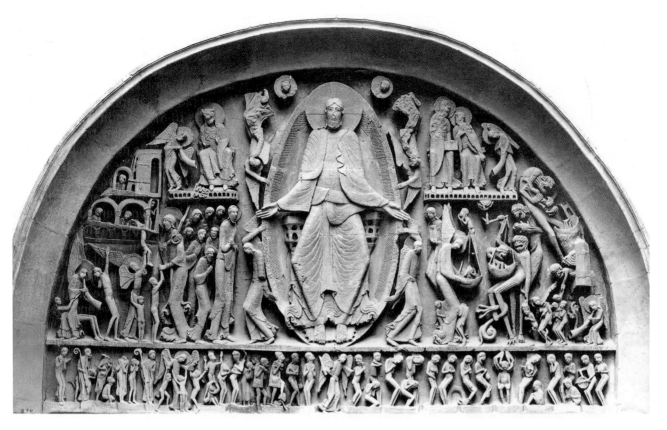

10-7. **Gislebertus.** *Last Judgment*, tympanum of the west portal, Cathedral of Saint-Lazare, Autun, Burgundy, France. c. 1120–35

who created the Ebbo Gospel (see fig. 8-10) or the narrative drama of the Ottonian Hildesheim doors (see fig. 8-13), the lives of the saints were painted by artists inspired by Byzantine art.

An apse painting from the Church of San Clemente (fig. 10-6) in Tahull, in the Catalonian Pyrenees of northern Spain, also shows the influence of Byzantium. The Romanesque artist has transformed the Byzantine Christ Pantokrator, ruler and judge of the world (see fig. 7-22). Byzantine features include the figure's frontal pose, its modeling from light to dark through the use of repeated colored lines of varying width and shades of color, and such iconographical features as the alpha and omega (the first and last letters of the Greek alphabet), and the inclusion of a Gospel inscribed *"ego sum lux mundi"* ("I am the light of the world"; John 8:12). The Western artist, however, has adapted the Byzantine style to the local taste for geometry and simplicity of form, turning facial features and draperies into elegant patterns. The refreshingly decorative feeling may have come from southern France, transmitted to the Pyrenees over pilgrimage routes.

The San Clemente Master, as the otherwise anonymous Tahull painter is known, is considered one of the finest Spanish painters of the Romanesque period. The artist's expressive figures, pointing toward Christ or interacting directly with the viewer; the inventive detailing of the draperies with their crinkles and loops; as well as the mosaic-like intensity of the colors

built up from many thin coats of paint, reflect the influence of a remarkable variety of artistic traditions, including Roman, Carolingian, Mozarabic, Italo-Byzantine, and southern French.

Not just painting, but also sculptural decoration enriched medieval churches. Portal sculpture (located around and above the main entrances) was one of the most notable features of Romanesque architecture. The most important carving was located on the **tympanum** (the semicircular area above the door lintel), on the archivolts (the moldings that follow the contour of the arch), and on the **trumeau** (the central supporting post) and jambs of the door. The tympanum above the west portal of the Cathedral of Saint-Lazare at Autun in France features a scene from the Last Judgment (fig. 10-7). Christ, enclosed in a mandorla (almond-shaped nimbus), presides in judgment over the cowering, naked figures of the resurrected dead at his feet. The Damned writhe in torment on the right, while the Saved, praying, reach toward heaven on the left. Below, angels help other souls to rise from their graves, while a pair of giant, pincerlike hands descends at the far right to snatch one of the Damned into hell. Above and to the left of these hands, in a scene reminiscent of the Egyptian Books of the Dead (see fig. 2-35), the archangel Michael oversees the weighing of souls on the scale of good and evil.

The tympanum at Saint-Lazare was designed and carved by an artist named Gislebertus, who may also have carved the pilaster capitals lining

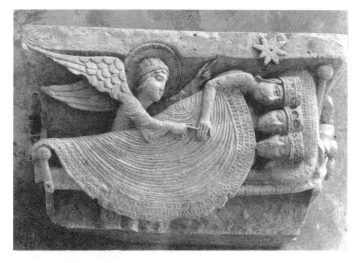

10-8. *The Magi Asleep*, capital from the nave, Cathedral of Saint-Lazare. c. 1120–32. Musée Lapidaire, Autun

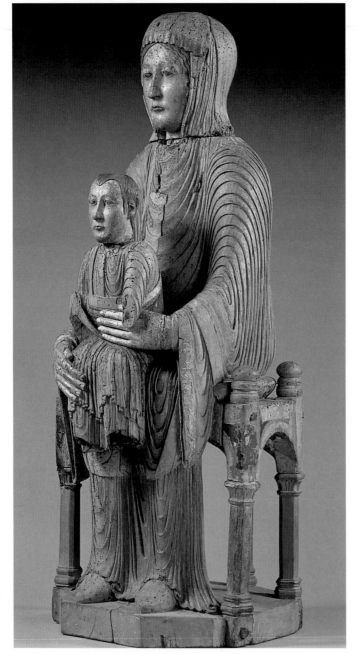

10-9. *Virgin and Child*, from the Auvergne region, France. c. 1150–1200. Oak with polychromy, 31 x 12³/₄" (78.7 x 32.4 cm). The Metropolitan Museum of Art, New York
Gift of J. Pierpont Morgan, 1916 (16.32.194)

the nave and aisles of the church. The creation of lively narrative scenes within the geometric confines of column capitals was an important Romanesque contribution to architectural decoration. One example is the capital depicting the sleeping Magi (fig. 10-8). According to the Gospels, three Magi, or wise men, traveled from the East to bring gifts to the newborn Jesus and acknowledge him as King of the Jews. Medieval tradition identified the Magi as kings, and gave them the names Caspar, Melchior, and Balthasar. The eldest, Caspar, is shown bearded here; Melchior has a mustache; and Balthasar, the youngest, is clean-shaven. An angel awakens the Magi and points to the Star of Bethlehem that will guide their journey. The sculptor's simultaneous use of two vantage points—the Magi and the head of the bed viewed from above and the angel and foot of the bed from the side—communicates the key elements of the story with wonderful economy and clarity. This capital, one of a series illustrating events related to the birth of Jesus, may have reminded worshipers that they were embarking on a metaphorically parallel journey to find Christ.

INDEPENDENT SCULPTURE

Reliquaries, altar frontals (the cloth hanging over the front of an altar), crucifixes, devotional images, and other sculpture once filled medieval churches. One form of devotional image that became increasingly popular during the later Romanesque period was that of the Virgin Mary holding the Christ Child on her lap. This particular type, used earlier by Byzantine and Ottonian artists (see fig. 7-18), is known as the Throne of Wisdom, for in it Mary actually is the throne of Jesus, who is seated on his mother's lap. It shows Mary as Theotokos (Greek for "bearer of God"), revered increasingly in the West from the twelfth century on as the nurturing, ever-merciful intercessor, second in heavenly power only to the Trinity. In the Auvergne region of France, such images became a local specialty. The well-preserved example in painted wood illustrated in figure 10-9 was made in Auvergne in the second half of the twelfth century. Mother and Child sit erect in a frontal pose, as rigid as they are regal, but appearing less remote than in earlier representations. Mary, seated on a thronelike bench, protectively supports the Christ Child, who raises his (now missing) right hand in a blessing. Recent cleaning has revealed the colorful blues, reds, and cream colors of the original surface. The sweet, slightly pouting expressions and softly modeled faces are typical of Auvergne figures.

Painted wood became an increasingly common medium in the Romanesque period as abbeys and churches of limited means began commissioning hundreds of statues. At the same time, royal or aristocratic patrons continued to

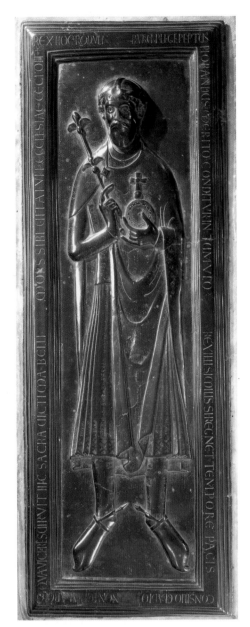

10-10. Tomb cover with effigy of Rudolf of Swabia, from Saxony, Germany. After 1080. Bronze with niello, approx. 6'5¹/₂" x 26¹/₂" (1.97 m x 68 cm). Cathedral, Merseburg, Germany

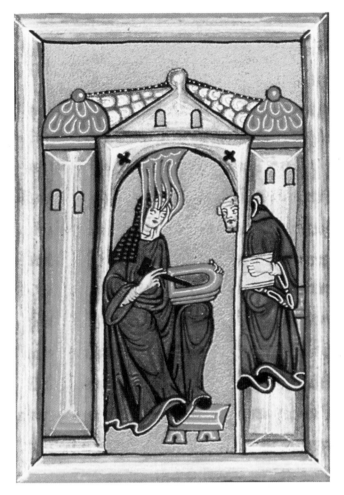

10-11. Page of facsimile with Hildegard's Vision, Liber Scivias. c. 1150–1200. Original manuscript lost during World War II

The text that accompanies this picture of Hildegard of Bingen reads: "In the year 1141 of the incarnation of Jesus Christ the Son of God, when I was forty-two years and seven months of age, a fiery light, flashing intensely, came from the open vault of heaven and poured through my whole brain. . . . And suddenly I could understand what such books as the psalter, the gospel and the other catholic volumes of the Old and New Testament actually set forth" (Liber Scivias, I, 1).

order works of art made of costly materials such as bronze, silver, or gold. For centuries, much of the best European sculpture in metal came from three areas of western Germany: Saxony, the Meuse Valley region (now in Belgium), and the lower Rhine Valley. In the late eleventh century, Saxon metalworkers, already known for their large-scale bronze casting, began making bronze **tomb effigies,** or portraits of the deceased. Thus began a tradition of funerary art that spread throughout Europe and persisted for hundreds of years. The oldest known bronze tomb effigy, the work of an artist originally from the Rhine region, is that of King Rudolf of Swabia (fig. 10-10). Made soon after the king's death in battle in 1080, the spurs on Rudolf's oversized feet identify him as a heroic warrior. In his hands he holds emblems of kingship, the scepter and orb. Like

the figures on the Hildesheim doors, the head of the nearly lifesize figure is modeled in higher relief than the body.

BOOK ART

The output of books, like other arts, increased dramatically in the eleventh and twelfth centuries. Monastic scriptoria, or workshops, continued to be centers of production. A painting on an opening page from the earliest illustrated copy of the Liber Scivias by Hildegard of Bingen (1098–1179) is as notable for the text it illustrates as for its artistic merit (fig. 10-11). Hildegard became one of the towering figures of her age. Like many aristocratic women, she entered a convent as a child. An able administrator, Hildegard became the convent's abbess in 1136, and about 1147 she founded a new convent near

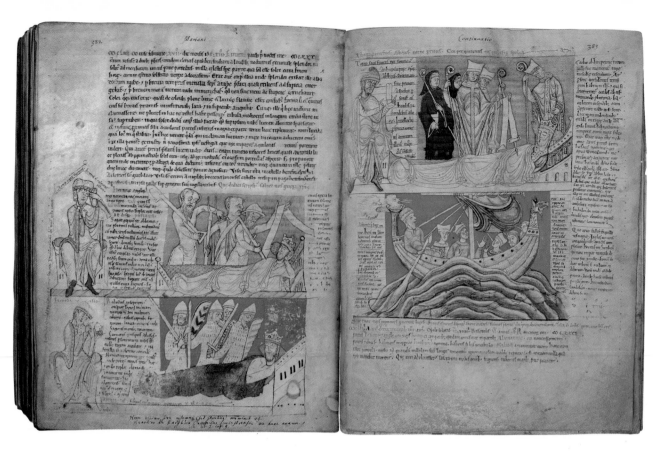

10-12. John of Worcester. Page with *Dream of Henry I*, *Worcester Chronicle*, Worcester, England. c. 1140. Ink and tempera on vellum, each page 12¾ x 9⅜" (32.5 x 23.7 cm). Corpus Christi College, Oxford

One of the most significant achievements of Henry I's father, William the Conqueror, was a comprehensive census of English property owners, the *Domesday Book*. Compiled into two huge volumes, this document was used to assess taxes and settle property disputes.

Bingen. When in her forties, with the assistance of the monk Volmar, she began to record her visions in a book, *Scivias* (translated from the Latin as "know the ways [of the light]"). She also wrote on medicine and natural science, and she composed music that is still performed today.

The opening page of *Scivias* shows Hildegard receiving a flash of divine insight, represented by the tongues of flame encircling her head. She records the vision on a tablet while Volmar waits outside with a stack of parchment. The original manuscript was lost in World War II, so we must depend on a copy to study the work of this remarkable woman.

In England, the great Anglo-Saxon tradition of book illumination, which declined for a time after of the Norman Conquest, revived after about 1130. The *Worcester Chronicle*, written by a monk named John, is the earliest known illustrated English history. The pages shown here concern Henry I (ruled 1100–1135), the second of William the Conqueror's sons to sit on the English throne (fig. 10-12). The text relates a series of dreams the king had on consecutive nights in 1130 in which his subjects demanded tax relief. The illustrations depict the dreams with energetic directness. On the first night, angry farmers confront the sleeping king; on the second, armed knights surround his bed, and on the third, monks, abbots, and bishops. In the fourth illustration, the king is in a storm-tossed

ship and saves himself by promising God to lower taxes for a period of seven years. The *Worcester Chronicle* assured its readers that this story came from a reliable source, the royal physician Grimbald, who appears in the margins next to most scenes.

The best-known narrative work of Norman art is, in fact, not a book but rather an **embroidered** wall hanging known as the *Bayeux Tapestry* (fig. 10-13). The work, which documents events surrounding the Norman Conquest of England in 1066, was embroidered in eight colors of wool on eight lengths of undyed linen, stitched together to form a hanging 230 feet long and 20 inches high. It was made for William the Conqueror's half brother Odo, Bishop of Bayeux in Normandy and Earl of Kent in southern England, who commissioned it for Bayeux Cathedral. It may have been completed in 1077, in time for the cathedral's consecration. According to an inventory made in 1476, it was "hung round the nave of the church on the Feast of relics."

The *Bayeux Tapestry* is a major political document, celebrating William's victory, validating his claim to the English throne, and promoting Odo's interests as a powerful leader himself. A Norman probably wrote the narrative of the story, and either an illuminator from a scriptorium or a specialist from an embroidery workshop provided drawings. Recent research suggests that the embroiderers were women. The scene

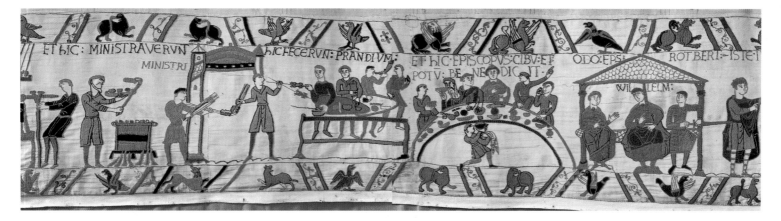

10-13. Bishop Odo Blessing the Feast, sections 47–48 of the *Bayeux Tapestry*, Norman–Anglo-Saxon embroidery from Canterbury, Kent, England, or Bayeux, Normandy, France. c. 1066–82. Linen with wool, height 20" (50.8 cm). Centre Guillaume le Conquérant, Bayeux, France

The top and bottom registers of the *Bayeux Tapestry* contain a variety of subjects separated by diagonal bars. These include heraldic beasts, stylized plants, and figures spilling over from the action in the central register, as well as a knight killing a tethered bear, a pair of naked lovers, and a farmer plowing. Such peripheral imagery was an English specialty throughout the Middle Ages. The sheer number of images in the *Bayeux Tapestry* is staggering: there are some 50 surviving scenes containing 623 human figures, 202 horses, 55 dogs, 505 other creatures, 37 buildings, 41 ships and boats, 49 trees, and nearly 2,000 inch-high letters.

10-14. Nave of Durham Cathedral. 1087–1133. Original apses replaced by a Gothic choir, 1242–c. 1280. View from the west

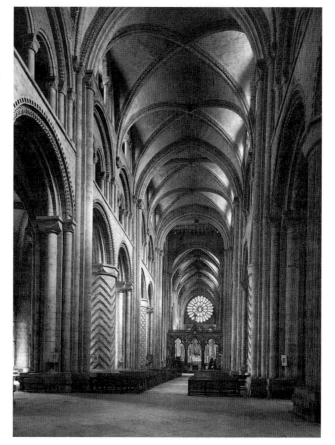

illustrated here shows Odo, William, and others feasting at a curved table on the eve of battle. At the left, attendants provide roasted birds on skewers, placing them on a makeshift table of knights' shields laid over trestles. A kneeling servant in the middle proffers a basin and towel so that the diners may wash their hands. A man seated next to Odo (the central figure) points impatiently to the next event, a council of war among three men of power: William, Odo, and a third man labeled "Rotbert," probably Robert of Mortain, another of William's half brothers.

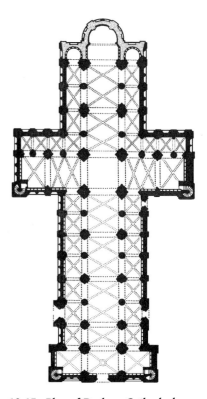

10-15. Plan of Durham Cathedral. Vaults constructed 1093–1133

ARCHITECTURE IN ENGLAND AND NORMANDY

Norman architects working in England and Normandy after the conquest of 1066 made major innovations in Romanesque religious architecture. Their sophisticated designs prepared the way for the architectural feats seen in Gothic cathedrals of the twelfth and thirteenth centuries. Durham Cathedral in England, begun in 1093, is one of the most impressive of all medieval churches as well as one of the most original (figs. 10-14, 10-15). Enormous compound piers alternating with robust columns support the nave arcade, gallery, and vaults. The columns are carved with **chevrons** (inverted Vs), spiral fluting, and diamond patterns, and some have scalloped, cushion-shaped capitals. All of this ornamentation was originally painted.

The masons at Durham developed a new system of vaulting. They modified the Romanesque ribbed groin vault by using two pairs of crisscrossing ribs in each bay. The complex

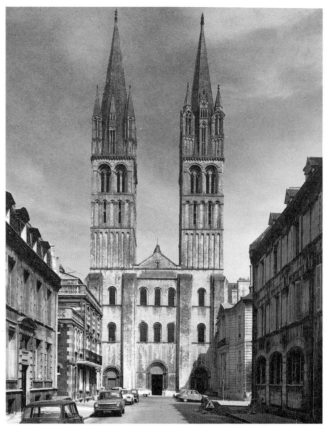

10-16. Church of Saint-Étienne, Caen, Normandy, France. Begun 1064; facade late 11th century; spires 13th century

patterns created by the ribs are visually compelling, and the diagonal movement helps to unify the separate bays. The architects also experimented with rectangular rather than square bays. Between 1093 and 1133, the Durham builders developed a system of vaulting that was carried to the Norman homeland in France, perfected in churches such as Saint-Étienne at Caen, and then adopted by French masons in the Gothic period (see "Rib Vaulting and Flying Buttresses," page 225).

Saint-Étienne at Caen in Normandy was begun nearly a generation before Durham Cathedral, originally with a wooden roof, but the work continued over a period of many years. The west facade of the church (fig. 10-16) was constructed at the end of the eleventh century, probably about 1096–1100 (the spires of the towers are thirteenth-century additions in Norman Gothic style). Tall wall buttresses divide the facade into three vertical sections. At each windowlevel, small **stringcourses**—horizontal cornicelike moldings—suggest the three stories of the building's interior. A product of the logic so characteristic of the Normans, the design of the facade reflects the plan and the elevation of the church itself, an idea that would be adopted by Gothic builders.

The Gothic Period

In the mid-twelfth century, a distinctive new architecture emerged in the Île-de-France region, a style now known as Gothic. From there it spread across Europe, taking on distinctive regional forms. Gothic architecture's elegant, soaring, light-filled interiors were adapted to all types of structures, including town halls, market buildings, residences, and synagogues, as well as churches and cathedrals. The influence of Gothic design extended beyond architecture and sculpture to all mediums.

During the flowering of the Gothic style in the twelfth and thirteenth centuries, Europe enjoyed a period of vigorous growth. Towns gained increasing prominence, becoming important centers of artistic patronage and intellectual life. Urban universities and cathedral schools supplanted rural monastic schools as centers of learning. The first European university, at Bologna, Italy, was founded in the eleventh century, and soon after, important universities were established in Paris, Cambridge, and Oxford. Two new religious orders arose to serve the new urban population, the Franciscans and the Dominicans. The friars, as these monks were called, went out into the world to preach and minister to those in need, rather than confining themselves to monasteries.

Crusades and pilgrimages continued throughout the thirteenth century. One of the benefits of the resulting contact with the Byzantine and Islamic worlds was that Europeans discovered many literary works from classical antiquity. These writings, particularly those of Aristotle, promoted rational inquiry rather than faith as the path to truth, which, at first, seemed incompatible with Christian emphasis on faith and spirituality. The thirteenth-century scholar Thomas Aquinas finally brought together faith and reason—traditional belief and the new logic—in Scholastic philosophy, which has endured as a basis of Catholic thought to this day.

The artists and master builders, like the Scholastic thinkers, saw divine order in geometric relationships and expressed these in their art. Unlike their Romanesque predecessors, who used stylization and distortion to achieve emotional impact, thirteenth-century sculptors created more naturalistic forms that reflect the idealism and reasoned analysis of Scholastic thought. Gothic religious imagery, like Romanesque imagery, aimed to instruct and persuade the viewer; however, its effects are more varied and subtle, and it incorporates a wide range of subjects drawn from the natural world. In the Gothic church, Scholastic logic and the new naturalism intermingle with the mysticism of light and color to create for the worshiper a direct, emotional, ecstatic experience of the church as the embodiment of God's house, filled with divine light.

GOTHIC ARCHITECTURE AND DECORATION

The birth of the Gothic style took place in France against the backdrop of the growing power of the French monarchy. Europe's first Gothic structure is arguably the Abbey Church of Saint-Denis, which had great symbolic significance for the French crown. Located a few miles north of central Paris, it housed the tombs of many French kings, the royal regalia, and the relics of Saint Denis, the patron saint of France. Construction began on a new church in the 1130s under the supervision of Suger, abbot of the Benedictine monastery there.

Abbot Suger was familiar with the latest architecture and sculpture of Romanesque Europe through his travels in France, the Rhineland, and Italy. He also turned for inspiration to the authority of Church writings, including treatises erroneously attributed to a first-century follower of Saint Paul named Dionysius, who identified radiant light with divinity. Through the centuries Dionysius had become confused with Saint Denis, so Suger, not unreasonably, adapted Dionysius's concept of divine luminosity to the redesign of the Abbey Church of Saint-Denis. When he began work on the choir after completing a magnificent Norman-inspired and structurally innovative facade, he created "a circular string of chapels" so that the whole church "would shine with the wonderful and uninterrupted light of most luminous windows, pervading the interior beauty" (cited in Panofsky, page 101).

The plan of the choir, built 1140–1144, superficially resembles that of a Romanesque pilgrimage church (fig. 10-17); that is, the semicircular sanctuary is surrounded by an ambulatory from which radiate seven chapels of uniform size. All the architectural elements of the choir had already appeared in Romanesque buildings, including pointed arches, ribbed groin vaults springing from cylindrical piers, and buttresses to relieve stress on the walls and to allow larger window openings. The dramatic achievement of Suger's master mason was to combine these features into a fully integrated architectural whole that emphasized open, flowing space (fig. 10-18). Sanctuary, ambulatory, and chapels open into one another, and the walls give the impres-

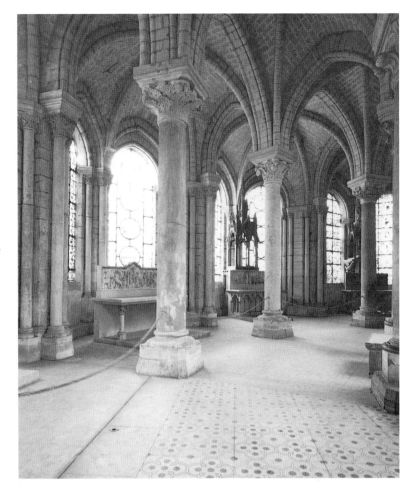

10-17. Ambulatory choir, Abbey Church of Saint-Denis, Saint-Denis, Île-de-France, France

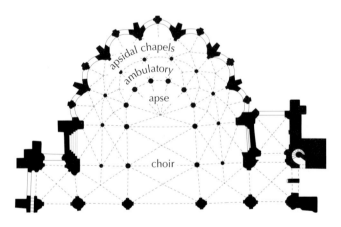

10-18. Plan of the sanctuary, Abbey Church of Saint-Denis. 1140–44

sion of being made of **stained glass** rather than masonry. Windows permit light to flood the interior with color. Suger saw light and color as a means of illuminating the soul and uniting it with God. The Abbey Church of Saint-Denis initiated a period of competitive experimentation in the Île-de-France and surrounding regions that resulted in ever-taller churches enclosing increasingly larger interior spaces walled with ever-greater expanses of colored glass.

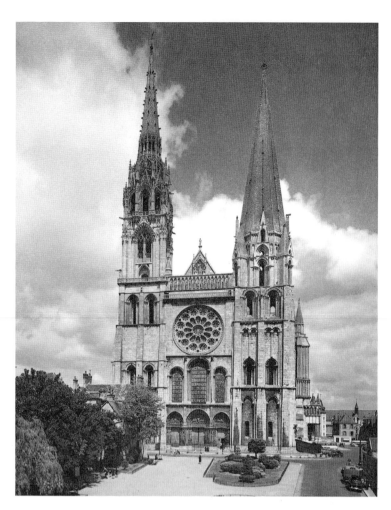

10-19. West facade, Chartres Cathedral. c. 1134–1220; south tower c. 1160; north tower 1507–13

At the Cathedral of Notre-Dame in Chartres (fig. 10-19), southwest of Paris, masons built on the concepts pioneered at Saint-Denis. Chartres Cathedral, constructed in several stages beginning in the mid-twelfth century and extending into the mid-thirteenth, illustrates both the early and the mature Gothic style. The facade survived a fire in 1194 and consequently represents a design contemporary with the church facade of Saint-Denis. Its three doors—the so-called Royal Portal (fig 10-20)—show Christ enthroned in majesty on the central tympanum, supported by his Old Testament precursors. The sculptors pose their high-relief figures naturally and comfortably in the architectural setting. The erect, frontal **column statues** with their elongated proportions and vertical drapery echo the cylindrical shafts from which they seem to emerge. Their heads are finely rendered with idealized features.

10-20. Royal Portal, west facade, Chartres Cathedral. c. 1145–55

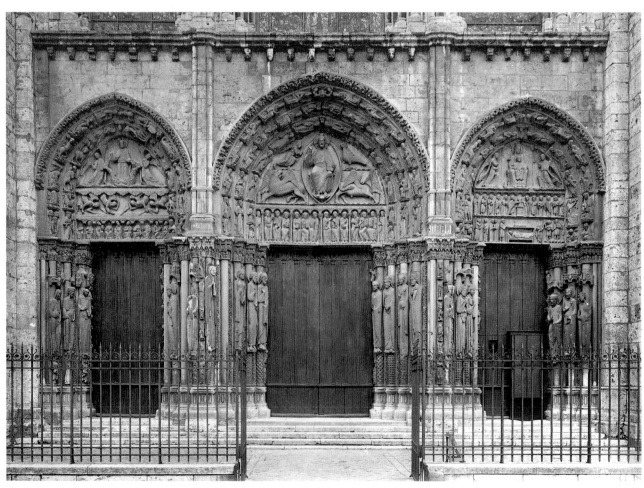

Elements of Architecture

THE GOTHIC CHURCH

Most large Gothic churches in western Europe were built on the **Latin-cross plan**, with a projecting **transept** marking the transition from nave to sanctuary. The main entrance **portal** was generally on the west, the **choir** and **apse** on the east. A **narthex** led to the nave and **side aisles**. An **ambulatory** with radiating chapels circled the apse and facilitated the movement of worshipers through the church. Above the nave were a **triforium** passageway and windowed **clerestory**. Narthex, side aisles, ambulatory, and nave usually had **rib vaults** in the Gothic period. Church walls were decorated inside and out with **arcades** of round and pointed arches, **engaged columns** and **colonnettes**, and horizontal moldings called **stringcourses**. The roof was supported by a wooden framework. A spire or **crossing** tower above the junction of the transept and nave was usually planned, though often never finished. The **apsidal chapels** ringing the apse were often visible on the exterior, as were the **buttress piers** and **flying buttresses** that countered the outward thrusts of the interior vaults. **Portal** facades were customarily marked by high, flanking towers or **gabled** porches ornamented with **pinnacles** and **finials**. Architectural sculpture covered each portal's **tympanum**, **archivolts**, and **jambs**. A magnificent stained-glass **rose window** typically formed the centerpiece of the portal facades. Stained glass filled the tall, pointed **lancets**.

Chartres Cathedral

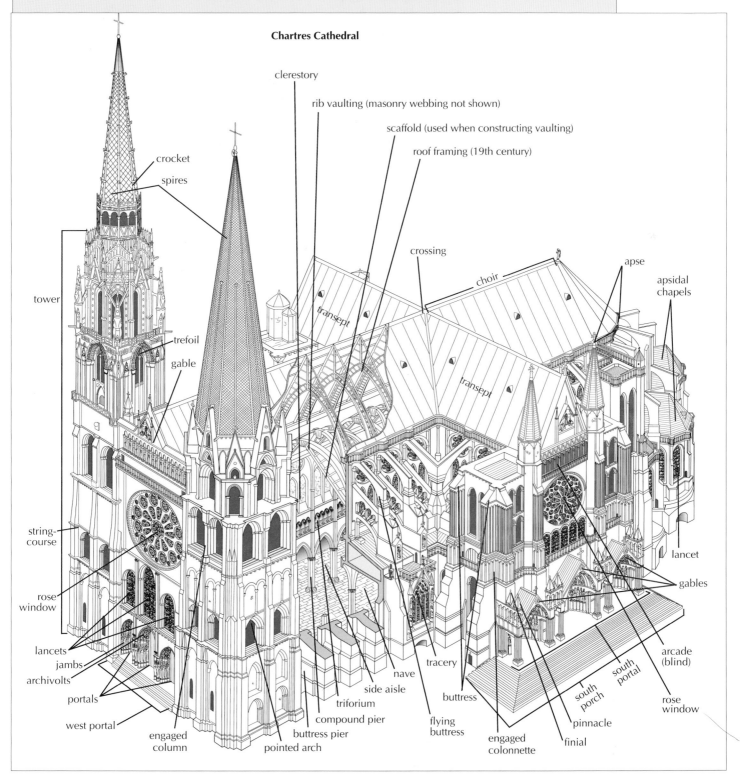

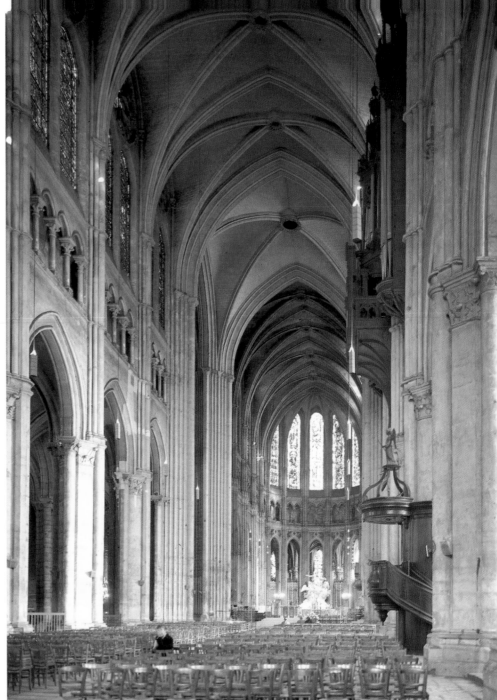

10-22. Nave, Chartres Cathedral. c. 1200–20

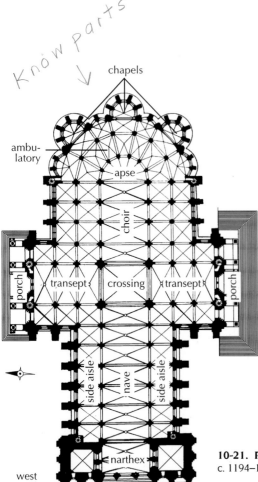

Know parts

10-21. Plan of Chartres Cathedral. c. 1194–1220

In the rest of the building, constructed after 1194 (fig. 10-21), the master mason and his men brought together what were to become the typical Gothic structural devices: pointed arches and ribbed groin vaulting rising from **compound piers** over rectangular bays, supported by flying buttresses, which permitted the masons to introduce huge windows into the upper walls (see "The Gothic Church," page 237). The **triforium** (series of arched openings under the clerestory) became a mid-level passageway overlooking the nave through an arcaded screen, rather than a flat wall (as in a basilica) or a full gallery. At Chartres, the elegant glass and masonry shell encloses an enor-

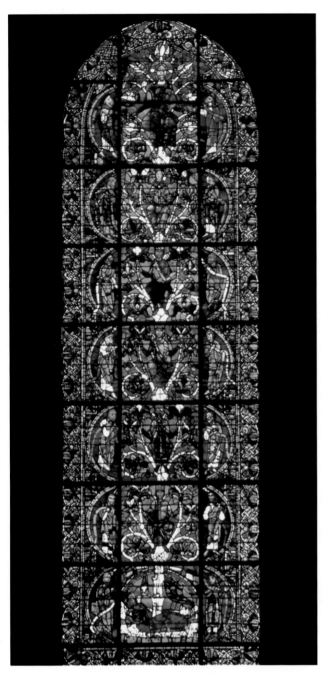

**10-23. *Tree of Jesse*, west facade, Chartres Cathedral.
c. 1150–70. Stained glass**

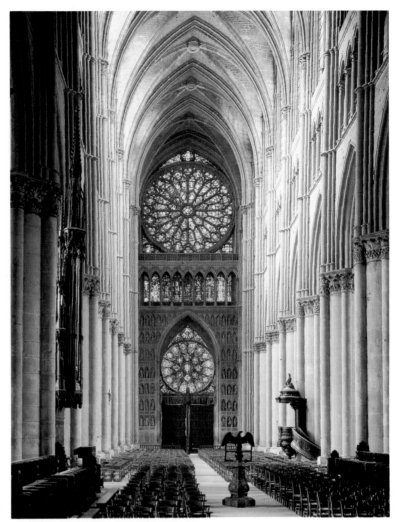

10-24. Nave, Cathedral of Notre-Dame at Reims, Île-de-France, France. 1211–60

mous open space. The building has one of the widest naves in Europe (45 1/2 feet) and vaults that soar 118–120 feet above the floor (fig. 10-22). The large and luminous clerestory is filled by pairs of tall, arched windows, called **lancets** surmounted by circular windows, or oculi. At a Romanesque church like Sainte-Foy (see fig. 10-4), the worshiper's gaze is mainly drawn forward toward the apse; at Chartres it is drawn upward as well, to the clerestory windows and the soaring vaults overhead.

Chartres is unique among French Gothic buildings in that most of its stained-glass windows have survived. The cathedral was famous for its glassmaking workshops, which by 1260 had installed about 22,000 square feet of stained glass. Most of the glass dates from between about 1210 and 1250, but a few earlier windows from around 1150 to 1170 have been preserved

in the west facade and elsewhere. The light from these windows changes constantly as sunlight varies with the time of day, the seasons, and the movement of clouds.

The *Tree of Jesse* window in the west facade of the cathedral dates from the mid-twelfth century (fig. 10-23). Jesse was the father of King David, who, according to the Gospels, was an ancestor of Mary and therefore of Jesus. A family tree literally connects Jesus with the house of David. At Chartres, Jesse is shown recumbent with the tree trunk growing from his body. In the branches above him appear four kings of Judaea, Christ's royal ancestors, then the Virgin Mary, and finally Christ himself. Fourteen prophets stand in the half-moons flanking the tree. The glass is set within a rectilinear iron armature, visible as silhouetted black lines filled with blues and reds.

Overlapping with the building of Chartres Cathedral was the construction of the Cathedral of Notre-Dame at Reims, where the kings of France were traditionally crowned. Construction began in 1211 and continued throughout the century. Artisans at each site borrowed from and influenced each other. The nave of Reims Cathedral, like Chartres, has a ribbed vault and a three-part elevation composed of a tall arcade, a triforium, and a windowed clerestory (fig. 10-24).

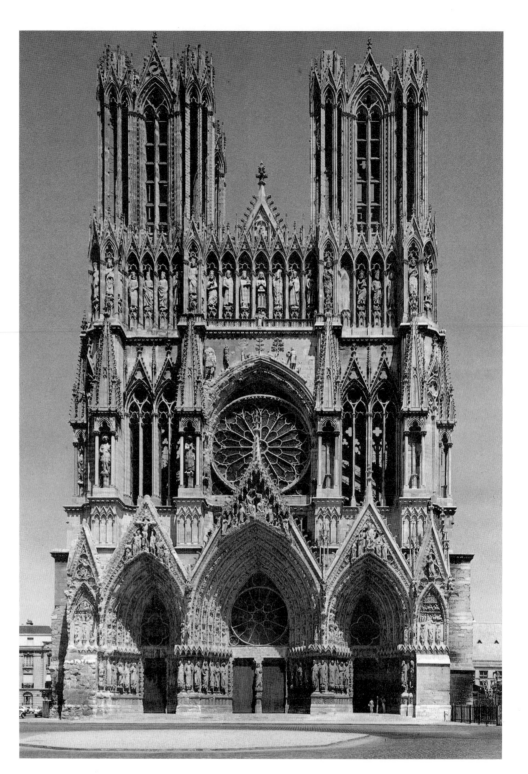

10-25. West facade, Reims Cathedral. 1230s–1260; towers mid-15th century

The cathedral was restored in the sixteenth century and again in the nineteenth and twentieth centuries. During World War I it withstood bombardment by some 3,000 shells, an eloquent testimony to the skills of its builders. It was recently cleaned.

In the west wall, the great **rose window** in the clerestory, a row of lancets at the triforium level, and windows over the portals replace the traditional stone of wall and tympana. A technique known as **bar tracery,** perfected at Reims, made possible this remarkable expanse of glass. In bar tracery, thin stone strips, called **mullions,** form a lacy matrix for the glass, replacing the older practice in which glass was inserted directly into window openings. Reims's wall of glass is anchored visually by a masonry screen around the doorway. Here, ranks of carved Old Testament prophets and ancestors of Christ serve as moral guides for the newly crowned monarchs who faced them after coronation.

A view of the magnificent west facade shows the massive gabled portals with their soaring peaks as well as the large stained-glass windows filling the portal tympana (fig. 10-25). In a departure from tradition, Marian (relating to Mary) rather than Christ-centered imagery prevails in the central portal, a reflection of the growing popularity of Mary's cult. The enormous rose window, the focal point of the facade, fills the entire clerestory level. The towers were later additions, as was the row of statues (the so-called Kings' Gallery) stretching across the facade at the base of the towers.

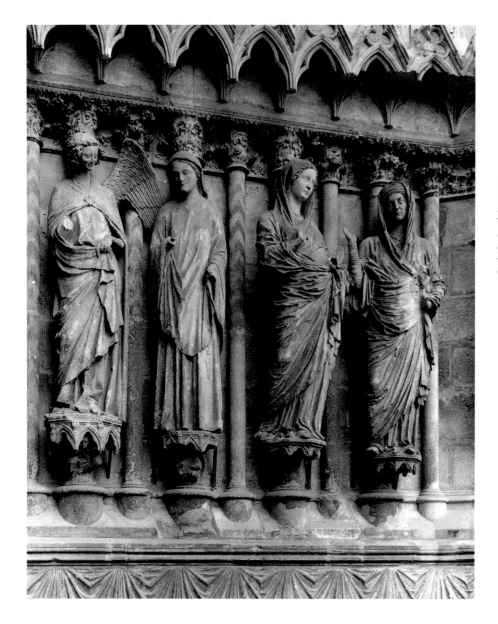

10-26. Annunciation (left pair: Mary c. 1245, angel c. 1255) **and Visitation** (right pair: c. 1230), right side, central portal, west facade, Reims Cathedral

Different workshops and individuals worked at Reims over a period of several decades. A group of four figures from the central portal of the western front illustrates some of the Reims styles (fig. 10-26). The subject of the pair on the right is the Visitation, in which Mary (left), pregnant with Jesus, visits her older cousin, Elizabeth (right), who is pregnant with Saint John the Baptist. These figures' sculptors, from the so-called classical Shop, which was active in Reims about 1230–1235, drew on classical sources. The heavy figures have the same solidity seen in Roman sculpture, and Mary's full face, wavy hair, and heavy mantle recall imperial portrait statuary (see fig. 6-9).

The pair on the left in figure 10-26 illustrates the Annunciation, in which the archangel Gabriel (left) announces to Mary that she will bear Jesus. The slight bodies, restrained gestures, and delicate features contrast markedly with the bold tangibility of the figures to the right. Gabriel is the work of an artist known today as the Master of the Smiling Angels or the Saint Joseph Master, after his most famous sculptures at Reims. This artist, whose work began to appear in the mid-thirteenth century, created tall, gracefully swaying figures whose aristocratic refinement became a guiding force in later Gothic sculpture and painting.

The royal palace chapel in Paris, called the Saint-Chapelle (built 1243–1248), took the use of stained glass to new heights. Constructed to house the French king Louis IX's prized collection of relics, the Sainte-Chapelle resembles a giant reliquary itself, one made of stone and glass instead of gold and gems. It was built in two stories, with a ground-level chapel accessible from a courtyard and a private upper chapel entered from the royal residence. Climbing up the narrow spiral stairs from the lower to the

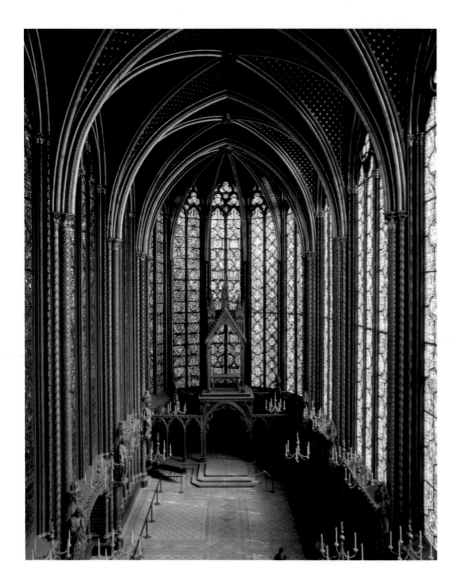

10-27. Interior, upper chapel, the Sainte-Chapelle, Paris. 1243–48

Louis IX avidly collected relics of the Passion, some of which became available in the aftermath of the Crusaders' sack of Constantinople. Those that Louis acquired were supposedly the crown of thorns that had been placed on Jesus' head before the Crucifixion, a bit of the metal lance tip that pierced his side, the vinegar-soaked sponge offered to wet his lips, a nail used in the Crucifixion, and a fragment of the True Cross. The king is depicted in the Sainte-Chapelle's stained glass walking out barefoot to demonstrate his piety and humility when his treasures arrived in Paris.

upper level is like emerging into a kaleidoscopic jewel box (fig. 10-27). The ratio of glass to stone is higher here than in any other Gothic structure, for the walls have been reduced to clusters of slender painted **colonnettes** framing tall windows filled with brilliant color. The stained glass illustrates narrative and symbolic scenes, including, among others, the Nativity and Passion (sufferings) of Christ, the life of Saint John the Baptist, and the story of Louis's acquisitions of his relics. This exquisite structure epitomizes a new Gothic style known as *Rayonnant* (a French term meaning "radiant" or "radiating") because of its radiating bar tracery, like that at Reims. It is also sometimes called the Court style because of its association with the royal courts of Paris and London.

Beginning in the late thirteenth century, France began to suffer from overpopulation and

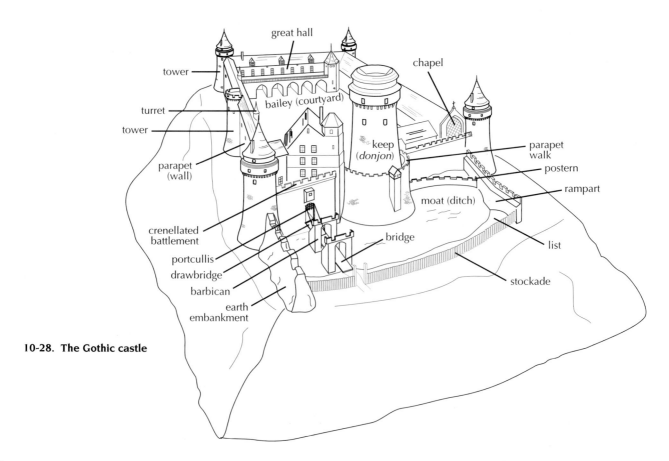

10-28. The Gothic castle

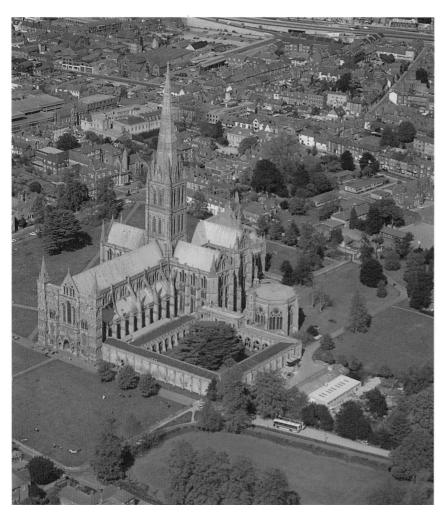

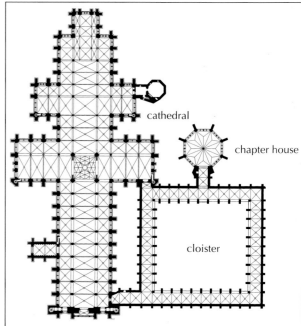

10-29. West facade, Salisbury Cathedral, Salisbury, Wiltshire, England. 1220–58; west facade 1265; spire c. 1320–30

10-30. Plan of Salisbury Cathedral

economic decline. The plague followed in the fourteenth century, along with a devastating conflict with England known as the Hundred Years' War. Large-scale cathedral construction generally ceased, although the Gothic style continued to develop in smaller churches, municipal and commercial buildings, and private residences.

Although the Gothic style is most studied in religious architecture, it is also seen in such secular structures as castles, which during the turbulent Middle Ages were necessary fortress-residences. Castles evolved during the Romanesque and Gothic periods from enclosed strongholds to elaborate fortified residential complexes (fig. 10-28). Since a castle needed a site that gave it a defensive, military advantage, the best sites were hilltops or cliffs along a river where the water formed a natural moat.

Medieval warfare consisted of long sieges. Castle defenses included ditches, or moats, and heavy walls and towers with stone battlements designed to shield defenders standing on parapet walks, which allowed the troops to repel attacks by shooting through notched crenellations. The most secure spot in the castle, and the final refuge of the defenders, was a massive tower called the keep in England, or the *donjon* in France. Inside the walls a large courtyard (the bailey) contained wooden structures including living quarters, great hall, stables, and the chapel. The castle was entered through a heavily defended gate that might include a drawbridge over the moat, an iron portcullis (a grating set into the doorway), and even a separate defensive structure called a barbican. All of these elements, which seem so picturesque today, had a military function.

GOTHIC ART OUTSIDE FRANCE

As the Gothic style spread outside of France, it not only became an international style in Europe but also took on innovative regional forms in the thirteenth and fourteenth centuries. In England, for instance, cathedral builders were less concerned with height than were their French counterparts, and they constructed long, broad naves, Romanesque-type galleries, and clerestory-level passageways. The English builders focused their decorative efforts on the cathedral walls, which retained a Romanesque solidity. Salisbury Cathedral, because its principal structure was built in a relatively short period of time (1220–1258), has a consistency of style that makes it an ideal representative of English Gothic architecture (fig. 10-29). Typically English is the parklike setting (the cathedral close) and attached **cloister** and chapter house for the cathedral clergy (fig. 10-30). The width of the massive west facade is underscored by tier upon tier of blind tracery and arcaded niches. In contrast to French cathedral facades, which suggest the entrance to paradise with their mighty towers flanking deep portals,

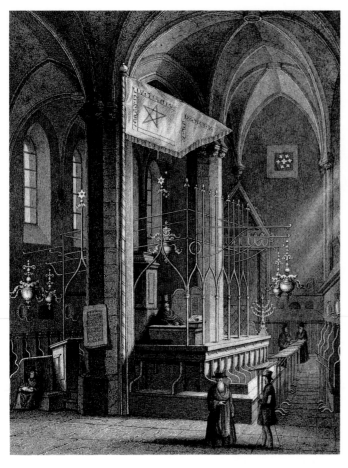

10-31. Interior, Altneuschul, Prague, Bohemia (Czech Republic). c. late 13th century; later additions and alterations. Engraving from *Das Historisches Prag in 25 Stahlstichen,* 1864

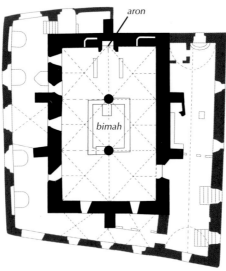

10-32. Plan of Altneuschul

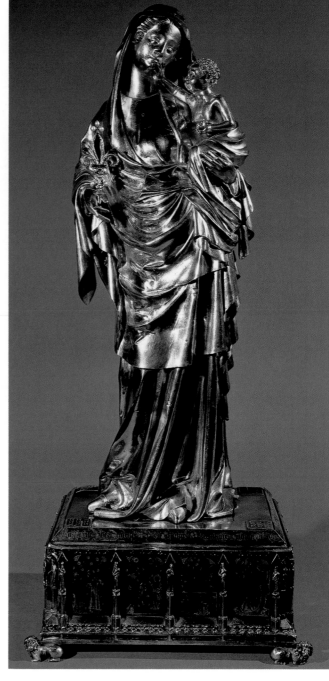

10-33. *Virgin and Child,* from the Abbey Church of Saint-Denis. c. 1339. Silver gilt and enamel, height 27 1/8" (69 cm). Musée du Louvre, Paris

English facades like the one at Salisbury suggest a jeweled wall around paradise. The huge crossing tower and its 400-foot spire are later additions, as are the flying buttresses that were added to stabilize the tower.

In Germany, a new type of Gothic church, the **hall church**, developed in the thirteenth century in response to the increasing importance of sermons within church services. The hall church featured a nave and side aisles with vaults of the same height, creating a spacious and open interior that could accommodate the large crowds drawn by charismatic preachers.

The flexible design of these "great halls" was also widely adopted for civic and residential buildings and even for Jewish religious structures. The oldest functioning synagogue in Europe, Prague's Altneuschul (Old-New Synagogue), was built in the style of a Gothic great hall, probably in the late thirteenth or fourteenth century (fig. 10-31). As in a hall church, the vaults of the synagogue are all the same height. But unlike a church, with its nave and side aisles, the Altneuschul has two central aisles with six bays (fig. 10-32). The bays have four-part vaulting with a decorative fifth rib.

The synagogue had two focal points, the *aron*, or shrine for the Torah scrolls, located on the east wall, toward Jerusalem, and a central raised reading platform called the *bimah*. The

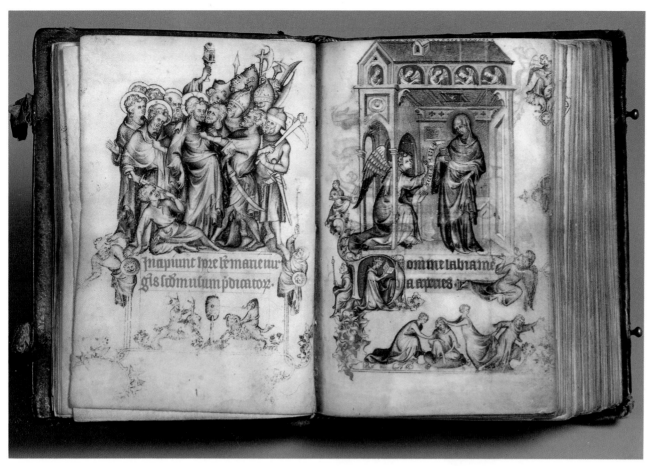

10-34. Jean Pucelle. Pages with *Betrayal and Arrest of Christ*, folio 15v. (left) and *Annunciation*, folio 16r. (right), *Petites Heures of Jeanne d'Evreux*, from Paris. c. 1325–28. Grisaille and color on vellum, each page 3½ x 2¼" (8.2 x 5.6 cm). The Metropolitan Museum of Art, New York
The Cloisters Collection, 1954 (54.1.2)

This book was precious to the queen, who mentioned it in her will; she named its illuminator, an unusual tribute.

bimah can be seen in figure 10-32, straddling the two central bays. The interior of the synagogue was originally richly adorned with murals. Men worshiped and studied in the principal space; women were sequestered in annexes.

INDEPENDENT SCULPTURE

Besides carving the sculptural ornament for churches, Gothic sculptors also found a lucrative new outlet for their work in a growing demand for small religious statues intended for homes and personal chapels or as donations to favorite churches. Among the treasures of the Abbey Church of Saint-Denis is a silver-gilt image, slightly more than 2 feet tall, of a standing Virgin and Child (fig. 10-33). An inscription on the base bears the date 1339 and the name of Queen Jeanne d'Evreux, wife of Charles IV of France (ruled 1322–1328). The Virgin holds her son in her left arm, her weight on her left leg, creating the graceful S-curve pose that was a stylistic signature of the period. She holds a scepter topped with an enameled and jeweled fleur-de-lis, the heraldic symbol of French royalty, and she originally had a crown on her head. The scepter served as a reliquary for hairs said to come from Mary's head. Despite this figure's clear association with royalty, the Virgin's simple clothing and sweet, youthful face anticipates a type of the ideally beautiful mother that emerged in the later fourteenth and fifteenth centuries in northern France, Flanders, and Germany.

MANUSCRIPT ILLUMINATION AND EMBROIDERY

France and England gained renown in the thirteenth and fourteenth centuries not only for the new Gothic architectural style but also for book and textile arts. Books ranged from practical manuals for artisans to elaborate devotional works illustrated with exquisite miniatures. Beginning in the late thirteenth century, private prayer books became popular among those who could afford them. Such books came to be called Books of Hours because they contained special prayers to be recited at the eight canonical "hours," literally around the clock. Books of Hours were most commonly devoted to the Virgin, but they could be personalized for individual patrons with prayers to patron saints, a calendar of saints' church festivals, and other offices, such as that said for the dead.

A tiny, exquisite Book of Hours given by Charles IV to his wife, Queen Jeanne d'Evreux, shortly after their marriage in 1325 is the work of an illuminator named Jean Pucelle (fig. 10-34). Instead of the intense colors used by earlier illuminators, Pucelle worked in a technique called **grisaille**—monochromatic painting in shades of gray with delicate touches of color. The pages shown here are part of a narrative cycle juxtaposing scenes from the Infancy and the Passion of Christ, a form known as the Joys and Sorrows of the Virgin. Here, the "Joy" of the *Annunciation*

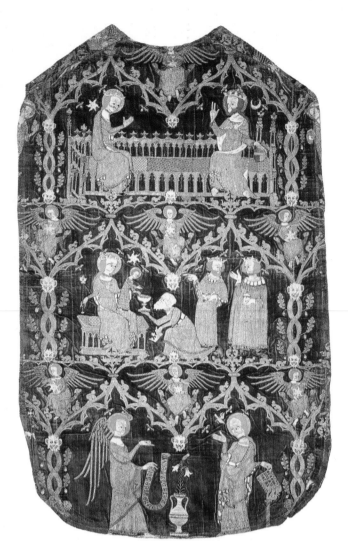

10-35. *Life of the Virgin* (Chichester-Constable chasuble back, from a set of vestments embroidered in *opus anglicanum*), from southern England. 1330–50. Red velvet with silk and metallic thread; length 5'6" (1.64 m), width 30" (76 cm). The Metropolitan Museum of Art, New York
Fletcher Fund, 1927 (2.7 162.1)

The Game of Love

The idea of gallant knights serving refined ladies, who bestowed tokens of affection on their chosen suitors or cruelly withheld their love, captures the popular imagination. The battle of love, played out over a chessboard, or in the pageantry of tournaments, provided the secular arts of the Middle Ages with some of their most popular secular themes.

The ideal of courtly love arose in southern France in the early twelfth century and gained impetus at the court of Eleanor of Aquitaine (1122–1204). Eleanor had been married first to the king of France and then to King Henry II of England. She was the mother of one of the most romantic figures in history, Richard the Lion-Hearted. As dowager queen, she presided over one of the most cultivated courts in Europe, at Poitiers, in Aquitaine.

The primary theme of courtly love involved the passionate devotion of lover and loved one. The relationship was almost always illicit—for example, that of a married woman and a lover—and its consummation was usually impossible. The love of the knight Lancelot for Guinevere, the wife of King Arthur, is still a compelling story, as the success of the musical *Camelot* shows. The literature of courtly love was initially spread by the musician-poets known as troubadours, who included women among their members. They sang of love's joys and heartbreaks in daring terms and extolled the ennobling effects of the lovers' selfless devotion. In these songs, love often ends in tragedy. Our own popular and country-western music continues this tradition today.

---

on the right is paired with the "Sorrow" of the *Betrayal and Arrest of Christ* on the left.

In the *Annunciation*, Mary receives the archangel Gabriel in her Gothic-style home, as rejoicing angels look on from windows under the eaves. Queen Jeanne appears in the initial below the *Annunciation*, kneeling before a lectern and reading from her Book of Hours. This inclusion of the patron in prayer within a scene, a practice that continued in monumental painting and sculpture in the fifteenth century, conveyed the idea that the scenes were "visions" inspired by meditation rather than records of historical events. In the Betrayal scene on the left page, the traitorous disciple Judas Iscariot embraces Jesus, thus identifying him to soldiers who have come to seize him and setting in motion the events that lead to the Crucifixion. The spoof of military training sketched below, showing "knights" riding goats and jousting at a barrel stuck on a pole, is perhaps a comment on the lack of valor of the soldiers assaulting Jesus.

Both pages show Pucelle adapting the sculptural style of the French court to manuscript illustration. Softly modeled, voluminous draperies are gathered around tall, elegantly curved figures with curly hair and broad foreheads. Jesus on the left and Mary on the right stand in the swaying S-curve pose typical of Court style works, such as the *Virgin and Child* from Saint-Denis, commissioned by the same queen (see fig. 10-33). The earnest face of the Annunciation archangel resembles that of the angel Gabriel at Reims (see fig. 10-26).

The English also made richly decorated books, but they became renowned throughout Europe for their pictorial needlework using colored silk and gold thread. The art came to be called *opus anglicanum* (English work). The names of several prominent embroiderers are known, but in her own day no one surpassed Mabel of Bury Saint Edmunds, who worked for King Henry III. She created both religious and secular pieces for him, and the grateful king paid her in money and rich gifts.

None of Mabel's work has been identified, but it must have resembled the embroidery seen on a chasuble—garment worn by priests while celebrating the Mass—known as the Chichester-Constable chasuble (fig. 10-35). Here, the images are formed by fine gradations of colored silk as subtle as the finest painting. Three Marian scenes—the Annunciation, the Adoration of the Magi, and the Coronation of the Virgin—are arranged in three registers framed by cusped, crocketed S-shaped arches and twisting branches sprouting oak leaves with seed-pearl acorns. This vestment would have glinted in the candlelight amid the other treasures of the altar. So heavy did such gold and bejeweled garments become that their wearers often needed help to move.

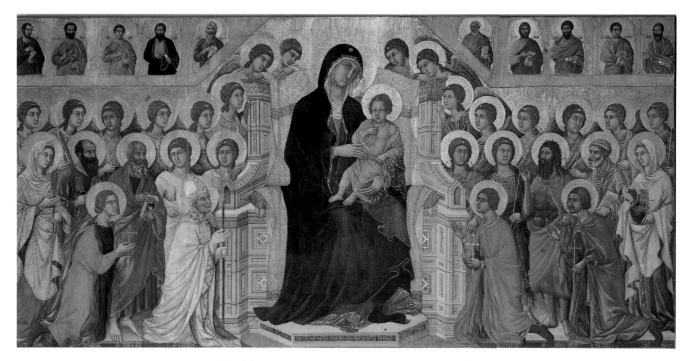

10-36. Duccio di Buoninsegna. *Virgin and Child in Majesty (Maestà)*, main panel of *Maestà Altarpiece*, from Siena Cathedral. 1308–11. Tempera and gold on wood, 7' x 13'6¼" (2.13 x 4.12 m). Museo dell'Opera del Duomo, Siena

"On the day that it was carried to the [cathedral] the shops were shut, and the bishop conducted a great and devout company of priests and friars in solemn procession, accompanied by . . . all the officers of the commune, and all the people, and one after another the worthiest with lighted candles in their hands took places near the picture, and behind came the women and children with great devotion. And they accompanied the said picture up to the [cathedral], making the procession around the Campo [square], as is the custom, all the bells ringing joyously, out of reverence for so noble a picture as is this" (Holt, page 69).

Italian Panel and Mural Painting

The elegant Court style seen in manuscript illustrations and embroideries also influenced Gothic **panel painting**. **Altarpieces**, or large-scale paintings on wood panels, made to decorate church altars, began to appear in the twelfth century and proliferated throughout Europe in the thirteenth century. Important schools of Gothic painting emerged in the Italian cities of Florence and Siena. Italian painters at this time worked in a kind of paint known as **tempera** (see "Cennini on Panel Painting," right).

Siena's foremost painter was Duccio di Buoninsegna (active 1278–1318), whose synthesis of Byzantine and northern Gothic influences transformed the tradition in which he worked. Duccio and his studio assistants painted a huge altarpiece for Siena Cathedral, known as the *Maestà* (Majesty) *Altarpiece*, between 1308 and 1311. Because the *Maestà* was broken up in the eighteenth century, its power and beauty can only be imagined from scattered parts. The main scene, depicting the *Virgin and Child in Majesty* (fig. 10-36), was once accompanied above and below by narrative scenes from the Life of the Virgin and the Infancy of Christ. On the back were scenes from the Life and Passion of Christ. In this altarpiece, Duccio has combined a softened Italo-Byzantine figure style (an Italian adaptation of later Byzantine art) with the linear grace and easy relationship between figures

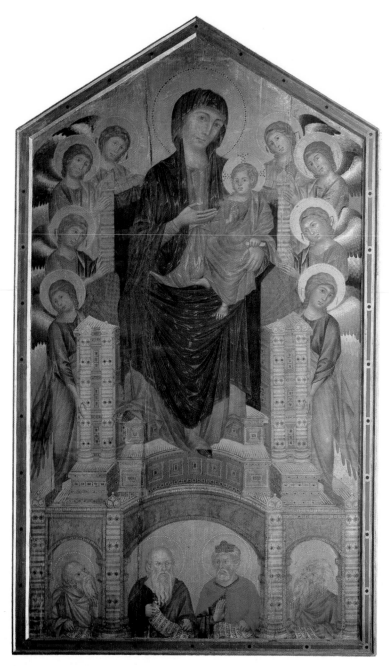

10-37. Cimabue. *Virgin and Child Enthroned,* from the Church of Santa Trinità, Florence. c. 1280. Tempera and gold on wood, 12'7½" x 7'4" (3.9 x 2.2 m). Galleria degli Uffizi, Florence

and their settings characteristic of the Gothic art of France. The central, most holy figures retain an iconic Byzantine solemnity and immobility, but those adoring them reflect a more naturalistic, courtly style that became the hallmark of the Sienese school for years to come. The ornate **punchwork**, or tooled designs in gold leaf, is also characteristically Sienese.

In Florence, Duccio's counterpart was an older painter named Cenni di Pepi (active c. 1272–1302), better known by his nickname, Cimabue. Cimabue is believed to have painted the *Virgin and Child Enthroned* (fig. 10-37) in about 1280 for the main altar of the Church of the Santa Trinità (Holy

Trinity) in Florence. At more than 11½ feet high, this enormous panel painting seems to have set a precedent for monumental altarpieces. In it, Cimabue combines two iconographic types: the Virgin as the Throne of Wisdom (see fig. 10-9) and the Virgin Pointing the Way—that is, pointing to the infant Jesus as the path to salvation.

Cimabue employed Byzantine formulas in determining the proportions of the figures. To render the draperies (and to suggest divinity), he used the Byzantine technique of highlighting the base color with thin lines of gold where the folds break. Mary's huge throne, painted to represent gold with inset enamels and gems, provides an

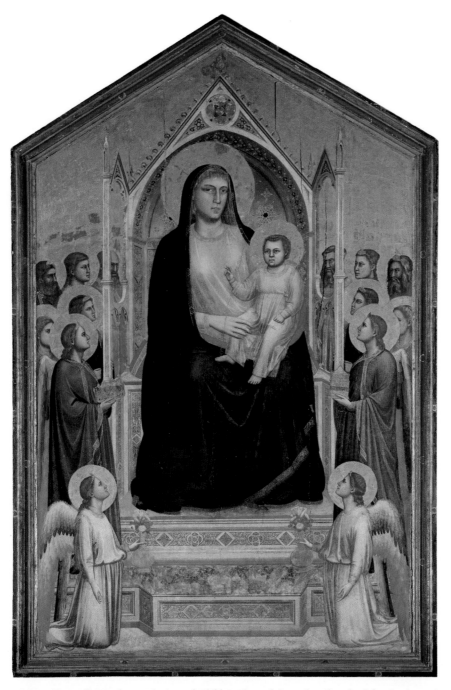

10-38. Giotto di Bondone. *Virgin and Child Enthroned,* from the Church of the Ognissanti, Florence. c. 1310. Tempera and gold on wood, 10'8" x 6'8¼" (3.53 x 2.05 m). Galleria degli Uffizi, Florence

architectural framework for the figures. The vantage point suspends the viewer in space in front of the image, simultaneously looking down on the projecting elements of the throne and Mary's lap, but straight at the prophets at the base of the throne and the splendid winged seraphim who appear one above another on either side. These spacial ambiguities, as well as subtle asymmetries throughout the composition, the Virgin's thoughtful gaze, and the well-observed faces of the old men, are all departures from tradition that serve to enliven the picture.

Cimabue's pupil Giotto (active c. 1300–1337) shared his master's concern for spatial volumes,

solid forms, and warmly naturalistic human figures. Giotto's 1310 painting of the *Virgin and Child Enthroned* (fig. 10-38) for the Church of the Ognissanti (All Saints) in Florence reflects Cimabue's influence in its largely symmetrical composition, the rendering of the angels' wings, and Mary's Byzantine facial type. Gone, however, are the Virgin's modestly inclined head and delicate gold-lined drapery; instead, light and shadow play across her substantial form. This colossal Mary seems to overwhelm her slender Gothic throne. Despite Giotto's retention of hierarchical scale and the formal, enthroned image type, he has created the sense that his figures are fully

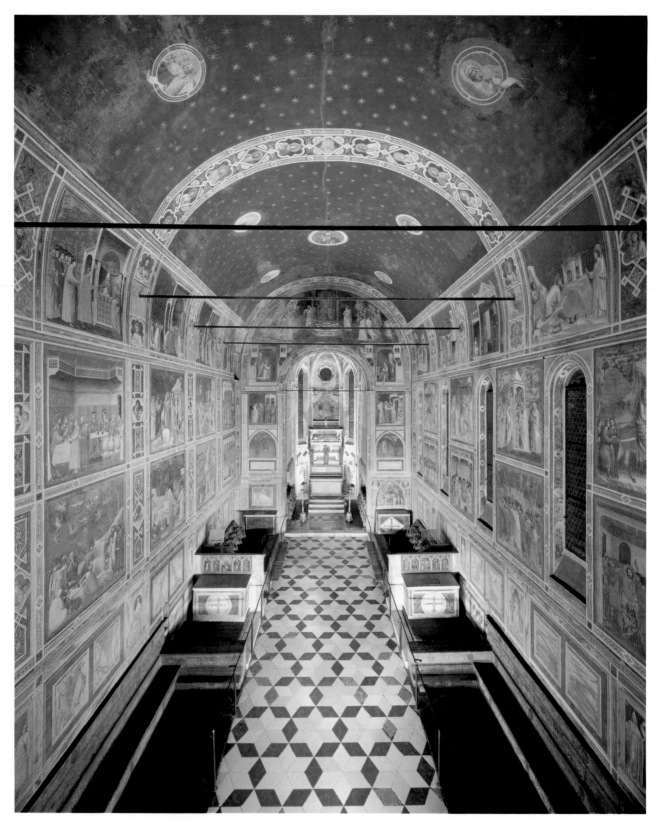

10-39. Giotto di Bondone. Frescoes, Arena Chapel, Padua. View toward the east wall, 1305–6

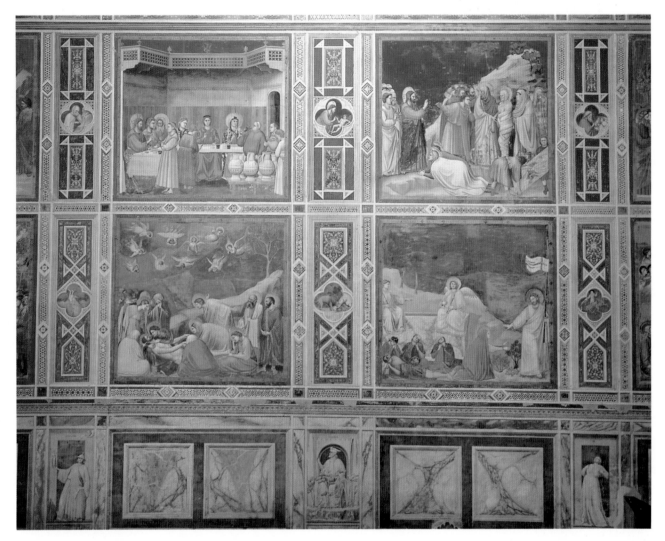

10-40. Giotto di Bondone. *Marriage at Cana,* *Raising of Lazarus,* *Resurrection and* *Noli Me Tangere,* **and** *Lamentation* (clockwise from top left), frescoes on north wall of Arena Chapel, Padua

three-dimensional beings inhabiting real space.

The most famous among Giotto's works is the frescoed interior of the Arena Chapel at Padua, painted about 1305–1306 (fig. 10-39). Giotto rendered his bulky figures as pure color masses by painting the deepest shadows with the most intense hues and highlighting shapes with lighter shades mixed with white. These sculpturally modeled figures enabled Giotto to convey a sense of depth in landscape settings without relying on the traditional convention of an architectural framework, although he did make use of that convention as well.

Both Giotto's narrative skills and his use of **typology**—in which earlier events presage later ones—are apparent in the paintings on the side walls (fig. 10-40). Events in the life of the Virgin

Mary and in the ministry of Jesus are depicted in three registers that circle the room. In the section illustrated here, the first miracle, the event of Jesus' changing water to wine at the wedding feast at Cana (in an event that prefigures the Last Supper) is followed by the raising of Lazarus (a reference to the Resurrection, which is depicted below).

Sienese painting was a key contributor to the development of the mainstream of Gothic art in Europe, but Florentine painting, in the style originated by Giotto and kept alive by his pupils and their followers, was fundamental to the development of Italian Renaissance art over the next two centuries. With Giotto, art moved toward the depiction of a humanized world anchored in three-dimensional form.

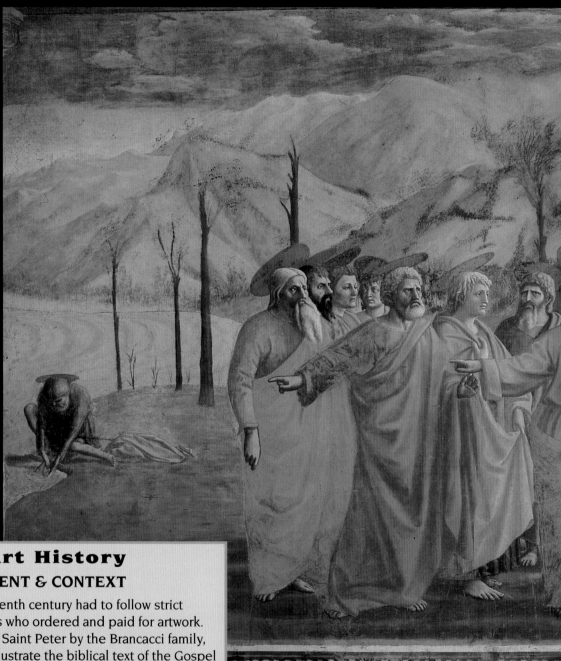

Masaccio. *Tribute Money,*
fresco in the Brancacci Chapel,
Church of Santa Maria del
Carmine, Florence. c. 1427.
8'1" x 19'7" (2.3 x 6 m)

Narrative

The story of Peter, Jesus, and the tax collector begins with the confrontation between Jesus and the tax man in the center of the painting. The tax collector stands in front of all twelve apostles and demands the temple tax. Jesus tells Peter not to offend the officials but instead to cast a line into the sea and to take the first fish he hooks, then to give the coin—worth twice the temple tax—that he will find in the fish's mouth to the state. Peter is pictured on the left as he pulls the coin from the fish's mouth. At the right, Peter gives the tax collector the coin. The three events take place in the same space. Many cultures use this convention to illustrate an unfolding narrative.

Context

The story takes place in Roman Judea, yet the tax man wears contemporary fifteenth-century clothing, and the porticoed building is Early Renaissance in style. Jesus and his apostles wear vaguely classicizing robes and cloaks, giving the painting a timeless quality. Neither the artist nor his public was concerned with historical accuracy. Although artists and patrons ignored the historical context of the events pictured, they were not quite prepared to place Jesus and Peter in the dress of their own day. Today we see the painting in its fifteenth-century context.

K E Y S to Art History
NARRATIVE, CONTENT & CONTEXT

Artists before the nineteenth century had to follow strict instructions from patrons who ordered and paid for artwork. In a chapel dedicated to Saint Peter by the Brancacci family, Masaccio was asked to illustrate the biblical text of the Gospel of Matthew, which tells the story of Jesus and the tax collector. The Gospel story forms the *narrative content*. In his painting, Masaccio creates recognizable subject matter—three groups of male figures standing in front of a classically proportioned building in a stark landscape. More important, however, is another dimension of content, the idea expressed by the narrative. Completing the definition of content as it is used by many art historians is the notion of *context*, the ways in which the time and place influenced the artist.

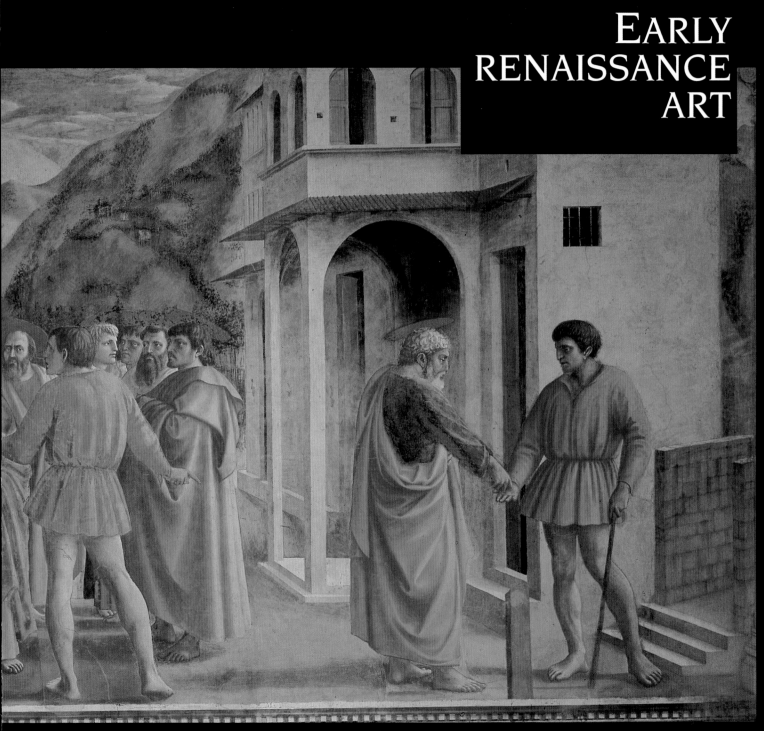

EARLY RENAISSANCE ART

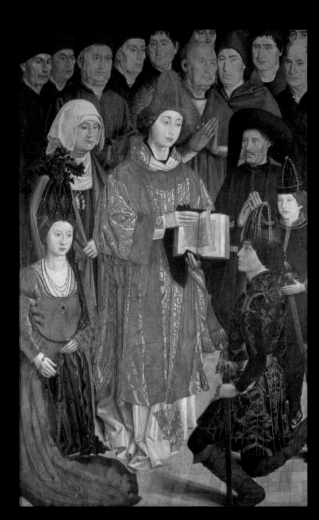

11-1. Nuño Gonçalvez. *Saint Vincent with the Portuguese Royal Family,* panel from *the Altarpiece of Saint Vincent.* c. 1471–81. Oil on panel, 6'9¾" x 4'2⅝" (2.07 x 1.28 m). Museu Nacional de Arte Antiga, Lisbon

With furrowed brow and eyes fixed on a distant goal, Prince Henry the Navigator stands next to Saint Vincent, a patron saint of the royal house of Portugal (fig. 11-1). Prince Henry (1394–1460), the third son of King João I of Portugal, was a crusading soldier who fought against Islamic forces in North Africa; he was also a classical scholar, a prince and statesman, an intensely religious Catholic who wore a hair shirt beneath his clothes, and a remarkable catalyst of the Age of Exploration. Although he never journeyed on a voyage of discovery himself, he founded an observatory and a school for the study of geography and navigation and spent some forty years sponsoring the expeditions of mariners who explored the African coast in search of a sea route to India and the Far East. He was motivated by both the love of pure knowledge and a desire for riches to fill Portuguese coffers. He almost certainly believed the words of his personal motto, "the desire to do good."

Discovery, not just physical but also intellectual discovery, was the guiding theme of the *Renaissance,* or "rebirth." During the Middle Ages, European scholars had studied the work of Greek and Roman philosophers, poets, rhetoricians, and historians. In the fifteenth and early sixteenth centuries, a group of scholars of antiquity, known as humanists, rediscovered the equally remarkable accomplishments of the ancient mathematicians, astronomers, geographers, physicians, naturalists, artists, and architects. Encouraged by these examples, Renaissance scholars and artists tried to understand, describe, and reproduce the appearance of the natural world in a rational and scientific way. In Italy, Renaissance artists developed a system known as **linear perspective** (see "Renaissance Perspective Systems," opposite), which allowed them to represent three-dimensional reality convincingly, and architects revived features of classical architecture, including the classical orders, and borrowed designs and decorative motifs from ruins of Roman temples, triumphal arches, and tombs. Both painters and sculptors tried to portray the human body accurately, and they even depicted the nude in secular works of art for the first time since classical antiquity. The methods of seeing and reproducing the visual world that Renaissance artists revived prevailed across Europe as late as the nineteenth century. The Renaissance viewpoint survives in "realistic" art and in the conventions of popular art, especially in advertising, today.

Renaissance Art in the Low Countries

Renaissance art followed slightly different paths in Italy and north of the Alps. The French Gothic style had never taken deep root in Italy, where artists continued to be influenced by Byzantine art and were surrounded by the ruins of Roman antiquity. Thus, the Italian Renaissance was less a reaction to the Gothic past than a return to a classical tradition that had never been completely forgotten.

In northern Europe, in contrast, where the Gothic style had emerged from native traditions, artists came to the Renaissance by way of an intense interest in the natural world. Gothic artists in France, Germany, and the Low Countries had depicted birds, plants, and animals with breathtaking accuracy in manuscript painting, textiles, and sculpture. In the fourteenth century, they enlarged on these developments by accurately portraying such things as reflections on water, steamy breath on a cold winter's day, and the sheen of a metal basin. In the fifteenth century, they learned to place these details convincingly in scenes from the material world. Similarly, fifteenth-century portraits seem astonishingly lifelike (see fig. 10), and even in religious paintings, saints and angels often seem to have distinct personalities.

TECHNIQUE
RENAISSANCE PERSPECTIVE SYSTEMS

In the fifteenth century, Italian humanists developed a system known as **linear**, or **mathematical, perspective** that enabled artists to represent the visible world in a convincingly illusionistic way. The architect Filippo Brunelleschi first demonstrated the system about 1420, and the scholar and architect Leon Battista Alberti codified it in 1436 in his treatise *Della Pittura* (*On Painting*).

For Alberti, a picture's surface was a flat plane that intersected the viewer's field of vision at right angles. This highly artificial concept presumed a one-eyed viewer standing dead center at a prescribed distance from a work of art. From this fixed vantage point, every-thing would appear to recede into the distance at the same rate, shaped by imaginary lines called **orthogonals** that met at a single **vanishing point**, often on the horizon. The use of orthogonals replicated the optical illusion that things grow smaller and closer together as they get farther away from us.

Linear perspective has the advantage of making the pictorial space seem almost like an extension of the real space, creating a compelling, even exaggerated sense of depth (see fig. 11-17). In the course of the fifteenth century, however, many artists adopted multiple vanishing points, which gave their work a more relaxed, less tunnel-like feeling.

Meanwhile, in the north, artists such as Jan van Eyck (see fig. 11-3) continued to employ older visual systems known as **atmospheric** and **intuitive perspective**. In atmospheric perspective, variations in color and clarity convey the feeling of distance. In intuitive per-spective, artists use visual devices, such as making background figures smaller, to convey spatial depth, but do not follow a consistent mathematical system such as linear perspective.

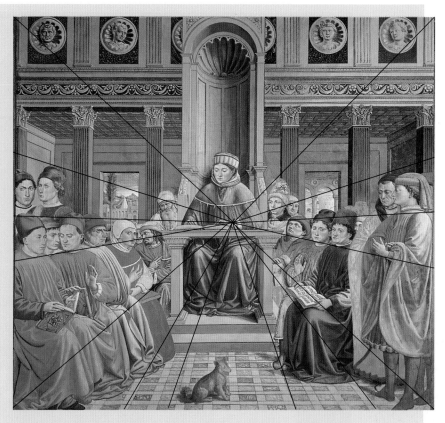

Benozzo Gozzoli. *Saint Augustine Teaching in Rome.* 15th century

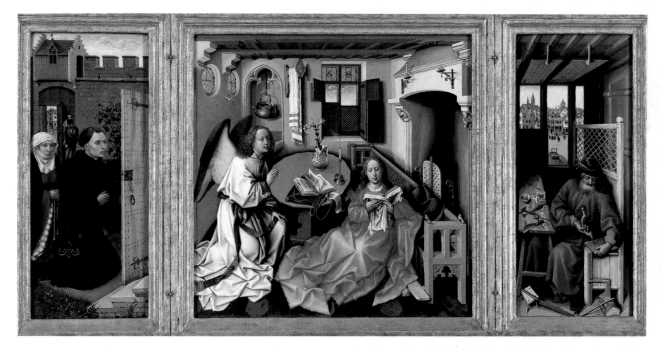

11-2. Robert Campin. *Mérode Altarpiece* (Triptych of the Annunciation) (open). c. 1425–28. Oil on panel, center 25¼ x 24⅞" (64.1 x 63.2 cm); each wing approx. 25⅜ x 10⅞" (64.5 x 27.6 cm). The Metropolitan Museum of Art, New York The Cloisters Collection, 1956 (56.70)

Throughout most of the fifteenth century, the artists of Flanders were considered the best in Europe. The art produced in the Low Countries and Burgundy during this period is commonly called *Flemish* because its greatest exponents lived in the province of Flanders (roughly equivalent to the western part of modern Belgium and a small area of northern France), part of the domain of the duke of Burgundy. Flanders, with its major seaport and commercial center at Bruges, was the com-mercial power of northern Europe, rivaling the Italian city-states of Florence and Venice.

The most outstanding exponents of the new Flemish style were Robert Campin (documented from 1406; d. 1444), Jan van Eyck (c. 1370/90–1441), and Rogier van der Weyden (c. 1399–1464). About 1425–1428, Campin painted an altarpiece now known as the *Mérode Altarpiece* (fig. 11-2) after

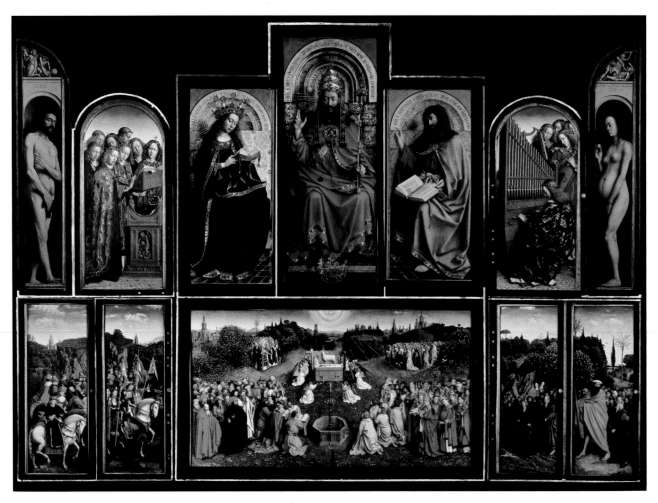

11-3. **Jan and Hubert van Eyck.** *Ghent Altarpiece* (open), Cathedral of Saint-Bavo, Ghent, Flanders (Belgium). 1432. Oil on panel, 11'5¾" x 15'1½" (3.5 x 4.6 m)

TECHNIQUE

PAINTING ON PANEL

Painting pictures on wood has an ancient history, and wood panels were particularly favored by European painters and their patrons in the fifteenth century for works ranging from enormous altarpieces to small portraits. First the wood surface was prepared to make it smooth and non-absorbent. After being sanded, the panel was coated—in Italy with **gesso**, a fine solution of plaster, and in northern Europe with a solution of chalk. These coatings soaked in and closed the pores of the wood. Fine linen was often glued down over the whole surface or over the joining lines on large panels made of two or more pieces of wood. The cloth was then also coated with gesso or chalk.

Once the surface was ready, the artist could paint on it with either a water-soluble color, called **tempera**, or **oil paint**. Italian artists favored tempera, using it almost exclusively for panel painting until the end of the fifteenth century. Northern European artists preferred the oil technique that Flemish painters so skillfully exploited at the begin-

ning of the century. In some cases, wood panels were first painted with oil, then given fine detailing with tempera, a technique especially popular for small portraits.

Tempera had to be applied in a very precise manner, because it dried almost as quickly as it was laid down. Shading had to be done with careful overlying strokes in tones ranging from white and gray to dark brown and black. Because tempera is opaque—light striking its surface does not penetrate to lower layers of color and reflect back—the resulting surface was **matte**, or dull, and had to be varnished to give it a sheen. Oil paint, on the other hand, took much longer to dry, and while it was still wet, errors could simply be wiped away with a cloth. Oil could also be made translucent by applying it in very thin layers, called glazes. Light striking a surface built up of glazes penetrates to the lower layers and is reflected back, creating the appearance of glowing from within. In both tempera and oil the desired result in the fifteenth century was a smooth surface that betrayed no brush-strokes and somewhat resembled enamel.

the name of its former owners. Its relatively small size—slightly more than 2 feet tall and about 4 feet wide with the wings open—suggests that it was made for a private chapel. Campin portrayed the Annunciation as if the Virgin lived in a Flemish home. Into this contemporary setting he brought normal household objects that could also be seen as religious symbols. The lilies on the table, for example, were a traditional element of Annunciation imagery symbolizing Mary's virginity. The hanging waterpot and towel (actually a Jewish prayer shawl) in the niche refer to Mary's purity and her sacred role as the vessel for the Incarnation of Christ. Such objects are often referred to as "hidden" symbols because they are treated as a normal part of the scene, but their religious meanings would have been understood by most contemporary viewers.

In the right-hand panel, the mousetraps in Joseph's carpentry shop are a reference to a passage written by the theologian Saint Augustine, referring to Christ as the bait in a trap set by God to catch Satan. In the left-hand panel, the altarpiece's donors kneel in front of the open door of the house where the Annunciation takes place, suggesting that the scene is a vision induced by their prayers. Such a presentation, often used by Flemish artists, allowed the donors of a religious work to appear in the same space and time,

11-4. Jan van Eyck. *Portrait of Giovanni Arnolfini (?) and His Wife, Giovanna Cenami (?).* 1434. Oil on panel, 33 x 22½" (83.8 x 57.2 cm). The National Gallery, London

Jan is famous for his talent with the technique of painting with oil on wood panel—so much so that he is sometimes mistakenly called the "inventor" of oil painting. Oils had been known as a medium for several centuries but had been used for practical purposes, for example, for painting that would be exposed to the weather. Jan perfected the technique by building up his images in transparent oil layers, a procedure called glazing, using tiny, carefully applied brushstrokes to render detail.

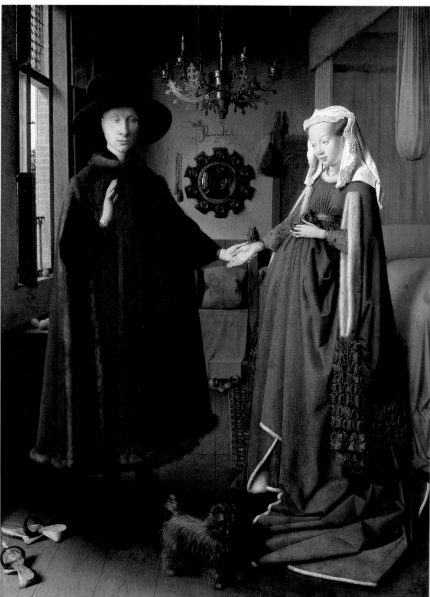

and often on the same scale as the figures of the saints represented. The view out of Saint Joseph's window in the right panel, however, depicts a realistic Flemish street scene.

The complex treatment of light in the *Mérode Altarpiece* is an example of the innovation of the Flemish painters. The strongest illumination comes from an unseen source at the upper left in front of the **picture plane** (picture surface), apparently the sun entering through the miraculously transparent wall that allows the viewer to observe the scene. More light comes from the rear windows, and a few rays from the round window at left are a symbolic vehicle for the Christ Child's descent. Jesus seems to slide down the rays of light joining God and Mary, carrying the cross of human salvation. The light falling on the Virgin's lap emphasizes this connection.

Campin's contemporary Jan van Eyck was a court painter to Philip the Good, duke of Burgundy, the uncle of the king of France and one of the wealthiest and most sophisticated men in Europe. He made Jan van Eyck one of his confidential employees and even sent him on an embassy to Portugal. The duke was not Jan's only patron. Civic leaders, town councils, and rich merchants were also important art patrons in the Low Countries, where cities were largely independent of the landed nobility.

Jan's most important early painting was the *Ghent Altarpiece*, completed in 1432 for a wealthy official of Ghent and his wife. When the altarpiece is closed (see fig. 10), the patrons appear to be kneeling at each side of Mary and Gabriel, in effect, looking into the Virgin's chamber at the moment of the Incarnation.

The brilliantly painted interior panels of the *Ghent Altarpiece* (fig. 11-3), which was opened only at Easter, present the Adoration of the Lamb of God by all the saints, accompanied by angel musicians and the towering figures of God, the Virgin Mary, and Saint John the Baptist. The jewels and embroidery, meticulously re-created gem by gem and stitch by stitch, are superb examples of Jan's characteristic technique (see "Painting on Panel," opposite). On the outermost panels, the nude figures of Adam and Eve—whose disobedience to God was humankind's Original Sin, which

Christians believe was redeemed by the sacrifice of Christ—contrast shockingly with the richly dressed figures between them.

Below these figures, in a panoramic landscape, is the Communion of Saints, based on a passage in the Book of Revelation that describes the Lamb of God venerated by a multitude of believers (Revelation 14:1). Despite its visionary subject, Jan's painting is firmly grounded in the terrestrial world. The meadow and woods, painted leaf by leaf and petal by petal, testify to his careful observation of nature. Jan noted, for example, that the farther the colors are from a viewer, the more muted they seem, so he painted the more distant objects with a grayish or bluish cast and the sky paler toward the horizon, a treatment called **atmospheric perspective**. A truly realistic atmospheric perspective would include the blurring of objects, but Jan paints objects as sharply in the distance as in the foreground.

Jan's best-known painting today is an elaborate portrait of a couple, traditionally identified as Giovanni Arnolfini and his wife Giovanna Cenami (fig. 11-4). Early interpreters suggested

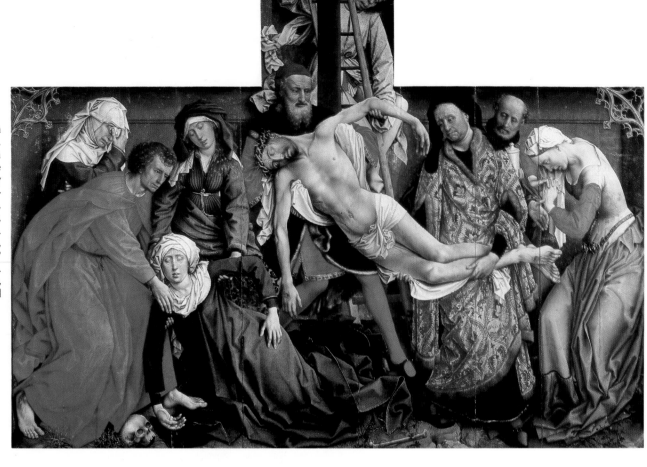

11-5. Rogier van der Weyden. *Deposition*, from an altarpiece commissioned by the Crossbowmen's Guild, Louvain, Brabant, Belgium. c. 1442. Oil on panel, 7'2⅝" x 8'7⅛" (2.2 x 2.62 m). Museo del Prado, Madrid

that this fascinating work represents a wedding or betrothal. Below the mirror on the back wall, the artist inscribed the words: *Johannes de eyck fuit hic 1434* ("Jan van Eyck was here, 1434"). Normally, a work of art in fifteenth-century Flanders would have been signed "Jan van Eyck made this." The wording here is that used by witnesses to legal documents, and indeed, two witnesses to the scene are reflected in the mirror, a man in a red turban—perhaps the artist—and one other. They watch the richly dressed man in the portrait raise his right hand to take an oath while holding the woman's right hand in his left. The scene takes place in the principal room of a house filled with impressive furniture, including a luxurious bed. (The modern idea of rooms performing a single specific function did not yet exist.) The furnishings in Jan's painting may have hidden significance. The crystal prayer beads on the wall suggest the couple's piety; the dog is a symbol of fidelity; the single candle and the round mirror, the presence of God.

One of the least known of the major early Flemish artists is Rogier van der Weyden. Although he maintained a large workshop in Brussels, attracting apprentices and assistants from as far away as Italy, not a single existing

work of art bears his name or has an undisputed connection with him. The work scholars use to establish the thematic and stylistic characteristics for Rogier's art is a large panel (more than 7 by 8 feet), depicting the Deposition, or removal of Christ's body from the Cross (fig. 11-5). The central panel of an altarpiece, commissioned by the Louvain Crossbowmen's Guild sometime around 1442, it originally was accompanied by **wings** representing the Four Evangelists and Christ's Resurrection.

The Deposition was a popular theme in the fifteenth century because of its dramatic, personally engaging character. Here Jesus' suffering and death are made palpably real by the display of the lifesize corpse at the center of the composition. Rogier has arranged the figure in a graceful curve framed by a jarringly angular pattern of arms, echoed by the form of the fainting Virgin. The highly emotional treatment of both mother and son encourages the viewer to identify with both of them. Red and white color accents focus attention on the main subject. The whites of the winding cloth and the tunic of the youth on the ladder set off Jesus' pale body, as the white veil wrapped like a turban and shawl emphasizes the ashen face of Mary. The solid, three-dimensional

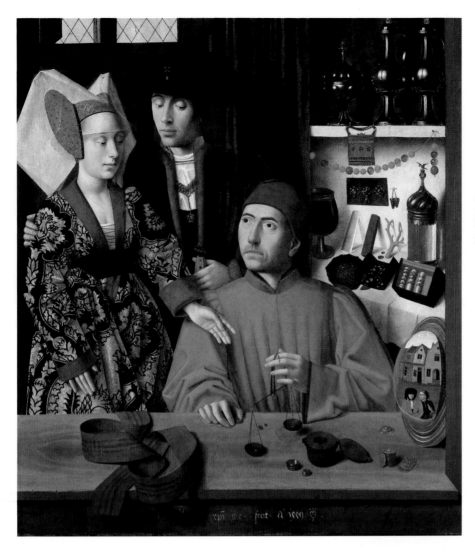

11-6. Petrus Christus. *Saint Eloy (Eligius) in His Shop.* 1449. Oil on oak panel, 38⅝ x 33½" (98 x 85 cm). The Metropolitan Museum of Art, New York

Robert Lehman Collection, 1975 (1975.1.110)

figures, compressed in a shallow space in front of a gilded wood backdrop, press toward the viewer, allowing no escape from their expressions of intense grief. Many scholars see the emotionality of Rogier's work as a tie with the Gothic past, but the intense feelings evoked by his painting can also be interpreted as an example of fifteenth-century humanistic concern for the individual. Although united by their sorrow, the mourning figures react in personal ways, Jesus' friend Mary Magdalen wringing her hands in anguish at the right, and Saint John the Evangelist looking sorrowfully down at the Virgin, whom he supports on the left.

The extraordinary achievements of Robert Campin, Jan van Eyck, and Rogier van der Weyden attracted many followers. A number of this second generation of Flemish painters received their training in the Dutch provinces of the Low Countries, where local schools of painting had developed strong followings. Petrus Christus (documented from 1444; d. c. 1475), who worked in Bruges beginning about 1444, probably came from the northern duchy of Brabant. In 1449, Christus painted one of his most admired works, *Saint Eloy (Eligius) in His Shop* (fig. 11-6). According to Christian legend, Eloy, a seventh-century

ecclesiastic and a goldsmith and mintmaster for the French court, used his wealth to ransom Christian captives. Here he weighs a ring to determine its value, as a handsome couple looks on. A stock of similar rings rests on a shelf in the background, affording us a remarkable view of a fifteenth-century goldsmith's wares. The painting may record a specific betrothal or wedding, or the couple may be idealized figures personifying marital love in general.

As in Jan van Eyck's *Portrait of Giovanni Arnolfini (?) and His Wife, Giovanna Cenami (?)* (see fig. 11-4), a convex mirror extends the viewer's field of vision, in this case showing two men on the street outside. The young couple is dressed in the height of Burgundian court fashion. The woman wears a rich Italian brocade gown and jeweled headdress; the man, fur-lined black wool. The emphasis on everyday details is so strong that the presence of the saint seems more a pretext for a secular subject rather than an integral part of a religious scene. In fact, this painting provided the precedent for a long line of clearly secular pictures showing businesspeople in their shops, which persisted well into the sixteenth century.

The painter Hugo van der Goes (c. 1440–1482) brought together the intellectualism of Jan van

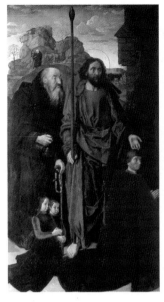
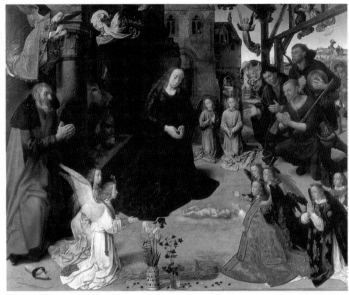
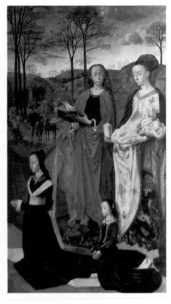

11-7. Hugo van der Goes. *Portinari Altarpiece* (open). c. 1474–76. Tempera and oil on panel, center 8'3¹/₂" x 10' (2.53 x 3.01 m); wings each 8'3¹/₂" x 4'7¹/₂" (2.53 x 1.41 m). Galleria degli Uffizi, Florence

Women Artists in the Late Middle Ages and the Renaissance

Since most formal apprenticeships were closed to women, medieval and Renaissance women artists learned their trade either from family members or in convents. Despite the obstacles, however, a few highly skilled women received major commissions. In the fourteenth century, Bourgot, the daughter of the miniaturist Jean le Noir, illuminated books for Charles V of France and Jean, duke of Berry. Christine de Pisan supported herself and her children by writing for these same patrons. She oversaw the production of her books and wrote of one artist named Anastaise, "who is so learned and skillful in painting manuscript borders and miniature backgrounds that one cannot find an artisan who can surpass her . . . nor whose work is more highly esteemed" (*Le Libre de la Cité des Dames*, I.41.4, translated by Earl J. Richards).

Also in the fourteenth century, Jeanne de Montbaston and her husband, Richart, worked together as book illuminators under the auspices of the University of Paris. After Richart's

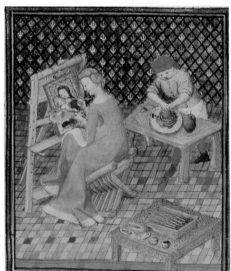

Page with Thamyris, from Giovanni Boccaccio's *De Claris Mulieribus (Concerning Famous Women)*. 1402. Ink and tempera on vellum. Bibliothèque Nationale, Paris

death, Jeanne continued the workshop and was sworn in as a *libraire* (publisher) by the university in 1343.

In the fifteenth century, women were admitted to the artists' guilds (professional organizations) in some cities, including the Flemish towns of Ghent, Bruges, and Antwerp. The painter Agnes van den Bassche of Ghent, for example, operated a painting workshop with her artist husband and became a free master of the painters' guild after his death. A study of the painters' guild of Bruges has shown that by the 1480s one-quarter of its membership was female.

The position of women artists in Italy was not as strong as in Flanders. The humanists' emphasis on academic study rather than apprenticeship for artists, the tie between mathematics and the new linear perspective, and the emphasis on anatomical study—forbidden to women—and realistic figure drawing, prevented women from following careers in painting. Some women nevertheless learned from their fathers or husbands and helped in the family business.

Eyck and the emotionalism of Rogier van der Weyden in an entirely new style. Hugo's major work was an exceptionally large altarpiece, more than 8 feet tall, commissioned by Tommaso Portinari for the family chapel in Florence and probably painted between 1474 and 1476 (fig. 11-7). Portinari, a Florentine living in Bruges, was the local manager of the bank owned by the powerful Medici family. He and his wife, Maria Baroncelli, kneel on the wing interiors with their three eldest children, accompanied by patron saints. The central panel represents the Adoration of the new-born Jesus by Mary and Joseph, a host of angels, and a few shepherds who have rushed in from the fields. Although the brilliant palette and meticulous accuracy recall Jan van Eyck, and the intense but controlled feelings suggest the emotional content of Rogier van der Weyden's works, the composition and interpretation of the altarpiece are entirely Hugo's. The monumental figures of Joseph, Mary, and the shepherds dominating the central panel are the same size as the patron saints on the wings; the Portinari family and the angels are small in comparison.

In the center of the composition, the Christ Child rests naked and vulnerable on the ground with rays of light emanating from his body. The source of this image was the visionary writing of the medieval Swedish mystic Bridget (declared a saint in 1391), which specifically mentions Mary kneeling to adore the Child immediately after giving birth. Hugo's complex symbolism recalls Jan's *Ghent Altarpiece*. The glass vessel in the foreground still life alludes to Christ's entry into Mary's womb without destroying her virginity, the way light passes through glass without breaking it. The three red carnations in the glass (barely visible here) may refer to the Trinity; the seven blue columbines symbolize the Virgin's future sorrows; and the violets scattered on the ground symbolize humility. The **majolica** (glazed earthenware) *albarelo*, or drug jar, a luxury ceramic imported from Spain, holds three irises—white for purity and purple for Christ's royal ancestry—and a red lily, representing the blood of Christ. Hugo's artistic vision goes far beyond this formal religious symbolism. For example, the shepherds, who stand in unaffected awe before the miraculous event, are among the most sympathetically rendered images of common people to be found in the art of this, or any, period.

FLEMISH-INFLUENCED ART OUTSIDE THE LOW COUNTRIES

The style of northern masters such as Hugo van der Goes and Jan van Eyck influenced many artists outside the Low Countries. Spanish and Portuguese painters quickly absorbed the new Flemish style to such an extent that the term *Hispano-Flemish* is applied to their works in the second half of the fifteenth century. Nuño Gonçalvez, a major artist connected with the court of Portugal, painted monumental figures with an intensity of detail and a richness of color that recalls the style of Jan van Eyck. Gonçalvez was renowned for his portraiture and for his virtuoso rendering of costumes and draperies. Sadly, the only paintings that are surely his own are six panels from a **polyptych** (multiple-panel work) made for the Lisbon Convent of Saint Vincent de Fora between 1471 and 1481. In one of the two largest panels (see fig. 11-1), Saint Vincent, magnificent in red and gold vestments, appears with the Portuguese royal family and a row of courtiers. With the exception of the saint, whose features are idealized, all are portraits: at the right, in front of Saint Vincent, kneels King Alfonso V, while his young son and late uncle, Henry the Navigator, look on. At the left are Alfonso's wife and mother, their right hands wrapped in rosary beads. Saint Vincent is clearly a vision, brought on by the intense prayer of the royal family. This altarpiece may have been created to commemorate a Portuguese crusade against the Muslims in Morocco undertaken in 1471 under Saint Vincent's flag.

In France, the Flemish style was particularly influential in manuscript **illumination**, a field in which women excelled (see "Women Artists in the Late Middle Ages and the Renaissance," opposite). Anastaise, who worked for Christine de Pisan, gained considerable renown (see fig. 11). At the beginning of the fifteenth century, the most famous northern illuminators were three brothers, Paul, Herman, and Jean, commonly known as the Limbourg brothers because they came from the region of Limbourg in the Low Countries. In the fifteenth century, people generally did not have family names, but were known instead by their first names, often followed by a reference

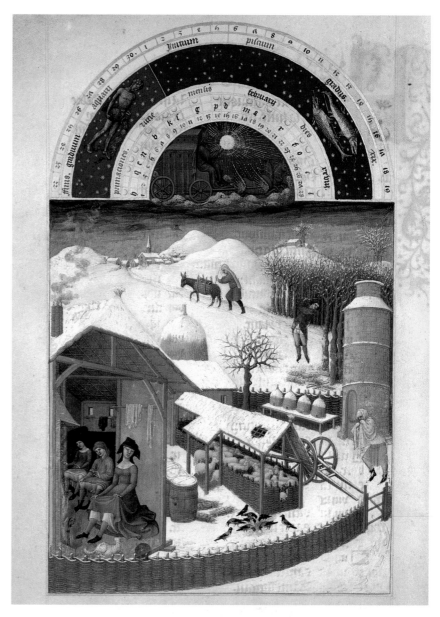

11-8. Paul, Herman, and Jean Limbourg. *Page with February, Très Riches Heures.* 1413–16. Musée Condé, Chantilly, France

to their place of origin, parentage, or occupation. For instance, Jan van Eyck means "Jan from [the town of] Eyck."

The Limbourg brothers are first recorded as apprentice goldsmiths in Paris about 1390. About 1404, they entered the service of the duke of Berry, for whom they produced their major work, the so-called *Très Riches Heures* (*Very Sumptuous Hours*), between 1413 and 1416. This Book of Hours included a calendar section with full-page paintings introducing each month. The subjects alternated between peasants' labors and aristocratic pleasures. In the *February* page (fig. 11-8), farm people relax before a blazing fire. Although many country people at this time lived in hovels, this farm looks comfortable and well maintained, with timber-framed buildings, a row of beehives, a sheepfold, and woven fences.

Most remarkably, the details of the painting convey the feeling of the cold winter weather: the breath of the bundled-up worker turning to

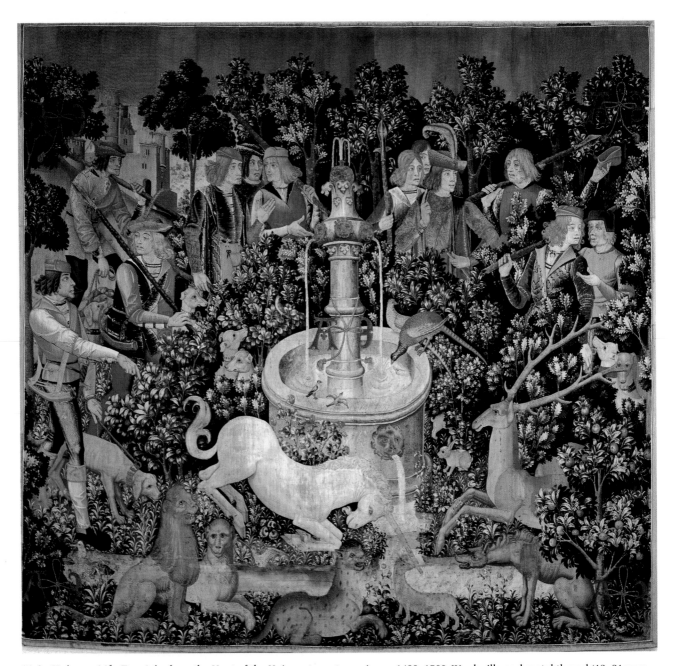

11-9. Unicorn at the Fountain, from the Hunt of the Unicorn tapestry series. c. 1498–1500. Wool, silk, and metal thread (13–21 warp threads per inch), 12'1" x 12'5" (3.68 x 3.78 m). The Metropolitan Museum of Art, New York
Gift of John D. Rockefeller, the Cloisters Collection (37.80.2)

The price of a tapestry depended on the materials used. Rarely was a fine, commissioned series woven only with wool; instead, tapestry producers enhanced it to varying degrees with silk, silver, and gold threads. The richest kind of tapestry was one made entirely of silk and gold. Because the silver and gold threads used silk wrapped with real metal, people later burned many tapestries in order to retrieve the precious materials. As a result of this practice, few French royal tapestries survived the French Revolution. Many existing works show obvious signs, however, that the metallic threads were painstakingly pulled out in order to preserve the tapestries.

steam as he blows on his hands; the leaden sky, bare trees, and soft snow. The painting clearly shows several Gothic conventions (seen, for example, in the *Petites Heures of Jeanne d'Evreux;* see fig. 10-34), which persisted in northern Renaissance art into the first half of the fifteenth century. These include the missing front wall of the house, the attention to detail, and the high placement of the **horizon line**. The integration of figures and animals into the landscape has been accomplished within the prevailing Gothic style, but on a more believable scale, with a landscape receding continuously from foreground to middle-ground to background.

The importance of textiles in the fifteenth century cannot be overemphasized. Major weaving centers arose in Brussels, Tournai, Arras, and in the Loire Valley, where Flemish and French artists produced outstanding tapestries that served both as sumptuous wall coverings and as a form of portable wealth. Indeed, the wealth of individuals can often be judged from the number of tapestries listed in their household inventories. The Christine de Pisan painting (see fig. 11) gives a good idea of the effect achieved by luxurious wall hangings.

One of the finest tapestry suites of the period is the Hunt of the Unicorn, probably made for royal patrons around 1500 (fig. 11-9). The unicorn, a mythical horselike beast with a single horn, could be captured only by a young virgin, to whom it came willingly. The animal symbolized the Incarnation, with Christ as the unicorn captured by the Virgin Mary; in the secular world, the unicorn hunt became a metaphor for romantic love and a suitable subject for wedding tapestries. The unicorn's horn was believed to be an antidote for poison; thus, the unicorn here is shown dipping its horn into the stream and so purifying the water from the fountain.

The figures in the Unicorn tapestry appear in a dense forest, filled with flowers, with a distant view of a castle. The many birds and animals shown have symbolic meanings: the lion represents valor and faith; the stag, the Resurrection and protection against evil; rabbits, fertility; and dogs, fidelity. Among the birds, the pheasants are emblems of human love and marriage, and the goldfinch is another fertility symbol. The plants, depicted with botanical accuracy, reinforce the theme of protective and curative powers: the strawberry stands for sexual love, the pansy for remembrance, the oak for fidelity, the holly for protection, and the orange for fertility. The tapestry captures the vision of the biblical Song of Songs (4:12–13). "You are an enclosed garden, my sister, my bride, an enclosed garden, a fountain sealed."

Renaissance Art in Italy

In the fifteenth century, Flemish art was so admired that many artists came to Flanders from abroad to study the work of the Flemish painters. Only at the end of the century did European patrons begin to favor the new styles of art and architecture developed in Italy beginning around 1400. At that time, Italian painters and sculptors, like their Flemish counterparts, began to move toward a greater precision in rendering the illusion of physical reality, building on the achievements of the great Florentine artist Giotto (see fig. 10-39). Rather than replicating the smallest details of appearance with perfect fidelity to nature, like the Flemings, Italian artists aimed instead at achieving anatomically correct but idealized figures—perfected, generic types—set within a rationally, rather than intuitively, defined space, organized through the use of linear perspective (see "Renaissance Perspective Systems," page 255). At the same time, Italian architects began to use mathematically derived design principles and the classical architectural orders to create buildings expressing the ideals of symmetry and restraint.

ARCHITECTURE AND SCULPTURE

Two towering figures of early Renaissance art, the sculptor Donatello and the architect Brunelleschi, came from Florence, the birthplace

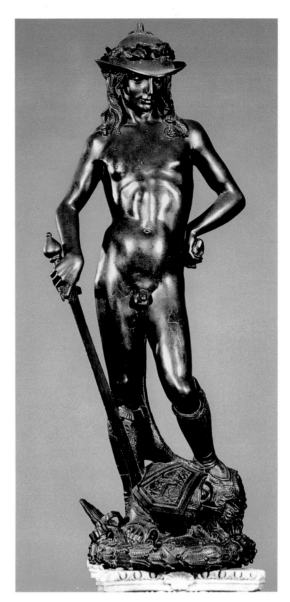

11-10. Donatello. David. After 1428. Bronze, height 5'2¼" (1.58 m). Museo Nazionale del Bargello, Florence

of the Italian Renaissance. The two visited Rome together to study the physical remains of classical antiquity, and they integrated detailed knowledge of the past into their own highly original works. Donatello, born Donato di Niccolo Bardi (c. 1386–1466), executed each commission as if it were a new experiment in expression. His sculpture is like an encyclopedia of techniques and ideas, with nearly every piece breaking new ground. For example, Donatello's rendition of the biblical hero David, who slew the giant Goliath with a slingshot, is the earliest known lifesize freestanding bronze nude in European art since antiquity (fig. 11-10). The sculpture was first recorded in 1469 in the courtyard of the palace owned by the ruling Medici family of Florence, where it stood on a base engraved with an inscription extolling Florentine heroism and virtue. Although the work clearly draws on the classical tradition of heroic nudity, this portrayal of a sensuous, adolescent boy in a

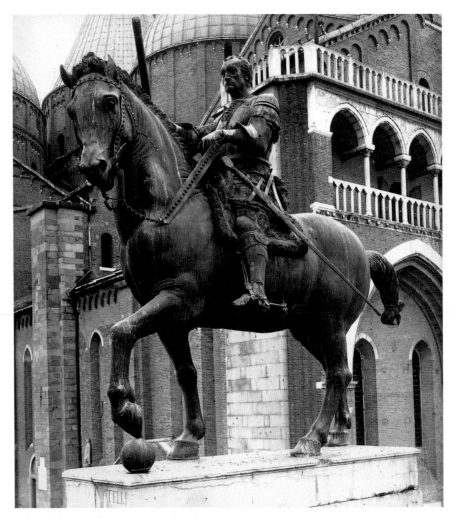

11-11. Donatello. Equestrian monument of Erasmo da Narni (*Gattamelata*), Piazza del Santo, Padua. 1443–53. Bronze, height approx. 12'2" (3.71 m)

jaunty hat and boots, standing on his enemy's severed head, is utterly original. David's angular pose, his underdeveloped torso, and the sensation of his wavering between childish interests and adult responsibility heighten his heroism in challenging and defeating the giant warrior.

Donatello influenced other artists both in and outside Florence. He worked for a decade in Padua, where he was called in 1443 to execute an equestrian statue commemorating the Venetian general Erasmo da Narni, nicknamed *Gattamelata* (Honeyed Cat) (fig. 11-11). The sources for this statue were two surviving Roman bronze equestrian portraits, one (now lost) in the north Italian city of Pavia, the other of the emperor Marcus Aurelius (see fig. 6-24), which the sculptor certainly saw and probably sketched during his youthful stay in Rome. The completed monument, installed on a high base in front of the church dedicated to the beloved Italian Franciscan Saint Anthony, was the first large-scale bronze equestrian portrait since antiquity. Viewed from a distance, this man-animal juggernaut seems capable of thrusting forward at the first threat. Seen from up close, however, the man's sunken cheeks, sagging jaw, ropey neck, and stern but sad expression suggest a war machine now grown old and tired. Such **expressionism** was a recurring theme in Donatello's portrayals.

Donatello's friend Filippo Brunelleschi (1377–1446), a young sculptor-turned-architect, was one of the major pioneers of Renaissance architectural design in Florence. His design for the vast dome of Florence Cathedral (fig. 11-12) was a great technical accomplishment. The dome had an octagonal outer shell, essentially a Gothic construction based on the pointed arch, and used ribs to support the vault. The lower inner shell is connected to the outer one through a system of arches and horizontal sandstone rings. Brunelleschi invented an ingenious structural system by which each portion of the dome reinforced the next one as it was built up layer by layer (fig. 11-13). When completed, this self-buttressed unit required no external support. The dome is still the source of immense local pride.

Brunelleschi also produced remarkably innovative plans for smaller projects. Around 1421, he was commissioned to rebuild the Church of San Lorenzo in Florence. San Lorenzo is an austere basilica-plan church with elements of Early

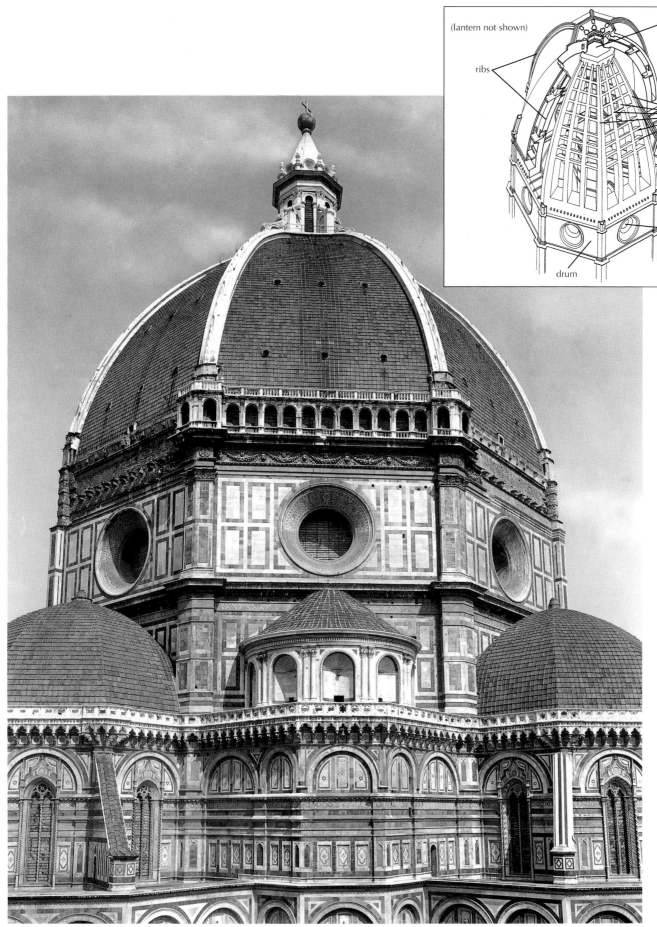

11-13.
(*above*)
Cutaway drawing of Brunelleschi's dome, Florence Cathedral (Drawing by P. Sanpaolesi)

11-12. Filippo Brunelleschi. Dome of Florence Cathedral. 1417–36; lantern completed 1471

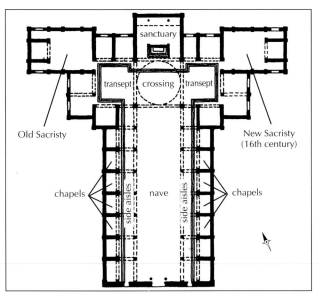

11-14. Filippo Brunelleschi. Plan of the Church of San Lorenzo, Florence. c. 1421–46; plan includes later additions and modifications

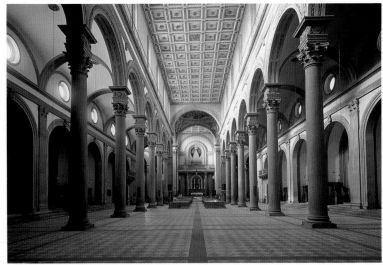

11-15. Filippo Brunelleschi. Nave, Church of San Lorenzo

Christian design (fig. 11-14). The long nave, flanked by single side aisles opening into shallow chapels, is intersected by a short transept with a square crossing. Beyond the crossing is a square sanctuary, flanked by chapels. Two **sacristies** (rooms housing ritual attire and vessels) project from the transept. Brunelleschi designed the Old Sacristy as a chapel and mausoleum for the Medici family; the New Sacristy was built in the sixteenth century.

Brunelleschi, like many Romanesque and Gothic builders before him, worked out his church plans on a module, or basic unit of measure, that could be multiplied or divided and applied to every element of the design. The result was a series of clear, rational interior spaces in harmony with one another. Unlike the Romanesque and Gothic system, however, the result was architecture on a human scale.

The nave of the church (fig. 11-15) has a flat ceiling inset with coffers, like a Roman basilica; a hemispherical dome on pendentives covers the crossing. Each nave arch springs from an **impost block**, or section of entablature, resting on slender Corinthian columns. With this arrangement, Brunelleschi managed to bend, without exactly breaking, the rules of classical architecture, in which piers, rather than columns, supported arches, and columns only supported entablatures (see fig. 6-11). In the side aisles, the arched openings to the chapels are surmounted by arched lunettes that mirror the shape of the nave arcade. The Church of San Lorenzo was an experimental building combining old and new

elements, but Brunelleschi's rational approach, unique sense of order, and innovative incorporation of classical motifs inspired later Renaissance architects, many of whom learned from his work firsthand by completing his unfinished projects.

Leon Battista Alberti (1404–1472), a humanist-turned-architect, wrote about his classical theories on art before ever designing a building. His various writings, including books on painting and sculpture and a ten-volume treatise on architecture, present the first coherent exposition of early Italian aesthetic theory. Like Brunelleschi, Alberti integrated classical forms into his works. In one of his relatively few actual building projects, a palace commissioned by the Rucellai family in Florence, Alberti dealt with one of the continuing challenges faced by Renaissance architects: the relationship (or more often, the lack of one) of a facade to the building behind it. He designed the facade—begun in 1455 but never finished—to be the unifying front for a planned merger of eight adjacent houses acquired by Giovanni Rucellai (fig. 11-16). The simple rectangular front suggests a single, cubical three-story building capped with an overhanging cornice, or heavy projecting horizontal molding, at the top of the wall. The stone blocks in the facade are lightly **rusticated** (left rough or textured), in a style derived from fortifications that was popular in Florentine town house exteriors. Inspired by the ancient Colosseum in Rome (see fig. 6-11), Alberti organized the surface of the wall with a horizontal-vertical pattern of pilasters and architraves that superimposed the Classical orders: Doric on the ground floor, Ionic on the second, and Corinthian on the third. Thus the Palazzo Rucellai provided a visual lesson for later architects in the use of classical elements and mathematical proportions.

The intellectual ferment surrounding architecture and urban planning in Renaissance Italy inspired artists to design ideal, and often imaginary, cities. The anonymous central Italian artist who painted an ideal city-center around 1500 included a triumphal arch and a mini-Colosseum amid contemporary town houses (fig. 11-17). The octagonal church or baptistry in the right background suggests the influence of Alberti's theories. In his treatise *De re aedificatoria* (*On Architecture*, 1452), Alberti expressed his preference, based on his understanding of classical buildings such as the Pantheon, for churches that were either circular or polygonal, because "most things which are generated, made or directed by Nature are round." The streets in this view are unnaturally wide and clean—surely totally unlike the crowded and twisted alleyways that crisscrossed virtually all fifteenth-century cities. The roofs of the houses are the same height, as Alberti recommended in a description of an ideal city. The Four Cardinal Virtues—Justice, Prudence, Patience, and Fortitude—stand on columns in the four corners of the square, a reminder of the dreams of Renaissance theorists, who predicted that ideal surroundings would bring out the best qualities in a city's people.

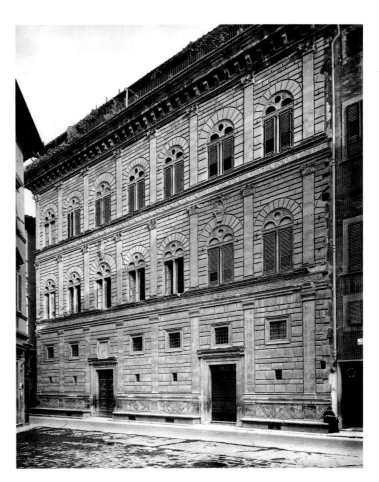

11-16. Leon Battista Alberti. Palazzo Rucellai, Florence. 1455–70

PAINTING

One of the major achievements of Italian Renaissance artists was the convincing integration of human figures into rational architectural settings. This accomplishment can be seen early on in the works of the Florentine artist Maso di Ser Giovanni di Mone Cassai (1401–1429?), nicknamed Masaccio ("big, ugly Tom"), one of the most innovative of early Italian Renaissance painters. The exact chronology of his works is uncertain, and his fresco painting of the Trinity in the Church of Santa Maria Novella in Florence

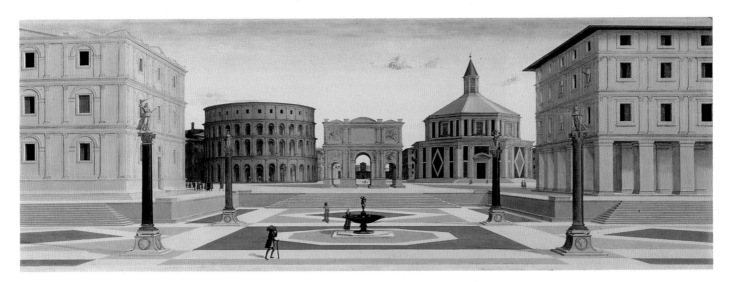

11-17. Anonymous. *Ideal City with a Fountain and Statues of the Virtues.* c. 1500. Oil on panel, 30½" x 7'1⅝" (77.4 cm x 2.17 m). Walters Art Gallery, Baltimore

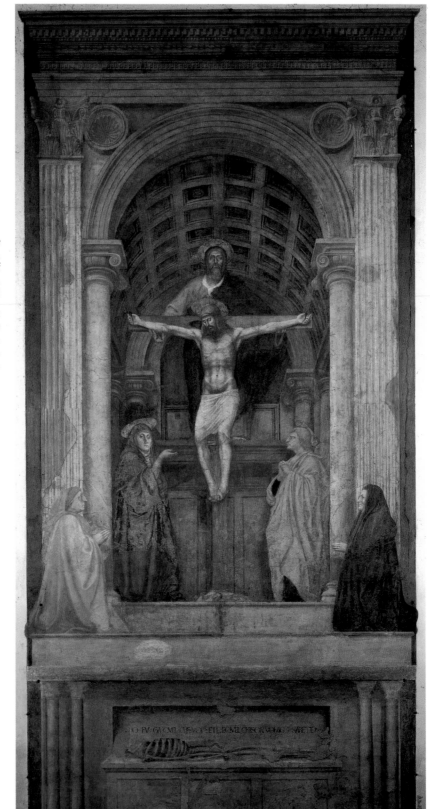

11-18. Masaccio. *Trinity with the Virgin, Saint John the Evangelist, and Donors,* fresco in the Church of Santa Maria Novella, Florence. c. 1425–28(?). 21' x 10'5" (6.4 x 3.2 m)

The inscription over the skeleton under the altar reads, "I was once that which you are, and what I am, you also will be" (trans. Hartt, *Italian Renaissance Art*, p. 211).

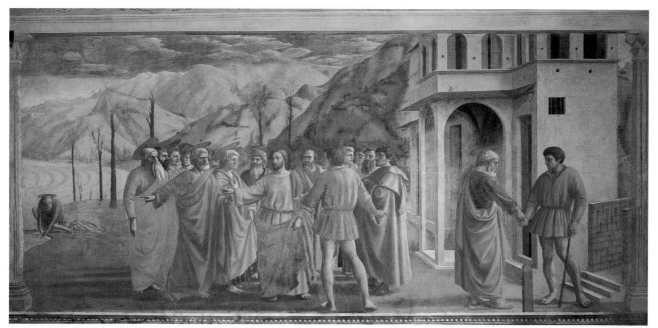

11-19. Masaccio. *Tribute Money,* fresco in the Brancacci Chapel, Church of Santa Maria del Carmine, Florence. c. 1427. 8'1" x 19'7" (2.46 x 6 m)

Much valuable new information about the Brancacci Chapel frescoes was discovered during the course of a cleaning and restoration carried out between 1981 and 1991. Art historians now have a more accurate picture of how the frescoes were done and in what sequence, as well as which artist did what. One interesting discovery was that all of the figures in the *Tribute Money*, except those of the temple tax collector, originally had gold-leaf halos, several of which had flaked off. Rather than silhouette the heads against flat gold circles in the medieval manner, Masaccio conceived of the halo as a gold disk hovering in space above each head and subjected it to perspective foreshortening depending on the position of the figure.

falls sometime between 1425 and 1428 (fig. 11-18).

The *Trinity* fresco was meant to give the illusion of a stone funerary monument and altar table set in a deep **aedicula** (framed niche) in the wall. Masaccio created the appearance of the niche through precisely rendered linear perspective. The vanishing point is centered on a horizon line at the eye level of an adult viewer just above the base of the cross. The niche itself resembles the architecture of San Lorenzo (see fig. 11-15). Thus, the painting demonstrates Masaccio's intimate knowledge of both Brunelleschi's perspective experiments (see "Renaissance Perspective Systems," page 255) and his architectural style. In Masaccio's painting, God the Father holds the cross on which Jesus hangs, while the dove of the Holy Spirit seems poised in downward flight between Jesus' tilted halo and the head of God the Father. Mary and Saint John the Evangelist stand at the foot of the cross, and outside the niche the donors kneel in prayer. The apparent source of the consistent light that models the figures and illuminates the coffers lies in front of the picture.

Masaccio's brief six- or seven-year career

reached its height in his collaboration with a painter known as Masolino (c. 1400–1440/47) on the fresco decoration of the Brancacci Chapel in the Church of Santa Maria del Carmine in Florence. In the scene of the *Tribute Money* (fig. 11-19), Masaccio illustrates an incident in which a collector of Jewish temple taxes demands payment from the apostle Peter, shown in the central group with Jesus and the other disciples (Matthew 17:24–7). Jesus instructs Peter to "go to the sea, drop in a hook, and take the first fish that comes up," which Peter does at the far left. In the fish's mouth, Peter finds a coin worth twice the tax demanded, which he gives to the tax collector at the far right.

The *Tribute Money* is particularly remarkable for its use of both linear and atmospheric perspective to integrate the figures, architecture, and landscape into a consistent whole. The lines of the house converge on the head of Jesus, which Masaccio emphasized by diminishing the sizes of the barren trees and reducing Peter's size at the left. There is a second vanishing point for the steps and stone rail at the right. Masaccio

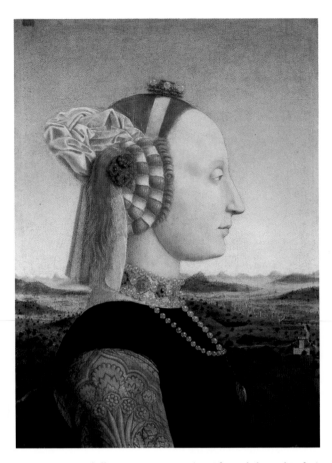
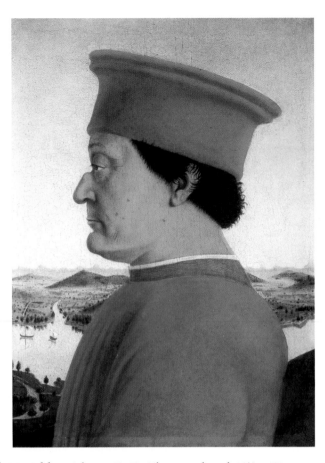

11-20. Piero della Francesca. Battista Sforza (left) and **Federico da Montefeltro** (right). 1472–73. Oil on panel, each 18½ x 13" (47 x 33 cm). Galleria degli Uffizi, Florence

also used atmospheric perspective in his rendering of the distant landscape, where the mountains fade from grayish green to greenish white, and the house and trees on their slopes become increasingly obscure.

The volumetric solidity of the foreground figures testifies to Masaccio's intimate knowledge of Roman sculpture as well as earlier Italian painters, such as Giotto. They are modeled with strong highlights and cast their long shadows on the ground toward the left, implying a light source at the far right, as if the scene were lit by the actual window in the rear wall of the chapel. As in Giotto's frescoes at the Arena Chapel in Padua (see fig. 10-39), the colors of the figures' robes vary in tone according to the strength of the illumination.

Masaccio's powerful modeling of forms and masterful handling of linear and atmospheric perspective strongly influenced Piero della Francesca (c. 1406/12–1492). Piero, born in Borgo San Sepolcro, a small Tuscan hill town, worked in Florence in the 1430s. There he studied Masaccio's frescoes and Brunelleschi's system of spatial illusion and linear perspective and became acquainted with Alberti's theories. He later wrote his own treatise on perspective and in his painting stressed the three-dimensional construction of forms and spaces.

Commissions took Piero to the court of Federico da Montefeltro at Urbino. There, in 1472–1473, he painted a pair of companion portraits of Federico and his recently deceased wife, Battista Sforza (fig. 11-20). Like portraits on Roman coins and cameos, the figures are portrayed in strict profile, as remote from the viewer as icons. Piero emphasized the underlying geometry of the forms, rendering the figures with an absolute stillness. At the same time, his use of the northern technique of atmospheric perspective, with the landscape features becoming lighter and paler as they recede, resulted in a highly believable illusion of space. Piero used another northern European device in the harbor view near the center of Federico's panel: the water narrows into a river and leads the eye into the distant landscape. The portraits may have been hinged as a **diptych** (a pair of panels, usually hinged together), since the landscape appears continuous across the two panels. On the back of the panels, the couple ride in triumphant chariots through another continuous landscape.

Contrasting sharply with Piero's sober monumentality is the fluid, linear grace characteristic

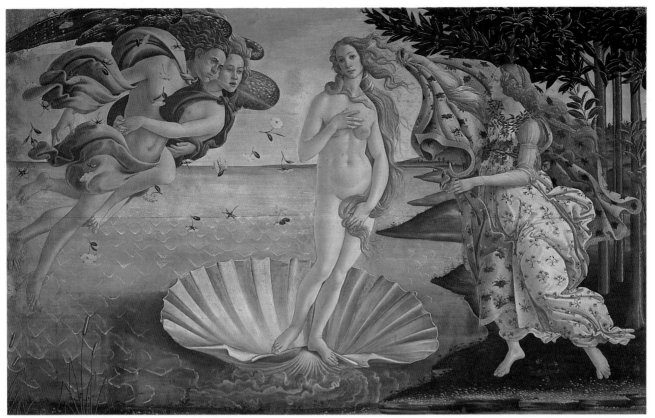

11-21. Sandro Botticelli. *Birth of Venus.* c. 1484–86. Panel, 5'8⁷/₈" x 9'1⁷/₈" (1.8 x 2.8 m). Galleria degli Uffizi, Florence

of the Florentine painter Sandro Botticelli (1445–1510). Botticelli's best-known works are paintings of mythological subjects, among them the *Birth of Venus* (fig. 11-21). According to the later Roman poets, the goddess Venus was born from the foaming waves of the sea. Mild winds, known as Zephyrs, wafted her to shore on the island of Cyprus, where the Seasons met her, clothed her, and took her to join the other gods. Here the Zephyrs hovering at left look like angelic visitants, while Venus's pose recalls Classical statuary (see fig. 4-37). Spring, draperies aflutter, stands ready to wrap the young goddess in a flower-sprigged cloak. The date of this lovely painting is controversial, but it was probably made around 1484–1486 for the private collection of Lorenzo de' Medici, who had become ruler of Florence in 1469.

The meaning of Botticelli's mythological paintings is probably related to Neoplatonism, a philosophy favored by the Medicis. Cosimo de' Medici the Elder (1389–1464) had founded an academy in Florence devoted to the study of classical texts, especially the works of Plato and his followers, the Neoplatonists. Neoplatonism is highly complex, but most basically it is characterized by a sharp opposition of the spiritual (the Ideal or Idea) and the carnal (Matter) that can be overcome by severe discipline and aversion to the world of the senses. Neoplatonists conceived of Venus as having two natures, one terrestrial and the other celestial. The first ruled over earthly, human love and the second over universal love. For the Florentine Neoplatonists, the celestial Venus was a classical equivalent of the Virgin Mary.

In northern Italy, the Renaissance appeared first in Venice and in Padua, where both Giotto (in the fourteenth century) and Donatello (in the early fifteenth) had lived and worked. Donatello was working in Padua during the formative years of the young artist Andrea Mantegna (1431–1506). Mantegna absorbed the system of linear perspective used by Donatello and pushed it to its limits with his own radical perspective views and strongly foreshortened figures.

Mantegna's mature style is exemplified by the frescoes of the Camera Picta (Painted Room) in the Ducal Palace of Mantua. The artist decorated this tower chamber between 1465 and 1474 for Ludovico Gonzaga, the ruler of Mantua. On the vaulted ceiling, the artist painted a tour de force of perspective, called *di sotto in sù* (seen directly from below), which began a long tradition

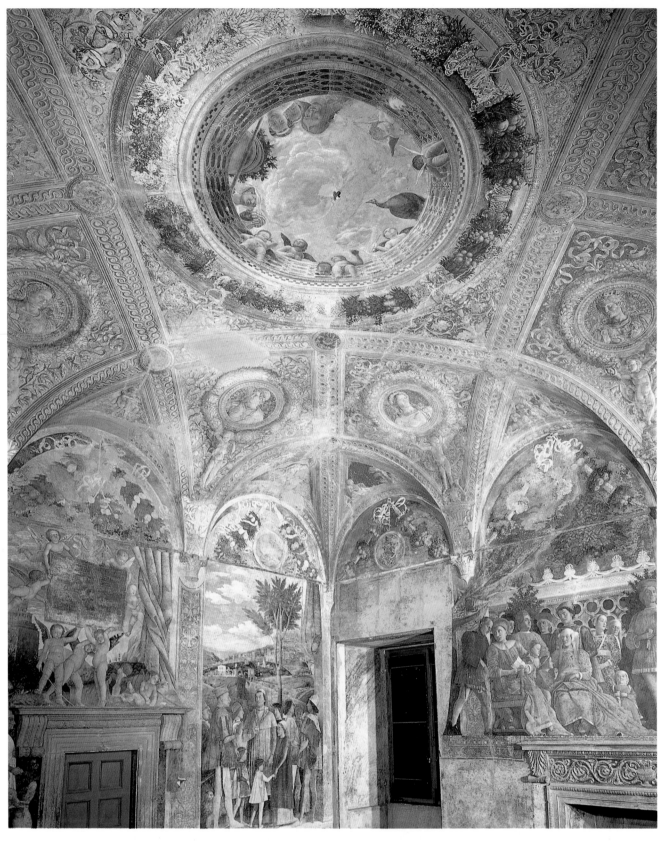

11-22. Andrea Mantegna. *Frescoes in the Camera Picta*, Ducal Palace, Mantua. 1465–74

of illusionistic ceiling painting (fig. 11-22). The room appears to be open to a cloud-filled sky through a large oculus in a simulated marble and mosaic-covered vault. On each side of a precariously balanced planter, three young women and an exotically turbaned African man peer over a marble railing. A fourth young woman in a veil looks dreamily upward. Joined by a large peacock, several

winged **putti** (naked little boys) frolic around the **balustrade** (supports topped by a rail). Mantegna completed the decoration of the room with two wall frescoes (not illustrated here) featuring portraits of members of the Gonzaga family.

In the last quarter of the fifteenth century, Venice—once a center of Byzantine art—emerged as a major center of Renaissance painting. From

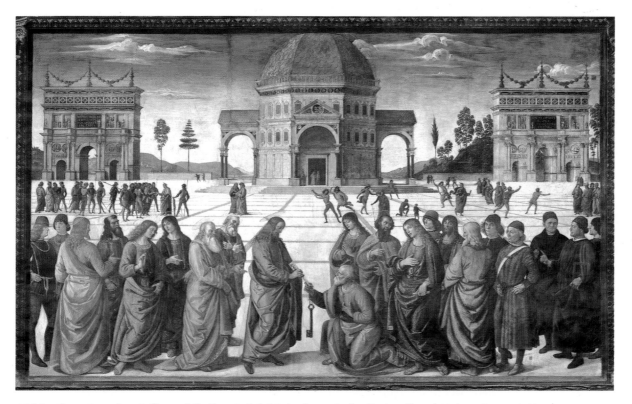

11-23. Pietro Perugino. *Delivery of the Keys to Saint Peter,* fresco in the Sistine Chapel, Vatican, Rome. 1482.
11'5¹/₂" x 18'8¹/₂" (3.48 x 5.70 m)

Modern eyes accustomed to gigantic parking lots would not find a large open space in the middle of a city extraordinary, but in the fifteenth century this great piazza was purely the product of artistic imagination. A real piazza this size would have been very impractical. In summer sun or winter wind and rain, such spaces would have been extremely unpleasant for a pedestrian population, but, more important, no city could afford such extravagant use of valuable land within its walls.

the late 1470s on, Venetian artists embraced the oil medium for works on both panel and canvas. The most important of these painters were members of the Bellini family, Jacopo and his sons Gentile and Giovanni. Andrea Mantegna was also part of this circle, for he married one of Jacopo Bellini's daughters. Gentile Bellini (c. 1429–1507) celebrated the daily life of the city in large and lively narrative scenes, such as the *Procession of the Relic of the True Cross before the Church of San Marco* (see fig. 7-21). We have already studied this work for what it tells us about Byzantine art in Venice.

Late in the fifteenth century, the city of Rome became a magnet for Renaissance artists because of Pope Sixtus IV's decision to summon the best painters he could find to decorate the walls of his newly built Sistine Chapel. Among those who went to Rome was Pietro Vannucci, called Perugino (c. 1445–1523), who was active in Florence but came originally from near the town of Perugia in Umbria. His contribution to the Sistine wall frescoes, painted in 1482, was a rendition of the *Delivery of the Keys to Saint Peter* (fig. 11-23). In an event not actually described in the Bible but suggested in Matthew 16:19— and which provided the justification for the supremacy of papal authority—Christ is shown giving the keys to the kingdom of heaven to the

apostle Peter, the first bishop of Rome.

Delivery of the Keys is a remarkable study in accurate linear perspective. The banded paving stones of the piazza provide a geometric grid for perspectival recession. The figures stand like chess pieces on the squares, scaled to size according to their distance from the picture plane and **modeled** by a consistent light source from the upper left. Horizontally, the composition is divided between the foreground frieze of figures and the widely spaced background buildings, vertically by the open space at the center between Christ and Peter and by the symmetrical architectural forms on either side of this central axis. Perugino's painting is, among other things, a representation of Alberti's ideal city (see fig. 11-17), described in his treatise on architecture as having a "temple" (that is, a church) at the very center of a great open space raised on a dais and separate from any other buildings that might obstruct its view (see "Renaissance Perspective Systems," page 255).

Printmaking in Renaissance Europe

The achievements of Renaissance painters, sculptors, and architects were disseminated across Europe through single-sheet prints and printed books. Printmaking emerged in Europe with the wider availability of paper at the end

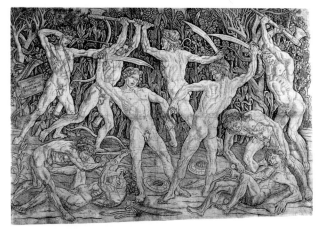

11-24. Antonio del Pollaiuolo. *Battle of the Ten Nudes.*
c. 1465–70. Engraving, 15¹⁄₈ x 23¹⁄₄" (38.3 x 59 cm). Cincinnati Art Museum, Ohio

Bequest of Herbert Greer French. 1943.118

of the fourteenth century. The major types of prints produced during the Renaissance were **woodcuts** and **engravings** (see "Woodcuts and Engravings on Metal," below). In the beginning, woodcuts were often made by woodworkers with no training in drawing, but very quickly artists began to draw images for them to cut from the block. Engravings, on the other hand, seem to have developed from the metalworking techniques of goldsmiths and armorers. Sometimes these artisans made prints as personal studies, in the manner of drawings, or for use in their shops as models.

The Florentine goldsmith and sculptor Antonio del Pollaiuolo (c. 1432–1498) may have intended his only known—but highly influential—print, *Battle of the Ten Nudes*, an engraving done about 1465–1470, as a study in composition involving the human figure in action (fig. 11-24). The naked men fighting each other ferociously against a tapestry-like background of foliage seem to have been drawn from a single model in a variety of poses, many of which were taken from classical sources. Much of our fascination with the print lies in how Pollaiuolo depicts the muscles of the male body reacting under tension.

The German painter Martin Schongauer, who learned engraving from his goldsmith father, was an immensely skillful printmaker who excelled in drawing and the difficult technique of shading from deep blacks to the faintest grays. One of his best-known prints today is the *Temptation of Saint Anthony*, engraved about 1480 to 1490 (fig. 11-25). Schongauer illustrated the original biblical meaning of temptation, expressed in the Latin world *tentatio*, as a physical assault rather than a subtle inducement. Wildly acrobatic, slithery, spiky demons lift Anthony off the ground to torment and terrify him in midair. The engraver intensified the horror of the moment by condensing the action into a swirling vortex of figures beating, scratching, poking, tugging, and no doubt shrieking at the stoical saint, who remains impervious to all by reason of his faith.

The prevalence of religious prints made for private devotion, whether simple woodcuts or highly sophisticated engravings like Schongauer's, are an important reminder that the rise of

---

TECHNIQUE
WOODCUTS AND ENGRAVINGS ON METAL

An artist making a **woodcut** draws a design on a smooth block of wood, then cuts away all the areas around the lines, leaving them in **high relief**. When the block's surface is inked and a piece of paper pressed down hard on it, the ink on the relief areas is transferred to the paper to create a reverse image.

Engraving on metal, in contrast, requires a technique called **intaglio**, in which lines are cut into the plate with tools called gravers or **burins**, while the surface remains flat. Ink is applied over the whole plate and forced down into the lines, after which the surface of the plate is carefully wiped clean. The ink in the lines prints onto a sheet of paper pressed hard against the metal plate.

Whichever technique is used, the great advantage of printmaking is that woodblocks and metal plates can be used repeatedly to make nearly identical images.

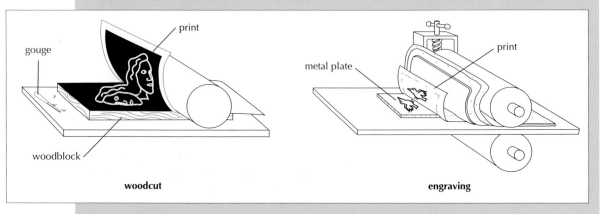

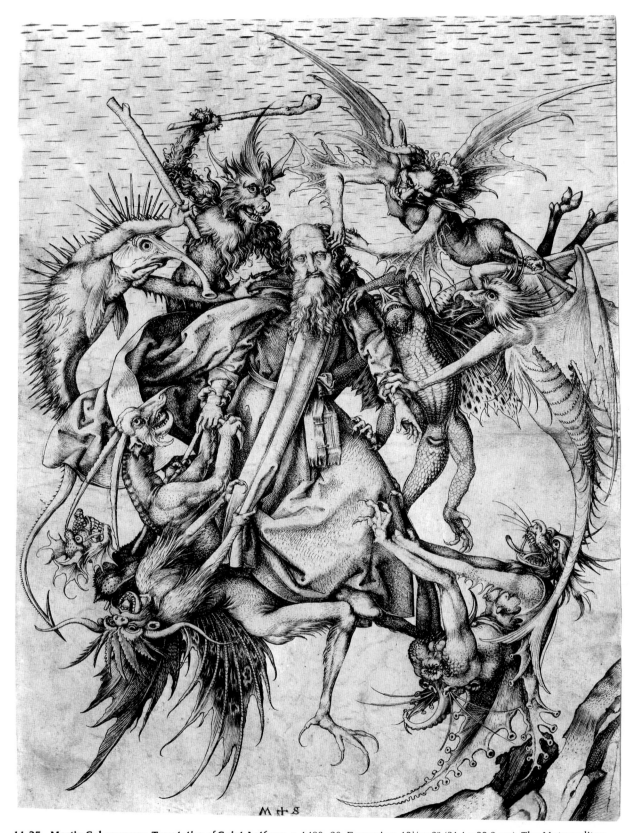

11-25. Martin Schongauer. *Temptation of Saint Anthony.* c. 1480–90. Engraving, 12¼ x 9" (31.1 x 22.9 cm). The Metropolitan Museum of Art, New York

Rogers Fund, 1920 (20.5.2)

humanism did not signify a decline in the importance of Christian belief. In fact, an intense spirituality continued to inspire European art throughout the fifteenth century, and long after.

As the High Renaissance dawned in the sixteenth century, Christianity remained deeply central to a Europe exploding with intellectual, social, geographic, and religious ferment.

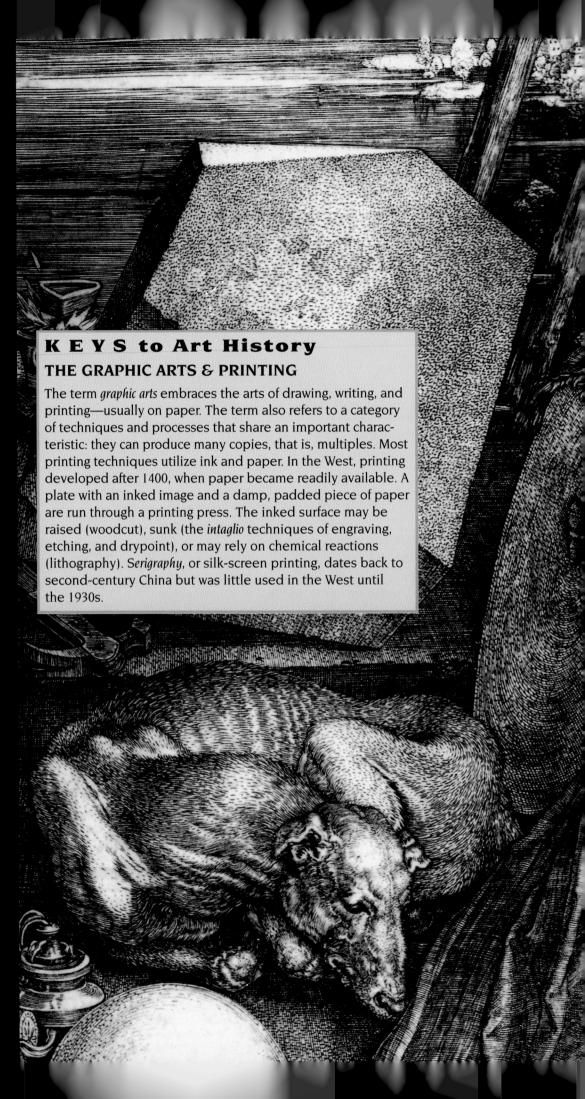

Prints

Melencolia I is an engraving. The same image exists in many *impressions*, that is, a number of other sheets taken from the same printing surface—the copper plate engraved by Dürer. From just one plate, Dürer and his assistants "pulled" many impressions of the same design. The total number of impressions made from a printing surface constitutes an *edition*. An artist may make changes to the design and may pull trial proof sheets to see the result. Each of these versions is called a *state* of the print.

Dürer's Master Engravings

In the years 1513–1514, Dürer produced three engravings that are known as the *Master Engravings*. While each is distinctive, they all display the artist's interest in classical form and perspective, and also his sophisticated understanding of philosophy and theology. The first of the three is *Knight, Death, and the Devil* (representing the active life, according to one scholar); the second is *St. Jerome in His Study* (the contemplative life); and the third is *Melencolia* I (pictured here). *Melencolia* I is the most enigmatic of the three. Many scholars interpret it as a study of the frustration felt by the secular intellect. The image abounds with symbols of and references to Humanism's scientific inquiry, such as the caliper and book in the winged figure's right hand, the sphere and polyhedron, and the hourglass and balance scale (not visible). Dürer captured the terrible lethargy of a huge figure weighed down by self-imposed intellectual burdens, in short, by melancholy.

K E Y S to Art History
THE GRAPHIC ARTS & PRINTING

The term *graphic arts* embraces the arts of drawing, writing, and printing—usually on paper. The term also refers to a category of techniques and processes that share an important characteristic: they can produce many copies, that is, multiples. Most printing techniques utilize ink and paper. In the West, printing developed after 1400, when paper became readily available. A plate with an inked image and a damp, padded piece of paper are run through a printing press. The inked surface may be raised (woodcut), sunk (the *intaglio* techniques of engraving, etching, and drypoint), or may rely on chemical reactions (lithography). *Serigraphy*, or silk-screen printing, dates back to second-century China but was little used in the West until the 1930s.

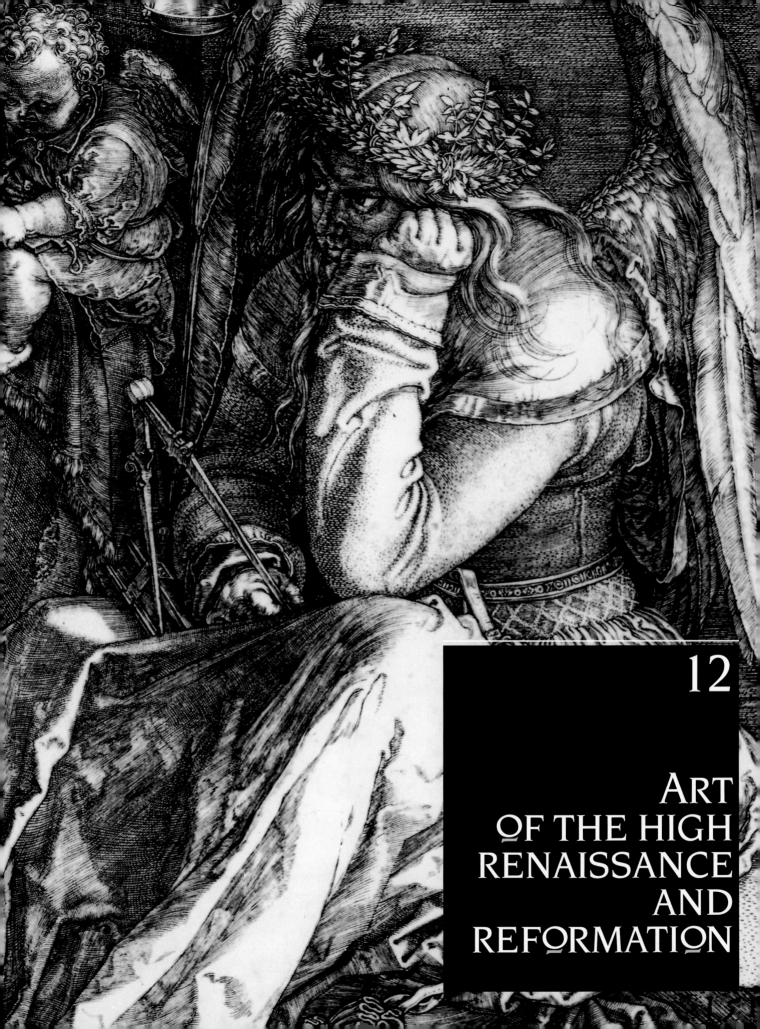

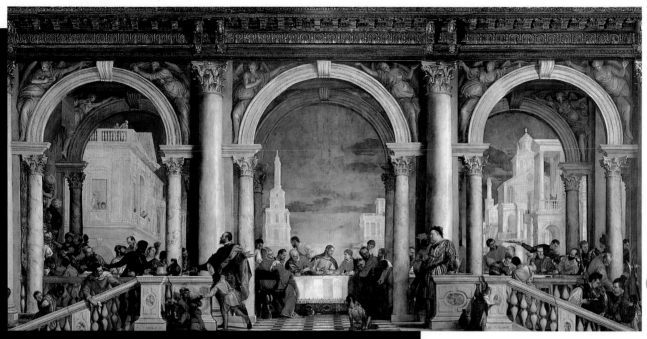

12-1. Veronese. *Feast in the House of Levi,* from the Monastery of Santi Giovanni e Paolo, Venice. 1573. Oil on canvas, 18'3" x 42' (5.56 x 12.8 m). Galleria dell'Accademia, Venice

According to the New Testament, Jesus revealed his impending death to his disciples during a seder, a meal celebrating the Jewish festival of Passover. This occasion, known to Christians as the Last Supper, and which, according to the Gospels, took place the evening before the Crucifixion, was a popular subject in sixteenth-century European art. But in 1573, when the painter Veronese delivered an enormous canvas of this subject to fulfill a commission (fig. 12-1), the Venetian clergy were shocked. Some were offended by the grandiose pageantry of the scene. Others protested the impiety of surrounding Jesus with a man picking his teeth, scruffy dogs, and foreign soldiers. As a result of the furor, Veronese was called before the Inquisition. There he justified himself first by asserting that the picture actually depicted not the Last Supper, but rather the Feast in the House of Simon, a small dinner held shortly before Jesus' final entry into Jerusalem. He also noted that artists customarily invent details in their pictures and that he had received a commission to paint the piece "as I saw fit." His argument fell on unsympathetic ears, and he was ordered to change the painting. Later he sidestepped the issue by changing its title to that of another banquet, one given by the tax collector Levi, whom Jesus had called to follow him (Luke 5:27–32).

The Inquisitors who scrutinized paintings such as Veronese's *Feast in the House of Levi* (fig. 12-1) for heretical or profane content, the artist who defended his craft, and the very size, medium, and style of the painting itself—all were products of the extraordinarily complex and diverse currents of sixteenth-century European culture. During the century's course, the humanism of the early Renaissance, with its medieval roots and often uncritical acceptance of the authority of classical texts, slowly gave way to an intensified spirit of inquiry. This impulse led scholars to investigate the natural world around them, to conduct scientific and mechanical experiments, to explore lands in Africa, Asia, and the Americas previously unknown to Europeans, and even to question the authority of the pope and the Church hierarchy in a movement known as the Reformation. The influential writings and leadership of important reformers, especially Martin Luther (1483–1546), led to the establishment of Protestant churches in Germany, Scandinavia, France, England, and the Netherlands. In response, at the Council of Trent (1545–1563), the Roman Catholic hierarchy formulated a program to counter the Reformation, including the Inquisition, with its special tribunals to root out heresy.

The effects of the Reformation on art were significant and sometimes even violent. Some Protestants considered religious imagery to be idolatrous and in some areas actually destroyed religious art and whitewashed church interiors. As a result, many artists turned to portraiture and other secular subjects to make their livings. In Catholic regions, people still venerated traditional images of Christ and the saints, but officials from the Church scrutinized works of art for heretical or profane subject matter.

Artists became increasingly mobile, traveling from city to city and from one country to another; consequently, styles and techniques

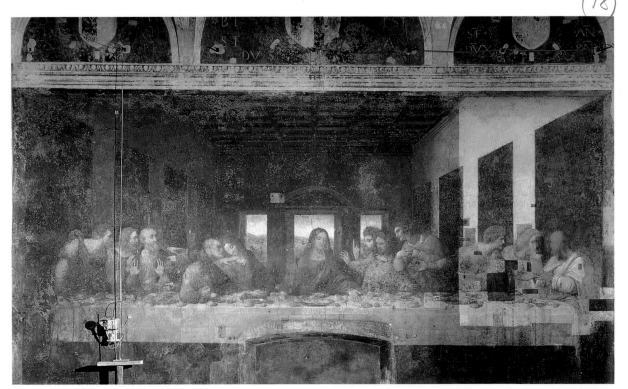

12-2. Leonardo da Vinci. Last Supper, wall painting in the Refectory, Monastery of Santa Maria delle Grazie, Milan. 1495–98. Tempera and oil on plaster, 15'2" x 28'10" (4.6 x 8.8 m)

Instead of painting in fresco, Leonardo devised an experimental technique for this mural. Hoping to achieve the freedom and flexibility of painting on panel, he worked directly on dry *intonaco*—a thin layer of smooth plaster—with an oil tempera paint, whose formula is unknown. The result was disastrous. Within a short time, the painting began to deteriorate, and by the middle of the sixteenth century its figures could be seen only with difficulty. In the seventeenth century, the monks saw no harm in cutting a doorway through the lower center of the composition. Since then the work has barely survived, despite many attempts to halt its deterioration and restore its original appearance. The painting narrowly escaped complete destruction in World War II, when the refectory was bombed to rubble around its heavily sandbagged wall. The restoration shown here is from 1983 (equipment is visible at left). Completion is expected in 1999.

became less regional and more international. The materials artists worked with changed. Fresco painting was still common, but more and more artists painted in oils on canvases, which they could produce in their studios and easily transport and install anywhere. Artists of stature became sought-after international celebrities, and their social status rose as painting, sculpture, and works of architecture came to be seen as liberal rather than manual arts.

Italian Art

The painting, sculpture, and architecture produced during the early sixteenth century reflect a self-confident humanism, an abiding admiration for classical forms, and a dominating sense of stability and order. These characteristics are found above all in the work of four towering figures: Leonardo da Vinci, Raphael Sanzio, Michelangelo Buonarotti, and Titian Vecelli. The achievements of these artists are so remarkable that nineteenth-century scholars called the period from 1500 to 1520 in Italy the High Renaissance.

Leonardo da Vinci (1452–1519) received his artistic training in Florence in the workshop of the painter and sculptor Verrocchio. Leonardo's fame as an artist is based on only a few known works of art, for his fertile mind jumped from one subject to another, and he seldom finished his projects. He had a passion for the study of mathematics, science, and engineering, and he compiled volumes of detailed drawings and notes on anatomy, botany, geology, meteorology, architectural design, and mechanics (see "The Vitruvian Man," below). At the court of Duke Ludovico Sforza of Milan, where he worked from 1482 or 1483 until 1498, he spent much of his time on military and civil engineering projects, including an urban renewal plan for the city. But at Duke Ludovico's request, Leonardo also created one of the defining monuments of Renaissance art: an image of the Last Supper painted on the wall of the dining room in the Monastery of Santa Maria delle Grazie in Milan (fig. 12-2).

The Vitruvian Man

Artists throughout history have turned to geometric shapes and mathematical proportions to seek the ideal representation of the human form. Leonardo da Vinci, and before him the first-century BCE Roman architect and engineer Marcus Vitruvius Pollio, equated the ideal man with both circle and square.

In his ten-volume *De Architectura* (*On Architecture*), Vitruvius wrote: "For if a man be placed flat on his back, with his hands and feet extended, and a pair of compasses centered at his navel, the fingers and toes of his two hands and feet will touch the circumference of a circle described therefrom. And just as the human body yields a circular outline, so too a square figure may be found from it. For if we measure the distance from the soles of the feet to the top of the head, and then apply that measure to the outstretched arms, the breadth will be found to be the same as the height" (Book III, Chapter 1, Section 2). Vitruvius determined that the body should be eight heads high. Leonardo added his own observations in the reversed writing he always used for his notebooks when he created his well-known diagram for the ideal male figure, called the *Vitruvian Man*.

Leonardo da Vinci. Vitruvian Man. c. 1490. Ink, approx. 13½ x 9⅝" (34.3 x 24.5 cm). Galleria dell'Accademia, Venice

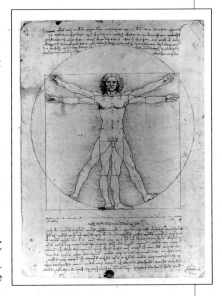

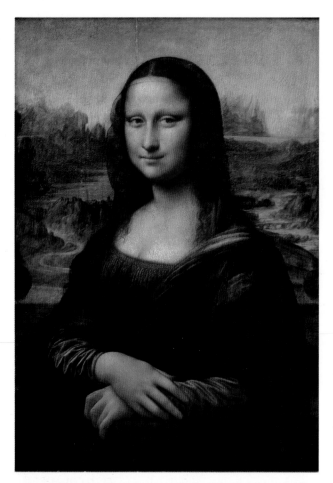

12-3. Leonardo da Vinci. *Mona Lisa.* c. 1503–6. Oil on panel, 30¼ x 21" (76.8 x 53.3 cm). Musée du Louvre, Paris

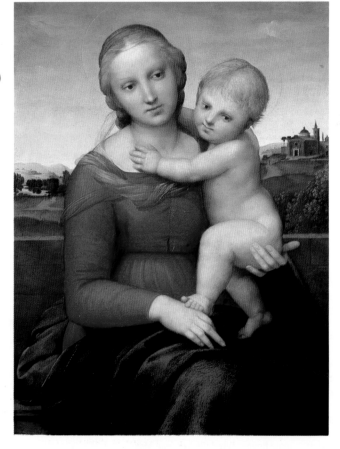

12-4. Raphael. *The Small Cowper Madonna.* c. 1505. Oil on panel, 23⅜ x 17⅜" (59.4 x 44.1 cm). National Gallery of Art, Washington, D.C. Widener Collection

On one level, Leonardo painted a narrative, showing the moment when Jesus tells his companions that one of them will betray him. They react with shock, disbelief, and horror, presenting a study of human emotions. Leonardo modeled

the disciples on real people he knew. He is said to have found his Judas (the disciple who betrayed Jesus) in the thieves' quarter of Milan. On another level, the *Last Supper* is replete with timeless symbolism. The disciples are arranged in four groups of three around the stable, pyramidal form of Jesus, who sits calmly in the middle of the general commotion. Leonardo placed Judas in the first triad to the left of Jesus, along with the young John the Evangelist and the elderly Peter. Judas, Peter, and John were each to play essential roles in Jesus' mission: Judas, to set in motion the events leading to the Crucifixion; Peter, to lead the Church after Jesus' death; and John, the visionary, to foretell the Second Coming of Christ and the Last Judgment in the Apocalypse. By arranging the disciples and architectural elements in groups of three and four, Leonardo incorporated a medieval tradition of numerical symbolism related to the three persons of the Trinity, the three Theological Virtues, the four Cardinal Virtues, the four seasons, and the four elements (earth, air, fire, and water).

The composition enhances the meaning. The scene is set in a stagelike space defined by the horizontals of table and coffered ceiling; the one-point linear perspective is emphasized by the tapestries on the side walls. These orthogonals, or perspective lines, converge on the head of Jesus. A triple window behind Jesus' head forms a natural halo of light. Leonardo modeled the figures in a rich **chiaroscuro** (light and shadow), which is somewhat obscured by the deterioration of the experimental medium, but now recaptured in a recent restoration.

In 1498, Leonardo left Milan and resettled in Florence. There he painted his renowned portrait *Mona Lisa* (fig. 12-3), between about 1503 and 1506. The subject was twenty-four-year-old Lisa Gherardini del Giocondo, the wife of a prominent Florentine merchant. The solid, pyramidal form of her half-length figure is silhouetted against distant mountains, whose desolate grandeur reinforces the mysterious atmosphere of the painting. Leonardo achieved this atmosphere and unified his compositions partly by covering them with a thin, lightly tinted varnish, which helped to create the effect of a smoky overall haze, or **sfumato**, a refinement of his masterful use of chiaroscuro. Because early evening light is likely to produce a similar effect naturally, he considered dusk the finest time of day and recommended that painters set up their studios in a courtyard with black walls and a linen sheet stretched overhead to reproduce the effects of twilight.

Mona Lisa's facial expression has been called enigmatic because her gentle smile is not accompanied by the warmth one would expect to see in her eyes. The contemporary fashion for plucked eyebrows and a shaved hairline to

Saint Peter's Basilica

The original church of Saint Peter's was built in the fourth century CE by Constantine, the first Christian Roman emperor, to mark the grave of the apostle Peter, the first bishop of Rome and therefore the first pope. Because this site was considered one of the holiest in the world, Constantine's architect had to build a monumental structure both to house Saint Peter's tomb and to accommodate the large crowds of pilgrims who came to visit it. A huge terrace was cut into the side of the Vatican Hill in the midst of a cemetery across the Tiber River from the city. Here Constantine's architect erected a **basilica**, a type of Roman building used for law courts, markets, and other public gatherings. Like most basilicas, Saint Peter's had a **nave**, with flanking side aisles set off by **colonnades**, and an **apse**. To allow large numbers of visitors to approach the shrine, a **transept** was added. The rest of the church was, in effect, a covered cemetery, carpeted with the tombs of believers who wanted to be buried near the grave of the apostle. In front of the church was a walled **atrium**. When it was built, Constantine's basilica was one of the largest buildings in the world (interior length 368 feet; width 190 feet),

and for more than a thousand years it was the most important pilgrim shrine in Europe.

In 1506, Pope Julius II made the decision to demolish the Constantinian basilica, which had fallen into disrepair, and to replace it with a new building. That anyone, even a pope, had the nerve to pull down such a venerated building is an indication of the extraordinary sense of assurance of the age—and of Julius himself. To design and build the new church, the pope appointed Donato Bramante. The architect envisioned the new Saint Peter's as a grander version of the Tempietto, a small, round, domed shrine he had designed for the site of Saint Peter's martyrdom. His Greek-cross plan was intended to continue the ancient Roman tradition of domed temples and round **martyria**, which had been revived by Filippo Brunelleschi in Florence Cathedral (see fig. 11-12). In Renaissance thinking, the central plan and dome also symbolized the perfection of God.

The deaths of both pope and architect in 1513–1514 put a temporary halt to the project. Successive plans by Raphael and others changed the Greek cross to a Latin cross in order to provide the church with a full-length nave. However, when Michelangelo was appointed architect in 1546, he returned to

the Greek-cross plan. Michelangelo simplified Bramante's design to create a single, unified space. The dome was finally completed some years after Michelangelo's death by the Baroque architect Giacomo della Porta, who retained Michelangelo's basic design but gave the dome a taller and slimmer profile.

By the early seventeenth century the needs of the basilica had changed. During the Counter Reformation, the Church emphasized congregational worship, so more space was needed for people and processions. Moreover, it was felt that the new church should more closely resemble Old Saint Peter's and should extend over roughly the same area, including the ground covered by the atrium. In 1606, more than a hundred years after Julius II had initiated the project, Pope Paul V commissioned the architect Carlo Maderno to change Michelangelo's Greek-cross plan to a Latin-cross plan. Maderno extended the nave to its final length of slightly more than 636 feet and added a Baroque facade (see fig. 12-10), thus completing Saint Peter's as it is today. Later in the seventeenth century, the sculptor and architect Gianlorenzo Bernini monumentalized the square in front of the basilica by surrounding it with a great colonnade (see fig. 13-3).

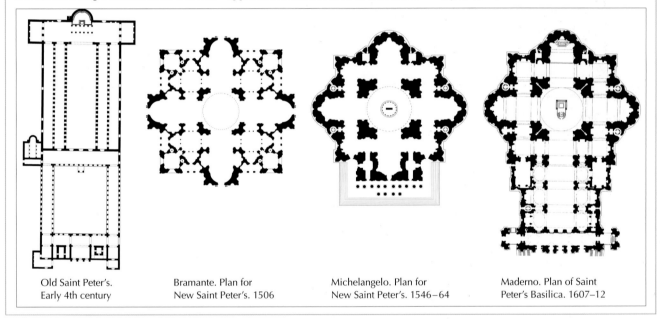

Old Saint Peter's. Early 4th century

Bramante. Plan for New Saint Peter's. 1506

Michelangelo. Plan for New Saint Peter's. 1546–64

Maderno. Plan of Saint Peter's Basilica. 1607–12

increase the height of the forehead adds to her arresting appearance. Perhaps most unsettling is the bold way her gaze has shifted toward the right to look straight out at the viewer. The implied challenge of her direct stare, contrasting with her apparent serenity, has made the Mona Lisa one of the most studied and written about, and best-known, works in the history of art.

In 1504, Leonardo's contemporary, Raphael Sanzio (1483–1520), arrived in Florence from his native Urbino. Raphael had studied in Perugia with the leading artist of that city, Perugino. Raphael soon achieved success in Florence. His paintings of the Virgin and Child, such as The Small Cowper Madonna (named for a modern owner) of about 1505 (fig. 12-4) brought him fame and attracted patrons. The monumental, pyramidal

form of the Virgin and Child, the naturalistic draperies, and the rich, concentrated colors show that Raphael must have studied the work of Leonardo and Michelangelo. However, the clear, even light that softly but solidly models the figures contrasts with the sfumato Leonardo favored. It recalls instead the atmospheric clarity and lovely colors of Perugino's paintings (see fig. 11-23).

In the distance on a hilltop, Raphael has painted a scene he knew well from his childhood, the domed Church of San Bernardino, two miles outside Urbino. The church contains the tombs of the dukes of Urbino, Federico and Guidobaldo da Montefeltro, and their wives. Donato Bramante (1444–1514), who worked in Urbino before settling in Rome in 1499, may have designed the church (see "Saint Peter's Basilica," above).

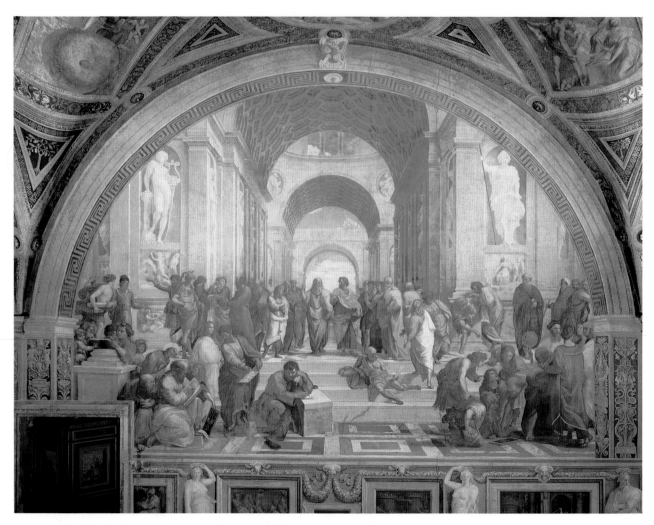

12-5. Raphael. *School of Athens*, fresco in the Stanza della Segnatura, Vatican, Rome. 1510–11. 19 x 27' (5.79 x 8.24 m)

Raphael gave many of the figures in his imaginary gathering of philosophers the features of his friends and colleagues. Plato, standing immediately to the left of the central axis and pointing to the sky, was said to have been modeled after Leonardo da Vinci; Euclid, shown inscribing a slate with a compass at the lower right, was a portrait of Raphael's friend the architect Donato Bramante. Michelangelo, who was at work on the Sistine Ceiling only steps away from the *stanza* (room) where Raphael was painting his fresco, is shown as the solitary figure at the lower left center, leaning on a block of marble and sketching, in a pose reminiscent of the figures of sibyls and prophets on his great ceiling. Raphael's own features are represented on the second figure from the front group at the far right, as the face of a young man listening to a discourse by the astronomer Ptolemy.

Raphael's greatest achievements came during a dozen years spent in Rome, where he arrived around 1509. As the fortunes of the ruling families of Florence and Milan fluctuated sharply because of political struggles, Rome rose to become the most active artistic and intellectual center in Italy. Pope Julius II (elected in 1503) began a campaign to rebuild Rome and the Vatican and put Raphael to work almost immediately decorating the papal apartments. Raphael's most outstanding achievement in these rooms was the *School of Athens* (fig. 12-5), painted during 1510–1511 for the pope's library. The painting seems to summarize the ideals of the Renaissance papacy in its grand conception of harmoniously arranged forms and rational space, as well as the calm dignity of the figures.

The viewer gazes at the scene through an illusionistic arch. The Classical Greek philosophers Plato and Aristotle command center stage. At the left, Plato gestures toward the heavens as the ultimate source of his philosophy, while Aristotle, his outstretched hand palm down, seems to emphasize the importance of gathering empirical knowledge from observing the natural world. Looking down from niches in the walls are Minerva (on the right), the Roman goddess of wisdom, and Apollo (holding a lyre), the Greek and Roman god of sun, rationality, poetry, and music. Around Plato and Aristotle are mathematicians, naturalists, astronomers, geographers, and other philosophers. The scene, flooded with light from a single source, takes place in an immense barrel-vaulted interior possibly inspired by the new design for Saint Peter's, which was being rebuilt on a plan by the architect Bramante. The grandeur of the building is matched by the monumental dignity of the philosophers themselves and the sweeping arcs of the composition, which link the figures in a dramatic unity.

Like many Renaissance artists, Raphael was a master of several arts. He provided **cartoons** (full-scale paintings or drawings to be used as models) for a series of Brussels tapestries for

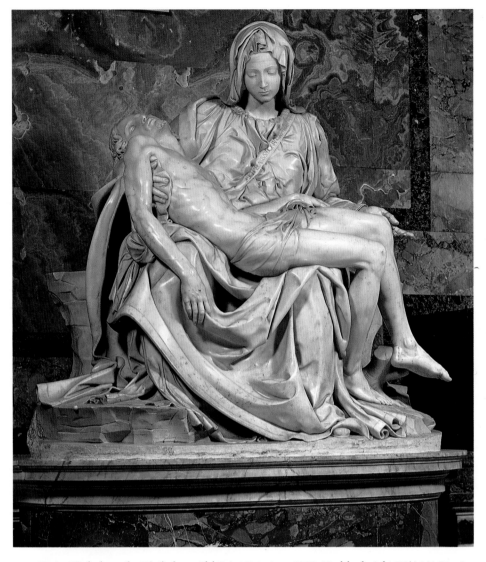

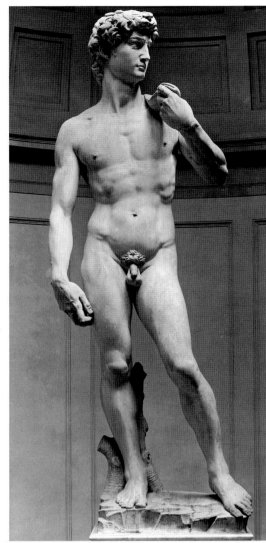

12-6. Michelangelo. *Pietà*, from Old Saint Peter's. c. 1500. Marble, height 5'8¹/₂" (1.74 m). Saint Peter's, Vatican, Rome

12-7. Michelangelo. *David*. 1501–4. Marble, height 13'5" (4.09 m). Galleria dell'Accademia, Florence

the Sistine Chapel. He was the director of all archeological and architectural projects in Rome for the Medici pope, Leo X. When he died after a short illness at age thirty-seven, he was buried in the Pantheon. His death in 1520 marks the end of the High Renaissance in many people's view.

Michelangelo Buonarroti (1475–1564), like Raphael, spent part of his early career in Florence and later worked for Pope Julius II in Rome. Born in the Tuscan town of Caprese, Michelangelo grew up in Florence and was apprenticed at age thirteen to the painter Domenico del Ghirlandaio. He soon joined the household of Lorenzo Medici the Magnificent, where he studied sculpture with Bertoldo di Giovanni, a pupil of Donatello. Bertoldo's sculptures were primarily in bronze, and Michelangelo later claimed that he had taught himself to carve marble by studying the Medici collection of classical statues.

Michelangelo's major early work was a **pietà**—an image of the Virgin supporting and mourning the body of the dead Christ—of about 1500, commissioned by a French cardinal and installed as a tomb monument in Old Saint Peter's in the Vatican (fig. 12-6). Pietàs had long

been popular in northern Europe but were rare in Italian art at the time. Michelangelo traveled to the marble quarries at Carrara in central Italy to select the block from which to make this large work, a practice that he was to follow for nearly all of his sculpture. The choice of the stone was important because he envisioned the image as already existing within the marble and needing only to be "set free" from it.

Michelangelo's Virgin is a very young, sweet-faced woman of heroic stature holding the smaller, smoothly modeled body of her grown son. The artist's compelling vision of beauty is meant to be seen up close at the statue's own level, so that the viewer can look into Jesus' face. The sculptor's name is carved prominently on the strap across the Virgin's breast. The twenty-five-year-old artist is said to have done this after the statue was finished, stealing into the church at night to provide the answer to the many questions about its creator.

In 1501, Michelangelo accepted a commission for a statue of the biblical hero David (fig. 12-7) for an exterior buttress of the Florence Cathedral. When it was finished in 1504, the

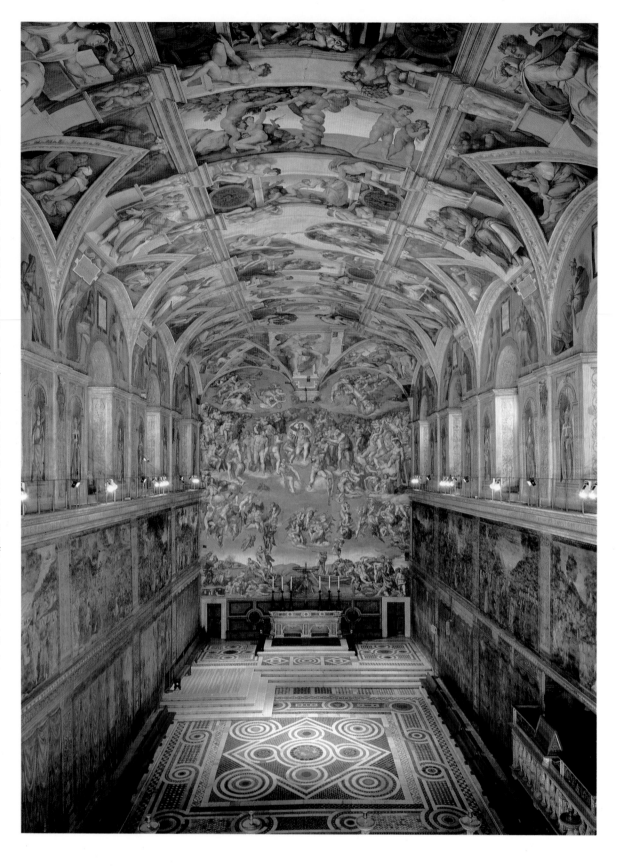

12-8. Interior, Sistine Chapel, Vatican, Rome. Built 1475–81. Ceiling painted 1508–12

Named after its builder, Pope Sixtus (Sisto) IV, the chapel is slightly more than 130 feet long and about 43½ feet wide, approximately the same measurements recorded in the Old Testament for the Temple of Solomon. The floor mosaic was recut from the colored stones used in the floor of an earlier papal chapel. The plain walls were painted in fresco between 1481 and 1483 with scenes from the life of Moses and the life of Christ by Perugino, Botticelli, Ghirlandaio, and others. Below these are trompe l'oeil painted draperies, where Raphael's tapestries illustrating the Acts of the Apostles once hung. Michelangelo's famous ceiling frescoes begin with the lunette scenes above the windows (see fig. 12-9). On the end above the altar is his *Last Judgment*, finished in 1541.

David was so admired that the Florentine city council placed it in the principal city square, next to the Palazzo della Signoria, the building housing the city's government. Although the statue embodies the antique ideal of the athletic, nude male, the emotional power of its facial expression and concentrated gaze is new. Unlike Donatello's bronze *David* (see fig. 11-10), this is not a triumphant hero with the head of the giant Goliath under his feet. Slingshot over his shoulder and a rock in his right hand, Michelangelo's *David* frowns and stares into space, seemingly preparing himself psychologically for the danger ahead. No match for his opponent in experience, weaponry, or physical strength, David represents the power of right over might. He was a

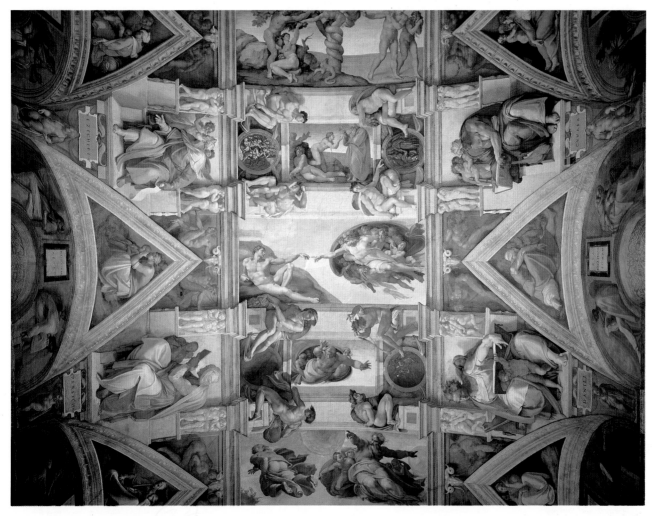

12-9. Michelangelo. Sistine Ceiling. Top to bottom: *Expulsion* (center); *Creation of Eve* with *Ezekiel* (left) and *Cumaean Sibyl* (right); *Creation of Adam*; *God Gathering the Waters* with *Persian Sibyl* (left) and *Daniel* (right); and *God Creating the Sun, Moon, and Planets*. Frescoes on the ceiling, Sistine Chapel. 1508–12

perfect emblematic figure for the Florentines, who twice drove out the powerful Medici and reinstituted short-lived republics in the early years of the sixteenth century.

Michelangelo had a contract to make other statues for the cathedral, but in 1505 Pope Julius II arranged for him to come to Rome. The sculptor's first undertaking was the pope's future tomb, but Julius set this commission aside in 1506 and ordered Michelangelo to redecorate the ceiling of the most important chapel in the Vatican, the Sistine Chapel (fig. 12-8). Julius's initial directions for the ceiling specified a simple architectural decoration; later he added the Twelve Apostles. When Michelangelo objected to the limitations of Julius's plan, the pope told him to paint whatever he liked on the ceiling. This he presumably did, although he probably had an adviser in theology.

Michelangelo's design for the Sistine Ceiling consists of an illusionistic, painted architectural framework, including a ribbed vault and a cornice running completely around the ceiling (fig. 12-9). Figures of nude young men sit in a variety of poses on projections of this fictive cornice. Rising behind the youths the ribs of the vault divide the center of the ceiling into compartments. The scenes in these compartments depict the Creation, the Fall of Man (the disobedience of Adam and Eve), and the story of Noah and the Flood, as told in Genesis. The triangular spandrels contain paintings of the ancestors of Jesus. Between the spandrels are figures of Old Testament prophets and classical sibyls (female prophets), who were believed to have foretold Jesus' birth.

Perhaps the most familiar scene on the ceiling is the Creation of Man, in which Michelangelo depicts the moment when God charges the

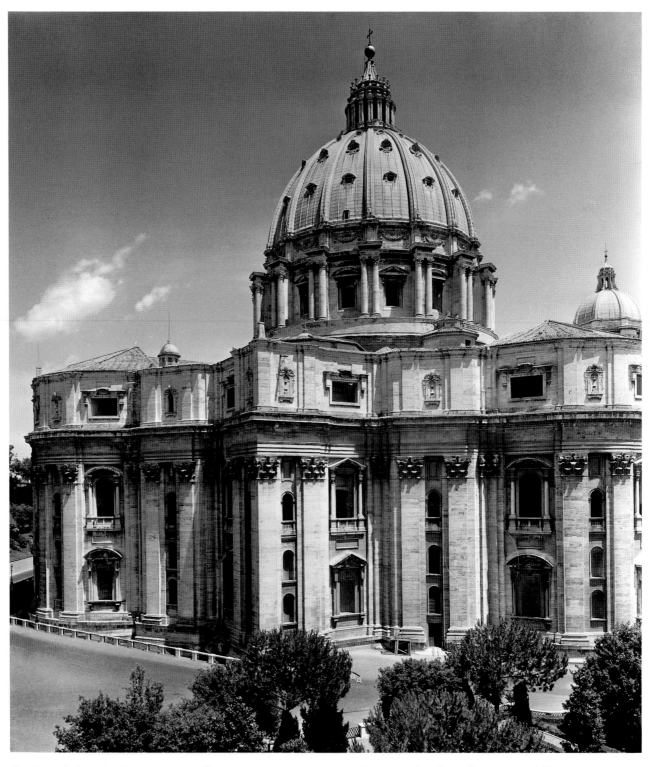

12-10. Michelangelo. Saint Peter's Basilica, Vatican, Rome. c. 1546–64 (dome completed 1590 by Giacomo della Porta). View from the southwest

languorous Adam with the spark of life. As if to echo the biblical text, Adam's heroic body and pose mirror those of God, in whose image he has been created. Directly below Adam is a youth grasping a bundle of oak leaves and giant acorns, which refer to Julius's family name (della Rovere, or "of the oak"), and possibly also to a passage in the Old Testament prophecy of Isaiah (61:3): "They will be called oaks of justice, planted by the Lord to show his glory."

A quarter of a century later, Michelangelo

again went to work in the Sistine Chapel, this time on the *Last Judgment,* painted between 1536 and 1541 on the large end wall behind the altar (see fig. 12-8). Michelangelo, now entering his sixties, had complained of feeling old for years, yet he accepted this important and demanding task, which took him two years to finish.

Michelangelo painted a writhing swarm of resurrected humanity with the Saved dragged from their graves and pushed up into a vortex of figures around Christ. Despite the efforts of several saints to save them at the last minute, the Damned plunge toward hell on the right. To the right of Christ's feet is Saint Bartholomew, who in legend was martyred by being skinned alive, holding his flayed skin, the face of which is painted with Michelangelo's own distorted features. On the lowest level of the mural, directly above the altar, is the gaping, fiery Hell-mouth, toward which the demonic boatman Charon propels his craft on the River Styx, which encircles the underworld. The painting is a grim and constant reminder to the celebrants of the Mass—the pope and his cardinals—that ultimately they will be judged for their deeds.

Besides being a sculptor and painter, Michelangelo was also an architect of genius. More than thirty years after the completion of the Sistine Chapel ceiling in 1512, the artist took on his most important building commission, the rebuilding of Saint Peter's in Rome. The project had begun in 1506, when Pope Julius II made the astonishing decision to demolish the vener-ated but crumbling Constantinian basilica hous-ing Saint Peter's tomb (see fig. 7-6). The pope appointed the architect Donato Bramante, who like Raphael came from Urbino, to design and build a magnificent new church. Bramante envi-sioned the new Saint Peter's as a central-plan building, a Greek cross (a cross with four arms of equal length) crowned with an enormous dome (see "Saint Peter's Basilica," page 281). The design was intended to continue the ancient Roman tra-dition of domed temples and round tombs; in Renaissance thinking, the central plan and dome also symbolized the perfection of God.

The deaths of the pope in 1513 and the architect in 1514 halted the project temporarily. Successive plans by Raphael and others changed the Greek cross to a Latin cross (one with three shorter arms and one long one) in order to provide the church with a full-length nave. However, when Michelangelo was appoint-ed architect in 1546, he returned to the Greek-cross plan, tearing down or canceling those parts of the previous design that he found with-out merit. Ultimately, Michelangelo transformed the building into a central-plan church of mag-nificent proportions and superhuman scale (fig. 12-10). Seventeenth-century additions and reno-vations dramatically changed the original plan of the church and the appearance of its interior. However, Michelangelo's Saint Peter's can still be seen in the contrasting forms of the flat and angled walls and the three **hemicycles** (semicir-cular structures). Within this arrangement, the colossal pilasters (engaged columnar elements extending through two or more stories), **blind windows** (having no openings), and niches form the sanctuary of the church. The level above the heavy entablature was later given windows of a different shape. How Michelangelo would

have built the great dome is not known; most scholars believe that he would have made it hemispherical. The dome that was actually erected, by Giacomo della Porta in 1588–1590, retains Michelangelo's basic design: it is a seg-mented dome with regularly spaced openings, resting on a high drum with pedimented win-dows between paired columns, and surmounted by a tall lantern shaped like a circular temple. Della Porta raised the dome's height, narrowing its segmental bands and changing the shape of its openings.

VENICE AND THE VENETO

In the last quarter of the fifteenth century, Venice emerged as a major artistic center. Vene-tian painters embraced the oil medium earlier than most other Italian artists, working with oil on both panel and canvas from the late 1470s on. Oil pigments were particularly suited to the brilliant color and lighting effects of Venice's most famous sixteenth-century painters: Titian, Tintoretto, and Veronese.

The early life of Titian (Tiziano Vecelli, c. 1478?–1576) is obscure. He supposedly began an apprenticeship as a mosaicist, then studied painting under the Venetian painters Gentile and Giovanni Bellini (Chapter 7). In 1507 Titian began working as an assistant to another Venetian artist, Giorgio da Castelfranco, called Giorgione (c. 1477–1510). Besides portraits, altarpieces, and frescoes, Giorgione made a few paintings showing figures placed in mysterious, intensely observed landscapes. Their meaning is uncertain, and scholars have theorized that Giorgione approached his work as many modern-day artists do, by selecting subjects in response to personal, private impulses, which he then expressed through his paintings.

The painting known as the *Pastoral Concert* (see fig. 2) is one of these mysterious paintings. Perhaps Giorgione began the painting and Titian completed it after Giorgione's death, or Titian, inspired by Giorgione, painted it alone. In this puzzling picture, two young men, one richly dressed, the other a barefoot peasant, relax in a verdant landscape. They seem almost oblivious to the two nude women beside them and the shepherd tending his flock in the background. While the meaning of the juxtaposition of the nude and clothed figures is obscure, in a general sense this scene of an outdoor concert evokes the romantic ideal of a lost golden age, some misty time in remote antiquity when people led a carefree pastoral life, a theme much loved by classical and early Renaissance poets. The sub-ject also permitted Titian to display his incom-parable talent for painting female nudes, whose flesh seems to glow with an incandescent light. The relaxed pose of the seated woman with the pipe contrasts with the complicated stance of

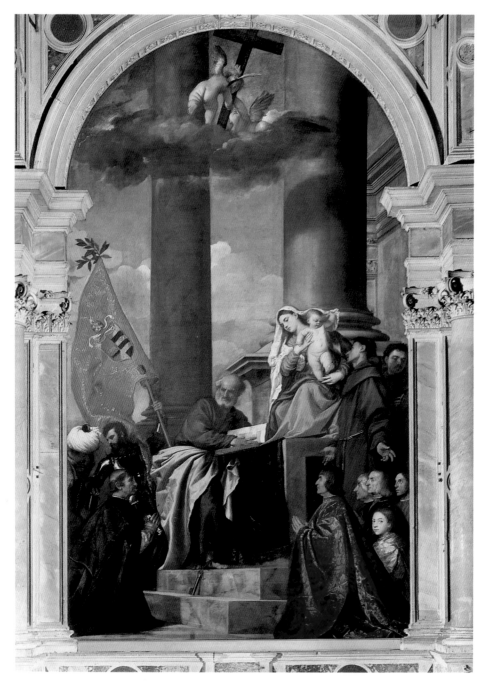

12-11. Titian. *Pesaro Madonna*. 1519–26. Oil on canvas, 15'11" x 8'10" (4.85 x 2.69 m). Pesaro Chapel, Santa Maria Gloriosa dei Frari, Venice

the woman at the well. Her tightly crossed legs and the swiveling twist of her body are impractical if her aim is to fill the glass pitcher but function admirably to focus the viewer's attention on the swelling forms of her stomach and thighs. The sensuous quality of this work suggests that Titian was as inspired by flesh-and-blood beauty as by any source from poetry or the history of art.

Titian was made official painter to the Republic of Venice in 1516. Three years later, the powerful Pesaro family commissioned him to paint an altarpiece for Santa Maria Gloriosa dei Frari in Venice. The subject was the traditional Madonna and Child, but Titian surrounded them by proud members of the Pesaro family (fig. 12-11). In the right foreground, Benedetto Pesaro,

garbed in red brocade, kneels in front of other family members: Vittorio, Antonio, Fantino, and Giovanni. In the left foreground, Jacopo Pesaro, Bishop of Paphos, kneels directly in front of the Virgin. No doubt he merited this honored spot because he had led a victory over the Turks in 1502. A turbaned Turkish captive stands behind him, and a knight holds a banner incorporating the arms of Jacopo Pesaro and Alexander VI, who was pope at the time of the battle. Saint Peter, a monumental figure with the key of heaven at his feet, looks approvingly at Jacopo, while Saint Francis, at right, gazes upward at the Cross. The grandeur of the scene, with its massive columns and marble staircase, must have reminded the viewer of the power and glory of the Pesaros. No photograph can convey the vibrancy of the paint surfaces, which Titian built up in layers of individual brushstrokes in pure colors, chiefly red, white, yellow, and black. The powerful intersecting diagonals of the composition, reaching from Jacopo Pesaro to the Virgin (innovatively placed off-center), and from Benedetto to the tilting banner at the upper left, strongly influenced other Venetian painters such as Veronese (see fig. 12-1) and led the way to the compositions based on sweeping diagonals that would later become a staple of Baroque art.

Titian's skill as a portrait painter led the most powerful and distinguished people of the time, including Emperor Charles V, to seek him out. Titian skillfully represented his sitters as they wanted to be remembered, at their best. The great humanist and patron of the arts, Isabella d'Este, was sixty years old when Titian painted her portrait, but he had studied an earlier portrait of the lady in order to capture her youthful beauty (see illustration for "Women Patrons of the Arts," right).

Paolo Caliari (1528–1588), called Veronese after his home town of Verona, carried on Titian's vision of the glories of both Venice and the Church. Like Titian, Veronese employed elaborate architectural settings and costumes for religious images, but he also added still lifes, anecdotal vignettes, and other details unconnected with the main subject that proved immensely appealing to Venetian patrons. One of Veronese's most famous works is the religious painting of 1573 now called *Feast in the House of Levi* (see fig. 12-1), painted for the Dominican Monastery of Santi Giovanni e Paolo, Venice. At first glance the true subject of this painting seems to be architecture, with the inhabitants of the space secondary to it. Beyond the enormous **loggia** (covered open-air gallery), entered through colossal triumphal arches, an imaginary city of white marble gleams in the distance. The size of the canvas allowed Veronese to make his figures realistically proportional to the architectural setting without losing their substance. He also maintained visual balance by giving the figures exaggerated, theatrical gestures and poses.

Jacopo Robusti (1518–1594), called Tintoretto ("little dyer") after his father's trade, carried Venetian Renaissance painting in another direc-

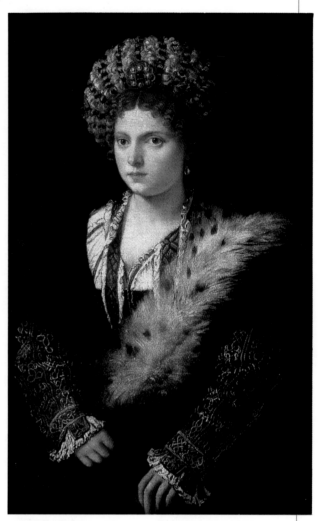

Women Patrons of the Arts

In the sixteenth century, many wealthy women, from both the aristocracy and the merchant class, were enthusiastic patrons of the arts. Two English queens, the Tudor half sisters Mary I and Elizabeth I, glorified their combined reigns of half a century with the aid of court artists, as did most sovereigns of the period. The Habsburg princesses Margaret of Austria and Mary of Hungary presided over brilliant humanist courts when they were regents of the Netherlands. But perhaps the Renaissance's greatest woman patron of the arts was the marchesa of Mantua, Isabella d'Este (1474–1539), who gathered painters, musicians, composers, writers, and literary scholars around her. Married to Francesco II Gonzaga at age fifteen, she had great beauty, great wealth, and a brilliant mind that made her a successful diplomat and administrator. A true Renaissance woman, her motto was the epitome of rational thinking—"Neither Hope nor Fear." An avid reader and collector of manuscripts and books, she sponsored an edition of Virgil while still in her twenties. She also collected ancient art and objects, as well as works by contemporary Italian artists such as Botticelli, Mantegna, Perugino, Correggio, and Titian. Her *grotto*, or cave, as she called her study in the Mantuan palace, was a veritable museum for her collections. The walls above the storage and display cabinets were painted in fresco by Mantegna, and the carvedwood ceiling was covered with mottoes and visual references to Isabella's impressive literary interests.

Titian. *Isabella d'Este.* 1534–36. Oil on canvas, 40¹/₆ x 25¹/₄" (102 x 64.1 cm). Kunsthistorisches Museum, Vienna

tion entirely. He is said to have been an apprentice in Titian's shop, where he proclaimed as his goal the combination of his master's color with the drawing of Michelangelo. The speed with which Tintoretto drew and painted was the subject of comment in his own time and of legends thereafter. He may have seemed to paint so rapidly because he employed a large workshop, which included other members of his family. Of his eight children, four became artists. His oldest child, Marietta Robusti, worked with him as a portrait painter, and two or perhaps three of his sons also joined the shop. Another daughter, famous for her needlework, became a nun. Marietta, in spite of her fame and many commissions, stayed in her father's shop until she died, at the age of thirty. So skillfully did she capture her father's style and technique that today art historians cannot be certain which paintings are hers.

With his visibly dynamic technique, strong colors, and bright highlights, Tintoretto created a pictorial mood of intense spirituality. The *Last*

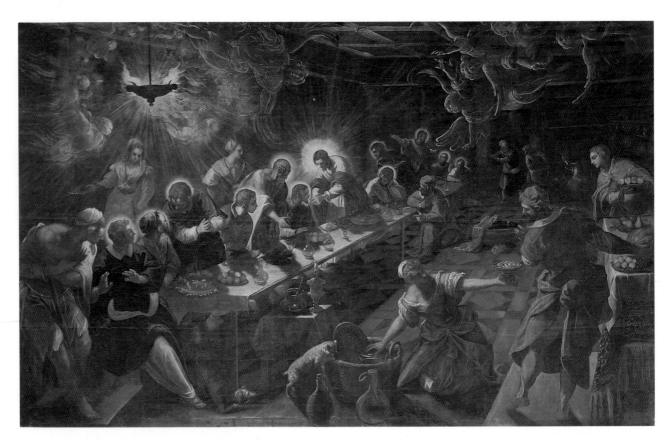

12-12. Tintoretto. *Last Supper.* 1592–4. Oil on canvas, 12' x 18'8" (3.7 x 5.7 m). Church of San Giorgio Maggiore, Venice

Tintoretto often developed a composition by creating a small-scale model like a miniature stage set, which he populated with wax figures. He then adjusted the positions of the figures and the lighting until he was satisfied with the entire scene. Using a grid of horizontal and vertical threads placed in front of this model, he could easily sketch the composition onto squared paper for his assistants to recopy onto a large canvas. His assistants also primed the canvas, blocking in the areas of dark and light, before the artist himself, now free to concentrate on the most difficult passages, finished the painting.

Supper (fig. 12-12), one of his final paintings, is filled with the kind of everyday details that Veronese also included, such as a servant kneeling by a basket of provisions, which is inspected by a curious cat. But these realistic elements are transformed by the plunging, off-center perspective and by the brilliant, otherworldly light emanating from Jesus and the disciples, which takes the place of simple halos. Bands of angels swoop in from above as the supernatural and secular worlds become one. Compared with the timeless, rigorous geometry of Leonardo da Vinci's *Last Supper* (see fig. 12-2), Tintoretto's composition is all sweeping motion and twisting, gesturing figures. The spectator is drawn irresistibly inward, caught up in the sacred drama.

Tintoretto painted the *Last Supper* and a companion painting, the *Gathering of Manna*, for the walls of the sanctuary of the church of San Giorgio Maggiore in Venice, designed by the architect Antonio Palladio (Andrea di Pietro, 1508–1580). Palladio, probably born in Padua, began his career as a stonecutter but became one of the foremost architects in Italy. After moving to Vicenza in the Veneto (the mainland region ruled by Venice), he became the protégé of a humanist scholar and amateur architect,

Giangiorgio Trissino. He learned Latin at Trissino's small academy, and he accompanied his benefactor on three trips to Rome, where he made drawings of Roman monuments.

Palladio's diversity can best be seen in numerous villas (country houses) built early in his career. Around 1550 he started his most famous villa, just outside Vicenza (fig. 12-13). Although most rural villas were working farms, Palladio designed this one as a retreat for relaxation. To afford views of the countryside, he placed an Ionic-order porch on each face of the building, with a wide staircase leading up to it. Upon its completion in 1569, the building was dubbed the Villa Rotonda because it had been inspired by another rotonda (round hall), the Roman Pantheon (see fig. 6-20). After its purchase in 1591 by the Capra family, it became known as the Villa Capra.

The villa plan (fig. 12-14) shows the geometrical clarity of Palladio's conception: a circle inscribed in a small square inside a larger square; with symmetrical rectangular rooms and identical rectangular projections from each of its faces. The use of a central dome on a domestic building was a daring innovation that effectively secularized the dome. The Villa Rotonda was the first of what

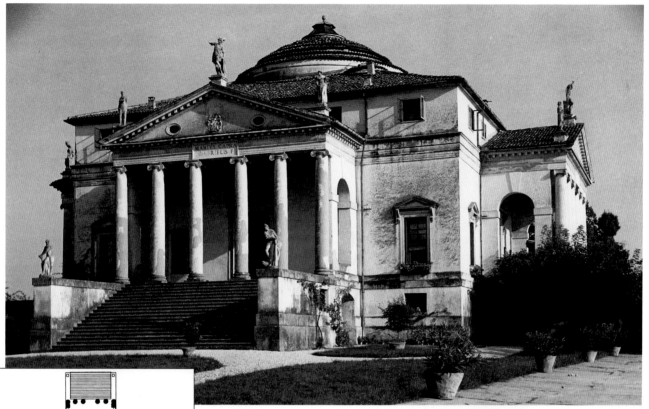

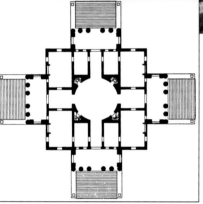

12-13. Palladio. Villa Rotonda (Villa Capra), Vicenza, Venetia, Italy. Begun 1550

12-14. Palladio. Plan of the Villa Rotonda.

was to become a long tradition of domed country houses, particularly in England and the United States, including Monticello, Thomas Jefferson's country house in Virginia (see fig. 16-13).

MANNERISM

The term *Mannerism* comes from the Italian *maniera*, a term used in the sixteenth century to mean charm, grace, or even courtly behavior. It suggests art concerned with formal beauty for its own sake rather than idealized nature according to Renaissance conventions. As a stylistic movement, Mannerism arose in Florence and Rome in the 1520s, first in painting and then in other mediums. Any attempt to define Mannerism as a single style is futile, but common Mannerist characteristics included figures with elongated proportions and enigmatic facial expressions, compositions with irrational spacial treatment, unusual colors and color juxtapositions, and obscure, unsettling, and often erotic imagery.

An early leader of the Mannerist movement, Jacopo da Pontormo (1494–1557) painted the *Entombment* (fig. 12-15) during 1525–1528 for the Church of Santa Felicità in Florence. Pontormo

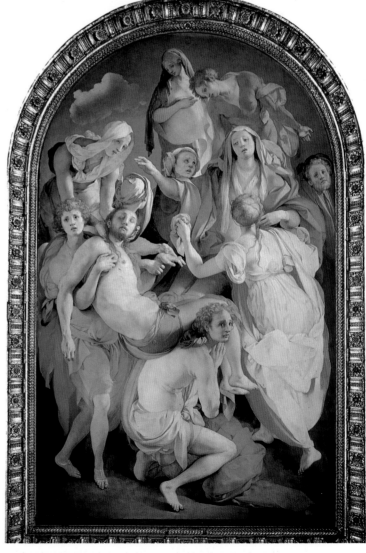

12-15. Pontormo. Entombment. 1525–28. Oil on panel, 10'3" x 6'4" (3.12 x 1.93 m). Capponi Chapel, Church of Santa Felicità, Florence

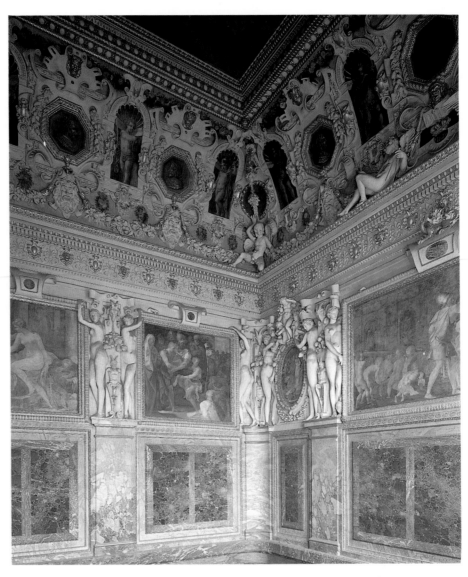

12-16. Primaticcio. Stucco and wall painting, Chamber of the Duchess of Étampes, Château of Fontainebleau. 1540s

Primaticcio worked on the decoration of Fontainebleau from 1532 until his death in 1570. During that time, he also commissioned and imported a large number of copies and casts made from original Roman sculpture, including the *Apollo Belvedere* in the Vatican gardens, the newly discovered *Laocoön* (see fig. 3), and even the relief decoration on the Column of Trajan. These works provided an invaluable visual source for the northern artists employed on the project.

seems to have chosen a moment just after Jesus' removal from the Cross, when the youths who have lowered him have paused to regain their composure. The large green bundle of cloth below Jesus apparently represents the shroud brought for his entombment. Only the faintest sense of location in space, which is immediately confused by the arrangement of the figures, who are either levitating or standing on a ring of boulders in the rocky terrain, is indicated by the rocky ground and cloudy sky. The emotional atmosphere of the scene is poignantly expressed by the dramatic use of color. Blue and pink with

accents of olive green, gray, scarlet, and creamy white dominate the palette. The overall tone of the picture is set by the color treatment of the crouching youth, whose bright pink torso is shaded in iridescent, pale gray-green.

Painters from Italy carried the Mannerist style to France, where King Francis I (ruled 1515–1547) was an important patron of the arts and enthusiastic supporter of the Italian Renaissance style. Francis even persuaded Leonardo da Vinci to join him at Amboise in the Loire River valley of France, where the artist spent the last two years of his life.

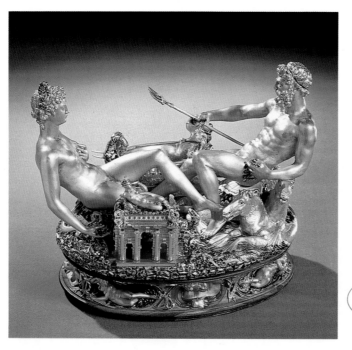

12-17. Benvenuto Cellini. *Saltcellar of Francis* I. 1539–43. Gold with enamel, 10¼ x 13⅛" (26 x 33.3 cm). Kunsthistorisches Museum, Vienna

Having chosen as his primary residence a medieval hunting lodge at Fontainebleau, Francis began transforming it in 1526 into a grand country palace, or **château**. In 1530, the king appointed a Florentine artist, the Mannerist painter Rosso Fiorentino (1495–1540), as the first artistic director of the project. After Rosso died, he was succeeded by his Italian colleague Francesco Primaticcio (1504–1570), who spent the rest of his career at Fontainebleau.

Among Primaticcio's first projects was the redecoration, in the 1540s, of the chambers of the king's official mistress, Anne, duchess of Étampes (fig. 12-16). The artist combined the arts of woodworking, stucco relief, and fresco painting in his complex but lighthearted and graceful interior design. The lithe figures of his stucco nymphs recall Pontormo's painting style (see fig. 12-15), with their elongated bodies and small heads. Their spiraling postures and the bits of clinging drapery are playfully sexual. The wall surface is almost overwhelmed with garlands, mythological figures, and Roman architectural ornament, and the total visual effect is extraordinarily confident and joyous. The first School of Fontainebleau, as this Italian phase of the palace decoration is called, established a tradition of Mannerism in painting and interior design that spread to other centers in France and the Netherlands.

Italian craftspeople began to move north after the end of the fifteenth century, and the Fontainebleau treasury includes some of the finest work of the Florentine goldsmith and sculptor Benvenuto Cellini (1500–1571). Cellini worked from just before 1540 to 1545 at Fontainebleau, where he made the famous *Saltcellar of Francis* I (fig. 12-17).

This utilitarian table piece, dated 1539–1543, was transformed into an elegant sculptural ornament through the artist's fanciful imagery and superb execution in gold and enamel. The Roman sea god, Neptune, representing the source of salt, sits next to a tiny boat-shaped container that carries the seasoning. Opposite him, a personification of the earth guards the plant-derived pepper, contained in the triumphal arch. The Seasons and the Times of Day on the base refer to both daily meal schedules and festive seasonal celebrations. The two main figures, their poses mirroring each other's with one bent and one straight leg, lean out from the center at impossible angles; they are nevertheless connected and visually balanced by glances and gestures. Their supple elongated bodies and small heads reflect the Mannerist conventions also followed by Primaticcio.

The architect Giacomo Barozzi (1507–1573), called Vignola after his native town, worked with Primaticcio in France from 1541 to 1543. His later work, however, is more expressive of Renaissance than Mannerist ideals. In Rome he designed the headquarters church for the Society of Jesus, or Jesuit order. The simplicity and practical planning of the Church of Il Gesù (Jesus), completed after Vignola's death by Giacomo della Porta in 1584, influenced church design for more than a century. As conceived by Vignola, the church fit compactly into a city block, its interior essentially a hall for preaching, with shallow side chapels. Even the traditional Christian desire for an east-west-oriented building gave way to the practical considerations of theatrical oratory and urban space.

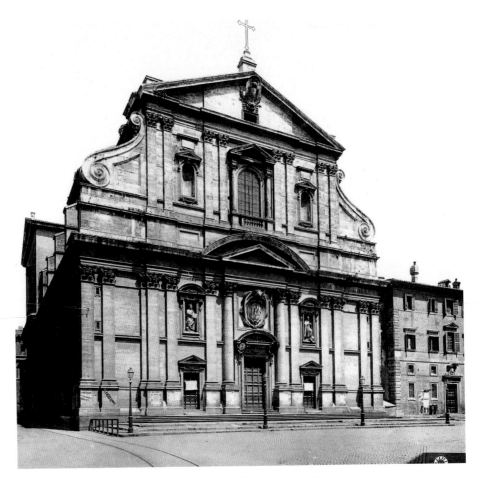

12-18. Giacomo da Vignola and **Giacomo della Porta. Facade of the Church of Il Gesù,**
Rome. Begun on Vignola's design in 1568; completed by della Porta c. 1575–84

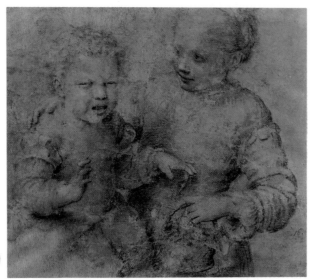

12-19. Sofonisba Anguissola. *Child Bitten by a Crayfish.*
c. 1558. Black chalk, 12³⁄₈ x 13³⁄₈" (31.5 x 34 cm). Galleria
Nazionale de Capodimonte, Naples

The facade (fig. 12-18), planned by Vignola
but altered by della Porta during construction,
followed a general design established by Renaissance architects: paired colossal orders visually
tying together the first and second stories; a second order superimposed on the third story; and
large volutes (scroll forms) to ease the transition
between the wide lower levels and the narrow

third level by masking the sloping roofs of the
side aisles (see "Baroque and Rococo Church
Facades," opposite). The central axis of the building was stressed by gradually moving the orders
on the lower level forward, from the relatively flat
pilasters at the corners to the engaged half-
columns at the center; by crowning the central
door with a double pediment (a triangle inside a
semicircle); and by enlarging the central window
on the upper level. The intrusion of the double
pediment into the story above it emphasizes the
verticality of the facade.

Many sixteenth-century Italian artists
continued to be inspired by the great leaders
of the earlier generation—Leonardo da Vinci,
Raphael, and Michelangelo—rather than adopt-
ing Mannerist principles. The father of the
gifted portrait painter from Cremona, Sofonisba
Anguissola (1528–1625), consulted Michelangelo
about her artistic talents in 1557. He asked
Michelangelo for a drawing that she might copy
and return to be critiqued. Michelangelo not only
obliged but also set another task for Anguissola:
she was to send him a drawing of a crying boy.

Elements of Architecture

BAROQUE AND ROCOCO CHURCH FACADES

The two facades featured here demonstrate the shift of taste in architecture—from classicistic to expressionistic—between the beginning of the Baroque and the end of the Rococo. At one end of the spectrum is Giacomo da Vignola and Giacomo della Porta's Roman Baroque facade for Il Gesù (see fig. 12-18), of about 1575–1584, which, like Renaissance and Mannerist buildings, is still firmly grounded in the clean articulation and vocabulary of classical architecture. At the other end is Pedro de Ribera's portal for the Hospicio de San Fernando (see fig.13-16), now a municipal museum in Madrid, which was designed about 150 years later, in 1722. Ribera's portal is Rococo taken to extremes, in which there is nearly a meltdown of heavily encrusted, highly elaborated ornament in the **churrigueresque** style.

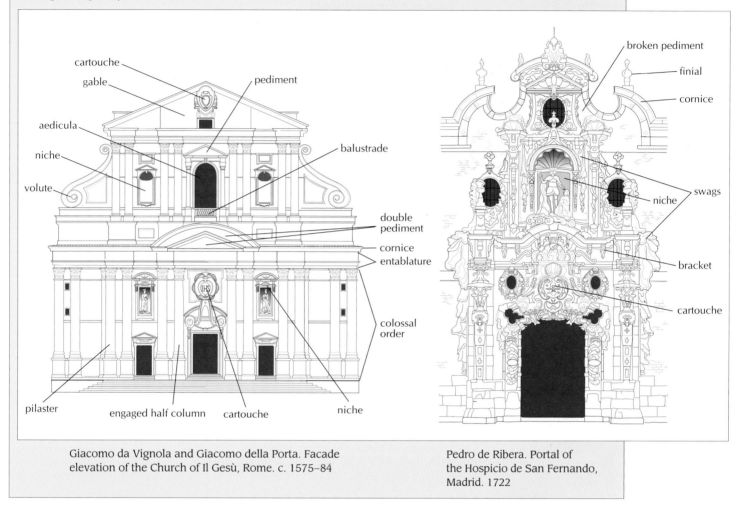

Giacomo da Vignola and Giacomo della Porta. Facade elevation of the Church of Il Gesù, Rome. c. 1575–84

Pedro de Ribera. Portal of the Hospicio de San Fernando, Madrid. 1722

Michelangelo and his contemporary, Leonardo da Vinci, were both intensely interested in the expression of human emotion, and both made many drawings of faces showing specific emotional states.

Anguissola took the concept one step further. She turned the assignment into an excuse for a charming **genre scene**, or picture of everyday life, a type of subject matter that would become popular in seventeenth-century painting. A young boy, perhaps Sofonisba's brother, wails because a crayfish is biting his finger, while a slightly older girl attempts to comfort him (fig. 12-19). The sketch, with its naturalistic treatment of the two children, so impressed Michelangelo that he gave it as a gift to his closest friend. This friend later presented it to Cosimo I de' Medici, along with a drawing by Michelangelo. From 1560, Anguissola served as an official court painter to the queen of Spain, a post she held for twenty years. Unfortunately, most of her Spanish works were lost in a seventeenth-century palace fire.

Another northern Italian, Lavinia Fontana (1552–1614), learned to paint from her father, a Bolognese follower of Raphael. By the 1570s, she was a highly respected painter of narrative as well as of portraits, the more usual field for women artists of the time. Her success was so well rewarded, in fact, that her husband, the painter Gian Paolo Zappi, eventually gave up his own career to care for their large family and help Lavinia with such technical aspects of her work as framing. This situation was unusual even in Bologna, which boasted some two dozen women painters as well as a number of women scholars who lectured at the university in a variety of subjects, including law.

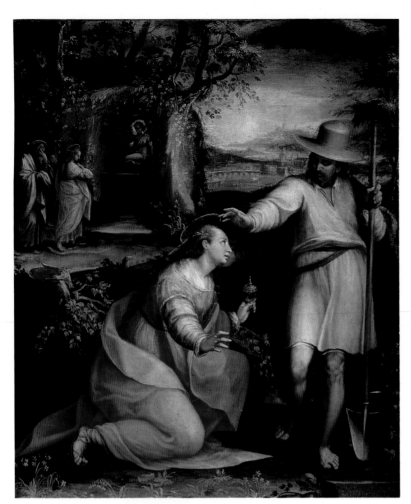

12-20. Lavinia Fontana. *Noli Me Tangere.* 1581. Oil on canvas, 47³/₈ x 36⁵/₈" (120.3 x 93 cm). Galleria degli Uffizi, Florence

While still in her twenties, Lavinia painted the *Noli Me Tangere* of 1581 (fig. 12-20), illustrating the biblical story of Christ revealing himself for the first time to Mary Magdalen following his Resurrection (Mark 16:9, John 20:17). The Latin title of the painting means "Do not touch me," Christ's words when the Magdalen moved to embrace him, explaining that he now existed in a new form somewhere between physical and spiritual. Christ's costume refers to the passage in the Gospel of John that says that the Magdalen at first mistook Him for a gardener.

In 1603, Lavinia moved to Rome as an official painter to the papal court. She also soon came to the attention of the Habsburgs, who paid large sums for her work. In 1611, she was honored with a commemorative medal portraying her in a bust as a dignified, elegantly coiffed woman on one side and as an intensely preoccupied artist with rolled-up sleeves and wild, uncombed hair on the other.

German and English Art

In Germany, the first decades of the sixteenth century were dominated by two very different artists, Matthias Gothardt, known as Matthias Grünewald (c. 1480–1528), and Albrecht Dürer

(1471–1528). Grünewald's style expressed the continuing currents of medieval German mysticism and emotionalism, while Dürer's intense observation of the natural world represented the scientific Renaissance interest in empirical observation, perspective, and a reasoned canon of human proportions.

Grünewald is best known today for his *Isenheim Altarpiece* (fig. 12-21), painted between about 1510 and 1515 for the Community of Saint Anthony in Isenheim, whose hospital specialized in diseases of the skin, including plague and leprosy. The altarpiece was thought to have healing properties, and viewing it was part of the treatment given to patients who entered the hospital.

The altarpiece, which had both fixed and movable wings, was displayed in different configurations depending upon the Church calendar. On normal weekdays, when it was closed, as illustrated here, viewers saw a shocking image of the Crucifixion in a darkened landscape, a Lamentation below, and lifesize figures of Saints Sebastian and Anthony Abbot standing like statues on trompe l'oeil pedestals on the fixed wings. Grünewald represented in the most horrific detail the tortured body of Jesus covered with gashes from being beaten and pierced by the thorns used mockingly to form a crown for his head. Not only do his ashen color, open mouth, and blue lips indicate that he is dead, but he also already appears to be decaying, an effect enhanced by the palette of putrescent greens, yellows, and purplish red. A ghostlike Virgin Mary has collapsed in the arms of an emaciated John the Evangelist, and Mary Magdalen has fallen in anguish to her knees. In the **predella**, or supporting platform, below, Jesus' bereaved mother and friends prepare his body for burial, a scene that must have been familiar indeed in the hospital. The saints on the wings serve as models for a life of Christian devotion and as intercessors for the sick and dying.

Grünewald's personal identification with the struggles of the peasants in the social and religious turmoil of the 1520s damaged his artistic career. After actively supporting the peasants, who, because of economic and religious oppression, rose up against their feudal overlords in the Peasants' War in 1525, he left Mainz and spent his last years in Halle, whose ruler was the chief protector of Martin Luther and a longtime patron of Grünewald's contemporary, Albrecht Dürer.

Dürer, one of eighteen children of a Nuremberg goldsmith, served apprenticeships in painting, stained-glass design, and the making of woodcuts. He later took up engraving and became familiar with the latest trends in Renaissance art during two trips to Italy, in 1494–1495 and 1505–1506. Thereafter, he seems to have resolved to reform the art of his own country by publishing theoretical writings and manuals

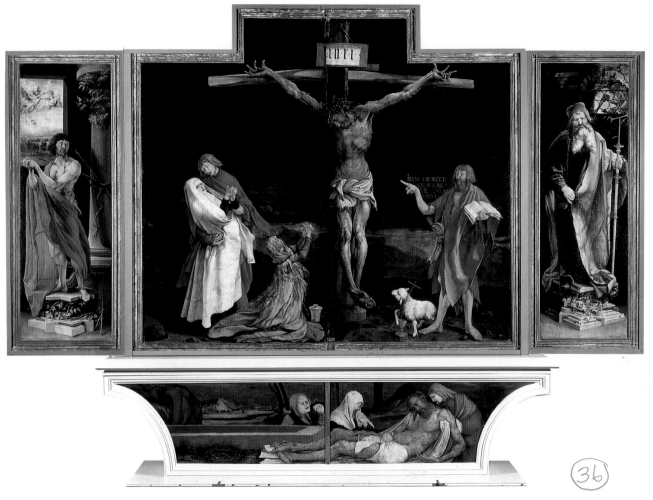

12-21. **Matthias Grünewald.** *Isenheim Altarpiece*, closed, from the Community of Saint Anthony, Isenheim, Alsace, France. Center panels: *Crucifixion*; predella: *Lamentation*; side panels: Saints Sebastian and Anthony Abbot. c. 1510–15. Oil on panel, center panels 9'9" x 10'9" (2.97 x 3.28 m); each wing 8'2" x 3'1/2" (2.49 x 0.93 m); predella 2'5½" x 11'2" (0.75 x 3.40 m). Musée d'Unterlinden, Colmar, France

that discussed Renaissance problems of perspective, ideal human proportions, and the techniques of painting.

Dürer's early interest in Italian art and theoretical investigations is apparent in his 1504 engraving of *Adam and Eve* (fig. 12-22). These nudes, rendered with his first documented use of a canon of ideal human proportions, were based on Roman copies of Greek statues, probably known to him through prints or small sculpture in the antique manner. As idealized as the human figures may be, the flora and fauna are recorded with typically northern European microscopic detail. Dürer embedded the landscape with symbols related to the medieval theory that after Adam and Eve disobeyed God, they and their descendants became vulnerable to imbalances in body fluids that altered human temperament: an excess of black bile from the liver produced melancholy, despair, and greed; yellow bile caused anger, pride, and impatience; phlegm in the lungs resulted in lethargy, disinterest, and a lack of emotion; and an excess of blood made a person unusually optimistic but

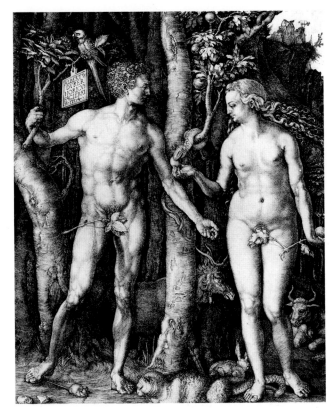

12-22. **Albrecht Dürer.** *Adam and Eve.* 1504. Engraving, 9⅞ x 7⅝" (25.1 x 19.4 cm). Philadelphia Museum of Art
Purchased: Lisa Nora Elkins Fund

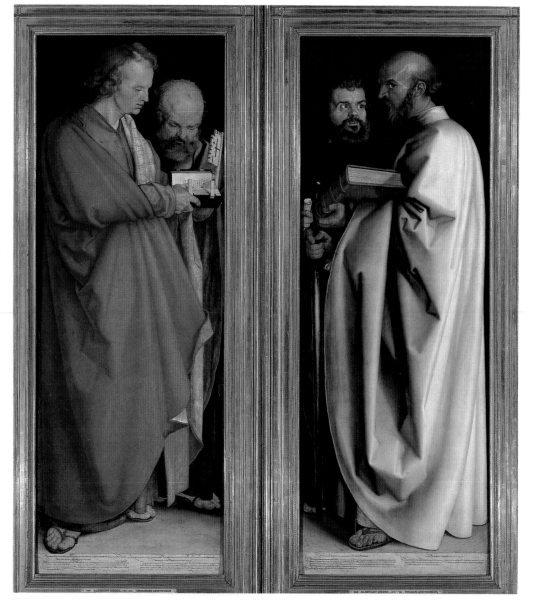

12-23. Albrecht Dürer.
Four Apostles. 1526.
Oil on panel, each panel
7'1/2" x 2'6" (2.15 x 0.76 m).
Alte Pinakothek, Munich

also compulsively interested in the pleasures of the flesh. These four human temperaments are symbolized here by the melancholy elk, the choleric cat, the phlegmatic ox, and the sensual rabbit. The mouse is an emblem of Satan, and the parrot may symbolize false wisdom, since it can only repeat mindlessly what is said to it.

In the 1520s, as the Protestant Reformation began to gain political power in Germany, religious upheavals and iconoclastic purges of religious images began to take a toll on artistic activity. Martin Luther, however, never supported the destruction of religious art, and Dürer, who admired Luther's writings, may have painted a pair of inscribed panels commonly referred to as the *Four Apostles* (fig. 12-23) in order to demonstrate that Protestant imagery was possible. The paintings depict the Saints John, Peter, Paul, and Mark the Evangelist. On the left panel, the elderly Saint Peter, the first pope, seems to shrink behind the young Saint John, Luther's favorite evangelist.

On the right panel, Saint Mark is nearly hidden behind Saint Paul, whose teachings and epistles were greatly admired by the Protestants. Dürer presented the panels, painted in 1526, to the city of Nuremberg, which had already adopted Lutheranism (then almost synonymous with Protestantism) as its official religion.

German sculptors had to face even greater problems of theme and patronage than German painters, since their principal commissions had been for altarpieces and tombs. Nevertheless, they worked in every medium, and they produced some of their finest and most original work in this period in limewood, from the linden or lime tree, which grew abundantly in central and southern Germany. Tilman Riemenschneider (active 1483–1531), after about 1500, ran the largest sculpture workshop in Würzburg; he was also politically active in the city's government. Riemenschneider's work attracted patrons from other cities, and in 1501 he signed a contract

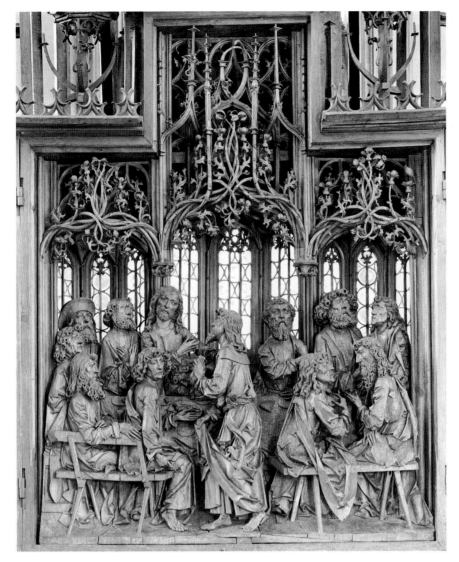

12-24. Tilman Riemenschneider. *Last Supper,* center of the *Altarpiece of the Holy Blood,* Sankt Jakobskirche, Rothenburg ob der Tauber, Germany. c. 1499–1505. Limewood, height of tallest figure 39" (99.1 cm); height of altar 29'6" (9 m)

for one of his major creations, the *Altarpiece of the Holy Blood,* for the Church of Saint James in Rothenburg. The most important relic in the church was a drop of what was believed to be Jesus' blood. The altarpiece was to be nearly 30 feet high and made entirely of limewood. A specialist in wood shrines began work on the frame in 1499, while Riemenschneider later provided the figures. The relative value of their contributions in contemporary thinking can be judged from the fact that the frame carver received fifty florins and Riemenschneider sixty.

The main panel of the altarpiece represents the *Last Supper* (fig. 12-24). Like his Italian contemporary Leonardo da Vinci (see fig. 12-2), Riemenschneider depicted the moment of Jesus' revelation that one of his disciples would betray him. Unlike Leonardo, however, Riemenschneider composed his group with Jesus off-center at the left and the disciples packed around him. Judas, at center stage, holds a money bag as a symbol

of the thirty pieces of silver he received for his treachery. Jesus extends a morsel of food to Judas, signifying that he is the one destined to set in motion the events that will lead to Jesus' death (John 13:21–30). One apostle points down toward the altar where the relic of the Holy Blood would have been displayed.

The scene is set in a stagelike space with windows in the back wall glazed with bull's-eye glass. Natural light from the church's windows illuminates the scene with constantly changing effects, according to the time of day and weather. Although earlier sculpture had been painted and gilded, Riemenschneider introduced the use of a natural wood finish. Rather than creating individual portraits, he tended to repeat a limited number of types. His figures have large heads, prominent features, and elaborate hair treatments with thick wavy locks and deeply drilled curls. The muscles, tendons, and raised veins of hands and feet are especially lifelike, as are the

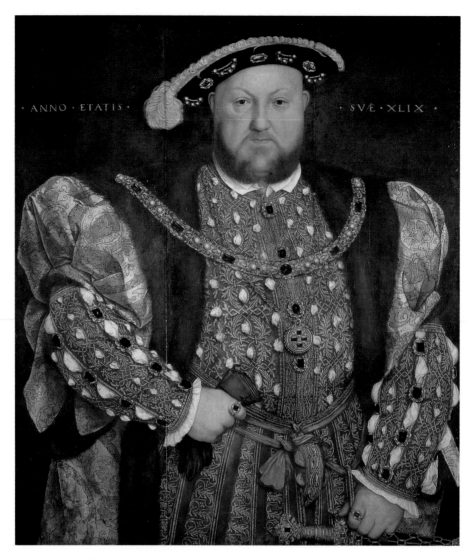

12-25. Hans Holbein the Younger. *Henry* **VIII.** c. 1540. Oil on panel, 32¹/₂ x 29¹/₂" (82.6 x 75 cm). Galleria Nazionale d'Arte Antica, Rome

pronounced cheekbones, sagging jowls, and baggy eyes. Voluminous draperies cover the slim figures; the deep folds and active patterning create strong highlights and dark shadows that unify the narrative and the intricate carving of the framework. Despite the success of his religious images, Riemenschneider's career ended when his support of the 1525 Peasants' War led to his being fined and imprisoned. He survived, but died just six years later.

The successors of Grünewald and Dürer often had to compromise and to take drastic measures to navigate the radically changed German social and political scene. Some artists, like Tilman Riemenschneider, found their careers at a standstill because of their sympathies for rebels and reformers. Others left their homes to seek patronage abroad because of their support for the Roman Catholic Church. Hans Holbein the Younger (1497–1543), born in Augsburg, spent much of his early career in Basel, Switzerland, but worked in Antwerp and London from 1526 to 1528 to escape religious turmoil. Although he

had officially become a Protestant by 1532, harassment from reformers sent him once again to England, where he served as court painter to the Tudor monarch Henry VIII (ruled 1509–1547). The Tudors so favored Netherlandish, German, and French artists that a vigorous native school of painters did not emerge in England until the eighteenth century.

One of Holbein's official portraits of Henry at age thirty-nine (fig. 12-25) was painted about 1540. The dress and appearance of the king had already been established in an earlier prototype based on sketches of the king's features. Henry's huge frame—he was well over 6 feet tall and had a 54-inch waist in his maturity—is covered by the latest style of dress, a short puffed-sleeved cloak of heavy brocade trimmed in dark fur, a narrow, stiff white collar fastened at the front, and a doublet slit to expose his silk shirt and encrusted with gemstones and gold braid. Henry, quite vain, was so fascinated by the elegant French king Francis I that he attempted to emulate and even surpass him in appearance.

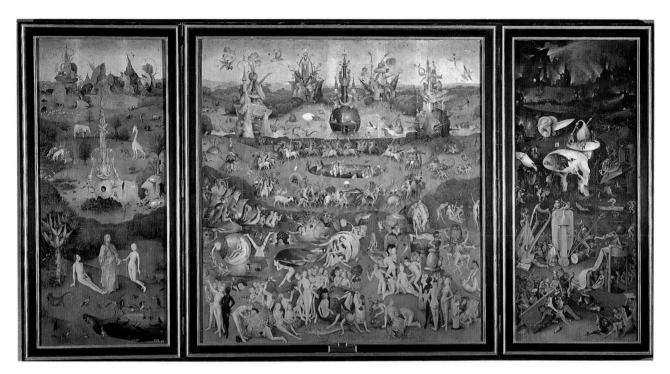

12-26. Hieronymus Bosch. *Garden of Earthly Delights*. c. 1505–15. Oil on panel, center panel 7'2¹/₂" x 6'4³/₄" (2.20 x 1.95 m); each wing 7'2¹/₂" x 3'2" (2.20 x 0.97 m). Museo del Prado, Madrid

The triptych format that the artist chose may be an understated irony. Before the Reformation, the altarpiece had been synonymous with religious imagery in northern Europe, but this work was commissioned by an aristocrat for his Brussels town house. As a secular work, the *Garden of Earthly Delights* may well have inspired lively discussion and even ribald comment, much as it does today in its museum setting.

After Francis set a new style by growing a beard, Henry also grew one, as shown in this portrait.

Netherlandish and Spanish Art

Politically the Netherlands and Spain were united under the Habsburg Empire during the sixteenth century. The art made there, however, followed several different directions and was affected to varying degrees by developments in Italian art. Some artists continued the styles of the late fifteenth century; others looked back to earlier Flemish painters for models; some became Mannerists in the Italian mode. A few artists, perhaps the best known today, were such individualists that they must be considered unique.

The Netherlandish artist Hieronymus Bosch (c. 1450–1516) certainly falls into the latter category. He created a world of fantastic imagery associated with medieval art in paintings such as his triptych, the *Garden of Earthly Delights* (fig. 12-26). There are many interpretations of the *Garden*, but a few broad conclusions can be drawn with certainty. The subject of the overall work seems to be the Christian belief in humanity's natural state of sinfulness. The triptych begins with the Creation of the World (on the wing exteriors, not shown), continues with the Creation

of Adam and Eve on the left wing, and ends with the Last Judgment on the right. The fact that only the Damned and not the Saved are shown in the Judgment scene suggests that Bosch might have meant to caution that damnation is the natural outcome of a life lived in ignorance and folly. The central panel illustrates the activities that condemn humanity, which include seemingly harmless diversions such as games, romance, and music, and sins such as lust, gluttony, and sloth. Luscious fruits—strawberries, cherries, grapes, and pomegranates—appear everywhere in the *Garden*, serving as food, as shelter, and even as a boat. Herbalists believed these fruits enhanced fertility. In the painting they also suggest that life is as fleeting and insubstantial as the taste of a strawberry.

The works of Hieronymus Bosch were so popular that the painter Pieter Brueghel the Elder (c. 1525–1569), nearly half a century later, began his career by imitating his work. Fortunately, Brueghel's talents went far beyond those of a copyist, and he soon developed his own style and themes. Working first in Antwerp and then in Brussels, he produced artfully composed works that reflected contemporary social, political, and religious conditions. Brueghel's inspiration came from visits to country fairs, where he

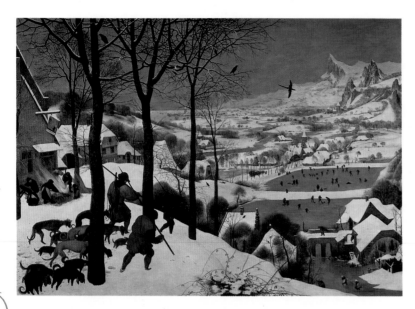

12-27. Pieter Brueghel the Elder. *Return of the Hunters.* 1565. Oil on panel, 3'10½" x 5'3¾" (1.18 x 1.61 m). Kunsthistorisches Museum, Vienna

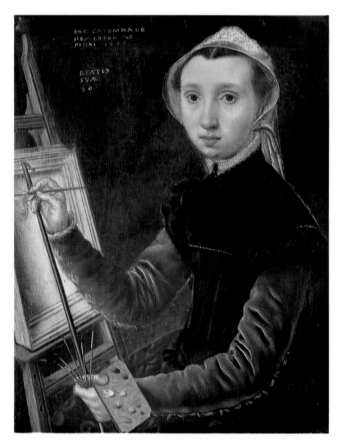

12-28. Caterina van Hemessen. *Self-Portrait.* 1548. Oil on panel, 12¼ x 9¼" (31.1 x 23.5 cm). Öffentliche Kunstsammlung, Basel, Switzerland

sketched the farmers and townspeople who became the focus of both his religious and secular painting.

Cycles, or series, of paintings on a single allegorical subject such as the Times of Day, the Seasons, or the Five Senses were popular decorations in Flemish upper-class homes. Brueghel's *Return of the Hunters* (fig. 12-27) of 1565 is one of a cycle of six panels, each representing two months of the year. In this November–December scene, the artist captures the damp, cold winter weather much as his compatriots the Limbourgs did 150 years earlier (see fig. 11-8). In contrast to much Renaissance and Mannerist art, the subject matter in this painting appears neutral and realistic. The hunters slog stoically by, trailed by their dogs, while workers at an inn singe a pig in a fire before finishing butchering it. The viewer's eye, plunging across the wide valley toward the distant peaks, is deliberately slowed by the careful balance of the vertical tree trunks and the horizontal rectangles of frozen water.

As a depiction of Flemish life, this scene represents a relative calm before the storm. Two years after it was painted, the northern provinces of the Low Countries, which would eventually become the independent country of the Netherlands, began their struggle for independence from Spain. But even during the long years of political and social turmoil, which divided the Low Countries along religious lines, people found the resources to patronize artists.

Caterina van Hemessen (1528–1587) of Antwerp developed an illustrious international reputation. She learned to paint from her father, a Flemish Mannerist with whom she collaborated on large commissions, but her quiet realism had Renaissance roots. Her portraits typically depict the subject in three-quarter view, carefully including background elements that could be shown perspectively, such as the easel in her *Self-Portrait* (fig. 12-28). In delineating her own features, Caterina presented a serious young person without personal vanity yet seemingly already self-assured about her artistic abilities. The inscription on the painting reads: "I Caterina van Hemessen painted myself in 1548. Her age 20."

Early in van Hemessen's career, she became a favored court artist of Mary of Hungary, regent of the Netherlands. When Mary ceased to be regent in 1556, the artist accompanied her to Spain, where Flemish painting had been popular since the fifteenth century. She arrived at the outset of the long reign of Philip II (ruled 1556–1598). Under Philip's direction, Spain halted the advance of Islam in the Mediterranean and secured control of most of the Americas. Despite enormous effort and expense, however, Philip could not suppress the revolt in the Spanish Netherlands, and his navy, the famous Spanish Armada, was destroyed by the English in 1588.

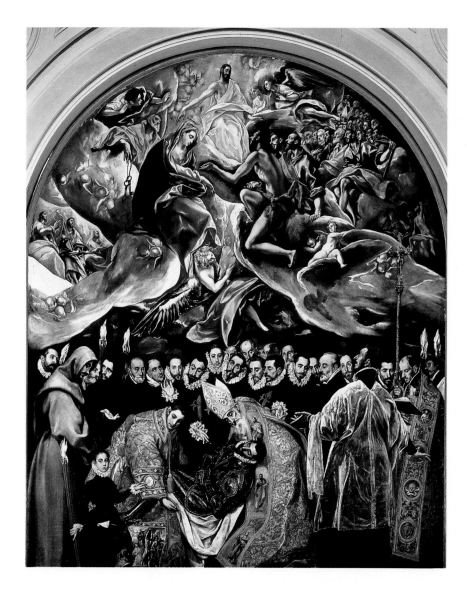

12-29. El Greco. *Burial of Count Orgaz,* Church of Santo Tomé, Toledo, Spain. 1586. Oil on canvas, 16' x 11'10" (4.88 x 3.61 m)

Philip was a serious art collector from an early age, supporting artists in Spain and abroad for more than half a century. He did not, however, appreciate the works of the man who became one of Spain's most famous painters. This was the Greek painter Kyriakos (Domenikos) Theotokopoulos (1541–1614), who arrived in Spain in 1577 after working for ten years in Italy. El Greco ("the Greek"), as he was called, began as a Byzantine-style icon painter in his native Crete and then entered Titian's shop in Venice in about 1566. His mature style united the intense emotionalism of Byzantine religious art with rich color and loose brushwork reminiscent of Tintoretto. This pictorial vision ideally suited the needs of patrons in late-sixteenth-century Spain, which was undergoing a fervent religious revival.

In 1586, the artist was commissioned by the Orgaz family to paint a large canvas illustrating a legend from the fourteenth century, the *Burial of Count Orgaz* (fig. 12-29). The count had been a great benefactor of the Church, and at his funeral Saints Augustine and Stephen were said to have appeared and lowered his body into his tomb while his soul was seen ascending to heaven. In El Greco's painting, an angel in the center lifts Orgaz's tiny ghostly soul as the miraculous burial takes place below. Portraits of local aristocrats and religious notables fill the background of the picture, which is painted, in the Mannerist tradition, without specific reference to the spatial setting (see fig. 12-15). El Greco placed his eight-year-old son at the lower left next to Saint Stephen and signed the painting on the boy's white kerchief. He may have put his own features on the man just above the saint's head, the only one who looks straight out at the viewer.

El Greco distinguished between earth and heaven in this painting by creating a separate light source above in the figure of Christ, who sheds an otherworldly luminescence quite unlike the natural light below. The dramatic lighting effects and emotionalism of El Greco's work would be echoed by an increasing number of painters in the early seventeenth century, as European art entered the Baroque era.

READING A PAINTING

Sometimes, paintings seem to have been created to be read as documents rather than to be enjoyed primarily in visual terms. When Jan Brueghel painted allegories of the five senses—sight, touch, hearing, taste, and smell—he invited the viewer to wander in an imaginary space and to enjoy and inventory an amazing collection of works of art and scientific equipment—a display of wealth, scholarship, and connoisseurship.

Gathered in a huge vaulted room are paintings, sculpture, furniture, objects in gold and silver, books and prints, scientific instruments—all under a magnificent bronze chandelier adorned with the double-headed eagle of the Habsburgs. The painting *Sight* can be "read" by the viewer like an illustrated catalogue of the ducal collection.

Jan Brueghel and Peter Paul Rubens. *Sight,* from Allegories of the Five Senses. c. 1617–18. Oil on panel, 25⅝ x 43" (65 x 109 cm). Museo del Prado, Madrid

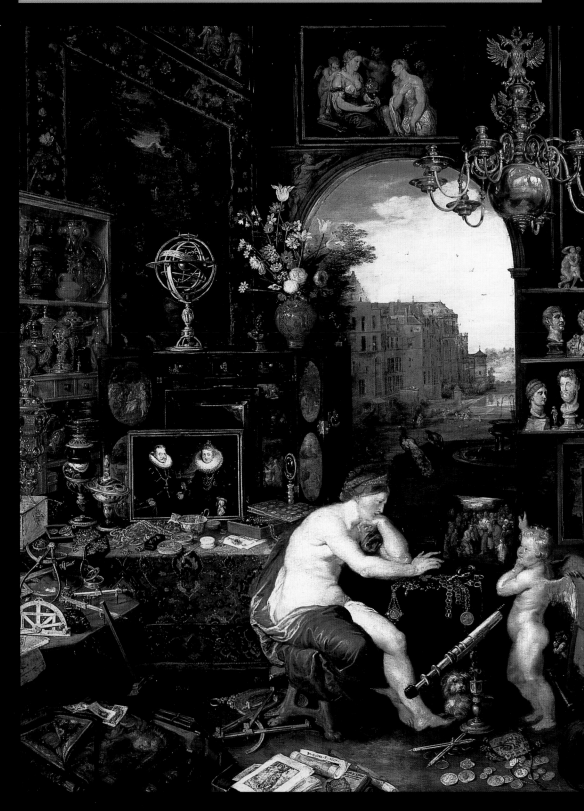

Taking a Visual Inventory

We look over the painting inch by inch, almost as if we were reading a book or a palace inventory. We can begin with Brueghel's copies of Rubens's portraits of Archduke Albert and Princess Isabel Clara Eugenia on the table and the duke's portrait on the floor. (Rubens and Brueghel were friends and neighbors in Antwerp, and they often worked together, as they did here, with Rubens painting figures and Brueghel painting settings.) Besides the portraits we can find *Daniel in the Lions' Den* (upper-left corner), *The Lion and Tiger Hunt* (top center), and *The Drunken Silenus* (lower right). The *Madonna and Child in a Wreath of Flowers* (far right) was a popular subject in which Rubens usually painted Mary and the Child, and Brueghel painted the flower wreath. Brueghel also included Raphael's *St. Cecilia* (behind the globe) and Titian's *Venus and Psyche* (over the door).

Reading and Seeing: Religion, Fine Arts, and Science

The classical goddess Venus, attended by Cupid (both figures painted by Rubens), has put aside her mirror to contemplate Jan Brueghel's painting *Christ Healing the Blind*. She has also rejected Pieter Brueghel's painting *The Blind Leading the Blind* (on the floor at the back). The equipment needed to see and study surrounds Venus. The huge globe at the right and the armillary sphere with its gleaming rings (at the upper left) symbolize the extent of humanistic learning. Books and prints, ruler, compasses, magnifying glass, and the more complex astrolabe and telescope are scattered on the floor and tables. The monkeys playing with the telescope and eyeglasses refer to spiritual blindness, to those who look but do not see.

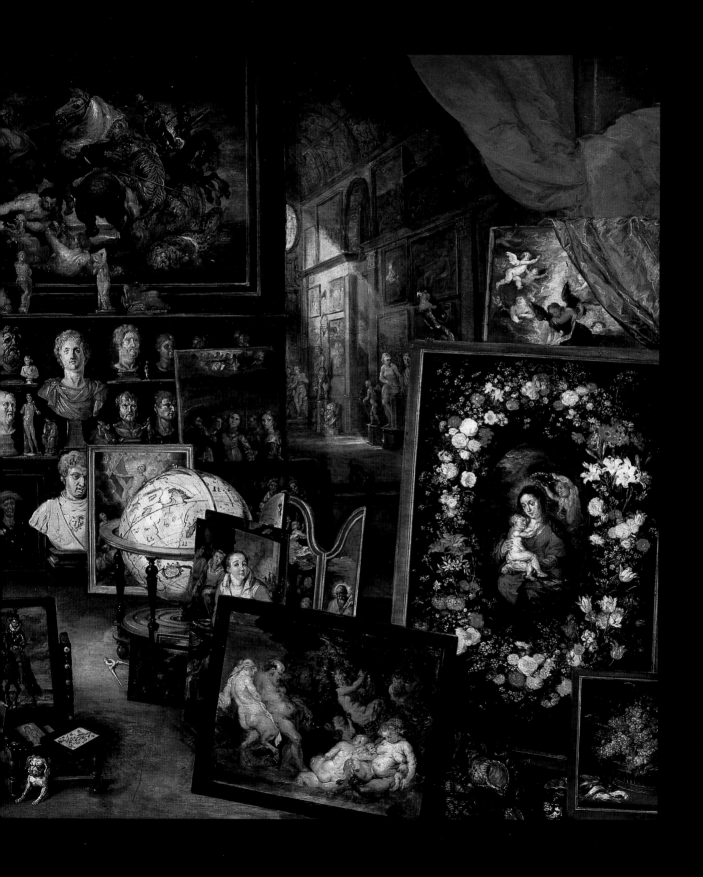

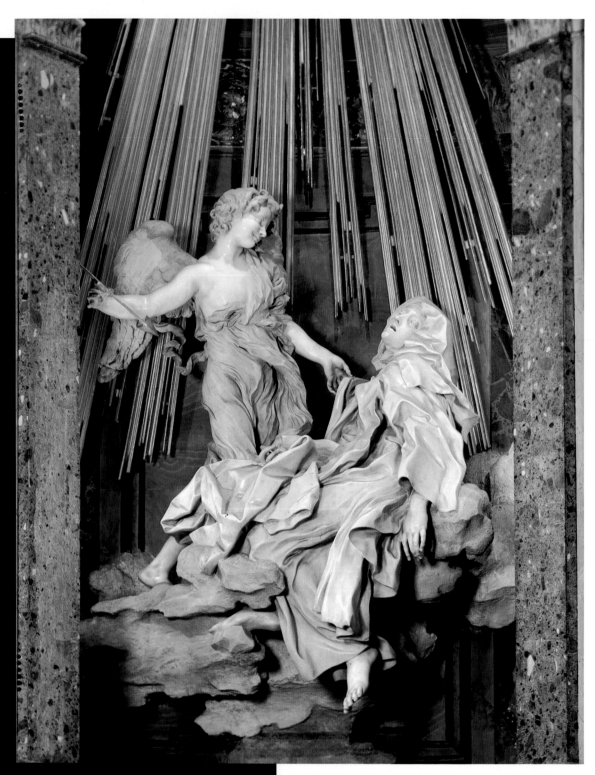

13-1. Gianlorenzo Bernini. *Saint Teresa of Ávila in Ecstasy.* 1645–52. Marble, height of the group 11'6" (3.5 m). Cornaro Chapel, Church of Santa Maria della Vittoria, Rome

In the Church of Santa Maria della Vittoria in Rome, the sixteenth-century Spanish mystic Saint Teresa of Ávila swoons in ecstasy on a bank of billowing clouds (fig. 13-1). A youthful angel plucks open her robe, aiming a gilded arrow at her breast. Gilt bronze rays of supernatural light descend, even as actual light illuminates the figures from a hidden window above. This dramatic scene, created by Gianlorenzo Bernini (1598–1680) between 1645 and 1652, represents a famous vision Teresa described, in which an angel pierced her body repeatedly with an arrow, transporting her to a state of ecstatic oneness with God.

Bernini's *Saint Teresa of Ávila in Ecstasy* is one of the great works of the Baroque, the prevailing artistic style in much of Europe in the seventeenth and early eighteenth centuries. Common Baroque features (all of which are seen here) include the deliberate evocation of intense emotional responses in the viewer; the creation of dramatically lit, often theatrical compositions; the use of diverse media such as bronze and marble within a single artwork; and a spectacular technical virtuosity. The Baroque also has its own version of classicism, a more emotional and dramatic variant of Renaissance ideals and principles. Baroque classicism featured idealization based on observation of the material world;

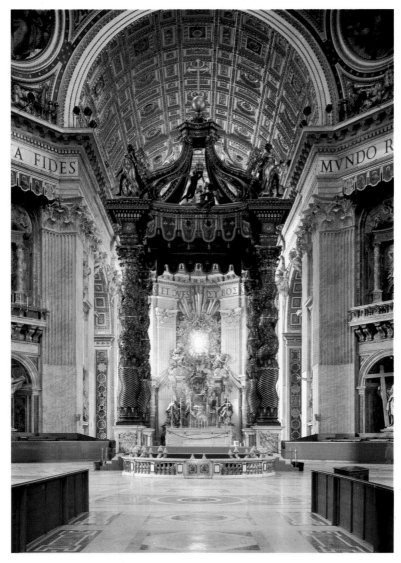

13-2. **Gianlorenzo Bernini.**
Baldacchino. 1624–33. Gilt
bronze, height approx. 100'
(30.48 m). Chair of Peter.
1657–66. Gilt bronze, marble,
stucco, and glass. Pier decorations. 1627–41. Gilt bronze
and marble. Crossing, Saint
Peter's Basilica, Vatican,
Rome

balanced (al-
though often
asymmetrical)
compositions;
the sense
of diagonal
movement in
space; rich, harmonious colors; and the inclusion
of visual references to ancient Greece and Rome.
Many Baroque artists achieved their ends through
naturalism, the true-to-life depiction of the world
that led to the popularity of portraiture, genre
paintings (scenes from everyday life), still life
(paintings of inanimate objects such as food, fruit,
or flowers), and religious paintings featuring
ordinary people and settings. Intense emotional
involvement, naturalistic rendering, and classicism or classical references may exist in the same
work. Many of the best examples of Baroque art
combine all of these elements.

Late in the period, a refined Baroque manner
known as the Rococo emerged. Developing in
Italy at the beginning of the eighteenth century,
this style soon spread into France, central
Europe, and even Russia. The Rococo, characterized by fanciful architectural decoration, a light
palette, and, often, a mood of playful melancholy,
remained popular along with earlier Baroque
styles until the rise of Neoclassicism in the third
quarter of the eighteenth century.

Art for the Counter-Reformation Church: Roman Baroque

The patronage of the Church and the aristocratic
families allied with the papacy—the Borghese,

the Barberini,
the Farnese—
dominated Ital-
ian art from the
late sixteenth to
the late seven-
teenth century.
A major program of the Counter-Reformation (the
official Catholic reaction to the rise of Protestantism, Chapter 12) was to build churches with
splendid architecture embellished with painting.
In Rome, Pope Paul V (Borghese, papacy 1605–
1621) ordered the expansion and modernization
of Saint Peter's Basilica. In 1606, he commissioned
the architect Carlo Maderno (1556–1629) to add
a longer nave and a new facade to Michelangelo's
Greek-cross plan of only a half century before
(see "Saint Peter's Basilica," page 281). During
the Counter-Reformation the Church emphasized
congregational worship, so more space was
needed for people and processions. Moreover, it
was felt that the new church should more closely
resemble the ancient basilica of Old Saint Peter's
(see fig. 7-6) and should extend over roughly
the same area.

When Urban VIII (Barberini, papacy 1623–
1644) was elected pope in 1623, he unhesitatingly
gave the young Bernini the task of designing an
enormous cast-bronze **baldachin**, or canopy, for
the main altar of Saint Peter's. The resulting
Baldacchino (fig. 13-2), which stands about 100
feet high, exemplifies the Baroque tendency to
combine materials so that a work cannot be categorized as being in one set medium or another.
The twisted columns decorated with winding

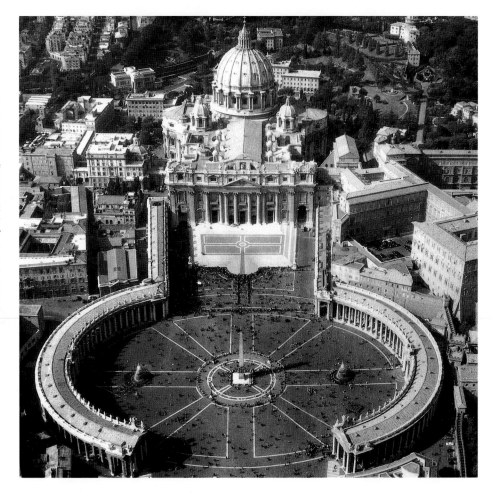

13-3. Gianlorenzo Bernini. Saint Peter's Basilica and Square, Vatican, Rome. Carlo Moderno, facade 1607–15; Bernini, square designed c. 1656–57

Perhaps only a Baroque artist of Bernini's talents could have unified the many artistic periods and styles that come together in Saint Peter's Basilica. The visitor today does not see a piecing together of parts made by different builders at different times, starting with Bramante's original design for the building in the sixteenth century, but rather encounters a triumphal unity of all the parts in one coherent whole.

bronze vines were inspired by columns supposed to have come from Solomon's Temple in Jerusalem, and the grapevines are an ancient symbol of the wine of the Eucharist. Thus, the columns combine symbolism from both the Old and New Testaments. Crowning the structure is an orb and a cross representing the universe and the reign of Christ. The angels and putti, as well as the tasseled panels on the entablature, are all of bronze. These elements not only mark the tomb of Saint Peter but also serve as a tribute to Urban VIII and his family, the Barberini, whose emblems—honeybees, suns, laurel leaves—are prominently displayed.

Visible through the *Baldacchino* is the reliquary containing the throne of Saint Peter, an ancient wooden chair, encased in bronze. Known as the Chair of Peter, it symbolizes the direct descent of Christian authority from the apostle Peter to the reigning pope. This belief was rejected by Protestants and therefore deliberately emphasized in Counter-Reformation Catholicism. The chair is lifted upward by four theologians amid a surge of gilded clouds toward an explosion of angels, putti, and gilt-bronze rays of glory. These elements surround a stained-glass window depicting the dove of the Holy Spirit. The actual sunlight, and the flickering of candles, reflected and multiplied by the polished bronze, are a calculated part of the sculpture. Here Bernini has combined nature and art just

as he did in the *Saint Teresa of Ávila in Ecstasy* (see fig. 13-1).

When Maderno died in 1629, Saint Peter's Basilica was complete as we know it today. However, Bernini, Maderno's collaborator of five years, later designed and supervised the building of a colonnade to enclose the square in front of the church (fig. 13-3). The space that Bernini had to work with was irregular and already contained an Egyptian obelisk (moved there in 1586) and to the right a fountain (made by Maderno in 1613), which had to be incorporated into the overall plan. In a remarkable design, Bernini framed the square with two enormous, curved porticoes, or covered walkways, supported by Doric columns. These connect with two straight but diverging porticoes that lead up a slight incline to the two ends of Maderno's church facade. Later, in 1675, Bernini added a matching fountain at the left of the obelisk, which serves to further define the vast space.

Bernini spoke of his conception as representing the "motherly arms of the church" reaching out to the world. He intended to build a third section of the colonnade closing the open side facing the church so that pilgrims, after crossing the Tiber River bridge and passing through the narrow streets, would suddenly emerge into the enormous open space before the church. Encountered this way, the great church, colonnade, and square, with its towering

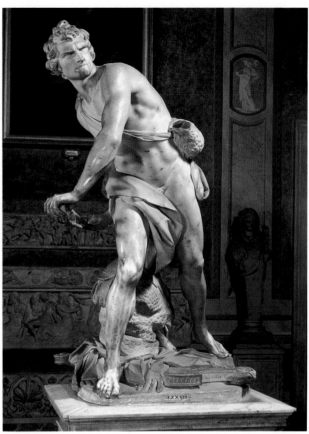

13-4. Gianlorenzo Bernini. David. 1623. Marble, height 5'7" (1.7 m). Galleria Borghese, Rome

obelisk and monumental fountains, would have been an awe-inspiring sight.

Bernini began not as an architect, but as a sculptor, and continued to work in that medium throughout his career for both the papacy and private clients. His *David* (fig. 13-4), made for the nephew of Pope Paul V in 1623, introduced a new type of three-dimensional composition that intrudes forcefully on the viewer's space. The young hero bends at the waist and twists far to one side, ready to launch the fatal rock. Unlike Donatello's introspective adolescent (see fig. 11-10) or Michelangelo's composed youth (see fig. 12-7), this more mature David, with his lean, sinewy body, is all tension and determination. His tightly clenched mouth and straining muscles echo his frame of mind, and the energetic figure activates its surrounding space by implying the presence of an unseen adversary.

Even after Bernini's appointment as Vatican architect in 1629, his large workshop enabled him to accept outside commissions, such as the decoration of the funerary chapel of Cardinal Federigo Cornaro in the Church of Santa Maria della Vittoria (fig. 13-5). For this project, carried out from 1642 to 1652, Bernini covered the walls of the tall, shallow chapel with colored marble panels and created the sculptural group of *Saint Teresa of Ávila in Ecstasy* (see fig. 13-1) for a huge oval niche above the altar. On the chapel's back wall, the curved ceiling surrounding the window appears to dissolve into a painted vision of clouds and angels, and on the side walls, kneeling against what appear to be balconies, are portrait statues of members of the Cornaro family. Two are reading from their prayer books; others converse; and one leans out from his seat, apparently to look at someone entering the chapel. Bernini's complex, theatrical interplay of the various levels of illusion in the chapel was imitated by sculptors throughout Europe.

Baroque illusionism reached its peak in ceiling decorations for churches, civic buildings, palaces, and villas. Many ceilings were done entirely in trompe l'oeil painting, but some were complex constructions combining architecture, painting, and stucco sculpture. A ceiling painted by Annibale Carracci (1560–1609) in the Roman palace of the powerful Farnese family is considered the major monument of early Baroque classicism. Commissioned to celebrate the wedding of Duke Ranuccio Farnese of Parma, it presents an exuberant mythological tribute to earthly love

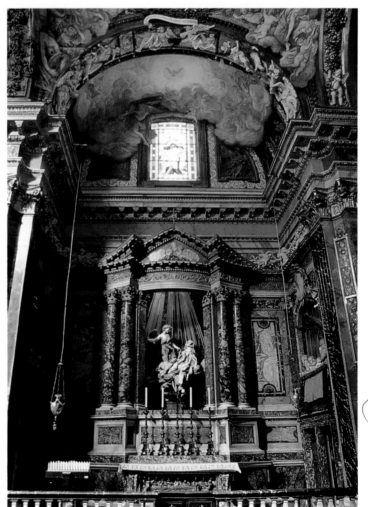

13-5. Gianlorenzo Bernini. Cornaro Chapel, Church of Santa Maria della Vittoria, Rome. 1642–52

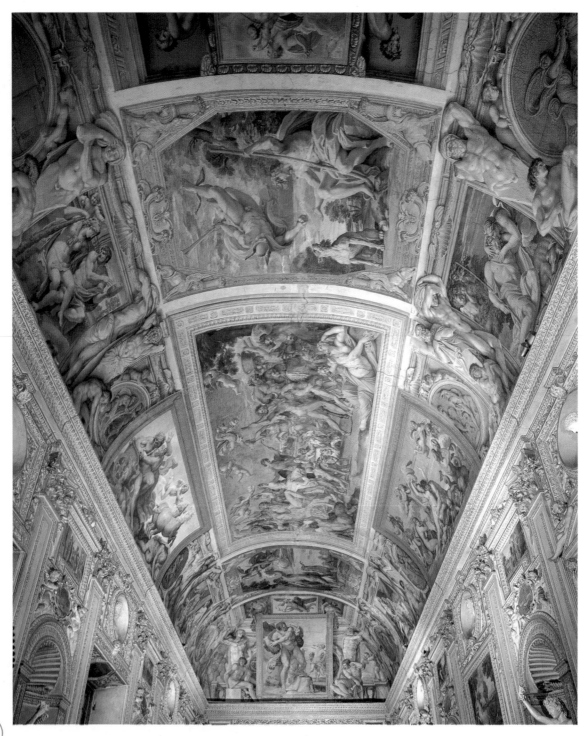

13-6. Annibale Carracci. Farnese Ceiling, fresco in main gallery, Palazzo Farnese, Rome. 1597–1601

(fig. 13-6). Annibale, cofounder with his family of an art academy in Bologna, was assisted by his brother Agostino (1557–1602) on this spectacular project, painted at the turn of the century (1597–1601). The ceiling painting creates the illusion of framed paintings, stone sculpture, bronze medallions, and nude youths in an architectural framework, clearly inspired by Michelangelo's Sistine Ceiling (see figs. 12-8, 12-9). But instead of Michelangelo's cool illumination and intellectual detachment, the Farnese Ceiling glows with a warm light that recalls the work of the Venetian painters Titian and Veronese. The primary image, set in the center of the vault, is *The Triumph of Bacchus and Ariadne,* a joyous

procession celebrating the wine god's love for Ariadne, a mortal princess. The ceiling was greatly admired and became famous almost immediately. The Farnese family, proud of the gallery, were generous in allowing young artists to sketch the figures there, so that Annibale Carracci's great work influenced Italian classicism well into the seventeenth century.

Perhaps the ultimate illusionistic Baroque ceiling is the *Triumph of the Name of Jesus* (fig. 13-7), which fills the vault of the nave of the Church of Il Gesù, mother church of the Society of Jesus (the Jesuits), in Rome (Chapter 12; see fig. 12-18). Giovanni Battista Gaulli (1639–1709), also called Baciccio, painted the fresco between 1676 and

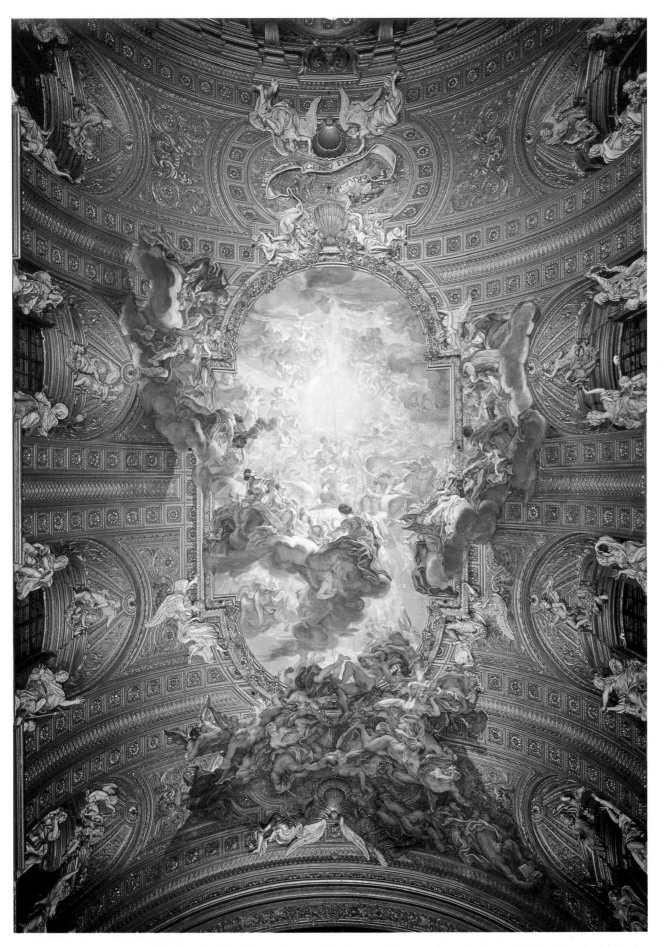

13-7. Giovanni Battista Gaulli. *Triumph of the Name of Jesus,* ceiling fresco with stucco figures in the vault of the Church of Il Gesù, Rome. 1676–79

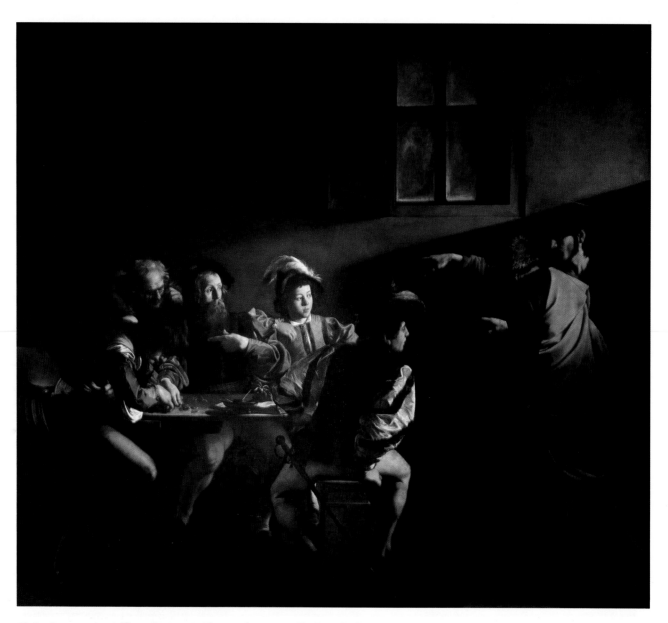

13-8. **Caravaggio.** *Calling of Saint Matthew*, in the Contarelli Chapel, Church of San Luigi dei Francesi, Rome. 1599–1600. Oil on canvas, 11'1" x 11'5" (3.4 x 3.5 m)

1679 in an interior that was originally rather austere, since the vault had remained unpainted. The artist had worked in his youth for Bernini, from whom he absorbed a Baroque taste for drama and multimedia spectacle.

Gaulli's astonishing creation went beyond anything that had preceded it in unifying architecture, sculpture, and painting. Every element is dedicated to the illusion that clouds and angels have floated down through an opening in the church's vault into the upper reaches of the nave. The whole composition, a Last Judgment, focuses off-center on the golden aura around the letters *IHS* (barely visible in fig. 13-7), a Greek abbreviation for "Jesus," the Holy Name and symbol of the Jesuits. The Elect rise toward the name of God and the Damned plummet through the ceiling toward the nave floor. The powerful and exciting appeal to the viewer's emotions and the nearly total unity of visual effect have never been surpassed.

Not all Roman Baroque art was meant to overwhelm the viewer by sheer spectacle. Michelangelo Merisi (1571–1610), known as Caravaggio after his birthplace in northern Italy, introduced an intense new realism and a dramatic use of light and gesture to Italian Baroque art. After his arrival in Rome in 1592, Caravaggio painted for a small circle of sophisticated patrons. His subjects from the 1590s include still lifes and scenes featuring fortune-tellers, cardsharpers, and street urchins dressed as musicians or mythological figures. Most of his commissions after 1600 were for religious art, and reactions to these paintings were mixed. On occasion his powerful, sometimes brutal, naturalism was rejected by patrons as unsuitable to the subject's dignity. However, this very realism was closely allied with Counter-Reformation ideas of spirituality, including the meditations, or *Spiritual Exercises*, of Saint Ignatius Loyola (1491–1556), the founder of the Jesuit order. It was also connected to the populist theology of the preacher Filippi Neri, later canonized as Saint Philip Neri (1515–1595), who consciously strove to make Christian history and doctrine meaningful to common people.

One of Caravaggio's earliest religious commissions, the *Calling of Saint Matthew* (fig. 13-8), was painted during the years 1599–1600 for the private chapel of the Cointrel family (Contarelli in Italian) in the French community's church in Rome. The painting depicts the moment recorded in the Gospels when Jesus called the tax collector Levi to become one of his apostles (Mark 2:14, Matthew 9:9). Nearly hidden behind the beckoning Saint Peter, the gaunt-faced Jesus dramatically points toward Levi—who will become Saint Matthew—but who is now surrounded by overdressed young men in plumed hats, velvet doublets, and satin shirts. For all the naturalism of these figures, Caravaggio also used antique and Renaissance sources. Jesus' outstretched arm, for example, recalls God's gesture of giving life to Adam in Michelangelo's *Creation of Adam* on the Sistine Ceiling (see fig. 12-9). The future Saint Matthew responds by pointing to himself in surprise, a gesture emphasized by the descent of the raking light that enters the painting from a high, unseen source at the right. The dramatic contrast of light and dark is a heightened variant of chiaroscuro known as **tenebrism**, which was introduced by Caravaggio.

Artemisia Gentileschi (1593–c. 1653) was one of Caravaggio's most successful Italian followers. Born in Rome, Artemisia first studied and worked under her father, himself a follower of Caravaggio. She later worked in Florence, where she was elected at age twenty-three to the Florentine Academy of Design. After assisting her father in England, she eventually settled in Naples. Her paintings, like Caravaggio's, feature large figures set close to the picture plane and strong contrasts of light and dark, the light often from a source outside the picture.

In 1630 she painted *La Pittura*, an **allegory** of the art of painting (fig. 13-9). The image of a woman richly dressed, her hair loose, wearing a gold necklace with a mask pendant, came from the *Iconologia* by Cesare Ripa, a popular sourcebook for images during the Baroque period. According to Ripa, wild hair denotes inspiration, the mask imitates the human face as painting imitates nature, and the gold chain symbolizes the continuous chain of relationships as each artist builds on the work of predecessors and carries this achievement into the future. Artemisia's allegory is a self-portrait; thus, she not only commemorated her profession but also paid tribute to her father and first teacher.

Art for the Secular State

The princes of the Church were not the only patrons of the arts in the seventeenth century,

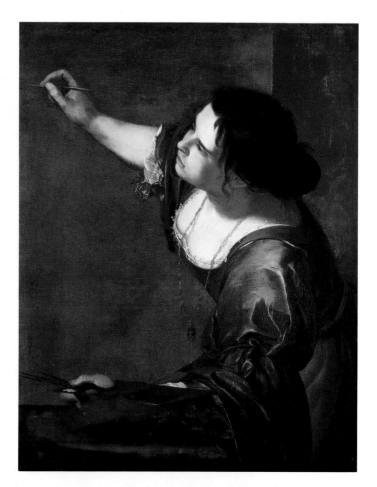

13-9. **Artemisia Gentileschi.** *La Pittura,* a self-portrait. 1630. Oil on canvas, 38 x 29" (96.5 x 73.7 cm). The Royal Collection, Windsor Castle, Windsor, England

which saw the growth of the nation-state and absolute monarchy. Kings and nobles realized that impressive buildings and splendid portraits could secure and enhance their status by surrounding them with an aura of power. Patronage of the arts became expected of an absolute monarch, and following the example of King Louis XIV of France, the rulers of Europe built and rebuilt their palaces, planted vast gardens, and spent fortunes on paintings, sculpture, and the decorative arts.

FRENCH BAROQUE ART

The early seventeenth century was a difficult period in France, marked by almost continuous foreign and civil wars. King Henry IV was assassinated in 1610, and the country endured a long regency during the minority of Henry's nine-year-old heir, Louis XIII (ruled 1610–1643). Louis XIV (ruled 1643–1715) also inherited the throne as a youth, beginning his personal rule only in 1661.

An absolute monarch whose reign was the longest in European history, Louis XIV became known as *le Roi Soleil*, or "the Sun King." He was sometimes glorified in art through parallels drawn between him and the classical sun god, Apollo. In a 1701 portrait by the French court painter

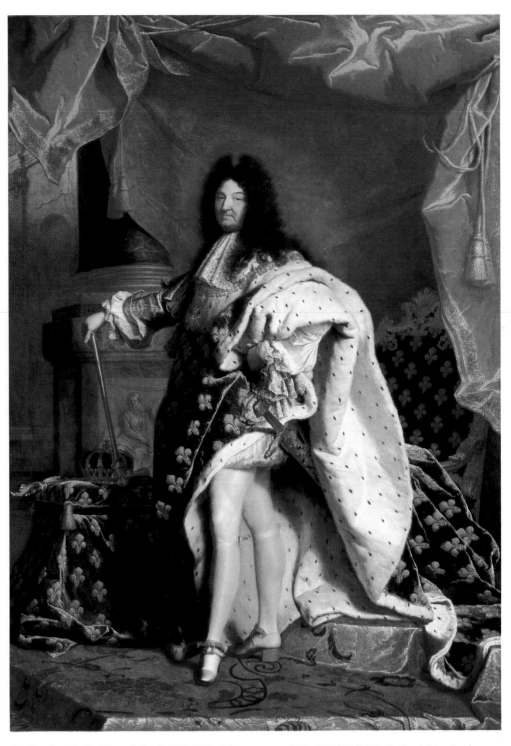

13-10. Hyacinthe Rigaud. *Louis* XIV. 1701. Oil on canvas, 9'2" x 7'10½" (2.79 x 2.40 m). Musée du Louvre, Paris

Hyacinthe Rigaud (1659–1743), the richly costumed monarch is revealed by an unseen hand pulling aside a billowing curtain (fig. 13-10). Showing off his elegant legs, of which he was quite proud, the sixty-three-year-old Louis XIV poses in a robe trimmed with gold fleurs-de-lis and white ermine and wears the high-heeled shoes he invented to compensate for his shortness. Despite the commanding pose and magnificent surroundings, the directness of the king's gaze and the realism of his aging face make him movingly human and testify to Rigaud's genius for portraiture.

Under Louis XIV's lavish patronage of the arts, the French court became the envy of every ruler in Europe. The Royal Academy of Painting and Sculpture, founded in 1648, maintained strict national control over the arts, and membership ensured an artist lucrative royal and civic commissions. Although the French Academy was not the first in Europe, none before it had exerted such dictatorial authority—an authority that lasted in France until the late nineteenth century (see "Grading the Old Masters," opposite). Classicism enjoyed particular favor in the

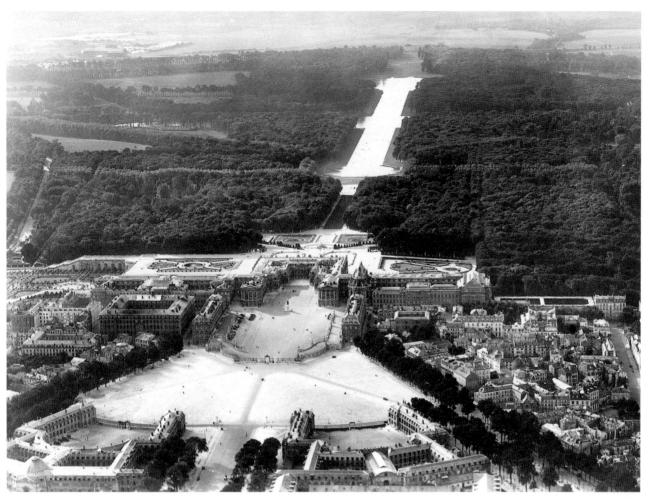

13-11. Louis Le Vau and Jules Hardouin-Mansart. Palais de Versailles, Versailles, France. Gardens by André Le Nôtre. 1668–85

academy and permeates French Baroque painting, sculpture, and architecture. When the Royal Academy of Architecture was founded in 1671, its members developed guidelines for architectural design based on the belief that mathematics was the true basis of beauty, with Vitruvius (see "Vitruvian Man," page 279) and Palladio as their models.

In 1668, Louis XIV turned his attention to enlarging a small hunting lodge, a château built by Louis XIII at Versailles. The changes Louis XIV commanded consumed the energy of France's greatest painters, sculptors, designers, and architects for decades. For both political and sentimental reasons, the old Versailles château was left standing, and the new building went up around it under the direction first of Louis Le Vau (1612–1670) beginning in 1668, and then after his death, of Jules Hardouin-Mansart (1646–1708) (fig. 13-11). Concurrently, André Le Nôtre (1613–1700), who planned the gardens, turned the terrain around the palace into an extraordinary work of art, destined to have a powerful influence on urban as well as garden design. Neatly contained stretches of lawn and broad, straight vistas seem to stretch to the horizon, while the formal gardens immediately behind

Grading the Old Masters

The members of the French Royal Academy of Painting and Sculpture considered ancient classical art the standard by which contemporary art should be judged. By the 1680s, however, younger artists began to argue that modern art might equal and even surpass the art of the ancients. A debate also arose over the relative merits of drawing and color in painting. The conservatives argued that drawing was superior because it appealed to the mind, while color appealed to the senses. They saw the work of Nicolas Poussin as perfectly embodying the classical principles of subject and design. The young artists, who admired the

vivid colors of Titian, Veronese and Peter Paul Rubens, claimed that painting should deceive the eye, and since color achieves this deception more convincingly than drawing, color should be valued over drawing. The two factions were called the *poussinistes* (in honor of Poussin) and the *rubénistes* (for Rubens).

The portrait painter and critic Roger de Piles (1635–1709) published his views in a series of pamphlets, in which he took up the cause of the *rubénistes*. In *The Principles of Painting*, de Piles evaluated the most important painters on a scale of 0 to 20. He gave no score higher than 18, since no mortal could achieve perfection. Caravaggio received the lowest grade, a 0 in expression

and 6 in drawing, while Michelangelo and Leonardo both got a 4 in color and Rembrandt a 6 in drawing. Top grades (18) went to Titian for color, Rubens for composition, and Raphael for drawing and expression.

If we work out the "grades" using the traditional scale of 90% = A, 80% = B, and so forth, most of the painters we have studied don't do very well. Raphael and Rubens get As; but no one seems to get a B, although Van Dyck might be considered close with a C plus. Poussin and Titian earn solid Cs, while Rembrandt slips by with a C minus. Leonardo gets a D, and Michelangelo, Dürer, and Caravaggio all are resounding failures in Piles's view.

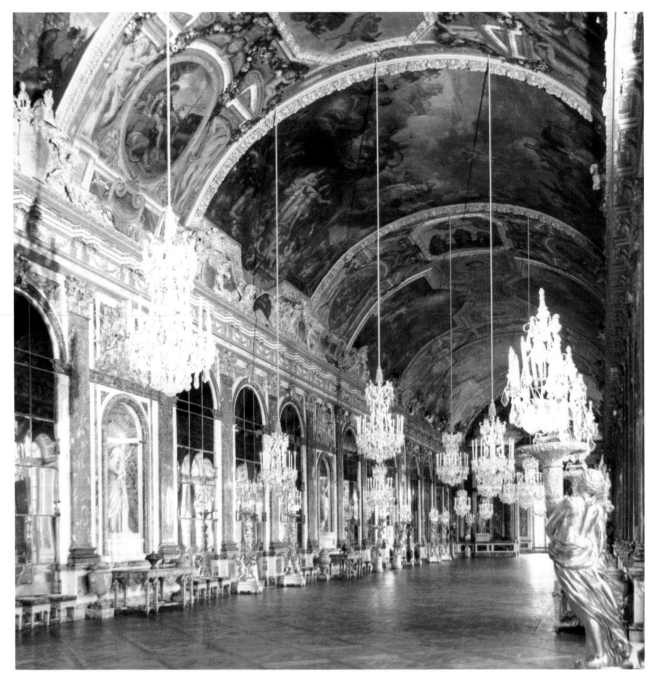

13-12. Jules Hardouin-Mansart and Charles Le Brun. Hall of Mirrors, Palais de Versailles. Begun 1678

the palace are an exercise in precise geometry. From these gardens, a series of terraces descends to controlled, shaped, wooded areas and the mile-long Grand Canal. Classically harmonious and restful in their symmetrical, geometric design, the Versailles gardens are Baroque in their vast size and extension into the surrounding countryside.

Visitors to the château could admire the gardens from an arcaded rear terrace designed by Le Vau. In his renovations, Hardouin-Mansart enclosed this previously open space, turning it into an immense gallery known as the Hall of Mirrors (fig. 13-12). He lit the hall, which is about 240 feet long, with seventeen immense arched windows, lining the opposite wall with

Venetian glass mirrors—enormously expensive in the seventeenth century—of exactly the same size and shape. The mirrors reflect the natural light from the windows and give the impression of an even larger space. In a tribute to Carracci's Farnese Ceiling (see fig. 13-6), the painter Charles Le Brun (1619–1690), a founding member of the Royal Academy of Painting and Sculpture, decorated the vaulted ceiling with paintings glorifying the reign of Louis XIV. The underlying theme for the design and decoration of the palace was the glorification of the king as the sun god Apollo.

French seventeenth-century painting was much affected by developments in Italian art. The important history painter Nicolas Poussin

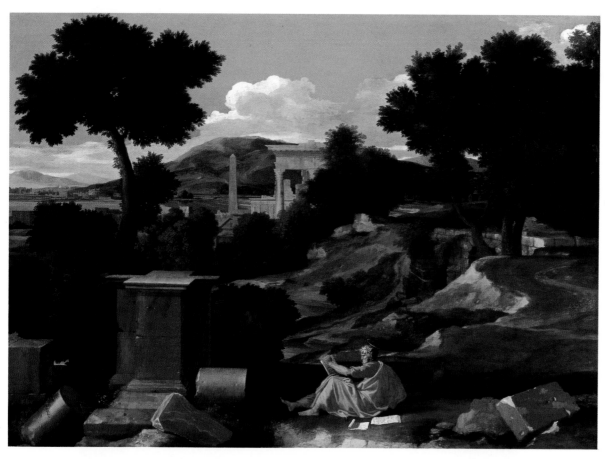

13-13. Nicolas Poussin. *Landscape with Saint John on Patmos.* 1640. Oil on canvas, 40 x 53½" (101.8 x 136.3 cm). The Art Institute of Chicago
A. A. Munger Collection, 1930.500

(1594–1665) worked for French patrons but pursued his career in Italy. As a dedicated classicist, he did not paint the landscape as he saw it but instead organized nature, buildings, and figures into idealized compositions. Thus, Poussin's *Landscape with Saint John on Patmos* (fig. 13-13), from 1640, appears orderly and admirably arranged. The artist has created a consistent perspective progression from the picture plane back into the distance through a clearly defined **foreground**, **middle ground**, and **background**. These zones are marked by alternating sunlight and shade, as well as by architectural elements in the Roman or Renaissance styles. Some of Poussin's landscapes are of identifiable sites, but this scene incorporates both real and imaginary buildings. In the middle distance are a ruined temple and an obelisk, while the round building set down in the distant city is Hadrian's Tomb from Rome (barely visible here). Precisely placed trees, hills, mountains, water, and even clouds have a solidity of form that suggests architecture. The reclining Saint John, and his symbol, the eagle, to the right of him, seem almost incidental to this perfect landscape. The subject of Poussin's painting is in effect the balance and order of nature rather than the story of the saint.

SPANISH BAROQUE ART

Spain's Habsburg kings in the seventeenth century—Philip III, Philip IV, and Charles II—presided over the political and economic decline of the Spanish Empire. Agriculture, industry, and trade all suffered, and there were repeated local rebellions, culminating in 1640, when Portugal reestablished its independence. Protestant England and the Dutch Republic were an increasingly serious threat to Spanish trade and colonial possessions, and what had seemed an endless flow of gold and silver from the Americas diminished. Nevertheless, writers and artists produced much of what is considered the greatest Spanish literature and art, and the century is often called the Spanish golden age.

One of the most brilliant Spanish painters of the period was Diego Rodríguez de Silva y Velázquez (1599–1660), who entered the painters' guild of Seville in 1617. He was influenced at the beginning of his career by the style of Caravaggio, like many artists in Spain and Spanish-ruled Naples in the early seventeenth century. During his youth, Velázquez painted figural works set in taverns, markets, or kitchens, showing people with still lifes of various foods and kitchen utensils. Velázquez was devoted to

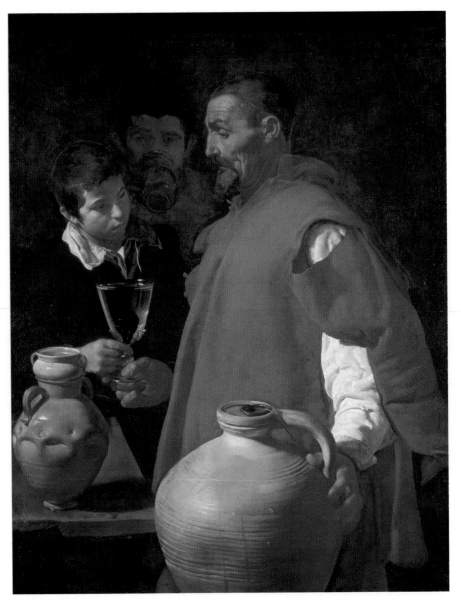

13-14. Diego Velázquez. *Water Carrier of Seville.* c. 1619. Oil on canvas, 41¹/₂ x 31¹/₂" (105.3 x 80 cm). Wellington Museum, London

In the oppressively hot climate of Seville, Spain, where this painting was made, water vendors walked the streets selling their cool liquid from large clay jars like the one in the foreground. In this scene, the clarity and purity of the water are proudly attested to by its seller, who offers the customer a sample poured into a glass goblet. The jug contents were usually sweetened by the addition of a piece of fresh fruit or a sprinkle of aromatic herbs.

sketching from life, and the model for the *Water Carrier of Seville* (fig. 13-14), of about 1619, was a well-known Sevillian water seller. The objects and figures in the painting, arranged with an almost mathematical rigor, allowed the artist to exhibit his virtuosity in rendering sculptural volumes and contrasting textures such as pottery and glass. All the elements in the picture are illuminated by dramatic natural light, in Velázquez's version of Caravaggio's tenebrism.

In 1623, Velázquez moved to Madrid, where he became court painter to the young Habsburg monarch Philip IV (ruled 1621–1665), a powerful position that he maintained until his death in

1660. The artist's style evolved significantly over his long career, stimulated in part by visits to Italy in 1629–1631 and 1649–1651.

Perhaps Velázquez's most striking and enigmatic work is the enormous multiple portrait, nearly 10¹/₂ feet tall and 9 feet wide, known as *Las Meninas*, or *The Maids of Honor* (fig. 13-15). Painted in 1656, near the end of the artist's life, this complex composition draws the spectator directly into its action, for the viewer is standing, apparently, in the space occupied by King Philip and his queen, whose reflections can be seen in the large mirror on the back wall. Velázquez himself is also present, brushes and palette in

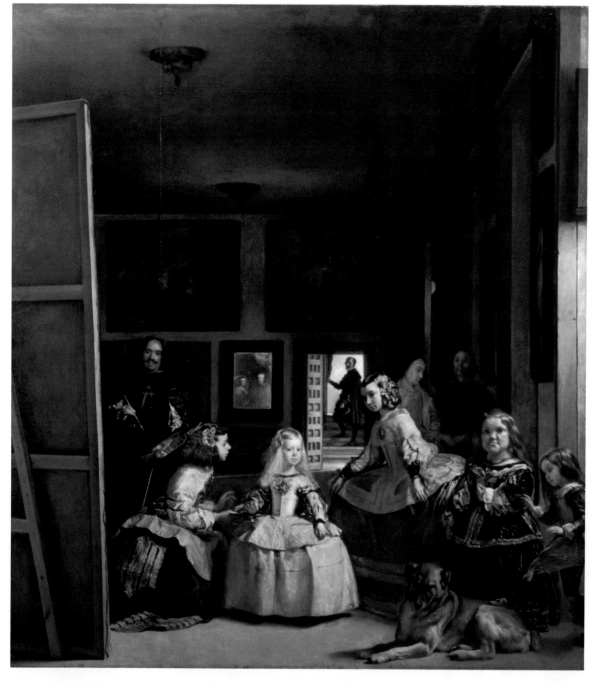

13-15. Diego Velázquez. *Las Meninas* **(*The Maids of Honor*).** 1656. Oil on canvas, 10'5" x 9'1/2" (3.18 x 2.76 m). Museo del Prado, Madrid

hand, beside a huge canvas. However, the central focus of the painting is on the royal couple's five-year-old daughter, the Infanta (Princess) Margarita. She is surrounded by her attendants, all of whom are identifiable portraits. In a bravura style of painting that fascinated the French Impressionist painters in the nineteenth century, Velázquez built up his forms with layers of loosely applied paint and finished off the surfaces with dashing highlights in white, lemon, and pale orange. His technique captures the appearance of light on surfaces, while on close inspection his forms dissolve into a complex maze of individual strokes of paint.

The sobriety and rigorous geometry of Velázquez's compositions contrast with later manifestations of Spanish Baroque art. In architecture, a profusion of ornament swept into fashion through the work of a family of architects and sculptors named Churriguera. The style, known as **churrigueresque**, found its most exuberant expression in the work of eighteenth-century architects such as Pedro de Ribera (c. 1638–1742) and in the architecture of the Spanish colonies of Mexico and Peru (Chapter 14). Ribera's 1722 facade for the Hospicio de San Fernando in Madrid concentrates an extraordinarily exuberant sculptural scheme on the portal

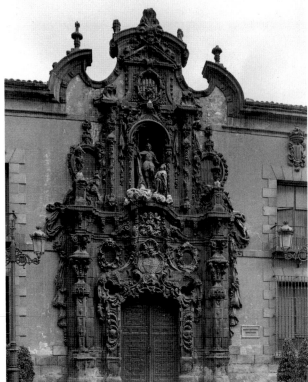

13-16. Pedro de Ribera. Portal of the Hospicio de San Fernando, Madrid. 1722

architecture are transformed into projecting and receding layers overlaid with foliage. Carved curtains loop back as if to reveal the doorway and central niche, which holds the figure of the hospital's patron saint.

FLEMISH BAROQUE PAINTING

Flanders was under direct Spanish rule during most of the Baroque period, after a period of relative autonomy under a Habsburg regent from 1598 to 1621. Artists of great talent flourished in Antwerp, the capital city and major art center. The painting of Peter Paul Rubens (1577–1640) has become nearly synonymous with the Flemish Baroque. Rubens was accepted into the Antwerp painters' guild at the age of twenty-one, and shortly thereafter, in 1600, he left for Italy, where he obtained a post with the duke of Mantua. Other than designs for court entertainment and occasional portraits, the duke never acquired a single original work of art by Rubens. Instead, he had him copy famous paintings in collections all over Italy to add to the ducal collection, and so inadvertently provided the young painter with an excellent education.

(fig. 13-16, and see "Baroque and Rococo Church Facades," page 295). Like a huge altarpiece, the portal soars upward, breaking through the roofline into segmental (semicircular) and triangular pediments. The structural forms of classical

Rubens returned in 1608 to Antwerp, where he accepted employment from the Habsburg governors of Flanders. His first major commission was a large canvas triptych for the main

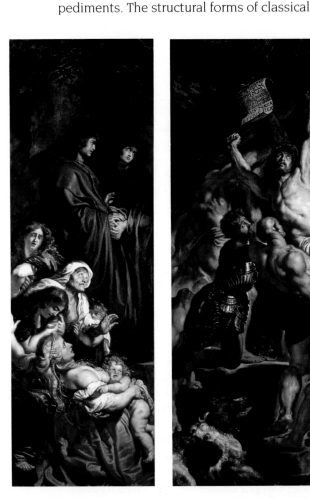
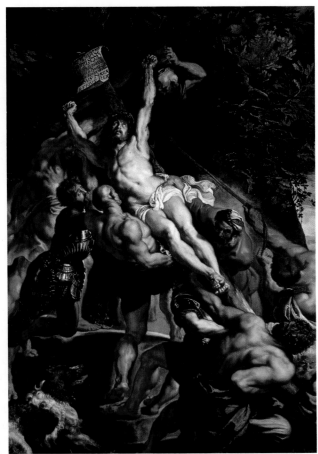
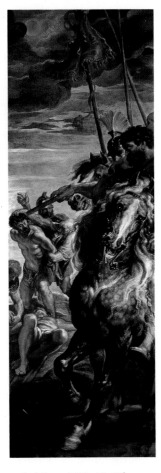

13-17. Peter Paul Rubens. *The Raising of the Cross*, painted for the Church of Saint Walpurga, Antwerp, Belgium. 1609–10. Oil on canvas, center panel 15'1⅞" x 11'1½" (4.62 x 3.39 m); each wing 15'1⅞" x 4'11⅞" (4.62 x 1.52 m). Cathedral of Our Lady, Antwerp

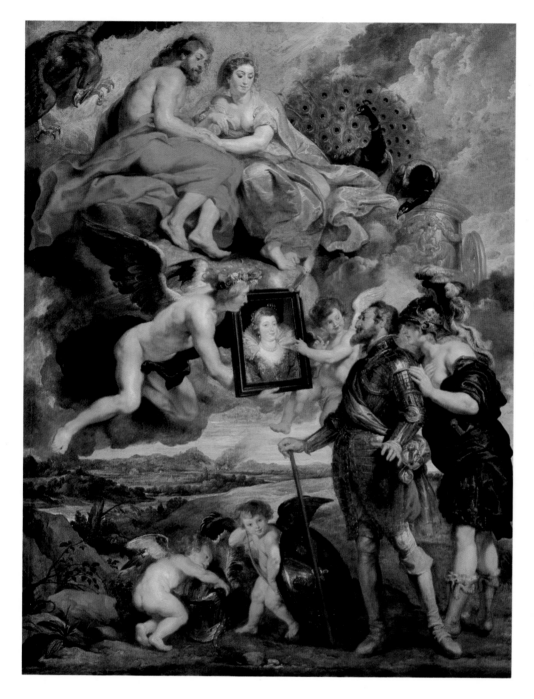

13-18. Peter Paul Rubens. *Henri IV Receiving the Portrait of Marie de' Medici.* 1621–25. Oil on canvas, 12'11⅛" x 9'8⅛" (3.94 x 2.95 m). Musée du Louvre, Paris

altar of the Church of Saint Walpurga, *The Raising of the Cross* (fig. 13-17), painted from 1609 to 1610. Unlike many earlier triptychs, where the side panels contained related but independent images, the wings here extend the action of the central scene and the surrounding landscape across the three vertical segments. At the center, Herculean figures strain to haul upright the wooden cross with Jesus already stretched upon it. The followers of Jesus mourn at left, and indifferent soldiers on the right supervise the execution. In this triptych, Rubens merges the drama and intense emotion of Caravaggio and the virtuoso technique of Annibale Carracci, but he transforms these qualities into a unity of his own. The heroic nude figures, dramatic lighting effects, dynamic diagonal composition, and intense emotions show the artist's debt to Italian art, but the rich colors and the realism of

the varied textures and forms belong to his native Flemish tradition.

Rubens's intelligence, courtly manners, and personal charm made him a valuable and trusted courtier to royal patrons, including Philip IV of Spain, Marie de' Medici of France, and Charles I of England. In 1621, Marie de' Medici, widow of King Henri IV and regent for her young son, Louis XIII, asked Rubens to paint the story of her life. In twenty-one paintings, Rubens glorified her role in ruling France and also commemorated the founding of the Bourbon dynasty, which began with Henri IV.

The lives and political careers of Marie and Henri appear as one continuous triumph overseen by the Roman gods. In the painting depicting the royal engagement (fig. 13-18), Henri IV falls in love with Marie as he gazes at her portrait, shown to him by Cupid and the god of marriage,

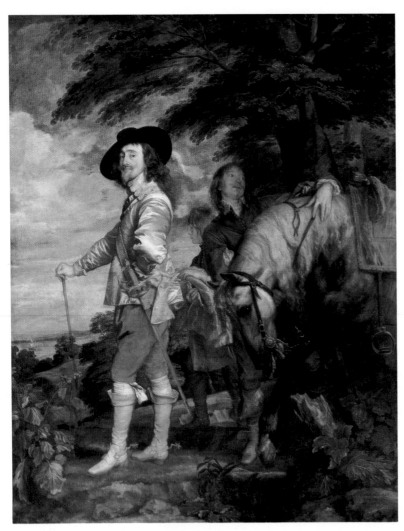

13-19. Anthony van Dyck. *Charles I at the Hunt.* 1635. Oil on canvas, 9 x 7'
(2.75 x 2.14 m). Musée du Louvre, Paris

pupils at age sixteen, although he did not become a member of the Antwerp painters' guild until 1618, the year after he began his association with Rubens as a painter of heads. Later in his career, Van Dyck became court painter to Charles I of England, by whom he was knighted and given a studio, a summer home, and a large salary.

In *Charles I at the Hunt* (fig. 13-19) of 1635, Van Dyck was able, by clever manipulation of the setting, to portray the king truthfully and yet as a quietly imposing figure. Dressed casually for the hunt and standing on a bluff overlooking a distant view, Charles, who was in fact a very small person, is shown as being taller than his pages and even than his horse, since its head is down and its heavy body is partly off the canvas. The viewer's gaze is diverted from the king's delicate frame to his pleasant features, framed by his jauntily cocked hat. As if in decorous homage, the tree branches bow gracefully toward him, echoing the circular lines of the hat.

BAROQUE ART IN ENGLAND

England and Scotland had been under the same rule since 1603, when James VI of Scotland ascended the English throne as James I (ruled 1603–1625). James's son, Charles I (ruled 1625–1649), was a better patron of the arts than he was a politician and king. Religious and political tensions, particularly a conflict between Charles and the religious reformers known as Puritans, resulted in a series of civil wars, beginning in 1642. Charles lost his throne, and his head, in 1649. Now in power, the Puritans, led by Oliver Cromwell as lord protector, stifled artistic expression. In 1660 the restoration of the Stuart dynasty under Charles II brought renewed patronage of foreign artists, especially portrait painters. In the eighteenth century, the Hanoverian kings, George I, II, and III, gave the name Georgian to art and architecture in the British Isles and the North American colonies.

In 1615 King James I appointed the architect Inigo Jones surveyor-general and commissioned him to design a residence, the Queen's House, in Greenwich, and a Banqueting House for the royal palace of Whitehall in London. Jones (1573–1652) introduced Renaissance classicism to England. His architectural style was based on the work of the Renaissance architect Andrea Palladio (Chapter 12). Jones had studied Palladio's buildings in Venice and owned a copy of the Italian architect's famous treatise, the *Four Books of Architecture*.

The Whitehall Banqueting House (fig. 13-20), constructed in 1619–1622 to replace an earlier building destroyed by fire, exemplifies the understated elegance of Jones's interpretation of Palladian design. The Banqueting House was used for court entertainments and ceremonies. The interior (fig. 13-21) is one large hall with

Hymen. The supreme Roman god, Jupiter, and his wife, Juno, look down approvingly from the clouds. Henri, silhouetted against a landscape in which the smoke of battle lingers, is encouraged by a personification of France to abandon war for love, as putti frolic with pieces of his armor. The sustained visual excitement of these enormous canvases makes them not only important works of art but political propaganda of the highest order.

Rubens, who accepted commissions from all over Europe, employed dozens of assistants as specialists in the painting of fruit and flowers, textiles, landscapes, even portraits. Using workshop assistants was standard practice among major artists, but Rubens was particularly efficient, and created something close to a painting factory. Working from his detailed sketches, his assistants completed giant canvases suitable for palatial rooms. Many of these assistants were, or became, important painters in their own right.

One of Rubens's collaborators, Anthony van Dyck (1599–1641), had an illustrious independent career as a portraitist. A precocious student at ten, he had his own studio and a roster of

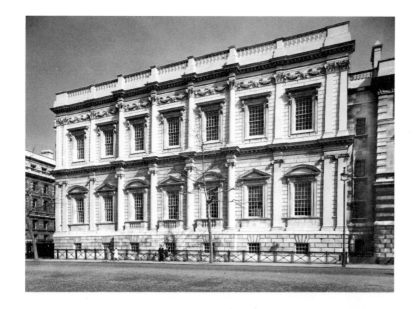

13-20. Inigo Jones. **Banqueting House,** Whitehall Palace, London. 1619–22

a balcony on the upper level, and ante-chambers at each end, one of which contains the entrance. Ionic pilasters suggest a colonnade but do not impinge on the ideal, double-cube space. In 1630, Charles I commissioned Peter Paul Rubens to decorate the ceiling. Jones had divided its flat surface into nine compartments, for which Rubens painted canvases glorifying the reign of James I, with a classical apotheosis of the king and the Stuart dynasty. So proud was Charles of the pictures, installed in 1635, that, rather than allow the smoke of candles and torches to darken them, he moved the evening entertainments to an adjacent pavilion.

Baroque Art in the Protestant Netherlands

Spain recognized Dutch sovereignty in 1648. Even before this official recognition, the Dutch Republic, as the united northern provinces of the Low Countries were officially known, managed not only to maintain its hard-won freedom but to prosper. Dutch artists found many eager patrons among the prosperous middle class of Amsterdam, Leiden, Haarlem, Delft, and Utrecht.

The most important painter working in the Netherlands in the seventeenth century was Rembrandt van Rijn (1606–1669). After studying painting in Amsterdam and Leiden and working as an artist in both cities, Rembrandt established a busy studio in Amsterdam. His repertoire included paintings and etchings of mythological subjects, religious scenes, and landscapes, but

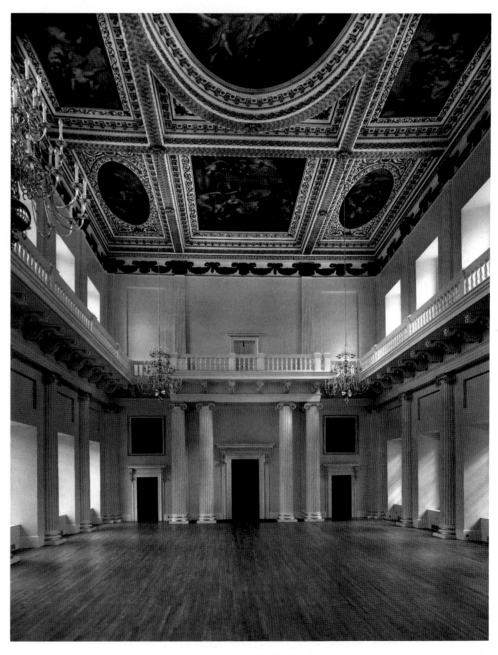

13-21. **Inigo Jones. Interior, Banqueting House,** Whitehall Palace. Ceiling paintings by Peter Paul Rubens. 1630–35

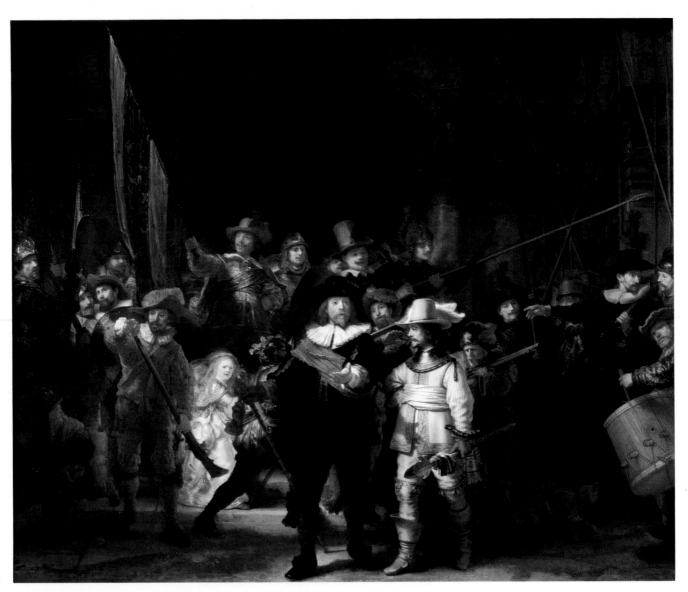

68

13-22. Rembrandt van Rijn. *Captain Frans Banning Cocq Mustering His Company (The Night Watch).* 1642. Oil on canvas (cut down from the original size), 11'11" x 14'4" (3.63 x 4.37 m). Rijksmuseum, Amsterdam

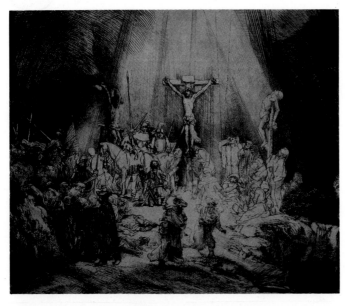

13-23. Rembrandt van Rijn. *Three Crosses* (first state). 1663. Drypoint and engraving, 15¹/₈ x 17³/₄" (38.5 x 45.0 cm). Rijksmuseum, Amsterdam

his primary source of income was portraiture.

In 1640 Rembrandt was commissioned by a civic guard company to create a large group portrait of its members for a new meeting hall. The result was *Captain Frans Banning Cocq Mustering His Company* (fig. 13-22), traditionally known as *The Night Watch* because a layer of dirt and old varnish obscured its colors in the nineteenth century and the painting was mistaken for a night scene. After recent cleaning and restoration, it now glows with a natural golden light that sets afire the palette of rich colors—browns, blues, olive green, orange, and red—around a central core of lemon yellow. As the company takes up its ranks, the crowd, including children, mill around. The surprising image of the running girl carrying a chicken with claws (*klauw* in Dutch) prominently displayed may be a pun on the name of the guns (*klover*) that gave the name Kloveniers to the company. The complex interactions of the figures and the vivid, individualized likenesses of the militiamen make this painting one of the greatest group of portraits of European art.

Rembrandt also created profoundly moving religious art. His **etchings** and **drypoints** (see "Etching and Drypoint," below) were sought after, widely collected, and brought high prices even in his lifetime. As he grew older, Rembrandt seems to have experienced a deepening religious belief, perhaps based on his study of the Bible. In a series of states (versions) of his print *Three Crosses*, Rembrandt tried to capture the moment during the Crucifixion described in the Gospels when Jesus cried out, "Father, into your hands I commend my spirit" (Luke 23:46). We can follow his intellectual process through four successive stages from the relatively anecdotal depiction of the crosses and the surrounding crowd in the first state (fig. 13-23) to the haunting blackness of the fourth and final state. As Jesus cries out, a mystical light illuminates the darkened scene. Mary, the apostles, and the Roman soldiers are captured and immobilized by the blinding light. Here Rembrandt has depicted the miracle of redemption and the power of God.

Rembrandt painted many self-portraits. In them, the evolution of his style can be traced. These images of himself became more searching as the artist aged and, like many of his paintings of other subjects, expressed a personal, internalized spirituality new in the history of art. In a self-portrait of 1659 (fig. 13-24), the half-length figure and the setting merge in a rich, luminous

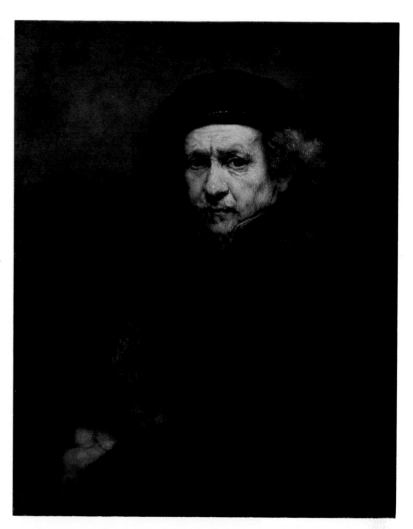

13-24. Rembrandt van Rijn. *Self-Portrait.* 1659. Oil on canvas, 33¼ x 26" (84.5 x 66 cm). National Gallery of Art, Washington, D.C. Andrew W. Mellon Collection

TECHNIQUE
ETCHING AND DRYPOINT

Rembrandt was the first artist to popularize **etching** as a major form of artistic expression. In the etching process, a metal plate is coated on both sides with an acid-resistant varnish that dries hard without being brittle. Then, instead of laboriously cutting the lines of the desired image directly into the plate, the artist draws through the varnish with a sharp needle to expose the metal. The plate is then covered with acid, which eats into the metal exposed by the drawn lines. By controlling the time the acid stays on different parts of the plate, the artist can make fine, shallow lines or heavy, deep ones. The varnish covering the plate is removed before an impression is taken. If a change needs to be made, the lines can be "erased" with a sharp metal scraper. Not surprisingly, a complex image with a wide range of tones requires many steps.

Another technique for registering images on a metal plate is called **drypoint**. A sharp needle is used to scratch lines in the metal. In drypoint, however, the burr, or metal thrown up by the drypoint needle, is left in place. Unlike in engraving, where the metal burr is scraped off, the burr, rather than the groove, holds the ink. Thus, under

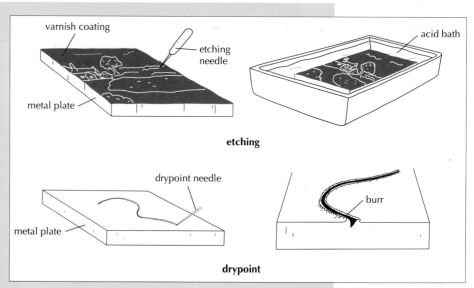

magnification, drypoint lines are white, with ink on both sides, but their rich black appearance when printed is impossible to achieve with engraving or etching. Unfortunately, drypoint burr is fragile, and only a few prints—a dozen or fewer—can be made before it flattens and loses its character. Rembrandt's earliest prints were pure etchings, but later he enriched his prints with drypoint to achieve greater tonal richness.

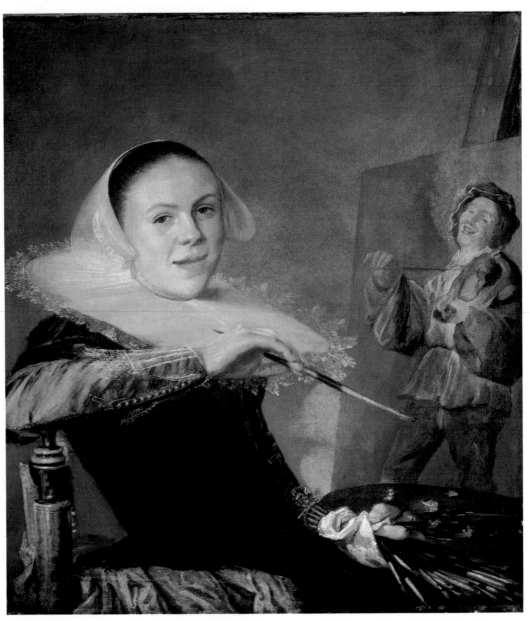

13-25. Judith Leyster. *Self-Portrait.* 1635. Oil on canvas, 29½ x 25¾" (74.9 x 65.4 cm). National Gallery of Art, Washington, D.C.
Widener Collection

chiaroscuro with the face and clasped hands emerging out of the darkness. A few well-placed brushstrokes suggest the physical tension in the fingers and the weariness of the soul in the deep-set eyes. Mercilessly analytical, the portrait depicts the furrowed brow, sagging flesh, and prematurely aged face (he was only fifty three) of one who has suffered deeply but retained his dignity.

More typical of Dutch painters, Judith Leyster (c. 1609–1660) painted boisterous genre scenes categorized in their own time by descriptive titles such as "merry company" or "garden party." In her lively *Self-Portrait* of 1635 (fig. 13-25), Leyster displays on her easel the type of work on which her popularity was based. The subject, a man playing a violin, may also be a visual pun on the painter's instruments, the palette and brush. To let the viewer immediately see the difference

between her painted portrait and the painted painting, she varied her technique, executing the image on her easel more loosely. The narrow range of colors sensitively dispersed in the composition and the warm spotlighting are typical of Leyster's mature style.

The art produced in the Netherlands of the seventeenth century shows that the Dutch delighted not only in depictions of themselves, but also of their country's landscape, cities, and domestic concerns. Jan Steen's The *Drawing Lesson* (see fig. 7) is typical of the beautifully painted scenes of daily life that appealed to middle-class patrons of the arts.

Perhaps the greatest Dutch genre painter, or painter of contemporary life, was Jan (Johannes) Vermeer of Delft (1632–1675). Vermeer produced few works. Many are enigmatic scenes of women in domestic settings, occupied with some

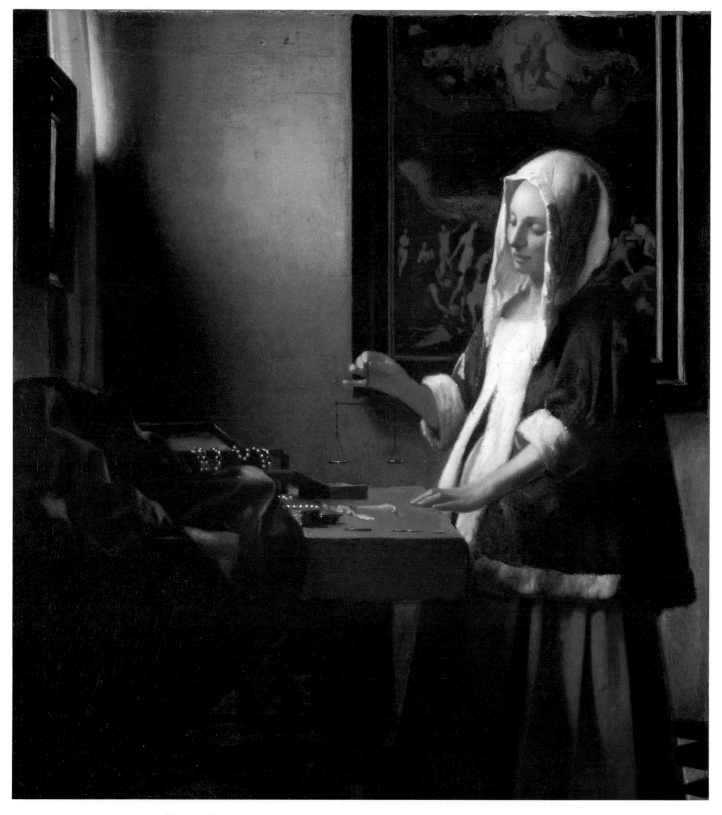

13-26. Jan Vermeer. _Woman Holding a Balance._ c. 1664. Oil on canvas, 16¾ x 15" (42.5 x 38.1 cm). National Gallery of Art, Washington, D.C. Widener Collection, 1942

cultivated activity such as writing, reading letters, or making music. Vermeer, a Catholic in a Protestant country, sometimes added a sobering religious reference to his work. Scholars of this period have noted that many of these works by Vermeer, like other Dutch genre paintings, contain apparently symbolic elements that suggest underlying meanings. For instance, Vermeer's _Woman Holding a Balance_ (fig. 13-26) of about 1664, once described in a sale simply as "a young lady weighing gold," can be understood straightforwardly as an exquisitely painted genre scene in which every object is carefully placed to achieve an overall balance and is illuminated

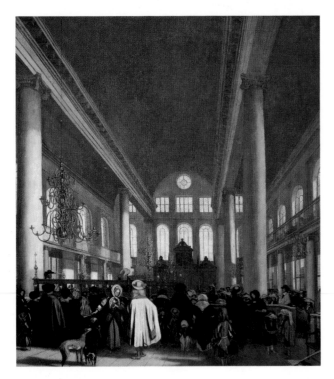

13-27. Emanuel de Witte. *Portuguese Synagogue, Amsterdam.* 1680. Oil on canvas, 43½ x 39" (110.5 x 99.1 cm). Rijksmuseum, Amsterdam

Architect Daniel Stalpaert built the synagogue in 1670–75.

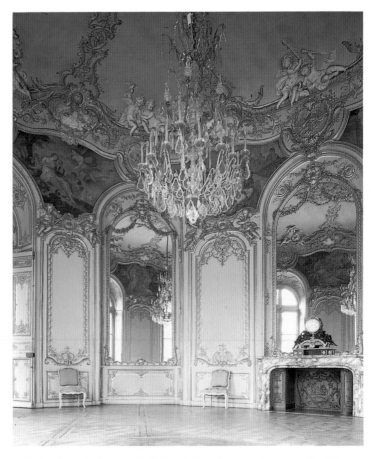

13-28. Germain Boffrand. Salon de la Princesse, Hôtel de Soubise, Paris. Begun 1732

by the clear, even light. However, the painting on the wall behind the young woman depicts the Last Judgment, suggesting that the empty balance in the woman's hand is more than a casual inclusion. The jewelry and coins on the table and the mirror on the wall were traditional elements in paintings with so-called ***vanitas*** subject matter, which stressed the fleeting nature of beauty, youth, and riches.

Another type of genre painting that achieved great popularity in the Baroque period was the architectural interior. These views seem to have been painted for their own special beauty, just as were exterior views of the land, cities, and harbors. Emanuel de Witte (c. 1617–1692) specialized in architectural painting in Delft and in Amsterdam. Many of his interiors, such as his *Portuguese Synagogue, Amsterdam* (fig. 13-27), are portraits of actual buildings. Today the painting is interesting not only as a work of art, but also as a record of seventeenth-century synagogue architecture and as evidence of Dutch religious tolerance in an age when Jews were often persecuted.

The building is a rectangular hall with women's galleries on both sides, roofed by three wooden barrel vaults and lit by large glass windows. In de Witte's painting, the caped figure in the foreground, the crowd, and the dogs suggest the size and popularity of the synagogue. The artist's shift of the straight-line viewpoint slightly to one side has created an interesting spatial composition, and strong contrasts of

light and shade add dramatic movement to the simple interior.

Still-life paintings—pictures of artfully arranged everyday objects—were a particular specialty in the Dutch Republic. The Dutch were so proud of their artists' still-life paintings that they presented one to the French queen Marie de' Medici when she made a state visit to Amsterdam. One of the most sought-after and highest-paid still-life painters in Europe was Rachel Ruysch (1663–1750), who worked in Amsterdam. During her seventy-year career, she specialized in **flower pieces**, or still-life paintings consisting predominantly of cut-flower arrangements (see fig. 13-33). Her works were highly prized for their sensitive, free-form arrangements and their unusual and beautiful color harmonies.

The Rococo Style

The Rococo style is characterized by pastel colors, delicately curving forms, dainty figures, and an apparently lighthearted mood. The Rococo manner may be seen partly as a reaction at all levels of society, even among kings and bishops, against the "grand manner" of Baroque art, identified with the formality and rigidity of seventeenth-century court life. The tendency toward a lighter, more delicate style appeared in Italian painting and pastels about 1700. By the end of Louis XIV's reign in 1715, the Rococo style dominated French architectural decoration, and it quickly spread across Europe.

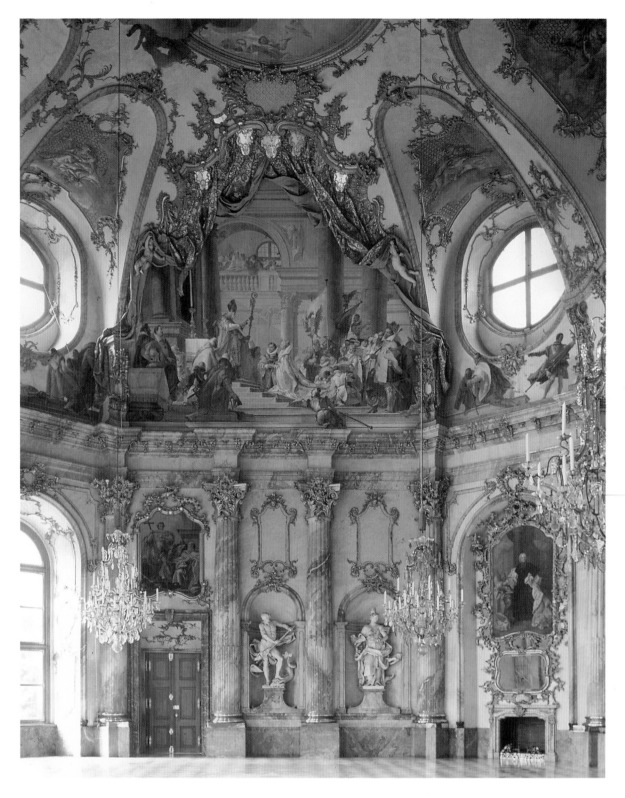

13-29. Johann Balthasar Neumann. Kaisersaal (Imperial Hall), Residenz, Würzburg, Bavaria, Germany. 1719–44. Fresco by Giovanni Battista Tiepolo. 1751–52

In France, the Rococo first appeared in the furnishings and decoration of the elegant Parisian town houses that are known in French as *hôtels*. The Salon de la Princesse in the Hôtel de Soubise in Paris (fig. 13-28), designed by Germain Boffrand beginning in 1732, is typical of French Rococo *hôtel* design of the 1730s. The glitter of silver or gold against expanses of white or pastel color, the visual confusion of mirror reflections, delicate ornament in sculpted stucco, carved wood panels called *boiseries*, and inlaid wood designs on furniture and floors were all part of the new look. In residential settings, pictorial themes were often taken from classical love stories, and sculpted ornaments were rarely devoid of putti, cupids, and clouds. In these elegant rooms, Parisian intellectuals gathered for conversation and entertainments presided over by accomplished, educated women of the upper class.

In Habsburg Germany and Austria, a major architectural project in the new Rococo style was the Residenz, a splendid palace built for the prince-bishop of Würzburg from 1719 to 1744 by Johann Balthasar Neumann (1687–1753). One of Neumann's great triumphs of planning and decoration is the oval Kaisersaal, or Imperial Hall (fig. 13-29). Although the clarity of the plan, the size and proportions of the marble columns, and

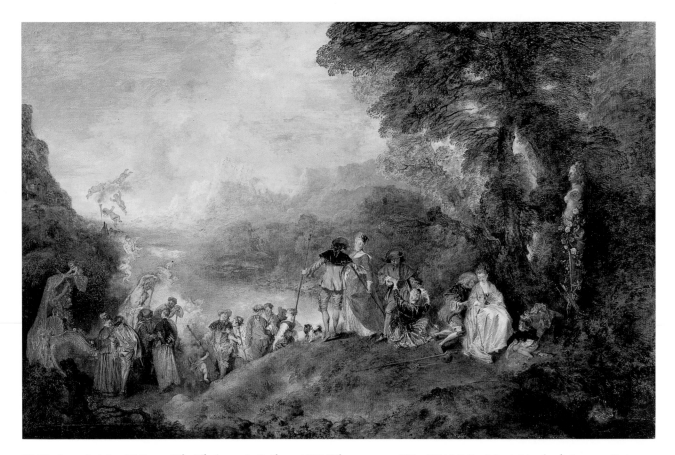

13-30. Jean-Antoine Watteau. *The Pilgrimage to Cythera*. 1717. Oil on canvas, 4'3" x 6'4½" (1.3 x 1.9 m). Musée du Louvre, Paris

the large windows recall the Hall of Mirrors at Versailles, the decoration of the Kaisersaal, with its white-and-gold color scheme and its profusion of delicately curved forms, embodies the Rococo spirit.

Neumann's collaborator on the Residenz was a brilliant Venetian painter, Giovanni Battista Tiepolo (1696–1770), who began to work there in 1750. Tiepolo was acclaimed internationally for his confident and optimistic expression of the illusionistic fresco painting pioneered by such sixteenth-century Venetians as Veronese (see fig. 12-1). Tiepolo's work in the Kaisersaal—three scenes glorifying the twelfth-century crusader-emperor Frederick Barbarossa, who had been a patron of the bishop of Würzburg—is a superb example of his architectural painting. *The Marriage of the Emperor Frederick and Beatrice of Burgundy* (seen on the vault at the far end of the hall in figure 13-29) is presented as if it were theater, with painted and gilded stucco curtains drawn back to reveal the splendor of an imperial wedding. Like Veronese's grand conceptions, Tiepolo's spectacle is populated with an assortment of character types, presented in dazzling light and sun-drenched colors.

The Rococo style of painting emerged with the career of the French artist Jean-Antoine Watteau (1684–1721). Watteau worked for a time as a decorator of interiors. In 1717, he was elected to membership in the Royal Academy of Paint-

ing and Sculpture on the basis of a painting for which there was no established category. The academicians created a new classification for it, called the **fête galante**, or elegant outdoor entertainment. The work he submitted, *The Pilgrimage to Cythera* (fig. 13-30), depicted a dreamworld in which an assortment of beautifully dressed couples depart for, or perhaps take their leave from, the mythical island of love. The lush landscape, which has no more reality than a painted theater backdrop, would never soil the characters' exquisite satins and velvets, nor would a summer shower ever threaten them. This idyllic vision, with its overtones of wistful melancholy, had a powerful attraction in early-eighteenth-century Paris and soon charmed the rest of Europe.

Jean-Honoré Fragonard (1732–1806) carried the French Rococo fantasies that Watteau pioneered into the second half of the eighteenth century. Fragonard's most memorable work is a group of fourteen canvases commissioned about 1771 by Madame du Barry, Louis XV's mistress. These marvelously free and seemingly spontaneous visions of lovers seem to explode in color and luxuriant vegetation. *The Meeting* (fig. 13-31) shows a secret encounter between a young man and his sweetheart, who looks back anxiously over her shoulder to be sure she has not been followed while clutching the letter arranging the tryst. The rapid brushwork that distinguishes Fragonard's technique is at its

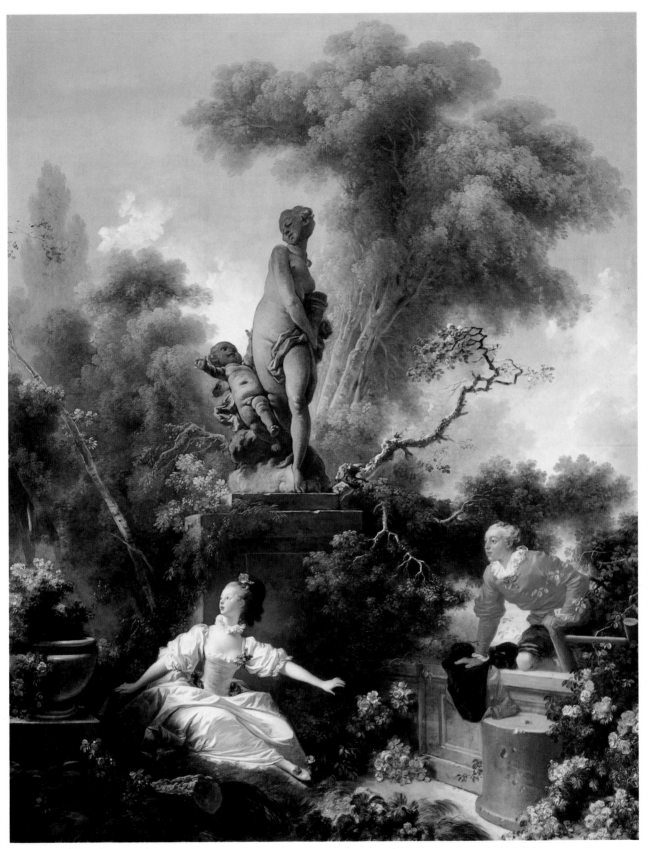

13-31. Jean-Honoré Fragonard. *The Meeting,* from The Progress of Love. 1771–73. Oil on canvas, 10'5¼" x 7'⅝" (3.18 x 2.15 m).
The Frick Collection, New York

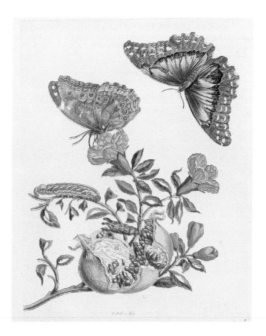

13-32. **Maria Sibylla Merian.** **Plate 9 from** *Dissertation in Insect Generations and Metamorphosis in Surinam.* 1719 (printed posthumously). Hand-colored engraving, 18⅞ x 13" (47.9 x 33 cm). National Museum of Women in the Arts, Washington, D.C. Gift of Wallace and Wilhelmina Holladay

Science and the Changing Worldview

During the seventeenth and eighteenth centuries, some of the new discoveries of the natural world brought a sense of the grand scale of the universe without, while others focused more precisely on the complexity of the world within. As frames of reference expanded and contracted, artists found new ways to mirror these changing perspectives in their own works.

Francis Bacon (1561–1626) in England and René Descartes (1596–1650) in France established a new scientific method of studying the world by insisting on scrupulous objectivity and logical reasoning. Bacon proposed that facts be established by observation and tested by controlled experiments. Descartes argued for the deductive method of reasoning, in which a conclusion was arrived at logically from basic premises, the most fundamental of which was "I think, therefore I am."

In 1543, the Polish scholar Nicolaus Copernicus (1473–1543) published *On the Revolutions of the Heavenly Spheres,* which contradicted the long-held view that Earth is the center of the universe (the Ptolemaic theory) by arguing instead that Earth and other planets revolve around the Sun. The Church viewed the Copernican theory as a challenge to its doctrines and put Copernicus's work on its Index of Prohibited Books in 1616. At the beginning of the seventeenth century, Johannes Kepler (1571–1630), the court mathematician and astronomer to Holy Roman Emperor Rudolf II, demonstrated that the planets revolve around the Sun in elliptical orbits. Kepler noted a number of interrelated dynamic geometric patterns in the universe, the overall design of which he believed was an expression of divine order.

Galileo Galilei (1564–1642), an astronomer, mathematician, and physicist, was the first to develop a tool for observing the heavens, the telescope. His findings provided further confirmation of the Copernican theory, and after the teaching of that theory was prohibited by the Church, Galileo was tried for heresy by the Inquisition. Under duress, he publicly rejected his views, although at the end of his trial, according to legend, he muttered, "Nevertheless it [Earth] does move." As the first person to see the craters of the moon through a telescope, Galileo began the exploration of space that would culminate in the first human steps on the moon in 1969.

The new seventeenth-century science turned to the study of the very small as well as to the vast reaches of space. This included the development of the microscope, developed by the Dutch lens maker and amateur scientist Anton van Leeuwenhoek (1632–1723). Leeuwenhoek perfected grinding techniques and increased the power of his lenses far beyond what was required for a simple magnifying glass. Ultimately, he was able to study the inner workings of plants and animals and even see microorganisms. Early scientists learned to draw or depended on artists to draw the images revealed by the microscope for further study and publication. Not until the discovery of photography in the nineteenth century could scientists communicate their discoveries without an artist's help.

freest and most lavish here. However, Madame du Barry rejected the paintings and commissioned another set in the newly fashionable Neoclassic style. Her view of Fragonard's ravishing visions as passé showed that the Rococo world was, indeed, at its end.

ART AND SCIENCE

Heralds of the future were the artists who worked with scientists (see "Science and the Changing Worldview," left) or carried on scientific investigations in their own right. Before the invention of photography, scientists relied on painters to illustrate their work. Maria Sibylla Merian (1647–1717) contributed to botany and entomology both as a researcher and as an artist. German by birth and Dutch by training, Merian was once described by a Dutch contemporary as a painter of worms, flies, mosquitoes, spiders, "and other filth." In 1699, Amsterdam subsidized Merian's research on plants and insects in the Dutch colony of Surinam in South America. She spent two years exploring the jungle and recording the insects there. On her return to Holland, she published the results of her research as *Dissertation in Insect Generations and Metamorphosis in Surinam,* illustrated with sixty large plates engraved after her watercolors (fig. 13-32).

Perhaps less daring but also scientific in her outlook, Rachel Ruysch made every flower in her still lifes a botanical study. Ruysch had learned botany as a girl, for her father was a professor of anatomy and botany in Amsterdam. Married with ten children, Ruysch never stopped painting and achieved considerable fame in her lifetime. Her work often brought higher prices than did paintings by Rembrandt.

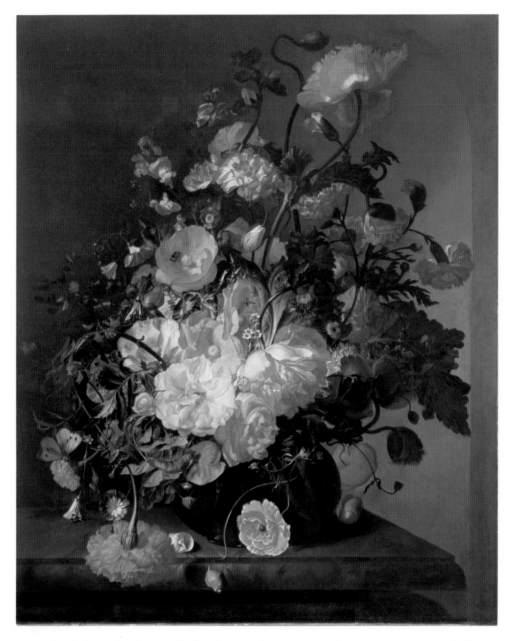

13-33. Rachel Ruysch. *Flower Still Life.* After 1700. Oil on canvas, 30 x 24" (76.2 x 61 cm). The Toledo Museum of Art, Ohio
Purchased with funds from the Libbey Endowment. Gift of Edward Drummond Libbey

Flower painting was a much-admired specialty in the Netherlands of the seventeenth and eighteenth century. Such paintings were almost never straightforward depictions of actual fresh flowers. Instead, artists made color sketches of fresh examples of each type of flower and studied scientifically accurate color illustrations in botanical publications. Using their sketches and notebooks, in the studio they could compose bouquets of perfect specimens of a variety of flowers that could never be found blooming at the same time.

In her *Flower Still Life* (fig. 13-33), painted after 1700, Ruysch created an asymmetrical arrangement of pale oranges, pinks, and yellows rising from the lower left to the top right of the picture, offset by the strong diagonal of the table edge. Ruysch often enlivened her compositions with reptiles or insects—in this case, two snail shells and a large gray moth—that give the paintings an unsettling feeling. Besides appreciating the beauty of such compositions, viewers may have seen the flaming tulips as a warning against the vanity of pride and greed, just as the short life of the cut flowers reminded them of the fleeting nature of beauty and human life. In Protestant Holland, even art informed by science carried a moral message in the Baroque and Rococo periods.

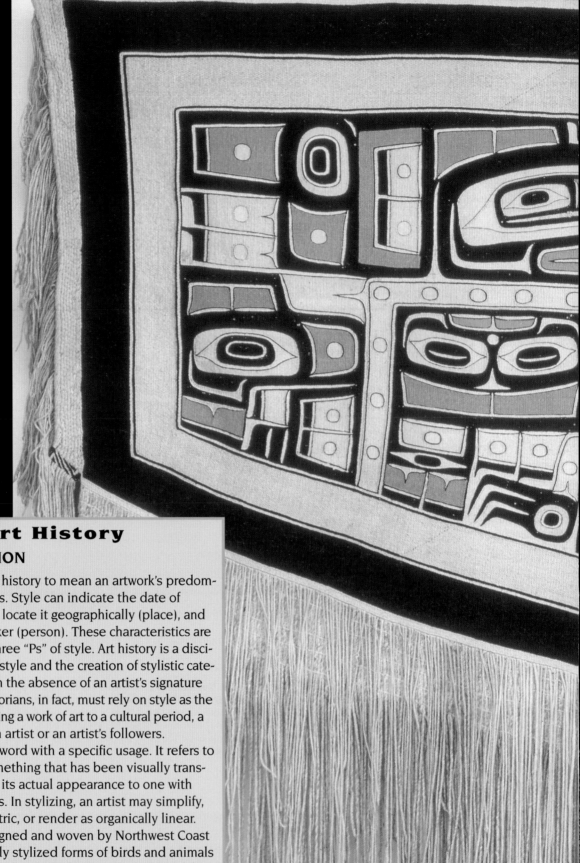

Chilkat blanket. Tlingit, before 1928. Mountain-goat wool and shredded cedar bark, 4'7¹/₂" x 5'3³/₄" (1.40 x 1.62 m). American Museum of Natural History, New York

KEYS to Art History
STYLE & STYLIZATION

Style is a word used in art history to mean an artwork's predominant visual characteristics. Style can indicate the date of a work of art (period), can locate it geographically (place), and can even identify the maker (person). These characteristics are popularly known as the three "Ps" of style. Art history is a discipline in which analysis of style and the creation of stylistic categories are fundamental. In the absence of an artist's signature or documentation, art historians, in fact, must rely on style as the main evidence for attributing a work of art to a cultural period, a region or country, or to an artist or an artist's followers.

Stylization is a related word with a specific usage. It refers to the representation of something that has been visually transformed by the artist from its actual appearance to one with certain visual conventions. In stylizing, an artist may simplify, exaggerate, make geometric, or render as organically linear. This fringed blanket designed and woven by Northwest Coast Tlingit weavers uses highly stylized forms of birds and animals (see page 352). The artists who made the design, working within a well-established Tlingit pictorial tradition, *abstracted* the bear and birds almost to the point of pure *pattern*. The large animal is made up of smaller ones. Here the body of the great bear is formed by a smaller bear's head. The stylized subjects are also *symbolic*: the bear has a specific meaning for the Tlingit. In this case, Tlingit *stylization* is a hallmark of Tlingit *style*.

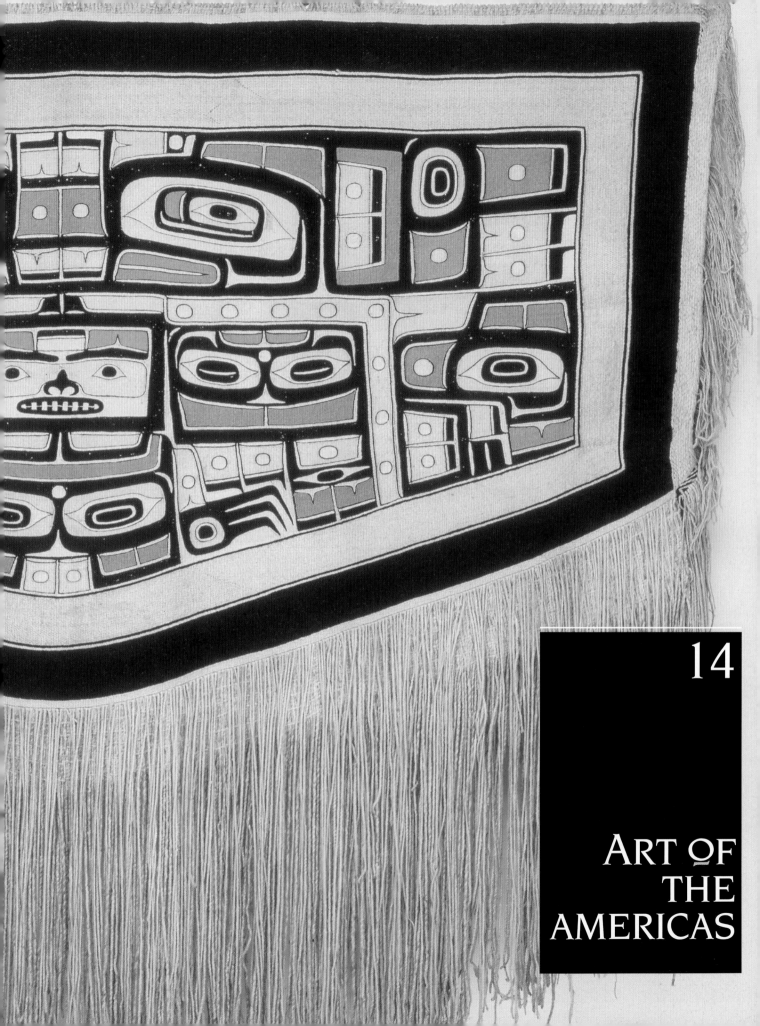

ART OF THE AMERICAS

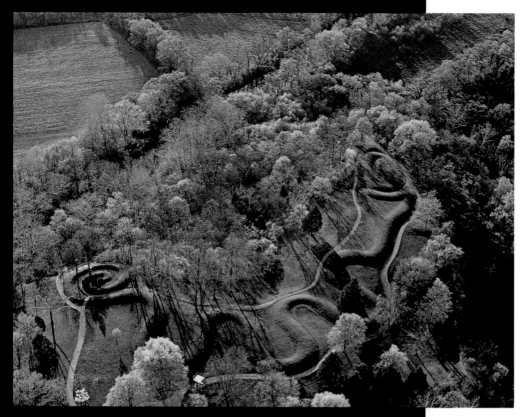

14-1. Great Serpent Mound, Adams County, Ohio. c. 1070 CE. Length 1,254'
(382.2 m)

Human beings first arrived in North and South America during the last Ice Age, when glaciers trapped enough of the world's water to lower the level of the oceans and expose a land bridge between Asia and North America. Sometime before about 12,000 years ago, perhaps as early as 20,000 to 30,000 years ago, Paleolithic hunter-gatherers crossed over this land bridge and began to spread out into two vast, uninhabited continents.

Between 10,000 and 12,000 years ago, bands of hunters roamed most of North America; a few reached the southern end of South America by 11,000 years ago. Although contact between Siberia and Alaska continued after the ice had retreated and rising oceans had flooded the Bering Strait, the people of the Western Hemisphere were essentially cut off from those of Africa and Eurasia until they were overrun by European invaders beginning in the late fifteenth century CE.

In this isolation, New World people experienced transformations similar to those that followed the end of the Paleolithic era elsewhere. In many regions, they developed an agricultural way of life, based on the cultivation of native plants: corn, beans, and squash. Other plants first domesticated in the New World included potatoes, tobacco, cacao (chocolate), tomatoes, and avocados. As elsewhere, the shift to agriculture in the Americas was accompanied by population growth and, in some places, the rise of hierarchical societies and the appearance of ceremonial centers and towns with monumental architecture. New World cities such as Teotihuacán in the Valley of Mexico rivaled those of the Old World, or Europe, in size and splendor. The people of Mesoamerica—the region that extends from central Mexico to northern Central America—developed writing, a complex and accurate calendar, and a sophisticated system of mathematics. Central and South American people developed an advanced metallurgy and produced exquisite gold, silver, and copper jewelry. In the American Southwest, Native American people built multistoried, apartment-like villages and cliff dwellings, as well as elaborate irrigation systems with canals.

The sudden incursion of Europeans from the fifteenth century onward had a dramatic and lasting impact on Native American people and their art. In some areas, highly advanced cultures, such as those of the Aztec and Inca, were destroyed. In other regions, such as the North

W hen eighteenth-century settlers in North America pushed beyond the Appalachian Mountains, they literally walked into a mystery. They found themselves facing, and in some cases climbing over or around, strange mounds of earth, large and small, that clearly had been created by human hands. The mounds take various forms. Some are shaped like birds or bears. One, in present-day Ohio, a writhing earthen snake 1,254 feet long and 20 feet wide, still winds along the crest of a ridge overlooking a stream, with its head at the highest point of the ridge (fig. 14-1).

Some of the mounds covered piles of refuse from permanent agricultural villages; others were burial sites where human skeletons had been interred. Theories abounded about the creators of these mounds—including speculations that they had been survivors from the lost island of Atlantis or one of the lost tribes of Israel. Just before he became president, Thomas Jefferson excavated a burial mound in Virginia and came close to the truth: that the monumental earthworks were creations of early residents of the Americas.

American plains, indigenous groups lost much of their land and saw their populations decimated yet retained their traditions and still exist as distinct cultural entities today.

Mesoamerica

Ancient Mesoamerica encompassed the area from north of the Valley of Mexico (the location of Mexico City) to modern Belize, Honduras, and western Nicaragua in Central America. The people of this physically diverse region, which included tropical rain forests and semiarid mountains, were linked by trade and cultural similarities. Among the shared features of the civilizations that arose in Mesoamerica were a complex calendrical system based on inter-locking 260-day and 365-day cycles, a ritual ball game with religious and political significance (see "The Cosmic Ball Game," right), and aspects of monumental ceremonial building construction. Mesoamerican society was also sharply divided into elite and commoner classes.

Archeologists have traditionally divided Mesoamerican history into three broad periods: the Formative or Preclassic (1500 BCE–250 CE), the Classic (250–900 CE), and the Postclassic (900–1500 CE). The Classic period brackets the time during which the Maya erected dated stone monuments. The term reflects the view of early Mayanists that the Classic period was a kind of golden age, the equivalent of the Classical period in ancient Greece (Chapter 4). Although this view is no longer current and the periods are only roughly applicable to other parts of Mesoamerica, the terminology has endured.

The earliest known major Mesoamerican civilization, that of the Olmec people, emerged during the Formative period along the Gulf of Mexico. In the swampy coastal jungles of the modern Mexican states of Veracruz and Tabasco, the Olmec cleared farmland, drained fields, and raised earth mounds on which they constructed religious and political centers. They created monumental works of basalt sculpture, such as colossal heads (see fig. 1-20), altars, and seated figures. The Olmecs also established trade contacts throughout Mesoamerica, importing goods not found in the Gulf region, such as obsidian, iron ore, and jade. Writing and calendrical systems first appeared around 600 to 500 BCE in areas with strong Olmec influence.

By 200 CE, forests and swamps began to reclaim Olmec sites, but Olmec civilization had spread widely throughout Mesoamerica and was to have an enduring influence on its successors. As the Olmec centers of the Gulf Coast faded, the great Classic period centers at Teotihuacán in the Valley of Mexico as well as in the Maya region were beginning their ascendancy.

Located some 30 miles northeast of present-day Mexico City, Teotihuacán experienced a

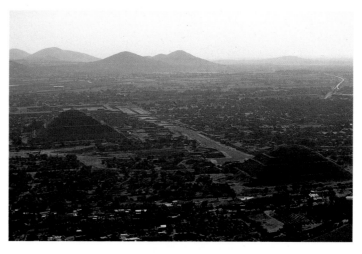

14-2. Ceremonial center of the city of Teotihuacán, Mexico. Teotihuacán culture, 350–650 CE

The Pyramid of the Moon is at the lower right, the Pyramid of the Sun at the middle left, and the Ciudadela and the Temple of the Feathered Serpent at the upper left.

The Cosmic Ball Game

The ritual ball game, which dates back at least to Olmec times, was one of the defining characteristics of Mesoamerican society. The game was generally played on a long, rectangular court. Players used their elbows, knees, or hips to direct a heavy rubber ball toward a goal or marker. The largest surviving ball court, at Chichén Itzá, Mexico, is about the size of a football field. The goals were stone rings set in the walls of the court about 25 feet above the field.

Figurines and stone votive sculpture depict ballplayers; relief sculpture show the game and its attendant rituals. The movements of the ball represented celestial bodies—the sun, moon, or stars—held aloft and directed by the skill of the players. The game was also associated with warfare. Captive warriors might have been forced to participate, and players were often sacrificed.

period of rapid growth early in the first millennium CE. By 200 it had emerged as a significant center of commerce and manufacturing, the first large city-state in the Americas. At its height, between 350 and 650 CE, Teotihuacán covered nearly 9 square miles and had a population of some 200,000, making it one of the largest cities in the world at that time (fig. 14-2). One reason for its dominance was its control of the market for high-quality obsidian. The stone, made into tools and pottery, was traded for luxury items such as the green feathers of the quetzal bird, used for priestly headdresses, and the spotted fur of the jaguar, used for ceremonial garments.

The name *Teotihuacán* is an Aztec word meaning "The City (gathering place) of the Gods." The people of Teotihuacán worshiped many deities that were recognizably similar to those worshiped by later Mesoamerican people, including the Aztec, who dominated central Mexico at the time of the Spanish Conquest. Among these are the Rain God (possibly also the god of fertility, war, and sacrifice), known to the Aztec as Tlaloc, and the Feathered Serpent, known to the Maya as Kukulcan and to the Aztec as Quetzalcoatl.

Teotihuacán's principal structures included the Pyramid of the Sun, the Pyramid of the

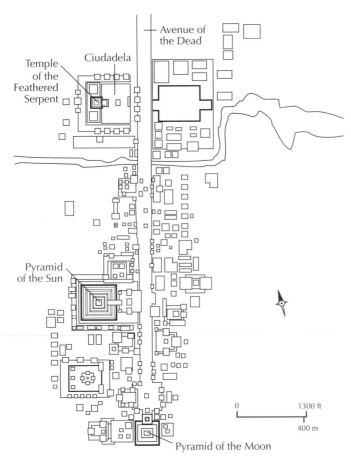

14-3. Plan of the ceremonial center of Teotihuacán

Labels on plan: Avenue of the Dead; Ciudadela; Temple of the Feathered Serpent; Pyramid of the Sun; Pyramid of the Moon; 0 — 1300 ft; 400 m

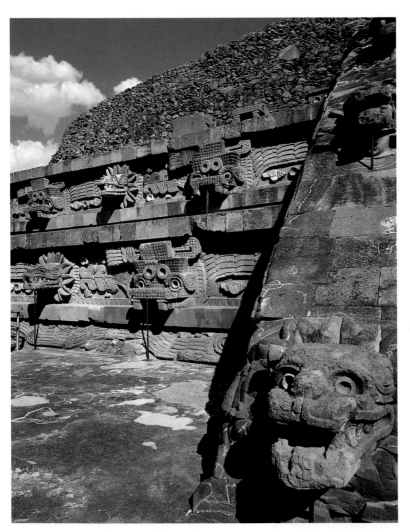

14-4. Temple of the Feathered Serpent, the Ciudadela, Teotihuacán, Mexico. Teotihuacán culture, c. 350 CE (?)

Moon, and the Ciudadela, a vast sunken plaza surrounded by temple platforms (fig. 14-3). One of the city's principal religious and political centers, the Ciudadela could accommodate an assembly of more than 60,000 people. Its focal point was the Temple of the Feathered Serpent. This structure exhibits the **talud-tablero** construction that is a hallmark of the Teotihuacán architectural style. The sloping base, or *talud*, of each platform supports a vertical *tablero*, or entablature, which is surrounded by a frame and often filled with sculptural decoration. The Temple of the Feathered Serpent was enlarged several times, and as was characteristic of Mesoamerican building practice, each completed enlargement enclosed the previous structure, like the concentric layers of an onion.

Archeological excavations of earlier-phase *tableros* and a stairway balustrade have revealed painted reliefs of the Feathered Serpent, the goggle-eyed Rain God (or Fire God, according to some), and aquatic shells and snails (fig. 14-4). Their flat, angular, abstract style, typical of Teotihuacán art, is in marked contrast to the three-dimensional, curvilinear style of Olmec art. The Rain God features a squarish, stylized head with protruding lips, huge, round eyes originally inlaid with obsidian and surrounded by colored circles, and large, circular earspools. The fanged serpent heads, perhaps composites of snakes and other creatures, emerge from an aureole of stylized feathers. The Rain God and the Feathered Serpent may be symbols of regeneration and cyclical renewal, perhaps representing the alternating wet and dry seasons.

Southeast of Teotihuacán was the homeland of the Maya people. In southern Mesoamerica, which includes present-day Guatemala, Yucatán peninsula, Belize, and the eastern part of Honduras and El Salvador, the Maya built imposing pyramids, temples, palaces, and administrative structures in densely populated cities. They developed the most advanced hieroglyphic writing in Mesoamerica and the most sophisticated version of the Mesoamerican calendrical system. In addition, they studied astronomy and the natural cycles of plants and animals, and they developed the mathematical concepts of zero and place value before they were known in Europe.

An increasingly detailed picture of the Maya has emerged from recent archeological research and progress in deciphering their writing. It shows a society divided into competing centers, each with a hereditary ruler and an elite class of nobles and priests supported by a far larger class of farmer-commoners. Rulers established their legitimacy, maintained links with their

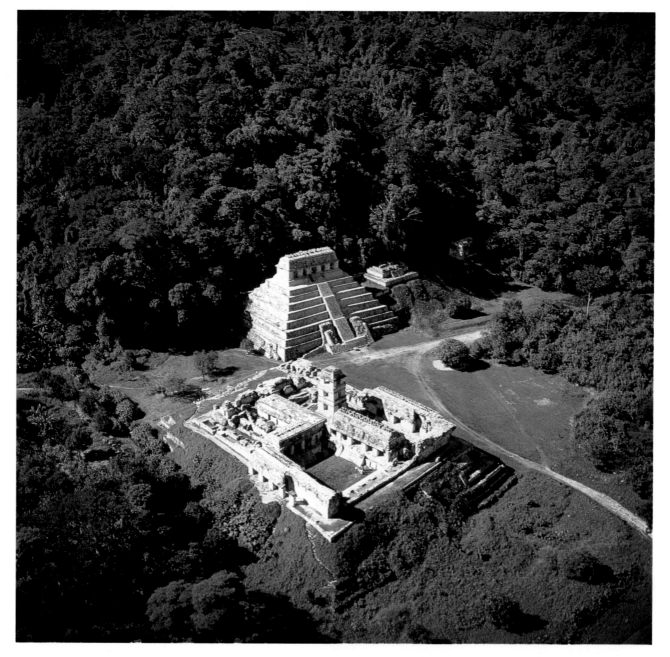

14-5. Palace (foreground) and Temple of the Inscriptions (tomb-pyramid of Lord Pacal), Palenque, Mexico. Maya culture, 7th century CE

divine ancestors, and venerated the gods through elaborate rituals, including ball games, bloodletting ceremonies, and human sacrifice. A complex pantheon of deities, many with several manifestations, presided over the Maya universe.

The Maya civilization, which emerged during the late Preclassic period (300 BCE–250 CE), reached its peak in the southern lowlands of Yucatán during the Classic period (250–900 CE), and shifted to northern Yucatán during the Postclassic period (900–1500 CE). In Palenque, a prominent city of the Classic period, the major buildings are grouped on high ground. The northern complex contains a group of five temples, with two additional temples nearby, and a ball court. A central group includes the so-called Palace (possibly an administrative rather than a residential structure), the Temple of the Inscriptions, and two other temples (fig. 14-5).

A third group of temples lies to the southeast. Most of the structures in these complexes were commissioned by a powerful ruler, Lord Pacal (Maya for "shield"), who ruled from 615 to 683 CE, and by Pacal's son, who succeeded him.

The Temple of the Inscriptions is a nine-level pyramid that rises to a height of about 75 feet. The consecutive layers probably reflect the belief, current among the Aztec and the Maya at the time of the Spanish Conquest, that the underworld had nine levels. Priests would climb the steep stone staircase on the exterior to the temple on top, which resembles the kind of pole-and-thatch houses the Maya still build in parts of Yucatán today. The roof of the temple is topped with a crest known as a **roof comb**, and the facade still retains much of its stucco sculpture. Inscriptions carved inside the temple gave the structure its name.

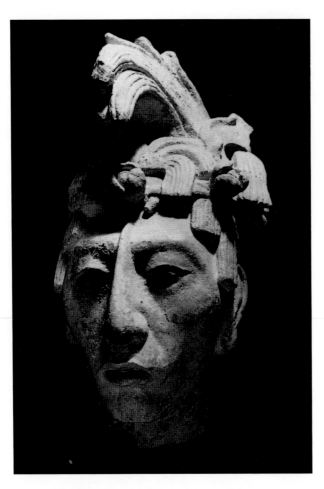

14-6. Portrait of Lord Pacal, from his tomb, Temple of the Inscriptions. Mid-7th century CE. Stucco, height 16⅞" (43 cm). Museo Nacional de Antropología, Mexico City

This portrait of the youthful Lord Pacal may have been placed in his tomb as an offering. Possibly it formed part of the original exterior decoration of the Temple of the Inscriptions.

of jade and flowers (fig. 14-6). His features are characteristic of the Maya ideal of beauty: a sloping forehead and elongated skull (babies had their heads bound to produce this shape), a large curved nose (enhanced by an ornamental bridge, perhaps of latex), full lips, and an open mouth. Traces of pigment indicate that this portrait, like much Maya sculpture, was colorfully painted.

As the focus of Maya civilization shifted northward in the Postclassic period, a northern Maya group called the Itzá rose to prominence. Their principal center, Chichén Itzá, which means "at the mouth of the well of the Itzá," flourished from the ninth to the thirteenth century CE, eventually covering about 6 square miles.

One of Chichén Itzá's most conspicuous structures is a massive, nine-level pyramid in the center of a large plaza (fig. 14-7). Embellished with figures of the Feathered Serpent, this structure is known today as the Castillo (Spanish for "castle"). A stairway on each side leads to a square temple on the pyramid's summit. At the spring and fall equinoxes, the rising sun casts an undulating, serpentlike shadow on the stairway balustrades.

Sculpture at Chichén Itzá includes half-reclining figures known as **Chacmools** (see fig. 14-7), which have the sturdy forms, proportions, and angularity of architecture. The Chacmools probably represent fallen warriors and were used to receive sacrificial offerings. They once typified pre-Columbian sculpture for many Westerners.

Maya civilization was in decline by the time of the Spanish Conquest. By the end of the fifteenth century, a people known as the Aztecs were rulers of much of Mexico. Their rise to power had been recent and swift. Only 400 years earlier, according to their own legends, they had been a nomadic people living on the shores of the mythological island called Aztlan somewhere to the northwest of the Valley of Mexico, where present-day Mexico City is located. They called themselves the M*exica*, hence the name *Mexico*. The term *Aztec* derives from the word *Aztlan*.

After a period of migration, the Aztecs arrived in the Valley of Mexico in the thirteenth century. There they eventually settled on an island in Lake Texcoco, where they had seen an eagle perching on a prickly pear cactus (*tenochtli*), a sign that Huitzilopochtli, their patron god, told them would mark the end of their wandering. They called the place Tenochtitlán. The city was situated on a collection of islands linked by canals.

In the fifteenth century, the Aztecs began an aggressive campaign of expansion. The tribute they exacted from all over Central Mexico transformed Tenochtitlán into a glittering capital. As the Spanish conquistador Hernán Cortés approached Tenochtitlán in November 1519, he and his soldiers marveled at the stone build-

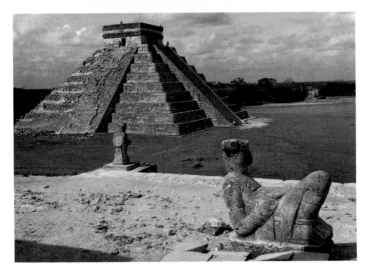

14-7. Castillo, with Chacmool in foreground, Chichén Itzá, Yucatán, Mexico. Maya culture, 9th–13th century CE

In 1952, an archeologist studying the Temple of the Inscriptions discovered a corbel-vaulted stairway beneath the summit shrine. This stairway descended almost 80 feet to a small subterranean chamber that contained the undisturbed tomb of Lord Pacal himself. The ruler lay in a monumental sarcophagus with a lid carved in low relief that showed him balanced between the spirit world and the earth. A stucco portrait of Lord Pacal found with the sarcophagus depicts him as a young man wearing a diadem

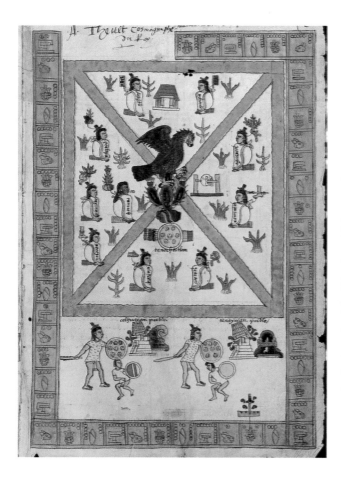

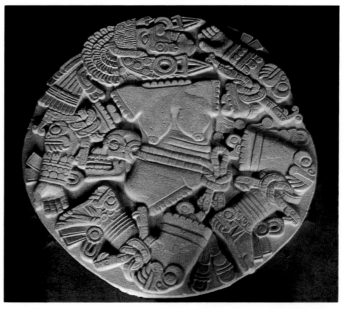

14-8. (*left*) ***The Founding of Tenochtitlán***, page from *Codex Mendoza*. Aztec, 16th century CE. Ink and color on paper, 8⁷/₁₆ x 12³/₈" (21.4 x 31.4 cm). The Bodleian Library, Oxford MS. Arch Selden. A.I.fol. 2r

14-9. (*above*) ***The Moon Goddess, Coyolxauhqui.*** Aztec, 15th century CE. Stone, diameter 11'6" (3.5 m)

This disk was discovered accidentally in 1978 by workers from a utility company who were excavating at a street corner in central Mexico City.

ings, towers, and temples that seemed from a distance to rise from the water like a mirage.

Most Aztec books were destroyed in the wake of the Spanish invasion, but the work of Aztec scribes appears in several **codexes** (manuscripts) created for Spanish administrators after the Conquest. The first page of the *Codex Mendoza*, prepared for the Spanish viceroy in the sixteenth century, can be interpreted as an idealized representation of the city of Tenochtitlán (fig. 14-8). An eagle perched on a prickly pear cactus—the symbol of the city— fills the center of the page. Waterways divide the city into four quarters, which are further subdivided into wards, as represented by the seated figures. The victorious warriors at the bottom of the page represent Aztec conquests.

Tenochtitlán had a sacred precinct, probably symbolized in figure 14-8 by the structure (a temple or house) at the top of the page. The focal point of the precinct was the Great Pyramid, a 130-foot-high stepped double pyramid with dual temples on top, one of which was dedicated to Huitzilopochtli (associated with the sun and warfare) and the other to Tlaloc, the god of rain and fertility. The Great Pyramid was an important site for ritual sacrifice. Victims climbed stairs on the exterior to the Temple of Huitzilopochtli at the summit, where several priests threw them over a stone and another quickly cut open their chests and pulled out their still-throbbing hearts. Their bodies were then rolled down the stairs and dis-

membered. Thousands of severed heads were said to have been kept on a skull rack in the plaza of the sacred precinct.

The Aztecs believed that human actions, including bloodletting and human sacrifice, were vital to the continued existence of the universe. Huitzilopochtli, son of the Earth Mother Coatlicue, was thought to require sacrificial victims so that he could, in a regular repetition of the events surrounding his birth, drive the stars and the moon from the sky at the beginning of each day. The stars were his half brothers, and the moon, Coyolxauhqui, was his half sister. According to myth, when Coatlicue conceived Huitzilopochtli by placing a ball of feathers in her bosom as she was sweeping, his jealous siblings conspired to kill her. When they attacked, Huitzilopochtli emerged from her body fully grown and armed, drove off his brothers, and destroyed his half sister, Coyolxauhqui.

A huge circular relief of the dismembered Coyolxauhqui once lay at the foot of the Great Pyramid, as if the enraged and triumphant Huitzilopochtli had cast her there like a sacrificial victim (fig. 14-9). Her torso is in the center, surrounded by her head and limbs. The rope around her waist is attached to a skull. She wears bells on her cheeks, a magnificent headdress, and distinctive ear ornaments composed of disks, rectangles, and triangles. The sculpture is two-dimensional in concept, with a deeply cut background.

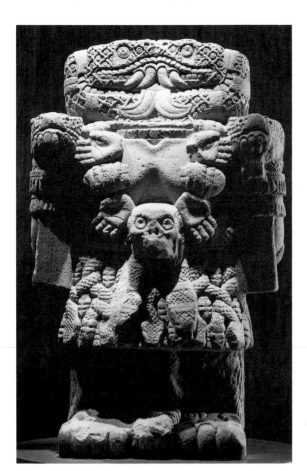

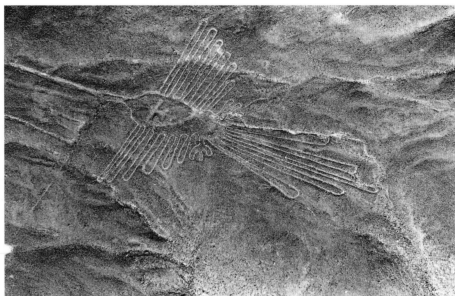

14-10. *The Mother Goddess, Coatlicue.* Aztec, 15th century CE. Stone, height 8'6" (2.59 m). Museo Nacional de Antropología, Mexico City

14-11. Earth drawing of a hummingbird, Nazca Plain, southwest Peru. Nazca culture, c. 200 BCE–200 CE. Length approx. 450' (137 m); wingspan approx. 200' (60.9 m)

Inside the Temple of Huitzilopochtli, an imposing statue of Coatlicue (fig. 14-10), mother of Huitzilopochtli, stood high above the vanquished Coyolxauhqui. One of the conquistadores who arrived at the site in the early sixteenth century described seeing such a statue covered with blood. Coatlicue means "she of the serpent skirt," and this broad-shouldered figure with clawed hands and feet wears a skirt of twisted snakes. A pair of serpents, symbols of gushing blood, rise from her neck to form her head. Around her stump of a neck hangs a necklace of sacrificial offerings—hands, hearts, and a dangling skull. Despite the surface intricacy, the sculpture's simple, bold, and blocky forms create a single visual whole. The colors with which it was originally painted would have heightened its dramatic impact.

The Spanish built their own capital, Mexico City, over the ruins of Tenochtitlán and built a cathedral on the site of Tenochtitlán's sacred precinct. The statue of Coatlicue was found near the cathedral during excavations there in the late eighteenth century.

South America: The Central Andes

Like Mesoamerica, the central Andes of South America—primarily present-day Peru and Bolivia—saw the development of complex hierarchical societies with rich and varied artistic traditions. The area is one of dramatic contrasts. The narrow coastal plain sandwiched between the Pacific Ocean and the soaring Andes is one of the driest deserts in the world. Life here depends on the rich marine resources of the

Pacific and the rivers that descend from the Andes. The Andes themselves are a region of snow-capped peaks, fertile river valleys, and high grasslands that support llamas, alpacas, vicuñas, and guanacos. The lush eastern slopes of the Andes descend to the tropical rain forest of the Amazon basin.

In the central Andes, the earliest evidence of monumental architecture dates to the third millennium BCE, contemporary with the earliest pyramids in Egypt. Sites with ceremonial mounds and plazas were discovered near the sea, while early centers in the highlands consisted of multi-roomed, stone-walled structures with sunken central fire pits in which ritual offerings were burned. Large, U-shaped ceremonial complexes with circular sunken plazas were built from the second millennium BCE. Some of the most enigmatic monumental constructions in Peru are the earthworks, or **geoglyphs**, first created by the people of the Nazca culture, who dominated the south coast of Peru from about 100 BCE to 700 CE. On great stretches of desert, they literally drew in the earth. By removing a layer of dark gravel, they exposed the lighter underlying soil, then edged the resulting lines with stones. In this way, they created gigantic images, including a hummingbird (fig. 14-11), a killer whale, a monkey, a spider, a duck, and other birds. They also made abstract patterns and groups of straight, parallel lines that extend for up to 12 miles. The beak of the hummingbird in figure 14-11 consists of two parallel lines, each 120 feet long. The purpose of these geoglyphs, which dwarf even the most ambitious

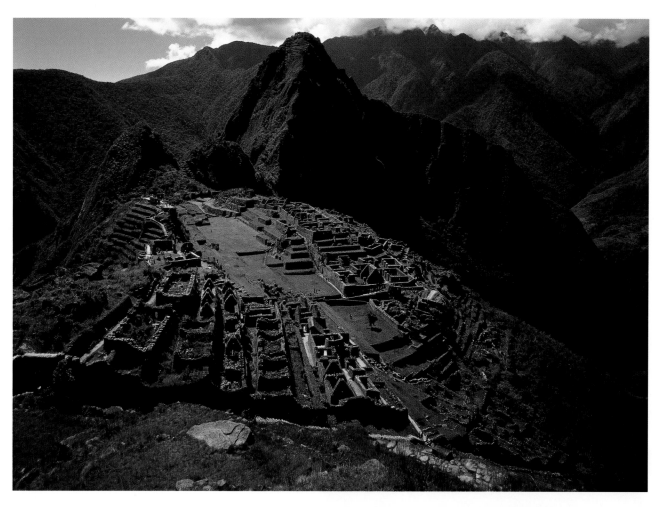

14-12.
Machu Picchu,
Peru. Inca,
15th–16th
century CE

twentieth-century environmental sculpture, is not known. Similar subject matter appears on a much smaller scale on multicolored pottery made by Nazca artisans.

The largest state in the Andes region in the pre-Columbian era was the Inca Empire, which rivaled China in size at the beginning of the sixteenth century. It extended for more than 2,600 miles along western South America, encompassing most of modern-day Peru, Ecuador, Bolivia, northern Chile, and reaching into Argentina. The Inca called their empire the Land of the Four Quarters. At its center was their capital, Cuzco, "the navel of the world," located high in the Andes Mountains. The early history of the Inca people is obscure. The Cuzco region had been under the control of the earlier Wari Empire, and the Inca state was probably one of many small competing kingdoms that emerged in the highlands in the wake of the Wari collapse. In the fifteenth century, the Inca, like the Aztec in the Valley of Mexico, began suddenly and rapidly to expand. Through conquest, alliance, and intimidation, they subdued most of their vast domain by 1500. To hold together the linguistically and ethnically diverse empire, the Inca relied on an overarching state religion, a hierarchical bureaucracy, and various forms of labor taxation, satisfied by a set amount of time spent performing tasks for the state. To speed transport and communication, the Inca built nearly 15,000 miles of roads, with more than a thousand lodgings

Elements of Architecture
INCA MASONRY

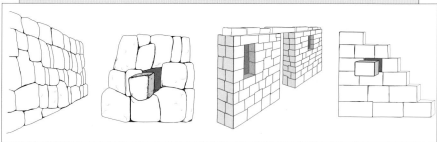

Working with the simplest of tools—mainly heavy stone hammers—and using no mortar, Inca builders created stonework of great refinement and durability: roads and bridges that linked the entire empire, built-up terraces for growing crops, and structures both simple and elaborate. At Machu Picchu (fig. 14-12), all buildings and terraces within its 3-square-mile extent were made of granite, the hard stone indigenous to the site. Commoners' houses and some walls were constructed of irregular stones that were carefully fitted together. Other walls and certain domestic and religious structures were erected using squared-off, smooth-surfaced stones laid in even rows. At a few Inca sites, the stones were boulder-size: up to 27 feet tall.

spaced a day's journey apart and a relay system of waiting runners to carry messages. In common with other Native American civilizations, the Inca had no wheeled vehicles. Travelers went on foot, and llamas were used as pack animals.

Inca builders created stonework structures of great refinement and durability (see "Inca Masonry," above). The most spectacular example is Machu Picchu (fig. 14-12). At 9,000 feet

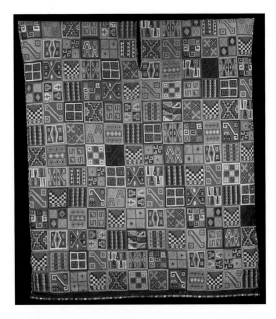

14-13. Tunic, from Peru. Inca, c. 1500 CE. Wool and cotton, 35⅞ x 30" (91.1 x 76.2 cm). Dumbarton Oaks Research Library and Collections, Washington, D.C.

Textile patterns and colors were standardized, like European heraldry or the uniforms of today's sports teams, to convey information at a glance.

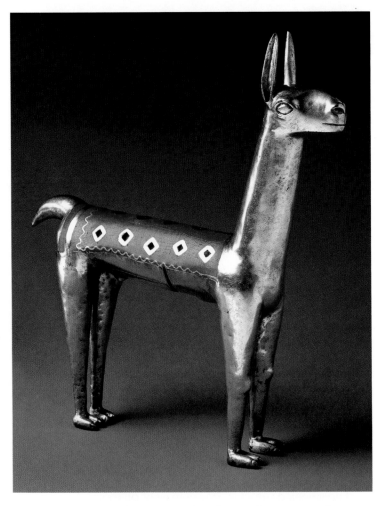

14-14. Llama, from Bolivia or Peru, found near Lake Titicaca, Bolivia. Inca, 15th century CE. Cast silver with gold and cinnabar, 9 x 8½ x 1¾" (22.9 x 21.6 x 4.4 cm). American Museum of Natural History, New York
Trans. #5003

above sea level, the site straddles a ridge between two high peaks in the eastern slopes of the Andes. Machu Picchu's location, near the eastern limits of the empire, suggests that it may have been a frontier outpost. Its temples and carved sacred stones imply it may also have had an important religious function.

The production of textiles is an ancient art in the Andes. As one of the primary forms of wealth for the Inca, cloth was a fitting offering for the gods. Fine garments were draped around golden statues, and complex images were woven of cloth. Garments also carried important symbolic messages. Their patterns and designs indicated, among other things, a person's ethnic identity and social rank. Each square in the tunic shown in figure 14-13 represents a miniature tunic, but the meaning of the individual patterns is not yet completely understood. The checkerboard pattern designated military officers and royal escorts. The four-part motifs may refer to the Land of the Four Quarters.

THE AFTERMATH OF THE SPANISH CONQUEST

Hernán Cortés arrived off the coast of Mexico from the Spanish colony in Cuba in 1519. He forged alliances with the Aztecs' enemies and, within two years after, took Tenochtitlán. Over the next several years, Spanish forces subdued much of the rest of Mexico and established it as a colony of Spain. In 1532, Francisco Pizarro, following Cortés's example, led an expedition to the land of the Inca. He and his men seized the Inca ruler Atahualpa, held him for a huge ransom in gold, then treacherously strangled him. They marched on to Cuzco and seized it in 1533.

The Spanish who conquered the Inca Empire were obsessed with amassing gold and silver. They melted down whatever they could find to enrich themselves and the royal coffers of Spain. The Inca, in contrast, valued gold and silver not as precious metals in themselves, but as symbols of the sun and the moon. Some small figures, buried as offerings, escaped the invaders' treasure hunt. A small llama was found near Lake Titicaca (fig. 14-14). To the Inca, the llama had a special connection with the sun, with rain, and with fertility. In Cuzco, a llama was sacrificed to the sun every morning and evening. Dressed in a red tunic and wearing gold jewelry, this llama would be paraded through the streets during April celebrations. According to Spanish commentators, these processions included lifesize gold and silver images of llamas, people, and gods.

Native American populations in Mexico and Peru declined sharply after the conquest because of the exploitive policies of the Conquerors and the ravages of smallpox and other diseases they imported, against which the indigenous people had no immunity. European

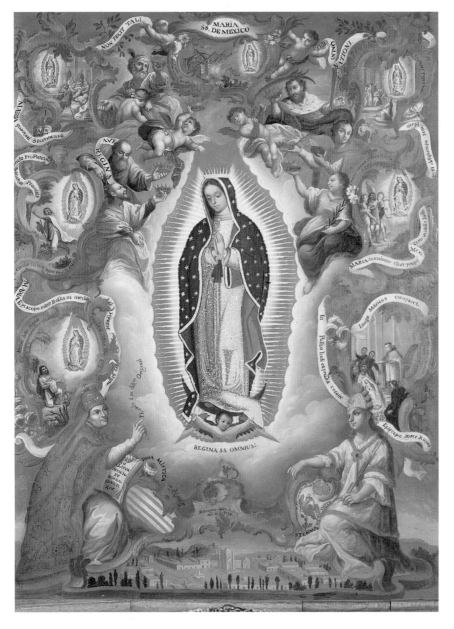

14-15. Sebastián Salcedo.
Our Lady of Guadalupe. 1779.
Oil on panel and copper,
24³/₄ x 18¹¹/₁₆" (62.9 x 47.5 cm).
The Denver Art Museum

Museum Purchase with funds
contributed by Mr. and
Mrs. George G. Anderman
and an anonymous donor

missionaries suppressed local beliefs and practices and spread Roman Catholicism throughout
Spanish America.

In 1531, converts in Mexico gained their own
patron saint when the Virgin Mary appeared as
an Indian to an Indian named Juan Diego. Mary
is said to have asked that a church be built on a
hill where the Aztec Mother Goddess (see fig.
14-10) had once been worshiped. As evidence of
this vision, Juan Diego brought flowers that the
Virgin had caused to bloom, wrapped in a cloak,
to the archbishop. When he opened the bundle,
the cloak bore the likeness of a dark-skinned
Virgin Mary, an image popular in Spain (with a
light-skinned Virgin) and known as the Woman of
the Apocalypse or the Virgin of the Immaculate
Conception. The site of the vision was renamed
Guadalupe, after Our Lady of Guadalupe in Spain,
and became a venerated pilgrimage center. In
1754, the pope declared the Virgin of Guadalupe
to be the patron saint of the Americas (fig. 14-15).
In 1990 Pope John Paul II beatified Juan Diego,
marking the first step to sainthood.

North America

Compared with the densely inhabited agricultural regions of Mesoamerica and South America,
much of North America remained sparsely populated until the arrival of European settlers in
the fifteenth century. In the Northeast, people
lived primarily by hunting, fishing, and gathering
edible plants. In the Southeast and in the lands
drained by the Mississippi and Missouri river
systems, agriculture emerged, and nomadic
hunting and gathering gave way to more settled
communities by 1000 BCE or possibly even earlier.
Toward the end of the first millennium BCE,
people in the American Southwest also began
to adopt an agricultural way of life.

THE SOUTHEAST AND THE SOUTHWEST

In the fertile lands near the Ohio, Illinois,
Mississippi, and Missouri rivers, the people of
the Adena, Hopewell, and Mississippian cultures
cultivated maize (corn) and other crops. They
began building monumental **earthworks** and

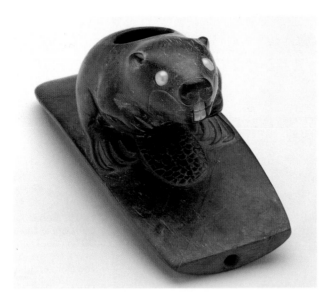

14-16. Beaver effigy platform pipe, from Bedford Mound, Pike County, Illinois. Hopewell culture, c. 100–200 CE. Pipestone, pearl, and bone, length 4¹/₂" (11.4 cm). Gilcrease Museum, Tulsa, Oklahoma

bowl—a hole in the beaver's back—could be filled with dried leaves (the Hopewell may not have grown tobacco), the leaves lighted, and smoke drawn through a hole in the stem. A second way that these pipes were used was to blow smoke inhaled from another vessel through the pipe to envelop the animal carved on it. Hopewell pipes and pipestone have been found from Lake Superior to the Gulf of Mexico.

The people of the Mississippian culture (800–1500 CE) continued the mound-building tradition of the Adena, Hopewell, and other early southeastern cultures. One of the most impressive Mississippian-period earthworks is the Great Serpent Mound in present-day Adams County, Ohio (see fig. 14-1). Carbon-14 dating of wood charcoal samples from the mound suggests that the earthwork was built about 1070 CE. It was probably the work of the people of the Fort Ancient culture (900–1600 CE), a Mississippian group of the Ohio Valley. There have been many interpretations of the writhing snake form, especially the "head" at the highest point, which some see as opening its jaws to swallow a huge egg formed by a heap of stones.

The Mississippian peoples built a major urban center known as Cahokia near the juncture of the Illinois, Missouri, and Mississippi rivers (now East Saint Louis, Illinois). Cahokia was founded about 900 CE, but most construction took place between about 1050 and 1250. At its height, the city had a population of between 10,000 and 20,000 people, with another 10,000 in the surrounding countryside (fig. 14-17).

burying their leaders with valuable grave goods sometime before 1000 BCE. Objects discovered in these burials show that the people of the Mississippi and Ohio Valleys traded widely with other regions. For example, burials of the mound-building Adena (600 BCE–200 CE) and Hopewell (200 BCE–200 CE) cultures contained jewelry made with copper from Michigan's upper peninsula and silhouettes cut in sheets of mica from the Appalachian Mountains.

The Hopewell people made pipes of fine-grain pipestone carved with realistic representations of forest animals and birds, sometimes with inlaid eyes and teeth of freshwater pearls and bone. A pearl-eyed beaver crouching on a platform forms the bowl of a pipe found in Illinois (fig. 14-16). As in a modern pipe, the

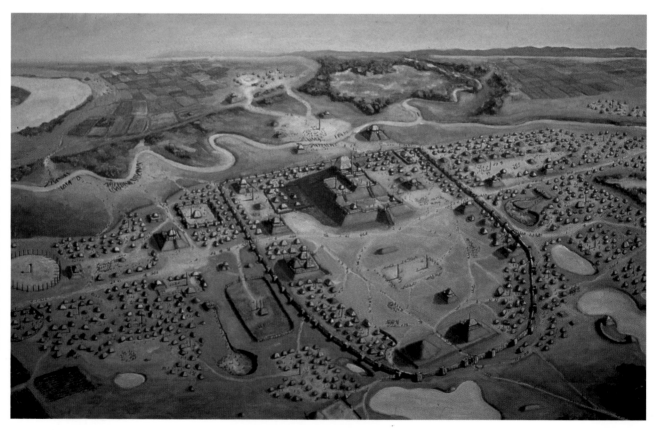

14-17. Reconstruction of central Cahokia, East Saint Louis, Illinois. Mississippian culture, c. 1150 CE. Earth mounds and wooden structures; east-west length approx. 3 miles (4.84 km), north-south length approx. 2¹/₄ miles (3.63 km); base of great mound, 1,037 x 790' (316 x 241 m), height approx. 100' (30 m). Painting by William R. Iseminger

The most prominent feature of Cahokia is an enormous earth mound covering 15 acres. A small, conical platform on its summit originally supported a wooden fence and a rectangular temple or house. Smaller rectangular and conical mounds in front of the principal mound surrounded a large, roughly rectangular plaza. The city's entire ceremonial center was protected by a **stockade**, or fence, of upright wooden posts—a sign of increasing warfare. In all, the walled enclosure contained more than 500 mounds, platforms, wooden enclosures, and houses. The various earthworks functioned as tombs and as bases for palaces and temples. A conical burial mound, for example, was located next to a platform that may have been used for sacrifices.

Farming cultures were slower to arise in the arid southwestern region of what is now the United States. The Hohokam culture, centered in central and southern Arizona, emerged around 200 BCE and endured until sometime after 1200 CE. The Hohokam built large-scale irrigation systems with canals made deep and narrow to reduce evaporation and lined with clay to reduce seepage. In the Four Corners region, where Colorado, Utah, Arizona, and New Mexico meet, the Anasazi (a Navajo word meaning "the ancient ones") adopted this irrigation technology to produce food for settled communities. Around 750 CE they began building elaborate, multistoried structures with many rooms for specialized purposes, including communal food storage and ritual. The Spaniards called these communities pueblos, or "towns." The descendants of the Anasazi, including the Hopi and

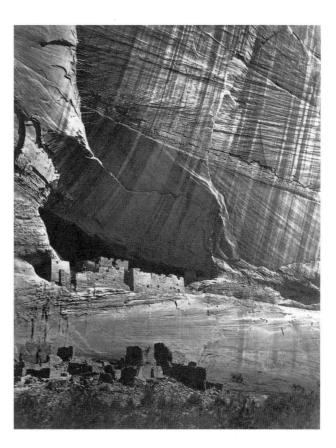

14-18. Timothy H. O'Sullivan. *Ancient Ruins in the Cañon de Chelley, Arizona.* 1873. Albumen print. National Archives, Washington, D.C.

Zuni, still occupy similar communities in the Four Corners area. An early photograher, Timothy O'Sullivan, recorded Anasazi ruins in the Cañon de Chelley, in Arizona, while accompanying a geological expedition in 1873 (fig. 14-18).

The largest known ancient Anasazi center is Pueblo Bonito in Chaco Canyon, which was built in stages from the tenth to mid-thirteenth century CE (fig. 14-19). This remarkable, D-shaped structure had hundreds of rooms and rose four

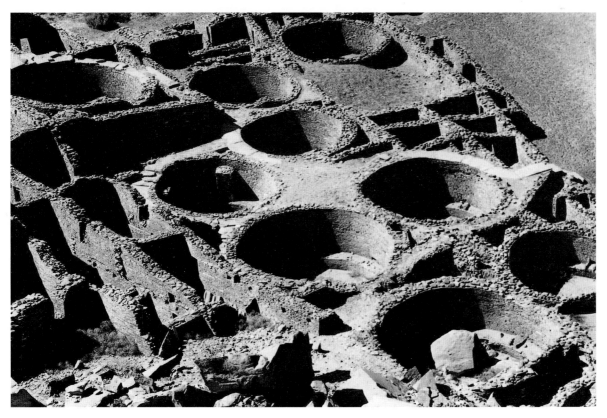

14-19. **Pueblo Bonito, Chaco Canyon,** New Mexico. Anasazi culture, c. 900–1250 CE

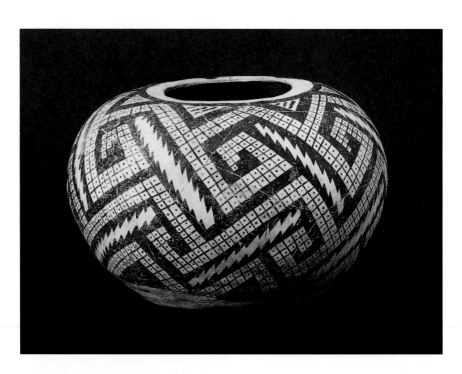

14-20. Seed jar. Anasazi culture, 1100–1300 CE. Earthenware and black-and-white pigment, diameter 14½" (36.8 cm). The St. Louis Art Museum, St. Louis, Missouri
Purchase: Funds given by the Children's Art Festival 175:1981

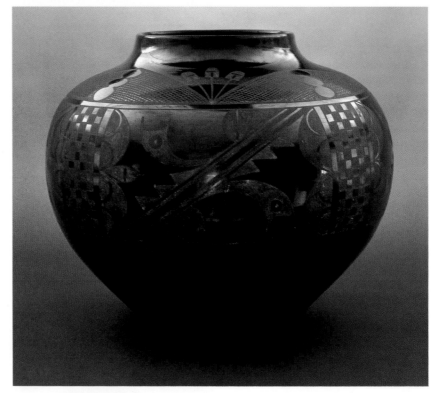

14-21. Maria Montoya Martinez and Julian Martinez. Blackware storage jar, from San Ildefonso Pueblo, New Mexico. Hopi, c. 1942. Ceramic, height 18¾" (47.6 cm), diameter 22½" (57.1 cm). Museum of Indian Arts and Culture/Laboratory of Anthropology, Museum of New Mexico, Santa Fe

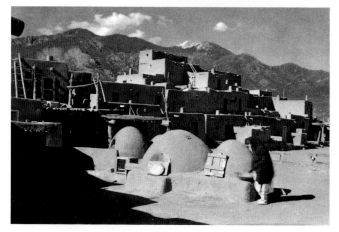

14-22. (*left*) **Taos Pueblo,** Tewa, Taos, New Mexico. Photographed by Laura Gilpin. 1947. Amon Carter Museum, Fort Worth, Texas
Laura Gilpin Collection (neg. # 2528.1)

stories high. Its outer perimeter wall was 1,300 feet long. The sandstone masonry walls on the ground floor were 4 feet thick, and trunks of ponderosa pines were used for roof beams. As new rooms were added over time, older rooms lost access to natural light. Amazingly, all aspects of construction—including quarrying, timber cutting, and transport—were done without draft animals, wheeled vehicles, or metal tools.

Pueblo Bonito stood at the center of a network of wide, straight roads, in some places with curbs and paving. The builders made no effort to avoid topographic obstacles; when they encountered cliffs, they ran stairs up them. This practice suggests that the roads served as processional routes rather than practical thoroughfares.

Women were the potters in Anasazi society. In the eleventh century, these potters perfected a functional, aesthetically pleasing, coil-built earthenware, or ceramic fired at a low temperature. The wide-mouthed seed jar shown in figure 14-20 is decorated with black-and-white checkerboard and zigzag patterns that conform to the body of the jar and, in spite of their angularity, enhance its curved shape. The intricate play of dark and light, positive and negative, suggests lightning flashing over a grid of irrigated fields.

The ceramic tradition of the Anasazi continues today among the Pueblo people of the Southwest. One of the best-known twentieth-century Pueblo potters is Maria Montoya Martinez (1887–1980) of San Ildefonso Pueblo. Inspired by prehistoric **blackware** pottery that was unearthed at nearby archeological excavations, she and her husband, Julian Martinez (1885–1943), developed a distinctive new ware decorated with **matte** (nongloss) black forms on a lustrous black background (fig. 14-21). Their decorative patterns were inspired by both traditional Pueblo imagery and the then-fashionable Euro-American Art Deco style.

Other traditional practices have survived today (see "Basketry," right). Some contemporary Pueblo villages, like those of their Anasazi forebears, consist of multistoried, apartment-like dwellings. One of these, Taos Pueblo, shown here in a mid-twentieth-century photograph (fig. 14-22), is located in north-central New Mexico. The northernmost of the surviving Pueblo communities, Taos once served as a trading center between Plains and Pueblo peoples. It burned in 1690 but was rebuilt about 1700 and has been modified often since. Its great multifamily "houses" stand on either side of Taos Creek, rising in a stepped fashion to form a series of roof terraces. The houses border a plaza that opens toward the neighboring mountains. The plaza and roof terraces are centers of communal life and ceremony.

THE EASTERN WOODLANDS AND THE GREAT PLAINS

When European settlement began in earnest in North America around the late 1500s to the early 1600s, forests stretched from the Hudson Bay to the Gulf of Mexico and from the Atlantic coast to the Mississippi River and Missouri River watersheds. Between this Eastern Woodlands region and the Rocky Mountains to the west lay an area of prairie grasslands now known as the Great Plains.

In the Eastern Woodlands, Native American peoples supported themselves by a combination of hunting and agriculture. Living together in villages, they cultivated corn, squash, and beans. They used waterproof birchbark to construct their homes and to make the watercraft known as the canoe. In the sixteenth century, one Eastern Woodlands group, the Iroquois, formed a powerful confederation of northeastern Native American nations that played a prominent military and political role until after the American Revolution.

TECHNIQUE
BASKETRY

Basketry involves weaving reeds, grasses, and other materials to form containers. The three principal basket-making techniques are: **coiling**, or sewing together a spiraling foundation of rods with some other material; **twining**, or sewing together a vertical **warp** of rods; and **plaiting**, which involves weaving strips over and under each other. In North America the earliest evidence of basketwork, found in Danger Cave, Utah, dates to as early as 8400 BCE. Over the subsequent centuries Native American women, notably in California and the Southwest, developed basketry into an art form that combined utility with great beauty.

The coiled basket shown here was made by the Pomo of California. According to Pomo legend, the earth was dark until their ancestral hero stole the sun and brought it to earth in a basket. He hung the basket first just over the horizon, but, dissatisfied with the light it gave, he kept suspending it in different places across the dome of the sky. He repeats this process every day, which is why the sun moves across the sky from east to west. In the Pomo basket the structure of coiled willow and bracken fern root produces a spiral surface into which the artist worked sparkling pieces of clamshell, trade beads, and the soft tufts of woodpecker and quail feathers. Such baskets were treasured possessions, often cremated with their owners at death.

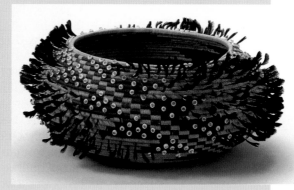

Wedding basket. Pomo, c. 1877. Willow, bracken fern root, clamshell, trade beads, woodpecker and quail feathers, height 5½" (14 cm), diameter 12" (30.5 cm). Philbrook Museum of Art, Tulsa, Oklahoma
Clark Field Collection

On the Great Plains, two differing ways of life developed, one nomadic—dependent on the region's great migrating herds of buffalo for food, clothing, and shelter—and the other sedentary and agricultural. Horses, introduced by Spanish explorers in the late seventeenth century, and later, firearms, made buffalo hunting vastly more efficient than before and attracted more people to the nomadic way of life.

As European settlers on the eastern seaboard began to turn forests into farms, they put increasing pressure on the Eastern Woodlands peoples, seizing their lands and forcing them westward. The resulting interaction of Eastern

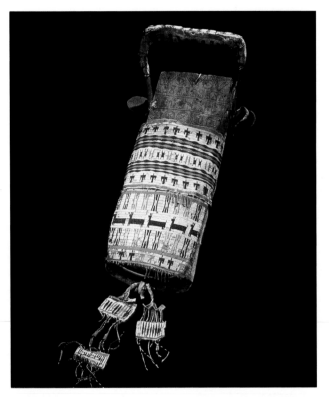

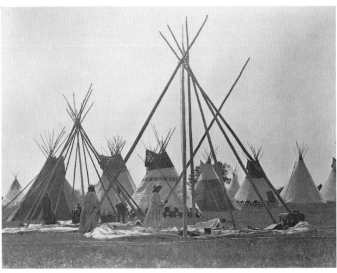

14-24. Blackfoot women raising a tepee. Photographed c. 1900. Montana Historical Society, Helena

14-23. Baby carrier, from the Upper Missouri River area. Eastern Sioux, 19th century. Board, buckskin, porcupine quill, length 31" (78.7 cm). Smithsonian Institution Libraries, Washington, D.C.

Woodlands artists with one another and with Plains artists led to the emergence of the Prairie style among numerous groups.

One distinctively Eastern Woodlands medium that found its way to the Plains was **quillwork** embroidery. Quillwork involved soaking porcupine and bird quills to soften them, dyeing them, and then working them into rectilinear, ornamental surface patterns on deerskin clothing and on birchbark artifacts like baskets and boxes. A legend of the Plains people known as the Sioux recounts how a mythical ancestor, Doublewoman ("double" because she was both beautiful and ugly, benign and dangerous), appeared to a Sioux woman in a dream and taught her the art of quillwork. As this legend suggests, quillwork was a woman's art form. The Sioux baby carrier shown in figure 14-23 is richly decorated with symbols of protection and well-being, including bands of antelopes in profile and thunderbirds with their heads turned and their tails outspread. The thunderbird was an especially beneficent symbol, thought to be capable of protecting against both human and supernatural adversaries.

The nomadic Plains peoples developed a light, portable dwelling known as a **tepee** (fig. 14-24), which was sturdily constructed to withstand the wind, dust, and rain of the prairies. Hides (or later, canvas) covered a framework of poles to form an almost conical structure that leaned slightly in the direction of the prevailing wind. The flap-covered door and smoke hole (the opening at the top above the central hearth) usually faced away from the wind. A typical tepee required about eighteen hides, the largest about thirty-eight hides. An inner lining covered the lower part of the walls and the perimeter of the floor to protect the occupants from drafts. When packed to be dragged by a horse, the tepee served as a platform for transporting other possessions as well.

Tepees were the property and responsibility of women. Blackfoot women could set up their huge tepees in less than an hour. The bottom of a tepee was usually covered with a group's traditional motifs and the center section with personal images.

Men of the Plains recorded their exploits in symbolic and narrative form in paintings on tepee linings and covers and on buffalo-hide robes. The earliest known surviving painted buffalo-hide robe illustrates a battle fought in 1797 between the Mandan of North Dakota and their allies against the Sioux (fig. 14-25). The painter, trying to capture the full extent of a conflict in which five nations took part, shows a party of warriors in twenty-two separate episodes. Their leader appears with a pipe and wears an elaborate eagle-feather headdress. Lines were pressed into the hide, and black, red, green, yellow, and brown pigments added. A strip of porcupine quills runs down the spine. The robe would have been worn draped over the shoulders of the powerful warrior whose deeds it commemorates. As he moved, the painted horses

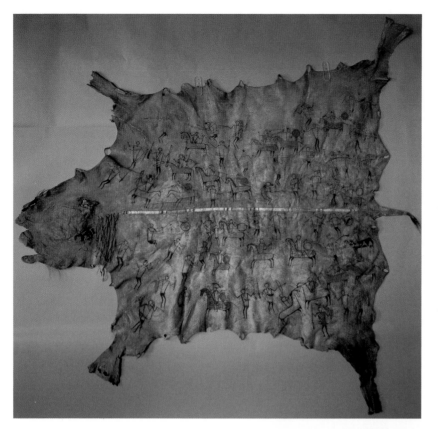

14-25. Battle-scene hide painting, from North Dakota. Mandan, 1797–1805. Tanned buffalo hide, dyed porcupine quills, and black, red, green, yellow, and brown pigment, 7'10" x 8'6" (2.38 x 2.59 m). Peabody Museum of Archaeology, Harvard University, Cambridge, Massachusetts (99-12-10/53121)

This robe, collected by Meriwether Lewis and William Clark on their 1803–1806 expedition into western lands acquired by the United States in the Louisiana Purchase, is the earliest documented example of Plains painting. The robe was one of a number of Native American artworks that Lewis and Clark sent to President Thomas Jefferson. Jefferson displayed the robe in the entrance hall of his home at Monticello, Virginia.

and warriors would have come alive, transforming him into a living representation of his exploits.

THE NORTHWEST COAST

Before the arrival of European explorers, the Native American peoples of the Northwest Coast—among them the Chilkat Tlingit, the Haida, and the Kwakiutl—lived on the Pacific coast of North America from southern Alaska to northern California. Their major food source was salmon from the region's many rivers. Harvested and dried, the fish could sustain large populations throughout the year.

Northwest Coast peoples lived in extended family groups in large, elaborately decorated communal houses made of massive timbers and thick planks. Family groups claimed descent from a mythic animal or animal-human ancestor. Chiefs, who were in the most direct line of descent from the ancestor, validated their status and garnered prestige for themselves and their families by holding ritual feasts during which they gave valuable gifts to the guests. Shamans, who were sometimes also chiefs, mediated between the human and spirit worlds.

The participants who danced in Northwest Coast ceremonies wore elaborate costumes and striking carved masks. Among the most elaborate masks were those used by the Kwakiutl in the Winter Dance for initiating new members into the shamanistic Hamatsa society (fig. 14-26). The dance reenacted the taming of Hamatsa, a

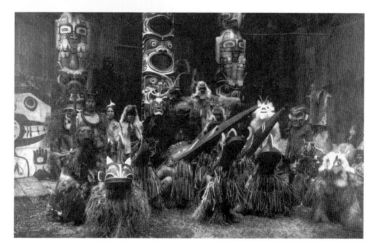

14-26. Hamatsa dancers, Kwakiutl, Canada. Photographed by Edward S. Curtis 1914

The photographer Edward S. Curtis (1868–1952) devoted thirty years to documenting the lives of Native Americans. This photograph shows participants in a film he made about the Kwakiutl. For the film, his Native American informant and assistant, Richard Hunt, borrowed family heirlooms and commissioned many new pieces from the finest Kwakiutl artists. Most of the pieces are now in museum collections. The photograph shows carved and painted posts, masked dancers (including those representing cannibal birds), a chief at the left (holding a speaker's staff and wearing a cedar neck ring), and spectators at the right.

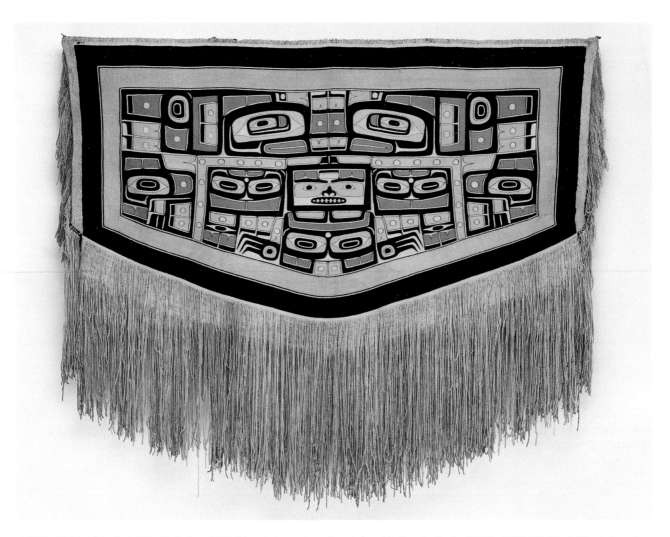

14-27. Chilkat blanket. Tlingit, before 1928. Mountain-goat wool and shredded cedar bark, 4'7⅛" x 5'3¾" (1.40 x 1.62 m). American Museum of Natural History, New York
Trans. #3804

people-eating spirit, and his three attendant bird spirits. Magnificent carved and painted masks transformed the dancers into Hamatsa and the bird attendants, who searched for victims to eat. Strings allowed the dancers to manipulate the masks so that the beaks snapped open and snapped shut with spectacular effect.

Blankets and other textiles produced by the Chilkat Tlingit had great prestige throughout the Northwest Coast (fig. 14-27). Chilkat men drew the patterns on boards, and women did the weaving. Instead of using looms, the weavers hung **warp** (vertical) threads from a rod and twisted colored threads back and forth through them to make the pattern. The ends of the warp formed the fringe at the bottom of the blanket.

The stylized creature in the center of this blanket is perhaps a sea bear or a standing eagle. The legs and claws are placed on either side of

the blocky body. The images on the blanket are composed of two basic Northwest Coast elements: the ovoid, a slightly bent rectangle with rounded corners, and the **formline**, a continuous, shape-defining line. Here, swelling black formlines define structures with gentle curves, ovoids, and rectangular C shapes. When the blanket was worn, its two-dimensional forms would have become three-dimensional, with the dramatic central figure curving over the wearer's back.

The contemporary Canadian Haida artist Bill Reid (1920–1998) sought to sustain and revitalize the traditions of Northwest Coast art in his work. Trained as a wood carver, painter, and jeweler, Reid revived the art of carving dugout canoes and totem poles in the Haida homeland of Haida Gwaii—"Islands of the People"—known on maps today as the Queen Charlotte Islands. Late in life he began to create

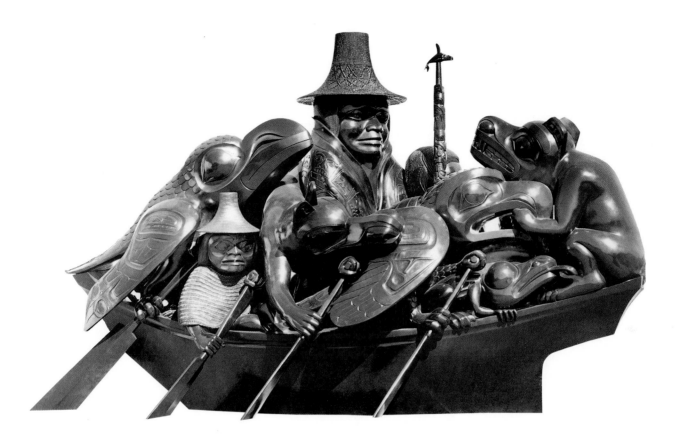

14-28. **Bill Reid. T***he* **Spirit** *of* **Haida** **Gwaii.** Haida, 1991. Bronze, approx. 13 x 20' (4 x 6 m). Canadian Embassy, Washington, D.C.

large-scale sculpture in bronze. With their black patina, these works recall traditional Haida carvings in argillite, a shiny black stone. One of them, *The Spirit of Haida Gwaii*, now stands outside the Canadian Embassy in Washington, D.C. (fig. 14-28). This sculpture, which Reid viewed as a metaphor for modern Canada's multi-cultural society, depicts a collection of figures from the natural and mythic worlds struggling to paddle forward in a canoe. The dominant figure in the center is a shaman in a spruce-root basket hat and Chilkat blanket holding a speaker's pole, a staff that gives him the right to speak with authority. In the prow, the place

reserved for the chief in a war canoe, is the Bear. The Bear faces backward rather than for-ward, however, and is bitten by the Eagle, with formline-patterned wings. The Eagle, in turn, is bitten by the Seawolf. In the stern, steering the canoe, is the Raven, the trickster in Haida mythology. The Raven is assisted by Mouse-woman, the traditional guide and escort of humans in the spirit realms. According to Reid, the work represents a "mythological and envi-ronmental lifeboat," where "the entire family of living things . . . whatever their differences, . . . are paddling together in one boat, headed in one direction."

Head of an *oba* (king), from Benin. c. 1700–1897 CE (Late Period). Brass, height 17¼" (45 cm). Museum für Völkerkunde, Vienna/Musée Dapper, Paris

General and Officers, from Benin. c. 1550–1650 CE (Middle Period). Brass, height 21" (53.5 cm). National Museum, Lagos, Nigeria

Mask representing an *iyoba*, from Benin. c. 1550 CE. Ivory, iron, and copper, height 9¼" (23.4 cm). The Metropolitan Museum of Art, New York

Cast-metal Sculpture

Almost all Benin metal sculpture was made by the *lost-wax casting* process (see "Starter Kit"). Although Benin sculptures are popularly referred to as "bronze," an alloy of copper and zinc (brass) rather than of copper and tin (bronze) was used.

Mixed-media Sculpture

The sculptor of the ivory face added iron pupils and copper rims to the eyes. The rectangular marks on the forehead are also of iron. When artists combine several different materials in a piece, we refer to it as *mixed media*.

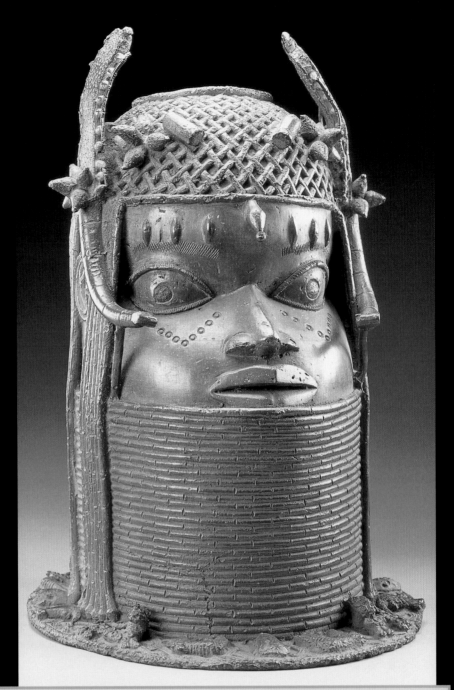

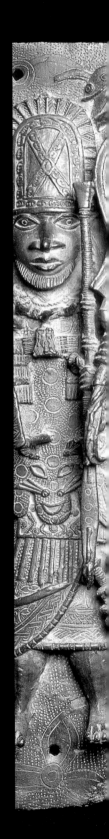

K E Y S to Art History

SCULPTURE & THE FINE ARTS

In Western cultures, the *fine arts* traditionally encompass painting, sculpture, and architecture. Since the sixteenth century, *painting* has been considered the most important medium. At other times (for example, during the ancient and medieval periods) and in other places (including much of Africa), *sculpture* has traditionally been regarded as the most important. Perhaps sculpture's attraction lies in its absolute physicality; it takes up space the same way we do, and it is made of materials that appeal to our tactile sense (even if, in museums, we cannot satisfy the urge to touch).

Sculpture is classified in a number of ways: as additive or reductive or assembled; freestanding or relief; independent or architectural; monumental or small scale. *Additive sculpture* is created with a malleable material that can be built up and shaped (modeled). Such materials include terra-cotta and other clays, plaster and stucco, gesso, and wax. Often these materials are used to make a mold so that metals in a molten state can be *cast* to create the final image. *Reductive sculpture* is carved: the image takes shape as the sculptor removes or carves away material. Stone and marble, wood, ivory, even precious stones are carved. Some materials, such as wax or plaster, can be worked both additively and reductively. *Assembled sculpture* is put together from preexisting parts.

Independent sculpture is *freestanding*; it is usually referred to as *sculpture in the round*. In contrast, in *relief sculpture* the images remain part of the original material, the ground. *Architectural sculpture* is often created in relief and is integrated into the design and decoration of a building. *Monumental* describes large-scale sculpture or pieces that give an impression of grandeur and excellence. *Small scale* implies a work significantly smaller than *lifesize*.

AFRICAN ART

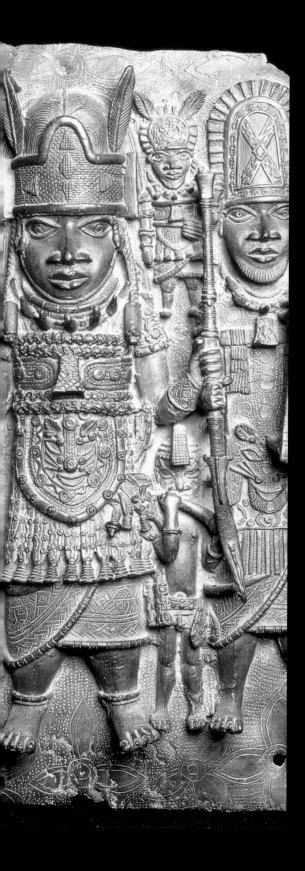

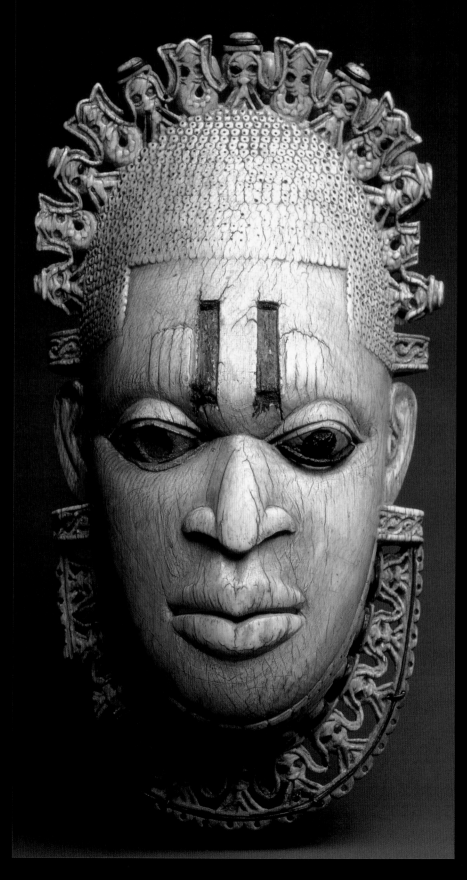

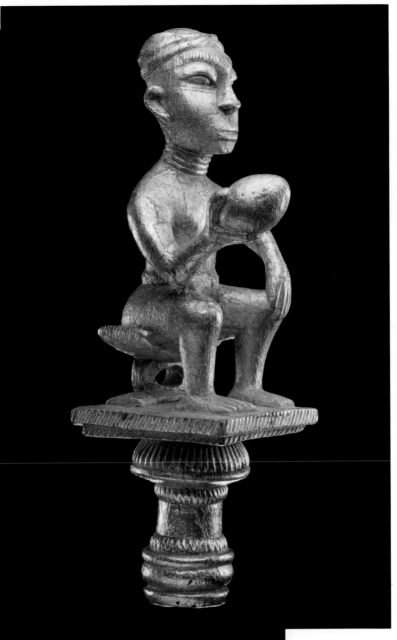

15-1. Finial of a spokesperson's staff (*okyeame poma*), from Ghana. Asante culture, 20th century. Wood and gold, height 11¼" (28.57 cm). Musée Barbier-Mueller, Geneva

Political power is like an egg, says an Asante proverb. Grasp it too tightly and it will shatter in your hand; hold it too loosely and it will slip from your fingers. Whenever the *okyeame*, or spokesperson, for one twentieth-century Asante ruler was conferring with that ruler or communicating the ruler's words to others, he held before him a staff with this symbolic caution on the use and abuse of power prominently displayed on the gilded finial (fig. 15-1).

From the time of the first European explorations of Africa, quantities of artworks—such as this staff—were shipped back to Western museums of natural history or ethnography, where the works were exhibited as curious artifacts of "primitive" cultures (see "The Myth of 'Primitive' Art," opposite). Toward the end of the nineteenth century, however, profound changes in Western thinking about art gradually led more and more people to appreciate the inherent aesthetic qualities of these unfamiliar objects and at last to embrace them fully as art (see "African Furniture and the Art Deco Style," page 358). In recent years, scholars have further enriched the world's vision of traditional African arts by exploring their rich meaning from the point of view of the people who made and used them. If we are to attempt to understand artwork such as this staff on its own terms, we must first take it out of the glass museum case where we usually encounter it and imagine it playing a vital role in human life.

Early African Art

Africa is a land of enormous diversity. Geographically, it ranges from enormous deserts to tropical rain forests, from flat grasslands to spectacular mountains and dramatic rift valleys. Human diversity in Africa is equally impressive. More than 1,000 languages have been identified, representing a seemingly infinite variety of cultures, each with its own history, customs, and art forms. Africa is the site of one of the great ancient civilizations, that of Egypt (Chapter 2), and North Africa later contributed prominently to the development of Islamic art and culture.

As we saw in Chapter 1, the history of African art begins in the Paleolithic era. Like prehistoric people around the world, early Africans painted and inscribed an abundance of images on the walls of the caves and rock shelters in which they sought refuge. The mountains of the central Sahara have especially fascinating examples of rock art, with the earliest images dating from at least 8000 BCE. At that time, the Sahara was a great grassy plain, perhaps much like the game-park areas of modern East Africa. Vivid images of hippopotamuses, elephant, giraffe, antelope, and other animals incised into rock surfaces testify to the abundant wildlife that roamed the region.

By 4000 BCE, hunting had given way to herding as the Saharan climate became more arid. Rock art from the herding period shows scenes of sheep, goats, and cattle and the people who tended them (see fig. 1-12). The desiccation of the Sahara coincided with the rise of Egyptian civilization along the Nile Valley to the east. As the Saharan grasslands dried up, some of their inhabitants may have migrated to the Nile Valley region in search of arable land and pasture. Perhaps this migration, by greatly expanding the population of the valley, contributed to the tensions that resulted in the emergence of complex forms of social organization there.

Saharan people presumably migrated southward as well, into the Sudan, the broad belt of grassland that stretches across Africa south of the Sahara desert, bringing with them knowledge of settled agriculture and animal husbandry. Agriculture reached the Sudan by at least 3000 BCE,

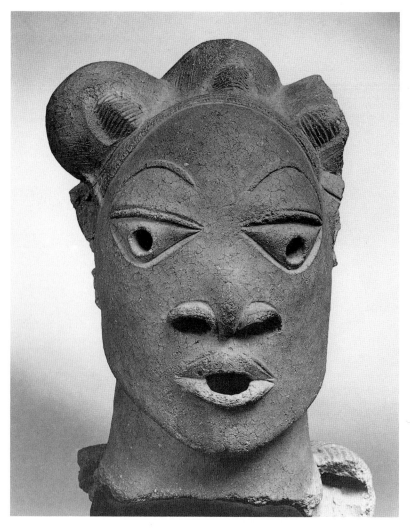

15-2. Head. Nok culture, c. 500 BCE–200 CE. Terra-cotta, height 14³/₁₆" (36 cm). National Museum, Lagos, Nigeria

and knowledge of ironworking spread across the Sudan toward the middle of the first millennium BCE.

Some of the earliest evidence of iron technology in sub-Saharan Africa comes from the so-called Nok culture, which arose in the western Sudan, in present-day Nigeria, as early as 500 BCE. The Nok people were farmers who grew grain and oil-bearing seeds; they were also smelters with the technology for refining ore. In addition, they created the earliest known sculpture of sub-Saharan Africa, producing accomplished **terra-cotta** figures of human and animal subjects between about 500 BCE and 200 CE.

The Nok head shown here (fig. 15-2), slightly larger than lifesize, originally formed part of a complete figure. The triangular or D-shaped eyes are characteristic of Nok style and appear also on sculpture of animals. Each of the large buns of the elaborate hairstyle is pierced with a hole that may have held ornamental feathers. Other Nok figures boast large quantities of beads and other prestige ornaments. Nok sculpture may represent ordinary people dressed up for a special occasion, or it may portray people of high status, providing evidence of social stratification in this early farming society.

The Nok region of present-day Nigeria remained a vigorous cultural and artistic center after this culture disappeared. The city of Ife, which was, and remains, the sacred city of the Yoruba people, arose in the southern, forested part of that region by about 800 CE. Yoruba myth tells how at Ife the gods descended from heaven

In some African cultures, elaborate stools or chairs were created not only to indicate their owners' status but also to serve as altars for their souls after death. Thrones and other important seats in Africa are often carved from a single block of wood. This is the case with a chair taken from the Ngombe people, who live along the Congo River in the former Zaire. The back is cantilevered out from the seat, which is in turn supported by four massive, braced legs. The rich surface decoration consists of European brass carpet tacks and darker iron tacks arranged in parallel lines and diamond patterns. The use of the tacks (imported goods) indicates that the owner had access to the extensive trade routes linking people of the inland forest to people of the coast. Both copper and iron were precious materials in central Africa: they were used as currency long before contact with Europe, and they were associated with both high social status and spirituality. The chair was thus an object of both beauty and power.

France began to colonize Africa in the late

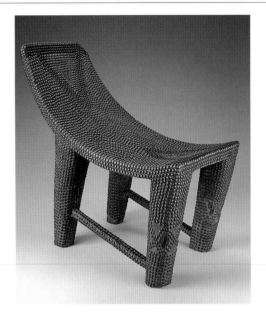

Chair, Ngombe people, Democratic Republic of the Congo. Wood, brass, and iron tacks, 25⅝" (65.1 cm). National Museum of African Art, Washington, D.C. Museum Purchases, 90-4-1

nineteenth century, and African objects were brought to France by soldiers, administrators, and adventurers. Colonial expositions held in France in 1919 and 1923 displayed trophies from the newly vanquished territories, including household objects and artworks from African courts. Just as painters and sculptors such as Picasso and Matisse were inspired by the formal power of African masks, the French designer Pierre Legrain (1889–1929) recognized

the aesthetic excellence of African furniture. Legrain made a fairly faithful reproduction of this Ngombe chair but adapted the simple, elegant forms of other African furniture to French taste. His Africa-inspired pieces appeared in the definitive 1925 exhibition, *Exposition Internationale des Arts Décoratifs et Industriels Modernes*, where the term Art Deco was given to describe the geometric quality of many of the objects displayed there.

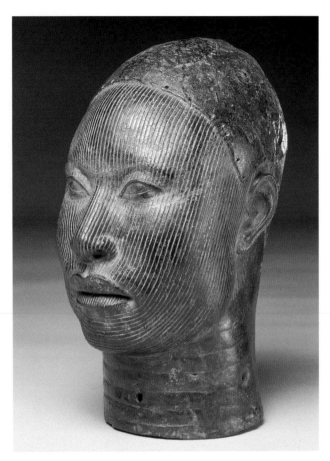

15-3. Head of a king, from Ife. c. 13th century CE. Brass, height 11⁷/₁₆" (29 cm). Museum of Ife Antiquities, Ife, Nigeria

The naturalism of Ife sculpture contradicted everything Europeans thought they knew about African art. The German scholar who "discovered" Ife sculpture in 1910 suggested that it had been created not by Africans but by survivors from the legendary lost island of Atlantis. Later scholars speculated that influence from ancient Greece or Renaissance Europe must have reached Ife. Scientific dating methods, however, finally put such misleading comparisons and prejudices to rest. When naturalism flowered in Ife, the ancient Mediterranean world was long gone and the European Renaissance still to come. In addition, the proportions of the few known full figures are characteristically African, with the head composing as much as one quarter of the total height. These proportions probably reflect a belief in the head's importance as the abode of the spirit and the focus of individual identity.

on iron chains to create the world. Ife artists created remarkable, naturalistic works of sculpture. The Ife sculptural tradition began about 1050 CE and flourished for some four centuries.

A lifesize brass head of an *oni* (king) shows the extraordinary artistry achieved by Ife sculptors (fig. 15-3). The modeling of the flesh is extremely sensitive, especially around the nose and mouth. The eyes are strikingly similar in shape to those of some modern Yoruba, and the face is covered with decorative parallel **scarification** patterns (decorations made by scarring). Holes along the scalp apparently permitted the attachment of hair or a crown or perhaps a beaded veil. The head may have been attached to a wooden mannequin using the large holes at the base of

the neck. The mannequin was probably dressed in a deceased *oni*'s robes and used for display during his memorial services.

It is likely that Ife was the artistic parent of the great city-state of Benin, which arose some 150 miles to the southeast. According to oral histories, the earliest kings of Benin belonged to the Ogiso, or Skyking, dynasty. After a long period of misrule, however, the people of Benin asked the *oni* of Ife for a new ruler. The *oni* sent Prince Oranmiyan, who founded a new dynasty in 1170 CE. Some two centuries later, the fourth king, or *oba*, of Benin decided to start a tradition of memorial sculpture like that of Ife. He sent to Ife for a master metal caster named Iguegha. The tradition of casting memorial heads for the shrines

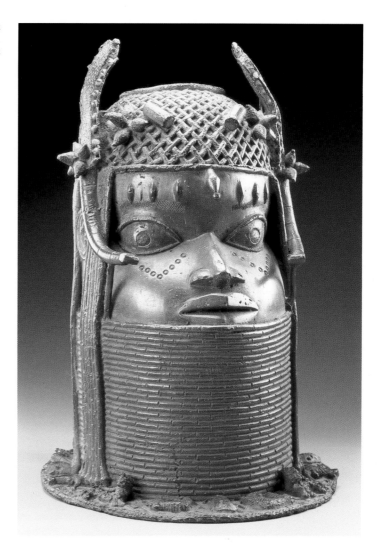

15-4. Head of an *oba* (king), from Benin. C. 1700–1897 CE (Late Period). Brass, height 17¾" (45 cm). Museum für Völkerkunde, Vienna/Musée Dapper, Paris

of royal ancestors endures among the successors of Oranmiyan to this day.

Benin brass heads range from small, thinly cast, naturalistic images to large, thickly cast, highly stylized representations. The dating of these works is controversial, but many scholars have concluded that the smallest, most naturalistic heads were created during a so-called Early Period (1400–1550 CE), when Benin artists were still heavily influenced by those of Ife. The memorial heads grew increasingly stylized during the Middle Period (1550–1700 CE), becoming very large and heavy during the ensuing Late Period (1700–1897 CE), with angular, stylized features and an elaborate beaded crown (fig. 15-4). A similar crown is still worn by the present-day *oba*.

All of the heads include representations of coral-bead necklaces, which have been part of the royal costume from earliest times to the present day. In Late Period sculpture, the necklaces form a tall, cylindrical mass that obscures the chin and greatly adds to the weight of the sculpture. The increase in size and weight of Benin memorial heads over time may reflect the growing power and wealth of the *oba* deriving from Benin's expanding trade with Europe. Benin traded with Portugal from the late fifteenth century, first in ivory and forest products and later, tragically, in slaves. Commerce between Benin and Europe flourished until 1897, when, in reprisal for the massacre of a party of trade negotiators, British troops sacked and burned the royal palace of Benin, sending the *oba* into an exile from which he did not return until 1914.

The metal sculpture of Benin is a royal art; only the *oba* could commission works in brass. Among the most remarkable visual records of court life are the hundreds of brass plaques, each about 2 feet square, that once decorated the walls and columns of the royal palace. The plaques, produced during the Middle Period, are sometimes in such high relief that the figures are almost freestanding. An exceptionally detailed example (fig. 15-5) shows a general holding a

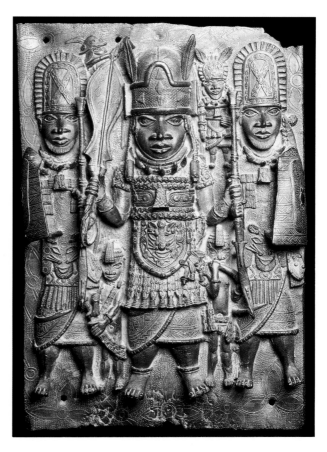

15-5. *General and Officers*, from Benin. C. 1550–1650 CE. Brass, height 21" (53.5 cm). National Museum, Lagos, Nigeria

The general wears an elaborate, appliqué apron depicting the head of a leopard, and the flanking officers wear leopard pelts. Leopards were symbols of royalty in Benin. Live leopards were kept at the royal palace, where they were looked after by a special keeper. Water pitchers in the form of leopards were cast in bronze and placed on altars dedicated to ancestors. An engraving from a European travel book of the sixteenth century depicts a procession of courtiers in Benin led by a pair of magnificent leopards.

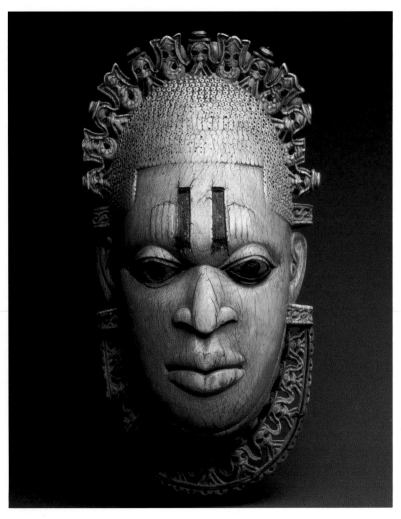

15-6. Mask representing an *iyoba*, from Benin. c. 1550 CE. Ivory, iron, and copper, height 9¼" (23.4 cm). The Metropolitan Museum of Art, New York
The Michael C. Rockefeller Memorial Collection, Gift of Nelson A. Rockefeller, 1972 (1978.412.323)

spear in one hand and a ceremonial sword in the other. Flanking him, two officers brandish spears and shields. Their helmets indicate their rank. Above the tip of the general's sword is a small figure of a Portuguese soldier.

Obas also commissioned important works in ivory. One example is a beautiful ornamental mask (fig. 15-6) that represents an *iyoba*, or queen mother. The *iyoba* was the woman who had borne the previous *oba*'s first male child and thus was the mother of the current *oba*. She ranked as the senior female member of the court. This mask may represent Idia, the first and best-known *iyoba*. She is particularly remembered for raising an army and using her magical powers to help her son Esigie (ruled 1504–1550 CE) defeat his enemies.

The mask, a belt or hip ornament, was probably worn at the *oba*'s waist. There were originally iron inlays in the pupils and in the scarification patterns on the forehead. The *iyoba*'s necklace represents heads of Portuguese soldiers with beards and flowing hair. (The Portuguese also helped Esigie expand his kingdom.) In her crown,

more Portuguese heads alternate with figures of mudfish, which in Benin iconography symbolized Olokun, the Lord of the Great Waters. Mudfish lived on the riverbanks, mediating between water and land, just as the *oba*, who was viewed as semidivine, mediated between the human world and the supernatural world of Olokun.

Ife and Benin were but two of the many cities that arose in ancient Africa. The first European visitors to the West African coast at the end of the fifteenth century were impressed not only by Benin, but also by the cities of Loango and Luanda near the mouth of the Congo River. Foreign ships exploring the East African coastline happened on cosmopolitan cities that had been busily carrying on long-distance trade across the Indian Ocean and with countries as far away as China and Indonesia for hundreds of years.

Important centers also arose in the interior, especially across the central and western Sudan. Wealth flowed from the trans-Saharan trade that had linked West Africa and the Mediterranean from at least the first millennium BCE. Among the most significant goods traded were salt from

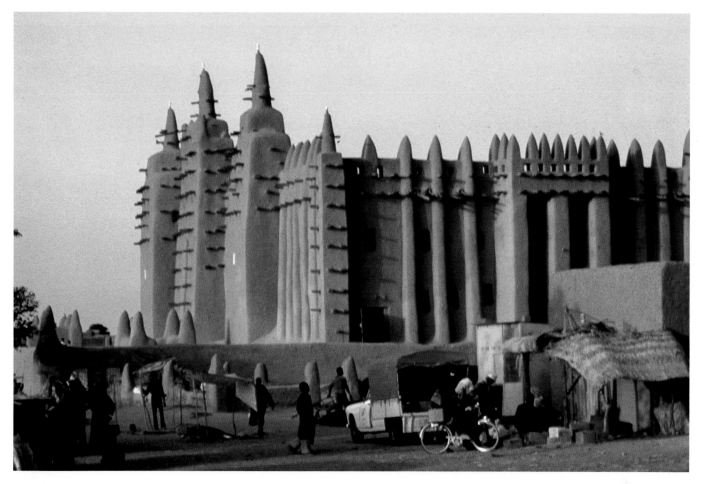

15-7. Great Friday Mosque, Djenné, Mali, showing the eastern and northern facades. Rebuilding of 1906–7, in the style of 13th-century original structure

The plan of the mosque is quite irregular. Instead of a rectangle, the building forms a parallelogram. Inside, nine long rows of heavy adobe columns some 33 feet tall run along the north-south axis, supporting a flat ceiling of palm logs. A pointed arch links each column to the next in its row, thereby forming nine east-west archways facing the *mihrab*, the niche that indicates the direction of Mecca. The mosque is augmented by an open courtyard for prayer on the west side, which is enclosed by a great double wall only slightly lower than the walls of the mosque itself.

the north and gold from West Africa. Along the banks of the Niger River, fabled cities such as Mopti, Timbuktu, and Djenné became great centers of commerce, where merchants from all over West Africa met caravans arriving from the Mediterranean coast. With this contact came the spread of Islam. By the ninth century CE, North Africa and the northern terminals of the trans-Saharan trade route were part of the Islamic empire. By the thirteenth century CE, a new language, Swahili, had developed from the longtime mingling of Arabic with local African languages.

Djenné, in present-day Mali, was one of the greatest markets in the Islamic world. Established by the third century CE, it was a major urban center by the ninth century. Koi Konboro, the twenty-sixth king of Djenné, converted to Islam in the thirteenth century and transformed his palace into the first of three successive mosques in the city. Like the two that followed, the first mosque was built of **adobe** brick, a sun-dried mixture of clay and straw. With its great surrounding wall and tall towers, it was said to have been more beautiful and more lavishly decorated than the Kaaba, the central shrine of Islam at Mecca.

The mosque eventually attracted the attention of austere Muslim rulers, who objected to its sumptuous furnishings. The early-nineteenth-century ruler Sekou Amadou had it razed and a far more humble structure erected on a new site. This second mosque was in turn replaced by the current grand mosque, constructed between 1906 and 1907 on the ancient site and in the style of the original. The architect Ismaila Traoré, the head of the Djenné guild of masons, supervised the reconstruction.

The mosque's eastern, or "marketplace," facade boasts three tall towers (fig. 15-7). The finials at the top of each tower bear ostrich eggs, symbols of fertility and purity. Tall, narrow engaged columns act as buttresses on the facade and sides of the building. These columns are characteristic of West African mosque architecture, and their cumulative rhythmic effect is one of great verticality and grandeur. The most unusual feature of West African mosques are the **torons**, wooden beams projecting from the walls. *Torons* provide permanent supports for the scaffolding erected each year so that the exterior of the mosque can be replastered.

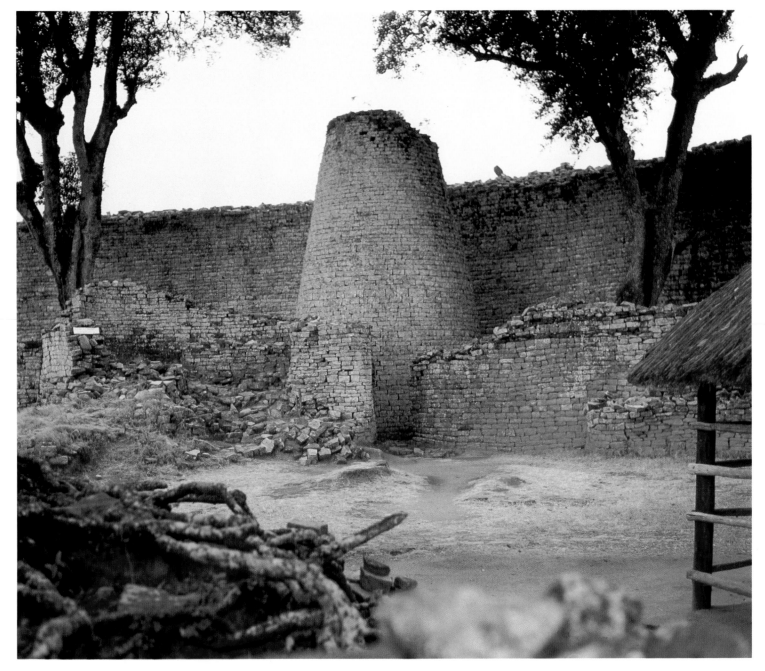

15-8. Conical Tower, Great Zimbabwe. Before 1450 CE

Several thousand miles from Djenné, in southeastern Africa, an extensive trade network developed along the Zambezi, Limpopo, and Sabi Rivers. Its purpose was to funnel gold, ivory, and exotic skins to coastal trading towns. Between 1000 and 1500 CE, this trade was largely controlled by the Shona people from a site called Great Zimbabwe. It is estimated that at the height of its power in the fourteenth century, Great Zimbabwe and its surrounding city housed a population of more than 10,000 people. A large cache of goods containing items such as Portuguese medallions, Persian pottery, and Chinese porcelain testifies to the extent of trade at Great Zimbabwe.

The word *zimbabwe* derives from the Shona term for "venerated houses" or "houses of stone," and, indeed, much of Great Zimbabwe was built

of stone. Scholars agree that the stone buildings were constructed by the ancestors of the present-day Shona people, who still live in the region. The earliest construction at the site took advantage of the enormous boulders abundant in the vicinity. Masons used the uniform granite blocks that split naturally from the boulders to build a series of tall enclosing walls high on a hilltop. Each enclosure defined a family's living or ritual space and housed dwellings made of adobe with conical thatched roofs.

The largest building complex at Great Zimbabwe is located in a broad valley below the hilltop enclosures. Known as Imba Huru, or the Big House, it was probably a royal residence or palace complex. It is ringed by a massive masonry wall constructed without mortar. This wall is more than 800 feet long, 32 feet high, and 17 feet thick at the base. Inside the outer wall are numerous smaller stone enclosures and adobe foundations representing various additions and extensions built over the centuries. As the artisans grew more skillful, they used dressed, or smoothly finished, stones and laid them in fine, level courses. A fascinating structure known simply as the Conical Tower (fig. 15-8) is one of these later additions. Some 18 feet in diameter and 30 feet high, the tower was originally capped with three courses of ornamental stonework. Resembling a large version of a present-day Shona granary, it may have represented the good harvest and prosperity believed to result from allegiance to the ruler of Great Zimbabwe.

Among the many interesting finds at Great Zimbabwe are a series of carved soapstone birds (fig. 15-9). The carvings, which originally crowned tall **monoliths**, seem to depict birds of prey, perhaps eagles. They may, however, represent mythical creatures, for the species cannot be identified. Traditional Shona beliefs include an eagle called *shiri ye denga*, or "bird of heaven," who brings lightning, a metaphor for communication, between the heavens and earth. These soapstone birds may have represented such messengers from the spirit world, or they may have served as symbols of royalty, expressing the king's power to mediate between his subjects and the supernatural world of spirits.

During the twentieth century, the sculpture of traditional African societies—wood carvings of astonishing formal inventiveness and power—have found admirers the world over. Wood decays rapidly, however, and little of African wood sculpture remains from before the nineteenth century. As a result, much of ancient Africa's artistic heritage has probably been as irretrievably lost, as have, for example, the great monuments of wooden architecture of dynastic China. Yet the beauty of ancient African creations in such durable materials as terra-cotta, stone, and bronze bears eloquent witness to the skill of ancient African artists and the splendor of the civilizations in which they worked.

African Art in the Modern Era: Living Traditions and New Trends

European exploration and subsequent colonization of the African continent brought its flourishing and diverse societies into sudden and traumatic contact with the "modern," largely European, world. European ships first visited sub-Saharan Africa in the fifteenth century, but for the next several hundred years, European contact with Africa was almost entirely limited to coastal areas, where trade, including the devastating slave trade, was carried out. During the nineteenth century, however, as the trade in

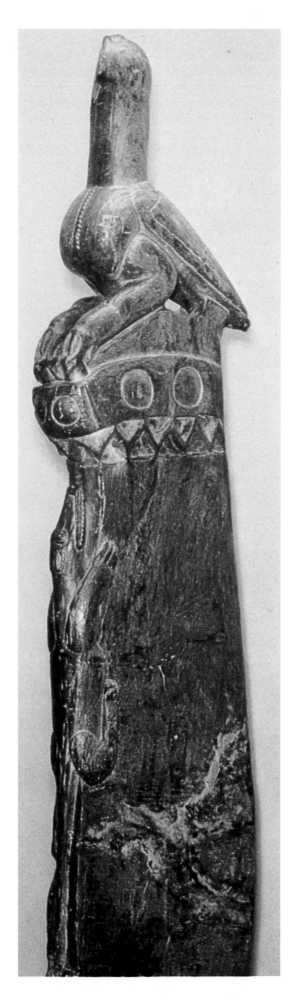

15-9. **Bird, top part of a monolith, from Great Zimbabwe.** c. 1200–1400 CE. Soapstone, height 14¹/₂" (36.8 cm). Great Zimbabwe Site Museum, Zimbabwe

slaves to the West was gradually eliminated, European explorers, soon followed by Christian missionaries, began to investigate the unmapped African interior. Drawn by the potential wealth of Africa's natural resources, European governments began to seek territorial concessions from African rulers. Diplomacy soon gave way to force, and, toward the end of the century, competition among rival powers fueled the so-called

---

Numumusow and West African Ceramics

In many West African cultures, fired ceramics are made exclusively by women. Among the Mande-speaking people of Mali, Burkina Faso, Guinea, and Ivory Coast, potters are *numumusow*, female members of *numu* lineages, and hold an important place in society. Women from these families may resolve disputes and initiate girls; their husbands, fathers, and sons are the sculptors and blacksmiths of the Mande.

Numumusow make a wide selection of vessels, including huge storage jars. The shapes of these pots reflect their intended use, from wide bowls and cooking pots to narrow-necked stoppered water bottles, from large storage vessels to small eating dishes. The *numumusow* form the soft and sticky clay by coiling and modeling with their fingers. They decorate their vessels by burnishing (polishing), engraving, or by adding pellets or coils of clay or by coloring with slip (a wash of colored clay). The vessels are fired at low temperatures in a shallow pit or in the open: this produces a ware that can be used to cook over an open fire without breaking.

Even though most urban Africans use metal and plastic dishes and cook-ware today, large earthenware jars still keep water cool and clean in areas where refrigeration is expensive. In the past, water-storage jars were public display pieces, standing near the entrance to the house, where a guest would be offered a drink of cool water as an essential part of hospitality. Mande vessels for drinking water are often decorated with incised lines and molded ridges. On older wares such as this example, raised images of figures or lizards might have referred to Mande myths or to philosophical concepts.

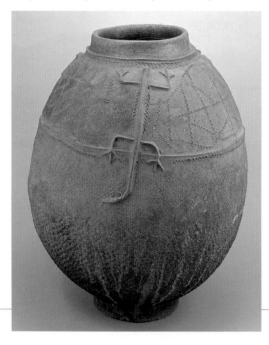

Jar, from Bamana, Mali.
20th century. Earthenware, 23½ x 18¾" (59.7 x 47.6 cm). The Nelson-Atkins Museum of Art, Kansas City, Missouri Purchase: The George H. and Elizabeth O. Davis Fund

---

scramble for Africa, when European leaders raced to lay claim to whatever portion of the continent they were powerful enough to seize. By 1914, virtually all of Africa was under colonial rule.

In the years following World War I, nationalistic movements arose across Africa. From 1945 through the mid-1970s, one colony after another gained its independence, and the map of modern African nations took substantial shape. Many contemporary African artists, including Ouattara, Magdalene Odundo, and Cheri Samba, have come of age in a postcolonial culture that mingles European and African elements. Drawing on these diverse influences, they have established a place in the lively international art scene along with their European, American, and Asian counterparts, and their work is shown as readily in Paris, Tokyo, and Los Angeles as it is in the African cities of Abidjan, Kinshasa, and Dakar.

At the same time, other African artists have continued to create the traditional art objects that play a vital part in the spiritual and social life of the community (see "Numumusow and West African Ceramics," left). The living arts of traditional cultures today, together with collections of African art in both Africa and the West, enable us to better understand the historic role of these enduring objects in the cycle of daily life.

Much traditional African art is devoted to dealings with the spirit world. Spirits are believed to inhabit the fields that produce crops, the rivers that provide fish, the forests that are home to game, the land that must be cleared in order to build a new village. A family, too, includes spirits—those of its ancestors as well as those of children yet unborn. In the blessing or curse of these myriad spirits lies the difference between success and failure in life.

To communicate with these all-important spirits, African societies usually rely on a specialist in ritual—a person known elsewhere in the world as priest, minister, rabbi, pastor, imam, or shaman. Each African people has its own name for this specialist, but for simplicity we can refer to them all as diviners. Diviners open the lines of communication between the supernatural and human worlds through such techniques as prayer, sacrifice, offerings, magic, divination, and even the creation of images that give spirits a physical form.

Among the most potent images of power in African art are the *nkisi*, or spirit, figures made by the Kongo and Songye people of the Democratic Republic of the Congo (formerly Zaire). The best known of these are the large wooden *nkonde* figures, which bristle with nails, pins, blades, and other sharp objects (fig. 15-10). A *nkisi nkonde* begins its life as a simple, unadorned wooden figure that may be purchased from a carver at a market or commissioned by a diviner on behalf of a client who has encountered some adversity or who faces some important turning point in his or her life. Drawing on vast knowledge, the diviner prescribes certain magical/medicinal ingredients, called *bilongo*, that will help solve the client's problem. These *bilongo*, which may include human hair, nail clippings, and other animal, plant, or mineral ingredients, are added to the figure, either mixed with white clay and plastered directly onto the body or held in a packet suspended from the neck or waist.

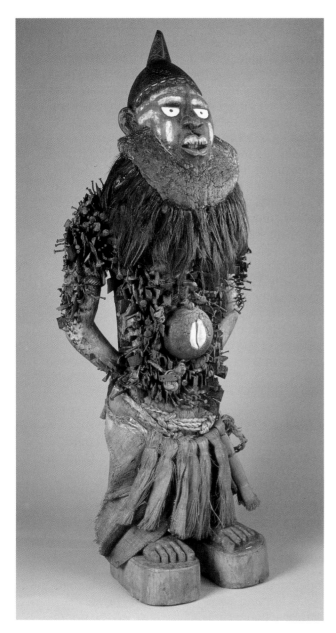

15-10. Power figure (*nkisi nkonde*), from the Democratic Republic of the Congo (formerly Zaire). Kongo culture, 19th century. Wood, nails, pins, blades, and other materials, height 44" (111.7 cm). The Field Museum, Chicago
Acquisition A109979 c

Who Made African Art?

On label after label identifying African artworks exhibited in museums, a standard piece of information is missing. Where are the artists' names? Who made this art?

Until quite recently, Westerners tended to see Africa as a single country and not as an immense continent of vastly diverse cultures. Morover, they perceived artists working in Africa as obedient craftspeople, bound to styles and images dictated by village elders and producing art that was anonymous and interchangeable. Explorers, colonial officers, and missionaries who filled the storerooms of European museums rarely asked who had made or owned the objects they were acquiring.

Over the past several decades, however, these misconceptions have begun to crumble. One of the first non-Africans to understand that African art, as much as European art, was the work of identifiable artists was the Belgian art historian Frans Olbrechts. During the 1930s, while assembling a group of objects from present-day Democratic Republic of the Congo for an exhibition, Olbrechts noted that as many as ten figures had been carved in a very distinctive style. A look at the labels revealed that two of the statues had been collected in the same town, Buli, in eastern Congo. Accordingly, Olbrechts named the unknown African artist the Master of Buli. In the late 1970s, the owners of an object in the style of the Master of Buli identified the artist as Ngongo ya Chintu, of Kateba village. Kateba villagers in turn remembered Ngongo ya Chintu as an artist of great skill. The story of Ngongo ya Chintu showed clearly that African artists did not work anonymously and that Africans were fully aware of the names of their artists. Art historians and anthropologists have now identified numerous African artists and compiled catalogs of their work. Certainly we will never known the names of the vast majority of African artists of the past, just as we do not know the names of the sculptors responsible for the portrait busts of ancient Rome or the monumental reliefs of the Hindu temples of South Asia. But as elsewhere, the greatest artists in Africa were famous and sought after, while innumerable others labored honorably and not at all anonymously.

The *bilongo* transform the *nkonde* into a living being with frightful powers, ready to attack the forces of evil on behalf of a human client. Each *bilongo* ingredient has a specific role in activating the figure. For example, the Kongo people admire the quickness and agility of a particular species of mouse. Tufts of this mouse's hair included in the *bilongo* ensure that the *nkisi nkonde* will act rapidly when its powers are activated.

To mobilize the figure's powers, clients drive a nail or other pointed object into the *nkisi nkonde*, which may serve many private and public functions. Two warring villages might agree to end their conflict by swearing an oath of peace in the presence of the *nkonde* and then driving a nail into it to seal the agreement. A mother might invoke the power of the *nkonde* to heal her sick children. Two merchants might agree to a partnership by driving two small nails into the figure side by side and then make their pact binding by wrapping the nails together with a stout cord.

Some African people conceive of the spirit world as a parallel realm in which spirits may have families, attend markets, live in villages, and possess personalities complete with faults and virtues. The Baule people in Ivory Coast believe that each of us lived in the spirit world before we were born. While there, we had a spirit spouse, whom we left behind when we entered this life. A person who has difficulty assuming his or her gender-specific role as an adult Baule—a man who has not married, for example, or a woman who has not borne children—may dream of his or her spirit spouse.

For such a person, the diviner may prescribe the carving of an image of the spirit spouse

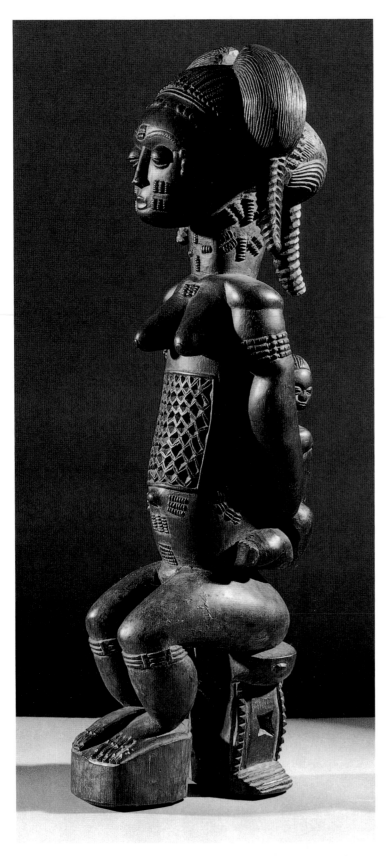

15-11. Spirit spouse (blolo bla), from Ivory Coast. Baule culture, early 20th century. Wood, height 17¹/₈" (43.5 cm). University Museum, University of Pennsylvania, Philadelphia

(fig. 15-11)—either a female figure (blolo bla) for a man or a male figure (blolo bian) for a woman. The figures display the most admired and desirable marks of beauty so that the spirit spouses may be encouraged to enter and inhabit them. The owner keeps the figure in his or her room, dressing it in beautiful textiles and jewelry, washing it, anointing it with oil, feeding it, and caressing it. The Baule hope that by caring for and pleasing their spirit spouse a balance may be restored that will free their human life to unfold smoothly.

As in societies throughout the world, art in Africa is also used to identify those who hold power, to validate their right to kingship or their authority as representatives of the family or community. The gold-and-wood spokesperson's staff with which this chapter opened is an example of the art of leadership (see fig. 15-1). It belongs to the culture of the Asante people of Ghana, in West Africa, and was probably carved in the 1960s or 1970s by Kojo Bonsu (see "Who Made African Art?," page 365). The son of a famous carver, Osei Bonsu, Kojo Bonsu lives in the Asante city of Kumasi and continues to carve prolifically. He decorated the staff with **gold leaf**, a sign of the object's importance. Gold was a major source of power for the Asante, who traded it for centuries, first across the Sahara to the Mediterranean world, and then directly to Europeans on the West African coast.

Yoruba kings manifested their power through the large, complex palaces in which they lived. In a typical palace plan, the principal rooms opened onto a veranda with elaborate figured posts fronting a courtyard. Dense, highly descriptive figure carving also covered the doors. The finest architectural sculptor of modern times was Olówè of Isè, who carved doors and veranda posts for the rulers of the Ekìtì-Yoruba kingdoms in southwestern Nigeria.

The door of the royal palace in Ikéré (fig. 15-12) illustrates Olówè's artistry. Its asymmetrical composition combines narrative and symbolic scenes in horizontal rectangular panels. Tall figures carved in profile end in heads facing out to confront the viewer. Their long necks and elaborate hairstyles make them appear even taller, unlike typical Yoruba sculpture, which uses short static figures. The figures are in such high relief that the upper portions are actually carved in the round. The figures move energetically against an underlying decorative pattern, and the entire surface of the doors is also painted.

Olówè seems to have worked from the early 1900s until his death in 1938. Although famous throughout Yorubaland and called upon by patrons as distant as 60 miles from his home, few records of his activities remain, and only one European, Philip Allison, wrote of meeting him and watching him work. Allison described Olówè

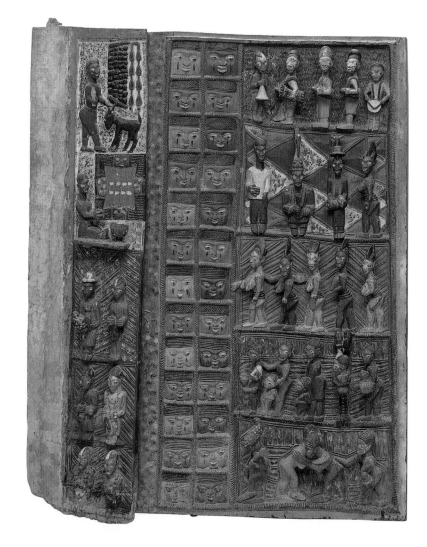

15-12. **Olówè of Isè, from Yoruba. Door from royal palace in Ikéré.** c. 1925. Wood, pigment, height 6'2⁷/₈" (1.9 m). The Detroit Institute of the Arts Acc. 1997.80 .A & .B. Gift of Bethea and Irwin Green in honor of the 20th anniversary of the Department of African, Oceanic and New World Cultures

carving the iron-hard African oak "as easily as [he would] a calabash [gourd]."

Woven textiles, called **kente**, also once signaled status in West Africa (fig. 15-13). The pattern of the Asante kente cloth here, known as *oyokoman ogya da mu*—meaning "there is a fire between two factions of the Oyoko clan"—refers to the civil war that followed the death of the Asante king Osei Tutu in about 1730. Traditionally, only the king of the Asante was allowed to wear this pattern. Other patterns were reserved for members of the royal family or the court. Commoners who dared to wear a restricted pattern were severely punished.

Kente cloth is made on small, light looms that produce long, narrow strips of fabric. Asante weavers begin by laying out the long **warp** (vertical) threads in a brightly colored pattern. Today the threads are likely to be rayon. Formerly, however, they were silk, which the Asante produced by unraveling Chinese cloth obtained through European trade. **Weft** threads woven through the warp produce complex patterns, including double weaves in which the front and back of the cloth display different patterns. The long strips

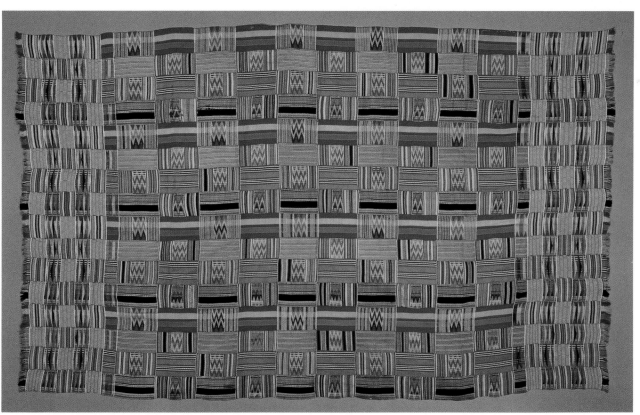

15-13. Kente cloth, from Ghana. Asante culture, 20th century. Silk, 6'10⁹/₁₆" x 4'3⁹/₁₆" (2.10 x 1.31 m). National Museum of African Art and National Museum of Natural History, Washington, D.C.
Purchased with funds provided by the Smithsonian Collections Acquisition Program, 1983–85, EJ 10583

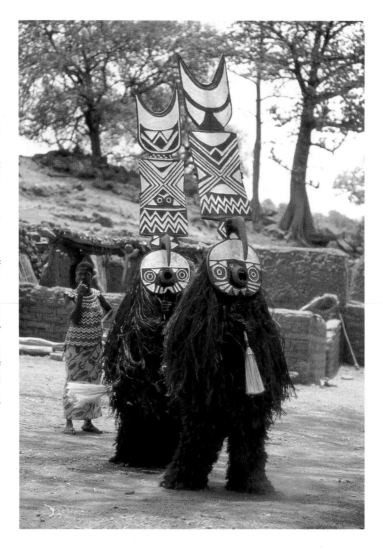

15-14. Two masks in performance, from Dossi, Burkina Faso. Bwa culture, 1984. Wood, mineral pigments, and fiber, height approx. 7' (2.13 m)

The Bwa have been making and using such masks since well before Burkina Faso achieved its independence in 1960. We might assume their use is centuries old, but in this case, the masks are a comparatively recent innovation. The elders of the Bwa family who own these masks state that they, like all Bwa, once followed the cult of the spirit of Do, who is represented by masks made of leaves. In the last quarter of the nineteenth century, the Bwa were the targets of slave raiders from the north and east. Their response to this new danger was to acquire wooden masks from their neighbors, for such masks seemed a more effective and powerful way of communicating with spirits who could help them. Thus, faced with a new form of adversity, the Bwa sought a new tradition to cope with it.

produced on the loom are then cut to size and sewn together to form large rectangles of finished *kente* cloth. In present-day Ghana, the wearing of *kente* and other traditional textiles is encouraged, and patterns are no longer restricted to a particular person or group.

Traditional clothes, costumes, and, particularly, masks of many varieties play an important role in African life today. Among the Bwa people of central Burkina Faso, masks depicting spirits are used regularly in ceremonies. When young Bwa men and women are initiated into adulthood following the onset of puberty, they are taught about the world of nature spirits and about the wooden masks that represent them.

The initiates are first separated from younger playmates by older relatives who "kidnap" them and explain their disappearance in the community by saying that they have been devoured by wild beasts. The initiates are stripped of their clothing and made to sleep on the ground without blankets. Isolated from the community, they are taught about the spirit world invoked by the masks. Although they have seen these masks all their lives, they learn for the first time that they

are made of wood and have been worn by their older brothers and cousins. They learn of the spirit each mask represents, and they memorize the story of each spirit's encounter with the founding ancestors of the clan. Returning to the community, the initiates display their new knowledge in a public ceremony. Each boy performs with one of the masks, in a dance that expresses the character and personality the mask represents. The girls, who are not allowed to wear the masks, sing the songs that accompany each one. At the end of the ceremony, the young men and women rejoin their families as adults, ready to marry, start farms, and begin families of their own.

Most Bwa masks depict spirits in human or animal form. Among the most spectacular masks, however, are abstract examples crowned with a tall, narrow plank, which represent spirits that have taken neither animal nor human form (fig. 15-14). The patterns of these abstract masks convey a message about the proper moral conduct of life. The white crescent at the top represents the quarter moon, under which initiations are held. The large central X represents the scar that every initiated Bwa wears as a mark of devotion. The horizontal zigzags at the bottom represent the path of ancestors and symbolize adherence to traditional ways. The hooked shape that projects in front of the face is said to represent the beak of the hornbill, a bird associated with the supernatural world and believed to be an intermediary between the living and the dead.

Africa also has a rich tradition of funerary art, of which that of Egypt is probably the best known in the West (Chapter 2). All over Africa, when death comes, special ceremonies and rituals help the community to mourn. The death of a child is a particularly traumatic event. The Yoruba people of Nigeria have one of the highest rates of twin births in the world. The birth of twins is a joyful occasion, yet it is troubling as well, for twins are more delicate than single babies, and one or both may well die. When a Yoruba twin dies, the parents consult a diviner, who may tell them that an image of a twin, or *ere ibeji*, must be carved (fig. 15-15).

The mother cares for the "birth" of this image by sending the artist food while the image is being carved and gifts when it is finished. Then she dances home, carrying the figure as she would a living child, accompanied by the singing of neighborhood women. She places the figure in a shrine in her bedroom and lavishes care upon it, feeding it, dressing it richly, and anointing it with cosmetic oils. The Yoruba believe that the spirit of a dead twin thus honored may bring its parents wealth and good luck.

The female twins in figure 15-15, which may be the work of the Yoruba artist Akiode (d. 1936), radiate health and well-being. Their beautiful, glossy surfaces and rings of fat indicate that they

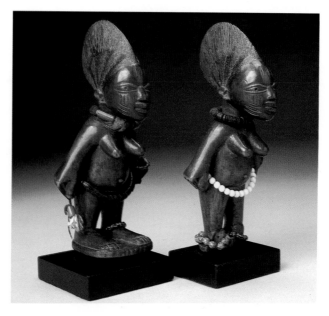

15-15. Twin figures (*ere ibeji*), from Nigeria. Yoruba culture, 20th century. Wood, height 7⅞" (20 cm). The University of Iowa Museum of Art, Iowa City
The Stanley Collection

As with other African sculpture, patterns of use result in particular signs of wear. The facial features of *ere ibeji* are often worn down or even obliterated by repeated feedings and washings. Camwood powder applied as a cosmetic builds to a thick crust in areas that are rarely handled. Even the blue indigo dye regularly applied to the hair eventually builds to a thin layer.

are well fed; breasts and other attributes signal the mature adulthood that will one day be achieved. They represent hope for survival, for the future, and for prosperity. Figures such as these reflect the enduring cycle of life that is such a vital part of African art.

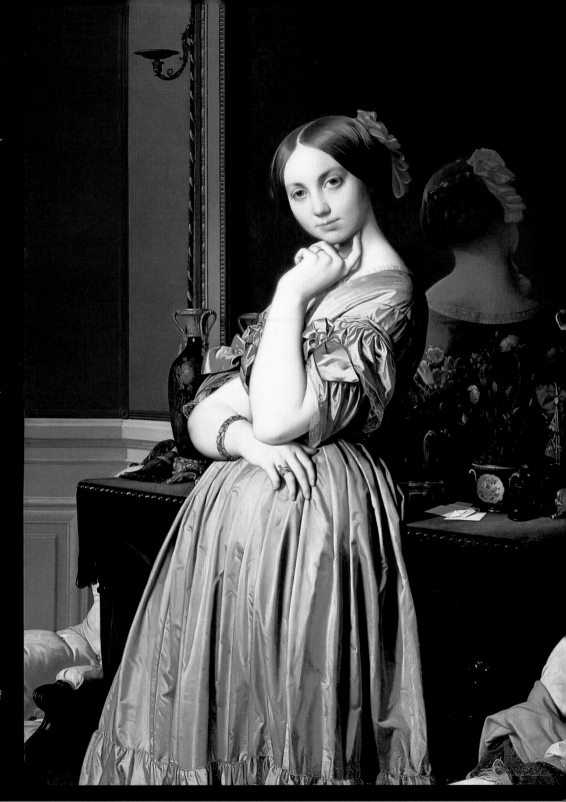

Jean-Auguste-Dominique Ingres.
The Comtesse d'Haussonville.
Dated 1845. Oil on canvas,
51⅞" x 36¼" (131.8 x 92.1 cm).
The Frick Collection, New York

Francisco Goya. *Family
of Charles* **IV.** 1800. Oil on canvas,
9'2" x 11' (2.79 x 3.36 m).
Museo del Prado, Madrid

Linear

In a linear work, *outline* (contour) defines the forms; shadow is used to help ground objects in space and to suggest their almost sculptural three-dimensionality. In this mid-nineteenth-century Neoclassical portrait by Jean-Auguste-Dominique Ingres, line is the undisputed means of definition. Ingres relies on it to delineate the beautiful head and shoulders of the countess (also reflected in the mirror behind her) as well as the interior setting. In this painting, we are hardly aware of the physical medium of paint. It is as if drawing dominates the painting. Wölfflin recognized linearity both in classical art and in all forms of Neoclassicism.

Painterly

What makes this royal family portrait by Francisco Goya a painterly work is the blending of individual forms into the larger composition through the use of brushwork and color. Goya's loose brushwork, the visible marks he makes with his brush as opposed to the seamless quality of Ingres's painted surface, is seen in the women's dresses and in the flesh tones of the figures. The turned head of the princess to the left of the queen is defined by color much more than by line. Shadows are part of the overall pattern of the design and are less important as delineators of space than is customary in a more linear painting. (Goya's self-portrait emerges from shadow near the left margin.)

K E Y S to Art History

LINEAR & PAINTERLY

In 1915, Swiss art historian Heinrich Wölfflin (1864–1945), a scholar of Renaissance and Baroque art, published his *Principles of Art History*. Wölfflin was a formalist (his approach to art was based almost solely on considerations of form), not a contextualist (one who focuses on the cultural backdrop of an art object). He wrote *Principles of Art History* to explain the change of styles on a purely visual basis from what he saw as the clear, balanced Early Renaissance style through a visually complex Baroque style.

Wölfflin set up five contrasting pairs of style characteristics: *linear* and *painterly*; plane and depth; closed form and open form; multiplicity and unity; and clarity and unclarity (roughly the difference between explicitness and implication). The first term in each pair describes the classical or Renaissance style; the second, the Baroque. Of all the pairs, the *linear/painterly* pair has proved the most enduring and became a key concept in the art history of the twentieth century. Both terms are now applied to art before and after the Renaissance and Baroque periods in Europe as well as to the arts of many cultures around the world.

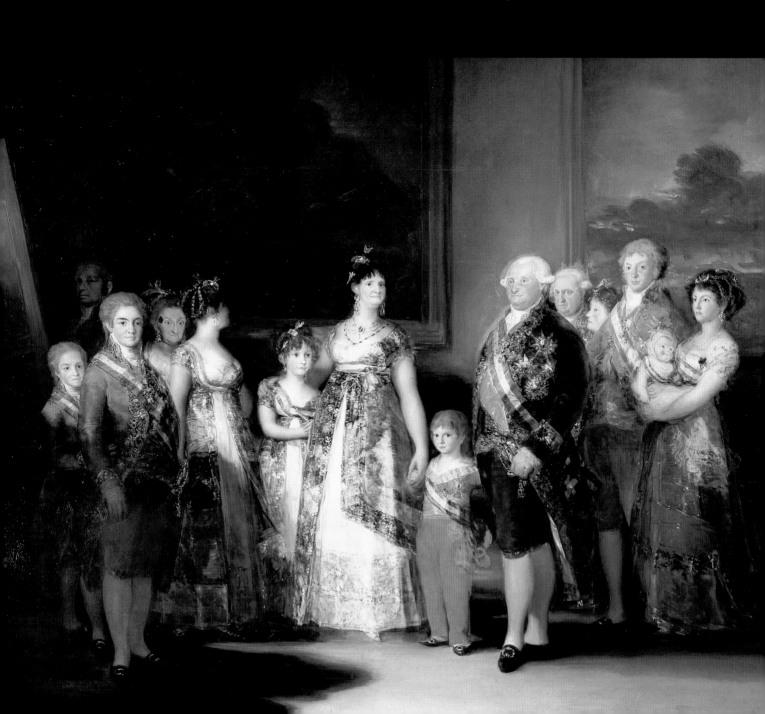

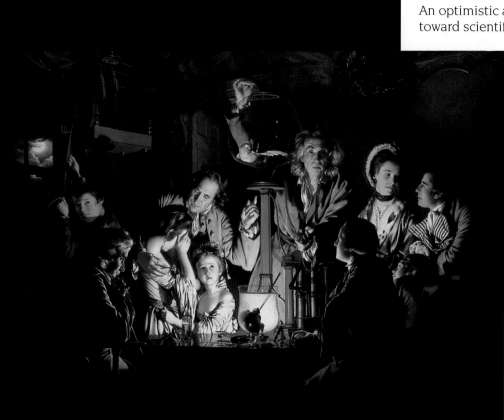

16-1. Joseph Wright. *An Experiment on a Bird in the Air-Pump.* 1768. Oil on canvas, 6 x 8' (1.83 x 2.44 m). The National Gallery, London

I n a series of paintings of scientific experiments, Joseph Wright of Derby (1734–1797) captured the romance of science and technology (fig. 16-1). While Maria Sibylla Merian and Rachel Ruysch had used their research in biology to produce Baroque botanical fantasies, Joseph Wright, in contrast, glorified the scientist as a modern wizard. In *An Experiment on a Bird in the Air-Pump*, a scientist looms over his "experiment"—the air pump featured in the scene, used to study the properties of gases. The air pump was widely featured in public demonstrations because of its dramatic possibilities. Here, the scientist has pumped air out of a glass bowl, and the bird inside has collapsed from lack of oxygen. Before the animal dies, the scientist will reintroduce air by adjusting a simple mechanism and assume the role of the great magician who resurrects the bird.

From about 1765 Joseph Wright illuminated modern scenes of science and industry with nocturnal lighting effects borrowed from seventeenth-century art (see fig. 13-22). The dramatic chiaroscuro, which recalls Baroque religious painting (see fig. 13-8), not only underscores the life-and-death aspect of the bird's fate but also suggests that science brings light into a world of darkness and ignorance. The devout expressions of some of the observers intimate that science had begun to replace religion as the hope of humanity.

An optimistic and even reverential attitude toward scientific inquiry developed in the West during the eighteenth century. Reason became the touch-stone for evaluating nearly every civilized endeavor, including philosophy, art, and politics. By extension, nature, which was thought to embody reason, was invoked to cor-roborate the correctness—and goodness—of everything from political systems to architectural designs. These beliefs led cultural historians to call the eighteenth century the Age of Enlightenment, or the Age of Reason.

An eighteenth-century manifestation that profoundly affected art was the devel-opment of historicism, or the consciousness of history. Partly as a result of this new awareness and partly stimu-lated by new discoveries in the excavations of Pompeii (Chapter 6) and Herculaneum, two Roman cities buried by the first-century eruption of Mount Vesuvius, Neoclassicism emerged in Rome in the 1760s. Neoclassicism was characterized by subject matter borrowed from ancient Greek and Roman art, stylistic dependence on antique sources, heroic nudity in sculpture and sometimes painting, classical orders in architecture, and the use of pure line in painting and drawing. These qualities were accompanied by an underlying moralism that exalted virtues popularly attributed to Republican Rome: moral incorruptibility, patriotism, and courage. In art and architecture, light and playful Rococo tendencies gave way to a general long-ing for a noble and serious mode of expression.

Neoclassicism was the dominant European artistic style in the late eighteenth and early nineteenth centuries, but running parallel with it was another strain of expression called Roman-ticism. Romantic painting and sculpture might feature fantastic or novelistic themes, perhaps set in a remote time or place and infused with a spirit of poetic fancy or melancholy. But Roman-ticism was less a specific style than an imagina-tive and "irrational" approach to art, centered in the strong subjective feelings of the artist. Many artworks of the period combine elements of Neoclassicism and Romanticism; some Neo-classic art exhibits such clearly Romantic qualities as eroticism, violence, and expressive formal distortions. At the same time, older Baroque and Rococo forms persisted. Some artists frequently moved from one style to

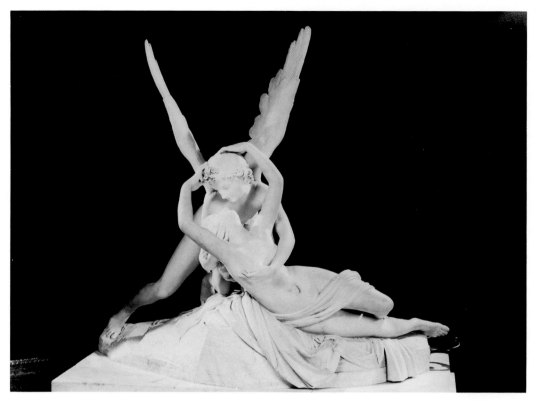

16-2. Antonio Canova. *Cupid and Psyche.* 1787–93. Marble, 5'1" x 5'8¹/₈" (1.55 x 1.73 m). Musée du Louvre, Paris

another, painting in a Baroque vein for one work, then in a Neoclassic manner for the next.

Neoclassicism and Its Heritage

Eighteenth-century Italy, with its wealth of antique ruins, was the birthplace of the Neoclassic movement. Few Italian artists, however, were stylistic innovators, although Italy could proudly point to Antonio Canova (1757–1822), the foremost Neoclassic sculptor in Europe. Born into a family of stonemasons near Venice, Canova settled in Rome in 1781, rapidly achieving such renown that critics compared him with Michelangelo. One of Canova's most admired works is the erotic mythological subject *Cupid and Psyche* (fig. 16-2). Condemned to a deathlike sleep by a jealous Venus, Psyche revives at Cupid's kiss. Here Canova combined a Romantic interest in emotion with a more typically Neoclassical appeal to the senses of sight and touch. Cupid's wings offset the rounded forms of the two linked bodies, and the lustrous off-white finish of the marble skin is played against the textures of drapery and rocks. The sculptor is said to have finished his surfaces by candlelight so that no subtlety would be lost, enabling him to produce the almost miraculously delicate shading evident in this work. Although carved fully in the round, the figures are meant to be seen in an almost two-dimensional way, as a symmetrical series of interlocking triangles and ovals. The piece also recalls the classical sculpture that attracted so many aesthetes to Rome.

Forty Years of Revolution: 1775–1815	
1775	First skirmishes of the American Revolution, Lexington and Concord, Massachusetts; George III, king of England, 1760–1820
1776	American Declaration of Independence
1781	Victory of the Americans over the English at Yorktown, New York
1787	Constitution of the United States is signed
1789	Storming of the Bastille in Paris and beginning of the French Revolution; George Washington, first president of the United States, 1789–1797
1793	Execution of Louis XVI and Marie Antoinette in Paris
1799	Napoleon takes over French government
1801–1809	Thomas Jefferson, third president of the United States
1802	Napoleon becomes life consul; emperor, 1804
1808–1814	Spanish war for independence
1812	Napoleon defeated in Russia; British-American War of 1812
1814	Napoleon abdicates and is exiled
1815	Return of Napoleon; defeat at Waterloo, second exile; Congress of Vienna divides up Europe

The end of an era: 1820, death of George III of England; 1821, death of Napoleon; 1826, death of Jefferson

PORTRAIT PAINTING

In the mid-eighteenth century many French artists began to work in a classicizing mode. For some years this was expressed primarily as a new sobriety in subject matter and treatment imposed upon Rococo forms and coloring. Marie-Louise-Élisabeth Vigée-Lebrun's 1787 portrait of the French queen, Marie Antoinette,

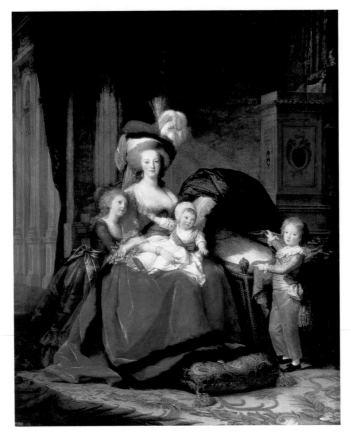

16-3. Marie-Louise-Élisabeth Vigée-Lebrun. *Portrait of Marie Antoinette with Her Children*. 1787. Oil on canvas, 9'1/4" x 7'5/8" (2.75 x 2.15 m). Musée National du Château de Versailles

As the favorite painter to the queen, Vigée-Lebrun escaped from Paris with her daughter on the eve of the Revolution of 1789 and fled to Rome. After a very successful self-exile working in Italy, Austria, Russia, and England, the artist finally resettled in Paris in 1804 at the invitation of Napoleon I and again became popular with Parisian art patrons. Over her long career, she painted around 800 portraits in a vibrant style that changed very little over the decades.

and her children falls into this mode (fig. 16-3). Painted two years before the outbreak of the French Revolution spelled the end of the Bourbon monarchy, it was hoped that the queen's depiction as a devoted mother would counter her public image as immoral, extravagant, and conniving. Marie Antoinette's youngest son squirms on her lap, and her daughter leans affectionately against her. In a poignant touch, the little dauphin—the eldest son and heir to a throne that he would never ascend—points to the empty cradle of a recently deceased sibling. Even though the French upper classes routinely used wet nurses and governesses, the image of a loving mother surrounded by children represented an ideal in the work of many Neoclassic artists (see fig. 16-8). The portrait thus identified the queen as a sister to women everywhere, united to them in sacred motherhood.

Vigée-Lebrun (1755–1842), the painter of this well-known image, was one of the most famous portraitists in France in the last quarter of the eighteenth century. In 1783 she was elected to one of the four places in the French Academy available to women (see "Art Academies in the Eighteenth Century," below). Also elected that year was Adélaïde Labille-Guiard (1749–1803), who in 1790 successfully petitioned to end the restriction on entry for women.

Art Academies in the Eighteenth Century

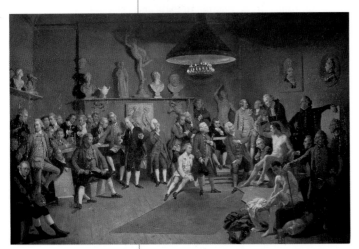

Johann Zoffany. *Academicians of the Royal Academy*. 1771–72. Oil on canvas, 47 1/2 x 59 1/2" (120.6 x 151.2 cm). The Royal Collection, Windsor Castle, New Windsor, England

During the seventeenth century, the French government founded royal academies for the instruction and encouragement of artists and architects, writers, scientists, musicians, and dancers. In 1667 the Royal Academy of Painting and Sculpture began to mount occasional exhibitions of the members' recent work.

These exhibitions came to be known as the Salons because they were held in the Salon d'Apollon (Salon of Apollo) in the Palais du Louvre. From 1737, the Salons were mounted every other year, with a jury of members selecting the works that would be shown. As the only public art exhibitions of any importance in Paris, the Salons were enormously influential in establishing officially approved styles and in molding public taste.

In England, the Royal Academy of Arts was different, in that it was a private institution independent of any interference from the Crown. Founded in 1768, it had only two functions: to operate an art school and to hold two annual exhibitions, one of art of the past and the other of contemporary art, which was open to any exhibitor on the basis of merit alone. The Royal Academy continues to function in this way today.

Besides the influential French and British academies, other art academies, public and private, sprang up throughout Europe in the eighteenth century. They primarily welcomed male artists; the number of women members was often restricted or women were welcomed only as honorary members. In France only seven women were awarded the title of academician (full member) between 1648 and 1706, and then the Royal Academy declared itself closed to women. Nevertheless, four women had been admitted by 1770, when the men again became worried that women members would become "too numerous" and declared four women would be the limit at any one time. Women were not admitted to the Academy's school or allowed to compete for Academy prizes, both of which were nearly indispensable for professional success.

Women fared even worse at London's Royal Academy. After the Swiss painters Angelica Kauffmann and Mary Moser were named founding members in 1768, no other women were elected until 1922, and then only as associates. In a 1771–1772 portrait of the London Academicians (see figure), Johann Zoffany showed the men grouped around two nude male models. Propriety prohibited the presence of women in this setting, so Zoffany painted the portraits of the female members hanging on the wall.

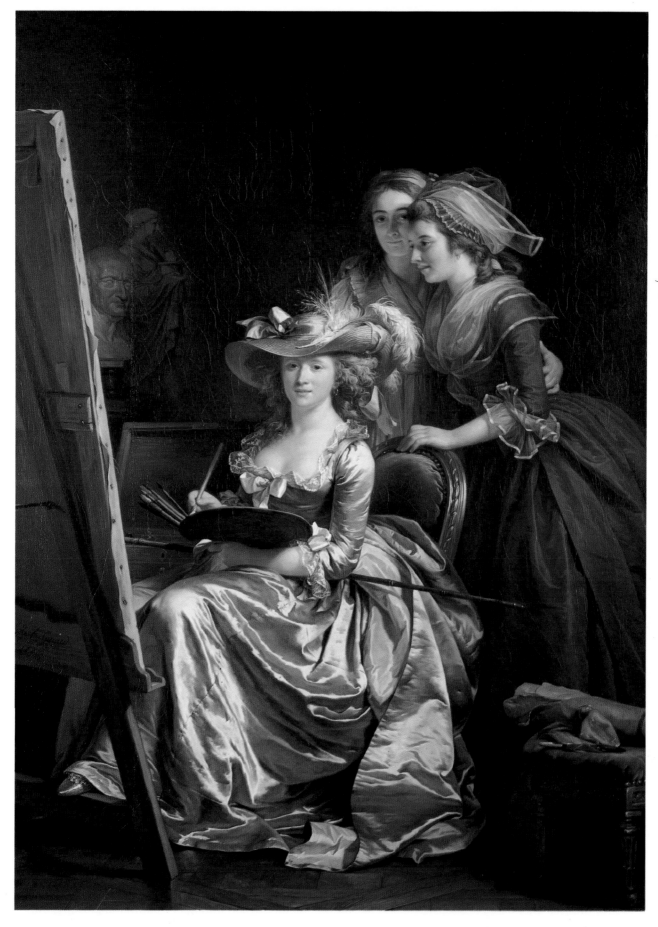

16-4. Adélaïde Labille-Guiard. *Self-Portrait with Two Pupils.* 1785. Oil on canvas, 6'11" x 4'11½" (2.11 x 1.51 m). The Metropolitan Museum of Art, New York

Gift of Julia A. Berwind, 1953

Labille-Guiard's commitment to training and promoting the interests of women painters is reflected in her *Self-Portrait with Two Pupils* (fig. 16-4). Exhibited in 1785 at the Salon, the biennial exhibition open to members of the French Academy, this monumental image of the artist at her easel was also meant to answer sexist rumors that her paintings had been painted by men. In a witty role reversal, the only male in her work is *her* muse—her father, whose portrait bust is at her

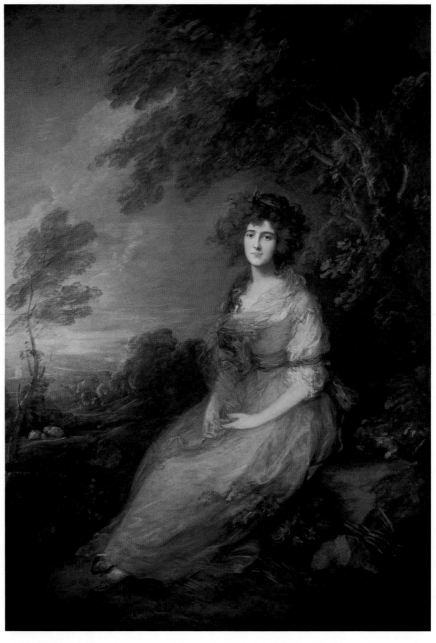

16-5. Thomas Gainsborough. *Portrait of Mrs. Richard Brinsley Sheridan.* 1785–87. Oil on canvas, 7'2¹/₂" x 5'¹/₂" (2.2 x 1.54 m). National Gallery of Art, Washington, D.C. Andrew W. Mellon Collection

side. As for style, Labille-Guiard's self-portrait, like many other paintings produced in France just before the Revolution, is relaxed, elegant, and urbane rather than severe or academic.

In England at this time, the portrait painter Thomas Gainsborough (1727–1788) achieved great success with a mode of portraiture featuring informal poses against natural vistas, derived from the kind of portraiture Van Dyck had brought to England in the 1620s. Gainsborough's *Portrait of Mrs. Richard Brinsley Sheridan* (fig. 16-5) shows the professional singer and wife of the celebrated playwright seated informally outdoors. The distant landscape view and the use of a tree to frame the sitter's head recall Van Dyck (see fig. 13-19), but the formula is updated through feathery brushwork and a lighter, Rococo palette. Innova-

tively, Gainsborough identifies the woman with the landscape, matching her windblown hair to the foliage of the tree overhead. The work illustrates one of the new values of the Enlightenment: the emphasis on nature and the natural as the sources of goodness and beauty.

In colonial North America, the taste of the settlers was generally conservative, and styles often lagged behind the European mainstream. John Singleton Copley (1738–1815), the stepson of an English immigrant painter-engraver, grew up to be North America's first portrait painter of genius. Copley's sources of inspiration were meager, but his work was already drawing attention by the time he was fifteen. He learned his craft by studying his stepfather's engravings and portraits by other immigrant painters.

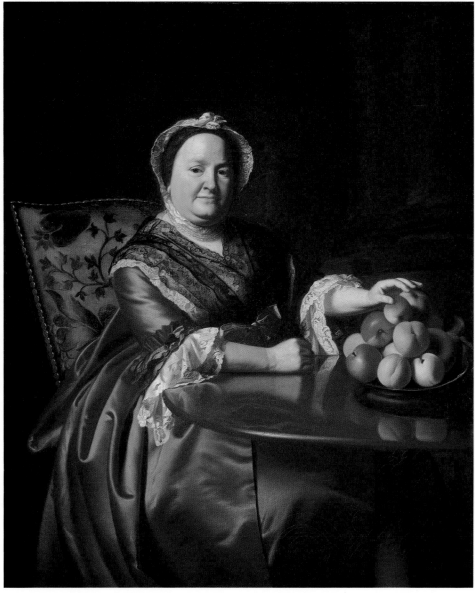

16-6. **John Singleton Copley. Mrs. Ezekiel Goldthwait (Elizabeth Lewis).** 1771. Oil on canvas, 50³/₈ x 40¹/₄" (128 x 102.2 cm). Museum of Fine Arts, Boston
Bequest of John T. Bowen in memory of Eliza M. Bowen, 1941

Copley's clients valued not only his excellent technique, which equaled that of European artists, but also his ability to dignify them while recording their features with unflinching realism. In his portrait of *Mrs. Ezekiel Goldthwait* (*Elizabeth Lewis*) (fig. 16-6), painted in 1771, Copley displayed the sitter's prosperity by painting her dressed in a lace-trimmed silk dress and seated at a mahogany table. But her open, amiable features, strong, thick wrists, and large, capable hands show a lack of vanity and a commitment to hard work that seem to personify the spirit of Puritan New England.

Copley's talents so outdistanced those of his colonial contemporaries that the artist aspired to a larger reputation. In June 1774, he sailed for Europe, where he visited London, Paris, and Italy. He spent the rest of his life in London, where he settled in 1775. For over a century, many of the most talented artists of the young United States followed in Copley's footsteps, going to Europe to obtain the best training and to forward their careers.

MORALIZED GENRE PAINTING

Mrs. Sheridan and Mrs. Goldthwait were members of the growing middle class made up of newly prosperous merchants and professionals. Many now had the money to commission portraits just as their upper-class contemporaries did, and they also helped to fuel the market for a type of painting known as moralized genre painting, first developed in the Netherlands in the seventeenth century. Pictures of this type featured scenes from everyday life that conveyed clear, didactic messages.

Earlier, the British theorists Colin Campbell (d. 1729) and Jonathan Richardson the Elder (1665–1745) had called for reform in art because of the moral decay and disillusionment they

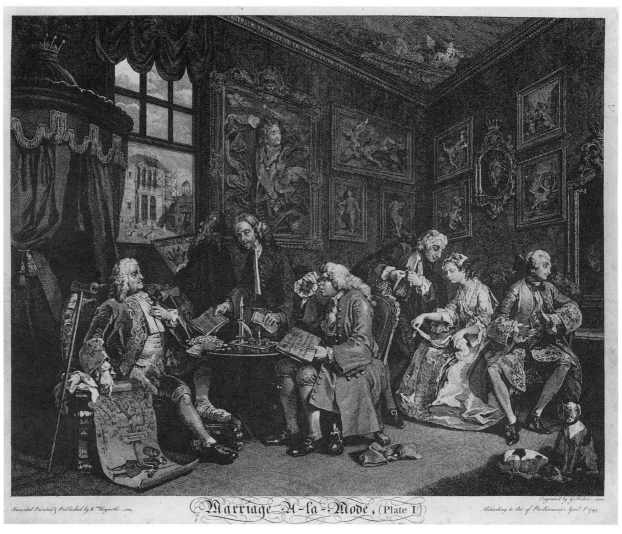

**16-7. William Hogarth. T*he Marriage Contract*, from Marriage à la Mode. 1745. Engraving, 15³/₁₆ x 18⁷/₁₆" (38.6 x 46.8 cm).
The Metropolitan Museum of Art, New York**

Harris Brisbane Dick Fund, 1932

found in Britain. They believed that art should promote and support "civic humanism," or public virtue and integrity, and for this they favored a restrained, classical style.

Although not a classicist in style, William Hogarth (1697–1764) was the most important practitioner of moralized genre painting in England. About 1730, Hogarth, trained as a portrait painter, began illustrating moralizing tales of his own invention in sequences of four to six paintings. He then reproduced the canvases in sets of prints, both to maximize his profits and to influence as many people as possible.

Hogarth's Marriage à la Mode series (1743–1745) was inspired by an essay written by the English essayist and poet Joseph Addison promoting the concept of marriage based on love. The opening scene, *The Marriage Contract* (fig. 16-7), shows the gout-ridden and bankrupt Lord Squanderfield pointing proudly to his family tree as he arranges his son's marriage to the daughter of a

wealthy merchant. Sitting back to back on the sofa are the loveless couple who will be sacrificed to their fathers' greed and pride. The young Squanderfield admires himself in a mirror as the lawyer Silvertongue whispers blandishments to the unhappy bride-to-be and suggestively sharpens his pen. Five more scenes (not illustrated here) show the progressively disastrous results of such a union, culminating in murder and suicide.

British patrons tended to favor amusing and easily understandable satirical and moralizing scenes over high-minded history paintings with subjects drawn from mythology, the Bible, or classical literature. By doing so, they contradicted art theorists of their time and earlier, who had long considered **history painting** the highest form of artistic endeavor. When British buyers did acquire historical canvases, they tended to purchase them from Italy, the cradle of the Neoclassic movement, rather than to patronize artists of their own country.

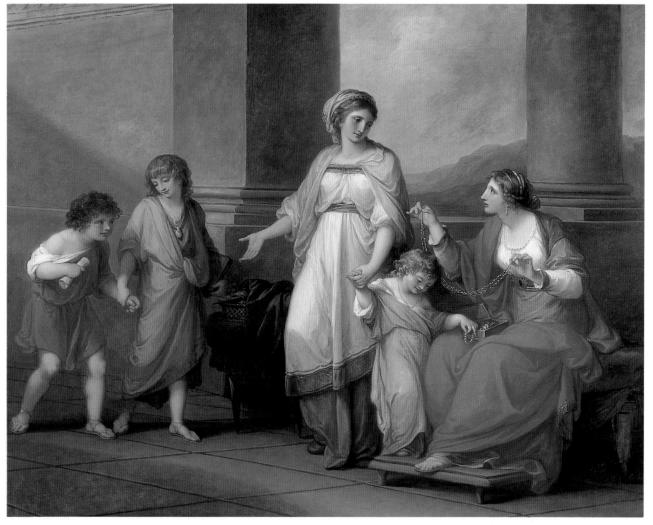

16-8. Angelica Kauffmann. *Cornelia Pointing to Her Children as Her Treasures.* 1785. Oil on canvas, 40 x 50" (101.6 x 127 cm).
Virginia Museum of Fine Arts, Richmond, Virginia
The Adolph D. and Wilkins C. Williams Fund

The Italian-trained Swiss artist Angelica Kauffmann (1741–1807) became one of the leading Neoclassic history painters in England when she was invited to Britain in 1766 by a wealthy client. In 1768 she was one of only two women artists named among the founding members of the Royal Academy in London (see "Art Academies in the Eighteenth Century," page 374). In her painting *Cornelia Pointing to Her Children as Her Treasures* (fig. 16-8), Kauffmann illustrated a moral lesson. The scene takes place in Republican Rome, during the second century BCE. A woman visitor has been showing Cornelia her jewels and then requests to see those of her hostess. In response, Cornelia gestures to her children and states, *"These* are my jewels." The setting is classically simple, and the figures are based loosely on those found in Roman wall paintings. The sentiment, however—the glorification and idealization of the good mother—belongs unmistakably to the eighteenth century. Enlightenment

philosophers, especially the influential French-Swiss theorist Jean-Jacques Rousseau (1712–1778), concluded that men and women should conform to the roles assigned to them by nature (i.e., biology), with women tending to the home and raising children, and men practicing learned professions, governing the state, and taking other active roles in public life.

NEOCLASSICAL ARCHITECTURE IN ENGLAND AND NORTH AMERICA

In architecture, as in history painting, the British looked to Italy for inspiration. Richard Boyle, third earl of Burlington (1695–1753), who promoted classicism in English architecture, made two trips to Italy, one to study the works of the sixteenth-century architect Palladio (see fig. 12-13). The best-preserved of Burlington's works is an annex to his residence at Chiswick, in West London, designed in 1724. This building (figs.

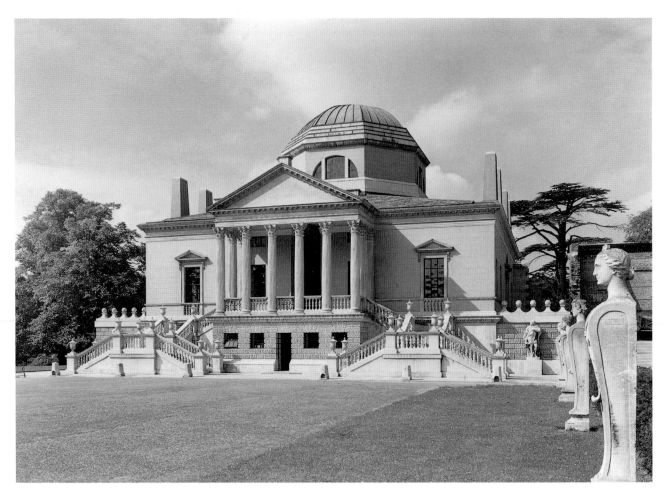

16-9. **Richard Boyle, Lord Burlington. Chiswick House,** West London, England. 1724–29

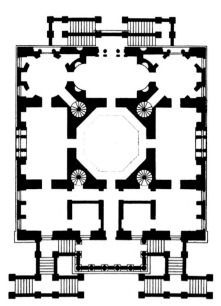

16-10. **Plan of Chiswick House.** 1724

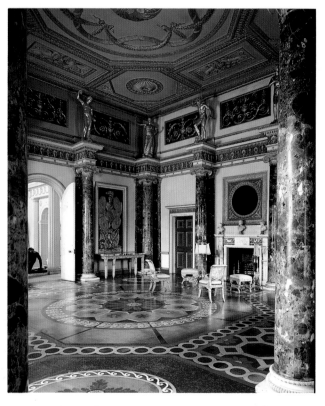

16-11. **Robert Adam. Anteroom, Syon House,** Middlesex, England. 1760–69

16-9, 16-10) recalls Palladio's Villa Rotunda (see fig. 12-14), although its central core is octagonal rather than round. Its elevation is characteristically Palladian, with a main floor resting on a basement, and tall rectangular windows with triangular pediments. However, Lord Burlington

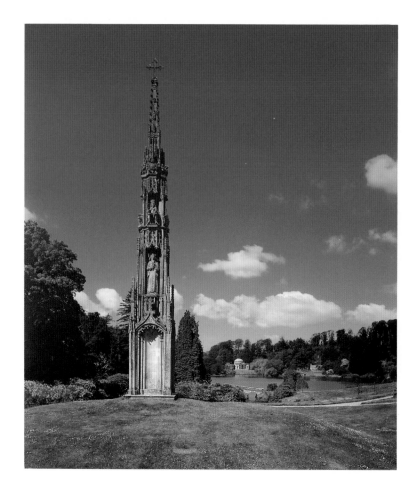

16-12. Henry Flitcroft and Henry Hoare. The Park at Stourhead, Wiltshire, England. Laid out 1743; executed 1744–65, with continuing additions

introduced a staircase on each side of the porch rather than a single steep flight at the center. The result is a lucid evocation of Palladio's design, whose few but crisp details seem perfectly suited to the refined proportions of the whole.

Wealthy Britains turned to a Scot, Robert Adam (1728–1792), and his brothers to create Neoclassic interiors, which became the height of fashion in the late eighteenth century. During a period of study in Rome, Robert Adam became enthralled with the remains of classical antiquity. The influence of Roman architecture and its decoration is readily apparent in the interiors Adam designed between 1760 and 1769 for the duke of Northumberland's country estate, Syon House, near London. The anteroom, a square chamber between the entrance hall and the dining room, remains today a prime example of Adam's brilliance (fig. 16-11). The opulent colored marbles, gilded relief panels and statues, spirals, garlands, rosettes, and carved **moldings** are profuse, yet restrained by the strong geometric order imposed on them and by the visual relief of the plain wall and ceiling surfaces. Adam's great gift was the seeming effortlessness with which he combined a variety of classical motifs into elegant and original designs.

In the art of landscape design, the British could claim true innovation. They created a style that contrasted sharply with the rigid formality of Baroque gardens (see fig. 13-11) and became known throughout Europe as the English land-scape garden. One of the earliest such gardens took shape in 1743, when the banker Henry Hoare redid the grounds of his estate at Stourhead in Wiltshire (fig. 16-12) with the assistance of Henry Flitcroft, a protégé of the earl of Burlington. Winding paths, irregular plantings of shrubs, and other effects imitated the appearance of the natural rural landscape, carefully and discreetly "improved" by orchestrated views. To further engage and intrigue the eye, Flitcroft and Hoare dotted the landscape with Greek and Roman temples, a grotto with copies of antique statues, and such added delights as a rural cottage, a Chinese bridge, a Turkish tent, and the Gothic spire pictured here. While the antique structures and statues relate to the taste for Neoclassicism and nostalgically evoke an idyllic classical past, the exotic elements here are an early indication of Romantic taste in Britain, with its eagerness for the novel and the strange.

In America, Thomas Jefferson, a political leader and the principal author of the Declaration of Independence, believed fervently in architecture as a means of expressing the nation's ideals and in Neoclassicism as the style appropriate for its public buildings. A talented amateur architect himself, Jefferson made designs based on Roman temples for Virginia's State Capitol at Richmond and the library and academic buildings of the University of Virginia at Charlottesville (1817–1826). Jefferson's first attempt at architectural design was at his own home,

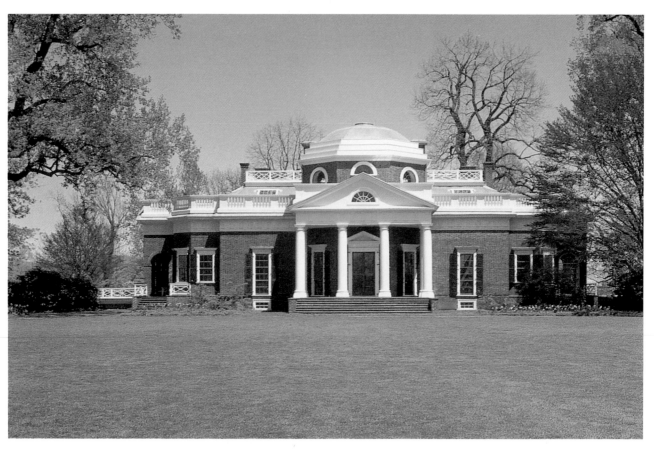

16-13. Thomas Jefferson. Monticello, Charlottesville, Virginia. 1770–84, 1796–1806

Monticello, near Charlottesville (fig. 16-13). He based the first version of the house, built during the 1770s and early 1780s, on a design in the *Four Books on Architecture*, an architectural treatise by Palladio. But when Jefferson went to Paris in 1785 as the American minister to France, he discovered an elegant domestic architecture that made his home seem crude and provincial.

After his return in 1793, Jefferson completely redesigned Monticello, using french doors, tall narrow windows, and a balustrade above the unifying cornice to mask the second floor. Despite these French elements and his stated rejection of the British Palladian mode, the building's simplicity and its combination of temple front and dome remain closer to Burlington's Chiswick House (see fig. 16-9) than to contemporary French buildings. Compared with Chiswick House, however, Monticello seems less aristocratic as a result of its humbler building materials (brick with wooden trim and columns formed of stuccoed and painted bricks) and its extended, low-lying profile.

HISTORY AND NARRATIVE PAINTING IN FRANCE AND SPAIN

In the 1770s, the French history painter Jacques-Louis David (1748–1825) developed a truly Neoclassical painting style. In 1774 David had won the Prix de Rome, a competitive scholarship for study in Italy awarded to the top graduating students from the French Academy's art school. During six

years in Rome, David studied Raphael and Michelangelo, the Baroque classicism of Poussin and the Carracci, and above all, ancient Roman sculpture and frescoes. After his return to Paris he produced a series of severe, anti-Rococo paintings that extolled the antique virtues of moral incorruptibility, stoicism, courage, and patriotism.

The first of these, painted as a royal commission, was the *Oath of the Horatii* of 1784–1785 (fig. 16-14). The subject, taken from Roman history, is a duel to the death fought by three Roman brothers (the Horatii) and three brothers from nearby Alba (the Curatii) to settle a dispute between their native cities. David's painting was inspired by Pierre Corneille's seventeenth-century drama *Horace*. Somewhat surprisingly, however, David chose to depict an incident that is not part of the story in any known source: the Horatii taking an oath to fight to the death for Rome. The message of the finished painting—the value of putting patriotic duty above personal interests and even family obligations—is expressed with such clarity and power that it created a sensation when David exhibited it in Rome and Paris in early 1785. The young men's father, Horace, standing at the center, administers the oath to his sons. To the right of him, Horace's daughter Camillia, who is betrothed to one of the Curatii, and his daughter-in-law Sabina, a Curatii herself, weep together, knowing that whatever the outcome of the battle, they will inevitably lose someone dear to them. The ener-

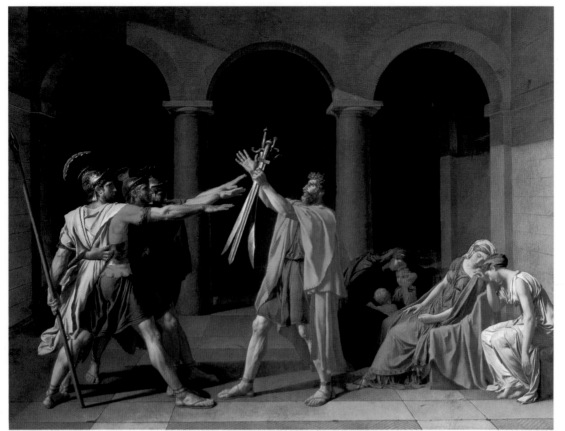

16-14. Jacques-Louis David. _Oath of the Horatii._ 1784–85. Oil on canvas, 10'8³/₈" x 14' (3.26 x 4.27 m). Musée du Louvre, Paris

getic young men with their glittering swords are a powerful contrast to the swooning women already mourning the tragedy to come.

David's _Oath_ soon became an emblem of the French Revolution of 1789. Its harsh lesson in republican citizenship effectively captured the mood of the Jacobins, the new leaders of the French state who came to power in 1793. The Jacobins executed King Louis XVI and Marie Antoinette, drafted a new constitution, and ruthlessly disposed of all opponents, aristocratic or republican, supposedly for the greater good of the nation. More than 1,300 men and women died on the guillotine in 1794 in the final six weeks of Jacobin rule. David, a Jacobin himself, painted portraits of the Revolution's own martyrs and became propaganda minister and director of public festivals.

The initial French Republic ended in 1799 when the government was reorganized under Napoleon Bonaparte, a popular and successful general. David admired the general and became his court painter after Napoleon was named emperor in 1804. Even before that time, David produced canvases that turned Napoleon into a larger-than-life figure. _Napoleon Crossing the Saint-Bernard_ (fig. 16-15), painted during 1800–1801, is an idealized vision of a military campaign that took place in 1800. David shows the future emperor leading his troops across the Alps into Italy. Although he actually made the crossing on a donkey, here he charges up the mountain on a rearing horse, past rocks incised with his

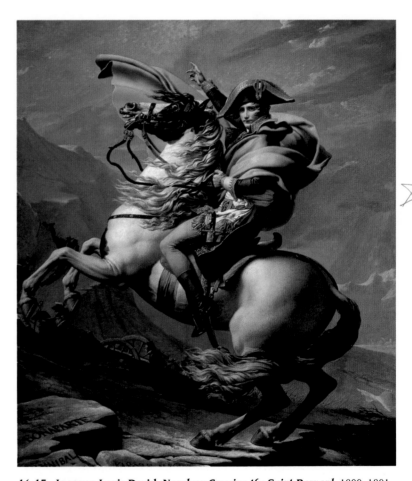

16-15. Jacques-Louis David. _Napoleon Crossing the Saint-Bernard._ 1800–1801. Oil on canvas, 8'10¹/₄" x 7'6¹/₂" (2.7 x 2.3 m). Musée National du Château de la Malmaison, Rueil-Malmaison

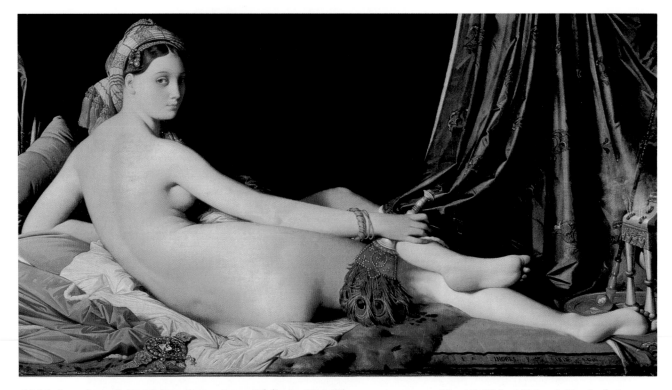

16-16. **Jean-Auguste-Dominique Ingres.** *Large Odalisque.* 1814. Oil on canvas, approx. 35 x 64" (88.9 x 162.5 cm). Musée du Louvre, Paris

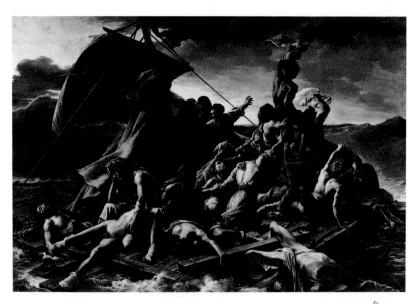

16-17. **Théodore Géricault.** *Raft of the "Medusa."* 1818–19. Oil on canvas, 16'1" x 23'6" (4.9 x 7.16 m). Musée du Louvre, Paris

At the Salon of 1819, this painting was retitled A *Shipwreck Scene*, to avoid the politically inflammatory aspects of the event. Because the monarchy refused to buy the painting, Géricault took it on a two-year tour of England and Ireland, where he exhibited it commercially following the example pioneered by the American John Singleton Copley in the 1780s. While in England, Géricault did a number of naturalistic lithographs recording London slum life. Géricault produced the first important artistic lithographs, a printmaking technique invented by a music publisher in 1798.

name and those of Hannibal and Charlemagne— a reference to military heroes who had preceded him. A strong wind whips his cloak and the horse's mane and tail into a passionate frenzy. With its sweeping diagonals and flowing draperies, this painting of contemporary history owes as much to the idealized grand manner of the Baroque as it does to David's Neoclassicism.

David was the leading force in French painting during the Revolutionary and Napoleonic eras and trained many young artists of the succeeding generation. Jean-Auguste-Dominique Ingres (1780–1867), one of David's most talented pupils, thoroughly absorbed his master's Neoclassical vision but interpreted it in a new manner. Inspired by Raphael rather than by antique art, Ingres emulated the Renaissance artist's graceful lyricism, precise drawing, and idealized forms.

Ingres's *Large Odalisque* of 1814, despite its cool and precise treatment, is in many respects anticlassical (fig. 16-16). The exotic subject is an **odalisque**—that is, any woman living in the women's quarter of a Turkish house (*oda*). The artist paints the full nude, but the odd distortions of her body seem akin to the Mannerist art of the late sixteenth century. To make this figure conform to his idiosyncratic aesthetic, Ingres has given her several extra vertebrae and tiny, boneless feet scarcely capable of supporting her weight. This cool, languorous woman radiates an elegant eroticism in her remote and imaginary world.

As a teacher and theorist, Ingres became the most influential artist of his time, helping to formulate the taste of a generation. He helped to ensure the dominance of classicism over a strong subcurrent of Romanticism in France well into the mid-nineteenth century. Nevertheless, Romanticism ultimately became the dominant style.

Romanticism

French Romantic painting was characterized by loose, fluid brushwork, dramatic contrasts of light and dark, and expressive poses and gestures. Already anticipated during Napoleon's reign, it flowered during the restoration of the French

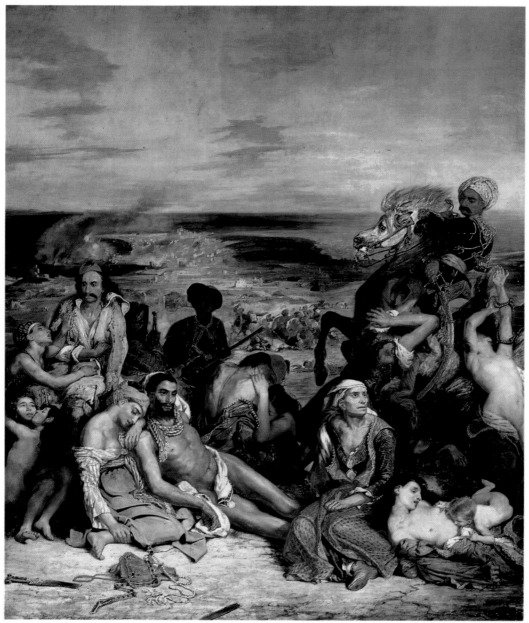

16-18. Eugène Delacroix.
The Massacre at Chios.
1822–24. Oil on canvas,
13'10⅛" x 11'7" (4.22 x 3.53 m).
Musée du Louvre, Paris

monarchy that lasted from 1815 to 1848. The Romantic style became identified with a type of social commentary in which the dramatic presentation was intended to stir public emotions, especially in the work of its chief exponents, Théodore Géricault (1791–1824) and Eugène Delacroix (1798–1863).

Géricault began his career painting works inspired by Napoleonic military campaigns. During a brief stay in Rome between 1816 and 1817, he studied the work of Michelangelo. Géricault returned to Paris determined to paint a great contemporary history painting and finally decided to treat the scandalous and sensational shipwreck of the *Medusa* (fig. 16-17). In 1816 a ship of colonists headed for Madagascar foundered near its destination; its captain was an incompetent aristocrat appointed by the newly restored monarchy for political reasons. Because there were insufficient lifeboats, the commander ordered 149 passengers and crew onto a small raft, which tossed about on stormy seas for nearly

two weeks before it was found. The fifteen survivors had subsisted for the last days of their horrific voyage on human flesh.

Géricault decided to show the moment when the survivors first spotted their rescue ship, but survival was not yet assured. The outstretched arms of the victims lead the viewer's eye to the climactic figure of an African held aloft by other men. He waves a cloth to attract the attention of a ship that is still only a speck on the horizon. Géricault's academic training underlies the painting's organization as a series of interlocking triangles, through which he illustrates this human tragedy and injustice with indignant compassion.

Eugène Delacroix, who modeled for one of the nude victims on the raft, followed Géricault as the inspirational leader of the Romantic movement. One of the first paintings he exhibited at the Salon (the Academy's official exhibition) was *The Massacre at Chios* (fig. 16-18), an event even more terrible than the shipwreck of the

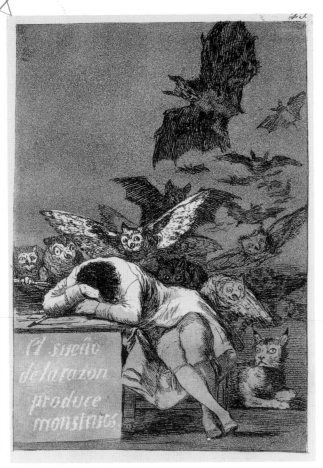

16-19. Francisco Goya. *The Sleep of Reason Produces Monsters*, No. 43 from *Los Caprichos* (*The Caprices*). 1796–98. Etching and aquatint, 8½ x 6" (21.6 x 15.2 cm). Published 1799. The Hispanic Society of America, New York

After printing about 300 sets of this series, Goya offered them for sale in 1799. He withdrew them from sale two days later without explanation. Historians believe that he was probably warned by the Church that if he did not do so he might have to appear before the Inquisition, because of his unflattering portrayal of the Church in some of the etchings. In 1803, Goya donated the plates to the Royal Printing Office in Madrid.

Medusa. In January 1822, the Greeks began a struggle for independence from the Turks that aroused the sympathies of many western Europeans. While returning from a naval defeat in April of that year, the Turkish fleet stopped at the peaceful Greek island of Chios and took its revenge. About 20,000 of the 100,000 inhabitants were killed, and the rest were taken to North Africa and sold into slavery.

Delacroix's painting focuses on the exhausted victims, quietly and sadly awaiting their fate. Despite the fighting in the rear, the painting is oddly tranquil and, as Delacroix himself insisted, "beautiful." The horror of what we know is overcome by visual pleasure in what we see—an inventory of handsome and picturesquely dressed figures, rich colors, and fluid brushwork. Here Delacroix has effectively translated the horrors of life into the beauty of art.

In the mid-eighteenth century, Spanish patrons looked primarily to foreign artists, such as Giovanni Battista Tiepolo (Chapter 13), to execute major commissions. Not until late in the century did a native painter emerge whose achievements were comparable to those of Spain's great seventeenth-century painter, Velázquez. This new master was Francisco Goya y Lucientes (1746–1828), who would become one of the major figures of the Romantic movement.

Goya began his career painting portraits and genre scenes, the latter used as tapestry designs by the Royal Manufactory in Madrid. Around the turn of the nineteenth century, the artist's study of Velázquez and Rembrandt began to be manifest in his work in a darker tonality, freer brushwork, and dramatic presentation. In 1799 Goya published *Los Caprichos* (*The Caprices*), the first of several suites of etchings he created. These prints exhibit a bitterness of outlook that is absent from his earlier Rococo genre paintings. Setting the tone for the eighty etchings is the print originally intended as its **frontispiece**, *The Sleep of Reason Produces Monsters* (fig. 16-19). Although the text published with the print sounds a hopeful note ("Imagination abandoned by reason produces impossible monsters; united with her, she is the mother of the arts and the source of their wonders"), the images are an angry attack on contemporary Spanish manners and morals. In comparison, Hogarth's satire (see fig. 16-7) seems tame. Goya did not share the Enlightenment faith in the ultimate rationality and goodness of humanity. On the contrary, he believed that the violence, greed, and foolishness of his society had to be examined mercilessly if it were to be changed in any way.

Goya made another attempt to awaken Spanish reason in a series of works produced at the end of the Napoleonic War of 1808–1814. In 1808 Napoleon conquered Spain and placed his brother Joseph Bonaparte on its throne. Many Spaniards, including Goya, at first welcomed the French because of the liberal reforms they inaugurated, but soon a new authoritarianism appeared. On May 2, 1808, however, a rumor spread in Madrid that the French planned to kill the royal family. The populace rose up and a day of bloody street fighting ensued. Hundreds of Spanish people were taken to a convent and executed the following morning. The fighting soon spread to the countryside, and for the next six years the Spanish conducted guerilla warfare against the French occupying forces.

After the war, Goya made a series of etchings documenting the atrocities on both sides and a pair of paintings to commemorate the events of May 2 and May 3. The more famous of the two paintings shows a French firing squad executing helpless Spanish prisoners in the predawn hours of May 3 (fig. 16-20). The violent gestures of the terrified rebels and the mechanical efficiency of the firing squad seem to be scenes from a nightmare. The man in the white shirt, confronting his faceless killer with outstretched arms suggesting the crucified Jesus, is an image of particular horror and pathos. When asked why he painted such a brutal scene, Goya responded: "To warn men never to do it again."

The Neoclassic and the Romantic modes flourished side by side in England in the second half of the eighteenth century and the early nineteenth century. The Swiss-born artist John Henry Fuseli (born Johann Heinrich Füssli; 1741–1825), a true Romantic, found as congenial

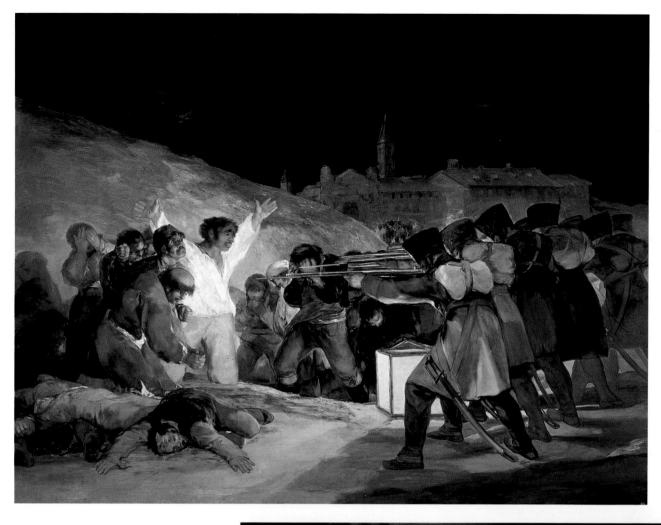

16-20.
Francisco
Goya. *Third of
May, 1808.*
1814–15.
Oil on canvas,
8'9" x 13'4"
(2.67 x 4.06 m).
Museo del
Prado, Madrid

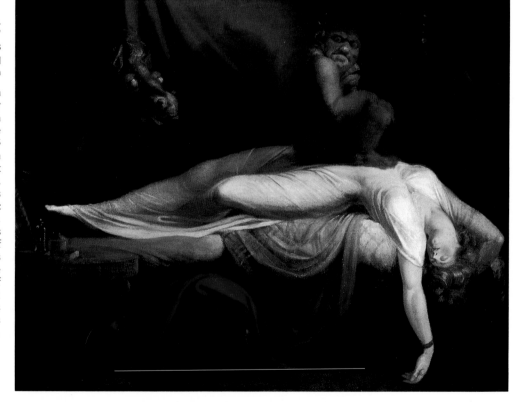

16-21. John Henry Fuseli. *The Nightmare.*
1781. Oil on canvas, 39³/₄ x 49¹/₂"
(101 x 126 cm). The Detroit Institute of Arts
Gift of Mr. and Mrs. Bert Smokler and Mr. and
Mrs. Lawrence A. Fleischmann

Fuseli was not popular with the English critics. One writer said Fuseli's 1780 entry in the London Royal Academy exhibition "ought to be destroyed," and Horace Walpole called another painting in 1785 "shockingly mad, mad, mad, madder than ever." Even after achieving the highest official acknowledgment of his talents, Fuseli was called the Wild Swiss and Painter to the Devil. But the public appreciated his work, and *The Nightmare*, exhibited at the Academy in 1782, was repeated in at least six versions, all of which were sold to commercial engravers for reproduction in prints. One of these prints would one day hang in the office of the Austrian psychoanalyst Sigmund Freud, who believed that dreams were manifestations of the dreamer's repressed desires.

a home in Britain as did his Neoclassic country-woman Angelica Kauffmann (see fig. 16-8). Fuseli, originally trained as a minister, arrived in London in 1764, eventually settled there, and quickly became a member of the city's intellectual elite.

As a painter, Fuseli developed an unusual style that seems to have originated in his own psyche.

One of Fuseli's best-known paintings, *The Nightmare* (fig. 16-21), combines the irrational and the erotic, two persistent themes in most of his work. The subject was inspired by an old and widespread belief in the incubus, a demon who was believed to alight upon sleeping virgins to have sexual intercourse with them, or cause them to have erotic nightmares. The content of this sleeper's dream is suggested by the way the "night mare," on which the incubus travels, breaks through the curtains of her room.

William Hackwood, for Josiah Wedgwood. "Am I Not a Man and a Brother?" 1787. Black-and-white jasperware, 1⅜ x 1⅜" (3.5 x 3.5 cm). The Wedgwood Museum, Barlaston, Staffordshire, England

"Am I Not a Man and a Brother?"

For two centuries the name *Wedgwood* has been synonymous with fine English ceramics, especially tableware. But there was another side to Josiah Wedgwood. He was active in the international effort to halt the African slave trade and abolish slavery. To publicize the abolitionist cause, he asked the sculptor William Hackwood to design an emblem for the British Committee to Abolish the Slave Trade, formed in 1787. The compelling image created by Hackwood had the likeness of a black African man kneeling in chains, with the legend, "Am I Not a Man and a Brother?" Wedgwood sent copies of the medallion to Benjamin Franklin, the president of the Philadelphia Abolition Society, and to others in the movement. In the nineteenth century, the women's suffrage movement in the United States adapted the image by representing a woman in chains with the motto, "Am I Not a Woman and a Sister?"

A work of art as explicitly political as this was unusual in the eighteenth century. Nevertheless, artists like Goya in both Europe and America responded to the tumultuous social changes and political events with powerful and courageous works of art.

ROMANTIC REALISM

In the early nineteenth century, Romantic taste in England found a major outlet in landscape painting. Of the two great landscapists of the period, John Constable (1776–1837) specialized in naturalistic scenes of rural stability, while Joseph Mallord William Turner (1775–1851) focused on mood, light, and drama.

The son of a successful miller, Constable claimed that the landscape of his youth in southern England had made him a painter before he ever picked up a brush. In spite of his training at the Royal Academy, where landscape was considered an inferior art, he was greatly impressed by the work of seventeenth-century Dutch landscapists, and theirs was the example he followed. Constable's *The White Horse* (fig. 16-22) of 1819 draws on his intense observation of every facet of the natural landscape, recorded in sketches he made on walking tours. As a storm passes away to the right, a farmer and his helpers ferry a workhorse across a river. Sunlight glistens off the water and foliage, an effect Constable achieved through tiny dabs of white paint.

Constable detested what he called "cold, trumpery stuff" and "bravura" in other landscape painters' work, by which he meant Romantic effects of drama and grandeur. The naturalistic stylistic current to which his pastoral idylls belong is sometimes referred to as Romantic naturalism. The figures in his landscapes are harmoniously one with nature; the artist omitted from his rural idylls any references to the civil unrest among agrarian workers that was then being experienced in England.

Turner, Constable's contemporary, imbued his early works with a pleasant, picturesque quality not far removed from Constable's and rapidly won public acclaim. At twenty-seven, Turner was elected a full member of the Royal Academy, and he later became a professor at the Royal Academy school. As Turner's personal style matured, the phenomena of colored light and atmospheric movement became the true subjects of his paintings. To the **academicians** his works increasingly looked like sketches or preliminary underpainting of unfinished canvases, but to his admirer Constable they were "golden visions, glorious and beautiful," painted with "tinted steam." Between 1819 and 1840 Turner made four trips to Italy, where he was strongly affected by the technique and coloration of Venetian Renaissance paintings and by Venice's own watery brilliance and glowing atmosphere.

Turner's *The Fighting "Téméraire," Tugged to Her Last Berth to Be Broken Up* (fig. 16-23) of 1838 is both a history painting and a study in the optical effects of the setting sun over water. The *Téméraire* had been the second-ranking British ship at the Battle of Trafalgar in 1805, a great British naval victory over the combined fleets of Spain and Napoleon's France. Some thirty-three years later, however, the ship was ready for the scrap heap, and Turner watched as it was towed away to be destroyed. Some have interpreted

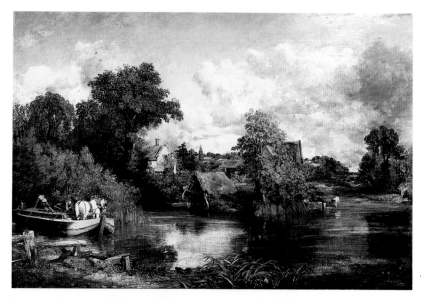

16-22. John Constable. *The White Horse.* 1819. Oil on canvas, 4'3³/₄" x 6'2¹/₈" (1.31 x 1.88 m). The Frick Collection, New York

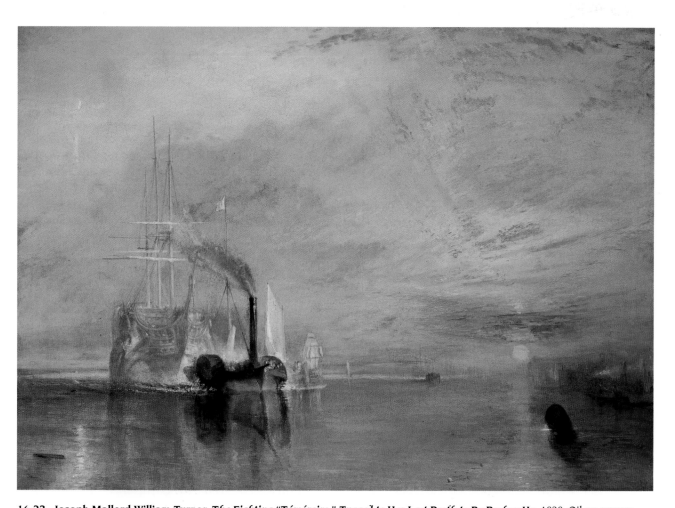

16-23. Joseph Mallord William Turner. *The Fighting "Téméraire," Tugged to Her Last Berth to Be Broken Up.* 1838. Oil on canvas, 35¹/₄ x 48" (89.5 x 121.9 cm). The National Gallery, London

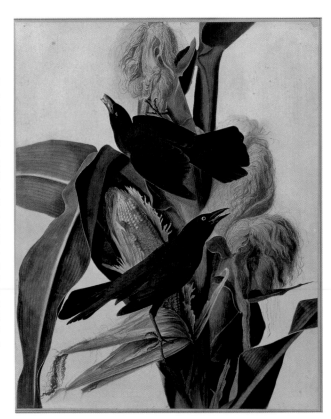

16-24. John James Audubon. *Common Grackle*, for *The Birds of America*. 1826–39. Watercolor, graphite, and selective glazing, 23⅞ x 18½" (60.6 x 47.0 cm). Collection of the New York Historical Society, New York City

To create Audubon's *The Birds of America* (1826–39), his watercolors, like this one of grackles, were copied by the London print-maker Robert Havell using the aquatint process. Broad areas of neutral color were inked on the plates and the rest added by hand on the prints themselves. This bird encyclopedia was Audubon's first success-ful business venture. The cost to him of the first issue was $100,000, and 2,000 sets were eventually sold at $1,000 each. Between 1840 and 1844, before his health and eyesight began to fail, he supervised the production of *Birds* with reduced-size illustrations.

the scene as a symbol of the passing of the old order, the sailing ship destroyed by the steam-engine-driven tug. But the narrative content is entirely overwhelmed by light and color; the glowing red sun creates an apotheosis for the dying ship.

While Europe suffered through the Napoleonic Wars, the United States was entering an era of great optimism. The new country emerged from its war for independence from Britain with sufficient resources, technology, and entrepreneurs to move into the forefront of the industrialized world. Many American painters, sculptors, and architects looked to Europe for their inspiration in the nineteenth century, but others found everything they needed in their native landscape and took pride in the American scene. These artists and their patrons tended to favor a detailed realism over high-minded Neoclassic scenes drawn from ancient history.

John James Audubon (1785–1851), a French immigrant, set out to make accurate watercolors of the birds of America. Like Merian (see fig. 13-32) before him, he reproduced his work in prints and published hand-colored impressions of them in portfolios. He solicited subscriptions for the portfolios in advance, even traveling to Europe in the late 1820s to sign up subscribers. From a financial point of view, the trip was not very successful, but Audubon was proud to have

received compliments on his work from the French Neoclassic master, Jacques-Louis David.

To complete his bird encyclopedia, Audubon traveled and sketched from Labrador to Florida, and southwest as far as Texas. Ultimately he made 435 watercolor studies of birds. Combining close observation with an artist's eye for design, he showed the birds in their natural habitats, often whimsically or dramatically. In his *Common Grackle* (fig. 16-24), these sleek and fearless birds are shown assaulting ears of corn.

The first major painter to live and work west of the Mississippi River was George Caleb Bingham (1811–1879), who began his career as an itinerant portrait painter. He also sketched and painted scenes of everyday life along the river, such as his *Fur Traders Descending the Missouri* (fig. 16-25), painted in about 1845. With this canvas, Bingham began an association with the newly formed American Art-Union in New York. As a way to promote American painters, the union purchased works for a flat fee, then reproduced prints to be sold by subscription. The paintings themselves were awarded through a lottery, which allowed people of modest means to own original works of art. *Fur Traders Descending the Missouri*, which Bingham sold to the union for $25, is an idyllic scene of a French trapper and his son with their pet bear cub in a dugout canoe. As they glide through the early-morning

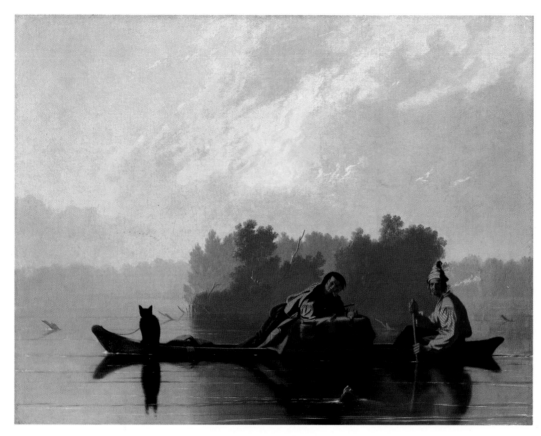

16-25. George Caleb Bingham. *Fur Traders Descending the Missouri*. c. 1845. Oil on canvas, 29 x 36" (73.7 x 91.4 cm). The Metropolitan Museum of Art, New York
Morris K. Jesup Fund, 1933

stillness, the still-hidden sun tinges the clouds with rosy gold, and morning mists shroud the river landscape in mystery. Despite the peacefulness of the scene, there is an underlying ominousness. Branches and rocks stick out of the water, reminders of the hazards the boatmen faced, and the mysterious black shape of the chained bear mirrored in the glassy water surface produces an eerie effect reminiscent of the demon in Fuseli's *The Nightmare* (see fig. 16-21).

Bingham's idyllic visions of life in the West

appeared just as America's open spaces began to face threats from industrial development and urbanization. The Industrial Revolution, the flurry of technological progress and mechanization that began in Europe in the mid-eighteenth century, reached the United States by the early nineteenth century. A transcontinental railroad was completed in 1869, and by the 1890s the frontier had disappeared. By the second half of the nineteenth century, both the United States and Europe were ready for an art of the modern age.

Rosa Bonheur. *Plowing in the Nivernais: The Dressing of the Vines.* 1849. Oil on canvas, 5'9" x 8'8" (1.75 x 2.64 m). Musée d'Orsay, Paris

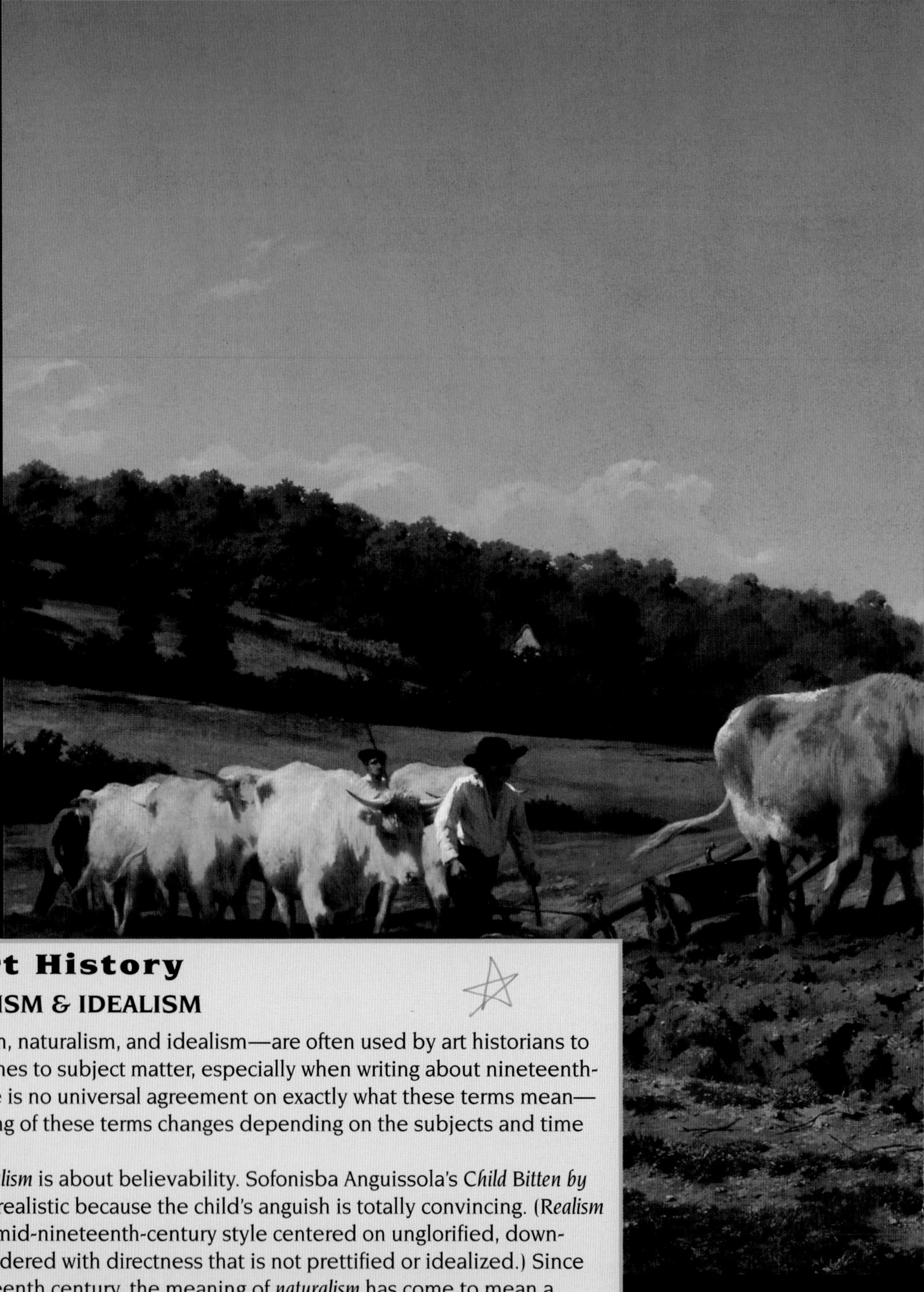

Realism

Rosa Bonheur's *Plowing in the Nivernais*, seen here, is highly *realistic* in its treatment of animals, people, and landscape. The artist's rendering of the scene satisfied expectations of what plowing in that part of nineteenth-century France really looked like at midcentury.

Naturalism

Bonheur's painting is *naturalistic* as well as realistic in its closely observed, convincing details, such as the plodding gait of the pairs of oxen, the texture of their coats, and the type of plow and prod.

Idealism

A farmer might see the beautiful, clean, white oxen and the sparkling white shirts of the men as an urban middle-class *ideal* of rural life and labor. How neat and regular the furrows! How sunny the gentle landscape!

K E Y S to Art History
REALISM, NATURALISM & IDEALISM

These three -isms—realism, naturalism, and idealism—are often used by art historians to describe styles or approaches to subject matter, especially when writing about nineteenth-century art. Ironically, there is no universal agreement on exactly what these terms mean—in part because the meaning of these terms changes depending on the subjects and time periods.

In the largest sense, *realism* is about believability. Sofonisba Anguissola's *Child Bitten by a Crayfish* (see fig. 12-19) is realistic because the child's anguish is totally convincing. (*Realism* with a capital *R* refers to a mid-nineteenth-century style centered on unglorified, down-to-earth subject matter rendered with directness that is not prettified or idealized.) Since the beginning of the nineteenth century, the meaning of *naturalism* has come to mean a close, sometimes even minute, observation of the natural world.

Idealism can be thought of as a counterpart to *realism*. Artists who believe that art can inspire its viewers to noble thoughts and actions select and represent just the "best" elements of a given subject. They then render images that serve as the most perfect or excellent examples of the original source. In the early nineteenth century, the Neoclassical movement was the chief vehicle for idealism.

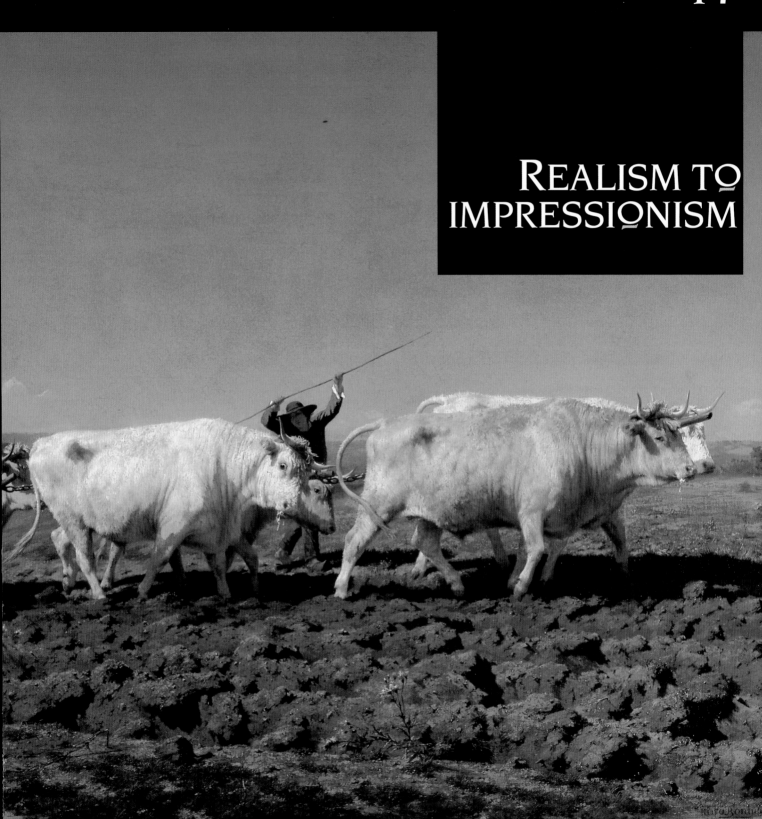

REALISM TO IMPRESSIONISM

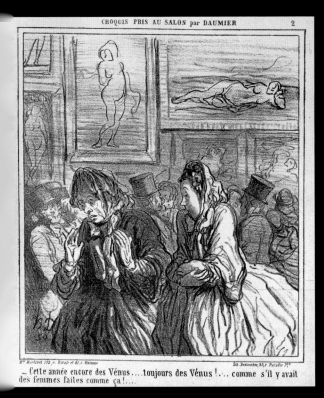

_ Cette année encore des Vénus....toujours des Vénus !... comme s'il y avait
des femmes faites comme ça!....

**7-1. Honoré Daumier. *This Year, Venuses Again . . . Always
Venuses*!** No. 2 of the sketches made at the Salon, from *Le
Charivari*, May 10, 1864

e second half of the nineteenth century, art in Europe
the United States fluctuated uneasily between two
ergent poles. At the one side were academic artists and
cts who used classical forms and even classical
matter, building on the achievements of antiquity
Italian Renaissance. At the other side were those who
d that art and architecture must invent new forms and
matter to speak to the realities of contemporary life.
noré Daumier (1808–1879) highlighted this tension
ped to usher in the new taste for Realism through biting
of academic art and its upper-middle-class audience. For
e, in *This Year, Venuses Again . . . Always Venuses* (fig. 17-1),
orously contrasts academic standards of ideal female
with the appearance of two quite ordinary women visit-
Paris Salon. One of them turns away from a wall of aca-
nudes with the comment, "Cette année encore des
. . toujours des Vénus! . . . comme s'il y avait des
s faites comme ça!" ("This year, Venuses again . . . always
s! . . . as if there were really women built like that!")
ntings on the walls seem to have little to do with the
n-going public, at least in the view of these proper
ives.

The latter half of the nineteenth century has
been called the positivist age, an age of faith
in the positive consequences of what can be
achieved through close observation of the
natural and the human realms. In the visual arts,
the positivist spirit is most obvious, perhaps,
in the widespread rejection of Romantic subjec-
tivism and imagination in favor of the accurate
and apparently objective description of the ordinary, observable world. This new emphasis on
descriptive accuracy, **realism**, had its roots in the
approach to art known as naturalism—in use
since ancient times. (In fact, the terms *realism*
and *naturalism* are often used interchangeably.)
Beginning in the 1830s in France and culminating
in the Revolution of 1848, the tendency became
the recognizable style known as Realism. With
the rise of middle-class patronage beginning in
the Baroque period, the subjects of painting
underwent a shift. While not entirely supplanted,
historical and literary subjects were joined by
works of landscape, genre, portrait, and still life.
At the height of Realism, Gustave Courbet expressed his sympathy for working people through
his painting. Later in the nineteenth century,
Realism became less aligned with liberal social
concern, which for some artists seemed more in
keeping with its original aim of objectivity.

Positivist thinking is evident not only in the
growth of Realism but also in the full range
of artistic developments of the period after 1850.
Included among these are the application of
new technologies in architecture, the highly
descriptive style of academic art, the development of early photography, and the Impressionist
emphasis on the phenomenon of light.

Architecture

Major works of public architecture in the nineteenth century tended to be based on historical
models. But if revival styles, such as Neoclassicism, Gothic Revival, and Neo-Romanesque, were
popular, modern conditions and materials had
an increasing impact on construction. Building
techniques introduced in the late eighteenth and
nineteenth centuries ultimately led to the aban-
donment of architectural **historicism**—dependence on architectural styles used in the past.

Bridge designers rather than architects
pioneered the use of the most important new
building materials: cast iron, wrought iron, and
steel. In England in 1776–1779, Abraham Darby III
built the first cast-iron bridge at an industrial
site known as Coalbrookdale (fig. 17-2). In this
groundbreaking use of structural metal on a large
scale, iron replaced the heavy, hand-cut stone
voussoirs used to construct earlier bridges. The
skeletal structure desired by builders since
the twelfth century was at last possible, enabling
the qualities of light, space, and movement to
be incorporated into building designs.

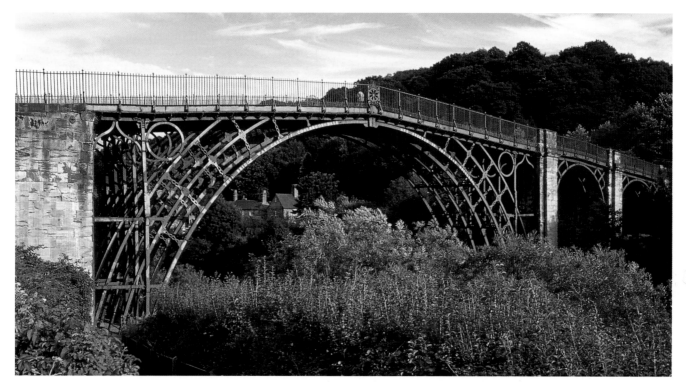

17-2. Abraham Darby III. The Severn River Bridge, Coalbrookdale, England. Completed 1779

Beginning in the mid-nineteenth century, there was a short-lived vogue for iron-framed buildings in the United States. Many of the first examples also had cast-iron facade elements. These structures were soon found to have a fatal susceptibility to fire; exposed to intense heat, iron will warp, buckle, collapse, or melt altogether. The solution was to encase the internal iron supports in fireproof materials and return to masonry sheathing. This suited the tastes of architects trained in traditional historical styles, such as the American architect Henry Hobson Richardson (1838–1886).

Richardson absorbed the conventions of historicism at the architecture school of the École des Beaux-Arts (School of Fine Arts; the Academy's school) in Paris, an important training ground for European and American architects. After his return from Paris in 1865, Richardson worked in many styles but became famous for a simplified Romanesque style known as Richardsonian Romanesque. His best-known building is probably the Marshall Field Warehouse in Chicago (fig. 17-3). Although it is reminiscent of Renaissance palaces in form and of Romanesque churches in its heavy stonework and arches, it had no precise historical antecedents. Richardson all but eliminated applied ornament in favor of the intrinsic appeal of the rough stone and the subtle harmony between the red sandstone and the darker red granite of the base. The solid corner piers (the vertical architectural supports) gave way to the regular rhythm of the broad arches of the middle floors, which were doubled in the smaller arches above,

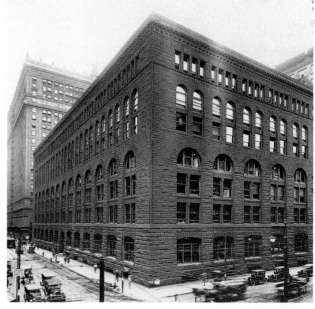

17-3. Henry Hobson Richardson. Marshall Field Warehouse, Chicago. 1885–87. Demolished c. 1935

then doubled again in the square windows of the attic. The clean, crisp line of a simple cornice crowned the whole. Richardson's plain, sturdy building helped shape an emerging desire for a distinctly American architecture.

The perfection of a technique for making inexpensive steel (an alloy of iron and carbon, stronger and lighter than pure iron) introduced new architectural possibilities. Steel was first used for buildings in 1884 by young midwestern architects soon grouped under the label of the Chicago School. The material's light weight combined with strength made taller buildings feasible, as did the introduction of passenger elevators, the first of which was installed in the United States in 1857.

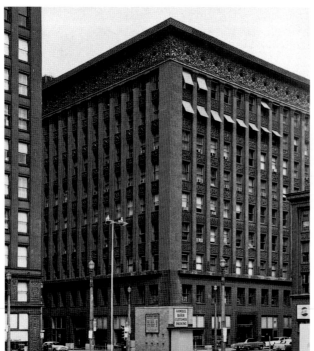

17-4. Louis Sullivan. Wainwright Building, St. Louis, Missouri. 1890–91

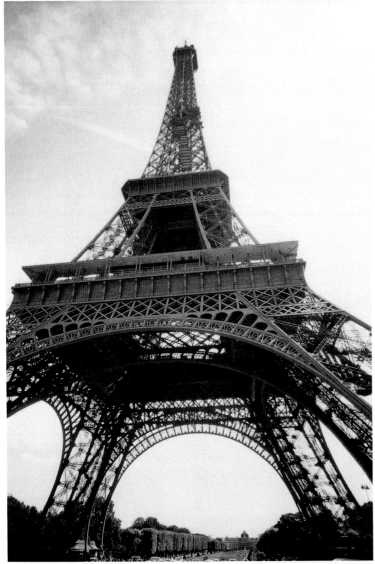

17-5. Gustave Eiffel. Eiffel Tower, Paris. 1887–89

Equipped with these new technologies and inspired by Richardson's radical departure from Beaux-Arts historicism, the Chicago School architects produced a new kind of building, the skyscraper. A fine example of their early work, and evidence of its rapid spread throughout the Midwest, is the Wainwright Building in St. Louis, Missouri (fig. 17-4), built by Louis Sullivan (1856–1924).

Like Richardson's Marshall Field Warehouse, Sullivan's ten-story office building adapts the formal vocabulary of the Beaux-Arts tradition. Its organization into three parts respects the basic compositional rule taught at the French Academy. What is entirely new is the building's vertical emphasis. Unlike Richardson's warehouse, this structure is taller than it is wide; whereas Richardson tried to make his building look shorter by grouping multiple floors into single arcades and by organizing his dominant rhythms horizontally, Sullivan used governing verticals to emphasize height. The corner piers rise in uninterrupted lines to the cornice, their verticality echoed and reinforced by small piers between the windows, designed to suggest the steel framing beneath them.

While the Chicago School was looking for an American alternative to the Beaux-Arts tradition, its European counterparts had likewise been calling for an end to historicism and the invention of an architectural and design style appropriate to the modern age. The search would lead eventually to the frank acceptance of new industrial materials and techniques, like those that first appeared in structures such as the Eiffel Tower (fig. 17-5).

The tower is named after the civil engineer Gustave Eiffel (1832–1923), who built it for the Paris Universal Exposition of 1889 after winning a competition for the design of a monument that would symbolize French industrial progress. Composed of iron latticework, the tower stands on four huge legs reinforced by trussed (braced) arches such as those used in railway bridges. Passenger elevators allowed fairgoers to ascend to the top of what was then, at 984 feet, the tallest structure in the world.

Although the French public loved the tower, most architects, artists, and writers found it completely lacking in beauty. They dolefully predicted that it would have a brutalizing effect on the future of architecture in Paris. One response to this concern was the birth of Art Nouveau, a style stressing flowing curves and organic forms that attempted to be modern without losing a preindustrial sense of beauty.

This application of fluid linear arabesques and organic forms to all aspects of design began a vogue that lasted for more than a decade. In Italy this movement was known as *Stile floreale* (Floral Style) and *Stile Liberty* (after the Liberty department store in London); in Germany, *Jugend-*

stil (Youth Style); in Spain, *Modernismo* (Modernism); in France it had a number of names, including *moderne*. The name eventually accepted in most countries derived from a shop, La Maison de l'Art Nouveau (The House of the New Art), which opened in Paris in 1895.

The man who launched the Art Nouveau style of the 1890s was a Belgian architect, Victor Horta (1861–1947). In 1892 Horta received his first independent commission, to design Tassel House, a private residence in Brussels. The result, especially the house's entry hall and staircase (fig. 17-6), was strikingly original. Horta laid out the wall decoration, floor tile, and ironwork (used instead of stone or wood) in an intricate series of long, graceful curves to integrate interior design and architecture into an exquisite and unified whole.

The Catalan architect Antoni Gaudí i Cornet (1852–1926) created particularly spectacular examples of Art Nouveau in Spain. His work paralleled developments in the work of Horta and others but did not depend on them. Almost ten years before Horta's decorative ironwork at the Tassel House in Brussels, Gaudí had produced similar work in Barcelona.

Unlike his contemporaries in architecture, Gaudí attempted to introduce the organic principle into the very structure of his buildings. Many of these, such as his residential complexes and churches in Spain, reflect his concern for integrating natural forms into daily life. In Güell Park, around a public plaza in the ideal commu-

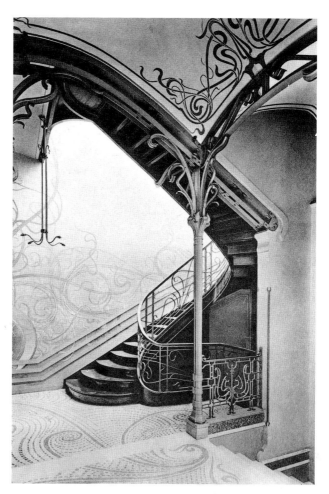

17-6. Victor Horta. Stairway, Tassel House, Brussels. 1892–93

nity he designed on the outskirts of Barcelona, a continuous, serpentine bench serves as a boundary wall (fig. 17-7). Its surface is a glittering mosaic of broken pottery and tiles in homage to

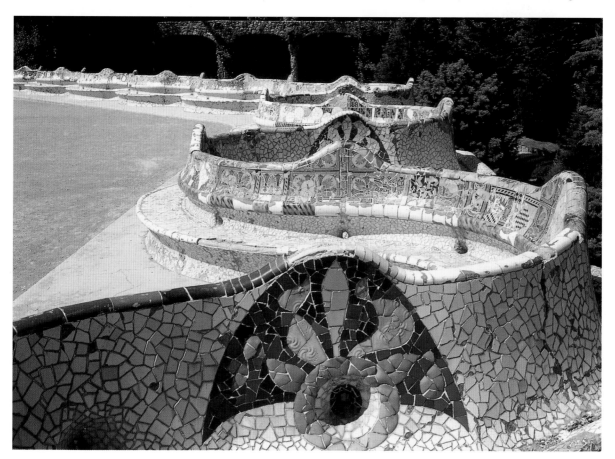

17-7. Antoni Gaudí. Serpentine bench, Güell Park, Barcelona. 1900–14

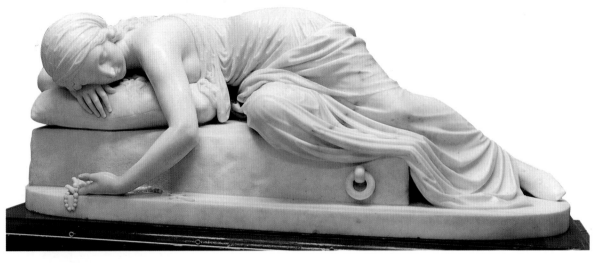

17-8. Harriet Hosmer. *Beatrice Cenci.* 1853–55. Marble, 28" x 5'2" (71 cm x 1.57 m). The St. Louis Mercantile Library Association, St. Louis, Missouri

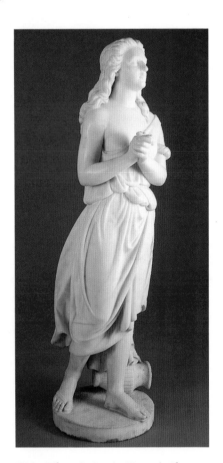

17-9. Edmonia Lewis. *Hagar in the Wilderness.* 1875. Marble, 52⅝ x 15¼ x 17" (133.6 x 38.7 x 43.2 cm). National Museum of African Art, Smithsonian Institution, Washington, D.C.

the long tradition of ceramic work in Spain. Like a strange flowering vine, the bench-wall seems to combine architecture and sculpture. This is a national as well as a personal alternative to historicism and industrialization, reflecting Gaudí's affinity for Spanish Gothic architecture as well as his concern for modern everyday life.

Academic Art

Historicism in nineteenth-century architecture had its counterpart in academic art: painting and sculpture that followed the conservative principles of the French Academy, which exerted enormous influence over artistic matters. Students at the École des Beaux-Arts began their training by copying prints and plaster casts of classical and Renaissance sculpture; then they studied live models posed like classical sculpture. The objective was to develop technical skill and detailed knowledge of the human form. When artists finally began making actual paintings or works of sculpture, they were expected to recall their earlier immersion in classical art and "correct" ordinary nature against its higher ideal.

As a sequel to study at the Academy, or sometimes as an alternative to it, sculptors in particular often visited or settled in Italy. Italy was the wellspring of Neoclassical inspiration in sculpture, and it was also the source of the materials and skilled workers needed to assist in the execution of large commissions. From about 1825, many sculptors from the United States went to Italy for training, and there were bustling American artists' colonies in Rome and Florence by the 1840s.

The American sculptor Harriet Hosmer (1830–1908) arrived in Rome in 1852, after studying with a Boston sculptor and taking anatomy classes in a St. Louis medical school. When her father's financial problems ended his ability to support her, she made a small marble of Shakespeare's character Puck sitting on a toadstool, the sale of which brought her about $50,000—a tremendous sum at a time when skilled American artisans earned about $400 to $500 a year. Among her many idealized works is her *Beatrice Cenci* (fig. 17-8) of 1853–1855. Beatrice, the daughter of a Roman nobleman, conspired with her mother and brothers to murder her tyrannical father. At Beatrice's trial, her lawyer defended her on the grounds that she had been a victim of attempted incest, but she was nevertheless convicted and beheaded in 1599. Hosmer's vision of Beatrice, asleep in her cell after exhausting herself in prayer, is emphatically sensuous. The contrasts of flesh, hair, and drapery folds recall the work of Canova (see fig. 16-2). Discreet eroticism such as this, prudently justified by historical subject matter, held enormous appeal to a certain audience in the nineteenth century.

Edmonia Lewis (1845–1890), who was born to a Chippewa mother and an African-American father, was another American sculptor who worked in Italy. The abolitionist William Lloyd Garrison arranged for her to study with a Neoclassical sculptor. In 1862 she sculpted a bust of Robert Gould, the white colonel of the famed African-American Fifty-fourth Massachusetts Regiment, which fought in the Civil War. The sale of plaster replicas of the Shaw portrait earned her enough money to travel to Rome in 1867, where she sculpted portrait busts and idealized works on African and Native American themes. Two years after returning to the United States in 1873, she sculpted one of her important works on a biblical subject, *Hagar in the Wilderness* (fig. 17-9).

Hagar was the Egyptian concubine of the biblical patriarch Abraham, given to him by his childless wife, Sarah, so that he might have a son. When Sarah later gave birth to a son of her own, Isaac, she became jealous of Hagar and Hagar's son, Ishmael. Sarah demanded that Abraham drive them into the desert to survive as best they could. When the two outcasts were dying of thirst, an angel led Hagar to a well and foretold that Ishmael's descendents would become a great nation (Genesis 16:1–16, 18:1–21). Lewis shows Hagar standing with her hands clasped in prayer for her rescue, an overturned water pitcher at her foot. Her hair and tunic are blown back, as if from a rush of wind from the angel's wings, while she gazes into the distance.

Neoclassical idealism remained a powerful force in both sculpture and painting well into the nineteenth century, but a new taste for descriptive accuracy gradually emerged. The bankers and businesspeople who came to dominate French society and politics in the years after 1830 were, as patrons, generally less interested in art that idealized than in art that brought the ideal down to earth.

Even painters who treated subjects remote from contemporary life showed a growing inter-

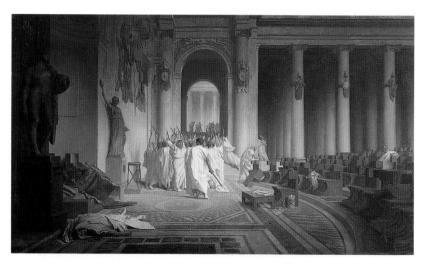

17-10. Jean-Léon Gérôme. *Death of Caesar.* 1859. Oil on canvas, 33⅝ x 57¼" (85.4 x 145.4 cm). Walters Art Gallery, Baltimore

Gérôme was one of the leading antagonists of innovative art forms. As a member of the Salon jury during the last four decades of the nineteenth century, he skillfully opposed the acceptance of much of the new art, especially that of the Impressionists, which he considered "the disgrace of French art." In 1884 he fought the installation of the Manet memorial exhibition at the École, and in 1895–1897 he led the fight against the acceptance by the government of Gustave Caillebotte's bequest of Impressionist works.

est in realistic detail. In *Death of Caesar*, for example, Jean-Léon Gérôme (1824–1904) attempted an objective and archaeologically correct recreation of a historical event (fig. 17-10). He depicts not the moment of the assassination in 44 BCE in Rome but instead the sudden calm that follows as the conspirators rush out to announce their action to the city. With a reporter's concern for the facts, he carefully researched the building where Caesar died, the Theater of Pompey, in order to situate it properly. From historical accounts he learned that the conspirators gave Caesar a petition scroll to distract him, that he knocked over a chair during the assassination, and that he struggled to the base of the statue of Pompey, which he grasped with his bloodied hands before succumbing. Gérôme made sure that the painting included each of those details. Compared with Neoclassic artists such as Jacques-Louis David, Gérôme and his contemporaries began to think of history more as a set of objective facts than as something from which to learn moral lessons.

Early Photography

The development of photography, which had a profound impact on the arts, was another expression of the new interest in descriptive accuracy. Photography developed essentially as a way to fix, that is, to make permanent, images produced on light-sensitive material (see "How Photography Works," page 400).

The first person to achieve this goal was the "gentleman inventor" Joseph-Nicéphore Niépce (1765–1833). Using metal-and-glass plates covered with a kind of light-sensitive asphalt called bitumen, and a camera, he succeeded

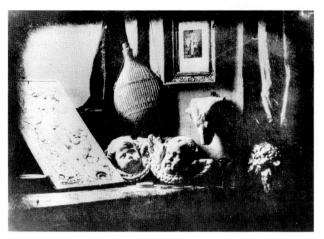

17-11. Louis-Jacques-Mandé Daguerre. *The Artist's Studio.* 1837. Daguerreotype, 6⅝ x 8⅝" (17 x 22 cm). Société Française de Photographie, Paris

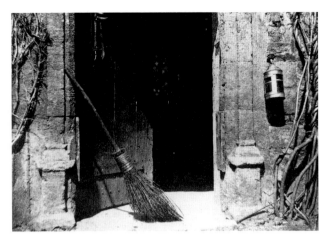

17-12. William Henry Fox Talbot. *The Open Door.* 1843. Salt-paper print from a calotype negative. Science Museum, London
Fox Talbot Collection

TECHNIQUE
HOW PHOTOGRAPHY WORKS

A camera is essentially a lightproof box with a hole, called an aperture, which is usually adjustable in size and which regulates the amount of light that strikes the film. The aperture is covered with a lens, which focuses the image on the film, and a shutter, a kind of door that opens for a controlled amount of time, to regulate the length of time that the film is exposed to light—usually a small fraction of a second. Modern cameras also have a viewer that permits the photographer to see virtually the same image that the film will "see."

Photography is based on the principle that certain substances are sensitive to light and react to light by changing **value**. In modern black-and-white photography, silver halide crystals (silver combined with iodine, chlorine, or other halogens) are suspended in a gelatin base to make an emulsion that coats the film (in early photography, before the invention of plastic, a glass plate was used with a variety of emulsions). The film is then exposed. Light reflected off objects enters the camera and strikes the film. Pale objects reflect more light than do dark ones. The silver in the emulsion collects most densely where it is exposed to the most light, producing a "negative" image on the film. Later, when the film is placed in a chemical bath (developed), the silver deposits turn black, as if tarnishing. The more light the film receives, the denser the black tone created. A positive image is created from the negative in a darkroom; then the film negative is placed over a sheet of paper that, like the film, has been treated to be light-sensitive, and light is directed through the negative onto the paper. Thus, a multiple number of positive prints are able to be generated from a single beginning negative.

around 1826 in making the first positive-image photographs at his estate at Le Gras, France.

While seeking financial help to develop his discovery, Niépce met Louis-Jacques-Mandé Daguerre (1787–1851), a Parisian painter who was experimenting in creating images for his **diorama** (a theater built for the display of huge, dramatically lit, illusionistic paintings on semi-transparent fabric). Working with a lens maker, Daguerre had developed an improved camera. After Niépce's death in 1833, Daguerre continued their research using copper plates coated in iodized silver, long known to be light-sensitive. In 1835 he left one of the plates he had been working on in a cupboard. When he returned several days later, he was amazed to find an image on it. Through a process of elimination, he determined that the vapor of a few drops of spilled mercury from a broken thermometer had produced the effect. Thus Daguerre discovered that an exposure to light of only twenty to thirty minutes would produce a latent image on one of his silvered plates treated with iodine fumes, which could then be made visible through an after-process involving mercury vapor. By 1837 he had developed a method of fixing the image by bathing the plate in a strong solution of common salt after exposure. Daguerre's first picture of this type, a still life of plaster casts and a framed drawing (fig. 17-11), makes the earliest claim for photography as an art form through its specifically "artistic" subject matter.

The 1839 announcement of Daguerre's invention prompted the English scientist William Henry Fox Talbot (1800–1877) to publish the results of his own work on what he called the **calotype** (from the Greek term for "beautiful image"). Talbot's process, even more than Daguerre's, became the basis of modern photography because, unlike Daguerre's, which produces a single, positive image, Talbot's calotype is a negative image from which an unlimited number of positives can be printed.

Beginning in the mid-1830s, Talbot copied engravings, pieces of lace, and leaves in negative by placing them on paper impregnated with silver chloride and exposing them to light. By the summer of 1835 he was using this chemically treated paper in both large and small cameras. Then, in 1840, he discovered, independently of Daguerre, that latent images resulting from exposure to the sun for short periods of time could be developed chemically. Applying the technique he had earlier used with engravings and leaves, Talbot was able to make positive prints from the calotype negatives.

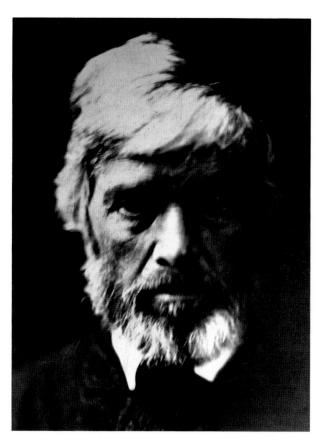

17-13. Julia Margaret Cameron. *Portrait of Thomas Carlyle.*
1863. Silver print, 10 x 8" (25.4 x 20.3 cm). The Royal Photographic Society, London

Talbot's book *The Pencil of Nature* (issued in six parts, 1844–1846) was the first book to be illustrated with photographs. The subjects of the photographs were often rural; Talbot, along with a number of his contemporaries, seems to have been distressed by the growing industrialization of Britain. In *The Open Door* (fig. 17-12), which appeared in *The Pencil of Nature*, the photographer evoked an agrarian way of life that was fast disappearing. A traditional, handcrafted broom—of a type that mass production was beginning to make obsolete—rests against the doorway of a timeworn cottage. The photographer carefully positioned the broom's handle to parallel the shadows on the door.

In 1851, Frederick Scott Archer, a British sculptor and photographer, took the final step in the development of early photography. Archer found that silver nitrate would adhere to glass if it was mixed with collodion, a combination of guncotton, ether, and alcohol used in medicinal bandages. When wet, this collodion-silver nitrate mixture needed only a few seconds' exposure to light to create an image. The result was a glass negative, from which countless positive proofs with great tonal subtleties could be made.

Once this practical photographic process had been invented, the question became how to use it. For some, the photograph was a convenience, replacing a live model; for others, it was a threat or cheap substitute for painting, especially portraiture. Those in the sciences agreed on its value for recording data, but artists were less certain how to take advantage of it. Julia Margaret Cameron (1815–1879) was one of the pioneers of photography as an art form in its own right. Cameron's principal subjects were the great men of British arts, letters, and sciences, many of whom had long been family friends.

Cameron's portrait of the famous British historian Thomas Carlyle is slightly out of focus (fig. 17-13). Cameron produced this blurred effect deliberately in her works, consciously rejecting the precision of popular portrait photography, which she felt neglected a subject's inner character. By blurring the details she sought to call attention to the light that suffused her subjects—an artistic metaphor for creative genius. Carlyle's concentrated expression is so intense that the dramatic lighting of his hair, face, and beard almost seems to emanate from within. With regard to her medium Cameron said: "My aspirations are to ennoble Photography and to secure for it the character and uses of High Art by combining the real and ideal."

Realism and Its Outgrowths in Europe

Painting of all types, whether academic or **avant-garde**, increasingly shared with photography an allegiance to factual accuracy. In the second quarter of the nineteenth century, innovative English artists such as Constable pioneered a naturalist credo that art should faithfully record ordinary life. In France this naturalistic current was represented by the Barbizon School, a group of painters working around the quiet village of Barbizon in the 1830s and 1840s. Academic jurors and conservative critics initially attempted to bar their naturalistic landscapes and rural scenes from the Salons, but after about 1850 the critical fortunes of the members of the Barbizon School soared. To those living in a rapidly urbanizing Europe, the image of a peaceful and contented country life began to grow in appeal.

Rosa Bonheur (1822–1899), though not a member of the Barbizon School, was one of the most popular French painters to address the taste for rural scenes. In order to achieve realistic depictions of the farm animals she loved, she read zoology books and made detailed studies in the countryside and in slaughterhouses. Although Bonheur received some critical praise for her animal portraits in the 1840s, her success dates from the Salon of 1848, where she showed eight paintings and won a first-class medal. As a result, the government commissioned a work from her, *Plowing in the Nivernais: The Dressing of the*

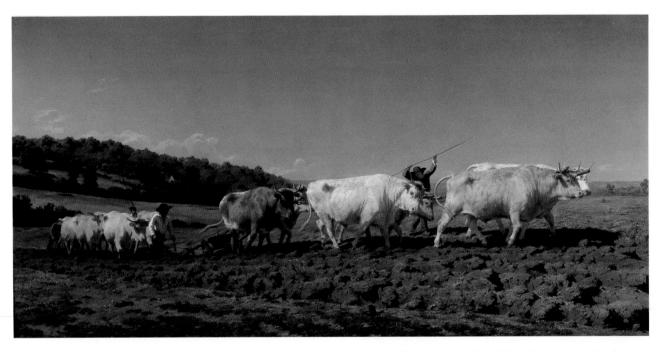

17-14. Rosa Bonheur. ***Plowing in the Nivernais: The Dressing of the Vines.*** 1849. Oil on canvas, 5'9" x 8'8" (1.75 x 2.64 m). Musée d'Orsay, Paris

Bonheur was often compared with Georges Sand, a contemporary woman writer who adopted a male name as well as male dress. Sand devoted several of her novels to the humble life of farmers and peasants. Critics at the time noted that *Plowing in the Nivernais* may have been inspired by a passage in Sand's *The Devil's Pond* (1846) that begins: "But what caught my attention was a truly beautiful sight, a noble subject for a painter. At the far end of the flat ploughland, a handsome young man was driving a magnificent team [of] oxen."

Vines (fig. 17-14). In this monumental painting, powerful beasts, anonymous workers, and fertile soil offer a reassuring image of the continuity of agrarian life. If the choice of a rural scene populated by agricultural laborers is a manifestation of new nineteenth-century tastes, the stately movement of people and animals reflects the kind of carefully balanced compositional schemes taught in the Academy and echoes scenes of processions found in classical art (see fig. 6-8).

A defining moment in Realism as we understand it today grew out of the Revolution of 1848 in France. In February of that year, Parisian workers overthrew the monarchy and established the Second Republic (1848–1851). Its founders' socialist goals, including collective ownership of the means of production and distribution, were abandoned when conservative factions won elections that summer. Fear of further disruptions continued to trouble many, while others, including the painter Gustave Courbet (1819–1877), became converts to the radicals' visions of social change. Courbet proclaimed his new political commitment in three large paintings he submitted to the Salon of 1850–1851.

One of these, *A Burial at Ornans* (fig. 17-15), is a monumental canvas showing the funeral of Courbet's grandfather Oudot, who had died in 1847. Conservative critics hated the work for its focus on common people and for its disrespect for traditional composition and standards of beauty. Instead of arranging figures in a conven-

tional pyramid that would indicate a hierarchy of importance, Courbet lined them up in rows across the picture plane—an arrangement he considered more democratic. The artist's respect and affinity for the people is expressed in the vast scale of the work—a size ordinarily reserved for the depiction of major historical events. It is also shown in the way the mourners' genuine sorrow is contrasted with the apparent indifference of the two Church officials dressed in red behind the officiating priest.

Partly for convenience, Bonheur, Courbet, and the other country-life naturalists and Realists who emerged in the 1850s are sometimes referred to as the generation of 1848 (named for the year of the Revolution). Because he had liberal political views and sympathized with working-class people, the somewhat older Honoré Daumier (see fig. 17-1) is grouped with this generation. Besides the French, artists of other Western nations also embraced Realism in the period after 1850. In Russia, Realism developed in relation to a new concern for the peasantry. In 1861 the czar abolished serfdom, emancipating Russia's peasants from the virtual slavery they had endured on the large estates of the aristocracy. Two years later, a group of painters inspired by the emancipation declared allegiance to the peasant cause and freedom from the St. Petersburg Academy of Art, which had controlled Russian art since 1754. Rejecting what they considered the ideal-

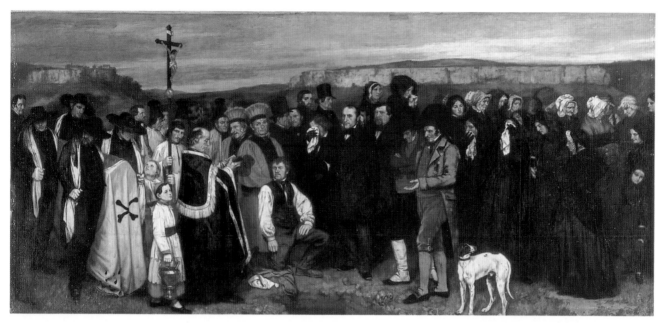

17-15. Gustave Courbet. *A Burial at Ornans.* 1849. Oil on canvas, 10'2" x 21'8" (3.1 x 6.6 m). Musée du Louvre, Paris

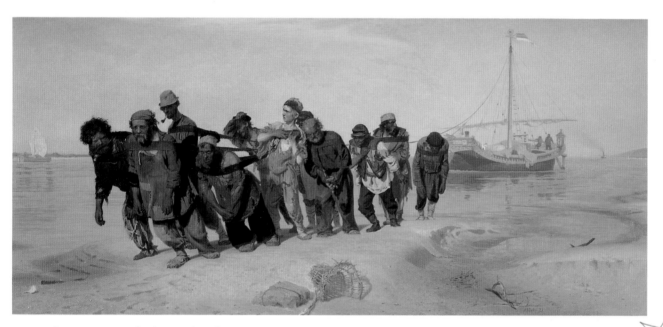

17-16. Ilya Repin. *Bargehaulers on the Volga.* 1870–73. Oil on canvas, 4'3¹/₆" x 9'2⁵/₈" (1.3 x 2.81 m). Russian State Museum, St. Petersburg

ized "art for art's sake" **aesthetics** of the Academy, the members of the group, calling themselves the Wanderers, dedicated themselves to bringing a socially relevant art to the people in traveling exhibitions.

Ilya Repin (1844–1930), who attended the St. Petersburg Academy and won a scholarship to study in Paris, joined the Wanderers on his return to Russia in 1878. He painted a series of works illustrating the social injustices then prevailing in his homeland, the first and most famous of which was *Bargehaulers on the Volga* (fig. 17-16). The painting features a group of wretchedly dressed peasants condemned to the brutal work of pulling ships up the Volga River.

In order to heighten our sympathy for these workers, Repin placed a youth in the center of the group, a young man who will soon look as old and tired as his companions unless something is done to rescue him. In this way, the painting is a cry for action.

In England, as in Russia, social concerns were expressed by a group of artists who broke away from a traditionalist academy. In 1848 seven young artists formed the Pre-Raphaelite Brotherhood to counter what they considered misguided practices of contemporary British art. Instead of the idealized Raphaelesque conventions taught at the Royal Academy, they advocated the naturalistic, descriptive approach to

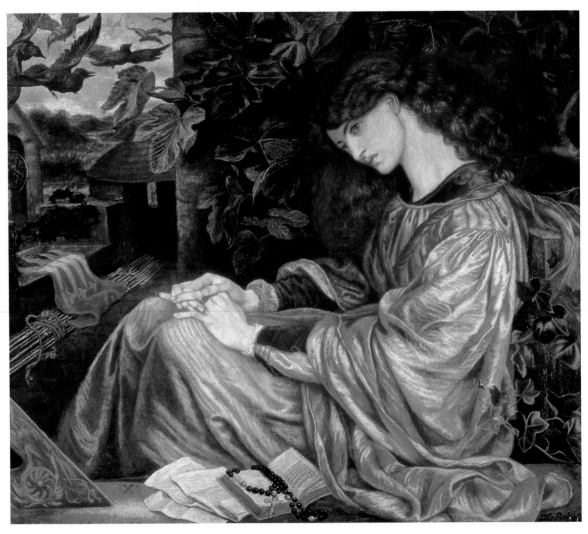

17-17. **Dante Gabriel Rossetti. La Pia de' Tolomei.** 1868–69. Oil on canvas, 41½ x 47½" (105.4 x 120.6 cm). Spencer Museum of Art, University of Kansas, Lawrence

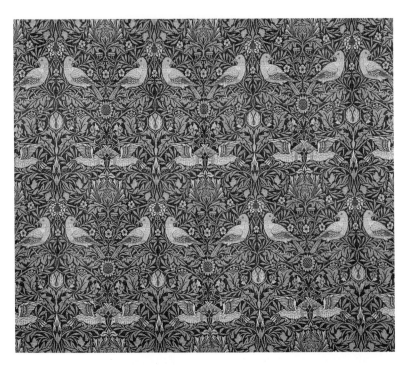

17-18. **William Morris. Bird Woolen** double cloth, designed for the drawing-room tapestry for Kelmscott House, Hammersmith. 1878. Victoria and Albert Museum, London

the human body and to nature used by certain early Renaissance masters, especially those of northern Europe. They advocated as well a moral approach to art, in keeping with a long tradition in Britain established by Hogarth (see fig. 16-7). As they were especially attracted to medieval themes, their brand of naturalism or realism was apparent more in the carefully factual rendition of figures and settings than in the use of contemporary subject matter.

Dante Gabriel Rossetti (1828–1882), a leading member of the Pre-Raphaelite Brotherhood, looked to the Middle Ages for a spiritual beauty and meaning he found lacking in the present. His painting La Pia de' Tolomei (fig. 17-17) illustrates an incident from Dante's Purgatory and is filled with the type of symbolism found in medieval paintings. La Pia (Pious One), locked up by her husband in a castle, is soon to die. The rosary and prayer book to the side of her refer to the piety from which she takes her name. The sundial and ravens apparently allude to her impending death. Her continuing love for her husband, whose freshly read letters lie under

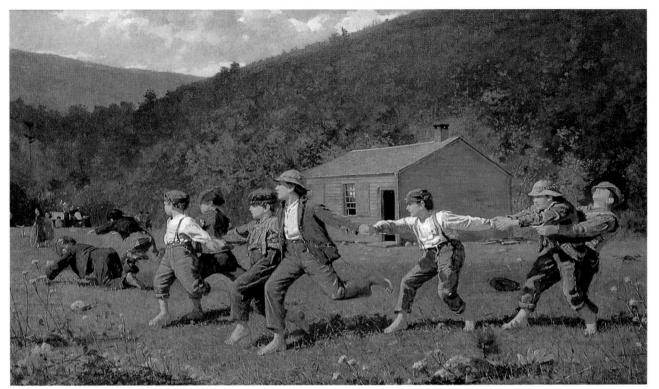

17-19. Winslow Homer. *Snap the Whip*. 1872. Oil on canvas, 22¼ x 36½" (57.1 x 92.7 cm). The Butler Institute of American Art, Youngstown, Ohio

the prayer book, is symbolized by the evergreen ivy behind her. However, the luxuriant fig leaves that surround her, traditionally associated with the Fall, have no source in Dante's tale. In fact, the painting is not simply an idealized transcription of a text but a metaphor for Rossetti's own unhappy situation. Jane Burden, Rossetti's model for this and many other paintings, was at once the wife of Rossetti's friend William Morris and also Rossetti's lover. Here she fingers her wedding ring, a captive not so much of her husband as of her marriage.

William Morris (1834–1896), a Pre-Raphaelite follower of Rossetti, was less interested in painting than in handcrafts and book design. His interest in handcrafts developed in the context of a widespread reaction against the gaudy design of industrially produced goods. Unable to find satisfactory furnishings for a new home, Morris, with the help of a number of friends, designed and made them himself. He then founded a decorating firm, Morris, Marshall & Faulkner (later changed to Morris & Company), to produce a full range of medieval-inspired objects. *Bird Woolen* (fig. 17-18) is typical of his fabric design in its use of flattened motifs consistent with the two-dimensional medium. The organic subjects, the decorative counterparts of those of naturalistic landscape painting, were meant to provide relief from modern urban existence. Morris also saw a social component in the skilled craftwork needed to produce handcrafts such as these. He wanted to eliminate the machine not only because he found its products ugly but also because of its deadening influence on the worker. With craftwork, he maintained, the laborer gets as much satisfaction as the consumer does. Unlike his Pre-Raphaelite friends, who wished to escape into idealizations of the Middle Ages, Morris saw the preindustrial era as a model for economic and social reform.

REALISM IN THE UNITED STATES

In the United States in the nineteenth century, the context surrounding Realism was far less revolutionary than it was in Europe. The United States had an unbroken tradition of realism stretching back to Colonial portrait painters such as John Singleton Copley (Chapter 16). The advocates of Realism had long considered it distinctly American and democratic, even though others saw the academic ideal as a link to a higher western European culture.

Winslow Homer (1836–1901), who worked in a naturalistic mode, began painting rural subjects about 1870. Works such as *Snap the Whip* (fig. 17-19), with its depiction of boys playing outside a one-room schoolhouse in the Adirondack Mountains, evoke the innocence of childhood and the imagined charms of a preindustrial America for an increasingly urbanized audience. Many of Homer's paintings were reproduced as wood engravings for illustrated books and magazines, reflecting the popular appeal of his subject matter.

Another famous American Realist to emerge after the Civil War, Thomas Eakins (1844–1916)

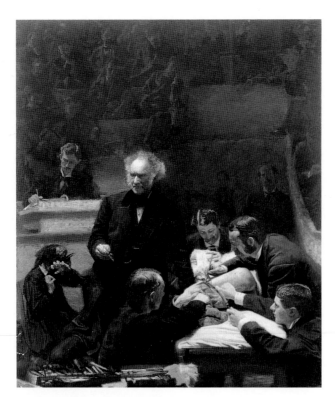

17-20. Thomas Eakins. *The Gross Clinic*. 1875. 8' x 6'5"
(2.44 x 1.96 m). Jefferson Medical College of Thomas Jefferson
University, Philadelphia

In 1876 Eakins joined the staff of the Pennsylvania Academy
of the Fine Arts, where he taught anatomy and figure drawing.
He disapproved of the academic technique of drawing from
plaster casts. In an interview in 1879, he said, "At best, they are
only imitations, and an imitation of an imitation cannot have
so much life as an imitation of nature itself." He added, "The
Greeks did not study the antique . . . the draped figures in
the Parthenon pediment were modeled from life, undoubtedly."
Eakins introduced the study of the nude model, which
shocked many in staid Philadelphia society. In 1886 he caused
a further scandal when he allowed female students to study
from male models. He was given the choice of changing his
teaching policy or resigning. He chose the latter.

studied for three years at the French École des
Beaux-Arts under Jean-Léon Gérôme (see fig.
17-10). Afterward, he spent six months in Spain,
where he was heavily influenced by the works
of Diego Velázquez (see fig. 13-15) and Jusepe
de Ribera. After he returned to Philadelphia in
1870 he specialized in frank portraits and genre
scenes whose lack of conventional charm generated little popular interest.

One work that did attract attention, *The
Gross Clinic* (fig. 17-20), was severely criticized for
offensive bluntness. The painting shows Dr.
Samuel Gross performing an operation in front
of medical students at the Jefferson Medical
College, which commissioned the work. The
doctor's hand is bloodstained, and Eakins, who
had attended Gross's lectures, did not shrink
from delineating the gory details of the operation.
The dramatic use of light, borrowed—like the
theme—from paintings of anatomy lessons by
Rembrandt, is not meant to stir emotions but
to make a point: from the darkness of ignorance
and fear, modern science is bringing forth the
light of knowledge.

Impressionism

In France the artists that matured around 1870
preferred a less austere realism. They painted
scenes of leisure in the city and the country and
depicted the pleasures of life among the upper
middle class. The leader of this loosely knit group
was Édouard Manet (1832–1883). Once classified
as an Impressionist, Manet is now generally considered a Realist. While never actually exhibiting
with the Impressionists, he was influenced by
their work, particularly their lighter palette. They
in turn were much indebted to Manet for his
sketchy, visible brushwork.

A close friend of the poet Charles Baudelaire, Manet seems to have responded to Baudelaire's call for an artist who would be the painter
of contemporary manners, "the painter of the
passing moment and of all the suggestions of
eternity that it contains." *Le Déjeuner sur l'Herbe*
(*The Luncheon on the Grass*) (fig. 17-21) was one of
Manet's most famous and controversial paintings. When the jury for the official Salon of 1863
turned down nearly 3,000 works, including
Manet's, a storm of protest erupted, prompting
the French emperor Napoleon III to order an
exhibition of the refused works called the Salon
des Refusés (Salon of the Rejected Ones). In
that exhibition, *Le Déjeuner sur l'Herbe* provoked a
critical avalanche that was a mixture of shock
and bewilderment.

Part of the problem was that Manet ignored
the basic tenets of academic painting. To a viewer
used to traditional perspective and the rounded
modeling of forms using gradations of shadow,
the stark lighting of Manet's nude and the flat,
cutout quality of his figures were jarring. The
figures are not integrated into their natural surroundings but seem to stand out against them,
as if before a painted backdrop.

Nor did critics understand why Manet had
chosen the scandalous subject of well-dressed
men relaxing with scantily clad women, although
the artist had thought that his basic intent
would be fairly obvious to viewers. According
to a close friend, Manet intended to make a
modern version of a highly respectable painting
in the Louvre, Titian's *Pastoral Concert* (see fig. 2).
Even with this information, however, what Manet
meant by his radical remake of the earlier painting remains a matter of considerable debate.
Several details in the picture suggest that
he may have intended to make a contemporary
interpretation of the popular Renaissance theme
of sacred and profane love, a contrast between
spiritual love and that of the flesh. For example,
the man on the right makes a curious hand gesture, with his thumb pointing to the clothed
woman in the stream and his index finger pointing to the nude. Above the woman in the water,
itself a symbol of purity, is a bird, traditionally

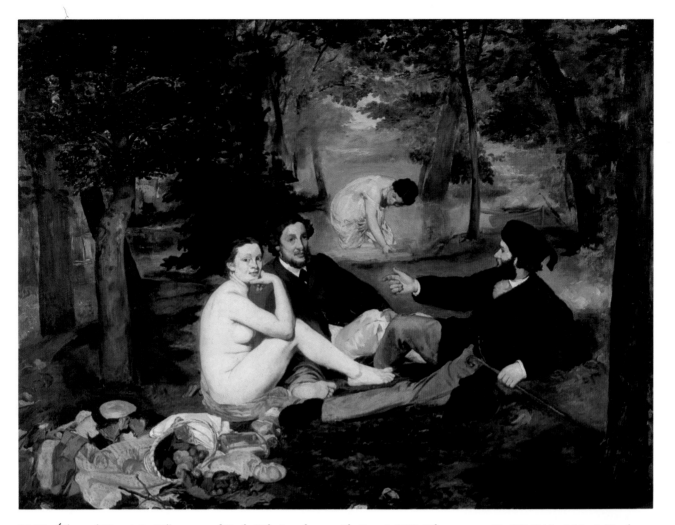

17-21. Édouard Manet. *Le Déjeuner sur l'Herbe* (*The Luncheon on the Grass*). 1863. Oil on canvas, 7' x 8'8" (2.13 x 2.64 m). Musée d'Orsay, Paris

associated with the spirit. In the lower left corner, next to the nude's discarded garments, is a frog, often an emblem of the flesh or the devil.

While Manet was attempting to paint modern life without breaking entirely with the great art of the past, most of his slightly younger associates sought a completely fresh and unmediated vision. The leader in this quest was Claude Monet (1840–1926). Whereas earlier landscape painters had conceived nature essentially as a "site"—that is, a place—Monet learned to approach it largely as a "sight," something to stimulate the eye (see fig. 16). He advised a friend in a letter to forget the subject matter when he went out to paint: "Merely think, Here is a little square of blue, here an oblong of pink, here a streak of yellow, and paint it just as it looks to you, the exact color and shape, until it gives your own naive impression of the scene before you" (*The American Magazine of Art*, 18 [March 1927]). Monet even titled one of his pictures *Impression, Sunrise* (1872). A critic, seeing it at an independent exhibition organized by Monet and others in 1874, titled his review "Exhibition of Impressionists," and the term *Impressionist* was quickly adopted as a convenient, if not entirely accurate, label for all thirty artists who participated in the show and the seven subsequent

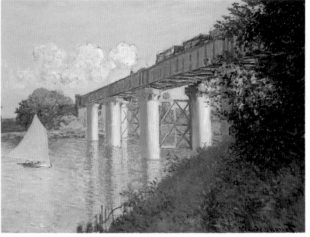

17-22. Claude Monet. *The Railroad Bridge*. 1874. Oil on canvas, 21³⁄₄ x 28⁷⁄₈" (55.2 x 73.3 cm). Philadelphia Museum of Art
The John G. Johnson Collection

exhibitions Monet and his circle organized between 1874 and 1886.

Monet's early way of looking at the world is especially evident in the works he produced in the 1870s while living in Argenteuil, a flourishing Parisian suburb. Paintings such as *The Railroad Bridge* (fig. 17-22) display heightened color and broken brushstrokes intended to capture more accurately the shifting surface of natural appearance. Because of the bright sunny colors

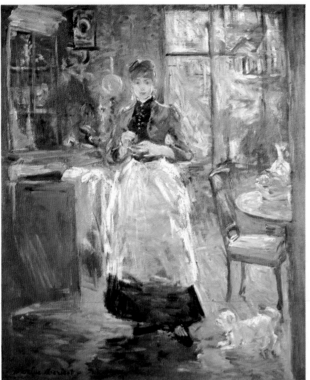

17-23. Berthe Morisot. In the Dining Room. 1886. Oil on canvas, 24¹/₈ x 19³/₄" (61.3 x 50.2 cm). National Gallery of Art, Washington, D.C.
Chester Dale Collection

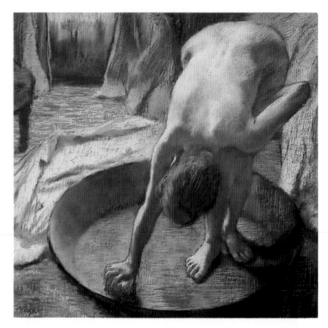

17-24. Edgar Degas. The Tub. c. 1885–86. Pastel, 27¹/₂ x 27¹/₂" (69.9 x 69.9 cm). Hill-Stead Museum, Farmington, Connecticut

and the emphasis on summertime pleasures, one tends not to notice how often these works feature industrial subjects, such as the railway bridge that overshadows the sailboat. As Monet seems to have understood, the two themes are complementary: modern industrial progress provided the economic basis for the new leisure pursuits of the middle class.

Monet's fellow Impressionist Berthe Morisot (1841–1895), who participated in seven of the group's eight exhibitions, focused on women and domestic scenes. The vigorous and varied brushwork of In the Dining Room (fig. 17-23) calls attention to the act of painting itself. The palette of pastel colors, and especially the lavish use of white, are characteristic of Morisot's work. In her painting, Morisot sought an equality for women that she felt men refused to cede. Late in life she commented: "I don't think there has ever been a man who treated a woman as an equal, and that's all I would have asked, for I know I'm worth as much as they" (cited in Higonnet, page 19).

Unlike Morisot, not all of the painters who are grouped with the Impressionists (because they participated in some or all of the exhibitions organized by Monet and his friends) really worked in an Impressionist style. The artist whose work most severely tests the legitimacy of

the Impressionist label is Edgar Degas (1834–1917). His friendship with Manet, whom he met in 1862, and with the realist critics in his circle turned him gradually toward the depiction of contemporary life. Unlike Monet and some of the other Impressionists, however, he avoided the complete dissolution of form into light, and he remained deeply concerned with the careful delineation of the human figure. He drew regularly from live models throughout his career.

Part of Degas's intent was to counter the clichés of academic training by revealing the truths obscured by them. In his pastel The Tub (fig. 17-24), for example, the bather is off-center and is viewed obliquely from above because things often appear to us that way. Instead of moving gracefully and effortlessly in accord with academic standards, she reaches awkwardly, almost uncomfortably, for her soap. Degas meant such works to be both naturalistic and to serve as a visual antidote to the tired formulas of conventional art and illustration.

It could be argued, based on works such as The Tub, that Degas never truly adopted an Impressionist mode. Other artists passed through an Impressionist phase but then went on to explore varied stylistic ideas. In the years after 1880, in particular, a number of artists began to reconsider their earlier approaches or make

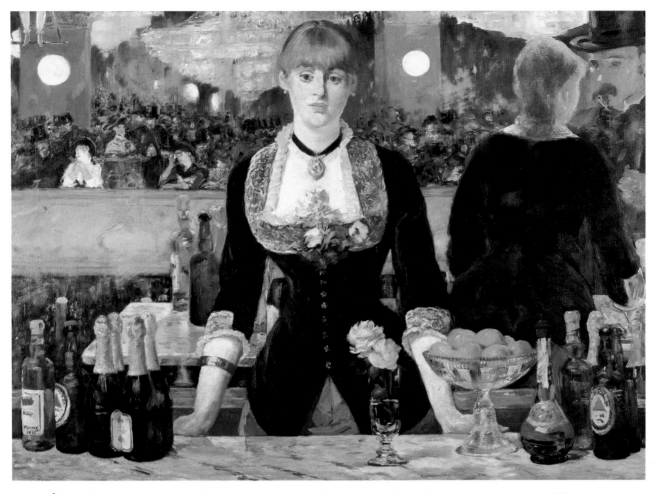

17-25. Édouard Manet. A Bar at the Folies-Bergère. 1881–82. Oil on canvas, 37³/₄ x 51¹/₆" (95.9 x 130 cm). Courtauld Institute Galleries, London
Home House Collection

important adjustments to them. Manet, for instance, had embraced his younger colleagues' brighter palette about 1870, but his late paintings, such as A Bar at the Folies-Bergère (fig. 17-25), contradict the happy aura of works such as Monet's The Railroad Bridge (see fig. 17-22). Manet's painting features one of the barmaids at the Folies-Bergère, a large nightclub with a series of bars arranged around a theater that offered vaudeville acts. A performer on a trapeze, whose legs can be seen at the upper left, entertains the elegant crowd reflected in the mirror behind the bar. Manet puts the viewer directly in front of the barmaid, in the position of her customer. From the front, the woman appears self-absorbed and downcast, but her mirrored reflection and that of her customer suggest a different story. There she leans toward the patron, whose intent gaze she appears to meet; the physical and

psychological distance between them has vanished. Exactly what Manet meant to suggest by this juxtaposition has been much debated. One possibility is that he wanted to contrast poignantly the longing for happiness and intimacy with the disappointing reality of everyday existence.

What many of the Impressionists found missing in their art of the 1870s was not truth value but permanence. Pierre-Auguste Renoir (1841–1919) wanted to turn Impressionism into a style that could compete with the classic art of the Renaissance and antiquity. Despite his continued use of sensual brushwork and lush color, Renoir's paintings from about 1880 onward present firmly modeled figures and relatively conservative compositions. In Luncheon of the Boating Party of 1881, for example, a variation on the traditional pyramidal structure advocated by the academies underlies the apparent informality

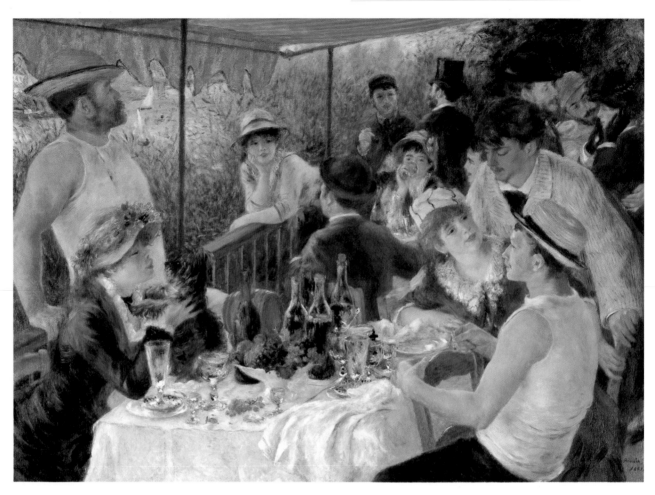

17-26. Pierre-Auguste Renoir. *Luncheon of the Boating Party.* 1881. Oil on canvas, 4'3" x 5'8" (1.29 x 1.73 m). The Phillips Collection, Washington, D.C.

of the summer scene (fig. 17-26). A small triangle whose apex is the woman leaning on the rail is set within a larger, somewhat looser one that culminates in the two men at the rear. Thus, instead of a moment quickly scanned in passing (an impression), Renoir created a more stable and permanent scene.

Mary Cassatt (1845–1926), who, like Renoir, exhibited with the Impressionists, also moved toward a firmer handling of form and more classic subjects in the period after 1880. In the *Maternal Caress* (fig. 17-27), one of the many colored prints she produced in her later career, Cassatt offers a sensitive response to the tradition of the Madonna and Child. The plump infant, apparently fresh from the bath, shares a tender moment with its adoring mother. The flat decorative patterns, simple contours, and sharply sloping floor derive from Japanese prints (see fig. 9-24), which became very popular among

French artists in the late nineteenth century.

By the early twentieth century, of the survivors of the original group of artists designated as Impressionists, Monet remained closest to the original roots of the style, with its flickering brushstrokes designed to capture the passing moment. During the last two decades of his life, Monet found endless subject matter in the gardens and the lily pond at Giverny, his country home. In most of his paintings of the lily pond, there is neither a horizon line nor a place for the viewer to stand. We are in the midst of the pool, between water and sky, adrift among floating blossoms and reflections of leaves and clouds. The largest of these water-lily canvases, such as one in the Museum of Modern Art in New York (fig. 17-28), are almost a contradiction in terms. They dwarf us, envelop us, even engulf us completely in what began as a single fleeting moment of time.

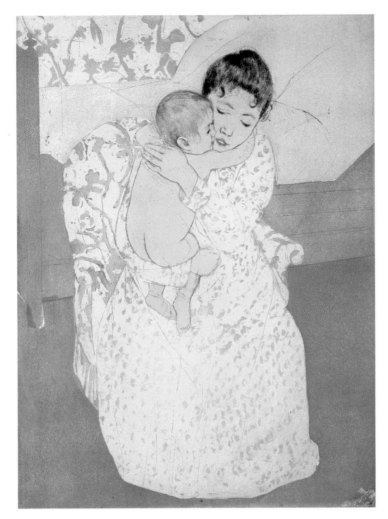

17-27. Mary Cassatt.
Maternal Caress. 1891.
Drypoint, soft-ground
etching, and aquatint,
14³/₄ x 10³/₄"
(37.5 x 27.3 cm).
National Gallery of Art,
Washington, D.C.
Rosenwald Collection

17-28. Claude Monet. *Water Lilies.* c. 1920. Oil on canvas, 6'5¹/₂" x 19'7¹/₂" (1.97 x 5.98 m). The Museum of Modern Art, New York
Mrs. Simon Guggenheim Fund

Vasily Kandinsky. *Improvisation*
No. 30 (*Cannons*). 1913. Oil on
canvas, 43¹/₄" x 43¹/₄" (109.9 x 109.9 cm).
The Art Institute of Chicago

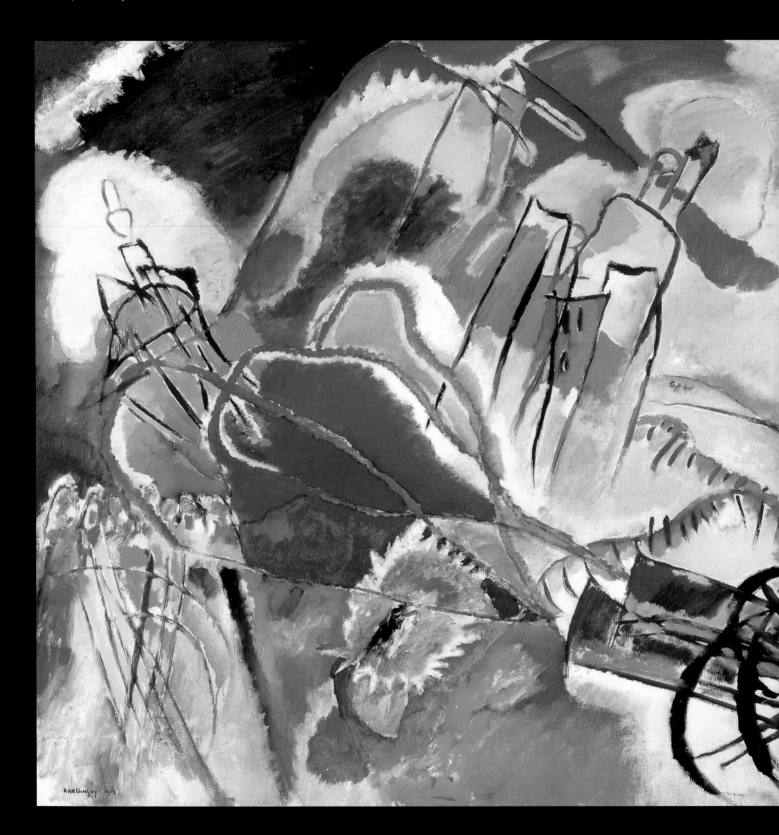

Representational

At first glance, this painting looks *nonrepresentational* (without recognizable subject matter). A closer look reveals otherwise. In the lower-right corner you can find the abstracted forms of cannons. Although the cannons are representational enough to be identifiable, the outlined vertical forms in the middle ground are less specific, perhaps suggesting buildings or churches. Above and behind the cannons you can find what might represent fences in a field or on dunes, although the rest of the composition and imagery gives few clues as to how these elements might fit together.

Abstract

This is an *abstract* painting with a few forms that refer to objects. Line and color have powerful lives of their own, ones that are independent of subject matter. Kandinsky believed that color possesses special emotional and spiritual powers. By the time he was painting in a purely abstract style (around 1914), the formal elements of color and line had themselves become his subject matter.

POST-IMPRESSIONISM THROUGH EARLY MODERN ART

K E Y S to Art History

REPRESENTATIONAL, NONOBJECTIVE, & ABSTRACT ART

Representational art, which has recognizable subject matter, has overwhelmingly dominated the history of art since the Renaissance (or fifteenth century). *Abstraction*, first introduced on page 30, has been present in greater and lesser degrees as well. The art of Vasily Kandinsky (1866–1944) was pivotal to Modernism's transition from representational to abstract art. What makes Kandinsky's work *abstract* in the context of modern art is that the artist eventually gave up all references to objects and made *nonobjective* art. The year he painted *Improvisation No. 30 (Cannons)*—1913—was a turning-point year for modern art in Europe and America. It was the year of the International Exhibition of Modern Art at the 69th Regiment Armory (known popularly as the Armory Show) in New York (see page 432), the first full-scale exhibition of modern European and American painting and sculpture in America. Kandinsky was represented by one painting there. *Improvisation No. 30* is not wholly abstract, but it is an abstraction of objects and forms expressive of a theme.

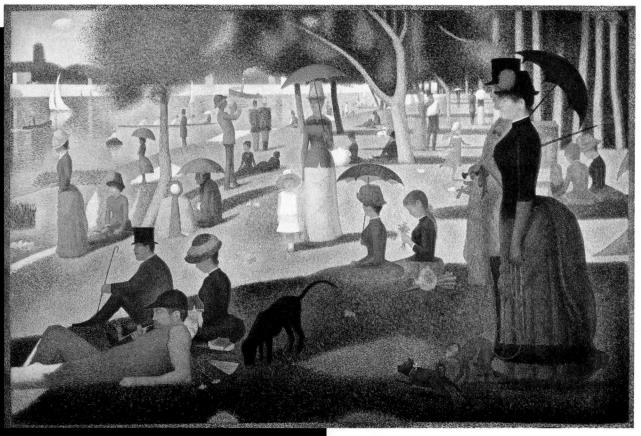

18-1. Georges Seurat. *A Sunday Afternoon on the Island of La Grande Jatte.* 1884–86. Oil on canvas, 6'9½" x 10'1¼" (2.07 x 3.08 m). The Art Institute of Chicago Helen Birch Bartlett Memorial Collection

In *A Sunday Afternoon on the Island of La Grande Jatte* (fig. 18-1), Georges Seurat (1859–1891) took a typical Impressionist subject, weekend leisure activities, and gave it an entirely new handling. An avid reader of scientific color theory, he applied his paint in small dots of pure color in the belief that when they are "mixed" in the eye—as opposed to being mixed on the palette—the resulting colors would be more luminous. He used upward-moving lines (seen in the angle of the coastline) and warm bright colors, presuming that these elements created "happy" paintings. During the months he spent visiting the island, he studied the people he found there and the way the light fell on the figures and the landscape. Every character in the final painting—even the woman with the monkey—was based on his observations at the site.

The style Seurat developed, known as Pointillism, was only one of a dizzying array of western European and American artistic styles that began in the time period known as Neo-Impressionism. These various trends, often consciously at odds with one another, are nevertheless grouped under a common label, *modernism*. In many ways, modernism is an attitude, not a look. Beginning with Manet, the artist who self-consciously strove to create something new by using and building on the past, the process of painting—the materials and their handling—began to assume a much larger role in the work of art. Some of these styles were directed at self-expression, others at the suppression of human feeling. Many artists saw the need to communicate deep-felt social concerns. A sometimes unbridled utopianism often stood in direct counterpoint to the political crises of the age. And as if to defy all consistency, yet another group of artists saw the artwork as a unique experience in which the materials and process of painting, carving, or printmaking was primary, leading ultimately to abstraction.

Like the word *Romanticism*, the term *modernism* is a disputed one, with neither an authoritative definition nor an entirely agreed-upon time frame. While definitions for this term are constantly undergoing revision, one traditional but still useful way of looking at modern art was popularized by the art historian Alfred H. Barr, Jr., director for many years at the Museum of Modern Art in New York. Barr saw two broad tendencies as standing out in the work of modernist artists: loosely articulated, these are **expressionism** and **formalism**. Expressionism is the manipulation of formal (visual) components or representational elements in a work of art to convey intense feeling. Formalism is the aesthetic arrangement of shapes, colors, and forms. In a modernist artwork, the play of these so-called formal elements may take precedence over the naturalistic or realistic representation of a subject as it appears in real life. Expressionist and formalist currents may intermingle in modernist artworks, just as Neoclassic and Romantic currents did in the period around 1800.

The culmination of modernism, in the view of the important modernist critic Clement Greenberg, was the development of **abstraction**. Greenberg saw in the history of modern art the gradual shift away from the representation of specific things, whether imaginary or real, in favor of an emphasis on the intrinsic characteristics of an artistic medium. In painting, this shift meant an increasing concern with colored

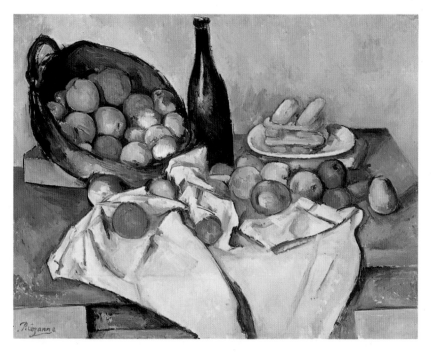

18-2. Paul Cézanne. *Still Life with Basket of Apples.* 1890–94. Oil on canvas, 24³/₈ x 31" (61.9 x 78.7 cm). The Art Institute of Chicago
Helen Birch Bartlett Memorial Collection

paint and its two-dimensional canvas support. However, many modernist artists—the Surrealists, for example (Chapter 19)—rejected abstraction, and most critics and art historians now agree that **nonrepresentational** art (not attempting to reproduce the appearance of the natural world) was only one facet, if a very important one, of modernism.

Post-Impressionism

Many scholars date the beginnings of modernism to the flattening of form in the work of Manet (see fig. 17-21) or to the stylistic innovations of the Impressionists. Others locate its origins in the work of the Post-Impressionists. Narrowly defined, *Post-Impressionism* refers to the work of five painters who assimilated much from Impressionism but in the end moved on to develop five quite different styles. These five artists are Paul Cézanne (1839–1906), Georges Seurat (1859–1891), Paul Gauguin (1848–1903), Vincent van Gogh (1853–1890), and Henri de Toulouse-Lautrec (1864–1901). In a broader sense, however, *Post-Impressionist* refers to the period when these five artists were either active or still influential. Thus the term encompasses the entire generation of diverse innovators, including sculptors and photographers as well as painters, whose principal work falls between about 1880 and 1910.

Paul Cézanne, ignored or misunderstood in his own day by all but a few perceptive collectors

and fellow artists, was the Post-Impressionist artist whose work most greatly changed the future of Western art. His radical stylistic innovations paved the way for abstraction. In his early works, beginning around 1870, Cézanne treated a number of violently Romantic themes in a purposefully dark, crude style. Soon after, he discovered Impressionism and renounced this mode for the objective transcription of what he called his "sensations" of nature. Unlike his Impressionist colleagues, however, Cézanne resisted thinking about landscape in terms of its human uses, and his "sensations" went beyond optical effects. In *Still Life with Basket of Apples* (fig. 18-2), for example, an apparently conventional studio arrangement of fruit, biscuits, and wine bottle is, on closer examination, on the verge of collapse. As he shifts his viewpoint to capture every aspect of the objects, the bottle seems to tilt precariously on a tabletop whose two sides do not match. The dynamic folds of the white cloth add considerably to the work's instability; only the small tucks in the fabric prevent the apples from cascading to the floor. The strained balance in such studio works suggests that Cézanne was moving beyond a faithful reproduction of objects in his still lifes; he was re-creating and reconstructing nature.

In Cézanne's late period (c. 1895–1906), his favorite subject was Mont Sainte-Victoire, a large mountain in the vicinity of his home. Judging from paintings of Mont Sainte-Victoire, such as the

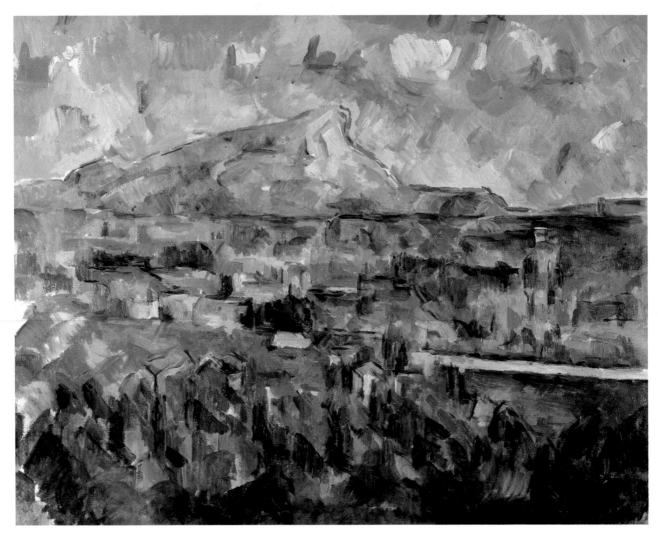

18-3. Paul Cézanne. *Mont Sainte-Victoire*. 1904–6. Oil on canvas, 25¹/₂ x 32" (65 x 81 cm). Private collection, Pennsylvania

After receiving a considerable inheritance in 1886, Cézanne returned to his hometown, Aix-en-Provence, in the south of France. In 1901–1902 he built a studio in the countryside with a large window facing Mont Sainte-Victoire, to facilitate painting the subject that had increasingly come to preoccupy him.

one illustrated in figure 18-3, Cézanne saw in nature not only the shifting, ever-changing surface so ably captured by the Impressionists but also the solidity and constancy that lay beneath it. Although it is tempting to see in *Mont Sainte-Victoire* evidence of Cézanne's ultimate rejection of Impressionist aesthetics for an interest in solid form, this and works like it remain firmly grounded in the understanding of the individual brush mark as a record of the artist's immediate "sensation" of nature. In the middle section, for example, the solid rectangular strokes, generally applied according to a rigid grid of vertical and horizontal lines, nevertheless form dynamic and irregular contours. The juxtaposition of warm colors like red and yellow, which appear to come forward, with cool colors like blue, which appear to recede, creates a spatial tension that is heightened by the contradiction between the presumed depth and distance of the landscape features depicted in the painting and the flat painted surface the viewer actually sees. Pablo Picasso, Georges Braque, and others would later view this move away from three-dimensional illusionism and descriptive accuracy as evidence of a pioneering interest in abstraction, but producing nonrepresentational art was never

Cézanne's intention. Rather, he *abstracted* what he considered nature's deepest truth—its essential tension between stasis and change.

Cézanne's Post-Impressionist colleagues Georges Seurat and Paul Gauguin continued a different, distinctive aspect of modernist art: the belief in art as a force for social change. The word that came into general use to describe such art was *avant-garde*. Originally a military term meaning "advance guard," it was used in 1825 by a French socialist, the Comte de Saint-Simon, to refer to those artists whose visual expression would prepare people to accept the social changes he and his colleagues envisioned. The idea of producing a socially revolutionary art had briefly attracted such artists as Courbet, but the real popularity of this notion dates from the Post-Impressionist era.

Georges Seurat was apparently one of the first in his generation to think of himself in these terms. After studying at the École des Beaux-Arts, he devoted his energies to "correcting" Impressionism, which he found too intellectually shallow and too improvisational. In the mid-1880s he gathered around him a circle of young artists who became known as the Neo-Impressionists. The work that became the centerpiece of the

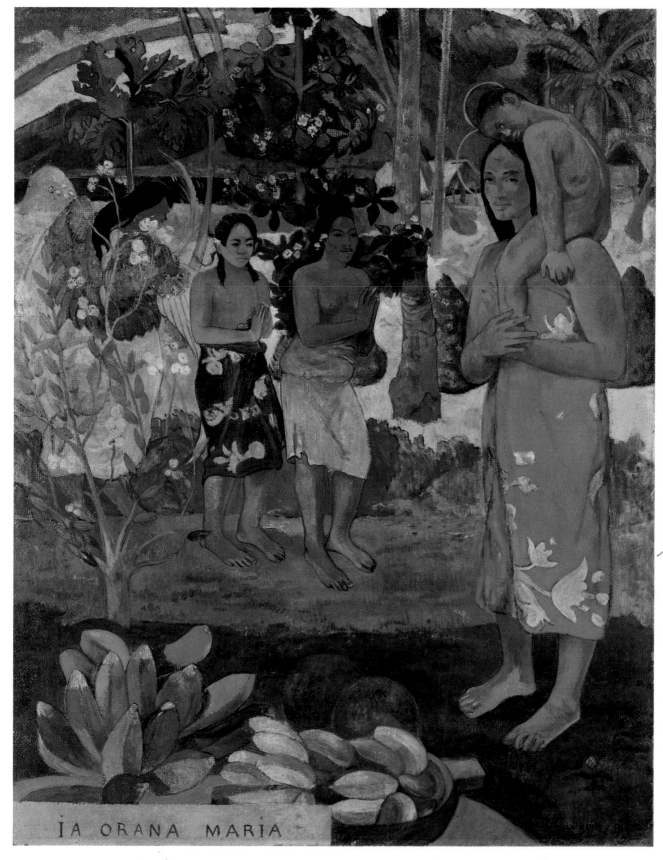

IA ORANA MARIA

18-4. Paul Gauguin. Ia Orana Maria (We Hail Thee Mary). c. 1891–92. Oil on canvas, 44³/₄ x 34¹/₂" (113.7 x 87.6 cm). The Metropolitan Museum of Art, New York Bequest of Samuel A. Lewisohn, 1951

new movement and made his reputation was *A Sunday Afternoon on the Island of La Grande Jatte* (see fig. 18-1).

From its first appearance, the painting, with its curiously formal and stylized figures, gave rise to a number of conflicting interpretations. Contemporary accounts of the island indicate that on Sundays it was noisy, littered, and chaotic. By painting it the way he did, Seurat may have intended to show how tranquil it could be. Was he merely criticizing the middle class or was he trying to establish a social ideal—a model for a more civilized way of life in the modern city? The key perhaps lies in the composure of the two central figures, the mother and child around which the others move. The child, in particular, is a model of self-restraint. She may even represent Seurat's sense of the progress of human evolution,

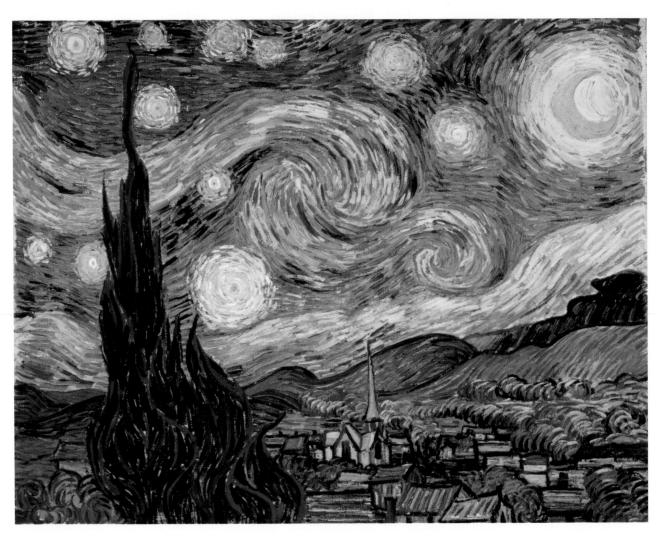

18-5. Vincent van Gogh. *The Starry Night*. 1889. Oil on canvas, 28³/₄ x 36¹/₂" (73 x 93 cm). The Museum of Modern Art, New York
Acquired through the Lillie P. Bliss Bequest

as obliquely suggested by the contrasting presence of the monkey in the right foreground. The growth of massive industrial cities was thought by many to have terrible personal consequences for its citizens. When people moved to the urban centers to find work, their old family and community ties were often strained or broken, and they found themselves surrounded by strangers, feeling alienated and alone.

Whereas Seurat seems to have believed that people were not civilized enough, the French painter Paul Gauguin held the opposite view. At the age of thirty-seven, Gauguin gave up a conventional existence as a Paris stockbroker and left his wife and children to pursue a full-time painting career. In 1891, in an extreme reaction against the modern world, he moved to Tahiti, an island in the South Pacific Ocean, in the belief that he could return to what he thought was a more idyllic state.

The first picture Gauguin painted in Tahiti was *Ia Orana Maria* (*We Hail Thee Mary*) (fig. 18-4). The new Mary, a strong Polynesian woman holding a contented and robust child, stands in sharp contrast to the crucified Christs and mourning

Marys that dominated French Catholicism. Gauguin even wrote in an essay that what the modern world needed was Adam and Eve's blissful ignorance before the Temptation. He thought that he could reenter the Garden of Paradise among the Tahitians, a people he and other Europeans imagined were childlike and close to nature. The warm, rich colors and decorative patterns in the painting underscore the message that life in this supposedly uncivilized world is sweet and harmonious. The fresh-plucked fruits on the table in the foreground invite the viewer to leave a chaotic industrial society and enjoy the bounty of a primeval Paradise.

Among the artists in Gauguin's circle before his departure for Tahiti was the Dutch painter Vincent van Gogh. Van Gogh shared Gauguin's preference for a simple, preindustrial life, and the two planned to move to the south of France and establish a commune of like-minded artists. In the spring of 1888, Van Gogh moved to Arles, where the radiant sun and the lush farmland prompted him to create such dazzling images as his famous *Sunflowers* (see fig. 17). However, when Gauguin joined him late in the year, con-

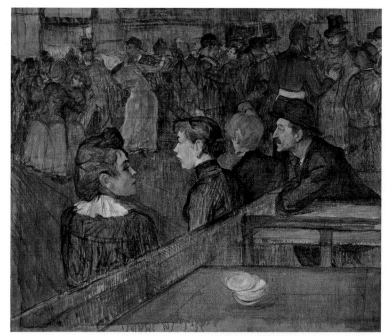

**18-6. Henri de Toulouse-Lautrec.
*At the Moulin de la Galette.***
1889. Oil on canvas, 35¹/₂ x 39¹/₄"
(90.2 x 99.7 cm). The Art Institute
of Chicago
Mr. and Mrs. Lewis L. Coburn Memorial
Collection

stant quarrels led to a violent confrontation in which Van Gogh threatened Gauguin with a razor. After Gauguin fled, Van Gogh turned the instrument on himself and cut off the lobe of his right ear. This was the first of a series of psychological crises that led to the artist's eventual suicide in July 1890.

The paintings Van Gogh produced during the last year and a half of his life testify to his heightened emotional state. At the same time, they contributed significantly to the emergence of the expressionistic tradition, in which the intensity of an artist's feelings overrides fidelity to the actual appearance of things. One of the earliest and most famous examples of expressionism is *The Starry Night* (fig. 18-5), which Van Gogh painted from the window of his cell in a mental asylum. The sky pulsating with exploding stars high above the quiet town is clearly a record of what Van Gogh felt, not a record of what he saw. The painting may give expression to the then-popular theory that after death people journeyed to a star, where they continued their lives. Contemplating immortality in a letter, Van Gogh wrote: "Just as we take the train to get to Tarascon or Rouen, we take death to reach a star." In the painting, a cypress tree, a traditional symbol of both death and eternal life, dramatically links the terrestrial world and the heavens.

Expressionism was one way to communicate the psychological impact of life in the modern world. Another artistic response to these concerns was simply to document them, a tactic followed by the Post-Impressionist Henri de Toulouse-Lautrec in his paintings and prints (see "Lithography," right). From the late 1880s, Toulouse-Lautrec dedicated himself to visually chronicling life in Montmartre, a part of Paris devoted to entertainment and inhabited by many who lived

TECHNIQUE
LITHOGRAPHY

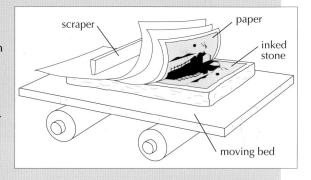

Aloys Senefelder invented **lithography** in Bavaria, Germany, in 1796 and registered for an exclusive right to the process the following year. Lithography is a planographic process— that is, the printing is done from a flat surface. It was the first wholly new printing process to be introduced since the fifteenth century, when the **intaglio**, or **incising**, process was developed.

Lithography, still popular today, is based on the natural antagonism between oil and water. The artist draws on a flat surface—traditionally, fine-grained stone—with a greasy, crayonlike instrument. The stone's surface is wiped with water, then with an oil-based ink. The ink adheres to the greasy areas but not to the damp ones. A sheet of paper is laid facedown on the inked stone, which is passed through a flatbed press. A scraper applies light pressure from above as the stone and paper pass under it, transferring ink from stone to paper, thus making lithography a direct method of creating a printed image. Francisco Goya, Honoré Daumier, and Henri de Toulouse-Lautrec exploited the medium to great effect.

on the fringes of society. *At the Moulin de la Galette* (fig. 18-6) depicts the sad reality of the festivities at a popular dance hall. The happy couples in the background are only foils for the four lonely, dispirited figures in the front. A diagonal rail creates a barrier between the sexes, and the rail and a foreground table separate the viewer from the scene. In these ways, the painting reveals the artist's sensitivity to a new kind of loneliness: the modern feeling of alienation.

Auguste Rodin (1840–1917) was the most important sculptor of the Post-Impressionist era. His status was confirmed in 1884, when he won

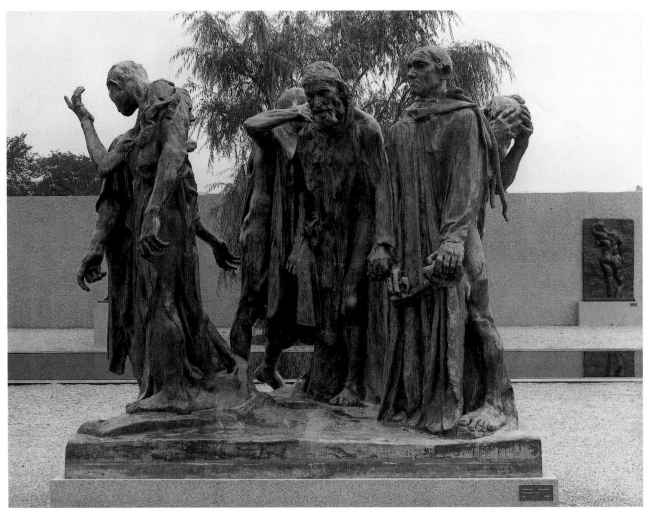

18-7. Auguste Rodin. *Burghers of Calais*. 1884–86. Bronze, 6'10½" x 7'11" x 6'6" (2.1 x 2.4 x 2.0 m). Hirshhorn Museum and Sculpture Garden, Smithsonian Institution, Washington, D.C.

a competition for a French monument for his *Burghers of Calais* (fig. 18-7), commissioned to commemorate an event from the Hundred Years' War. In 1347 King Edward III of England had besieged Calais but offered to spare the city if six leading citizens (or burghers) would surrender themselves to him for execution. Rodin shows the six volunteers—dressed only in sackcloth with rope halters and carrying the keys to the city—marching out to what they assume will be their deaths.

The officials at Calais were upset to find that their chosen sculptor produced not calm, idealized heroes but rather ordinary-looking men in various attitudes of resignation and despair. Rodin expressively lengthened their arms, greatly enlarged their hands and feet, and changed the light fabric he knew they wore into a much heavier one, showing not only how they may have looked but how they must have felt as they forced themselves to take one difficult step after another. He placed the figures on a low base, almost at street level, to suggest to viewers that ordinary people like themselves were capable of noble acts.

Expressionism

From the Post-Impressionist period onwards, a great many artists assumed that the chief func-

tion of art was to express their intense feelings to the world. The Norwegian painter and print-maker Edvard Munch (1863–1944) was one such artist. When Munch was five, he witnessed his mother's death from tuberculosis. In 1875 he nearly died of the same disease. Three years later, his favorite sister hemorrhaged to death just as his mother had. As an artist he was rejected for his frank treatments of death and sex, not only by a general audience but by progressive artists and critics as well.

Munch's personal and professional anxiety found expression in his most famous work, *The Scream* (fig. 18-8). Munch recorded the painting's genesis in his diary: "One evening I was walking along a path; the city was on one side, and the fjord below. I was tired and ill. . . . I sensed a shriek passing through nature. . . . I painted this picture, painted the clouds as actual blood." The tormented figure in the painting, hands clasped over its ears, attempts to shut out the primal scream. The skull-like head suggests that the overwhelming anxiety Munch expressed was chiefly a dread of death.

Another artist of intense feelings was the American visionary painter Albert Pinkham Ryder (1847–1917). By the early 1880s he had evolved a distinctive approach to landscapes and sea-

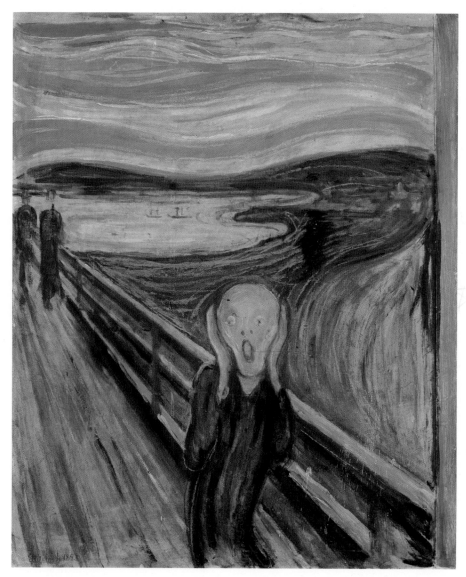

18-8. Edvard Munch. *The Scream.* 1893. Tempera and casein on cardboard, 36 x 29" (91.3 x 73.7 cm). Nasjonalgalleriet, Oslo

scapes, inspired in part by the European Romantic painting tradition, especially as represented by Delacroix and Turner (Chapter 16). In a painting of about 1885 (fig. 18-9), Ryder portrayed a scene from the biblical story of Jonah, who was thrown overboard from a ship and swallowed by a great fish. The immense billows of the sea, representing hostile nature, are intensified through dynamic curves and sharp contrasts of light and dark. In the end, Jonah was forgiven and saved by the loving God, shown holding an orb, the symbol of divine power, in a blaze of redemptive light.

The paths toward expressionism were many and varied, as the vast difference between Munch's and Ryder's works makes clear. In Germany, Paula Modersohn-Becker (1876–1907) took yet another tack. Working as a painter in the rustic village of Worpswede, a famous artist's retreat, she initially adopted a naturalistic approach to rural life. Dissatisfied with the results, she made four trips to Paris between 1900 and her death in 1907 to assimilate developments in Post-Impressionist

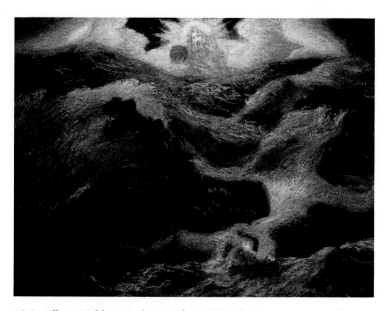

18-9. Albert Pinkham Ryder. *Jonah.* c. 1885. Oil on canvas, mounted on fiberboard, 27¼ x 34⅜" (69.2 x 87.3 cm). National Museum of American Art, Smithsonian Institution, Washington, D.C. Gift of John Gellatly

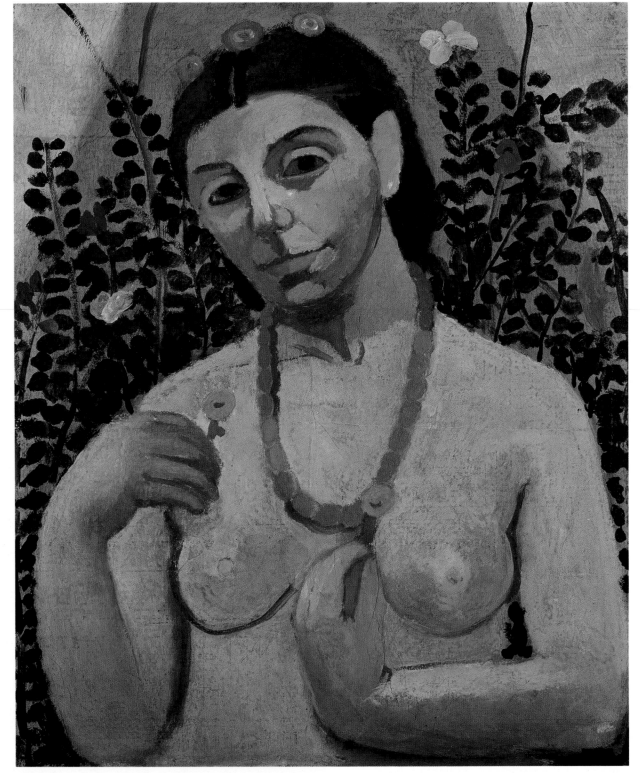

18-10. Paula Modersohn-Becker. *Self-Portrait with an Amber Necklace.* 1906. Oil on canvas, 24 x 19³/₄" (61 x 50 cm). Öffentliche Kunstsammlung, Kunstmuseum, Basel, Switzerland

painting. Her *Self-Portrait with an Amber Necklace* of 1906 (fig. 18-10) testifies to the inspiration she found in Gauguin's formal simplicity and Edenic themes. The basic shapes and crude outlines of the portrait suggest the influence of African and Oceanic sculpture, while her bare figure, decorated only with flowers and a necklace, carries on the "primitive" theme. Standing before a screen of flowering plants, tenderly holding two small blooms, she shows herself at one with nature.

Another German who was an important expressionist of the early modern period is Käthe Schmidt Kollwitz (1867–1945). Raised in a socialist household, she studied at the Berlin School of Art for Women and at a similar school in Munich. In 1891 she married a doctor who shared her leftist political views, and they settled in a working-class neighborhood of Berlin. Art for her was a political tool, and to reach as many people as possible, she became a printmaker.

Using a stark graphic style, Kollwitz aimed to win sympathy for working-class people. Between 1902 and 1908, she produced the Peasants' War series, seven etchings that depict events in the sixteenth-century peasant rebellion. *The Outbreak* (fig. 18-11) shows the peasants' built-up fury from years of mistreatment exploding in mass action against their oppressors. To the artist's contemporaries, the work was a lesson in the power of group action. In the front, with her back to us, is Black Anna, the leader of the revolt. Kollwitz said that she modeled the figure of Anna after herself.

EXPRESSIONIST MOVEMENTS

Van Gogh, Ryder, Munch, Modersohn-Becker, and others developed personal versions of expressionism between the 1880s and the turn of the century. Interest in this artistic idiom spread more widely in the years just before and after 1910, as three major groups of artists in France, Germany, and Russia evolved expressionist styles.

The first of these groups emerged in France around 1905. Henri Matisse (1869–1954) and the leading members of his circle, including André Derain (1880–1954) and Maurice de Vlaminck (1876–1958), combined the dynamic brushwork of Van Gogh with bold **primary colors** (red, yellow, and blue), often applied directly from the tube. The effect was explosive—"like sticks of dyna-

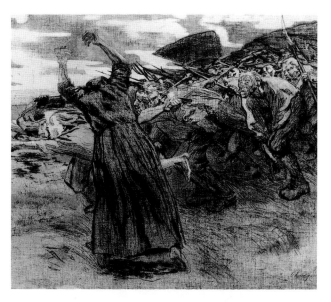

18-11. **Käthe Schmidt Kollwitz.** *The Outbreak,* from the Peasants' War. 1903. Etching. Staatliche Museen zu Berlin, Preussischer Kulturbesitz, Kupferstichkabinett

mite," Derain said—and won the style's practitioners the label of Fauves (French for "wild beasts"). Dynamic brushwork heightened the energy of the brilliant colors, conveying a new intensity of experience.

Matisse's *The Joy of Life* (fig. 18-12) treats hedonistic pursuits in a pastoral realm animated

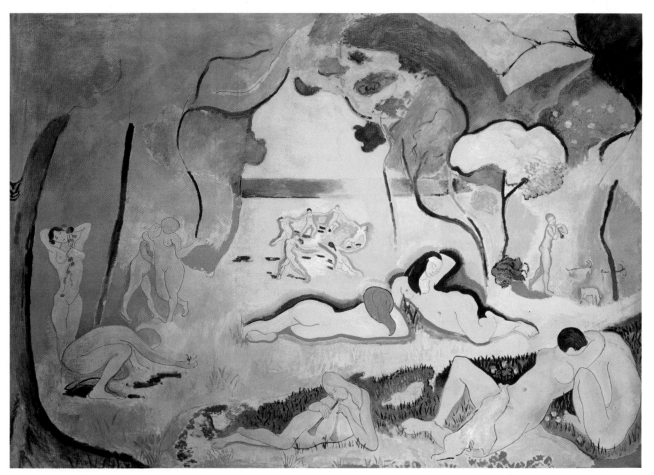

18-12. **Henri Matisse.** *The Joy of Life.* 1905–6. Oil on canvas, 5'8½" x 7'9¾" (1.74 x 2.38 m). The Barnes Foundation, Merion, Pennsylvania

During an illness in his youth, Matisse was given a box of paints by his mother, a moment that he recalled as fundamental to his later concerns as a painter: "When I started to paint, I felt transported into a kind of paradise. . . . In everyday life, I was usually bored and vexed by the things that people were always telling me I must do. Starting to paint, I felt gloriously free, quiet and alone." The reference to paradise, in particular, suggests that his mature paintings, such as *The Joy of Life,* are not concerned simply with the escapist Western myth of Arcadia but with painting itself as an ideal realm.

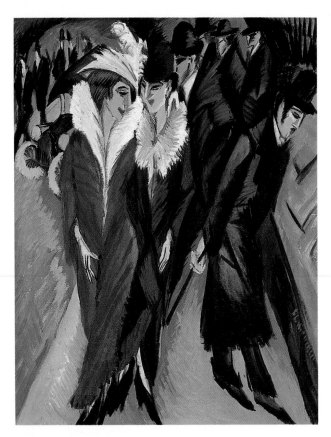

18-13. Ernst Ludwig Kirchner. *Street, Berlin.* 1913. Oil on canvas, 47¹/₂ x 35⁷/₈" (120.6 x 91.1 cm). The Museum of Modern Art, New York
Purchase

by a bouquet of luscious colors. Uninhibited, naked revelers dance, make love, commune with nature, or simply stretch out in their idyllic glade by the Mediterranean. Colors freed from naturalistic constraints convey the joyous mood, as do the undulating rhythms of the trees and body contours. In an essay titled "Notes of a Painter," which Matisse published in 1908, he expressed his allegiance to "an art . . . devoid of troubling or depressing subject matter . . . which might be for every mental worker, be he businessman or writer, like . . . a mental comforter, something like a good armchair in which to rest."

The German counterpart to Fauvism was Die Brücke (German for "the bridge"). In 1905, the same year the Fauves were so famously named by the French art critic Louis Vauxcelles, three architecture students at the Dresden Technical College—Ernst Ludwig Kirchner (1880–1938), Karl Schmidt-Rottluff (1884–1976), and Erich Heckel (1883–1970)—decided to take up painting and form a brotherhood. They took their collective name from a passage in Nietzsche's *Thus Spake Zarathustra* (1883) in which the prophet Zarathustra speaks of contemporary humanity's potential

to be the evolutionary "bridge" to a more perfect specimen of the future, the U*bermensch* ("beyond man," but usually translated as "superman").

In their art, however, the group demonstrated little interest in advancing the evolutionary process. Their paintings, sculpture, and graphics suggest, instead, a Gauguinesque yearning to return to nature, and the images they made of cities offer powerful arguments against living in them. Kirchner's *Street, Berlin* (fig. 18-13), for example, forcefully demonstrates the isolation that can occur in cities. Although crowded together physically, the well-dressed men and women are psychologically distant. The artist presents them as a series of independent vertical elements, an accumulation of isolated individuals, not a tight-knit community. The angular, brittle shapes and the sharp contrast of predominantly cool colors formally underscore the message.

The last of the important pre–World War I expressionist groups to come out of the crucible of late-nineteenth-century painting formed in Munich around the Russian painter Vasily Kandinsky (1866–1944). In 1895, after seeing a Monet painting whose color moved him deeply, Kandinsky gave up a law professorship in Moscow in order to devote himself fully to art. Choosing to study in Munich because of the research being done there on the effects of color and form on the human psyche, Kandinsky also traveled often to Paris and other European centers to familiarize himself with the latest artistic currents. The development of his own style depended not only on the contemporary art he saw but also on the folk art and children's art he collected. In 1911 Kandinsky organized Der Blaue Reiter (German for "the blue rider"), a group of nine artists who shared his interest in the power of color. *Der Reiter* was the popular name for the image of Saint George, mounted on a horse and slaying a dragon, that appeared on the Moscow city emblem. The rider was blue because Kandinsky considered that color to be the male principle and to represent spirituality.

Millennial and apocalyptic imagery appeared often in Kandinsky's art in the years just prior to World War I. According to a long Russian tradition, revived around 1900, Moscow would be the capital of the world during the millennium, the thousand years of Christ's reign on earth that would follow the Apocalypse, as prophesied by Saint John the Divine. In *Improvisation* No. 30 (*Cannons*) (fig. 18-14), the firing cannons in the lower right combine with the intense reds, a blackened sky, and precariously leaning mountains to suggest a scene from the end of the world. Such paintings, sometimes thought to reflect fear of the coming war, may instead be ecstatic visions of the destructive prelude to the Second Coming of Christ.

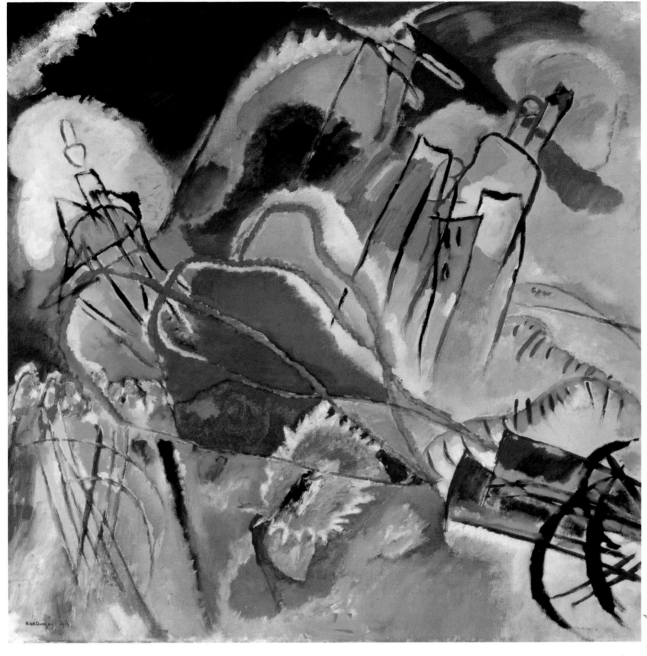

18-14. Vasily Kandinsky. *Improvisation No. 30 (Cannons).* 1913. Oil on canvas, 43¼ x 43¼" (109.9 x 109.9 cm). The Art Institute of Chicago
Arthur Jerome Eddy Memorial Collection

The traditional Russian idea that Moscow would be the "third Rome" was central to Kandinsky's art prior to World War I. The first center of Christianity had been Rome itself. The second Rome, according to Russian Orthodox tradition, had been Constantinople, the capital of the Christian world until 1453, when the Muslim Turks conquered it. The third and final Rome would be Moscow, according to the vision of a sixteenth-century monk, whose descriptive letter to the grand prince of Moscow led the prince's successor, Ivan the Terrible, to assume the title *czar*, Russian for "Caesar."

Kandinsky never expected his viewers to understand his symbolism. Instead, he intended to awaken their spirituality through the sheer force of color. As he explained it: "[C]olor directly influences the soul. Color is the keyboard, the eyes are the hammers, the soul is the piano with many strings. The artist is the hand that plays, touching one key or another purposively, to cause vibrations in the soul" (cited in Chipp, pages 154–155).

The Swiss-born Paul Klee (1879–1940) was among the best-known artists associated with Der Blaue Reiter, but his involvement with the group was never more than tangential. It was not Der Blaue Reiter but a 1914 trip to Tunisia that inspired Klee's interest in the expressive potential of color. On his return, Klee painted a series of watercolors based on his memories of North Africa, among them *Hammamet with Its*

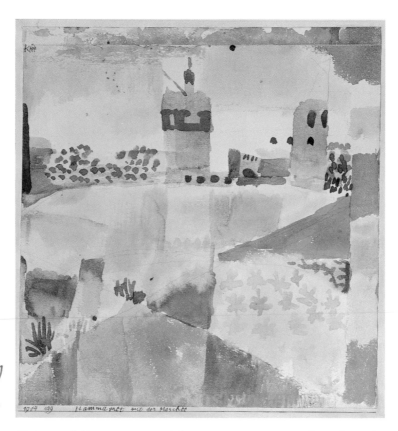

18-15. Paul Klee. *Hammamet with Its Mosque.* 1914. Watercolor and pencil on two sheets of laid paper mounted on cardboard, 8¹⁄₈ x 7⁵⁄₈" (20.6 x 19.4 cm). The Metropolitan Museum of Art, New York
The Berggruen Klee Collection, 1984

Mosque (fig. 18-15). The play between geometric composition and irregular brushstrokes in this watercolor is reminiscent of Cézanne's work, which Klee had recently seen. The luminous colors and delicate washes, or applications of dilute watercolor, result in a gently shimmering effect. The subtle modulations of red across the bottom, especially, are positively melodic. Klee, who played the violin and belonged to a musical family, seems to have wanted to use color the way a musician would use sound, not to describe appearances but to evoke subtle nuances of feeling.

Cubism

Hammamet with Its Mosque reflects the influence of the most radical, innovative, and influential *ism* of twentieth-century art, Cubism. The complete flattening of space and the use of independent facets or blocks of color in Klee's painting derive from the Cubist art he had seen in Paris. Cubism was the joint invention of two men, Pablo Picasso (1881–1973) and Georges Braque (1882–1963).

Picasso, born in Spain, studied at the art academies in Barcelona and Madrid. In 1900 he began to make frequent extended visits to Paris, and he moved there early in 1904. Initially drawn to the socially conscious tradition in French painting that included artists such as Toulouse-

Lautrec (see fig. 18-6), Picasso went through an extraordinary and complex transformation between early 1905 and the winter of 1906–1907. Wanting to produce art of greater formal and psychological strength, he began to study classical sculpture at the Louvre. In 1906 the Louvre installed a newly acquired collection of sculpture from Iberia (as ancient Spain and Portugal were known) that dated to the sixth and fifth centuries BCE. Inspired by these archaic figures, which became the chief influence on his work for the next several years, Picasso spent the summer of 1906 rediscovering his roots in a small village in the Spanish Pyrenees. Another important influence came from sculpture made by Gauguin in a "primitive" style, which Picasso also studied at this time.

Picasso's Iberian period culminated in 1907 in *Les Demoiselles d'Avignon* (fig. 18-16). The painting is Picasso's response to Matisse's *Joy of Life* (see fig. 18-12), exhibited the year before, and to the French classical tradition, which to Picasso was embodied in Ingres's paintings of harems (see fig. 16-16), which had been exhibited in a 1905 retrospective. Picasso, however, substituted a bordello for a harem. The term *demoiselles* is a euphemism for prostitutes, and Avignon refers not to the French town but to a street in the red-light district of Barcelona.

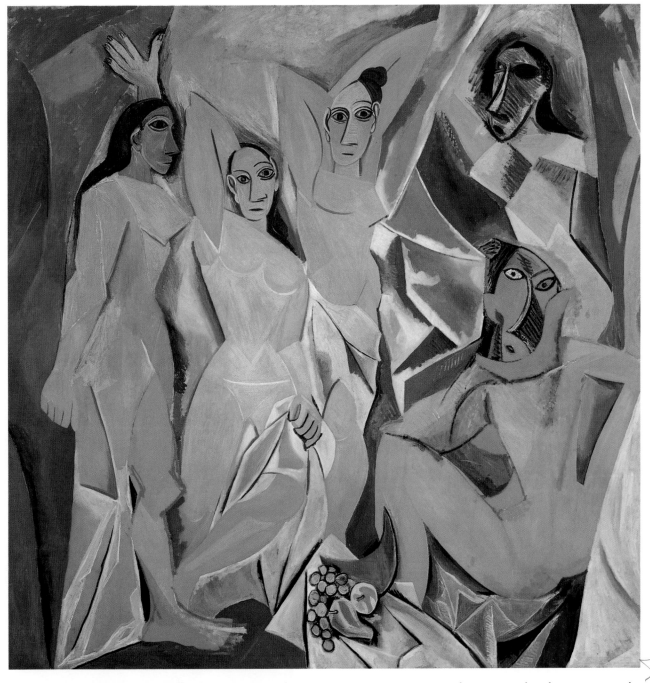

18-16. Pablo Picasso. *Les Demoiselles d'Avignon.* 1907. Oil on canvas, 8' x 7'8" (2.43 x 2.33 m). The Museum of Modern Art, New York
Acquired through the Lillie P. Bliss Bequest

Picasso makes the viewer an uneasy participant in the painting. The women pose for and look directly at us, but they hardly present a conventional picture of yielding femininity. The artist flattened the figures and transformed the entire space into a turbulent series of sharp curves and angles, conveying what one art historian has called "a tidal wave of aggression." The central pair of women raise their arms in a traditional gesture of accessibility but contradict it with their hard, piercing gazes and firm mouths. Even the fruit displayed in the foreground, a symbol of female sexuality, here seems hard and dangerous. Women, Picasso suggests, are not the gentle and passive creatures men would like

them to be. With this viewpoint he contradicts practically the entire Western tradition of erotic imagery since the Renaissance.

Picasso's friends were horrified by his new work. Matisse, for example, accused Picasso of making a joke of modern art and threatened to break off their friendship. Only one artist, the French painter Georges Braque, responded positively, and he saw in *Les Demoiselles d'Avignon* a potential that Picasso probably had not fully intended. Using broken and flattened forms to express his view of women, Picasso was not consciously trying to break with the Western pictorial tradition that dated back to the early-fourteenth-century painter Giotto. Yet it was this

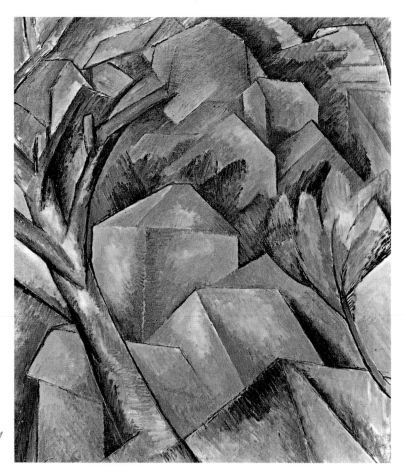

18-17. George Braque. *Houses at L'Estaque.* 1908. Oil on canvas, 36¼ x 23⅝"
(92 x 60 cm). Kunstmuseum, Bern, Switzerland
Collection Hermann and Magrit Rupf-Stiftung

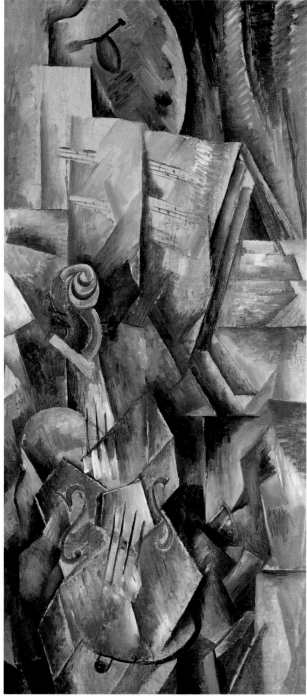

18-18. Georges Braque. *Violin and Palette.* 1909–10.
Oil on canvas, 36⅛ x 16⅞" (91.8 x 42.9 cm). Solomon R.
Guggenheim Museum, New York

formal innovation that Braque responded to in this proto-Cubist work: Picasso, Braque observed, had flattened space and taken liberties with form much as Cézanne had in his late landscapes (see fig. 18-3).

In a landscape by Braque himself, *Houses at L'Estaque* of 1908 (fig. 18-17), we see the emergence of early Cubism. Braque reduced nature's many colors to its essential browns and greens, and he eliminated detail to emphasize basic geometric forms. Arranging the buildings into an approximate pyramid, he reduced them to a kind of Platonic "houseness." The painting seems not so much a landscape as an arrangement of form and color.

When *Houses at L'Estaque* went on view in Picasso's studio, Matisse explained to a puzzled critic that Braque had made the painting out of "small cubes." The critic Louis Vauxcelles later described the painting in print using those words, and the term Cubism was born. Braque's painting also pointed Picasso in a new artistic direction. By the end of 1908, the two artists had begun an intimate working relationship that lasted until Braque went off to war in 1914.

The move toward abstraction begun in Braque's landscapes in 1908 continued in a series of still lifes the two artists produced over the next two and a half years. In Braque's *Violin and Palette* (fig. 18-18), the gradual elimination of space and clearly recognizable subject matter is well under way. The still-life items are not arranged on a table using illusionistic depth but are placed parallel to the picture plane in a shallow space. Using the **passage** technique developed by Cézanne, in which shapes closed on one side are open on another so that they can merge with adjacent shapes, Braque knit the various elements together into a single shifting surface of forms and colors.

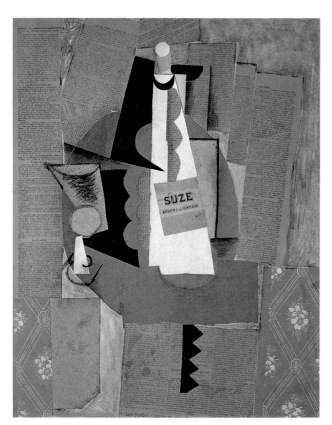

18-19. Pablo Picasso. *Glass and Bottle of Suze.*
1912. Pasted paper, gouache, and charcoal, 25¾ x 19¾"
(65.4 x 50.2 cm). Washington University Gallery of Art,
St. Louis, Missouri
University Purchase, Kende Sale Fund, 1946

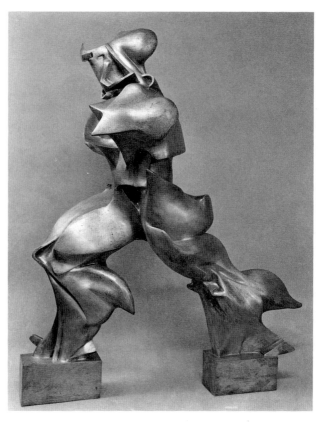

18-20. Umberto Boccioni. *Unique Forms of Continuity in Space.* 1913. Bronze, 43⅞ x 34⅞ x 15¾" (111 x 89 x 40 cm).
The Museum of Modern Art, New York
Acquired through the Lillie P. Bliss Bequest

Boccioni and the Futurist architect Antonio Sant'Elia were both
killed in World War I. The Futurists had ardently promoted
Italian entry into the war on the side of France and England.
After the war, Marinetti's movement, still committed to nation-
alism and militarism, supported the rise of fascism under
Benito Mussolini, although a number of the original members
of the group rejected their radical values.

In works such as *Violin and Palette*, Braque
and Picasso were moving toward the complete
disintegration of subject matter. Yet, having
reached the brink of total abstraction, they
retreated; in the spring of 1912, they began to
create works with more clearly discernible subjects. Rather than rendering subjects naturalistically, however, they suggested them, generally
through the use of **collage** (a technique in which
cutout paper forms are pasted onto another
surface).

At the center of Picasso's collage *Glass and
Bottle of Suze* (fig. 18-19) are pieces of newsprint
and construction paper. Assembled in a composition on the canvas, they suggest a tray or round
table supporting a glass and bottle of liquor
with an actual label. Around this arrangement,
Picasso pasted larger pieces of newspaper and
wallpaper. The elements together evoke not only
a place—a bar—but an activity: the viewer
alone with a newspaper, enjoying a quiet drink.

As variations on Cubism emerged from the
studios of Picasso and Braque, it became clear
to the art world that something of great significance was happening. The radical innovations of
the new style confused and upset the public
and most critics, but the avant-garde saw in them
the future of art.

CUBIST-RELATED STYLES

In Italy, Cubism led to another twentieth-century
ism: Futurism emerged on February 20, 1909,
when a Milanese literary magazine editor, Filippo
Marinetti, published his "Foundation and Manifesto of Futurism" in a Paris newspaper. An
outspoken attack against everything old, dull,
"feminine," and safe, Marinetti's manifesto (declaration of his principles) promoted the supposedly
exhilarating "masculine" experiences of warfare
and reckless speed to liberate Italy from its out-
worn past.

A number of artists and poets gathered
around Marinetti to create art forms for a modern
and revitalized Italy. Prominent among the artists
was the sculptor and painter Umberto Boccioni
(1882–1916), whose major sculptural work was
Unique Forms of Continuity in Space (fig. 18-20).
Cubist still lifes and figure studies that Boccioni
saw in Paris in 1911 inspired the exaggerated
muscular curves and countercurves of this
powerful nude figure. Yet whereas the Cubists had
broken forms to integrate their compositions,

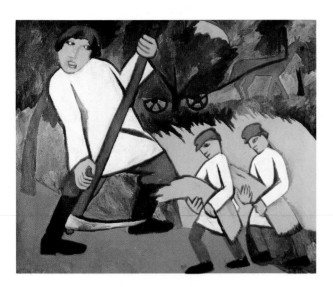

18-21. Natalia Goncharova. Haycutting. 1910. Oil on canvas, 38⅝ x 46¼" (98 x 117 cm). Private collection

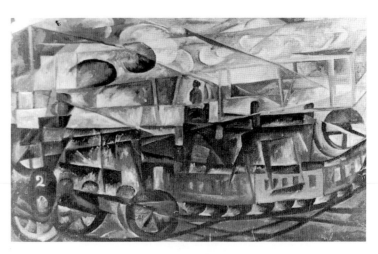

18-22. Natalia Goncharova. Aeroplane over Train. 1913. Oil on canvas, 21⅝ x 32⅞" (55 x 83.5 cm). Kazan-skil Muzej, Russia

Boccioni dynamically stretched and swelled them to express the figure's force and speed. This sculpted form personifies the new Italian man envisioned by the group, a strong male figure rushing headlong into the future.

Many Russian artists adopted French artistic currents with more ambivalence than the Italian Futurists had. They were torn between the desire to develop a native, characteristically Russian art and the wish to keep up with and even surpass western European artistic developments. The work of Natalia Goncharova (1881–1962) illustrates these tensions. By the early 1900s, Goncharova had come under the influence of Moscow's pro-Russian (or Slavophile) movement. She and her friends were convinced that in order to participate in the international avant-garde, they would, ironically, have to return to their own roots. With *Haycutting*, 1910 (fig. 18-21), and similar paintings that she had exhibited in Moscow in 1908, she created a sensation and launched the Russian Neo-Primitive movement.

In *Haycutting* Goncharova expresses the Slavophile view that the simple virtues of the provincial peasant represented the best of Russia. The crude style, meant to communicate the rough but authentic quality of peasant life, was based on cheap woodblock prints of religious and political scenes that decorated peasant homes. The disregard for scale, as seen in the figures of Goncharova's painting, was characteristic of these prints.

If *Haycutting* seems to support a negative attitude toward the industrialization of Russia, Goncharova's viewpoint seems to have changed completely in the ensuing years. Only three years later, she produced a painting titled *Aeroplane over Train* in a new Russian style, known as Cubo-Futurist, which melded Cubism and Futurism (fig. 18-22).

The brief time between *Haycutting* and *Aeroplane over Train* suggests the considerable confusion that many Russian artists felt over the questions of rural versus urban, agrarian versus industrial, and Russian versus French. The one issue Goncharova and the Cubo-Futurists were in agreement about was artistic progress. They embraced Cubism and Futurism out of a commitment to "advance" art, and they were not satisfied with simply keeping up with the new advances: they wanted to contribute to them.

Indeed, Kazimir Malevich (1878–1935), the first Russian to go beyond Cubo-Futurism, did so—spectacularly and unforgettably. Malevich is recognized as the modernist artist who produced the first truly abstract work of art. According to

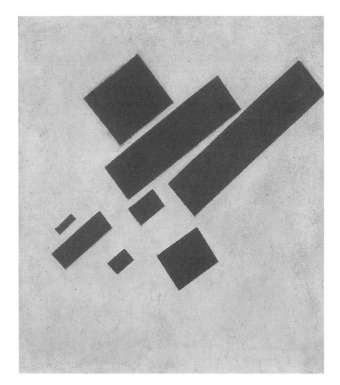

18-23. Kazimir Malevich. *Suprematist Painting (Eight Red Rectangles)*. 1915. Oil on canvas, 22¹/₂ x 18⁷/₈" (57 x 48 cm). Stedelijk Museum, Amsterdam

Malevich's Suprematist works, like many abstract paintings, do not reproduce well—their aesthetically appealing subtleties of texture, line, and color are not readily apparent in photographs. Even more than other artworks, they need to be seen firsthand to be fully appreciated.

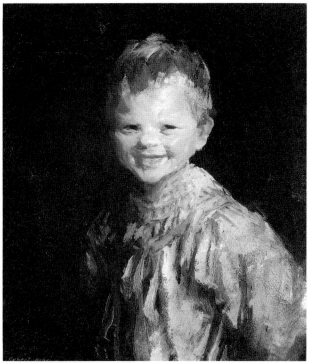

18-24. Robert Henri. *Laughing Child*. 1907. Oil on canvas, 24 x 20" (61 x 50.8 cm). Whitney Museum of American Art, New York
Lawrence H. Bloedel Bequest

his later reminiscences, "in the year 1913, in my desperate attempt to free art from the burden of the object, I took refuge in the square form and exhibited a picture which consisted of nothing more than a black square on a white field." Because he did not exhibit such a work until 1915, there is some question about the exact date of his first completely nonrepresentational work. Whatever the case, Malevich exhibited thirty-nine works in this radically new and highly controversial vein in Saint Petersburg in the winter of 1915–1916. One work, *Suprematist Painting (Eight Red Rectangles)* (fig. 18-23), consists simply of rectangles arranged diagonally on a white painted ground.

Malevich called this art Suprematism, short for "the supremacy of pure feeling in creative art." Although he sometimes spoke of this feeling in terms of technology ("the sensation of flight . . . of metallic sounds . . . of wireless telegraphy"), a later essay suggests that what motivated these works was "a pure feeling for plastic [that is, formal] values." By eliminating objects and focusing entirely on formal issues, Malevich thought that he was "liberating" the essential beauty of all great art. At the same time, he freed twentieth-century artists to explore the previously untapped potential of nonrepresentational forms.

Modernist Tendencies in the United States

At the end of the nineteenth century, American artists sought a purely "American" style, free from what they saw as European domination. The artist and teacher Robert Henri (1865–1929) spoke out against both the academic conventions and the impressionistic style then dominating American art. He told his students: "Paint what you see. Paint what is real to you."

In 1908, Henri organized an exhibition of a group of artists who came to be known as The Eight, many of whom were former newspaper illustrators. The show, which took place at the Macbeth Galleries in New York, was a gesture of protest against the conservative exhibition policies of the National Academy of Design, the American counterpart of the French École des Beaux-Arts. Because of their interest in depicting scenes of often gritty urban life in New York City, five of the group's original eight members became a part of what was later dubbed the Ashcan School. Henri and his followers succeeded in developing a confident, American brand of realism in painting (fig. 18-24) and printmaking.

The American artist Alfred Stieglitz (1864–1946) chose a different approach in photographing the quintessentially modern city of New York. In *Spring Showers* of 1901 (fig. 18-25), he hides the new skyscrapers in an atmospheric haze, employing photography not for documentation but rather as a means of creating purely aesthetic pleasure. The sanitation worker behind the tree is not the subject of the image; he is there only to balance the composition. The off-center placement of the leaning tree and the diagonal of the curb, inspired by the example of Japanese prints, would be aesthetically disturbing without the visual weight of the man's presence. The appeal of the photograph also depends on the contrast between the indefinite forms of the horse-drawn vehicles seen through the drizzle and the sharper forms of the tree and the fence in front.

In 1905 Stieglitz opened a New York gallery for exhibitions of both modern art and photography in order to help break down what he considered the artificial barrier between the two. Located at 291 Fifth Avenue, the Little Galleries of the Photo-Secession soon became known simply as 291 after its address. In the years around 1910, 291 became the American focal point not only for the advancement of photographic art but also for the larger cause of European modernism. In collaboration with another American photographer, Edward Steichen (1879–1973), who then lived in Paris, Stieglitz arranged exhibitions unlike any seen before in the United States, including works by Cézanne, Toulouse-Lautrec, Picasso, Braque, Matisse, Brancusi, and Rodin.

The event that climaxed Stieglitz's pioneering efforts on behalf of European modernism was the International Exhibition of Modern Art, held in 1913 at the 69th Regiment Armory in New York City, and so known as the Armory Show. The aim of the exhibition, arranged not by Stieglitz but by Walt Kuhn and Arthur B. Davies, a member of The Eight, was to demonstrate how outmoded the views of the National Academy of Design were. Unhappily for the Henri group, the Armory Show also demonstrated how old-fashioned their realistic approach was.

Of the more than 1,300 works in the show, only about a third were by Europeans, but it was to these works that primary attention was paid. Critics claimed that Matisse, Kandinsky, Braque, and others were the agents of "universal anarchy." The American academic painter Kenyon Cox called them mere "savages." When a selection of works continued on to Chicago, civic leaders there called for a morals commission to investigate the show.

A number of younger artists, however, responded positively. Indicative of the work produced by Americans in the aftermath of the Armory Show is that of Max Weber (1881–1961). In the new climate established by the exhibition,

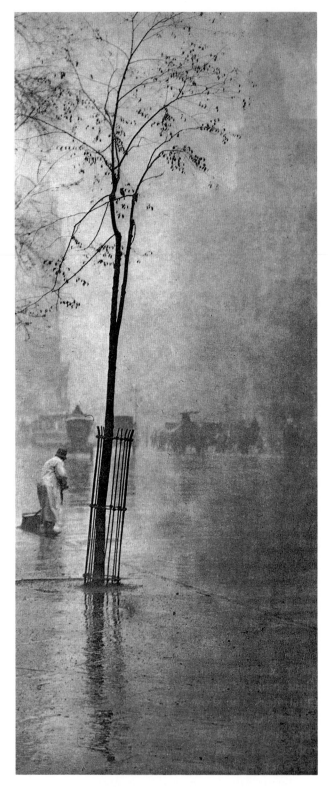

18-25. Alfred Stieglitz. *Spring Showers.* 1901. The Art Institute of Chicago

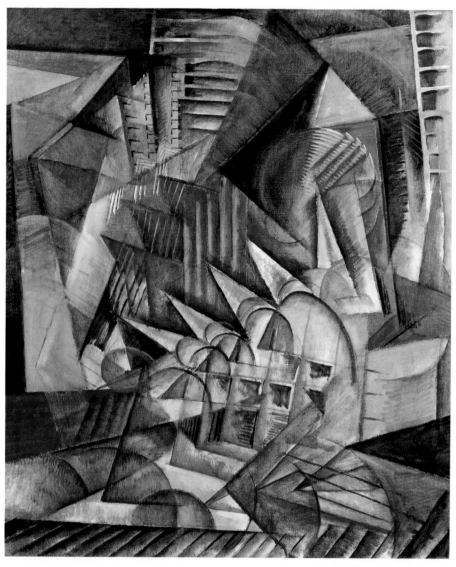

18-26. Max Weber. *Rush Hour, New York.* 1915. Oil on canvas, 36¼ x 30¼" (92 x 76.8 cm).
National Gallery of Art, Washington, D.C.
Gift of the Avalon Foundation

he produced an American version of Cubo-Futurism, although no one called it that. *Rush Hour, New York* (fig. 18-26), for example, at first seems a fairly typical example of the Futurist embrace of city life. The tightly packed surface of angular and curvilinear elements suggests the noisy and crowded rush hour, but the harmony of soft grays, blues, browns, and greens undercuts that effect considerably and produces an aesthetically pleasing formal symphony as well.

The Armory Show marks an important turning point in the history of art in the United States. In the ten years after the Armory Show, Americans assimilated the most recent developments in European art. The issue of realism versus academicism, so critical before 1913, suddenly seemed inconsequential. For the first time in their history, American artists at home began fighting their provincial status.

Artist. The first name usually appears first, though sometimes the last name appears first.

Country of citizenship and life dates of the artist. It happens that this brilliant French Dada artist became an American. The label lists the name of the country in which he became naturalized, as well as his place of birth. Birth and death dates often appear on a line with the artist's name.

Name of work and date of creation. The name a museum gives an artwork at any one time is regarded as its authoritative title. This is followed by the date the work was made.

Materials and medium. The Bride is a mixed-media work, and the materials Duchamp used to create this piece even include dust.

Donor or purchase information and accession number. Katherine Sophie Dreier (1877–1952) was a New York–born collector, painter, and writer. She met Duchamp in 1920 and with him founded the Société Anonyme, a group of influential intellectuals and artists who promoted international modernism in the United States. She owned The Bride, which she left to the Philadelphia Museum of Art on her death (with many more great works) in the form of a bequest. The records of the Société Anonyme now belong to Yale University.

Every single piece of art acquired by an institution has a unique number, called an accession number. The first group of numbers (1952) tells when the museum acquired The Bride. The accession number appears as the last item of information on a label.

Marcel Duchamp

United States, born France 1887–1968

The Bride Stripped Bare by Her Bachelors, Even (The Large Glass)

1915–1923

Oil, varnish, lead foil, lead wire, and dust on two glass panels

Bequest of Katherine S. Dreier, 1952–098–001

K E Y S to Art History
READING MUSEUM LABELS

Around the world, most museums provide labels for the artworks they display. Some are brief, giving only the artist's name and the name of the work, its *title*. Some museums provide additional information on a *wall text*—sometimes it is factual, sometimes anecdotal. When museums give only the most basic data in their labels, it is frequently because they believe that reading a long label distracts the art lover from directly experiencing art on its own, unmediated terms.

Usually today a museum label gives the name(s) of the artist or period; the name of the work; the date of the work; the materials and technique (oil on canvas, for example, or silkscreen); and the work's accession number and information telling how the museum acquired the work. You may find other information on a label such as measurements in feet/inches and often also in meters/centimeters, with height before width and width before depth for three-dimensional works. Labels may also be bilingual. You will find that captions to illustrations of art in books such as this one have many of the same elements as museum labels.

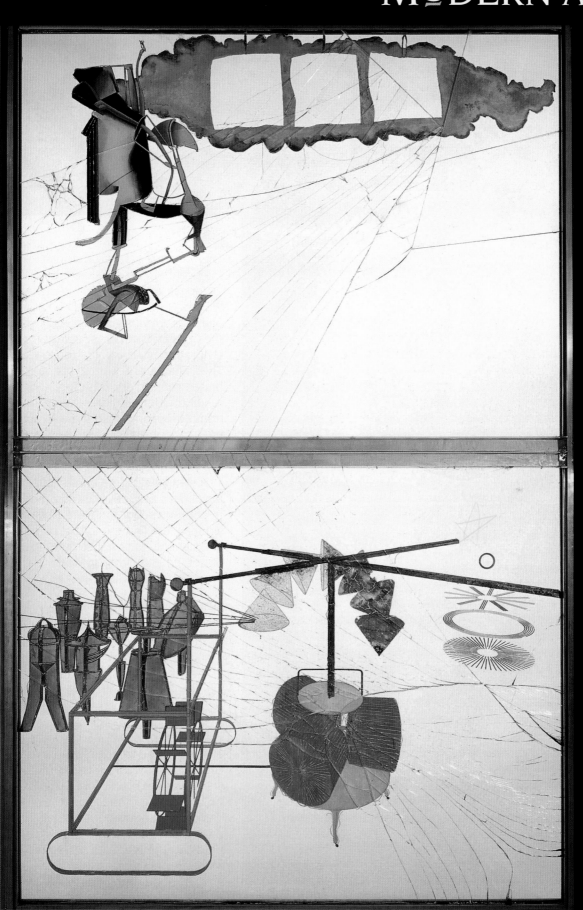

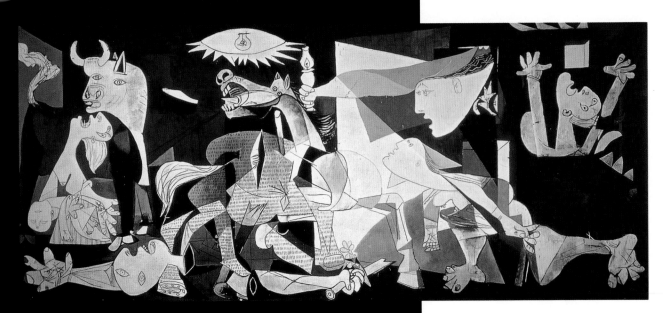

19-1. Pablo Picasso. *Guernica.* 1937. Oil on canvas, 11'5³/₄" x 25'7" (3.5 x 7.8 m). Museo Nacional Centro de Arte Reina Sofía, Madrid. On permanent loan from the Museo del Prado, Madrid

In April 1937, German pilots of the famous Condor Legion flying for the Spanish fascist leader General Francisco Franco bombed the Basque city of Guernica, killing more than 1,600 men, women, and children. Countries all over the globe were shocked by the world's first aerial bombing of civilians. The Spanish Civil War between Republicans and fascists had begun in 1936. Some historians, in retrospect, see this air attack as a prelude to World War II. Pablo Picasso, who was living in Paris at the time, reacted to the massacre by creating a painting (fig. 19-1) that has become a symbol of the brutality of war and humanity's struggle for freedom from oppression.

In a damning indictment of the fascists, Picasso painted *Guernica* as a stark, hallucinatory nightmare, focusing on its victims. He restricted his palette to black, gray, and white—the tones of the newspaper photographs that publicized the atrocity. Expressively distorted women, one holding a dead child and another in a burning house, wail in desolation at the carnage. The suffering Spanish Republic takes the form of a screaming horse, an image also taken to represent betrayed innocence. To the left is a bull, thought to symbolize either Franco or Spain. An electric light and a woman holding a lantern suggest Picasso's desire to reveal the event in all its horror.

The painting, commissioned by the short-lived Spanish Republican government for the Spanish pavilion at the world's fair in Paris in 1937, became a famous symbol of the inhumanity of fascism and war. (That same summer Hitler held the infamous exhibition of "degenerate art" in Munich; see "Suppression of the Avant-Garde in Germany," opposite.) During World War II, which Picasso spent in Paris, a Nazi officer showed him a reproduction of *Guernica* and asked, "Is that you who did that?" Picasso is said to have replied, "No, it is you."

The wars that ravaged Europe in the first half of the twentieth century had a profound effect on European artists and architects. After the Great War, as World War I was then known, members of artists' groups such as the Dutch de Stijl and the German Bauhaus sought the basis for a new civilization in severely rational beauty and order. The Dadaists and Surrealists, in contrast, celebrated subjectivity, intuition, and chance.

In the United States, many artists retreated from European-inspired modernism into a documentary portrayal of the American scene. There were a few experiments in an abstract vein in the teens and twenties, but it was only in the late 1930s and 1940s that artists and architects fleeing Hitler's Europe renewed American interest in nonrepresentational art. Abstract Expressionism, the first modernist painting style of international importance developed in the United States, emerged during World War II and the immediate postwar period.

Art after World War I

The dizzying array of *isms* that fragmented the European art world before World War I offered many formal options to postwar innovators. Some artists were even ready to reevaluate the classical tradition. In the late 1920s, the British sculptor Henry Moore (1898–1986) attempted to reinvigorate classicism with the strength and power of "primitive" art. His *Reclining Figure* (fig. 19-2) combines a pose found in some Classical Greek sculptures from the Parthenon (see fig. 4-29) with the blocky formal language of pre-Columbian art of the Americas (see fig. 14-7). The erotic connotations of the figure's reclining pose seem at odds with her psychological and physical strength. With its imposing monumentality, Moore's work comforts the modern viewer anxious about the human capacity to endure.

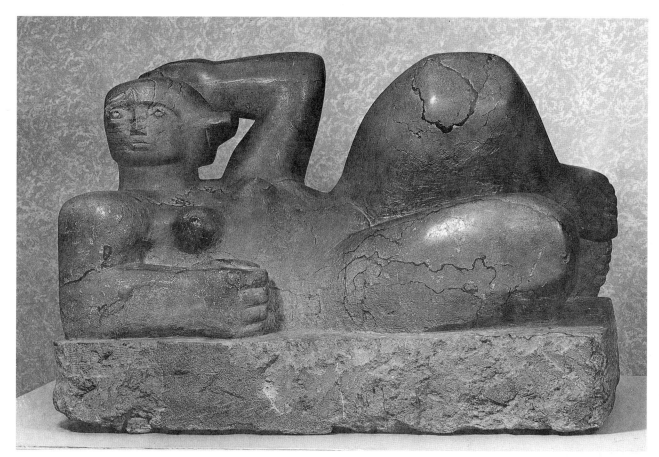

19-2. Henry Moore. _Reclining Figure_. 1929. Brown Hornton stone, 22$^{1}/_{2}$ x 33 x 15" (57 x 83.8 x 38 cm). Leeds City Art Gallery, England

In Russia, the most dynamic artistic achievements of the immediate postwar period came from avant-garde artists who enthusiastically supported the revolution: the overthrow of the czar in March 1917 and the rise of the Bolsheviks ("radical socialists") under Vladimir Lenin in November 1917. The artists of the Russian Revolution were committed to the notion that the artist leave the studio and "go into the factory, where the real body of life is made." The Con-

structivists, as they were known, envisioned politically engaged artists devoted to creating useful objects and promoting the aims of the collective. In their ideal of artistic production, forms would be perfectly suited to their functions and to the mechanical processes appropriate to their making.

One of the members of this socially visionary movement was El Lissitzky (1890–1941), who trained as an engineer in Germany. After the

Suppression of the Avant-Garde in Germany

During the 1930s in Germany a serious political reaction against avant-garde art arose, and eventually a concerted effort was made to suppress it. One of the principal targets was the Bauhaus (see fig. 19-7), the art and design school founded in 1919 by Walter Gropius, where Paul Klee, Vasily Kandinsky, Josef Albers, Ludwig Mies van der Rohe, and many other luminaries taught (see figs. 18-14, 18-15). Through much of the 1920s the Bauhaus had been struggling against an increasingly hostile and reactionary political climate. As early as 1924, conservatives had accused the Bauhaus of being not only educationally unsound but also politically subversive. In order to avoid having the school shut down by this opposition, Gropius moved it from Weimar to Dessau in 1926, at the invitation of Dessau's liberal mayor, but left soon after the relocation. His successors faced increasing political pressure on the school because it was a prime center of modernist practice, and the Bauhaus was again forced to move in 1932, this time to Berlin.

After Adolf Hitler came to power in 1933, the Nazi Party mounted an aggressive campaign against modern art. In his youth Hitler himself had been a mediocre academic painter, and he had developed an intense hatred of the avant-garde. During the first year of his regime, the Bauhaus was forced to close for good. A number of the artists, designers, and architects who had been on its faculty immigrated to the United States, including Albers, Gropius, and Mies van der Rohe.

The Nazis also launched attacks against the German Expressionists, whose often intense depictions of German soldiers defeated in World War I and of the economic depression following the war were considered unpatriotic. Most of all, the treatment of the human form in these works, such as the expressionistic exaggeration of facial features, was deemed offensive. The works of these and other artists were removed from museums, while the artists themselves were subjected to public ridicule and often forbidden to buy canvas or paint.

As a final move against the avant-garde, in 1937 the Nazi leadership organized a notorious

exhibition of banned works. The "Degenerate Art" exhibition was intended to erase modernism once and for all from the artistic life of the nation. Seeking to brand all the advanced movements of art as sick and degenerate, it presented modern artworks as if they were specimens of pathology. As part of the exhibition, the organizers printed derisive slogans and comments to that effect on the gallery walls. The 650 paintings, sculpture, prints, and books confiscated from German public museums were viewed by 2 million people in the four months the exhibition was on view in Munich and by another million during its subsequent three-year tour of German cities.

By the time World War II broke out, the authorities had confiscated countless works from all over the country. Most were publicly burned, though the Nazi officials sold much of the looted art at public auction in Switzerland to obtain foreign currency. Among the many artists crushed by the Nazi suppression was Ernst Ludwig Kirchner, whose _Street, Berlin_ (see fig. 18-13) was included in "Degenerate Art." The state's open animosity was a factor in his suicide in 1938.

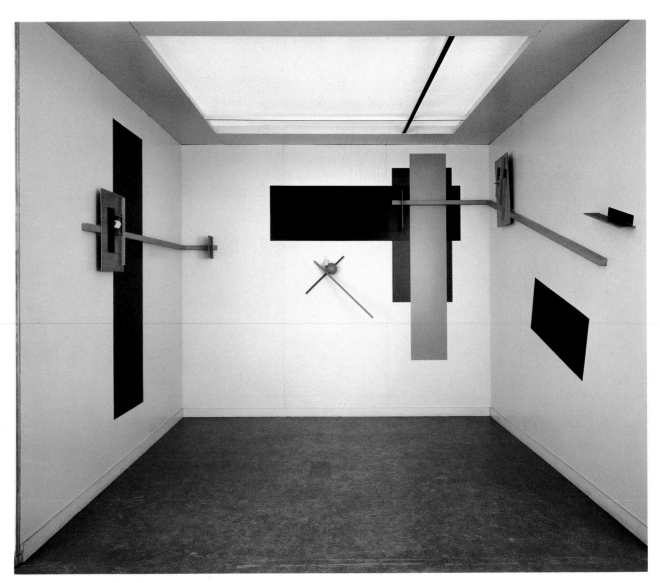

19-3. El Lissitzky. Proun space created for a Berlin art exhibition. 1923, reconstruction 1965. Stedelijk Van Abbemuseum, Eindhoven, the Netherlands

revolution, he was invited to teach architecture and graphic arts at the Vitebsk School of Fine Arts, where he came under the influence of a fellow professor, Kazimir Malevich (Chapter 18). By 1919 he was using Malevich's formal vocabulary for propaganda posters and for artworks he called Prouns, an acronym for "Project for the Affirmation of the New." Most are paintings, but a few, like one made for an exhibition in Germany (fig. 19-3), were Proun spaces. Lissitzky, who rejected conventional painting tools as too personal and imprecise, produced his Prouns with the aid of mechanical instruments. Their engineered look is meant not merely to celebrate industrial technology but to encourage precise thinking among the public.

In the Netherlands the counterpart to the inspired formalism of Lissitzky was the de Stijl (the Style) group, led by Piet Mondrian (1872–1944). The de Stijl movement was grounded in the conviction that there are two kinds of beauty: a sensual or subjective one and a higher, rational, or objective—"universal"—kind. In his mature

works, Mondrian sought the second type of beauty, eliminating representational elements because of their subjective associations. In paintings such as *Composition with Red, Blue, and Yellow* (fig. 19-4), he restricted his formal vocabulary to the three **primary colors** (red, yellow, and blue), the two primary **values** (black and white), and to horizontal and vertical lines. The heavier weight of the red threatens to tip the painting to the right, but the placement of the tiny rectangle of yellow at the lower right prevents this imbalance by supporting the red's weight. This effect, what Mondrian called dynamic equilibrium, was achieved among the elements through the precise arrangement of color areas of different visual weight. Mondrian and his colleagues hoped that this style based on ideas of balance would help to stabilize the viewer as well, "purifying" humankind's chaotic natural instincts.

The major architect and designer of the de Stijl movement was Gerrit Rietveld (1888–1964), whose famous "red and blue" chair is shown here in the bedroom of his most important project,

19-4. Piet Mondrian. *Composition with Red, Blue, and Yellow.* 1930. Oil on canvas, 20 x 20" (50.8 x 50.8 cm). Private collection

the Schröder House (fig. 19-5) in Rietveld applied Mondrian's design aesthetic—the dynamic symmetry of rectangular planes of color—to the entire house and its built-in furnishings. Sliding partitions on the interior, the idea of the house's owner, Truus Schröder, allowed modifications in the spaces used for sleeping, working, and entertaining. Schröder, a wealthy woman, wanted her home to suggest not luxury but an elegant austerity, with the basic necessities sleekly integrated into a meticulously restrained whole.

Like the Dutch proponents of de Stijl, followers of a movement known as Purism, which developed in France, firmly believed in the power of art to change the world. The leading Purist figure was the Swiss-born Charles-Édouard Jeanneret (1887–1965), a largely self-taught architect and designer who moved to Paris in 1917. Three years later, Jeanneret, partly to demonstrate his faith in the ability of individuals to remake themselves, renamed himself Le Corbusier, a play on the French word for raven.

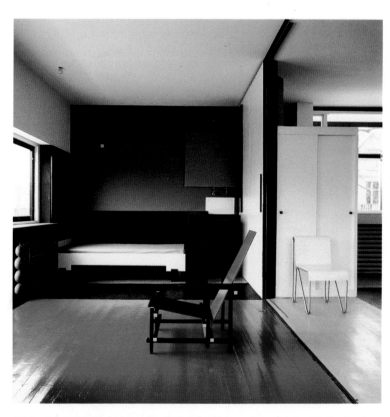

19-5. Gerrit Rietveld. Interior, Schröder House, Utrecht, the Netherlands. 1924

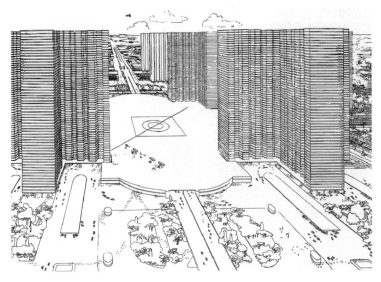

19-6. Charles-Édouard Jeanneret (Le Corbusier). Plan for a Contemporary City of Three Million Inhabitants. 1922

In 1925 Le Corbusier devised a similar plan for Paris, convinced that the center of the city needed to be torn down and rebuilt to accommodate automobile traffic. The Parisian street was a "Pack-Donkey's Way," he said: "Imagine all this junk . . . cleared off and carried away and replaced by immense clear crystals of glass, rising to a height of over six hundred feet!"

One of Le Corbusier's first projects as a mature architect was his plan for a Contemporary City of Three Million Inhabitants (fig. 19-6), which he exhibited in Paris in 1922. Le Corbusier hated the crowded, noisy, and polluted places that cities had become in the late nineteenth century. What he envisioned for the future was a city of uniform style, laid out on a grid, and dominated by skyscrapers (see "The Skyscraper," page 442), with wide traffic arteries that often passed beneath ground level. Large expanses of parkland would surround strictly functional buildings. The result, Le Corbusier thought, would be a new,

clean, and efficient city filled with light, air, and greenery. Le Corbusier's vision had a profound effect on later city planning, especially in the United States.

The German counterpart to the total, rational planning envisioned by de Stijl and Le Corbusier was carried out between 1919 and 1933 at the Bauhaus (House of Building). The Bauhaus was the brainchild of Walter Gropius (1883–1969), one of the founders of modernist architecture. Gropius, who belonged to several utopian groups, including one in sympathy with the Russian Revolution, admired the spirit of the medieval building guilds, or *Bauhütten*, that had erected the great German cathedrals. He sought to revive their cooperative spirit and bring together modern art and industry by combining the schools of art and craft in the city of Weimar into a single institution.

The Bauhaus had no formal architectural curriculum. Gropius felt that students needed to demonstrate proficiency in workshop courses in construction, metalwork, carpentry, interior design (including mural painting), and furniture making—all of which emphasized an understanding of materials—before going on to study architecture. Bauhaus masters aimed to train a generation of architects dedicated to "a clear, organic architecture, whose inner logic will be radiant and naked, unencumbered by lying facades and trickeries; we want an architecture adapted to our world of machines, radios and fast motor cars, an architecture whose function is clearly recognizable in the relation of its forms" (cited in Bayer, Gropius, and Gropius, page 27).

Gropius's design for the new Dessau Bauhaus, built in 1925–1926 (fig. 19-7), illustrates his

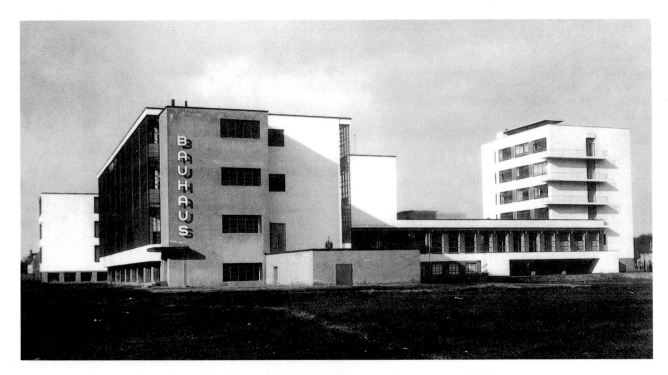

19-7. Walter Gropius. Bauhaus Building, Dessau, Germany. 1925–26

theories. The building frankly acknowledges the reinforced concrete, steel, and glass of which it is built; Gropius made no attempt to cover or decorate his building materials. A glass-panel wall that wraps around two sides of the workshop wing exposes and lights the industrial activities of the workshop. The corner piers standard in earlier buildings have been eliminated as unneeded references to outmoded tradition. Modern engineering methods made it possible to replace walls as massive structural supports and to create light, airy spaces.

The sans-serif (without serifs) letters of the Bauhaus sign announce the new clean lines and functional ideals of the group. This typography style was comparatively new, for it had only been in use since 1816, with a string of new sans-serif faces created in rapid succession in the 1920s. One of the enduring contributions of the Bauhaus was to graphic design, and the sans-serif letters of the Bauhaus sign communicate this sense of modernity.

From 1930 until the Nazis closed it in 1933, the Bauhaus was directed by Ludwig Mies van der Rohe (1886–1969). Mies had a passion for realizing the subtle perfection of structure, proportion, and detail, using sumptuous materials such as travertine, richly veined marbles, tinted glass, and bronze. His abilities and interests are evident in the elegantly simple entrance pavilion to the German exhibits (fig. 19-8) that he designed for the 1929 world's fair, held in Barcelona. For its construction, Mies relied on the so-called domino system developed by Le Corbusier. A system of slender piers supports floor and ceiling slabs. **Curtain walls**, walls that bear no weight but simply separate the inside from the outside or partition interior spaces, divide and enclose the spaces. The design of the interior, based on the de Stijl conception of harmoniously balanced rectangles, resembles a Mondrian painting (see fig. 19-4).

Mies also designed furniture for the pavilion: a pair of elegantly simple, leather-upholstered, stainless-steel chairs for the king and queen of Spain to sit in during their official visit, as well as a number of ottomans for their entourage. Although the handmade originals were designed for ceremonial use, they were later mass-produced and are still a status symbol in many homes and offices today.

After the Bauhaus closed (see "Suppression of the Avant-Garde in Germany," page 437), Mies moved to the United States, where he was named director of the Armour Institute in Chicago, which later became the Illinois Institute of Technology. In his designs for schools, apartments, and office buildings, Mies used the same rectilinear industrial vocabulary pioneered by Le Corbusier and Walter Gropius. This style dominated urban architecture in much of the world after World War II

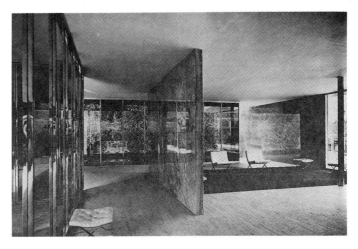

19-8. Ludwig Mies van der Rohe. Interior, German pavilion, International Exposition, Barcelona, 1929

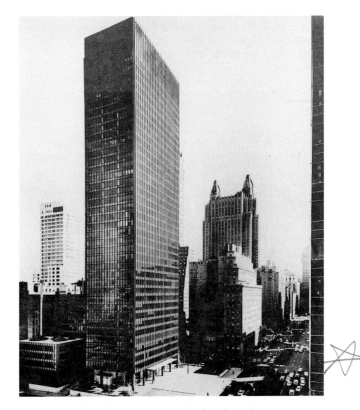

19-9. Ludwig Mies van der Rohe and Philip Johnson. Seagram Building, New York City. 1954–58

and came to be known as the International Style. One of the most well-known practitioners of this style is Philip Johnson (b. 1906), with whom Mies designed the Seagram Building in New York City (fig. 19-9). Mies's buildings are distinguished by his attention to detail. Because he had a large budget for the Seagram Building, he used custom-made bronze instead of standardized steel beams on the exterior. He would have preferred to have visible steel supports for the structure, but building codes required him to encase them in concrete. The ornamental beams on the outside stand in for the functional girders inside. Tall, narrow windows with discreet dark glass emphasize the skyscraper's height. Set back from the street,

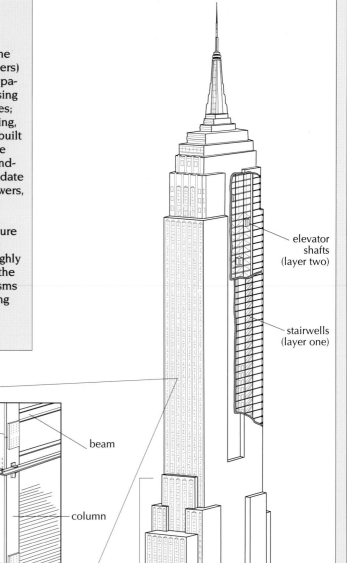

Elements of Architecture

THE SKYSCRAPER

The United States gave birth to the skyscraper—a big building for a big country. Its evolution depended on the development of these essentials: metal beams (or girders) and columns for the structural-support skeleton; the separation of the building-support structure from the enclosing layer (the cladding); fireproofing materials and measures; elevators; and plumbing, central heating, artificial lighting, and ventilation systems. First-generation skyscrapers, built between about 1880 and 1900, were concentrated in the Midwest, especially Chicago (see figs. 17-3, 17-4). Second-generation skyscrapers, with more than twenty stories, date from 1895. At first the tall buildings were freestanding towers, sometimes with a base. New York City's Building Zone Resolution of 1916 introduced mandatory setbacks—recessions from the ground-level building line—to ensure light and ventilation of adjacent sites. Built in 1931, the 1,250-foot, setback-form Empire State Building is thoroughly modern in having a streamlined exterior that conceals the great complexity of the internal structure and mechanisms that make its height possible. The Empire State Building is still one of the tallest building in the world.

elevator shafts (layer two)

stairwells (layer one)

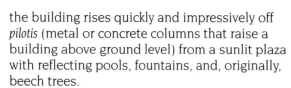

masonry wall

girder

cladding

heat source

beam

column

concrete slab flooring

setbacks

the building rises quickly and impressively off *pilotis* (metal or concrete columns that raise a building above ground level) from a sunlit plaza with reflecting pools, fountains, and, originally, beech trees.

Business leaders embraced the International Style, which seemed to epitomize the efficiency, standardization, and impersonality that had become synonymous with the modern corporation itself. At the same time, critics called for an architecture that would provide spiritual nourishment to those starved by the severity of recent building styles. Frank Lloyd Wright (1867–1959), the most celebrated American architect of the Chicago School, had been advocating an "organic" approach that integrated architecture

with nature since as early as 1900. When asked what could be done to improve the modern industrial city, he bluntly responded: "Tear it down."

Wright's most famous architectural expression of his conviction that buildings ought to be a part of nature—*in* it, not simply on it—is Fallingwater, in rural Pennsylvania (fig. 19-10). The site of this country house was notable for the existence of a waterfall that fed into a pool where the owners, the Edgar Kaufmann family, played and swam. Wright decided to build the house into the cliff over the pool, allowing the waterfall to flow around and under the house. In a daring engineering move that experts questioned, he cantilevered a series of broad terraces out from the cliffside, echoing the great

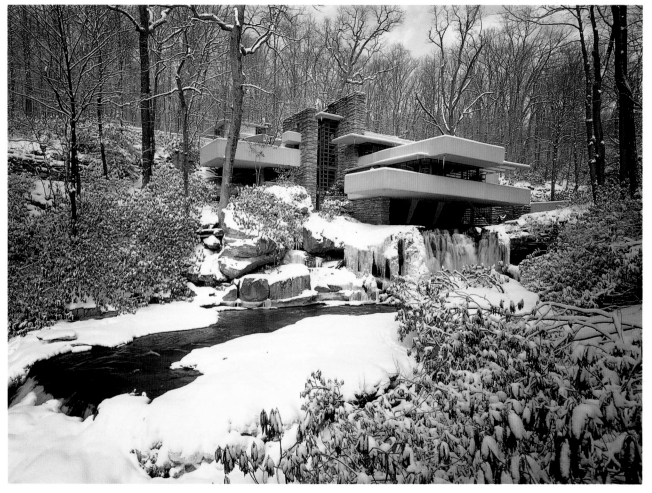

19-10. Frank Lloyd Wright. Fallingwater, Mill Run (Bear Run), Pennsylvania. 1937

slabs of rocks below (fig. 19-11). The rocks on which the family had once lounged in the sun became the hearthstone of the fireplace. He added long bands of windows and glass doors that offer spectacular views and practically bring nature into the house. Today most engineers would probably agree that no city in the United States would grant a building permit to erect Fallingwater.

DADA AND SURREALISM

If the formalist aspects of modernism led to new developments after World War I, expressionist currents also flourished. The Dada movement, which began with the opening of the Cabaret Voltaire in Zürich on February 5, 1916, was a remarkable theatrical manifestation of the disillusioned mood of the times, as artists and writers failed to conjure a rationale for the thousands killed in World War I. The cabaret's founders, the German actor and artist Hugo Ball (1886–1927) and his companion, Emmy Hennings, a nightclub singer, invited "young artists of Zürich, whatever their orientation . . . to come along with suggestions and contributions of all kinds." They immediately attracted a circle of

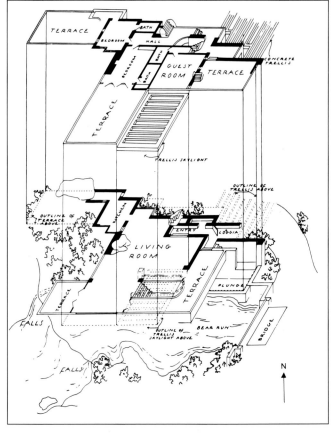

19-11. Plan of Fallingwater

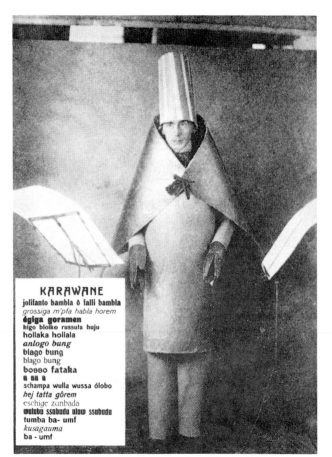

KARAWANE

jolifanto bambla ô falli bambla
grossiga m'pfa habla horem
égiga goramen
higo bloiko russula huju
hollaka hollala
anlogo bung
blago bung
blago bung
bosso fataka
ü üü ü
schampa wulla wussa ólobo
hej tatta gôrem
eschige zunbada
wulubu ssubudu uluw ssubudu
tumba ba- umf
kusagauma
ba - umf

19-12. Hugo Ball reciting the sound poem "Karawane."
Photographed at the Cabaret Voltaire, Zürich, 1916

avant-garde writers and artists of various nationalities who shared in Ball's and Henning's disgust with bourgeois culture.

Ball's performance while reciting one of his sound poems, "Karawane" (fig. 19-12), reflects the spirit of the place. His legs and body were encased in blue cardboard tubes, and his head was surmounted by a white-and-blue "witch-doctor's hat," as he called it. Meanwhile his shoulders were covered with a huge cardboard collar that flapped when he moved his arms. Dressed in this manner, he slowly and solemnly recited the poem, which consisted entirely of nonsense sounds. As was typical of Dada, this performance involved both critical and playful aims. One goal, as Ball said, was to renounce "the language devastated and made impossible by journalism." In other words, by retreating into sound alone, he avoided language, which had been spoiled by the lies and excesses of journalism and advertising. Another end was simply to amuse his audience by introducing the healthy play of children back into what he considered overly restrained adult lives. The flexibility of interpretation inherent in Dada extended to its name. In German the term signifies "baby talk"; in French it means "hobbyhorse," in Russian, "yes, yes"; and in Romanian, "no, no." The name and therefore the movement could be defined as the individual wished.

The Dada movement first spread to New York and Barcelona; then to Berlin, Cologne, and Paris. French and American artists living in New York produced work similar to that of the European Dadaists. The leading figure in this group was the French artist Marcel Duchamp (1887–1968). Duchamp and his friends maintained that art should appeal to the mind rather than to the senses. His most intellectually challenging work is probably *The Bride Stripped Bare by Her Bachelors, Even* (fig. 19-13), also known as *The Large Glass*. Notes that Duchamp made while working on the piece confirm that it is enormously complex in conception and operates on several intellectual and aesthetic levels. Most fundamentally it is a pessimistic statement of the insoluble frustrations of male-female relations. Tubular elements encased in the top half of the glass represent the bride. She releases a large romantic sigh, which stimulates the bachelors below, represented by nine different costumes attached to a waterwheel. The wheel resembles and is attached to a chocolate grinder, a reference to a French euphemism for masturbation. A bar separates the males from the female, preventing the fulfillment of their respective sexual desires.

Another European movement, Surrealism, also resisted the rationalist tide of post–World War I art and architecture. Surrealism began as a literary movement and was popularized by the French writer André Breton (1896–1966). Breton, involved in the Paris Dada movement after the war, became dissatisfied with the playful nonsense activities of his colleagues and focused on other means to free human behavior from the constrictions of reason and bourgeois morality. In 1924 he published his "Manifesto of Surrealism," outlining his own view of Freud's theory that the human psyche is a battleground where the rational, civilized forces of the conscious mind struggle against the irrational, instinctual urges of the unconscious. Breton and his followers employed a number of techniques for liberating the individual unconscious, including dream analysis, free association, automatic writing, word games, and hypnotic trances. Their aim was to help people discover the larger reality, or "surreality," that lay beyond conventional notions of what was real. Even artists such as Pablo Picasso, who was not actually part of the Surrealist group, profited from the approaches and techniques pioneered by the Surrealists. The expressive forms of *Guernica* (see fig. 19-1)— fragmented, distorted, and evocative of much more than words can say—would not have been possible without the lessons of Surrealism.

Among the writers and artists around Breton was the Spanish painter and printmaker Salvador Dalí (1904–1989). Dalí contributed the "paranoiac-critical method" to Surrealist practice. In this approach, the sane man or woman cultivates the

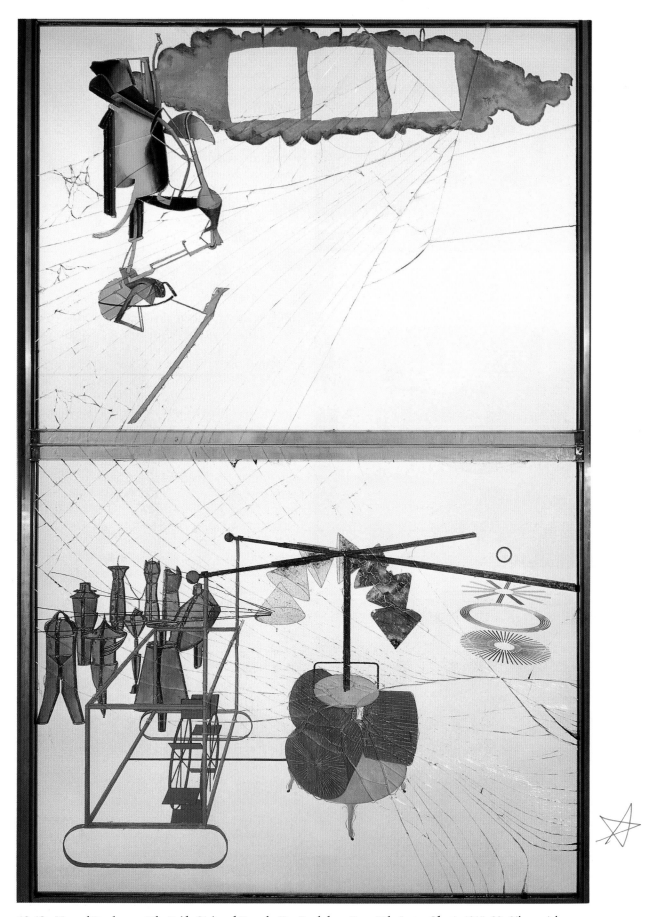

19-13. Marcel Duchamp. *The Bride Stripped Bare by Her Bachelors, Even (The Large Glass).* 1915–23. Oil, varnish, lead foil, lead wire, and dust on two glass panels, 9'1¼" x 5'9¼" (2.77 x 1.76 m). Philadelphia Museum of Art
Bequest of Katherine S. Dreier

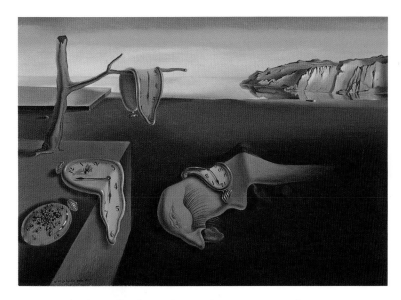

19-14. Salvador Dalí. *The Persistence of Memory.* 1931. Oil on canvas, 9½ x 13" (24.13 x 33.02 cm). The Museum of Modern Art, New York Given anonymously. © Demart Pro Arte/Artists Rights Society (ARS), New York

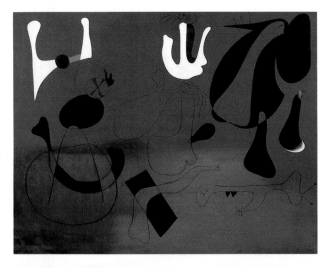

19-15. Joan Miró. *Painting.* 1933. Oil on canvas, 4'3¼" x 5'3½" (1.30 x 1.61 m). Wadsworth Atheneum, Hartford, Connecticut The Ella Gallup Sumner and Mary Catlin Sumner Collection Fund

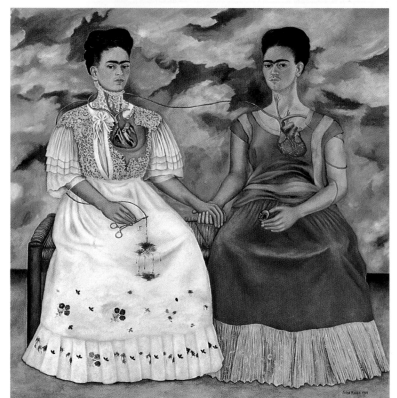

ability of the paranoiac to misread ordinary appearances in order to free himself or herself from the shackles of conventional thought. Dalí demonstrated this method at work in *The Persistence of Memory* (fig. 19-14). The Bay of Rosas near the painter's birthplace in Catalonia provides the setting for a painting based on a childhood memory of a doctor who asked to see his tongue. The French words *montrer* (to show) and *langue* (tongue), according to the paranoiac-critical method, easily become *montre* (watch) and *langueur* (languid). One of the soft watches drapes over a fetal image of the artist himself, who claimed to have a classic Oedipal love for his mother. The fetus belongs in the mother's womb, where Dalí longed to return. The ants on the hardening watch in the foreground become an expression of the anxieties that attended his Oedipal love, namely, the fears of his father's anger. Finally, Dalí chose a highly realistic style in order to make his irrational world seem more convincing and more unsettling.

Another Catalan artist associated with Surrealism was Joan Miró (1893–1983). Miró developed works such as *Painting* (fig. 19-15) by freely drawing a series of lines without considering what they might be or become, a popular Surrealist technique called **automatism**. The loosely drawn figures or forms made by this method often reside in shallow space. Next he consciously reworked the lines into the fantastic animal and vegetable forms that they suggested to his imagination. The result is an assortment of delicate flora and fauna that seem to float gracefully and effortlessly across a dry landscape inspired by Miró's native Catalonia and Mallorca.

Surrealism influenced artists in the Americas as well as in Europe. André Breton claimed the Mexican artist Frida Kahlo (1910–1954) as a natural Surrealist, although she herself said: "I never painted dreams. I painted my own reality." That reality included her mixed German and Mexican ancestry, and a nearly fatal trolley accident at the age of fifteen that left her crippled and in pain for the rest of her life. In *The Two Fridas* (fig. 19-16), Kahlo presented her two ethnic selves: the European one, in a Victorian dress, and the Mexican one, wearing a traditional Mexican peasant skirt and blouse. The painting also reflects her stormy relationship with a fellow Mexican artist, Diego Rivera. The two married in 1929 but were in the process of obtaining a divorce when Kahlo was painting *The Two Fridas.* She told an art historian at the time that the European image was the Frida whom Diego loved and the Mexican image was the Frida he did not. An artery linking the alter egos

19-16. Frida Kahlo. *The Two Fridas.* 1939. Oil on canvas, 5'8½" x 5'8½" (1.74 x 1.74 m). Museo de Arte Moderno, Instituto Nacional de Bellas Artes, Mexico City

begins at a miniature of Rivera as a boy that the Mexican Frida holds and ends in the lap of the European Frida, who attempts without success to stem the flow of blood from it.

The Surrealists also influenced the American sculptor Alexander Calder (1898–1976). Calder, originally trained as an engineer, made contact with members of the Dada and Surrealist groups on visits to Paris in the 1920s and 1930s. He also visited Mondrian's studio, where he was impressed by the rectangles of colored paper that Mondrian had tacked up everywhere on the walls. What would it be like, he wondered, if the flat shapes were moving freely in space, interacting in not just two but three dimensions? The experience inspired Calder to begin creating mobiles, sculptures like his *Lobster Trap and Fish Tail* (fig. 19-17) of 1939 in which the individual parts float and bob in response to shifting currents of air. At first, this mobile seems almost completely abstract, but Calder's title works on our imagination, helping us to find the oval trap awaiting unwary crustaceans at the right and the delicate wires at the left that suggest the backbone of a fish. The term *mobile*, which in French means both "moving body" and "motive," or "driving force," came from Calder's friend Marcel Duchamp, who no doubt relished the double meaning of the word.

ART IN THE UNITED STATES BETWEEN THE WARS

In the early decades of the twentieth century, American artists such as Calder who were interested in contemporary art had to go to Europe if they wanted to keep abreast of developments. Alfred Stieglitz's 291 (Chapter 18) was one of the few galleries in the United States exhibiting the more radical manifestations of contemporary European art. Besides showing European art, Stieglitz also exhibited the work of many pioneering American modernists. Among the artists whose careers Stieglitz supported were Arthur Dove, Marsden Hartley, John Marin, and Georgia O'Keeffe.

Georgia O'Keeffe (1887–1986) adopted the formal qualities of Cubism and the energy of Futurism to her own vision of America. In drawings and paintings of New York and the southwestern United States, she captured on canvas the basic forces of nature that would characterize all her mature art. O'Keeffe and Stieglitz lived together from 1920 and were married in 1924. Although they continued to reside in New York until his death in 1946, O'Keeffe began in 1928 to make yearly trips to New Mexico, where she eventually settled. Moved by the austere grandeur of the New Mexican landscape, she considered the arid land her spiritual home. In *The Lawrence Tree* (fig. 19-18), O'Keeffe painted an experience she had one evening while visiting

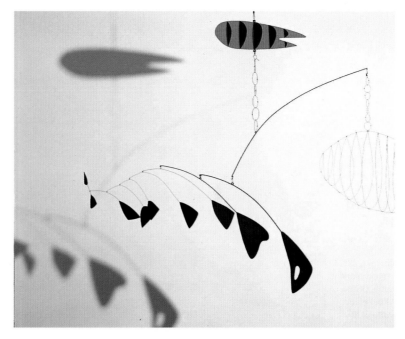

19-17. Alexander Calder. *Lobster Trap and Fish Tail.* 1939. Hanging mobile: painted steel wire and sheet aluminum, approx. 8'6" x 9'6" (2.60 x 2.90 m). The Museum of Modern Art, New York
Commissioned by the Advisory Committee for the stairwell of the Museum

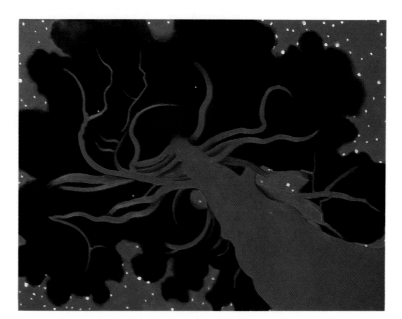

19-18. Georgia O'Keeffe. *The Lawrence Tree.* 1929. Oil on canvas, 31¹/₁₆ x 39³/₁₆" (79.0 x 99.5 cm). Wadsworth Atheneum, Hartford, Connecticut
Ella Gallup and Mary Catlin Sumner Collection. © 1996
The Georgia O'Keeffe Foundation/Artists Rights Society (ARS), New York

the writer D. H. Lawrence, who owned a ranch near Taos. Beneath a giant pine, she lay down on a bench to look up at the stars in the sky. With minimal detail, she recorded from memory the essence of that sublime sight.

The entry of the United States into World War I in 1917 promised to further stimulate the new American fascination with contemporary European art. Instead, the country entered a period of isolationism that lasted from about 1920 to the bombing of Pearl Harbor in 1941 and had a powerful effect on its artists. In the 1920s and 1930s, the majority of American artists

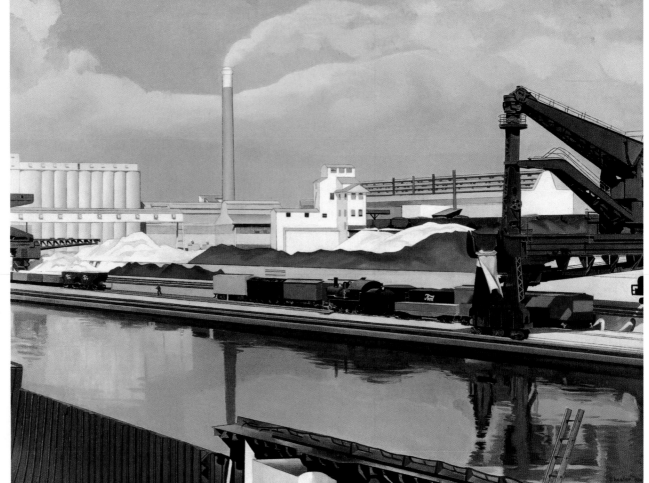

**19-19.
Charles Sheeler.
*American
Landscape.*
1930. Oil on
canvas, 24 x 31"
(61.0 x 78.7 cm).
The Museum
of Modern Art,
New York
Gift of Abby Aldrich
Rockefeller**

returned to realism, which they used to chronicle American life.

The shift back to realism is evident in the work of Charles Sheeler (1883–1965), who began his career painting Fauvist still lifes and landscapes inspired by Cubism and Cézanne. By the early 1920s, he had adopted a highly descriptive realism, partly as a result of a growing interest and business in commercial photography. In 1927, for example, an advertising firm hired him to take photographs of the new Ford Motor Company plant outside Detroit. In 1930 he used one of these photographs as the source for *American Landscape* (fig. 19-19), a seemingly faithful transcription of the photograph. The title of the work, considered separately from the painting, suggests a rural view rather than the industrial site actually portrayed. The careful attention Sheeler gives to the subject, however, suggests that his intent was not to make a caustic joke but rather to share a little gentle humor with the viewer. Recently, art historians have examined the extent to which Sheeler's paintings are indeed literal transcriptions of their subjects. A careful look at some of his paintings suggests that he may have subtly rearranged reality rather than faithfully recorded it.

Sheeler's choice of subject reflects the fact that the United States was an increasingly indus-

trialized nation. The 1920 census demonstrated that for the first time in history, more Americans were living in urban centers than rural areas. Individuals had left their hometowns and their roots in search of better opportunities. During World War I, for instance, thousands of African Americans left the rural South for jobs in northern defense plants. The Great Migration, as it is known, created racial tensions over housing and employment that in turn fostered a concern for the rights of African Americans. It produced as well new explorations of Black experience and identity, above all by the African-American writers, artists, and musicians who contributed to what became known as the Harlem Renaissance of the 1920s.

Alain Locke, an influential voice in the Harlem Renaissance, encouraged younger black artists and writers to seek their contemporary cultural identity in their African and African-American heritage. The influence of this advice can be seen in depictions of Harlem in the 1930s by the artist Jacob Lawrence (b. 1917). The bright colors and flat areas in *Interior Scene* (fig. 19-20) recall exuberant southern folk art. The lively patterning and cheerful palette lend an almost playful air to what is otherwise a grim scene of a brothel infested with flies and rats. Neighbor-

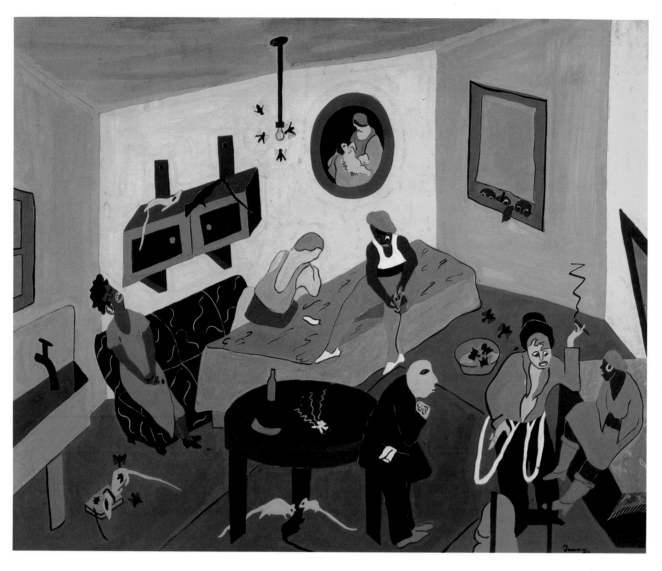

19-20. Jacob Lawrence. *Interior Scene.* 1937. Tempera on paper, 28½ x 33¾" (72.4 x 85.7 cm). Collection Philip J. and Suzanne Schiller

hood children peak through the window at the women and their disheveled white patrons. Below a picture of the Madonna and Child, a woman tucks her recently earned money into a stocking. The unstable composition and steep perspective suggest a world out of kilter. Lawrence's purposes here are unclear. Are we to be amused, appalled, or both?

Many Americans shrank from facing the realities of urban life in the nation's growing cities. In the late 1920s and 1930s, a small group of painters, known collectively as the Regionalists, instead celebrated, sometimes nostalgically, the country's rural heartland. One prominent Regionalist artist was John Steuart Curry (1897–1946), who often painted Kansas farm life.

19-21. John Steuart Curry. Baptism in Kansas. 1928. Oil on canvas, 40 x 50" (101.6 x 127.0 cm). Whitney Museum of American Art, New York
Gift of Gertrude Vanderbilt Whitney

Curry painted this work in his Westport, Connecticut, studio. He did not revisit the Midwest until the summer of the next year. Between that date and his appointment as artist-in-residence at the College of Agriculture at the University of Wisconsin, he made annual sketching trips to the Midwest for the paintings he produced in his East Coast studio during the winter.

His canvas *Baptism in Kansas* (fig. 19-21) is based on an incident from rural life. It shows a woman being baptized in a farm trough, surrounded by the members of the local community. Rays of

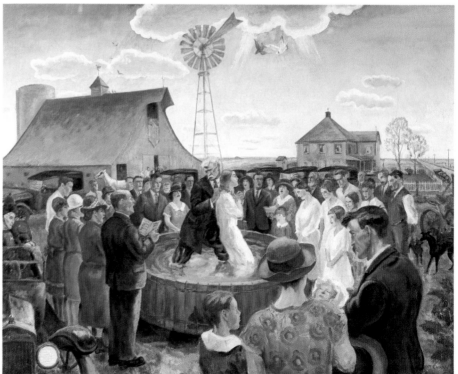

19-22. Dorothea Lange. *Migrant Mother, Nipomo, California.* February 1936. Gelatin-silver print. Library of Congress, Washington, D.C.

sunshine and flying doves, Christian symbols of the Divine Spirit, appear in the sky above the woman. Automobiles circle the group, recalling the protective circles of wagons formed at resting places during the early western migrations. Although some critics have seen the man at the right and woman in the car at the left as "skeptical outsiders," the overall mood of the painting seems to glorify a stable agrarian way of life.

In spite of the largely positive visions of the Regionalists, the economic hardships of the Great Depression, which began with the stock market crash of 1929, made it clear to most Americans that an agricultural lifestyle was no panacea for the country's woes. Many farmers faced bankruptcy, and rural regions suffered great poverty. In 1935, a newly established government agency, the Farm Securities Administration (FSA), began to hire photographers to document the problems of farmers and migrant workers.

Dorothea Lange (1895–1965) played a major role in the formation of the FSA photography program. Lange, who worked in San Francisco as a freelance photographer and portraitist, was touched by the struggles of the city's poor and unemployed during the Depression. She began to photograph their plight. After seeing some of these photographs in 1934, Paul S. Taylor, an economics professor at the University of California at Berkeley, asked her to collaborate on a report on migrant farm laborers in California. The report, which helped persuade state officials to build migrant labor camps, was also influential in the federal government's decision to include a photographic unit in the FSA. Lange was hired as one of the unit's first photographers in 1935.

Perhaps her most famous photograph is *Migrant Mother, Nipomo, California* (fig. 19-22). The woman in the picture is Florence Thompson, a thirty-two-year-old mother of ten children. Drawn and prematurely aged, she gazes past the viewer into an uncertain future. The fears of all disenfranchised people, perpetually shunted to the margins of society, seem crystallized in her worried face.

Abstract Expressionism and the New York School

Although realism dominated American art in the period between the two world wars, some artists of the period maintained an interest in the nonrepresentational styles of European art. A group of these men and women banded together in 1937 to form the American Abstract Artists. This group of about forty artists dedicated itself to promoting the abstract tradition of the European avant-garde and so helped to pave the way for Abstract Expressionism, the dominant style of the late 1940s and 1950s.

America's living link with the modernist tradition in Europe was Hans Hofmann (1880–1966), a German-born teacher and painter who had studied in both Paris and Munich before World War I. The rise of fascism in Europe and the outbreak of World War II led a number of leading European artists and writers to move to the United States. By 1940, for example, André Breton, Salvador Dalí, and Piet Mondrian were all living in New York. Although many of the émigrés kept to themselves, their very presence provoked fruitful discussions among American abstract artists.

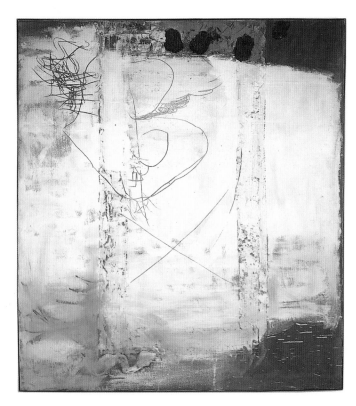

**19-23. Antoni Tàpies.
*White with Graphism.***
1957. Mixed media on
canvas, 6'3⅞" x 5'8¾"
(1.93 x 1.75 m).
Washington University
Gallery of Art, St. Louis,
Missouri
Gift of Mr. and Mrs. Richard
Weil, 1963

In Europe the most distinctive postwar approach was called *art informel* ("formless" art) or Lyrical Abstraction or *tachisme* (*tache* is French for "spot" or "stain"). If Dada and the two world wars had discredited all notions of humanity as reasonable, artists had the duty to discover or invent a new and more authentic concept of our species. They believed they were able to do so by returning to the origins of art as expressed in the simple, honest mark. One of the many artists who participated in this movement was the Catalan painter Antoni Tàpies (b. 1923). In works such as *White with Graphism* (fig. 19-23), he attempted to recover the primordial language of art with crudely drawn and incised marks on a white ground that recalled a plaster wall. Tàpies did not mean to communicate a particular message but rather to record the fundamental human urge to self-expression. In 1953, when he visited New York, he found that American artists were assuming similar approaches to their art.

In New York, American artists, deeply affected by the ideas of Surrealism and the teaching of Hans Hofmann, began working in a style collectively called Abstract Expressionism. This term designates a wide variety of work produced in New York between 1940 and roughly 1960. By the late 1940s, two major approaches to abstract art emerged: Color Field painting, distinguished by broad sweeping fields of color, and action painting, or **gesturalism**, characterized by active paint handling. Because not all Abstract Expressionist work was abstract or expressionistic, some art historians prefer to refer to the art simply as the New York School (see "Clement Greenberg and the New York School," page 453).

The Abstract Expressionists gained from the Surrealists both a commitment to examining the unconscious and techniques for doing so. But whereas the European Surrealists had derived their notion of the unconscious from Sigmund Freud, many of the Americans subscribed to the thinking of Swiss psychoanalyst Carl Jung (1875–1961). His theory of the "collective unconscious" holds that beneath one's private memories is a storehouse of feelings and symbolic associations common to all humans.

The action painter Jackson Pollock (1912–1956) was the most famous of the Jung-inspired Abstract Expressionists. Undergoing Jungian analysis between 1939 and 1941, the alcoholic and self-destructive artist made little progress with his personal problems. The sessions greatly affected his work, however, giving him a new vocabulary of signs and symbols and a belief in the therapeutic role of the artist in society.

In the mid-1940s, Pollock replaced those painted symbols with freely applied paint, working on large canvases spread out on the floor. He began to employ enamel house paints along with conventional oils sometime in the winter of 1946–1947, dripping them onto his canvases with sticks and brushes using a variety of fluid arm and wrist movements. The result over the next four years was a series of graceful linear abstractions such as *Autumn Rhythm* (*Number* 30) (fig. 19-24). As the titles of this and others of his paintings suggest, Pollock seems to have felt that in the free, unselfconscious act of painting he was giving vent to primal, natural forces.

In 1945 Pollock married Lee Krasner (1908–1984), a member of the original American Abstract

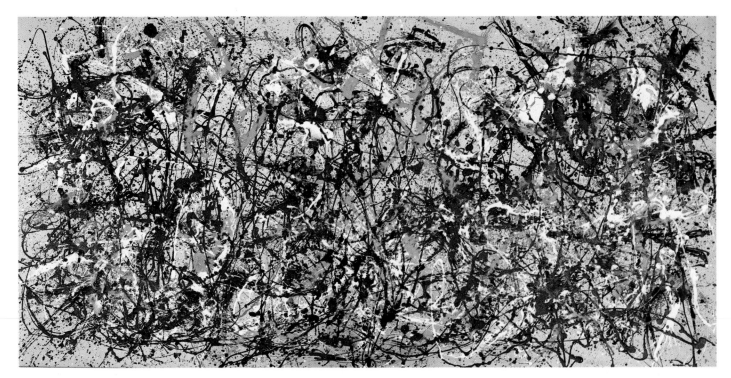

19-24. Jackson Pollock. *Autumn Rhythm (Number 30).* 1950. Oil on canvas, 8'9" x 17'3" (2.66 x 5.25 m). The Metropolitan Museum of Art, New York
George A. Hearn Fund

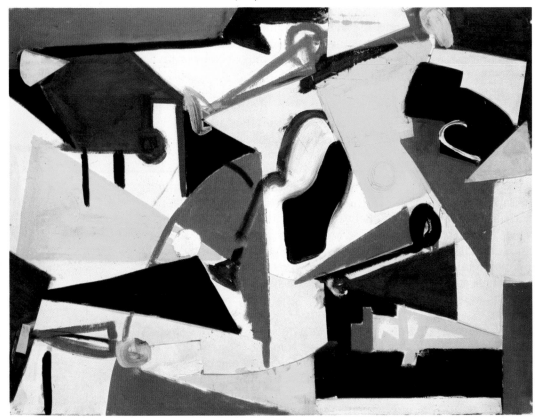

19-25. Lee Krasner. *Red, White, Blue, Yellow, Black.* 1939. Collage of oil on paper, 19 x 25" (48.5 x 63.5 cm). Thyssen-Bornemisza Collection, Lugano, Switzerland

Artists group and a student of Hofmann's (fig. 19-25). When Krasner began living with Pollock in 1942, she virtually stopped painting in order to devote herself to the conventional role of a supporting wife. In 1946–1947, however, she began to produce her first mature statement. Despite marital problems caused by Pollock's alcoholism, she created significant works in the medium of collage. After Pollock's death in an automobile crash in 1956, Krasner took over his studio and during the next year and a half produced a dazzling group of monumental gestural paintings. Works from this period are painted in bold sweeping curves that express not only her sense of grief but also her identification with the forces of nature suggested by the bursting rounded forms.

In contrast to Pollock, who said that he found "pure harmony" when at work on his drip paintings, his contemporary Willem de Kooning (1904–1997) insisted, "Art never seems to make me peaceful or pure." De Kooning, born in the Netherlands, immigrated to the United States in 1926. After a period of painting in a nonrepresentational mode, he shocked the New York art world in the early 1950s by returning to the figure with a series of paintings of women. The first of the

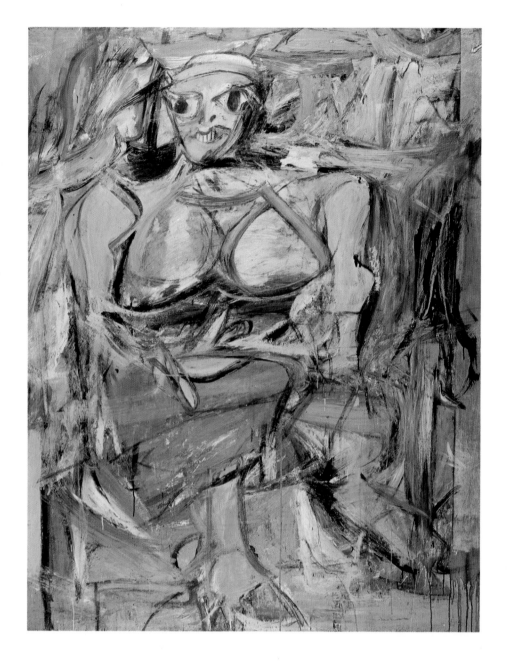

19-26. Willem de Kooning.
Woman I. 1950–52. Oil on canvas, 6'3⅞" x 4'10" (1.93 x 1.47 m). The Museum of Modern Art, New York Purchase

Dissatisfied with the results of his extended work on this painting, de Kooning left it outside his studio, where Meyer Schapiro, a Columbia University art historian and supporter of the New York School, found it when he came to visit. He admired the work and convinced de Kooning that it was worth keeping and exhibiting.

series, *Woman* I (fig. 19-26), took him almost two years to paint. His wife, the artist Elaine de Kooning (1918–1989), said that he painted it, scraped it, and repainted it several dozen times at least. Part of de Kooning's dissatisfaction stemmed from the way his figure, inspired by conventionally pretty images of women seen in American advertising, kept veering away from those models. What emerges in *Woman* I is not the elegant companion of Madison Avenue fantasy but a powerful adversary, more dangerous than alluring. Only the soft pastel colors and luscious paint surface give any hint of de Kooning's original sources, and these qualities are nearly lost in the furious slashing of the paint. "Women irritate me sometimes," de Kooning said in response to critics who questioned his

Clement Greenberg and the New York School

Perhaps more than any other single critic, Clement Greenberg (1909–1994) defined European modernism for American artists, art historians, and the informed public. After World War II he identified Abstract Expressionism as the dominant style of the late 1940s and 1950s and championed the New York School of painting. Inspired in part by Hans Hofmann's teaching, he demanded close analysis of the work of art and judgments based on visual perception alone. As he argued for the value of pure abstraction, he focused public attention on the large, colorful, abstract paintings of artists such as Jackson Pollock and, later, Helen Frankenthaler.

The reaction against Greenberg began in the 1970s. By the 1980s to argue against *Greenbergian formalism* identified the art historian or critic as a postmodernist, a member of the new avant-garde. Most art historians now acknowledge that there are a variety of categories and ways of looking at modern art. Ironically, Greenberg continues to influence critical theory by forcing others to study his writings, if only to disavow them.

19-27. Mark Rothko.
Homage to Matisse. 1953.
Oil on canvas,
8'10" x 4'3" (2.7 x 1.3 m).
Collection the Edward
R. Broida Trust

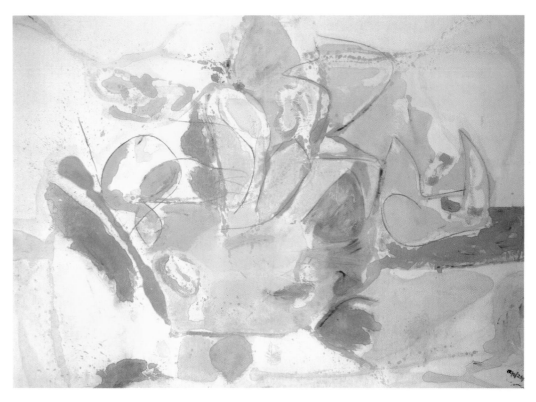

19-28. Helen Frankenthaler. *Mountains and Sea.* 1952. Oil on canvas, 7'2¾" x 9'8¼" (2.20 x 2.95 m). Collection of the artist on extended loan to the National Gallery of Art, Washington, D.C.

feelings toward women. "I painted that irritation in the Woman series." But he also added: "I was painting the woman in me."

During the 1950s, de Kooning dominated the avant-garde in New York. Among the handful of modernist painters who resisted his influence was Mark Rothko (1903–1970), a pioneering Color Field painter who used large rectangles of color to evoke transcendent emotional states. In works such as *Homage to Matisse* (fig. 19-27), Rothko consciously sought a profound harmony between the two divergent human tendencies that German philosopher Friedrich Nietzsche (1844–1900) called the Dionysian (after the Greek god of wine, the harvest, and inspiration) and the Apollonian (after the Greek god of light, music, and truth). The painting's rich color is its Dionysian element, the emotional and instinctive side of human nature, while the simple compositional structure underlying the coloristic virtuosity is its rational and disciplined Apollonian counterpart. Together they form a deeply satisfying unity, which hints at a momentary resolution of our fundamental human duality. The painting's title refers to Rothko's great predecessor, Henri Matisse, who also created harmonious, color-saturated works that celebrate the joys of human existence (see fig. 18-12).

Elements from Color Field paintings like Rothko's intermingled with the gesturalism of action painting in the early work of the Abstract Expressionist Helen Frankenthaler (b. 1928). Frankenthaler, like Pollock, worked on the floor, drawn to what she described as Pollock's "dance-like use of arms and legs." She produced a huge canvas, *Mountains and Sea* (fig. 19-28), in this way, working from watercolor sketches she had made in Nova Scotia. Instead of using thick, full-bodied paint, as Pollock did, Frankenthaler thinned her oils and applied them in washes that soaked into the raw canvas, producing an effect that somewhat resembles watercolor but also evokes Color Field painting. A few delicate contour lines suggest not only the mountains of the painting's title but also less translatable, dream-inspired Surrealistic forms.

Frankenthaler and her contemporaries who emerged in the 1950s, such as Joan Mitchell (1922–1992) and Grace Hartigan (b. 1922), were the second and last generation of Abstract Expressionists. By the end of the decade, some artists and theorists were complaining that Abstract Expressionism had lost its innovative edge. Critic Harold Rosenberg, who disagreed with this emerging critical consensus, nevertheless summed it up succinctly in a published article: "Today it is felt that a new art mode is long overdue, if for no other reason than that the present avant-garde has been with us for fifteen years. . . . No innovating style can survive that long without losing its radical nerve and turning into an Academy." Amid the growing critical conviction that Abstract Expressionism was no longer fresh, the next matter on the agenda would be to choose among the many competing styles on the periphery.

Maya Ying Lin.
tnam Veterans Memorial. 1982.
ck granite, length 500' (152 m).
The Mall, Washington D.C.

wentieth-Century
bute

power of Maya Lin's monu-
t lies in its understatement.
ple, dark, polished stone
ngraved with the names of
dead—names so numerous
they lose individuality
become a surface texture.
wall is a statement of
, sorrow, and the futility of
Like a black mirror, it
ects back shadowy images
he mourners. It is a timeless
ument to suffering humanity,
less in sacrifice.

K E Y S to Art History

PUBLIC ART

Writing about Michelangelo in 1568, the architectect and biog-
rapher of artists Giorgio Vasari reported, "He went to see
a sculpture which was to be put out of doors, and the sculptor
was taking pains to arrange the lights of the windows to show it
to advantage. Michelangelo said, 'Do not trouble, the light of
the piazza is what you have to fear,' meaning that the popular
opinion decides the worth of public works."

Art created for spaces accessible to the public is public art.
(Art historians do not regard art in churches, temples, and
synagogues as public art, even though most of these spaces are
open to the public. Likewise, art made for private individuals,
whether of the nobility or the middle class, is not public art
because, originally, it was not available for the public to view.)
Most often, public art is sculpture or a mural painted in a public
building. Until the modern era, most public art celebrated and
commemorated political and social leaders and aspects of war:
officers and soldiers—both victorious and slain—in large, freestanding monuments. The motives of those who have commissioned public art have ranged from civic pride, to the wish to
honor heroes, to political propaganda and social intimidation.
Maya Lin's memorial in Washington, D.C. to the American men
and women who died in the Vietnam War is among the most
visited works of public art of the twentieth century and is certainly among the most affecting war monuments ever conceived.

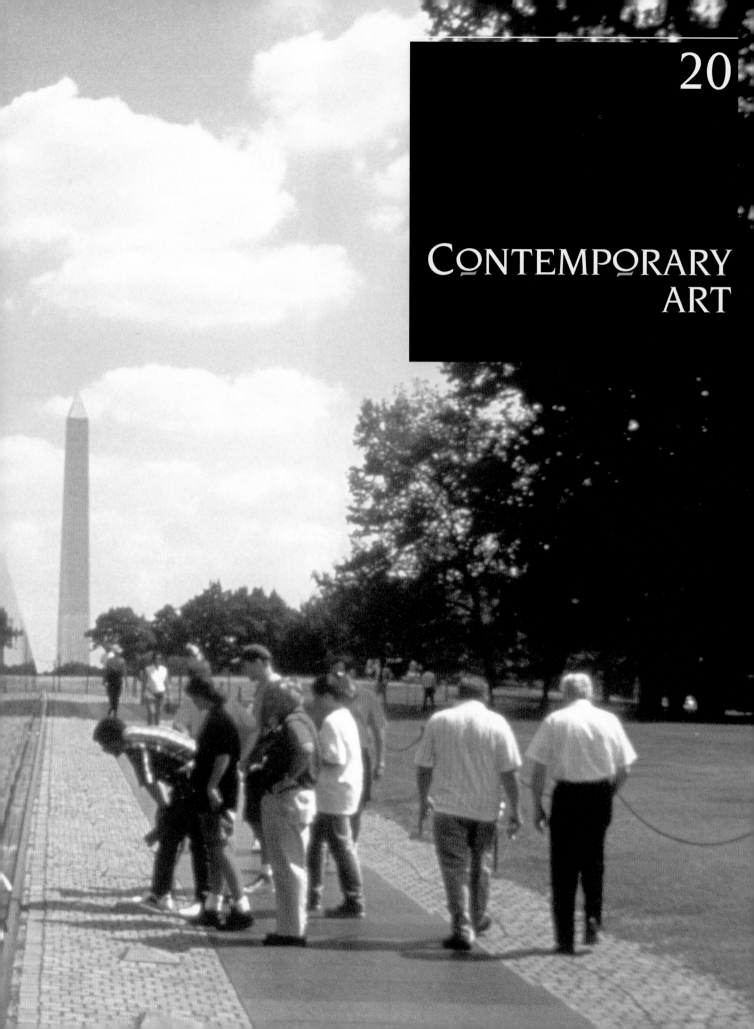

CONTEMPORARY ART

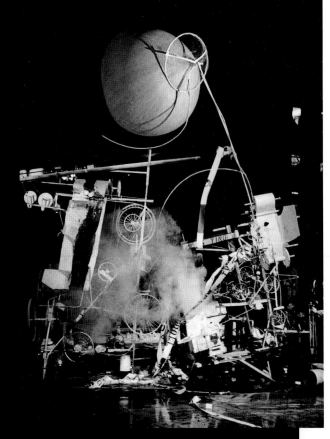

20-1. Jean Tinguely. *Homage to New York.* 1960. Self-destroying sculpture in the garden of the Museum of Modern Art, New York

O n the evening of March 17, 1960, a distinguished group of guests, including Governor Nelson Rockefeller of New York, gathered in the sculpture garden of the Museum of Modern Art in New York City. Awaiting them was an unlikely construction titled *Homage to New York* (fig. 20-1) by the Swiss-born artist Jean Tinguely (1925–1991). The work was assembled from yards of metal tubing, several dozen bicycle and baby-carriage wheels, a washing-machine drum, an upright piano, a radio, several electric fans, a noisy old Addressograph machine, a bassinet, numerous small motors, two motor-driven devices that produced abstract paintings by the yard, several bottles of chemical inks, and various noisemakers. White paint covered everything except the crowning element—an inflated orange meteorological balloon.

The machine, designed to destroy itself when activated, was plugged in in front of the expectant guests. As smoke poured out of the machinery and covered the crowd, parts of the contraption broke free and scuttled off in various directions, sometimes threatening the onlookers. A device meant to douse the burning piano—which kept playing only three notes—failed to work, and firefighters had to be called in. They extinguished the blaze and finished the work's destruction to boos from the crowd, which, with the exception of the museum officials present, had been delighted by the spectacle.

This new kind of art, dramatic but transitory, prefigured a question and answer raised by musician and philosopher John Cage. Surveying art and music in 1961, he asked, "Where do we go from here," and his answer was, "Towards theater." Such questions about what art is and what role it plays in society have marked the richly innovative period since 1960.

Alternative Styles Following Abstract Expressionism

By the end of the 1950s, many artists and critics were ready for a change from Abstract Expressionism (Chapter 19). One alternative path was **assemblage**, putting together disparate elements to construct a work of art, as Tinguely did in his *Homage to New York.* Tinguely, an anarchist, wanted to free the machine, to let it play. "Art hasn't been fun for a long time," he said. Not since Dada, he might have added. Like the creations of his Dada forebears, Tinguely's work was implicitly critical of an overly restrained and practical bourgeois mentality.

By 1950 Louise Nevelson (1899–1988) had developed a Cubist-inspired version of assemblage that prefigured the Minimalist (stripped to essentials) focus on formal concerns. Prowling the streets of downtown Manhattan, she collected discarded packing boxes in which she would carefully arrange chair legs, broom handles, cabinet doors, spindles, and other wooden refuse. She painted her assemblages a matte black, both to obscure the identity of the individual elements and to integrate them formally.

After stacking several of these boxes together against a studio wall, Nevelson realized that the resulting accumulation made a more powerful effect than the individual units. One of her first monumental wall assemblages was *Sky Cathedral* (fig. 20-2). What she particularly liked about the new schema was the way it could transform ordinary space into another, higher realm—just as the prosaic elements she worked with had themselves been transformed into something finer. In order to complete this process, and to add a further poetic dimension, Nevelson first displayed *Sky Cathedral* bathed in a soft blue light like moonlight. (An equally evocative use of assemblage can be seen in James Hampton's work; see fig. 5.)

Another artist, Robert Rauschenberg (b. 1925), evolved a distinctive style of assemblage by chaotically mixing painted and found elements

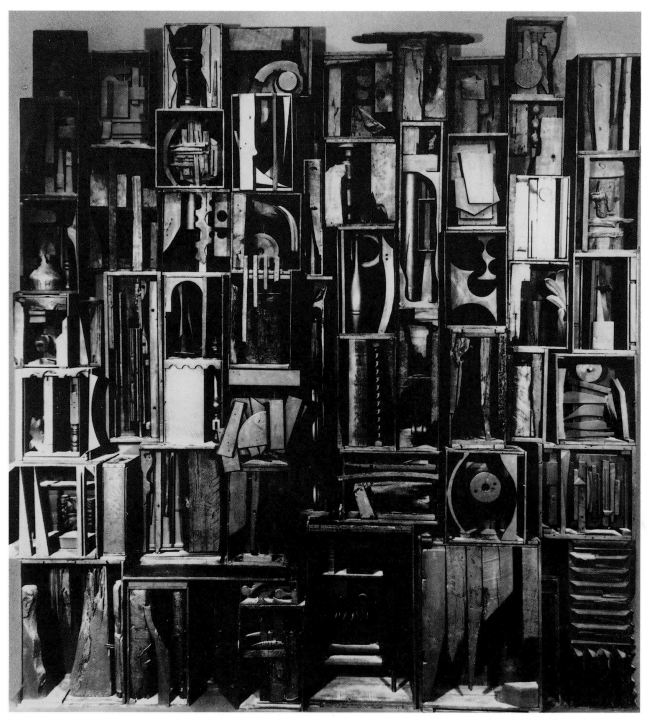

20-2. Louise Nevelson. *Sky Cathedral*. 1958. Assemblage of wood construction, painted black, 11'3¹/₂" x 10'¹/₄" x 18" (3.44 m x 3.05 m x 45.7 cm). The Museum of Modern Art, New York

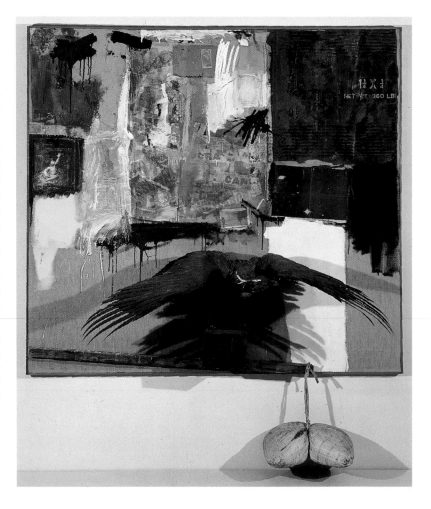

20-3. Robert Rauschenburg. *Canyon.*
1959. Combine painting: oil, pencil, paper, metal, photograph, fabric, wood on canvas, plus buttons, mirror, stuffed eagle, pillow tied with cord, and paint tube, 6'1" x 5'6" x 24¾" (1.85 m x 1.68 m x 63 cm). Collection Mr. and Mrs. Michael Sonnabend, on infinite loan at the Baltimore Museum of Art

Avant-garde critics were not bothered by the fact that much of Rauschenberg's and the other assemblers' materials were drawn from popular culture. Many of the early-twentieth-century collagists, including Picasso and Braque, had worked with similar materials. However, critics such as Hilton Kramer (at the *New York Times*) and Thomas Hess (at *Artnews*) pointed out that whereas earlier artists had aesthetically coordinated such elements, transforming the crude materials of life into the finer ones of art, Rauschenberg and his associates left them in their raw, "unpurified" condition. In this view, therefore, such works as this one were not art at all.

in artworks he called *combines. Canyon* (fig. 20-3), one of these combines, features an assortment of old family photographs (the boy with the upraised arm is Rauschenberg), public imagery (the Statue of Liberty, which echoes the boy's pose), fragments of political posters (in the middle), and various objects salvaged from the trash (the flattened steel drum at upper right) or donated by friends (the stuffed eagle). The artist meant his work to be open to various readings, choosing material that each viewer might interpret differently. Cheerfully accepting the chaos and unpredictability of modern urban experience, he tried to find artistic metaphors for it. "I only consider myself successful," he said, "when I do something that resembles the lack of order I sense."

In 1961 the Museum of Modern Art organized an exhibition titled "The Art of Assemblage." Rauschenberg was one of two major American artists included in the show; the other was his close friend Jasper Johns (b. 1930). Inspired by the example of Marcel Duchamp (see fig. 19-13), Johns produced conceptually challenging works that seemed to bear on issues raised in contemporary art. For instance, art historians and critics had praised the evenly dispersed, "nonhierarchical" or "allover" quality of so much Abstract Expressionist painting, particularly the late work

of Pollock (see fig. 19-24). The target in *Target with Four Faces* (fig. 20-4), an emphatically hierarchical, organized image, can be seen as a response and a rebuttal to this position.

Target also has a psychological dimension that may stem from the artist's own anxieties and fears. Above the target are four faces, casts taken at different times from the same model. Cut off below eye level and thus made anonymous, they are as blank and empty as the target itself. The viewer can complete the process of depersonalization by closing the lid over the faces, obliterating the human presence. The work of Johns had a powerful effect on the artists who matured around 1960. His interest in Duchamp helped elevate that artist to a place of importance previously reserved for Picasso. In addition, his conceptually intriguing use of subjects from ordinary life, a feature also evident in the work of Rauschenberg, helped to open the way for a new development, Pop art.

POP ART

Pop art, as its name suggests, took its style and subject matter from popular culture: its sources were comic books, advertisements, movies, and television. One of the best-known American Pop artists, Roy Lichtenstein (1923–1997), used imagery found in cartoons and advertisements.

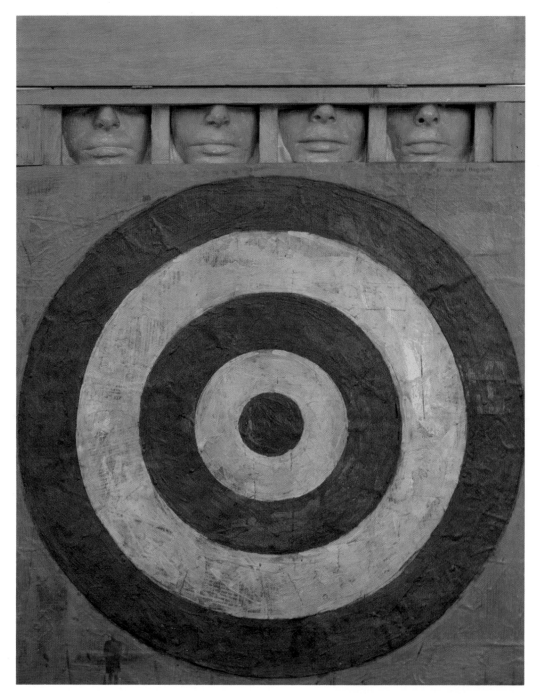

20-4. **Jasper Johns.** *Target with Four Faces.* 1955. Assemblage: encaustic on newspaper and cloth over canvas, surmounted by four tinted plaster faces in wood box with hinged front, overall, with box open, 33⅝ x 26 x 3" (85.4 x 66 x 7.6 cm). The Museum of Modern Art, New York
Gift of Mr. and Mrs. Robert C. Scull

He adopted as well their heavy outlines and imitated the **Benday dots** used to add tone in offset printing. Although many assume that he merely copied from the comics, in fact he made numerous subtle yet important formal adjustments that tightened, clarified, and strengthened the final image. *Oh, Jeff . . . I Love You, Too . . . But . . .* (fig. 20-5) compresses into a single frame the soap opera story of two people who fall in love, face some sort of crisis or "but" that temporarily threatens their relationship, and then live happily ever after. Lichtenstein reminds the grown-up viewer, however, that this plot is only an adolescent fiction; real-life relationships like his own marriage, then in the process of dissolving, end, as here, with the "but."

Another of the Pop artists who veiled personal meditations behind the impersonal veneer of American popular imagery was Andy Warhol

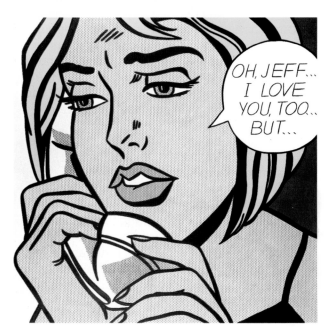

20-5. **Roy Lichtenstein.** *Oh, Jeff . . . I Love You, Too . . . But . . .* 1964. Oil on Magna on canvas, 4 x 4' (1.22 x 1.22 m). Private collection

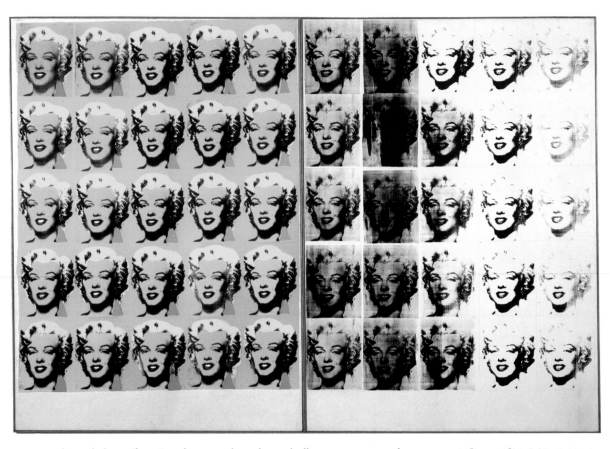

20-6. Andy Warhol. *Marilyn Diptych*. 1962. Oil, acrylic, and silk screen on enamel on canvas, 6'8⅞" x 4'8⅝" (2.05 x 1.44 m). Tate Gallery, London

Warhol assumed that all Pop artists shared his affirmative view of ordinary culture. In his account of the beginnings of the Pop movement, he wrote: "The Pop artists did images that anybody walking down Broadway could recognize in a split second—comics, picnic tables, men's trousers, celebrities, shower curtains, refrigerators, Coke bottles—all the great modern things that the Abstract Expressionists tried so hard not to notice at all."

(1928?–1987). A successful commercial illustrator in New York City during the 1950s, Warhol grew envious of Rauschenberg's and Johns's emerging "star" status and decided in 1960 to pursue a career as an artist along the general lines suggested by their work. His decision to focus on popular culture was more than a careerist move, however; it also allowed him to celebrate the middle-class social and material values he had absorbed growing up amid the hardships of the Great Depression.

A number of these values may be discerned in the *Marilyn Diptych* (fig. 20-6), even in its industrial mode of production. The painting, produced in Warhol's studio called The Factory, is one of the first in which Warhol turned from conventional modes of hand painting to the assembly-line technique of silk-screening photo-images onto canvas. The method was faster and thus more profitable, and Warhol could also produce many versions of the subject—all of which he considered good business. The subject of the work is also telling. Like so many Americans,

Warhol was fascinated by American movie stars such as Marilyn Monroe. The strip of pictures in this work suggests the sequential images of film, the medium that made Monroe famous. The face Warhol portrays, taken from a publicity photograph (see "Appropriation," opposite), is not that of Monroe the person but of Monroe the star, since Warhol was interested in her public mask, not in her personality or character. He borrowed the diptych format from the Byzantine icons of Christian saints he saw at the Greek Orthodox church services he attended every Sunday. By symbolically treating the famous actress as a saint, Warhol shed light on his own fascination with fame. Not only does fame bring wealth and transform the ordinary into the beautiful, it also confers, like holiness for a saint, a kind of immortality.

MINIMALISM

In contrast with the emphasis on content and recognizable subject matter in assemblage and Pop art, Minimalism, another style that

Appropriation

During the late 1970s and 1980s, **appropriation**, or the presentation of a preexisting image as one's own, became a popular technique among postmodernists in both the United States and Western Europe. The borrowing of figures or compositions has been an essential technique throughout the history of art (see figs. 2, 17-21), but the emphasis had always been on changing or personalizing the source. A copy or reproduction was not considered a legitimate work of art until Marcel Duchamp changed the rules with his **"readymades"** (see image within this box). *Fountain* caused a sensation when it was discovered that the work, signed "R. Mutt" and accompanied by an entry fee for the first annual exhibition of the American Society of Independent Artists, was actually a urinal mounted on its side. Duchamp's insistence that the quality of an artwork depends not on formal invention but on the ideas that stand behind it established the theoretical basis for the recent popularity of the technique. Duchamp's own type of appropriations first inspired the Pop artists Andy Warhol (see fig. 20-6) and Roy Lichtenstein (see fig. 20-5), whose reuse of imagery from popular culture, high art, ordinary commerce, and the tabloids, in turn, helped point the way for the artists of the 1970s and 1980s.

Unfortunately, perhaps, critics and historians now use the term *appropriation* to describe the activities of two distinct groups. To the first belong artists who combine and shape their borrowings in personal ways. These artists, along with earlier ones such

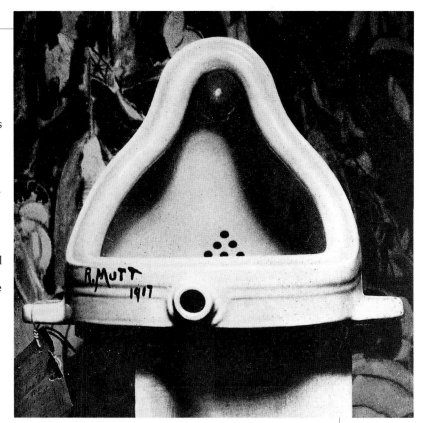

Marcel Duchamp. *Fountain.* 1917. Porcelain plumbing fixture and enamel paint, height 24⅝" (62.5 cm). Photographed by Alfred Stieglitz. Philadelphia Museum of Art
Louise and Walter Arensberg Collection

as Robert Rauschenberg (see fig. 20-3), might be called "collage appropriators." "Straight appropriators," on the other hand, are those who simply repaint or rephotograph imagery from commerce or the history of art and present it as their own.

The work of the latter is grounded not only in the Duchampian tradition but also in the recent ideas of the French literary critics known collectively as the Post-Structuralists. Of particular importance was their critique of certain basic and unexamined assumptions about art. In "Death of the Author"

(1968), for example, Roland Barthes argued that the meaning of a work of art depends not on what the author meant (which Jacques Derrida and others argued was neither certain nor entirely recoverable) but on what the reader understands. Furthermore, Barthes questioned the modernist notion of originality, of the author as a creator of an entirely new meaning. The author, Barthes argued, merely recycles meanings from other sources, saying that a "text is a tissue of quotations drawn from the innumerable centers of culture" (cited in Fineberg, page 454).

emerged in the wake of Abstract Expressionism, focused on stripping all extra-artistic meanings from artworks and reducing them to their technical essentials.

An important proponent of this style was the sculptor Donald Judd (1928–1994). Convinced along with Clement Greenberg and others that Abstract Expressionism had deteriorated into a set of techniques for faking both the subjective and the transcendent, Judd began around 1960

to search for an art free of falsehood. By the early 1960s he had decided that sculpture offered a better medium than painting for creating literal, matter-of-fact art. Rather than depicting shapes, which Judd thought smacked of illusionism and therefore fakery, he would create actual shapes. In search of simplicity and clarity, he soon evolved a formal vocabulary featuring identical rectangular units arranged in rows and constructed of industrial materials, especially

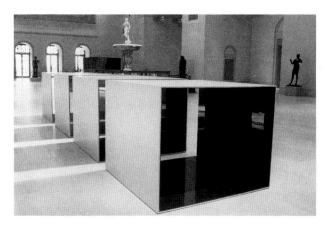

20-7. Donald Judd. Untitled. 1969. Anodized aluminum and blue Plexiglas, each 3'11½" x 4'11⅞" x 4'11⅞" (1.2 x 1.5 x 1.5 m); overall 3'11½" x 4'11⅞" x 23'8½" (1.2 x 1.5 x 7.2 m). The Saint Louis Art Museum, St. Louis, Missouri
Purchase funds given by the Shoenberg Foundation, Inc.

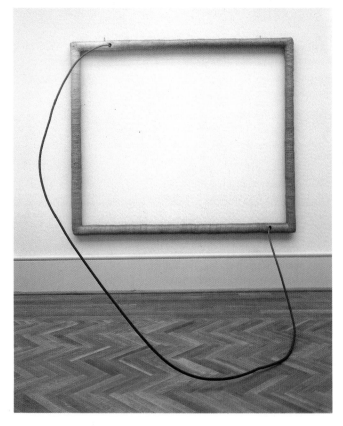

20-8. Eva Hesse. Hang-Up. 1965–66. Acrylic on cloth over wood and steel, 6' x 7' x 6'6" (1.83 x 2.13 x 1.98 m). The Art Institute of Chicago
Through prior gift of Arthur Keating and Mr. and Mrs. Edward Morris, 1988

anodized aluminum and Plexiglas. *Untitled* (fig. 20-7) is a typical example of his mature work.

Approaches to Minimalism varied from artist to artist. Eva Hesse (1936–1970) countered the rigid prefabricated forms of Minimalism with the incorporation of malleable techniques such as sewing, lacing, and bandaging into her work. In that sense, Hesse was one of the first artists to move beyond the austerity of Minimalism. Instead of sleek surface, her work shows the actual process of art making. In *Hang-Up* (fig. 20-8), contradictions abound—the self-contained and the protruding, the regular and the organic, order and chaos. In the face of the severe exactitude of serial Minimalism, Hess provided an alternative in her choice of materials and in their inherent capacity for movement and change.

Postmodernism

Many Minimalists, inspired by the theories of art critics such as Greenberg, believed that art represented a pure realm outside ordinary existence and that the history of art followed a coherent, progressive trajectory culminating in modernism and abstraction. To most of the artists who followed them, by contrast, the concepts of artistic purity and the mainstream seemed naive. Critics and artists recognized that they lived in the midst of artistic **pluralism**, the presence of a variety of artistic intentions and styles. The generation that grew to maturity around 1970 had been the first to accept pluralism in its own right as a manifestation of our culturally heterogeneous age.

The decline of the concept of modernism in the various arts was neither uniform nor sudden. Its gradual erosion occurred over a long period and was the result of many individual transformations. The many approaches to art that emerged at the end of the twentieth century are designated by the catchall term *postmodernism*.

ARCHITECTURE

Postmodernism manifested itself first in architecture, in the late 1960s in the work of Robert Venturi (b. 1925) and his associates (see fig. 14). In the pioneering publication *Complexity and Contradiction in Architecture* (1966), Venturi argued that the problem with Mies van der Rohe and other International Style architects (Chapter 19) was their impractical unwillingness to accept the modern city for what it is: a complex, contradictory, and heterogeneous collection of "high" and "low" architectural forms. Taking these ideas further in the book *Learning from Las Vegas* (1972), he and his colleagues suggested that rather than turning their backs in disdain at ordinary commercial buildings, architects should get in "the habit of looking nonjudgmentally" at them. "Main Street is almost all right," Venturi observed. We "look backward at history and tradition to go forward; we can also look downward to go upward."

The postmodernist Frank Gehry (b. 1929) was one architect who was willing to look downward at the chaotic heterogeneity of urban life as well as the architecture of the past. One of the most dramatic buildings created at the end of the twentieth century is his Guggenheim Museum for the Basque city of Bilbao, Spain (fig. 20-9). Although Gehry had made a reputation during the late 1970s and 1980s based on his use of vernacular forms and cheap materials, his guiding concern in Bilbao was to reconcile the client's needs with his own interest in sculptural form. The commission for the Guggenheim Museum Bilbao provided him with an extraordinary opportunity to realize that goal.

The Solomon R. Guggenheim Museum in New York had become one of the most famous in the world, as much for its innovative architecture designed by Frank Lloyd Wright as for its collection of abstract art. Like Wright's spiraling design, Gehry's sprawling, organic plan resembles a living organism, like some gigantic metallic flower growing along the bank of a river. Gehry covered the building's complex steel skeleton with a thin skin of silvery titanium that shimmers gold or silver depending on the light. From many vantage points, however, the building resembles a giant ship, a reference to the shipbuilding and port facilities so important to the economy of the northern Spanish city. Inside, the museum features a giant atrium, which both pays homage to Wright's famous design and attempts to outdo it in size and effect. In competing with Wright, Gehry said he meant to provide for the needs of the artists. "Artists want to be in great buildings," he claimed.

PHOTOGRAPHY

In photography, a major change, perhaps as great as that in architecture, became evident in the postmodern period. Post–World War II photography before about 1970 can be divided into three categories: abstract, fantastic, and photodocumentary. All three shared both a belief in photography's access to a higher truth (whether aesthetic, personal, or social) and a commitment to a formally handsome finished product. By about 1970, however, a shift from what might be called high-art photography to deliberately bad, low-art photography took place.

Among the postmodernist heirs to this tradition, perhaps the most radical was Duane Michals (b. 1932). An art director at *Dance Magazine* and *Time*, Michals became dissatisfied with photography's inability to deal with the inner life. Inspired by the Surrealist paintings of René Magritte, whom he came to know well, Michals began at the end of the 1960s to fabricate photographic sequences, often accompanied by written narratives. In some cases Michals tells the story in a single frame, as in *This Photograph Is My Proof* (fig. 20-10).

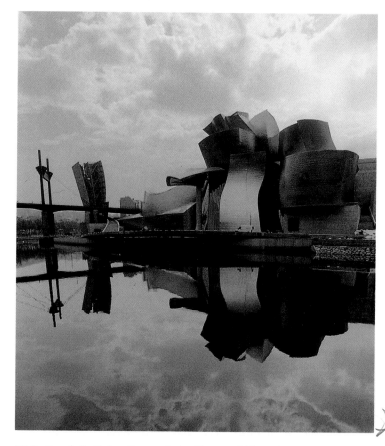

20-9. Frank O. Gehry. Guggenheim Museum Bilbao, Spain. 1997

Philip Johnson, the dean of American architects (see fig. 19-9), called the Guggenheim Museum Bilbao "the greatest building of our century."

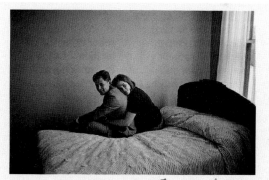

This photograph is my proof. There was that afternoon, when things were still good between us; and she embraced me, and we were so happy. It had happened. She did love me. Look, see for yourself.

20-10. Duane Michals. *This Photograph Is My Proof.*
Gelatin-silver print with text
Courtesy the artist

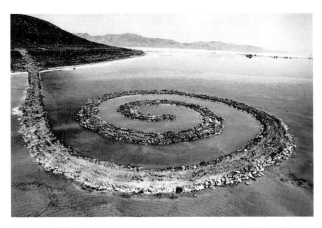

20-11. Robert Smithson. *Spiral Jetty.* 1969–70. Black rock, salt crystal, and earth spiral, length 1,500' (457.2 m). Great Salt Lake, Utah

Meant to resemble a snapshot in a personal photo album, the work purports to record a young man's attempt to cope with unrequited love. Convinced by the conventional notion that photographs do not lie, the man in the photograph tries to persuade himself, and the viewer, that the woman hugging him once really did love him. This picture—a record of a single moment in a bleak little room—is his best and only proof. Michals's deliberate use of amateurish-looking photographs with scratchy writing on them underscores his banal stories and completes the shift from high-art photography to the era of so-called bad photography.

EARTHWORKS

Artists who would define themselves as sculptors also participated in the retreat from Minimalism that characterized the advent of the postmodern era. Robert Smithson (1938–1973) was among a number of sculptors who sought to take art back to nature and out of the marketplace, where it seemed to have become a commodity judged by its monetary value rather than by its intrinsic worth (see "Patronage and Commerce," left). Because they often used raw materials found at a specific location, the works of artists such as Smithson are known as **earthworks**.

In his mature work, Smithson sought to illustrate what he called the "ongoing dialectic" in nature between constructive forces—those that build and shape form—and destructive forces—those that destroy it. *Spiral Jetty* (fig. 20-11), a 1,500-foot spiraling stone and earth platform extending into the Great Salt Lake in Utah, reflects these ideas. To Smithson, the salty waters and the algae of the lake suggested the primordial ocean where life began, and the abandoned oil rigs dotting the lakeshore brought to mind both prehistoric dinosaurs and some vanished civilization. He used the spiral because it is an archetypal shape that appears throughout the natural world, in galaxies and seashells, for example, and in salt crystals. Also, unlike modernist squares, circles, and straight lines, it is a "dialectical" shape, one that opens and closes, curls and uncurls endlessly. More than any other shape, it suggested to him the perpetual "coming and going of things." Algae turned the water into a harmony of ephemeral colors, and eventually the action of the water caused the earthwork to erode and disappear.

Another earthworks artist to carry modernist concerns into the postmodernist era is Nancy Holt (b. 1938). Since visiting the Nevada desert in 1968 with Michael Heizer, one of the leaders of the earthworks movement, and her husband, Robert Smithson, Holt has specialized in making intimate spaces for viewing the tranquil, sublime beauties of the natural world, especially the sky. In 1977–1978 she built *Stone Enclosure: Rock*

Rings (fig. 20-12) on the campus of Western Washington University, Bellingham. The work consists of two concentric 10-foot-high stone rings, the outer one about 40 feet in diameter. Four aligned doorways suggestive of processional entryways give access to the interior of the rings. Strong, secure, and snug, the interior provides a number of impressive vistas—into the woods, across the campus, or into the heavens. *Stone Enclosure: Rock Rings* is meant to remind the viewer of a variety of prehistoric and historic forms, from the Neolithic Stonehenge (see fig. 1-16) to the Roman Colosseum (see fig. 6-10). As Holt says, "I'm interested in conjuring up a sense of time that is longer than the built-in obsolescence we have all around us."

FEMINIST AND AUTOBIOGRAPHICAL TENDENCIES

Feminist artists initiated an even more ambitious attempt to break down barriers. During the 1970s, almost entirely as a result of the feminist movement, women finally began to achieve increased recognition in the American art world. The watershed event was a march in August 1970 commemorating the fiftieth anniversary of the Nineteenth Amendment to the Constitution, which guaranteed women the right to vote. The anniversary gave women an opportunity to assess their progress in various fields since 1920, and they were disappointed by what they found. Women constituted half the nation's practicing artists, but only 18 percent of commercial New York galleries carried the work of any women at all. Of the 151 artists in the 1969 Whitney Annual, one of the country's most prominent exhibitions of the work of living artists, only 8 were women. Few women served as museum directors, and few achieved the rank of full professor in art history departments.

To focus more attention on women in the arts, feminist artists began organizing women's cooperative galleries; feminist art historians, such as Eleanor Tufts and Linda Nochlin, wrote about women artists in journals; and feminist curators and critics promoted the work of emerging women artists and long-neglected earlier ones. In 1971, two feminist artists and teachers, Judy Chicago (b. 1939) and Miriam Schapiro (b. 1923), established the Feminist Art Program, dedicated to training women artists, at the California Institute of the Arts (CalArts).

Schapiro was a champion of the theory that women have a distinct artistic sensibility that can be distinguished from that of men, and hence a specifically feminine aesthetic. During the late 1950s and 1960s she made explicitly female versions of the dominant modernist styles, including reductive, hard-edged abstractions of the female form: large X shapes with openings at their centers. In the 1970s she began to create works such as *Heartfelt* (fig. 20-13)

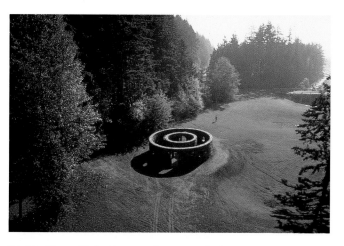

20-12. Nancy Holt. *Stone Enclosure: Rock Rings*. 1977–78. Brown Mountain stone, height 10' (3.05 m), outer ring diameter 40' (12.2 m), inner ring 20' (6.1 m). Western Washington University, Bellingham
Funding from the Virginia Wright Fund, the National Endowment for the Arts, Washington State Arts Commission, Western Washington University Art Fund, and the artist's contributions

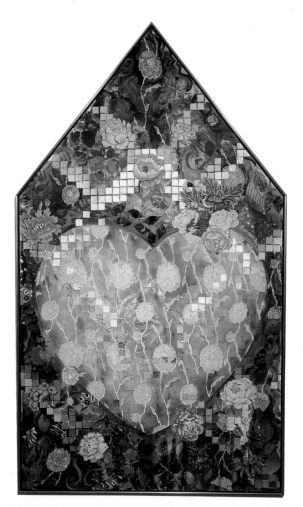

20-13. Miriam Schapiro. *Heartfelt*. 1979. Acrylic and fabric on canvas, 5'10" x 40" (1.8 m x 101 cm). Collection the Norton Neuman Family
Courtesy Steinbaum Krauss Gallery, New York

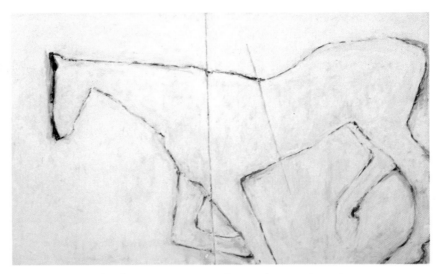

20-14. Susan Rothenberg. Axes. 1976. Synthetic polymer paint and gesso on canvas, 5'4⅝" x 8'8⅞" (1.64 x 2.66 m). The Museum of Modern Art, New York
Purchased with the aid of funds from the National Endowment for the Arts

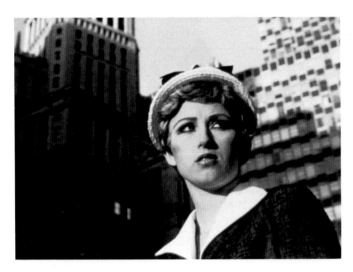

20-15. Cindy Sherman. Untitled Film Still. 1978. Black-and-white photograph, 8 x 10" (20.3 x 25.4 cm). The Museum of Modern Art, New York

using a method of construction she called fem-mage (from *female* and *collage*). Combining painting and fabrics, these works celebrate traditional women's craftwork. *Heartfelt* was shaped like a house because that was where most women worked, and its patterns suggested curtains, wallpapers, quilts, and other decorative forms women make or use in their domestic spheres. The heart within evokes women's concern for others, which Schapiro associated with the idea of home. Both the formal and emotional richness of *Heartfelt* were meant to counter the Minimalist aesthetic of the 1960s, which Schapiro and other feminists considered typically male.

Susan Rothenberg (b. 1945) took a different tack. Among those who exhibited in the 1978 "New Image Painting" exhibition at the Whitney Museum of American Art, Rothenberg developed a self-referential imagery. One day in 1973, she had doodled a horse's profile on a small piece of

unstretched canvas and something clicked. The horse became her alter ego—a way, perhaps, of dealing with the self while maintaining a distance from the subject. The humanization of the horse—or vice versa—is suggested in some 1974 Polaroids she took of a friend on all fours, which resulted in a series of paintings titled *Mary*.

Rothenberg's horses may at first seem somewhat ungainly. For example, because of its off-center placement in the picture frame, the horse in *Axes* (fig. 20-14) appears to be stumbling. The two straight lines, one dividing the picture frame and the other dividing the horse, are the axes of the painting's title. If the canvas is reoriented so that the axis that divides the horse in half becomes the vertical axis, the animal would be upright, in midstride. The painting's 'awkward' aspects are countered by the rich, appealing buildup of painting strokes and the low-key harmony of its creams and blacks—derived, like its simple forms, from the Minimalist aesthetic of the 1960s.

A second generation of feminist artists, those who emerged in the 1980s, tended to believe that the differences between the sexes were not intrinsic but fabricated, or "socially constructed." They argued that media images and other cultural forces worked against women to suit the needs of those in power. According to this view, young people learn how to behave from the role models they see heralded in magazines, movies, and other sources of mass culture. A major task of feminism and feminist art should, these artists believed, be to resist the power of these forces.

In 1977 one of the most prominent of these later feminists, Cindy Sherman (b. 1954), began work on a series of black-and-white photographs

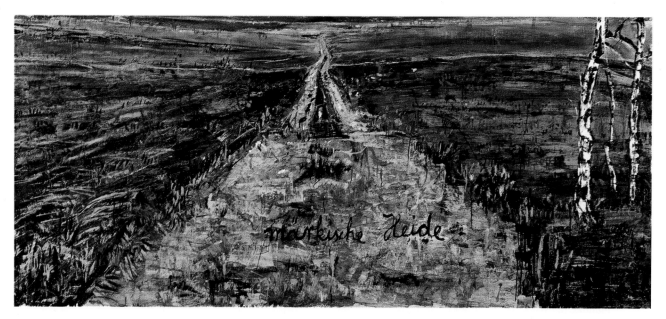

20-16. Anselm Kiefer. *Heath of the Brandenburg March*. 1984. Oil, acrylic, and shellac on burlap, 3'10½" x 8'4" (1.18 x 2.54 m). Stedelijk Van Abbemuseum, Eindhoven, the Netherlands

of herself in various assumed roles. The images simulate stills from B-grade movies of the 1940s and 1950s. In one of these photographs (fig. 20-15), Sherman plays a perplexed young innocent apparently recently arrived in a big city, its buildings looming threateningly behind her. The image suggests a host of films in which some such character is overwhelmed by dangerous forces, perhaps to be destroyed, or perhaps to be rescued by some hero. While Sherman's motives are complex, many observers have suggested that in these works she indicts Hollywood's stereotypical images of women and femininity by showing how one can "invent" onself in a variety of roles.

The emphasis on personal feeling in feminist art helped to inspire a renewed interest in expressionism, a stylistic option long thought dead. Many recent avant-garde styles implicitly acknowledge the exhaustion of the old modernist faith in innovation—and in what it implied about the "progressive" course of history—by reviving older styles. The names of these styles often begin with the prefix *neo*, denoting a new form of something that already exists.

A number of shows in leading New York art galleries in 1980 signaled the emergence of Neo-Expressionism, the first of these revival styles. About the same time, various European artists working in a similar vein gained critical recognition in the United States. One was the German artist Anselm Kiefer (b. 1945), who has long sought to revisit his country's Nazi past. The burned and barren landscape in *Heath of the Brandenburg March* (fig. 20-16) evokes the ravages of war that the Brandenburg area, near Berlin, has frequently experienced, most recently in World War II. The road lures us into the landscape,

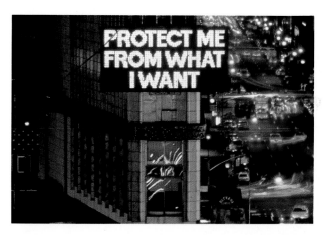

20-17. Jenny Holzer. *Protect Me from What I Want*, excerpt from Survival series. 1985–86. Spectacolor board, Times Square, New York
Courtesy Barbara Gladstone Gallery, New York

a standard device often used in nineteenth-century landscape paintings. Kiefer's works compel viewers to ponder troubling historical and social realities, "in order," he said, "to understand the madness."

ART AND THE PUBLIC

The issue of art's potential social mission and the desire to make art meaningful to a larger public took on a new prominence in the 1990s. Contemporary artists experimented with new media, such as video monitors (see "Video Art," page 470), to connect with modern audiences saturated by a media-oriented culture.

Jenny Holzer (b. 1950) turned to some of advertising's more pervasive tools, including electronic signage, to reach out to people who do not go to galleries and museums. She prefers to use popular media devices already in place. In her Survival series (fig. 20-17), for example, she used the Spectacolor board in New York

Video Art

Among the many new mediums of art making created by the technology revolution of the twentieth century, the video monitor is one of the most provocative. The content of the video form, like that of film, can range from raw documentary material to scripted theatrical performance, from animation to pure abstraction. Images may last only seconds or add up to a full-length feature.

Video art is often political in content, and like some experimental dance and theater, it links the performing arts with the visual arts. Because video has developed in a period in which many artists are self-consciously avant-garde, many video artists pay particular attention to the relationship between the imagery of popular culture (commercial television, advertising) and the traditional arts of painting and sculpture.

The video monitor itself is often a visible part of the artwork. Monitors may be inserted as elements within larger sculptures, such as Nam June Paik's (b. 1932) *Electronic Superhighway.* Installations may be accompanied by sound, music, or a voice-over, and some are interactive, including cameras that permit the viewer to enter the artwork by appearing on the monitor. The images on the screen may be austere and minimal, or quite ornate, as in Paik's colorful, rapidly flickering multiple patterns, which are often computer generated or manipulated.

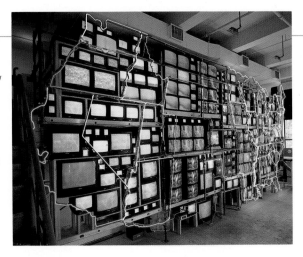

Nam June Paik. *Electronic Superhighway.* 1995. Installation: multiple television monitors, laser disk images, and neon, 15 x 32' (4.57 x 9.75 m). Holly Solomon Gallery, New York
Courtesy Holly Solomon Gallery, New York

City's Times Square to flash a series of short, provocative messages. The one illustrated here, *Protect Me from What I Want*, is a reference to the way advertising generates a desire in people for products and services they may not need. Holzer phrased her messages as one-liners suited to the reading habits of Americans raised on advertising sound bites.

In recent years, art designed for public spaces rather than for museum walls or private collectors' homes has provoked many sensational controversies involving public funding, censorship, and individual rights. The *Vietnam Veterans Memorial* (fig. 20-18), now widely admired as a fitting and moving testament to the Americans who died in that conflict, was originally a lightning rod for contention. The request for proposals for the design of the monument stipulated that the memorial be without political or military content, that it be reflective in character, that it harmonize with its surroundings, and that it include the names of the more than 58,000 dead and missing. In 1981 the Vietnam Veterans Memorial Fund awarded the commission to Maya Ying Lin (b. 1960), then an undergraduate in the architecture department at Yale University. Her Minimalist-inspired design called for two 200-foot-long walls (later expanded to almost 250 feet) of polished black granite, set into rising ground on the Mall in Washington, D.C., and meeting at a 136-degree angle at the point where the walls and slope would be at their full

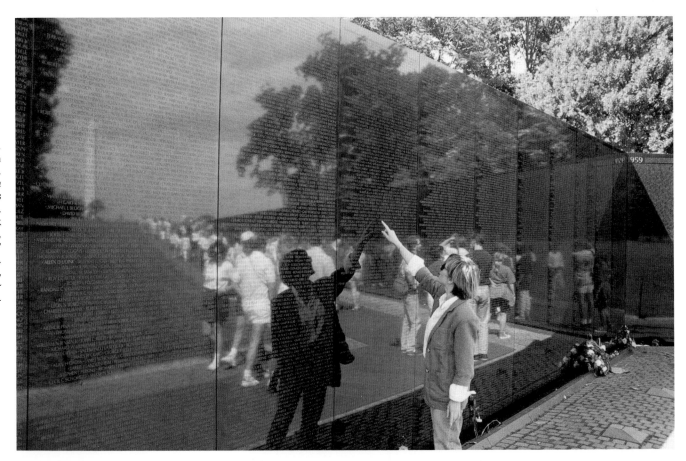

20-18. Maya Ying Lin. *Vietnam Veterans Memorial.* 1982. Black granite, length 500' (152 m). The Mall, Washington, D.C.

10-foot height. The names of the dead were to be incised into the stone in the order in which they died.

While construction was under way, several veterans groups—who had provided much of the approximately $8 million for the project and who originally had supported the Lin proposal—asked that a realistic 8-foot sculpture of three soldiers on patrol be added toward the apex of the memorial and that a 50-foot flagpole be raised some distance behind. The veterans felt that in this way the survivors, too, would be honored at the site. After much negotiation, a compromise provided that the additions would be made farther from the Lin design, at one entrance to the memorial grounds. In the end, the memorial as designed by Lin became one of the most compelling monuments in the United States. Quiet and solemn, it creates an understated encounter between the living, reflected in the mirrorlike polished granite, and the dead, whose names are etched into the black stone.

Not all art with social impact is public on the scale of the *Vietnam Veterans Memorial*. Artists like Roger Shimomura (b. 1939) turn painting and prints into powerful statements. American citizens of Japanese ancestry were forcibly confined in internment camps during World War II. Shimomura based his 1978 painting *Diary* (fig. 20-19) on his grandmother's record of the family's experience in an internment camp in Idaho. Shimomura painted his grandmother writing while he (the toddler) and his mother stand by an open door—a door that opens onto a barbed-wire-enclosed compound. In his painting, Shi-

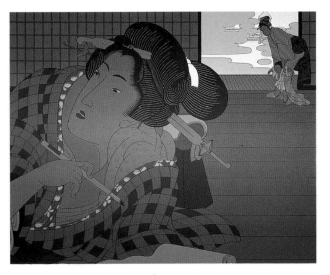

20-19. Roger Shimomura. *Diary* (Minidoka Series #3). 1978. Acrylic on canvas, 4'11⅞" x 6'1/16" (1.52 x 1.83 m). Spencer Museum of Art, University of Kansas, Lawrence

momura has combined two formal traditions— the Japanese art of color woodblock prints (see figs. 9-24, 9-25) and American Pop art (see fig. 20-5)—to create a personal style that expresses his own dual heritage as it makes a powerful political statement.

Jaune Quick-to-See Smith (b. 1940), who was raised on Flatrock Reservation in Montana and numbers among her ancestors the Salish, Shoshone, and Cree American Indians, also combines traditional and contemporary forms to convey political and social messages. During the United States' quincentennial celebration of Columbus's arrival in the Americas—in her words, the beginning of "the age of tourism"— Quick-to-See Smith created paintings and collages that confronted viewers with their own, perhaps unwitting, stereotypes. In *Trade* (*Gifts for Trading Land with White People*) (fig. 20-20), a stately

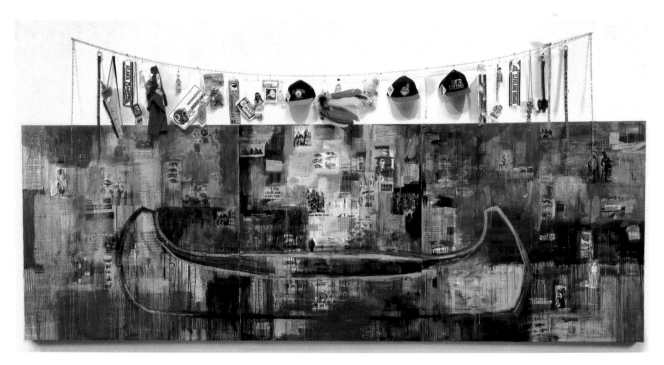

20-20. Jaune Quick-to-See Smith. *Trade (Gifts for Trading Land with White People).* Salish-Cree-Shoshone, 1992. Oil and collage on canvas, 5' x 14'2" (1.52 x 4.32 m). Chrysler Museum of Art, Norfolk, Virginia
Courtesy Steinbaum Krauss Collection, New York City

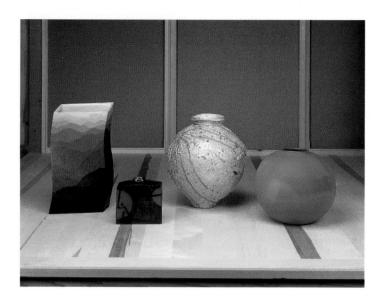

20-21. From left: Miyashita Zenji, Morino Hiroaki, Tsujimura Shiro, Ito Sekisui. Four ceramic vessels. After 1970. Spencer Museum of Art, University of Kansas, Lawrence
Gift of the Friends of the Art Museum/Helen Foresman Spencer Art Acquisition Fund

canoe floats over a richly colored and textured field, which on closer inspection proves to be a dense collage of newspaper clippings from Native American newspapers. On a chain above the painting hangs a collection of Amerindian cultural artifacts, including tomahawks, beaded belts, feather headdresses, and sports memorabilia for teams with names like the Atlanta Braves, the Washington Redskins, and the Cleveland Indians that many people today find offensive. Surely, the painting suggests, Native Americans could trade these goods to retrieve their lost lands, just as European settlers traded trinkets to acquire Native American lands in the first place.

THE INTERNATIONALIZATION OF CONTEMPORARY ART

The mix of elements from different cultures seen in the works of Shimomura and Quick-to-See Smith reflects the internationalization of art in the postmodern era. Increasingly, artists from diverse backgrounds are combining traditional art forms with contemporary forms and materials developed primarily in the United States and Europe. They may choose among, or meld, more than one artistic heritage. In Japan, for instance, artists may decide whether to work in an East Asian style, a Western style, or some combination of the two. Their creativity in embracing these diverse options stands out in contemporary ceramics. Some ceramists continue to create **raku** teabowls and other traditional wares, while others experiment with new styles and new techniques. Figure 20-21 shows the work of four contemporary potters, from left to right, Miyashita

Zenji (b. 1939), Morino Hiroaki (b. 1934), Tsujimura Shiro (b. 1947), and Ito Sekisui (b. 1941).

Miyashita's work is modern in shape, yet also traditional in its evocation of nature. The varied colors of the clay seem to form a landscape, with layers of mountains leading up to the sky. On the other hand, Morino's works are often abstract and sculptural, without any reference to nature or function. But he has also made vases that showcase his ability to create quirky and playful designs in glaze. Tsujimura, in contrast, makes pieces that are always functional, and part of their beauty comes from their suitability for holding food, flowers, or tea. He values the natural ash finish that comes with wood firing, and he creates jars, vases, bowls, and cups with rough exteriors covered by rivulets of flowing green glaze that are often truly spectacular.

Ito demonstrates the Japanese love of natural materials by presenting the essential nature of fired clay in his works. The warm tan, orange, and reddish colors of the clay reveal themselves in irregularly flowing and changing tones created by allowing different levels of oxygen into the kiln when firing.

Some contemporary artists adopt modern media and techniques but retain traditional subject matter. In Australia, Aborigine artists have adopted canvas and acrylic paint for rendering imagery traditionally associated with more ephemeral mediums like bark, sand, and body painting. Under the influence of Geoff Bardon, an art teacher who introduced them to new media, a group of Aborigines expert in **sand painting**—an ancient ritual art form that involves creating large colored designs on the

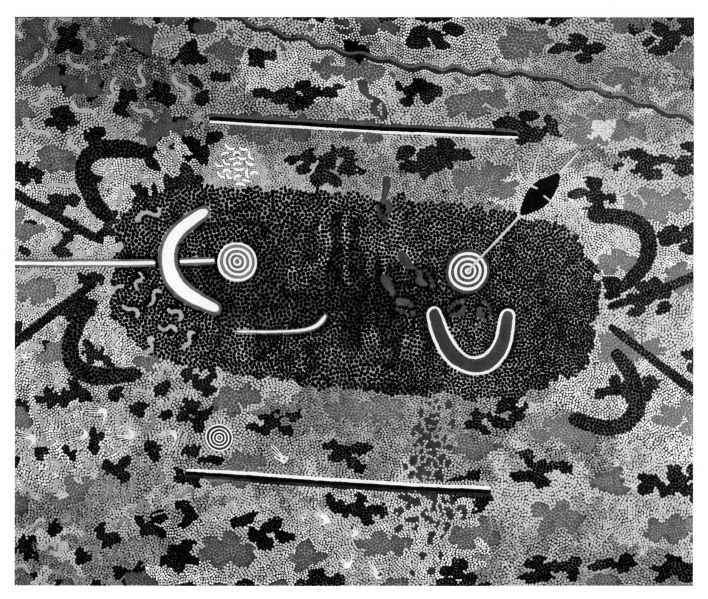

20-22. Clifford Possum Tjapaltjarri. _Man's Love Story._ 1978. Papunya, Northern Territory, Australia. Synthetic polymer paint on canvas, 6'11¾" x 8'4¼" (2.13 x 2.55 m). Art Gallery of South Australia, Adelaide
Visual Arts Board of the Australia Council Contemporary Art Purchase Grant, 1980

ground—formed an art cooperative in 1971 in Papunya, in central Australia. Painting soon became an economic mainstay for many Aboriginal groups in the region.

Clifford Possum Tjapaltjarri, a founder of the Papunya cooperative, gained an international reputation after an exhibition of his paintings in 1988. As in the technique of sand painting, he works with his canvases on the floor, using traditional patterns and colors (red and yellow ochers), as well as touches of blue. His paintings, like _Man's Love Story_ (fig. 20-22), may at first seem entirely abstract, but they actually convey complex narratives. This painting tells a story involving two mythical ancestors. One man came to

Papunya in search of honey ants; the white U shape on the left represents him seated in front of a water hole with an ants' nest, represented by concentric circles. His digging stick lies to his right, and white sugary leaves lie to his left. The straight white "journey line" represents his trek from the west. The second man, represented by the brown-and-white U-shape form, came from the north, leaving footprints, and sat down by another water hole nearby. He began to spin a hair string (a string made from human hair) on a spindle (the form leaning toward the upper right of the painting) but was distracted by thoughts of the woman he loved, who belonged to a kinship group into which he could not marry. When

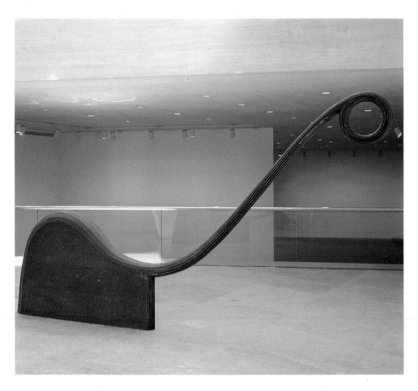

20-23. Martin Puryear. *Lever No. 3.* 1989. Wood, carved and painted,
7'1/2" x 13'5" x 13" (2.15 m x 4.09 m x 33 cm). National Gallery of Art, Washington, D.C.
Gift of the Collectors Committee

she approached, he let his hair string blow away (represented by the brown flecks below him) and lost all his work. Four women (the dotted U shapes) from the group into which he could marry came with their digging sticks and sat around the two men.

Rich symbolism fills other areas of the painting. For instance, the wiggly shapes represent caterpillars and the dots represent seeds, both forms of food. What seemed to be a richly decorative surface pattern is in fact a visual recording of the ephemeral impressions left on the earth by the figures—their tracks, direction lines, and the U-shaped marks they left when sitting.

Western interest in artists such as Clifford Possum Tjapaltjarri who are working with traditional, narrative subject matter reflects in part a modern yearning toward continuity in an era of rapid change. This same concern for continuity can be seen in the 1980s work of a number of painters and sculptors working in a contemporary, nonrepresentational mode, among them the African-American sculptor Martin Puryear (b. 1941).

Puryear studied preindustrial woodworking methods in Sierra Leone and cabinetmaking in Sweden before encountering the works of a number of Minimalist sculptors during graduate studies in sculpture at Yale. He combined these formative influences into the distinctive personal style exemplified in works such as *Lever No. 3* (fig. 20-23). The work evokes both organic and inorganic forms, including an animal with a long neck, a plant, and even the prow of a ship. The beauty of the piece lies in its swelling curves and its completion in the perfection of a circle. Puryear does not begin with a particular theme in mind but claims to discover his final image in the process of making it. The simple form of the carefully fitted pieces of wood conveys a sense of connection with both the natural world and the sculpture of the early-twentieth-century modernists.

Interest in natural forms and natural materials, such as that seen in contemporary sculpture by Puryear and others, has helped to break down long-standing barriers between art and craft. Since the Renaissance, Western artists, critics, and art historians have generally maintained a distinction between the so-called high or fine arts—painting, sculpture, and architecture— and the so-called minor or decorative arts— such as glass, fiber, ceramics, even graphic arts and photography. In recent years, the notion that one medium is intrinsically superior to another has come under scrutiny. For instance, the work of Dale Chihuly (see fig. 6) in glass or of the Polish sculptor Magdalena Abakanowicz (b. 1930) challenges conventional distinctions between craft and sculpture.

Typical of Abakanowicz's work is *Backs* (fig. 20-24), eighty headless, limbless, genderless, and hollow-front impressions made on a single mold over a five-year period. When shown in nature, as here, the figures appear to grow out of and form a part of the setting, a result of their

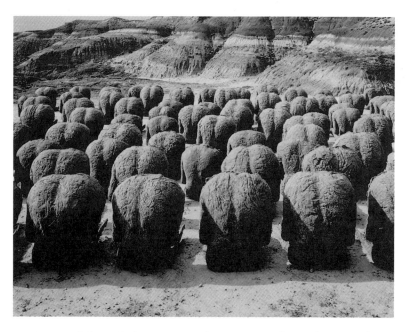

20-24. Magdalena Abakanowicz. *Backs.* 1976–80. Burlap and resin, each piece approximately 25³/₄ x 21³/₄ x 23³/₄" (65.4 x 55.3 x 60.3 cm). Installed near Calgary, Canada, 1982. Collection of Museum of Modern Art, Pusan, South Korea

organic shapes as well as their materials: coarse, brown, resin-impregnated burlap and twine meant to resemble soil and roots. The anonymous forms appear to be both resigned and worshiping. "People ask me," Abakanowicz says, "is this the concentration camp in Auschwitz or is it a religious ceremony in Peru . . . and I answer all these questions, 'yes,' because it is . . . about existence in general" (cited in Wheeler, page 322).

What art means, and what its function should be, have always been vital questions in human society. Some artists have sought to comfort us, others to unsettle us. Both of these positions demonstrate the continuing relevance of art to our lives. The case for art and the artist was made eloquently at a congressional subcommittee hearing by Robert Motherwell (1915–1991), a major New York School painter:

> Most people ignorantly suppose that artists are the decorators of our human existence, the esthetes to whom the cultivated may turn when the real business of the day is done. But actually what an artist is, is a person skilled in expressing human feeling. . . . Far from being merely decorative, the artist's awareness . . . is one . . . of the few guardians of the inherent sanity and equilibrium of the human spirit that we have.

Glossary

abacus The flat, usually square slab forming the top of a capital, directly under the entablature.

abstract, abstraction Any art that does not represent observable aspects of nature or transforms visible forms into a pattern resembling the original model. Also: the formal qualities of this process.

academy, academician An institutional group established for the training of artists. Most academies date from the Renaissance and after; they were particularly powerful state-run institutions in the seventeenth and eighteenth centuries. In general, academies replaced guilds as the venue where students learned the craft of art and were also provided with a complete education, including art theory and artistic rules. The academies helped artists to be seen as trained specialists, rather than as craftspeople, and promoted the change in the social status of the artist. An academician is an official academy-trained artist, whose work conforms to the accepted style of the day.

acanthus A plant whose foliage inspires a leaflike architectural ornamentation used in the Corinthian and Composite orders.

acropolis The citadel of an ancient Greek city, located at its highest point and consisting of temples, a treasury, and sometimes a royal palace. The most famous is the Acropolis in Athens, where the ruins of the Parthenon can be found.

adobe Sun-baked blocks made of clay mixed with straw. Also: the buildings made with this material.

aedicula (aediculae) A type of decorative architectural frame, usually found around a niche, door, or window. An aedicula is made up of a pediment and entablature supported by columns or pilasters.

aesthetics The philosophic theories relating to the concept of beauty in art and, by extension, to the history of art appreciation and taste.

album A book consisting of blank pages (leaves) on which typically an artist may sketch, draw, or paint.

album leaves See **album**.

allegory The representation in a work of art of an abstract concept or idea using specific objects or human figures.

altar A tablelike structure where religious rites are performed. In Christian churches, the altar is the site of the rite of the Eucharist.

altarpiece A painted or carved panel or winged structure placed at the back of or behind an altar. Contains religious imagery, often specific to the place of worship for which it was made.

ambulatory The passage walkway around the apse in a basilican church or around the central space in a centrally planned building.

amphora An ancient Greek jar for storing oil or wine, with an egg-shaped body and two curved handles.

aniconic A term describing a representation without images of human figures, often found in Islamic cultures.

animal interlace Decoration made up of interwoven animal or serpent forms, often found in Celtic and northern European art of the medieval period.

animal style A type of imagery popular in Europe and western Asia during the ancient and medieval periods, characterized by linear, animal-like forms arranged in intricate patterns or combats.

apotheosis Deification of an individual. In painting, often shown as an ascent to heaven, borne by angels or putti.

apprentice A student artist or craftsperson in training. In a system of artistic training established under the guilds and still in use today, master artists took on apprentices (who usually lived with the master's family) for several years. The apprentice was taught every aspect of the artist's craft, and he or she participated in the master's workshop or atelier.

appropriation Term used to describe an artist's practice of borrowing from another source for a new work of art. While in previous centuries artists often copied one another's figures, motifs, or compositions, in modern times the sources for appropriation extend from material culture to works of art.

apse, apsidal A large semicircular or polygonal (and usually vaulted) niche protruding from the end wall of a building. In the Christian church, it contains the altar. Apsidal is an adjective describing the condition of having such a semicircular or polygonal space.

aquatint A type of intaglio printmaking developed in the eighteenth century that produces an area of even tone without laborious cross-hatching. Basically similar in technique to an etching, the aquatint is made through use of a porous resin coating of a metal plate, which, when immersed in acid, allows an even, allover biting of the plate. When printed, the end result has a granular, textural effect.

aqueduct A trough to carry flowing water, if necessary, supported by arches. Under the Romans, built over long distances at a gradually decreasing incline.

arabesque A type of linear surface decoration based on foliage and calligraphic forms, usually characterized by flowing lines and swirling shapes.

arcade A series of arches, carried by columns or piers and supporting a common wall or lintel. In a blind arcade, the arches and supports are engaged (attached to the background wall) and have a decorative function.

arch In architecture, a curved structural element that spans an open space. Built from wedge-shaped stone blocks called voussoirs, which, when placed together and held at the top by a trapezoidal keystone, form an effective weight-bearing unit. Requires buttresses for support at either side to contain outward thrust of structure. Found in a variety of shapes and sizes, depending upon style of period. **Corbel arch**: arch or vault formed by courses of stones, each of which projects beyond the lower course until the space is enclosed; usually finished with a capstone. **Horseshoe arch**: an arch with a rounded horseshoe shape; the standard arch form in western Islamic architecture. **Ogival arch**: a pointed arch created by S curves. **Relieving arch**: an arch built into a heavy wall just above a post-and-lintel structure (such as a gate, door, or window) to help support the wall above. Relieves some of the weight on the lintel by transferring the load to the side walls.

Archaic smile The curved lips of an ancient Greek statue, usually interpreted as a half smile.

architrave The bottom layer of an entablature, beneath the frieze and the cornice.

assemblage An artwork created by gathering and manipulating found objects and other three-dimensional items. The technique of assemblage was especially popular in the first half of the twentieth century.

atmospheric perspective See **perspective**.

atrium An unroofed interior courtyard or room in a Roman house, sometimes having a pool or garden. Also: the open courtyard in front of a Christian church, or an entrance area in modern architecture.

attic story The top story of a building. In classical architecture, the level above the entablature, often decorated or carrying an inscription.

attribute The symbolic object or objects that identify a particular deity, saint, or personification in art.

automatism A technique whereby the usual intellectual control of the artist over his or her brush or pencil is forgone. The artist's aim is to allow the subconscious to create the artwork without rational interference. Also called automatic writing, automatism was developed by the Surrealists in the 1910s, and it was influential for later movements such as Abstract Expressionism.

avant-garde A term derived from the French military word meaning "before the group," or "vanguard." Avant-garde denotes those artists or concepts of a strikingly new, experimental, or radical nature for the time.

axis mundi A concept of an axis of the world, which denotes important sacred sites and provides a link between the human and celestial realms. For example, in Buddhist art, the axis mundi can be marked by monumental freestanding decorated pillars.

background Within the depicted space of an artwork, the area of the image at the greatest distance from the picture plane.

baldachin A canopy (whether suspended from the ceiling, projecting from a wall, or supported by columns) placed over an honorific or sacred space such as a throne or church altar.

balustrade A series of short circular posts (called balusters), with a rail on top. Sometimes balusters are replaced by decorated panels or ironwork under the rail.

baptistry A building used for the Christian ritual of baptism. It is usually separate from the main church and often octagonal or circular in shape.

barrel vault See **vault**.

bar tracery See **tracery**.

base A slab of masonry supporting a statue or the shaft of a column (also called a plinth).

basilica A large rectangular building. Often built with a clerestory and side aisles separated from the center nave by colonnades. Used in Roman times as centers for administration or justice and later adapted to Christian church use. A basilica-plan structure incorporates the essential elements of this plan.

basilica plan See **basilica**.

bas-relief See **relief sculpture**.

bay One unit of a construction system of a building. Bays divide the space of a building into regular spatial units marked by elements such as columns, piers, buttresses, windows, or vaults.

beehive tomb A corbel vaulted tomb, conical in shape like a beehive, and covered by an earthen mound.

Benday dots In modern printing and typesetting, the individual dots that, together with many others, make up lettering and images. Often machine- or computer-generated, the dots are very small and closely spaced to give the effect of density and richness of tone.

bird's-eye view Painting, drawing, or print that incorporates high-level perspective.

black-figure A decorative style of ancient Greek pottery in which black figures are painted on a red clay background.

blackware An ancient ceramic technique that produced pottery with a primarily black surface. As rediscovered and adapted by Maria Montoya Martinez, a Native American potter in the United States, blackware exhibits alternating matte and glossy patterns on the black surfaces of the objects.

blind window The outlining elements of a window applied to a solid wall, often to help create symmetry on a facade, but without the actual window opening.

block printing A printed image, such as a woodcut or wood engraving, made from a carved wooden block.

bodhisattva A deity that is far advanced in the long process of transforming itself into a buddha. While seeking enlightenment or emancipation from this world (nirvana), bodhisattvas help others attain this same liberation.

bracket, bracketing An architectural element that projects from a wall and that often helps support a horizontal part of a building, such as beams or the eaves of a roof.

bronze A metal made from copper alloy, usually mixed with tin. Also: any sculpture or object made from this substance.

buon fresco See **fresco**.

burin A metal instrument used in the making of engravings to cut lines into the metal plate. The sharp end of the burin is trimmed to give a diamond-shaped cutting point, while the other end is finished with a wooden handle that fits into the engraver's palm.

buttress, buttressing A type of architectural support. Usually consists of massive masonry with a wide base built against an exterior wall to brace the wall and strengthen the vaults. Acts by transferring the weight of the building from a higher point to the ground. **Flying buttress**: An arch built on the exterior of a building that transfers the thrust of the roof vaults at important stress points through the wall to a detached buttress pier leading to the wall buttress.

cairn A pile of stones or earth and stones that served both as a prehistoric burial site and as a marker of underground tombs.

calligraphy The art of highly ornamental handwriting.

calotype The first photographic process utilizing negatives and paper positives. It was invented by William Henry Fox Talbot in the late 1830s.

came (cames) A lead strip used in the making of leaded or stained-glass windows. Cames have an indented vertical groove on the sides into which the separate pieces of glass are fitted to hold the design together.

camera obscura An early cameralike device used in the Renaissance and later for capturing images of nature. Made from a dark box (or room) with a hole in one side (sometimes fitted with a lens), the camera obscura operates when bright light shines through the hole, casting an upside-down image of an object outside onto the inside wall of the box. This image then can be traced.

canon of proportions A set of ideal mathematical ratios in art, especially sculpture, originally applied by the Egyptians and later the ancient Greeks to measure the various parts of the human body in relation to each other.

capital The sculpted block that tops a column. According to the conventions of the orders, capitals include different decorative elements. See **order**. Also: a historiated capital in medieval art is a capital displaying a narrative.

capstone The final, topmost stone in a corbel arch or vault, which joins the sides and completes the structure.

caricature An artwork that exaggerates a person's features or individual peculiarities, usually with humorous or satirical intent.

cartoon A full-scale drawing used to transfer the outline of a design onto a surface (such as a wall, canvas, or panel) to be painted.

cartouche A frame for a hieroglyphic inscription formed by a rope design surrounding an oval space. Used to signify a sacred or honored name. Also: in architecture, a decorative device or plaque, usually with a plain center and rolled or sculpted edges, used for inscriptions or epitaphs.

caryatid A sculpture of a draped female figure acting as a column that supports an entablature.

catacomb An underground cemetery; also called a hypogeum. Urns and busts of the dead were placed in niches along the tunnels, which crisscrossed the area under an existing cemetery and often incorporated rooms (cubicula) and several different levels.

cella The principal interior structure at the center of a Greek or Roman temple within which the cult statue was usually housed. Also called the naos.

central-plan building Any structure designed with a primary central space surrounded by symmetrical areas on each side. For example, Greek-cross plan (equal-armed cross).

Chacmool In Mayan sculpture, a half-reclining figure, often monumental in scale and carved in a blocky style. Probably representing offering bearers. Chacmools can be found at Chichen Itza.

château (châteaux) The country house or castle of a French aristocrat. Usually built on a grand scale, châteaux are luxurious homes intended for an elegant lifestyle (although many do incorporate defensive fortifications such as moats and towers).

cherub (cherubim) The second-highest order of angels. Popularly, an idealized small child, usually depicted naked and with wings.

chevron A decorative motif made up of repeated inverted Vs.

chiaroscuro An Italian word designating the relative contrast of dark and light in a painting, drawing, or print. Artists use chiaroscuro to create spatial depth and volumetric forms through slight gradations in the intensity of light and shadow.

choir The section of a church, usually between the crossing and the apse, where the clergy officiate.

churrigeresque A showy, painterly style of Baroque architecture and ornament seen in Spain, Portugal, and Latin America, named after the Spanish architect José Benito de Churriguera (1665–1725).

Classical A term referring to the art and architecture of ancient Greece between c. 480–320 BCE.

classical, classicism Any aspect of later art or architecture reminiscent of the rules, canons, and examples of the art of ancient Greece and Rome. Also: in general, any art aspiring to the qualities of restraint, balance, and rational order exemplified by the ancients.

clerestory The topmost zone of a wall with windows (especially of a church or temple), when it extends above any abutting aisles or secondary roofs. Provides direct light into the central interior space.

cloison See **cloisonné**.

cloisonné A technique in enameled decoration of metal involving metal wire (filigree) that is affixed to the surface in a design. The resulting areas (cloisons) are filled with decorative enamel.

cloister An open space, part of a monastery or church, surrounded by an arcaded or colonnaded walkway, often having a fountain and garden, and dedicated to nonliturgical activities and the secular life of the religious. Members of a cloistered order do not interact with outsiders.

codex (codices) A book, or a group of manuscript pages, held together by stitching or other binding on one side.

coffer A recessed decorative panel that, with many other similar ones, is used to decorate ceilings or vaults. The use of coffers is called coffering.

coiling A technique in basketry. Coiled baskets are made from a spiraling structure to which another material is sewn.

collage A technique in which cutout paper forms (often painted or printed) are pasted onto another surface in a composition. Also: an image created using this technique.

colonnade A sequence or row of columns, supporting a straight lintel (as in a porch or portico) or a series of arches (an arcade).

colonnette A small columnlike vertical element, usually found attached to a pier. Colonnettes are decorative features, and they can reach into the vaulted sections of the building, contributing to the vertical effect of a Gothic cathedral.

colophon The data placed at the end of a book, especially a late medieval manuscript, listing the book's author, publisher, illuminator, and other information related to its production.

column An architectural element used for support and/or decoration. Consists of a rounded vertical shaft placed on a block (base) topped by a larger, usually decorative block (capital). Usually built in accordance with the rules of one of the architectural orders. Although usually freestanding, columns can be attached to a background wall (engaged).

column statue A carved column, depicting usually a religious person but also allegorical or mythological themes.

complementary color The primary and secondary colors across from each other on the color wheel (red and green, blue and orange, yellow and purple). When juxtaposed, the intensity of both colors increases.

Composite order See **order**.

composition The arrangement of elements in an artwork.

compound pier Typically found in a Romanesque or Gothic church, a compound pier is a pier or large column with multiple shafts, pilasters, or colonnettes attached to it on one or all sides.

conch A semicircular recess, such as an apse or niche, with a half-dome vault.

concrete A building material invented by the Romans, which is easily poured or molded when wet and hardens into a particularly strong and durable stonelike substance. Made primarily from lime, sand, cement, and rubble mixed with water.

cone mosaic An early type of surface decoration created by pressing colored cones of baked clay into prepared wet plaster; associated with Sumerian architecture.

connoisseur See **connoisseurship**

connoisseurship A term derived from the French word *connoisseur*, meaning "an expert," and signifying the practice of art history based primarily on formal, visual, and stylistic analysis. A connoisseur studies the style and technique of an object to deduce its relative quality and possible maker. This is done through visual association with other, similar objects and styles the connoisseur has seen in his or her study. See also **contextualism**, **formalism**.

content When discussing a work of art, the term can include all of the following: its subject matter; the ideas contained in the work; the artist's intention; and even its meaning for the beholder.

contextualism A methodological approach in art history which focuses on the cultural background of an art object. Unlike connoisseurship, contextualism utilizes the literature, history, economics, and social developments (among others) of a period, as well as the object itself, to explain the meaning of an artwork. See also **connoisseurship**.

contrapposto A way of representing the human body so that its weight appears to be borne on one leg. Contrapposto first appears in sculpture from ancient Greece, where sculptors adopted a great degree of naturalism in their works.

corbel, corbeling Early roofing and arching technique in which each course of stone projects inward and slightly beyond the previous layer (a corbel) until the uppermost corbels meet. Results in a high, narrowly pointed arch or vault. A corbel table is a table supported underneath by corbels.

corbel arch See **arch**.

corbel vault See **vault**.

Corinthian order See **order**.

cornice The uppermost section of a Classical entablature. More generally, any horizontally projecting element of a building, usually found at the top of a wall or a pedestal. A raking cornice is formed by the junction of two slanted cornices, most often found in pediments.

course A horizontal layer of stone used in building.

crenellation A pattern of open notches built into the top parapets and battlements of many fortified buildings for the purposes of defense.

cross-hatching A technique primarily used in printmaking and drawing, in which a set of parallel lines (hatching) is drawn across a previous set, but from a differing (usually right) angle. Cross-hatching gives a great density of tone and allows the artist to create the illusion of shadows efficiently.

crossing The part of a cross-shaped church where the nave and the transept meet, often marked on the exterior by a tower or dome.

cruciform A term describing anything that is cross-shaped, as in the cruciform plan of a church.

cubiculum (cubicula) A private chamber for burial in the catacombs. The sarcophagi of the affluent were housed there in arched wall niches.

cuneiform writing An early form of writing with wedge-shaped marks; impressed into wet clay with a stylus, primarily by ancient Mesopotamians.

curtain wall A wall in a building that does not support any of the weight of the structure. Also: the freestanding outer wall of a castle, usually encircling the inner bailey and keep.

cycle A series of paintings, frescoes, or tapestries depicting a single story or theme intended to be displayed together.

cyclopean construction A prehistoric method of building, utilizing megalithic blocks of rough-hewn stone. Any large-scale, monumental building project that impresses by sheer size. Named after one-eyed giants of legendary strength from Greek myths.

cylinder seal A small cylindrical stone decorated with incised patterns. When rolled across soft clay or wax, a raised pattern or design (relief) is made, which served in Mesopotamian and Indus Valley cultures as an identifying signature.

dado (dadoes) The lower part of a wall, differentiated in some way (by a molding or different color) from the upper section. Also: the part of a pedestal between the base and the cornice, usually constructed of plain stone without decoration.

daguerreotype An early photographic process invented and marketed in 1839 by Louis-Jacques Mondé Daguerre. The first practically possible photographic system, a daguerreotype was a positive print made on a light-sensitized copperplate.

demotic writing An informal script developed by the ancient Greeks in about the eighth century BCE and used exclusively for nonsacred texts.

diorama A large painting made to create an environment, giving the viewer an impression of being at the site depicted. Usually hung on several walls of a room and specially lit, the diorama was a popular attraction in the nineteenth century and was sometimes exhibited with sculpted figures.

diptych Two panels of equal size (usually decorated with paintings or reliefs) hinged together.

dolmen A prehistoric structure made up of two or more large (often upright) stones supporting a large, flat, horizontal slab or slabs (called capstones).

dome A round vault, usually over a circular space. Consists of the supporting vertical wall (drum), from which the vault springs, and a curved masonry vault of shapes and cross sections that can vary from hemispherical to bulbous to ovoidal. May be crowned by an open space (oculus) and/or an exterior lantern. When a dome is built over a square space, an intermediate element is required to make the transition to a circular drum. There are two types: A dome on pendentives (spherical triangles) incorporates arched, sloping intermediate sections of wall that carry the weight and thrust of the dome to heavily buttressed supporting piers. A dome on squinches uses an arch built into the wall (squinch) in the upper corners of the space to carry the weight of the dome across the corners of the square space below.

Doric order See **order**.

dressed stone A highly finished, precisely cut block of stone. When laid with others in even courses, dressed stone creates a uniform face with fine joints. Most often used as a facing on the visible exterior of a building, especially as a veneer for the facade. Also called ashlar.

drillwork The technique of using a drill for the creation of certain effects in sculpture.

drum The wall that supports a dome. Also: a segment of the circular shaft of a column.

drypoint An intaglio printmaking process by which a metal (usually copper) plate is directly inscribed by means of a pointed instrument (stylus). The resulting design of scratched lines is inked, wiped, and printed. Also: the print made by this process.

earthworks Artwork and/or sculpture, usually on a large scale, created by manipulating the natural environment. Also: the earth walls of a fort.

echinus A cushionlike circular element found below the abacus of a Doric capital. Also: a similarly shaped molding (usually with egg-and-dart motifs) underneath the volutes of an Ionic capital.

edition A single printing of a book or print. An edition can be of differing numbers but includes only what is printed at a particular moment, usually pulled from the same press by the same publisher.

elevation The arrangement, proportions, and details of any vertical side or face of a building. Also: an architectural drawing showing an exterior or interior wall of a building. A building's main elevation is usually its facade.

embroidery The technique in needlework of decorating fabric by stitching designs and figures of colored threads of fine material (such as silk) into another material (such as cotton, wool, leather, or paper). Also: the material produced by this technique.

enamel A technique in which powdered glass is applied to a metal surface in a decorative design. After firing, the glass forms an opaque or transparent substance that is fixed to the metal background. Also: an object created with enamel technique.

enamelwork See **enamel**.

encaustic A type of painting technique utilizing pigments mixed with a medium of hot wax. Encaustic paintings were typically made in ancient times, particularly in Egypt, Greece, and Rome.

engaged column See **column**.

engraving An intaglio printmaking process of inscribing an image, design, or letters onto a metal or wood surface from which a print is made. An engraving is usually drawn with a sharp implement (burin) directly onto the surface of the plate. Also: the print made from this process.

entablature In the Classical orders, the horizontal elements above the columns and capitals. The entablature consists of, from top to bottom, a cornice, frieze, and architrave.

entasis A slight bulge built into the shaft of a Greek column. The optical illusion of entasis makes the column appear from afar to be straight.

etching An intaglio printmaking process, in which a metal plate is coated with acid-resistant resin and then inscribed with a stylus in a design, revealing the plate below. The plate is then immersed in acid, and the design of exposed metal is eaten away by the acid. The resin is removed, leaving the design etched permanently into the metal and the plate ready to be inked, wiped, and printed.

Eucharist The central rite of the Christian church, from the Greek word "thanksgiving." Also known as the Mass or Holy Communion, it is based on the Last Supper. According to traditional Catholic Christian belief, consecrated bread and wine become the body and blood of Christ; in Protestant belief, bread and wine symbolize body and blood.

exedra (exedrae) In architecture, a semicircular niche. On a small scale, often used as decoration, whereas larger exedrae can form interior spaces (such as an apse).

expressionism Terms describing a work of art in which forms are created primarily to evoke subjective emotions rather than to portray objective reality.

facade The face or front wall of a building.

faience A glazing technique for ceramic vessels, utilizing a glass paste that, upon firing, acquires a lustrous shine and smooth texture.

fête galante A subject in painting depicting well-dressed people at leisure in a park or country setting. It is most often associated with eighteenth-century French Rococo painting and the work of Antoine Watteau.

finial A knoblike architectural decoration usually found at the top point of a spire, pinnacle, canopy, or gable. Also found on furniture.

flower piece Any painting with flowers as the primary subject. Still lifes of flowers became particularly popular in the seventeenth century in the Netherlands and Flanders.

flying buttress See **buttress**.

folio A large sheet of paper, which, when folded and cut, becomes four separate or parchment pages in a book. Also: a page or leaf in a manuscript or book; more generally, any large book.

foreground Within the depicted space of an artwork, the area that is closest to the picture plane.

foreshortening The illusion created on a flat painted or drawn surface in which figures and objects appear to recede or project sharply into space. Often accomplished according to the rules of perspective.

form In speaking of a work of art or architecture, the term refers to purely visual components: line, color, shape, texture, mass, spatial qualities, and composition—all of which are called formal elements.

formal elements See **form**.

formalism, formalist An approach to the understanding, appreciation, and valuation of art based almost solely on considerations of form. This approach tends to regard an artwork as independent of its time and place of making.

formline In Native American works of art, a line that defines a space or form.

forum The central square of a Roman town, often used as a market or gathering area for the citizens. Site of most community temples and administrative buildings.

fresco A painting technique in which water-based pigments are applied to a surface of wet plaster (called *buon fresco*). *Fresco a secco* is created by painting on dried plaster. Murals made by both these techniques are called frescoes.

fresco a secco See **fresco**.

frieze The middle element layer of an entablature, between the architrave and the cornice. Usually decorated with sculpture, painting, or moldings. Also: any continuous flat band with relief sculpture or painted decorations.

frontispiece An illustration opposite or preceding the title page of a book. Also: the primary facade or main entrance bay of a building.

fusuma Sliding doors covered with paper, used in an East Asian house. *Fusuma* are often highly decorated with paintings and colored backgrounds.

gable The triangular wall space found on the end wall of a building between the two sides of a pitched roof. Also: a triangular decorative panel that has a gablelike shape.

galleria In church architecture, the story found above the side aisles of a church, usually open to and overlooking the nave. Also: in secular architecture, a long room, usually above the ground floor in a private house or a public building, used for entertaining, exhibiting pictures, or promenading. In English, gallery.

gallery See **galleria**

genre A type or category of artistic form, subject, technique, style, or medium. See also **genre scene**.

genre scene A term used to loosely categorize paintings depicting scenes of everyday life, including (among others) domestic interiors, merry companies, inn scenes, and street scenes.

geoglyphs Earthen designs on a colossal scale, often created in a landscape as if to be seen from an aerial viewpoint.

geometric A term describing Greek art, especially pottery, from about 1100 to 600 BCE, characterized by patterns of rectangles, squares, and other abstract shapes. Also: any style or art using primarily these shapes.

gesso A thick medium usually made from glue, gypsum, and/or chalk and often forming the ground, or priming layer, of a canvas. A gesso ground gives a smooth surface for painting and seals the absorbency of the canvas.

gesturalism The motivation behind painting and drawing in which the brushwork or line visibly records the artist's physical gesture at the moment the paint was applied or the lines laid down. Associated especially with expressive styles, such as European Baroque, Zen painting, and Abstract Expressionism.

gilded See **gilding.**

gilding The application of paper-thin gold leaf to an object made from another medium (for example, a sculpture or painting). Usually used as a decorative finishing detail.

giornata Adopted from the Italian term meaning "a day's work," a *giornata* is the section of a fresco plastered and painted in a single day.

glaze See **glazing.**

glazing In ceramics, a method of treating earthenwares with an outermost layer of vitreous liquid (glaze) that, upon firing, renders a waterproof and decorative surface. In painting, a technique particularly used with oil mediums in which a transparent layer of paint (glaze) is laid over another, usually lighter, painted or glazed area.

gold leaf Paper-thin sheets of hammered gold that are used in gilding. In some cases (such as Byzantine icons), also used as a ground for paintings.

graffiti Imposed on public structures by anonymous persons, graffiti usually consists of drawings and/or text of an obscene, political, or violent nature and can be found in all periods and all mediums.

Grand Manner A grand and elevated style of painting popular in the Neoclassical period of the eighteenth century. An artist working in the Grand Manner looked to the ancients and to the Renaissance for inspiration; for portraits as well as history painting, the artist would adopt the poses, compositions, and attitudes of Renaissance and antique models.

granulation A technique for decorating gold in which tiny balls of the precious metal are fused to the main surface in a pattern.

graphic arts A term referring to those branches of the arts that utilize paper as primary support. The graphic arts, whether drawn, typeset, or printed, often have a heavy emphasis on linear means of expression.

graphic design A concern in the visual arts for shape, line, and two-dimensional patterning, often especially apparent in works including typography and lettering.

Greek-cross plan See **central-plan building.**

grid A system of regularly spaced horizontally and vertically crossed lines that gives regularity to an architectural plan. Also: in painting, a grid enables designs to be enlarged or transferred easily.

grisaille A painting executed primarily in various tones of gray.

groin vault See **vault.**

groundline The solid baseline that indicates the ground plane of an image on which the figure stands. In ancient representations, such as those of the Egyptians, the figures and the objects are placed on the groundline without reference to their actual spatial relationships.

grout A soft cement placed between the tesserae of a mosaic to hold the design together. Also used in tiling.

guild An association of craftspeople. The medieval guild had great political power, as it controlled the selling and marketing of its members' products, and it provided economic protection, political solidarity, and training in the craft to its members. An artists' guild was usually dedicated to Saint Luke, the patron saint of artists.

hall church A church (typified by those in the Gothic style in Germany), with a nave and aisles that are all the same height, giving the impression of a large, open hall.

handscroll A long, narrow, horizontal painting or text (or combination thereof) common in Chinese and Japanese art and of a size intended for individual use. A handscroll is stored wrapped tightly around a wooden pin and is unrolled for viewing or reading.

hanging scroll In Chinese and Japanese art, a vertically oriented painting or text mounted within sections of silk. At the top is a semicircular rod; at the bottom is a round dowel. Hanging scrolls are kept rolled and tied except for special occasions, when they are hung for display, contemplation, or commemoration.

haniwa Pottery figures that were placed on top of Japanese tombs or burial mounds.

happening A type of art form incorporating performance, theater, and visual images developed in the 1960s. A happening was organized without a specific narrative or intent; with audience participation, the event proceeded according to chance and individual improvisation.

hemicycle A semicircular interior space or structure.

henge A circular area enclosed by stones or wood posts set up by Neolithic peoples. It is usually bounded by a ditch and raised embankment.

hieratic In painting and sculpture, when the concern to communicate spiritual values results in a formalized, grand style for representing rulers or sacred or priestly figures. Can also be seen in the use of different scales for holy figures and those of the everyday world.

hieratic scale The larger the figure, the greater the importance.

hieroglyphic Picture-writing signs rendered in the form of pictorial symbols, utilized primarily for sacred names and ceremonial inscriptions (cartouches) by the ancient Egyptians.

high relief See **relief sculpture.**

historicism A nineteenth-century consciousness of and attention to the newly available and accurate knowledge of the past, made accessible by historical research, textual study, and archeology.

history painting The term used to denote those paintings that include figures in any kind of historical, mythological, or biblical narrative. Considered since the Renaissance (until the twentieth century) as the noblest form of art, history paintings generally convey a high moral or intellectual idea and are often painted in a grand pictorial style.

hollow-casting See **lost-wax casting.**

horizon line A horizontal "line" formed by the actual or implied meeting point of earth and sky. In linear perspective, the vanishing point or points are located on this line.

horseshoe arch See **arch.**

house-church In early Christian times, any small and relatively secret church located in a private home.

house-synagogue A Jewish place of worship located in a private home.

hue Pure color. The saturation or intensity of the hue depends on the purity of the color. Its value depends on its lightness or darkness.

hydria A large ancient Greek and Roman jar with three handles (horizontal ones at both sides and one vertical at the back), used for storing water.

hypogeum (hypogea) See **catacomb.**

hypostyle hall Marked by numerous rows of tall, closely spaced columns. In ancient Egyptian architecture, a large interior room of a temple complex preceding the sanctuary.

icon A painted, low relief, or mosaic image representing a sacred figure or event in the Byzantine, and later the Orthodox, church. Icons were venerated by the faithful, who believed them to have miraculous powers.

iconoclasm The banning or destruction of icons and religious art. Iconoclasm in eighth- and ninth-century Byzantium and sixteenth- and seventeenth-century Protestant territories arose from differing beliefs about the power, meaning, function, and purpose of imagery in religion.

iconography In the visual arts, the study of the subject matter of a representation and its meaning.

iconology The study of the significance and interpretation of the subject matter of art. Iconology often incorporates contextual evidence regarding traditions of representation of specific subjects to aid in understanding.

idealization A process in art through which artists strive to make their forms and figures attain perfection, based on pervading cultural values or their own mental image of what the ideal is.

idealized See **idealization**.

illumination A painting on paper or parchment used as illustration and/or decoration for manuscripts or albums. Usually done in rich colors, often supplemented by gold and other precious materials. The illustrators are referred to as illuminators. Also: the technique of decorating manuscripts with such paintings.

illusionism, illusionistic An appearance of reality in art created by the use of certain pictorial means, such as perspective and foreshortening. Also: the quality of having this type of appearance.

impost, impost block A block, serving to concentrate the weight above, imposed between the capital of a column and the springing of an arch above.

impression Any single printing of an intaglio print (engraving, drypoint, or etching). Each and every impression of a print is by nature different, given the possibilities for variation inherent in the printing process, which requires the plate to be inked and wiped between every impression.

incising A technique in which a design or inscription is cut into a hard surface with a sharp instrument.

ink painting A style of painting developed in China using only monochrome colors, usually black ink with gray washes. Ink painting was often used by artists of the literati painting tradition and is connected with Zen Buddhism.

inlay A decorative process in which pieces of one material are set into the surface of an object fashioned from a different material.

intaglio Term used for a technique in which the design is carved out of the surface of an object, such as an engraved seal stone. In the graphic arts, intaglio includes engraving, etching, and drypoint—all processes in which ink transfers to paper from incised, ink-filled lines cut into a metal plate.

interlace A type of linear decoration particularly popular in early medieval art, in which ribbonlike bands are illusionistically depicted as if woven under and over one another.

intuitive perspective See **perspective**.

Ionic order See **order**.

iwan A large, vaulted chamber in a mosque with a monumental arched opening on one side.

jamb In architecture, the vertical element found in pairs on both sides of an opening in a wall, such as a door or window.

japonisme A style in nineteenth-century French and American art that was highly influenced by Japanese art, especially prints.

joined-wood sculpture A method of constructing large-scale wooden sculpture developed in Japan. The entire work is constructed from smaller hollow blocks, each individually carved and assembled when complete. The joined-wood technique allowed the production of larger sculpture, as the multiple joints alleviate the problems of drying and cracking found with sculpture carved from a single block.

kente A woven cloth made by the Ashanti peoples of Africa. *Kente* cloth is woven in long, narrow pieces in complex and colorful patterns, which are then sewn together.

key block A key block is the master block in the production of a colored woodcut, which requires different blocks for each color. The key block is a flat piece of wood with the entire design carved or drawn on its surface. From this, other blocks with partial drawings are made for printing the areas of different colors.

keystone The topmost voussoir at the center of an arch, usually the last block to be placed. The pressure of this block holds the arch together. Often of a larger size and/or highly decorated.

kiln An oven designed to produce enough heat for the baking, or firing, of clay.

kore An archaic Greek statue of a young woman.

kouros An archaic Greek statue of a young man or boy.

krater An ancient Greek vessel for mixing wine and water, with many subtypes that each have a distinctive shape. **Calyx krater**: a bell-shaped vessel with handles near the base that resemble a flower calyx. **Volute krater**: a type of krater with handles shaped like scrolls.

kylix A shallow Greek vessel or cup, used for drinking, with a wide mouth and small handles near the rim.

lacquer A type of hard, glossy surface varnish used on objects in East Asian cultures. Lacquer can be layered and manipulated or combined with pigments and other materials for various decorative effects.

lancet A tall narrow window crowned by a sharply pointed arch, typically found in Gothic architecture.

lantern A cylindrical turretlike structure situated on top of a dome, with windows that allow light into the space below.

Latin-cross plan A cross-shaped building plan, incorporating one longer arm (nave) and three arms of equal length.

linear, linearity A descriptive term indicating an emphasis on line, as opposed to mass or color, in art.

linear perspective See **perspective**.

lintel A horizontal element of any material carried by two or more vertical supports to form an opening.

literati painting A style of painting that reflects the taste of the educated class of East Asian intellectuals and scholars. Aspects include an appreciation for the antique, smaller scale, and an intimate connection between maker and audience.

lithograph A print made from a design drawn on a flat stone block with greasy crayon. Ink is applied to the stone and, when printed, adheres only to the open areas of the design.

loggia Italian term for a covered open-air gallery. Often used as a corridor between buildings or around a courtyard, loggias usually have arcades or colonnades and an upper story.

lost-wax casting A method of casting metal, such as bronze, by a process in which a wax mold is covered with clay and plaster, then fired, melting the wax and leaving a hollow form. Molten metal is then poured into the hollow space and slowly cooled. When the hardened clay and plaster exterior shell is removed, a solid metal form remains to be smoothed and polished.

lunette A semicircular wall area, framed by an arch over a door or window. Can be either plain or decorated.

madrasa An Islamic institution of higher learning, where teaching is focused on theology, law, and the sciences.

majolica Pottery painted with a tin glaze that, when fired, gives a lustrous and colorful surface.

mandala An image of the cosmos represented by an arrangement of circular or concentric geometric shapes containing diagrams or images. Used for meditation and contemplation, mandalas are most often found in Buddhist places of worship.

mandorla An almond-shaped area in which a sacred figure, such as Christ, is represented.

manuscript A handwritten book or document.

martyrium (martyria) In Christian architecture, a church, chapel, or shrine built over the grave of a martyr or the site of a great miracle.

mastaba A flat-topped, one-story building with slanted walls. Invented by the ancient Egyptians to mark a part of underground tombs.

mathematical perspective See **perspective**.

matte A surface that is smooth but without shine or luster.

mausoleum A monumental building used as a tomb. Named after the tomb of Mausolos erected at Halikarnassos around 350 BCE.

medallion In architecture, any round ornament or decoration. Also: a large medal.

medium (mediums, media) In general, the material from which any given object is made. In painting, the liquid substance in which pigments are suspended.

memento mori From Latin phrase meaning "reminder of death." An object, such as a skull or extinguished candle, typically found in an image, symbolizing the transience of life.

menhir A megalithic stone block, placed by prehistoric peoples in an upright position.

menorah A Jewish lamp, usually in the form of a candelabrum, divided into seven or nine branches; the nine-branched menorah is used during the celebration of Hanukkah. Representations of the seven-branched menorah, once used in the Temple of Jerusalem, became in general a symbol of Judaism.

metope The rectangular spaces, sometimes decorated but often plain, between the triglyphs of a Doric frieze.

middle ground Within the depicted space of an artwork, the area that takes up the middle distance of the image. See also **foreground**.

mihrab A recess or niche that distinguishes the wall oriented toward Mecca (*qibla*) in a mosque.

minaret A tall slender tower on the exterior of a mosque from which believers are called to prayer.

minbar A high platform or pulpit in an Islamic mosque.

modeling In painting, the process of creating the illusion of three-dimensionality on a two-dimensional surface by use of light and shade. In sculpture, the process of molding a three-dimensional form out of a malleable substance.

molding A shaped or sculpted strip with varying contours and patterns. Used as decoration on architecture, furniture, frames, and other objects.

monolith A single stone, often very large. Monoliths may be set up as focal points for rituals or to define a ritual space.

monoprint A single print pulled from a hard surface (such as a blank plate or stone) that has been prepared with a painted design. Each print is an individual artwork, as the original design is a transient one, lost in the printing process.

monumental A term used to designate a project or object that, whatever its physical size, gives an impression of grandeur and excellence.

mosaic Images formed by small colored stone or glass pieces (tesserae), affixed to a hard, stable surface.

mosque An edifice used for communal Muslim worship.

motif Any recurring element of a design or composition. Also: a recurring theme or subject in artwork, often referring to those that can be easily separated from the whole for the purposes of copying or study.

mudra A symbolic hand gesture in Indian art. The many different *mudras* each denotes certain behaviors, actions, or feelings.

mullion A slender vertical element or colonnette that divides a window into subsidiary sections.

muqarna The geometric patterning used in Islamic architecture to smooth the transition between decorative flat and rounded surfaces; usually found on the vault of a dome.

mural A large painting or decoration, done either directly on the wall or separately and affixed to it.

naos In ancient art, see **cella**. In a Byzantine church, the nave and sanctuary.

narthex The rectangular vestibule at the main (usually western) entrance of a church. In Early Christian architecture, it can also be an entrance porch with columns on the outside of a church.

naturalism, naturalistic A style of depiction in which the physical appearance of the rendered image in nature is the primary inspiration. A naturalistic work appears to resemble visible nature.

nave The rectangular central aisle of a basilica, two or three stories high and flanked by aisles.

necropolis A large cemetery or burial area.

niche A hollow or recess in a wall or other solid architectural element. Niches can be of varying size and shape, and may be intended for many different uses, from display of objects to housing of a tomb.

nonrepresentational A term describing any artwork of an abstract nature. Nonrepresentational art does not attempt to reproduce the appearance of the natural world.

obelisk A tall stone shaft of four-sided rectangular shape, hewn from a single block, that tapers at the top and is completed by a pyramidion. Erected by the ancient Egyptians in ceremonial spaces (such as entrances to temple complexes). Today used as commemorative monuments and sun symbols.

oculus (oculi) In architecture, a circular opening. Oculi are usually found either as windows or at the apex of a dome. When at the top of a dome, an oculus is either open to the sky or covered by a decorative exterior lantern.

odalisque A subject in painting of a reclining female nude, usually shown among the accoutrements of an exotic, haremlike environment.

oil painting Any painting executed with the pigments floating in a medium of oil. Oil paint has particular properties that allow for greater ease of working (among others, a slow drying time, which allows for corrections, and a great range of relative opaqueness of paint layers, which permits a high degree of detail and luminescence). It was adopted on a wide scale in Europe after about 1450.

orant The representation, usually in ancient or Early Christian art, of a standing figure praying with outstretched arms.

order A system of proportions in Classical architecture. **Composite**: a combination of the Ionic and the Corinthian orders. The capital combines acanthus leaves with volute scrolls. **Corinthian**: the most ornate of the orders, the Corinthian includes a base, a fluted column shaft with a capital elaborately decorated with acanthus leaf carvings. Its entablature consists of an architrave decorated with moldings, a frieze often containing sculptured reliefs, and a cornice with dentils. **Doric**: the column shaft of the Doric order can be fluted or smooth-surfaced and has no base. The Doric capital consists of an undecorated echinus and abacus. The Doric entablature has a plain architrave, a frieze with metopes and triglyphs, and a simple cornice. **Ionic**: the column of the Ionic order has a base, a fluted shaft and a capital decorated with volutes. The Ionic entablature consists of an architrave of two panels and moldings, a frieze usually containing sculpted relief ornament, and a cornice with dentils. **Tuscan**: a variation of Doric characterized by a smooth-surfaced column shaft with a base, a plain architrave, and an undecorated frieze. A **colossal order** is any of the above built on a large scale, rising through several stories in height and often raised from the ground by a pedestal.

orthogonal Any line running back into the represented space of a picture perpendicular to the imagined picture plane. In linear perspective, all orthogonals converge at a single vanishing point in the picture and are the basis for a grid that maps out the internal space of the image. An orthogonal plan is any plan for a building or city that is based exclusively on right angles, such as the grid plan of many modern cities.

pagoda An East Asian temple in the form of a tower built with successively smaller, repeated stories. Each story is usually marked by an elaborate projecting roof.

painterly A style of painting, which emphasizes the techniques and surface effects of brushwork (also light and shade).

palette A handheld support used by artists for the storage and mixing of paint during the process of painting. Also: the choice of a range of colors made by an artist in a particular work, or typical of his or her style.

panel painting Any painting executed on a wood support. The wood is usually planed to provide a smooth surface. A panel can consist of several boards joined together.

parapet A low wall at the edge of a balcony, bridge, roof, or other place from which there is a steep drop, built for safety. A parapet walk is the passageway, usually open, immediately behind the uppermost exterior wall or battlement of a fortified building.

parchment A writing surface made from treated skins of animals and used during antiquity and the Middle Ages.

Paris Salon The annual display of art by French artists in Paris during the eighteenth and nineteenth centuries. Established in the seventeenth century as a venue to show the work of members of the French Academy, the Salon and its judges established the accepted official style of the time.

passage In painting, passage refers to any particular area within a work, often those where painterly brushwork or color changes exist. Also: a term used to describe Paul Cézanne's technique of blending adjacent shapes.

passage grave A prehistoric tomb under a cairn, reached by a long, narrow, slab-lined access passageway or passageways.

pedestal A platform or base supporting a sculpture or other monument. Also: the block found below the base of a classical column (or colonnade), serving to raise the entire element off the ground.

pediment A triangular gable found over major architectural elements such as Classical Greek porticoes, windows, or doors. Formed by an entablature and the ends of a sloping roof or a raking cornice. A similar architectural element is often used decoratively above a door or window, sometimes with a curved upper molding. A broken pediment is a variation on the traditional pediment, with an open space at the center of the topmost angle and/or the horizontal cornice. Often filled with a decorative element, such as a cartouche.

pendentive The concave triangular section of a wall that forms the transition between a square or polygonal space and the circular base of a dome.

performance art An artwork based on a live, sometimes theatrical performance by the artist.

peristyle A surrounding colonnade in Greek architecture. A peristyle building is surrounded on the exterior by a colonnade. Also: a peristyle court is an open colonnaded courtyard, often having a pool and garden.

perspective A system for representing three-dimensional space on a flat surface. **Atmospheric perspective**: A method of rendering the effect of spatial distance on a two-dimensional plane by subtle variations in color and clarity of representation. **Intuitive perspective**: A method of representing three-dimensional space on a two-dimensional surface by the use of formal elements that act to give the impression of recession. This impression, however, is achieved by visual instinct, not by the use of an overall system or program (usually involving scientific principles or mathematics) for depicting the appearance of spatial depth. **Oblique perspective**: An intuitive spatial system used in painting, in which a building or room is placed with one corner in the picture plane, and the other parts of the structure all recede to an imaginary vanishing point on its other side. Oblique perspective is not a comprehensive, mathematical system. **One-point and multiple-point perspective** (also called **linear**, **scientific**, or **mathematical perspective**): A method of creating the illusion of three-dimensional space on a two-dimensional surface by delineating a horizon line and multiple orthogonal lines. These recede to meet at one or more points on the horizon (called vanishing points), giving the appearance of spatial depth. Called scientific or mathematical because its use requires some knowledge of geometry and mathematics, as well as optics. **Reverse perspective**: A Byzantine perspective theory in which the orthogonals or rays of sight do not converge on a vanishing point in the picture, but are thought to originate in the viewer's eye in front of the picture. Thus, in reverse perspective the image is constructed with orthogonals that diverge, giving a slightly tipped aspect to objects.

pictograph A highly stylized depiction serving as a symbol for a person or object. Also: a type of writing utilizing such symbols.

picture plane The theoretical spatial plane corresponding with the actual surface of a painting (usually vertical).

picture stone A stone used in medieval northern Europe as a commemorative monument, which is carved or inscribed with representations of human figures or symbolic forms.

picturesque A term describing the taste for the familiar, the pleasant, and the pretty, popular in the eighteenth and nineteenth centuries in Europe. When contrasted with the sublime, the picturesque stood for all that was ordinary but pleasant.

pier A masonry support made up of many stones, or rubble and concrete (in contrast to a column shaft, which is formed by a single stone or a series of drums), often square or rectangular in plan and capable of carrying very heavy architectural loads. See also **compound pier**.

pietà A devotional subject in Christian religious art. After the Crucifixion the body of Jesus was laid across the lap of his grieving mother, Mary. When others are present the subject is called the Lamentation.

pilaster An engaged columnar element that is rectangular in format and used for decoration in architecture.

pinnacle In Gothic architecture, a steep pyramid decorating the top of another element such as a buttress.

plaiting In basketry, the technique of weaving strips of fabric or other flexible substances under and over each other.

plan A graphic convention for representing the arrangement of the parts of a building.

plinth The slablike base or pedestal of a column, statue, wall, building, or piece of furniture.

pluralism A social structure or goal that allows members of diverse ethnic, racial, or other groups to exist within the society while continuing to practice the customs of their own divergent cultures. Also: an adjective describing the state of having many valid contemporary styles available at the same time to artists.

podium A raised platform that acts as the foundation for a building. Most often used for Etruscan, Greek, and Roman temples.

polychromy The multicolored painted decoration applied to any part of a building, sculpture, or piece of furniture.

polyptych An altarpiece constructed from multiple panels, sometimes with hinges to allow for movable wings.

porcelain A type of extremely hard and fine ceramic made from a mixture of kaolin and other minerals. Porcelain is fired at a very high heat, and the final product has a translucent surface.

portal A grand entrance, door, or gate, usually to an important public building, and often decorated with sculpture.

portico In architecture, a projecting roof or porch supported by columns, often marking an entrance.

post-and-lintel construction An architectural system of construction with two or more vertical elements (posts) supporting a horizontal element (lintel).

predella The lower zone, or base, of an altarpiece, decorated with painting or sculpture related to the main iconographic theme of the altarpiece.

primary colors Blue, red, and yellow, the three colors from which all others are derived.

pronaos The enclosed vestibule of a Greek or Roman temple, found in front of the cella and marked by a row of columns at the entrance.

proscenium The stage of an ancient Greek or Roman theater. In modern theater, the area of the stage in front of the curtain. Also: the framing arch that separates a stage from the audience.

provenance The history of ownership of a work of art from the time of its creation to the present.

punchwork Decorative designs that are stamped onto a surface, such as metal or leather, using a punch (a handheld metal implement).

putto (putti) A divine creature in the form of a plump, naked little boy, often with wings. In classical art, called a cupid or cherub (secular).

pylon A massive gateway formed by a pair of tapering walls of oblong shape. Erected by ancient Egyptians to mark the entrance to a temple complex.

qibla The mosque wall oriented toward Mecca that includes the mihrab.

quadrant vault See **vault**.

quillwork A Native American decorative craft technique. The quills of porcupines and bird feathers are dyed, woven together in patterns, and attached to fabric, birch bark, or other material.

raku A type of ceramic pottery made by hand, coated with a thick, dark glaze, and fired at a low heat. The resulting vessels are irregularly shaped and glazed and are highly prized. Raku ware is used in the Japanese tea ceremony.

readymade An object from popular or material culture presented without further manipulation as an artwork by the artist.

realism A term first used in Europe around 1850 to designate a kind of naturalism with a social or political message, which soon lost its didactic import and became synonymous with naturalism.

recto The right-hand page in the opening of a book or manuscript. Also: the principal or front side of a leaf of paper, as in the case of a drawing.

red-figure A style of ancient Greek vase painting made in the sixth and fifth centuries BCE. Characterized by red-clay-colored figures on a black background.

register A device used in systems of spatial definition. In painting, a register indicates the use of differing groundlines to differentiate layers of space within an image. In sculpture, the placement of self-contained bands of reliefs in a vertical arrangement. In printmaking, the marks at the edges used to align the print correctly on the page, especially in multiple-block color printing.

relief sculpture A sculpted image or design whose flat background surface is carved away to a certain depth, setting off the figure. Called high or low (bas) depending upon the extent of projection of the image from the background. Called sunken relief when the image is modeled below the original surface of the background, which is not cut away.

reliquary A container, often made of precious materials, used as a repository for sacred relics.

repoussé A technique by which metal reliefs are created. Thin sheets of metal are gently hammered from the back to create a protruding image. More elaborate reliefs are created with wooden forms against which the metal sheets are pressed.

representational Any art that attempts to depict an aspect of the external, natural world in a visually understandable way.

ribbon interlace A linear decoration made up of interwoven bands, often found in Celtic and northern European art of the medieval period.

rib vault See **vault**.

roof comb In a Mayan building, a masonry wall along the apex of a roof that is built above the level of the roof proper. Roof combs support the highly decorated false facades that rise above the height of the building at the front.

rosette A round or oval ornament resembling a rose.

rose window A round window, often filled with stained glass, with tracery patterns in the form of wheel spokes. Large, elaborate, and finely crafted, rose windows are usually a central element of the facade of French Gothic cathedrals.

rotunda Any building (or part thereof) constructed in a circular (or sometimes polygonal) shape, usually producing a large open space crowned by a dome.

roundel Any element with a circular format, often placed as a decoration on the exterior of architecture.

rune stone A stone used in early medieval northern Europe as a commemorative monument, which is carved or inscribed with ancient German or Scandinavian writing, or runes.

rustication In building, the rough, irregular, and unfinished effect deliberately given to the exterior facing of a stone edifice. Rusticated stones are often large and used for decorative emphasis around doors or windows or across the entire lower floors of a building, probably deriving from fortifications.

sacristy In a Christian church, the room in which the priest's robes and the sacred vessels are housed. Sacristies are usually located close to the sanctuary and often have a place for ritual washing as well as a private door to the exterior.

sahn The central courtyard of a Muslim mosque.

sanctuary In Greek architecture, a sacred or holy enclosure used for worship consisting of one or more temples and an altar. Also: the space around the altar in a church, usually at the east end (also called the chancel or presbytery).

sand painting Ephemeral religious designs created with different colored sands by Native Americans of North America, Australian Aborigines, and other peoples in Japan and Tibet.

sarcophagus (sarcophagi) A rectangular stone coffin. Often decorated with relief sculpture.

scarification Ornamental marks, scars, or scratches made on the human body.

scriptorium (scriptoria) A room in a monastery for writing or copying manuscripts.

sculpture in the round Three-dimensional sculpture that is carved free of any attaching background or block.

segmental pediment A pediment formed when the upper cornice is a shallow arc.

sfumato In painting, the effect of haze in an image.

Resembling the color of the atmosphere at dusk, *sfumato* gives a smoky effect.

shade Any area of an artwork that is shown through various technical means to be in shadow. Also: the technique of making such an effect.

shading See **shade**.

shaft The main vertical section of a column between the capital and the base, usually circular in cross section.

shater A type of roof or dome used in Russia and the Near East with a steep pitch and tentlike shape.

shikhara In the architecture of northern India, a conical (or pyramidal) spire found atop a Hindu temple.

site-specific sculpture A sculpture commissioned and designed for a particular spot. Most site-specific sculpture requires the location for which it was designed in order to be complete.

slip A mixture of clay and water applied to a ceramic object as a final decorative coat. Also: a solution that binds different parts of a vessel together, such as the handle and the main body.

spandrel The area of wall adjoining the exterior curve of an arch between its springing and the keystone, or the area between two arches, as in an arcade.

squinch An arch or lintel built over the upper corners of a square space, allowing a circular or polygonal dome to be more securely set above the walls.

stained glass A decorative process in glassmaking by which glass is given a color (whether intrinsic in the material or painted onto the surface). Stained glass is most often used in windows, for which small pieces of differently colored glass are precisely cut and assembled into a design, held together by cames.

stela (stelae) A stone slab placed vertically and decorated with inscriptions or reliefs. Used as a grave marker or memorial.

still life A type of painting that has as its subject inanimate objects (such as food, dishes, fruit, or flowers).

stretcher The wooden framework on which an artist's canvas is attached, usually with tacks, nails, or staples. Also: a reinforcing horizontal brace between the legs of a piece of furniture, such as a chair. Also: in building, a brick laid so that its longer edge is parallel to the wall.

stringcourse A continuous horizontal band, such as a molding, decorating the face of a wall.

stucco A mixture of lime, sand, and other ingredients into a material that can be easily molded or modeled. When dry, produces a very durable surface used for covering walls or for architectural sculpture and decoration.

stupa In Buddhist architecture, a bell-shaped or pyramidal religious monument, made of piled earth or stone and containing sacred relics.

style A particular manner, form, or character of representation, construction, or expression typical of an individual artist or of a certain school or period.

stylization A manner of representation that conforms to an intellectual or artistic idea rather than to naturalistic appearances.

stylized See **stylization**.

stylobate In Classical architecture, the stone foundation on which a temple colonnade stands.

stylus An instrument with a pointed end (used for writing and printmaking), which makes a delicate line or scratch. Also: a special writing tool for cuneiform writing with one pointed end and one triangular wedge end.

subject matter See **content**.

sunken relief See **relief sculpture**.

swag A decorative device in architecture or interior ornament (and in paintings), in which a loosely hanging garland is made to look as if constructed of flowers or gathered cloth.

talud-tablero A design characteristic of Mayan architecture at Teotihuacan in which a sloping talud at the base of a building supports a wall-like tablero, where ornamental painting and sculpture are usually placed.

tempera A painting medium made by blending egg yolks with water, pigments, and occasionally other materials, such as glue. The technique was often used during the fourteenth and fifteenth centuries to paint frescoes and panel paintings.

tenebrism A term signifying the prevalent use of dark areas in a painting. A tenebrist style, such as Caravaggism, uses strong chiaroscuro and artificially illuminated areas to create a dramatic contrast of light and dark.

tepee A dwelling constructed from hides stretched on a structure of poles set at the base in a circle and leaning against one another at the top. Tepees were typically found among the nomadic Native Americans of the North American plains.

terra-cotta A medium made from clay fired over a low heat and usually left unglazed. Also: the orange-brown color typical of this medium.

tessera (tesserae) The small piece of stone, glass, or other object that is pieced together with many others to create a mosaic.

tint The dominant color in an object, image, or pigment.

tomb effigy A sculpted portraitlike image on a tomb or sarcophagus that represents a deceased individual.

tondo A painting or relief of circular shape.

tone The overall degree of brightness or darkness in an artwork. Also: saturation, intensity, or value of color and its effect.

torana In Indian architecture, an ornamented gateway arch in a temple, usually leading to the stupa.

toron In West African mosque architecture, the wooden beams that project from the walls. Torons are used as support for the scaffolding erected annually for the replastering of the building.

tracery The thin stone or wooden bars in a Gothic window, screen, or panel, which create an elaborate decorative matrix or pattern.

transept The arm of a cruciform church, perpendicular to the nave. The point where the nave and transept cross is called the crossing. Beyond the crossing lies the sanctuary, whether apse, choir, or chevet.

triforium The element of the interior elevation of a church, found directly below the clerestory and consisting of a series of arched openings. The triforium can be made up of openings from a passageway or gallery or can be a purely decorative device built into the wall.

triglyph Rectangular blocks between the metopes of a Doric frieze. Identified by the three carved vertical grooves, which approximate the appearance of the ends of wooden beams.

triptych An artwork made up of three panels. The panels are often hinged together so the side segments (wings) fold over the central area.

triumphal arch A freestanding, massive stone gateway with a large central arch, built as urban ornament and/or to celebrate military victories (as by the Romans).

trompe l'oeil A manner of representation in which the appearance of natural space and objects is re-created with the express intention of fooling the eye of the viewer, who may be convinced that the subject actually exists as three-dimensional reality.

trumeau A column, pier, or post found at the center of a large portal or doorway, supporting the lintel.

Tuscan order See **order**.

twining A basketry technique in which short rods are sewn together vertically. The panels are then joined together to form a vessel.

tympanum In Classical architecture, the vertical panel of the pediment. In medieval and later architecture, the area over a door enclosed by an arch and a lintel, often decorated with sculpture or mosaic.

typology The study of symbolic types of representation in art history, especially of Old Testament events of the Bible as they prefigure those of the New Testament.

ukiyo-e A Japanese term for a type of popular art that was favored from the sixteenth century, particularly in the form of color woodblock prints. Ukiyo-e prints often depicted the world of the common people in Japan, such as courtesans and actors, as well as landscapes and myths.

undercutting A technique in sculpture by which a form is carved to project outward, then under. Undercutting gives a highly three-dimensional effect with deep shadows behind the form.

underglaze Color or decoration applied to a ceramic piece before glazing.

value The darkness or lightness of a color (hue).

vanishing point In a perspective system, the point on the horizon line at which orthogonals meet. A complex system can have multiple vanishing points.

vanitas An image, especially popular in Europe during the seventeenth century, in which all the objects symbolize the transience of life. Vanitas paintings are usually of still lifes or genre subjects.

vault An arched masonry structure covering that spans an interior space. In different shapes, called by different names. **Barrel or tunnel vault**: a continuous semicircular vault. **Corbel vault**: a vault made by the technique of corbeling. **Groin or cross vault**: a vault created by the intersection of two barrel vaults of equal size. **Quadrant or half-barrel vault**: a vault with two diagonally crossed ribs, which creates four side compartments of equal size and shape. **Rib vault**: a rib vault is found when the joining of curved sides of a groin vault is demarcated by a raised rib.

vellum A fine animal skin prepared for writing and painting. See **parchment**.

veneer In architecture, the exterior facing of a building, often in decorative patterns of fine stone or brick. In decorative arts, a thin exterior layer for decoration laid over wooden objects or furniture. Made of fine materials such as rare wood, ivory, metal, and semiprecious stones.

verism A style in which artists concern themselves with capturing the exterior likeness of an object or person, usually by rendering its visible details in a finely executed, meticulous manner.

veristic See **verism**.

verso The (reverse) left-hand page of the opening of a book or manuscript. Also: the subordinate or back side of a leaf of paper, as in the case of drawings.

volumetric A term indicating the concern for rendering the impression of three-dimensional volumes in painting, usually achieved through modeling and the manipulation of light and shadow (chiaroscuro).

volute A spiral scroll, most often decoration on an Ionic capital.

votive figure An image created as a devotional offering to a god or other deity.

voussoirs The oblong, wedge-shaped stone blocks used to build an arch. The topmost voussoir is called a keystone.

wall painting See **mural**.

ware A general term designating the different techniques by which pottery is produced and decorated. Different wares utilize different procedures to achieve different decorative results. See also **black-figure**, **red-figure**.

warp The vertical threads in a weaver's loom. Warp threads make up a fixed framework that provides the structure for the entire piece of cloth, and are thus often thicker than weft threads. See also **weft**.

wash A diluted watercolor. Often washes are applied to drawings or prints to add tone or touches of color.

weft The horizontal threads in a woven piece of cloth. Weft threads are woven at right angles to and through the warp threads to make up the bulk of the decorative pattern. In carpets, the weft is often completely covered or formed by the rows of trimmed knots that form the carpet's soft surface.

westwork The monumental, west-facing entrance section of a Carolingian, Ottonian, or Romanesque church. The exterior consists of multiple stories between two towers; the interior includes an entrance vestibule, a chapel, and a series of galleries overlooking the nave.

wing A side panel of a triptych or polyptych (usually found in pairs), which was hinged to fold over the central panel. Wings often held the depiction of the donors and/or subsidiary scenes relating to the central image.

woodblock print A print made from a block of wood that is carved in relief or incised.

woodcut A type of print made by carving a design into a wooden block. The ink is applied to the plate with a roller. As the ink remains only on the raised areas between the carved-away lines, these carved-away areas and lines provide the white areas of the print. Also: the process by which the woodcut is made.

x-ray style In Aboriginal art, a manner of representation in which the artist depicts a figure or animal by illustrating its outline as well as essential internal organs and bones.

zeitgeist From the German word for "spirit of the time," the term means cultural and intellectual aspects of a time period that pervade human experience and are expressed in all creative and social endeavors.

ziggurat In Mesopotamia, a human-made mountain; a tall stepped tower of earthen materials, often supporting a shrine.

Selected Bibliography

General

Adams, Laurie Schneider. A History of Western Art. 2nd ed. Madison, Wis.: Brown and Benchmark, 1997.

Anderson, Richard L. Art in Small-Scale Societies. 2nd ed. Englewood Cliffs, N.J.: Prentice Hall, 1989.

Bazin, Germain. A Concise History of World Sculpture. London: David & Charles, 1981.

Bearden, Romare. A History of African American Artists: From 1792 to the Present. New York: Pantheon, 1993.

Becatti, Giovanni. The Art of Ancient Greece and Rome, from the Rise of Greece to the Fall of Rome. New York: Abrams, 1967.

Berlo, Janet Catherine, and Lee Ann Wilson. Arts of Africa, Oceania, and the Americas: Selected Readings. Englewood Cliffs, N.J.: Prentice Hall, 1993.

Brown, Milton W. American Art: Painting, Sculpture, Architecture, Decorative Arts, Photography. New York: Abrams, 1979.

Brownston, David M., and Ilene Franck. Timelines of the Arts and Literature. New York: HarperCollins, 1994.

Bull, Stephen. An Historical Guide to Arms and Armor. Ed. Tony North. New York: Facts on File, 1991.

Chadwick, Whitney. Women, Art, and Society. New York: Thames and Hudson, 1990.

Chipp, Herschel Browning. Theories of Modern Art: A Source Book by Artists and Critics. California Studies in the History of Art. Berkeley: Univ. of California Press, 1984.

Cole, Bruce, and Adelheid Gealt. Art of the Western World: From Ancient Greece to Post-Modernism. New York: Summit, 1989.

Craven, Wayne. American Art: History and Culture. New York: Abrams, 1994.

Crouch, Dora P. A History of Architecture: Stonehenge to Sky-scrapers. New York: McGraw-Hill, 1985.

Dictionary of Art, The. 34 vols. New York: Grove's Dictionaries, 1996.

Eitner, Lorenz. An Outline of Nineteenth Century European Painting: From David to Cézanne. 2 vols. New York: Harper & Row, 1987.

Encyclopedia of World Art. 16 vols. New York: McGraw-Hill, 1972–83.

Ferrier, Jean Louis, ed. Art of Our Century: The Chronicle of Western Art, 1900 to the Present. New York: Prentice Hall, 1989.

Fleming, John, Hugh Honour, and Nikolaus Pevsner. The Penguin Dictionary of Architecture. 4th ed. New York: Penguin, 1991.

Frampton, Kenneth. Modern Architecture: A Critical History. World of Art. New York: Oxford Univ. Press, 1980.

Gardner, Helen. Gardner's Art through the Ages. 9th ed. Ed. Horst de la Croix, Richard G. Tansey, and Diana Kirkpatrick. San Diego: Harcourt Brace College, 1991.

Groenewegen-Frankfort, H. A., and Bernard Ashmole. Art of the Ancient World: Painting, Pottery, Sculpture, Architecture from Egypt, Mesopotamia, Crete, Greece, and Rome. Library of Art History. Englewood Cliffs, N.J.: Prentice Hall, 1972.

Hall, James. Dictionary of Subjects and Symbols in Art. Rev. ed. New York: Harper & Row, 1979.

Hamilton, George Heard. 19th and 20th Century Art: Painting, Sculpture, Architecture. Library of Art History. New York: Abrams, 1972.

Handlin, David P. American Architecture. World of Art. London: Thames and Hudson, 1985.

Harris, Ann Sutherland, and Linda Nochlin. Women Artists: 1550–1950. Los Angeles: Los Angeles County Museum of Art, 1976.

Harrison, Charles, and Paul Wood, eds. Art in Theory, 1900–1990: An Anthology of Changing Ideas. Cambridge, Mass.: Blackwell, 1992.

Hartt, Frederick. Art: A History of Painting, Sculpture, Architecture. 4th ed. New York: Abrams, 1993.

Heller, Nancy G. Women Artists: An Illustrated History. New York: Abbeville, 1987.

Heydenreich, Ludwig Heinrich. Architecture in Italy, 1400 to 1600. Pelican History of Art. Harmondsworth, Eng.: Penguin, 1966.

Hitchcock, Henry Russell. Architecture: Nineteenth and Twentieth Centuries. 4th ed. Pelican History of Art. Harmondsworth, Eng.: Penguin, 1977.

Holt, Elizabeth Gilmore, ed. A Documentary History of Art. 3 vols. New Haven, Conn.: Yale Univ. Press, 1986.

Honour, Hugh, and John Fleming. The Visual Arts: A History. 4th ed. New York: Abrams, 1995.

Hunter, Sam, and John Jacobus. American Art of the 20th Century: Painting, Sculpture, Architecture. New York: Abrams, 1973.

———. Modern Art: Painting, Sculpture, Architecture. 3rd ed. New York: Abrams, 1992.

Huyghe, René. Larousse Encyclopedia of Renaissance and Baroque Art. Art and Mankind. New York: Prometheus, 1964.

Janson, H. W. History of Art. 5th ed. Rev. and exp. Anthony F. Janson. New York: Abrams, 1995.

Jeffrey, Ian. Photography: A Concise History. London: Thames and Hudson, 1981.

Jones, Lois Swan. Art Information: Research Methods and Resources. 3rd ed. Dubuque, Iowa: Kendall/Hunt, 1990.

Kostof, Spiro. A History of Architecture: Settings and Rituals. New York: Oxford Univ. Press, 1985.

Kubler, George, and Martin Soria. Art and Architecture in Spain and Portugal and Their American Dominions, 1500–1800. Pelican History of Art. Harmondsworth, Eng.: Penguin, 1959.

Kurtz, Bruce D. Visual Imagination: An Introduction to Art. Englewood Cliffs, N.J.: Prentice Hall, 1987.

Langer, Suzanne. Feeling and Form. Upper Saddle River, N.J.: Prentice Hall, 1990.

Larousse Encyclopedia of Byzantine and Medieval Art. London: Hamlyn, 1963.

Lee, Sherman E. A History of Far Eastern Art. 5th ed. New York: Abrams, 1994.

Lindemann, Gottfried. Prints and Drawings: A Pictorial History. Trans. Gerald Onn. Oxford: Phaidon, 1976.

Lynton, Norbert. The Story of Modern Art. 2nd ed. Oxford: Phaidon, 1989.

Mason, Penelope. History of Japanese Art. New York: Abrams, 1993.

Mayor, A. Hyatt. Prints and People: A Social History of Printed Pictures. New York: Metropolitan Museum of Art, 1971.

McConkey, Wilfred J. Klee as in Clay: A Pronunciation Guide. Lantham, Md.: Univ. Press of America, 1985.

McCoubrey, John W. American Art, 1700–1960: Sources and Documents. Englewood Cliffs, N.J.: Prentice-Hall, 1965.

Myers, Bernard, ed. McGraw-Hill Dictionary of Art. 5 vols. New York: McGraw-Hill, 1969.

Newhall, Beaumont. The History of Photography: From 1839 to the Present. Rev. ed. New York: Museum of Modern Art, 1982.

Rosenblum, Robert, and H. W. Janson. 19th Century Art. New York: Abrams, 1984.

Rothberg, Robert I., and Theodore K. Rabb, eds. Art and History: Images and Their Meaning. Cambridge: Cambridge Univ. Press, 1988.

Saggs, H. W. F. Civilization before Greece and Rome. New Haven, Conn.: Yale Univ. Press, 1989.

Schapiro, Meyer. Modern Art: 19th and 20th Century Art. New York: Braziller, 1978.

Seckel, Dietrich. Art of Buddhism. Art of the World. New York: Crown, 1964.

Selz, Peter. Art in Our Times: A Pictorial History 1890–1980. New York: Abrams, 1981.

Snyder, James. Medieval Art: Painting, Sculpture, Architecture, 4th–14th Century. New York: Abrams, 1989.

Stangos, Nikos. The Thames and Hudson Dictionary of Art and Artists. Rev ed. World of Art. New York: Thames and Hudson, 1994.

———, ed. Concepts of Modern Art. 3rd ed. World of Art. New York: Thames and Hudson, 1994.

Stechow, Wolfgang. Northern Renaissance, 1400–1600: Sources and Documents. Englewood Cliffs, N.J.: Prentice Hall, 1966.

Steer, John, and Antony White. Atlas of Western Art History: Artists, Sites and Movements from Ancient Greece to the Modern Age. New York: Facts on File, 1994.

Tafuri, Manfredo. Modern Architecture. 2 vols. History of World Architecture. New York: Electa/Rizzoli, 1986.

Trachtenberg, Marvin, and Isabelle Hyman. Architecture, from Prehistory to Post-Modernism: The Western Tradition. New York: Abrams, 1986.

Tufts, Eleanor. Our Hidden Heritage: Five Centuries of Women Artists. New York: Paddington, 1974.

Wilkins, David G., Bernard Bichultz, and Katheryn M. Linduff. Art Past/Art Present. 3rd ed. New York: Abrams, 1997.

Wilmerding, John. American Art. Pelican History of Art. Harmondsworth, Eng.: Penguin, 1976.

Chapter 1 Art Before the Written Word

Amiet, Pierre. Art in the Ancient World: A Handbook of Styles and Forms. New York: Rizzoli, 1981.

Anati, Emmanuel. Camonica Valley: A Depiction of Village Life in the Alps from Neolithic Times to the Birth of Christ, as Revealed by Thousands of Newly Found Rock Carvings. Trans. Linda Asher. New York: Knopf, 1961.

Blocker, H. Gene. The Aesthetics of Primitive Art. Lantham, Md.: Univ. Press of America, 1994.

Castleden, Rodney. The Making of Stonehenge. London: Routledge, 1993.

Chippindale, Christopher. Stonehenge Complete. New York: Thames and Hudson, 1994.

Clewlow, C. William. Colossal Heads of the Olmec Culture. Contributions of the Univ. of California Archaeological Research Facility. Berkeley: Archaeological Research Facility, Univ. of California, 1967.

Dawn of Art: The Chauvet Cave. New York: Abrams, 1996.

Flood, Josephine. Archaeology of the Dreamtime: The Story of Prehistoric Australia and Its People. Rev. ed. New Haven, Conn.: Yale Univ. Press, 1990.

Graziosi, Paolo. Paleolithic Art. New York: McGraw-Hill, 1960.

Guidoni, Enrico. Primitive Architecture. Trans. Robert Erich Wolf. History of World Architecture. New York: Rizzoli, 1987.

Heyerdahl, Thor. The Art of Easter Island. Garden City, N.Y.: Doubleday, 1975.

Huyghe, René. Larousse Encyclopedia of Prehistoric and Ancient Art. Art and Mankind. New York: Prometheus, 1966.

Kenrick, Douglas Moore. Jomon of Japan: The World's Oldest Pottery. London and New York: Kegan Paul International, 1995.

Laing, Lloyd Robert, and Jennifer Laing. Ancient Art: The Challenge to Modern Thought. Dublin: Irish Academic, 1993.

Layton, Robert. Australian Rock Art: A New Synthesis. New York: Cambridge Univ. Press, 1992.

Leroi-Gourhan, André. Treasures of Prehistoric Art. New York: Abrams, 1967.

Lhote, Henri. The Search for the Tassili Frescoes: The Story of the Prehistoric Rock-Painting of the Sahara. 2nd ed. Trans. Alan Houghton Brodrick. London: Hutchinson, 1973.

Lloyd, Seton, and Hans Wolfgang Muller. Ancient Architecture. New York: Rizzoli, 1986.

Oliphant, Margaret. The Atlas of the Ancient World: Charting the Great Civilizations of the Past. New York: Simon & Schuster, 1992.

Powell, Ann. Origins of Western Art. London: Thames and Hudson, 1973.

Powell, T. G. E. Prehistoric Art. World of Art. New York: Oxford Univ. Press, 1966.

Ruspoli, Mario. The Cave of Lascaux: The Final Photographs. New York: Abrams, 1987.

Scranton, Robert L. Aesthetic Aspects of Ancient Art. Chicago: Univ. of Chicago Press, 1964.

Wilcox, A. R. The Rock Art of Africa. London: Croon Helm, 1984.

Chapter 2 The Art of Mesopotamia and Egypt

Aldred, Cyril. Egyptian Art in the Days of the Pharaohs, 3100–320 B.C. World of Art. London: Thames and Hudson, 1980.

Amiet, Pierre. Art of the Ancient Near East. Trans. John Shepley and Claude Choquet. New York: Abrams, 1980.

Andrews, Carol. Ancient Egyptian Jewelry. New York: Abrams, 1991.

Bierbrier, Morris. Tomb-Builders of the Pharaohs. London: British Museum, 1982.

Bottero, Jean. Mesopotamia: Writing, Reasoning, and the Gods. Trans. Zainab Bahrani and Marc Van De Mieroop. Chicago: Univ. of Chicago Press, 1992.

Brier, Bob. Egyptian Mummies. New York: Morrow, 1994.

Edwards, I. E. S. The Pyramids of Egypt. Rev. ed. Harmondsworth, Eng.: Penguin, 1985.

Egyptian Book of the Dead, The: The Book of Going Forth by Day: Being the Papyrus of Ani (Royal Scribe of the Divine Offerings). Trans. Raymond O. Faulkner. San Francisco: Chronicle, 1994.

James, T. G. H., and W. V. Davies. Egyptian Sculpture. Cambridge, Mass.: Harvard Univ. Press, 1983.

Kozloff, Arielle P., and Betsy M. Bryan. Egypt's Dazzling Sun: Amenhotep III and His World. Cleveland: Cleveland Museum of Art, 1992.

Kramer, Samual Noah. *History Begins at Sumer: Thirty-Nine Firsts in Man's Recorded History.* 3rd rev. ed. Philadelphia: Univ. of Pennsylvania Press, 1981.

———. *The Sumerians, Their History, Culture, and Character.* Chicago: Univ. of Chicago Press, 1963.

Martin, Geoffrey Thorndike. *The Hidden Tombs of Memphis: New Discoveries from the Time of Tutankhamun and Ramesses the Great.* London: Thames and Hudson, 1991.

Mellaart, James. *The Earliest Civilization of the Near East.* London: Thames and Hudson, 1965.

Montet, Pierre. *Everyday Life in Egypt in the Days of Ramesses the Great.* Trans. A. R. Maxwell-Hysop and Margaret S. Drower. Philadelphia: Univ. of Pennsylvania Press, 1981.

Parrot, André. *The Arts of Assyria.* Trans. Stuart Gilbert and James Emmons. Arts of Mankind. New York: Golden, 1961.

Roaf, Michael. *Cultural Atlas of Mesopotamia and the Ancient Near East.* New York: Facts on File, 1990.

Smith, William Stevenson. *The Art and Architecture of Ancient Egypt.* Rev. ed. Pelican History of Art. Harmondsworth, Eng.: Penguin, 1981.

———. *Interconnections in the Ancient Near East: A Study of the Relationships between the Arts of Egypt, the Aegean, and Western Asia.* New Haven, Conn.: Yale Univ. Press, 1965.

Reeves, C. N. *The Complete Tutankhamun: The King, the Tomb, the Royal Treasure.* London: Thames and Hudson, 1990.

Winstone, H. V. F. *Howard Carter and the Discovery of the Tomb of Tutankhamun.* London: Constable, 1991.

Woldering, Irmgard. *The Art of Egypt: The Time of the Pharaohs.* Trans. Ann E. Keep. Art of the World. New York: Crown, 1963.

Wolkstein, Dianne, and Samuel Noah Kramer. *Inanna: Queen of Heaven and Earth.* New York: Harper & Row, 1983.

Chapter 3 Early Asian Art

Ackerman, Phyllis. *Ritual Bronzes of Ancient China.* New York: Dryden, 1945.

Arts of China. 3 vols. Tokyo: Kodansha International, 1968–70.

Berkson, Carmel. *Elephanta: The Cave of Shiva.* Princeton, N.J.: Princeton Univ. Press, 1983.

Bussagli, Mario. *Oriental Architecture.* 2 vols. History of World Architecture. New York: Electa/Rizzoli, 1989.

Chandra, Pramod. *The Sculpture of India, 3000 B.C.–1300 A.D.* Washington, D.C.: National Gallery of Art, 1985.

Craven, Roy C. *Indian Art: A Concise History.* World of Art. New York: Thames and Hudson, 1985.

Egami, Namio. *The Beginnings of Japanese Art.* Trans. John Bester. Heibonsha Survey of Japanese Art, vol. 2. New York: Weatherhill, 1973.

Elisseeff, Danielle, and Vadime Elisseeff. *Art of Japan.* Trans. I. Mark Paris. New York: Abrams, 1985.

Errington, Elizabeth, and Joe Cribb, eds. *The Crossroads of Asia: Transformation in Image and Symbol in the Art of Ancient Afghanistan and Pakistan.* Cambridge, Eng.: Ancient India and Iran Trust, 1992.

Fong, Wen, ed. *The Great Bronze Age of China: An Exhibition from the People's Republic of China.* New York: Metropolitan Museum of Art, 1980.

Frankfort, Henri. *Art and Architecture of the Ancient Orient.* 4th ed. Pelican History of Art. Harmondsworth, Eng.: Penguin, 1970.

Goetz, Hermann. *The Art of India: Five Thousand Years of Indian Art.* 2nd ed. Art of the World. New York: Crown, 1964.

Harle, James C. *Gupta Sculpture.* Oxford: Clarendon, 1974.

Kidder, J. Edward. *Early Buddhist Japan.* Ancient People and Places. New York: Praeger, 1972.

Kurata, Bunsaku. *Horyu-ji, Temple of the Exalted Law: Early Buddhist Art from Japan.* New York: Japan Society, 1981.

Martynov, Anatolii Ivanovich. *Ancient Art of Northern Asia.* Urbana: Univ. of Illinois Press, 1991.

Paine, Robert Treat, and Alexander Soper. *Art and Architecture of Japan.* 3rd ed. Pelican History of Art. Harmondsworth, Eng.: Penguin, 1981.

Sickman, Lawrence, and Alexander Soper. *Art and Architecture of China.* Pelican History of Art. Harmondsworth, Eng.: Penguin, 1971.

Suzuki, Kakichi. *Early Buddhist Architecture in Japan.* Trans. and adapted by Mary Neighbor Parent and Nancy Shatzman Steinhardt. Japanese Arts Library, vol. 9. New York: Kodansha International, 1980.

Tregear, Mary. *Chinese Art.* World of Art. New York: Oxford Univ. Press, 1980.

Varley, H. Paul. *Japanese Culture.* 3rd ed. Honolulu: Univ. of Hawaii Press, 1984.

Watanabe, Yasutada. *Shinto Art: Ise and Izumo Shrines.* Trans. Robert Ricketts. Heibonsha Survey of Japanese Art, vol. 3. New York: Weatherhill, 1974.

Weiner, Sheila L. *Ajanta: Its Place in Buddhist Art.* Berkeley: Univ. of California Press, 1977.

Whitfield, Roderick, and Anne Farrer. *Caves of the Thousand Buddhas: Chinese Art from the Silk Route.* London: British Museum, 1990.

Chapter 4 Art of the Aegean World

Adam, Robert. *Classical Architecture: A Comprehensive Handbook to the Tradition of Classical Style.* New York: Abrams, 1991.

Akurgal, Ekrem. *The Art of Greece: Its Origins in the Mediterranean and Near East.* Trans. Wayne Dynes. Art of the World. New York: Crown, 1968.

Arias, Paolo. *A History of 1000 Years of Greek Vase Painting.* New York: Abrams, 1962.

Ashmole, Bernard. *Architect and Sculptor in Classical Greece.* Wrightsman Lectures. New York: New York Univ. Press, 1972.

Avery, Catherine, ed. *The New Century Handbook of Greek Mythology and Legend.* New York: Appleton-Century Crofts, 1972.

Barber, R. L. N. *The Cyclades in the Bronze Age.* Iowa City: Univ. of Iowa Press, 1987.

Boardman, John. *Greek Art.* 4th ed. rev. and exp. New York: Thames and Hudson, 1996.

———. *Greek Sculpture: The Archaic Period: A Handbook.* World of Art. New York: Oxford Univ. Press, 1978.

———. *Greek Sculpture: The Classical Period: A Handbook.* London: Thames and Hudson, 1985.

Charbonneaux, Jean, Robert Martin, and François Villard. *Archaic Greek Art (620–480 B.C.).* Trans. James Emmons and Robert Allen. Arts of Mankind. New York: Braziller, 1971.

———. *Classical Greek Art (480–330 B.C.).* Trans. James Emmons. Arts of Mankind. New York: Braziller, 1972.

Chitham, Robert. *The Classical Orders of Architecture.* New York: Rizzoli, 1985.

Fitton, J. Lesley. *Cycladic Art.* Cambridge, Mass.: Harvard Univ. Press, 1990.

Francis, E. D. *Image and Idea in Fifth-Century Greece: Art and Literature after the Persian Wars.* London: Routledge, 1990.

Higgins, Reynold. *Minoan and Mycenean Art.* Rev. ed. World of Art. New York: Oxford Univ. Press, 1981.

Hurwit, Jeffrey M. *The Art and Culture of Early Greece 1100–480 B.C.* Ithaca, N.Y.: Cornell Univ. Press, 1985.

Jenkins, Ian. *The Parthenon Frieze.* Austin: Univ. of Texas Press, 1994.

Lawrence, A. W. *Greek Architecture.* 4th ed. Pelican History of Art. Harmondsworth, Eng.: Penguin, 1983.

Marinatos, Spyridon, and Max Hirmer. *Crete and Mycenae.* New York: Abrams, 1960.

Martin, Roland. *Greek Architecture: Architecture of Crete, Greece, and the Greek World.* History of World Architecture. New York: Electa/Rizzoli, 1988.

Papaioannou, Kostas. *The Art of Greece.* Trans. I. Mark Paris. New York: Abrams, 1989.

Pedley, John Griffiths. *Greek Art and Archaeology.* New York: Abrams, 1993.

Roes, Anna. *Greek Geometric Art: Its Symbolism and Its Origin.* London: Oxford Univ. Press, 1933.

Scully, Vincent. *The Earth, the Temple, and the Gods: Greek Sacred Architecture.* Rev. ed. New Haven, Conn.: Yale Univ. Press, 1979.

Stewart, Andrew F. *Greek Sculpture: An Exploration.* 2 vols. New Haven, Conn.: Yale Univ. Press, 1990.

Chapter 5 The Spread of Greek Art and Culture

Bloch, Raymond. *Etruscan Art.* Greenwich, Conn.: New York Graphic Society, 1965.

Brendel, Otto J. *Etruscan Art.* Pelican History of Art. Harmondsworth, Eng.: Penguin, 1978.

Charbonneaux, Jean, Robert Martin, and François Villard. *Hellenistic Art (330–50 B.C.).* Trans. Peter Green. Arts of Mankind. New York: Braziller, 1973.

Collon, Dominique. *First Impressions: Cylinder Seals in the Ancient Near East.* Chicago: Univ. of Chicago Press, 1987.

Ferrier, R. W., ed. *Arts of Persia.* New Haven, Conn.: Yale Univ. Press, 1989.

Ghirshman, Roman. *The Arts of Ancient Iran from Its Origins to the Time of Alexander the Great.* Trans. Stuart Gilbert and James Emmons. Arts of Mankind. New York: Golden, 1964.

Havelock, Christine Mitchell. *Hellenistic Art: The Art of the Classical World from the Death of Alexander the Great to the Battle of Actium.* 2nd ed. New York: Norton, 1981.

Onians, John. *Art and Thought in the Hellenistic Age: The Greek World View 350–50 B.C.* London: Thames and Hudson, 1979.

Pollitt, J. J. *Art in the Hellenistic Age.* Cambridge: Cambridge Univ. Press, 1986.

Porada, Edith. *The Art of Ancient Iran: Pre-Islamic Cultures.* Art of the World. New York: Crown, 1965.

Roux, Georges. *Ancient Iraq.* 3rd ed. London: Penguin, 1992.

Saggs, H. W. F. *Everyday Life in Babylonia and Assyria.* New York: Dorset, 1987.

Smith, R. R. R. *Hellenistic Sculpture: A Handbook.* World of Art. New York: Thames and Hudson, 1991.

Sprenger, Maja, and Gilda Bartolini. *The Etruscans: Their History, Art, and Architecture.* New York: Abrams, 1983.

Webster, T. B. L. *The Art of Greece: The Age of Hellenism.* Art of the World. New York: Crown, 1966.

Woolley, Leonard. *The Art of the Middle East including Persia, Mesopotamia and Palestine.* Trans. Ann E. Keep. Art of the World. New York: Crown, 1961.

Chapter 6 Art of the Roman Republic and Empire

Andreae, Bernard. *The Art of Rome.* Trans. Robert Erich Wolf. New York: Abrams, 1977.

Balsdon, J. P. V. D. *Roman Women: Their History and Habits.* London: Bodley Head, 1962.

Bianchi Bandinelli, Ranuccio. *Rome: The Centre of Power: Roman Art to A.D. 200.* Trans. Peter Green. Arts of Mankind. London: Thames and Hudson, 1970.

Breeze, David John. *Hadrian's Wall.* London: Allen Lane, 1976.

Brown, Peter. *The World of Late Antiquity: A.D. 150–750.* New York: Norton, 1989.

Christ, Karl. *The Romans: An Introduction to Their History and Civilization.* Berkeley: Univ. of California Press, 1984.

Guilland, Jacqueline, and Maurice Guilland. *Frescoes in the Time of Pompeii.* New York: Potter, 1990.

Heintze, Helga von. *Roman Art.* New York: Universe, 1990.

L'Orange, Hans Peter. *The Roman Empire: Art Forms and Civic Life.* New York: Rizzoli, 1985.

MacDonald, William L. *The Architecture of the Roman Empire: An Introductory Study.* Rev. ed. 2 vols. Yale Publications in the History of Art. New Haven, Conn.: Yale Univ. Press, 1982.

———. *The Pantheon: Design, Meaning, and Progeny.* Cambridge, Mass.: Harvard Univ. Press, 1976.

Pollitt, J. J. *The Art of Rome, c. 753 B.C.–337 A.D.: Sources and Documents.* Englewood Cliffs, N.J.: Prentice-Hall, 1966.

Ramage, Nancy H., and Andrew Ramage. *Roman Art: Romulus to Constantine.* New York: Abrams, 1991.

Strong, Donald. *Roman Art.* 2nd ed. Pelican History of Art. Harmondsworth, Eng.: Penguin, 1988.

Ward-Perkins, J. B. *Roman Architecture.* History of World Architecture. New York: Electa/Rizzoli, 1988.

Chapter 7 Jewish, Early Christian, and Byzantine Art

Age of Spirituality: Late Antique and Early Christian Art, Third to Seventh Century. New York: Metropolitan Museum of Art, 1979.

Carr, Annemarie Weyl. *Byzantine Illumination, 1150–1250: The Study of a Provincial Tradition.* Chicago: Univ. of Chicago Press, 1987.

Christe, Yves. *Art of the Christian World, A.D. 200–1500: A Handbook of Styles and Forms.* New York: Rizzoli, 1982.

Cutler, Anthony. *The Hand of the Master: Craftsmanship, Ivory, and Society in Byzantium (9th–11th Centuries).* Princeton, N.J.: Princeton Univ. Press, 1994.

Demus, Otto. *Byzantine Mosaic Decoration: Aspects of Monumental Art in Byzantium.* New Rochelle, N.Y.: Caratzas, 1976.

Ferguson, George Wells. *Signs and Symbols in Christian Art.* New York: Oxford Univ. Press, 1967.

Krautheimer, Richard. *Early Christian and Byzantine Archi-*

tecture. 4th ed. Pelican History of Art. Hamondsworth, Eng: Penguin, 1986.

Lane Fox, Robin. *Pagans and Christians.* Harmondsworth, Eng.: Viking, 1986.

Mainstone, R. J. *Hagia Sophia: Architecture, Structure and Liturgy of Justinian's Great Church.* London: Thames and Hudson, 1988.

Manicelli, Fabrizio. *Catacombs and Basilicas: The Early Christians in Rome.* Florence: Scala, 1981.

Milburn, R. L. P. *Early Christian Art and Architecture.* Berkeley: Univ. of California Press, 1988.

Rice, David Talbot. *Art of the Byzantine Era.* New York: Praeger, 1963.

Schapiro, Meyer. *Late Antique, Early Christian, and Mediaeval Art.* New York: Braziller, 1979.

Simson, Otto Georg von. *Sacred Fortress: Byzantine Art and Statecraft in Ravenna.* Chicago: Univ. of Chicago Press, 1948.

Stevenson, James. *The Catacombs: Rediscovered Monuments of Early Christianity.* Ancient Peoples and Places. London: Thames and Hudson, 1978.

Weitzmann, Kurt. *Late Antique and Early Christian Book Illumination.* New York: Braziller, 1977.

Wharton, Annabel Jane. *Art of Empire: Painting and Architecture of the Byzantine Periphery: A Comparative Study of Four Provinces.* University Park: Pennsylvania State Univ. Press, 1988.

Chapter 8 Early European and Islamic Art

Akurgal, Ekrem, ed. *The Art and Architecture of Turkey.* New York: Rizzoli, 1980.

Alexander, J. J. G. *Medieval Illuminators and Their Methods of Work.* New Haven, Conn.: Yale Univ. Press, 1992.

Atasoy, Nurhan. *Splendors of the Ottoman Sultans.* Ed. and trans. Tulay Artan. Memphis, Tenn.: Lithograph, 1992.

Atil, Esin. *The Age of Sultan Suleyman the Magnificent.* Washington, D.C.: National Gallery of Art, 1987.

Backes, Magnus, and Regine Dolling. *Art of the Dark Ages.* Trans. Francisca Garvie. Panorama of World Art. New York: Abrams, 1971.

Backhouse, Janet, D. H. Turner, and Leslie Webster. *The Golden Age of Anglo-Saxon Art, 966–1066.* Bloomington: Indiana Univ. Press, 1984.

Beckwith, John. *Early Medieval Art: Carolingian, Ottonian, Romanesque.* World of Art. New York: Oxford Univ. Press, 1974.

Blair, Sheila S., and Jonathan M. Brown. *The Art and Architecture of Islam 1250–1800.* New Haven, Conn.: Yale Univ. Press, 1994.

Brend, Barbara. *Islamic Art.* Cambridge, Mass.: Harvard Univ. Press, 1991.

Conant, Kenneth John. *Carolingian and Romanesque Architecture, 800–1200.* 3rd ed. Pelican History of Art. Harmondsworth, Eng.: Penguin, 1973.

Dodds, Jerrilynn D., ed. *al-Andalus: The Art of Islamic Spain.* New York: Metropolitan Museum of Art, 1992.

Evans, Angela Care. *The Sutton Hoo Ship Burial.* London: British Museum, 1986.

Frishman, Martin, and Hasan-Uddin Khan. *The Mosque: History, Architectural Development and Regional Diversity.* London: Thames and Hudson, 1994.

Grabar, Oleg. *The Alhambra.* Cambridge, Mass.: Harvard Univ. Press, 1978.

——. *The Mediation of Ornament.* A. W. Mellon Lectures in the Fine Arts. Princeton, N.J.: Princeton Univ. Press, 1992.

Henderson, George. *Early Medieval.* Style and Civilization. Harmondsworth, Eng.: Penguin, 1972.

Hubert, Jean, Jean Porcher, and W. F. Volbach. *Carolingian Renaissance.* Arts of Mankind. New York: Braziller, 1970.

Jones, Dalu, and George Mitchell, eds. *The Arts of Islam.* London: Arts Council of Great Britain, 1976.

Khatibi, Abdelkebir, and Mohammed Sijelmassi. *The Splendour of Islamic Calligraphy.* New York: Rizzoli, 1977.

Koran, The. Rev. ed. Trans. N. J. Dawood. London: Penguin, 1993.

Laing, Lloyd. *Art of the Celts.* World of Art. New York: Thames and Hudson, 1992.

Megaw, Ruth, and Vincent Megaw. *Celtic Art: From Its Beginnings to the Book of Kells.* New York: Thames and Hudson, 1989.

Nordenfalk, Carl Adam Johan. *Early Medieval Book Illumination.* New York: Rizzoli, 1988.

Papadopoulo, Alexandre. *Islam and Muslim Art.* Trans. Robert Erich Wolf. New York: Abrams, 1979.

Petsopoulos, Yanni, ed. *Tulips, Arabesques and Turbans: Decorative Arts from the Ottoman Empire.* New York: Abbeville, 1982.

Rice, David Talbot. *Islamic Art.* World of Art. New York: Thames and Hudson, 1965.

Schimmel, Annemarie. *Calligraphy and Islamic Culture.* New York: New York Univ. Press, 1983.

Verzone, Paola. *The Art of Europe: The Dark Ages from Theodoric to Charlemagne.* Art of the World. New York: Crown, 1968.

Wilson, David M. *Anglo-Saxon Art: From the Seventh Century to the Norman Conquest.* London: Thames and Hudson, 1984.

——, and Ole Klindt-Jensen. *Viking Art.* 2nd ed. Minneapolis: Univ. of Minnesota Press, 1980.

Chapter 9 Later Asian Art

Addiss, Stephen. *The Art of Zen: Painting and Calligraphy by Japanese Monks, 1600–1925.* New York: Abrams, 1989.

Asher, Catherine B. *Architecture of Mughal India.* New York: Cambridge Univ. Press, 1992.

Barnhart, Richard M. *Painters of the Great Ming: The Imperial Court and the Zhe School.* Dallas, Tex.: Dallas Museum of Art, 1993.

Beach, Milo Cleveland. *Grand Mogul: Imperial Painting in India, 1600–1660.* Williamstown, Mass.: Sterling and Francine Clark Art Institute, 1978.

——. *Mughal and Rajput Painting.* New York: Cambridge Univ. Press, 1992.

Billeter, Jean François. *The Chinese Art of Writing.* New York: Skira/Rizzoli, 1990.

Blurton, T. Richard. *Hindu Art.* Cambridge, Mass.: Harvard Univ. Press, 1993.

Bush, Susan, and Hsui-yen Shih, eds. *Early Chinese Texts on Painting.* Cambridge, Mass.: Harvard Univ. Press, 1985.

Cahill, James. *The Distant Mountains: Chinese Painting in the Late Ming Dynasty, 1580–1644.* New York: Weatherhill, 1982.

——. *Hills beyond a River: Chinese Painting of the Y'uan Dynasty, 1279–1368.* New York: Weatherhill, 1976.

Fisher, Robert E. *Buddhist Art and Architecture.* World of Art. New York: Thames and Hudson, 1993.

Forrer, Matthi. *Hokusai.* New York: Rizzoli, 1988.

Fukuyama, Toshio. *Heian Temples: Byudo-in and Chuson-ji.* Trans. Ronald K. Jones. Heibonsha Survey of Japanese Art, vol. 9. New York: Weatherhill, 1976.

Hayakawa, Masao. *The Garden Art of Japan.* Trans. Richard L. Gage. Heibonsha Survey of Japanese Art, vol. 28. New York: Weatherhill, 1973.

Hayashiya, Tatsusaburo, Masao Nakamura, and Seizo Hayashiya. *Japanese Arts and the Tea Ceremony.* Trans. and adapted by Joseph P. Macadam. Heibonsha Survey of Japanese Art, vol. 15. New York: Weatherhill, 1974.

In Pursuit of the Dragon: Traditions and Transitions in Ming Ceramics: An Exhibition from the Idemitsu Museum of Arts. Seattle: Seattle Art Museum, 1988.

Keswick, Maggie. *The Chinese Garden: History, Art and Architecture.* New York: Rizzoli, 1978.

Liu, Laurence G. *Chinese Architecture.* New York: Rizzoli, 1989.

Losty, Jeremiah P. *The Art of the Book in India.* London: British Library, 1982.

Michener, James A. *The Floating World.* New York: Random House, 1954.

Mitchell, George. *The Royal Palaces of India.* London: Thames and Hudson, 1994.

Murase, Miyeko. *Iconography of the Tale of Genji: Genji Monogatari Ekotoba.* New York: Weatherhill, 1983.

——. *Masterpieces of Japanese Screen Painting: The American Collections.* New York: Braziller, 1990.

Ng, So Kam. *Brushstrokes: Styles and Techniques of Chinese Painting.* San Francisco: Asian Art Museum of San Francisco, 1993.

Nou, Jean-Louis. *Taj Mahal.* Text by Amina Okada and M. C. Joshi. New York: Abbeville, 1993.

Okawa, Naomi. *Edo Architecture: Katsura and Nikko.* Trans. Alan Woodhull and Akito Miyamoto. Heibonsha Survey of Japanese Art, vol. 20. New York: Weatherhill, 1975.

Okudaira, Hideo. *Narrative Picture Scrolls.* Trans. Elizabeth ten Grutenhuis. Arts of Japan, 5. New York: Weatherhill, 1973.

Ooka, Minoru. *Temples of Nara and Their Art.* Trans. Dennis Lishka. Heibonsha Survey of Japanese Art, vol. 7. New York: Weatherhill, 1973.

Pal, Pratapaditya. *Court Paintings of India, 16th–19th Centuries.* New York: Navin Kumar, 1983.

——, et al. *Romance of the Taj Mahal.* Los Angeles: Los Angeles County Museum of Art, 1989.

Polo, Marco. *The Travels of Marco Polo.* Trans. Teresa Waugh and Maria Bellonci. New York: Facts on File, 1984.

Rosenfield, John M., Fumiko E. Cranston, and Edwin A. Cranston. *Japanese Arts of the Heian Period: 794–1185.* New York: Asia Society, 1967.

Rowland, Benjamin. *Art and Architecture of India: Buddhist,*

Hindu, Jain. Pelican History of Art. Hamondsworth, Eng.: Penguin, 1977.

Sullivan, Michael. *Symbols of Eternity: The Art of Landscape Painting in China.* Stanford: Stanford Univ. Press, 1979.

Takahashi, Seiichiro. *Traditional Woodblock Prints of Japan.* Trans. Richard Stanley-Baker. Heibonsha Survey of Japanese Art, vol. 22. New York: Weatherhill, 1972.

Tanaka, Ichimatsu. *Japanese Ink Painting: Shubun to Sesshu.* Trans. Bruce Darling. Heibonsha Survey of Japanese Art, vol. 12. New York: Weatherhill, 1972.

Terada, Toru. *Japanese Art in World Perspective.* Trans. Thomas Guerin. Heibonsha Survey of Japanese Art, vol. 25. New York: Weatherhill, 1976.

Thompson, Sarah E., and H. D. Harpptunian. *Undercurrents in the Floating World: Censorship and Japanese Prints.* New York: Asia Society Gallery, 1992.

Vainker, S. J. *Chinese Pottery and Porcelain: From Prehistory to the Present.* London: British Museum, 1991.

Weidner, Marsha, ed. *Latter Days of the Law: Images of Chinese Buddhism, 850–1850.* Lawrence: Spencer Museum of Art, Univ. of Kansas, 1994.

Welch, Stuart Cary. *The Emperors' Album: Images of Mughal India.* New York: Metropolitan Museum of Art, 1987.

——. *India: Art and Culture 1300–1900.* New York: Metropolitan Museum of Art, 1985.

Yamane, Yuzo. *Momoyama Genre Painting.* Trans. John M. Shields. Heibonsha Survey of Japanese Art, vol. 17. New York: Heibonsha, 1973.

Yu, Zhuoyun, comp. *Palaces of the Forbidden City.* Trans. Ng Mau-Sang, Chan Sinwai, and Puwen Lee. New York: Viking, 1984.

Chapter 10 Romanesque and Gothic Art

Andrews, Francis B. *The Mediaeval Builder and His Methods.* New York: Barnes & Noble, 1993.

Armi, C. Edson. *Masons and Sculptors in Romanesque Burgundy: The New Aesthetics of Cluny III.* 2 vols. University Park: Pennsylvania State Univ. Press, 1983.

——. *The "Headmaster" of Chartres and the Origins of "Gothic" Sculpture.* University Park: Pennsylvania State Univ. Press, 1994.

Aubert, Marcel. *The Art of the High Gothic Era.* Rev. ed. Art of the World. New York: Greystone, 1966.

Bogin, Magda. *The Women Troubadours.* New York: Norton, 1980.

Bony, Jean. *French Gothic Architecture of the 12th and 13th Centuries.* California Studies in the History of Art. Berkeley: Univ. of California Press, 1983.

Borsook, Eve, and Fiorella Superbi Gioffredi. *Italian Altarpieces, 1250–1550: Function and Design.* Oxford: Clarendon, 1994.

Branner, Robert. *Manuscript Painting in Paris during the Reign of Saint Louis: A Study of Styles.* California Studies in the History of Art. Berkeley: Univ. of California Press, 1977.

Busch, Harald, and Bernd Lohse. *Romanesque Sculpture.* London: Batsford, 1962.

Cahn, Walter. *Romanesque Bible Illumination.* Ithaca, N.Y.: Cornell Univ. Press, 1982.

Calkins, Robert C. *Monuments of Medieval Art.* New York: Dutton, 1979.

Chiellini, Monica. *Cimabue.* Trans. Lisa Pelletti. Florence: Scala, 1988.

Cole, Bruce. *Giotto and Florentine Painting, 1280–1375.* New York: Harper & Row, 1975.

Crosby, Sumner McKnight. *The Royal Abbey of Saint-Denis from Its Beginnings to the Death of Suger, 475–1151.* Yale Publications in the History of Art. New Haven, Conn.: Yale Univ. Press, 1987.

Duby, Georges. *Sculpture: The Great Art of the Middle Ages from the Fifth to the Fifteenth Century.* New York: Skira/Rizzoli, 1990.

Erlande-Brandenburg, Alain. *Gothic Art.* Trans. I. Mark Paris. New York: Abrams, 1989.

Favier, Jean. *The World of Chartres.* Trans. Francisca Garvie. New York: Abrams, 1990.

Focillon, Henri. *The Art of the West in the Middle Ages.* 2 vols. Ed. Jean Bony. Trans. Donald King. London: Phaidon, 1963.

Forsyth, Ilene H. *The Throne of Wisdom: Wood Sculptures of the Madonna in Romanesque France.* Princeton, N.J.: Princeton Univ. Press, 1972.

Gantner, Joseph, and Marvel Pobe. *Romanesque Art in France.* London: Thames and Hudson, 1956.

Grape, Wolfgang. *The Bayeux Tapestry: Monument to a Norman Triumph.* New York: Prestel, 1994.

Grodecki, Louis. *Gothic Architecture.* Trans. I. Mark Paris. History of World Architecture. New York: Electa/Rizzoli, 1985.

——, and Catherine Brisac. *Gothic Stained Glass, 1200–1300.* Ithaca, N.Y.: Cornell Univ. Press, 1985.

Hurlimann, Martin, and Jean Bony. *French Cathedrals.* Boston: Houghton Mifflin, 1951.
Husband, Timothy. *Wild Man: Medieval Myth and Symbolism.* New York: Metropolitan Museum of Art, 1980.
Jantzen, Hans. *High Gothic: The Classic Cathedrals of Chartres, Reims, Amiens.* Trans. James Palmes. New York: Pantheon, 1962.
Kenyon, John. *Medieval Fortifications.* Leicester: Leicester Univ. Press, 1990.
Kubach, Hans Erich. *Romanesque Architecture.* History of World Architecture. New York: Electa/Rizzoli, 1988.
Kunstler, Gustav. *Romanesque Art in Europe.* Greenwich, Conn.: New York Graphic Society, 1969.
Labarge, Margaret Wade. *A Small Sound of the Trumpet: Women in Medieval Life.* London: Hamilton, 1990.
Mâle, Emile. *Religious Art in France: The Late Middle Ages: A Study of Medieval Iconography and Its Sources.* Princeton, N.J.: Princeton Univ. Press, 1986.
Martindale, Andrew. *Gothic Art.* World of Art. London: Thames and Hudson, 1967.
Panofsky, Erwin. *Abbot Suger on the Abbey Church of St.-Denis and Its Art Treasures.* 2nd ed. Ed. Gerda Panofsky-Soergel. Princeton, N.J.: Princeton Univ. Press, 1979.
———. *Gothic Architecture and Scholasticism.* Latrobe, Penn.: Archabbey, 1951.
Pevsner, Nikolaus, and Priscilla Metcalf. *The Cathedrals of England.* 2 vols. Harmondsworth, Eng.: Viking, 1985.
Radding, Charles M., and William W. Clark. *Medieval Architecture, Medieval Learning: Builders and Masters in the Age of Romanesque and Gothic.* New Haven, Conn.: Yale Univ. Press, 1992.
Sauerlander, Willibald. *Gothic Sculpture in France,* 1140–1270. Trans. Janet Sandheimer. London: Thames and Hudson, 1972.
Schapiro, Meyer. *Romanesque Art.* New York: Braziller, 1977.
Simson, Otto Georg von. *The Gothic Cathedral: Origins of Gothic Architecture and the Medieval Concept of Order.* 3rd ed. Bollingen Series. Princeton, N.J.: Princeton Univ. Press, 1988.
Smart, Alastair. *The Dawn of Italian Painting,* 1250–1400. Ithaca, N.Y.: Cornell Univ. Press, 1978.
Stoddard, Whitney. *Art and Architecture in Medieval France: Medieval Architecture, Sculpture, Stained Glass, Manuscripts. The Art of the Church Treasuries.* New York: Harper & Row, 1972.
Stokstad, Marilyn. *Medieval Art.* New York: Harper & Row, 1986.
Swarzenski, Hanns. *Monuments of Romanesque Art: The Art of Church Treasures of North-Western Europe.* 2nd ed. Chicago: Univ. of Chicago Press, 1967.
White, John. *Art and Architecture in Italy, 1250 to 1400.* 3rd ed. Pelican History of Art. Harmondsworth, Eng.: Penguin, 1993.
———. *Duccio: Tuscan Art and the Medieval Workshop.* New York: Thames and Hudson, 1979.
Wieck, Roger S. *Time Sanctified: The Book of Hours in Medieval Art and Life.* New York: Braziller, 1988.
Wilson, Christopher. *The Gothic Cathedral: The Architecture of the Great Church,* 1130–1530. New York: Thames and Hudson, 1990.
Wilson, David M. *The Bayeux Tapestry: The Complete Tapestry in Color.* New York: Random House, 1985.
Year 1200, The. 2 vols. New York: Metropolitan Museum of Art, 1970.
Zarnecki, George. *Romanesque Art.* New York: Universe, 1971.
———. *The Art of the Medieval World: Architecture, Sculpture, Painting, the Sacred Arts.* New York: Abrams, 1975.

Chapter 11 Early Renaissance Art

Ainsworth, Maryan Wynn. *Petrus Christus: Renaissance Master of Bruges.* New York: Metropolitan Museum of Art, 1994.
Art and Politics in Late Medieval and Early Renaissance Italy, 1250–1500. South Bend, Ind.: Univ. of Notre Dame Press, 1990.
Baxandall, Michael. *Painting and Experience in Fifteenth-Century Italy: A Primer in the Social History of Pictorial Style.* Oxford: Clarendon, 1972.
Campbell, Lorne. *Renaissance Portraits: European Portrait-Painting in the 14th, 15th, and 16th Centuries.* New Haven, Conn.: Yale Univ. Press, 1990.
Christianity and the Renaissance: Image and Religious Imagination in the Quattrocento. Syracuse. N.Y.: Syracuse Univ. Press, 1990.
Christiansen, Keith. *Andrea Mantegna: Padua and Mantua.* New York: Braziller, 1994.
———, Laurence B. Kanter, and Carl Brandon Strehlke. *Painting in Renaissance Siena,* 1420–1500. New York: Metropolitan Museum of Art, 1988.
Circa 1492: Art in the Age of Exploration. Washington, D.C.: National Gallery of Art, 1991.
Cole, Bruce. *Italian Art, 1250–1550: The Relation of Renaissance Art to Life and Society.* New York: Harper & Row, 1987.
———. *Masaccio and the Art of Early Renaissance Florence.* Bloomington: Indiana Univ. Press, 1980.
Davies, Martin. *Rogier van der Weyden: An Essay, with a Critical Catalogue of Paintings Assigned to Him and to Robert Campin.* London: Phaidon, 1972.
de Pisan, Christine. *Le Livre de la Cité des Dames (The Book of the City of Ladies).* Trans. Earl J. Richards. New York: Persea, 1982.
Dhanens, Elisabeth. *Van Eyck: The Ghent Altarpiece.* New York: Viking, 1973.
Freeman, Margaret B. *The Unicorn Tapestries.* New York: Metropolitan Museum of Art, 1976.
Goffen, Rona. *Giovanni Bellini.* New Haven, Conn.: Yale Univ. Press, 1989.
Hartt, Frederick. *History of Italian Renaissance Art: Painting, Sculpture, Architecture.* 4th ed. New York: Abrams, 1994.
Hind, Arthur M. *An Introduction to a History of Woodcut.* New York: Dover, 1963.
Krautheimer, Richard. *Ghiberti's Bronze Doors.* Princeton, N.J.: Princeton Univ. Press, 1971.
Lane, Barbara G. *The Altar and the Altarpiece: Sacramental Themes in Early Netherlandish Painting.* New York: Harper & Row, 1984.
Levey, Michael. *Early Renaissance.* Harmondsworth, Eng.: Penguin, 1967.
Lightbown, Ronald. *Piero della Francesca.* New York: Abbeville, 1992.
———. *Sandro Botticelli: Life and Work.* New ed. New York: Abbeville, 1989.
Lloyd, Christopher. *Fra Angelica.* Rev. ed. London: Phaidon, 1992.
Pacht, Otto. *Van Eyck and the Founders of Early Netherlandish Painting.* Ed. Maria Schmidt-Dengler. Trans. David Britt. London: Miller, 1994.
Panofsky, Erwin. *Early Netherlandish Painting: Its Origins and Character.* 2 vols. Cambridge, Mass.: Harvard Univ. Press, 1966.
Pope-Hennessy, Sir John. *Donatello: Sculptor.* New York: Abbeville, 1993.
Saalman, Howard. *Filippo Brunelleschi: The Buildings.* University Park: Pennsylvania State Univ. Press, 1993.
Snyder, James. *Northern Renaissance Art: Painting, Sculpture, the Graphic Arts from 1350 to 1575.* New York: Abrams, 1985.

Chapter 12 Art of the High Renaissance and Reformation

Baldini, Umberto. *The Sculpture of Michelangelo.* Trans. Clare Coope. New York: Rizzoli, 1982.
Baxandall, Michael. *The Limewood Sculptors of Renaissance Germany.* New Haven, Conn.: Yale Univ. Press, 1980.
Beck, James H. *Raphael.* New York: Abrams, 1994.
Bier, Justus. *Tilman Riemenschneider, His Life and Work.* Lexington: Univ. of Kentucky Press, 1989.
Blunt, Anthony. *Art and Architecture in France: 1500–1700.* 4th ed. Pelican History of Art. Harmondsworth, Eng.: Penguin, 1981.
Boucher, Brude. *Andrea Palladio: The Architect in His Time.* New York: Abbeville, 1994.
Bronstein, Leo. *El Greco (Domenicos Theotocopoulos).* New York: Abrams, 1990.
Chastel, André. *The Age of Humanism: Europe,* 1480–1530. Trans. Katherine M. Delavenay and E. M. Gwyer. London: Thames and Hudson, 1963.
Cuttler, Charles D. *Northern Painting from Pucelle to Bruegel: Fourteenth, Fifteenth and Sixteenth Centuries.* New York: Holt, Rinehart and Winston, 1973.
Freedberg, S. J. *Painting in Italy, 1500 to 1600.* 3rd ed. Pelican History of Art. New Haven, Conn.: Yale Univ. Press, 1993.
Goldschneider, Ludwig. *Leonardo da Vinci: Life and Work, Paintings and Drawings.* 7th ed. London: Phaidon, 1964.
Hartt, Frederick. *Michelangelo.* New York: Abrams, 1984.
Hayum, André. *The Isenheim Altarpiece: God's Medicine and the Painter's Vision.* Princeton Essays on the Arts. Princeton, N.J.: Princeton Univ. Press, 1989.
Heydenreich, Ludwig H. *Leonardo: "The Last Supper."* Art in Context. London: Allen Lane, 1974.
Hollingsworth, Mary. *Patronage in Renaissance Italy: From 1400 to the Early Sixteenth Century.* London: Murray, 1994.
Huizinga, Johan. *Waning of the Middle Ages: A Study of the Forms of Life, Thought, and Art in France and the Netherlands in the XIVth and XVth Centuries.* Garden City, N.Y.: Doubleday, 1954.
Jones, Roger, and Nicholas Penny. *Raphael.* New Haven, Conn.: Yale Univ. Press, 1983.
Landau, David, and Peter Parshall. *The Renaissance Print: 1470–1550.* New Haven, Conn.: Yale Univ. Press, 1994.
Langdon, Helen. *Holbein.* 2nd ed. London: Phaidon, 1993.
Linfert, Carl. *Hieronymus Bosch.* Masters of Art. New York: Abrams, 1989.
Martineau, Jane, and Charles Hope, eds. *The Genius of Venice, 1500–1600.* New York: Abrams, 1984.
McMullen, Roy. *Mona Lisa: The Picture and the Myth.* Boston: Houghton Mifflin, 1975.
Murray, Linda. *Late Renaissance and Mannerism.* World of Art. London: Thames and Hudson, 1967.
Murray, Peter. *Renaissance Architecture.* History of World Architecture. Milan: Electa, 1985.
———, and Linda Murray. *The Art of the Renaissance.* World of Art. London: Thames and Hudson, 1963.
Olson, Roberta J. M. *Italian Renaissance Sculpture.* World of Art. New York: Thames and Hudson, 1992.
Osten, Gert von der, and Horst Vey. *Painting and Sculpture in Germany and the Netherlands, 1500–1600.* Pelican History of Art. Harmondsworth, Eng.: Penguin, 1969.
Perlingieri, Ilya Sandra. *Sofonisba Anguissola: The First Great Woman Artist of the Renaissance.* New York: Rizzoli, 1992.
Pietrangeli, Carlo, et al. *The Sistine Chapel: The Art, the History, and the Restoration.* New York: Harmony, 1986.
Pope-Hennessy, Sir John. *Cellini.* New York: Abbeville, 1985.
———. *Italian High Renaissance and Baroque Sculpture.* 3rd ed. Oxford: Phaidon, 1986.
Rearick, William R. *The Art of Paolo Veronese, 1528–1588.* Washington, D.C.: National Gallery of Art, 1988.
Rosand, David. *Painting in Cinquecento Venice: Titian, Veronese, Tintoretto.* New Haven, Conn.: Yale Univ. Press, 1982.
Russell, Francis. *The World of Dürer,* 1471–1528. New York: Time-Life, 1967.
Shearman, John. *Mannerism.* Harmondsworth, Eng.: Penguin, 1967.
Stechow, Wolfgang. *Pieter Bruegel the Elder.* Masters of Art. New York: Abrams, 1990.
Tavernor, Robert. *Palladio and Palladianism.* World of Art. New York: Thames and Hudson, 1991.
Vasari, Giorgio. *The Lives of the Artists.* Trans. Julia Conaway Bondanella and Peter Bondanella. New York: Oxford Univ. Press, 1991.
Verheyen, Egon. *The Paintings in the Studiolo of Isabella d'Este at Mantua.* Monographs on Archaeology and Fine Arts. New York: New York Univ. Press, 1971.
Vitruvius Pollio. *Vitruvius: The Ten Books on Architecture.* Trans. Morris Hicky Morgan. New York: Dover, 1960.
Whiting, Roger. *Leonardo: A Portrait of the Renaissance Man.* London: Barrie and Jenkins, 1992.

Chapter 13 Baroque and Rococo Art

Ackley, Clifford S. *Printmaking in the Age of Rembrandt.* Boston: Museum of Fine Arts, 1981.
Age of Caravaggio, The. New York: Metropolitan Museum of Art, 1985.
Bazin, Germain. *Baroque and Rococo.* Trans. Jonathan Griffin. World of Art. New York: Praeger, 1964.
Berger, Robert W. *Versailles: The Chateau of Louis XIV.* Monographs on the Fine Arts. University Park: Pennsylvania State Univ. Press, 1985.
Blunt, Anthony, et al. *Baroque and Rococo Architecture and Decoration.* New York: Harper & Row, 1982.
Brown, Christopher. *Scenes of Everyday Life: Dutch Genre Painting of the Seventeenth Century.* London: Faber & Faber, 1984.
Brown, Jonathan. *The Golden Age of Painting in Spain.* New Haven, Conn.: Yale Univ. Press, 1991.
———. *Velázquez, Painter and Courtier.* New Haven, Conn.: Yale Univ. Press, 1986.
Fuchs, R. H. *Dutch Painting.* World of Art. New York: Oxford Univ. Press, 1978.
Grasselli, Margaret Morgan, and Pierre Rosenberg. *Watteau,* 1684–1721. Washington, D.C.: National Gallery of Art, 1984.
Haak, Bob. *The Golden Age: Dutch Painters of the Seventeenth Century.* Trans. and ed. Elizabeth Willems-Treeman. New York: Abrams, 1984.
Held, Julius Samuel, and Donald Posner. *17th and 18th Century Art: Baroque Painting, Sculpture, Architecture.* Library of Art History. New York: Abrams, 1971.
Kalnein, Wend, and Michael Levey. *Art and Architecture of the Eighteenth Century in France.* Pelican History of Art. Harmondsworth, Eng.: Penguin, 1972.
Lagerlof, Margaretha Rossholm. *Ideal Landscape: Annibale Caracci, Nicolas Poussin, and Claude Lorrain.* New Haven, Conn.: Yale Univ. Press, 1990.
Moir, Alfred. *Anthony Van Dyck.* New York: Abrams, 1994.

———. *Caravaggio*. Library of Great Painters. New York: Abrams, 1982.

Norberg-Schulz, Christian. *Baroque Architecture*. New York: Rizzoli, 1986.

Rosenberg, Pierre. *Fragonard*. New York: Metropolitan Museum of Art, 1988.

Russell, H. Diane. *Claude Lorrain, 1600–1682*. Washington, D.C.: National Gallery of Art, 1982.

Schwartz, Gary. *Rembrandt, His Life, His Paintings*. New York: Penguin, 1991.

Scribner, Charles, III. *Gianlorenzo Bernini*. Masters of Art. New York: Abrams, 1991.

———. *Peter Paul Rubens*. Masters of Art. New York: Abrams, 1989.

Summerson, John. *Inigo Jones*. Harmondsworth, Eng.: Penguin, 1966.

Sutton, Peter. *The Age of Rubens*. Boston: Museum of Fine Arts, 1993.

Welu, James A., and Pieter Biesboer, eds. *Judith Leyster: A Dutch Master and Her World*. New York: Yale Univ. Press, 1993.

Wheelock, Arthur K., Jr. *Jan Vermeer*. New York: Abrams, 1988.

———, Susan J. Barnes, and Julius S. Held. *Anthony Van Dyck*. Washington, D.C.: National Gallery of Art, 1990.

White, Christopher. *Peter Paul Rubens: Man & Artist*. New Haven, Conn.: Yale Univ. Press, 1987.

———. *Rembrandt*. World of Art. London: Thames and Hudson, 1984.

Wittkower, Rudolf. *Art and Architecture in Italy, 1600 to 1750*. 3rd ed. Pelican History of Art. Harmondsworth, Eng.: Penguin, 1982.

Chapter 14 Art of the Americas

Baquedano, Elizabeth. *Aztec Sculpture*. London: British Museum, 1984.

Berdan, Frances F. *The Aztecs of Central Mexico: An Imperial Society*. New York: Holt, 1982.

Bringhurst, Robert. *The Black Canoe: Bill Reid and the Spirit of Haida Gwaii*. Seattle: Univ. of Washington Press, 1991.

Coe, Ralph. *Lost and Found Traditions: Native American Art 1965–1985*. Ed. Irene Gordon. Seattle: Univ. of Washington Press, 1986.

Feest, Christian F. *Native Arts of North America*. Updated ed. World of Art. New York: Thames and Hudson, 1992.

Hemming, John. *Monuments of the Incas*. Boston: Little, Brown, 1982.

Jonaitis, Aldona. *Art of the Northern Tlingit*. Seattle: Univ. of Washington Press, 1986.

Kahlenberg, Mary Hunt, and Anthony Berlant. *The Navajo Blanket*. New York: Praeger, 1972.

Levi-Strauss, Claude. *Way of the Masks*. Trans. Sylvia Modelski. Seattle: Univ. of Washington Press, 1982.

McNair, Peter L., Alan L. Hoover, and Kevin Neary. *Legacy: Tradition and Innovation in Northwest Coast Indian Art*. Vancouver: Douglas and McIntyre, 1984.

Mexico: Splendors of Thirty Centuries. New York: Metropolitan Museum of Art, 1990.

Nicholson, H. B., and Eloise Quinones Keber. *Art of Aztec Mexico: Treasures of Tenochtitlan*. Washington, D.C.: National Gallery of Art, 1983.

Pasztory, Esther. *Aztec Art*. New York: Abrams, 1983.

Stierlin, Henri. *Art of the Aztecs and Its Origins*. New York: Rizzoli, 1982.

———. *Art of the Incas and Its Origins*. New York: Rizzoli, 1984.

Trimble, Stephen. *Talking with the Clay: The Art of Pueblo Pottery*. Santa Fe: School of American Research Press, 1987.

Wade, Edwin, and Carol Haralson, eds. *The Arts of the North American Indian: Native Traditions in Evolution*. New York: Hudson Hills, 1986.

Walters, Anna Lee. *Spirit of Native America: Beauty and Mysticism in American Indian Art*. San Francisco: Chronicle, 1989.

Wood, Nancy C. *Taos Pueblo*. New York: Knopf, 1989.

Chapter 15 African Art

Abiodun, Rowland, Henry J. Drewal, and John Pemberton III, eds. *The Yoruba Artist: New Theoretical Perspectives on African Arts*. Washington, D.C.: Smithsonian Institution, 1994.

Adler, Peter, and Nicholas Barnard. *African Majesty: The Textile Art of the Ashanti and Ewe*. New York: Thames and Hudson, 1992.

Biebuyck, Daniel P. *Lega Culture: Art, Initiation, and Moral Philosophy among a Central African People*. Berkeley: Univ. of California Press, 1973.

Brincard, Marie-Thérèse, ed. *The Art of Metal in Africa*. Trans. Evelyn Fischel. New York: African-American Institute, 1984.

Cole, Herbert M. *Icons: Ideals and Power in the Art of Africa*.

Washington, D.C.: National Museum of African Art, Smithsonian Institution, 1989.

D'Azevedao, Warren L. *The Traditional Artist in African Societies*. Bloomington: Indiana Univ. Press, 1989.

Drewal, Henry, and John Pemberton III. *Yoruba: Nine Centuries of African Art and Thought*. New York: Center for African Art, 1989.

Fagg, William Buller, and John Pemberton III. *Yoruba Sculpture of West Africa*. Ed. Bryce Holcombe. New York: Knopf, 1982.

Gilfoy, Peggy S. *Patterns of Life: West African Strip-Weaving Traditions*. Washington, D.C.: National Museum of African Art, Smithsonian Institution, 1992.

Glaze, Anita. *Art and Death in a Senufo Village*. Bloomington: Indiana Univ. Press, 1981.

Laude, Jean. *African Art of the Dogon: The Myths of the Cliff Dwellers*. Trans. Joachim Neugroschell. New York: Brooklyn Museum, 1973.

Leiris, Michel, and Jacqueline Delange. *African Art. Arts of Mankind*. London: Thames and Hudson, 1968.

Martin, Phyllis, and Patrick O'Meara, eds. *Africa*. 2nd ed. Bloomington: Indiana Univ. Press, 1986.

Mbiti, John S. *African Religions and Philosophy*. 2nd ed. Oxford: Heinemann, 1990.

McNaughton, Patrick R. *The Mande Blacksmiths: Knowledge, Power and Art in West Africa*. Bloomington: Indiana Univ. Press, 1988.

Murray, Jocelyn, ed. *Cultural Atlas of Africa*. New York: Facts on File, 1981.

Perrois, Louis, and Marta Sierra Delage. *The Art of Equatorial Guinea: The Fang Tribes*. New York: Rizzoli, 1990.

Picon, John, and John Mack. *African Textiles*. New York: Harper & Row, 1989.

Price, Sally. *Primitive Art in Civilized Places*. Chicago: Univ. of Chicago Press, 1989.

Schildkrout, Enid, and Curtis A. Keim. *African Reflections: Art from Northeastern Zaire*. Seattle: Univ. of Washington Press, 1990.

Sieber, Roy. *African Furniture and Household Objects*. Bloomington: Indiana Univ. Press, 1980.

———, and Roslyn Adele Walker. *African Art in the Cycle of Life*. Washington, D.C.: National Museum of African Art, Smithsonian Institution, 1987.

Vogel, Susan. *Africa Explores: 20th Century African Art*. New York: Center for African Art, 1991.

Willett, Frank. *African Art: An Introduction*. Rev ed. World of Art. New York: Thames and Hudson, 1993.

Chapter 16 Neoclassicism and Romanticism

Age of Neoclassicism. London: Arts Council of Great Britain, 1972.

Bindman, David. *William Blake: His Art and Time*. New Haven, Conn.: Yale Center for British Art, 1982.

Boime, Albert. *Art in an Age of Bonapartism, 1800–1815*. Chicago: Univ. of Chicago Press, 1990.

Byson, Norman. *Tradition and Desire: From David to Delacroix*. New York: Cambridge Univ. Press, 1984.

Clark, Kenneth. *The Romantic Rebellion: Romantic versus Classic Art*. New York: Harper & Row, 1973.

Cooper, Wendy A. *Classical Taste in America 1800–1840*. Baltimore: Baltimore Museum of Art, 1993.

Eitner, Lorenz. *Neoclassicism and Romanticism, 1750–1850: An Anthology of Sources and Documents*. New York: Harper & Row, 1989.

Harris, Enriqueta. *Goya*. Rev. ed. London: Phaidon, 1994.

Honour, Hugh. *Neo-Classicism*. Harmondsworth, Eng.: Penguin, 1968.

———. *Romanticism*. London: Allen Lane, 1979.

Kroeber, Karl. *British Romantic Art*. Berkeley: Univ. of California Press, 1986.

Manners and Morals: Hogarth and British Painting 1700–1760. London: Tate Gallery, 1987.

Mayoux, Jean-Jacques. *English Painting*. Trans. James Emmons. New York: Grove, 1975.

Middleton, Robin, and David Watkin. *Neoclassical and 19th Century Architecture*. 2 vols. History of World Architecture. New York: Electa/Rizzoli, 1987.

Novotny, Fritz. *Painting and Sculpture in Europe, 1780–1880*. Pelican History of Art. Harmondsworth, Eng.: Penguin, 1980.

Paulson, Ronald. *The Art of Hogarth*. London: Phaidon, 1975.

Perez Sanchez, Alfonso E., and Eleanor A. Sayre. *Goya and the Spirit of Enlightenment*. Boston: Museum of Fine Arts, 1989.

Roberts, Warren E. *Jacques-Louis David, Revolutionary Artist: Art, Politics, and the French Revolution*. Chapel Hill: Univ. of North Carolina Press, 1989.

Rosenblum, Robert. *Jean-Auguste-Dominique Ingres*. Masters of Art. New York: Abrams, 1990.

Rousseau, Jean-Jacques. *Emile*. Ed. F. and P. Richard. New York: French & European, 1962.

Roworth, Wendy Wassyng. *Angelica Kauffman: A Continental Artist in Georgian England*. London: Reaktion, 1992.

Rykwert, Joseph, and Anne Rykwert. *Robert and James Adam: The Men and the Style*. New York: Rizzoli, 1985.

Shapiro, Michael Edward. *George Caleb Bingham*. New York: Abrams, 1993.

Vaughan, William. *German Romantic Painting*. New Haven, Conn.: Yale Univ. Press, 1980.

Walker, John. *John Constable*. New York: Abrams, 1991.

Wilton, Andrew. *Turner in His Time*. New York: Abrams, 1987.

Wolf, Bryan Jay. *Romantic-Revision: Culture and Consciousness in Nineteenth-Century American Painting and Literature*. Chicago: Univ. of Chicago Press, 1986.

Chapter 17 Realism to Impressionism

Adams, Steven. *The Barbizon School and the Origins of Impressionism*. London: Phaidon, 1994.

Ades, Dawn. *Photomontage*. Rev ed. World of Art. New York: Thames and Hudson, 1986.

Ashton, Dore. *Rosa Bonheur: A Life and a Legend*. New York: Viking, 1981.

Barger, M. Susan, and William B. White. *The Daguerreotype: Nineteenth-Century Technology and Modern Science*. Washington, D.C.: Smithsonian Institution, 1991.

Baudelaire, Charles. *The Painter of Modern Life, and Other Essays*. Trans. and ed. Jonathan Mayne. London: Phaidon, 1964.

Boime, Albert. *The Academy and French Painting in the Nineteenth Century*. London: Phaidon, 1971.

Cachin, Françoise, Charles S. Moffett, and Michel Melot, eds. *Manet, 1832–1883*. New York: Metropolitan Museum of Art, 1983.

Clark, T. J. *The Absolute Bourgeois: Artists and Politics in France, 1848–1851*. London: Thames and Hudson, 1973.

———. *Image of the People: Gustave Courbet and the 1848 Revolution*. London: Thames and Hudson, 1973.

Cumming, Elizabeth, and Wendy Caplan. *Arts and Crafts Movement*. World of Art. New York: Thames and Hudson, 1991.

Duncan, Alastair. *Art Nouveau*. World of Art. New York: Thames and Hudson, 1994.

Faxon, Alicia Craig. *Dante Gabriel Rossetti*. Oxford: Phaidon, 1989.

Gordon, Robert, and Andrew Forge. *Degas*. Trans. Richard Howard. New York: Abrams, 1988.

Harding, James. *Artistes Pompiers: French Academic Art in the 19th Century*. New York: Rizzoli, 1979.

Hargrove, June, ed. *The French Academy: Classicism and Its Antagonists*. Newark: Univ. of Delaware Press, 1990.

Higonnet, Anne. *Berthe Morisot's Images of Women*. Cambridge, Mass.: Harvard Univ. Press, 1992.

Homer, William Innes. *Thomas Eakins: His Life and Art*. New York: Abbeville, 1992.

Mathews, Nancy Mowll. *Mary Cassatt*. Library of American Art. New York: Abrams, 1987.

Needham, Gerald. *19th-Century Realist Art*. New York: Harper & Row, 1988.

Nochlin, Linda. *Impressionism and Post-Impressionism, 1874–1904: Sources and Documents*. Englewood Cliffs, N.J.: Prentice-Hall, 1966.

———. *Realism and Tradition in Art, 1848–1900: Sources and Documents*. Englewood Cliffs, N.J.: Prentice-Hall, 1966.

O'Gorman, James F. *Three American Architects: Richardson, Sullivan, and Wright, 1865–1915*. Chicago: Univ. of Chicago Press, 1991.

Rouart, Denis. *Renoir*. New York: Skira/Rizzoli, 1985.

Schaaf, Larry J. *Out of the Shadows: Herschel, Talbot and the Invention of Photography*. New Haven, Conn.: Yale Univ. Press, 1992.

Spate, Virginia. *Claude Monet: Life and Work*. New York: Rizzoli, 1992.

Stansky, Peter. *Redesigning the World: William Morris, the 1880s, and the Arts and Crafts*. Princeton, N.J.: Princeton Univ. Press, 1985.

Touissaint, Hélène. *Gustave Courbet, 1819–1877*. London: Arts Council of Great Britain, 1978.

Valkenier, Elizabeth Kridl. *Ilya Repin and the World of Russian Art*. New York: Columbia Univ. Press, 1990.

Chapter 18 Post-Impressionism Through Early Modern Art

Barr, Alfred H., Jr. *Cubism and Abstract Art: Painting, Sculpture, Constructions, Photography, Architecture, Industrial Arts, Theatre, Films, Posters, Typography*. Cambridge, Mass.: Belknap, 1986.

Brown, Milton. *Story of the Armory Show: The 1913 Exhibition That Changed American Art*. 2nd ed. New York: Abbeville, 1988.

Champigneulle, Bernard. *Rodin*. World of Art. New York: Oxford Univ. Press, 1980.

Cowling, Elizabeth. *Picasso: Sculptor/Painter.* London: Tate Gallery, 1994.

Davidson, Abraham A. *Early American Modernist Painting, 1910–1935.* New York: Harper & Row, 1981.

Denvir, Bernard. *Toulouse-Lautrec.* World of Art. New York: Thames and Hudson, 1991.

Dube, Wolf-Dieter. *Expressionism.* Trans. Mary Whittall. World of Art. New York: Praeger, 1973.

Freeman, Judi. *The Fauve Landscape.* Los Angeles: Los Angeles County Museum of Art, 1990.

Fry, Edward. *Cubism.* New York: McGraw-Hill, 1966.

Glackens, Ira. *William Glackens and the Ashcan Group: The Emergence of Realism in American Art.* New York: Crown, 1957.

Golding, John. *Cubism: A History and an Analysis, 1907–1914.* Cambridge, Mass.: Belknap, 1988.

Gordon, Donald E. *Expressionism: Art and Idea.* New Haven, Conn.: Yale Univ. Press, 1987.

Gowing, Lawrence. *Matisse.* World of Art. New York: Oxford Univ. Press, 1979.

Gray, Camilla. *Russian Experiment in Art, 1863–1922.* New York: Abrams, 1970.

Hahl-Koch, Jelena. *Kandinsky.* New York: Rizzoli, 1993.

Harrison, Charles, Francis Frascina, and Gill Perry. *Primitivism, Cubism, Abstraction: The Early Twentieth Century.* New Haven, Conn.: Yale Univ. Press, 1993.

Herbert, James D. *Fauve Painting: The Making of Cultural Politics.* New Haven, Conn.: Yale Univ. Press, 1992.

Homer, William Innes. *Alfred Stieglitz and the American Avant-Garde.* Boston: New York Graphics Society, 1977.

Hulsker, Jan. *The Complete Van Gogh: Paintings, Drawings, Sketches.* New York: Abrams, 1980.

Lloyd, Jill. *German Expressionism: Primitivism and Modernity.* New Haven, Conn.: Yale Univ. Press, 1991.

McQuillan, Melissa. *Van Gogh.* World of Art. New York: Thames and Hudson, 1989.

Norman, Dorothy. *Alfred Stieglitz, an American Seer.* New York: Aperture, 1990.

Post-Impressionism: Cross-currents in European and American Painting, 1880–1906. Washington, D.C.: National Gallery of Art, 1980.

Rewald, John. *Post-impressionism: From Van Gogh to Gauguin.* 3rd ed. New York: Museum of Modern Art, 1978.

Rosenblum, Robert. *Cubism and Twentieth-Century Art.* Rev. ed. New York: Abrams, 1984.

Rubin, William. *Picasso and Braque: Pioneering Cubism.* New York: Museum of Modern Art, 1989.

———, ed. *Pablo Picasso, A Retrospective.* New York: Museum of Modern Art, 1980.

Russell, John. *Seurat.* World of Art. London: Thames and Hudson, 1965.

Spate, Virginia. *Orphism: The Evolution of Non-Figurative Painting in Paris, 1910–1914.* Oxford Studies in the History of Art and Architecture. Oxford: Clarendon, 1979.

Thomson, Belinda. *Gauguin.* World of Art. New York: Thames and Hudson, 1987.

Verdi, Richard. *Cézanne.* World of Art. New York: Thames and Hudson, 1992.

Wilkin, Karen. *Georges Braque.* New York: Abbeville, 1991.

Zhadova, Larissa A. *Malevich: Suprematism and Revolution in Russian Art.* Trans. Alexander Lieven. London: Thames and Hudson, 1982.

Chapter 19 Modern Art

Alexandrian, Sarane. *Surrealist Art.* World of Art. London: Thames and Hudson, 1970.

Anfam, David. *Abstract Expressionism.* World of Art. New York: Thames and Hudson, 1990.

Arnason, H. H., and Marla F. Prather. *History of Modern Art: Painting, Sculpture, Architecture, Photography.* 4th ed. New York: Abrams, 1998.

Art into Life: Russian Constructivism, 1914–32. New York: Rizzoli, 1990.

Ashton, Dore. *American Art since 1945.* New York: Oxford Univ. Press, 1982.

Baigell, Matthew. *The American Scene: American Painting of the 1930's.* New York: Praeger, 1974.

Banham, Reyner. *Theory and Design in the First Machine Age.* 2nd ed. Cambridge, Mass.: MIT Press, 1980.

Barron, Stephanie, ed. *Degenerate Art: The Fate of the Avant-Garde in Nazi Germany.* Los Angeles: Los Angeles County Museum of Art, 1991.

Bayer, Herbert, Walter Gropius, and Ise Gropius. *Bauhaus, 1919–1928.* New York: Museum of Modern Art, 1975.

Blake, Peter. *No Place Like Utopia: Modern Architecture and the Company We Kept.* New York: Knopf, 1993.

Canaday, John. *Mainstreams of Modern Art.* 2nd ed. New York: Holt, Rinehart and Winston, 1981.

Castleman, Riva, ed. *Art of the Forties.* New York: Museum of Modern Art, 1991.

Cernuschi, Claude. *Jackson Pollock: Meaning and Significance.* New York: Icon Editions, 1992.

Curtis, James. *Mind's Eye, Mind's Truth: FSA Photography Reconsidered.* Philadelphia: Temple Univ. Press, 1989.

Curtis, William J. R. *Le Corbusier: Idea and Forms.* New York: Rizzoli, 1986.

Dachy, Marc. *The Dada Movement, 1915–1923.* New York: Skira/Rizzoli, 1990.

Eldredge, Charles C. *Georgia O'Keeffe.* Library of American Art. New York: Abrams, 1991.

Gay, Peter. *Art and Act: On Causes in History—Manet, Gropius, Mondrian.* New York: Harper & Row, 1976.

Haiko, Peter, ed. *Architecture of the Early XX Century.* Trans. Gordon Clough. New York: Rizzoli, 1989.

Hammacher, A. M. *Modern Sculpture: Tradition and Innovation.* Enlg. ed. New York: Abrams, 1988.

Herrera, Hayden. *Frida Kahlo: The Paintings.* New York: HarperCollins, 1991.

Hobbs, Robert Carleton, and Gail Levin. *Abstract Expressionism: The Formative Years.* Ithaca, N.Y.: Cornell Univ. Press, 1981.

Jaffe, Hans L. C. *De Stijl, 1917–1931: The Dutch Contribution to Modern Art.* Cambridge, Mass.: Belknap, 1986.

Kingsley, April. *The Turning Point: The Abstract Expressionists and the Transformation of American Art.* New York: Simon & Schuster, 1992.

Kuenzli, Rudolf, and Francis M. Naumann. *Marcel Duchamp: Artist of the Century.* Cambridge, Mass.: MIT Press, 1989.

Kuspit, Donald B. *Clement Greenberg, Art Critic.* Madison: Univ. of Wisconsin Press, 1979.

Lane, John R., and Susan C. Larsen. *Abstract Painting and Sculpture in America 1927–1944.* Pittsburgh: Museum of Art, Carnegie Institute, 1984.

Larkin, David, and Bruce Brooks Pfeiffer. *Frank Lloyd Wright: The Masterworks.* New York: Rizzoli, 1993.

Overy, Paul. *De Stijl.* World of Art. New York: Thames and Hudson, 1991.

Picon, Gaetan. *Surrealists and Surrealism, 1919–1939.* Trans. James Emmons. New York: Rizzoli, 1977.

Sandler, Irving. *The New York School: The Painters and Sculptors of the Fifties.* New York: Harper & Row, 1978.

———. *The Triumph of American Painting: A History of Abstract Expressionism.* New York: Harper & Row, 1976.

Shapiro, David, and Cecile Shapiro. *Abstract Expressionism: A Critical Record.* New York: Cambridge Univ. Press, 1990.

Spaeth, David A. *Mies van der Rohe.* New York: Rizzoli, 1985.

Stich, Sidra. *Anxious Visions: Surrealist Art.* New York: Abbeville, 1990.

Waldman, Diane. *Willem de Kooning.* Library of American Art. New York: Abrams, 1988.

Weaver, Mike, ed. *The Art of Photography, 1939–1989.* London: Royal Academy of Arts, 1989.

Weiss, Jeffrey S. *The Popular Culture of Modern Art: Picasso, Duchamp, and Avant-Gardism.* New Haven, Conn.: Yale Univ. Press, 1994.

Whitford, Frank. *Bauhaus.* World of Art. London: Thames and Hudson, 1984.

Chapter 20 Contemporary Art

Alloway, Lawrence. *Roy Lichtenstein.* New York: Abbeville, 1983.

Atkins, Robert. *Artspeak: A Guide to Contemporary Ideas, Movements, and Buzzwords.* New York: Abbeville, 1990.

Baker, Kenneth. *Minimalism: Art of Circumstance.* New York: Abbeville, 1988.

Battcock, Gregory. *Idea Art: A Critical Anthology.* New York: Dutton, 1973.

———, and Robert Nickas. *The Art of Performance: A Critical Anthology.* New York: Dutton, 1984.

Beardsley, John. *Earthworks and Beyond: Contemporary Art in the Landscape.* New York: Abbeville, 1984.

Bolton, Richard, ed. *Culture Wars: Documents from the Recent Controversies in the Arts.* New York: New Press, 1992.

Bourdon, David. *Warhol.* New York: Abrams, 1989.

Broude, Norma, and Mary D. Garrard. *The Power of Feminist Art: The American Movement of the 1970s, History and Impact.* New York: Abrams, 1994.

Dormer, Peter. *Design Since 1945.* World of Art. New York: Thames and Hudson, 1993.

Endgame: Reference and Simulation in Recent Painting and Sculpture. Boston: Institute of Contemporary Art, 1986.

Ferguson, Russell, ed. *Discourses: Conversations in Postmodern Art and Culture.* Documentary Sources in Contemporary Art. Cambridge, Mass.: MIT Press, 1990.

Fineberg, Jonathan. *Art Since 1940: Strategies of Being.* New York: Abrams, 1995.

Goldberg, Rose Lee. *Performance Art: From Futurism to the Present.* Rev. ed. New York: Abrams, 1988.

Green, Jonathan. *American Photography: A Critical History since 1945 to the Present.* New York: Abrams, 1984.

Grundberg, Andy. *Photography and Art: Interactions since 1945.* New York: Abbeville, 1987.

Hays, K. Michael, and Carol Burns, eds. *Thinking the Present: Recent American Architecture.* New York: Princeton Architectural, 1990.

Henri, Adrian. *Total Art: Environments, Happenings, and Performance.* World of Art. New York: Oxford Univ. Press, 1974.

Hertz, Richard. *Theories of Contemporary Art.* 2nd ed. Englewood Cliffs, N.J.: Prentice Hall, 1993.

Hoffman, Katherine. *Explorations: The Visual Arts since 1945.* New York: HarperCollins, 1991.

Jencks, Charles. *What Is Post-Modernism?* 3rd rev. ed. London: Academy Editions, 1989.

Johnson, Ellen H., ed. *American Artists on Art from 1940 to 1980.* New York: Harper & Row, 1982.

Kaprow, Allan. *Assemblage, Environments & Happenings.* New York: Abrams, 1965.

Kramer, Hilton. *The Age of the Avant-Garde: An Art Chronicle of 1956–1972.* New York: Farrar, Straus & Giroux, 1973.

Lewis, Samella S. *African American Art and Artists.* Rev. ed. Berkeley: Univ. of California Press, 1994.

Lippard, Lucy. *Pop Art.* World of Art. New York: Praeger, 1966.

Livingstone, Marco. *Pop Art: A Continuing History.* New York: Abrams, 1990.

Lucie-Smith, Edward. *Art in the Eighties.* Oxford: Phaidon, 1990.

———. *Art Today: From Abstract Expressionism to Superrealism.* 3rd ed. Oxford: Phaidon, 1989.

Manhart, Marcia, and Tom Manhart, eds. *The Eloquent Object: The Evolution of American Art in Craft Media since 1945.* Tulsa, Okla.: Philbrook Museum of Art, 1987.

Meisel, Louis K. *Photo-Realism.* New York: Abrams, 1989.

Morgan, Robert C. *Conceptual Art: An American Perspective.* Jefferson, N.C.: McFarland, 1994.

Rosen, Randy, and Catherine C. Brawer, comps. *Making Their Mark: Women Artists Move into the Mainstream, 1970–85.* New York: Abbeville, 1989.

Sandler, Irving. *American Art of the 1960's.* New York: Harper & Row, 1988.

Sayre, Henry M. *The Object of Performance: The American Avant-Garde since 1970.* Chicago: Univ. of Chicago Press, 1989.

Smith, Jaune Quick-to-See, and Harmony Hammond. *Women of Sweetgrass: Cedar and Sage.* New York: American Indian Center, 1984.

Stich, Sidra. *Made in USA: An Americanization in Modern Art, the '50s & '60s.* Berkeley: Univ. of California Press, 1987.

Taylor, Paul, ed. *Post-Pop Art.* Cambridge, Mass.: MIT Press, 1989.

Waldman, Diane. *Collage, Assemblage, and the Found Object.* New York: Abrams, 1992.

———. *Jenny Holzer.* New York: Abrams, 1989.

Wallis, Brian, ed. *Art after Modernism: Rethinking Representation.* Documentary Sources in Contemporary Art. New York: New Museum of Contemporary Art, 1984.

Wheeler, Daniel. *Art since Mid-Century: 1945 to the Present.* Englewood Cliffs, N.J.: Prentice Hall, 1991.

Word as Image: American Art, 1960–1990. Milwaukee: Milwaukee Art Museum, 1990.

Index

Credits